AMERICAN CONSTITUTIONAL INTERPRETATION

By

WALTER F. MURPHY
Princeton University

JAMES E. FLEMING, Esq.
Cravath, Swaine & Moore

WILLIAM F. HARRIS, II
University of Pennsylvania

Mineola, New York
THE FOUNDATION PRESS, INC.
1986

Library of Congress Cataloging in Publication Data

Murphy, Walter F., 1929–
   American constitutional interpretation.

   Includes bibliographies and index.
   1. United States—Constitutional law—Interpretation
and construction—Cases. 2. Law and politics—Cases.
I. Fleming, James E., 1954– II. Harris, William F. II, 1949–
III. Title.

KF4549.M87 1986   342.73'023   86–6240
ISBN 0–88277–321–6   347.30223

M., F. & H. Amer.Const.Inter. FP

*For Sidney M. Davis,
A Friend of the Constitution*

*

PREFACE

We began this volume because we felt that, despite the existence of a wealth of casebooks dealing with constitutional law, there was a great need for a collection of essays, cases, and other materials that directly confronted the problems of constitutional interpretation. At the outset, we should candidly state some of the concerns that gnawed at us during the years this book was gestating.

First, though one of us is also an attorney, we are all political scientists. We want to learn about politics, to teach students about politics, and to share ideas with colleagues with similar interests. That one cannot understand the political system of the United States or of most industrialized nations outside the Soviet sphere without understanding its "constitution" seems self-evident. Our primary purpose in this book is thus to bring together materials that will help students understand the American polity and some of the interactions between law and politics.

Second, we have a deep interest in constitutional interpretation; we find it intellectually fascinating and believe, we hope not solely for self-serving reasons, it to be practically important. Although we do not harbor any illusions that consitutional interpretation can ever be a hard science in the sense of chemistry or physics, it need not be a mere reflexive response to particular practical problems any more than it need be applied ideology. In sum, while we believe that constitutional interpretation is an art, we also believe that it is an art that can become disciplined. This view is not universally shared among political scientists, practicing lawyers, elected public officials, or even members of the U.S. Supreme Court. But it is a belief that is hardly unique to the three of us. We hope to convince others of its validity. Thus our second purpose is to further comprehension of what it means to interpret a constitution.

We are often explicitly and even more often implicitly critical of much constitutional interpretation. We criticize not out of a sense of epistemological skepticism or some sophisticated version of the belief that constitutional interpretation is a function of election returns—related to, yes; determined by, no. Rather, we criticize because we see missed opportunities to discipline the art, for interpreters to bring their assumptions and hidden premises out into the open so they can be evaluated on their own merits and for their effects on the constitutional order, on its ideals and aspirations, on its overarching structures, as well as on immediate public policies.

We propose to accomplish these tasks not by what has become the standard approach of casebooks, by focusing on legal doctrine. Rather, we try to analyze the enterprise of constitutional interpretation itself.

We hope to show students that constitutional interpretation is a necessary part of the study of politics, connecting the abstractions of political theory to the concrete realities of public policy. Constitutional interpretation usually produces legal doctrine; it always interacts with other forces in the political system to help shape public policies, perhaps even to transform the nature of the system itself. In turn, those other forces act on the interpretive enterprise, sometimes changing the sort of decisions it yields, sometimes modifying the nature of the enterprise.

To facilitate understanding, we have organized the book around three basic interrogatives:

(1) WHAT is the Constitution?

(2) WHO are the Constitution's authoritative interpreters?

(3) HOW should interpreters interpret the Constitution?

Any answers to these questions will be difficult and controversial, but no intellectually serious effort to understand or engage in constitutional interpretation can avoid them. And answers may have enormous consequences for the entire polity. A public official who believes "the Constitution" is totally contained within the plain words of the document of 1787 and its amendments is very apt to see both the rules of the political system as well as its values and goals very differently from an official who believes that "the Constitution" includes traditions, practices, and perhaps even political theories that bind and loose as authoritatively as does the document. So, too, a response to the WHO interrogative that Congress or the President has authority equal or superior to that of the judiciary in interpreting the Constitution has massive implications not only for public policy, but also for the nature of the political system. Similarly significant consequences follow from responses about the HOW of interpretation.

In examining these basic questions, we recognize that students both want and need to understand substance. We have therefore organized analyses of these interrogatives around customary categories of constitutional law. For example, in dealing with questions of HOW to interpret, we look at several modes of interpretation such as structural analysis and applications of theories of representative democracy and constitutionalism. To clarify structuralism we first use cases and materials dealing with problems of sharings of power among the presidency, Congress, and the judiciary and then with problems of federalism. To illustrate interpretive applications of a theory of representative democracy we use cases dealing with freedom of political communication and participation; for constitutionalist theory, cases dealing with rights to privacy and personal liberty. We have designed this book so that no one who uses it can avoid learning a great deal of constitutional law. We intend, however, that users will also learn much more.

Instructors will thus find in these pages much that is familiar, but they will find it organized, we hope, in ways that are more enlightening to students about the nature and relevance of constitutional interpretation. We should caution, however, that we have edited some traditional material to include sections that have traditionally been omitted because editors were more concerned with legal doctrine than linkages between political theory and public policy.

To guide students, we have begun Parts and chapters with introductory essays and have included bibliographies there as well as after some of the cases. Because we know that many instructors will not assign all pages of this book, we have built in a degree of redundance so that some important points will not be lost. After many of the readings we have also appended additional pieces of information and queries. Some of this apparatus may be of use to busy instructors as well as beginning students.

To allow students to savor how judges justify their work, we have retained most of their references to previous decisions. But to make the cases more legible, we have eliminated the citations to those cases without burdening the text with ellipses. The Table of Cases at the end of this volume includes citations to all the cases reprinted here as well as those discussed in the essays and notes; it does not, however, include all the cases mentioned by the justices.

This book is large. It provides more than enough readings—and we hope ideas—to energize a two-semester course. By judicious selection, the materials can also nourish a one-semester course. Indeed, the book has been used for the shorter course at Michigan, Princeton, and South Florida. And, if we take democractic theory seriously, having a choice is not a bad thing.

We are grateful to many people for years of assistance, some of it unwitting. This book began at Princeton as the core of readings in a course begun by Edward S. Corwin and continued by Alpheus Thomas Mason; it spread to Michigan (where Corwin had been President of the class of 1900) when William F. Harris, II, joined the faculty there in 1982. As a result, several generations of undergraduates at both institutions put up with Xeroxed versions of much of what is here. Their sharp criticisms helped make this a better book. We are grateful to them, though they might not believe it. We are also indebted to Sotirios A. Barber for using an early version at the University of South Florida and John E. Finn, Esq., for using the penultimate version at the University of Michigan and offering their criticisms together with those of their students. People who taught with us at Princeton and Michigan, some of them as visiting faculty, also liberally offered time and ideas:

Sotirios A. Barber, University of Notre Dame

Mark E. Brandon, Esq., University of Michigan

Gregory C. Keating, Esq.

John E. Finn, Esq., Wesleyan University

Suzette Hemberger, Princeton University

Jennifer Nedelsky, University of Toronto

Jeffrey Tulis, Princeton University

the late Clement E. Vose, Wesleyan University

Paul K. Warr, Esq., Texas A & M University

Thomas H. Wright, Esq., Princeton University

When they were graduate students, John E. Finn, Suzette Hemberger, and Gregory C. Keating, Esq., also acted as valuable research assistants as did Bonnie Berry of the Princeton Class of 1984 and Kathleen T. Neeff of Griggstown, N.J. Stacie Scofield of Princeton photocopied all the material that we have included, along with thousands of other pages that now lie fallow in our files. As always, Rosemary Allen Little cheerfully and efficiently opened the resources of Firestone Library to us. Her assistant Carole Simmons was also generous with her time and knowledge. Prof. Karen Flax of the Villanova Law School read portions of the manuscript and corrected some of our errors. Ronald Kahn of Oberlin College read an earlier draft of the entire manuscript with a thoughtfulness that proved enormously helpful to us. Stephen L. Wasby of SUNY at Albany provided useful additional criticisms.

We acknowledge full responsibility for errors that remain. If, however, there were a way of graciously sharing blame with those commentators and public officials who have so often misinterpreted the Constitution, we would most assuredly seize it.

W.F.M.
J.E.F.
W.F.H.

April, 1986

SUMMARY OF CONTENTS

C. Keeping Political Processes Open

D. Treating Equals Equally

E. Discovering Fundamental Rights

PART V

CONSTITUTIONAL DEMOCRACY IN THE CRUCIBLE OF CRISIS

APPENDICES

TABLE OF CONTENTS

PART II

WHAT IS THE CONSTITUTION?

PART IV

<u>HOW</u> TO INTERPRET THE CONSTITUTION?

E. DISCOVERING FUNDAMENTAL RIGHTS

PART V

CONSTITUTIONAL DEMOCRACY IN THE CRUCIBLE OF CRISIS

AMERICAN CONSTITUTIONAL INTERPRETATION

*

1

Introduction: Interpreting a Constitution

A constitution can perform many functions in a modern state. One of these tasks may be to serve as a deposit for a cluster of a society's fundamental political values. A constitution can reflect these values in substantive ways, as in forbidding governmental interferences with freedom of religion, and in procedural ways, as in providing that government can punish people for criminal actions only after trial by jury at which the defendant has been represented by counsel. A constitution can also reflect society's fundamental values in "allocative" ways. By denying governmental authority to make some kinds of decisions, dividing authority to make other kinds of decisions among various institutions,[1] and in determining how officials of those institutions shall be chosen, a constitution not only structures a system of government, it also mirrors basic values about who shall govern and how.

In addition to structuring, allocating, and limiting power, a constitution can perform an aspirational function. Through its institutional arrangements and commandments about rights, duties, and prohibitions, it can reflect a particular vision of a good and achievable community life. The Preamble to the American constitutional document, for instance, lists the overarching goals of the founding generation:

> to form a more perfect Union, establish Justice, insure domestic Tranquility, provide for the common defense, promote the general Welfare, and secure the blessings of liberty to ourselves and our Posterity. . ..

Thus a constitution can be more than a set of statements about relations to be protected, regulated, or left alone; it is also a continuing statement about society's fundamental purposes. The "only way to make complete sense of the Constitution," Professor Sotirios A. Barber has argued about the United States, "is to understand it in light of what our best thinking shows Americans do and ought to stand for as a people—past, present, and future."[2]

---

1. The term "separation of powers" is misleadingly simple here. See the discussions in Chapters 6 and 9.

2. *On What the Constitution Means* (Baltimore: Johns Hopkins University Press, 1984), p. 9.

1

To perform these functions a constitution must include, though it need not do so in explicit terms, a political theory or a set of political theories. For a constitution's functions concern politics not merely in the earthy sense of shaping "Who gets what, when, and how,"[3] but also in the more abstract sense of expressing a society's general aspirations and more specific goals, and how it may, consistently with those aspirations and goals, utilize its resources and distribute costs, benefits, rewards, and punishments among its members.[4]

The complexities of a constitution's functions make its interpretation an intricate, arduous, and inherently controversial process. It involves much more than translating the general rules of a document so they can be applied to specific problems of public policy. It also requires finding and justifying one's understanding of the fundamental values and aspirations the constitution may reflect, then explaining how they, along with the constitution's more specific rules and procedures, fit concrete problems. As in religious,[5] musical,[6] or literary interpretation,[7] these are often creative acts. These are also typically political acts, and in trying to understand constitutional interpretation one should never permit those stark facts of creativeness and "politicalness" to move far from the center of one's focus.

Moreover, interpretation is more than sophisticated application of rules to facts because it may travel in two directions. A constitution may be quite different after interpretation from what it was before. By explaining what a constitution means in the context of a particular problem, an interpreter can shape what that constitution will mean in the future—what fundamental values it will enshrine, what aspirations it will encourage, and what concrete policies its more particular rules will nourish or stifle.

---

3. Harold Lasswell, *Politics: Who Gets What, When, and How* (New York: McGraw-Hill, 1936).

4. See Walter F. Murphy and Michael N. Danielson, *American Democracy* (10th ed.; New York: Holmes-Meier, 1983), chap. 1.

5. For attempts to link interpretation of religious and legal texts, see, for example: Milner S. Ball, *The Promise of American Law* (Athens, Ga.: University of Georgia Press, 1981); Ronald R. Garet, "Comparative Normative Hermeneutics: Scripture, Literature, Constitution," 58 *So. Cal. L. Rev.* 35 (1985); Sanford V. Levinson, " 'The Constitution' in American Civil Religion," 1979 *Sup. Ct. Rev.* 123; and Michael J. Perry, "The Authority of Text, Tradition, and Reason: A Theory of Constitutional 'Interpretation,' " 58 *So. Cal. L. Rev.* 551 (1985). For a more general analysis linking biblical with other forms of interpretation, see Raymond F. Collins, *Introduction to the New Testament* (New York: Doubleday, 1983).

6. For an effort to draw analogies between muscial and legal interpretation, see Jerome Frank, "Words and Music," 47 *Colum. L. Rev.* 1259 (1947); a slightly revised version appears in his *Courts on Trial* (Princeton, N.J.: Princeton University Press, 1949), chap. 21.

7. There is a growing literature on the similarities and differences between legal and literary interpretation; see, for example, Symposium: Law and Literature, 60 *Tex. L. Rev.* 373 (1982); Interpretation Symposium, 58 *So. Cal. L. Rev.* 1 (1985); John Brigham, *Constitutional Language* (Westport, Con.: Greenwood Press, 1978); Lief H. Carter, *Contemporary Constitutional Lawmaking* (New York: Pergamon Press, 1985), chap. 6; Robert M. Cover, "Nomos and Narrative," 97 *Harv. L. Rev.* 4 (1984); William F. Harris, II, "Bonding Word & Polity: The Logic of American Constitutionalism," 76 *Am. Pol. Sci. Rev.* 34 (1982); James Boyd White, *When Words Lose Their Meaning* (Chicago: University of Chicago Press, 1984); and White, "The Judicial Opinion and the Poem," 82 *Mich. L. Rev.* 1669 (1984).

In the United States, the impact of these and other aspects of constitutional interpretation on collective and individual lives can be profound. Boundaries between the President's power as commander in chief of the armed forces and Congress' power to declare war, or between the power of the state and federal governments to regulate commerce, depend on interpretations of the Constitution no less than do questions about whether a woman has a right to an abortion, a pacifist to a draft exemption, a city dweller to a vote equal in weight to that of a farmer, a person to marry someone of a different race, or any citizen to travel freely across state lines.

For our time, the School Segregation Cases (reprinted below, pp. 768 and 774) provide the most dramatic example of constitutional interpretation's impact on society. In 1954 the justices held, in effect, that governmentally imposed segregation in public schools stigmatized black children and therefore violated the general value of equality that infuses the American Constitution as well as the specific prohibition of the Fourteenth Amendment against a state's denying "to any person within its jurisdiction the equal protection of the laws." Spurred by the Court, a powerful coalition of white liberals and blacks, and the symbol of a martyred President, Congress and a new President agreed in the Civil Rights Act of 1964 that government's requiring or even supporting separation by race was constitutionally anathema. The 1964 Act went even further and outlawed some forms of racial discrimination by private citizens.

The importance of these interpretations of the Constitution was not merely that it eventually allowed blacks to attend "white" schools or sit at lunch counters beside whites. They also revolutionized the United States, changing it from a society in which caste was legally sanctioned to one that is, at least as a matter of law, open. Racial discrimination became morally wrong, a violation of fundamental values of human dignity and equality. And public acknowledgement of the evil of racial discrimination has cast a moral shadow over discrimination based on religion, ethnic origin, sex, and to a lesser extent wealth. The point is not that discrimination has ended. Certainly it has not; but now society stigmatizes the discriminators rather than their victims.

In sum, constitutional interpretation links the political theories and ideals on which the nation is founded—the Constitution's, and thus our own, vision of the good society—to the legitimacy of concrete public policies. And constitutional interpretation performs this function through the medium of a written document that points to, without precisely defining, the content either of underlying political theories and ideals or of particular public policies. The process, moreover, does not occur once and then harden forever on any particular issue. The changing nature of the problems the nation faces demands that interpreters frequently reexamine their own and the country's values as well as its traditions, thus producing a dynamic process that will end only when the Constitution itself ends.

I. WHY INTERPRET THE CONSTITUTION?

Even granting that constitutional interpretation shapes and re-shapes our lives, why should this be so? The American Constitution, after all, is supposedly a model of clear, concise prose. Its sentences are crisp, its words carefully chosen. The skeleton of its "architectural scheme" provides strong support for the muscle of its words. All public officials and many private citizens take an oath to support the Constitution, and the overwhelming majority of them seem to think they do so faithfully.

These claims for clarity and dutiful compliance are not mere pious myth. The document's words are often precise and they have been precisely followed. Free elections take place at regular intervals, every two years for representatives, every four for presidents, every six for senators. No party has ever nominated for the presidency a person who was less than thirty-five or not a native-born citizen. More important, no candidate whom the electorate rejected has ever tried to seize the White House or a seat in Congress.[8] Other constitutional provisions seem equally exact and have been as uniform-ly followed. Congress, for example, has never conferred a title of nobility and in that respect has been true both to the document's terms and to an underlying concern for equal citizenship.

Without a doubt, then, the constitutional document settles many potentially dangerous issues so that they seldom rise to the level of public consciousness. Nevertheless, with this much said and empha-sized, serious problems remain, problems of clarity, of conflict, of omission, and of developments not "foreseen by the most gifted of [the Constitution's] begetters."[9]

A. Clarity

Although many clauses of the constitutional document are models of specificity, some admit of several meanings.[10] James Madison conceded as much in *Federalist* No. 37 and noted that the problem was not unique to politics:

> When the Almighty himself condescends to address mankind in their own language, his meaning, luminous as it must be, is ren-dered dim and doubtful by the cloudy medium through which it is communicated.

---

8. Losers, of course, often contest the validity of particular elections; but, with a few exceptions in state politics, most notably Rhode Island and Georgia, losers do so in the courts or before boards of election commissioners, not in the streets.

9. Missouri v. Holland (1920; reprinted below, p. 132).

10. Even the most seemingly obvious textual clauses may admit of several equally defensible meanings. See, for instance, Mark V. Tushnet's discussion of the constitutional provision specifying 35 as the minimum age for presidents, "A Note on the Revival of Textualism in Constitutional Theory," 58 *So.Cal.L.Rev.* 683, 686–687 (1985).

For human affairs, Madison identified three sources of the difficulty: the complexity of the relations to be regulated, the imperfections of human notions about politics, and the inadequacy of words to convey complex ideas with precision and accuracy.

For the constitutional document of 1787 and its amendments, he might have added several other sources of difficulty. Not only has the English language changed over time,[11] but also the framers: (1) frequently found it necessary to compromise among themselves as well as between what they wanted and what they believed the larger community would accept; (2) were sometimes unsure in their own minds exactly what it was they wished to establish, either because their vision was cloudy or because some of the values they shared were not easily adjusted to each other; and, (3) like the men who sat in the ratifying conventions and their successors who have proposed and approved constitutional amendments—indeed, like all of us—lacked both the time and capacity to arrange their competing values in a systematic hierarchical order.

Either because of these difficulties, or because as wise men they knew that a workable constitution would have to be flexible, or for both reasons, the framers often adopted abstract principles rather than detailed rules. They frequently spoke, as Ronald Dworkin says, in general concepts rather than in specific conceptions. ("Taking Rights Seriously"; reprinted below, p. 168.) The Eighth Amendment, for instance, forbids "cruel and unusual punishments"; it does not offer a word of explanation or even a single example of what might be either "cruel" or "unusual." The Fourth Amendment prohibits "unreasonable searches and seizures," but does not define or illustrate what is reasonable. Moreover, the framers expressly conferred general powers, leaving it to governmental institutions to work out the implications. Thus, the "sweeping clause" of Article I majestically authorizes Congress to "make all laws which shall be necessary and proper for carrying into execution" powers delegated to the federal government.

Determining what these and similar phrases import for specific political problems such as capital punishment, "stop and frisk" laws, or congressional requirements that state governments pay their employees at least minimum wages is not a mechanical task. A great deal of thought, adjustment, compromise, and explanation must come first. Many clauses of the document, Felix Frankfurter wrote when he was still a professor, "leave the individual [interpreter] free, if indeed they do not compel him, to gather meaning not from reading the Constitu-

---

11. For an effort to reconstruct an eighteenth century legal dictionary as *the* tool for constitutional interpretation, see William W. Crosskey, *Politics and the Constitution* (Chicago: University of Chicago Press, 1953), 2 vols. In 1980, after Crosskey's death, Chicago published a third volume, co-authored by William Jeffery, Jr. The first two volumes created a seismic tremor in academic circles. For citations to many of these reactions, see David Fellman, "Constitutional Law in 1952–1953," 48 *Am.Pol.Sci.Rev.* 63, 63n (1954); and Fellman, "Constitutional Law in 1953–1954," 49 *Am.Pol.Sci.Rev.* 63, 64n (1955). Among the reviewers who engaged Crosskey on the accuracy of his definitions was Henry M. Hart, Jr., "Professor Crosskey and Judicial Review," 67 *Harv.L.Rev.* 1456 (1954).

tion, but from reading life."[12]   He might have put it another way:
Not from reading specific clauses of the constitutional document, but
from reading "the Constitution" understood more broadly.

B. Conflict

Some clauses in the document stand in potential conflict with each
other.   In clashes between the states and the national government, the
"sweeping clause" may be pitted against the Tenth Amendment:

> The powers not delegated to the United States by the Constitu-
> tion, nor prohibited by it to the States, are reserved to the States
> respectively, or to the people.

A claim for congressional power under the "sweeping clause" may
also conflict with the Ninth Amendment's protection of individual
rights:

> The enumeration in the Constitution, of certain rights, shall not
> be construed to deny or disparage others retained by the people.

In addition, some parts of the document read as if they take away
what other parts give.   Article I empowers Congress "to raise and
support armies" and so might appear to authorize a draft.   But the
Thirteenth Amendment forbids not only slavery but also "involuntary
servitude, except as punishment for crime whereof the party shall have
been duly convicted."   The *U.S. Code* does not list being a healthy
young male as a crime, and no court has yet "duly convicted" anyone
for enduring such a condition; yet from time to time Congress, at the
urging of the President and with the approval of the Supreme Court,[13]
has forced young men to serve in the armed forces.

The collection of clauses lumped under the term "war powers"
(see Chapter 18) exemplifies how the document lays the groundwork
for further disputes.   Article I allocates to Congress power to declare
war, to make regulations for the armed forces, to appropriate (or not
appropriate) money to carry on the government's operations, and to
organize federal agencies; and to the Senate authority to "advise and
consent" to the President's nominations of executive officials, including those who deal with defense and diplomacy.   On the other hand,
Article II vests "the executive power" in the President and designates
him commander in chief of the armed forces and chief diplomat.   This
blending of authority provides the setting for bitterly self-righteous
disputes between the President and Congress over the constitutional
legitimacy as well as the wisdom of foreign policies.   (See the War
Powers Resolution of 1973, reprinted below, p. 351.)

Reconciling implied powers in the national government either
with a reservoir of retained state authority or with unlisted individual
rights may not be impossible.   After all, the country has been living

---

12. *Law and Politics,* eds. E.F. Pritchard and A. MacLeish (New York: Harcourt, Brace,
1939), p. 30.

13. Selective Draft Law Cases (1918).

with and formulating solutions, however delicate, to those problems for almost 200 years. The same thing could be said about finding allocations of power between Congress and the President that the two institutions—and the nation—can live with, at least for a time. None of these efforts, however, is any more likely to be a mechanical task than is divining the meaning of the document's general concepts.

C. Omissions

The constitutional document, Justice William O. Douglas once observed, "is a compendium, not a code; a declaration of articles of faith, not a compilation of laws." [14]   Although in many ways the document's brevity is a blessing, this brevity means that much is left completely unsaid or only hinted at. Because it is a declaration of faith rather than an elaborate treatise, it is more like "a system of signs" [15] than a detailed map. Nowhere in the document, for instance, is there specific authorization for Congress to create anything like the Federal Reserve System or even a bank to enable it to discharge its fiscal responsibilities, establish a national police force like the Federal Bureau of Investigation, or establish an agency like the Federal Communications Commission to regulate use of airwaves by the mass media. Nor are there references to many kinds of intragovernmental authority, such as executive privilege, senatorial courtesy, or judicial review. There is no mention of some rights that most of us consider basic, such as to a presumption of innocence if accused of crime or to privacy or to marry or to move our place of residence. There is not even a positive declaration of a right to vote, only prohibitions against denials of the ballot because of race, sex, age (for those over 18), or failure to pay a tax.

Obviously, much filling in is essential and, one can argue, the document's general concepts, such as those contained in the sweeping clause and the Ninth Amendment, provide textual licenses for such work. [16]   But, even accepting that claim—and not all constitutional interpreters accept it—does little to lessen the complexity of determining what powers are "necessary and proper," what rights, though unlisted, are fundamental, or settle whose institutional task it is to make such decisions.

D. Unforeseen Developments

Among the more remarkable aspects of the American constitutional document is that so much of its language fits an industrialized world of television, microchips, antibiotics, organ transplants, supersonic transports, and space exploration, as closely as it did the relatively primitive world of the eighteenth century. The framers could not

---

14. *We, the Judges* (New York: Doubleday, 1956), p. 429.

15. Harris, supra note 7.

16. But, again, the limitations of the plain words are not always plain. See Perry, supra note 5; Tushnet, supra note 10; and Sanford V. Levinson, "On Interpretation: The Adultery Clause of the Ten Commandments," 58 *So.Cal.L.Rev.* 719 (1985).

foresee a polyglot society like ours, which would bring people of all races and religions of the world together—and not to work the land, but to live in sprawling metropolises, earn wages, luxuriate in dividends from multinational corporations, or exist off welfare. Nor did the people of 1787 imagine a culture that would provide twelve or more years of free public schooling, the uplifting effects of television, the safety net of innoculations, the availability of clinics for abortion, or the convenience of no-fault divorce.

But at a higher level of abstraction, the framers did foresee as constants in a changing universe struggles for money and power, peace, and justice among fallible and sinful human beings. And they built to cope with the perennial problems of people who are, as Hamilton asserted in *Federalist* No. 6, "ambitious, vindictive, and rapacious," and yet, as he claimed in *Federalist* No. 1, also open to "philanthropy and patriotism."

Despite the framers' collective genius for political engineering, we sometimes encounter grave difficulties in inferring from their specific conceptions and even general concepts solutions to our problems. How does the existence of ICBMs affect Congress' power to declare war? Electronic surveillance the Fourth Amendment's protections against "unreasonable searches and seizures"? Or computers and telecommunications the scope of what is protected against searches and seizures? Does the complexity of modern social and economic problems require Congress to delegate some of its power to expert but unelected officials who have the technical knowledge necessary for intelligent decision making? If so, can Congress exercise a "legislative veto" over their actions lest experts negate public policy made by elected officials?

One may answer these and similar problems, but those answers require thought, research, and analysis; and the resulting "interpretation" might well be closer to adaptation. Moreover, any answer to these sorts of questions will be controversial in the sense that, even after careful study, reasonable people can reasonably disagree. But any procedure less sophisticated is likely to turn the Constitution into a suicide pact or a "splendid bauble."

E. Reaffirmation

These are all good and important reasons for constitutional interpretation. There is, however, another that may be primary: to reaffirm our commitment to the Constitution. That the Constitution constitutes us as a people is a common claim. It is also easy to respond that "the Constitution constituted *them,* the people of 1787–88, as a people, not us, the 'we, the people' of today. We cannot be ruled by the dead." The problem is that of consent. How do we agree to live under this system and owe allegiance to it and its Constitution?

Some answers are obvious. First, we do not choose to leave the country, though we are all, if we are not in jail or accused of crime, legally free to do so. Second, at some time in our lives, most us take oaths to support and defend the Constitution—when we enter the armed forces, serve as jurors or as one of millions of minor and not so minor governmental officials, party officers, or even play some professional roles in private life. Third, through the electoral processes we may take part in amending the Constitution by choosing officials who will—or will not—change it.

There is yet another way of affirming our commitment to the Constitution: by interpreting it, by discovering, translating, justifying, and applying its values and principles to our public problems. Only a few of us perform those acts directly, but all of us can perform them indirectly by communicating with public officials and holding them or their superiors responsible at elections for their interpretations, or even by writing books or articles on the subject.

II. THE ENTERPRISE CALLED CONSTITUTIONAL INTERPRETATION

Because constitutional interpretation has enormous consequences for our lives and because it is apt to be a creative rather than a mechanical act, the next question becomes: What is that enterprise all about? It is a difficult and complex process, forming a link, at one extreme, between the general principles of political theory that underlie the larger political culture as well as the constitutional document and, at the other, the day-to-day public policies that governmental agencies try to carry out.

We think the most effective, though surely not the quickest, way to explain constitutional interpretation is to invite readers to share in that process by confronting the central problems with which constitutional interpreters grapple. Accordingly, we have structured this book around three interrelated interrogatives that are fundamental to all constitutional interpretation:

1. WHAT is the Constitution that is to be interpreted?
2. WHO are the Constitution's authoritative interpreters?
3. HOW can/should/do those interpreters accomplish their tasks?

A. WHAT is the Constitution?

This question is more tangled than it may at first seem. One set of concerns involves the nature of the Constitution: Is it a compact among sovereign states or among a larger community of private citizens who style themselves "the people of the United States"? Or is it merely a hortatory resolution that we hope to follow? Or is it a solemn charter that constitutes us as a people, states our purposes and values, distributes powers, rights, and duties to achieve those goals, and also binds us together with the strongest of moral and legal chains?

For most Americans approaching the end of the twentieth century, the answers may seem obvious. We should not forget, however, that our ancestors fought a bloody civil war over whether the Constitution was a treaty among states or a solemn charter of a people. We should also be aware that, as a practical matter, the issue of the Constitution's binding power will always be with us. "What's the Constitution between friends?" is sometimes more than a bad joke. Furthermore, the degree to which the people of the United States form a "community" for any purpose other than income taxes and vulnerability to Hydrogen bombs remains an open question.

A second concern involves what the term "the Constitution" includes. So far we have not challenged identifying "the Constitution" as the document of 1787 and its formal amendments. But that identification is a debatable assumption, not a self-evident fact. We have already mentioned significant gaps in the document, some of which interpreters have filled in. If the document of 1787 is incomplete, one must ask whether other documents—the Declaration of Independence, for example—might have constitutional status. So, too, one cannot exclude *a priori* the possibility that certain aspects of political theory—of constitutionalism or representative democracy, for instance—might be parts of a larger "constitution," or that, over the decades, some practices like judicial review or executive privilege might have taken on a constitutional status, whether or not sanctioned by the document.

Closely related is a third query: Is "the Constitution" unchanging in its meaning except insofar as it is formally amended? If the Constitution is not permanent in meaning, what does an oath to support it imply? If a society's credo of fundamental values and aspirations fluctuates, does it form a community or simply a collection of individuals bound together by force and fear? On the other hand, if the Constitution's meaning were frozen in time, could it or the nation survive? Must a "constitution intended to endure for ages to come," as John Marshall claimed, be "adapted to the various *crises* of human affairs"? If so, WHO adapts it and HOW?

Problems about what the Constitution includes and how it may be legitimately changed are difficult, and we do not mean to offer solutions so much as to raise questions that thoughtful constitutional interpretation must address. The cases and materials in Part II of this book confront these problems.

B. WHO Shall Interpret?

"[U]nder the Constitution," Justice William H. Rehnquist has remarked, "the first question to be answered is not whose plan is best, but in what branch of the Government is lodged the authority initially to devise the plan." [17] Most Americans who have taken high school courses in civics or college courses in American government are likely to respond that, regardless of who has initial authority, the Supreme Court has the final word on constitutional interpretation. And,

----

17. Bell v. Wolfish (1979).

without doubt, in practice the Court is the most visible interpreter. Yet every public official, state or federal, takes an oath to support the Constitution; none, as President Andrew Jackson once observed (see below, p. 225), takes an oath to support the Supreme Court's interpretations of the Constitution. And the document itself is wonderously taciturn about who its authoritative interpreters are to be. Appeals to a long established tradition of judicial review, of an authority in courts to invalidate executive and legislative actions that judges believe violate the Constitution's terms, are themselves appeals to something outside the document.

At times, presidents, senators, representatives, and state officials have asserted interpretive authority at least equal if not superior to that of judges. Thomas Jefferson, for example, formulated a coherent theory of American politics around a claim of coordinate authority. (See his arguments reprinted below, pp. 190 and 218.) And, the Supreme Court itself has usually been reluctant to make explicit claims to bind the President and Congress by its interpretations. The justices, however, have flatly insisted on their authority to oblige state officials and have implied more authority over other branches of the federal government than they have openly proclaimed.

Questions of WHO shall interpret have had and will continue to have obvious and critical implications for the country. Visions of the Constitution vary from time to time, and at the same time from judge to judge, from legislator to legislator, and presidential adviser to presidential adviser. And differences in institutional competence and perspective may make important differences in the values various branches of government accept as fundamental.

Presidents of the Virginia dynasty of Jefferson, James Monroe, and even Madison were not nearly so nationalistic as was the Supreme Court under John Marshall. For a decade after the Civil War, Congress was far more concerned to protect the rights of blacks than was the Court, though both soon became almost equally indifferent. The Court from the turn of the century until 1937 was usually uncaring about the effects of industrialization on workers, while Congress and state legislators showed a real measure of sympathy if not full understanding. The Court's primary goal was to safeguard what it conceived to be the fundamental right of "freedom of contract," which the justices found in the Fifth and Fourteenth amendments' protection of "liberty"; legislators were more worried about sweatshops, child labor, and the growing voting power of workers. In 1937 the justices changed their minds after a battle with Franklin D. Roosevelt and his New Deal.

Since 1937 and especially under Earl Warren (1953–1969), the Supreme Court has been untroubled by tight governmental regulation of contract and property, but has been far more distressed than Congress about impediments to free speech, violations of the guarantees of the Bill of Rights to the criminally accused, and for a time about problems of racial equality.

Part III addresses the question of WHO shall interpret.   An adequate theory of constitutional interpretation must propose an answer to this problem and do so consistently with solutions to other basic interrogatives.

C. HOW to Interpret?

Any serious attempt to answer the question of HOW will be complex.   The very necessity of interpretation implies that there is a substantive problem that the plain words of the document do not solve.   At very least—and there may be a great deal more—those plain words need definitions.   WHO defines those words and determines WHAT the Constitution includes can make a critical difference, just as can HOW an interpreter goes about the basic task of milking meaning from, or perhaps even pumping meaning into, "the Constitution."

Part IV, by far the largest share of this book, takes up the HOW of interpretation.   It opens in Chapter 8 with a general essay discussing some of the basic *approaches, modes,* and *techniques* of interpretation. Subsequent sets of chapters analyze such broad interpretative *modes* to determine the implications of the Constitution's structure—its basic arrangement of offices and institutions—or the requirements of fundamental rights.

Each of these chapters focuses on specific sets of substantive problems.   When we discuss structural analysis, for instance, one chapter deals with the sharing of power among the branches of the federal government, another with sharing of power between state and nation; in discussing the maintenance of constitutional democracy one set of chapters deals with problems of free speech and press, and the rights to vote, to participate in political campaigns, and to influence public officials.   Another set attacks problems of equality; yet another focuses on identifying and safeguarding fundamental substantive rights such as those to privacy and bodily integrity.   Thus the reader should emerge from those chapters knowing something substantive about the Supreme Court's rulings in constitutional law.

Even more, however, we hope the reader will learn a great deal about the nature of the enterprise of constitutional interpretation and understand not merely what doctrines it has produced, but also how the process operates and what are its relations to political theory, to a long history, and to current public policy.   In sum, we hope the reader will appreciate more than the "output" of constitutional interpretation and come to understand how it helps discover, articulate, and translate abstract principles into viable public policy.

III. CONSTITUTIONAL LITERACY

Whatever their intellectual objectives and however they approach the subject, students of constitutional interpretation must acquire a new form of literacy.   They must learn to "read" the Constitution, to interpret the very special form of language of the constitutional document as well as the theories, practices, traditions, values, and glosses that have developed in the name of the Constitution's authority.   Insofar as we explore the wider field of constitutional interpretation, we are attempting to interpret the American constitutional order. In so doing we shall be imposing a form on constitutional interpretation.   And to impose a form on that enterprise it is necessary to show that there is a *structure* (to use what will become a familiar metaphor) both to that intellectual process (although judges seldom show any more awareness of it than do legislative or executive officials) and to the political system itself.   All of these activities are highly controversial, and we urge readers to be aware of the controversy and to prepare to challenge what seems obvious.

Most educated people can rather easily understand presidential addresses and legislative debates.   Elected officials may use more than a fair share of blather and blarney and be adept at evasion, but by and large they employ forms of discourse with which we are familiar. Most of us can, if we are willing to take the time, sort out spurious from valid arguments and reach our own conclusions.   But reading judicial opinions and other forms of systematic constitutional argument poses more difficult problems.   Judges use a style as well as a format that is quite different from ordinary discourse.   And skill in reading these opinions is indispensable, if readers are to go beyond simply *covering* the material.   The sooner readers achieve this facility, the sooner they will be able to argue cogently about the issues raised by the cases and employ the methods of interpretation in their own treatment of constitutional problems.

A. Purposes in Reading Judicial Opinions

Judicial opinions share at least one element with presidential addresses and legislative speeches: none of them is basically an explanation of how the author arrived at a decision, though it may purport to be.   Rather, each is a reasoned justification for a decision.

How we read something is strongly dependent on the purposes for which we read it.   Many instructors in this field have found that, in the beginning, students who have read—even conscientiously studied—the material feel at a loss when asked to analyze cases.   If one is not looking for something, he or she is not apt to find it.   This section tries to help identify what readers should be looking for.

We should first consider the various purposes one might have in reading a constitutional case.   The possibilities include:

1. LEGAL SUBSTANCE. What is the *holding* of the judges in this case?   How does it fit into or change legal doctrine on this subject matter, such as free speech or federalism?   Here one is concerned with the principles or rules that the case stands for.   This preoccupation is the usual focus of courses in constitutional *law*.

2.   METHOD.   What intellectual processes does this case
illustrate? The central concerns here are with the nature, intellectual power, or persuasiveness of the justification(s) for an interpretation. The reader looks for *models of argument,* with close attention to
how opinion writers move from step to step in reaching their
conclusions. On what points does their logic turn? Where do they
get the authoritative material they use? What factors do they
incorporate in their reasoning to ground the next stage of argument,
and how do they consolidate all of their logical maneuverings to
support their conclusions? Where do they leave gaps?

3.   HISTORY.   One might see judicial opinions as "period
pieces"—evidence of values long cherished, or long since tarnished
or repudiated, or stepping stones toward currently accepted political
goals. Here one might ask how constitutional interpretation affects
and is affected by the course of history. To accomplish these aims,
it is necessary to know something of the general context of a
constitutional problem.

4.   STRATEGY.   Judicial opinions may shape public policy.
As do most public officials and private citizens, judges usually want
to convince others. To be persuasive may require cautious compromise as well as learning and eloquence. Analysis may reveal efforts
to win the votes of other justices or even to convince other public
officials and groups of citizens outside the Court. Again like a
presidential or legislative speech, a judicial opinion may also evade
some issues. The opinion writer may not have been able to muster
a majority of the Court on the point, or the justices may have
believed that enough support from those who must live with and
enforce the decision would not be forthcoming. Thus one might
look at judicial opinions as sharing with other forms of political
rhetoric the goal of welding coalitions and unifying majorities
within and outside an institution.[18]

5.   DEBATE ON INSTITUTIONAL ROLES.   Almost every
piece of constitutional interpretation must make peace with concepts
of institutional roles proper to the American political system.
Therefore much of constitutional law addresses this problem either
directly or indirectly. To do so usually requires interpreters to
confront important questions of political theory. Not only do they
involve critical substantive questions such as equality and dignity,
but they also deal with allocative questions: Who, for instance, shall
make decisions about the existence and/or extent of a constitutional
right to an abortion, public officials' protection against libel and
slander, the power of communities to ban books, movies, or stage
shows that feature explicit sexual activity? Citizens? State legislators? Congress? Federal judges?

6.   POLITICAL IMPACT.   This aspect of constitutional interpretation is the functional equivalent of the bottom line in business.
Any responsible interpreter must always worry about the practical
implications, long and short range, for the nation and its people.
Neither a conscientious official nor a reflective citizen can be
indifferent to the possible effects of an interpretation. We lack

---

18.   See Walter F. Murphy, *Elements of Judicial Strategy* (Chicago: University of Chicago Press,
1964).

space fully to explore such issues;[19] but the reader might gain perspective by looking at judicial opinions as parables, moral fables, efforts to reshape the polity by appeals to abstract principles that at first glance seem to have little relation to the grubby world of day-to-day politics. (One must also realize that reactions to a particular interpretation may cut its life short.)

In analyzing the materials in this book, readers should be attentive to these concerns. They interact with one another to such an extent that there is little hope of fully understanding what is going on without considering all of them. Many of them also represent specific aspects of the three interrogatives around which this book is organized. But we need to move beyond these specific concerns, for our objective is to achieve a comprehensive understanding of the enterprise of constitutional interpretation. We must focus on these interrogatives because interpreters must respond to them, either consciously or unconsciously. These interrogatives are more abstract than the specific concerns we just listed; they provide us with a model of constitutional interpretation at a level that allows us to be more comprehending and our criticisms to be more trenchant.

For interpretation in a constitutional scheme of government does not confer a license to impose one's personal preferences about what is politically good. Rather, it imposes rigorous demands that we understand and articulate the nature of the political system and its constitution and craft an appropriate jurisprudence. The three interrogatives of WHAT, WHO, and HOW suggest an order for constitutional interpretation that allows it to be conducted on a principled and publicly defensible basis. They make constitutional decision making more open to rational debate and help reveal the stakes involved.

These interrogatives connect broad theories of the nature of the American constitutional order to specific constitutional controversies. The answer to any particular interrogative may dispose of a problem; more likely a combination of answers may be necessary. Thus many pieces of constitutional interpretation will orchestrate answers to several interrogatives. Organizing answers to all three forms the basis of a systematic jurisprudence.

Thus students should be attentive to the ways in which constitutional decision makers are answering—whether they realize it or not—these interrogatives. Students should also ponder the effects these answers and the ways in which they are orchestrated have not only for settling the controversy at hand but also for visualizing what the society should become.

To organize this casebook we have classified each entry, whether case, statute, debate, or executive pronouncement, under a particular interrogative of WHAT, WHO, or HOW; but, as we have suggested,

---

19. For studies of the impact of judicial decisions, see espec. Charles A. Johnson and Bradley C. Cannon, *Judicial Policies: Implementation and Impact* (Washington, D.C.: Congressional Quarterly Press, 1984); and the discussion and bibliography in Walter F. Murphy and C. Herman Pritchett, *Courts, Judges, & Politics* (4th ed.; New York: Random House, 1986), chap. 8.

each item will usually address more than one of those interrogatives. Constitutional interpretation is characterized by complexity not simplicity, by interrelationships not isolation. And it will soon be apparent that dissenting and concurring opinions may be at least as enlightening as majority opinions; and that outside protests against what the Court has said, such as those by Thomas Jefferson or John C. Calhoun (reprinted below, p. 1181 and p. 272), offer valuable, and arguably authoritative, insights into constitutional interpretation.

B. Briefing a Case

One must keep in mind that constitutional adjudication is only a subset of constitutional interpretation. Still, for a bevy of historical reasons, judicial opinions form the principal lode for systematic study of the larger enterprise. It helps to keep in mind that judges write opinions—just as elected officials make speeches—to convince an audience that they have not made a mistake in this instance. Unlike a literary text, which describes an event or tells a story, an opinion justifies a result, the application of political power to resolve a controversy.

To understand and evaluate a justification, one must take the opinion apart and then put it back together again. To accomplish these goals, most students have found it useful to write out a "brief" of each case, a summary outline of a page or two to provide a framework for analysis and to refresh memories at the end of the term. Standards instructions include the following format:

(1) The facts (the context). What is the case all about? What governmental policy has conflicted with what asserted individual right, or what pair of policies have clashed with each other, or what pair of rights are in opposition? What are the terms of the statutes, executive orders, or constitutional clauses involved? What is/are the shape(s) of the alleged right(s)?

(2) The fundamental question or questions the case presents. What is the controversy really all about? Is more involved than a state's having convicted a doctor for giving advice on contraception?

(3) The holding of the case—i.e., the answer(s) to the constitutional question(s) posed by the controversy. If one phrases (2) properly, the answer(s) will be simply "yes" or "no."

(4) A summary of the reasoning behind the decision. How does the opinion writer get from the question(s) to the answer(s)?

(5) An analysis of dissenting and concurring opinions, much like those in (4). If one's interest is primarily in doctrine, then this part can be very short. But if one's interest is in the enterprise of constitutional interpretation, separate opinions may be even more valuable than those of the majority, for, when speaking only for him- or herself, a judge can often be more candid than when he or she has to accommodate the views of four or more colleagues.

(6) The general constitutional principle(s) for which the case stands, i.e., the substantive doctrine the case produced.

(7) The answers that various opinions give or imply to any (or all) of the three central interrogatives as well as the ways in which these opinions orchestrate these answers.

(8) Some analysis (or informed speculation) of what the decision's immediate effects on public policy are likely to be; and how the several opinions illuminate the nature of the American polity.

In their initial efforts at reading cases, students often do not get close enough to the text of the opinion in dissecting its argument, nor do they move far enough away from it in their understanding of what it represents for constitutional interpretation. In reading a case, it is important to conduct both a close analysis that is attentive to details of various arguments as well as a more abstract assessment that gets away from a purely internal perspective. After careful examination of the words and organization of the opinions, the analyst should ask: "What else is going on here?" It is, therefore, necessary when reading to move back and forth in distance from the opinion itself. In the beginning, this sort of work may well seem extraordinarily difficult. Within a few weeks, it will become easier; soon it will become a natural and valuable part of one's intellectual style.

C. Problems of Omnicompetence

People beginning constitutional interpretation often feel overwhelmed. Not only do judges use jargon, they often simultaneously address several questions, each of them highly technical. Furthermore, a style of writing that requires appending references to earlier decisions every few lines often seems to the novice to clutter rather than clarify reasoning—though, as shorthand encapsulations of earlier lines of reasoning, these citations are frequently a boon to more practiced readers.

These are facts of life that we are powerless to change. The situation, however, is far from hopeless. As editors, we have tried to help by excluding much discussion from the opinions, by providing introductory essays at the beginning of each Chapter and Part of the book, and by appending headnotes and hindnotes to cases. Some of these notes are explanatory, some interrogatory. The first are designed to soothe by providing additional information, the second to irritate by goading readers toward deeper understanding.

Because problems of constitutional interpretation, like all important problems of life, are interrelated, because it often seems that one must understand everything at once, we have liberally, even lavishly, cross referenced material. The phrase "reprinted above, p. ——" will become familiar. Its purpose is to allow readers immediately to turn to matter that is relevant to what they are now analyzing.

Nevertheless, no editorial effort, however heroic, can change the hard fact that constitutional interpretation is intellectually demanding. It requires careful reading and rereading, close analysis, concentrated thought, and a willingness to imagine other worlds. For those willing to make the effort, few enterprises are more challenging, important, or rewarding.

APPENDIX:

Deciphering the Numbers

The first thing a reader notices about a case is, of course, its title, indicating who is taking legal action against whom. Somebody against (v.) somebody else is the typical form, though very famous cases may acquire a descriptive title—Brown v. Board of Education is often referred to as the School Segregation Cases.

The next and possibly confusing item that one notices about a case is a string of numbers and abbreviations following the title. These are the "citations," references to where the case can be found in its original form. The Government Printing Office publishes the official reports of opinions by the Supreme Court. These are called the *United States Reports* and are cited as U.S. The number that precedes U.S. is the volume and the number that follows is the page at which the case begins in that volume. The date in parentheses is the year in which the Court announced its decision. Thus the citation to the School Segregation Cases, Brown v. Board of Education, is 347 U.S. 483 (1954), meaning that the cases can be found in volume 347 of the *United States Reports*, beginning at p. 483, and that the decisions were announced in 1954.

Several commercial publishers also print the Supreme Court's opinions. The *United States Law Week*, distributed by the Bureau of National Affairs, Washington, D.C., puts out a loose leaf copy within a week or ten days of the decision, as does the Commerce Clearing House. Slower but more widely used are volumes compiled by the West Publishing Co. of St. Paul, Minn., and the Lawyers Cooperative Publishing Co. of Rochester, N.Y. West's volumes are called the *Supreme Court Reporter* and are abbreviated as S.Ct. *Brown*'s citation is 74 S.Ct. 686, meaning that it appears in volume 74 of the *Supreme Court Reporter*, beginning at p. 686. The Lawyers Cooperative version is called the *Lawyers' Edition* and is cited as L.Ed. *Brown*'s citation is 98 L.Ed. 873, meaning it appears in volume 98, beginning at p. 873. (After volume 100 came out, the *Lawyers' Edition* went into a second series, so that cases decided after November, 1956 appear in volumes with a "2d"; for example, 6 L.Ed.2d means that the case appears in the sixth volume of the second series of the *Lawyers' Edition*.)

Both West and the Lawyers Cooperative put additional material into their volumes. The latter, for example, reprints precis of the briefs for each side and for any amici curiae (friends of the court whom the justices allow to intervene) in each case and often includes "annotations," that is, summaries and analyses of earlier rulings on the same point and perhaps discussions of where the Court seems to be heading. Both publishers have copious references to multi-volume encyclopedias they publish that collate summaries of the Court's opinions on particular points of law.

West also selects for publication some opinions of federal district courts and courts of appeal. The first are now contained in either the *Federal Supplement* (cited as F.Supp.) or the *Federal Rules Decisions* (cited as F.R.D.) and the latter in the *Federal Reporter,* now in its second series, cited as F.2d. The first series is cited as Fed. Early decisions of lower federal courts are collected in a set of volumes called Federal Cases, cited as Fed. Cases. Most states publish some of the rulings by their own tribunals, and West puts out a series of regional reporters that reprint most of the opinions by the highest courts in states in the region and occasionally a lower court ruling.

Before 1816, we have unofficial and possibly incomplete reports of the U.S. Supreme Court's opinions, first under the name of A.J. Dallas (cited as Dall.) then William Cranch (cited as Cr.). In 1816 Congress created the office of Reporter for the Court; [20] and from then until 1875, opinions were published under his name:

Dates	Reporter	Citation
1816–1827	Wheaton	Wh.
1828–1843	Peters	Pet.
1843–1860	Howard	How.
1861–1862	Black	Bl.
1863–1874	Wallace	Wall.

Thus the citation to Marbury v. Madison is 1 Cr. 137 (1803), meaning it appears in the first volume of Cranch's Reports, beginning at p. 137. (Early on, there might be several years' opinions in one volume.) Beginning in 1875, the Court's reporter began to use the current system, titling the volumes *United States Reports.*

SELECTED BIBLIOGRAPHY

Anastaplo, George. *The Constitutionalist* (Dallas: Southern Methodist University Press, 1971).

Barber, Sotirios A. *On What the Constitution Means* (Baltimore: Johns Hopkins University Press, 1984).

Ball, Milner S. *The Promise of American Law* (Athens, Ga.: University of Georgia Press, 1981).

Brest, Paul. "The Fundamental Rights Controversy," 90 *Yale L.J.* 1063 (1981).

Brigham, John. *Constitutional Language* (Westport, Conn.: Greenwood Press, 1978).

Carter, Lief H. *Contemporary Constitutional Lawmaking* (New York: Pergamon Press, 1985).

Choper, Jesse H. *Judicial Review and the National Political Process* (Chicago: University of Chicago Press, 1980).

Corwin, Edward S. *Liberty Against Government* (Baton Rouge, La.: Louisiana State University Press, 1948). (See also the entries under Loss and Mason and Garvey.)

---

20. See Charles Warren, *The Supreme Court in United States History* (Rev. ed.; Boston: Little, Brown, 1926), I, 454–455.

Dworkin, Ronald M. *Taking Rights Seriously* (Cambridge, Mass.: Harvard University Press, 1977).

————. *A Matter of Principle* (Cambridge, Mass.: Harvard University Press, 1985).

Eidelberg, Paul. *The Philosophy of the American Constitution* (New York: The Free Press, 1968).

Ely, John Hart. *Democracy and Distrust* (Cambridge: Harvard University Press, 1980).

Flathman, Richard. *The Practice of Rights* (Cambridge: Cambridge University Press, 1976).

Fleming, James E. "A Critique of John Hart Ely's Quest for the Ultimate Constitutional Interpretivism of Representative Democracy," 80 *Mich.L.Rev.* 634 (1982).

Grey, Thomas. "Do We Have an Unwritten Constitution?" 27 *Stan. L.Rev.* 703 (1975).

Harris, William F., II. "Bonding Word & Polity: The Logic of American Constitutionalism," 76 *Am.Pol.Sci.Rev.* 34 (1982).

Interpretation Symposium. 58 *So.Cal.L.Rev.* 1 (1985).

Loss, Richard. *Corwin on the Constitution* (Ithaca, N.Y.: Cornell University Press, 1981).

Mason, Alpheus Thomas. *The Supreme Court: Palladium of Freedom* (Ann Arbor, Mich.: University of Michigan Press, 1962).

———— and Gerald Garvey, eds. *American Constitutional History: Essays by Edward S. Corwin* (New York: Harper & Row, 1964).

Murphy, Walter F. "The Art of Constitutional Interpretation," in M. Judd Harmon, ed., *Essays on the Constitution of the United States* (Port Washington, N.Y.: Kennikat Press, 1978).

————. "Constitutional Interpretation: The Art of the Historian, Magician, or Statesman?" 87 *Yale L.J.* 1752 (1978).

————. "Constitutional Interpretation: Text, Values, and Processes," 9 *Revs. in Am. Hist.* 7 (1981).

———— and Joseph Tanenhaus. *Comparative Constitutional Law* (New York: St. Martin's, 1977).

Perry, Michael J. *The Constitution, the Courts and Human Rights* (New Haven, Conn.: Yale University Press, 1982).

Powell, Thomas Reed. "The Logic and Rhetoric of Constitutional Law," 15 *Jo. of Phil., Psych., and Sc'fc Method* 654 (1918); reprinted in Robert G. McCloskey, ed., *Essays in American Constitutional Law* (New York: Knopf, 1957).

————. *Vagaries and Varieties in Constitutional Interpretation* (New York: Columbia University Press, 1956).

Pritchett, C. Herman. *Constitutional Law of the Federal System* (Englewood Cliffs, N.J.: Prentice-Hall, 1984).

————. *Constitutional Civil Liberties* (Englewood Cliffs, N.J.: Prentice-Hall, 1984).

Tribe, Laurence H. *American Constitutional Law* (Mineola, N.Y.: Foundation Press, 1978).

————. *Constitutional Choices* (Cambridge, Mass.: Harvard University Press, 1985).

I

The Context of Constitutional Interpretation

At the end of the great battle over constitutional interpretation between the Supreme Court and President Franklin D. Roosevelt, Max Lerner quipped that "judicial decisions are not babies brought by judicial storks, but are born out of the travail of economic circumstance." [1] He might have added that all constitutional interpretation is born out of travail, not merely economic but also political. It is also the product of the intellectual travail of trying to solve an immediate problem of public policy while remaining true to overarching principles—or perhaps even while creating new general principles.

How interpreters face these sorts of problems depends on many factors. This Part looks first, in Chapter 2, at the theoretical context of constitutional interpretation. Here we examine the sometimes reinforcing, sometimes competing, and sometimes conflicting theories of democracy and constitutionalism that underpin the American political system. Their implications for constitutional interpretation are individually important; how an interpreter combines their elements or chooses between them may be profoundly significant.

Chapter 3 analyzes the institutional setting in which governmental agencies interact. It provides a brief overview of the structure of the political system and looks at the implications for constitutional interpretation of relations between the federal and state governments and, at the national level, among the presidency, Congress, and the judiciary. More particularly, it focuses on decision making and persuasion within the Supreme Court.

These two chapters provide a basis for understanding much of the controversy about constitutional interpretation that the rest of the book develops. They also help further understanding of the nature of the solutions interpreters offer and provide a partial explanation of why so many of those solutions seem less than logically complete.

---

1. *Ideas for the Ice Age* (New York: Viking, 1941), p. 259.

2

The Theoretical Context of Constitutional Interpretation

The governmental system of the United States does not fit a model of representative democracy in which elected officials rule in the name of the people. The United States—like Australia, Canada, Japan, and most nations of western Europe—is a political hybrid of constitutionalism and democracy, that is, a constitutional democracy. Its formal political structures and the political theories on which they are based combine rule by popularly chosen representatives with government limited by institutional checks on their power.

The two kinds of political theory on which the American system rests, democracy and constitutionalism, coexist, sometimes in harmony, often in competition, and occasionally in conflict. The notion that the people should govern through those whom they elect sometimes blends lumpily with the notion that there are critical limitations on both what government—however democratically chosen—may validly do and on how it may carry out its legitimate powers.

I. COMPETING POLITICAL THEORIES

A. Representative Democracy

Although the social and economic prerequisites for a successful representative democracy are complex and the actual functioning of a democratic system wonderfully elaborate, only five formal, institutional conditions need obtain: (1) Popular election for limited terms of most of the important policy makers to governmental institutions that allow the majority's representatives to govern in fact and not merely in name; (2) Universal adult suffrage with only minimal restrictions to protect against fraud; (3) Electoral districts of approximately equal population that are not skewed to give disproportionate advantage to particular areas or interests; (4) Free entry of citizens to candidacy for elective office, again with only minimal restrictions to prevent overcrowding the ballot with frivolous candidates; (5) and Freedom of political communication—written and oral—so that private citizens, public officials, and candidates can be as informed as they care to be about politics, can discuss issues and personalities with each other, and can try to persuade each other.

23

These five conditions, if operative, create a free market place of political ideas and encourage civic participation. As Justice Hugo L. Black said for the Supreme Court in 1964:

> No right is more precious in a free country than that of having a voice in the election of those who make the laws under which, as good citizens, we must live. Other rights, even the most basic, are illusory if the right to vote is undermined.[1]

But even more, these conditions allow citizens to act together to form groups to express shared economic and social interests and so increase their political influence. As Alexis de Tocqueville noted in 1835: "The most natural privilege of man, next to the right of acting for himself, is that of combining his exertions with those of his fellow creatures and of acting in common with them."[2] Further, the Court held in 1958, "freedom to engage in association for the advancement of beliefs and ideas is an inseparable aspect of the 'liberty' assured by the Due Process Clause of the Fourteenth Amendment";[3] as such, it is protected against state as well as federal infringement.

Most modern democratic theorists stress the value of political participation and the centrality of the political processes to community life—in sum, the right to participate politically is a, if not the, fundamental right. Open discussion, the ability to associate with others, and the right to vote mean that, for democratic theorists, the ballot box supplies legitimacy to decisions of public officials. Judge Hans Linde of the Oregon Supreme Court has extolled

> the primacy of process over product in a free society, the knowledge that no ends can be better than the means of their achievement. "The highest morality is almost always the morality of process," Professor [Alexander] Bickel wrote . . . . If this republic is remembered in the distant history of law, it is likely to be for its enduring adherence to legitimate institutions and processes, not for its perfection of unique principles of justice and certainly not for the rationality of its laws.[4]

For most democratic theorists, what obliges citizens to obey "the law" is the fact that officials chosen under an open system operating under the five rules made the decisions. Democratic theorists tend toward legal positivism, the view that law has no necessary connection with principles of morality or justice, but is grounded in specific enactments of the "sovereign" or its representatives. And for democratic theorists, the people are sovereign and therefore their representatives partake of that sovereign legitimacy.

There is no assumption here that individuals or the citizenry as a whole will never make mistakes or that all people have equal capaci-

---

1. Wesberry v. Sanders (1964).

2. *Democracy in America,* Philips Bradley, ed. (New York: Vintage Books, 1959), I, 203.

3. NAACP v. Alabama (1958).

4. "Due Process of Lawmaking," 55 *Neb.L.Rev.* 197, 255 (1976).

ties to understand and choose among the options open to them. "The claim is most persuasively put," Michael Walzer says, "not in terms of what the people know, but in terms of who they are. They are the subjects of the law, and if the law is to bind them as free men and women, they must also be its makers." [5]

The basic assumption, therefore, need only be that all sane adults can cope with political problems to the extent of being able to recognize their own self interests, join with others who share those interests, and choose among candidates. Frequently, however, one also hears echoes of Aristotle's argument that the people's collective wisdom and morality may exceed that of any individual or small group of individuals. It is, of course, such a belief, coupled with an understanding of the complexity of political issues, that provides the main theoretical justification for equal public education in a representative democracy.[6] "At its core," Professor Joseph Tussman has written about democratic theory,

> is the significance it gives to universal (normal adult) participation in the political process, and the faith that men can, if encouraged and given the opportunity, develop the arts, the skills and habits necessary for a life of responsible deliberation and decision making. Democracy seeks to universalize the parliamentary state of mind.[7]

The chief check that most democratic theory posits against tyranny is that the people will not tyrannize themselves. Therefore they will vote out of office officials who try to enact oppressive measures. The "mass of citizens," Jefferson once claimed, is "the safest depository for their own rights." [8] Foreknowledge of the likelihood of defeat for reelection will keep most officials from infringing civil rights.

Many theorists find an effective second check in what they perceive to be the way in which democratic politics operates. Echoing Madison in *Federalist* No. 10, they argue that, in a large and diverse nation, the population will seldom be divided between those who fervently favor a particular policy and those who adamantly oppose it. Rather, more typically, coalitions of minority groups form and reform as different issues arise. On a particular matter, some group or groups care very deeply, while others are more or less indifferent but are willing to trade their support in exchange for backing on different issues that they deem critical.

These theorists stress the claim that political cleavages are seldom cumulative.[9] That is, alliances of groups organize and dissolve as issues change, rather than the same interests always finding themselves

---

5. "Philosophy and Democracy," 9 *Political Theory* 379, 383 (1981).

6. See Justice Thurgood Marshall's dissent in San Antonio v. Rodriguez (1973; reprinted below, p. 858).

7. *Government and the Mind* (New York: Oxford University Press, 1977), p. 143.

8. To John Taylor, May 28, 1816; Paul L. Ford, ed., *The Works of Thomas Jefferson* (New York: Putnam's Sons, 1905), XI, 527.

9. Robert A. Dahl has done much theoretical and empirical work here. See his *A Preface to Democratic Theory* (Chicago: University of Chicago Press, 1956); "Decision-Making in a

in coalition with and opposition to the same other groups. On this view, democratic politics is characterized by shifting coalitions of minorities rather than by a more or less constant division between an equally passionate majority and minority.

In addition, the existence of open political processes makes it difficult if not impossible for one set of groups to coalesce without alerting others with conflicting interests to form an opposing alliance. As a result, public officials who wish to be reelected will be forced, or at very least strongly pushed, to mediate interests, to act as brokers and compromise clashes rather than adjudicate winner-take-all struggles.

Some theorists add a third check. In a representative democracy, they assert, professional politicians develop and internalize a political subculture that constrains them from trying to tyrannize their constituents. Fear of being voted out of office is not a trivial restraint, nor are crosspressures from competing alliances, actual and latent; but also quite effective is acceptance of rules of the political game that "some things are not done." [10] And it is difficult to argue with the claim that for American presidents, if not other leading public officials, the "judgment of history" has been a strong factor in decision making.

Some proponents of democracy add a limitation that may link it with constitutionalism: To be legitimate, the popular will must will generally; that is, valid laws may not merely reflect prejudices against minorities by imposing burdens only or principally on minorities.[11] Such a limiting principle may flow from the premise that the people *as a whole* are sovereign, but it is problematic how much it is compatible with majority rule.[12]

B. Constitutionalism

Democratic theory focuses on how the system chooses decision makers and makes public policy. To generate public policy and protect civil rights, it relies mainly on process. Constitutionalists share these concerns as well as many of the values, such as protection of human dignity, that most democratic theorists believe open political processes protect. There are, however, significant differences between several thrusts of the two theories.

First, at a psychological level, constitutionalists tend to be more pessimistic about human nature and the efficacy of the checks of

Democracy: The Supreme Court as a National Policy-Maker," 6 *J. of Pub.L.* 279 (1957); and *Democracy in the United States* (4th ed.; Boston: Houghton-Mifflin, 1981), espec. chap. 18.

10. See again the various writings of Robert A. Dahl, espec. *Who Governs?* (New Haven, Conn.: Yale University Press, 1961), chaps. 27–28; and *Dilemmas of Pluralist Democracy* (New Haven, Conn.: Yale University Press, 1982).

11. See espec. Walzer, supra note 5, and John Hart Ely, *Democracy and Distrust* (Cambridge, Mass.: Harvard University Press, 1980).

12. Madison was concerned in *Federalist* No. 10 with the possibility that in a democratic system a majority could oppress the whole society as well as minorities: "When a majority is included in a faction, the form of popular government . . . enables it to sacrifice to its ruling passion or interest, both the *public good* and *the rights of other citizens.*" (Italics supplied.)

democratic political processes as protectors of fundamental rights: People are often sufficiently clever to oppress others without hurting themselves. Constitutionalism is thus constantly concerned with the human penchant to act selfishly and abuse power. On an empirical level, it is also less optimistic about the claim that cleavages within a polity will not be cumulative and so create permanent divisions between a majority and a minority or that the shifting alliances of interests that do occur will protect the fundamental rights of those, like the poor and elderly, who lack both political savvy and political clout. As John Rawls has put it:

> [T]he democratic political process is at best regulated rivalry; it does not even . . . have the desirable properties that price theory ascribes to truly competitive markets. Moreover, the effects of injustices in the political system are much more grave and long lasting than market imperfections. Political power rapidly accumulates and becomes unequal; making use of the coercive apparatus of the state and its law, those who gain the advantage can often assure themselves of a favored position . . . . Universal suffrage is an insufficient counterpoise; for when parties and elections are financed not by public funds but by private contributions, the political forum is so constrained by the wishes of the dominant interests that the basic measures needed to establish just constitutional rule are seldom seriously presented.[13]

Most important, perhaps, constitutionalism rejects the primacy of process. Where individual rights are concerned, the legitimacy of public policy depends, constitutionalism contends, not merely on the authenticity of decision makers' credentials but also on the substance of their work. There are some fundamental rights that government may not trample on, even with the active support of the overwhelming majority of the population, whether aggregated individually or by groups. For a constitutionalist, a law unanimously enacted by a Congress chosen after long, open public debate and free elections and signed by a President similarly chosen would have no legitimacy if the statute invaded individual autonomy or violated human dignity.

There is, constitutionalism claims, a zone of autonomy, of privacy, and of dignity surrounding each individual that should be immune from governmental regulation, even regulation that an overwhelming majority of society considers wise and just. At the heart of constitutionalism, as perhaps of democratic theory, is a belief in the intrinsic moral worth of each person. That belief, to be sure, is the result of a value judgment, but so is the belief that the people *should* govern. The "core objective" of constitutionalism, Professor Carl J. Friedrich once wrote,

> is that of safeguarding each member of the political community as a political person, possessing a sphere of genuine autonomy. The constitution is meant to protect the *self* in its dignity and

---

13. *A Theory of Justice* (Cambridge, Mass.: Harvard University Press, 1971), p. 226.

worth. . . . The prime function of a constitutional political order has been and is being accomplished by means of a system of regularized restraints imposed upon those who exercise political power.[14]

Lord Byron expressed the constitutionalist's fear of unlimited popular sovereignty when he wrote:

> What from this barren being do we reap?
> Our senses narrow, and our reason frail,
> Life short, and truth a gem which loves the deep,
> And all things weigh'd in custom's falsest scale;
> Opinion an omnipotence,—whose veil
> Mantles the earth with darkness, until right
> And wrong are accidents, and men grow pale
> Lest their own judgments should become too bright,
> And their free thoughts be crimes, and earth have too much light.[15]

For the constitutionalist, political morality cannot be weighed on a scale in which "opinion is an omnipotence," but only against the moral criteria of individual rights. And the constitutionalist insists on institutional limitations beyond those of open political processes to curb government. After all, a constitutionalist would argue, totalitarian democracy in which a government, elected by, responsible to, and responsive to a majority, controls all aspects of behavior except those relating to the five conditions for representative democracy is a logical possibility. Further, oppressive popular government is a practical as well as logical possibility. As James Madison wrote to Jefferson:

> In our Governments the real power lies in the majority of the Community, and the invasion of private rights is chiefly to be apprehended, not from acts of Government contrary to the sense of its constituents, but from acts in which Government is the mere instrument of the major number of its constituents.[16]

While totalitarian democracy is a possibility, totalitarian constitutionalism is a contradiction in terms, though a constitutional government in an extreme form might become anarchistic just as it might, like any other government, betray its fundamental principles and become tyrannical. A constitutional democracy, blending popular government with limited government, may require some logical legerdemain; but it is a practical, if fragile, reality.

One must be very careful in defining the differences between constitutionalism and democratic theory. Modern constitutionalism does not reject the democratic processes, it treats them as a means— and though necessary, still an insufficient means—to achieve what it

14. *Transcendent Justice* (Durham, N.C.: Duke University Press, 1964), pp. 16–17.

15. "Childe Harold's Pilgrimmage," Canto IV, xciii; Frederick Page, ed., *Byron's Poetical Works* (London: Oxford University Press, 1970), p. 239.

16. October 17, 1788. A convenient source for this letter is Marvin Meyers, ed., *The Mind of the Framer* (Indianapolis, Ind.: Bobbs-Merrill, 1973), pp. 206–209.

considers the ultimate civic purpose of protecting individual liberty. Nor does constitutionalism reject the notion of community or the importance of civil society; it is merely suspicious of the claims of these concepts when pitted against those of individual autonomy. Moreover, constitutionalism is committed to its own kind of process: When government acts within its proper sphere, it must respect certain procedural rights—for example, to a fair trial—again even when the people and their representatives wish otherwise. In short, by limiting government, constitutionalism attempts to limit the risks of being a member of civil society.

The basic difference between constitutionalism and democratic theory lies not in a dispute over the importance of human dignity but on how best to protect that value. Because of its distrust of human nature, constitutionalism cannot accept the workings of political processes, even if they are open, as *sufficient* criteria of legitimate public policy. Because of its belief in the primacy of self-government, democratic theory can accept no other standard as of more or even equal importance.

II. THE "PURE CONSTITUTIONALIST" v. THE "PURE REPRESENTATIVE DEMOCRAT"

One can visualize the attitudes of constitutionalism and democratic theory toward a system's basic law as falling along a spectrum ranging from an imaginary Pure Constitutionalist at one end to an equally imaginary Pure Representative Democrat at the other:

+————————————————————————————+

Pure Constitutionalist   Pure Representative Democrat

The Pure Constitutionalist would see a written constitution as surrounded by "an ocean of rights." The fundamental assumption would be that people are by nature free and only to protect their rights do they give limited authority to society. Government, as Tom Paine said, "has of itself no rights; they are altogether duties." [17] To legitimate its action, government would have to point to language in the constitutional document granting the power it asserts. Individual liberty, on the other hand, would need no justification. Its preservation is the purpose of a constitution. Those who defend governmental authority would carry the burden of proof. As Edward S. Corwin put it:

> From this point of view . . . governmental authority . . . is a trust which, save for the grant of it effected by the written constitution, was non-existent, and private rights, since they precede the constitution, gain nothing of authoritativeness from being enumerated in it, though possibly something of security. *These rights are not, in other words, fundamental because they find mention in the written*

17. *The Rights of Man,* Part II, chap. 4; Henry Collins, ed. (Baltimore: Pelican Books, 1969), p. 187.

instrument; they find mention there because fundamental . . . . The written constitution is, in short, but a nucleus or core of a much wider region of private rights, which, though not reduced to black and white, are as fully entitled to the protection of government as if defined in the minutest detail.[18]

Madison used similar language when he introduced what became the Bill of Rights in the first session of Congress:

> It has been objected also against a bill of rights, that, by enumerating particular exceptions to the grant of power, it would disparage those rights which were not placed in that enumeration; and it might follow by implication, that those rights which were not singled out, were intended to be assigned into the hands of the General Government, and were consequently insecure. This is one of the most plausible arguments I have ever heard urged against the admission of a bill of rights into this system; but, I conceive, that it may be guarded against. I have attempted it, as gentlemen may see by turning to the last clause of the fourth resolution.[19]

That clause of the fourth resolution ultimately became the Ninth Amendment:

> The enumeration in the Constitution, of certain rights, shall not be construed to deny or disparage others retained by the people.

In contrast, the Pure Representative Democrat would see all power as vested in the people and, through their votes, in their representatives. Whatever those representatives would do, provided they remained within the five conditions specified earlier, would be legitimate. At most, a written constitution would provide a set of rules for elections and express national ideals. No document, no matter how solemn or ancient, could define rights and duties beyond free political participation; only the people's will, as expressed through their elected representatives, could perform those functions.

In the modern world, the Pure Constitutionalist's attitude would, if dominant, cripple government. On the other hand, Pure Representative Democracy would be unacceptable to a nation that endorsed values like religious freedom, personal privacy, private property, or a right to "equal concern and respect."[20] Even the British qualify parliamentary sovereignty by placing it within a political culture in which some things are supposedly not done. Most American public officials and most private citizens who have thought about the matter would probably align themselves at various points near the center of the spectrum.

Those people somewhat closer to the democratic pole would view a constitution as a plenary grant of power to government, although

---

18. "The Basic Doctrine of American Constitutional Law," 12 *Mich.L.Rev.* 247, 247–248 (1914). (Italics supplied.)

19. *Annals,* 1st Cong., 1st sess., I, 456.

20. Ronald Dworkin, *Taking Rights Seriously* (Cambridge, Mass.: Harvard University Press, 1977), p. 180; see also Ely, supra note 11, p. 82.

they might differ widely among themselves about which level or branch of government possessed which power. The only exclusions would be those explicitly listed or clearly implicit in those listed by the democratic authority of the ratifiers of the Constitution. The relevant credo might read: "The voice of the people's elected representatives is sovereign except when speaking either on an issue or in a manner explicitly forbidden by the constitutional document." Justice William H. Rehnquist of the U.S. Supreme Court put it succinctly:

> If such a [democratic] society adopts a constitution and incorporates in that constitution safeguards for individual liberty, these safeguards indeed do take on a generalized moral rightness or goodness. They assume a general social acceptance neither because of any intrinsic worth nor because of unique origins in someone's idea of natural justice but instead simply because they have been incorporated in the constitution by the people.[21]

As we have noted, scholars and jurists who hold these views have faith in open political processes as both protecting fundamental rights and creating viable public policies. For people near the democratic end of the spectrum, constitutional interpretation consists of reading the terms of the actual document and its amendments, ascertaining the meaning of its words, and applying them to the factual matrix of the current problem. To be legitimate, a public policy must meet several sets of criteria that relate mainly to process. It must:

> 1) Be enacted by a majority of the people's representatives, chosen according to the rules of representative democracy listed above, and operating in conformity with the processes established in the constitutional document; *and*
> 2) Be authorized *either* by:
>   a) the explicit powers delegated by the constitutional document, *or*
>   b) the powers reasonably implied by the constitutional document's terms; *or*
>   c) the residuum of inherent power on which government may call to preserve the polity; *and*
> 3) Violate *neither:*
>   a) any of the specific prohibitions of the constitutional document, *nor*
>   b) any of the rights clearly implied in the constitutional document.

Testing a policy's legitimacy by the first set of criteria might appear a simple task. In fact, of course, numerous problems swiftly arise, not least of which are how to determine who is qualified to vote and how to apportion electoral districts fairly.

Testing under 2(a) and 3(a) is even more difficult. As the cases reprinted in this book will demonstrate, reading the Constitution's

---

21. "Observation: The Notion of a Living Constitution," 54 *Tex.L.Rev.* 693, 704 (1976); we reprint part of this article below, p. 163.

"plain words" is far less easy than it initially might seem. The basic document is now almost 200 years old. Does an interpreter try to discover the original meanings such words had or the meanings those words have taken on as the American version of the English language has developed? Whatever the answer to that question, whose usage does the interpreter adopt, that of lawyers or ordinary people on whose authority the document claims to speak? Assuming a satisfactory answer to that query, how does the interpreter choose among popular dictionaries or among expert interpretations of such words?

Such questions only begin to chart the difficulties. The "plain words" of the constitutional document are often not very plain. The Fourth Amendment forbids only "unreasonable" searches and seizures; the Fifth Amendment orders the federal government to pay "just compensation" if it takes private property for public use; the Eighth bans "cruel and unusual punishments." What is "reasonable," "just," "cruel," "unusual," or "public use" is often controversial. The Fourteenth Amendment forbids states to deny any person "the equal protection of the laws." But laws frequently must discriminate among people. No one would contend that a state should permit the blind to drive automobiles or demand that the elderly or infirm serve in the militia.

Testing under 2(b) and 3(b) opens a new universe of problems. Still taking only the document's own words, an interpreter must confront, sooner or later, the "necessary and proper" clause as well as the Ninth Amendment, with its explicit protection of unlisted constitutional rights. These clauses are such stuff as legal positivists' nightmares are made of.

Interpreters somewhat closer to the Pure Constitutionalist's end of the spectrum also face great difficulties. In general, they insist on testing a public policy by its conformity to constitutionalist values of individual rights, values that may well go beyond the words of the constitutional document—precisely what Justice Rehnquist rejects. They accept the notion of implied governmental powers, but they also embrace the idea that a constitution is surrounded by "an ocean of rights" and that, as the Ninth Amendment explicitly says, these rights need not be mentioned in the document to be worthy of, even demanding of, protection by all branches of government, including a non-elected judiciary.

For such people—"constitutionalists" as distinguished from Pure Constitutionalists—to be legitimate a public policy must meet all the criteria just listed plus one other:

3) Not violate . . .
    c)   any of "the ocean of rights" that surround the constitutional document and so are actually part of the Constitution itself and just as binding as the document's plain words.

It is this position of the moderate "constitutionalist," with all its complexities and uncertainties, that the U.S. Supreme Court has typically taken. The justices' visions of the size and depth of that "ocean of rights" have varied; sometimes that ocean has seemed like a vast sea, at other times more like a lake, at still others like a mere puddle. But it has been a rare Court that has not seen "the Constitution" as being girded by at least a moat of some unlisted rights, whether to "freedom of contract" or privacy.

For all those who find themselves near the center of the spectrum, whether somewhat more constitutionalist or somewhat more democratic, political life is not a matter of simple choices. On the one hand, the people, through their elected representatives, must govern if government is to retain popular support. In addition, the people must govern, at least indirectly, if they are to be autonomous individuals. The right to participate in one's government is a mark of human dignity, a fundamental claim that all sane adults can make against their society.

On the other hand, to have a life worth living, citizens must retain a sphere of dignity, privacy, and autonomy, even in times of crisis. The authority of the people to govern must be limited if society is to fulfill its purpose of making it possible for men and women to live as free human beings. "What," a constitutionalist might ask, "doth it profit a nation to survive if the price is the loss of what the nation holds most dear?"

On many of the abstract and concrete issues here, the demands of constitutionalism and those of democracy are likely to conflict. And solutions are not likely to be obvious or easy. With that much said, there are also ways in which the two philosophies, if joined in a given polity, can reinforce one another. Both, for instance, look to the dignity and freedom of the individual person as the great public good; both preach the equal worth of citizens; and both try to limit governmental power—democracy by requiring open political processes, constitutionalism by other institutional checks. At minimum, this mutual nurturing of values should affect the political culture by discouraging many potentially oppressive demands from ever being voiced.

To understand how the American system blends constitutionalism and democracy, it would be helpful to look first at the general scheme of government that the framers created in Philadelphia and then at how the system has developed over the years.

III. FREE GOVERNMENT: THE FOUNDING GENERATION

The delegates to the Philadelphia Convention of 1787 were largely members of the establishment; some enjoyed wealth, all had social status and power. Despite their constitutional prohibition of titles of nobility, it would not be unfair to say that they considered themselves a natural aristocracy. Partly because of their social and economic position, most of them were deeply troubled by government under the Articles of Confederation. The national government was both "national" and a "government" more in name than in fact. Lacking central direction, the separate states went their own ways. Many of the states had democractic political systems that responded to the wishes of the majority by easing contractual obligations, favoring debtors over creditors, and printing bales of paper money and making it legal tender. Some states were also erecting barriers against the products and people of sister states. The framers saw this bundle of policies as menacing the institution of private property and not only depriving them and people like them of wealth but threatening the prosperity of the whole nation by destroying investors' confidence.

The weakness of the central government compounded problems. It could neither command the respect of foreign nations necessary to negotiate treaties to assist international trade, nor could it enforce uniform rules of commerce within the so-called United States.

To minimize these difficulties, the framers strove for two objectives. First, they tried to construct a national government that was much stronger than that which existed under the Articles, a government that would take over many important functions from the states. The delegates' second objective complemented the first. As men of wealth and property, they knew that they and people like them were apt to remain a minority. Furthermore, not only were the excesses of democratically elected state governments causing immediate distress, but so had, only a few years earlier, the rule of a British monarch. Thus the framers' second fundamental objective was not merely to limit the states, but also to organize national power in a manner that would protect property rights at all levels and so prevent the most likely form of tyranny.

Before the Convention, James Madison published a booklet in which he explained the dual objective in constructing a constitution:

> The great desideratum of Government is such a modification of the sovereignty as will render it sufficiently neutral between the different interests and factions, to controul one part of the society from invading the rights of another, and at the same time sufficiently controuled itself from setting up an interest adverse to that of the whole Society.[22]

After the Convention, he described these objectives in similar terms, "combining the requisite stability and energy in government, with the inviolable attention due to liberty and the republican form."[23] And, without being troubled by false modesty, he boasted that the delegates at Philadelphia had improved on the efforts of the leaders of the revolt against England to carry out "a revolution which has no parallel

---

22. "Vices of the Political System of the United States," (1787), reprinted in Meyers, supra note 16, pp. 83–92.

23. Benjamin F. Wright, ed., *The Federalist,* No. 37 (Cambridge, Mass.: The Belknap Press of Harvard University Press, 1961), p. 267.

in the annals of human society. They reared the fabrics of governments which have no model on the face of the globe." [24]

There was some truth in Madison's bravado. The new constitutional document did outline a much more powerful central government than the Articles of Confederation had allowed. At the same time, however, the terms of that document and the frictions it would generate might well keep political power at all levels of government faithful to its appointed, and limited, tasks, especially protecting, as Madison said in *Federalist* No. 10, "diversity in the faculties of men" to acquire property.

Unlike the old government, which lacked an effective executive and a judiciary and could really only recommend action to the states, the new national government had its own executive and judicial systems and would operate directly on the people of the United States. New powers included those of taxing and spending; of regulating commerce among the several states, with foreign nations, and with the Indian tribes; of coining and borrowing money, establishing postal services and post roads, and enacting uniform rules of bankruptcy; of conducting foreign relations, raising armies and navies, waging war, and concluding treaties; and, under the so-called "sweeping clause," of making "all Laws which shall be necessary and proper for carrying into Execution" the enumerated powers.

The constitutional document also expressly denied many powers to the states, such as authority to enter into a treaty or alliance, enact ex post facto laws [25] or bills of attainder,[26] or grant titles of nobility. More directly related to the policies that had aroused the framers were prohibitions against states' impairing the obligations of contracts, issuing bills of credit, making anything but gold or silver legal tender, or taxing (without congressional approval) exports or imports. Further, the supremacy clause proclaimed the Constitution, along with "the laws of the United States which shall be made in Pursuance thereof, and all Treaties made, or which shall be made, under the authority of the United States" to be the "supreme Law of the Land" and decreed that "Judges in every State shall be bound thereby, any Thing in the Constitution or Laws of any State to the Contrary notwithstanding."

A. The Grand Strategy of Checks and Counterchecks [27]

When the framers undertook to limit power, they did not deem elections to be *the* solution. Making public officials responsible to their constituencies was by no means insignificant; but it was insuffi-

---

24. *The Federalist,* No. 14, p. 154.

25. As construed by Calder v. Bull (1798; reprinted below, p. 86), a statute that makes an act that was lawful when committed a crime, retroactively increases the penalty for a crime, or, again retroactively, lowers the conditions of proof to establish guilt.

26. A legislative act that convicts a person of crime and punishes that person.

27. We are especially indebted in this section to Paul Eidelberg, *The Philosophy of the American Constitution* (New York: The Free Press, 1968).

cient.   The injustice of recent state laws regarding property, Madison wrote before the Convention, was alarming because it brought into question whether "the majority . . . are the safest Guardians both of public Good and private rights."   Like a good constitutionalist, he went on to speculate:

> A succeeding election it might be supposed, would displace the offenders, and repair the mischief.   But how easily are base and selfish measures, masked by pretexts of public good and apparent expediency?   How frequently will a repetition of the same arts and industry which succeeded in the first instance, again prevail on the unwary to misplace their confidence? [28]

Madison saw the source of the evil in human nature, in the propensity of all men, individually and collectively, to act selfishly, a flaw that neither philosophy nor religion could eradicate.   As a result, the gravest danger of oppression in a society that allowed wide popular participation would come not from a government that ignored or violated the will of the majority, but from one that followed the majority will.[29]   As he wrote in Federalist No. 51:

> It is of great importance in a republic, not only to guard against the oppression of its rulers; but to guard one part of society against the injustice of the other part. . . . If a majority be united by a common interest, the rights of the minority will be insecure.

Initially, the framers chose not to rely on a bill of rights as the main protection against governmental abuses of power.   They included some taboos, especially, as we have just seen, where the states were concerned but also a few against national action, such as bans against ex post facto laws, bills of attainder, taxes on exports, and prohibition of the slave trade before 1808.   On the whole, however, the framers believed, as John Randolph later expressed it: "You may cover whole skins of parchment with limitations but power alone can limit power." [30]

Madison explained to Jefferson that there were many reasons not to include a Bill of Rights against the national government:

1.   Because I conceive that in a certain degree, though not to the extent argued by Mr. [James] Wilson [of Pennsylvania], the rights in question are reserved by the manner in which the federal powers are granted.

2.   Because there is great reason to fear that a positive declaration of some of the most essential rights could not be obtained in the requisite latitude.   I am sure that the rights of conscience in particular, if submitted to public definition, would be narrowed much more than they are likely ever to be by an assumed

28.   "Vices of the Political System," in Meyers, supra note 16, p. 89.

29.   See his letter to Jefferson, October 17, 1788; Meyers, supra note 16, p. 206.

30.   Quoted in William Bruce, *John Randolph of Roanoke* (New York: Putnam's, 1922), II, 211.

power. One of the objections in New England was, that the Constitution, by prohibiting religious tests, opened a door for Jews, Turks, and infidels.

3. Because the limited power of the federal Government, and the jealousy of the subordinate Governments, afford a security which has not existed in the case of the State Governments, and exists in no other.

4. Because experience proves the inefficacy of a bill of rights on those occasions when its controul is most needed. Repeated violations of these parchment barriers have been committed by overbearing majorities in every State.[31]

Later, after ratification, partly because of Jefferson's arguments and partly because of concerns expressed in state ratifying conventions, Madison changed his mind about a bill of rights. But in 1787 most of the framers put their main reliance for limiting governmental power on geographic, social, and institutional strategies that recognized human selfishness and sinfulness and tried to play groups of selfish sinners off against each other.

B. Geographic Strategy

The geographic strategy was to widen the scope of the political unit and so the number of citizens as well as the diversity of their interests—in sum, to make the entire nation a meaningful political arena of widely diverse interest groups. In *Federalist* No. 10, Madison argued that a large as opposed to a small republic would make it easier for the people to choose men of character as their representatives and more difficult for a majority to coalesce to oppress smaller groups.

> The smaller the society, the fewer probably will be the distinct parties and interests composing it; the fewer the distinct parties and interests, the more frequently will a majority be found of the same party; and the smaller the number of individuals composing a majority, the more easily will they concert and execute their plan of oppression. Extend the sphere, and you take in a greater variety of parties and interests; you make it less probable that a majority of the whole will have a common motive to invade the rights of other citizens; or if such a common motive exists, it will be more difficult for all who feel it to discover their own strength, and to act in unison with each other . . . .

C. Socio-Economic Strategy

In a related fashion, the framers devised a socio-economic strategy to divide power among economic interests in society by providing different constituencies for various federal offices. Membership in the House of Representatives would be apportioned among the states according to population, terms would run for only two years, and all

31. To Jefferson, October 17, 1788; Meyers, supra note 16, p. 206.

persons eligible to vote for the most numerous house of the state's legislature could vote for candidates for the House.

"Here, sir," Hamilton claimed, "the people govern" [32]—though more in a negative than a positive sense because, acting alone, the House cannot enact legislation. The broad nature of its electorate and the requirement of frequent elections could mean, however, that the House would represent the policies of the less affluent and require the more affluent, represented in the Senate, to compromise if they wished to enact legislation.

Senators—two from each state, originally chosen by its legislature—would be more insulated from the popular will. Their overrepresenting the smaller states, indirect election, relatively long terms of office (six years), and the fact that only one-third of them would come up for election in the same year in which the entire House or the House and the President were chosen further detached senators from the popular will. And many of the framers were quite candid in their image of the Senate as an institution that would represent the policies of the more affluent and stable elements in society. Edmund Randolph of Virginia told his fellow delegates that the Senate was needed to restrain "the turbulence and follies of democracy." [33] John Dickenson of Delaware made a more extreme argument: "In the formation of the Senate we ought to carry it through such a refining process as will assimilate it as near as may be to the House of Lords of England." [34] Few delegates wanted to adopt a British model, but Madison agreed that the "Senate shd. come from, and represent, the wealth of the Nation . . . ." [35]

The President was also to be indirectly chosen through the Electoral College. Each state would have a number of electors equal to its combined representation in the House and Senate (and so smaller states would have a relative advantage over the more populous), and every state could decide how it would choose its electors.

---

32. Speech in New York's ratifying convention, in Jonathan Elliot, ed., *Debates in The Several State Conventions on the Adoption of the Federal Constitution* (Philadelphia: Lippincott, 1901), II, 348. (Orig. published, 1836.)

33. "Debates in the Federal Convention of 1787 as Reported by James Madison," reprinted in Charles C. Tansill, ed., *Documents Illustrative of the Formation of the Union of the United States* (Washington, D.C.: Government Printing Office, 1927), p. 128. At least seven of the framers took more or less extensive notes of the debates. Tansill reprints in their entirety those of Alexander Hamilton, Rufus King, James McHenry, James Madison, William Paterson, and Robert Yates. Robert Lansing also kept a set of notes, first published in 1939 and republished in 1967: Joseph R. Strayer, ed., *The Delegate from New York* (Port Washington, N.Y.: Kennikat Press, 1967). None of these is a "record" in any formal sense or even an informal shorthand transcript, but notes written in longhand by participants during and sometimes well after the debates. Not only are they individually and collectively incomplete, they also sometimes disagree with each other on what was said. Madison, for example, accused Yates, who published his notes during Madison's lifetime, of perverting the historical record for partisan political purposes. Madison's own notes were published in 1840, after his death. In sum, one should treat these notes of debates with the same caution that one treats the notes that justices of the Supreme Court take of the secret conferences in which they discuss cases. See below, Chapter 3.

34. Tansill, supra note 33, p. 163.

35. "Notes of Rufus King in the Federal Convention of 1787," reprinted in Tansill, supra note 33, p. 853.

The people so selected would meet in their own state capitals, cast their ballots, then send them to Congress to be counted. (Some framers seem to have expected this process to be more one of nomination than election, for political parties as we have them were unknown and communications slow). If no candidate received an absolute majority of electoral votes, the House would choose (initially among the five leading candidates, but since adoption of the Twelfth Amendment in 1804, the top three), with each state having one vote regardless of the size of its congressional delegation.

Federal judges, nominated by an indirectly elected President and confirmed by an indirectly elected Senate, would serve for "good Behaviour"—a term that in practice has usually meant until the judge decides to retire or is overtaken by death. Only the most naive populist would have expected that men so chosen would, in the political context of the last decade of the eighteenth century, have supported the economic policies of state legislatures under the Articles of Confederation.

In this network of competing constituencies, the more affluent had great advantage. They could reasonably expect to control the executive, the judiciary, and the Senate—expectations that escaped few Anti-Federalists. Even that avid defender of the Constitution, Alexander Hamilton, conceded that through "the natural operation of the different interests and views of the various classes of the community," federal legislators would "consist almost entirely of proprietors of land, of merchants, and of members of the learned professions"; but, he insisted, such men would represent different interests and views.[36]

Nevertheless, even if one could not accept Hamilton's hope for "virtual representation" of most interests, control of the House with its exclusive authority to initiate tax bills would allow the common people's actual representatives to block any positive policy their "betters" wished to enact into law—always providing, of course, that the common people could in fact exercise their potential power to choose their congressmen and hold them to account.

D. Institutional Strategy

The institutional web the framers spun fit the same strategy as the geographic and social arrangements—playing off sets of officials and interests against each other. Basically, the constitutional document fractured formal governmental power and gave overlapping pieces to different officials. The constitutional structure explicitly provided for the states to continue as important political entities. The document required the federal government to guarantee to every state "a Republican Form of Government," to protect each against invasion and insurrection, and to insure that none lost any of its territory without its consent. Furthermore, grants of power to the national government were seldom exclusive, leaving it open how much authority states retained.

---

36. *Federalist*, No. 36, p. 259.

More consequential than specific references to the states was the assumption that the federal government was to be one of delegated powers. "The Powers not delegated to the United States by the Constitution," as the Tenth Amendment later said, "nor prohibited by it to the States, are reserved to the States respectively, or to the people." Like the rest of the document, however, that provision offers a general guide rather than a precise formula for federal-state relations. For, in proposing the Tenth Amendment, Congress three times rejected the wording "expressly delegated" and thus left intact Article I's grant of implied powers in its conferring on Congress all powers "necessary and proper" to carry out powers expressly delegated to the national government.

By drawing only vague verbal boundaries and leaving both national and state officials with tracts of apparently overlapping powers, the framers insured enduring rivalry and constant friction among the representatives of various geographic and socio-economic interests. That same pattern reappears in the fabric of the federal government itself. Article I begins: "All legislative Powers herein granted shall be vested in a Congress of the United States"; then Article II makes the President part of the legislative process by allowing him, among other things, to recommend and veto legislation. So, too, that Article allows the Senate a share in executive power by confirming the President's nominees to all important offices, including his own cabinet; and Article I confers on Congress authority to organize the entire executive branch and makes all federal programs dependent on congressional appropriations of money. Similarly, Article II's grant of executive power to the President includes quasi-judicial authority to nominate judges and to pardon people convicted of crimes.

Article III establishes a Supreme Court and empowers Congress to institute a system of lower federal courts and to make exceptions to the appellate jurisdiction of the Supreme Court. On these tribunals Article III conferred but did not define "the judicial power of the United States."

If, as seems probable, the framers thought that judges would share in interpreting the Constitution, they left wide room for judicial discretion; indeed, they required judicial discretion. Many constitutional clauses are couched in broad language that demands creative interpretation. What powers are "necessary and proper" to carry out those specifically delegated to the national government is far from obvious, and many of the expressly delegated powers are hardly specific. What is "commerce" is no easier to define than it is in an interdependent society to distinguish commerce "among the several states" from local businesses.

E. Sentinels Over Public Rights

The system that the Convention produced seems chaotic and devoid of any master plan. But that assessment would be wrong. Many of the framers, most especially Madison, consciously tried to knit networks of tensions and jealousies among competing public officials, whose inexact grants of power would make them insecure and thus zealous watchdogs against efforts of rivals to aggrandize power. "Ambition," Madison explained, "must be made to counteract ambition. The interest of the man must be connected with the constitutional rights of the place." He continued:

> the constant aim is to divide and arrange the several offices in such a manner as that each may be a check on the other—that the private interest of every individual may be a sentinel over the public rights.[37]

IV. THE DEVELOPING SYSTEM

We have been careful not to speak of the "intent of the framers," but instead of the larger architectural scheme they created. We can discuss broad "purposes" with some confidence, but if we try to determine the exact meaning the framers intended for specific clauses—what, for instance, they *and* the ratifiers had precisely in mind when they proposed and approved congressional authority to regulate "commerce among the several states"—difficulties multiply. In the first place, we lack a complete and accurate "record" of debates either at Philadelphia or at the state ratifying conventions. More fundamentally, it is open to doubt whether future generations are bound by the framers' (or ratifiers') specific intentions, even if we knew what they were, rather than by the document and the constitutional order to which it gave birth.

That order has developed in ways the framers could not have possibly foreseen. The most dramatic political changes have involved democratization not merely of government but of the entire society. The political and social cultures of the nation have become far more egalitarian; the right to vote has been broadened; slavery has been abolished; and the notion of the equal moral and legal worth of every human being has come closer to being an accepted political value.

Constitutional amendments have at times recognized these changes, at other times precipitated them. The Thirteenth Amendment's outlawing of slavery culminated a long campaign for freedom; it owes as much to constitutionalist as to democratic theory and most of all to military victory in the Civil War. The Fifteenth Amendment forbids denials of suffrage based on race. It came into being after a long history of struggle and took more than a century to become effective. More recent voting amendments have reflected growing democratic sentiment: The Nineteenth Amendment forbids denying a person the ballot because of his or her sex, the Twenty-Fourth because of failure to pay a tax, the Twenty-Sixth because of age, for those over 18; the Seventeenth made senators directly elected by popular vote; and the Twenty-Third gave citizens of the District of Columbia the franchise in presidential elections. In addition, without amendment to

---

37. Ibid., No. 51, p. 356.

the U.S. Constitution, every state now chooses its presidential electors by popular vote, and none retains a property qualification for general elections.

Even the least democratic among the framers believed that a free and stable government must rest on the consent of the governed. And, they explicitly provided that the new Constitution's fate was to be determined by *conventions* chosen in the states (qualifications of electors for the conventions were not specified), not by state legislatures. Furthermore, as already noted, the House was to be chosen by a broad constituency.

Madison expressed a common sentiment when he wrote that it was a "fundamental principle that men cannot be justly bound by laws in [the] making of which they have no part." [38]   But, believing in government by consent is not equivalent to believing in representative as distinguished from constitutional democracy. And, as we have seen, the formal and informal structures created at Philadelphia in 1787 hedged all political power within mazes of checks and counterchecks. "One person, one vote" was not a value originally embodied in the letter or spirit of the constitutional document; even "one vote for each white, male, adult citizen" did not find strong support among the delegates.

Part of the opposition to democracy was undoubtedly due to fear that elected representatives would govern at the national level as they had in the states and further endanger property and progress. Another part of the opposition came from a more deeply rooted distrust, a doubt that people without property could be sufficiently autonomous to vote in their own self interest. As John Dickenson remarked, "No one could be considered as having an interest in the government unless he possessed some of the soil." [39]   Gouverneur Morris added another kind of objection:

> If the suffrage was to be open to all *freemen* —the government would indubitably be an aristocracy .   .   .   It [would] put in the power of opulent men whose business created numerous dependents to rule at all elections. Hence so soon as we erected large manufactories and our towns became more populous—wealthy merchants and manufacturers would elect the house of representatives. This was an aristocracy. This could only be avoided by confining the suffrage to *free holders.* [40]

(Morris's remarks make more sense when one realizes that at the time voting was typically both public and oral. The secret ballot did not

---

38. Madison appended these words in a "Note" to his speech of August 7, 1787; reprinted in Max Farrand, ed., *The Records of the Federal Convention of 1787* (New Haven, Conn.: Yale University Press, 1911), II, 204. (Despite the title, Farrand's volumes are not "records," but, like Tansill's volume, supra note 33, collections of notes various delegates jotted down.)

39. "Papers of Dr. James McHenry on the Federal Convention of 1787," Tansill, supra note 33, p. 934.

40. Ibid., pp. 934–935. McHenry added: "Mr. Maddison [sic] supported similar sentiments."

come into widespread use in the United States until almost a century had passed.)

Despite dramatic democratization, the roots of the American system still run deeply into constitutionalism. Industrialization has helped multiply the number and kinds of interest groups, but development of instant mass communications and democratization of the political processes have weakened the grand strategy of geographic, socio-economic, and institutional checks. And, today, federal judges, especially justices of the Supreme Court, have had thrust on them or have taken on themselves the duty of functioning as the most visible if not the principal defenders of constitutionalism.

Curiously, it was Jefferson, who was to become the foe of the federal judiciary led by John Marshall, who planted some of the most intellectually fruitful seeds for the growth of judicial authority. After the Revolution, he complained about the almost unlimited power Virginia's constitution gave the legislature: "One hundred and seventy-three despots would surely be as oppressive as one . . . . An elective despotism was not the government we fought for . . . ." [41] After the Convention, he urged Madison to fight for a national bill of rights. It was, Jefferson claimed, "what the people are entitled to against every government on earth, general or particular, and what no just government should refuse, or rest on inference." [42]

Madison at first resisted for the reasons noted above, though he conceded that a bill of rights might "acquire by degrees the character of fundamental maxims of *free* governments, and as they become incorporated with the national sentiment"—modern scholars would say become part of the political culture—"counteract the impulses of interest and passion." He also admitted that such a bill would be useful to the extent that tyranny sprang from government alone, rather than from government's obeying a popular mandate.

In response Jefferson said he approved of Madison's arguments *for* a bill of rights, but:

> you omit one which has great weight with me, the legal check which it puts into the hands of the judiciary. This is a body, which if rendered independent, and kept strictly to their own department merits great confidence for their learning and integrity.

When he introduced in the House of Representatives the amendments that became the Bill of Rights, Madison polished Jefferson's reasoning:

---

41. "Notes on Virginia," (1784), Andrew A. Lipscomb, ed., The *Writings of Thomas Jefferson* (Washington, D.C.; The Thomas Jefferson Memorial Association, 1903), II, 163. Compare Tom Paine, *The Rights of Man* (New York: Dutton, 1951), Part II, p. 192: "It is not because a part of the Government is elective that makes it less a despotism, if the persons so elected possess afterwards, as a Parliament, unlimited powers."

42. The exchange of letters is reprinted in Julian P. Boyd, ed., *The Papers of Thomas Jefferson* (Princeton, N.J.: Princeton University Press, 1955) XII, 439–442; ibid. (1958), XIV, 18–21, 656–661. A more convenient source for these and many other documents in American constitutional history is Alpheus T. Mason and Gordon E. Baker, eds., *Free Government in the Making* (4th ed; New York: Oxford University Press, 1985), pp. 285–294.

> If they are incorporated into the constitution, independent tribunals of justice will consider themselves in a peculiar manner the guardians of those rights; they will be an impenetrable bulwark against every assumption of power in the legislative or executive; they will be naturally led to resist every encroachment upon the rights expressly stipulated for in the constitution by the declaration of rights.[43]

Judicial protection against legislative or executive tyranny was quite compatible with the other checks that Madison had persuaded the Convention to adopt, but it was not an arrangement that he had earlier stressed. To show that he saw a bill of rights as also fitting into his strategic scheme, he quickly added:

> Besides this security, there is a great probability that such a declaration in the federal system would be enforced; because the State Legislatures will jealously and closely watch the operations of this Government, and be able to resist with more effect every assumption of power, than any other power on earth can do; and the greatest opponents to a Federal Government admit the State Legislatures to be sure guardians of the people's liberty.[44]

The proposition that federal judges, appointed for what amounts to life terms, should sometimes stand with, and at other times stand against, elected legislators as bulwarks of individual liberty against the will of the people silhouettes the potential conflict between constitutionalism and democracy. And it is important to understand the precise nature of that conflict. It is undemocratic for a group of appointed officials to declare invalid decisions reached by the people's elected representatives. But federalism is similarly undemocratic. The democratic ideal of equal electoral districts is incompatible with giving more than 22 million people in California the same number of senators as fewer than a half million in Alaska, or for the Electoral College to overweight small states in presidential elections. Neither is it democratic for the people to be unable to elect a majority of senators in any given election, or for the Electoral College to be able to frustrate a numerical majority in choosing a President—or, when no candidate receives a majority of electoral votes, for the House, voting by states with Alaska having the same single vote as California, to select a President.

These sorts of potential conflict have occasionally become very real. They indicate the differing demands that constitutionalism and democracy may make on the political system and the differing ways in which the system accommodates those competing demands. The relationship between the two is conceptually as well as practically difficult. Yet the system has survived its inner tensions and perhaps prospered because of those tensions.

---

43. *Annals,* 1st Cong., 1st sess., I, 457.

44. Ibid.

V. CONCLUSION

As we have seen, most of the framers would have arrayed themselves much closer to the Pure Constitutionalist's end of the spectrum than to the Pure Representative Democrat's. We have also noted that the system has become more democratic, eroding some geographic, socio-economic, and institutional checks. At the same time, the sheer size of government has increased enormously along with its reach into once private affairs. These changes have heightened concern for some check on the huge, faceless power of government. In the place of these eroded checks, judicial review has blossomed as the most important institutional protector of individual rights in particular and constitutionalism in general, so much so that most Americans probably look on the justices of the U.S. Supreme Court as the true guardians of their constitutional chastity.

Because American legislators and executives have tended to shunt off on judges the duty to interpret the Constitution and reconcile democracy and constitutionalism, the study of constitutional interpretation has largely become the study of what the U.S. Supreme Court says and does. But the occasions on which Congress, the President, or the states challenge the Court's role as ultimate interpreter of the Constitution provide magnificent debates on political fundamentals, as Chapters 6 and 7 will demonstrate.

By deciding what the Constitution allows and forbids—defining unplain "plain words" and specifying implied powers and implied rights—judges inevitably have a great impact on public policy. In determining who may vote, what restrictions any level of government may put on political communications, or what differences in population among electoral districts are permissible, judicial decisions affect who will be elected to office, what demands will be given favorable hearings, and what policies will be enacted into law. More immediate are the policy effects of decisions like those regarding the authority of the President to seize vital industries that have been crippled by strikes [45] or to contract with a foreign government to suspend lawsuits by American citizens against that government; [46] or the authority of Congress to command, as part of its power to "regulate commerce among the several states," hotels and restaurants to serve all customers without regard to race; [47] or state authority to regulate abortions [48] or impose capital punishment.[49]

Public officials and private citizens who lose such cases often cry foul and complain that judges are acting "undemocratically" in overturning decisions of the people's representatives. The charge may be basically correct—although it is not always correct that elections have

45. Youngstown Sheet & Tube Co. v. Sawyer (1952).

46. Dames & Moore v. Regan (1981).

47. Heart of Atlanta Motel v. United States (1964).

48. Roe v. Wade (1973); reprinted below, p. 1109.

49. Compare Furman v. Georgia (1972), with Gregg v. Georgia (1976).

been truly free, that debate on a particular policy has been full and open, or that "the people," and at times even their representatives, have understood what the legislature did. Further, as we have just seen, a cluster of institutional arrangements including federalism, staggered elections, and the staffing of the Senate limits the capacity of the people to choose officials who can actually govern at the national level.

Despite these qualifications, there can be no doubt that judicial decisions have often frustrated the popular will. But that statement says very little. Indeed, to focus on a conflict between judicial review and democratic government is to miss much of what is interesting and important about the American political system. The tension is between democracy and constitutionalism. Judicial review, like each of the other institutional restraints on popular rule, is only one aspect of constitutionalism's larger effort to limit government.

SELECTED BIBLIOGRAPHY

Anastaplo, George. *The Constitutionalist* (Dallas, Tex.: Southern Methodist University Press, 1971).

Agresto, John. *The Supreme Court and Constitutional Democracy* (Ithaca, N.Y.: Cornell University Press, 1984).

Ball, Milner S. *The Promise of American Law* (Athens, Ga.: University of Georgia Press, 1981).

Barber, Sotirios A. *On What the Constitution Means* (Baltimore: Johns Hopkins Press, 1984).

Brest, Paul. "The Fundamental Rights Controversy," 90 *Yale L.J.* 1063 (1981).

Carter, Lief H. *Contemporary Constitutional Lawmaking* (New York: Pergamon Press, 1985).

Corwin, Edward S. "The Basic Doctrine of American Constitutional Law," 12 *Mich.L.Rev.* 247 (1914).

———. *The "Higher Law" Background of American Constitutional Law* (Ithaca, N.Y.: Cornell University Press, 1955).

———. *Liberty Against Government* (Baton Rouge, La.: Louisiana State University Press, 1948).

Dahl, Robert A. *A Preface to Democratic Theory* (Chicago: University of Chicago Press, 1956).

———. *Polyarchy: Participation and Opposition* (New Haven, Conn.: Yale University Press, 1971).

———. *Dilemmas of Pluralist Democracy: Autonomy vs. Control* (New Haven, Conn.: Yale University Press, 1982).

Dworkin, Ronald. *Taking Rights Seriously* (Cambridge, Mass.: Harvard University Press, 1977), espec. chap. 5.

———. *A Matter of Principle* (Cambridge, Mass.: Harvard University Press, 1985).

Eidelberg, Paul. *The Philosophy of the American Constitution* (New York: The Free Press, 1968).

Ely, John Hart. *Democracy and Distrust* (Cambridge, Mass.: Harvard University Press, 1980).

Friedrich, Carl J. *Constitutional Reason of State* (Providence, R.I.: Brown University Press, 1957).

————. *Transcendent Justice: The Religious Dimension of Constitutionalism* (Durham, N.C.: Duke University Press, 1964).

————. *Constitutional Government and Democracy* 4th ed.; (Waltham, Mass.: Blaisdell, 1968), espec. chaps. 1, 7–11, 13, 25.

Hallowell, John H. *The Moral Foundation of Democracy* (Chicago: University of Chicago Press, 1954).

Hirschman, Albert O. *The Passions and the Interests: Political Arguments for Capitalism before Its Triumph* (Princeton, N.J.: Princeton University Press, 1977).

McIlwain, Charles H. *Constitutionalism: Ancient & Modern* (Ithaca, N.Y.: Cornell University Press, 1947).

MacPherson, C.B. *Democratic Theory* (London: Oxford University Press, 1973).

Maddox, Graham. "A Note on the Meaning of 'Constitution,' " 76 *Am.Pol.Sci.Rev.* 805 (1982).

Parker, Richard D. "The Past of Constitutional Theory—And Its Future," 42 *Ohio St.L.J.* 223 (1981).

Pennock, J. Roland. *Democratic Political Theory* (Princeton, N.J.: Princeton University Press, 1979).

———— and John W. Chapman, eds. *Constitutionalism* ((New York: New York University Press, 1979).

————. *Liberal Democracy* (New York: New York University Press, 1983).

Perry, Michael J. *The Constitution, the Courts, and Human Rights* (New Haven, Conn.: Yale University Press, 1982).

Sartori, Giovanni. *Democratic Theory* (New York: Praeger, 1965), espec. chaps. 12–13, 15.

Smith, Rogers M. "The Constitution and Autonomy," 60 *Tex.L.Rev.* 175 (1982).

————. *Liberalism and American Constitutional Law* (Cambridge, Mass.: Harvard University Press, 1985).

Storing, Herbert, J. *What the Anti-Federalists Were For* (Chicago: University of Chicago Press, 1981).

Tribe, Laurence H. "The Puzzling Persistence of Process-Based Constitutional Theories," 89 *Yale L.J.* 1063 (1980); reprinted as chap. 2 in his *Constitutional Choices* (Cambridge, Mass.: Harvard University Press, 1985).

Tushnet, Mark. "The Dilemmas of Liberal Constitutionalism," 42 *Ohio St.L.J.* 411 (1981).

————. "Following the Rules Laid Down, A Critique of Interpretivism and Neutral Principles," 96 *Harv.L.Rev.* 781 (1983).

Wheeler, Harvey. "Constitutionalism," in Fred I. Greenstein and Nelson W. Polsby, eds., *Handbook of Political Science* (Reading, Mass.: Addison-Wesley, 1975), vol. V.

3

The Political and Institutional Contexts of Constitutional Interpretation

"Jurisprudence" is a compound word blending the notion of "right" or "justice" on the one hand, with "practical wisdom" on the other. That verbal union symbolizes the dual role of constitutional interpretation in keeping the political system both true to its ideals and practically viable. Thus, to understand constitutional interpretation, one needs to understand not only the theoretical but also the political and institutional contexts in which it takes place.

This Chapter looks at these latter contexts mainly from the perspective of the Supreme Court. We adopt that perspective not because the Court is the exclusive constitutional interpreter, but because it has become the most visible of constitutional interpreters. We do not prejudge Part III's interrogative of WHO are the authoritative interpreters of the Constitution.

I. THE POLITICAL SYSTEM

The framers at Philadelphia did not design a scheme of government to transform selfish human beings into saints, but to allow people to survive in liberty by pitting power against power and ambition against ambition. As we have already noted, the system has developed in many ways the Framers could not have foreseen, but it continues to function as a network of checks and counterchecks restraining power and ambition. The official who thinks that he or she has a monopoly of any form of political power, including constitutional interpretation, is doomed to be frustrated.

A. Sharing Powers Within the National System of Government

The widely repeated term "separation of powers" is misleading. The structure of the constitutional document has combined with long usage to produce a system that Richard E. Neustadt has far more accurately described as one of "separated institutions *sharing* powers." [1]

---

1. *Presidential Power* (New York: Wiley, 1960), p. 33.

Article I begins "All legislative power herein granted shall be vested in a Congress of the United States"; but both Article I and II make the President a critical part of the legislative process. He can propose legislation and veto bills, call Congress into special session and adjourn the two houses when they cannot agree on a date. Presidents have used those formal powers in expansive ways to create a long tradition that has become part of the system. Many, perhaps most, public laws are initially drafted by executive agencies; executive officials are among the most numerous lobbyists on Capitol Hill; and the President can be the most influential lobbyist of all, if he chooses to prod Congress by using his nominating power, his authority "to take care that the laws be faithfully executed," and his capacity to shape general public opinion. In short, he is as much "chief legislator" as he is "chief executive."

Article II vests "the executive power" in the President, but Articles I and II also give Congress some of that power. Together, the two houses create the executive departments; establish lines of authority among those agencies; enact rules for selecting, promoting, and firing officials; and appropriate money to carry out policies. The Senate can refuse to consent to presidential choices of people for the more important executive positions. The President also finds himself forced to share power by unwritten constitutional rules. For instance, "senatorial courtesy"—the custom that the Senate will not confirm a nominee over the disapproval of a senator from the President's party in whose state the nominee is to serve—often allows senators to share in the power to select as well as to confirm federal officials. And not infrequently officials so chosen feel stronger loyalty to a senator than to a President.

Control over the budget gives legislators an even greater share of executive power. The President often confronts an iron triangle: a tight alliance among an interest group, a congressional subcommittee, and an executive agency. In such situations, bureaucrats are as likely to follow the wishes of the subcommittee chairman (who in turn may be following the wishes of the interest group) as of the President, lest their operating funds be drastically reduced.[2]

Both Congress and the President exercise some judicial powers. Most European countries pretty much allow judges to determine who may join their ranks. In the United States, however, the President nominates federal judges and the Senate confirms or rejects their appointments. At least that is the formula the constitutional document presents. In fact, under the tradition of senatorial courtesy, senators from the President's party play a very active role in selecting federal district judges who will serve in their states and a smaller, though not necessarily insignificant role in choosing judges of the U.S. courts of appeals, whose jurisdiction includes several states. Here as elsewhere in selecting federal officials, the process tends to be one of negotia-

2. The classic study is Arthur Maass, *Muddy Waters* (Cambridge, Mass.: Harvard University Press, 1951).

tion, with the President typically getting more than the senators, but not always all that he would like.

The President is also formally responsible for initiating law suits—civil or criminal—in the name of the United States and for carrying out judicial decisions. His discretion in these areas is wide. Moreover, he may pardon anyone convicted of a federal crime, including criminal contempt of court. Perhaps most significant, the President may be able to persuade Congress to use (or not use) its quasi-judicial powers.

And Congress's potential to affect the federal judiciary is vast. First is the matter of jurisdiction, the authority of a court to hear and decide cases. Questions of jurisdiction are always issues of power; without jurisdiction a court is impotent. Article III, § 2, ¶ 1—as modified by the Eleventh Amendment's withdrawal of authority to hear suits brought against a state by foreigners or out-of-state citizens [3]—details the sorts of issues and parties to which federal jurisdiction "shall extend." [4] It was not, however, until after the Civil War that Congress conferred on federal courts the bulk of this jurisdiction; and it has never seen fit to give federal courts exclusive jurisdiction over all these matters. In sum, Congress has claimed that "shall extend" is permissive rather than mandatory, allowing it discretion to grant, not grant, and even remove jurisdiction from federal courts. Two centuries of practice, accepted by federal judges [5] no less than by presidents, have probably—but not certainly—validated that interpretation. As the Supreme Court said in 1938: "There can be no question of the power of Congress thus to define and limit the jurisdiction of the inferior courts of the United States." [6]

The language of Article II, § 2, ¶ 2 regarding congressional power to make "exceptions" to and "regulations" for the appellate jurisdiction of the Supreme Court is even more problematic. ("Original" jurisdiction refers to the authority of a court to hear a case in the first instance, "appellate" to the authority of one court to review rulings of a court farther down the judicial hierarchy.) The crucial disputes revolve around when an "exception" becomes so wide or a "regulation" so restrictive as to deprive the Court of its fundamental

---

3. Hans v. Louisiana (1890) held that the framers of the Eleventh Amendment erred: They had meant to deprive federal courts of jurisdiction to hear cases brought either by in- or by out-of-state citizens as well as by foreigners. And, the Court ruled, what the framers had meant to ask the states to ratify took precedence over what they actually asked the states to ratify. Green v. Mansour (1985) affirmed this rule, but four justices dissented and would have overturned *Hans*.

4. "The judicial power shall extend to all cases, in law and equity, arising under this Constitution, the laws of the United States, and treaties made, or which shall be made, under their authority;—to all cases affecting ambassadors, other public ministers and consuls;—to all cases of admiralty and maritime jurisdiction;—to controversies to which the United States shall be a party;—to controversies between two or more states;—. . . between citizens of different states;—between citizens of the same state claiming lands under grant of different states;—and between a state, or the citizens thereof, and foreign states, citizens or subjects."

5. See espec. Durousseau v. United States (1810) and Martin v. Hunter's Lessee (1816; reprinted below, p. 266).

6. Lauf v. Shinner & Co.

character as the head of the branch of government entrusted with "the judicial power."

Chapter 6 discusses these issues in some detail. Here we note only that, after the Civil War, Congress used this authority to prevent the Court's deciding a critical issue regarding the constitutionality of the centerpiece of Reconstruction, military rule in the South. With only Justice Grier dissenting, the Court meekly acquiesced,[7] setting a precedent that has haunted the justices, when opponents of decisions—such as those defending free speech during the McCarthy era or, more recently, defining a woman's right to abortion—have generated bills in Congress to remove the Court's jurisdiction to hear controversial matters.

Congress also has authority to determine the organization of lower federal courts, the number of Supreme Court justices—which has varied over American history from five to ten—the compensation that federal judges shall receive, as well as the rules under which all federal courts operate.[8] And the content of the criminal law that federal judges interpret and apply is contained in acts of Congress, just as is most federal civil law.

What should not be lost in a discussion of specific checks is that any time Congress passes a bill it at least implicitly—and often after lengthy, heated, and learned debate—interprets the Constitution, for, in effect, it says: "We think that making this kind of public policy falls within our authority and the means we have chosen to carry out that policy meet constitutional standards." In addition, Congress may propose constitutional amendments. Four of these—the Eleventh, Fourteenth, Sixteenth, and Twenty-sixth—changed the Supreme Court's interpretations of the Constitution;[9] and one, the Eleventh, struck directly at federal judicial authority.[10]

Further, the money to carry out the Supreme Court's decisions—indeed to operate the entire judicial system—comes only from con-

---

7. Ex parte McCardle (1868 and 1869). The Court's reporter did not publish Justice Grier's bitter dissenting opinion, though several newspapers printed excerpts. See Charles Warren, *The Supreme Court in United States History* (Rev. ed.; Boston: Little, Brown, 1926), II, 482.

8. Congress has chosen to delegate its rule-making authority to the Supreme Court, subject to congressional approval; but INS v. Chadha (1983; reprinted below, p. 383) casts a constitutional pall over this delegation. In any event, Congress may revoke that delegation by passing a new statute, which, like all statutes including those relating to jurisdiction and organization, is subject to a presidential veto.

9. The Eleventh changed the interpretation in Chisholm v. Georgia (1793) that citizens of one state could sue another state in a federal court; the Fourteenth reversed the holding of Dred Scott v. Sanford (1857) that a black person could not be a citizen of the United States; the Sixteenth displaced the decision in the Income Tax Cases (1895) that a federal income tax was a direct tax and so had, by the terms of Art. I, § 2, to be apportioned among the states by population; and the Twenty-sixth changed the interpretation of Oregon v. Mitchell (1970) that Congress could not set 18 as the minimum voting age for state elections.

10. For an argument that the Eleventh Amendment "merely requires a narrow construction of constitutional language affirmatively authorizing federal jurisdiction and . . . did nothing to prohibit federal court jurisdiction," see William A. Fletcher, "A Historical Interpretation of the Eleventh Amendment," 35 *Stan.L.Rev.* 1033 (1983).

gressional appropriations. In a much more constitutionally problematic fashion, congressional investigations may also exercise a form of judicial power. Committees have often paraded witnesses' sins before television cameras and so punished them in a very real sense. As a final judicial power, the House may impeach any federal judge for "treason, bribery, or other high crimes and misdemeanors," and he or she will be removed if the Senate convicts.

For their part, judges exercise some legislative and executive as well as judicial authority. Most basically, interpreting "the law," especially the law of the Constitution with its references in the Ninth Amendment, for example, to unlisted rights and (in the necessary and proper clause) to unenumerated powers, may require creating that law. We need not repeat what Chapter 1 argued at length about the inevitability of discretion and creativity in interpreting the Constitution.

Statutes are often even more difficult to decipher, requiring judges to rethink thoughts legislators were trying or should have been trying to think. Congressional and presidential efforts to placate assorted interest groups while grappling with difficult practical problems typically result in obtuse language that forces judges, if they are to make sense of those words, to become part of the legislative process. Much the same sort of thing can happen with executive orders, more of which qualify as grammarians' nightmares than as models of clear prose.

B. Sharing Powers Within the Federal System of Government

As Chapter 2 pointed out, the constitutional document looks to a federal system in which the national government is supreme within a sphere only inexactly sketched, and in which states also function as important political units with broad, though undefined, residual powers. The result is a further sharing of power and pitting of ambition against ambition.

For our purposes three points are critical. First, states may compete with federal power, even in the field of constitutional interpretation. (See Chapter 7 for a detailed discussion.) Second, as the ratifiers of proposed constitutional amendments, states may participate directly in changing the document's provisions and indirectly the system's traditions. Third, and perhaps most important, state officials may influence senators, congressmen, and presidents, all of whom are to some extent dependent for reelection on the good will of officials in their home states.

C. The Checking of Sharing

The result of these separate institutions sharing powers is a messy, rather than a neat political system. Not only do governmental institutions compete, but they check and countercheck each other.

Each can use its own power as well as the power it shares with another branch to thwart another branch's action. This network of restraints often deadlocks government; and were each branch to unleash its weapons against the others, the system would self-destruct. Recognizing these dangers, most politicians who become national leaders have the good sense to use their power with caution. Friction is continual and conflict frequent, but all-out-war is rare. The norm is a process of accommodation, negotiation, and compromise with the resulting public policy, including constitutional interpretation, often being fuzzily rather than sharply defined.

Yet, even when conflict stops short of war, it can change, at least temporarily, the balance of power within the system. The scandals of Watergate and an imminent threat of impeachment led to Richard Nixon's resignation in 1974 from an "imperial presidency"; his next two successors inherited a much weaker office. It was not until Ronald Reagan that the White House regained much of its former power. Similarly, in 1937, the likelihood of some form of curb on its power nudged the Supreme Court to change its constitutional interpretation and to demote "freedom of contract" from its former status as a fundamental right. That shift, which Edward S. Corwin termed a "constitutional revolution," [11] was dramatic; but, each time a President nominates a new justice, he tries to affect the Court's constitutional interpretation. And similar hopes have usually fired Congress when it has deployed its quasi-judicial powers.

D. The Capacity of Interest Groups to Trigger Checks

The very nature of a constitution means that almost every piece of constitutional interpretation will, in the long run, have some impact on a wide spectrum of values, people, and very tangible interests. Even in the short run, the effects are usually broad. Statutes and administrative orders are aimed at wide audiences. And, though a judicial decision formally binds only the parties to a case, its reasoning is likely to ripple across the community. A decision about the validity of governmental regulations of economic affairs will encourage business, labor, and consumers to bring fresh lawsuits and/or pressure executive and legislative officials; rulings about reapportionment immediately shape the electoral structure in the state involved and flash omens to other states; constitutional standards concerning the rights of the criminally accused may not only change the treatment accorded those people, but may also influence the degree of liberty as well as "domestic tranquility" the entire population can enjoy.

Thus whenever a governmental institution interprets the Constitution, some interests are likely to be furthered and others injured; and the same people—the general public, for instance, in matters of criminal justice—may find some of their rights enhanced at the same time as others are diminished. Because of the open nature of the

---

11. *Constitutional Revolution, Ltd.* (Claremont, Cal.: The Claremont Press, 1941).

political processes, individuals and groups aggrieved by an interpretation of the Constitution may utilize their access to one or another governmental institution to frustrate or reverse policies they do not like or to reinforce those they like.

Not only can individuals and groups lobby senators, representatives, federal executive officials, or state legislators and administrators to counter judicial decisions, but they can also go to court—again as individuals or as members of a group—to block (or, under some circumstances, to validate) legislative or executive action, state or federal. Litigation designed to affect public policy, the Supreme Court has said, is "a form of political expression." As such, it is fully protected from federal or state interference by the First and Fourteenth amendments. This right can be especially important to people who lack the numbers, organization, or prestige to influence popularly elected officials. "[U]nder the conditions of modern government," the Court has added, "litigation may well be the sole practical avenue open to a minority to petition for redress of grievances." [12]

Because one can so readily challenge governmental action, constitutional interpretation, again like public policy generally, is often unsettled. But, if the system's open nature offers many routes to governmental power, it does not guarantee success in effecting substantive change. For, just as any particular constitutional interpretation will anger some groups, that same interpretation is likely to please others who are not apt to watch passively while their opponents try to rechange it. Open access insures only the availability of additional arenas for peaceful struggle.

It is also important to keep in mind that open access does not insure that all groups will have an equal chance in each arena. Money, education, organization, prestige, and particular skills, whether in obtaining publicity, mustering blocs of voters, bargaining, or legal reasoning, confer great advantages; and none of these is evenly distributed among the population.

E. An Open System of Checks and Counterchecks

In sum, when a judge, a President, a senator, a representative, or state official interprets the Constitution, he or she must realize that other officials may also be engaged in that enterprise. Moreover, constitutional interpretation affects the short and long term interests of human beings who have needs and rights and wants and demands and access to other political institutions. Thus, not only is any interpretation to some extent subject to modification or even reversal by other interpreters, but the institution making an interpretation is also vulnerable to being curbed by one or both of the other branches. That an

---

12. NAACP v. Button (1963). See also Bounds v. Smith (1977), which spoke of "the fundamental constitutional right of access to the courts" in the context of a duty on the part of prison officials to provide inmates with adequate law libraries or professional assistance to help them appeal their convictions or seek habeas corpus.

interpreter may ride out any particular storm is very possible, indeed likely, but the threat of shipwreck is always present.

The reality of the political system does not force justices continually to look over their shoulders to see what Congress and the President are doing, nor do they need to hire a polling agency to keep them in touch with public opinion. As a practical matter, however, judges are not free to interpret the Constitution as they wish. That reality also means that, however much they want what they honestly believe to be the most justifiable interpretation of the Constitution to prevail, they may have to settle for less than the best. Neither constitutional nor democratic theory prescribes total judicial freedom; and the political system limits both the good and evil that any set of public officials can accomplish.

In essence, constitutional interpretation is a theoretical process, a search for the best in our past to guide our present and shape our future; but it is more than an abstract intellectual process. It is also one aspect of the practical process of governing a nation, an integral part of the art of politics.

II. THE JUDICIAL PROCESS: PROCEDURAL DIFFERENCES

In their operations courts differ from other governmental institutions in several consequential ways. First, judges have "no self-starting capacity." [13] When legislators or executive officials perceive a problem, they can attack it directly by passing new legislation, prosecuting, investigating, or merely generating publicity to embarrass wrongdoers. Judges, however, cannot initiate action. They must wait until someone formally brings a lawsuit before them.

Second, that lawsuit must display certain characteristics. It must present a "case or controversy," that is, a real dispute between genuinely adverse parties involving injury, or immediate threat of injury, to a legally protected right. Furthermore, that person must show that this case raises a legal issue over which the court has jurisdiction, that is, authority to decide. The litigant must also meet technical rules relating to "standing." Essentially, these require a person bringing suit to show that: (a) the legally protected right involved is a personal one, not someone else's right or a right shared by the public generally; (b) the dispute is "justiciable," that is, a matter that, judges have said, the Constitution assigns to them; (c) if governmental action is challenged, the action is sufficiently "final" to be "ripe" for judicial determination, and sufficiently "live" not to be moot; and (d) the judicial decision will be binding between the

---

13. Robert H. Jackson, *The Supreme Court in the American System of Government* (Cambridge, Mass.: Harvard University Press, 1955), p. 24. But see Abram Chayes, "The Role of the Judge in Public Law Litigation," 89 *Harv.L.Rev.* 1281 (1976), for a model of the judicial role as declaring law rather than merely as resolving disputes.

parties to the case, that is, it will not merely be a piece of advice that the litigants are legally free to ignore.[14]

A third peculiarity of judicial operations relates to the limited number and kinds of remedies that a judge can fashion. More of these are negative than positive. A court can hold a particular criminal statute constitutional, but it cannot force the attorney general to prosecute those who violate that law. It may invalidate a statute for failing to protect the rights of minorities, but it cannot directly compel either Congress or the states to enact a law that protects minority rights.

Fourth, although the influence of an opinion as a precedent may be far flung, a formal judicial decree is quite limited in its reach. Unlike a statute, which may obligate everyone in the United States and its possessions, an order of a court binds only the parties to the case, their employees, agents, successors in office, and those who, knowing an order is in force, conspire with the litigants to violate that order. Thus the Supreme Court's decision that school segregation in Topeka, Kansas, was unconstitutional (see Brown v. Board [1954; reprinted below, p. 768]) did not legally require officials anywhere else to desegregate, at least not until someone brought and won a new law suit against them.

The fifth and perhaps the most obvious difference between courts and other institutions lies in procedure. In court, each side is entitled to be represented by a lawyer, to present full evidence and argument to support its position, to compel witnesses to testify about what they know, to hear all opposing evidence and have an opportunity to rebut it, including a right to cross examine opposing witnesses. The proceeding takes place in public before a judge, who must be neutral between the litigants, and sometimes before a jury, whose members are also chosen to insure impartiality. If the matter is criminal in nature, the government must prove guilt "beyond a reasonable doubt" and must further show that during the period before the trial it respected all of the accused's constitutional rights.

After the verdict, the loser normally has a right to appeal to a higher court to correct any alleged errors at the trial. The loser also has a right to expect that the trial judge and any appellate judges who have reviewed the case will justify their decisions by legal principles, not merely by expediency or wise public policy. In sum, "a day in court" has become another way of saying "fair play." Other institutions may also operate fairly, but they do not do so with such fastidious regard for formal procedures as do courts.

III. PROCEDURES WITHIN THE SUPREME COURT

The Supreme Court's procedures can effect the substance of its decisions. Appendix A pp. 1213–1220 explains in detail how litigants

---

14. For a fuller discussion of standing, see Walter F. Murphy and C. Herman Pritchett, *Courts, Judges, & Politics* (4th ed.; New York: Random House, 1986), chap. 5 and literature cited.

bring cases to the justices. For our immediate purposes, it is sufficient to understand that most cases come up as "petitions for certiorari," that is, as requests that the Court review decisions of lower federal courts or state judicial rulings on federal questions. The person asking for the writ (the petitioner) must succinctly set out the pertinent facts of the dispute, the questions of law, and a justification for the Court's hearing the case. The other party (the respondent) has 30 days in which to file counterargument.

The justices have complete discretion to grant or deny these petitions. In fact, they deny more than 95 per cent of them and seldom offer any reason whatsoever. That statistic does not mean the justices treat petitions cavalierly, though their sheer number—more than 4,000 a year—demands efficiency. When a petition arrives, the Clerk of the Court assigns the case a docket number and sends a copy of all papers to every justice. The next step varies among the justices. Some read all or most of these petitions themselves; others divide them among their personal clerks;[15] and several have agreed to share their clerks' recommendations.

The following memorandum, written by Justice Hugo L. Black for his own use, is typical of these recommendations:

NO. 788
HARRY BRIDGES v. I.F. WIXON, AS DISTRICT DIRECTOR,
    IMMIGRATION AND NATURALIZATION SERVICE
Cert. to CCA 9th
In this case Harry Bridges has been ordered deported by the Attorney General after hearings before an appointed Commissioner. Hearings before a previous Commissioner, Dean Landis, had decided that the evidence failed to show that Bridges was a member of the Communist Party. Thereafter Congress amended the law, expressly intending to hit Bridges, so that deportation could be brought about for past membership in the Communist Party. It is under this new legislation that the deportation was ordered here.

Questions are raised with reference to the absence of evidence to support the finding and which involved freedom of speech and association. They are of sufficient importance that I think we should grant certiorari on all the points requested.
    GRANT.

                                                    H.L.B.

Every week or so the chief justice circulates a "discuss list," the petitions for certiorari that he recommends for debate at the Court's next conference. All other petitions received during the period covered by the list are automatically denied. If any justice wishes to discuss a petition not on the list, he or she merely so notes and those items are automatically added.

---

15. Each justice has four clerks, typically young men or women who recently graduated at or near the top of their classes at the most prestigious law schools. Because of his heavy administrative burdens, the chief justice also has a more senior lawyer and an experienced judicial administrator as assistants.

The Supreme Court's term begins on the first Monday in October and, until 1981, ran until early summer. The Court still recesses then, but the term does not end until the following October, just before the new one begins. During vacations as well as term time, petitions for certiorari roll endlessly in. Oliver Wendell Holmes, who gave them the nickname "bloody certs," used to greet new members of the Court with a cheery "Welcome to our chain gang."

During term, the Court usually is in session for two weeks, hearing oral arguments on Mondays, Tuesdays, and Wednesdays from 10 a.m. until noon, and from 1 until 3 p.m. Then the justices recess for two weeks to continue arguing among themselves and to write opinions. During the weeks when the Court is sitting, the justices meet in conference late on Wednesday afternoons and all day Friday. It is here that they debate petitions on the "discuss list" and decide cases just argued. It takes a vote of four, one less than a majority, to grant certiorari.

When the Court grants certiorari it agrees only to hear the case (though it is statistically more likely that the Court will reverse than affirm cases it has agreed to hear). Each side may then submit a brief on the merits, more fully stating its arguments, and a reply brief, responding to the other's arguments. Either at this stage or when the petition for certiorari is filed, other parties may also present briefs to the Court as *amici curiae,* friends of the court. Such individuals or organizations must show that they, too, have interests at stake in the litigation and wish to present arguments different from those of either side. On occasion, the Court will invite someone to appear as an *amicus,* usually the Solicitor General of the United States or an attorney general of a state.

If the justices grant certiorari, the Clerk sets a date for oral argument. Each side is allowed 30 minutes, although in cases whose impact is likely to be especially far reaching, the Court may grant additional time. Normally, *amici* are not allowed to participate in oral argument, though the Court often allows the solicitor general or sometimes state attorneys general to do so.

Counsel stands at a lectern facing the bench and begins "Chief Justice, may it please the Court . . . ." Frequently, these are his or her last prepared words. In italics the Court's rules say: *"The Court looks with disfavor on any oral argument that is read from a prepared text."* Instead of a lecture, the justices want a discussion, in which they can sate their appetites for information. Most lawyers who argue before the Court do not do so on a regular basis and wrongly assume the justices want explanations of their own previous decisions. Counsel find themselves constantly interrupted, as two or three justices simultaneously push for responses to questions that range in sweep from a decision's potential effects on public policy to more details about the factual background of the case.

When an attorney has five minutes remaining, a white light flashes on the lectern. When time is up, a red light goes on.

Argument must immediately stop. There is a story that Chief Justice Hughes once cut a famous lawyer off in the middle of the word "if."

Later that week when the justices meet in conference, no one except the nine members of the Court is allowed into the room. Messengers are met at the door by the junior justice in time of service on the Court. The only outsider to get as much as a foot inside is the man who pushes a coffee cart, and he seldom makes it farther than the threshold before the justices wheel his wagon from him.

The chief justice opens discussion by summarizing the case and explaining his views. Then the justices speak in order of seniority. The Court keeps no formal record of these debates, but some justices scribble notes either to refresh their memories or to enlighten history. We have used in this book some of the notes that Frank Murphy, Harold Burton, and William O. Douglas left. We should treat these with caution because the people who took them were usually hotly engaged in discussion themselves. Still, all three sets provide the same general picture of intense, informed, and wide-ranging debate.

Justices use the conference either to try to persuade their colleagues or, if they are undecided, to learn from them. At times tempers flash. "We do take our jobs seriously," one justice has said in private, "and we do get angry. Any judge who didn't get angry when he saw the Constitution misinterpreted ought to be impeached."

The style of conferences has varied with the personality of the chief justice. Charles Evans Hughes (1930–41) and Harlan Fiske Stone (1941–46) represent opposite extremes. Hughes disciplined himself to speak only a few minutes, and he expected similar self control from his colleagues. He would cut off a speech with a curt "thank you" and nod to the justice next in seniority to begin. He preferred rapid disposition of cases to debate. Stone, a former professor, rankled under Hughes's management; and, when he became chief, he tried to turn the conference into a seminar. His colleagues sometimes turned it into a shouting match. Business that took several hours under Hughes usually took several days under Stone, but no one complained that issues were not thoroughly aired.

When the chief believes that further discussion would be fruitless, he calls for a vote. From John Marshall to Earl Warren, the justices voted in reverse order of seniority, increasing the power of the more senior members, especially of the chief since by voting last he could always be in the majority. Warren felt that procedure was unfair and persuaded the justices to vote in the same order as they had spoken.

Being in the majority is important, for the chief has the prerogative of assigning the task of writing the opinion of the Court unless he votes with the minority. If the chief is in the minority, the senior associate justice in the majority makes the assignment. The person who assigns the opinion may, of course, keep it himself or give it to the justice whom he thinks most likely to reflect the views he wants to prevail. Some chief justices—Marshall, Taft, and Hughes, for instance—almost never dissented; others—such as Warren and Burger—frequently did so.

Being assigned the task of writing the Court's opinion does not guarantee that the opinion written will be that of the Court. To be so labelled and carry the institutional authority of the Supreme Court rather than merely be an expression of personal views, an opinion must have the approval of at least five justices; and all justices are free to write their own opinions, either concurring or dissenting, to join in whichever other opinion(s) suit(s) them, and to change their votes up to the minute the Court announces its decision. Even afterward, if the losing party asks for a rehearing, justices can change their minds.

The opinion writer prepares a manuscript, and when he or she thinks it ready, circulates it in the form of a printed "slip opinion" to the rest of the Court, usually referred to as "the Conference." Each justice is supposed to give such drafts immediate attention, and few have been bashful about suggesting changes. Sometimes these are minor; sometimes they involve recasting the entire reasoning; and sometimes suggestions from different justices are mutually incompatible. If the last is true, the opinion writer has to convert others or decide which colleague's vote to lose.

At the same time, the dissenters, acting alone or together, may circulate their opinion(s), although they may wait until the majority's opinion is approaching final form. Dissents are also circulated to every member of the Court, and sometimes they persuade justices to change their votes. It is uncommon but not unheard of for what began as a dissent to end up as the opinion of the Court. It is more common for the Court's opinion writer to try to accommodate some of the dissenters' views and win them over. Indeed, circulation of a dissent can be a means of tacit negotiation, one that Louis D. Brandeis used with great effectiveness.[16]

Like the larger political system of which it is a part, the intra-Court process encourages compromise, even bargaining of a sort. First, there is the magic goal of five votes. The justice who refuses to compromise seldom writes for the Court in important cases. Sometimes the price of compromise is high. Holmes complained that "the boys generally cut one of the genitals" out of his opinions.[17] Some of the cases reprinted in this book contain incompatible, incomplete, and at times even illogical arguments. On occasion, the opinion writer has erred; but more often to achieve a majority, the justice has incorporated differing views.

Second, the justices realize that they will be working together over a long period. The average tenure on the Court is almost 20

16.   See Alexander M. Bickel, *The Unpublished Opinions of Mr. Justice Brandeis* (Cambridge, Mass.: The Belknap Press of Harvard University Press, 1957). For more general discussions of judicial strategy, see Walter F. Murphy, *Elements of Judicial Strategy* (Chicago: University of Chicago Press, 1964), and David M. O'Brien, *Storm Center: The Supreme Court in American Politics* (New York: Norton, 1986).

17.   Holmes to Sir Frederick Pollock, Jan. 24, 1918; Mark DeWolf Howe, ed., *Holmes-Pollock Letters* (Cambridge, Mass.: Harvard University Press, 1942), II, 258.

years. The person who graciously concedes a point today can expect similar treatment tomorrow; just as the person who refuses to compromise when in the majority may face a similar stonewall the next week. Thus, as Felix Frankfurter once said, an opinion for the Court often involves "an orchestral and not a solo performance." [18]

IV. THE INFLUENCE OF PERSONAL VALUES

In a post-Freudian world, there can be no serious doubt that a judge's—or a senator's, representative's, governor's, President's, police officer's, professor's, or student's—personal values influence the way in which he or she interprets the Constitution. Society can require that judges be neutral between parties to a case; but no one can ask a mature adult to be neutral between ideas that go to the heart of political philosophy. Not only do we all carry the effects of early childhood, religious and moral instruction, family relations, and social class, but we are affected by our more formal education and our experiences through life. These factors shape the values that we apply to choices; they also influence the way in which we selectively perceive "facts" from which we make choices.

The political system puts one set of limitations on judicial choices, the rules of the judicial process impose another, and the internal operating procedures of the Supreme Court yet a third set. Of comparable significance are the restraints implanted by political culture, especially as transmitted through training in law school, law practice, and practical political experience. Still, these are limitations, not iron fetters. The American political system is flexible; rules of law—in particular of constitutional law—are often open-ended; and political culture is a force that is felt rather than read in black letters. There is, in short, much room for the play of individual values, not only among judges but among other public officials as well. It does make a difference whether Earl Warren or Warren Earl Burger is Chief Justice, whether the Court is composed of William J. Brennans or William H. Rehnquists, just as it matters whether James Earl Carter or Ronald Reagan is President.

The procedures of the Court also make it probable that the justices will influence each other—and not always positively. Feuds and friendships sometimes develop on the Court. Frankfurter and Douglas detested each other, as did Black and Jackson. McReynolds, a blatant anti-semite, refused to have anything to do "with the Orient" and so never spoke to Brandeis or Cardozo unless absolutely necessary. On the other hand, Holmes and Brandeis enjoyed a close relationship and later brought Stone in as a third musketeer.

All such human interactions influence opinions. It is normal to listen more sympathetically to arguments of friends than to those of foes. With some justification, Taft complained that Brandeis's friend-

---

18. *The Commerce Clause under Marshall, Taney* and *Waite* (Chapel Hill, N.C.: University of North Carolina Press, 1937), p. 43.

ship with Holmes often gave him two votes; and Stone freely conceded that the warmth of Holmes and Brandeis helped move him away from Taft's conservative views of the Constitution. Justice Brennan's genial nature allowed him to play the role of an intellectual bridge between the more and less libertarian justices on the Warren Court. Conversely, Brandeis and McReynolds could never negotiate except through intermediaries, nor could Black and Jackson, Douglas and Frankfurter.

It is important to keep in mind, however, that affection or animosity seldom *causes* agreement or disagreement on matters of jurisprudence. Douglas and Rehnquist had great mutual respect, but they voted against each other in almost every non-unanimous decision in which they both participated. So, too, Douglas and his dear friend Sherman Minton seldom agreed on constitutional issues. On the other hand, jurisprudential agreement or disagreement can form the basis of friendship or enmity. Because justices feel so deeply about their work, it is sometimes difficult for them to leave their battles in the conference room.

V. *KOREMATSU*: A CASE STUDY

We have been speaking of the contexts in which constitutional interpretation, as performed by justices of the Supreme Court, takes place. In this section, we shall go through one case, Korematsu v. United States (1944), to illustrate how various political and institutional factors interact with personal values to produce decisions. (We reprint the opinions in that case, below at p. 1197.)

A. General Background

On December 7, 1941, while their special emissaries were in Washington supposedly negotiating, the Japanese attacked Pearl Harbor and wiped out a large part of the American fleet. They then swept across the western Pacific, quickly conquering Wake, Guam, the Philippines, Malaya, Singapore, and the Dutch East Indies; invaded New Guinea, the Solomon Islands, and Burma, threatening Australia to the south and India to the west. There was panic among some American civilian and military leaders that the west coast was also in danger.

Agitation for some kind of action against both alien Japanese and American citizens of Japanese descent (Nisei) began within weeks of the attack on Pearl Harbor. Some military leaders, most notably General John L. DeWitt, commanding the west coast area, wanted to intern these people. (He was also worried about the large number of "colored troops" under his command.) Others, such as the Office of Naval Intelligence, thought that the Nisei posed no danger to the national safety—a view in which the FBI concurred. But more was involved than a dispute about national security. Racism, evidenced on the west coast by anti-oriental more than by anti-black prejudice, was hardly unknown in the United States. The Japanese government's treachery and their troops' torturing and murdering civilians and prisoners of war provided a license to hate. Some public officials honestly, if incorrectly, feared mass violence against people of Japanese extraction and raised the argument that the Nisei as well as enemy aliens should be locked up for their own good.

Economic self interests encouraged radical governmental action against Japanese Americans. Their work ethic had made them tough competitors in farming, fishing, and small businesses. It did not escape notice that if they were forcibly removed, their competition would be destroyed—and their homes and businesses perhaps sold at fire-sale prices. Legislators, especially from the west, were soon swamped with demands from individuals and interest groups for action against all people of Japanese ancestry. Other groups, the American Civil Liberties Union and the Japanese American Citizens League, for example, fought back; but their prestige was low, their numbers few, and their influence small. Even the doubts publicly expressed by ONI and the FBI about the need for a restrictive program and the misgivings of some officials about the constitutionality of incarcerating people because their ancestors had emigrated from a country with whom we were now at war could not stop a juggernaut fed by fear, hate, and economic self interest.[19]

On March 27, 1942, Franklin Roosevelt signed into law a bill which made it a crime to remain in a "military zone" designated by a commander acting under authority of the Secretary of War or, for those allowed to remain in such a zone, to disobey the commander's regulations. This statute legitimated an earlier executive order authorizing the Secretary of War to designate military zones "from which any and all persons" might be excluded. The statute also retroactively validated the curfew that General DeWitt had imposed on enemy aliens and Nisei living in the Pacific states.

Pursuant to this new authority, the Army required all persons of Japanese ancestry to report to designated centers for transportation to and imprisonment in concentration camps. General DeWitt explained that it was legitimate to put the Nisei behind barbed wire while allowing German and Italian aliens to remain free because "a Jap is a Jap" and World War II was "a war of the white race against the yellow race."

B. Hirabayashi v. United States (1943)

By disobeying both the curfew and the order to report for evacuation, Gordon Hirabayashi, a student at the University of Washington, provided the first judicial test of the statute as applied to an American citizen. A federal district court convicted him on both counts. He lost in the court of appeals and obtained certiorari from

---

19. The ugly story is most fully told in Morton Grodzins, *American Betrayed: Politics and the Japanese Evacuation* (Chicago: University of Chicago Press, 1949); see also Peter Irons, *Justice at War* (New York: Oxford University Press, 1983).

the U.S. Supreme Court.   The justices held oral argument in May, 1943, and discussed and voted on the case a few days later.

Chief Justice Stone opened the conference.   According to Justice Frank Murphy's notes, the Chief stressed that, although Hirabayashi had been convicted on counts of violating both the curfew and evacuation, the trial judge had imposed concurrent sentences.   Thus affirming a conviction on either count would mean that Hirabayashi would have to serve the full sentence, and so the Chief thought there was no need for the Court to go beyond the validity of the curfew.

Stone saw three major constitutional problems: 1.   Had Congress unconstitutionally delegated legislative power to executive officials? He believed not.   Congress had known what action the executive would take and approved it.   The debate went on:

> CHIEF JUSTICE STONE: "2.   So you come to whether it was within [the] constitutional power of Congress and [the] President together.   3.   Then you come to discrimination against Japanese. All this depends [on] whether there was a reasonable basis at the time government took action.   It is jarring to me that U.S. citizens were subjected to this treatment, but I can't say [that] . . . it was unconstitutional.   They [the military] conducted a war under peculiar danger and great treachery . . . .   Our safety was involved. They could draw [a] distinction between an Italian and [a] Japanese. You cannot say that it was an unconstitutional measure during wartime.   It is a power about which I am abhorrent and mistrustful. [But] we can't walk through fire lines even at misconvenience . . . .   [W]e should not deal with second count."
> ROBERTS: "I take the narrow ground that you do, if we can pass the destruction of citizens' rights in camp."
> BLACK: "I want it done on narrowest possible points."
> REED: "The curfew is the same as concentration camp.   The difficulty is [that] it is applied to certain types of citizens."
> FRANKFURTER: "I am for deciding this case on narrow grounds . . . ."
> JACKSON: "I don't think [a] military commander is bound by due process.   [But] can you make as simple a test as who is [an] ancestor?"
> ROBERTS: "If applied to all citizens, it would be all right."

Murphy did not record Douglas as speaking.   It is quite possible, given that justice's taciturn nature, that he said little, for he was nursing serious doubts.   Murphy noted that he himself was concerned about racial discrimination.

Fear of dividing a nation at war reinforced the normal desire of a chief justice to mass the Court in important cases.   Thus Stone assumed the task of writing the Court's opinion and sought to mute conflict by considering only the validity of the curfew.   He wrote that the Court would not in 1943 say that in 1942, only months after the disaster at Pearl Harbor, it had been unreasonable for the military to fear espionage and sabotage and to doubt there was time to separate the loyal from the disloyal among groups most likely to contain enemy sympathizers. It had been legitimate, therefore, to require such people to remain in their homes after dark.

The Chief insisted that "it is not for any court to sit in review" of the wisdom of the military's choices. And, toward the close of his opinion, he re-emphasized the limited nature of the Court's holding: "it is unnecessary to consider whether or to what extent such findings [of military peril] would support orders differing from the curfew order."

Hugo Black and Felix Frankfurter were generally satisfied with the draft, and three others, Owen Roberts, Stanley Reed, and Robert H. Jackson, swallowed their doubts. Reed remarked to Stone that his task had been "thankless," but he had "done it well."

On the other hand, Wiley Rutledge, Frank Murphy, and William O. Douglas still had serious reservations. Murphy was the most outspoken. Not only was he angered by DeWitt's crass racism, he was also worried that Stone's opinion undercut judicial authority by requiring the military to meet only a test of "reasonableness" to justify its actions, rather than the stricter test that Stone himself had suggested for "insular minorities" in United States v. Carolene Products (1938; reprinted below, p. 482) and the Court had strengthened in Skinner v. Oklahoma (1942; reprinted below, p. 868). "While this Court sits," Murphy said, "it has the inescapable duty of seeing that the mandates of the Constitution are obeyed."

Learning of Murphy's plans to dissent, Frankfurter urged him to negotiate with Stone:

> Please, Frank, with your eagerness for the austere functions of the Court and your desire to do all that is humanly possible to maintain and enhance the corporate reputation of the Court, why don't you take the initiative with the Chief Justice in getting him to take out everything that either offends you or that you would want to express more irenically?

Even after an exchange of several notes, Stone and Murphy remained far apart, and the latter circulated a blistering opinion branding the army's program as "utterly inconsistent with our ideals and traditions" and "at variance with the principles for which we are fighting." Frankfurter read Murphy's draft in horror and immediately wrote another plea:

> Of course I shan't try to dissuade you from filing a dissent . . . not because I do not think it highly unwise but because I think you are immovable. But I would like to say two things to you about the dissent: (1) it has internal contradictions which you ought not to allow to stand, and (2) do you really think it is conducive to the things you care about, including the great reputation of this Court, to suggest that everybody is out of step except Johnny, and more particularly that the Chief Justice and seven other Justices of this Court are behaving like the enemy and thereby playing into the hands of the enemy?

Murphy had second thoughts. Within a few days he modified his dissent into a concurrence. Still, he felt obliged to say publicly:

> We give great deference to the judgment of the Congress and of the military authorities as to what is necessary in the effective prosecution of the war, but we can never forget that there are constitutional boundaries which it is our duty to uphold. . . . Under the curfew order . . . no less than 70,000 American citizens have been placed under a special ban and deprived of their liberty because of their particular racial inheritance. In this sense, it bears a melancholy resemblance to the treatment accorded to members of the Jewish race in Germany and in other parts of Europe.

Douglas also tried to negotiate with Stone. He had some success in persuading the Chief to remove a reference to the "ethnic solidarity" of the Nisei that smacked to Douglas of racism and, for a brief time, to include a hint that the Court would require individual judicial hearings before allowing internment. But several other members of the majority complained; Justice Black went so far as to state that, if he were the commanding general, he would refuse to allow the Nisei to return to the West Coast even if a court so ordered. Stone then explained to Douglas he feared that "if I accepted your suggestions very little of the structure of my opinion would be left, and that I should lose most of my adherents. It seems to me, therefore, that it would be wiser for me to stand by the substance of my opinion and for you to express your views in your concurring opinion."

As published, Douglas' concurrence noted that he agreed "substantially" with the opinion of the Court that, in 1942, the curfew had not been unreasonable. He insisted, however, that "[l]oyalty is a matter of mind and of heart not race."

Wiley Rutledge confessed to Stone that "I have had more anguish over this case than any I have ever decided, save possibly one death case in the Court of Appeals." And in an early draft of a concurring opinion he wrote:

> I have very strong sympathies with Mr. Justice Murphy's views. Next to totalitarian power, sheer racial discrimination goes to the heart of the Nazi-Fascist political policy that we now fight.[20]

Eventually, however, Rutledge removed this statement and contented himself with a notation that he did not join in the suggestion,

> if that is intended, that the courts have no power to review any action a military officer may "in his discretion" find it necessary to take with respect to civilian citizens . . . . [It] does not follow that there may not be bounds beyond which he cannot go and, if he oversteps them, that courts may not have power to protect the civilian citizen.

---

20. Quoted in Fowler V. Harper, *Justice Rutledge and the Bright Constellation* (Indianapolis: Bobbs, Merrill, 1965), p. 176.

C. *Korematsu* and *Endo* (1944) Reach the Court

The Court announced its decision in *Hirabayashi* in June, 1943. In the fall of 1944, Fred Korematsu, a young Nisei who had been unwilling to leave his sweetheart, brought the issue of concentration camps before the Court. He had been convicted on the single count of not reporting for evacuation, and the circuit court of appeals had sustained his conviction. Korematsu then petitioned the Supreme Court for certiorari. According to Justice Douglas's notes, Stone did not vote at all on the question of granting the writ. Black voted against, but the others agreed to take the case.

On the same day the Court heard argument in both *Korematsu* and Ex parte Endo. The latter was a challenge by a Nisei to her continued detention in a camp after a governmental board had found that she was not even suspected of disloyalty. Logically—and, it turned out, tactically—her suit was closely tied to Korematsu's. The government argued that danger to the Nisei from other American citizens made it necessary to keep them imprisoned until some "orderly" way of resettling them could be found.

Murphy's notes on the conference for *Korematsu* are sparse, perhaps because he himself was heavily engaged in the debate. The way in which the justices spoke out of turn indicates something of the heat.

> JACKSON: "I would limit this to sabotage. It was a state of war. I don't think [DeWitt] could exclude [people of] Japanese ancestry. I stop with H[irabayashi] last year and [go] no further. They say the courts have got to become a part of it. I don't accept [a] military order as something we have got to accept without any inquiry into [its] reasonableness."
> CHIEF JUSTICE: "You are saying that the Congress and President acting together are unable to create zones to protect us against military espionage and sabotage. If you can do it for curfew you can do it for exclusion."
> RUTLEDGE: "I had to swallow H[irabayashi]. I didn't like it. At that time I knew if I went along with that order I had to go along with detention for [a] reasonably necessary time. Nothing but necessity would justify it . . . . And so I vote to affirm."
> CHIEF JUSTICE: "I affirm on this record."

Douglas recalled that Black "was very much on Stone's side, very eloquent in defense of the power of the military to do what they did. And he had no doubts, no reservations." [21]

The initial vote was 5–4. Black, Reed, Frankfurter, and, sadly, Rutledge, agreed with Stone that *Hirabayashi,* despite all its careful disclaimers of upholding no more than the curfew, disposed of *Korematsu.* On the other hand, Roberts, never before known as a crusader for civil liberty, voted with Douglas, Murphy, and Jackson to

---

21. "Transcriptions of Conversations between William O. Douglas and Walter F. Murphy," (Tape recorded during 1961–63), Mudd Library, Princeton University, pp. 165–66.

reverse. Stone assigned the opinion to Black, a staunch libertarian who was on close personal terms with two of the dissenters, Douglas and Murphy.

Discussion at conference focused rather than ended wrangling. *Korematsu* "was very much discussed, very much considered," Douglas remembered, "very much debated up and down the halls of the, the corridors of the Court." Pens cut eloquent phrases; and tempers—of clerks as well as justices—flared.

As in *Hirabayashi,* Black, like Stone, wanted a very narrow opinion, and he tried to stick to this plan, despite prodding by some of his other colleagues. Probably at Stone's suggestion, he asserted that the charge against Korematsu had only been failing to report to a relocation center. Thus Black hoped to avoid the issue of the camps altogether and simply say that the Court could not know that Korematsu would have been imprisoned. No one, however, except Stone and Black took this reasoning seriously. Even the government's brief conceded that if Korematsu had reported to the center he would have been interned.

Jackson, who detested Black, quickly circulated a withering opinion that, in effect, charged the majority with bad faith and shoddy logic in relying on *Hirabayashi.* Quoting copiously from Stone's restrictive sentences in the earlier opinion, Jackson pointed out: "The Court is now saying that in *Hirabayashi* we did decide the very things we there said we were not deciding." On the merits, his tone was no less scathing, alleging that the decision violated the fundamental constitutional principle that guilt was personal and distorted the Constitution to rationalize racism.[22] By ignoring its own claim that such invasions of rights had to be subjected to "the strictest scrutiny," and by refusing to examine the reasons behind the military's decision, the majority, Jackson wrote, "for all time has validated the principle of racial discrimination in criminal procedure and of transplanting American citizens. The principle . . . lies about like a loaded weapon ready for the hand of any authority that can bring forward a plausible claim of urgent need."

Murphy had been busy with his law clerk preparing his own dissent, an opinion that made heavy use of the amicus curiae brief of the Japanese American Citizens League. He gleefully read Jackson's draft and sent it to his clerk, Eugene Gressman, with a brief note:

Gene—
Read this and perish!
The Court has blown up over the Jap case—just as I expected it would.

Murphy's own dissent was even more impassioned than Jackson's. He opened by asserting that "exclusion goes over 'the very brink of constitutional power' "—a phrase he had used in *Hirabayashi* —"and

---

22. Perhaps Jackson knew that General DeWitt and Black were old friends and was, for a select audience, tarring Black with the same brush as DeWitt.

falls into the ugly abyss of racism." His closing paragraph stated his personal ideals, earlier versions of which had earned him Felix Frankfurter's sarcastic rebaptism as "St. Francis":

> I dissent . . . from this legalization of racism. Racial discrimination in any form and in any degree has no justifiable part whatever in our democratic way of life. It is unattractive in any setting but it is utterly revolting among a free people who have embraced the principles set forth in the Constitution of the United States.

Meanwhile, Roberts circulated a short dissent, arguing that Korematsu had been caught in a trap. Had he left his home to report to the center, he would have violated the curfew; had he not reported to the center, he would have violated the exclusion order.

Frankfurter wrote several memoranda to inform and stiffen Black. Their essential reasoning was: "To find that the Constitution does not forbid the military measures now complained of does not carry with it approval of that which Congress and the Executive did. That is their business not mine." Circulation of the dissents, however, especially Jackson's, led Frankfurter to write a full scale concurrence.

Stone was concerned that Black, despite his initial resolve, was not sufficiently emphasizing the narrowness of the Court's decision. The Chief followed his usual practice of writing a draft of a concurrence and sending it to the author of the Court's opinion for his enlightenment.

> Mr. Chief Justice **STONE** concurring.
> I concur in the opinion of the Court and add a word only because it seems desirable, and a matter of some importance, to state explicitly the reasons why we are not free to decide petitioner's main contention that a relocation order applied to him would be unconstitutional.
> Petitioner has not been convicted of violating a relocation order and in fact has never been subjected to such an order. He has been convicted of violating an Act of Congress which penalizes his disobedience of an order which in effect required him, pending further orders, to enter and remain in an assembly center . . . . The conviction is plainly sustained by the reasoning of the opinion in the *Hirabayashi* case . . . .
> It was no necessary consequence of obedience to enter the assembly center that petitioner would ever be subjected to a relocation order. For it does not follow, either as a matter of fact or of law, that his presence in the assembly center would result in his detention under a relocation order. Many who were sent to the assembly center were not sent to relocation centers, but instead were released and sent out of the military area. We cannot say that petitioner would not have been released, as others were. We do not and cannot know the terms of any relocation order to which he might be but has not been subjected. For there is nothing to preclude the radical modification or complete abandonment of the

relocation scheme at any time before petitioner could have been subjected to it.

This Court does not decide moot cases or give advisory opinions. It will be time enough to decide the serious constitutional issue which petitioner seeks to raise here when a relocation order is in fact applied or is certain to be applied to him, and we are advised of its terms.

Douglas circulated a dissent, based on statutory rather than constitutional interpretation. Given his strong antipathy to racism, it was a surprisingly mild document. But he was not only a civil libertarian, he also deeply loved his country and, as a close friend of President Roosevelt, trusted its leaders. As a former executive official, Douglas could also sympathize with the sense of urgency that decent and patriotic military officers might have felt in early 1942, as the United States and its allies suffered disaster after disaster. While he could recognize and despise the racism of DeWitt and the leaders of interest groups who had lobbied against the Nisei, Douglas was hesitant to ascribe that racism to the political system as a whole.

D. Negotiations Within the Court

A unanimous Court would have made such a shaky constitutional decision seem less tortured, but that possibility did not exist. Next best would be to pick off several of the dissenters, but the majority had no real hope of winning over anyone except Douglas. He accepted the difficulties that the military faced in 1942, as they confronted a victorious enemy. Moreover, he and Black were friends and, more important, jurisprudential allies. Each thought of the other as an ardent defender of civil liberties.

By nature a self-contained and independent man, Douglas usually resented efforts to persuade him to change his vote. Ex parte Endo, however, presented a potential avenue of indirect communication. The Court had voted in conference to hold that the government was obliged to release Miss Endo; and Stone, perhaps sensing early that there were grounds for negotiating with Douglas, had assigned him the task of writing the opinion of the Court. Douglas wanted, he later said, "to put it [Endo] on the constitutional grounds, but I couldn't get a court [a majority] to do that. Black, Frankfurter, [and] Stone were very clear that that [keeping Nisei imprisoned even after the government's own processes had shown them to be loyal] was not unconstitutional, but that this would have to turn, Endo would have to turn, upon the construction of the regulations."

Now, even while Korematsu was churning up the Court, Douglas, who always wrote swiftly and was typically impatient to secure agreement, was getting anxious about when Endo could come down. Black was delaying the case, even though Douglas had reluctantly agreed to restrict the opinion to holding that Congress had not authorized detention of any citizen whom the government conceded to be loyal.

Stone tried to persuade Douglas that *Endo*, not *Korematsu*, was the critical case, at least if the latter ruling clearly stated that the Court's sustaining exclusion did not legitimate detention. So restricted, Stone reasoned, *Korematsu* would uphold only authority to exclude potentially dangerous people from a war zone during a state of emergency. *Endo*, on the other hand, would compel the government to release all Nisei who were not charged with disloyalty—and, of course, almost no Nisei was so charged. *Endo* would be the great ruling; *Korematsu*, a narrow, technical decision.

Black had also been talking to Douglas. Eventually, they sat down in Black's chambers with Black's clerk to seek accommodation. To meet many of Douglas' objections, Black heavily edited the draft of his opinion for the Court. But the changes, though numerous, were largely in tone—for instance, stressing the Court's rejection of racism as a justification for evacuation. He did not retreat from his position that the power to evacuate the Nisei fell within Congress' power to wage war.

With Douglas now a member of the majority, Black recirculated his amended opinion. After only minor changes, the Conference approved the final draft. The vote was now 6–3 to place the mantle of constitutionality on forced evacuation of the Nisei—and despite what Stone pretended to believe—imprisonment, without charge or trial, in concentration camps. For his part, Black withdrew whatever reservations he had about *Endo*, and the Court announced the two decisions on the same Monday, a week before Christmas, 1944.

E. Aftermath

Korematsu quickly became and remains an important case in American constitutional law, indicating just how far the Court may be willing to bend the Constitution to rationalize governmental power in time of war. As Douglas ruefully mused in 1963, "I think that those cases, like *Korematsu* and *Hirabayashi*, probably would have been decided the same way by any Court that I have sat on in the twenty-three years [I've been a justice]." [23] In contrast to *Korematsu*'s notoriety, *Endo* belongs in the domain of esoteric historians.

Shortly before his death in 1971, Hugo Black still stoutly maintained that his opinion in *Korematsu* had been constitutionally correct and that he would make the same choice if faced with the problem again. Douglas, on the other hand, came to regard *Korematsu* as a tragic, even shameful, mistake. "I caved in," he remarked as he expressed bitter regret at having suppressed his dissent. *Endo*, too, continued to gnaw at his conscience.

> I think perhaps the biggest disappointment to me was the fact that they couldn't, the Court wouldn't, in *Endo*, go to the constitutional ground but just stick to the conventional way of deciding the case, strain to construe a regulation to avoid a constitutional question.

---

23. Douglas-Murphy Conversations, supra note 21, p. 172.

I'm the author of that, but I did it under the necessities of the situation. But it seemed to me to be a much more wholesome thing, from the point of view of the Court as an educating influence, just to say what you can and can't do.

During the war, others were even more insensitive. As attorney general of California, Earl Warren, whose tenure as Chief Justice would become synonymous with civil liberty, strongly urged evacuation of the Nisei in 1942 and, the following year, adamantly opposed release and resettlement in the state of even those Japanese-Americans who had been cleared by loyalty-security programs. Later, he confessed profound regret at denying

> our American concept of freedom and the rights of citizens . . . . It was wrong to react so impulsively, without positive evidence of disloyalty, even though we felt we had a good motive in the security of our state.[24]

The economic harm the Nisei suffered was staggering. They were forced to abandon their homes and businesses, and, to sell for whatever they could immediately get, almost everything they had worked all their lives to accumulate. Far worse was the psychological injury of being denied the most basic rights of citizenship. They were herded like criminals behind barbed wire enclosures and deprived of liberty and dignity without any process of law whatsoever other than General DeWitt's savage scream, "A Jap is a Jap," and Hugo Black's nostrum that "hardships are part of war, and war is an aggregation of hardships."

VI. CONCLUSION

Writing in *Federalist* No. 72, Alexander Hamilton asserted that "the best security for the fidelity of mankind is to make their interest coincide with their duty." That hard-headed psychology underlies the American constitutional structure. To a large extent the political processes are open, though money, education, and experience confer great advantages on some people and interests over others. And as Chapter 2 pointed out, democracy in the United States is also curtailed in other consequential ways. National public policy is made in arenas subject to pressures, crosspressures, checks, and counterchecks—some more democratic in character, some more constitutionalist.

In an important sense, *Korematsu* highlights the constitutionalist's fear of representative democracy. Here there can be little doubt that an overwhelming majority of the nation approved the decision to fill up concentration camps with American citizens of Japanese descent. Open political processes, institutional access, crosspressures, political culture, and the potential judgment of history did nothing to sway Congress, the President, the War Department, or General DeWitt

---

24. *The Memoirs of Chief Justice Earl Warren* (New York: Doubleday, 1977), p. 149.

from violating the basic right of the Nisei to be treated by their government with equal dignity and respect.

In an important sense, however, *Korematsu* also highlights the democrat's fear of the futility, if not the undesirability, of checks on popular government. For even federal judges, those people whom James Wilson thought would be "the noble guards" of the Constitution, caved in. Their reason may have been respect for military judgment at a time of crisis rather than fear of defeat at the polls, but the result was still surrender. For the Nisei, the Bill of Rights was no more than a parchment barrier. Madison would have understood, even if he would have been appalled.

Yet as it illustrates a failure of the system, *Korematsu* also illustrates the way the system works. Freely elected officials approved the underlying policy, though they did not initiate it. The Nisei found a few allies and they had access to the congressional phase of decision making as well as to the courts. Curiously, however, negotiation and compromise—the supposed hallmarks of the legislative process—occurred mostly in the judicial process, and on issues that were of little help to the Nisei. And for all the shame that the evacuation policy earned, even *Korematsu* did not end the matter. (See Eds.' notes 1 and 5 to *Korematsu*, below, p. 1197.) First, in 1948 Congress enacted a reparations bill that, in token form, acknowledged guilt and offered small economic recompense. Second, Fred Korematsu returned to court and had his conviction vacated. (As this book went to press, Gordon Hirabayashi's suit to vacate his conviction was still pending.)

Third, and with marvelous irony, the Supreme Court has also acted. Early in his opinion in *Korematsu*, Black offered a bit of constitutional law that he promptly ignored: "[A]ll legal restrictions which curtail the civil rights of a single racial group are immediately suspect." The justices, of course, have never again faced the spectacle of American concentration camps, but time after time they have plucked Black's sentence out of context and used it to justify striking down various sorts of racial and ethnic discrimination. (See Chapter 14 for the development of the doctrine of "suspect classifications," for which the Court often cites *Korematsu* as an authority.) If one did not read the actual opinion and decision in *Korematsu* but only looked at the way the Court has used it, it would be quite reasonable to conclude that it must have been a courageous ruling upholding the rights of all Americans to equal justice under law.

SELECTED BIBLIOGRAPHY

Abraham, Henry. *Justices & Presidents* (2d ed.; New York: Oxford University Press, 1985).

————. *The Judicial Process* (4th ed.; New York: Oxford University Press, 1980).

Bessette, Joseph M., and Jeffrey Tulis, eds. *The Presidency in the Constitutional Order* (Baton Rouge, La.: Louisiana State University Press, 1981).

Beveridge, Albert J. *The Life of John Marshall* (Boston: Houghton Mifflin, 1916), 4 vols.

Bickel, Alexander M. *The Least Dangerous Branch: The Supreme Court at the Bar of Politics* (Indianapolis, Ind.: Bobbs-Merrill, 1962).

————. *The Supreme Court and the Idea of Progress* (New York: Harper & Row, 1970).

Commission on Wartime Relocation and Internment of Civilians. *Report: Personal Justice Denied* (Washington, D.C.: Government Printing Office, 1982).

Cox, Archibald. *The Role of The Supreme Court in American Government* (New York: Oxford University Press, 1976).

Danelski, David J. *A Supreme Court Justice Is Appointed* (New York: Random House, 1964).

Fish, Peter G. *The Office of Chief Justice* (Charlottesville, Va.: White Burkett Miller Center of Public Affairs, 1984).

Fisher, Louis. *Constitutional Conflicts Between Congress and the President* (Princeton, N.J.: Princeton University Press, 1985).

Grodzins, Morton. *American Betrayed: Politics and the Japanese Evacuation* (Chicago: University of Chicago Press, 1949).

Howard, J. Woodford. *Mr. Justice Murphy* (Princeton, N.J.: Princeton University Press, 1968).

Jackson, Robert H. *The Supreme Court in the American System of Government* (Cambridge, Mass.: Harvard University Press, 1955).

Irons, Peter. *Justice at War: The Story of the Japanese American Internment Cases* (New York: Oxford University Press, 1983).

Kluger, Richard. *Simple Justice: The History of Brown v. Board of Education and Black America's Struggle for Equality* (New York: Knopf, 1976).

McCloskey, Robert. *The American Supreme Court* (Chicago: University of Chicago Press, 1960).

Mason, Alpheus Thomas. *Harlan Fiske Stone* (New York: Viking, 1956).

Murphy, Walter F. *Congress and the Court* (Chicago: University of Chicago Press, 1962).

————. *Elements of Judicial Strategy* (Chicago: University of Chicago Press, 1964).

———— and Joseph Tanenhaus. *The Study of Public Law* (New York: Random House, 1972).

———— and C. Herman Pritchett. *Courts, Judges, & Politics* (4th ed.; New York: Random House, 1986).

O'Brien, David M. *Storm Center: The Supreme Court in American Politics* (New York: Norton, 1986).

Pritchett, C. Herman. *The Roosevelt Court* (Chicago: Quadrangle Books, 1969; originally published, 1948).

————. *Congress versus the Supreme Court* (Minneapolis: University of Minnesota Press, 1961).

Schubert, Glendon A. *The Judicial Mind* (Evanston, Ill.: Northwestern University Press, 1965).

_____. *The Judicial Mind Revisited* (New York: Oxford University Press, 1974).

Schwartz, Bernard. *Super Chief: Earl Warren and His Supreme Court* (New York: New York University Press, 1983).

_____. *The Unpublished Opinions of the Warren Court* (New York: Oxford University Press, 1985).

Tribe, Lawrence H. *God Save This Honorable Court* (New York: Random House, 1985).

Ulmer, S. Sidney. *Courts, Law and Judicial Processes* (New York: The Free Press, 1981).

*

II

What is the Constitution?

Part I sketched the intellectual, institutional, and political frameworks within which constitutional interpretation operates. We now turn to more substantive problems surrounding that enterprise. The interrogative one must confront is: WHAT is it that is to be interpreted? WHAT precisely is the Constitution? One should keep in mind that, like each of the other basic interrogatives around which this book is organized, the problem of deciding WHAT the Constitution is permeates not merely these pages but all of constitutional debate, whether carried on in private homes, universities, Congress, the White House, state governments, courtrooms, or barrooms. The answer to any specific query about what the Constitution means in particular circumstances depends in large part on WHAT the Constitution is.

This basic interrogative has several dimensions. First, what sort of "thing" is a constitution? Is it like a contract between private citizens or is it something different (and more)? Second, what are a constitution's principal functions? How is it supposed to operate within society? Third, what does a constitution include? Only a document so labeled along with any of its amendments? Does it include other documents—for instance, in the American case, the Declaration of Independence? Or does it (also) include various practices, understandings, and/or political theories? Fourth, does a constitution change over time? If it does change, how does it do so?

The answer to some questions along the first dimension seem easy to us, in fact, so easy that we may have difficulty articulating answers. A constitution is, in John Marshall's term (McCulloch v. Maryland [1819]; reprinted below, p. 413), "a constituent act," one that creates a new regime, not merely fresh offices but a different political system. It constitutes (or reconstitutes) the people of the United States as a political community.

Thus a constitution is hardly equivalent to a contract between individuals. Not only is it quantitatively different in that it is done in the name of the entire society rather than of a few individual members, it is also qualitatively different because of its sweeping implications for that society. It creates and marks off the powers of particular organs of government, and specifies the processes by which government shall arrive at and carry out decisions.

The effects of a constitution range far beyond recognizing a set of reciprocal rights and obligations among a limited number of citizens. It also establishes rules and procedures to locate, protect, and control all rights, powers, and obligations in a society; and, consistent with the individualistic tradition of Classical Liberalism, it attempts to draw lines to distinguish that which is of public concern from that which is private.

In the American context, the Constitution is not a compact among the several states. To use Marshall's words in *McCulloch* again, it "proceeds directly from the people" and "is 'ordained and established' in the name of the people." As the government created by the Constitution—and thus by the agreement of the people—the federal government is not the creature of state governments. That statement may seem obvious to us today, but we should not forget that it took a bloody civil war to settle the issue. And that fact alone should make us slow to accept easy answers to any problem of constitutional interpretation, most especially about WHAT the Constitution is, WHO interprets it, and HOW.

The second dimension of subquestions asks about a constitution's functions and raises more complex problems. Chapter 2 discussed the two principal political theories, constitutionalism and representational democracy, that underlie the American political system. Both theories stress the necessity of limiting government and value the utility of a constitution in accomplishing this task. But the two theories see a constitution as functioning in different ways to achieve this goal. For a representational democrat, process is primary. A constitution mainly establishes a set of procedures specifying who shall participate in choosing public officials and how public officials shall arrive at and carry out decisions. For a constitutionalist, a constitution performs those tasks and more: It also recognizes certain rights of citizens as setting substantive, not merely procedural, limitations on government. Process, while important, remains secondary.

In a sometimes awkward and not always logically consistent fashion, a constitutional democracy must try to accommodate these two competing and occasionally conflicting theories. One result we have already noted is a constitutional jurisprudence that is lumpy rather than smooth, producing decisions that cry out, seemingly in vain, for systematic explanation.

The third dimension of subquestions relates to inclusion: What ideas, practices, and things comprise the constitution that it is to be interpreted? Chapter 4 shows the U.S. Supreme Court grappling— not always consciously and certainly never systematically—with that sort of issue.

In reading these cases, it is easy to miss a critical point: Implicit in all of these opinions is a vision of the good society. This sort of vision—and it is not of a wispy utopia, but of what the United States should and can be—is probably a necessity if constitutional interpretation is to make sense as a coherent whole. Certainly both democratic theories and the theories of constitutionalism offer such visions, and here the two differ more in means than in objectives. Each sees the good society as consisting of free, self-governing men and women enjoying not only specific liberties but, more basically, the status of human beings equal in worth and dignity, able to choose, without interference from government or society, their lives and life styles, as long as they respect the equal rights and dignity of others in making the same sorts of choices. What is evident here is a reflection of a larger reality: A constitution is an integral part of a way of life; indeed, it is an effort to shape a way of life.

The cases in Chapter 5 address a fourth dimension of subquestions about the nature of a constitution, that of constitutional change. No political order could "endure for ages to come" were its provisions incapable of adjustment. Thus most constitutions include procedures for amendment. But are these sorts of procedures sufficient? Can a constitution endure if its terms are so rigid as to be incapable of being "adapted to the various *crises* of human affairs" by other than cumbersome formal amendment? Alternatively, if constitutional change is easy, will the constitution be taken seriously as establishing fundamental rules that must be followed? Can, for example, rights be eliminated or powers expanded because of a crisis of a sort for which the doucment's terms do not explicitly provide? In short, can a constitution be legitimately changed by interpretation? If so, what are the limits on such a means of change? And who has authority to effect such changes? Immediately we find ourselves facing questions not only of WHAT the Constitution is but also questions that flow from our second basic interrogative, WHO shall interpret? And, although those kinds of questions form the focus of Part III of this book, we cannot avoid at least raising them here.

4

What is the Constitution?
Problems of Inclusion

Professor Sanford V. Levinson has likened various views of WHAT the Constitution includes to the differences between Fundamentalist Protestant and Roman Catholic theologians. The archetypal Fundamentalist Protestant sees the revealed word of God as fully contained in the books of the Bible. So, too, some judges and commentators view "the Constitution" as including no more than the document produced at Philadelphia in 1787 together with its amendments.[1] In his definition of the Constitution, Justice Hugo L. Black spoke as a model "Fundamentalist Protestant." The text, the whole text, and nothing but the text was his usual refrain. Thus he would angrily dissent when he thought the Court was adding to or subtracting from the document's plain words, even when his own values would have led him to agree with the majority's decision had he been drafting a new constitution. (See his dissent in Griswold v. Connecticut [1965; reprinted below, p. 113].)

In sharp contrast, Catholic theologians believe that the Bible is only one source, though a very important one, of revelation. God's truth, they argue, is also found in a tradition and in "authoritative" interpretations of that tradition as well as in Scripture. So, too, many judges and commentators have argued for a "living" tradition that exists alongside the constitutional text. Courts commonly regard as "authoritative" previous judicial interpretations of the Constitution, and Justice Frankfurter claimed in the Steel Seizure Case (1952; reprinted below, p. 339) that long and unchallenged usages of other branches of government would qualify for constitutional status. Even more broadly, Justice Harlan claimed in his dissent in Poe v. Ullman (1961; reprinted below p. 106 that:

> Due process has not been reduced to any formula; its content cannot be determined by reference to any code. The best that can be said is that through the course of this Court's decisions it has represented the balance which our Nation, built upon postulates of respect for the liberty of the individual, has struck between that liberty and the demands of organized society. . . . The balance of which I speak is the balance struck by this country, having regard

---

1. Sanford V. Levinson, " 'The Constitution' in American Civil Religion," 1979 *Sup. Ct. Rev.* 123.

to what history teaches are the traditions from which it broke. That
tradition is a living thing.

Although judges seldom admit it, they, like other interpreters,
often read political theory into as well as out of the document. Chief
Justice Earl Warren used a theory of representative democracy to hold
that the Constitution required electoral districts to conform to the
principle of "one person, one vote." (Reynolds v. Sims [1964;
reprinted below, p. 632].) And many of the Court's rulings about the
substance of such "fundamental rights" as those to marriage, travel,
and privacy depend at least as heavily on a theory of constitutionalism
as on the words of the text. (See especially the cases reprinted in
Chapter 17, below.)

Almost as frequently as a majority of justices finds a tradition,
hallows a practice, or utilizes a political theory, a group of dissenting
justices will question the legitimacy of such "interpretation." Similarly where the Court sticks to the plain words of the text, other
dissenters will protest against "mechanical interpretation." This disagreement over WHAT "the Constitution" includes began shortly after
ratification, as illustrated by the debate between Justices Chase and
Iredell in Calder v. Bull (1798; reprinted below, p. 86, the very first
case in this chapter. That debate echoes through the next 500
volumes of the United States Reports.

The notion of a "living Constitution" or an "unwritten Constitution" is wonderfully open-ended. Not only is there doubt, even
confusion, about WHAT is included in the Constitution, but constitutional interpretation also lacks "rules of recognition," [2] standards to
determine when and how a practice, tradition, or political theory
becomes part of the constitutional canon. These are serious deficiencies, for it may be a long and widely accepted practice—segregation
by race, for example—that generates the constitutional problem.

A textualist would respond by saying that constitutional interpretation does have one rule of recognition, the only one needed:
Inclusion in the words of the document or its amendments makes a
practice, tradition, or theory part of the canon; exclusion makes it
apocryphal, unless it is part of the definition of the words of the text.

At first glance, those who would restrict "the Constitution" to the
document and its amendments have the tidier argument. The text is
tangible, bounded, set in hard print, and reproduced on pages that can
be read and explained. And the single "rule of recognition" seems to
provide a clear standard. Yet the textualist position has problems of
its own. As we saw in Chapter 1, some clauses of the document cry
out for interpretations that go beyond parsing sentences and looking
up definitions in a dictionary. The words of the Preamble setting
such goals as justice, liberty, and domestic tranquility no more lend

---

2. See H.L.A. Hart, *The Concept of Law* (Oxford: Clarendon Press, 1961), chap. 6; and
Richard S. Kay, "Preconstitutional Rules," 42 *Ohio St.L.J.* 187 (1981).

themselves to rigid application than do the terms of the "sweeping clause" of Article I.

Thus even people who believe in literal rather than creative interpretation concede that sometimes it is necessary to go behind (though not beyond) the document to find the meaning of its words. Hugo Black, the greatest of the textualists, sought help when plain words failed by trying to reconstruct the "intent of the framers." He was fond of quoting from Ex parte Bain (1887): [3]

> It is never to be forgotten that, in the construction of the language of the Constitution . . . as indeed in all other instances where construction becomes necessary, we are to place ourselves as nearly as possible in the condition of the men who framed the instrument.

But "intent" adds something to the words of the document. And, as Marsh v. Chambers (1983; reprinted below, p. 158) will indicate and Chapter 8 will develop in detail, questing for "intent of the framers" is usually as open-ended as for the contents of the "unwritten constitution." Indeed, the two may be only different aspects of the same project. What the framers, whether of 1787 or of later amendments had in mind, is seldom crystal clear. Moreover, as Felix Frankfurter noted when Black claimed to have discovered the intent of the Fourteenth Amendment in the speeches of one of the proposal's managers in Congress: "What was submitted for ratification was his proposal, not his speech." [4]

More generally, the document is riddled with language that, in Ronald Dworkin's phrase (see his "Taking Rights Seriously," reprinted below, p. 168), expresses broad "concepts" rather than specific "conceptions." These terms make sense, one might well argue, only when understood as products of a political theory or set of political theories, with constitutionalism and representative democracy being the most serious contenders for interpretive honors.

To a strict legal positivist, one, that is, who believes only in following the black letter of the law, the Ninth Amendment presents the most troublesome problem of broad language. For that amendment's specific terms command interpreters to read "the Constitution" as including more than the words of the document: "The enumeration in the Constitution, of certain rights, shall not be construed to deny or disparage others retained by the people." The language here is obligatory: The Constitution "shall not be construed," not "should not" or "need not" be construed to exclude unlisted rights. One can, as Justice Black did in *Griswold*, try to dismiss these words as not being cognizable by judges, but that reasoning seems circular. At root it argues:

---

3. He quoted this passage, for instance, in his *A Constitutional Faith* (New York: Knopf, 1969), p. 8; and in his dissent in Adamson v. California (1947).

4. Adamson v. California, concur. op. (1947).

Because judges only interpret the words of the written Constitution, when the words of the written Constitution say there is more to the Constitution than the words, judges must ignore those words.

In addition, the document presents, as Chief Justice Marshall asserted in McCulloch v. Maryland (1819; reprinted below, p. 413), only the framework of a political system, one that must be filled in by practice. As we saw in Chapter 1, some of the most important parts of the constitutional system are not found in the text—for example: the right to a presumption of innocence in a criminal trial or the necessity of government's proving guilt beyond a reasonable doubt to secure a criminal conviction.[5]

There is also the matter of long practice having filled in the gaps between words and having supplied meanings—perhaps conflicting meanings—to words within the document. Among the many problems the dramatic case of United States v. Nixon (1974; reprinted below, p. 234) presented the Supreme Court was WHAT the Constitution included. On the one hand, Nixon was asserting the Constitution contained the doctrine of executive privilege, the President's authority to maintain the confidentiality of conversations and papers relating to the executive department. In the abstract, such a claim seems reasonable, but it is nowhere specified in the constitutional text.

On the other hand, Nixon's former aides were asking the Court to exercise judicial review, the authority of judges to declare unconstitutional acts of coordinate officials (here the President's refusal to make documents available to a court in a criminal case). And the constitutional text is as silent about judicial review as it is about executive privilege. Thus, either to uphold the President or to uphold those who wanted access to the tapes of their conversations with the President, the Court would have had to move beyond the plain words of the written Constitution. (That Nixon had chosen Warren Earl Burger to be Chief Justice of the United States because, Nixon said, Burger was a strict constructionist only heightened the irony of the drama.)

The cases and notes in this chapter teach much about substantive constitutional law—for example, the meaning of such terms as "ex post facto" law or "self-incrimination," the existence of a right to privacy, the limits on any right to bodily integrity, some of the wide-ranging implications of the phrase "due process of law," and the extent to which the Fourteenth Amendment's due process clause "incorporates" the Bill of Rights. These are interesting issues in themselves, and they are important to WHAT the Constitution means and how it constrains public policy. They do not, however, form the focal point of this chapter. What is critical is that constitutional interpretation—and thus also public policy—must continually grapple with the fundamental question of WHAT the Constitution includes.

---

5. For discussions of these two closely related "constitutional rights," see In re Winship (1970), Estelle v. Williams (1976), Sandstrom v. Montana (1979), Jackson v. Virginia (1979), and Francis v. Franklin (1985).

And, despite the fact that neither judges nor commentators have solved the problem of convincingly justifying their answers, how they have tried to solve it is significant. For we can learn from failures as well as from successes. And learn we must, for the basic question is not about to disappear or to become less decisive to the life of the political system.

SELECTED BIBLIOGRAPHY

Barber, Sotirios A. *On What the Constitution Means* (Baltimore: The Johns Hopkins University Press, 1984).

Black, Hugo L. *A Constitutional Faith* (New York: Knopf, 1968).

Bobbitt, Philip. *Constitutional Fate* (New York: Oxford University Press, 1982), especially chaps. 2–4, 13–15, 17.

Cortner, Richard C. *The Supreme Court and the Second Bill of Rights* (Madison, Wisc.: University of Wisconsin Press, 1981).

Corwin, Edward S. "The Constitution *versus* Constitutional Theory," in Alpheus Thomas Mason and Gerald Garvey, eds., *American Constitutional History* (New York: Harper & Row, 1964).

Douglas, William O. *We, the Judges* (New York: Doubleday, 1956), especially chaps. 1 & 12.

Ely, John Hart. *Democracy and Distrust* (Cambridge, Mass.: Harvard University Press, 1979), chaps 1–3.

Grey, Thomas. "Do We Have an Unwritten Constitution?" 27 *Stan. L.Rev.* 703 (1975).

Hart, H.L.A. *The Concept of Law* (Oxford: Clarendon Press, 1961), chap. 6.

Harris, William F., II. "Bonding Word & Polity: The Logic of American Constitutionalism." 76 *Am.Pol.Sci.Rev.* 34 (1982).

Horwill, Herbert A. *The Usages of the American Constitution* (Port Washington, N.Y.: Kennikat Press, 1969) (first published 1925), chap. 1.

Kay, Richard S. "Preconstitutional Rules," 42 *Ohio St.L.J.* 187 (1982).

Levinson, Sanford V. "The 'Constitution' in American Civil Religion," 1979 *Sup.Ct.Rev.* 123.

Maddox, Graham. "A Note on the Meaning of 'Constitution,'" 76 *Am.Pol.Sci.Rev.* 805 (1982).

Monaghan, Henry P. "Our Perfect Constitution," 56 *N.Y.U.L.Rev.* 353 (1981).

Parker, Richard D. "The Past of Constitutional Theory—And its Future," 42 *Ohio St.L.J.* 223 (1981).

Peltason, J.W. *Corwin & Peltason's Understanding the Constitution*, 10th ed., (New York: Holt, Rinehart & Winston, 1985), pp. 1–16.

Perry, Michael J. "The Authority of Text, Tradition, and Reason: A Theory of Constitutional 'Interpretation,'" 58 *So.Cal.L.Rev.* 551 (1985).

Richards, David A.J. "Moral Philosophy and the Search for Fundamental Values in Constitutional Law," 42 *Ohio St.L.J.* 319 (1981).

Story, Justice Joseph. *Commentaries on the Constitution of the United States* (Boston: Hilliard, Grey & Co., 1833) Book III, chap. 3.

Tribe, Laurence H. *American Constitutional Law* (Mineola, N.Y.: The Foundation Press, 1978), chaps. 1–3.

————. *Constitutional Choices* (Cambridge, Mass.: Harvard University Press, 1985), chap. 2.

Tushnet, Mark V. "A Note on the Revival of Textualism in Constitutional Theory," 58 *So.Cal.L.Rev.* 683 (1985).

"There are certain vital principles in our free republican governments which will determine and overrule an apparent and flagrant abuse of legislative power . . . ."— Justice CHASE.

"If . . . the legislature of the Union, or the legislature of any member of the Union, shall pass a law, within the general scope of their constitutional power, the court cannot pronounce it void, merely because it is, in their judgment, contrary to the principles of natural justice."— Justice IREDELL.

CALDER v. BULL

3 U.S. (Dall.) 386, 1 L.Ed. 648 (1798).

The legislature of Connecticut passed a law setting aside a decree of a probate court disapproving and refusing to record a will. The statute granted a new hearing, after which the probate court approved and recorded the will. Calder, who would have inherited the property had the probate court disapproved the will, contended that the statute granting a new hearing was an ex post facto law, prohibited by Article I, § 10 of the U.S. Constitution. The state superior court rejected the argument, as did the Connecticut Supreme Court of Errors. Calder obtained a writ of error from the U.S. Supreme Court.

CHASE, Justice . . . . .

It appears to me a self-evident proposition, that the several state legislatures retain all the powers of legislation, delegated to them by the state constitutions; which are not expressly taken away by the constitution of the United States . . . . All the powers delegated by the people of the United States to the federal government are defined, and NO CONSTRUCTIVE powers can be exercised by it, and all the powers that remain in the state governments are indefinite . . . . The sole inquiry is, whether this resolution or law of Connecticut . . . is an ex post facto law, within the prohibition of the federal constitution?

 . . . I cannot subscribe to the omnipotence of a state legislature, or that it is absolute and without controul; although its authority should not be expressly restrained by the constitution, or fundamental law of the state. The people of the United States erected their constitutions or forms of government, to establish justice, to promote the general welfare, to secure the blessings of liberty, and to protect their persons and property from violence. The purposes for which men enter into society will determine the nature and terms of the social compact; and as they are the foundation of the legislative power, they will decide what are the proper objects of it. This fundamental principle flows from the very nature of our free republican government, that no man should be compelled to do what the laws do not require, nor to refrain from acts which the laws permit. There are acts which the federal or state legislatures cannot do, without exceeding their authority. There are certain vital principles in our free republican governments which will determine and overrule an apparent and flagrant abuse of legislative power; as to authorize manifest injustice by positive law; or to take away that security for personal liberty, or private property, for the protection whereof government was established. An act of the legislature (for I cannot call it a law), contrary to the great first principles of the social compact, cannot be considered a rightful exercise of legislative authority. The obligation of a law in governments established on express compact, and on republican principles, must be determined by the nature of the power on which it is founded.

A few instances will suffice to explain what I mean. A law that punished a citizen for an innocent action, or, in other words, for an act which, when done, was in violation of no existing law; a law that destroys, or impairs, the lawful private contracts of citizens; a law that makes a man a judge in his own cause; or a law that takes property from A, and gives it to B. It is against all reason and justice for a people to intrust a legislature with such powers; and, therefore, it cannot be presumed that they have done it. The genius, the nature, and the spirit of our state governments amount to a prohibition of such acts of legislation; and the general principles of law and reason forbid them. The legislature may enjoin, permit, forbid and punish; they may declare new crimes, and establish rules of conduct for all its citizens in future cases; they may command what is right, and prohibit what is wrong; but they cannot change innocence into guilt, or punish innocence as a crime; or violate the right of an antecedent lawful private contract; or the right of private property. To maintain that our federal or state legislature possesses such powers, if they had not been expressly restrained, would, in my opinion, be a political heresy altogether inadmissible in our free republican governments . . . .

The Constitution of the United States . . . lays several restrictions on the legislatures of the several states; and among them, "that no state shall pass any *ex post facto* law." . . .

I will state what laws I consider *ex post facto* laws, within the words and the intent of the prohibition. 1st. Every law that makes an action done before the passing of the law, and which was innocent when done, criminal; and punishes such action. 2d. Every law that aggravates a crime, or makes it greater than it was, when committed. 3d. Every law that changes the punishment, and inflicts a greater punishment, than the law annexed to the crime, when committed. 4th. Every law that alters the legal rules of evidence, and receives less, or different testimony, than the law required at the time of the commission of the offense, in order to convict the offender. All these, and similar laws, are manifestly unjust and oppressive. In my opinion, the true distinction is between an *ex post facto* laws, and retrospective laws. Every *ex post facto* law must necessarily be retrospective; but every retrospective law is not an *ex post facto* law; the former only are prohibited. Every law that takes away or impairs rights vested, agreeably to existing laws, is retrospective, and is generally unjust, and may be oppressive; and it is a good general rule, that a law should have no retrospect; but there are cases in which laws may justly, and for the benefit of the community, and also of individuals, relate to a time antecedent to their commencement; as statutes of oblivion or of pardon. They are certainly retrospective, and literally both concerning and after the facts committed. But I do not consider any law *ex post facto*, within the prohibition, that mollifies the rigor of the criminal law; but only those that create or aggravate the crime; or increase the punishment, or change the rules of evidence, for the purpose of conviction . . . . There is a great and apparent difference between making an unlawful act lawful; and the making an innocent action criminal, and punishing it as a crime. The expressions "*ex post facto* laws" are technical, they had been in use long before the revolution, and had acquired an appropriate meaning by legislators, lawyers and authors. The celebrated and judicious Sir William Blackstone, in his *Commentaries*, considers an *ex post facto* law precisely in the same light I have done. His opinion is confirmed by his successor, Mr. Wooddeson; and by the author of *The Federalist*, who I esteem superior to both, for his extensive and accurate knowledge of the true principles of government . . . . If the term *ex post facto* law is to be construed to include and to prohibit the enacting any law after the fact, it will greatly restrict the power of the federal and state legislatures; and the consequences of such a construction may not be foreseen. . . .

It is not to be presumed that the federal or state legislatures will pass laws to deprive citizens of rights vested in them by existing laws; unless for the benefit of the whole community; and on making full satisfaction. The restraint against making any *ex post facto* laws was not considered, by the framers of the constitution, as extending to prohibit the depriving a citizen even of a vested right to property; or the provision, "that private property should not be taken for public use, without just compensation," was unnecessary. . . .

It seems to me, that the *right of property,* in its origin, could only arise from *compact express,* or *implied,* and I think it the better opinion, that the *right,* as well as the *mode,* or *manner,* of acquiring property, and of alienating or transferring, inheriting, or transmitting it, is conferred by society . . . and is always subject to the rules prescribed by *positive* law . . . .

I am of opinion that the decree of the supreme court of errors of Connecticut be affirmed, with costs.

PATERSON, Justice . . . .

IREDELL, Justice . . . .

If . . . a government composed of legislative, executive and judicial departments, were established by a constitution which imposed no limits on the legislative power, the consequence would inevitably be, that whatever the legislative power chose to enact, would be lawfully enacted, and the judicial power could never interpose to pronounce it void. It is true, that some speculative jurists have held, that a legislative act against natural justice must, in itself, be void; but I cannot think that, under such a government any court of justice would possess a power to declare it so. Sir William Blackstone, having put the strong case of an act of parliament, which authorizes a man to try his own cause, explicitly adds, that even in that case, "there is no court that has power to defeat the intent of the legislature, when couched in such evident and express words, as leave no doubt whether it was the intent of the legislature or no." 1 Bl.Com. 91.

In order, therefore, to guard against so great an evil, it has been the policy of all the American states, which have, individually, framed their state constitutions, since the revolution, and of the people of the United States, when they framed the federal constitution, to define with precision the objects of legislative power, and to restrain its exercise within marked and settled boundaries. If any act of congress, or of the legislature of a state, violates those constitutional provisions, it is unquestionably void; though, I admit, that as the authority to declare it void is of a delicate and awful nature, the court will never resort to that authority, but in a clear and urgent case. If, on the other hand, the legislature of the Union, or the legislature of any member of the Union, shall pass a law within the general scope of their constitutional power, the court cannot pronounce it to be void, merely because it is, in their judgment, contrary to the principles of natural justice. The ideas of natural justice are regulated by no fixed standard; the ablest and purest men have differed upon the subject; and all that the court could properly say, in such an event, would be that the legislature (possessed of an equal right of opinion) had passed an act which, in the opinion of the judges, was inconsistent with the abstract principles of natural justice. There are then but two lights, in which the subject can be viewed: 1st. If the legislature pursue the authority delegated to them, their acts are valid. 2d. If they transgress the boundaries of that authority, their acts are invalid. In the former case, they exercise the discretion vested in them by the people, to whom alone they are responsible for the faithful discharge of their trust: but in the latter case, they violate a fundamental law, which must be our guide, whenever we are called upon as judges, to determine the validity of a legislative act.

Still, however, in the present instance, the act or resolution of the legislature of Connecticut, cannot be regarded as an *ex post facto* law; for the true construction of the prohibition extends to criminal, not to civil issues . . ..

The policy, the reason and humanity of the prohibition, do not . . . extend to civil cases, to cases that merely affect the private property of citizens. Some of the most necessary and important acts of legislation are, on the contrary, founded upon the principle, that private rights must yield to public exigencies. Highways are run through private grounds; fortifications, lighthouses, and other public edifices, are necessarily sometimes built upon the soil owned by individuals. In such, and similar cases, if the owners should refuse voluntarily to accommodate the public, they must be constrained, so far as the public necessities require; and justice is done, by allowing them a reasonable equivalent. Without the possession of this power, the operations of government would often be obstructed, and society itself would be endangered. It is not sufficient to urge, that the power may be abused, for such is the nature of all power—such is the tendency of every human institution . . . .. We must be content to limit power, where we can, and where we cannot, consistently with its use, we must be content to repose a salutary confidence. It is our consolation, that there never existed a government, in ancient or modern times, more free from danger in this respect, than the governments of America . . ..

CUSHING, Justice. The case appears to me to be clear of difficulty, taken either way. If the act is a judicial act, it is not touched by the Federal Constitution; and, if it is a legislative act, it is maintained and justified by the ancient and uniform practice of the state of Connecticut.

JUDGMENT *affirmed.*

Editors' Note

Until the early years of John Marshall's tenure as chief justice (1801–1835), each justice usually wrote his own opinion or joined in one of the several opinions filed by other justices. In 1798 there were six members of the Court. Apparently two of them, Chief Justice Ellsworth and Justice Wilson, did not participate in this case.

"There are manifold restraints to which every person is necessarily subject for the common good."

JACOBSON v. MASSACHUSETTS

197 U.S. 11, 25 S.Ct. 358, 49 L.Ed. 643 (1905).

The Massachusetts legislature authorized localities to require vaccinations when they thought it necessary for public health. After an increase in smallpox, Cambridge in 1902 ordered all residents to be vaccinated. Jacobson refused and was prosecuted. At the trial he attacked the law's constitutionality and tried unsuccessfully to introduce evidence that such vaccinations often had injurious and sometimes fatal side effects and that both he and one of his sons had earlier become seriously ill after being vaccinated. The trial court found him guilty, a decision that state appellate courts affirmed. Jacobson then appealed to the U.S. Supreme Court.

Mr. Justice **HARLAN** delivered the opinion of the Court.

We pass without extended discussion the suggestion that the particular section of the statute of Massachusetts . . . is in derogation of rights secured by the Preamble of the Constitution of the United States. Although that Preamble indicates the general purposes for which the people ordained and established the Constitution, it has never been regarded as the source of any substantive power conferred on the Government of the United States or on any of its Departments. . . .

We also pass without discussion the suggestion that the above section of the statute is opposed to the spirit of the Constitution. Undoubtedly, as observed by Chief Justice Marshall, speaking for the court in Sturges v. Crowninshield, [1819] "the spirit of an instrument, especially of a constitution, is to be respected not less than its letter, yet the spirit is to be collected chiefly from its words." We have no need in this case to go beyond the plain, obvious meaning of the words in those provisions of the Constitution which, it is contended, must control our decision. . . .

The authority of the State to enact this statute is to be referred to what is commonly called the police power—a power which the State did not surrender when becoming a member of the Union under the Constitution . . . . According to settled principles the police power of a State must be held to embrace, at least, such reasonable regulations established directly by legislative enactment as will protect the public health and the public safety. . . . It is equally true that the State may invest local bodies . . . with authority in some appropriate way to safeguard the public health and the public safety . . . . Gibbons v. Ogden [1824]; Lawton v. Steele [1894].

We come, then, to inquire whether any right given, or secured by the Constitution, is invaded by the statute . . . . The defendant insists that his liberty is invaded when the State subjects him to fine or imprisonment for neglecting or refusing to submit to vaccination; that a compulsory vaccination law is unreasonable, arbitrary, and oppressive, and, therefore, hostile to the inherent right of every freeman to care for his own body and health in such way as to him seems best; and that the execution of such a law against one who objects to vaccination, no matter for what reason, is nothing short of an assault upon his person. But the liberty secured by the Constitution . . . does not import an absolute right in each person to be, at all times and in all circumstances, wholly freed from restraint. There are manifold restraints to which every person is necessarily subject for the common good. On any other basis organized society could not exist with safety to its members. Society based on the rule that each one is a law unto himself would soon be confronted with disorder and anarchy . . . . This court has more than once recognized it as a fundamental principle that "persons and property are subjected to all kinds of restraints and burdens in order to secure the general comfort, health, and prosperity of the State . . .." In Crowley v. Christensen [1890] we said: "The possession and enjoyment of all rights are subject to such reasonable conditions as may be deemed by the governing authority of the country, essential to the safety, health, peace, good order and morals of the community. Even liberty itself, the greatest of all rights, is not unrestricted license to act according to one's own will. It is only freedom from restraint under conditions essential to the equal enjoyment of the same right by others. It is then liberty regulated by law." . . .

Applying these principles to the present case, it is to be observed that the legislature of Massachusetts required the inhabitants of a city or town to be vaccinated only when, in the opinion of the Board of Health, that was necessary for the public health or the public safety. . . . Upon the principle of self-defense, of paramount necessity, a community has the right to protect itself against an epidemic of disease which threatens the safety of its members . . . . Smallpox being prevalent and increasing at Cambridge, the court would usurp the functions of another branch of government if it adjudged, as matter of law, that the mode adopted under the sanction of the State, to protect the people at large, was arbitrary and not justified by the necessities of the case. We say necessities of the case, because it might be that an acknowledged power of a local community to protect itself against an epidemic threatening the safety of all, might be exercised in particular circumstances and in reference to particular persons in such an arbitrary, unreasonable manner, or might go so far beyond what was reasonably required for the safety of the public, as to authorize or compel the courts to interfere for the protection of such persons. . . . There is, of course, a sphere within which the individual may assert the supremacy of his own will and rightfully dispute the authority of any human government, especially of any free government existing under a written constitution, to interfere with the exercise of that will. But it is equally true that in every well-ordered society . . . the rights of the individual in respect of his liberty may at times, under the pressure of great dangers, be subjected to such restraint, to be enforced by reasonable regulations, as the safety of the general public may demand. . . .

The liberty secured by the Fourteenth Amendment, this court has said, consists, in part, in the right of a person "to live and work where he will," Allgeyer v. Louisiana [1897] and yet he may be compelled, by force if need be, against his will and without regard to his personal wishes or his pecuniary interests, or even his religious or political convictions, to take his place in the ranks of the army of his country and risk the chance of being shot down in its defense. . . .

[The Court then discussed Jacobson's effort to present medical evidence attacking the effectiveness of vaccination in preventing small-pox.]

. . . We must assume that when the statute in question was passed, the legislature of Massachusetts was not unaware of these opposing theories, and was compelled . . . to choose between them . . . . It is no part of the function of a court or a jury to determine which one of two modes was likely to be the most effective for the protection of the public against disease. That was for the legislative department to determine in the light of all the information it had or could obtain. . . . If there is any such power in the judiciary to review legislative action in respect of a matter affecting the general welfare, it can only be when that which the legislature has done comes within the rule that if a statute purporting to have been enacted to protect the public health, the public morals or the public safety, has no real or substantial relation to those objects, or is, beyond all question, a plain, palpable invasion of rights secured by the fundamental law, it is the duty of the courts to so adjudge, and thereby give effect to the Constitution. . . .

We are not prepared to hold that a minority, residing or remaining in any city or town where smallpox is prevalent, and enjoying the general protection afforded by an organized local government, may thus defy the will of its constituted authorities, acting in good faith for all, under the legislative sanction of the State. If such be the privilege of a minority then a like privilege would belong to each individual of the community, and the spectacle would be presented of the welfare and safety of an entire population being subordinated to the notions of a single individual who chooses to remain a part of that population . . . . While this court should guard with firmness every right appertaining to life, liberty or property as secured to the individual by the Supreme Law of the Land, it is of the last importance that it should not invade the domain of local authority except when it is plainly necessary to do so in order to enforce that law. . . .

Before closing this opinion we deem it appropriate, in order to prevent misapprehension as to our views, to observe—perhaps to repeat a thought already sufficiently expressed, namely—that the police power of a State, whether exercised by the legislature, or by a local body acting under its authority, may be exerted in such circumstances or by regulations so arbitrary and oppressive in particular cases as to justify the interference of the courts to prevent wrong and oppression . . . . .

The judgment of the court below must be affirmed.

It is so ordered.

Mr. Justice **BREWER** and Mr. Justice **PECKHAM** dissent.

Editors' Note

By the mid-1970s most U.S. public health officials believed that smallpox had become so rare that the danger of an adverse reaction to the vaccination—something the Court in *Jacobson* weighed lightly—was many times greater than that of contracting the disease. As a result, it has become difficult in the United States to be vaccinated against smallpox.

"If the Fourteenth Amendment has absorbed them [portions of the Bill of Rights], the process of absorption has had its source in the belief that neither liberty nor justice would exist if they were sacrificed."

PALKO v. CONNECTICUT
302 U.S. 319, 58 S.Ct. 149, 82 L.Ed. 288 (1937).

For several generations, a majority of the Supreme Court held that the Fourteenth Amendment did not make the Bill of Rights binding on the states. Hurtado v. California (1884) ruled that the Fifth Amendment's requirement of indictment by grand jury did not apply to the states; In re Kemmler (1890) decided that the Eighth Amendment did not forbid states to use electrocution as a method of execution; Maxwell v. Dow (1900) reaffirmed *Hurtado*; and Twining v. New Jersey (1908) said the Fourteenth Amendment did not extend to the states the Fifth's ban against compulsory self-incrimination.

On the other hand, after 1890 the Court extended the Fourteenth Amendment's protection of property and "liberty of contract" under the proposition that these were included under the general term "liberty" in the due process clause. More specifically, Chicago, Burlington & Quincy R.R. v. Chicago (1897) applied to the states the Fifth Amendment's requirement of payment of "just compensation" for private property taken for public use. Then, without further warning, in 1925 Gitlow v. New York held that the First Amendment's protection of freedom of speech restricted the states. This ruling was followed by others that included in the Fourteenth Amendment freedom of the press, Near v. Minnesota (1931); under certain circumstances, the Sixth Amendment's guarantee of the right to counsel, Powell v. Alabama (1932); and, the Sixth Amendment's requirement of a trial by "an impartial jury," at least where a state chose to use juries, Norris v. Alabama (1935).

By the mid-1930s the whole question of which of the Bill of Rights were included in the Fourteenth was thoroughly confused. Palko v. Connecticut presented the Court with an opportunity to clarify the situation. A state statute allowed a prosecutor in a criminal case to appeal rulings of law and so seek to retry a defendant who had been acquitted under a mistaken interpretation of the law. Palko was tried for first degree murder, but the jury returned a verdict of guilty only of second degree murder. The prosecutor appealed, and the state supreme court ordered a new trial, holding that the trial judge had erred in excluding certain testimony as well in instructing the jury. At the second trial, the jury found Palko guilty of murder in the first degree, and he was sentenced to death. He lost in the state appellate courts and appealed to the U.S. Supreme Court.

Mr. Justice **CARDOZO** delivered the opinion of the Court. . . .

1. The execution of the sentence will not deprive appellant of his life without the process of law assured to him by the Fourteenth Amendment of the Federal Constitution.

The argument for appellant is that whatever is forbidden by the Fifth Amendment is forbidden by the Fourteenth also. The Fifth Amendment, which is not directed to the states, but solely to the federal government, creates immunity from double jeopardy. No person shall be "subject for the same offense to be twice put in jeopardy of life or limb." The Fourteenth Amendment ordains, "nor shall any State deprive any person of life, liberty, or property, without due process of law." To retry a defendant, though under one indictment and only one, subjects him, it is said, to double jeopardy in violation of the Fifth Amendment, if the prosecution is one on behalf of the United States. From this the consequence is said to follow that there is a denial of life or liberty without due process of law, if the prosecution is one on behalf of the People of a State . . . ..

We do not find it profitable to mark the precise limits of the prohibition of double jeopardy in federal prosecutions. The subject was much considered in Kepner v. United States, decided in 1904 by a closely divided court. The view was there expressed for a majority of the court that the prohibition was not confined to jeopardy in a new and independent case. It forbade jeopardy in the same case if the new trial was at the instance of the government and not upon defendant's motion. All this may be assumed for the purpose of the case at hand, though the dissenting opinions show how much was to be said in favor of a different ruling. Right-minded men, as we learn from those opinions, could reasonably, even if mistakenly, believe that a second trial was lawful in prosecutions subject to the Fifth Amendment, if it was all in the same case. Even more plainly, right-minded men could reasonably believe that in espousing that conclusion they were not favoring a practice repugnant to the conscience of mankind. Is double jeopardy in such circumstances, if double jeopardy it must be called, a denial of due process forbidden to the states? The tyranny of labels, Snyder v. Massachusetts, [1934], must not lead us to leap to a conclusion that a word which in one set of facts may stand for oppression or enormity is of like effect in every other.

. . . [I]n appellant's view the Fourteenth Amendment is to be taken as embodying the prohibitions of the Fifth. His thesis is even broader. Whatever would be a violation of the original bill of rights (Amendments I to VIII) * if done by the federal government is now

---

* **Eds.' Query:** Why only amendments 1–8? Why not the Ninth Amendment as well? Or even the Ninth and the Tenth? The Tenth relates only in part to powers reserved to the states; it also speaks of powers reserved "to the people."

equally unlawful by force of the Fourteenth Amendment if done by a state. There is no such general rule.

The Fifth Amendment provides, among other things, that no person shall be held to answer for a capital or otherwise infamous crime unless on presentment or indictment of a grand jury. This court has held that, in prosecutions by a state, presentment or indictment by a grand jury may give way to informations at the instance of a public officer. Hurtado v. California [1884]. The Fifth Amendment provides also that no person shall be compelled in any criminal case to be a witness against himself. This court has said that, in prosecutions by a state, the exemption will fail if the state elects to end it. Twining v. New Jersey [1908]. The Sixth Amendment calls for a jury trial in criminal cases and the Seventh for a jury trial in civil cases at common law where the value in controversy shall exceed twenty dollars. This court has ruled that consistently with those amendments trial by jury may be modified by a state or abolished altogether.

On the other hand, the due process clause of the Fourteenth Amendment may make it unlawful for a state to abridge by its statutes the freedom of speech which the First Amendment safeguards against encroachment by the Congress, De Jonge v. Oregon [1937]; Herndon v. Lowry [1937]; or the like freedom of the press, Grosjean v. American Press Co. [1936]; Near v. Minnesota [1931]; or the free exercise of religion Pierce v. Society of Sisters [1925]; or the right of peaceable assembly, without which speech would be unduly trammeled, *De Jonge; Herndon;* or the right of one accused of crime to the benefit of counsel, Powell v. Alabama [1932]. In these and other situations immunities that are valid as against the federal government by force of the specific pledges of particular amendments have been found to be implicit in the concept of ordered liberty, and thus, through the Fourteenth Amendment, become valid as against the states.

The line of division may seem to be wavering and broken if there is a hasty catalogue of the cases on the one side and the other. Reflection and analysis will induce a different view. There emerges the perception of a rationalizing principle which gives to discrete instances a proper order and coherence. The right to trial by jury and the immunity from prosecution except as the result of an indictment may have value and importance. Even so, they are not of the very essence of a scheme of ordered liberty. To abolish them is not to violate a "principle of justice so rooted in the traditions and conscience of our people as to be ranked as fundamental." *Snyder.* Few would be so narrow or provincial as to maintain that a fair and enlightened system of justice would be impossible without them. What is true of jury trials and indictments is true also, as the cases show, of the immunity from compulsory self-incrimination. This too might be lost, and justice still be done. Indeed, today as in the past there are students of our penal system who look upon the immunity as a mischief rather than a benefit, and who would limit its scope, or destroy it altogether. No doubt there would remain the need to give protection against torture, physical or mental. Justice, however, would not perish if the accused were subject to a duty to respond to orderly inquiry. The exclusion of these immunities and privileges from the privileges and immunities protected against the action of the states has not been arbitrary or casual. It has been dictated by a study and appreciation of the meaning, the essential implications, of liberty itself.

We reach a different plane of social and moral values when we pass to the privileges and immunities that have been taken over from the earlier articles of the federal bill of rights and brought within the Fourteenth Amendment by a process of absorption. These in their origin were effective against the federal government alone. If the Fourteenth Amendment has absorbed them, the process of absorption has had its source in the belief that neither liberty nor justice would exist if they were sacrificed. *Twining.* This is true, for illustration, of freedom of thought, and speech. Of that freedom one may say that it is the matrix, the indispensable condition, of nearly every other form of freedom. With rare aberrations a pervasive recognition of that truth can be traced in our history, political and legal. So it has come about that the domain of liberty, withdrawn by the Fourteenth Amendment from encroachment by the states, has been enlarged by latter-day judgments to include liberty of the mind as well as liberty of action. The extension became, indeed, a logical imperative when once it was recognized, as long ago it was, that liberty is something more than exemption from physical restraint, and that even in the field of substantive rights and duties the legislative judgment, if oppressive and arbitrary, may be overridden by the courts. Fundamental too in the concept of due process, and so in that of liberty, is the thought that condemnation shall be rendered only after trial. The hearing, moreover, must be a real one, not a sham or a pretense. For that reason, ignorant defendants in a capital case were held to have been condemned unlawfully when in truth, though not in form, they were refused the aid of counsel. *Powell.* The decision did not turn upon the fact that the benefit of counsel would have been guaranteed to the defendants by the provisions of the Sixth Amendment if they had been prosecuted in a federal court. The decision turned upon the fact that in the particular situation laid before us in the evidence the benefit of counsel was essential to the substance of a hearing.

Our survey of the cases serves, we think, to justify the statement that the dividing line between them, if not unfaltering throughout its course, has been true for the most part to a unifying principle. On which side of the line the case made out by the appellant has appropriate location must be the next inquiry and the final one. Is that kind of double jeopardy to which the statute has subjected him a hardship so acute and shocking that our polity will not endure it? Does it violate those "fundamental principles of liberty and justice which lie at the base of all our civil and political institutions"? Hebert v. Louisiana [1926]. The answer surely must be "no." What the answer would have to be if the state were permitted after a trial free from error to try the accused over again or to bring another case against him, we have no occasion to consider. We deal with the statute before us and no other. The state is not attempting to wear the accused out by a multitude of cases with accumulated trials. It asks no more than this, that the case against him shall go on until there shall be a trial free from the corrosion of substantial legal error. This is not cruelty at all, nor even vexation in any immoderate degree. If the trial had been infected with error adverse to the accused, there might have been review at his instance, and as often as necessary to purge the vicious taint. A reciprocal privilege, subject at all times to the discretion of the presiding judge, . . . has now been granted to the state. There is here no seismic innovation. The edifice of justice stands, its symmetry, to many, greater than before.

2. The conviction of appellant is not in derogation of any privileges or immunities that belong to him as a citizen of the United States . . . .

The judgment is affirmed.

Mr. Justice **BUTLER** dissents.

Editors' Note

"INCORPORATION" OF THE BILL OF RIGHTS

The plain words of the Fourteenth Amendment indicate that, if any of its clauses "incorporates" some or all of the Bill of Rights so as to make them applicable against the states, it is the so-called "privileges or immunities clause": "No State shall make or enforce any law which shall abridge the privileges or immunities of citizens of the United States . . . ." The amendment's legislative history, though complex and confused, gives far stronger support to such a claim for this clause than for the so-called "due process clause," which forbids states to "deprive any person of life, liberty, or property without due process of law . . . ."

But in the Slaughter-House Cases (1873; reprinted below, p. 435), the very first judicial interpretation of the amendment, the Supreme Court gutted the privileges or immunities clause. Thus, to make any part of the Bill of Rights applicable to the states, the Court either had to overrule much of *Slaughter-House,* find another clause to bear the burden, or look beyond the constitutional document for justification. Despite occasional protests, the justices have opted to use the due process clause as the instrument of incorporation.

The opinion for the Court in *Slaughter-House,* as did the debate in Congress on the Fourteenth Amendment, utilized an opinion by Justice Bushrod Washington, while sitting as a circuit judge, in Corfield v. Coryell (1823), in which he discussed the meaning of the very similar clause in Article IV. Dicta in Twining v. New Jersey (1908) listed as among the privileges and immunities of citizens of the United States rights to: travel interstate, petition Congress, vote for national officials, enter public lands, inform federal officials of crimes, and be protected against violence when in federal custody. During the great battle between the Court and the New Deal, Colgate v. Harvey (1935) tried to resurrect privileges and immunities for use as a defense against governmental regulation of business, but the attempt was short-lived. Only five years later Madden v. Kentucky (1940) overruled *Colgate.*

The Court has now held that the due process clause of the Fourteenth Amendment incorporates most of the Bill of Rights:

1) First Amendment: Free speech—Gitlow v. New York (1925); freedom of the press—Near v. Minnesota (1931); free exercise of religion—Hamilton v. Regents (1934), Cantwell v. Connecticut (1940); ban against establishment of religion—Everson v. Ewing Township (1947); freedom of assembly—DeJonge v. Oregon (1937); right to petition government for redress of grievances—NAACP v. Button (1963).

2) Fourth Amendment: General protection of a right to privacy: Griswold v. Connecticut (1965); protection against "unreasonable searches and seizures"—Wolf v. Colorado (1949); exclusion of unconstitutionally seized evidence—Mapp v. Ohio (1961); exclusion of illegally seized evidence—Berger v. New York (1967), Terry v. Ohio (1968); requirement of probable cause to arrest a suspect—Terry v. Ohio (1968).

3) Fifth Amendment: Protection against taking private property without "just compensation"—Chicago, Burlington & Quincy R.R. v. Chicago (1897); protection against self-incrimination—Malloy v. Hogan (1964), overruling Twining v. New Jersey (1908) and Adamson v. California (1947); protection against double jeopardy—Benton v. Maryland (1969), overruling the specific holding of Palko v. Connecticut (1937), but not *Palko* 's general approach to the problem of incorporation.

4) Sixth Amendment: Gideon v. Wainwright (1963), Miranda v. Arizona (1966), and Argersinger v. Hamlin (1972); trial by jury for serious offenses—Duncan v. Louisiana (1968); right to a speedy trial—Klopfer v. North Carolina (1967); right to be informed of the nature of the charge—Connally v. General Construction Co. (1926), Lanzetta v. New Jersey (1939), and Winters v. New York (1948) (Actually the Court has often decided such cases on the basis of the "void for vagueness rule," that is, to be valid a criminal statute must be sufficiently clear and specific to give fair warning of what it outlaws.); right to confront and cross examine witnesses—Pointer v. Texas (1965); right to compulsory processes (subpoenas) to require attendance of witnesses at a criminal trial—Washington v. Texas (1967).

5) Eighth Amendment: Protection against "cruel and unusual" punishment—Louisiana ex rel. Francis v. Resweber (1947) and Robinson v. California (1962). (There are also dicta in In re Kemmler [1878] as well as clear logical implications of the Court's specific holding that this protection was included under the general rubric of due process.)

6) Ninth Amendment: Protection of unlisted fundamental rights—Griswold v. Connecticut (1965) and Roe v. Wade (1973).

Not included have been the Fifth Amendment's right to indictment by grand jury and the Seventh's right to a jury trial in civil cases where the amount in controversy exceeds $20. There has been no specific ruling on the Third Amendment's protection against quartering of troops in civilian homes in time of peace, but *Griswold,* a case involving state action, cited this guarantee as part of the general right to privacy. So, too, the Court has not specifically held that the Eighth Amendment's ban against excessive bail binds the states, but the logic of recent criminal justice decisions indicates that the Court would so rule. The Second Amendment's guarantee of "the right of the people to keep and bear Arms" is preceded by the words: "A well regulated militia, being necessary to the security of a free State"; and to date the Court has treated this right as that of a state to maintain a militia, not of individual citizens to own or carry weapons. See United States v. Cruikshank (1875); United States v. Miller (1939); Lewis v. United States (1980); and the discussion in C. Herman Pritchett, *Constitutional Civil Liberties* (Englewood Cliffs, N.J.: Prentice-Hall, 1984), p. 3n.

There have been at least four approaches to the general problem of the Bill of Rights and the due process clause of the Fourteenth Amendment: (1) Due process incorporates all of the Bill of Rights, at least all of the first eight (though why not the Ninth and Tenth as well?)—Justice Black; (2) Due process incorporates all of the Bill of Rights plus some other "fundamental" rights not listed there—Justices Murphy and Rutledge, dissenting in Adamson v. California (1947); Justice Douglas, dissenting in Poe v. Ullman (1961) and speaking for the Court in Griswold v. Connecticut (1965); (3) Due process "selectively" incorporates only those parts of the Bill of Rights that are "of the very essence of a scheme of ordered liberty"—Justice Cardozo in *Palko* and, generally, the Court since; (4) Due process includes none of the Bill of Rights, and so the states are pretty much free from the *particular* restraints of the Bill of Rights—a view, not altogether unfairly, Justice Black attributed to the Court in Hurtado v. California (1884) and Twining v. New Jersey (1908).

Justice John Marshall Harlan, II, offered a variation on the fourth theme: The Fourteenth Amendment "incorporates" none of the Bill of Rights; rather, "due process" includes restrictions very much like those contained in some of the clauses of the Bill of Rights. Thus it is "due process" the Court must interpret, not the Bill of Rights. See his dissent in Poe v. Ullman (1961; reprinted, p. 106) and his concurring opinion in Griswold v. Connecticut (1965; reprinted, p. 113). See also Sanford Kadish, "Methodology and Criteria in Due Process Analysis—A Survey and Criticism," 66 *Yale L.J.* 319 (1957):

> The consequence of requiring due process to be measured precisely by the provisions of the Bill of Rights is not to eliminate broad judicial inquiry, but rather to change its focus from due process to freedom of speech or freedom from double jeopardy and the rest, and to disguise its essential character.

"The vague contours of the Due Process Clause do not leave judges at large. . . . [Its] limits are derived from considerations that are fused in the whole nature of our judicial process . . . considerations deeply rooted in reason and in the compelling traditions of the legal profession."

ROCHIN v. CALIFORNIA

342 U.S. 165, 72 S.Ct. 205, 96 L.Ed. 183 (1952).

Suspecting Antonio Rochin of dealing in narcotics, Los Angeles police forcibly entered his room. Before they could seize the two capsules they spotted, Rochin swallowed them. After failing to extract this evidence from Rochin's mouth, the officers took him to a hospital and, against Rochin's will, directed a physician to pump the suspect's stomach. The vomited matter contained the remains of the capsules, which the state used to convict Rochin of possessing morphine. The California supreme court refused review, and the U.S. Supreme Court granted certiorari.

Mr. Justice **FRANKFURTER** delivered the opinion of the Court
. . . .

In our federal system the administration of criminal justice is predominantly committed to the care of the States . . . . Accordingly, in reviewing a State criminal conviction under a claim of right guaranteed by the Due Process Clause of the Fourteenth Amendment . . . , "we must be deeply mindful of the responsibilities of the States for the enforcement of criminal laws, and exercise with due humility our merely negative function in subjecting convictions from state courts to the very narrow scrutiny which the Due Process Clause of the Fourteenth Amendment authorizes." Malinski v. New York [1945]
. . . .

However, this Court too has its responsibility. Regard for the requirements of the Due Process Clause "inescapably imposes upon this Court an exercise of judgment upon the whole course of the proceedings [resulting in a conviction] in order to ascertain whether they offend those canons of decency and fairness which express the notions of justice of English-speaking peoples . . . ." Ibid. These standards of justice are not authoritatively formulated anywhere as though they were specifics. Due process of law is a summarized constitutional guarantee of respect for those personal immunities which, as Mr. Justice Cardozo twice wrote for the Court, are "so rooted in the traditions and conscience of our people as to be ranked as fundamental," Snyder v. Massachusetts [1934], or are "implicit in the concept of ordered liberty." Palko v. Connecticut [1937].

The Court's function in the observance of this settled conception of the Due Process Clause does not leave us without adequate guides in subjecting State criminal procedures to constitutional judgment. In dealing not with the machinery of government but with human rights, the absence of formal exactitude, or want of fixity of meaning, is not an unusual or even regrettable attribute of constitutional provisions. Words being symbols do not speak without a gloss. On the one hand the gloss may be the deposit of history, whereby a term gains technical content . . . . On the other hand, the gloss of some of the verbal symbols of the Constitution does not give them a fixed technical content. It exacts a continuing process of application.

When the gloss has thus not been fixed but is a function of the process of judgment, the judgment is bound to fall differently at different times and differently at the same time through different judges. Even more specific provisions, such as the guaranty of freedom of speech and the detailed protection against unreasonable searches and seizures, have inevitably evoked as sharp divisions in this Court as the least specific and most comprehensive protection of liberties, the Due Process Clause.

The vague contours of the Due Process Clause do not leave judges at large. We may not draw on our merely personal and private notions and disregard the limits that bind judges in their judicial function. Even though the concept of due process of law is not final and fixed, these limits are derived from considerations that are fused in the whole nature of our judicial process. See Cardozo, *The Nature of the Judicial Process*. These are considerations deeply rooted in reason and in the compelling traditions of the legal profession. The Due Process Clause places upon this Court the duty of exercising a judgment, within the narrow confines of judicial power in reviewing State convictions, upon interests of society pushing in opposite directions.

Due process of law thus conceived is not to be derided as resort to a revival of "natural law." To believe that this judicial exercise of judgment could be avoided by freezing "due process of law" at some fixed stage of time or thought is to suggest that the most important aspect of constitutional adjudication is a function for inanimate machines and not for judges . . . .. Even cybernetics has not yet made that haughty claim. To practice the requisite detachment and to achieve sufficient objectivity no doubt demands of judges the habit of self-discipline and self-criticism, incertitude that one's own views are incontestable and alert tolerance toward views not shared. But these are precisely the presuppositions of our judicial process. They are precisely the qualities society has a right to expect from those entrusted with ultimate judicial power.

Restraints on our jurisdiction are self-imposed only in the sense that there is from our decisions no immediate appeal short of impeachment or constitutional amendment. But that does not make due process of law a matter of judicial caprice. The faculties of the Due Process Clause may be indefinite and vague, but the mode of their ascertainment is not self-willed. In each case "due process of law" requires an evaluation based on a disinterested inquiry pursued in the spirit of science, on a balanced order of facts exactly and fairly stated, on the detached consideration of conflicting claims, on a judgment not ad hoc and episodic but duly mindful of reconciling the needs both of continuity and of change in a progressive society.

Applying these general considerations to the circumstances of the present case, we are compelled to conclude that the proceedings by which this conviction was obtained do more than offend some fastidious squeamishness or private sentimentalism about combatting crime too energetically. This is conduct that shocks the conscience. Illegally breaking into the privacy of the petitioner, the struggle to open his mouth and remove what was there, the forcible extraction of his stomach's contents—this course of proceeding by agents of government to obtain evidence is bound to offend even hardened sensibilities. They are methods too close to the rack and the screw to permit of constitutional differentiation.

. . . Due process of law, as a historic and generative principle, precludes defining, and thereby confining, these standards of conduct more precisely than to say that convictions cannot be brought about by methods that offend "a sense of justice." . . .

. . . Use of involuntary verbal confessions in State criminal trials is constitutionally obnoxious not only because of their unreliability. They are inadmissible under the Due Process Clause even though statements contained in them may be independently established as true. Coerced confessions offend the community's sense of fair play and decency. So here, to sanction the brutal conduct which naturally enough was condemned by the court whose judgment is before us, would be to afford brutality the cloak of the law. Nothing would be more calculated to discredit law and thereby to brutalize the temper of a society . . . .

Reversed.

Mr. Justice **MINTON** took no part in the consideration or decision of this case.

Mr. Justice **BLACK**, concurring.

Adamson v. California [1947] sets out reasons for my belief that state as well as federal courts and law enforcement officers must obey the Fifth Amendment's command that "No person . . . shall be compelled in any criminal case to be a witness against himself." I think a person is compelled to be a witness against himself not only when he is compelled to testify, but also when as here, incriminating evidence is forcibly taken from him by a contrivance of modern science . . . . I believe that faithful adherence to the specific guarantees in the Bill of Rights insures a more permanent protection of individual liberty than that which can be afforded by the nebulous standards stated by the majority.

What the majority hold is that the Due Process Clause empowers this Court to nullify any state law if its application "shocks the conscience," offends "a sense of justice" or runs counter to the "decencies of civilized conduct." The majority emphasize that these statements do not refer to their own consciences or to their senses of justice and decency. For we are told that "we may not draw on our merely personal and private notions"; our judgment must be grounded on "considerations deeply rooted in reason, and in the compelling traditions of the legal profession." We are further admonished to measure the validity of state practices, not by our reason, or by the traditions of the legal profession, but by "the community's sense of fair play and decency"; by the "traditions and conscience of our people"; or by "those canons of decency and fairness which express the notions of justice of English-speaking peoples." These canons are made necessary, it is said, because of "interests of society pushing in opposite directions."

If the Due Process Clause does vest this Court with such unlimited power to invalidate laws, I am still in doubt as to why we should consider only the notions of English-speaking peoples to determine what are immutable and fundamental principles of justice. Moreover, one may well ask what avenues of investigation are open to discover "canons" of conduct so universally favored that this Court should write them into the Constitution? All we are told is that the discovery must be made by an "evaluation based on a disinterested inquiry pursued in the spirit of science on a balanced order of facts."

Some constitutional provisions are stated in absolute and unqualified language such . . . as the First Amendment stating that no law shall be passed prohibiting the free exercise of religion or abridging the freedom of speech or press. Other constitutional provisions do require courts to choose between competing policies, such as the Fourth Amendment which, by its terms, necessitates a judicial decision as to what is an "unreasonable" search or seizure. There is, however, no express constitutional language granting judicial power to invalidate *every* state law of *every* kind deemed "unreasonable" or contrary to the Court's notion of civilized decencies; yet the constitutional philosophy used by the majority has, in the past, been used . . . to nullify state legislative programs passed to suppress evil economic practices. . . . Of even graver concern . . . is the use of the philosophy to nullify the Bill of Rights. I long ago concluded that the accordion-like qualities of this philosophy must inevitably imperil all the individual liberty safeguards specifically enumerated in the Bill of Rights. . . .

Mr. Justice DOUGLAS, concurring.

The evidence obtained from this accused's stomach would be admissible in the majority of states where the question has been raised. So far as the reported cases reveal, the only states which would probably exclude the evidence would be Arkansas, Iowa, Michigan, and Missouri. Yet the Court now says that the rule which the majority of the states have fashioned violates the "decencies of civilized conduct." To that I cannot agree. It is a rule formulated by responsible courts with judges as sensitive as we are to the proper standards for law administration.

As an original matter it might be debatable whether the provision in the Fifth Amendment that no person "shall be compelled in any criminal case to be a witness against himself" serves the ends of justice. Not all civilized legal procedures recognize it. But the choice was made by the Framers, a choice which sets a standard for legal trials in this country. . . . I think that words taken from [an accused's] lips, capsules taken from his stomach, blood taken from his veins are all inadmissible provided they are taken from him without his consent. They are inadmissible because of the command of the Fifth Amendment.

That is an unequivocal, definite and workable rule of evidence for state and federal courts. But we cannot in fairness free the state courts from that command and yet excoriate them for flouting the

"decencies of civilized conduct" when they admit the evidence. That is
to make the rule turn not on the Constitution but on the idiosyncrasies
of the judges who sit here. . . .

Editors' Notes

(1) **Query:** To what extent is *Rochin* compatible with Jacobson v. Massachusetts (1905), reprinted above, p. 91? To put the question another way,
was the Court in *Rochin* finding a right to bodily integrity in the "whole nature
of the judicial process" and/or "the compelling traditions of the legal profession"? Or was it merely setting outer limits to such terms in the constitutional
document as "self-incrimination" and "unreasonable searches and seizures"?
Whatever one believes the majority to have been doing in *Rochin,* the
concurring opinions of Black and Douglas were much more limited and
positivistic in their reasoning. The reasoning of several more recent opinions
of the Court dealing with efforts to obtain evidence from the bodies' of
suspects has been more positivistic than that of the Court in *Rochin,* but Black
and Douglas dissented against those results, while they were still on the Court:

  (i) Breithaupt v. Abram (1957) sustained a conviction for drunken
  driving based on a test done on a sample of blood taken from a
  suspect while he was unconscious. The majority found nothing
  "brutal" or "offensive" in such procedures: "As against the right of
  an individual that his person be held inviolable even against so slight
  an intrusion as is involved in applying a blood test of the kind to which
  millions of Americans submit as a matter of course nearly every day,
  must be set the interests of society in the scientific determination of
  intoxication, one of the great causes of the mortal hazards of the
  road."

  (ii) Schmerber v. California (1966) upheld a conviction based on
  a similar test, even though conducted on a conscious and protesting
  suspect. The majority conceded that the basic reason underlying
  constitutional protections against self-incrimination and unreasonable
  searches was concern for human dignity: "If the scope of the
  privilege [against self-incrimination] coincided with the complex of
  values it helps to protect, we might be obliged to conclude that the
  privilege was violated." The majority, however, found the privilege
  more limited and chose to follow *Breithaupt.* Nevertheless, the Court
  added: "The integrity of the individual is a cherished value of our
  society. That we today hold that the Constitution does not forbid the
  State's minor intrusion into an individual's body under stringently
  limited conditions in no way indicates that it permits more substantial
  intrusions or intrusions under other conditions."

  (iii) South Dakota v. Neville (1983) allowed use in evidence of a
  defendant's refusal to take a blood test to determine sobriety.

(2) The Supreme Court does not currently have the reputation of being
especially sympathetic to individual rights. Reality is more compliated, however. See Vincent Blasi, ed., *The Burger Court: The Counter-Revolution That
Wasn't* (New Haven, Conn.: Yale University Press, 1983). It is quite possible
that the Court will hold that "the Constitution" protects a right to bodily

integrity.   Much earlier, Skinner v. Oklahoma (1942; reprinted below, p. 868) struck down as a denial of equal protection of the laws a state statute sterilizing people convicted three times for some offenses but not for others no less serious.   More recently, Roe v. Wade (1973; reprinted below, p. 1109), reaffirmed in Akron v. Akron Center for Reproductive Health (1983; reprinted below, p. 1122), held that the constitutional right to privacy—first identified by the Court in Griswold v. Connecticut (1965; reprinted below, p. 113), but nowhere specifically mentioned in the constitutional document—includes a woman's right, at least during the first trimester of her pregnancy, to have an abortion.   On the other hand, Bell v. Wolfish (1979; reprinted below, p. 1134) ruled that defendants being detained in jail awaiting trial could be subjected to routine searches of bodily cavities to detect smuggling of contraband.

See also:

(i) Mills v. Rogers (1982) involved a challenge by patients in a Massachusetts mental institution protesting against being compelled to take certain kinds of drugs.   The Supreme Court remanded (sent back) the case to the U.S. court of appeals for reconsideration in light of a ruling by the Massachusetts supreme court that non-institutionalized mental patients have a right to refuse such treatment.

(ii) Youngberg v. Romeo (1982) held that patients involuntarily institutionalized for mental illness have rights to safe conditions, to freedom from restraints except as necessary to protect them or others, and to such training as may be necessary to ensure their safety or to enable them to live safely without restraints.

Among the leading cases in this field is O'Connor v. Donaldson (1975), holding that a state cannot institutionalize against their will mentally disturbed people who are not dangerous to themselves or others.

(3) For general efforts by the justices to explain how they discover rights not listed in the constitutional document as well as attacks on such efforts, see not only the various opinions in *Griswold* but also the dissenting opinions of Douglas and Harlan in Poe v. Ullman (1961; reprinted below, p. 106), and the opinions of Powell and White in Moore v. East Cleveland (1977; reprinted below, p. 1145).

—————

"This notion of privacy is not drawn from the blue.   It emanates from the totality of the constitutional scheme under which we live."—Justice DOUGLAS.

"[We must approach] the text which is the only commission for our power not in a literalistic way, as if we had a tax statute before us, but as the basic charter of our society, setting out in spare but meaningful terms the principles of government."—Justice HARLAN.

POE v. ULLMAN
367 U.S. 497, 81 S.Ct. 1752, 6 L.Ed.2d 989 (1961).

In 1879 Connecticut adopted a statute making it a crime to use or aid in using contraceptives.   As technology and notions about sexual morality changed, so did the composition of the state's population. In the nineteenth century, a heavily Protestant majority had apparently supported the law; by the middle of the twentieth century, it was the large Catholic population who were, officially at least, in favor of the statute. Thus repeal was politically unlikely.

In the 1940s a group advocating birth control went to court to attack the law as violating the Fourteenth Amendment. A doctor challenged the statute as depriving his patients of life and liberty without due process by preventing his giving them medical advice that might save their lives. State courts sustained the law, and the U.S. Supreme Court dismissed the action on grounds that the doctor lacked standing to assert his patients' rights. Tileston v. Ullman (1943). In the late 1950s, the group tried again. This time the plaintiffs were married couples and a physician. They, too, lost in state courts, and once more the Supreme Court dismissed the suit. For four justices, Felix Frankfurter concluded that there was no imminent threat to any putative right: In the 82 years the statute had been on the books, Connecticut had only once tried to enforce it. Justice Brennan concurred separately on similar grounds, while Justices Black and Stewart dissented for procedural reasons. Justices Douglas and Harlan also dissented.

We reprint here only parts of the latter two opinions dealing with substantive issues.

Mr. Justice **DOUGLAS**, dissenting. . . .

. . . [T]his Connecticut law as applied to this married couple deprives them of "liberty" without due process of law, as that concept is used in the Fourteenth Amendment.

The first eight Amendments to the Constitution have been made applicable to the States only in part. My view has been that when the Fourteenth Amendment was adopted, its Due Process Clause incorporated all of those Amendments. See Adamson v. California [1947] (dissenting opinion [by Black, J.]). Although the history of the Fourteenth Amendment may not be conclusive, the words "due process" acquired specific meaning from Anglo-American experience. . . . When the Framers wrote the Bill of Rights they enshrined in the form of constitutional guarantees those rights—in part substantive, in part procedural—which experience indicated were indispensable to a free society. Some would disagree as to their importance; the debate concerning them did indeed start before their adoption and has continued to this day. Yet the constitutional conception of "due process" must, in my view, include them all until and unless there are amendments that remove them. That has indeed been the view of a full court of nine Justices, though the members who make up that court unfortunately did not sit at the same time.

Though I believe that "due process" as used in the Fourteenth Amendment includes all of the first eight Amendments, I do not think it is restricted and confined to them. We recently held that the undefined "liberty" in the Due Process Clause of the Fifth Amendment includes freedom to travel. Kent v. Dulles [1958]. Cf. Edwards v. California [1941] (concurring opinion [by Douglas, J.]). The right "to marry, establish a home and bring up children" was said in Meyer v.

Nebraska [1923] to come within the "liberty" of the person protected by
the Due Process Clause of the Fourteenth Amendment. As I indicated
in my dissent in Public Utilities Com. v. Pollak [1952], "liberty" within
the purview of the Fifth Amendment includes the right of "privacy"
. . . . "Liberty" is a conception that sometimes gains content from
the emanations of other specific guarantees (National Asso. for Advancement of Colored People v. Alabama [1958]) or from experience
with the requirements of a free society.

For years the Court struck down social legislation when a particular law did not fit the notions of a majority of Justices as to legislation
appropriate for a free enterprise system. . . .

The error of the old Court, as I see it, was not in entertaining
inquiries concerning the constitutionality of social legislation but in
applying the standards that it did. Social legislation dealing with
business and economic matters touches no particularized prohibition of
the Constitution, unless it be the provision of the Fifth Amendment
that private property should not be taken for public use without just
compensation. If it is free of the latter guarantee, it has a wide scope
for application. Some go so far as to suggest that whatever the
majority in the legislature says goes. . . . That reduces the legislative power to sheer voting strength and the judicial function to a
matter of statistics. . . . While the legislative judgment on economic
and business matters is "well-nigh conclusive" (Berman v. Parker
[1954]), it is not beyond judicial inquiry.

The regime of a free society needs room for vast experimentation.
. . . Yet to say that a legislature may do anything not within a
specific guarantee of the Constitution may be as crippling to a free
society as to allow it to override specific guarantees so long as what it
does fails to shock the sensibilities of a majority of the Court.

The present legislation is an excellent example. If a State banned
completely the sale of contraceptives in drug stores, the case would be
quite different. It might seem to some or to all judges an unreasonable
restriction. Yet it might not be irrational to conclude that a better way
of dispensing those articles is through physicians. The same might be
said of a state law banning the manufacture of contraceptives. Health,
religious, and moral arguments might be marshalled pro and con. Yet
it is not for judges to weigh the evidence. Where either the sale or the
manufacture is put under regulation, the strictures are on business and
commercial dealings that have had a long history with the police power
of the States.

The present law, however, deals not with sale, not with manufacture, but with *use*. . . .

The regulation . . . reaches into the intimacies of the marriage
relationship. If we imagine a regime of full enforcement of the law in
the manner of an Anthony Comstock we would reach the point where
search warrants issued and officers appeared in bedrooms to find out
what went on. It is said that this is not that case. And so it is not.
But when the State makes "use" a crime and applies the criminal

sanction to man and wife, the State has entered the innermost sanctum
of the home. If it can make this law, it can enforce it. And proof of its
violation necessarily involves an inquiry into the relations between
man and wife.

That is an invasion of the privacy that is implicit in a free society.

.   .   .

This notion of privacy is not drawn from the blue. It emanates
from the totality of the constitutional scheme under which we live.

.   .   .

Can there be any doubt that a Bill of Rights that in time of peace
bars soldiers from being quartered in a home "without the consent of
the Owner" should also bar the police from investigating the intimacies
of the marriage relation? The idea of allowing the State that leeway is
congenial only to a totalitarian regime. .   .   .

Mr. Justice **HARLAN,** dissenting .   .   .   .

.   .   . I believe that a statute making it a criminal offense for
married couples to use contraceptives is an intolerable and unjustifiable
invasion of privacy in the conduct of the most intimate concerns of an
individual's personal life .   .   .   .

I

In reviewing state legislation .   .   . in provision for the health,
safety, morals or welfare of its people, it is clear that what is concerned
are "the powers of government inherent in every sovereignty." License
Cases [1847]. Only to the extent that the Constitution so requires may
this Court interfere with the exercise of this plenary power of government. Barron v. Baltimore [1833]. But precisely because it is the
Constitution alone which warrants judicial interference in sovereign
operations of the State, the basis of judgment as to the Constitutionality
of state action must be a rational one, approaching the text which is the
only commission for our power not in a literalistic way, as if we had a
tax statute before us, but as the basic charter of our society, setting out
in spare but meaningful terms the principles of government.
M'Culloch v. Maryland [1819]. But as inescapable as is the rational
process in Constitutional adjudication in general, nowhere is it more so
than in giving meaning to the prohibitions of the Fourteenth Amendment and, where the Federal Government is involved, the Fifth Amendment, against the deprivation of life, liberty or property without due
process of law.

It is but a truism to say that this provision of both Amendments is
not self-explanatory. As to the Fourteenth, which is involved here, the
history of the Amendment also sheds little light on the meaning of the
provision. It is important to note, however, that two views of the
Amendment have not been accepted by this Court .   .   .   . One view
.   .   . sought to limit the provision to a guarantee of procedural
fairness. The other view .   .   . would have it that the Fourteenth
Amendment .   .   . applied against the States only and precisely those

restraints which had prior to the Amendment been applicable merely to federal action. However, "due process" in the consistent view of this Court has ever been a broader concept than the first view and more flexible than the second. . . .

. . . [I]t is not the particular enumeration of rights in the first eight Amendments which spells out the reach of Fourteenth Amendment due process, but rather . . . those concepts which are considered to embrace those rights "which are . . . *fundamental;* which belong . . . to the citizens of all free governments." Corfield v. Coryell [1823], for "the purposes [of securing] which men enter into society," Calder v. Bull [1798]. Again and again this Court has resisted the notion that the Fourteenth Amendment is no more than a shorthand reference to what is explicitly set out elsewhere in the Bill of Rights. Slaughter House Cases [1873]; Palko v. Connecticut [1937]. Indeed the fact that an identical provision limiting federal action is found among the first eight Amendments, applying to the Federal Government, suggests that due process is a discrete concept which subsists as an independent guaranty of liberty and procedural fairness, more general and inclusive than the specific prohibitions.

Due process has not been reduced to any formula; its content cannot be determined by reference to any code. The best that can be said is that through the course of this Court's decisions it has represented the balance which our Nation, built upon postulates of respect for the liberty of the individual, has struck between that liberty and the demands of organized society. If the supplying of content to this Constitutional concept has of necessity been a rational process, it certainly has not been one where judges have felt free to roam where unguided speculation might take them. The balance of which I speak is the balance struck by this country, having regard to what history teaches are the traditions from which it developed as well as the traditions from which it broke. That tradition is a living thing. A decision of this Court which radically departs from it could not long survive, while a decision which builds on what has survived is likely to be sound. No formula could serve as a substitute, in this area, for judgment and restraint.

It is this outlook which has led the Court continuingly to perceive distinctions in the imperative character of Constitutional provisions, since that character must be discerned from a particular provision's larger context. And inasmuch as this context is one not of words, but of history and purposes, the full scope of the liberty guaranteed by the Due Process Clause cannot be found in or limited by the precise terms of the specific guarantees elsewhere provided in the Constitution. This "liberty" is not a series of isolated points pricked out in terms of the taking of property; the freedom of speech, press, and religion; the right to keep and bear arms; the freedom from unreasonable searches and seizures; and so on. It is a rational continuum which, broadly speaking, includes a freedom from all substantial arbitrary impositions and purposeless restraints and which also recognizes, what a reasonable and sensitive judgment must, that certain interests require particularly careful scrutiny of the state needs asserted to justify their abridgment. Cf. Skinner v. Oklahoma [1942]; Bolling v. Sharpe [1954].

As was said in *Meyer*, "this Court has not attempted to define with exactness the liberty thus guaranteed . . . . Without doubt, it denotes not merely freedom from bodily restraint . . . ." Thus, for instance, when in that case and in Pierce v. Society of Sisters [1925] the Court struck down laws which sought not to require what children must learn in schools, but to prescribe, in the first case, what they must *not* learn, and in the second, *where* they must acquire their learning, I do not think it was wrong to put those decisions on "the right of the individual to . . . establish a home and bring up children," or on the basis that "The fundamental theory of liberty upon which all governments in this Union repose excludes any general power of the State to standardize its children by forcing them to accept instruction from public teachers only." I consider this so, even though today those decisions would probably have gone by reference to the concepts of freedom of expression and conscience assured against state action by the Fourteenth Amendment, concepts that are derived from the explicit guarantees of the First Amendment against federal encroachment upon freedom of speech and belief.* For it is the purposes of those guarantees and not their text, the reasons for their statement by the Framers and not the statement itself, see *Palko;* United States v. Carolene Products Co. [1938], which have led to their present status in the compendious notion of "liberty" embraced in the Fourteenth Amendment.

Each new claim to Constitutional protection must be considered against a background of Constitutional purposes, as they have been rationally perceived and historically developed. Though we exercise limited and sharply restrained judgment, yet there is no "mechanical yardstick," no "mechanical answer." The decision of an apparently novel claim must depend on grounds which follow closely on well-accepted principles and criteria. . . .

III

Precisely what is involved here is this: the State is asserting the right to enforce its moral judgment by intruding upon the most intimate details of the marital relation with the full power of the criminal law. . . .

. . . The statute must pass a more rigorous Constitutional test than that going merely to the plausibility of its underlying rationale. This enactment involves what, by common understanding throughout the English-speaking world, must be granted to be a most fundamental aspect of "liberty," the privacy of the home in its most basic sense, and it is this which requires that the statute be subjected to "strict scrutiny." *Skinner.*

---

* **Eds.' Note:** Compare Justice Douglas's opinion for the Court in Griswold v. Connecticut (1965; reprinted below, p. 113), interpreting *Meyer* and *Pierce* in light of the First Amendment rather than "substantive due process."

That aspect of liberty which embraces the concept of the privacy of the home receives explicit Constitutional protection at two places only. These are the Third Amendment, relating to the quartering of soldiers, and the Fourth Amendment, prohibiting unreasonable searches and seizures. While these Amendments reach only the Federal Government, this Court has held . . . that the concept of "privacy" embodied in the Fourth Amendment is part of the "ordered liberty" assured against state action by the Fourteenth Amendment. See Wolf v. Colorado [1949]; Mapp v. Ohio [1961] . . . .

Perhaps the most comprehensive statement of the principle of liberty underlying these aspects of the Constitution was given by Mr. Justice Brandeis, dissenting in Olmstead v. United States [1928]:

> The makers of our Constitution undertook to secure conditions favorable to the pursuit of happiness. . . . They conferred, as against the Government, the right to be let alone—the most comprehensive of rights and the right most valued by civilized men. To protect that right, every unjustifiable intrusion by the Government upon the privacy of the individual, whatever the means employed, must be deemed a violation of the Fourth Amendment. . . .

I think the sweep of the Court's decisions . . . amply shows that the Constitution protects the privacy of the home against all unreasonable intrusion of whatever character. "[These] principles . . . affect the very essence of constitutional liberty and security. They . . . apply to all invasions on the part of the government and its employes of the sanctity of a man's home and the privacies of life . . . ." Boyd v. United States [1886]. "The security of one's privacy against arbitrary intrusion by the police—which is at the core of the Fourth Amendment—is basic to a free society." *Wolf.*

It would surely be an extreme instance of sacrificing substance to form were it to be held that the Constitutional principle of privacy against arbitrary official intrusion comprehends only physical invasions by the police. To be sure, the times presented the Framers with two particular threats to that principle, the general warrant and the quartering of soldiers in private homes. But . . . "a principle to be vital must be capable of wider application than the mischief which gave it birth." Weems v. United States [1910].

. . . [T]here is another sense in which it could be argued that this intrusion on privacy differs from what the Fourth Amendment, and the similar concept of the Fourteenth, were intended to protect: here we have not an intrusion into the home so much as on the life which characteristically has its place in the home. But to my mind such a distinction is so insubstantial as to be captious . . . . Certainly the safeguarding of the home does not follow merely from the sanctity of property rights. The home derives its preminence as the seat of family life. And the integrity of that life is something so fundamental that it has been found to draw to its protection the principles of more than one explicitly granted Constitutional right . . . .

Of this whole "private realm of family life" [Prince v. Massachusetts (1944)] it is difficult to imagine what is more private or more intimate than a husband and wife's marital relations . . ..

Of course, just as the requirement of a warrant is not inflexible in carrying out searches and seizures, so there are countervailing considerations at this more fundamental aspect of the right involved. "[T]he family . . . is not beyond regulation," *Prince,* and it would be an absurdity to suggest either that offenses may not be committed in the bosom of the family or that the home can be made a sanctuary for crime. The right of privacy most manifestly is not an absolute. Thus, I would not suggest that adultery, homosexuality, fornication and incest are immune from criminal enquiry, however privately practiced . . ..

Adultery, homosexuality and the like are sexual intimacies which the State forbids altogether, but the intimacy of husband and wife is necessarily an essential and accepted feature of the institution of marriage, an institution which the State . . . always . . . has fostered and protected . . ..

. . . I must agree with Mr. Justice Jackson that "There are limits to the extent to which a legislatively represented majority may conduct . . . experiments at the expense of the dignity and personality" of the individual. *Skinner.* In this instance these limits are, in my view, reached and passed. . . .

———

"[S]pecific guarantees in the Bill of Rights have penumbras, formed by emanations from those guarantees that help give them life and substance."

GRISWOLD v. CONNECTICUT
381 U.S. 479, 85 S.Ct. 1678, 14 L.Ed.2d 510 (1965).

This case marked a further stage in the long struggle against the Connecticut law of 1879 that made it a crime to use or to aid, abet, or counsel use of "any drug, medicinal article or instrument for the purpose of preventing conception." After the decision in Poe v. Ullman (1961); reprinted above, p. 106), dismissing a suit against the constitutionality of this statute on grounds that the plaintiffs had not shown that the state was likely to enforce it against them, the Director of the Planned Parenthood League of Connecticut and a physician flouted the law by publicly advising married persons about the use of contraceptives. They were arrested, tried, convicted, and fined $100 each. State courts sustained the convictions, and the two men appealed to the U.S. Supreme Court.

Mr. Justice **DOUGLAS** delivered the opinion of the Court . . . .

[W]e are met with a wide range of questions that implicate the Due Process Clause of the Fourteenth Amendment. Overtones of some arguments suggest that Lochner v. New York [1905] should be our guide. But we decline that invitation as we did in West Coast Hotel Co.

v. Parrish [1937]. We do not sit as a super-legislature to determine the
wisdom, need, and propriety of laws that touch economic problems,
business affairs, or social conditions. This law, however, operates
directly on an intimate relation of husband and wife and their physician's role in one aspect of that relation.

The association of people is not mentioned in the Constitution nor
in the Bill of Rights. The right to educate a child in a school of the
parents' choice—whether public or private or parochial—is also not
mentioned. Nor is the right to study any particular subject or any
foreign language. Yet the First Amendment has been construed to
include certain of those rights.

By Pierce v. Society of Sisters [1925], the right to educate one's
children as one chooses is made applicable to the States by the force of
the First and Fourteenth Amendments. By Meyer v. Nebraska [1923],
the same dignity is given the right to study the German language in a
private school. In other words, the State may not, consistently with
the spirit of the First Amendment, contract the spectrum of available
knowledge. The right of freedom of speech and press includes not only
the right to utter or to print, but the right to distribute, the right to
receive, the right to read (Martin v. Struthers [1943]) and freedom of
inquiry, freedom of thought, and freedom to teach (see Wieman v.
Updegraff [1952])—indeed the freedom of the entire university community. Sweezy v. New Hampshire [1957]; Barenblatt v. United States
[1959]. Without those peripheral rights the specific rights would be
less secure. And so we reaffirm the principle of the Pierce and the
Meyer cases.

In NAACP v. Alabama [1958], we protected the "freedom to associate and privacy in one's associations," noting that freedom of association was a peripheral First Amendment right. Disclosure of membership lists of a constitutionally valid association, we held, was invalid "as
entailing the likelihood of a substantial restraint upon the exercise by
petitioner's members of their right to freedom of association." In other
words, the First Amendment has a penumbra where privacy is protected from governmental intrusion. In like context, we have protected
forms of "association" that are not political in the customary sense but
pertain to the social, legal, and economic benefit of the members.
NAACP v. Button [1963]. In Schware v. Board of Bar Examiners
[1957], we held it not permissible to bar a lawyer from practice, because
he had once been a member of the Communist Party. The man's
"association with that Party" was not shown to be "anything more than
a political faith in a political party" and was not action of a kind
proving bad moral character.

Those cases involved more than the "right of assembly"—a right
that extends to all irrespective of their race or ideology. De Jonge v.
Oregon [1937]. The right of "association," like the right of belief (Board
of Education v. Barnette [1943]), is more than the right to attend a
meeting; it includes the right to express one's attitudes or philosophies
by membership in a group or by affiliation with it or by other lawful

means. Association in that context is a form of expression of opinion; and while it is not expressly included in the First Amendment its existence is necessary in making the express guarantees fully meaningful.

The foregoing cases suggest that specific guarantees in the Bill of Rights have penumbras, formed by emanations from those guarantees that help give them life and substance. See Poe v. Ullman [1961] (dissenting opinion [by Douglas, J.]). Various guarantees create zones of privacy. The right of association contained in the penumbra of the First Amendment is one, as we have seen. The Third Amendment in its prohibition against the quartering of soldiers "in any house" in time of peace without the consent of the owner is another facet of that privacy. The Fourth Amendment explicitly affirms the "right of the people to be secure in their persons, houses, papers, and effects, against unreasonable searches and seizures." The Fifth Amendment in its Self-Incrimination Clause enables the citizen to create a zone of privacy which government may not force him to surrender to his detriment. The Ninth Amendment provides: "The enumeration in the Constitution, of certain rights, shall not be construed to deny or disparage others retained by the people."

The Fourth and Fifth Amendments were described in Boyd v. United States [1886] as protection against all governmental invasions "of the sanctity of a man's home and the privacies of life." We recently referred in Mapp v. Ohio [1961] to the Fourth Amendment as creating a "right to privacy, no less important than any other right carefully and particularly reserved to the people." See Beaney, The Constitutional Right to Privacy, 1962 Sup.Ct. Rev. 212; Griswold, The Right to be Let Alone, 55 Nw.U.L.Rev. 216 (1960).

We have had many controversies over these penumbral rights of "privacy and repose." See, e.g., Public Utilities Com. v. Pollak [1952]; Skinner v. Oklahoma [1942]. These cases bear witness that the right of privacy which presses for recognition here is a legitimate one.

The present case, then, concerns a relationship lying within the zone of privacy created by several fundamental constitutional guarantees. And it concerns a law which, in forbidding the *use* of contraceptives rather than regulating their manufacture or sale, seeks to achieve its goals by means having a maximum destructive impact upon that relationship. Such a law cannot stand in light of the familiar principle, so often applied by this Court, that a "governmental purpose to control or prevent activities constitutionally subject to state regulation may not be achieved by means which sweep unnecessarily broadly and thereby invade the area of protected freedoms." NAACP v. Alabama. Would we allow the police to search the sacred precincts of marital bedrooms for telltale signs of the use of contraceptives? The very idea is repulsive to the notions of privacy surrounding the marriage relationship.

We deal with a right of privacy older than the Bill of Rights—older than our political parties, older than our school system. Marriage is a

coming together for better or for worse, hopefully enduring, and intimate to the degree of being sacred. It is an association that promotes a
way of life, not causes; a harmony in living, not political faiths; a
bilateral loyalty, not commercial or social projects. Yet it is an
association for as noble a purpose as any involved in our prior decisions.

Reversed.

Mr. Justice **GOLDBERG**, whom the Chief Justice [**WARREN**] and Mr.
Justice **BRENNAN** join, concurring.

     . . . Although I have not accepted the view that "due process" as
used in the Fourteenth Amendment incorporates all of the first eight
Amendments, I do agree that the concept of liberty protects those
personal rights that are fundamental, and is not confined to the specific
terms of the Bill of Rights. My conclusion that the concept of liberty is
not so restricted and that it embraces the right of marital privacy
though that right is not mentioned explicitly in the Constitution is
supported both by numerous decisions of this Court, referred to in the
Court's opinion, and by the language and history of the Ninth Amendment. . . . I add these words to emphasize the relevance of that
Amendment to the Court's holding . . ..

     This Court, in a series of decisions, has held that the Fourteenth
Amendment absorbs and applies to the States those specifics of the first
eight amendments which express fundamental personal rights. The
language and history of the Ninth Amendment reveal that the Framers
of the Constitution believed that there are additional fundamental
rights, protected from governmental infringement, which exist alongside those fundamental rights specifically mentioned in the first eight
constitutional amendments . . ..

     In presenting the proposed Amendment, Madison said:

> It has been objected also against a bill of rights, that, by enumerat-
> ing particular exceptions to the grant of power, it would disparage
> those rights which were not placed in that enumeration; and it might
> follow by implication, that those rights which were not singled out,
> were intended to be assigned into the hands of the General Govern-
> ment, and were consequently insecure. This is one of the most
> plausible arguments I have ever heard urged against the admission of
> a bill of rights into this system; but, I conceive, that it may be guarded
> against. I have attempted it, as gentlemen may see by turning to the
> last clause of the fourth resolution [the Ninth Amendment]. . . .

     While this Court has had little occasion to interpret the Ninth
Amendment, "[i]t cannot be presumed that any clause in the constitution is intended to be without effect." Marbury v. Madison [1803].
. . . The Ninth Amendment to the Constitution may be regarded by
some as a recent discovery and may be forgotten by others, but since
1791 it has been a basic part of the Constitution which we are sworn to
uphold. To hold that a right so basic and fundamental and so deep-
rooted in our society as the right of privacy in marriage may be

infringed because that right is not guaranteed in so many words by the first eight amendments to the Constitution is to ignore the Ninth Amendment and to give it no effect whatsoever. Moreover, a judicial construction that this fundamental right is not protected by the Constitution because it is not mentioned in explicit terms by one of the first eight amendments or elsewhere in the Constitution would violate the Ninth Amendment, which specifically states that "[t]he enumeration in the Constitution, of certain rights, shall not be *construed* to deny or disparage others retained by the people." (Emphasis added.)

A dissenting opinion suggests that my interpretation of the Ninth Amendment somehow "broaden[s] the powers of this Court." . . . With all due respect, I believe that it misses the import of what I am saying. . . . [I do not mean] to state that the Ninth Amendment constitutes an independent source of rights protected from infringement by either the States or the Federal Government. Rather, the Ninth Amendment . . . simply shows the intent of the Constitution's authors that other fundamental personal rights should not be denied such protection or disparaged in any other way simply because they are not specifically listed in the first eight constitutional amendments. I do not see how this broadens the authority of the Court; rather it serves to support what this Court has been doing in protecting fundamental rights.

Nor am I turning somersaults with history in arguing that the Ninth Amendment is relevant in a case dealing with a *State's* infringement of a fundamental right. While the Ninth Amendment—and indeed the entire Bill of Rights—originally concerned restrictions upon *federal* power, the subsequently enacted Fourteenth Amendment prohibits the States as well from abridging fundamental personal liberties. And, the Ninth Amendment, in indicating that not all such liberties are specifically mentioned in the first eight amendments, is surely relevant in showing the existence of other fundamental personal rights, now protected from state, as well as federal, infringement. In sum, the Ninth Amendment simply lends strong support to the view that the "liberty" protected by the Fifth and Fourteenth Amendments from infringement by the Federal Government or the States is not restricted to rights specifically mentioned in the first eight amendments.

In determining which rights are fundamental, judges are not left at large to decide cases in light of their personal and private notions. Rather, they must look to the "traditions and [collective] conscience of our people" to determine whether a principle is "so rooted [there] . . . as to be ranked as fundamental." Snyder v. Massachusetts [1934]. The inquiry is whether a right involved "is of such a character that it cannot be denied without violating those "fundamental principles of liberty and justice which lie at the base of all our civil and political institutions'. . .." Powell v. Alabama [1932]. "Liberty" also "gains content from the emanations of . . . specific [constitutional] guarantees" and "from experience with the requirements of a free society." *Poe* (dissenting opinion of Mr. Justice Douglas).

I agree fully with the Court that, applying these tests, the right of privacy is a fundamental personal right, emanating "from the totality of the constitutional scheme under which we live." *Ibid.* . . .

The entire fabric of the Constitution and the purposes that clearly underlie its specific guarantees demonstrate that the rights to marital privacy and to marry and raise a family are of similar order and magnitude as the fundamental rights specifically protected . . . .

In a long series of cases this Court has held that . . . fundamental personal liberties . . . may not be abridged by the States simply on a showing that a regulatory statute has some rational relationship to the effectuation of a proper state purpose. "Where there is a significant encroachment upon personal liberty, the State may prevail only upon showing a subordinating interest which is compelling." Bates v. Little Rock [1960]. The law must be shown "necessary, and not merely rationally related, to the accomplishment of a permissible state policy." McLaughlin v. Florida [1960].

Although the Connecticut birth-control law obviously encroaches upon a fundamental personal liberty, the State . . . at most, argues that there is some rational relation between this statute and what is admittedly a legitimate subject of state concern—the discouraging of extra-marital relations. It says that preventing the use of birth-control devices by married persons helps prevent the indulgence by some in such extra-marital relations. The rationality of this justification is dubious, particularly in light of the admitted widespread availability to all persons in the State of Connecticut, unmarried as well as married, of birth-control devices for the prevention of disease, as distinguished from the prevention of conception. But, in any event, it is clear that the state interest in safeguarding marital fidelity can be served by a more discriminately tailored statute, which does not, like the present one, sweep unnecessarily broadly, reaching far beyond the evil sought to be dealt with and intruding upon the privacy of all married couples. Here, as elsewhere, "[p]recision of regulation must be the touchstone in an area so closely touching our most precious freedoms." NAACP v. Button. The State of Connecticut does have statutes, the constitutionality of which is beyond doubt, which prohibit adultery and fornication. These statutes demonstrate that means for achieving the same basic purpose of protecting marital fidelity are available to Connecticut without the need to "invade the area of protected freedoms." NAACP v. Alabama.

Finally, it should be said of the Court's holding today that it in no way interferes with a State's proper regulation of sexual promiscuity or misconduct [e.g., homosexuality and extra-marital sexuality]. . . .

Mr. Justice **HARLAN**, concurring in the judgment.

I fully agree with the judgment of reversal, but find myself unable to join the Court's opinion. The reason is that it seems to me to evince an approach to this case very much like that taken by my Brothers Black and Stewart in dissent, namely: the Due Process Clause of the

Fourteenth Amendment does not touch this Connecticut statute unless the enactment is found to violate some right assured by the letter or penumbra of the Bill of Rights.

In other words, what I find implicit in the Court's opinion is that the "incorporation" doctrine may be used to *restrict* the reach of Fourteenth Amendment Due Process. For me this is just as unacceptable constitutional doctrine as is the use of the "incorporation" approach to *impose* upon the States all the requirements of the Bill of Rights as found in the provisions of the first eight amendments and in the decisions of this Court interpreting them.

In my view, the proper constitutional inquiry in this case is whether this Connecticut statute infringes the Due Process Clause of the Fourteenth Amendment because the enactment violates basic values "implicit in the concept of ordered liberty," Palko v. Connecticut [1937]. For reasons stated at length in my dissenting opinion in *Poe*, I believe that it does. While the relevant inquiry may be aided by resort to one or more of the provisions of the Bill of Rights, it is not dependent on them or any of their radiations. The Due Process Clause of the Fourteenth Amendment stands, in my opinion, on its own bottom.

A further observation seems in order respecting the justification of my Brothers Black and Stewart for their "incorporation" approach to this case. Their approach does not rest on historical reasons, which are of course wholly lacking (see Fairman, Does the Fourteenth Amendment Incorporate the Bill of Rights? The Original Understanding, 2 Stan.L.Rev. 5 (1949)), but on the thesis that by limiting the content of the Due Process Clause of the Fourteenth Amendment to the protection of rights which can be found elsewhere in the Constitution, in this instance in the Bill of Rights, judges will thus be confined to "interpretation" of specific constitutional provisions, and will thereby be restrained from introducing their own notions of constitutional right and wrong into the "vague contours of the Due Process Clause." Rochin v. California [1952].

While I could not more heartily agree that judicial "self restraint" is an indispensable ingredient of sound constitutional adjudication, I do submit that the formula suggested for achieving it is more hollow than real. "Specific" provisions of the Constitution, no less than "due process," lend themselves as readily to "personal" interpretations by judges whose constitutional outlook is simply to keep the Constitution in supposed "tune with the times". . ..

Judicial self-restraint will not, I suggest, be brought about in the "due process" area by the historically unfounded incorporation formula. . . . It will be achieved in this area, as in other constitutional areas, only by continual insistence upon respect for the teachings of history, solid recognition of the basic values that underlie our society, and wise appreciation of the great roles that the doctrines of federalism and separation of powers have played in establishing and preserving American freedoms. See Adamson v. California [1947] (Mr. Justice Frankfurter, concurring). Adherence to these principles will not, of

course, obviate all constitutional differences of opinion among judges,
nor should it. Their continued recognition will, however, go farther
toward keeping most judges from roaming at large in the constitutional
field than will the interpolation into the Constitution of an artificial
and largely illusory restriction on the content of the Due Process
Clause.

Mr. Justice **WHITE**, concurring in the judgment . . ..

Mr. Justice **BLACK**, with whom Mr. Justice **STEWART** joins, dissenting.

. . . I do not to any extent whatever base my view that this
Connecticut law is constitutional on a belief that the law is wise or that
its policy is a good one. . . . There is no single one of the graphic
and eloquent strictures and criticisms fired at the policy of this Connecticut law either by the Court's opinion or by those of my concurring
Brethren to which I cannot subscribe—except their conclusion that the
evil qualities they see in the law make it unconstitutional. . . .

The Court talks about a constitutional "right of privacy" as though
there is some constitutional provision or provisions forbidding any law
ever to be passed which might abridge the "privacy" of individuals.
But there is not. There are, of course, guarantees in certain specific
constitutional provisions which are designed in part to protect privacy
at certain times and places with respect to certain activities. Such, for
example, is the Fourth Amendment's guarantee against "unreasonable
searches and seizures." But I think it belittles that Amendment to talk
about it as though it protects nothing but "privacy." To treat it that
way is to give it a niggardly interpretation, not the kind of liberal
reading I think any Bill of Rights provision should be given. . . .

One of the most effective ways of diluting or expanding a constitutionally guaranteed right is to substitute for the crucial word or words
of a constitutional guarantee another word or words more or less
flexible and more or less restricted in meaning. . . . "Privacy" is a
broad, abstract and ambiguous concept which can easily be shrunken in
meaning but which can also, on the other hand, easily be interpreted as
a constitutional ban against many things other than searches and
seizures. . . . I get nowhere in this case by talk about a constitutional "right of privacy" as an emanation from one or more constitutional
provisions. I like my privacy as well as the next one, but I am
nevertheless compelled to admit that government has a right to invade
it unless prohibited by some specific constitutional provision. . . .

This brings me to the arguments made by my Brothers Harlan,
White and Goldberg . . .. I discuss the due process and Ninth
Amendment arguments together because on analysis they turn out to
be the same thing. . . .

The due process argument which my Brothers Harlan and White
adopt here is based . . . on the premise that this Court is vested with
power to invalidate all state laws that it considers to be arbitrary,

capricious, unreasonable, or oppressive, or this Court's belief that a particular state law under scrutiny has no "rational or justifying" purpose, or is offensive to a "sense of fairness and justice." If these formulas based on "natural justice," or others which mean the same thing are to prevail, they require judges to determine what is or is not constitutional on the basis of their own appraisal of what laws are unwise or unnecessary . . .. [P]erhaps it is not too much to say that no legislative body ever does pass laws without believing that they will accomplish a sane, rational, wise and justifiable purpose. . . . Such an appraisal of the wisdom of legislation is an attribute of the power to make laws, not of the power to interpret them. The use by federal courts of such a formula or doctrine or whatnot to veto federal or state laws simply takes away from Congress and States the power to make laws based on their own judgment of fairness and wisdom and transfers that power to this Court for ultimate determination—a power which was specifically denied to federal courts by the convention that framed the Constitution.

Of the cases on which my Brothers White and Goldberg rely so heavily, undoubtedly the reasoning of two of them supports their result here—as would that of a number of others which they do not bother to name, e.g., *Lochner* and Adkins v. Children's Hospital [1923]. The two they do cite and quote from, *Meyer* and *Pierce*, were both decided in opinions by Mr. Justice McReynolds which elaborated the same natural law due process philosophy found in *Lochner* . . . which many later opinions repudiated, and which I cannot accept.

My Brother Goldberg has adopted the recent discovery that the Ninth Amendment as well as the Due Process Clause can be used by this Court as authority to strike down all state legislation which this Court thinks violates "fundamental principles of liberty and justice," or is contrary to the "traditions and [collective] conscience of our people." He also states, without proof satisfactory to me, that in making decisions on this basis judges will not consider "their personal and private notions." One may ask how they can avoid considering them. Our Court certainly has no machinery with which to take a Gallup Poll. And the scientific miracles of this age have not yet produced a gadget which the Court can use to determine what traditions are rooted in the "[collective] conscience of our people." Moreover, one would certainly have to look far beyond the language of the Ninth Amendment to find that the Framers vested in this Court any such awesome veto powers over law-making, either by the States or by the Congress. Nor does anything in the history of the Amendment offer any support for such a shocking doctrine. The whole history of the adoption of the Constitution and Bill of Rights points the other way, and the very material quoted by my Brother Goldberg shows that the Ninth Amendment was intended to protect against the idea that "by enumerating particular exceptions to the grant of power" to the Federal Government, "those rights which were not singled out, were intended to be assigned into the hands of the General Government [the United States], and were consequently insecure." That Amendment was passed, not to broaden the powers of this Court or any other department of "the General Government," but, as every student of history knows, to assure the people that the Constitution in all its provisions was intended to limit the Federal Government to the powers granted expressly or by necessary implication. If any broad, unlimited power to hold laws unconstitutional because they offend what this Court conceives to be the "[collective] conscience of our people" is vested in this Court by the Ninth Amendment, the Fourteenth Amendment, or any other provision of the Constitution, it was not given by the Framers, but rather has been bestowed on the Court by the Court. . . . Use of any such broad, unbounded judicial authority would make of this Court's members a day-to-day constitutional convention. . . .

I realize that many good and able men have eloquently spoken and written, sometimes in rhapsodical strains, about the duty of this Court to keep the Constitution in tune with the times. The idea is that the Constitution must be changed from time to time and that this Court is charged with a duty to make those changes. For myself, I must with all deference reject that philosophy. The Constitution makers knew the need for change and provided for it. Amendments suggested by the people's elected representatives can be submitted to the people or their selected agents for ratification. That method of change was good for our Fathers, and being somewhat old-fashioned I must add it is good enough for me. And so, I cannot rely on the Due Process Clause or the Ninth Amendment or any mysterious and uncertain natural law concept as a reason for striking down this state law. The Due Process Clause with an "arbitrary and capricious" or "shocking to the conscience" formula was liberally used by this Court to strike down economic legislation in the early decades of this century, threatening, many people thought, the tranquility and stability of the Nation. See, e.g., *Lochner.* That formula, based on subjective considerations of "natural justice," is no less dangerous when used to enforce this Court's views about personal rights than those about economic rights. I had thought that we had laid that formula, as a means for striking down state legislation, to rest once and for all in cases like *West Coast Hotel* . . . .

[Justice Black quoted from Justice Iredell's opinion in Calder v. Bull (1798) and from his own dissenting opinion in *Adamson.*]

The late Judge Learned Hand, after emphasizing his view that judges should not use the due process formula suggested in the concurring opinions today or any other formula like it to invalidate legislation offensive to their "personal preferences," made the statement, with which I fully agree, that:

> For myself it would be most irksome to be ruled by a bevy of Platonic Guardians, even if I knew how to choose them, which I assuredly do not.

So far as I am concerned, Connecticut's law as applied here is not forbidden by any provision of the Federal Constitution as that Constitution was written, and I would therefore affirm.

Mr. Justice **STEWART**, whom Mr. Justice **BLACK** joins, dissenting.

. . . I think this is an uncommonly silly law. . . . But we are not asked in this case to say whether we think this law is unwise, or even asinine. We are asked to hold that it violates the United States Constitution. And that I cannot do. . . .

In the course of its opinion the Court refers to no less than six Amendments to the Constitution . . . [but] does not say which . . . , if any, it thinks is infringed by this Connecticut law. . . .

. . . [T]o say that the Ninth Amendment has anything to do with this case is to turn somersaults with history. The Ninth Amendment, like its companion the Tenth, which this Court held "states but a truism that all is retained which has not been surrendered," United States v. Darby [1941], was framed by James Madison and adopted by the States simply to make clear that the adoption of the Bill of Rights did not alter the plan that the *Federal* Government was to be a government of express and limited powers . . . . Until today no member of this Court has ever suggested that the Ninth Amendment meant anything else . . . .

What provision of the Constitution, then, does make this state law invalid? The Court says it is the right of privacy "created by several fundamental constitutional guarantees." With all deference, I can find no such general right of privacy in the Bill of Rights, in any other part of the Constitution, or in any case ever before decided by this Court.

At the oral argument in this case we were told that the Connecticut law does not "conform to current community standards." But it is not the function of this Court to decide cases on the basis of community standards. We are here to decide cases "agreeably to the Constitution and laws of the United States." . . . . If, as I should surely hope, the law before us does not reflect the standards of the people of Connecticut, the people of Connecticut can freely exercise their true Ninth and Tenth Amendment rights to persuade their elected representatives to repeal it. That is the constitutional way to take this law off the books.

Editors' Notes

(1) **Query:** To what extent were Douglas and Harlan consistent in Poe v. Ullman and in *Griswold?* Did Douglas' views in *Griswold* become more clear or merely more complex?

(2) Chap. 8 analyzes in detail various approaches, modes, and techniques of constitutional interpretation, but even before reading that chapter it should be apparent that the justices who wrote in *Griswold* looked at constitutional interpretation quite differently. Their opinions show the complex ways in which the question of HOW one interprets the Constitution interrelates with the

question of WHAT the Constitution includes. Douglas, in particular, was concerned with what might be called "the structure" of the Constitution, or as he phrased it in a different context, the Constitution's "architectural scheme." ("Stare Decisis," 4 *Rec. of the Assn. of the Bar of the City of New York* 152 [1949].)

Structural analysis looks at the thing to be interpreted as a whole rather than as a series of particular clauses. (See espec. Charles L. Black, *Structure and Relationship in Constitutional Law* [Baton Rouge: Louisiana State University Press, 1969].) In constitutional interpretation, it may limit itself to the document, to the document plus the larger political system, or to these plus the political theories on which the interpreter believes they are based. At which of these levels does Douglas operate?

(3) **Query:** Black was concerned with preserving the integrity of the words of individual clauses. What was Harlan's principal concern? Goldberg's?

(4) **Query:** Implicitly each justice who wrote in *Griswold* offered a definition of "the Constitution" that he was interpreting. How do those definitions differ from one another? Did those three members of the majority who wrote opinions—Douglas, Harlan, and Goldberg—agree on a definition, or did they differ among themselves as well as with Black and Stewart?

(5) **Query:** *Griswold* represents, as Black and Stewart noted, the first time the Court had cited the Ninth Amendment as a basis for striking down a statute, state or federal. Black, it will be recalled, had often argued—see especially Adamson v. California (1947)—that the Fourteenth Amendment "incorporates" the first eight amendments. By what logic, then, could he exclude the Ninth?

(6) **Query:** How did Douglas and Goldberg differ on their uses of the Ninth Amendment?

(7) The first draft of his opinion that Douglas circulated to the Court laid greater stress on the sacredness of the marital relationship, constitutionally protected as a form of association, and much less on the right of privacy—a curious orientation in light on his dissent in Poe v. Ullman. In a long memorandum Brennan urged Douglas to shift the emphasis to "an expansive interpretation" of privacy: "where fundamentals are concerned, the Bill of Rights guarantees are but expression or examples of those rights, and do not preclude applications or extensions of those rights to situations unanticipated by the framers." For a general discussion of the path of *Griswold* through the Court, see Bernard Schwartz, *The Unpublished Opinions of the Warren Court* (New York: Oxford University Press, 1985), pp. 227–239.

In an article Douglas cited, Prof. William M. Beaney had suggested such an approach a year earlier ("The Constitutional Right to Privacy," 1962 *Sup.Ct. Rev.* 212, 214):

> Why should one assume that the right to privacy is protected by fundamental law? . . . The answer in a few words must be that our Constitution and our system of constitutional government reflect a decision that government is limited in the powers and in the methods it may use. . . . "Liberty against government," a phrase used by Professor Corwin, expresses this idea forcefully. In this sense, virtually all enumerated rights in the Constitution can be described as

contributing to the right of privacy, if by the term is meant the integrity and freedom of the individual person and personality.

(8) Even as amended, Douglas' opinion for the Court (and also Harlan's concurrence) emphasized that *Griswold* involved advice given to married couples. In 1972 Eisenstadt v. Baird invalidated, as a violation of equal protection of the laws, Massachusetts' ban against distributing information about birth control to unmarried persons. For the Court, Justice Brennan wrote: "If the right of privacy means anything, it is the right of the *individual,* married or single, to be free from unwarranted governmental intrusion into matters so fundamentally affecting a person as the decision whether to bear or beget a child." Concurring, Douglas said he would strike the law down as interfering with freedom of speech.

Carey v. Population Services (1977) held unconstitutional a New York statute making it criminal for anyone: (i) To sell contraceptives to minors under 16; (ii) Except a licensed pharmacist to sell contraceptives to a person over 16; or (iii) To advertise or display contraceptives.

(9) The Court's decisions holding that the right to privacy includes a woman's right, at least during the first trimester of pregnancy, to obtain an abortion—see, espec. Roe v. Wade (1973; reprinted below, p. 1109)—build on *Griswold.* On the other hand, Doe v. Commonwealth's Attorney (1976; noted below, p. 1160) affirmed without opinion a lower court decision sustaining a state statute punishing homosexual relations, even in private between consenting adults. And, in rejecting a prison inmate's claim that he had a right to be protected against "shakedowns" designed merely to harass or humiliate and to keep certain "noncontraband items" as a picture of his family, Chief Justice Burger said for five members of the Court in Hudson v. Palmer (1984): "We hold that society is not prepared to recognize as legitimate any subjective expectation of privacy that a prisoner might have in his jail cell." See also Bell v. Wolfish (1979; reprinted below, p. 1134).

(10) For general discussions of the right to privacy, see: C. Herman Pritchett, *Constitutional Civil Liberties* (Englewood Cliffs, N.J.: Prentice-Hall, 1984), pp. 317–322; Laurence H. Tribe, *American Constitutional Law* (Mineola, N.Y.: Foundation Press, 1978), chap. 15; David M. O'Brien, *Privacy, Law, and Public Policy* (New York: Praeger, 1979); and Kenneth L. Karst, "The Freedom of Intimate Association," 89 *Yale L.J.* 624 (1980).

5

What is the Constitution? Problems of Continuity and Change

The spoken word evanesces as soon as it is uttered. In a general way, it can be recalled, but seldom with complete accuracy or in its entirety and exact context. In contrast, the written word seems permanent. Set in hard type, it can be visualized by audiences who live long after the author's death; its sentences can be parsed; its terms precisely defined; its meaning expounded with the constant assurance of relying on an exact replica of the author's creation rather than a hazy recollection of his or her message.

A *written* constitution is thus an effort to make a set of political relationships both explicit and permanent, to establish rights, duties, authorities, and processes in such a way that they will be comprehended not only by the present but also by the future. The goal, in the parlance of the ancient Common Law, is to create a situation in which all those "who run can read"—*and* understand *and* be bound. The Constitution, Justice Joseph Story wrote in his *Commentaries* (1833), "is to have a fixed, uniform, permanent construction."[1] Thomas Cooley, the great commentator of the next generation, expressed the same thought: "The meaning of the constitution is fixed when it is adopted, and it is not different at any subsequent time when a court has occasion to pass upon it."[2] Thus Hugo Black stood in a venerable tradition when he wrote that the notion of a "living Constitution" was "an attack not only on the great value of the Constitution itself, but also on the concept of a written constitution which is to survive through the years as originally written unless changed through the amendment process which the Framers wisely provided." (Harper v. Virginia, dis. op. [1966; reprinted below, p. 151].)

On the other hand—and in constitutional interpretation there is always another hand—the permanence and exactness conveyed by the written word are to a some extent misleading. Words can have a variety of meanings, and readers necessarily impose their own frameworks of understanding on a text, not so much, perhaps, as do

1. *Commentaries on the Constitution of the United States* (Boston: Hilliard, Gray & Co., 1833), I, § 426.

2. *A Treatise on Constitutional Limitations* (Boston: Little, Brown, 1868), p. 55.

126

listeners but significantly nonetheless. Language, whether written or spoken, is simply an inexact mode of transmitting complex ideas. "When the Almighty himself condescends to address mankind in their own language," James Madison observed in *Federalist* No. 37, "his meaning, luminous as it must be, is rendered dim and doubtful by the cloudy medium through which it is communicated." On a more mundane plane, Chief Justice Marshall noted that "Such is the character of human language, that no word conveys to the mind, in all situations, one single definite idea; and nothing is more common than to use words in a figurative sense." (McCulloch v. Maryland [1819; reprinted below, p. 413].)

Moreover, language evolves. As Chapter 1 pointed out and Chapter 8 will develop in greater detail, words assume new meanings that sometimes live alongside the old and sometimes replace them. Rules of grammar, syntax, and punctuation also mutate. Moreover, the real world, the world constitutions are meant to control, changes. The Constitution, Marshall also said in *McCulloch,* is "intended to endure for ages to come, and, consequently, to be adapted to the various *crises* of human affairs." None of the framers could have envisioned the dramatic developments in technology that have so revolutionized—and terrorized—human lives. Nor could the framers have anticipated the course American social and political development would take as the country has responded to change and adapted their words to our problems. As Oliver Wendell Holmes explained for the Court in 1920:

> [W]hen we are dealing with words that are also a constituent act, like the Constitution of the United States, we must realize that they have called into life a being the development of which could not have been foreseen completely by the most gifted of its begetters. It was enough for them to realize or to hope that they had created an organism; it has taken a century and cost their successors much sweat and blood to prove that they created a nation. The case before us must be considered in the light of our whole experience and not merely in that of what was said a hundred years ago. [Missouri v. Holland (reprinted below, p. 132).]

As conditions have changed, so have political institutions, ideas, and ideals. Therefore, defenders of informal constitutional change reason, notions prevalent in one era should not forever limit the reach of broad constitutional concepts like equal protection. For example, in 1868 when the Fourteenth Amendment was adopted, public education was neither so widespread nor so important in preparing young people to survive as it is today. Similarly, changes in the nature of most productive labor from muscle power to brain power have undercut historic justifications for discriminating against women in employment. So, too, notions about the legitimate linkage between a direct economic stake in a community and the right to vote have shifted. As William O. Douglas said for the Court in striking down Virginia's requirement that prospective voters in state elections pay a poll tax, the "Equal Protection Clause is not shackled to the political theory of a particular era.   .   .   .   Notions of what constitutes equal treatment for purposes of the Equal Protection clause *do* change." [3] Justice Black protested bitterly here against what he claimed was the Court's "consulting its own notions rather than following the original meaning" of the Fourteenth Amendment.

Social, economic, and technological developments have put enormous strains on the political system. That the system has survived is due in no small part to the fact that the Constitution has also developed. Problems of adaptation, as immense and fraught with uncertainty as they are, are further complicated by the question of WHAT is the Constitution that is being adapted.

For many if not most of those who deny judicial authority to adapt the Constitution, "the Constitution" is the text of 1787 and its amendments. Interpretation merely involves examining the document's specific words and clauses; discovering their meaning with the help of dictionaries, historical narratives of the times the particular clause was adopted, and, perhaps, previous judicial interpretations; and applying those meanings without regard to consequences, leaving such broader issues to officials who can enact statutes or amend the constitutional document.

Those who accept current authority to adapt the Constitution commonly see "the Constitution" as including much more than the document, though some may view the Ninth and Fourteenth Amendments as windows that let in a wider world. In any event, they tend to conceive of "the Constitution" as more than a concise and precise code and to look on constitutional interpretation as an effort, always struggling and often unsuccessful, to discover and apply imperfectly stated general principles to complex problems. Because they usually believe in constitutional democracy, because they visualize "the Constitution" as something more than the document, and because they accept human fallibility, changing the Constitution by interpretation is not especially bothersome to such people—though, like their opponents they may oppose particular changes.

Many who believe in the permanence of constitutional meaning would respond at this point that they accept the necessity for a changing constitution. They also accept as empirically true, though legally wrong, that the Supreme Court has often, in effect, amended the Constitution. Their objection to adaptation "under the guise of interpretation" is not grounded in a belief that the constitutional document of 1787 as amended is politically perfect, but in concern about WHO will do the adjusting, HOW those persons or institutions will adapt the Constitution, and WHAT the proposed changes would do to the system. Dissenting in *Griswold* (reprinted above, p. 113), Justice Black summed up the reasoning of those opposed to adaption by judicial interpretation:

---

3.   Harper v. Virginia (1966; reprinted below, p. 151); italics in original.

> [M]any good and able men have eloquently spoken and written
> . . . about the duty of this Court to keep the Constitution in tune
> with the times . . . . I must with all deference reject that
> philosophy. The Constitution makers knew the need for change
> and provided for it. Amendments suggested by the people's elect-
> ed representatives can be submitted to the people or their selected
> agents for ratification. That method of change was good for our
> Fathers, and . . . it is good enough for me.

Those who advocate change through judicial interpretation respond that almost all interpretation, including a quest for the "intent
of the framers," is creative. More basically, the adapters argue, the
system could not survive if before coping with each unforeseen
problem we first had to go through the cumbersome procedure of
formal amendment. Even if the world would stand still for that
period, the document would soon become so minutely detailed as to
be incomprehensible. People like Hugo Black would rejoin: First,
interpretation should involve no more than finding the meaning of
words, and the intent of the framers is open to dispassionate historical
inquiry; second, it has taken a relatively short time to amend the
Constitution;[4] and, third, formal amendment need seldom occur.
For, as Justice Sutherland wrote in his dissent in the Minnesota
Moratorium Case (1934; reprinted below, p. 136), applications of
constitutional principles can change, it is only the principles themselves that are permanent. And the obvious counterresponse to the
last point is that "adaptation of principles" is often also a creative act.

In recent decades, much but hardly all of the difference here has
been closely related to political philosophy: Those who oppose
change by judicial interpretation have tended to believe that the
United States is a representative democracy, while those who have
tended to be unconcerned about this method of change are more
likely to stress the system's constitutionalist underpinnings. Such an
explanation accounts for differences between Justices Black and Rehnquist, on the one hand, and Justice Douglas and Professor Ronald
Dworkin on the other. This relationship, however, may not always be
so neat. Even some constitutionalists oppose adaption by interpretation. They basically argue that, if judges create the principles they
interpret, they transform themselves into both makers of law and
interpreters of law. The political system degenerates into a judicial
oligarchy, and liberty becomes dependent on judges' wisdom and
benevolence. Either we have, one commentator asserts, "a fixed

---

4. If one counts the Bill of Rights, submitted together and ratified together, as one
amendment, the average length of time required for ratification has been only about fifteen
months. The longest time was for the Twenty-second, setting a two-term limit on the presidency
(three years and eleven months); and only the Bill of Rights (two years, three months) and the
Fourteenth (two years, one month) have taken longer than two years. The median time for
ratification has been slightly more than eleven months. These figures, however, do not count
the time the amendments spent in Congress. See Clement E. Vose, *Constitutional Change:
Amendment Politics and Supreme Court Litigation Since 1900* (Lexington, Mass.: Heath, 1972).

Constitution," or we "convert the chains of the Constitution to ropes of sand." [5]

There are other complications. Seldom has a judge so insistently and consistently opposed adaptation by interpretation as Hugo Black, and none has been so candid in support as Benjamin Cardozo in his *unpublished* slip opinion in the Minnesota Moratorium Case. At issue was the validity of a state law delaying for as long as two years the right of a creditor to foreclose on a defaulting debtor. This statute ran afoul not only of Article I's explicit prohibition against a state's "impairing the obligation of contracts," but also the framers' aim of protecting property against democratically elected legislators. But even in the face of the plain words of the document and weighty evidence about intent, Cardozo would have adapted the Constitution to sustain such legislation:

> To hold this may be inconsistent with things that men said in 1787 when expounding to compatriots the newly written constitution. They did not see the changes in the relation between states and nation or in the play of social forces that lay hidden in the womb of time. It may be inconsistent with things they believed or took for granted. [But] Their beliefs to be significant must be adjusted to the world they knew. It is not in my judgment inconsistent with what they would say today nor with what today they would believe, if they were called upon to interpret "in the light of our whole experience" the constitution they framed for the needs of an expanding future.

Most judges, like most commentators, would fall between the extremes of Black and Cardozo. That fact has clouded rather than clarified alternatives. Moreover, none of the participants in the debate has been concerned solely with the process of adjustment; all have also been deeply concerned about the substance of particular proposals. And faced with unwanted change, many interpreters will rely, however inconsistently, on procedural as much as or instead of substantive arguments.

Justice Sutherland, for example, was the epitome of a constitutionalist. He warmly endorsed fresh judicial interpretations, such as that in Lochner v. New York (1905), which he resurrected in Adkins v. Children's Hospital (1923), broadening (he would have said, "more accurately defining") rights of private property and freedom of contract. He opposed change by judicial interpretation when it weakened what he saw as the rights that constitutionalism protected—in the Minnesota Moratorium Case, the sanctity of contracts. On the other hand, President Franklin Roosevelt applauded broad judicial interpretations of federal power, but sharply attacked narrow interpretations of that power as "reading into the Constitution words and implications

---

5. Raoul Berger, *Government by Judiciary* (Cambridge, Mass.: Harvard University Press, 1977), p. 371.

which are not there, and which were never intended to be there."
(See his speech of March 9, 1937, reprinted below, p. 230.)

One should not, however, make too much of occasional inconsistency. Although few jurists have stated their views with the clarity of Black and Cardozo, positions in the debate are usually not simply functions of how a justice votes in particular cases or a President or commentator feels about a concrete issue of public policy.[6] Justice William H. Rehnquist's article on the living Constitution (reprinted below, p. 163) shows him to be the true heir of Justice Black on this issue; yet the two would have disagreed sharply on many specific substantive matters of constitutional law, most especially freedom of speech and press.

As Marsh v. Chambers (1983; reprinted below, p. 158) shows, the debate goes on, though judges, like commentators, sometimes talk past rather than at one another. That debate touches the heart of constitutional interpretation, for it also touches the heart of what a constitution, and constitutional democracy, are all about.

SELECTED BIBLIOGRAPHY

Barber, Sotirios A. *On What the Constitution Means* (Baltimore: John Hopkins University Press, 1984).

Berger, Raoul. *Government by Judiciary* (Cambridge: Harvard University Press, 1977).

Black, Hugo L. *A Constitutional Faith* (New York: Knopf, 1968).

Brest, Paul. "The Misconceived Quest for Original Understanding," 60 *Bost.U.L.Rev.* 204 (1980).

Cooley, Thomas M. *A Treatise on Constitutional Limitations* (Boston: Little, Brown, 1868).

Crosskey, William W. *Politics and the Constitution* (Chicago: University of Chicago Press, vols. 1 & 2, 1953; vol. 3 [with William Jeffrey, Jr.], 1980). (See also entry under Hart, below.)

Elliott, William Y. "The Constitution as the American Social Myth," in Conyers Read, ed., *The Constitution Reconsidered* (New York: Columbia University Press, 1938).

Grey, Thomas C. "Do We Have an Unwritten Constitution?" 27 *Stan.L.Rev.* 703 (1975).

Hart, Henry M. "Professor Crosskey and Judicial Review," 67 *Harv. L.Rev.* 1456 (1954).

Miller, Charles A. *The Supreme Court and the Uses of History* (Cambridge, Mass.: The Belknap Press of Harvard University Press, 1969).

---

6. Some commentators, however, have been almost as distinct in their divisions as Black and Cardozo. Compare the views of Berger, supra note 5, and Henry P. Monaghan, "Our Perfect Constitution," 56 *N.Y.U.L.Rev.* 353 (1981), with Michael J. Perry, *The Constitution, the Courts and Human Rights* (New Haven, Conn.: Yale University Press, 1982), Perry, "The Authority of Text, Tradition, and Reason." 58 *So.Cal.L.Rev.* 551 (1985), Richard D. Parker, "The Past of Constitutional Theory—And its Future," 42 *Ohio St.L.J.* 223 (1982), and Sotirios A. Barber, *On What the Constitution Means* (Baltimore: Johns Hopkins University Press, 1984).

Munzer, Stephen R., and James W. Nickel. "Does the Constitu-
    tion Mean What It Always Meant?" 77 *Colum.L.Rev.* 1029
    (1977).
Murphy, Walter F. "Constitutional Interpretation: The Art of
    the Historian, Magician, or Statesman?" 87 *Yale L.J.* 1752
    (1978).
Perry, Michael J. *The Constitution, the Courts, and Human Rights* (New
    Haven, Conn.: Yale University Press, 1982).
_____. "The Authority of Text, Tradition, and Reason: A Theory
    of Constitutional 'Interpretation,' " 58 *So.Cal.L.Rev.* 551 (1985).
Story, Justice Joseph. *Commentaries on the Constitution of the United
    States* (Boston: Hilliard, Gray & Co., 1833). 2 vols.
Vose, Clement E. *Constitutional Change: Amendment Politics and Su-
    preme Court Litigation Since 1900* (Lexington, Mass.: Heath,
    1972).

**"[W]hen we are dealing with words that also are a constit-
uent act, like the Constitution of the United States, we
must realize that they have called into life a being the
development of which could not have been foreseen completely by the most gifted of its begetters."**

MISSOURI v. HOLLAND

252 U.S. 416, 40 S.Ct. 382, 64 L.Ed. 641 (1920).

As a conservation measure, Congress in 1913 enacted a law limiting the
season during which migratory birds could be shot and the number of birds any
hunter could kill. Today this sort of federal law would seem unexceptional, but
it was unusual for the time. This was a period in which the Supreme Court
was largely, though not altogether consistently, following a doctrine known as
"dual federalism": State and nation were co-equals, each supreme within its
own sphere; thus all national powers, even those specifically delegated, had
to be interpreted against the Tenth Amendment's reservation of authority to
the states. More specifically, in Geer v. Connecticut (1896) the Court had
upheld a state law regulating hunting of wild game, ruling that such power had
inhered in colonial governments and had been passed on to the states upon
independence, "insofar as its exercise may not be incompatible with, or
restrained by, the rights conveyed to the Federal government by the Constitution." Following *Geer* a federal district judge held the 1913 act unconstitution-

al, and the Department of Justice was reluctant to press the case before the Supreme Court.[1]

Even the act's proponents had had some doubts about constitutionality, and Senator Elihu Root had suggested that the United States first sign a treaty protecting migratory birds. Shortly before the district court's decision, the Senate passed a resolution urging the administration to negotiate just such an agreement. The district court's decision made the treaty route appear more attractive, and Woodrow Wilson's diplomats began several years of negotiations with Britain, acting for Canada. The final treaty went into effect in 1916. Citing the value of migratory birds, including wild ducks, as both a direct source of food and effective in keeping down insects that attacked crops, Congress then passed a new statute to enforce the treaty by providing for, among other things, closed seasons on hunting.

Lobbied by hunters and concerned about state sovereignty, some state officials prepared to resist enforcement. In 1919, Missouri's legislature directed the state attorney general to "investigate the matter of enjoining the Federal game inspectors . . . from further interfering with or molesting any or all of our citizens in the exercise of their privileges" to hunt birds. Frank W. McAllister, Missouri's attorney general, added a note of personal drama. He was an avid duck hunter who opposed a long closed season on his sport. After being caught poaching by Ray Holland, the U.S. game warden, McAllister tried to get a state court to enjoin enforcement of the federal law, but local officials persuaded him to challenge the act's constitutionality in a federal district court. That tribunal sustained the statute, and McAllister appealed to the U.S. Supreme Court, arguing:

> If the Act of Congress now in question would have been unconstitutional when the Constitution and the first [ten] amendments were framed and ratified, it is unconstitutional now. The Constitution does not change.

Mr. Justice **HOLMES** delivered the opinion of the Court . . . .

. . . [T]he question raised is the general one whether the treaty and statute are void as an interference with the rights reserved to the states.

To answer this question it is not enough to refer to the Tenth Amendment, reserving the powers not delegated to the United States, because by Article II, § 2, the power to make treaties is delegated expressly, and by Article VI treaties made under the authority of the United States, along with the Constitution and laws of the United States made in pursuance thereof, are declared the supreme law of the land. If the treaty is valid there can be no dispute about the validity of the statute under Article I, § 8, as a necessary and proper means to execute the powers of the Government . . . .

It is said that a treaty cannot be valid if it infringes the Constitution; that there are limits, therefore, to the treaty-making power; and that one such limit is that which an act of Congress could not do

---

1. The "facts" offered in the U.S. Reports are sparse. In this headnote we summarize the account of Clement E. Vose, "State Against Nation: The Conservation Case of *Missouri v. Holland,*" *Prologue* (Winter, 1984), 233.

unaided, in derogation of the powers reserved to the States, a treaty cannot do. An earlier act of Congress that attempted by itself and not in pursuance of a treaty to regulate the killing of migratory birds within the states had been held bad in [two decisions of] the district court. These decisions were supported by the arguments that migratory birds were owned by the States in their sovereign capacity for the benefit of their people, and that under cases like Geer v. Connecticut [1896] this control was one that Congress had no power to displace. The same argument is supposed to apply now with equal force.

Whether the two cases . . . were decided rightly or not, they cannot be accepted as a test of the treaty power. Acts of Congress are the supreme law of the land only when made in pursuance of the Constitution, while treaties are declared to be so when made under the authority of the United States. It is open to question whether the authority of the United States means more than the formal acts prescribed to make the convention. We do not mean to imply that there are no qualifications to the treaty-making power; but they must be ascertained in a different way. It is obvious that there may be matters of the sharpest exigency for the national well being that an act of Congress could not deal with, but that a treaty followed by such an act could, and it is not lightly to be assumed that, in matters requiring national action, "a power which must belong to and somewhere reside in every civilized government" is not to be found. Andrews v. Andrews [1903] . . . .

We are not yet discussing the particular case before us but only are considering the validity of the test proposed. With regard to that we may add that when we are dealing with words that are also a constituent act, like the Constitution of the United States, we must realize that they have called into life a being the development of which could not have been foreseen completely by the most gifted of its begetters. It was enough for them to realize or to hope that they had created an organism; it has taken a century and has cost their successors much sweat and blood to prove that they created a nation. The case before us must be considered in the light of our whole experience and not merely in that of what was said a hundred years ago. The treaty in question does not contravene any prohibitory words to be found in the Constitution. The only question is whether it is forbidden by some invisible radiation from the general terms of the Tenth Amendment. We must consider what this country has become in deciding what that Amendment has reserved.

The State . . . founds its claim of exclusive authority upon an assertion of title to migratory birds . . . . No doubt it is true that as between a State and its inhabitants the State may regulate the killing and sale of such birds, but it does not follow that its authority is exclusive of paramount powers. To put the claim of the State upon title is to lean upon a slender reed. Wild birds are not in the possession of anyone; and possession is the beginning of ownership. The whole foundation of the State's rights is the presence within their jurisdiction of birds that yesterday had not arrived, tomorrow may be in another State and in a week a thousand miles away . . . .

As most of the laws of the United States are carried out within the States, and as many of them deal with matters which in the silence of such laws the State might regulate, such general grounds are not enough to support Missouri's claim. Valid treaties of course "are as binding within the territorial limits of the States as they are elsewhere throughout the dominion of the United States." No doubt the great body of private relations usually fall within the control of the State, but a treaty may override its power . . . .

Here a national interest of very nearly first magnitude is involved. It can be protected only by national action in concert with that of another power. The subject-matter is only transitorily within the State and has no permanent habitat therein. But for the treaty and the statute there soon might be no birds for any powers to deal with. We see nothing in the Constitution that compels the Government to sit by while a food supply is cut off and the protectors of our forests and our crops are destroyed . . . . We are of the opinion that the treaty and statute must be upheld.

Decree affirmed.

Mr. Justice **VAN DEVANTER** and Mr. Justice **PITNEY** dissent.

Editors' Notes

(1) In addition to the article by Vose, cited in the headnote, see Charles A. Lofgren, "Missouri v. Holland in Historical Perspective," 1975 *Sup.Ct.Rev.* 77.

(2) To what extent did Holmes address Missouri's argument about the unchanging nature of the Constitution? What line of reasoning did he use to support his claim that the Court must look to "our whole experience" to interpret the Constitution?

(3) Among the justices of his time, Holmes stands out as the most ardent supporter of national supremacy. But did his opinion waver between a broad assertion of federal power and a much more particularistic discussion of why federal power is valid under the peculiar circumstances of this case? If so, what could account for this ambivalence?

(4) "We do not mean to imply that there are no qualifications to the treaty-making power; but they must be ascertained in a different way," Holmes said here. That statement is less than precise, and the Court has not yet offered much clearer guidance. See, for example, Reid v. Covert (1957), and, more generally, Louis Henkin, *Foreign Affairs and the Constitution* (Mineola, N.Y.: Foundation Press, 1972). States-righters have frequently voiced fears about the havoc that power could wreak on federalism, and occasionally civil libertarians have speculated about the peril a treaty could present to the Bill of Rights as a bar to governmental action. During the late 1940s and early 1950s, there was a concerted effort to amend the Constitution to provide: "A treaty shall become effective as internal law in the United States only through legislation which would be valid in the absence of the treaty." In 1954, after a great constitutional debate, this so-called Bricker Amendment, named after its

principal sponsor Senator John Bricker of Ohio, was decisively defeated in the Senate.

————

> **"It is no answer to say that this public need was not apprehended a century ago, or to insist that what the provision of the Constitution meant to the vision of that day it must mean to the vision of our time."**

HOME BUILDING & LOAN ASSOCIATION v. BLAISDELL

(The Minnesota Moratorium Case) 290 U.S. 398, 54 S.Ct. 231, 78 L.Ed. 413 (1934).

During the Great Depression, tumbling prices and tidal waves of unemployment led to a massive inability to pay debts. Farmers, many of whom had large mortgages on their crops, animals, and equipment as well as on their homes, were especially hard hit. There were sporadic outbursts of violence in the Midwest against bankers' trying to foreclose. Under pressure from the governor and their own constituents, the Minnesota legislature adopted an emergency measure that allowed a judicial proceeding to place a moratorium on a foreclosure for as long as two years, with the debtor paying the creditor the functional equivalent of rent during that period. Bankers quickly challenged the constitutionality of the new statute, alleging that it violated the contract clause of Art. I, § 10. After losing in state courts, they appealed to the U.S. Supreme Court.

The vote among the justices at conference was 5–4 to uphold the statute. Chief Justice Charles Evans Hughes assigned himself the task of writing the opinion of the Court and promptly circulated a draft that evaded the central difficulty of the case: On the one hand, Article I, § 10 of the Constitution read: "No state shall . . . pass any . . . law impairing the obligation of contracts"; and, as Chapter 2 pointed out, the framers had inserted that clause specifically to prevent easing debtors' obligations to creditors. On the other hand, the country was in a depression that threatened to become a bottomless economic chasm, and refusal to permit some relief to debtors would insure chaos. Instead of confronting this dilemma, the Chief Justice tried to distinguish the *obligation* of a contract from the *remedy* for enforcement of a contract. Minnesota, Hughes reasoned, recognized the obligation of contracts and so did not violate the Constitution. It had merely changed the remedy open to creditors to enforce those obligations.

This reasoning had some basis in earlier opinions, but Justice Benjamin N. Cardozo thought it more clever than sound. He preferred to attack directly the underlying problem of continuity and change in constitutional interpretation. He wrote and circulated within the Court the following draft of a concurring opinion.

Mr. Justice **CARDOZO** concurring.

"We must never forget that it is a *constitution* we are expounding." Marshall, C.J., in McCulloch v. Maryland [1819]. "A constitution [is] intended to endure for ages to come, and, consequently, to be adapted to the various *crises* of human affairs." Ibid.

"The case before us must be considered in the light of our whole experience and not merely in that of what was said a hundred years ago" Holmes, J. in Missouri v. Holland [1920].

A hundred years ago . . . property might be taken without due process of law through the legislation of the states, and the courts of the nation were powerless to give redress, unless indeed they could find that a contract had been broken. Dartmouth College v. Woodward [1819]; Fletcher v. Peck [1810]. The judges of those courts had not yet begun to speak of the police power except in an off hand way or in expounding the effect of the commerce clause upon local regulations. The License Cases [1847]. Due process in the states was whatever the states ordained. In such circumstances there was jeopardy, or the threat of it, in encroachment, however slight, upon the obligation to adhere to the letter of a contract. Once reject that test, and no other was available, or so it might well have seemed. The states could not be kept within the limits of reason and fair dealing for such restraints were then unknown as curbs upon their power. It was either all or nothing.*

The Fourteenth Amendment came, and with it a profound change in the relation between the federal government and the governments of the states. No longer were the states invested with arbitrary power. Their statutes affecting property or liberty were brought within supervision of independent courts and subjected to the rule of reason. The dilemma of "all or nothing" no longer stared us in the face.

Upon the basis of that amendment, a vast body of law unknown to the fathers has been built in treatise and decision. The economic and social changes wrought by the industrial revolution and by the growth of population have made it necessary for government at this day to do a thousand things that were beyond the experience or the thought of a century ago. With the growing recognition of this need, courts have awakened to the truth that the contract clause is perverted from its proper meaning when it throttles the capacity of the states to exert their governmental power in response to crying needs. The early cases dealt with the problem as one affecting the conflicting rights and interests of individuals and classes. This was the attitude of the courts up to the Fourteenth Amendment; and the tendency to some extent persisted even later. The rights and interests of the state itself were involved, as it seemed, only indirectly and remotely, if they were thought to be involved at all. We know better in these days, with the passing of the frontier and of the unpeopled spaces of the west. With these and other changes, the welfare of the social organism in any of its parts is bound up more inseparably than ever with the welfare of the

* **Eds.' Query:** Was Cardozo correct on this point? See Justice Chase's opinion in Calder v. Bull (1798; reprinted above, p. 86) and Chief Justice Marshall's opinion for the Court in Fletcher v. Peck (1810; reprinted below, p. 956), holding that a Georgia law voiding sale of land by the state to a private company would have been invalid as violating "general principles which are common to our free institutions" even had the contract clause not been included in the Constitution. (See also Justice Johnson's concurring opinion, claiming that such principles even bound the Deity.)

whole. A gospel of *laissez-faire*—of individual initiative—of thrift and industry and sacrifice—may be inadequate in that great society we live in to point the way to salvation, at least for economic life. The state when it acts today by statutes like the one before us is not furthering the selfish good of individuals or classes as ends of ultimate validity. It is furthering its own good by maintaining the economic structure on which the good of all depends. Such at least is its endeavor, however much it miss the mark. The attainment of that end, so august and impersonal, will not be barred and thwarted by the obstruction of a contract set up along the way.

Looking back over the century, one perceives a process of evolution too strong to be set back. The decisions brought together by the Chief Justice [Hughes] show with impressive force how the court in its interpretation of the contract clause has been feeling its way toward a rational compromise between private rights and public welfare. From the beginning it was seen that something must be subtracted from the words of the Constitution in all their literal and stark significance. This was forcefully pointed out by Johnson, J., in Ogden v. Saunders [1827]. At first refuge was found in the distinction between right and remedy with all its bewildering refinements. Gradually the distinction was perceived to be inadequate. The search was for a broader base, for a division that would separate the lawful and the forbidden by lines more closely in correspondence with the necessities of government. The Fourteenth Amendment was seen to point the way. Contracts were still to be preserved. There was to be no arbitrary destruction of their binding force, nor any arbitrary impairment. There was to be no impairment, even though not arbitrary, except with the limits of fairness, of moderation, and of pressing an emergent need. But a promise exchanged between individuals was not to paralyze the state in its endeavor in times of direful crisis to keep its life-blood flowing.

To hold this may be inconsistent with things that men said in 1787 when expounding to compatriots the newly written constitution. They did not see the changes in the relation between states and nation or in the play of social forces that lay hidden in the womb of time. It may be inconsistent with things that they believed or took for granted. Their beliefs to be significant must be adjusted to the world they knew. It is not in my judgment inconsistent with what they would say today nor with what today they would believe, if they were called upon to interpret "in the light of our whole experience" the constitution that they framed for the needs of an expanding future. . . .

With this supplemental statement I concur in all that has been written in the opinion of the court.

As the last sentence of Cardozo's draft says, he was not threatening to reject Hughes's opinion. Had he not been willing to join, Hughes could not have spoken for the Court, since there were only five justices in the majority. The closeness of the vote, however, gave added weight to Cardozo's views. (Justice Harlan Fiske Stone was sympathetically revising and strengthening

Cardozo's concurrence—a fact the Chief Justice may not have known.) Hughes felt he had to placate Cardozo so he incorporated paragraphs from the daft concurrence into his own opinion, though still retaining his distinction between obligation and remedy. Cardozo did not wish to press his argument further and withdrew his concurrence. It was never published until many years after his death, when Prof. Alpheus Thomas Mason found a copy in Stone's private papers, now located in the Library of Congress.

Mr. Chief Justice **HUGHES** delivered the opinion of the Court . . . .

[We must determine] whether the provision for this temporary and conditional relief exceeds the power of the State by reason of the clause in the Federal Constitution prohibiting impairment of the obligations of contracts . . . .

Emergency does not create power. Emergency does not increase granted power or remove or diminish the restrictions imposed upon power granted or reserved. The Constitution was adopted in a period of grave emergency. Its grants of power to the Federal Government and its limitations of the power of the States were determined in the light of emergency and they are not altered by emergency. . . .

While emergency does not create power, emergency may furnish the occasion for the exercise of power . . . . The constitutional question presented in the light of an emergency is whether the power possessed embraces the particular exercise of it in response to particular conditions. . . . When the provisions of the Constitution, in grant or restriction, are specific, so particularized as not to admit of construction, no question is presented. . . . But where constitutional grants and limitations of power are set forth in general clauses, which afford a broad outline, the process of construction is essential to fill in the details. That is true of the contract clause. The necessity of construction is not obviated by the fact that the contract clause is associated in the same section with other and more specific prohibitions. Even the grouping of subjects in the same clause may not require the same application to each of the subjects, regardless of differences in their nature.

In the construction of the contract clause, the debates in the Constitutional Convention are of little aid. But the reasons which led to the adoption of that clause, and of the other prohibitions of Section 10 of Article 1, are not left in doubt and have frequently been described. . . . The widespread distress following the revolutionary period and the plight of debtors had called forth in the States an ignoble array of legislative schemes for the defeat of creditors and the invasion of contractual obligations. Legislative interferences had been so numerous and extreme that the confidence essential to prosperous trade had been undermined and the utter destruction of credit was threatened. . . . It was necessary to interpose the restraining power of a central authority in order to secure the foundations even of "private faith." . . .

But full recognition of the occasion and general purpose of the clause does not suffice to fix its precise scope. Nor does an examination of the details of prior legislation in the States yield criteria which can be considered controlling. To ascertain the scope of the constitutional prohibition we examine the course of judicial decisions in its application. These put it beyond question that the prohibition is not an absolute one and is not to be read with literal exactness like a mathematical formula. . . . [Chief Justice Hughes then reviewed decisions interpreting the contract clause].

. . . Chief Justice Marshall pointed out the distinction between obligation and remedy. Sturges v. Crowninshield [1819]: "The distinction between the obligation of a contract, and the remedy given by the legislature to enforce that obligation, has been taken at the bar, and exists in the nature of things. Without impairing the obligation of the contract, the remedy may certainly be modified as the wisdom of the nation shall direct." And in Von Hoffman v. Quincy [1867], . . . [the Court observed that:]

> It is competent for the States to change the form of the remedy, or to modify it otherwise, as they may see fit, provided no substantial right secured by the contract is thereby impaired. No attempt has been made to fix definitely the line between alterations of the remedy, which are to be deemed legitimate, and those which, under the form of modifying the remedy, impair substantial rights. Every case must be determined upon its own circumstances.

And Chief Justice Waite, quoting this language in Antoni v. Greenhow [1883], added: "In all such cases the question becomes therefore, one of reasonableness, and of that the legislature is primarily the judge." . . .

Not only is the constitutional provision qualified by the measure of control which the State retains over remedial processes, but the State also continues to possess authority to safeguard the vital interests of its people. It does not matter that legislation appropriate to that end "has the result of modifying or abrogating contracts already in effect." Stephenson v. Binford [1932]. Not only are existing laws read into contracts in order to fix obligations as between the parties, but the reservation of essential attributes of sovereign power is also read into contracts as a postulate of the legal order. The policy of protecting contracts against impairment presupposes the maintenance of a government by virtue of which contractual relations are worth while—a government which retains adequate authority to secure the peace and good order of society. This principle of harmonizing the constitutional prohibition with the necessary residuum of state power has had progressive recognition in the decisions of this Court. . . .

Undoubtedly, whatever is reserved of state power must be consistent with the fair intent of the constitutional limitation of that power. . . . They must be construed in harmony with each other. This principle precludes a construction which would permit the State to adopt as its policy the repudiation of debts or the destruction of contracts or the denial of means to enforce them. But it does not follow that conditions may not arise in which a temporary restraint of enforcement may be consistent with the spirit and purpose of the constitutional provision and thus be found to be within the range of the reserved power of the State to protect the vital interests of the community. . . .

It is manifest from [a] review of our decisions that there has been a growing appreciation of public needs and of the necessity of finding ground for a rational compromise between individual rights and public welfare. The settlement and consequent contraction of the public domain, the pressure of a constantly increasing density of population, the interrelation of the activities of our people and the complexity of our economic interests, have inevitably led to an increased use of the organization of society in order to protect the very bases of individual opportunity. Where, in earlier days, it was thought that only the concerns of individuals or of classes were involved, and that those of the State itself were touched only remotely, it has later been found that the fundamental interests of the State are directly affected; and that the question is no longer merely that of one party to a contract as against another, but of the use of reasonable means to safeguard the economic structure upon which the good of all depends.

It is no answer to say that this public need was not apprehended a century ago, or to insist that what the provision of the Constitution meant to the vision of that day it must mean to the vision of our time. If by the statement that what the Constitution meant at the time of its adoption it means to-day, it is intended to say that the great clauses of the Constitution must be confined to the interpretation which the framers, with the conditions and outlook of their time, would have placed upon them, the statement carries its own refutation. It was to guard against such a narrow conception that Chief Justice Marshall uttered the memorable warning—"We must never forget that it is a *constitution* we are expounding" (M'Culloch v. Maryland [1819])—"a constitution intended to endure for ages to come, and, consequently, to be adapted to the various *crises* of human affairs." When we are dealing with the words of the Constitution, said this Court in Missouri v. Holland [1920], "we must realize that they have called into life a being the development of which could not have been foreseen completely by the most gifted of its begetters . . . . The case before us must be considered in the light of our whole experience and not merely in that of what was said a hundred years ago."

Nor is it helpful to attempt to draw a fine distinction between the intended meaning of the words of the Constitution and their intended application. . . . The vast body of [contract clause] law which has been developed was unknown to the fathers but it is believed to have preserved the essential content and the spirit of the Constitution. With a growing recognition of public needs and the relation of individual right to public security, the court has sought to prevent the perversion of the clause through its use as an instrument to throttle the capacity of the States to protect their fundamental interests. This development is a growth from the seeds which the fathers planted. . . .

We are of the opinion that the Minnesota statute as here applied does not violate the contract clause of the Federal Constitution. Whether the legislation is wise or unwise as a matter of policy is a question with which we are not concerned. . . .

Judgment affirmed.

Mr. Justice **SUTHERLAND** dissenting . . . .

A provision of the Constitution, it is hardly necessary to say, does not admit of two distinctly opposite interpretations. It does not mean one thing at one time and an entirely different thing at another time. If the contract impairment clause, when framed and adopted, meant that the terms of a contract for the payment of money could not be altered *in invitum* by a state statute enacted for the relief of hardly pressed debtors to the end and with the effect of postponing payment or enforcement during and because of an economic or financial emergency, it is but to state the obvious to say that it means the same now . . . .

The provisions of the federal Constitution, undoubtedly, are pliable in the sense that in appropriate cases they have the capacity of bringing within their grasp every new condition which falls within their meaning. But, their *meaning* is changeless; it is only their *application* which is extensible. Constitutional grants of power and restrictions upon the exercise of power are not flexible as the doctrines of the common law are flexible. These doctrines, upon the principles of the common law itself, modify or abrogate themselves whenever they are or whenever they become plainly unsuited to different or changed conditions. . . .

The whole aim of construction, as applied to a provision of the Constitution, is to discover the meaning, to ascertain and give effect to the intent, of its framers and the people who adopted it. The necessities which gave rise to the provision, the controversies which preceded, as well as the conflicts of opinion which were settled by its adoption, are matters to be considered to enable us to arrive at a correct result . . . . As nearly as possible we should place ourselves in the condition of those who framed and adopted it. And if the meaning be at all doubtful, the doubt should be resolved, wherever reasonably possible to do so, in a way to forward the evident purpose with which the provision was adopted.

An application of these principles to the question under review removes any doubt, if otherwise there would be any, that the contract impairment clause denies to the several states the power to mitigate hard consequences resulting to debtors from financial or economic exigencies by an impairment of the obligation of contracts of indebtedness. A candid consideration of the history and circumstances which led up to and accompanied the framing and adoption of this clause will demonstrate conclusively that it was framed and adopted with the specific and studied purpose of preventing legislation designed to relieve debtors *especially* in time of financial distress. . . .

The present exigency is nothing new. From the beginning of our existence as a nation, periods of depression, of industrial failure, of financial distress, of unpaid and unpayable indebtedness, have alternated with years of plenty. . . .

The defense of the Minnesota law is made upon grounds which were discountenanced by the makers of the Constitution and have many times been rejected by this court. That defense should not now succeed because it constitutes an effort to overthrow the constitutional provision by an appeal to facts and circumstances identical with those which brought it into existence. With due regard for the processes of logical thinking, it legitimately cannot be urged that conditions which produced the rule may now be invoked to destroy it. . . .

The Minnesota statute either impairs the obligation of contracts or it does not. If it does not, the occasion to which it relates becomes immaterial, since then the passage of the statute is the exercise of a normal, unrestricted, state power and requires no special occasion to render it effective. If it does, the emergency no more furnishes a proper occasion for its exercise than if the emergency were non-existent. . . .

I quite agree with the opinion of the court that whether the legislation under review is wise or unwise is a matter with which we have nothing to do. . . . The only legitimate inquiry we can make is whether it is constitutional. If it is not, its virtues, if it have any, cannot save it; if it is, its faults cannot be invoked to accomplish its destruction. If the provisions of the Constitution be not upheld when they pinch as well as when they comfort, they may as well be abandoned. Being unable to reach any other conclusion than that the Minnesota statute infringes the constitutional restriction under review, I have no choice but to say so.

I am authorized to say that Mr. Justice **VAN DEVANTER,** Mr. Justice **McREYNOLDS** and Mr. Justice **BUTLER** concur in this opinion.

"The [Eighth] Amendment must draw its meaning from
the evolving standards of a maturing society."—Chief Justice WARREN.

"The awesome power of this Court to invalidate such
legislation, because in practice it is bounded only by our
own prudence in discerning the limits of the Court's
constitutional function, must be exercised with the utmost restraint."—Justice FRANKFURTER.

TROP v. DULLES
356 U.S. 86, 78 S.Ct. 590, 2 L.Ed.2d 630 (1958).

During World War II, Albert L. Trop served in the U.S. Army in North Africa.
In 1944 a court martial sentenced him to a term in a stockade in Casablanca.
Shortly after, he and a companion escaped. They were recaptured the next
day and tried for desertion. The second court martial convicted Trop and
sentenced him to three years at hard labor and ordered him dishonorably
discharged from the armed forces. In 1952 he applied for a passport, but the
Department of State refused the request because § 401q of the Nationality
Act of 1940 explicitly provided that persons convicted by courts martial for
desertion in time of war and dishonorably discharged lost their American
citizenship. Trop sued in a federal district court, asking for a declaratory
judgment that he was still a citizen of the United States. The district court
decided against him; the court of appeals affirmed that decision; and the
Supreme Court granted certiorari.

Mr. Chief Justice **WARREN** announced the judgment of the Court and
  delivered an opinion in which Mr. Justice **BLACK**, Mr. Justice
  DOUGLAS, and Mr. Justice **WHITTAKER** join . . . .

I

In Perez v. Brownell [1958] I expressed the principles that I believe
govern the constitutional status of United States citizenship. It is my
conviction that citizenship is not subject to the general powers of the
National Government and therefore cannot be divested in the exercise
of those powers. The right may be voluntarily relinquished or abandoned either by express language or by language and conduct that show
a renunciation of citizenship.

Under these principles, this petitioner has not lost his citizenship.
Desertion in wartime, though it may merit the ultimate penalty, does
not necessarily signify allegiance to a foreign state. Section 401(g) is
not limited to cases of desertion to the enemy, and there is no such
element in this case. This soldier committed a crime for which he
should be and was punished, but he did not involve himself in any way
with a foreign state. There was no dilution of his allegiance to this
country. The fact that the desertion occurred on foreign soil is of no
consequence. The Solicitor General acknowledged that forfeiture of
citizenship would have occurred if the entire incident had transpired in
this country.

Citizenship is not a license that expires upon misbehavior. The duties of citizenship are numerous, and the discharge of many of these obligations is essential to the security and well-being of the Nation. The citizen who fails to pay his taxes or to abide by the laws safeguarding the integrity of elections deals a dangerous blow to his country. But could a citizen be deprived of his nationality for evading these basic responsibilities of citizenship? In time of war the citizen's duties include not only the military defense of the Nation but also full participation in the manifold activities of the civilian ranks. Failure to perform any of these obligations may cause the Nation serious injury, and, in appropriate circumstances, the punishing power is available to deal with derelictions of duty. But citizenship is not lost every time a duty of citizenship is shirked. And the deprivation of citizenship is not a weapon that the Government may use to express its displeasure at a citizen's conduct, however reprehensible that conduct may be. As long as a person does not voluntarily renounce or abandon his citizenship, and this petitioner has done neither, I believe his fundamental right of citizenship is secure. . . .

. . . [W]e must face the question whether the Constitution permits the Congress to take away citizenship as a punishment for crime . . . . The question is whether this penalty subjects the individual to a fate forbidden by the principle of civilized treatment guaranteed by the Eighth Amendment.

At the outset, let us put to one side the death penalty as an index of the constitutional limit on punishment. Whatever the arguments may be against capital punishment, both on moral grounds and in terms of accomplishing the purposes of punishment—and they are forceful—the death penalty has been employed throughout our history, and, in a day when it is still widely accepted, it cannot be said to violate the constitutional concept of cruelty. But it is equally plain that the existence of the death penalty is not a license to the Government to devise any punishment short of death within the limit of its imagination.

The exact scope of the constitutional phrase "cruel and unusual" has not been detailed by this Court. But the basic policy reflected in these words is firmly established in the Anglo-American tradition of criminal justice. The phrase in our Constitution was taken directly from the English Declaration of Rights of 1688, and the principle it represents can be traced back to the Magna Carta. The basic concept underlying the Eighth Amendment is nothing less than the dignity of man. While the State has the power to punish, the Amendment stands to assure that this power be exercised within the limits of civilized standards. Fines, imprisonment and even execution may be imposed depending upon the enormity of the crime, but any technique outside the bounds of these traditional penalties is constitutionally suspect. This Court has had little occasion to give precise content to the Eighth Amendment, and, in an enlightened democracy such as ours, this is not surprising. But when the Court was confronted with a punishment of

12 years in irons at hard and painful labor imposed for the crime of falsifying public records, it did not hesitate to declare that the penalty was cruel in its excessiveness and unusual in its character. Weems v. United States [1910]. The Court recognized in that case that the words of the Amendment are not precise, and that their scope is not static. The Amendment must draw its meaning from the evolving standards of decency that mark the progress of a maturing society . . . .

. . . [D]enationalization as a punishment is barred by the Eighth Amendment. There may be involved no physical mistreatment, no primitive torture. There is instead the total destruction of the individual's status in organized society. It is a form of punishment more primitive than torture, for it destroys for the individual the political existence that was centuries in the development. The punishment strips the citizen of his status in the national and international political community. His very existence is at the sufferance of the country in which he happens to find himself. While any one country may accord him some rights, and presumably as long as he remained in this country he would enjoy the limited rights of an alien, no country need do so because he is stateless. Furthermore, his enjoyment of even the limited rights of an alien might be subject to termination at any time by reason of deportation. In short, the expatriate has lost the right to have rights.

This punishment is offensive to cardinal principles for which the Constitution stands. It subjects the individual to a fate of ever-increasing fear and distress. He knows not what discriminations may be established against him, what proscriptions may be directed against him, and when and for what cause his existence in his native land may be terminated. He may be subject to banishment, a fate universally decried by civilized people. He is stateless, a condition deplored in the international community of democracies. It is no answer to suggest that all the disastrous consequences of this fate may not be brought to bear on a stateless person. The threat makes the punishment obnoxious . . . .

In concluding as we do that the Eighth Amendment forbids Congress to punish by taking away citizenship, we are mindful of the gravity of the issue inevitably raised whenever the constitutionality of an Act of the National Legislature is challenged. No member of the Court believes that in this case the statute before us can be construed to avoid the issue of constitutionality. That issue confronts us, and the task of resolving it is inescapably ours. This task requires the exercise of judgment, not the reliance upon personal preferences. Courts must not consider the wisdom of statutes but neither can they sanction as being merely unwise that which the Constitution forbids.

We are oath-bound to defend the Constitution. This obligation requires that congressional enactments be judged by the standards of the Constitution. The Judiciary has the duty of implementing the constitutional safeguards that protect individual rights. When the Government acts to take away the fundamental right of citizenship, the safeguards of the Constitution should be examined with special diligence.

The provisions of the Constitution are not time-worn adages or hollow shibboleths. They are vital, living principles that authorize and limit governmental powers in our Nation. They are the rules of government. When the constitutionality of an Act of Congress is challenged in this Court, we must apply those rules. If we do not, the words of the Constitution become little more than good advice.

When it appears that an Act of Congress conflicts with one of these provisions, we have no choice but to enforce the paramount commands of the Constitution. We are sworn to do no less. We cannot push back the limits of the Constitution merely to accommodate challenged legislation. We must apply those limits as the Constitution prescribes them, bearing in mind both the broad scope of legislative discretion and the ultimate responsibility of constitutional adjudication. We do well to approach this task cautiously, as all our predecessors have counseled. But the ordeal of judgment cannot be shirked. In some 81 instances since this Court was established it has determined that congressional action exceeded the bounds of the Constitution. It is so in this case.
. . . .

Reversed and remanded.

Mr. Justice **BLACK**, whom Mr. Justice **DOUGLAS** joins, concurring.

While I concur in the opinion of The Chief Justice there is one additional thing that needs to be said.

Even if citizenship could be involuntarily divested, I do not believe that the power to denationalize may be placed in the hands of military authorities . . . .

Mr. Justice **BRENNAN**, concurring . . . .

. . . I can only conclude that the requisite rational relation between this statute and the war power does not appear—for in this relation the statute is not "really calculated to effect any of the objects entrusted to the government . . . ." M'Culloch v. Maryland— [1819]—and therefore that § 401(g) falls beyond the domain of Congress.

Mr. Justice **FRANKFURTER**, whom Mr. Justice **BURTON**, Mr. Justice **CLARK**, and Mr. Justice **HARLAN** join, dissenting . . . .

. . . What is always basic when the power of Congress to enact legislation is challenged is the appropriate approach to judicial review of congressional legislation. All power is, in Madison's phrase, "of an encroaching nature." *Federalist*, No. 48. Judicial power is not immune against this human weakness. It also must be on guard against encroaching beyond its proper bounds, and not the less so since the only restraint upon it is self-restraint. When the power of Congress to pass a statute is challenged, the function of this Court is to determine whether legislative action lies clearly outside the constitutional grant of power to which it has been, or may fairly be, referred. In making this determination, the Court sits in judgment on the action of a co-ordinate branch of the Government while keeping unto itself—as it must under our constitutional system—the final determination of its own power to act. No wonder such a function is deemed "the gravest and most delicate duty that this Court is called on to perform." . . .

Rigorous observance of the difference between limits of power and wise exercise of power—between questions of authority and questions of prudence—requires the most alert appreciation of this decisive but subtle relationship of two concepts that too easily coalesce. No less does it require a disciplined will to adhere to the difference. It is not easy to stand aloof and allow want of wisdom to prevail, to disregard one's own strongly held view of what is wise in the conduct of affairs. But it is not the business of this Court to pronounce policy. It must observe a fastidious regard for limitations on its own power, and this precludes the Court's giving effect to its own notions of what is wise or politic. That self-restraint is of the essence in the observance of the judicial oath, for the Constitution has not authorized the judges to sit in judgment on the wisdom of what Congress and the Executive Branch do.

One of the principal purposes in establishing the Constitution was to "provide for the common defence." To that end the States granted to Congress the several powers of Article 1, Section 8, clauses 11 to 14 and 18, compendiously described as the "war power." Although these specific grants of power do not specifically enumerate every factor relevant to the power to conduct war, there is no limitation upon it (other than what the Due Process Clause commands) . . . .

Probably the most important governmental action contemplated by the war power is the building up and maintenance of an armed force for the common defense. Just as Congress may be convinced of the necessity for conscription for the effective conduct of war . . . , Congress may justifiably be of the view that stern measures—what to some may seem overly stern—are needed in order that control may be had over evasions of military duty when the armed forces are committed to the Nation's defense, and that the deleterious effects of those evasions may be kept to the minimum. Clearly Congress may deal severely with the problem of desertion from the armed forces in wartime; it is equally clear—from the face of the legislation and from the circumstances in which it was passed—that Congress was calling upon its war powers when it made such desertion an act of expatriation . . . .

Possession by an American citizen of the rights and privileges that constitute citizenship imposes correlative obligations, of which the most indispensable may well be "to take his place in the ranks of the army of his country and risk the chance of being shot down in its defense," Jacobson v. Massachusetts [1905]. Harsh as this may sound, it is no more so than the actualities to which it responds. Can it be said that there is no rational nexus between refusal to perform this ultimate duty of American citizenship and legislative withdrawal of that citizenship? Congress may well have thought that making loss of citizenship a consequence of wartime desertion would affect the ability of the military authorities to control the forces with which they were expected to fight and win a major world conflict. It is not for us to deny that Congress might reasonably have believed the morale and fighting efficiency of our troops would be impaired if our soldiers knew that their fellows who had abandoned them in their time of greatest need were to remain in the communion of our citizens . . . .

This legislation is the result of an exercise by Congress of the legislative power vested in it by the Constitution and of an exercise by the President of his constitutional power in approving a bill and thereby making it "a law." To sustain it is to respect the actions of the two branches of our Government directly responsive to the will of the people and empowered under the Constitution to determine the wisdom of legislation. The awesome power of this Court to invalidate such legislation, because in practice it is bounded only by our own prudence in discerning the limits of the Court's constitutional function, must be exercised with the utmost restraint. Mr. Justice Holmes, one of the profoundest thinkers who ever sat on this Court, expressed the conviction that "I do not think the United States would come to an end if we lost our power to declare an Act of Congress void. I do think the Union would be imperiled if we could not make that declaration as to the laws of the several States." . . . He did not, of course, deny that the power existed to strike down congressional legislation, nor did he shrink from its exercise. But the whole of his work during his thirty years of service on this Court should be a constant reminder that the power to invalidate legislation must not be exercised as if, either in constitutional theory or in the art of government, it stood as the sole bulwark against unwisdom or excesses of the moment.

Editors' Notes

(1) **Query:** On the substance of the dispute on the constitutionality of the statute, what are the textual bases of the debate between Warren and Frankfurter? To what extent did either meet the other on his own textual grounds? Were textual grounds critical for either's argument?

(2) **Query:** Warren spoke of the Eighth Amendment as drawing "its meaning from the evolving standards of decency that mark the progress of a maturing society." How does he suggest that an interpreter find those standards? For an interesting effort to cope with this problem, see the dissenting opinion of Judge Jerome Frank of the U.S. Court of Appeals for the 2d Circuit in Repouille v. United States (1947).

(3) **Query:** To what extent can one argue that the terms of the Eighth Amendment are different from most other parts of the Constitution in that the word "unusual" in "cruel and unusual" requires interpreters to apply contemporary standards?

(4) Frankfurter and Warren sharply disagreed on the merits of the substantive issue before the Court. They did not basically disagree on the notion of the constitutional clauses meaning different things at different times. In a internal memorandum written during the Court's deliberation of the School Segregation Cases (1954), Frankfurter said:

> [T]he equality of laws enshrined in a constitution which was "made for an undefined and expanding future, and for a people gathered and to be gathered from many nations and many tongues," Hurtado v. California, is not a fixed formula defined with finality at a particular time. It does not reflect, as a congealed summary, the social arrangements and beliefs of a particular epoch. It is addressed to the changes wrought by time and not merely the changes that are the consequences of physical development. Law must respond to transformation of views as well as to that of outward circumstances. The effect of changes in men's feelings for what is right and just is equally relevant in determining whether a discrimination denies the equal protection of the laws. [Quoted in Richard Kluger, *Simple Justice* (New York: Knopf, 1976), p. 685.]

It was, of course, in the School Segregation Cases (Brown v. Board; reprinted below, p. 768) that Warren wrote for the Court: "[W]e cannot turn back the clock to 1868 when the [Fourteenth] Amendment was adopted . . . . We must consider public education in the light of its full development and its present place in American life throughout the Nation."

(5) *Trop* involved a substantive problem that was very real to people who had lived through the years when the Nazis ruled Germany. One of the standard techniques the Nazi used against dissenters, when they did not imprison or kill them, was to remove their citizenship and forcibly deport them. The Russians use similar tactics, but today most nations of the West welcome expelled Soviet dissidents. During the 1930s, however, Europeans were usually hostile to these outcasts, who were very often Jews, typically imprisoning them for illegal entry and then redeporting them to Germany or to a third nation, where they suffered the same fate over again and again. Erich Maria Remarque brilliantly captured the sufferings of these people in his novel *Arch of Triumph*, W. Sorrell & D. Lindley, trans., (New York: Appleton-Century, 1945), later made into a movie starring Ingrid Bergman and Charles Boyer.

(6) In *Trop* a majority of the justices could not agree on a single opinion. Thus Warren spoke for only four justices, not for the Court. It was not until 1967, in Afroyim v. Rusk, that a full majority held that government could not for any reason whatsoever take away an American's citizenship, though a citizen could voluntarily renounce that status.

"[T]he Equal Protection Clause is not shackled to the political theory of a particular era."—Justice DOUGLAS

"[W]hen a 'political theory' embodied in our Constitution becomes outdated . . . a majority of the nine members of this Court are not only without constitutional power but are far less qualified to choose a new constitutional political theory than the people of the country proceeding in the manner provided by Article V."—Justice BLACK

HARPER v. VIRGINIA STATE BOARD OF ELECTIONS

383 U.S. 663, 86 S.Ct. 1079, 16 L.Ed.2d 169 (1966).

The Twenty-Fourth Amendment, adopted in 1964, outlawed a poll tax as a requirement for voting for *federal* officials, but made no mention of such taxes as prerequisites for voting for *state* officials. Virginia continued to demand payment of an annual poll tax of $1.50 before voting in state elections. A group of citizens of Virginia filed suit in a federal district court, claiming the tax violated the equal protection clause of the Fourteenth Amendment. That court dismissed the case, saying it was bound by Breedlove v. Suttles (1937), in which the Supreme Court had unanimously sustained Georgia's poll tax against a similar attack. The litigants then appealed directly to the Supreme Court, as federal statutes permitted.

Mr. Justice **DOUGLAS** delivered the opinion of the Court . . . .

While the right to vote in federal elections is conferred by Art I, § 2, of the Constitution, the right to vote in state elections is nowhere expressly mentioned. It is argued that the right to vote in state elections is implicit, particularly by reason of the First Amendment and that it may not constitutionally be conditioned upon the payment of a tax or fee. We do not stop to canvass the relation between voting and political expression. For it is enough to say that once the franchise is granted to the electorate, lines may not be drawn which are inconsistent with the Equal Protection Clause of the Fourteenth Amendment. That is to say, the right of suffrage "is subject to the imposition of state standards which are not discriminatory and which do not contravene any restriction that Congress, acting pursuant to its constitutional powers, has imposed." Lassiter v. Northampton Election Board [1959]. We were speaking there of a state literacy test which we sustained, warning that the result would be different if a literacy test, fair on its face, were used to discriminate against a class. But *Lassiter* does not govern the result here, because, unlike a poll tax, the "ability to read and write . . . has some relation to standards designed to promote intelligent use of the ballot."

We conclude that a State violates the Equal Protection Clause of the Fourteenth Amendment whenever it makes the affluence of the voter or payment of any fee an electoral standard. Voter qualifications have no relation to wealth nor to paying this or any other tax. Our cases demonstrate that the Equal Protection Clause . . . restrains the

States from fixing voter qualifications which invidiously discriminate. Thus without questioning the power of a State to impose reasonable residence restrictions on the availability of the ballot, we held in Carrington v. Rash [1965] that a State may not deny the opportunity to vote to a bona fide resident merely because he is a member of the armed services . . . . Previously we had said that neither homesite nor occupation "affords a permissible basis for distinguishing between qualified voters within the State." Gray v. Sanders [1963]. We think the same must be true of requirements of wealth or affluence or payment of a fee.

Long ago in Yick Wo v. Hopkins [1886] the Court referred to "the political franchise of voting" as a "fundamental political right, because preservative of all rights." Recently in Reynolds v. Sims [1964], we said, "Undoubtedly, the right of suffrage is a fundamental matter in a free and democratic society. Especially since the right to exercise the franchise in a free and unimpaired manner is preservative of other basic civil and political rights, any alleged infringement of the right of citizens to vote must be carefully and meticulously scrutinized." There we were considering charges that voters in one part of the State had greater representation per person in the State Legislature than voters in another part of the State. We concluded: "A citizen, a qualified voter, is no more nor no less so because he lives in the city or on the farm. This is the clear and strong command of our Constitution's Equal Protection Clause . . . ."

We say the same whether the citizen, otherwise qualified to vote, has $1.50 in his pocket or nothing at all, pays the fee or fails to pay it. The principle that denies the State the right to dilute a citizen's vote on account of his economic status or other such factors by analogy bars a system which excludes those unable to pay a fee to vote or who fail to pay.

It is argued that a State may exact fees from citizens for many different kinds of licenses; that if it can demand from all an equal fee for a driver's license, it can demand from all an equal poll tax for voting. But we must remember that the interest of the State, when it comes to voting, is limited to the power to fix qualifications. Wealth, like race, creed, or color, is not germane to one's ability to participate intelligently in the electoral process. Lines drawn on the basis of wealth or property, like those of race (Korematsu v. United States [1944]), are traditionally disfavored. See Edwards v. California [1941] (Jackson, J., concurring); Griffin v. Illinois [1956]; Douglas v. California [1963]. To introduce wealth or payment of a fee as a measure of a voter's qualifications is to introduce a capricious or irrelevant factor. The degree of the discrimination is irrelevant. In this context—that is, as a condition of obtaining a ballot—the requirement of fee paying causes an "invidious" discrimination (Skinner v. Oklahoma [1942]) . . . . . Breedlove v. Suttles sanctioned its use as "a prerequisite of voting." To that extent *Breedlove* is overruled.

We agree, of course, with Mr. Justice Holmes that the Due Process Clause of the Fourteenth Amendment "does not enact Mr. Herbert

Spencer's Social Statics" (Lochner v. New York [1905]). Likewise, the Equal Protection Clause is not shackled to the political theory of a particular era. In determining what lines are unconstitutionally discriminatory, we have never been confined to historic notions of equality, any more than we have restricted due process to a fixed catalogue of what was at a given time deemed to be the limits of fundamental rights. See Malloy v. Hogan [1964]. Notions of what constitutes equal treatment for purposes of the Equal Protection Clause *do* change. This Court in 1896 held that laws providing for separate public facilities for white and Negro citizens did not deprive the latter of the equal protection and treatment that the Fourteenth Amendment commands. Plessy v. Ferguson . . . . When, in 1954 . . . we repudiated the "separate-but-equal" doctrine of *Plessy* as respects public education we stated: "In approaching this problem, we cannot turn the clock back to 1868 when the Amendment was adopted, or even to 1896 when *Plessy* was written." Brown v. Board of Education.

In [*Reynolds*], we held . . . that "the opportunity for equal participation by all voters in the election of state legislators" is required. We decline to qualify that principle by sustaining this poll tax.

Our conclusion, like that in *Reynolds,* is founded not on what we think governmental policy should be, but on what the Equal Protection Clause requires.

We have long been mindful that where fundamental rights and liberties are asserted under the Equal Protection Clause, classifications which might invade or restrain them must be closely scrutinized and carefully confined. See, e.g., *Skinner; Reynolds.*

Those principles apply here. For, to repeat, wealth or fee paying has, in our view, no relation to voting qualifications; the right to vote is too precious, too fundamental to be so burdened or conditioned.

Reversed.

Mr. Justice **BLACK,** dissenting . . . .

. . . . [T]he Court's decision is to no extent based on a finding that the Virginia law as written or as applied is being used as a device or mechanism to deny Negro citizens of Virginia the right to vote on account of their color . . . . If the record could support [such] a finding, the law would of course be unconstitutional as a violation of the Fourteenth and Fifteenth Amendments and also 42 USC § 1971(a)
. . . .

(1) . . . The mere fact that a law results in treating some groups differently from others does not, of course, automatically amount to a violation of the Equal Protection Clause. To bar a State from drawing any distinctions in the application of its laws would practically paralyze the regulatory power of legislative bodies . . . . Voting laws are no exception to this principle, All voting laws treat some persons differently from others in some respects. Some bar a person from voting who is under 21 years of age; others bar those under 18. Some bar convicted felons or the insane, and some have attached a freehold or other

property qualification for voting. *Breedlove* upheld a poll tax which was imposed on men but was not equally imposed on women and minors, and the Court today does not overrule that part of *Breedlove* which approved those discriminatory provisions. And in *Lassiter*, this Court held that state laws which disqualified the illiterate from voting did not violate the Equal Protection Clause. From these cases . . . it is clear that some discriminatory voting qualifications can be imposed without violating the Equal Protection Clause.

. . . The equal protection cases carefully analyzed boil down to the principle that distinctions drawn and even discriminations imposed by state laws do not violate the Equal Protection Clause so long as these distinctions and discriminations are not "irrational," "irrelevant," "unreasonable," "arbitrary," or "invidious." These vague and indefinite terms do not, of course, provide a precise formula or an automatic mechanism for deciding cases . . . . The restrictive connotations of these terms, however . . . , are a plain recognition of the fact that under a proper interpretation of the Equal Protection Clause States are to have the broadest kind of leeway in areas where they have a general constitutional competence to act. In view of the purpose of the terms to restrain the courts from a wholesale invalidation of state laws under the Equal Protection Clause it would be difficult to say that the poll tax requirement is "irrational" or "arbitrary" or works "invidious discriminations." State poll tax legislation can "reasonably," "rationally" and without an "invidious" or evil purpose to injure anyone be found to rest on a number of state policies including (1) the State's desire to collect its revenue, and (2) its belief that voters [who] pay a poll tax will be interested in furthering the State's welfare when they vote. Certainly it is rational to believe that people may be more likely to pay taxes if payment is a prerequisite to voting. And if history can be a factor in determining the "rationality" of discrimination in a state law . . . , then . . . history is on the side of "rationality" of the State's poll tax policy. Property qualifications existed in the Colonies and were continued by many States after the Constitution was adopted. Although I join the Court in disliking the policy of the poll tax, this is not in my judgment a justifiable reason for holding this poll tax law unconstitutional . . . .

(2) Another reason for my dissent . . . is that [the Court] seems to be using the old "natural-law-due-process formula" to justify striking down state laws as violations of the Equal Protection Clause. I have heretofore had many occasions to express my strong belief that there is no constitutional support whatever for this Court to use the Due Process Clause as though it provided a blank check to alter the meaning of the Constitution as written so as to add to it substantive constitutional changes which a majority of the Court at any given time believes are needed to meet present-day problems. Nor is there in my opinion any more constitutional support for this Court to use the Equal Protection Clause, as it has today, to write into the Constitution its notions of what it thinks is good governmental policy . . . .

The Court denies that it is using the "natural-law-due-process formula." It says that its invalidation of the Virginia law "is founded not on what we think governmental policy should be, but on what the Equal Protection Clause requires." I find no statement in the Court's opinion, however, which advances even a plausible argument as to why the alleged discriminations which might possibly be effected by Virginia's poll tax law are "irrational," "unreasonable," "arbitrary," or "invidious" or have no relevance to a legitimate policy which the State wishes to adopt . . . . The Court's failure to give any reasons . . . is a pretty clear indication to me that none exist. I can only conclude that the primary, controlling, predominate, if not the exclusive reason for declaring the Virginia law unconstitutional is the Court's deep-seated hostility and antagonism, which I share, to making payment of a tax a prerequisite to voting.

The Court's justification for consulting its own notions rather than following the original meaning of the Constitution, as I would, apparently is based on the belief of the majority of the Court that for this Court to be bound by the original meaning of the Constitution is an intolerable and debilitating evil; that our Constitution should not be "shackled to the political theory of a particular era," and that to save the country from the original Constitution the Court must have constant power to renew it and keep it abreast of this Court's more enlightened theories of what is best for our society. It seems to me that this is an attack not only on the great value of our Constitution itself but also on the concept of a written constitution which is to survive through the years as originally written unless changed through the amendment process which the Framers wisely provided. Moreover, when a "political theory" embodied in our Constitution becomes outdated, it seems to me that a majority of the nine members of this Court are not only without constitutional power but are far less qualified to choose a new constitutional political theory than the people of this country proceeding in the manner provided by Article V.

The people have not found it impossible to amend their Constitution to meet new conditions . . . . Moreover, the people, in § 5 of the Fourteenth Amendment, designated the governmental tribunal they wanted to provide additional rules to enforce the guarantees of that Amendment. The branch of Government they chose was not the Judicial Branch but the Legislative. I have no doubt at all that Congress has the power under § 5 to pass legislation to abolish the poll tax . . . . This Court had occasion to discuss this very subject in Ex parte Virginia (1880). There this Court said, referring to the first section of the Amendment:

> It is not said the *judicial power* of the general government shall extend to enforcing the prohibitions and to protecting the rights and immunities guaranteed. It is not said that branch of the government shall be authorized to declare void any action of a State in violation of the prohibitions. *It is the power of Congress which has been enlarged.*

Congress is authorized *to enforce* the prohibitions by appropriate legislation . . . . (Emphasis partially supplied.)

. . .

Mr. Justice **HARLAN,** whom Mr. Justice **STEWART** joins, dissenting.

The final demise of state poll taxes, already totally proscribed by
the Twenty-Fourth Amendment with respect to federal elections and
abolished by the States themselves in all but four States with respect to
state elections, is perhaps in itself not of great moment. But the fact
that the coup de grace has been administered by this Court instead of
being left to the affected States or to the federal political process should
be a matter of continuing concern to all interested in maintaining the
proper role of this tribunal under our scheme of government . . . .

The Equal Protection Clause prevents States from arbitrarily treating people differently under their laws. Whether any such differing
treatment is to be deemed arbitrary depends on whether or not it
reflects an appropriate differentiating classification among those affected; the clause has never been thought to require equal treatment of all
persons despite differing circumstances. The test evolved by this Court
for determining whether an asserted justifying classification exists is
whether such a classification can be deemed to be founded on some
rational and otherwise constitutionally permissible state policy. This
standard reduces to a minimum the likelihood that the federal judiciary will judge state policies in terms of the individual notions and
predilections of its own members and until recently it has been followed
in all kinds of "equal protection" cases.

Reynolds, among its other breaks with the past, also marked a
departure from these traditional and wise principles . . . . [W]hat
Reynolds really reflected was but this Court's own views of how modern
American representative government should be run. For it can hardly
be thought that no other method of apportionment may be considered
rational . . . . [Today] the Court reverts to the highly subjective
judicial approach manifested by *Reynolds.* In substance the Court's
analysis of the equal protection issue goes no further than to say that
the electoral franchise is "precious" and "fundamental," and to conclude that "[t]o introduce wealth or payment of a fee as a measure of a
voter's qualifications is to introduce a capricious or irrelevant factor."
These are of course captivating phrases, but they are wholly inadequate
to satisfy the standard governing adjudication of the equal protection
issue: Is there a rational basis for Virginia's poll tax as a voting
qualification? I think the answer to that question is undoubtedly "yes."

Property qualifications and poll taxes have been a traditional part
of our political structure. . . .

[I]t is only by fiat that it can be said, especially in the context of
American history, that there can be no rational debate as to their
advisability. Most of the early Colonies had them; many of the States
have had them during much of their histories, and, whether one agrees
or not, arguments have been and still can be made in favor of them.

For example, it is certainly a rational argument that payment of some minimal poll tax promotes civic responsibility, weeding out those who do not care enough about public affairs to pay $1.50 or thereabouts a year for the exercise of the franchise. It is also arguable, indeed it was probably accepted as sound political theory by a large percentage of Americans through most of our history, that people with some property have a deeper stake in community affairs, and are consequently more responsible, more educated, more knowledgeable, more worthy of confidence, than those without means, and that the community and Nation would be better managed if the franchise were restricted to such citizens. Nondiscriminatory and fairly applied literacy tests, upheld by this Court in *Lassiter,* find justification on very similar grounds.

These viewpoints, to be sure, ring hollow on most contemporary ears. Their lack of acceptance today is evidenced by the fact that nearly all of the States, left to their own devices, have eliminated property or poll-tax qualifications [and] by the cognate fact that Congress and three-quarters of the States quickly ratified the Twenty-Fourth Amendment . . . .

Property and poll-tax qualifications, very simply, are not in accord with current egalitarian notions of how a modern democracy should be organized. It is of course entirely fitting that legislatures should modify the law to reflect such changes in popular attitudes. However, it is all wrong, in my view, for the Court to adopt the political doctrines popularly accepted at a particular moment of our history and to declare all others to be irrational and invidious, barring them from the range of choice by reasonably minded people acting through the political process. It was not too long ago that Mr. Justice Holmes felt impelled to remind the Court that the Due Process Clause of the Fourteenth Amendment does not enact the laissez-faire theory of society. *Lochner.* The times have changed, and perhaps it is appropriate to observe that neither does the Equal Protection Clause of that Amendment rigidly impose upon America an ideology of unrestrained egalitarianism. . . .

Editors' Notes

(1) The four states that, when *Harper* was decided, still required payment of poll taxes for state elections were: Alabama, Mississippi, Texas, and Virginia.

(2) **Query:** To what extent can one say that "equal protection" is, like the ban against "cruel and unusual punishments," in a different category from most constitutional clauses in that its very terms require interpreters to impose current—and hence possibly changing—standards? What about "due process of law"?

(3) **Query:** See Note (4) to Trop v. Dulles (1958), above, at p. 144. Justice Black joined Warren's opinion for the Court in the School Segregation Cases (1954; reprinted below, p. 768). How does that choice square with Black's dissent in *Harper?*

"[H]istorical evidence sheds light not only on what the
draftsmen intended the Establishment Clause to mean,
but also on how they thought that Clause applied to the
practice authorized by the First Congress—their actions
reveal their intent."—Chief Justice BURGER

"[T]he Constitution is not a static document whose meaning on every detail is fixed for all time by the life experience of the Framers."—Justice BRENNAN

MARSH v. CHAMBERS
463 U.S. 783, 103 S.Ct. 3330, 77 L.Ed.2d 1019 (1983).

Under a long established practice, Nebraska's legislature, like the U.S.
Congress, opens each day's session with a prayer offered by a chaplain—for
almost twenty years the same Presbyterian minister—paid from money raised
by taxes. Ernest Chambers sued as a member of the legislature and as a
taxpayer for an injunction to forbid the practice as a violation of the Establishment Clause of the First Amendment, made applicable to the states by the
Fourteenth. The federal district judge held that the legislature's praying was
constitutional but paying the chaplain out of public funds was not. The U.S.
Court of Appeals for the Eighth Circuit ruled that both praying and paying
violated the Establishment Clause. Nebraska sought and obtained certiorari.

Chief Justice **BURGER** delivered the opinion of the Court . . . .

The opening of sessions of legislative and other deliberative public
bodies with prayer is deeply embedded in the history and tradition of
this country. From colonial times through the founding of the Republic and ever since, the practice of legislative prayer has coexisted with
the principles of disestablishment and religious freedom. In the very
courtrooms in which the United States District Judge and later three
Circuit Judges heard and decided this case, the proceedings opened with
an announcement that concluded, "God save the United States and this
Honorable Court." The same invocation occurs at all sessions of this
Court.

The tradition in many of the colonies was, of course, linked to an
established church, but the Continental Congress, beginning in 1774,
adopted the traditional procedure of opening its sessions with a prayer
offered by a paid chaplain. Although prayers were not offered during
the Constitutional Convention, the First Congress, as one of its early
items of business, adopted the policy of selecting a chaplain to open
each session with prayer. Thus, on April 7, 1789, the Senate appointed
a committee "to take under consideration the manner of electing
Chaplains." On April 9, 1789, a similar committee was appointed by
the House of Representatives. On April 25, 1789, the Senate elected its
first chaplain, the House followed suit on May 1, 1789. A statute
providing for the payment of these chaplains was enacted into law on
Sept. 22, 1789.

On Sept. 25, 1789, three days after Congress authorized the appointment of paid chaplains, final agreement was reached on the language of the Bill of Rights. Clearly the men who wrote the First Amendment Religion Clause did not view paid legislative chaplains and opening prayers as a violation of that Amendment, for the practice of opening sessions with prayer has continued without interruption ever since that early session of Congress. It has also been followed consistently in most of the states, including Nebraska, where the institution of opening legislative sessions with prayer was adopted even before the State attained statehood . . . .

Standing alone, historical patterns cannot justify contemporary violations of constitutional guarantees, but there is far more here than simply historical patterns. In this context, historical evidence sheds light not only on what the draftsmen intended the Establishment Clause to mean, but also on how they thought that Clause applied to the practice authorized by the First Congress—their actions reveal their intent. An act

> passed by the first Congress assembled under the Constitution, many of whose members had taken part in framing that instrument, . . . is contemporaneous and weighty evidence of its true meaning. Wisconsin v. Pelican Ins. Co. (1888).

In Walz v. Tax Comm'n (1970), we considered the weight to be accorded to history:

> It is obviously correct that no one acquires a vested or protected right in violation of the Constitution by long use, even when that span of time covers our entire national existence and indeed predates it. Yet an unbroken practice . . . is not something to be lightly cast aside.

No more is Nebraska's practice of over a century, consistent with two centuries of national practice, to be cast aside. It can hardly be thought that in the same week Members of the First Congress voted to appoint and to pay a Chaplain for each House and also voted to approve the draft of the First Amendment for submission to the States, they intended the Establishment Clause of the Amendment to forbid what they had just declared acceptable. In applying the First Amendment to the states through the Fourteenth Amendment, Cantwell v. Connecticut (1940), it would be incongruous to interpret that clause as imposing more stringent First Amendment limits on the States than the draftsmen imposed on the Federal Government.

This unique history leads us to accept the interpretation of the First Amendment draftsmen who saw no real threat to the Establishment Clause arising from a practice of prayer similar to that now challenged. We conclude that legislative prayer presents no more potential for establishment than the provision of school transportation, Everson v. Board of Education (1946), beneficial grants for higher education, Tilton v. Richardson (1971), or tax exemptions for religious organizations, *Walz*.

Respondent cites Justice Brennan's concurring opinion in Abington School Dist. v. Schempp (1963), and argues that we should not rely too heavily on "the advice of the Founding Fathers" because the messages of history often tend to be ambiguous and not relevant to a society far more heterogeneous than that of the Framers. Respondent also points out that John Jay and John Rutledge opposed the motion to begin the first session of the Continental Congress with prayer.

We do not agree that evidence of opposition to a measure weakens the force of the historical argument; indeed it infuses it with power by demonstrating that the subject was considered carefully and the action not taken thoughtlessly, by force of long tradition and without regard to the problems posed by a pluralistic society. Jay and Rutledge specifically grounded their objection on the fact that the delegates to the Congress "were so divided in religious sentiments . . . that [they] could not join in the same act of worship." Their objection was met by Samuel Adams, who stated that "he was no bigot, and could hear a prayer from a gentleman of piety and virtue, who was at the same time a friend to his country." . . .

This interchange emphasizes that the delegates did not consider opening prayers as a proselytizing activity or as symbolically placing the government's "official seal of approval on one religious view." Rather, the Founding Fathers looked at invocations as "conduct whose . . . effect . . . harmonize[d] with the tenets of some or all religions." McGowan v. Maryland (1961). The Establishment Clause does not always bar a state from regulating conduct simply because it "harmonizes with religious canons." Here, the individual claiming injury by the practice is an adult, presumably not readily susceptible to "religious indoctrination." . . .

In light of the unambiguous and unbroken history of more than 200 years, there can be no doubt that the practice of opening legislative sessions with prayer has become part of the fabric of our society. To invoke Divine guidance on a public body entrusted with making the laws is not, in these circumstances, an "establishment" of religion or a step toward establishment; it is simply a tolerable acknowledgment of beliefs widely held among the people of this country. As Justice Douglas observed, "[w]e are a religious people whose institutions presuppose a Supreme Being." Zorach v. Clauson (1952) . . . .

Framers can violate   Reversed.

Justice **BRENNAN**, with whom Justice **MARSHALL** joins, dissenting
. . . .

The Court's main argument for carving out an exception sustaining legislative prayer is historical. The Court cannot—and does not—purport to find a pattern of "undeviating acceptance," *Walz* (Brennan, J., concurring), of legislative prayer. It also disclaims exclusive reliance on the mere longevity of legislative prayer. The Court does, however, point out that, only three days before the First Congress reached agreement on the final wording of the Bill of Rights, it authorized the appointment of paid chaplains for its own proceedings, and the Court argues that in light of this "unique history," the actions of Congress reveal its intent as to the meaning of the Establishment Clause. I agree that historical practice is "of considerable import in the interpretation of abstract constitutional language." This is a case, however, in which—absent the Court's invocation of history—there would be no question that the practice at issue was unconstitutional. And despite the surface appeal of the Court's argument, there are at least three reasons why specific historical practice should not in this case override that clear constitutional imperative.

First, it is significant that the Court's historical argument does not rely on the legislative history of the Establishment Clause itself. Indeed, that formal history is profoundly unilluminating on this and most other subjects. Rather, the Court assumes that the Framers of the Establishment Clause would not have themselves authorized a practice that they thought violated the guarantees contained in the clause. This assumption, however, is questionable. Legislators, influenced by the passions and exigencies of the moment, the pressure of constituents and colleagues, and the press of business, do not always pass sober constitutional judgment on every piece of legislation they enact, and this must be assumed to be as true of the members of the First Congress as any other. Indeed, the fact that James Madison, who voted for the bill authorizing the payment of the first congressional chaplains, later expressed the view that the practice was unconstitutional is instructive on precisely this point. Madison's later views may not have represented so much a change of *mind* as a change of *role,* from a member of Congress engaged in the hurley-burley of legislative activity to a detached observer engaged in unpressured reflection. Since the latter role is precisely the one with which this Court is charged, I am not at all sure that Madison's later writings should be any less influential in our deliberations than his earlier vote.

Second, the Court's analysis treats the First Amendment simply as an Act of Congress, as to whose meaning the intent of Congress is the single touchstone. Both the Constitution and its amendments, however, became supreme law only by virtue of their ratification by the States, and the understanding of the States should be as relevant to our analysis as the understanding of Congress. This observation is especially compelling in considering the meaning of the Bill of Rights. The first 10 Amendments were not enacted because the members of the First Congress came up with a bright idea one morning; rather, their enactment was forced upon Congress by a number of the States as a condition for their ratification of the original Constitution. To treat any practice authorized by the First Congress as presumptively consistent with the Bill of Rights is therefore somewhat akin to treating any action of a party to a contract as presumptively consistent with the terms of the contract. The latter proposition, if it were accepted, would of course resolve many of the heretofore perplexing issues in contract law.

Finally, and most importantly, the argument tendered by the Court is misguided because the Constitution is not a static document whose meaning on every detail is fixed for all time by the life experience of the Framers. We have recognized in a wide variety of constitutional contexts that the practices that were in place at the time any particular guarantee was enacted into the Constitution do not necessarily fix forever the meaning of that guarantee. To be truly faithful to the Framers, "our use of the history of their time must limit itself to broad purposes, not specific practices." Abington School Dist. v. Schempp (Brennan, J., concurring). Our primary task must be to translate "the majestic generalities of the Bill of Rights, conceived as part of the pattern of liberal government in the eighteenth century, into concrete restraints on officials dealing with the problems of the twentieth century . . . ." West Virginia State Bd. of Education v. Barnette (1943).

The inherent adaptability of the Constitution and its amendments is particularly important with respect to the Establishment Clause. "[O]ur religious composition makes us a vastly more diverse people than were our forefathers . . . . In the face of such profound changes, practices which may have been objectionable to no one in the time of Jefferson and Madison may today be highly offensive to many persons, the deeply devout and the nonbelievers alike." *Schempp* (Brennan, J., concurring). President John Adams issued during his Presidency a number of official proclamations calling on all Americans to engage in Christian prayer. Justice Story, in his treatise on the Constitution, contended that the "real object" of the First Amendment "was, not to countenance, much less to advance Mahometanism, Judaism, or infidelity, by prostrating Christianity; but to exclude all rivalry among Christian sects . . . ." Whatever deference Adams' actions and Story's views might once have deserved in this Court, the Establishment Clause must now be read in a very different light. Similarly, the members of the First Congress should be treated, not as sacred figures whose every action must be emulated, but as the authors of a document meant to last for the ages. Indeed, a proper respect for the Framers themselves forbids us to give so static and lifeless a meaning to their work. To my mind, the Court's focus here on a narrow piece of history is, in a fundamental sense, a betrayal of the lessons of history . . . .

Justice **STEVENS** dissenting . . . .

> **"Once we have abandoned the idea that the authority of the courts to declare laws unconstitutional is somehow tied to the language of the Constitution . . . [judges become] a roving commission to second-guess Congress, state legislatures, and state and federal administrative officers concerning what is best for the country."**

THE NOTION OF A LIVING CONSTITUTION *

William H. Rehnquist.

At least one of the more than half-dozen persons nominated during the past decade to be an Associate Justice of the Supreme Court of the United States has been asked by the Senate Judiciary Committee at his confirmation hearings whether he believed in a living Constitution. It is not an easy question to answer; the phrase "living Constitution" has about it a teasing imprecision that makes it a coat of many colors.

. . .

. . . The phrase is really a shorthand expression that is susceptible of at least two quite different meanings.

The first meaning was expressed . . . by Mr. Justice Holmes in Missouri v. Holland [1920] . . . :

> When we are dealing with words that also are a constituent act, like the Constitution of the United States, we must realize that they have called into life a being the development of which could not have been foreseen completely by the most gifted of its begetters. It was enough for them to realize or to hope that they had created an organism; it has taken a century and has cost their successors much sweat and blood to prove that they created a nation.

. . . The framers of the Constitution wisely spoke in general language and left to succeeding generations the task of applying that language to the unceasingly changing environment in which they would live . . . . Merely because a particular activity may not have existed when the Constitution was adopted, or because the framers could not have conceived of a particular method of transacting affairs, cannot mean that general language in the Constitution may not be applied to such a course of conduct. . . .

. . . I have sensed a second connotation of the phrase "living Constitution." . . . Embodied in its most naked form, it recently came to my attention in some language from a brief that had been filed in a United States District Court on behalf of state prisoners asserting that the conditions of their confinement offended the United States Constitution . . . :

> We are asking a great deal of the Court because other branches of government have abdicated their responsibility. . . . Prisoners are

* Published originally in 54 Tex.L.Rev. 693 (1976). Copyright © 1976 by the *Texas Law Review*. Reprinted by permission.

William H. Rehnquist has been an associate justice of the U.S. Supreme Court since 1971.

like other "discrete and insular" minorities for whom the Court must spread its protective umbrella because no other branch of government will do so. . . . This Court, as the voice and conscience of contemporary society, as the measure of the modern conception of human dignity, must declare that the [named prison] and all it represents offends the Constitution of the United States and will not be tolerated.

Here we have a living Constitution with a vengeance. Although the substitution of some other set of values for those which may be derived from the language and intent of the framers is not urged in so many words, that is surely the thrust of the message. Under this brief writer's version of the living Constitution, nonelected members of the federal judiciary may address themselves to a social problem simply because other branches of government have failed or refused to do so. These same judges, responsible to no constituency whatever, are nonetheless acclaimed as "the voice and conscience of contemporary society."

. . . [T]hose who have pondered the matter have always recognized that . . . judicial review has basically antidemocratic and antimajoritarian facets that require some justification in this Nation, which prides itself on being a self-governing representative democracy . . . .

. . . John Marshall's classic defense of judicial review [is set forth] in Marbury v. Madison [1803] . . . [W]hile it supports the Holmes version of the phrase "living Constitution," it also suggests some outer limits for the brief writer's version.

The ultimate source of authority in this Nation, Marshall said, is not Congress, not the states, not for that matter the Supreme Court. . . . The people are the ultimate source of authority; they have parceled out the authority that originally resided entirely with them by adopting the original Constitution and by later amending it . . . .

In addition, Marshall said that if the popular branches of government . . . are operating within the authority granted to them by the Constitution, their judgment and not that of the Court must obviously prevail. When these branches overstep the authority given them by the Constitution . . . or invade protected individual rights, and a constitutional challenge to their action is raised in a lawsuit brought in federal court, the Court must prefer the Constitution to the government acts.

John Marshall's justification for judicial review makes the provision for an independent federal judiciary not only understandable but also thoroughly desirable. Since the judges will be merely interpreting an instrument framed by the people, they should be detached and objective. A mere change in public opinion since the adoption of the Constitution, unaccompanied by a constitutional amendment, should not change the meaning of the Constitution. . . .

Clearly Marshall's explanation contains certain elements of either ingenuousness or ingeniousness. . . . The Constitution is in many of its parts obviously not a specifically worded document but one couched in general phraseology.   There is obviously wide room for honest difference of opinion over the meaning of general phrases in the Constitution; any particular Justice's decision when a question arises under one of these general phrases will depend to some extent on his own philosophy of constitutional law.   One may nevertheless concede all of these problems . . . yet feel that [Marshall's] justification for nonelected judges exercising the power of judicial review is the only one consistent with democratic philosophy of representative government. . . .

One senses no . . . connection with a popularly adopted constituent act in . . . the brief writer's version of the living Constitution. [It] seems instead to be based upon the proposition that federal judges, perhaps judges as a whole, have a role . . . , quite independent of popular will, to play in solving society's problems.   Once we have abandoned the idea that the authority of the courts to declare laws unconstitutional is somehow tied to the language of the Constitution that the people adopted, a judiciary exercising the power of judicial review appears in a quite different light.   Judges then are no longer the keepers of the covenant;   instead they are a small group of fortunately situated people with a roving commission to second-guess Congress, state legislatures, and state and federal administrative officers concerning what is best for the country.   Surely there is no justification for a third legislative branch in the federal government, and there is even less justification for a federal legislative branch's reviewing on a policy basis the laws enacted by the legislatures of the fifty states . . . .   If there is going to be a council of revision, it ought to have at least some connection with popular feeling.   Its members either ought to stand for reelection on occasion, or their terms should expire and they should be allowed to continue serving only if reappointed by a popularly elected Chief Executive and confirmed by a popularly elected Senate.

The brief writer's version of the living Constitution is seldom presented in its most naked form, but is instead usually dressed in more attractive garb.   The argument in favor of this approach generally begins with a sophisticated wink—why pretend that there is any ascertainable content to the general phrases of the Constitution as they are written since, after all, judges constantly disagree about their meaning?   . . . We all know the basis of Marshall's justification for judicial review, the argument runs, but it is necessary only to keep the window dressing in place.   Any sophisticated student of the subject knows that judges need not limit themselves to the intent of the framers, which is very difficult to determine in any event.   Because of the general language used in the Constitution, judges should not hesitate to use their authority to make the Constitution relevant and useful in solving the problems of modern society . . . .

At least three serious difficulties flaw the brief writer's version of the living Constitution.   First, it misconceives the nature of the Constitution, which was designed to enable the popularly elected branches of government, not the judicial branch, to keep the country abreast of the times. Second, the brief writer's version ignores the Supreme Court's disastrous experiences when in the past it embraced contemporary, fashionable notions of what a living Constitution should contain. Third, however socially desirable the goals sought to be advanced by the brief writer's version, advancing them through a free-wheeling, nonelected judiciary is quite unacceptable in a democratic society.

It seems to me that it is almost impossible, after reading the record of the Founding Fathers' debates in Philadelphia, to conclude that they intended the Constitution itself to suggest answers to the manifold problems that they knew would confront succeeding generations. The Constitution that they drafted was indeed intended to endure indefinitely, but the reason for this very well-founded hope was the general language by which national authority was granted to Congress and the Presidency. These two branches were to furnish the motive power within the federal system, which was in turn to coexist with the state governments. . . . Limitations were indeed placed upon both federal and state governments. . . . These limitations, however, were not themselves designed to solve the problems of the future, but were instead designed to make certain that the constituent branches, when *they* attempted to solve those problems, should not transgress these fundamental limitations.

. . . . [T]he Civil War Amendments [XIII–XV] were designed more as broad limitations on the authority of state governments. . . . To the extent that the language of these amendments is general, the courts are of course warranted in giving them an application coextensive with their language. Nevertheless, I greatly doubt that even . . . leaders of the radical Republicans in Congress would have thought any portion of the Civil War Amendments, except section five of the fourteenth amendment,[1] was designed to solve problems that society might confront a century later. I think they would have said that those amendments were designed to prevent from ever recurring abuses in which the states had engaged prior to that time.

The brief writer's version of the living Constitution, however, suggests that if the states' legislatures and governors, or Congress and the President, have not solved a particular social problem, then the federal court may act. I do not believe that this argument will withstand rational analysis. Even in the face of a conceded social evil, a reasonably competent and reasonably representative legislature may decide to do nothing. It may decide that the evil is not of sufficient magnitude to warrant any governmental intervention. It may decide that the financial cost of eliminating the evil is not worth the benefit which would result from its elimination. It may decide that the evils which might ensue from the proposed solution are worse than the evils which the solution would eliminate . . . .

The second difficulty with the brief writer's version of the living Constitution lies in its inattention to or rejection of the Supreme

---

1. "The Congress shall have power to enforce, by appropriate legislation, the provisions of this article." U.S.Const. amend. XIV, § 5. [Footnote by Justice Rehnquist.]

Court's historical experience gleaned from similar forays into problem solving . . . [e.g., Dred Scott v. Sandford (1857) and Lochner v. New York (1905)].

. . . [Such] experimentation with [this] expansive notion of a living Constitution has done the Court little credit . . . . [Some] appear to cleave nevertheless to the view that [these] experiments . . . ended in failure not because they sought to bring into the Constitution a principle that . . . was not there but because they sought to bring into the Constitution the *wrong* extraconstitutional principle. This school of thought appears to feel that while added protection for slave owners . . . and safeguards for businessmen . . . were not desirable, expansion of the protection accorded to individual liberties against the state or to the interests of "discrete and insular" minorities, such as prisoners, must stand on a quite different, more favored footing. To the extent, of course, that such a distinction may legitimately be derived from the Constitution itself, these latter principles do indeed stand on an entirely different footing. To the extent that one must, however, go beyond even a generously fair reading of the language and intent of that document in order to subsume these principles, . . . they are not really distinguishable from those espoused in *Dred Scott* and *Lochner.*

The third difficulty with the brief writer's notion of the living Constitution is that it seems to ignore totally the nature of political value judgments in a democratic society. If such a society adopts a constitution and incorporates in that constitution safeguards for individual liberty, these safeguards indeed do take on a generalized moral rightness or goodness. They assume a general social acceptance neither because of any intrinsic worth nor because of any unique origins in someones' idea of natural justice but instead simply because they have been incorporated in a constitution by the people. Within the limits of our Constitution, the representatives of the people in the legislative branches of the state and national governments enact laws. The laws that emerge after a typical political struggle in which various individual value judgments are debated likewise take on a form of moral goodness. . . . It is the fact of their enactment that gives them whatever moral claim they have upon us as a society, however, and not any independent virtue they may have in any particular citizen's own scale of values.

Beyond the Constitution and the laws in our society, there simply is no basis other than the individual conscience of the citizen that may serve as a platform for the launching of moral judgments. There is no conceivable way in which I can logically demonstrate to you that the judgments of my conscience are superior to the judgments of your conscience, and vice versa. Many of us necessarily feel strongly and deeply about our own moral judgments, but they remain only personal moral judgments until in some way given the sanction of law. . . .

. . . Representative government is predicated upon the idea that one who feels deeply upon a question as a matter of conscience will seek

out others of like view or will attempt to persuade others who do not
initially share that view. When adherents to the belief become sufficiently numerous, he will have the necessary armaments required in a
democratic society to press his views upon the elected representatives of
the people, and to have them embodied into positive law.

Should a person fail to persuade the legislature, or should he feel
that a legislative victory would be insufficient because of its potential
for future reversal, he may seek to run the more difficult gauntlet of
amending the Constitution. . . .

I know of no other method compatible with political theory basic to
democratic society by which one's own conscientious belief may be
translated into positive law and thereby obtain the only general moral
imprimatur permissible in a pluralistic, democratic society. It is always time consuming, frequently difficult, and not infrequently impossible to run successfully the legislative gauntlet. . . . It is even more
difficult . . . to succeed in having such a value judgment embodied in
the Constitution. All of these burdens and difficulties are entirely
consistent with the notion of a democratic society. It should not be
easy for any one individual or group of individuals to impose by law
their value judgments upon fellow citizens who may disagree with those
judgments. Indeed, it should not be easier just because the individual
in question is a judge. . . .

The brief writer's version of the living Constitution, in the last
analysis, is a formula for an end run around popular government. To
the extent that it makes possible an individual's persuading one or
more appointed federal judges to impose on other individuals a rule of
conduct that the popularly elected branches of government would not
have enacted and the voters have not and would not have embodied in
the Constitution, the brief writer's version of the living Constitution is
genuinely corrosive of the fundamental values of our democratic society.

**"The constitutional theory on which our government
rests is not a simple majoritarian theory. The Constitution . . . is designed to protect individual citizens and
groups against certain decisions that a majority of citizens might want to make."**

TAKING RIGHTS SERIOUSLY: CONSTITUTIONAL CASES *
Ronald Dworkin.

1

. . . [I]n what follows I shall use the name "Nixon" to refer, not
to Nixon, but to any politician holding the set of attitudes about the

------

* Abridged by permission of the author and publishers from *Taking Rights Seriously* by
Ronald Dworkin, Cambridge, Mass.: Harvard University Press, Copyright © 1972, 1977 by
Ronald Dworkin. Ronald Dworkin, an American lawyer, is University Professor of
Jurisprudence, University of Oxford, and Professor of Law, New York University.

Supreme Court that he made explicit in his political campaigns. There was, fortunately, only one real Nixon, but there are, in the special sense in which I use the name, many Nixons.

What can be the basis of this composite Nixon's opposition to the controversial decisions of the Warren Court? He cannot object to these decisions simply because they went beyond prior law, or say that the Supreme Court must never change its mind. Indeed the Burger Court itself seems intent on limiting the liberal decisions of the Warren Court. . . . The Constitution's guarantee of "equal protection of the laws", it is true, does not in plain words determine that "separate but equal" school facilities are unconstitutional, or that segregation was so unjust that heroic measures are required to undo its effects. But neither does it provide that as a matter of constitutional law the Court would be wrong to reach these conclusions. It leaves these issues to the Court's judgment, and the Court would have made law just as much if it had, for example, refused to hold [segregation] unconstitutional. . . .

So we must search further to find a theoretical basis for Nixon's position. . . .

2

The constitutional theory on which our government rests is not a simple majoritarian theory. The Constitution, and particularly the Bill of Rights, is designed to protect individual citizens and groups against certain decisions that a majority of citizens might want to make, even when that majority acts in what it takes to be the general or common interest. Some of these constitutional restraints take the form of fairly precise rules . . . . But other constraints take the form of what are often called "vague" standards, for example, the provision that the government shall not deny men due process of law, or equal protection of the laws.

This interference with democratic practice requires a justification. The draftsmen of the Constitution assumed that these restraints could be justified by appeal to moral rights which individuals possess against the majority, and which the constitutional provisions, both "vague" and precise, might be said to recognize and protect.

The "vague" standards were chosen deliberately . . . in place of the more specific and limited rules that they might have enacted. But their decision . . . has caused a great deal of legal and political controversy, because even reasonable men of good will differ when they try to elaborate, for example, the moral rights that the due process clause or the equal protection clause brings into the law. They also differ when they try to apply these rights, however defined, to complex matters of political administration. . . .

The practice has developed of referring to a "strict" and a "liberal" side to these controversies, so that the Supreme Court might be said to have taken the "liberal" side in the segregation cases and its critics the "strict" side. Nixon has this distinction in mind when he calls himself a "strict constructionist". But the distinction is in fact confusing, because it runs together two different issues that must be separated. Any case that arises under the "vague" constitutional guarantees can be seen as posing two questions: (1) Which decision is required by strict, that is to say faithful, adherence to the text of the Constitution or to the intention of those who adopted that text? (2) Which decision is required by a political philosophy that takes a strict, that is to say narrow, view of the moral rights that individuals have against society? Once these questions are distinguished, it is plain that they may have different answers. The text of the First Amendment, for example, says that Congress shall make *no* law abridging the freedom of speech, but a narrow view of individual rights would permit many such laws. .   .   .

In the case of the "vague" provisions, however, like the due process and equal protection clauses, lawyers have run the two questions together because they have relied, largely without recognizing it, on a theory of meaning that might be put this way: If the framers of the Constitution used vague language .   .   . , then what they "said" or "meant" is limited to the instances of official action that they had in mind as violations, or, at least, to those instances that they would have thought were violations if they had had them in mind. .   .   .

This theory makes a strict interpretation of the text yield a narrow view of constitutional rights, because it limits such rights to those recognized by a limited group of people at a fixed date of history. It forces those who favor a more liberal set of rights to concede that they are departing from strict legal authority, a departure they must then seek to justify by appealing only to the desirability of the results they reach.

But the theory of meaning on which this argument depends is far too crude; it ignores a distinction that philosophers have made but lawyers have not yet appreciated. Suppose I tell my children simply that I expect them not to treat others unfairly. I no doubt have in mind examples of the conduct I mean to discourage, but I would not accept that my "meaning" was limited to these examples, for two reasons. First I would expect my children to apply my instructions to situations I had not and could not have thought about. Second, I stand ready to admit that some particular act I had thought was fair when I spoke was in fact unfair, or vice versa, if one of my children is able to convince me of that later; in that case I should want to say that my instructions covered the case he cited, not that I had changed my instructions. I might say that I meant the family to be guided by the *concept* of fairness, not by any specific *conception* of fairness I might have had in mind.

This is a crucial distinction .   .   .   .   Suppose a group believes in common that acts may suffer from a special moral defect which they call unfairness, and which consists in a wrongful division of benefits and burdens, or a wrongful attribution of praise or blame. Suppose also that they agree on a great number of standard cases of unfairness and use these as benchmarks against which to test other, more controversial cases. In that case, the group has a concept of unfairness, and its members may appeal to that concept in moral instruction or argument. But members of that group may nevertheless differ over a large number of these controversial cases, in a way that suggests that each either has or acts on a different theory of *why* the standard cases are acts of unfairness. They may differ, that is, on which more fundamental principles must be relied upon to show that a particular division or attribution is unfair. In that case, the members have different conceptions of fairness.

If so, then members of this community who give instructions or set standards in the name of fairness may be doing two different things. First they may be appealing to the concept of fairness, simply by instructing others to act fairly; in this case they charge those whom they instruct with the responsibility of developing and applying their own conception of fairness as controversial cases arise. That is not the same thing, of course, as granting them a discretion to act as they like; it sets a standard which they must try—and may fail—to meet . . . . The man who appeals to the concept in this way may have his own conception . . . but he holds this conception only as his own theory of how the standard he set must be met, so that when he changes his theory he has not changed that standard.

On the other hand, the members may be laying down a particular conception of fairness; I would have done this, for example, if I had listed my wishes with respect to controversial examples or if, even less likely, I had specified some controversial and explicit theory of fairness. . . . The difference is a difference not just in the *detail* of the instructions given but in the *kind* of instructions given. When I appeal to the concept of fairness I appeal to what fairness means, and I give my views on that issue no special standing. When I lay down a conception of fairness, I lay down what I mean by fairness, and my view is therefore the heart of the matter. . . .

Once this distinction is made it seems obvious that we must take what I have been calling "vague" constitutional clauses as representing appeals to the concepts they employ, like legality, equality, and cruelty. . . .

Those who ignore the distinction between concepts and conceptions, but who believe [for example] that the Court ought to make a fresh determination of whether the death penalty is cruel, are forced to argue in a vulnerable way. They say that ideas of cruelty change over time, and that the Court must be free to reject out-of-date conceptions; this suggests that the Court must change what the Constitution enacted. But in fact the Court can enforce what the Constitution says only by making up its own mind about what is cruel . . . . If those who enacted the broad clauses had meant to lay down particular conceptions, they would have found the sort of language conventionally used to do this, that is, they would have offered particular theories of the concepts in question.

Indeed the very practice of calling these clauses "vague" . . . can now be seen to involve a mistake. The clauses are vague only if we take them to be botched or incomplete or schematic attempts to lay down particular conceptions. If we take them as appeals to moral concepts they could not be made more precise by being more detailed.

The confusion I mentioned between the two senses of "strict" construction is therefore very misleading indeed. If courts try to be faithful to the text of the Constitution, they will for that very reason be forced to decide between competing conceptions of political morality. So it is wrong to attack the Warren Court, for example, on the ground that it failed to treat the Constitution as a binding text. On the contrary, if we wish to treat fidelity to that text as an overriding requirement of constitutional interpretation, then it is the conservative critics of the Warren Court who are at fault, because their philosophy ignores the direction to face issues of moral principle that the logic of the text demands.

I put the matter in a guarded way because we may not want to accept fidelity to the spirit of the text as an overriding principle of constitutional adjudication. It may be more important for courts to decide constitutional cases in a manner that respects the judgments of other institutions of government, for example. Or it may be more important for courts to protect established legal doctrines, so that citizens and the government can have confidence that the courts will hold to what they have said before. But it is crucial to recognize that these other policies compete with the principle that the Constitution is the fundamental and imperative source of constitutional law. They are not, as the "strict constructionists" suppose, simply consequences of that principle.

3

Once the matter is put in this light . . . we are able to assess these competing claims of policy, free from the confusion imposed by the popular notion of "strict construction". For this purpose I want now to compare and contrast two very general philosophies of how the courts should decide difficult or controversial constitutional issues. I shall call these two philosophies by the names they are given in the legal literature—the programs of "judicial activism" and "judicial restraint"—though it will be plain that these names are in certain ways misleading.

The program of judicial activism holds that courts should accept the directions of the so-called vague constitutional provisions in the spirit I described. . . . They should work out principles of legality, equality, and the rest, revise these principles from time to time in the light of what seems to the Court fresh moral insight, and judge the acts of Congress, the states, and the President accordingly . . . . .

The program of judicial restraint, on the contrary, argues that courts should allow the decisions of other branches of government to stand, even when they offend the judges' own sense of the principles required by the broad constitutional doctrines, except when these decisions are so offensive to political morality that they would violate the provisions on any plausible interpretation, or, perhaps, when a contrary decision is required by clear precedent. . . .

The Supreme Court followed the policy of activism rather than restraint in cases like the segregation cases because the words of the equal protection clause left it open whether the various educational practices of the states concerned should be taken to violate the Constitution, no clear precedent held that they did, and reasonable men might differ on the moral issues involved. . . . But the program of restraint would not always act to provide decisions that would please political conservatives. In the early days of the New Deal . . . it was the liberals who objected to Court decisions that struck down acts of Congress in the name of the due process clause.

It may seem, therefore, that if Nixon has a legal theory it depends crucially on some theory of judicial restraint. We must now, however, notice a distinction between two forms of judicial restraint, for there are two different, and indeed incompatible, grounds on which that policy might be based.

The first is a theory of political *skepticism* that might be described in this way. The policy of judicial activism presupposes a certain objectivity of moral principle; in particular it presupposes that citizens do have certain moral rights against the state, like a moral right to equality of public education or to fair treatment by the police. Only if such moral rights exist in some sense can activism be justified as a program based on something beyond the judge's personal preferences. The skeptical theory attacks activism at its roots; it argues that in fact individuals have no such moral rights against the state. They have only such *legal* rights as the Constitution grants them, and these are limited to the plain and uncontroversial violations of public morality that the framers must have had actually in mind, or that have since been established in a line of precedent.

The alternative ground of a program of restraint is a theory of judicial *deference*. Contrary to the skeptical theory, this assumes that citizens do have moral rights against the state beyond what the law expressly grants them, but it points out that the character and strength of these rights are debatable and argues that political institutions other than courts are responsible for deciding which rights are to be recognized.

This is an important distinction, even though the literature of constitutional law does not draw it with any clarity. The skeptical theory and the theory of deference differ dramatically in the kind of justification they assume, and in their implications for the more general moral theories of the men who profess to hold them. These theories are so different that most American politicians can consistently accept the second, but not the first.

A skeptic takes the view . . . that men have no moral rights against the state and only such legal rights as the law expressly provides. But what does this mean, and what sort of argument might the skeptic make for his view? . . . . I shall rely, in trying to answer

these questions, on a low-keyed theory of moral rights against the state.
. . . Under that theory, a man has a moral right against the state if
for some reason the state would do wrong to treat him in a certain way,
even though it would be in the general interest to do so. . . .

I want to say a word about the virtues of this way of looking at
moral rights against the state. . . . [I]t simply shows a claim of right
to be a special, in the sense of a restricted, sort of judgment about what
is right or wrong for governments to do.

Moreover, this way of looking at rights avoids some of the notorious
puzzles associated with the concept. It allows us to say, with no sense
of strangeness, that rights may vary in strength and character from
case to case, and from point to point in history. If we think of rights as
things, these metamorphoses seem strange, but we are used to the idea
that moral judgments about what it is right or wrong to do are complex
and are affected by considerations that are relative and that change.

The skeptic who wants to argue against the very possibility of
rights against the state of this sort has a difficult brief. He must rely, I
think, on one of three general positions: (a) He might display a more
pervasive moral skepticism, which holds that even to speak of an act
being morally right or wrong makes no sense. . . . (b) He might hold
a stark form of utilitarianism, which assumes that the only reason we
ever have for regarding an act as right or wrong is its impact on the
general interest. Under that theory, to say that busing may be morally
required even though it does not benefit the community generally
would be inconsistent. (c) He might accept some form of totalitarian
theory, which merges the interest of the individual in the good of the
general community, and so denies that the two can conflict.

Very few American politicians would be able to accept any of these
three grounds. . . .

I do not want to suggest, however, that no one would in fact argue
for judicial restraint on grounds of skepticism; on the contrary, some of
the best known advocates of restraint have pitched their arguments
entirely on skeptical grounds. In 1957, for example, the great judge
Learned Hand . . . argued for judicial restraint, and said that the
Supreme Court had done wrong to declare school segregation illegal.
. . . It is wrong to suppose, he said, that claims about moral rights
express anything more than the speakers' preferences. If the Supreme
Court justifies its decisions by making such claims, rather than by
relying on positive law, it is usurping the place of the legislature, for
the job of the legislature, representing the majority, is to decide whose
preferences shall govern.

This simple appeal to democracy is successful if one accepts the
skeptical premise. . . . But a very different, and much more vulnerable, argument from democracy is needed to support judicial restraint if
it is based not on skepticism but on deference, as I shall try to show.

4

. . . [A] theory of restraint based . . . on deference [holds] that
courts ought not to decide controversial issues of political morality

because they ought to leave such decisions to other departments of government. . . .

There is one very popular argument in favor of the policy of deference, which might be called the argument from democracy. It is at least debatable, according to this argument, whether a sound conception of equality forbids segregated education or requires measures like busing to break it down. Who ought to decide these debatable issues of moral and political theory? Should it be a majority of a court in Washington, whose members are appointed for life and are not politically responsible to the public whose lives will be affected by the decision? Or should it be the elected and responsible state or national legislators? A democrat, so this argument supposes, can accept only the second answer.

But the argument from democracy is weaker than it might first appear. The argument assumes, for one thing, that state legislatures are in fact responsible to the people in the way that democratic theory assumes. But in all the states, though in different degrees and for different reasons, that is not the case. . . . I want to pass that point, however, because it does not so much undermine the argument from democracy as call for more democracy. . . . I want to fix attention on the issue of whether the appeal to democracy in this respect is even right in principle.

The argument assumes that in a democracy all unsettled issues, including issues of moral and political principle, must be resolved only by institutions that are politically responsible in the way that courts are not. Why should we accept that view of democracy? To say that that is what democracy means does no good, because it is wrong to suppose that the word, as a word, has anything like so precise a meaning. Even if it did, we should then have to rephrase our question to ask why we should have democracy, if we assume that is what it means. Nor is it better to say that that view of democracy is established in the American Constitution, or so entrenched in our political tradition that we are committed to it. We cannot argue that the Constitution, which provides no rule limiting judicial review to clear cases, establishes a theory of democracy that excludes wider review, nor can we say that our courts have in fact consistently accepted such a restriction. . . .

So the argument from democracy is not an argument to which we are committed either by our words or our past. We must accept it, if at all, on the strength of its own logic. In order to examine the arguments more closely, however, we must make a further distinction. The argument . . . might be continued in two different ways: one might argue that judicial deference is required because democratic institutions, like legislatures, are in fact likely to make *sounder* decisions than courts . . . about the nature of an individual's moral right against the state.

Or one might argue that it is for some reason *fairer* that a democratic institution rather than a court should decide such issues.

. . . The distinction between these two arguments would make no sense to a skeptic, who would not admit that someone could do a better or worse job at identifying moral rights against the state, any more than someone could do a better or worse job of identifying ghosts. But a lawyer who believes in judicial deference rather than skepticism must acknowledge the distinction. . . .

I shall start with the second argument, that legislatures and other democratic institutions have some special title to make constitutional decisions. . . . One might say that the nature of this title is obvious, because it is always fairer to allow a majority to decide any issue than a minority. But that . . . ignores the fact that decisions about rights against the majority are not issues that in fairness ought to be left to the majority. Constitutionalism—the theory that the majority must be restrained to protect individual rights—may be a good or bad political theory, but the United States has adopted that theory, and to make the majority judge in its own cause seems inconsistent and unjust. So principles of fairness seem to speak against, not for, the argument from democracy.

Chief Justice Marshall recognized this . . . in Marbury v. Madison. . . . He argued that since the Constitution provides that the Constitution shall be the supreme law of the land, the courts . . . must have power to declare statutes void that offend that Constitution. Many legal scholars regard his argument as a *non sequitur,* because, they say, although constitutional constraints are part of the law, the courts, rather than the legislature itself, have not necessarily been given authority to decide whether in particular cases that law has been violated. But the argument is not a *non sequitur* if we take the principle that no man should be judge in his own cause to be so fundamental a part of the idea of legality that Marshall would have been entitled to disregard it only if the Constitution had expressly denied judicial review.

Some might object that it is simple-minded to say that a policy of deference leaves the majority to judge its own cause. Political decisions are made, in the United States, not by one stable majority but by many different political institutions each representing a different constituency which itself changes its composition over time. The decision of one branch of government may well be reviewed by another branch that is also politically responsible, but to a larger or different constituency. . . .

But this objection is itself too glib, because it ignores the special character of disputes about individual moral rights as distinct from other kinds of political disputes. Different institutions do have different constituencies when, for example, labor or trade or welfare issues are involved. . . . But this is not generally the case when individual constitutional rights, like the rights of accused criminals, are at issue. It has been typical of these disputes that the interests of those in political control of the various institutions of the government have been both homogeneous and hostile. Indeed that is why political theorists have conceived of constitutional rights as rights against the 'state' or the 'majority' as such, rather than against any particular body or branch of government. . . .

It does seem fair to say, therefore, that the argument from democracy asks that those in political power be invited to be the sole judge of their own decisions. . . . That is not a final proof that a policy of judicial activism is superior to a program of deference. . . . But the point does undermine the argument that the majority, in fairness, must be allowed to decide the limits of its own power.

We must therefore turn to the other continuation of the argument from democracy, which holds that democratic institutions, like legislatures, are likely to reach *sounder* results about the moral rights of individuals than would courts. In 1969 the late Professor Alexander Bickel . . . argued for the program of judicial restraint in a novel and ingenious way. He allowed himself to suppose, for purposes of argument, that the Warren Court's program of activism could be justified if in fact it produced desirable results. He appeared, therefore, to be testing the policy of activism on its own grounds, because he took activism to be precisely the claim that the courts have the moral right to improve the future, whatever legal theory may say. . . . Bickel accepted it, as least provisionally, but he argued that activism fails its own test.

The future that the Warren Court sought has already begun not to work, Bickel said. The philosophy of racial integration it adopted was too crude, for example, and has already been rejected by the more imaginative leaders of the black community. Its thesis of simple and radical equality has proved unworkable in many other ways as well; its simple formula for one-man-one-vote for passing on the fairness of election districting, for instance, has produced neither sense nor fairness.

Why should a radical Court that aims at improving society fail even on its own terms? Bickel has this answer: Courts, including the Supreme Court, must decide blocks of cases on principle, rather than responding in a piecemeal way to a shifting set of political pressures. They must do so not simply because their institutional morality requires it, but because their institutional structure provides no means by which they might gauge political forces even if they wanted to. But government by principle is an inefficient and in the long run fatal form of government, no matter how able and honest the statesmen who try to administer it. For there is a limit to the complexity that any principle can contain and remain a recognizable principle, and this limit falls short of the complexity of social organization.

The Supreme Court's reapportionment decisions, in Bickel's view, were not mistaken just because the Court chose the wrong principle. One-man-one-vote is too simple, but the Court could not have found a better, more sophisticated principle that would have served as a successful test for election districting across the country, or across the years, because successful districting depends upon accommodation with thousands of facts of political life, and can be reached, if at all, only by the chaotic and unprincipled development of history. Judicial activism cannot work as well as government by the more-or-less democratic institutions, not because democracy is required by principle, but, on the contrary, because democracy works without principle, forming institutions and compromises as a river forms a bed on its way to the sea.

What are we to make of Bickel's argument? His account of recent history can be, and has been, challenged. It is by no means plain, certainly not yet, that racial integration will fail as a long-term strategy; and he is wrong if he thinks that black Americans, of whom more still belong to the NAACP than to more militant organizations, have rejected it. No doubt the nation's sense of how to deal with the curse of racism swings back and forth as the complexity and size of the problem become more apparent, but Bickel may have written at a high point of one arc of the pendulum.

He is also wrong to judge the Supreme Court's effect on history as if the Court were the only institution at work, or to suppose that if the Court's goal has not been achieved the country is worse off than if it had not tried. . . . Nor do we have much basis for supposing that the racial situation in America would now be more satisfactory, on balance, if the Court had not intervened, in 1954 and later, in the way that it did.

But there is a very different, and for my purpose much more important, objection to take to Bickel's theory. His theory is novel because it appears to concede an issue of principle to judicial activism, namely, that the Court is entitled to intervene if its intervention produces socially desirable results. But the concession is an illusion, because his sense of what is socially desirable is inconsistent with the presupposition of activism that individuals have moral rights against the state. In fact, Bickel's argument cannot succeed, even if we grant his facts and his view of history, except on a basis of a skepticism about rights as profound as Learned Hand's.

I presented Bickel's theory as an example of one form of the argument from democracy, the argument that since men disagree about rights, it is safer to leave the final decision about rights to the political process, safer in the sense that the results are likely to be sounder. Bickel suggests a reason why the political process is safer. He argues that the endurance of a political settlement about rights is some evidence of the political morality of that settlement. He argues that this evidence is better than the sorts of argument from principle that judges might deploy if the decision were left to them. . . .

. . . [Bickel] argues that the organic political process will secure the genuine rights of men more certainly if it is not hindered by the artificial and rationalistic intrusion of the courts. On this view, the rights of blacks, suspects, and atheists will emerge through the process of political institutions responding to political pressures in the normal way. If a claim of right cannot succeed in this way, then for that reason it is, or in any event it is likely to be, an improper claim or right. But this bizarre proposition is only a disguised form of the skeptical point that there are in fact no rights against the state.

Perhaps, as Burke and his modern followers argue, a society will produce the institutions that best suit it only by evolution and never by radical reform. But rights against the state are claims that, if accepted, require society to settle for institutions that may not suit it so comfortably. The nerve of a claim of right . . . is that an individual is entitled to protection against the majority even at the cost of the general interest. Of course the comfort of the majority will require some accommodation for minorities but only to the extent necessary to preserve order; and that is usually an accommodation that falls short of recognizing their rights.

Indeed the suggestion that rights can be demonstrated by a process of history rather than by an appeal to principle shows either a confusion or no real concern about what rights are. A claim of right presupposes a moral argument and can be established in no other way. Bickel paints the judicial activists . . . as eighteenth-century philosophers who appeal to principle because they hold the optimistic view that a blueprint may be cut for progress. But this picture confuses two grounds for the appeal to principle and reform, and two senses of progress.

It is one thing to appeal to moral principle in the silly faith that ethics as well as economics moves by an invisible hand, so that individual rights and the general good will coalesce, and law based on principle will move the nation to a frictionless utopia . . . . But it is quite another matter to appeal to principle *as* principle, to show, for example, that it is unjust to force black children to take their public education in black schools, even if a great many people *will* be worse off if the state adopt the measures needed to prevent this.

This is a different version of progress. It is moral progress, and though history may show how difficult it is to decide where moral progress lies, and how difficult to persuade others once one has decided, it cannot follow from this that those who govern us have no responsibility to face that decision or to attempt that persuasion.

5

This has been a complex argument, and I want to summarize it. Our constitutional system rests on a particular moral theory, namely, that men have moral rights against the state. The difficult clauses of the Bill of Rights, like the due process and equal protection clauses, must be understood as appealing to moral concepts rather than laying down particular conceptions; therefore a court that undertakes the burden of applying these clauses fully as law must be an activist court, in the sense that it must be prepared to frame and answer questions of political morality.

It may be necessary to compromise that activist posture to some extent, either for practical reasons or for competing reasons of principle. But Nixon's public statements about the Supreme Court suggest that the activist policy must be abandoned altogether, and not merely compromised, for powerful reasons of principle. If we try to state these reasons of principle, we find that they are inconsistent with the assumption of a constitutional system, either because they leave the majority to judge its own cause, or because they rest on a skepticism about moral rights that neither Nixon nor most American politicians can consistently embrace.

So Nixon's jurisprudence is a pretense and no genuine theory at all . . . .

The academic debate about . . . judicial review must, however, have contributed to Nixon's confusion. The failure to draw the distinctions I have described . . . has posed a false choice between judicial activism as the program of moral crusade and judicial restraint as the program of legality . . . .

Neither [choice] forces lawyers to face the . . . issue of what moral rights an individual has against the state. The activists rest their case, when they argue it at all, on the assumption either that their social goals are self-evidently good or that they will in the long run work for the benefit of everybody . . . . Those who want restraint argue that some principle of legality protects constitutional lawyers from facing any moral issues at all.

Constitutional law can make no genuine advance until it isolates the problem of rights against the state and makes that problem part of its own agenda. That argues for a fusion of constitutional law and moral theory, a connection that, incredibly, has yet to take place . . . .

III

Who May Authoritatively Interpret the Constitution?

The materials in this Part focus on the interrogative "WHO shall interpret the Constitution?" The basic inquiry and its subqueries are both more subtle and complex than they may at first appear. At one level, it is a plain, if sometimes painful, fact of American political life that all public officials, state and federal, from presidents, senators, and representatives, to governors, state legislators, local district attorneys and police, may often have to interpret the Constitution. Deciding what policies government may legitimately pursue, how—or whether—to enforce a law, when to arrest and search a suspect, all create problems of constitutional interpretation.

Even if one were to concede what is not at all self-evident, that judges are the ultimate constitutional interpreters, if government had to stop and await a judicial decision every time a constitutional problem arose, we would have only grand anarchy. Every public official, after all, takes an oath to uphold the Constitution of the United States, to guide his or her actions by the commands of the Constitution. And, as we have seen, those commands are sometimes so general as to cry out for interpretation.

That oath is also one that millions of private citizens have taken. Moreover, the Preamble lodges responsibility for the Constitution in "the people of the United States." Thus, it is not far fetched to argue that, as its ultimate source of authority, "the people" can interpret the Constitution. Indeed, one could plausibly argue, they have the duty to do so, to consider carefully, when they cast their ballots, candidates' records and promises about how they will interpret the Constitution. Private citizens also have the same right and obligation when they speak out on political issues, lobby elected representatives, or utilize other means of advocating or opposing public policies.

Thus the central problem we face in this Part is not simply WHO shall interpret the Constitution, for the answer to that question is obvious: "Some of us most of the time, most of us some of the time." Rather, here we confront questions about the extent to which—as well as the circumstances under which—some governmental institutions should defer to the judgment of other institutions (and/or to those other institutions' claims to speak "for the people"), and, in cases of conflict, which institution's interpretation should prevail. In effect, this Part of the book searches not only for authoritative constitutional interpreters, but also for the relationships among those interpreters.

How an interpreter views the political system affects the direction he or she takes in that search. One who sees the Constitution as a compact among the states is likely to find answers at the state level; for, logically, it would be the parties to the compact who should determine its meaning. On the other hand, one who sees the Constitution as an agreement among the entire American people is likely to search at the national level, for the national government would be the direct creature of the people as a whole rather than of separate, sovereign states.

So, too, one who looks on the Constitution as establishing a representative democracy is apt to be more sympathetic toward elected officials as the ultimate interpreters. Conversely, as one puts more stress on constitutionalism, one is more likely to prefer the ultimate interpreters to be more removed from direct popular influences.

We have divided this Part into two chapters. Chapter 6 addresses the question of WHO should provide authoritative constitutional interpretation *within* the national system of government. Chapter 7 examines the question of an ultimate interpreter *between* the states and the national government. Cases and other materials in these two chapters also underline the additional and ever-present tensions between democracy and constitutionalism. And always part of any effort to answer the question of WHO must be the equally vexing question of WHAT is the Constitution that must be interpreted. The variety of responses to these inquiries points to continuing debates rather than to neatly packaged answers.

6

Who May Authoritatively Interpret the Constitution for the National Government?

The plain words of the constitutional document convey indirect but important messages about WHO shall interpret. In conferring on Congress authority to make "all laws necessary and proper" to carry out powers delegated to the national government, Article I, § 8 clearly implies that Congress (with the participation of the President since he is part of the legislative process) shall make judgments about the Constitution's meaning, for what laws are "proper" under the Constitution may be far from obvious. There are similar terms in the Thirteenth, Fourteenth, Fifteenth, Nineteenth, Twenty-fourth, and Twenty-sixth amendments, authorizing Congress to enact "appropriate legislation" to carry out the amendments' provisions.

In specifying the exact wording of the oath the President shall take to "preserve, protect, and defend the Constitution," Article II imposes on the chief executive additional responsibility for constitutional interpretation. He could hardly be expected to "preserve, protect, and defend" the Constitution without interpreting it to determine how or if it was being threatened. By extending "the judicial power" "to all cases, in law and equity, arising under this Constitution," Article III brings the courts into the processes of constitutional interpretation, as judges before and since Chief Justice John Marshall have modestly acknowledged.

These clauses place some interpretive authority in each of the three branches of national government. There is not, however, a single word about whose views should prevail in case of conflict among them. Jefferson's response was that the people should judge and that they could express their will by means of a national convention. As he explained to William Johnson, Marshall's colleague on the Court: "The ultimate arbiter is the people of the Union, assembled by their deputies in convention, at the call of Congress, or of two-thirds of the States." [1] But what happened in Philadelphia in 1787, when the convention the Continental Congress summoned to propose amendments to the Articles of Confederation drafted an

---

1. June 12, 1823; Andrew A. Lipscomb, ed., *Writings of Thomas Jefferson* (Washington, D.C.: Thomas Jefferson Memorial Association, 1903), XV, 451.

entirely new constitutional document, has not encouraged Congress to call such a body back into session.

Moreover, it would take some time and much deliberation to choose delegates to a national convention; additional time for them to debate and propose amendments, if, indeed, those were all the convention proposed, to the states; and yet more time for the states to vote on the proposals. For some crises, this solution would be too slow and cumbersome, even assuming senators and representatives were willing to accept the risks to their own careers and to the larger political system such a convention would entail.

The ballot box provides an institutional means for direct popular interpretation of the Constitution. Citizens are free—one might argue, are obliged—to judge candidates by the way they have or indicate they will interpret the Constitution. One can look at the election of 1936, in which the people of 46 of the then 48 states voted for Franklin Roosevelt and his New Deal despite the Supreme Court's decisions that most of his efforts to regulate the economy were unconstitutional, as a sort of constitutional referendum. Certainly it had that effect on the Court, for, six weeks after the election, the justices began to yield to the President's (and Congress') constitutional views. "Looking back," one member of the Old Court said fourteen years later, "it is difficult to see how the Court could have resisted the popular urge for uniform standards throughout the country—for what in effect was a unified economy." [2]

This example is dramatic, but one searches in vain for a close parallel. The most likely candidate would be the presidential election of 1940, in which the electorate decided that the tradition against a third term was no longer valid. But that decision was short-lived, for the Twenty-second Amendment, adopted in 1951, formally reimposed the old "unwritten" limit. In any event, not many voters often, consciously, or systematically utilize their ballots to express constitutional interpretations; and there is precious little evidence that many take the trouble even to formulate such views. This omission leaves officials to resolve most of their conflicts among themselves.

I. WHO IS THE ULTIMATE INTERPRETER?

Three theories compete for the honor of answering the question of WHO is the ultimate interpreter: judicial supremacy, legislative supremacy, and departmentalism. All, however, even judicial supremacy, draw heavily on democratic theory; and, in a sense, much of the debate rests on the possibility of an appeal to "the people," though seldom is that basis so clear as it was in Jefferson's plan to settle constitutional disputes by calling national conventions.

Even Hamilton in *Federalist* No. 78 (reprinted below, p. 195) rested his argument for judicial review—which, though not the same

---

2. Owen J. Roberts, *The Court and the Constitution* (Cambridge, Mass.: Harvard University Press, 1951), p. 61.

as judicial supremacy, forms a necessary basis for such a thesis—on democratic theory: Where "the will of the legislature, declared in its statutes, stands in opposition to that of the people, declared in the Constitution, the judges ought to be governed by the latter rather than the former." Such a power, he added, does not imply that judges are superior to legislators but that "the power of the people is superior to both."

A. Judicial Supremacy

Judicial supremacy is the theory most familiar to Americans. One justification for it rests on the sort of textual and functional grounds John Marshall used in Marbury v. Madison (1803; reprinted below, p. 211) for judicial review. The essential argument is: (1) Article VI says the Constitution is law; (2) "it is emphatically the province and duty of the judicial department to say what the law is"; and thus (3) judicial review must be an integral part of the political system. Then follows a smooth, though long, step from judicial review—the authority of a court, when deciding cases, to refuse to give force to an act of a coordinate branch of government—to judicial supremacy, the obligation of coordinate officials not only to obey that ruling but to follow its reasoning in future deliberations. Justice Joseph Story gladly took this step, but in his role as commentator and not as judge:

> Now, it is the proper function of the judicial department to inter-pret laws, and by the very terms of the constitution to interpret the supreme law. Its interpretation, then, becomes obligatory and conclusive upon all the departments of the federal government, and upon the whole people, so far as their rights and duties are derived from, or affected by that constitution.[3]

Story reinforced his conclusion with the claim that "[w]e find the power to construe the constitution expressly confined to the judicial department, without any limitation or qualification, as to its conclusiveness." [4]

Before accepting Story's conclusion, one should recognize that: (1) he did not point to any place in the constitutional text that "expressly confined" constitutional interpretation to the judiciary—indeed, we just saw the text's wording negates such a claim; (2) judicial review says nothing about the obligation of other branches of government either to obey that decision or to follow its reasoning in the future; and (3) Marshall himself did not draw Story's conclusion, though one might well argue that he approved of it and it is implicit in Marbury.

The practical need for an umpire provides a second and quite different justification for judicial supremacy. If there is a dispute

---

3. *Commentaries on the Constitution of the United States* (Boston: Hilliard, Gray, 1833), I, Bk. III, § 383.

4. Ibid., § 385.

among the branches of government, there must exist somewhere, so the argument goes, a final judge. As Story put it, "to produce uniformity of interpretation, and to preserve the constitution, as a perpetual bond of union, a supreme arbiter or authority of construing is, if not absolutely indispensable, at least of the highest practical utility and importance."[5] One might agree on the need for an umpire but disagree, as Jefferson did, that the judiciary best fulfills that function. One might also take the position that a system of fractured, separated, and shared powers is incongruent with the notion of a final umpire.[6]

The matter of institutional competence provides a third justification for judicial supremacy. The administrative and legislative processes, the argument runs, do not provide time for interpreters to research and engage in intellectual debate about underlying constitutional issues or settings that encourage dispassionate investigation and coherent, consistent, and systematic analysis.[7] This reasoning permeates Story's *Commentaries on the Constitution*. Charles Evans Hughes put it more bluntly a century later: "It is only from the Supreme Court that we can obtain a sane, well-ordered interpretation of the Constitution."[8]

There is ample room for reasonable doubt here. Many debates in Congress—see especially that on the Judiciary Act of 1802, reprinted below, p. 203—stand up well against the most sophisticated analyses by the justices. As for consistency and coherence, the Court has modified and reversed its interpretations sufficiently often that studying the malleable and sometimes swiftly changing substance of judge-made constitutional law is a full time profession.

There is a fourth, a constitutionalist, justification for judicial supremacy. It may partly rely on need, function, and competence, and it, of course, claims support in the text; but basically it rests on constitutionalism. In the debates on the Judiciary Act of 1802, Gouverneur Morris, who had chaired the Committee on Style at Philadelphia and had written much of the final draft of the document, made an unambiguous claim for judicial supremacy. Judges derive that power, he said, "from authority higher than this Constitution. They derive it from the constitution of man, from the nature of things, from the necessary progress of human affairs." He was arguing that human nature required that, if government were to be limited, some institution, removed from popular control, would have to check the

---

5. Ibid.

6. For a recent argument that courts should not act as constitutional judges between Congress and the President or between the nation and the states, see Jesse H. Choper, *Judicial Review and the National Political Process* (Chicago: University of Chicago Press, 1980).

7. See the attack on congressional interpretation by Circuit Judge (and former Congressman) Abner J. Mikva, "How Well Does Congress Support and Defend the Constitution?" 61 *No. Car. L. Rev.* 587 (1983) and the defense of congressional interpretation by Louis Fisher, "Constitutional Interpretation by Members of Congress," 63 ibid. 707 (1985).

8. Quoted in Carl Brent Swisher, *American Constitutional Development* (Boston: Houghton Mifflin, 1943), p. 773.

people and their representatives—the core of the constitutionalist position.

However convincing this sort of reasoning would be to the "pure constitutionalist" described in Chapter 2, it causes problems that increase in seriousness as one moves across the spectrum toward the "pure democrat." Even an interpreter who falls near the center, a constitutional democrat, could accept such an argument only with important qualifications relating to such matters as the nature of the substantive issue in dispute.

In sum, whether acceptance of judicial review necessarily carries acceptance of judicial supremacy is a matter about which public officials and commentators heatedly disagree. Certainly Jefferson, Jackson, Lincoln, and Franklin D. Roosevelt did not believe that they or Congress were bound by the Supreme Court's constitutional inter- pretations. And shortly after the Convention Madison most emphati- cally denied judicial supremacy. (See his letter to John Brown, 1788, reprinted below, p. 199, as well his comments quoted below, p. 190.)

The Court itself has seldom explicitly claimed judicial supremacy and has never articulated a full argument for it vis-á-vis Congress or the President. In Ableman v. Booth (1859; reprinted below, p. 274), a unanimous Court claimed:

> [N]o power is more clearly conferred by the Constitution and laws
> of the United States, than the power of this court to decide,
> ultimately and finally, all cases arising under such Constitution and
> laws . . . .

"To decide cases" under the Constitution is not quite the same as to interpret the Constitution in a manner that all other public officials must follow in situations other than the particular cases. Moreover, in *Ableman* the justices were asserting the interpretive authority of federal judges over that of state judges, not the superiority of federal judges over Congress or the presidency. The first modern, general claim by the Court to supremacy came in Cooper v. Aaron (1958; reprinted below, p. 281), where the justices said that "the federal judiciary is supreme in the exposition of the law of the Constitution"; and thus— "exposition of the Constitution" has far more sweeping implications than merely deciding a case under the Constitution—Brown v. Board (1954) was "the supreme law of the land."

Although *Cooper* spoke in broad terms, that case, like *Ableman,* involved only the authority of state versus federal officials. Similarly, only state officials were parties to Baker v. Carr (1962), where the Court first referred to itself as the "ultimate interpreter of the Constitution." It was not until Powell v. McCormack (1969) that the Court so designated itself in a dispute pertaining to its authority over Congress, an assertion the justices repeated about their relations to the President in United States v. Nixon (1974; reprinted below, p. 234) and reiterated about both in the Legislative Veto case, INS v. Chadha,

(1983; reprinted below, p. 383). *Powell,* however, addressed only
the authority of the House to exclude a duly elected member and did
not require that he be readmitted (his term had expired before the
decision) or that he be given back pay. *Nixon* upheld a subpoena to a
President whose political situation was desperate, and the fate of the
Legislative Veto remains in doubt. (See the notes to that case, at p.
234.)

B. Legislative Supremacy

Serious assertions of legislative supremacy in constitutional interpretation have been infrequent, though they have at times been
vigorously pushed, as after the Civil War when the Radical Republicans dominated Congress, impeached the President, and curbed the
Court. Early on, some Jeffersonians had also pressed for congressional supremacy. (See the debate on the Judiciary Act of 1802, reprinted
below, p. 203.) As Caesar Rodney of Delaware wrote in 1803:
"Judicial supremacy may be made to bow before the strong arm of
Legislative authority. We shall discover who is master of the ship."[9]
John Marshall was sufficiently frightened by threats to impeach and
remove Federalist judges that he was willing even to modify judicial
review. As he wrote a colleague:

> [T]he modern doctrine of impeachment should yield to an appellate
> jurisdiction in the legislature. A reversal of those legal opinions
> deemed unsound by the legislature would certainly better comport
> with the mildness of our character than [would] a removal of the
> Judge who has rendered them unknowing of his fault.[10]

This notion has been several times revived—usually with the proposed
appellate jurisdiction resting in the Senate alone—but, of course, has
never been formally adopted.

Even without appellate review, the basis of any claim that Congress' interpretation of the Constitution should prevail over that of
judges rests on legislators' connections to the people via the ballot.
As Justice Gibson, dissenting in Eakin v. Raub (1825; reprinted
below, p. 221), wrote: "It may be said, the power of the legislature
. . . is limited by prescribed rules. It is so. But it is nevertheless,
the power of the people, and sovereign as far as it extends . . . ."
Therefore, he concluded:

> it rests with the people, in whom full and absolute sovereign power
> resides, to correct abuses in legislation, by instructing their repre-
> sentatives to repeal the obnoxious act. What is wanting to plenary
> power in the government, is reserved to the people for their own
> immediate use; and to redress an infringement of their rights in this
> respect, would seem to be an accessory to the power thus reserved.

9. Quoted in Charles Warren, *The Supreme Court in United States History* (rev. ed.; Boston:
Little, Brown, 1926), I, 228–229.

10. Quoted in Albert J. Beveridge, *The Life of John Marshall* (Boston: Houghton Mifflin,
1919), III, 177.

Constitutionalism emphatically rejects any argument that popularly elected officials should have the final word in determining fundamental relations in the polity. Those officials, a constitutionalist would say, will be responsible to the people, who are themselves a potent source of danger to civil liberty. One does not, as the Italian proverb goes, make the goat one's gardener.

C. Departmentalism

No President has ever pressed a claim to supremacy in constitutional interpretation; but like many legislators, some presidents have asserted equality, at least where the issue involves their own authority. (See the opinions of Jefferson, Jackson, Lincoln, and Roosevelt, reprinted below, pp. 218–234.) Madison's position fluctuated as he faced various crises, but in the early days of the Republic he was clearly a departmentalist. His theory of allowing different social interests to dominate particular institutions and of pitting ambition against ambition and power against power pushes toward stalemate that can only be overcome by compromise, not by legal formulae. He was opposed to judicial supremacy, as he explained in 1788 (reprinted below, p. 198), just as he feared legislative supremacy.

Madison told the First Congress that the American constitutional system was departmentalist:

> There is not one Government . . . in the United States, in which provision is made for a particular authority to determine the limits of the constitutional division of power between the branches of the Government. In all systems, there are points which must be adjusted by the departments themselves, to which no one of them is competent.[11]

Jefferson was more consistent in his departmentalism. When he became President, he pardoned many people who had been convicted under the Sedition Act for libelling John Adams. Upset, John's wife Abigail wrote Jefferson and asked for an explanation. He replied:

> You seem to think it devolved on the judges to decide on the validity of the sedition law. But nothing in the Constitution has given them a right to decide for the Executive, more than the Executive to decide for them. Both magistrates are equally independent in the sphere of action assigned to them. The judges, believing the law constitutional, had a right to pass a sentence . . . . But the executive, believing the law to be unconstitutional, were bound to remit the execution of it because that power had been confined to them by the Constitution. That instrument meant that its coordinate branches should be checks on each other. But the opinion which gives to the judges the right to decide what laws are constitutional and what are not, not only for themselves in

---

11. *Annals of Congress* (1789), I.

their own sphere of action, but for the legislature and executive also in their spheres, would make the judiciary a despotic branch.[12]

Two decades later, Jefferson chided William Jarvis for considering "judges as the ultimate arbiters of all constitutional questions." Jefferson would agree only that they "have more frequent occasion to act on constitutional questions." That power, however, was neither exclusively nor finally theirs:

> The constitution has erected no such single tribunal, knowing that to whatever hands confided, with the corruptions of time and party, its members would become despots. It has more wisely made all the departments co-equal and co-sovereign within themselves.[13]

D. Resolution?

As for many of the basic questions in constitutional interpretation, the constitutional text does not offer a clear answer. One might argue, however, that whatever the ambiguities of the document, "the constitution," considered as including the political system's traditions, endorses judicial supremacy. The system accepts not only judicial review but also the obligation of Congress and the President to conform their actions to the Court's constitutional interpretations. The primary option open to Congress and the President when fundamentally disagreeing with the Court is to amend the Constitution. This tradition of amending the Constitution, which began in 1793 after Chisholm v. Georgia, one might reason, acknowledges that the Court's interpretations are so definitive as to require explicit, formal expunging to lose their validity.

It is true that the American system displays a general pattern of accepting the Court's constitutional interpretations. But, reasoning from this pattern raises at least three difficulties. Many constitutional problems, such as those involving foreign policy, do not lend themselves to judicial resolution. Second, judges also defer to Congress. The normal rule, subject to important exceptions as when a fundamental individual right is at stake or the government has used a "suspect" classification like race (see below, Chapters 13–14), is that courts "presume" an act of Congress is constitutional. In almost two centuries, the Supreme Court has invalidated less than a hundred provisions of federal law, few of them of great significance to the political system.

Third, as the readings in this Chapter illustrate, even where problems are amenable to judicial resolution and the issues have been significant, the general pattern of acceptance of the Court's interpretations has been broken often enough for a case for judicial supremacy on the basis of tradition to be shaky. Not only have presidents defied the Court, and not only did the election of 1936 constitute a sort of

---

12. Lipscomb, supra note 1, XI, 50–51.

13. September 28, 1820; Paul L. Ford, ed., *The Works of Thomas Jefferson* (New York: Putnam's, 1905), XII, 161–164; see also Jefferson's letter to Torrance, June 11, 1815; Lipscomb, supra note 1, XIV, 303–306.

constitutional referendum, but Congress has on occasion merely re-passed, in slightly modified form, a statute the Court has invalidated and watched the justices change their minds. Furthermore, presidents have frequently chosen men and women who, they thought, would speed the process of reshaping the judicial mind.

Nor does political theory supply *the* answer; instead, it provides several answers. Democratic theory favors legislative supremacy, constitutionalism judicial supremacy. A mixed theory of constitution-al democracy would tilt one way or the other, depending on whether the mix was more constitutionalist or democratic. Departmentalism might form a logical compromise. But accepting departmentalism would be recognizing the problem as much as solving it, especially given the impracticality of using Jefferson's suggestion for national conventions.

Perhaps the most fruitful way of beginning to solve the problem is to break it down into several subproblems. First would be the nature of the substantive issue. If the dispute concerned, for example, procedures that a judge must follow in conducting a criminal trial, the argument for judicial supremacy would be stronger than if the issue concerned the President's conduct of foreign relations. The question would become: Is there anything in the structure or tradition of the system or in the practicalities of political life as well as in the words of the document that indicates a particular agency of government should have the final word on specific sets of issues?

The vague and oft-maligned "doctrine of political questions," [14] that certain constitutional matters lie beyond the judiciary's institution-al authority and competence, makes some sense in this context. For example, after the tragic incident at Kent State University in 1970, at which Ohio National Guardsmen fired on students demonstrating against the war in Vietnam, killing and wounding a number of people, a group of students filed suit in a federal district court, asking the

---

14.   Marbury v. Madison (1803) hinted at the doctrine: "The province of the court is, solely, to decide on the rights of individuals, not to inquire how the executive, or executive officers, perform duties in which they have a discretion. Questions in their nature political, or which are, by the constitution and laws, submitted to the executive, can never be made in this court." Luther v. Borden (1849) is the classic, if murky, case. The Court has since made several heroic, if ultimately unsuccessful, efforts to distinguish "political" from "justiciable" questions. Perhaps the most useful was Justice Brennan's in Baker v. Carr (1962):

   (i) "Prominent on the surface of any case held to involve a political question is found a textually demonstrable constitutional commitment of the issue to a coordinate political department; or"

   (ii) "a lack of judicially discoverable and manageable standards for resolving it; or"

   (iii) "the impossibility of deciding without an initial policy determination of a kind clearly for non-judicial discretion; or"

   (iv) "the impossibility of a court's undertaking independent resolution without expressing a lack of the respect due coordinate branches of government; or"

   (v) "an unusual need for unquestioning adherence to a political decision already made; or"

   (vi) "the potentiality of embarrassment from multifarious pronouncements by various departments on one question."

See Fritz W. Scharf, "Judicial Review and the Political Question," 75 *Yale L.J.* 517 (1966), and Louis Henkin, "Is There a 'Political Question' Doctrine?" 85 *Yale L.J.* 597 (1976).

judge to restrain the governor from future "premature" use of the National Guard to cope with situations that could be handled by nonlethal force. The district court dismissed the case, but the court of appeals reversed in part and ordered the trial judge to determine if there was and had been a pattern of training for the National Guard that made inevitable the use of lethal force. When the case reached the Supreme Court, the majority noted that Article I, § 8 vested in Congress the authority "to provide for organizing, arming, and disciplining, the militia . . . ." Thus:

> It would be difficult to think of a clearer example of the type of governmental action that was intended by the Constitution to be left to the political branches . . . . Moreover, it is difficult to conceive of an area of governmental activity in which the courts have less competence. The complex, subtle, and professional decisions as to the composition, training, equipping, and control of a military force are essentially professional military judgments, subject *always* to civilian control of the Legislative and Executive Branches. The ultimate responsibility for these decisions is appropriately vested in branches of the government subject to electoral accountability.[15]

Another series of questions would deal with the range of judicial authority. Is there a difference in the obligation of other officials to obey a judicial decision in a specific case and their obligation to follow its reasoning in making future policy? Is there a difference in officials' obligations to obey a judicial decision when they themselves brought the lawsuit and when someone else sued them?

This sort of analysis transforms the question of WHO from one that might be expected to yield a universally applicable response, into a more complex set of queries for which one could provide replies about degrees of deference one institution owes another under varying circumstances.

II. DEFERENCE AND THE FOURTEENTH AMENDMENT

Among the more difficult contexts in which the question of deference arises concerns the Fourteenth Amendment. Section 5 reads: "The Congress shall have power to enforce, by appropriate legislation, the provisions of this article." Those provisions ban, among other things, state denials of "due process of law" and "the equal protection of the laws." And for the second half of the twentieth century, the most persistent and serious problems of domestic politics have been caused by a long history of discrimination based race, ethnicity, sex, and poverty. Thus those problems all raise questions about the meaning and application of equal protection.

For several decades, judges, with only occasional and not very effective help from the executive, fought for the constitutionalist's

---

15. Gilligan v. Morgan (1973).

ideal of "equal justice under law." Since the late 1950s, however, Congress has become more sensitive to such problems and has passed more than a dozen civil rights statutes that penalize various forms of discrimination by state and federal agencies as well as by private corporations and individual citizens. Furthermore, some of these statutes do not follow judicial interpretations about the reach of the Fourteenth Amendment. Given § 5, what deference, beyond the usual presumption of constitutionality, should judges accord to Congress, composed of people elected from all the states, when it interprets state obligations more stringently than have judges? When Congress interprets state obligations less stringently than have judges? Katzenbach v. Morgan (1966; reprinted below, p. 239) raises some of these questions.

Issues of equal protection do not exhaust the possibilities here. There are other clauses in the Fourteenth Amendment. In holding that that amendment acknowledged a woman's right to an abortion, at least during her first trimester of pregnancy, the Court said that a fetus was not a "person" and therefore not protected by the amendment. Might Congress, under § 5, validly define the term "person," which after all judges have said does include corporations and ships, to encompass fetuses and entitle them to governmental protection of a right to life and liberty? How much deference should Congress give to the Court's holding that a fetus is not a person? The Court to a congressional determination that a fetus is a person, at least for the purposes of the Fourteenth Amendment? The debate over the Right to Life Bill (reprinted below, p. 247) explores those questions.

SELECTED BIBLIOGRAPHY

Agresto, John. *The Supreme Court and Constitutional Democracy* (Ithaca, N.Y.: Cornell University Press, 1984).

Barber, Sotirios A. *On What the Constitution Means* (Baltimore, Md.: Johns Hopkins University Press, 1984), Chap. 6.

Brest, Paul. "Who Decides?" 58 *So.Cal.L.Rev.* 661 (1985).

————. "The Conscientious Legislator's Guide to Constitutional Interpretation," 27 *Stan.L.Rev.* 585 (1975).

Choper, Jesse H. *Judicial Review and the National Political Process* (Chicago: University of Chicago Press, 1980).

Cohen, William. "Congressional Power to Expand Judicial Definitions of the Substantive Terms of the Civil War Amendments," 67 *Minn.L.Rev.* 299 (1982).

Corwin, Edward S. "Marbury v. Madison and the Doctrine of Judicial Review," 12 *Mich.L.Rev.* 538 (1914).

Cox, Archibald. "Foreward: Constitutional Adjudication and the Protection of Human Rights," 80 *Harv.L.Rev.* 91 (1966).

————. "The Role of Congress in Constitutional Determinations," 40 *U. of Cinn.L.Rev.* 199 (1971).

————. *The Role of the Supreme Court in American Government* (New York: Oxford University Press, 1976).

Ely, John Hart, *Democracy and Distrust* (Cambridge, Mass.: Harvard University Press, 1980).

Monaghan, Henry P. "Constitutional Adjudication: The Who and the When," 82 *Yale L.J.* 1361 (1973).

Morgan, Donald G. *Congress and the Constitution* (Cambridge, Mass.: Harvard University Press, 1966).

Murphy, Walter F. *Congress and the Court* (Chicago: University of Chicago Press, 1962).

Note. "Congressional Reversal of Supreme Court Decisions: 1945–57," 71 *Harv.L.Rev.* 1324 (1958).

Pritchett, C. Herman. *Congress versus the Supreme Court, 1957–1960* (Minneapolis: University of Minnesota Press, 1961).

Schmidhauser, John R., and Larry L. Berg. *The Supreme Court and Congress: Conflict and Interaction, 1945–1968* (New York: The Free Press, 1972).

Warren, Charles. *Congress, the Constitution and the Supreme Court* (Boston: Little, Brown, 1925).

"A constitution is, in fact, and must be regarded by the judges, as a fundamental law. It therefore belongs to them to ascertain its meaning . . . ."

THE FEDERALIST, NO. 78

Alexander Hamilton (1788).

. . . Whoever attentively considers the different departments of power must perceive that, in a government in which they are separated from each other, the judiciary, from the nature of its functions, will always be the least dangerous to the political rights of the Constitution; because it will be least in capacity to annoy or injure them. The Executive not only dispenses honors, but holds the sword of the community. The legislature not only commands the purse, but prescribes the rules by which the duties and rights of every citizen are to be regulated. The judiciary, on the contrary, has no influence over either the sword or the purse; no direction either of the strength or of the wealth of the society; and can take no active resolution whatever. It may truly be said to have neither FORCE nor WILL, but merely judgment; and must ultimately depend upon the aid of the executive arm even for the efficacy of its judgment . . . .

Some perplexity respecting the rights of the courts to pronounce legislative acts void, because contrary to the constitution, has arisen from an imagination that the doctrine would imply a superiority of the judiciary to the legislative power. It is urged that the authority which can declare the acts of another void, must necessarily be superior to the one whose acts may be declared void. As this doctrine is of great importance in all the American constitutions, a brief discussion of the ground on which it rests cannot be unacceptable.

There is no position which depends on clearer principles, than that every act of a delegated authority, contrary to the tenor of the commission under which it is exercised, is void. No legislative act, therefore, contrary to the Constitution, can be valid. To deny this, would be to affirm that the deputy is greater than his principal; that the servant is above his master; that the representatives of the people are superior to the people themselves; that men acting by virtue of powers may do not only what their powers do not authorize, but what they forbid.

If it be said that the legislative body are themselves the constitutional judges of their own powers, and that the construction put on them is conclusive upon the other departments, it may be answered, that this cannot be the natural presumption, where it is not to be collected from any particular provisions in the Constitution. It is not otherwise to be supposed, that the Constitution could intend to enable the representatives of the people to substitute their *will* to that of their constituents. It is far more rational to suppose, that the courts were designed to be an intermediate body between the people and the legislature, in order, among other things, to keep the latter within the limits assigned to their authority. The interpretation of the laws is the proper and peculiar province of the courts. A constitution is, in fact, and must be regarded by the judges, as a fundamental law. It therefore belongs to them to ascertain its meaning, as well as the meaning of any particular act proceeding from the legislative body. If there should happen to be an irreconcilable variance between the two, that which has the superior obligation and validity ought, of course, to be preferred; or, in other words, the Constitution ought to be preferred to the statute, the intention of the people to the intention of their agents.

Nor does this conclusion by any means suppose a superiority of the judicial to the legislative power. It only supposes that the power of the people is superior to both; and that where the will of the legislature, declared in its statutes, stands in opposition to that of the people, declared in the Constitution, the judges ought to be governed by the latter rather than the former. They ought to regulate their decisions by the fundamental laws, rather than by those which are not fundamental . . . .

It can be of no weight to say that the courts, on the pretence of a repugnancy, may substitute their own pleasure to the constitutional intentions of the legislature. This might as well happen in the case of two contradictory statutes; or it might as well happen in every adjudication upon any single statute. The courts must declare the sense of the law; and if they should be disposed to exercise WILL instead of JUDGMENT, the consequence would equally be the substitution of their pleasure to that of the legislative body. The observation, if it prove any thing, would prove that there ought to be no judges distinct from that body.

If, then, the courts of justice are to be considered as the bulwarks of a limited Constitution against legislative encroachments, this consideration will afford a strong argument for the permanent tenure of judicial offices, since nothing will contribute so much as this to that independent spirit in the judges which must be essential to the faithful performance of so arduous a duty.

This independence of the judges is equally requisite to guard the Constitution and the rights of individuals from the effects of those ill humors, which the arts of designing men, or the influence of particular conjunctures, sometimes disseminate among the people themselves, and which, though they speedily give place to better information, and more deliberate reflection, have a tendency, in the meantime, to occasion dangerous innovations in the government, and serious oppressions of the minor party in the community. Though I trust the friends of the proposed Constitution will never concur with its enemies, in questioning that fundamental principle of republican government, which admits the right of the people to alter or abolish the established Constitution, whenever they find it inconsistent with their happiness, yet it is not to be inferred from this principle, that the representatives of the people, whenever a momentary inclination happens to lay hold of a majority of their constituents, incompatible with the provisions in the existing Constitution, would, on that account, be justifiable in a violation of those provisions; or that the courts would be under a greater obligation to connive at infractions in this shape, than when they had proceeded wholly from the cabals of the representative body. Until the people have, by some solemn and authoritative act, annulled or changed the established form, it is binding upon themselves collectively, as well as individually; and no presumption, or even knowledge, of their sentiments, can warrant their representatives in a departure from it, prior to such an act. But it is easy to see, that it would require an uncommon portion of fortitude in the judges to do their duty as faithful guardians of the Constitution, where legislative invasions of it had been instigated by the major voice of the community. . . .

There is yet a further and a weightier reason for the permanency of the judicial offices . . . . To avoid an arbitrary discretion in the courts, it is indispensable that they should be bound down by strict rules and precedents, which serve to define and point out their duty in every particular case that comes before them; and it will readily be conceived from the variety of controversies which grow out of the folly and wickedness of mankind, that the records of those precedents must unavoidably swell to a very considerable bulk, and must demand long and laborious study to acquire a competent knowledge of them. Hence it is, that there can be but few men in the society who will have sufficient skill in the laws to qualify them for the stations of judges. And making the proper deductions for the ordinary depravity of human nature, the number must be still smaller of those who unite the requisite integrity with the requisite knowledge. These considerations apprise us, that the government can have no great option between fit character; and that a temporary duration in office, which would naturally discourage such characters from quitting a lucrative line of practice to accept a seat on the bench, would have a tendency to throw the administration of justice into hands less able, and less well qualified, to conduct it with utility and dignity . . . .

"A law violating a constitution established by the people themselves, would be considered by the Judges as null & void."—MADISON at the Philadelphia Convention (1787)

"This makes the Judiciary Department paramount in fact to the Legislature, which was never intended and can never be proper."—MADISON to John Brown (1788)

"In all systems there are points which must be adjusted by the departments themselves . . . ."—MADISON in U.S. House of Representatives (1789)

JAMES MADISON ON JUDICIAL REVIEW AND JUDICIAL SUPREMACY

On July 23, 1787, at the Constitutional Convention, Oliver Ellsworth of Connecticut moved that the delegates reconsider their decision to have final ratification made by conventions in the several states and instead have state legislatures have the last word on accepting or rejecting the new constitution. According to Madison's notes of the debates:

Mr. **MADISON** thought it clear that the Legislatures were incompetent to the proposed changes. These changes would make essential inroads on the State Constitutions, and it would be a novel & dangerous doctrine that a Legislature could change the constitution under which it held its existence . . . . He considered the difference between a system founded on the Legislatures only, and one founded on the people, to be the true difference between a *league* or *treaty*, and a *Constitution*. The former in point of *moral obligation* might be as inviolable as the latter. In point of *political operation*, there were two important distinctions in favor of the latter. 1. A law violating a treaty ratified by a pre-existing law, might be respected by the Judges as a law, though an unwise or perfidious one. A law violating a constitution established by the people themselves, would be considered by the Judges to be null & void. 2. The doctrine laid down by the law of Nations in the case of treaties is that a breach of any one article by any of the parties, frees the other parties from their engagements. In the case of a union of people under one Constitution, the nature of the pact has always been understood to exclude such an interpretation . . . .[1]

Ellsworth's motion failed by a wide margin.

On August 27, the Convention took up William S. Johnson's proposal, now contained in broader form in Art. III, § 1, § 2, that the Supreme Court's jurisdiction should extend to cases arising under the Constitution. According to Madison's notes:

Mr. **MADISON** doubted whether it was not going too far to extend the jurisdiction of the [Supreme] Court generally to cases arising under the Constitution & whether it ought not to be limited to cases of a Judiciary Nature. The right of expounding the Constitution in cases not of this nature ought not to be given to that Department.

The motion of Docr. Johnson was agreed to nem: con [no one dissenting] it being generally supposed that the jurisdiction given was constructively limited to cases of a Judiciary nature.[2]

It is not altogether clear what "cases of a Judiciary Nature" means, but it implies at least that the Court could only interpret the Constitution in actual disputes that presented a problem of constituting meaning. One cannot help but wonder whether in fact the delegates "generally supposed" that the clause in Art. III had such a restricted meaning. None of the other delegates whose notes we have reports anything about this debate.

About fourteen months after the Convention adjourned and shortly after the Constitution had been ratified, John Brown, an old friend of Madison from his college days at Princeton, wrote to ask his views about proposals for a constitution for Kentucky, which was preparing for statehood. Brown enclosed a draft of a constitution that Jefferson had suggested for Virginia in 1783. Madison replied at length. We reprint here only his remarks dealing with constitutional interpretation.

A revisionary power is meant as a check to precipitate, to unjust, and to unconstitutional laws. These important ends would it is conceded by more effectually secured, without disarming the Legislature of its authority, by requiring bills to be separately communicated to the Exec: & Judic ʸ dep ᵗˢ If either of these object, let ²/₃, if both ³/₄ of each House be necessary to overrule the objection; and if either or both protest ag ˢᵗ a bill as violating the Constitution, let it moreover be suspended notwithstanding the overruling proportion of the Assembly, until there shall have been a subsequent election of the H[ouse] of D[elegate]ˢ and a re-passage of the bill by ²/₃ or ³/₄ of both Houses, as the case may be. It s[houl] ᵈ not be allowed the Judges or y ᵉ Executive to pronounce a law thus enacted unconstitu ¹ & invalid.

1. Charles C. Tansill, ed., *Documents Illustrative of the Formation of the Union of the American States* (Washington, D.C.: Government Printing Office, 1927), pp. 438–439.

2. Tansill, supra note 1, p. 625.

In the State Constitutions & indeed in the Fed[1] one also, no provision is made for the case of a disagreement in expounding them; and as the Courts are generally the last in making y[e] decision, it results to them by refusing or not refusing to execute a law, to stamp it with its final character. This makes the Judiciary Dep[t] paramount in fact to the Legislature, which was never intended and can never be proper.[3]

In June, 1789, during the first session of the First Congress, the House of Representatives debated a proposal to give (or acknowledge) in the President alone authority to remove officials whom he had appointed with the advice and consent of the Senate. Madison, now a congressman from Virginia, believed that the Constitution vested the removal power solely in the President, but he also wanted the House to address this constitutional issue.

Mr. **MADISON**— . . .

Another species of argument has been urged against this clause. It is said, that it is improper, or at least unnecessary, to come to any decision on this subject. It has been said by one gentleman, that it would be officious in this branch of the Legislature to expound the constitution, so far as it relates to the division of power between the President and Senate; it is incontrovertibly of as much importance to this branch of the Government as to any other, that the constitution should be preserved entire. It is our duty, so far as it depends upon us, to take care that the powers of the constitution be preserved entire to every department of Government; the breach of the constitution in one point, will facilitate the breach in another; a breach in this point may destroy that equilibrium by which the House retains its consequence and share of power; therefore we are not chargeable with an officious interference. Besides, the bill, before it can have effect, must be submitted to both those branches who are particularly interested in it; the Senate may negative, or the President may object, if he thinks it unconstitutional.

But the great objection drawn from the source to which the last arguments would lead us is, that the Legislature itself has no right to expound the constitution; that wherever its meaning is doubtful, you must leave it to take its course, until the Judiciary is called upon to declare its meaning. I acknowledge, in the ordinary course of Government, that the exposition of the laws and constitution devolves upon the Judiciary. But, I beg to know, upon what principle it can be contended, that any one department draws from the constitution greater powers than another, in marking out the limits of the powers of the several departments? The constitution is the charter of the people to the Government; it specifies certain great powers as absolutely granted, and marks out the departments to exercise them. If the

---

3. Madison to John Brown, October 12, 1788, "Observations on the 'Draught of a Constitution for Virginia,'" Gailliard Hunt, ed., *The Writings of James Madison* (New York: Putnam's Sons, 1904), V, 292–294.

constitutional boundary of either be brought into question, I do not see that any one of these independent departments has more right than another to declare their sentiments on that point.

Perhaps this is an omitted case. There is not one Government on the face of the earth, so far as I recollect, there is not one in the United States, in which provision is made for a particular authority to determine the limits of the constitutional division of power between the branches of the Government. In all systems there are points which must be adjusted by the departments themselves, to which no one of them is competent. If it cannot be determined in this way, there is no resource left but the will of the community, to be collected in some mode to be provided by the constitution, or one dictated by the necessity of the case. It is therefore a fair question, whether this great point may not as well be decided, at least by the whole Legislature as by a part, by us as well as by the Executive or Judiciary? As I think it will be equally constitutional, I cannot imagine it will be less safe, that the exposition should issue from the legislative authority than any other; and the more so, because it involves in the decision the opinions of both those departments, whose powers are supposed to be affected by it. Besides, I do not see in what way this question could come before the judges, to obtain a fair and solemn decision; but even if it were the case that it could, I should suppose, at least while the Government is not led by passion, disturbed by faction, or deceived by any discolored medium of sight, but while there is a desire in all to see and be guided by the benignant ray of truth, that the decision may be made with the most advantage by the Legislature itself.

My conclusion from these reflections is, that it will be constitutional to retain the clause; that it expresses the meaning of the constitution as must be established by fair construction, and a construction which, upon the whole, not only consists with liberty, but is more favorable to it than any one of the interpretations that have been proposed.[4]

Editors' Note

Query: How can one reconcile these varying opinions of Madison about constitutional interpretation?

---

4. *Annals of Congress*, I, 519–521 (June 17, 1789).

[T]he Legislature have the exclusive right to interpret the Constitution, in what regards the law-making power, and the judges are bound to execute the laws they make."— Senator John BRECKENRIDGE

"Why does a judge swear to discharge his duties agreeably to the constitution of the United States, if that constitution forms no rule for his government?"—Chief Justice John MARSHALL

THE GREAT DEBATE OF 1802-1803

Until adoption in 1933 of the Twentieth Amendment to the Constitution, the terms of incumbent presidents, senators, and congressmen did not expire until March of the year following an election, allowing the possibility of almost four months of rule by lame ducks. In the critical election of 1800, the Jeffersonians routed the Federalists under John Adams. The Federalists, however, took advantage of their period of grace to adopt the Judiciary Act of 1801, a law that, on the one hand, created sixteen circuit judgeships and, on the other hand, provided that, upon the next death or resignation on the Supreme Court, the number of justices would be reduced from six to five, thereby depriving Thomas Jefferson of an opportunity to choose a justice.

There were sound reasons for creating circuit judgeships. Earlier statutes had required justices of the Supreme Court to go around the country singly or in pairs to preside at trials. Not only was travel during that period always slow, often difficult, and sometimes perilous, the arrangement also caused awkward problems when a litigant appealed to the Supreme Court, for at least one of the justices had already heard the case and registered opinions about it. Nevertheless, coupled as it was with the reduction of the number of justices and recent experience under the Sedition Act of 1798—which many Federalist judges had been delighted to use to fine and imprison men who dared to criticize John Adams and support Thomas Jefferson—the Act of 1801 smacked of a crude power play. As Jefferson wrote to a confidante, the Federalists

> have retired into the judiciary as a stronghold. There the remains of federalism are to be preserved and fed from the treasury, and from that battery all the works of republicanism are to be beaten down and erased. By a fraudulent use of the Constitution, which has made judges irremovable, they have multiplied useless judges merely to strengthen their phalanx.

Not unexpectedly, repeal was one of the first objectives of the administration when the new Congress met in December, 1801 for its first session.

Meanwhile, the judiciary was also providing the stage for other scenes in the drama. After Jefferson's electoral victory, the Federalists persuaded the ailing Oliver Ellsworth to resign as Chief Justice while Adams was still in office and so deprive Jefferson of another opportunity to put one of his own men on the bench. For Ellsworth's place, Adams nominated and the Senate quickly confirmed his Secretary of State, John Marshall, a very healthy man not quite 46 years old.

On the evening before leaving office, Adams had signed commissions for 42 justices of the peace in the District of Columbia—the so-called "midnight judges." As required by law, the Secretary of State—still John Marshall, who had not thought it necessary to resign when accepting the chief justiceship—affixed the official seal and gave the commissions to his assistant, his brother James, to deliver. James, however, neglected to deliver them. When he assumed office the next day, Jefferson told his Secretary of State, James Madison, to withhold 17 of the commissions.

After some initial hesitation, William Marbury and three other men whose commissions had been withheld filed suit in the U.S. Supreme Court, asking for a mandamus—an order from a court to a public official commanding him to perform a non-discretionary act—directing James Madison to deliver the commissions. In December, 1801, just as the congressional session had begun, the Court ordered Madison to "show cause" why the justices should not grant Marbury's request.

The lawsuit and the Court's "show cause" order alarmed the Jeffersonians. On Christmas Eve, Senator John Breckenridge, one of Jefferson's staunchest supporters in Congress, wrote a friend that the Court's "show cause" order was "the most daring attack which the annals of Federalism have yet exhibited. I wish the subject of the Courts to be brought forward in the Senate next week . . . ." Breckenridge had his way. Repeal of the Judiciary Act of 1801 soon became the Senate's first order of business.

As drafted, the bill would not only have abolished the circuit courts but would also have turned out of office the sixteen circuit judges, all of whom had been serving for at least nine months on the federal bench. Immediately at issue was whether such dismissals without impeachment and trial violated the plain words of Article III of the Constitution that "judges shall hold their offices during good behavior." Jefferson's private comments indicate that, however angry he was at the Federalists' slickness, he thought removal unconstitutional. But, fortunately for his reputation as a strict constructionist, he allowed Senator Breckenridge and other friends on Capitol Hill to pit their interpretive ingenuity against that of the Federalists. Almost inevitably, discussion of judicial independence raised the more complex issue of the legitimacy of judicial review.

". . . I ask gentlemen to point out the clause [in the Constitution] which grants it [judicial review] . . . . Is it not extraordinary, that if this high power was intended, it should nowhere appear?"—Senator BRECKENRIDGE

"I answer, they [judges] derived that power from authority higher than this Constitution. They derive it from the constitution of man, from the nature of things, from the necessary progress of human affairs."—Senator MORRIS

A. THE SENATE DEBATES *

(1801–1802)

Mr. BRECKENRIDGE . . . .

. . . [T]here is little doubt indeed, in my mind, as to the power of Congress on this law. The first section of the third article [of the

---

* *Annals of Congress*, 7th Cong., 1st sess., pp. 27–183 (1802).

Constitution] vests the judicial power of the United States in one Supreme Court and such inferior courts as Congress may, from time to time, ordain and establish. By this clause Congress *may,* from time to time, establish inferior courts; but it is clearly a discretionary power, and they *may not* establish them. The language of the Constitution is very different when regulations are not left discretional. For example, "The trial," says the Constitution, "of all crimes (except in cases of impeachment) shall be by jury: representatives and direct taxes shall be apportioned according to numbers. All revenue bills shall originate in the House of Representatives," &c. It would, therefore, in my opinion, be a perversion, not only of language, but of intellect, to say, that although Congress may, from time to time, establish inferior courts, yet, when established, that they shall not be abolished by a subsequent Congress possessing equal powers. . . .

2d. As to the judges. The Judiciary department is so constructed as to be sufficiently secured against the improper influence of either the Executive or Legislative departments. The courts are organized and established by the Legislature, and the Executive creates the judges. Being thus organized, the Constitution affords the proper checks to secure their honesty and independence in office. It declares they shall not be removed from office during good behaviour; nor their salaries diminished during their continuance in office. From this it results, that a judge, after his appointment, is totally out of the power of the President, and his salary secured against legislative diminution, during his continuance in office. . . .

But because the Constitution declares that a judge shall hold his office during good behaviour, can it be tortured to mean, that he shall hold his office after it is abolished? Can it mean, that his tenure should be limited by behaving well in an office which did not exist? Can it mean that an office may exist, although its duties are extinct? . . . It must have intended all these absurdities, or it must admit a construction which will avoid them.

The construction obviously is, that a judge should hold an existing office, so long as he did his duty in that office . . . . Had the construction which I contend against been contemplated by those who framed the Constitution, it would have been necessary to have declared, explicitly that the judges should hold their offices and their salaries during good behaviour.

Such a construction is not only irreconcilable with reason and propriety, but is repugnant to the principles of the Constitution. It is a principle of our Constitution, as well as of common honesty, that no man shall receive public money but in consideration of public services. Sinecure offices, therefore, are not permitted by our laws or Constitution . . . .

Upon this construction, also, an infallibility is predicated. . . . On all other subjects of legislation we are allowed, it seems, to change our minds, except on judiciary subjects, which, of all others, is the most complex and difficult. I appeal to our own statute book to prove this difficulty; for in ten years Congress have passed no less than twenty-six laws on this subject.

I conceive, sir, that the tenure by which a judge holds his office, is evidently bottomed on the idea of securing his honesty and independence, whilst exercising his office . . . . . [I]f the construction now contended for shall prevail, we shall [establish] a judicial oligarchy

. . . .

. . . [A]s we have undeniable evidence before us that the creation of the courts now under consideration was totally unnecessary; and as no Government can . . . seriously deny that this Legislature has a right to repeal a law enacted by a preceding one, we will, in any event, discharge our duty by repealing this law; and thereby doing all in our power to correct the evil. If the judges are entitled to their salaries under the Constitution, our repeal will not affect them; and they will, no doubt, resort to their proper remedy. For where there is a Constitutional right, there must be a Constitutional remedy.

Mr. **J. MASON** of Massachusetts. . . .

The Constitution, in the construction of the Executive, Legislative, and Judiciary departments, had assigned to each a different tenure . . . . It says to the President at the expiration of every four years, you shall revert to the character of a private citizen, however splendid your talents or conspicuous your virtue. Why? Because you have assigned to you powers which it is dangerous to exercise. You have the power of creating offices and officers. You have prerogatives. The temptation to an abuse of your power is great. . . . The Constitution holds the same language to the Senate and House of Representatives

. . . .

To the Judiciary: What is the language applied to them? The judges . . . hold their appointments for life, unless they misbehave themselves. Why? For this reason: They are not the depositaries of the high prerogatives of Government. They neither appoint to office, or hold the purse-strings of the country, or legislate for it. They depend entirely upon their talents . . . . They cannot, therefore, be disposed to pervert their power to improper purposes. What are their duties? To expound and apply the laws. To do this, with fidelity and skill, requires a length of time. The requisite knowledge is not to be procured in a day . . . .

. . . [T]he people, in forming their Constitution, meant to make the judges as independent of the Legislature as of the Executive. Because the duties which they have to perform, call upon them to expound not only the laws, but the Constitution also; in which is involved the power of checking the Legislature in case it should pass any laws in violation of the Constitution. For this reason it was more important that the judges in this country should be placed beyond the control of the Legislature, than in other countries where no such power attaches to them. . . .

Thus [the Constitution] says "the judges *shall* hold their offices during good behaviour." How can this direction of the Constitution be complied with, if the Legislature shall, from session to session, repeal the law under which the office is held, and *remove the office?* He * did not conceive that any words, which human ingenuity could devise, could more completely get over the remarks that had been made by the gentleman from Kentucky. . . .

Besides, if Congress have the right to repeal the whole of the law, they must possess the right to repeal a section of it. If so, they may repeal the law so far as it applies to a particular district, and thus get rid of an obnoxious judge. . . . Would it not be absurd still to say, that the removed judge held his office during good behaviour? . . .

Mr. **MORRIS**,** of New York . . . .

. . . What will be the effect of the desired repeal? Will it not be a declaration to the remaining judges that they hold their offices subject to your will and pleasure? And what will be the result of this? It will be, that the check established by the Constitution, wished for by the people, and necessary in every contemplation of common sense, is destroyed. It had been said, and truly, too, that Governments are made to provide against the follies and vices of men. For to suppose that Governments rest upon reason is a pitiful solecism. If mankind were reasonable, they would want no Government. Hence, checks are required in the distribution of power among those who are to exercise it for the benefit of the people. Did the people of America vest all powers in the Legislature? No; they had vested in the judges a check intended to be efficient—a check of the first necessity, to prevent an invasion of the Constitution by unconstitutional laws—a check which might prevent any faction from intimidating or annihilating the tribunals themselves . . . .

Let us then, secondly, consider whether we have constitutionally a power to repeal this law. [Here Mr. Morris quoted the third article and first section of the Constitution.] I have heard a verbal criticism about the words *shall* and *may,* which appeared the more unnecessary to me, as the same word, *shall,* is applied to both members of the section. For it says "the judicial power, &c. *shall* be vested in one Supreme Court and such inferior courts as the Congress *may,* from time to time, ordain and establish." The Legislature, therefore, had, without doubt, the right of determining, in the first instance, what inferior courts should be established; but when established, the words are imperative, a part of the judicial power shall vest in them. And "the judges shall hold their offices during good behaviour." They shall receive a compensation which shall not be diminished during their continuance in office.

---

* **Eds.' Note:** The switch to the third person here illustrates difficulties stenographers had before invention of modern shorthand. They sometimes fell behind in recording the debates and had to summarize what had been said.

** **Eds.' Note:** Gouverneur Morris had been one of the more influential delegates at the Philadelphia Convention in 1787. He had been chairman of the Committee on Style and had written much of the final draft of the constitutional document.

Therefore, whether the remarks be applied to the tenure of office, or the quantum of compensation, the Constitution is equally imperative . . . .

But another criticism . . . has been made: the amount of which is, you shall not take the man from the office, but you may take the office from the man . . . . The Constitution secures to a judge his office, says he shall hold it, that is, it shall not be taken from him during good behaviour; the Legislature shall not diminish, though their bounty may increase, his salary; the Constitution provides perfectly for the inviolability of his tenure; but yet we may destroy the office which we cannot take away . . . . Is not this absurd? . . .

Mr. **JACKSON**, of Georgia . . . .

We have been asked, if we are afraid of having an army of judges? For myself, I am more afraid of an army of judges, under the patronage of the President, than of an army of soldiers. The former can do us more harm. . . . Have we not seen sedition laws? Have we not heard judges crying out through the land, sedition! . . .

Here then, said he, are two tribunals. First, the Supreme Court, the creature of the Constitution, the creature of the people; the other, the inferior jurisdictions, the creature of the Legislature . . . . The word *shall,* applied to the Supreme Court, is imperative and commanding, while the word *may,* applied to the inferior courts, is discretionary, and leaves to the Legislature a volition to act, or not to act, as it sees fit.

Again, why are the peculiar and exclusive powers of the Supreme Court designated in the following section of the Constitution, but because the Constitution considered that tribunal as absolutely established; while it viewed the inferior tribunals as dependent upon the will of the Legislature? And that this was the case was evident from the conduct of the Supreme Court on the pension act, which that court had some time since declared unconstitutional; and which declaration, he was convinced, would not have been hazarded by an inferior tribunal. . . .*

---

* **Eds.' Note:** The reference is probably either to Hayburn's Case (1792) or to United States v. Todd (decided in 1794 but not reported until 1852). The Invalid Pension Act of 1792 in effect authorized U.S. circuit courts—at that time the principal federal trial courts, staffed by two justices of the Supreme Court and one district judge—to act as commissioners and recommend to the Secretary of War awards for pensions to veterans of the Revolution. On circuit, four justices wrote to the President, protesting that such duties were nonjudicial and declining to perform them. One of these suits—Hayburn's Case—reached the Supreme Court, but before the Court reached a decision on the merits, Congress amended the statute. *Todd* questioned whether a recommendation actually given by a circuit court under the Act of 1792 was a legal judgment. The Supreme Court held, apparently unanimously, that that statute had attempted to confer nonjudicial duties on judges and was therefore unconstitutional. (One should note that *Todd* was brought under the Court's original jurisdiction, according to the terms of an Act of 1793. Cf. Marbury v. Madison [1803], which held that Congress could not add to the Court's original jurisdiction as spelled out in Article III of the Constitution.)

. . . Do not the observations of gentlemen, who insist upon the permanent tenure of the Judicial office, place the creature above its creator, man above his God, the model above its mechanic? . . .

But, upon the principles of gentlemen, the law which creates a judge cannot be touched . . . . What is the implication of this doctrine? To alter or amend what may greatly require alteration or amendment, it is necessary to return to the creator, and to inquire what this creator is. My principle is, that the creator is the people themselves; that very people of the United States whom the gentleman from New York [Sen. Morris] had declared ourselves to be the guardians of, to save the people themselves from their greatest enemies; and to save whom from destroying themselves he had invoked this House. Good God! is it possible that I have heard such a sentiment in this body? . . .

. . . Look to the Constitution, and see how it is to be amended.

There is required first, then, two-thirds of both Houses of Congress. Can this two-thirds be found now, or is there any probability of its being found for twenty years to come, who will concur in making the necessary alterations in the Judiciary system that are now, or may hereafter, be required? On this subject there are as many opinions as there are persons on this floor . . . . How, then, can we expect three-fourths of the Legislatures of the several States to agree when we cannot agree among ourselves. . . .

I am clearly, therefore, of opinion, that if the power to alter the Judiciary system vests not here, it vests no where. . . .

Mr. **MORRIS**, of New York . . . .

It is said, the judicial institution is intended for the benefit of the people, and not of the judge . . . . But the question remains, how will it be rendered most beneficial? Is it by making the judge independent, by making it *his* office, or is it by placing him in a state of abject dependence, so that the office shall be his to-day and belong to another to-morrow? Let the gentleman hear the words of the Constitution: It speaks of *their* offices; consequently, as applied to a single judge, of *his* office, to be exercised by him for the benefit of the people of America, to which exercise his independence is as necessary as his office . . . .

. . . In so far as they [judges] may be busied with the great mischief of checking the Legislative or Executive departments in any wanton invasion of our rights, I shall rejoice in that mischief. I hope, indeed, they will not be so busied, because I hope we shall give them no cause. But I also hope they will keep an eagle eye upon us lest we should. It was partly for this purpose they were established, and, I trust, that when properly called on, they will dare to act. I know this doctrine is unpleasant; I know it is more popular to appeal to public opinion—that equivocal, transient being, which exists nowhere and everywhere. But if ever the occasion calls for it, I trust the Supreme Court will not neglect doing the great mischief of saving this Constitution, which can be done much better by their deliberations, than by resorting to what are called revolutionary measures . . . .

. . . The Judicial power, that fortress of the Constitution, is now to be overturned . . . . I am too weak to defend the rampart against the host of assailants. I must call to my assistance their good sense, their patriotism, and their virtue. . . . Do not rely on that popular will, which has brought us frail beings into political existence. That opinion is but a changeable thing . . . . Do not, I beseech you, in reliance on a foundation so frail, commit the dignity, the harmony, the existence of our nation to the wild wind. Trust not your treasure to the waves. Throw not your compass and your charts into the ocean . . . . Cast not away this only anchor of our safety. I have seen its progress. I know the difficulties through which it was obtained. I stand in the presence of Almighty God, and of the world; and I declare to you, that if you lose this charter, never, no, never will you get another! We are now, perhaps, arrived at the parting point. Here, even here, we stand on the brink of fate. Pause—pause! For Heaven's sake, pause!

Mr. **BRECKENRIDGE** . . . .

I did not expect, sir, to find the doctrine of the power of the courts to annul the laws of Congress as unconstitutional, so seriously insisted on. . . . It is said that the different departments of Government are to be checks on each other, and that the courts are to check the Legislature. If this be true I would ask where they got that power, and who checks the courts when they violate the Constitution? Would they not, by this doctrine, have the absolute direction of the Government? To whom are they responsible? But I deny the power which is so pretended. If it is derived from the Constitution, I ask gentlemen to point out the clause which grants it. I can find no such grant. Is it not extraordinary, that if this high power was intended, it should nowhere appear? Is it not truly astonishing that the Constitution, in its abundant care to define the powers of each department, should have omitted so important a power as that of the courts to nullify all the acts of Congress, which, in their opinion, were contrary to the Constitution?

Never were such high and transcendent powers in any Government . . . claimed or exercised by construction only. The doctrine of constructions, not warranted by the letter of an instrument, is dangerous in the extreme. . . . Once admit the doctrine, that judges are to be indulged in these astute and wire-drawn constructions, to enlarge their own power, and control that of others, and I will join gentlemen of the opposition, in declaring that the Constitution is in danger.

To make the Constitution a practical system, this pretended power of the courts to annul the laws of Congress cannot possibly exist. My idea of the subject . . . is, that the Constitution intended a separation of the powers vested in the three great departments, giving to each exclusive authority on the subjects committed to it. That these departments are co-ordinate, to revolve each within the sphere of their own orbits, without being responsible for their own motion, and are not to direct or control the course of others. That those who made the laws are presumed to have an equal attachment to, and interest in the Constitution; are equally bound by oath to support it, and have an equal right to give a construction to it. That the construction of one department of the powers vested in it, is of higher authority than the construction of any other department; and that, in fact, it is competent to that department to which powers are confided exclusively to decide upon the proper exercise of those powers: that therefore the Legislature have the exclusive right to interpret the Constitution, in what regards the law-making power, and the judges are bound to execute the laws they make. For the Legislature would have at least an equal right to annul the decisions of the courts, founded on their construction of the Constitution, as the courts would have to annul the acts of the Legislature, founded on their construction.

Although, therefore, the courts may take upon them to give decisions which impeach the constitutionality of a law, and thereby, for a time, obstruct its operations, yet I contend that such a law is not the less obligatory because the organ through which it is to be executed, has refused its aid. A pertinacious adherence of both departments to their opinions, would soon bring the question to issue, in whom the sovereign power of legislation resided, and whose construction of the law-making power should prevail.

If the courts have a right to examine into, and decide upon the constitutionality of laws, their decision ought to be final and effectual. I ask then, if gentlemen are prepared to admit, that in case the courts were to declare your revenue, impost and appropriation laws unconstitutional, that they would thereby be blotted out of your statute book and the operations of Government be arrested? It is making, in my opinion, a mockery of the high powers of legislation. . . . Let gentlemen consider well before they insist on a power in the Judiciary which places the Legislature at their feet . . . .

Mr. **MORRIS**, of New York . . . .

. . . The honorable member tells us the Legislature have the supreme and exclusive right to interpret the Constitution, so far as regards the making of laws; which, being made, the judges are bound to execute. And he asks where the judges got their pretended power of deciding on the constitutionality of laws? . . . I answer, they derived that power from authority higher than this Constitution. They derive it from the constitution of man, from the nature of things, from the necessary progress of human affairs. When you have enacted a law, when process thereon has been issued, and suit brought it becomes eventually necessary that the judges decide on the case before them, and declare what the law is. They must, of course, determine whether that which is produced and relied on, has indeed the binding force of law. The decision of the Supreme Court is, and, of necessity, must be final. This, Sir, is the principle and the source of the right for which we contend. But it is denied and the supremacy of the Legislature insisted on. Mark, then, I pray, the result: The Constitution says, no bill of attainder, or *ex post facto* law shall be passed, no capitation or other direct tax shall be laid, unless in proportion to the census or enumeration to be taxed; no tax or duty shall be laid on articles exported from any State . . . . Suppose that, notwithstanding these prohibitions, a majority of the two Houses should (with the President) pass such laws. Suppose, for instance, that a capitation tax (not warranted by the Constitution) or a duty on exports were imposed. The citizen refuses to pay; but courts dependent on the will and pleasure of the Legislature are compelled to enforce the collection. Shall it be said, that there is an appeal to the Supreme Court? Sir, that appeal is subject to such exceptions and regulations as Congress shall make. Congress can, therefore, defeat the appeal, and render final the judgment of inferior tribunals, subjected to their absolute control. Nay, sir, to avoid all possible doubt or question, the honorable member last up has told us in so many words, that the Legislature may decide exclusively on the Constitution, and that the judges are bound to execute the laws which the Legislature enact. Examine then the state to which we are brought. If this doctrine be sustained . . . what possible mode is there to avoid the conclusion that the moment the Legislature of the Union declare themselves supreme, they become so? The analogies so often assumed to the British Parliament, will then be complete. The sovereignty of America will no longer reside in the people, but in the Congress, and the Constitution is whatever they choose to make it . . . .

The bill to repeal passed the Senate 16–15 and the House 59–32. It became law on March 31, 1802. The sixteen circuit judges lost their offices and their salaries. Although John Marshall thought that Congress could not constitutionally require justices of the Supreme Court to function also as trial judges, he acquiesced in the views of his colleagues and resumed circuit riding. A short time later, when a private litigant raised Marshall's point, the Court curtly and unanimously dismissed the issue as settled by long practice. Stuart v. Laird (1803).

"It is emphatically the province and duty of the judicial department to say what the law is."

B. MARBURY v. MADISON
5 U.S. (1 Cranch) 137, 2 L.Ed. 60 (1803).

Against the backdrop of debate and repeal, Marbury v. Madison continued its way through the Court's processes. It was scheduled to come up again in June, 1802; but, soon after repeal of the Judiciary Act of 1801, the Jeffersonians pushed through Congress a statute postponing the next sitting of the Supreme Court until February, 1803. The additional time was supposed to allow the justices to reflect on the distrust in which they were held by the new President and his Congress and dissuade them from issuing a mandamus to the Secretary of State. Indeed, rumors were rife in Washington that, were the Court to issue the writ, Jefferson would instruct Madison to ignore it; the question of judicial authority over elected officials would be determined on the scales of political power.

Mr. Chief Justice **MARSHALL** delivered the opinion of the Court

. . . .

In the order in which the court has viewed this subject, the following questions have been considered and decided.

1st. Has the applicant a right to the commission he demands?

2d. If he has a right, and that right has been violated, do the laws of his country afford him a remedy?

3d. If they do afford him a remedy, is it a mandamus issuing from this court?

The first object of inquiry is,

1st. Has the applicant a right to the commission he demands?

. . .

It is . . . decidedly the opinion of the court, that when a commission has been signed by the President, the appointment is made; and that the commission is complete when the seal of the United States has been affixed to it by the Secretary of State. . . .

The discretion of the executive is to be exercised until the appointment has been made. But having once made the appointment, his power over the office is terminated in all cases, where by law the officer is not removable by him. The right to the office is then in the person appointed, and he has the absolute, unconditional power of accepting or rejecting it.

Mr. Marbury, then, since his commission was signed by the President, and sealed by the Secretary of State, was appointed; and as the law creating the office, gave the officer a right to hold for five years, independent of the executive, the appointment was not revocable, but vested in the officer legal rights, which are protected by the laws of his country.

To withhold his commission, therefore, is an act deemed by the court not warranted by law, but violative of a vested legal right.

This brings us to the second inquiry; which is,

2d. If he has a right, and that right has been violated, do the laws of his country afford him a remedy?

The very essence of civil liberty certainly consists in the right of every individual to claim the protection of the laws, whenever he receives an injury. One of the first duties of government is to afford that protection. In Great Britain the king himself is sued in the respectful form of a petition, and he never fails to comply with the judgment of his court.

In . . . his *Commentaries* Blackstone states two cases in which a remedy is afforded by mere operation of law.

"In all other cases," he says, "it is a general and indisputable rule, that where there is a legal right, there is also a legal remedy by suit, or action at law, whenever that right is invaded." . . .

The government of the United States has been emphatically termed a government of laws, and not of men. It will certainly cease to deserve this high appellation, if the laws furnish no remedy for the violation of a vested legal right.

If this obloquy is to be cast on the jurisprudence of our country, it must arise from the peculiar character of the case . . . .

[Marshall then analyzed the "peculiar character" of the case and found nothing that exempted it from the usual rules of law.]

It is, then, the opinion of the Court,

1st. That by signing the commission of Mr. Marbury, the President of the United States appointed him a justice of peace for the county of Washington, in the District of Columbia; and that the seal of the United States, affixed thereto by the Secretary of State, is conclusive testimony of the verity of the signature, and of the completion of the appointment; and that the appointment conferred on him a legal right to the office for the space of five years.

2d. That, having this legal title to the office, he has a consequent right to the commission; a refusal to deliver which is a plain violation of that right, for which the laws of his country afford him a remedy.

It remains to be inquired whether,

3d. He is entitled to the remedy for which he applies. This depends on,

1st. The nature of the writ applied for; and,

2d. The power of this court.

1st. The nature of the writ . . . .

This writ [of mandamus], if awarded, would be directed to an officer of government [the Secretary of State], and its mandate to him would be, to use the words of Blackstone, "to do a particular thing therein specified, which appertains to his office and duty, and which the court has previously determined, or at least supposes, to be consonant to right and justice." . . .

These circumstances certainly concur in this case. . . .

. . . . The intimate political relation subsisting between the President of the United States and the heads of departments, necessarily renders any legal investigation of the acts of one of those high officers peculiarly irksome, as well as delicate; and excites some hesitation with respect to the propriety of entering into such investigation . . . .

It is scarcely necessary for the court to disclaim all pretensions to such jurisdiction. An extravagance, so absurd and excessive, could not have been entertained for a moment. The province of the court is, solely, to decide on the rights of individuals, not to inquire how the executive, or executive officers, perform duties in which they have a discretion. Questions in their nature political, or which are, by the constitution and laws, submitted to the executive, can never be made in this court . . . .

[But i]f one of the heads of departments commits an illegal act, under colour of his office, by which an individual sustains an injury, it cannot be pretended that his office alone exempts him from being sued in the ordinary mode of proceeding, and being compelled to obey the judgment of the law . . . .

The act to establish the judicial courts of the United States authorizes the Supreme Court "to issue writs of mandamus in cases warranted by the principles and usages of law, to any courts appointed, or persons holding office, under the authority of the United States."

The Secretary of State, being a person holding an office under the authority of the United States, is precisely within the letter of the description, and if this court is not authorized to issue a writ of mandamus to such an officer, it must be because the law is unconstitutional, and therefore absolutely incapable of conferring the authority, and assigning the duties which its words purport to confer and assign.

The constitution vests the whole judicial power of the United States in one Supreme Court, and such inferior courts as congress shall, from time to time, ordain and establish. This power is expressly extended to all cases arising under the laws of the United States; and, consequently, in some form, may be exercised over the present case; because the right claimed is given by a law of the United States.

In the distribution of this power it is declared that "the Supreme Court shall have original jurisdiction in all cases affecting ambassadors, other public ministers and consuls, and those in which a state shall be a party. In all other cases, the Supreme Court shall have appellate jurisdiction." . . .

If it had been intended to leave it in the discretion of the legislature to apportion the judicial power between the supreme and inferior courts according to the will of that body, it would certainly have been useless to have proceeded further than to have defined the judicial power, and the tribunals in which it should be vested. The subsequent part of the section is mere surplusage, is entirely without meaning, if such is to be the construction. If congress remains at liberty to give this court appellate jurisdiction, where the constitution has declared their jurisdiction shall be original; and original jurisdiction where the constitution has declared it shall be appellate; the distribution of jurisdiction, made in the constitution, is form without substance.

Affirmative words are often, in their operation, negative of other objects than those affirmed; and in this case, a negative or exclusive sense must be given to them, or they have no operation at all.

It cannot be presumed that any clause in the constitution is intended to be without effect; and, therefore, such a construction is inadmissible, unless the words require it. . . .

To enable this court, then, to issue a mandamus, it must be shown to be an exercise of appellate jurisdiction, or to be necessary to enable them to exercise appellate jurisdiction. . . .

It is the essential criterion of appellate jurisdiction, that it revises and corrects the proceedings in a cause already instituted, and does not create that cause. Although, therefore, a mandamus may be directed to courts, yet to issue such a writ to an officer for the delivery of a paper, is in effect the same as to sustain an original action for that paper, and, therefore, seems not to belong to appellate, but to original jurisdiction. . . .

The authority, therefore, given to the Supreme Court, by the act establishing the judicial courts of the United States, to issue writs of mandamus to public officers, appears not to be warranted by the constitution;* and it becomes necessary to inquire whether a jurisdiction so conferred can be exercised.

The question, whether an act, repugnant to the constitution, can become the law of the land, is a question deeply interesting to the United States; but, happily, not of an intricacy proportioned to its interest. It seems only necessary to recognize certain principles, supposed to have been long and well established, to decide it.

That the people have an original right to establish, for their future government, such principles, as, in their opinion, shall most conduce to their own happiness is the basis on which the whole American fabric has been erected. The exercise of this original right is a very great exertion; nor can it, nor ought it, to be frequently repeated. The principles, therefore, so established, are deemed fundamental. And as the authority from which they proceed is supreme, and can seldom act, they are designed to be permanent.

This original and supreme will organizes the government, and assigns to different departments their respective powers. It may either stop here, or establish certain limits not to be transcended by those departments.

The government of the United States is of the latter description. The powers of the legislature are defined and limited; and that those limits may not be mistaken, or forgotten, the constitution is written. To what purpose are powers limited, and to what purpose is that limitation committed to writing, if these limits may, at any time, be passed by those intended to be restrained? The distinction between a government with limited and unlimited powers is abolished, if those limits do not confine the persons on whom they are imposed, and if acts

---

* **Eds.' Note**—The relevant part of Section 13 of the Judiciary Act of 1789, the section that purportedly conferred authority on the Supreme Court to hear Marbury's case under the Court's original jurisdiction, read:

The Supreme Court shall also have appellate jurisdiction from the circuit courts [of the United States] and courts of the several states, in the cases herein after specifically provided for; and shall have power to issue writs of prohibition to the district courts [of the United States], when proceeding as courts of admiralty and maritime jurisdiction, and writs of mandamus, in cases warranted by the principles and usages of law, to any courts appointed, or persons holding office, under the authority of the United States.

Query: Is Marshall's contention that Section 13 attempted to confer additional original jurisdiction on the Supreme Court based on a fair reading of the plain words of the statute?

prohibited and acts allowed, are of equal obligation. It is a proposition too plain to be contested, that the constitution controls any legislative act repugnant to it; or, that the legislature may alter the constitution by an ordinary act.

Between these alternatives there is no middle ground. The constitution is either a superior paramount law, unchangeable by ordinary means, or it is on a level with ordinary legislative acts, and, like other acts, is alterable when the legislature shall please to alter it.

If the former part of the alternative be true, then a legislative act contrary to the constitution is not law: if the latter part be true, then written constitutions are absurd attempts, on the part of the people, to limit a power in its own nature illimitable.

Certainly all those who have framed written constitutions contemplate them as forming the fundamental and paramount law of the nation, and, consequently, the theory of every such government must be, that an act of the legislature, repugnant to the constitution, is void.

This theory is essentially attached to a written constitution, and, is consequently, to be considered, by this court, as one of the fundamental principles of our society . . . .

If an act of the legislature, repugnant to the constitution, is void, does it, notwithstanding its invalidity, bind the courts, and oblige them to give it effect? . . . This would be to overthrow in fact what was established in theory; and would seem, at first view, an absurdity too gross to be insisted on. It shall, however, receive a more attentive consideration.

It is emphatically the province and duty of the judicial department to say what the law is. Those who apply the rule to particular cases, must of necessity expound and interpret that rule. If two laws conflict with each other, the courts must decide on the operation of each.

So if a law be in opposition to the constitution; if both the law and the constitution apply to a particular case, so that the court must either decide that case conformably to the law, disregarding the constitution; or conformably to the constitution, disregarding the law; the court must determine which of these conflicting rules governs the case. This is of the very essence of judicial duty.

If, then, the courts are to regard the constitution, and the constitution is superior to any ordinary act of the legislature, the constitution, and not such ordinary act, must govern the case to which they both apply.

Those then who controvert the principle that the constitution is to be considered, in court, as a paramount law, are reduced to the necessity of maintaining that courts must close their eyes on the constitution, and see only the law.

This doctrine would subvert the very foundation of all written constitutions. It would declare that an act which, according to the principles and theory of our government, is entirely void, is yet, in practice, completely obligatory. It would declare that if the legislature shall do what is expressly forbidden, such act, notwithstanding the express prohibition, is in reality effectual. It would be giving to the legislature a practical and real omnipotence, with the same breath which professes to restrict their powers within narrow limits. . . .

That it thus reduces to nothing what we have deemed the greatest improvement on political institutions, a written constitution, would of itself be sufficient, in America, where written constitutions have been viewed with so much reverence, for rejecting the construction. But the peculiar expressions of the constitution of the United States furnish additional arguments in favour of its rejection.

The judicial power of the United States is extended to all cases arising under the constitution.

Could it be the intention of those who gave this power, to say that in using it the constitution should not be looked into? That a case arising under the constitution should be decided without examining the instrument under which it arises?

This is too extravagant to be maintained.

In some cases, then, the constitution must be looked into by the judges. And if they can open it at all, what part of it are they forbidden to read or to obey?

There are many other parts of the constitution which serve to illustrate this subject. . . .

The constitution declares "that no bill of attainder or ex post facto law shall be passed."

If, however, such a bill should be passed, and a person should be prosecuted under it; must the court condemn to death those victims whom the constitution endeavours to preserve?

"No person," says the constitution, "shall be convicted of treason unless on the testimony of two witnesses to the same overt act, or on confession in open court."

Here the language of the constitution is addressed especially to the courts. It prescribes, directly for them, a rule of evidence not to be departed from. If the legislature should change that rule, and declare one witness, or a confession out of court, sufficient for conviction, must the constitutional principle yield to the legislative act?

From these, and many other selections which might be made, it is apparent, that the framers of the constitution contemplated that instrument as a rule for the government of courts, as well as of the legislature.

Why otherwise does it direct the judges to take an oath to support it? This oath certainly applies, in an especial manner, to their conduct in their official character. How immoral to impose it on them, if they were to be used as the instruments, and the knowing instruments, for violating what they swear to support!

The oath of office, too, imposed by the legislature, is completely demonstrative of the legislative opinion on this subject. It is in these words: "I do solemnly swear that I will administer justice without respect to persons, and do equal right to the poor and to the rich; and that I will faithfully and impartially discharge all the duties incumbent on me as according to the best of my abilities and understanding, agreeably to the constitution and laws of the United States."

Why does a judge swear to discharge his duties agreeably to the constitution of the United States, if that constitution forms no rule for his government? . . .

If such be the real state of things, this is worse than solemn mockery. To prescribe, or to take this oath, becomes equally a crime.

It is also not entirely unworthy of observation, that in declaring what shall be the supreme law of the land, the constitution itself is first mentioned; and not the laws of the United States generally, but those only which shall be made in pursuance of the constitution, have that rank.

Thus, the particular phraseology of the constitution of the United States confirms and strengthens the principle, supposed to be essential to all written constitutions, that a law repugnant to the constitution is void; and that courts, as well as other departments, are bound by that instrument.

The rule must be discharged.

Editors' Notes

(1) **Query**: Does Marshall claim that the judiciary has an exclusive or even primary authority to interpret the Constitution? Does he claim that other branches of government, in their operations, are bound by judicial interpretations of the Constitution? Compare the reach of Marshall's reasoning with that of the Court in Cooper v. Aaron (1958), reprinted below, p. 281.

(2) For important analyses of *Marbury,* see especially: Albert J. Beveridge, *The Life of John Marshall* (Boston: Houghton Mifflin Co., 1919), III, ch. 3; Charles Warren, *The Supreme Court in United States History* (Rev. ed.; Boston: Little, Brown, and Co., 1926), I, chs. 4–5; Robert K. Faulkner, *The Jurisprudence of John Marshall* (Princeton, N.J.: Princeton University Press, 1968), pp. 192–223; William Van Alstyne, "A Critical Guide to Marbury v. Madison," 1969 *Duke L.J.* 1; George L. Haskins and Herbert A. Johnson, *History of the Supreme Court of the United States,* Vol. II: *Foundations of Power: John Marshall, 1801–1815* (New York: Macmillan, 1981), chs. 5–6.

"The Constitution intended that the three great branches of government should be co-ordinate, & independent of each other. As to acts, therefore, which are to be done by either, it has given no controul to another branch."

JEFFERSON INSTRUCTS A FEDERAL PROSECUTOR
(1807).

Marshall's cunning handling of Marbury v. Madison was a masterpiece of political strategy. He had, more firmly than the justices' letters to President Washington in Hayburn's Case (1792) or the judgment in United States v. Todd

(1794), proclaimed the doctrine of judicial review and had done so without issuing an order that Jefferson could flout. The reaction of the President's followers to *Marbury* was one of outrage; but, curiously, attention focused less on Marshall's assertion of judicial power to annul acts of Congress than on the opening sections of the opinion in which the Chief Justice had ruled that Jefferson had illegally withheld Marbury's commission.

Marbury chose not to seek redress in a lower court, and so the case quietly died. The Jeffersonians turned their energies to further cleansing the bench of Federalists. The House impeached and the Senate convicted and removed a district judge from New Hampshire. The House then impeached Justice Samuel Chase, one of Marshall's colleagues. In addressing grand and trial juries proceeding under the Sedition Act, Chase had flagrantly abused his power so as to ensure that Jeffersonians would be punished for their political views. Nevertheless, the President's men could not muster the necessary two-thirds vote in the Senate for conviction.

That same year, 1804, Marshall deftly advanced judicial power another long step by asserting authority to sit in constitutional judgment over presidential acts. In Little v. Barreme (reprinted below, p. 331) he held for the Court that President Adams had exceeded his lawful authority in carrying out the quasi-naval war with France in the late 1790s. The justices affirmed a district court order to a naval captain to return to its owners a ship seized in a blockade of French ports in the West Indies. Jefferson might have commanded the navy to ignore the order had it not been for the fact that, at the time Adams had ordered the blockade, Jefferson had openly opposed the policy. Thus Marshall had neatly skewered him again.

In 1807, Jefferson's decision to prosecute Aaron Burr, his former vice president, for treason provided another battlefield. The circuit court that had jurisdiction to conduct the trial was located in Virginia; and, because of the repeal of the Act of 1801, Supreme Court justices were again riding circuit, and Burr's tribunal was presided over by the Chief Justice. Anticipating that Marshall would issue a subpoena to the White House to forward various papers relating to earlier reports of a key witness for the government, Jefferson informed the prosecutor that he would "voluntarily" provide "whatever the purposes of justice may require," at the same time reserving "the necessary right of the President of the U S to decide, independently of all other authority, what papers, coming to him as President, the public interests permit to be communicated, & to whom . . . ." In addition, the President gave special instructions regarding the government's position about Marbury v. Madison:

WASHINGTON, June 2, 07.

DEAR SIR,—While Burr's case is depending before the court, I will trouble you, from time to time, with what occurs to me. I observe that the case of Marbury v. Madison has been cited, and I think it material to stop at the threshold the citing that case as authority, and to have it denied to be law. 1. Because the judges, in the outset, disclaimed all cognizance of the case, altho' they then went on to say what would have been their opinion, had they had cognizance of it. This, then, was confessedly an extrajudicial opinion, and, as such, of no authority. 2. Because, had it been judicially pronounced, it would have been against law; for to a commission, a deed, a bond, *delivery* is essential to give validity. Until, therefore, the commission is delivered out of the hands of the Executive & his agents, it is not his deed. He may withhold or cancel it at pleasure, as he might his private deed in the same situation. The Constitution intended that the three great branches of the government should be co-ordinate, & independent of each other. As to acts, therefore, which are to be done by either, it has given no controul to another branch. A judge, I presume, cannot sit on a bench without a commission, or a record of a commission; & the Constitution having given to the judiciary branch no means of compelling the executive either to *deliver* a commission, or to make a record of it, shews it did not intend to give the judiciary that controul over the executive, but that it should remain in the power of the latter to do it or not. Where different branches have to act in their respective lines, finally & without appeal, under any law, they may give to it different and opposite constructions. . . . . In the cases of Callendar & some others, the judges determined the sedition act was valid under the Constitution, and exercised their regular powers of sentencing them to fine & imprisonment. But the executive determined that the sedition act was a nullity under the Constitution, and exercised his regular power of prohibiting the execution of the sentence . . . .

On this construction I have hitherto acted; on this I shall ever act, and maintain it with the powers of the government, against any control which may be attempted by the judges, in subversion of the independence of the executive & Senate within their peculiar department. I presume, therefore, that in a case where our decision is by the Constitution the supreme one, & that which can be carried into effect, it is the constitutionally authoritative one, and that that by the judges was *coram non judice*, & unauthoritative, because it cannot be carried into effect. I have long wished for a proper occasion to have the gratuitous opinion in Marbury v. Madison brought before the public, & denounced as not law; & I think the present a fortunate one, because it occupies such a place in the public attention. I should be glad, therefore, if, in noticing that case, you could take occasion to express the determination of the executive, that the doctrines of that case were given extrajudicially & against law, and that their reverse will be the rule of action with the executive. . . .

Marshall did issue the subpoena. Not out of recognition of the court's authority but to promote justice, Jefferson complied with most of its terms. He also drafted a letter to the federal marshal of the circuit court instructing him not to try to enforce the subpoena. The Chief Justice did not press the matter, though Burr's attorneys asked the court to enforce full compliance with the writ.

"The grant of a power so extraordinary ought to appear so plain, that he who should run might read."

EAKIN v. RAUB

12 Sergeant & Rawle (Supreme Court of Pennsylvania) (1825).

To a large extent, the Jeffersonian senators in 1802 were arguing for departmental equality in constitutional interpretation. Several decades later, Justice John Gibson of the supreme court of Pennsylvania wrote a dissenting opinion that made a straightforward argument for legislative supremacy.

GIBSON, J. . . .

. . . I begin, then, by observing that in this country, the powers of the judiciary are divisible into those that are POLITICAL and those that are purely CIVIL. Every power by which one organ of the government is enabled to control another, or to exert an influence over its acts, is a political power . . . . [The judiciary's] civil, are its *ordinary* and *appropriate* powers; being part of its essence, and existing independently of any supposed grant in the constitution. But where the government exists by virtue of a *written* constitution, the judiciary does not necessarily derive from that circumstance, any other than its ordinary and appropriate powers. Our judiciary is constructed on the principles of the common law, which enters so essentially into the composition of our social institutions as to be inseparable from them, and to be, in fact, the basis of the whole scheme of our civil and political liberty. In adopting any organ or instrument of the common law, we take it with just such powers and capacities as were incident to it at the common law, except where these are expressly, or by necessary implication, abridged or enlarged in the act of adoption; and, that such act is a written instrument, cannot vary its consequences or construction. . . . Now, what are the powers of the judiciary at the common law? They are those that necessarily arise out of its immediate business; and they are therefore commensurate only with the judicial execution of the municipal law, or, in other words, with the administration of distributive justice, without extending to anything of a political cast whatever . . . . With us, although the legislature be the depository of only so much of the sovereignty as the people have thought fit to impart, it is nevertheless sovereign within the limit of its powers, and may relatively claim the same pre-eminence here that it may claim elsewhere. It will be conceded, then, that the ordinary and essential powers of the judiciary do not extend to the annulling of an act of the legislature . . . .

The constitution of *Pennsylvania* [like that of the United States] contains no express grant of political powers to the judiciary. But, to establish a grant by implication, the constitution is said to be a law of superior obligation; and, consequently, that if it were to come into collision with an act of the legislature, the latter would have to give way. This is conceded. But it is a fallacy, to suppose that they can come into collision *before the judiciary* . . . .

The constitution and the right of the legislature to pass the act, may be in collision. But is that a legitimate subject for judicial determination? If it be, the judiciary must be a peculiar organ, to revise the proceedings of the legislature, and to correct its mistakes; and in what part of the constitution are we to look for this proud pre-eminence? Viewing the matter in the opposite direction, what would be thought of an act of assembly in which it should be declared that the Supreme Court had, in a particular case, put a wrong construction on the constitution of the United States, and that the judgment should therefore be reversed? It would doubtless be thought a usurpation of judicial power. But it is by no means clear, that to declare a law void which has been enacted according to the forms prescribed in the constitution, is not a usurpation of legislative power . . . .

But it has been said to be emphatically the business of the judiciary, to ascertain and pronounce what the law is; and that this necessarily involves a consideration of the constitution. It does so: but how far? If the judiciary will inquire into anything besides the form of enactment, where shall it stop? There must be some point of limitation to such an inquiry; for no one will pretend that a judge would be justifiable in calling for the election returns, or scrutinizing the qualifications of those who composed the legislature . . . .

. . . In theory, all the organs of the government are of equal capacity; or, if not equal, each must be supposed to have superior capacity only for those things which peculiarly belong to it; and, as legislation peculiarly involves the consideration of those limitations which are put on the law-making power, and the interpretation of the laws when made, involves only the construction of the laws themselves, it follows that the construction of the constitution in this particular belongs to the legislature, which ought therefore to be taken to have superior capacity to judge of the constitutionality of its own acts. But suppose all to be of equal capacity in every respect, why should one exercise a controlling power over the rest? That the judiciary is of superior rank, has never been pretended, although it has been said to be coordinate. It is not easy, however, to comprehend how the power which gives law to all the rest, can be of no more than equal rank with one which receives it, and is answerable to the former for the observance of its statutes. Legislation is essentially an act of sovereign power; but the execution of the laws by instruments that are governed by prescribed rules and exercise no power of volition, is essentially otherwise . . . . It may be said, the power of the legislature, also, is limited by prescribed rules. It is so. But it is, nevertheless, the power of the people, and sovereign as far as it extends. It cannot be said, that the judiciary is co-ordinate merely because it is established by the constitution. . . . Inequality of rank arises not from the manner in which the organ has been constituted, but from its essence and the nature of its functions; and the legislative organ is superior to every other, inasmuch as the power to will and to command, is essentially superior to the power to act and to obey . . . .

. . . [H]ad it been intended to interpose the judiciary as an additional barrier, the matter would surely not have been left in doubt. The judges would not have been left to stand on the insecure and ever shifting ground of public opinion as to constructive powers; they would have been placed on the impregnable ground of an express grant. They would not have been compelled to resort to the debates in the convention, or the opinion that was generally entertained at the time . . . . The grant of a power so extraordinary ought to appear so plain, that he who should run might read . . . .

What I have in view in this inquiry, is the supposed right of the judiciary to interfere, in cases where the constitution is to be carried into effect through the instrumentality of the legislature, and where that organ must necessarily first decide on the constitutionality of its own act. The oath to support the constitution is not peculiar to the judges, but is taken indiscriminately by every officer of the government, and is designed rather as a test of the political principles of the man, than to bind the officer in the discharge of his duty: otherwise it is difficult to determine what operation it is to have in the case of a recorder of deeds, for instance, who, in the execution of his office, has nothing to do with the constitution. But granting it to relate to the official conduct of the judge, as well as every other officer, and not to his political principles, still it must be understood in reference to supporting the constitution, *only as far as that may be involved in his official duty;* and, consequently, if his official duty does not comprehend an inquiry into the authority of the legislature, neither does his oath . . . .

But do not the judges do a positive act in violation of the constitution, when they give effect to an unconstitutional law? Not if the law has been passed according to the forms established in the constitution. The fallacy of the question is, in supposing that the judiciary adopts the acts of the legislature as its own; whereas the enactment of a law and the interpretation of it are not concurrent acts, and as the judiciary is not required to concur in the enactment, neither is it in the breach of the constitution which may be the consequence of the enactment. The fault is imputable to the legislature, and on it the responsibility exclusively rests . . . .

But it has been said, that this construction would deprive the citizen of the advantages which are peculiar to a written constitution, by at once declaring the power of the legislature in practice to be illimitable . . . . But there is no magic or inherent power in parchment and ink, to command respect and protect principles from violation. In the business of government a recurrence to first principles answers the end of an observation at sea with a view to correct the dead reckoning; and for this purpose, a written constitution is an instrument of inestimable value. It is of inestimable value, also, in rendering its first principles familiar to the mass of people; for, after all, there is no effectual guard against legislative usurpation but public opinion, the force of which, in this country is inconceivably great.

. . . Once let public opinion be so corrupt as to sanction every misconstruction of the constitution and abuse of power which the temptation of the moment may dictate, and the party which may happen to be predominant, will laugh at the puny efforts of a dependent power to arrest it in its course.

For these reasons, I am of opinion that it rests with the people, in whom full and absolute sovereign power resides, to correct abuses in legislation, by instructing their representatives to repeal the obnoxious act. . . . On the other hand, the judiciary is not infallible; and an error by it would admit of no remedy but a more distinct expression of the public will, through the extraordinary medium of a convention; whereas, an error by the legislature admits of a remedy by an exertion of the same will, in the ordinary exercise of the right of suffrage,—a mode better calculated to attain the end, without popular excitement
. . . .

But in regard to an act of [a state] assembly, which is found to be in collision with the constitution, laws, or treaties of the *United States,* I take the duty of the judiciary to be exactly the reverse. By becoming parties to the federal constitution, the states have agreed to several limitations of their individual sovereignty, to enforce which, it was thought to be absolutely necessary to prevent them from giving effect to laws in violation of those limitations, through the instrumentality of their own judges. Accordingly, it is declared in the sixth article and second section of the federal constitution, that "This constitution, and the laws of the *United States* which shall be made in pursuance thereof, and all treaties made, or which shall be made under the authority of the *United States,* shall be the *supreme* law of the land; and the *judges* in every *state* shall be BOUND thereby: anything in the *laws* or *constitution* of any *state* to the contrary notwithstanding."

This is an express grant of a political power, and it is conclusive to show that no law of inferior obligation, as every state law must necessarily be, can be executed at the expense of the constitution, laws, or treaties of the *United States.* . . .

Editors' Notes

(1) In 1830 Gibson, who by then was chief justice of Pennsylvania, was touted by the states-rights faction led by John C. Calhoun for a vacancy on the U.S. Supreme Court. President Jackson, however, nominated Henry Baldwin. **Query:** Does the logic of Gibson's dissent in *Eakin* support a states-rights position?

(2) Gibson later changed his mind regarding the authority of Pennsylvania courts to declare acts of the state legislature unconstitutional. He explained the shift as due to the failure of the state constitutional convention that met after *Eakin* to change the clauses that a majority of the court had interpreted to imply that power. *Norris v. Clymer*, 2 Pa.St. 277 (1845). See Charles Warren, *The Supreme Court in United States History* (Rev. ed.; Boston: Little,

Brown, 1926), I, 711–713. Does that change logically affect his argument about authority of courts to declare acts of Congress unconstitutional?

"The Congress, the Executive, and the Court must each . . . be guided by its own opinion of the Constitution."

ANDREW JACKSON'S VETO OF THE BANK BILL *
(1932).

On July 4, 1832, Congress passed an act to continue the Bank of the United States. On July 10, 1832, President Andrew Jackson vetoed the bank bill as unwise, unfair, and unconstitutional. The portion of his veto message dealing with the argument that the constitutionality of the Bank had been definitively settled by the decision of the United States Supreme Court in McCulloch v. Maryland (1819) is reprinted here. This part of the message was largely drafted by Roger Brooke Taney, who was soon to succeed John Marshall as Chief Justice of the United States.

It is maintained by the advocates of the bank that its constitutionality in all its features ought to be considered as settled by precedent and by the decision of the Supreme Court. To this conclusion I can not assent. Mere precedent is a dangerous source of authority, and should not be regarded as deciding questions of constitutional power except where the acquiescence of the people and the States can be considered as well settled. So far from this being the case on the subject, an argument against the bank might be based on precedent. One Congress, in 1791, decided in favor of a bank; another, in 1811, decided against. One Congress, in 1815, decided against a bank; another, in 1816, decided in its favor. Prior to the present Congress, therefore, the precedents drawn from that source were equal. If we resort to the States, the expressions of legislative, judicial, and executive opinions against the bank have been probably to those in its favor as 4 to 1. There is nothing in precedent, therefore, which, if its authority were admitted, ought to weigh in favor of the act before me.

If the opinion of the Supreme Court covered the whole ground of this act, it ought not to control the coordinate authorities of this Government. The Congress, the Executive, and the Court must each for itself be guided by its own opinion of the Constitution. Each public officer who takes an oath to support the Constitution swears that he will support it as he understands it, and not as it is understood by others. It is as much the duty of the House of Representatives, of the Senate, and of the President to decide upon the constitutionality of any bill or resolution which may be presented to them for passage or approval as it is of the supreme judges when it may be brought before them for judicial decision. The opinion of the judges has no more authority over Congress than the opinion of Congress has over the judges, and on that point the President is independent of both. The

---

* James D. Richardson (ed.), *A Compilation of the Messages and Papers of the Presidents* (Washington, D.C.: Bureau of National Literature and Art, 1908), II, 581–582.

authority of the Supreme Court must not, therefore, be permitted to control the Congress or the Executive when acting in their legislative capacities, but to have only such influence as the force of their reasoning may deserve.

———

> "[I]f the policy . . . is to be irrevocably fixed by decisions of the Supreme Court . . . the people will have ceased, to be their own rulers . . . ."

ABRAHAM LINCOLN'S FIRST INAUGURAL ADDRESS *
March 4, 1861.

Believing Lincoln's election marked the start of a federal effort to end slavery, southern state legislatures began adopting resolutions of secession and setting about the business of establishing the Confederate States of America. A divided nation was becoming a reality.

Hovering in the background was the spectre of the Supreme Court's decision in Dred Scott v. Sanford (1857), which had helped polarize the country on the issue of slavery. The Court had ruled: (1) The Framers of the Constitution had meant to exclude blacks from citizenship; (2) Slaves were property; (3) The Fifth Amendment forbade Congress to take a person's property without due process of law, and "due process" had a substantive as well as a procedural aspect; thus Congress could not forbid a man to take his slave into any federal territory or legislate the slave's freedom if he travelled in federal territory; (4) Therefore, the Missouri Compromise and by implication all other political compromises, past and future, to control slavery in the territories were unconstitutional.

If Congress and the president accepted the authority of the Supreme Court to interpret the Constitution definitively for them, slavery could spread through the territories as the slaveholders themselves willed, something many if not most northern state officials were not willing to tolerate. It was widely expected, then, that Lincoln would have to attack the Court's authority, since he was on public record as saying that Dred Scott had been wrongly decided.

In addition to the tremendous practical problems of preventing disunion, Lincoln faced a difficult double problem of constitutional interpretation: Defining the nature of the Union and its distribution of authority between state and nation and, at the same time, defining the distribution of authority among the three branches of the federal government.

Fellow citizens of the United States . . . .

Apprehension seems to exist among the people of the Southern States, that by the accession of a Republican Administration, their property, and their peace, and personal security, are to be endangered. There has never been any reasonable cause for such apprehension. Indeed, the most ample evidence to the contrary has all the while existed . . . . It is found in nearly all the published speeches of him

* From *The Collected Works of Abraham Lincoln*, edited by Roy P. Basler, IV, 262–271. Copyright © 1953, by the Abraham Lincoln Association. Reprinted by permission of Rutgers University Press.

who now addresses you. I do but quote from one of those speeches when I declare that "I have no purpose, directly or indirectly, to interfere with the institution of slavery in the States where it exists. I believe I have no lawful right to do so, and I have no inclination to do so." Those who nominated and elected me did so with full knowledge that I had made this, and many similar declarations, and had never recanted them . . . .

There is much controversy about the delivering up of fugitives from service or labor. The clause I now read is as plainly written in the Constitution as any other of its provisions:

"No person held to service or labor in one State, under the laws thereof, escaping into another, shall, in consequence of any law or regulation therein, be discharged from such service or labor, but shall be delivered up on claim of the party to whom such service or labor may be due."

It is scarcely questioned that this provision was intended by those who made it, for the reclaiming of what we call fugitive slaves; and the intention of the law-giver is the law. All members of Congress swear their support to the whole Constitution—to this provision as much as to any other. To the proposition, then, that slaves whose cases come within the terms of this clause, "shall be delivered up," their oaths are unanimous. Now, if they would make the effort in good temper, could they not, with nearly equal unanimity, frame and pass a law, by means of which to keep good that unanimous oath?

There is some difference of opinion whether this clause should be enforced by national or by state authority; but surely that difference is not a very material one. . . .

Again, in any law upon this subject, ought not all the safeguards of liberty known in civilized and humane jurisprudence to be introduced, so that a free man be not, in any case, surrendered as a slave? And might it not be well, at the same time, to provide by law for the enforcement of that clause in the Constitution which guarranties that "The citizens of each State shall be entitled to all privileges and immunities of citizens in the several States?"

I take the official oath to-day, with no mental reservations, and with no purpose to construe the Constitution or laws, by any hypercritical rules. And while I do not choose now to specify particular acts of Congress as proper to be enforced, I do suggest that it will be much safer for all, both in official and private stations, to conform to, and abide by, all those acts which stand unrepealed, than to violate any of them, trusting to find impunity in having them held to be unconstitutional. . . .

I hold, that in contemplation of universal law, and of the Constitution, the Union of these States is perpetual. Perpetuity is implied, if not expressed, in the fundamental law of all national governments.
. . .

Descending from these general principles, we find the proposition that, in legal contemplation, the Union is perpetual, confirmed by the

history of the Union itself. The Union is much older than the Constitution. It was formed in fact, by the Articles of Association in 1774. It
was matured and continued by the Declaration of Independence in
1776. It was further matured and the faith of all the then thirteen
States expressly plighted and engaged that it should be perpetual, by
the Articles of Confederation in 1778. And finally, in 1787, one of the
declared objects for ordaining and establishing the Constitution, was "*to
form a more perfect union.*"

But if destruction of the Union, by one, or by a part only, of the
States, be lawfully possible, the Union is *less* perfect than before the
Constitution, having lost the vital element of perpetuity.

It follows from these views that no State, upon its own mere
motion, can lawfully get out of the Union,—that *resolves* and *ordinances* to that effect are legally void; and that acts of violence, within
any State or States, against the authority of the United States, are
insurrectionary or revolutionary, according to circumstances.

I therefore consider that, in view of the Constitution and the laws,
the Union is unbroken; and, to the extent of my ability, I shall take
care, as the Constitution itself expressly enjoins upon me, that the laws
of the Union be faithfully executed in all the States. Doing this I deem
to be only a simple duty on my part; and I shall perform it, so far as
practicable, unless my rightful masters, the American people, shall
withhold the requisite means, or, in some authoritative manner, direct
the contrary. I trust this will not be regarded as a menace, but only as
the declared purpose of the Union that it *will* constitutionally defend,
and maintain itself.

In doing this there needs to be no bloodshed or violence; and there
shall be none, unless it be forced upon the national authority. The
power confided to me, will be used to hold, occupy, and possess the
property, and places belonging to the government, and to collect the
duties and imposts; but beyond what may be necessary for these
objects, there will be no invasion—no using of force against, or among
the people anywhere. . . .

All profess to be content in the Union, if all constitutional rights
can be maintained. Is it true, then, that any right, plainly written in
the Constitution, has been denied? I think not . . . . Think, if you
can, of a single instance in which a plainly written provision of the
Constitution has ever been denied. If, by the mere force of numbers, a
majority should deprive a minority of any clearly written constitutional
right, it might, in a moral point of view, justify revolution—certainly
would, if such right were a vital one. But such is not our case. All the
vital rights of minorities, and of individuals, are so plainly assured to
them, by affirmations and negations, guarranties and prohibitions, in
the Constitution, that controversies never arise concerning them. But
no organic law can ever be framed with a provision specifically applicable to every question which may occur in practical administration. No
foresight can anticipate, nor any document of reasonable length contain
express provisions for all possible questions. Shall fugitives from labor

be surrendered by national or by State authority? The Constitution does not expressly say. *May* Congress prohibit slavery in the territories? The Constitution does not expressly say. *Must* Congress protect slavery in the territories? The Constitution does not expressly say.

From questions of this class spring all our constitutional controversies, and we divide upon them into majorities and minorities. If the minority will not acquiesce, the majority must, or the government must cease. There is no other alternative; for continuing the government, is acquiescence on one side or the other. If a minority, in such case, will secede rather than acquiesce, they make a precedent which, in turn, will divide and ruin them; for a minority of their own will secede from them, whenever a majority refuses to be controlled by such minority.

.   .   .

Plainly, the central idea of secession, is the essence of anarchy. A majority, held in restraint by constitutional checks, and limitations, and always changing easily, with deliberate changes of popular opinions and sentiments, is the only true sovereign of a free people. Whoever rejects it, does, of necessity, fly to anarchy or to despotism. Unanimity is impossible; the rule of a minority, as a permanent arrangement, is wholly inadmissible; so that, rejecting the majority principle, anarchy, or despotism in some form, is all that is left.

I do not forget the position assumed by some, that constitutional questions are to be decided by the Supreme Court; nor do I deny that such decisions must be binding in any case, upon the parties to a suit, as to the object of that suit, while they are also entitled to very high respect and consideration, in all parallel cases, by all other departments of the government. And while it is obviously possible that such decision may be erroneous in any given case, still the evil effect following it, being limited to that particular case, with the chance that it may be over-ruled, and never become a precedent for other cases, can better be borne than could the evils of a different practice. At the same time the candid citizen must confess that if the policy of the government, upon vital questions, affecting the whole people, is to be irrevocably fixed by decisions of the Supreme Court, the instant they are made, in ordinary litigation between parties, in personal actions, the people will have ceased, to be their own rulers, having, to that extent, practically resigned their government, into the hands of that eminent tribunal. Nor is there, in this view, any assault upon the court, or the judges. It is a duty, from which they may not shrink, to decide cases properly brought before them; and it is no fault of theirs, if others seek to turn their decisions to political purposes . . . .

The Chief Magistrate derives all his authority from the people, and they have conferred none upon him to fix terms for the separation of the States. The people themselves can do this also if they choose; but the executive, as such, has nothing to do with it. His duty is to administer the present government, as it came to his hands, and to transmit it, unimpaired by him, to his successor.

Why should there not be a patient confidence in the ultimate justice of the people? Is there any better, or equal hope, in the world? In our present differences, is either party without faith of being in the right? If the Almighty Ruler of nations, with his eternal truth and justice, be on your side of the North, or on yours of the South, that truth, and that justice, will surely prevail, by the judgment of this great tribunal, the American people. . . .

In *your* hands, my dissatisfied fellow countrymen, and not in *mine*, is the momentous issue of civil war. The government will not assail *you*. You can have no conflict, without being yourselves the aggressors. *You* have no oath registered in Heaven to destroy the government, while *I* shall have the most solemn one to "preserve, protect and defend" it.

I am loth to close. We are not enemies, but friends. We must not be enemies. Though passion may have strained, it must not break our bonds of affection. The mystic chords of memory, stretching from every battle-field, and patriot grave, to every living heart and hearthstone, all over this broad land, will yet swell the chorus of the Union, when again touched, as surely they will be, by the better angels of our nature.

"We must find a way to take an appeal from the Supreme Court to the Constitution itself."

FRANKLIN D. ROOSEVELT'S SPEECH ON REORGANIZING THE FEDERAL JUDICIARY *
(1937).

During 1935 and 1936, a majority of the Supreme Court waged what was, in effect, a constitutional war against the economic programs that FDR's administration in Washington and some state governments had enacted to cope with the Great Depression. As a result of these decisions, lower federal judges issued 1,600 injunctions against enforcement of federal statutes. Writing to his sister in June, 1936, Justice Harlan Stone commented sadly that "We seem to have tied Uncle Sam up in a hard knot." During the presidential campaign of 1936, Roosevelt was silent about the justices, but shortly after his second inauguration he announced a plan to authorize the President, with the advice and consent of the Senate, to appoint an additional member of the Supreme Court every time a sitting justice reached the age of 70 and did not retire; the maximum number of justices would be 16—a proposal, which, if enacted into law, would have immediately given FDR six nominations.

Roosevelt's plan encountered heavy and unexpected opposition in Congress; and, as was his custom, he took his case to the people.

In 1933 you and I knew that we must never let our economic system get completely out of joint again—that we could not afford to take the risk of another great depression.

------

* Speech of March 9, 1937. Senate Report No. 711, 75th Cong., 1st Sess., pp. 41–44.

We also became convinced that the only way to avoid a repetition of those dark days was to have a government with power to prevent and to cure the abuses and the inequalities which had thrown that system out of joint.

We then began a program of remedying those abuses and inequalities—to give balance and stability to our economic system—to make it bombproof against the causes of 1929.

Today we are only part way through that program—and recovery is speeding up to a point where the dangers of 1929 are again becoming possible, not this week or month perhaps, but within a year or two.

National laws are needed to complete that program. Individual or local or State effort alone cannot protect us in 1937 any better than 10 years ago. . . . The American people have learned from the depression. For in the last three national elections an overwhelming majority of them voted a mandate that the Congress and the President begin the task of providing that protection—not after long years of debate, but now.

The courts, however, have cast doubts on the ability of the elected Congress to protect us against catastrophe by meeting squarely our modern social and economic conditions.

We are at a crisis in our ability to proceed with that protection

. . . .

I want to talk with you very simply about the need for present action in this crisis—the need to meet the unanswered challenge of one-third of a nation ill-nourished, ill-clad, ill-housed.

Last Thursday I described the American form of government as a three-horse team provided by the Constitution to the American people so that their field might be plowed. The three horses are, of course, the three branches of government—the Congress, the executive, and the courts. Two of the horses are pulling in unison today; the third is not. Those who have intimated that the President of the United States is trying to drive that team overlook the simple fact that the President, as Chief Executive, is himself one of the three horses.

It is the American people themselves who are in the driver's seat.

It is the American people themselves who want the furrow plowed.

It is the American people themselves who expect the third horse to pull in unison with the other two.

I hope that you have reread the Constitution of the United States. Like the Bible, it ought to be read again and again.

It is an easy document to understand when you remember that it was called into being because the Articles of Confederation under which the Original Thirteen States tried to operate after the Revolution showed the need of a National Government with power enough to handle national problems. In its preamble the Constitution states that it was intended to form a more perfect Union and promote the general welfare; and the powers given to the Congress to carry out those purposes can be best described by saying that they were all the powers needed to meet each and every problem which then had a national character and which could not be met by merely local action.

But the framers went further. Having in mind that in succeeding generations many other problems then undreamed of would become national problems, they gave to the Congress the ample broad powers "to levy taxes . . . and provide for the common defense and general welfare of the United States."

That, my friends, is what I honestly believe to have been the clear and underlying purpose of the patriots who wrote a Federal Constitution to create a National Government with national power, intended as they said, "to form a more perfect union . . . for ourselves and our posterity." . . .

But since the rise of the modern movement for social and economic progress through legislation, the Court has more and more often and more and more boldly asserted a power to veto laws passed by the Congress and State legislatures in complete disregard of this original limitation.

In the last four years the sound rule of giving statutes the benefit of all reasonable doubt has been cast aside. The Court has been acting not as a judicial body, but as a policy-making body.

When the Congress has sought to stabilize national agriculture, to improve the conditions of labor, to safeguard business against unfair competition, to protect our national resources, and in many other ways to serve our clearly national needs, the majority of the Court has been assuming the power to pass on the wisdom of these acts of the Congress—and to approve or disapprove the public policy written into these laws.

That is not only my accusation. It is the accusation of most distinguished justices of the present Supreme Court. I have not the time to quote to you all the language used by dissenting justices in many of these cases. But in the case holding the Railroad Retirement Act unconstitutional, for instance, Chief Justice Hughes said in a dissenting opinion that the majority opinion was "a departure from sound principles," and placed "an unwarranted limitation upon the commerce clause." And three other justices agreed with him.

In the case holding the A[gricultural] A[djustment] A[ct] unconstitutional, Justice Stone said of the majority opinion that it was a "tortured construction of the Constitution." And two other justices agreed with him.

In the case holding the New York Minimum Wage Law unconstitutional, Justice Stone said that the majority were actually reading into the Constitution their own "personal economic predilections," and that if the legislative power is not left free to choose the methods of solving the problems of poverty, subsistence, and health of large numbers in the community, then "government is to be rendered impotent." And two other justices agreed with him. . . .

In the face of such dissenting opinions, it is perfectly clear that as Chief Justice Hughes has said, "We are under a Constitution, but the Constitution is what the judges say it is."

The Court in addition to the proper use of its judicial functions has improperly set itself up as a third House of the Congress—a super-legislature, as one of the justices has called it—reading into the Constitution words and implications which are not there, and which were never intended to be there.

We have, therefore, reached the point as a Nation where we must take action to save the Constitution from the Court and the Court from itself. We must find a way to take an appeal from the Supreme Court to the Constitution itself. We want a Supreme Court which will do justice under the Constitution—not over it. In our courts we want a government of laws and not of men.

I want—as all Americans want—an independent judiciary as proposed by the framers of the Constitution. That means a Supreme Court that will enforce the Constitution as written—that will refuse to amend the Constitution by the arbitrary exercise of judicial power—amendment by judicial say-so. It does not mean a judiciary so independent that it can deny the existence of facts universally recognized. . . .

What is my proposal? It is simply this: Whenever a judge or justice of any federal court has reached the age of seventy and does not avail himself of the opportunity to retire on a pension, a new member shall be appointed by the President then in office, with the approval, as required by the Constitution, of the Senate of the United States.

That plan has two chief purposes: By bringing into the judicial system a steady and continuing stream of new and younger blood, I hope, first, to make the administration of all federal justice speedier and therefore less costly; secondly, to bring to the decision of social and economic problems younger men who have had personal experience and contact with modern facts and circumstances under which average men have to live and work. This plan will save our National Constitution from hardening of the judicial arteries. . . .

Those opposing this plan have sought to arouse prejudice and fear by crying that I am seeking to "pack" the Supreme Court and that a baneful precedent will be established.

What do they mean by the words "packing the Court"?

Let me answer this question with a bluntness that will end all honest misunderstanding of my purposes.

If by that phrase "packing the Court" it is charged that I wish to place on the bench spineless puppets who would disregard the law and would decide specific cases as I wished them to be decided, I make this answer: That no President fit for his office would appoint, and no Senate of honorable men fit for their office would confirm, that kind of appointees to the Supreme Court.

But if by that phrase the charge is made that I would appoint and the Senate would confirm justices worthy to sit beside present members of the Court who understand those modern conditions; that I will appoint justices who will not undertake to override the judgment of the Congress on legislative policy; that I will appoint justices who will act as justices and not as legislators—if the appointment of such justices can be called "packing the Courts"—then I say that I, and with me the vast majority of the American people, favor doing just that thing—now. . . . Our difficulty with the Court today rises not from the Court as an institution but from human beings within it. But we cannot yield our constitutional destiny to the personal judgment of a few men who, being fearful of the future, would deny us the necessary means of dealing with the present.

This plan of mine is no attack on the Court; it seeks to restore the Court to its rightful and historic place in our system of constitutional government and to have it resume its high task of building anew on the Constitution "a system of living law." . . .

Editors' Note

Roosevelt's proposal was defeated in the Senate; but, as observed earlier, some of the justices had begun to change their minds shortly after the election of 1936 and before FDR announced his plan—though unfortunately for the Court's reputation the justices' change did not become public until well after FDR had launched his attack. The result was, as the saying went, that Roosevelt lost the battle but won the war against the Supreme Court.

"[W]e must weigh the importance of the general privilege of confidentiality of presidential communications . . . against the inroads of such a privilege on the fair administration of criminal justice."

UNITED STATES v. NIXON
418 U.S. 683, 94 S.Ct. 3090, 41 L.Ed.2d 1039 (1974).

Following the indictment of seven high-ranking White House officials—including former special presidential assistants H.R. Haldeman and John Ehrlichman and former attorney general John Mitchell—for conspiracy to defraud the U.S. government and obstruction of justice, the special prosecutor obtained a subpoena directing President Richard M. Nixon to deliver to the trial judge certain tape recordings and memoranda of conversations held in the White House. The trial judge would then examine those tapes and documents and give to the prosecution and defense those portions relevant to the issues at the trial. The remainder would be returned to the President. Nixon produced some of the subpoenaed material but withheld other portions, invoking executive privilege, which, he claimed, placed confidential presidential documents beyond judicial control. The trial judge denied the President's claim, and he appealed to the court of appeals. The special prosecutor asked the Supreme Court to review the case before the court of appeals had passed judgment, and the justices agreed.

Mr. Chief Justice **BURGER** delivered the opinion of the Court. . . .

A

. . . [W]e turn to the claim that the subpoena should be quashed because it demands "confidential conversations between a President and his close advisors that it would be inconsistent with the public interest to produce." . . . The first contention is a broad claim that the separation of powers doctrine precludes judicial review of a President's claim of privilege. The second contention is that if he does not prevail on the claim of absolute privilege, the court should hold as a matter of constitutional law that the privilege prevails over the subpoena *duces tecum*.

In the performance of assigned constitutional duties each branch of the Government must initially interpret the Constitution, and the interpretation of its powers by any branch is due great respect from the others. The President's counsel . . . reads the Constitution as providing an absolute privilege of confidentiality for all presidential communications. Many decisions of this Court, however, have unequivocally reaffirmed the holding of Marbury v. Madison [1803] . . . that "it is emphatically the province and duty of the judicial department to say what the law is." . . .

No holding of the Court has defined the scope of judicial power specifically relating to the enforcement of a subpoena for confidential presidential communications for use in a criminal prosecution, but other exercises of powers by the Executive Branch and the Legislative Branch have been found invalid as in conflict with the Constitution. Powell v. McCormack [1969] . . . Youngstown [Sheet & Tube Co. v. Sawyer (1952)]. . . . Since this Court has consistently exercised the power to construe and delineate claims arising under express powers, it must follow that the Court has authority to interpret claims with respect to powers alleged to derive from enumerated powers. . . .

B

In support of his claim of absolute privilege, the President's counsel urges two grounds one of which is common to all governments and one of which is peculiar to our system of separation of powers. The first ground is the valid need for protection of communications between high government officials and those who advise and assist them in the performance of their manifold duties; the importance of this confidentiality is too plain to require further discussion . . . . Whatever the nature of the privilege of confidentiality of presidential communications in the exercise of Art. II powers the privilege can be said to derive from the supremacy of each branch within its own assigned area of constitutional duties. Certain powers and privileges flow from the nature of enumerated powers; the protection of the confidentiality of presidential communications has similar constitutional underpinnings.

The second ground asserted by the President's counsel in support of the claim of absolute privilege rests on the doctrine of separation of powers. Here it is argued that the independence of the Executive

Branch within its own sphere . . . insulates a President from a judicial subpoena in an ongoing criminal prosecution. . . .

However, neither the doctrine of separation of powers, nor the need for confidentiality of high level communications, without more, can sustain an absolute, unqualified presidential privilege of immunity from judicial process under all circumstances. The President's need for complete candor and objectivity from advisers calls for great deference from the courts. However, when the privilege depends solely on the broad, undifferentiated claim of public interest in the confidentiality of such conversations, a confrontation with other values arises. Absent a claim of need to protect military, diplomatic or sensitive national security secrets, we find it difficult to accept the argument that even the very important interest in confidentiality of presidential communications is significantly diminished by production of such material for *in camera* inspection with all the protection that a district court will be obliged to provide.

The impediment that an absolute, unqualified privilege would place in the way of the primary constitutional duty of the Judicial Branch to do justice in criminal prosecutions would plainly conflict with the function of the courts under Art. III. In designing the structure of our Government and dividing and allocating the sovereign power among three coequal branches, the Framers of the Constitution sought to provide a comprehensive system, but the separate powers were not intended to operate with absolute independence.

> While the Constitution diffuses power the better to secure liberty, it also contemplates that practice will integrate the dispersed powers into a workable government. It enjoins upon its branches separateness but interdependence, autonomy but reciprocity. *Youngstown* (Jackson, J., concurring). . . .

C

Since we conclude that the legitimate needs of the judicial process may outweigh presidential privilege, it is necessary to resolve those competing interests in a manner that preserves the essential functions of each branch. The right and indeed the duty to resolve that question does not free the judiciary from according high respect to the representations made on behalf of the President. United States v. Burr (1807).

The expectation of a President to the confidentiality of his conversations and correspondence, like the claim of confidentiality of judicial deliberations, for example, has all the values to which we accord deference for the privacy of all citizens and added to those values the necessity for protection of the public interest in candid, objective, and even blunt or harsh opinions in presidential decision-making. . . . These are the considerations justifying a presumptive privilege for presidential communications. The privilege is fundamental to the operation of government and inextricably rooted in the separation of powers under the Constitution. In Nixon v. Sirica (1973), the Court of Appeals held that such presidential communications are "presumptively privileged," and this position is accepted by both parties in the present litigation. We agree with Mr. Chief Justice Marshall's observation, therefore, that "in no case of this kind would a court be required to proceed against the President as against an ordinary individual." *Burr.*

But this presumptive privilege must be considered in light of our historic commitment to the rule of law. This is nowhere more profoundly manifest than in our view that "the twofold aim [of criminal justice] is that guilt shall not escape or innocence suffer." Berger v. United States [1935]. We have elected to employ an adversary system of criminal justice in which the parties contest all issues before a court of law. The need to develop all relevant facts in the adversary system is both fundamental and comprehensive . . . . The very integrity of the judicial system and public confidence in the system depend on full disclosure of all the facts, within the framework of the rules of evidence. To ensure that justice is done, it is imperative to the function of courts that compulsory process be available for the production of evidence needed either by the prosecution or by the defense. . . .

In this case the President . . . does not place his claim of privilege on the ground they are military or diplomatic secrets. As to these areas of Art. II duties the courts have traditionally shown the utmost deference to presidential responsibilities. . . . No case of the Court . . . has extended this high degree of deference to a President's generalized interest in confidentiality. Nowhere in the Constitution . . . is there any explicit reference to a privilege of confidentiality, yet to the extent this interest relates to the effective discharge of a President's powers, it is constitutionally based.

The right to the production of all evidence at a criminal trial similarly has constitutional dimensions. The Sixth Amendment explicitly confers upon every defendant in a criminal trial the right "to be confronted with the witnesses against him" and "to have compulsory process for obtaining witnesses in his favor." Moreover, the Fifth Amendment also guarantees that no person shall be deprived of liberty without due process of law. It is the manifest duty of the courts to vindicate those guarantees and to accomplish that it is essential that all relevant and admissible evidence be produced.

In this case we must weigh the importance of the general privilege of confidentiality of presidential communications . . . against the inroads of such a privilege on the fair administration of criminal justice. The interest in preserving confidentiality is weighty indeed and entitled to great respect. However, we cannot conclude that advisers will be moved to temper the candor of their remarks by the infrequent occasions of disclosure because of the possibility that such conversations will be called for in the context of a criminal prosecution.

On the other hand, the allowance of the privilege to withhold evidence that is demonstrably relevant in a criminal trial would cut deeply into the guarantee of due process of law and gravely impair the basic function of the courts.   A President's acknowledged need for confidentiality in the communications of his office is general in nature, whereas the constitutional need for production of relevant evidence in a criminal proceeding is specific and central to the fair adjudication of a particular criminal case in the administration of justice.   Without access to specific facts a criminal prosecution may be totally frustrated . . . .

We conclude that when the ground for asserting privilege as to subpoenaed materials sought for use in a criminal trial is based only on the generalized interest in confidentiality, it cannot prevail over the fundamental demands of due process of law in the fair administration of criminal justice.   The generalized assertion of privilege must yield to the demonstrated, specific need for evidence in a pending criminal trial . . . .

E

Enforcement of the subpoena *duces tecum* was stayed pending this Court's resolution of the issues raised by the petitions for certiorari. Those issues now having been disposed of, the matter of implementation will rest with the District Court.   .   .   . Statements that meet the test of admissibility and relevance must be isolated; all other material must be excised . . . .   We have no doubt that the District Judge will at all times accord to presidential records that high degree of deference suggested in *Burr* . . . .

Affirmed.

Mr. Justice **REHNQUIST** took no part in the consideration or decision of these cases.

Editors' Notes

(1) Since the subpoenaed tapes revealed that he had publicly lied about his knowledge of and participation in felonious acts to obstruct justice, Nixon seriously considered disobeying the Court's ruling.   Shortly after the decision, however, the House Judiciary Committee favorably reported a bill of impeachment, and defiance of the Court would have probably meant even worse catastrophe.   Release of the tapes was quickly followed by Nixon's resignation on August 9, 1974, seventeen days after the Court's decision.   One of Gerald Ford's first acts as President was to pardon Nixon for all crimes he had committed while President.

(2) **Query:** Practical political considerations aside, would Nixon have been justified in terms of constitutional law in refusing to comply with the Court's mandate?

"It is not for us to review the congressional resolution of these factors."

KATZENBACH v. MORGAN

384 U.S. 641, 86 S.Ct. 1717, 16 L.Ed.2d 828 (1966).

In 1959, in Lassiter v. Northampton County, the Supreme Court unanimously sustained the constitutionality under the Fourteenth Amendment of a state requirement that voters be able to read and write English. Congress, however, included as § 4(e) of the Voting Rights Act of 1965 a ban against any state's denying the right to vote to any person who had completed the sixth grade in the United States or Puerto Rico, regardless of the language in which the school was taught and regardless of whether that person could read or write English. A group of registered voters in New York sued in a U.S. district court and obtained an injunction against enforcement of § 4(e) as a violation of the Tenth Amendment. The United States appealed directly to the Supreme Court.

Mr. Justice **BRENNAN** delivered the opinion of the Court . . . .

. . . We hold that, in the application challenged in these cases, § 4(e) is a proper exercise of the powers granted to Congress by § 5 of the Fourteenth Amendment and that by force of the Supremacy Clause, Article VI, the New York English literacy requirement cannot be enforced to the extent that it is inconsistent with § 4(e).

Under the distribution of powers effected by the Constitution, the States establish qualifications for voting for state officers, and the qualifications established by the States for voting for members of the most numerous branch of the state legislature also determine who may vote for United States Representatives and Senators, Art I, § 2; Seventeenth Amendment; Ex parte Yarbrough [1884]. But, of course, the States have no power to grant or withhold the franchise on conditions that are forbidden by the Fourteenth Amendment, or any other provision of the Constitution. . . .

. . . As was said with regard to § 5 [of the Fourteenth Amendment] in Ex parte Virginia [1880]:

> It is the power of Congress which has been enlarged. Congress is authorized to *enforce* the prohibitions by appropriate legislation. Some legislation is contemplated to make the amendments fully effective.

A construction of § 5 that would require a judicial determination that the enforcement of the state law precluded by Congress violated the Amendment, as a condition of sustaining the congressional enactment, would depreciate both congressional resourcefulness and congressional responsibility for implementing the Amendment. It would confine the legislative power in this context to the insignificant role of abrogating only those state laws that the judicial branch was prepared to adjudge unconstitutional, or of merely informing the judgment of the judiciary by particularizing the "majestic generalities" of § 1 of the Amendment. See Fay v. New York [1947].

Thus our task in this case is not to determine whether the New York English literacy requirement as applied to deny the right to vote to a person who successfully completed the sixth grade in a Puerto Rican school violates the Equal Protection Clause. Accordingly, our decision in Lassiter v. Northampton Election Bd. [1959] sustaining the North Carolina English literacy requirement as not in all circumstances prohibited by the first sections of the Fourteenth and Fifteenth Amendments, is inapposite. *Lassiter* did not present the question before us here: Without regard to whether the judiciary would find that the Equal Protection Clause itself nullifies New York's English literacy requirement as so applied, could Congress prohibit the enforcement of the state law by legislating under § 5 of the Fourteenth Amendment? In answering this question, our task is limited to determining whether such legislation is, as required by § 5, appropriate legislation to enforce the Equal Protection Clause.

By including § 5 the draftsmen sought to grant to Congress, by a specific provision applicable to the Fourteenth Amendment, the same broad powers expressed in the Necessary and Proper Clause, Art I, § 8, cl 18. The classic formulation of the reach of those two powers was established by Chief Justice Marshall in M'Culloch v. Maryland [1819].

> Let the end be legitimate, let it be within the scope of the constitution, and all means which are appropriate, which are plainly adapted to that end, which are not prohibited, but consist[ent] with the letter and spirit of the constitution, are constitutional. . . .

. . . Section 2 of the Fifteenth Amendment grants Congress a similar power to enforce by "appropriate legislation" the provisions of that amendment; and we recently held in South Carolina v. Katzenbach [1966] that "[t]he basic test to be applied in a case involving § 2 of the Fifteenth Amendment is the same as in all cases concerning the express powers of Congress with relation to the reserved powers of the States." That test was identified as the one formulated in *M'Culloch*.

We therefore proceed to the consideration whether § 4(e) is "appropriate legislation" to enforce the Equal Protection Clause, that is . . . whether it is "plainly adapted to that end" and whether it is not prohibited by but is consistent with "the letter and spirit of the constitution." [1]

There can be no doubt that § 4(e) may be regarded as an enactment to enforce the Equal Protection Clause. Congress explicitly declared that it enacted § 4(e) "to secure the rights under the fourteenth amendment of persons educated in American-flag schools in which the predominant classroom language was other than English." The persons referred to include those who have migrated from the Common-

---

1. Contrary to the suggestion of the dissent, § 5 does not grant Congress power to exercise discretion in the other direction and to enact "statutes so as in effect to dilute equal protection and due process decisions of this Court." We emphasize that Congress' power under § 5 is limited to adopting measures to enforce the guarantees of the Amendment; § 5 grants Congress no power to restrict, abrogate, or dilute these guarantees . . . . [Footnote by the Court.]

wealth of Puerto Rico to New York and who have been denied the right
to vote because of their inability to read and write English, and the
Fourteenth Amendment rights referred to include those emanating
from the Equal Protection Clause. More specifically, § 4(e) may be
viewed as a measure to secure for the Puerto Rican community residing
in New York nondiscriminatory treatment by government—both in the
imposition of voting qualifications and the provision or administration
of governmental services, such as public schools, public housing and law
enforcement.

Section 4(e) may be readily seen as "plainly adapted" to furthering
these aims of the Equal Protection Clause. The practical effect of
§ 4(e) is to prohibit New York from denying the right to vote to large
segments of its Puerto Rican community. Congress has thus prohibited
the State from denying to that community the right that is "preservative of all rights." Yick Wo v. Hopkins [1886]. This enhanced political
power will be helpful in gaining nondiscriminatory treatment in public
services for the entire Puerto Rican community . . . . It was for
Congress, as the branch that made this judgment, to assess and weigh
the various conflicting considerations . . . . It is not for us to
review the congressional resolution of these factors. It is enough that
we be able to perceive a basis upon which the Congress might resolve
the conflict as it did. There plainly was such a basis to support § 4(e)
in the application in question in this case. Any contrary conclusion
would require us to be blind to the realities familiar to the legislators.

The result is no different if we confine our inquiry to the question
whether § 4(e) was merely legislation aimed at the elimination of an
invidious discrimination in establishing voter qualifications . . . .

There remains the question whether the congressional remedies
adopted in § 4(e) constitute means which are not prohibited by, but are
consistent "with the letter and spirit of the constitution." The only
respect in which appellees contend that § 4(e) fails in this regard is that
the section itself works an invidious discrimination in violation of the
Fifth Amendment by prohibiting the enforcement of the English literacy requirement only for those educated in American-flag schools . . .
in which the language of instruction was other than English, and not
for those educated in schools beyond the territorial limits of the United
States in which the language of instruction was also other than English. This is not a complaint that Congress, in enacting § 4(e), has
unconstitutionally denied or diluted anyone's right to vote but rather
that Congress violated the Constitution by not extending the relief
effected in § 4(e) to those educated in non-American-flag schools. We
need not pause to determine whether appellees have a sufficient personal interest to have § 4(e) invalidated on this ground, see generally
United States v. Raines [1960], since the argument, in our view, falls on
the merits.

Section 4(e) does not restrict or deny the franchise but in effect
extends the franchise to persons who otherwise would be denied it by
state law. Thus we need . . . only decide whether the challenged

limitation on the relief effected in § 4(e) was permissible. In deciding that question, the principle that calls for the closest scrutiny of distinctions in laws *denying* fundamental rights . . . is inapplicable. . . . Rather . . . we are guided by the familiar principles that a "statute is not invalid under the Constitution because it might have gone farther than it did," Roschen v. Ward [1929], that a legislature need not "strike at all evils at the same time," Semler v. Dental Examiners [1935], and that "reform may take one step at a time, addressing itself to the phase of the problem which seems most acute to the legislative mind," Williamson v. Lee Optical Co. [1955].

Guided by these principles, we are satisfied that appellees' challenge to this limitation in § 4(e) is without merit. . . .

Reversed.

Mr. Justice **DOUGLAS** joins the Court's opinion except for the discussion . . . of the question whether the congressional remedies adopted in § 4(e) constitute means which are not prohibited by, but are consistent with "the letter and spirit of the constitution." On that question he reserves judgment until such time as it is presented by a member of the class against which that particular discrimination is directed.

Mr. Justice **HARLAN**, whom Mr. Justice **STEWART** joins, dissenting.

Worthy as its purposes may be, I do not see how § 4(e) of the Voting Rights Act of 1965 can be sustained except at the sacrifice of fundamentals in the American constitutional system—the separation between the legislative and judicial function and the boundaries between federal and state political authority. . . .

When recognized state violations of federal constitutional standards have occurred, Congress is of course empowered by § 5 to take appropriate remedial measures to redress and prevent the wrongs. See Strauder v. West Virginia [1880]. But it is a judicial question whether the condition with which Congress has thus sought to deal is in truth an infringement of the Constitution, something that is the necessary prerequisite to bringing the § 5 power into play at all. Thus, in Ex parte Virginia [1880] involving a federal statute making it a federal crime to disqualify anyone from jury service because of race, the Court first held as a matter of constitutional law that "the Fourteenth Amendment secures, among other civil rights, to colored men, when charged with criminal offences against a State, an impartial jury trial, by jurors indifferently selected or chosen without discrimination against such jurors because of their color." Only then did the Court hold that to enforce this prohibition upon state discrimination, Congress could enact a criminal statute of the type under consideration.

A more recent Fifteenth Amendment case also serves to illustrate this distinction. In South Carolina v. Katzenbach [1966], we held certain remedial sections of this Voting Rights Act of 1965 constitutional under the Fifteenth Amendment, which is directed against deprivations of the right to vote on account of race. In enacting those sections of the Voting Rights Act the Congress made a detailed investigation of various state practices that had been used to deprive Negroes of the franchise. In passing upon the remedial provisions, we reviewed first the "voluminous legislative history" as well as judicial precedents supporting the basic congressional finding that the clear commands of the Fifteenth Amendment had been infringed by various state subterfuges. Given the existence of the evil, we held the remedial steps taken by the legislature under the Enforcement Clause of the Fifteenth Amendment to be a justifiable exercise of congressional initiative.

Section 4(e), however, presents a significantly different type of congressional enactment. The question here is not whether the statute is appropriate remedial legislation to cure an established violation of a constitutional command, but whether there has in fact been an infringement of that constitutional command . . . . That question is one for the judicial branch ultimately to determine. Were the rule otherwise, Congress would be able to qualify this Court's constitutional decisions under the Fourteenth and Fifteenth Amendments, let alone those under other provisions of the Constitution, by resorting to congressional power under the Necessary and Proper Clause. In view of this Court's holding in *Lassiter* that an English literacy test is a permissible exercise of state supervision over its franchise, I do not think it is open to Congress to limit the effect of that decision as it has undertaken to do by § 4(e). In effect the Court reads § 5 of the Fourteenth Amendment as giving Congress the power to define the *substantive* scope of the Amendment. If that indeed be the true reach of § 5, then I do not see why Congress should not be able as well to exercise its § 5 "discretion" by enacting statutes so as in effect to dilute equal protection and due process decisions of this Court. In all such cases there is room for reasonable men to differ as to whether or not a denial of equal protection or due process has occurred, and the final decision is one of judgment. Until today this judgment has always been one for the judiciary to resolve.

I do not mean to suggest . . . that a legislative judgment of the type incorporated in § 4(e) is without any force whatsoever. Decisions on questions of equal protection and due process are based not on abstract logic, but on empirical foundations. To the extent "legislative facts" are relevant to a judicial determination, Congress is well equipped to investigate them, and such determinations are of course entitled to due respect. . . .

But no such factual data provide a legislative record supporting § 4(e) by way of showing that Spanish-speaking citizens are fully as capable of making informed decisions in a New York election as are English-speaking citizens. Nor was there any showing whatever to support the Court's alternative argument that § 4(e) should be viewed as but a remedial measure designed to cure or assure against unconstitutional discrimination of other varieties . . . .

Thus, we have here not a matter of giving deference to a congressional estimate, based on its determination of legislative facts, bearing upon the validity vel non of a statute, but rather what can at most be called a legislative announcement that Congress believes a state law to entail an unconstitutional deprivation of equal protection. Although this kind of declaration is of course entitled to the most respectful consideration, coming as it does from a concurrent branch and one that is knowledgeable in matters of popular political participation, I do not believe it lessens our responsibility to decide the fundamental issue of whether in fact the state enactment violates federal constitutional rights.

In assessing the deference we should give to this kind of congressional expression of policy, it is relevant that the judiciary has always given to congressional enactments a presumption of validity. The Propeller Genesee Chief v. Fitzhugh [1851]. However, it is also a canon of judicial review that state statutes are given a similar presumption, Butler v. Commonwealth [1850]. Whichever way this case is decided, one statute will be rendered inoperative in whole or in part, and although it has been suggested that this Court should give somewhat more deference to Congress than to a state legislature, such a simple weighing of presumptions is hardly a satisfying way of resolving a matter that touches the distribution of state and federal power in an area so sensitive as that of the regulation of the franchise. Rather it should be recognized that while the Fourteenth Amendment is a "brooding omnipresence" over all state legislation, the substantive matters which it touches are all within the primary legislative competence of the States. Federal authority, legislative no less than judicial, does not intrude unless there has been a denial by state action of Fourteenth Amendment limitations . . . . At least in the area of primary state concern a state statute that passes constitutional muster under the judicial standard of rationality should not be permitted to be set at naught by a mere contrary congressional pronouncement unsupported by a legislative record justifying that conclusion.

To deny the effectiveness of this congressional enactment is not of course to disparage Congress' exertion of authority in the field of civil rights; it is simply to recognize that the Legislative Branch like the other branches of federal authority is subject to the governmental boundaries set by the Constitution . . . .

Editors' Notes

(1) For analyses of Brennan's opinion and his use of the so-called "ratchet theory"—under § 5 Congress can add to but not take away from the liberties protected by the Fourteenth Amendment—see: William Cohen, "Congressional Power to Interpret Due Process and Equal Protection," 27 *Stan.L. Rev.* 603 (1975); and Jesse H. Choper, "Congressional Power to Expand

Judicial Definitions of the Substantive Terms of the Civil War Amendments,"
67 *Minn.L.Rev.* 299 (1982).

(2) The history of *Katzenbach* is checkered:

(a) *Oregon v. Mitchell (1970).* Here the Court sustained amendments to
the Voting Rights Act of 1965 that allowed 18-year-olds to vote for federal
officials, suspended all literacy tests for federal and state elections, and
regulated residency and absentee registration in presidential elections. By a
5–4 vote, however, the Court held that authorizing 18-year-olds to vote in *state*
elections exceeded congressional power both under Article I of the Constitution and § 5 of the Fourteenth Amendment.

There was no opinion for the Court, but five separate opinions that
consumed 185 pages of the U.S. Reports. Black announced the judgment of
the Court but wrote only for himself. He did not acknowledge that Congress
had the sweeping interpretive power that Brennan's opinion for the Court had
in *Katzenbach.* In particular, Black doubted congressional authority to regulate elections under the Fourteenth and Fifteenth amendments where there
was no issue of racial discrimination. More generally, he wrote:

> As broad as the congressional enforcement power is, it is not
> unlimited. Specifically, there are at least three limitations upon
> Congress' power to enforce the guarantees of the Civil War Amend-
> ments. First, Congress may not by legislation repeal other provisions
> of the Constitution. Second, the power granted to Congress was not
> intended to strip the States of their power to govern themselves or to
> convert our national government of enumerated powers into a central
> government of unrestrained authority. . . . Third, Congress may
> only "enforce" the provisions of the amendments and may do so only
> by "appropriate legislation." Congress has no power under the
> enforcement sections to undercut the amendments' guarantees of
> personal equality and freedom from discrimination, or to undermine
> those protections of the Bill of Rights which we have held the
> Fourteenth Amendment made applicable to the States.

Douglas, Brennan, White, and Marshall adhered to *Katzenbach's* broad
views of congressional interpretive power and would have sustained all the
amendments to the Voting Rights Act. Justice Harlan reiterated and amplified
his previous dissent:

> As the Court is not justified in substituting its own views of wise
> policy for the commands of the Constitution, still less is it justified in
> allowing Congress to disregard those commands as the Court under-
> stands them . . . . The reason for this goes beyond Marshall's
> assertion that: "It is emphatically the province and duty of the judicial
> department to say what the law is." Marbury v. Madison (1803). It
> inheres in the structure of the constitutional system itself. Congress
> is subject to none of the institutional restraints imposed on judicial
> decisionmaking. In Article V, the Framers expressed the view that
> the political restraints on Congress alone were an insufficient control
> over the process of constitution making. The concurrence of two-
> thirds of each House and of three-fourths of the States was needed
> for the political check to be adequate. To allow a simple majority of
> Congress to have final say on matters of constitutional interpretation
> is therefore fundamentally out of keeping with the constitutional

structure. Nor is that structure adequately protected by a requirement that the judiciary be able to perceive a basis for the interpretation . . . .

Stewart, joined by Burger and Blackmun, concurred in part and dissented in
part. They thought it would stretch *Katzenbach's* reasoning to sustain those
amendments to the Voting Rights Act relating to age requirements for either
federal or state elections.

(The Twenty-Sixth Amendment, ratified in 1971, disposed of the substantive issue of voting age: "The right of citizens of the United States, who are
eighteen years of age or older, to vote shall not be denied or abridged by the
United States or by any State on account of age." Sec. 2 repeats the formula
of § 5 of the Fourteenth Amendment, "The Congress shall have power to
enforce this article by appropriate legislation.")

(b) *Rome v. United States (1980).* If *Mitchell* seemed to signal a retreat
from *Katzenbach, Rome* appeared to move a step forward. In upholding
another provision of the Voting Rights Act of 1965, Justice Marshall's opinion
for the Court reasoned along lines that closely paralleled Brennan's in *Katzenbach:*

> It is clear, then, that under § 2 of the Fifteenth Amendment
> Congress may prohibit practices that in and of themselves do not
> violate § 1 of the Amendment, so long as the prohibitions attacking
> racial discrimination in voting are "appropriate" as that term is defined
> in McCulloch v. Maryland [1819] and Ex parte Virginia (1880).

(3) Critical to any analysis of *Katzenbach, Mitchell,* and *Rome* is the
question whether the phrase "prohibitions attacking racial discrimination"
merely reflects the fact that it was the Fifteenth Amendment that was before
the Court in *Rome* and not the Fourteenth, as in *Katzenbach,* or whether the
Court was adopting Black's doubts about congressional authority to regulate
elections under the Fourteenth and Fifteenth amendments where no racial
discrimination was present.

Whatever the answer to that question, Justice Rehnquist, who had joined
the Court five years after *Katzenbach* and a year after Oregon v. Mitchell,
thought his brethren were going too far in *Rome:*

> While the presumption of constitutionality is due to any act of a
> coordinate branch of the Federal Government or of one of the States,
> it is this Court which is ultimately responsible for deciding challenges
> to the exercise of power by those entities. Marbury v. Madison
> (1803). United States v. Nixon (1974). Today's decision is nothing
> less than a total abdication of that authority, rather than an exercise
> of the deference due to a coordinate branch of the government.

Stewart joined Rehnquist's dissent. Justice Powell, who had also not been on
the Court when *Katzenbach* or *Mitchell* was decided, dissented separately,
reasoning that the challenged section of the statute exceeded Congress'
powers. He did not, however, directly address the extent of deference the
Court owed congressional interpretations of the Civil War amendments.

(4) In 1975 Congress further amended the Voting Rights Act to outlaw
permanently all literacy tests as prerequisites for voting. 42 U.S.C. § 1971(a)
(2)(c).

———

"[I]f . . . Congress can redefine terms in this one area so as to entrust to a majority vote . . . a matter that the Supreme Court has held individual women entitled to resolve for themselves, then Congress has equal power to effectuate such a divestment of personal rights in other areas as well . . . ."—Professor Laurence H. TRIBE.

"A decision of the Supreme Court interpreting the Constitution is neither infallible nor eternal nor unchangeable. . . ."—Professor John T. NOONAN.

ABORTION, THE SUPREME COURT, AND CONGRESSIONAL AUTHORITY UNDER THE FOURTEENTH AMENDMENT TO DEFINE "PERSON"

Roe v. Wade (1973; reprinted below, p. 1109) held that, at least during the first three months of pregnancy, a woman had a constitutional right to an abortion. In reaching its decision, the Court held that a fetus was not a "person" protected by the Fourteenth Amendment, but conceded that if a fetus were a "person" much state regulation of abortion would be valid. Popular reactions ranged from effusive praise for recognizing women's rights to bitter condemnation for legalizing murder. As one would have guessed from reading Chapter 5, constitutional scholars were equally acerbic in their debates about the legitimacy of the Court's discovering such a right in the due process clause and/or in the Ninth Amendment. And, like others, commentators also sharply divided about the correctness of the substantive ruling. Additional state and federal legislation tried to counter Roe, but with the notable exception of withholding federal funding for abortions (see Harris v. McRae [1980; reprinted below, p. 898]), most of these proposals were struck down by judges. Among the efforts to disarm Roe was S. 158, introduced by Senator Jesse A. Helms (Rep., N.C.) in 1981. This bill tried to take advantage of Katzenbach v. Morgan and define "person" in the Fourteenth Amendment to include a fetus.

A. SENATE BILL 158

97th Congress, First Session.

To provide that human life shall be deemed to exist from conception

Be it enacted by the Senate and House of Representatives of the United States of America in Congress assembled, That title 42 of the United States Code shall be amended at the end thereof by adding the following new chapter:

CHAPTER 101

Sec. 1. The Congress finds that present day scientific evidence indicates a significant likelihood that actual human life exists from conception.

The Congress further finds that the fourteenth amendment to the Constitution of the United States was intended to protect all human beings.

Upon the basis of these findings, and in the exercise of the powers of the Congress, including its power under section 5 of the fourteenth amendment to the Constitution of the United States, the Congress hereby declares that for the purpose of enforcing the obligation of the States under the fourteenth amendment not to deprive persons of life without due process of law, human life shall be deemed to exist from conception, without regard to race, sex, age, health, defect, or condition of dependency; and for this purpose 'person' shall include all human life as defined herein.

Sec. 2.   Notwithstanding any other provision of law, no inferior Federal court ordained and established by Congress under article III of the Constitution of the United States shall have jurisdiction to issue any restraining order, temporary or permanent injunction, or declaratory judgment in any case involving or arising from any State law or municipal ordinance that (1) protects the rights of human persons between conception and birth, or (2) prohibits, limits, or regulates (a) the performance of abortions or (b) the provision at public expense of funds, facilities, personnel, or other assistance for the performance of abortions.

Sec. 3.   If any provision of this Act or the application thereof to any person or circumstance is judicially determined to be invalid, the validity of the remainder of the Act and the application of such provision to other persons and circumstances shall not be affected by such determination.

———

In the spring of 1981, the Senate's Subcommittee on Separation of Powers began holding hearings on the bill.

B. PREPARED STATEMENT OF LAURENCE H. TRIBE ON S. 158 *

. . . In substance, § 1 attempts to enshrine a congressional "theory of life" so as to "override the rights of the pregnant woman" under Roe v. Wade (1973)—precisely what the Supreme Court in *Roe* held a *state* powerless to do.

The fact that § 1 might operate merely as an authorization for the *states* to restrict the rights of pregnant women rather than as a direct restriction mandated by Congress itself is immaterial, since the Due Process Clause of the Fifth Amendment forbids Congress *either* to do by itself what the Fourteenth Amendment would prohibit states from doing *or* to license the states to do what, absent congressional permission, they would be prohibited by the Fourteenth Amendment from doing.

The only possible argument supporting the constitutionality of S. 158, § 1, is that Katzenbach v. Morgan somehow empowered Congress

---

* U.S. Senate, Subcommittee on Separation of Powers, *The Human Life Bill: Hearings on S. 158*, 97th Cong., 1st Sess., I, 249–252.
Laurence H. Tribe is Tyler Professor of Constitutional Law, Harvard Law School.

to restrict the rights of women, or to authorize states to do so, in circumstances where states would otherwise be constitutionally forbidden to take such action. Even if *Morgan* had not been considerably restricted by Oregon v. Mitchell . . . that decision obviously would *not* endow Congress with blank-check authority to restrict one set of judicially-declared rights upon Congress' decision, by majority vote, to proclaim another set of "rights" into existence.

This is so for three reasons. *First,* however expansive may be Congress' power, under § 5 of the Fourteenth Amendment, to make empirical determinations that might have eluded the courts or to create remedial structures that the courts may have been unprepared to require on their own, no corresponding power exists simply to reject, as a legislative matter, a legal conclusion reached by the Supreme Court as to the proper interpretation of constitutional language:

> It is emphatically the province and duty of the judicial department to say what the law is,

Marbury v. Madison (1803), a duty in which "the federal judiciary is supreme," Cooper v. Aaron (1958), see also United States v. Nixon (1974), not least because:

> Congress is subject to none of the institutional restraints imposed on judicial decisionmaking; it is controlled only by the political process. In Article V, the Framers expressed the view that the political restraints on Congress alone were an insufficient control over the process of constitution making. The concurrence of two-thirds of each House and of three-fourths of the States was needed for the political check to be adequate. To allow a simple majority of Congress to have final say on matters of constitutional interpretation is therefore fundamentally out of keeping with the constitutional structure.

Oregon v. Mitchell (Harlan, J., concurring in part and dissenting in part).

Second, the premise of S. 158, § 1 . . . . is the extraordinary proposition that the identification of human life or personhood, as a basis for justifying restraints upon the freedom, equality, and bodily integrity of a pregnant woman, is an empirical matter—one which "present-day scientific evidence" might somehow resolve. Suffice it to say, however, that such questions as when "human life" exists, or what is a "person," call at bottom for normative judgments no less profound than those involved in defining "liberty" or "equality." In this context, therefore, one cannot escape the conclusion that identifying "human life" and defining "person" entail "question[s] to which science can provide no answer," as the National Academy of Sciences itself acknowledged in a Resolution passed on April 28, 1981, during its 118th Annual Meeting. Congress cannot transform an issue of religion, morality, and law into one of fact by waving the magic wand of § 5. The section empowering Congress "to enforce, by appropriate legislation, the provisions of" the Fourteenth Amendment no more authorizes

Congress to transmute a matter of values into a matter of scientific observation than it authorizes Congress to announce a mathematical formula for human freedom.

Third, even if S. 158, § 1, were deemed to fall within the ambit of Congress' affirmative authority—under § 5 of the Fourteenth Amendment or otherwise—it would still be subject to judicial invalidation as a clear violation of the Liberty Clause of the Fifth Amendment, a clause that restricts Congress in precisely the same manner that, and to precisely the same degree as, its counterpart clause in the Fourteenth Amendment restricts the states. Any other approach would simultaneously denigrate the place of each state as "a coordinate element in the system established by the Framers for governing our Federal Union," National League of Cities v. Usery (1976), and jeopardize the personal rights and liberties whose fate the Framers wisely declined to leave entirely to a Congress unchecked by judicial review . . . .

Nor could the delegation of judicially unchecked power to Congress over such rights and liberties be confined to cases in which the judiciary has candidly confessed, as it did in Roe v. Wade its inability to give determinate meaning to constitutional terms like "life." For when Congress acts to override, or to invite states to override, the "liberty" of pregnant women, it does not merely "inform the judiciary" . . . of its legislative findings and views. Congress is empowered only to *make laws,* not to lobby or advise the courts. And if a law made by Congress can redefine terms in this one area so as to entrust to majority vote or other governmental determination a matter that the Supreme Court has held individual women entitled to resolve for themselves, then Congress has equal power to effectuate such a divestment of personal rights in other areas as well—regardless of the Supreme Court's degree of confidence or perplexity.

The only way to avoid that radical and profoundly threatening conclusion is to insist that *any* Act of Congress, even if that Act constitutes otherwise "appropriate legislation," be subject to judicial review for its consistency with the liberties secured by the Bill of Rights, under criteria no less demanding than those under which state legislation of similar effect would be scrutinized . . . .

C. PREPARED STATEMENT OF JOHN T. NOONAN, JR., ON § 158 *

II

THE FACT-FINDING AND DEFINITIONAL PROVISIONS OF THE ACT

The Act does four things. It finds "a significant likelihood that actual human life exists from conception." It finds that the Fourteenth

---

* U.S. Senate, Subcommittee on Separation of Powers, *The Human Life Bill: Hearings on S. 158,* 97th Cong., 1st Sess., I, 263–271.

John T. Noonan, Jr., is Professor of Law, University of California at Berkeley.

Amendment was "intended to protect all human beings." It declares that for the purpose of enforcing the obligation of the States "not to deprive persons of life without due process of law," human life "shall be deemed to exist from conception." For the same purpose it declares that "person" shall include all human life as so defined. Are these findings and declarations within the power of Congress?

1. *The Source of Congressional Power.* The Fourteenth Amendment, § 5 declares, "The Congress shall have power to enforce, by appropriate legislation, the provisions of this article." The key terms of this constitutional grant of power are "appropriate legislation" and "enforce." In general, there must be said of this part of the Constitution what Chief Justice Marshall said in McCulloch v. Maryland of congressional power under the "Necessary and Proper Clause of Article I: "1st. The clause is placed among the powers of Congress, not among the limitations on those powers. 2. Its terms purport to enlarge, not to diminish the powers vested in the government. It purports to be an additional power, not a restriction on those already granted."

The parallel in interpretation of Congress' power under § 5 and Congress' power under Article I has very recently been affirmed by Chief Justice Warren Burger in Fullilove v. Klutznick. The Court, he declared, had "equated the scope of this authority with the broad powers expressed in the Necessary and Proper Clause, U.S. Const., Act. 1, § 18, cl. 8." In the light of this interpretation, Congress has the power under § 5 to find facts, to adopt remedies, and to enact legislation it finds appropriate to secure the rights guaranteed by the Fourteenth Amendment.

It should be added that the enforcement of the Fourteenth Amendment by *congressional* action has solid historical roots. As the Supreme Court said unanimously in 1879 in Ex parte Virginia . . . : "It is not said that the *judicial power* of the government shall extend to enforcing the prohibitions and to protecting the rights and immunities guaranteed . . . . It is the power of Congress which has been enlarged." Even if today the judicial branch has taken to itself a more active part in enforcing the Amendments, surely its more assertive role cannot deprive Congress of the power which the framers of the Amendment intended to confer, as the 1879 Court acknowledged, and which the Court in 1980 has recognized to be as broad as Article I's fundamental grant of power to make "all laws which shall be necessary and proper for carrying into Execution the foregoing Powers."

2. *The Power of Congress Where the Supreme Court is in Doubt.* In Roe v. Wade the Supreme Court declared, "We need not resolve the difficult question of where life begins. When those trained in the respective disciplines of medicine, philosophy, and theology are unable to arrive at any consensus, the judiciary at this point in the development of man's knowledge, is not in a position to speculate as to the answer." . . .

Congress, as a coordinate branch of the national government, is of course in a position very different from any State vis-á-vis the Supreme

Court. In this area it is acting within the terms of power expressly conferred by the Fourteenth Amendment and expressly recognized by the Court itself. It is acting with better sources of information than the Court. . . . It is acting with a better ability than the Court to balance competing value considerations that go to the assessment of the facts. Further, Congress is performing an essential function in the enforcement of the Fourteenth Amendment; for if the judiciary is not "in a position to speculate" when life begins, the Fourteenth Amendment must fail, in a significant way, to be implemented, unless Congress draws on its power to supply an answer.

3. *The Power of Congress When the Supreme Court Has Made a Contrary Determination.* The objection will be raised, however, that the . . . Court in Roe v. Wade has formally held that "the word 'person' as used in the Fourteenth Amendment, does not include the unborn." Does not the proposed statute squarely conflict with this holding of the Court and, if it does so, is not the statute void?

It is clear that Congress will reach, if the proposed statute is enacted, a conclusion different from the Court's in Roe v. Wade on the meaning of person in the Fourteenth Amendment. It does not follow that the statute is void. It follows, rather, that the Court may, and should, change its mind, give deference to the congressional findings and declarations, and overrule Roe v. Wade.

In the area of the Fourteenth Amendment the Court has already provided just such an example of retreating from its own announced understanding of the Constitution in deference to congressional action taken after, and contrary to, the Court's announcement of what it found the Constitution to mean. In Lassiter v. Northampton Election Board (1959) the plaintiff complained that a literacy test for voting was unconstitutional. The Supreme Court, unanimously, held that Article 1, § 2 of the Constitution expressly reserves to the States the power to determine the qualifications of electors. Seven years later in Katzenbach v. Morgan (1966), the Court considered an Act of Congress eliminating literacy in English as a condition for voting . . . .

The Court . . . found *Lassiter* "inapposite." Speaking through Justice Brennan and quoting Ex parte Virginia of 1879, the Court held the congressional action a proper exercise of congressional power under § 5 of the Fourteenth Amendment. . . . The action of Congress, directly contrary to the interpretation of the Constitution by a unanimous Supreme Court, was upheld by the Court. In Oregon v. Mitchell (1970), while splitting on other issues, the Court unanimously upheld Congress' total elimination of literacy tests. . . .

4. *Congressional Action Affecting Personal Liberties.* In Shapiro v. Thompson, a case involving the welfare residency requirement of California, it was said by way of dictum that even if Congress had consented to the residency requirement—which the Court held it had not—the requirement was invalid, because "Congress may not authorize the States to violate the Equal Protection Clause." Similarly in a footnote to Katzenbach v. Morgan, Justice Brennan declared that § 5

"grants Congress no power to restrict, abrogate or dilute" the guarantees of the Fourteenth Amendment. . . . The question is thus presented whether the proposed Act authorizes states to violate the Equal Protection Clause, dilutes or abrogates Fourteenth Amendment guarantees, or is based on the same evidence on which state legislatures acted unreasonably.

In recognizing the unborn as persons, so far as protection of their lives is concerned, the proposed Act treats no one unequally but gives equal protection to one class of humanity now unequally treated. It does not dilute a Fourteenth Amendment guarantee, but expands the rights of a whole class. It is based not on evidence before the state legislatures—what that evidence was we do not know—but on evidence freshly taken from leading geneticists and physicians.

Yet the question will be pressed, "Does not the Act dilute or abrogate the right to an abortion?" Necessarily, the expression of the rights of one class of human beings has an impact on the rights of others. The elimination of literacy tests in this way "diluted" the voting rights of the literate. It is inescapable that congressional expression of the right to life will have an impact on the abortion right; but in the eyes of Congress, if it enacts this law, there will be a net gain for Fourteenth Amendment rights by the expansion and the attendant diminution. . . .

5. *Section 5 and Marbury v. Madison.* The cornerstone of the judicial power, Chief Justice Marshall's opinion in Marbury v. Madison, announces that the Constitution "controls any legislative act repugnant to it" and imposes on the judges the duty to determine this repugnancy. Does the proposed Act defy or subvert these fundamental principles?

Not in the least. Congress is not ousting the Court of jurisdiction, "overruling" the Court, or declaring its will superior to Constitution or Court. On the basis of hearings and fresh evidence, Congress is taking a position which in one important particular disagrees with the Court's interpretation of the Constitution in Roe v. Wade. Under the principles of Marbury v. Madison, it will be for the Court to decide whether, following such precedents as Katzenbach v. Morgan, it should now defer to Congress' interpretation.

To suppose that the statute proposed is a challenge to judicial review assumes a radical—I am inclined to say willful—misunderstanding of the functions of Court and Congress. A decision of the Supreme Court interpreting the Constitution is neither infallible nor eternal nor unchangeable. The Court has often been wrong. The Court has often corrected itself. There is nothing in our constitutional theory that says the Court must remain forever in a mistaken position, and much contrary example to its so doing. The proposed Act is an invitation to the Court to correct its error itself. . . .

The story is an old one, frequently retold. The Supreme Court is not immune to reason and to instruction. It reverses itself. It listens to Congress. Those who want an institution immoveable and beyond the reach of popular instruction must look elsewhere.

6. *Further Reasons for Congress to Exercise Its Section 5 Power Here.* "The *Morgan* case," Archibald Cox has written, "is soundly rooted in constitutional principles, yet it clears the way for a vast expansion of congressional legislation promoting human rights." This expansion, as Cox observes, can be achieved by any law which "may be viewed" as having a relation to an end specified by the Fourteenth Amendment. In the present context, the Fourteenth Amendment guarantees life to persons. But no one can enjoy adult life unless he or she is born. To protect the life guaranteed by the Amendment, Congress has the power under § 5 to protect the path to that life. The proposed legislation is readily seen as a way of protecting the means necessary to have life after birth.

Further, it is sometimes forgotten that the Court in Roe v. Wade, acknowledging that "the Constitution does not explicitly mention any right of privacy," finally located that right with some uncertainty in the Fourteenth Amendment "or, as the District Court determined, in the Ninth Amendment's reservation of rights to the people." To this point in this presentation, focus has been upon the Fourteenth Amendment. But if Justice Blackmun's other basis be accepted, Congress is better suited than the Court to make the determination as to the balance struck between the rights of the States and reserved Ninth Amendment rights. Such a determination requires political discretion. As Archibald Cox has written generally of why the Court should defer to Congress in its exercise of § 5 power, such judicial following of a congressional lead "rests upon application of the fact that the fundamental basis for legislative action is the knowledge, experience, and judgment of the people's representatives, only a small part, or even none of which may come from the hearings and reports of committees or debates upon the floor." As Ninth Amendment rights are reserved to the people, the people through its elected representatives can determine, better than a nonelected elite, where the line limiting governmental power should be drawn. . . .

7

Who May Authoritatively Interpret the Constitution for the Federal System?

Article VI of the Constitution explicitly declares its supremacy over all forms of state law:

> This Constitution, and the laws of the United States which shall be made in pursuance thereof; and all treaties made, or which shall be made, under the authority of the United States, shall be the supreme law of the land; and the judges in every state shall be bound thereby, any thing in the constitution or laws of any state to the contrary notwithstanding.

Yet as plain as they are about national supremacy, these words leave open the question of WHO should be the Constitution's authoritative interpreters in case of conflicts between state and nation. Binding judges [1] to prefer the Constitution, laws, and treaties of the United States over state laws and constitutions implies that judges will have to engage in some interpretation, but says nothing about whether the ultimate interpreters shall be state or federal officials. And the response to the question WHO shall interpret plays a critical role in determining the distribution of substantive powers between nation and state.

The debate has been sharp, and what has been written on all sides reads more like lawyers' briefs than closely reasoned scholarly arguments. That character is appropriate, because the issues have not been academic. As with disputes about the relative interpretive authority of the branches of the federal government, the stakes have been power and public policies that affect basic interests, economic, social, and political.

If we step back from the polemical rhetoric, however, we can see that the debate has assumed a shape similar to the pattern that Chapter 6 described for those who have offered rules for determining the ultimate interpreter among the branches of the federal government.

---

1. Here a problem with plain words arises. The text does not say "state judges shall be bound thereby," but rather "judges in every state" and so could include whatever federal judges Congress opted to provide for. Most of them (all of them initially because the United States did not obtain the District of Columbia from Maryland and Virginia until after ratification) sat in states, there being no other place except the territories.

255

Here again, three theories compete: state supremacy, confederational departmentalism, and national supremacy.

The choice among these is obvious to most Americans living near the end of the twentieth century. In the eighteenth and much of the nineteenth century, however, that choice was not obvious—or rather different answers appeared equally obvious to different segments of the population. We should never forget that it took a bloody civil war to resolve the issue in favor of national supremacy. And, indeed, all the details are not yet fully settled, as the generation of litigation and violence that followed the School Segregation Cases (1954) painfully demonstrates. (See, for example, the Southern Manifesto, reprinted below, p. 278.)

A. State Supremacy

The notion of state supremacy in constitutional interpretation was rarely stated in systematic form, probably because of the plain words of Article VI. But it was a mood that flashed in action, if not in academic writings or official pronouncements, and finally led to secession. Americans now celebrate their Constitution, but the document produced by the Philadelphia Convention was not greeted with universal enthusiasm. Persuading the country to ratify the new Constitution was no easy task. Whatever else its opponents had in common, they shared a deep-seated distrust of strong central government and an equally marked desire for local autonomy. In 1793, this mood moved the lower house of the Georgia legislature to threaten with death anyone who tried to take advantage of the Supreme Court's ruling in Chisholm v. Georgia that a state could be sued without its consent in a federal court. The actual resolution was more peaceful, adoption of the Eleventh Amendment, which denied jurisdiction to federal courts to hear suits against a state brought by citizens of another state or of foreign nations.[2]

B. Confederational Departmentalism

The term "confederational departmentalism" is awkward, but it is descriptive and points to parallels with the departmental theory that Jefferson and others espoused for constitutional interpretation among

---

2. Curiously, the wording of the amendment did not deny federal jurisdiction over suits brought against a state by its own citizens. The Supreme Court repaired that omission in Hans v. Louisiana (1890) by declaring it a mere oversight. The Fourteenth Amendment's prohibitions against certain kinds of state action, however, modify the Eleventh. Essentially the Court held in a line of decisions culminating in Ex parte Young (1908) that when state officials take life, liberty, or property without due process of law or deny equal protection of the laws, federal courts may have jurisdiction under congressional statutes enforcing the Fourteenth Amendment; those state officials do not have immunity under the Eleventh Amendment because insofar as they act unconstitutionally they cannot claim to act in the name of the state. "Logic," Justice Douglas once remarked, "cannot justify the rule of Ex parte Young. I have never thought it was in full harmony with the Eleventh Amendment. Ex parte Young and its offspring do, however, reflect perhaps an even higher policy: the belief that courts must be allowed in the interest of justice to police unruly, lawless government officials who seek to impose oppressive laws on the citizen." We, the Judges (Garden City, N.Y.: Doubleday, 1956), p. 75.

the three branches of the national government. The basis of this theory is that the Constitution is a compact not among the American people as a whole, but among sovereign states. Thus, as an interpreter of the Constitution—the compact to which it is a party—an individual state is equal in authority not only to any other state but also to the national government. Jefferson put the argument succinctly in the Kentucky Resolutions of 1798 (reprinted below, p. 261):

> *Resolved . . . .* That the Government created by this compact was not made the exclusive or final judge of the extent of the powers delegated to itself; since that would have made its discretion, and not the Constitution, the measure of its powers; but that as in all other cases of compact among parties having no common Judge, *each party has an equal right to judge for itself, as well of infractions as of the mode and measure of redress.* (Italics in original.)

From then until the eve of the Civil War at least seven states, including Pennsylvania and Wisconsin, repeated this sort of argument. Even James Madison, who at the Constitutional Convention had fought vehemently for national supremacy and in *Federalist* No. 39 had gone on public record as believing that the U.S. Supreme Court was the authoritative interpreter of the Constitution in disputes between state and nation, used language similar to that of Jefferson when writing the Virginia Resolutions of 1799. (Reprinted below, p. 409.) That Madison here contradicted his former self and then in later years changed again and tried valiantly to explain away his endorsement of confederational departmentalism only highlights the attractiveness of the doctrine to those who lost at the national level on important policy questions.

It was John C. Calhoun, of course, who most elaborately and systematically developed Jefferson's views in the Kentucky Resolutions. Calhoun's writings provided the theoretical basis for much of southern sectionalism in the years 1828–1861, reshaped nullification (or "interposition," as he preferred) into a powerful threat to the federal government, and eventually justified secession. (See his *Discourse on the Constitution of the United States,* reprinted below, p. 272.)

C. National Supremacy

Congress, presidents (including Madison), and the Supreme Court have all rejected both state supremacy and confederational departmentalism. They have opted for national supremacy, for a theory that not only is the Constitution "the supreme law of the land," but also that national officials are its authoritative interpreters. As we saw in Chapter 6, however, national officials have been less than unanimous in deciding which of the three national branches is the ultimate interpreter.

In enacting § 25 of the Judiciary Act of 1789 (reprinted below, p. 260), authorizing the U.S. Supreme Court to review and reverse state judges' constitutional interpretations, the very first Congress struck a decisive blow for national supremacy.   States-rights forces made repeated and unsuccessful efforts to repeal this section.   Later rulings by the Supreme Court, especially Martin v. Hunter's Lessee (1816; reprinted below, p. 266), McCulloch v. Maryland (1819; reprinted below, p. 413), and Ableman v. Booth (1859; reprinted below p. 274), upheld the constitutionality of § 25 and stressed the Court's own role as ultimate arbiter of the federal system.   Cooper v. Aaron (1958; reprinted below, p. 281) followed ineluctably in that tradition.

The most significant decisions, however, were by executive officials: Lincoln's first inaugural (reprinted above, p. 226) ranks among the most important pieces of constitutional interpretation in American history.   For, on his own authority as chief executive and commander in chief of the armed forces, he determined that the Constitution forbade secession.   Although he was a lawyer, he did not rely on or even cite any of the several Supreme Court rulings that supported his argument.   And on Lincoln's decision the continuation of the United States as a nation turned.   The next and only somewhat less crucial decision to use force to prevent disunion took final form when Ulysses S. Grant sat at Appomattox Courthouse.

Yet, like the question of the relative interpretive authority of the branches of the federal government, that between the nation and the states is more subtle and complex than legal rules might make it seem. Every senator and representative is elected from a constituency no broader than an individual state.   To return to Washington for another term, those legislators have to persuade their local constituencies—among whose most influential members are typically state officials—that they are protecting local interests, including as much freedom from "outside interference" as is feasible.   Presidents are less parochially bound, but they can seldom afford to alienate state officials en masse.   Thus these people have significant opportunities to persuade elected federal officials to lend a sympathetic ear, as well as their own interpretive authority and other potential weapons against judges, to arguments for "states rights."

Recognizing that the United States is "an indestructible union of indestructible states"[3] and not a unitary political system, the Supreme Court has traditionally accorded state constitutional interpretation considerable deference.   The justices take as definitive a state supreme court's interpretation of its own laws or constitution, and they often claim to indulge a presumption of constitutionality to state laws.[4]   This presumption is subject to the same exceptions for fundamental rights and suspect classifications as are acts of Congress;   and it is highly

---

3.   Texas v. White (1869; reprinted below, p. 429).

4.   The rhetoric goes back to the very early cases. See, for example, the Court claim in Fletcher v. Peck (1810; reprinted below, p. 956) and the Dartmouth College Case (1819) that it would never declare a doubtful state law invalid, only one that clearly violated the Constitution.   For more recent claims regarding economic regulation, see Williamson v. Lee Optical (1955; reprinted below, p. 763); for a more general statement of presumption of the validity of state laws, see Parham v. Hughes (1979).

doubtful as a matter of fact that, whatever the degree of presumption the justices do in fact and not merely in rhetoric accord state legislation, it is nearly so strong as that which they give to federal acts.

The Court has also developed an elaborate set of rules that it sometimes but not always deploys to avoid conflict with state constitutional interpretation. Probably the most important of these is the doctrine of "equitable abstention," under which federal judges should not pass on the constitutionality of a state statute whose meaning is not clear until state courts have had a chance to interpret the law and determine its validity.

In short, even at times when federal supremacy is secure and federal judicial supremacy over state constitutional interpretation equally firmly anchored in accepted norms, the Supreme Court has usually been respectful of the pride of state officials, especially state judges. Considerations of raw power encourage that attitude, but so do notions about democracy in that state legislators are popularly, if very locally, elected officials. And constitutionalism, recognizing federalism's potential to check oppressive national power, reinforces the attractiveness of a policy of diplomacy rather than domination.

SELECTED BIBLIOGRAPHY

Corwin, Edward S. "National Power and State Interposition, 1787–1861," 10 *Mich.L.Rev.* 535 (1912).

Douglas, William O. "Interposition and the Peters Case," 9 *Stan.L. Rev.* 3 (1956).

Koch, Adrienne, and Harry Ammon. "The Virginia and Kentucky Resolutions," 5 *Wm. & Mary Q.* (3rd Series) 145 (1948).

McKay, Robert B. "Georgia versus the United States Supreme Court," 4 *Jo. of Pub.L.* 285 (1955).

Madison, James. "On Nullification," originally published as a letter to the editor of the *North American Review* (1830). Reprinted in Marvin Meyers, ed., *The Mind of the Founder* (Indianapolis, Ind.: Bobbs, Merril, 1973).

Mason, Alpheus Thomas, ed. *The States Rights Debate* (2d ed.; New York: Oxford University Press, 1972).

Mathis, Doyle. "*Chisbom v. Georgia:* Background and Settlement," 54 *Jo. of Am. Hist.* 19 (1967).

Murphy, Walter F. *Elements of Judicial Strategy* (Chicago: University of Chicago Press, 1964), chaps. 4–6.

Note. "Judge Spencer Roane of Virginia: Champion of States' Rights—Foe of John Marshall," 66 *Harv.L.Rev.* 1242 (1953).

Note. "Interposition v. Judicial Power," 1 *Race Rel.L.Rep.* 464 (1956).

Storing, Herbert. *What the Anti-Federalists Were For* (Chicago: University of Chicago Press, 1981).

Warren, Charles. "Legislative and Judicial Attacks on the Supreme Court of the United States," 47 *Am.L.Rev.* 1, and 47 ibid. 161 (1913).

"[A state decision] may be re-examined and reversed or affirmed in the Supreme Court of the United States."

JUDICIARY ACT OF 1789, SECTION 25

Article III of the Constitution outlines the general jurisdiction of federal courts. Among the initial pieces of legislation adopted by the First Congress was the Judiciary Act of 1789, organizing and spelling out in detail the jurisdictions of various federal tribunals. Section 25 pertained to the authority of the Supreme Court to review decisions of state courts.

Sec. 1. *Be it enacted . . . .*

Sec. 25. That a final judgment or decree in any suit, in the high st court of law or equity of a State in which a decision in the suit cou.d be had, where is drawn in question the validity of a treaty or statute of, or an authority exercised under the United States, and the decision is against their validity; or where is drawn in question the validity of a statute of, or an authority exercised under any State, on the ground of their being repugnant to the constitution, treaties or laws of the United States, and the decision is in favour of their validity, or where is drawn in question the construction of any clause of the constitution, or of a treaty, or statute of, or commission held under the United States, and the decision is against the title, right, privilege or exemption specifically set up or claimed by either party, under such clause of the said constitution, treaty, statute or commission, may be re-examined and reversed or affirmed in the Supreme Court of the United States. . . .

"[E]ach party [to the Constitution] has an equal right to judge for itself, as well of infractions as of mode and measure of redress."

THE DEBATE OF 1798–99

In 1798, the Federalist majority in Congress, fearful of the spread of "radical" ideas, enacted the Alien and Sedition Acts. The first of the Alien Acts—there were two such statutes—authorized the President to deport "all such *aliens* as he shall judge dangerous to the peace and safety of the United States"; the second provided that all citizens of a nation with whom the United States might go to war "shall be liable to be apprehended, restrained, secured and removed" from this country.

The Sedition Act not only punished efforts to use violence to oppose or overthrow the federal government, but also put into statutory form the traditional British ban against "seditious libel." The law made it a crime to write or speak anything "false, scandalous and malicious" about the federal government in general, either house of Congress, or the President "with intent to defame . . . or to bring them, or either of them, into contempt or disrepute . . . ." In sum, the Act made it a crime to criticize in any but the most polite forms the national government or its officials. Federalist prosecutors promptly began cases against Jeffersonians, and many Federalist judges—and during this period justices of the Supreme Court spent most of their time as circuit judges, presiding with district judges over important federal trials around the country—delighted in delivering charges to juries about the evils of Jeffersonianism and the spirit of the French Revolution.[1]

Almost as promptly, Jefferson began drafting a series of resolutions attacking the constitutionality of the new statutes. Initially, he argued that protection against libel and slander fell under the jurisdiction of state legislatures, not Congress. The notion that freedom of speech and press as protected by the First Amendment forbade Congress to enact such legislation did not develop until the debate was well underway,[2] but it did find its way into a set of resolutions Jefferson prepared for state legislatures. He asked a friend to introduce his resolutions in North Carolina's legislature; but John Breckenridge,[3] who would later lead efforts in the Senate to repeal the Judiciary Act of 1801 (see above, p. 203), persuaded Jefferson to let him present the document to the Kentucky legislature. He, however, made a change of major importance, one that the Kentucky legislature adopted: He omitted Jefferson's claim that "every State has a natural right in cases not within the compact . . . to nullify of their own authority all assumptions of power by others within their limitations . . . ."

"In questions of power then let no more be heard of confidence in man, but bind him down from mischief by the chains of the Constitution."

A. THE KENTUCKY RESOLUTIONS OF 1798 *

I. *Resolved*, that the several States composing the United States of America, are not united on the principle of unlimited submission to their general government; but that by compact under the style and title of a Constitution for the United States and of amendments thereto, they constituted a general government for special purposes, delegated to that government certain definite powers, reserving each State to itself, the residuary mass of right to their own self-government; and that whensoever the general government assumes undelegated powers, its acts are unauthoritative, void, and of no force: That to this compact each State acceded as a State, and is an integral party, its co-States forming, as to itself, the other party: That the government created by this compact was not made the exclusive or final judge of the extent of the powers delegated to itself; since that would have made its discretion, and not the Constitution, the measure of its powers; but that as in

---

1. See J.C. Miller, *Crisis in Freedom: The Alien and Sedition Acts* (Boston: Little, Brown, 1951); and James Morton Smith, *Freedom's Fetters: The Alien and Sedition Laws and American Civil Liberties* (Ithaca, N.Y.: Cornell University Press, 1956).

2. See Leonard W. Levy, *Legacy of Suppression: Freedom of Speech and Press in Early American History* (Cambridge, Mass.: The Belknap Press of Harvard University Press, 1960), espec. chs. 1 and 6; see also Levy's somewhat revised thoughts: "*The Legacy* Reexamined," 37 *Stan.L.Rev.* 767 (1985).

3. In keeping with some of the loose standards of spelling of the times, he sometimes wrote his name "Breckinridge," at other times—and apparently more often—as "Breckenridge."

* Jonathan Elliot, ed., *The Debates in the Several State Conventions on the Adoption of the Federal Constitution* (2d ed.; Philadelphia: Lippincott, 1861), IV, 540–544.

all other cases of compact among parties having no common Judge, *each party has an equal right to judge for itself, as well of infractions as of the mode and measure of redress.*

II. *Resolved,* that the Constitution of the United States having delegated to Congress a power to punish treason, counterfeiting the securities and current coin of the United States, piracies and felonies committed on the high seas, and offenses against the laws of nations, and no other crimes whatever, and it being true as a general principle, and one of the amendments to the Constitution having also declared "that the powers not delegated to the United States by the Constitution, nor prohibited by it to the States, are reserved to the States respectively, or to the people," therefore also . . . [the Sedition Act of July 14, 1798]; as also the act . . . entitled "An act to punish frauds committed on the Bank of the United States" (and all other their acts which assume to create, define, or punish crimes other than those enumerated in the Constitution), are altogether void and of no force, and that the power to create, define, and punish such other crimes is reserved, and of right appertains solely and exclusively to the respective States, each within its own Territory.

III. *Resolved,* that it is true as a general principle, and is also expressly declared by one of the amendments to the Constitution that "the powers not delegated to the United States by the Constitution, nor prohibited by it to the States, are reserved to the States respectively or to the people;" and that no power over the freedom of religion, freedom of speech, or freedom of the press being delegated to the United States by the Constitution, nor prohibited by it to the States, all lawful powers respecting the same did of right remain, and were reserved to the States, or to the people: That thus was manifested their determination to retain to themselves the right of judging how far the licentiousness of speech and of the press may be abridged without lessening their useful freedom, and how far those abuses which cannot be separated from their use should be tolerated rather than the use be destroyed; and thus also they guarded against all abridgment by the United States of the freedom of religious opinions and exercises, and retained to themselves the right of protecting the same, as this State, by a law passed on the general demand of its citizens, had already protected them from all human restraint or interference: And that in addition to this general principle and express declaration, another and more special provision has been made by one of the amendments to the Constitution which expressly declares, that "Congress shall make no law respecting an establishment of religion, or prohibiting the free exercise thereof, or abridging the freedom of speech, or of the press" . . . and that libels, falsehoods, defamation equally with heresy and false religion, are withheld from the cognizance of Federal tribunals. That therefore . . . [the Sedition Act], which does abridge the freedom of the press, is not law, but is altogether void and of no effect . . . .

[Resolutions IV–VII detailed arguments against the constitutionality of the Alien Acts and the statute punishing fraud against the Bank of the United States.]

VIII. *Resolved,* that the preceding Resolutions be transmitted to the Senators and Representatives in Congress from this Commonwealth, who are hereby enjoined to present the same to their respective Houses, and to use their best endeavors to procure, at the next session of Congress, a repeal of the aforesaid unconstitutional and obnoxious acts.

IX. *Resolved,* lastly, that the Governor of this Commonwealth be, and is hereby authorized and requested to communicate the preceding Resolutions to the Legislatures of the several States, to assure them that this Commonwealth considers Union for specified National purposes, and particularly for those specified in their late Federal Compact, to be friendly to the peace, happiness, and prosperity of all the States; that faithful to that compact according to the plain intent and meaning in which it was understood and acceded to by the several parties, it is sincerely anxious for its preservation: that it does also believe, that to take from the States all the powers of self-government, and transfer them to a general and consolidated government, without regard to the special delegations and reservations solemnly agreed to in that compact, is not for the peace, happiness, or prosperity of these States . . . that it would be a dangerous delusion were a confidence in the men of our choice to silence our fears for the safety of our rights; that confidence is everywhere the parent of despotism—free government is founded in jealousy, not in confidence; it is jealousy and not confidence which prescribes limited constitutions, to bind down those whom we are obliged to trust with power: that our Constitution has accordingly fixed the limit to which, and no further, our confidence may go . . . . In questions of power, then, let no more be heard of confidence in man, but bind him down from mischief by the chains of the Constitution. That this commonwealth does therefore call on its co-States for an expression of their sentiments on the acts concerning aliens, and for the punishment of certain crimes herein before specified, plainly declaring whether these acts are or are not authorized by the Federal Compact . . . .

Madison drafted another set of resolutions for the Virginia legislature. Although similar to Jefferson's in proclaiming the unconstitutionality of the Alien and Sedition Acts, Madison's resolutions were more moderate in tone and substance, for, unlike Jefferson, Madison rejected the notion that a state legislature could nullify a federal statute.[4] The Virginia legislature "solemnly,"

---

4. Jefferson was displeased with what he thought was Madison's mincing on this issue. In response, Madison wrote to his mentor: "Have you ever considered thoroughly the distinction between the power of the *State,* & that of the *Legislature,* on questions relating to the federal pact. On the supposition that the former is clearly the ultimate Judge of infractions, it does not follow that the latter is the legitimate organ, especially as a convention was the organ by which the compact was made." Quoted in Nathan Schachner, *Thomas Jefferson: A Biography* (New York: Thomas Yoseloff, 1951), p. 617. At the Constitutional Convention Madison had been in favor of a very strong central government, one stronger than the structure that took shape. Later, when President, he faced an effort by Pennsylvania to nullify the Supreme Court's decision in United States v. Peters (1809). Madison not only refused to accept the state's assertion of authority, he insisted on his duty as President to use force, if necessary, to ensure compliance with the Court's ruling. His

if vaguely, appealed "to the like dispositions of the other states, in confidence that they will concur with this Commonwealth in declaring . . . that the acts aforesaid are unconstitutional; and that the necessary and proper measures will be taken by each for co-operating with this state, in maintaining unimpaired the authorities, rights, and liberties reserved to the states respectively, or to the people . . . ."

> **"[T]he Constitution . . . vests in the Federal Courts, exclusively, and in the Supreme Court of the United States, ultimately, the authority of deciding on the constitutionality of any act or law of the Congress of the United States."**

B. THE STATES RESPOND TO KENTUCKY AND VIRGINIA *

Seven state legislatures replied directly to the resolutions, three indirectly. All were negative. The other state legislatures were silent.

State of Rhode Island and Providence Plantations.

In General Assembly, *February, A.D.* 1799

Certain resolutions of the legislature of Virginia, passed on 21st of December last, being communicated to this Assembly,—

1. *Resolved,* That, in the opinion of this legislature, the second section of third article of the Constitution of the United States, in these words, to wit,—"The judicial power shall extend to all cases arising under the laws of the United States,"—vests in the federal courts, exclusively, and in the Supreme Court of the United States, ultimately, the authority of deciding on the constitutionality of any act or law of the Congress of the United States.

2. *Resolved,* That for any state legislature to assume that authority would be—

1st. Blending together legislative and judicial powers;

2d. Hazarding an interruption of the peace of the states by civil discord, in case of a diversity of opinions among the state legislatures; each state having, in that case, no resort, for vindicating its own opinions, but the strength of its own arm;—

3d. Submitting most important questions of law to less competent tribunals; and,

4th. An infraction of the Constitution of the United States, expressed in plain terms.

3. *Resolved,* That, although, for the above reasons, this legislature, in their public capacity, do not feel themselves authorized to consider and decide on the constitutionality of the Sedition and Alien laws, (so called,) yet they are called upon, by the exigency of this

---

firmness caused the governor, who had called out the militia to prevent execution of the Court's mandate, to beat a hasty retreat. For details, see Charles Warren, *The Supreme Court in U.S. History* (Rev. ed.; Boston: Little, Brown, 1926), I, 366ff.

* Jonathan Elliot, *The Debates in the Several State Conventions on the Adoption of the Federal Constitution* (2d ed.; Philadelphia: Lippincott, 1861), IV, 533–539.

occasion, to declare that, in their private opinions, these laws are within the powers delegated to Congress, and promotive of the welfare of the United States. . . .

Commonwealth of Massachusetts

In Senate, February 9, 1799.

The legislature of Massachusetts, having taken into serious consideration the resolutions of the state of Virginia, . . . deem it their duty solemnly to declare that, while they hold sacred the principle, that consent of the people is the only pure source of just and legitimate power, they cannot admit the right of the state legislatures to denounce the administration of that government to which the people themselves, by a solemn compact, have exclusively committed their national concerns. That, although a liberal and enlightened vigilance among the people is always to be cherished, yet an unreasonable jealousy of the men of their choice, and a recurrence to measures of extremity upon groundless or trivial pretexts, have a strong tendency to destroy all rational liberty at home, and to deprive the United States of the most essential advantages in relations abroad. That this legislature are persuaded that the decision of all cases in law and equity arising under the Constitution of the United States, and the construction of all laws made in pursuance thereof, are exclusively vested by the people in the judicial courts of the United States . . . . .

State of Vermont

In the House of Representatives, October 30, A.D. 1799.

The house proceeded to take under their consideration the resolutions of the General Assembly of Virginia, relative to certain measures of the general government, transmitted to the legislature of this state, for their consideration: Whereupon,—

Resolved, That the General Assembly of the state of Vermont do highly disapprove of the resolutions of the General Assembly of Virginia, as being unconstitutional in their nature, and dangerous in their tendency. It belongs not to state legislatures to decide on the constitutionality of laws made by the general government; this power being exclusively vested in the judiciary courts of the Union. . . . And that the same be sent to the governor and council for their concurrence.

In Council, October 30, 1799. Read and concurred unanimously.

Editors' Note

The strongly negative character of these responses pushed John Breckenridge and other political leaders in Kentucky to publish a counter-response.

In 1799, after a bitter debate, the state legislature repeated its condemnation of the federal legislation and added to its earlier resolution the sort of clause that Breckenridge had removed from Jefferson's draft:

> That the several states who formed that instrument [the Constitution] being sovereign and independent, have the unquestionable right to judge of the infraction; and, *That a nullification of those sovereignties, of all unauthorized acts done under color of that instrument is the rightful remedy.*

Madison managed to cool Jefferson down and persuade him that caution was wiser than confronting Federalist (and federal) power.   The Alien and Sedition Acts expired before Jefferson took office after winning the election of 1800. He pardoned three people still in prison under the acts, and Congress later remitted all the fines.   After 1828, when John C. Calhoun began to trumpet a new doctrine of nullification, Madison called it "a collosal heresy" and claimed it was false to associate Jefferson's name with such an "inlet to anarchy." [5]

"It is a mistake, that the constitution was not designed to operate upon states, in their corporate capacities."

MARTIN v. HUNTER'S LESSEE
14 U.S. (1 Wheat.) 304, 4 L.Ed. 97 (1816).

In 1813 the Supreme Court had reversed a decision of the Virginia Court of Appeals regarding the protection afforded land rights of British citizens by Jay's Treaty (1794). The Virginia Court of Appeals, however, responded by defying the U.S. Supreme Court:

> The court is unanimously of opinion that the appellate power of the Supreme Court of the United States does not extend to this court, under a sound construction of the constitution of the United States; that so much of the 25th section of the act of congress to establish the judicial courts of the United States, as extends the appellate jurisdiction of the supreme court to this court is not in pursuance of the constitution of the United States; that the writ of error, in this cause, was improvidently allowed under the authority of that act; that the proceedings thereon in the supreme court were *coram non judice* [in the presence of a person not a judge of competent jurisdiction], in relation to this court, and that obedience to its mandate be declined by the court.

Martin, who had won in the Supreme Court the first time, brought his case back to Washington.

STORY, J., delivered the opinion of the court . . . .

The constitution of the United States was ordained and established, not by the states in their sovereign capacities, but emphatically, as the

---

5. See vol. 4 of W. C. Rives and P. R. Fendall, eds., *Letters and Other Writings of James Madison* (Philadelphia: Lippincott, 1865), which collects a number of his letters and essays opposing nullification.

preamble of the constitution declares, by "the People of the United States." There can be no doubt, that it was competent to the people to invest the general government with all the powers which they might deem proper and necessary; to extend or restrain these powers according to their own good pleasure, and to give them a paramount and supreme authority. As little doubt can there be, that the people had a right to prohibit to the states the exercise of any powers which were, in their judgment, incompatible with the objects of the general compact; to make the powers of the state governments, in given cases, subordinate to those of the nation, or to reserve to themselves those sovereign authorities which they might not choose to delegate to either. The constitution was not, therefore, necessarily carved out of existing state sovereignties, nor a surrender of powers already existing in state institutions, for the powers of the states depend upon their own constitutions . . . . On the other hand, it is perfectly clear, that the sovereign powers vested in the state governments, by their respective constitutions, remained unaltered and unimpaired, except so far as they were granted to the government of the United States. These deductions do not rest upon general reasoning, plain and obvious as they seem to be. They have been positively recognised by one of the articles in amendment of the constitution, which declares, that "the powers not delegated to the United States by the constitution, nor prohibited by it to the states, are reserved to the states respectively, or to the people."

The government, then, of the United States can claim no powers which are not granted to it by the constitution, and the powers actually granted, must be such as are expressly given, or given by necessary implication. On the other hand, this instrument, like every other grant, is to have a reasonable construction, according to the import of its terms; and where a power is expressly given, in general terms, it is not to be restrained to particular cases, unless that construction grow out of the context, expressly, or by necessary implication. The words are to be taken in their natural and obvious sense, and not in a sense unreasonably restricted or enlarged.

The constitution unavoidably deals in general language . . . . Hence, its powers are expressed in general terms, leaving to the legislature, from time to time, to adopt its own means to effectuate legitimate objects, and to mould and model the exercise of its powers, as its own wisdom, and the public interests, should require. . . .

The third article of the constitution is that which must principally attract our attention. The 1st section declares, "the judicial power of the United States shall be vested in one supreme court, and in such other inferior courts as the congress may, from time to time, ordain and establish." The 2d section declares, that "the judicial power shall extend to all cases in law or equity, arising under this constitution, the laws of the United States, and the treaties made, or which shall be made, under their authority . . . ."

Such is the language of the article creating and defining the judicial power of the United States. It is the voice of the whole American people, solemnly declared, in establishing one great department of that government which was, in many respects, national, and in all, supreme. It is a part of the very same instrument which was to act, not merely upon individuals, but upon states; and to deprive them altogether of the exercise of some powers of sovereignty, and to restrain and regulate them in the exercise of others.

Let this article be carefully weighed and considered. The language of the article throughout is manifestly designed to be mandatory upon the legislature. Its obligatory force is so imperative, that congress could not, without a violation of its duty, have refused to carry it into operation. The judicial power of the United States *shall* be vested (not *may* be vested) in one supreme court, and in such inferior courts as congress may, from time to time, ordain and establish. Could congress have lawfully refused to create a supreme court, or to vest in it the constitutional jurisdiction? "The judges, both of the supreme and inferior courts, shall hold their offices during good behavior, and shall, at stated times, receive, for their services, a compensation which shall not be diminished during their continuance in office." Could congress create or limit any other tenure of the judicial office? Could they refuse to pay, at stated times, the stipulated salary, or diminish it during the continuance in office? But one answer can be given to these questions: it must be in the negative . . . .

The same expression, "shall be vested," occurs in other parts of the constitution, in defining the powers of the other co-ordinate branches of the government. The first article declares that "all legislative powers herein granted shall be vested in a congress of the United States." Will it be contended that the legislative power is not absolutely vested? . . . The second article declares that "the executive power shall be vested in a president of the United States of America." Could congress vest it in any other person . . . ? It is apparent, that such a construction, in either case, would be utterly inadmissible. Why, then, is it entitled to a better support, in reference to the judicial department?

If, then, it is a duty of congress to vest the judicial power of the United States, it is a duty to vest the whole judicial power. The language, if imperative as to one part, is imperative as to all. . . .

The next consideration is, as to the courts in which the judicial power shall be vested. It is manifest, that a supreme court must be established; but whether it be equally obligatory to establish inferior courts, is a question of some difficulty. If congress may lawfully omit to establish inferior courts, it might follow, that in some of the enumerated cases, the judicial power could nowhere exist. . . .

This construction will be fortified by an attentive examination of the second section of the third article. The words are "the judicial power shall extend," &c. . . . For the reasons which have been already stated, we are of opinion, that the words are used in an

imperative sense; they import an absolute grant of judicial power
. . . .

It being, then, established, that the language of this clause is imperative, the question is, as to the cases to which it shall apply. The answer is found in the constitution itself "the judicial power shall extend to all the cases enumerated in the constitution. . . .

This leads us to the consideration of the great question, as to the nature and extent of the appellate jurisdiction of the United States. . . . [A]ppellate jurisdiction is given by the constitution to the supreme court, in all cases where it has not original jurisdiction; subject, however, to such exceptions and regulations as congress may prescribe. It is, therefore, capable of embracing every case enumerated in the constitution, which is not exclusively to be decided by way of original jurisdiction . . . . The appellate power is not limited by the terms of the third article to any particular courts. The words are, "the judicial power (which includes appellate power) shall extend to all cases," &c., and "in all other cases before mentioned the supreme court shall have appellate jurisdiction." It is the case, then, and not the court, that gives the jurisdiction. If the judicial power extends to the case, it will be in vain to search in the letter of the constitution for any qualification as to the tribunal where it depends. It is incumbent, then, upon those who assert such a qualification, to show its existence, by necessary implication. If the text be clear and distinct, no restriction upon its plain and obvious import ought to be admitted, unless the inference be irresistible.

If the constitution meant to limit the appellate jurisdiction to cases pending in the courts of the United States, it would necessarily follow, that the jurisdiction of these courts would, in all the cases enumerated in the constitution, be exclusive of state tribunals . . . .

But it is plain, that the framers of the constitution did contemplate that cases within the judicial cognisance of the United States, not only might, but would, arise in the state courts, in the exercise of their ordinary jurisdiction. With this view, the sixth article declares, that "this constitution, and the laws of the United States which shall be made in pursuance thereof, and all treaties made, or which shall be made, under the authority of the United States, shall be the supreme law of the land, and the judges in every state shall be bound thereby, anything in the constitution or laws of any state to the contrary notwithstanding." It is obvious, that this obligation is imperative upon the state judges, in their official, and not merely in their private, capacities. . . . They were not to decide merely according to the laws or constitution of the state, but according to the constitution, laws and treaties of the United States—"the supreme law of the land." . . .

It must, therefore, be conceded, that the constitution not only contemplated, but meant to provide for cases within the scope of the judicial power of the United States, which might yet depend before state tribunals.

It has been argued, that such an appellate jurisdiction over state courts is inconsistent with the genius of our governments, and the spirit of the constitution. That the latter was never designed to act upon state sovereignties . . . . We cannot yield to the force of this reasoning; it assumes principles which we cannot admit, and draws conclusions to which we do not yield our assent.

It is a mistake, that the constitution was not designed to operate upon states, in their corporate capacities. It is crowded with provisions which restrain or annul the sovereignty of the states, in some of the highest branches of their prerogatives. The tenth section of the first article contains a long list of disabilities and prohibitions imposed upon the states. Surely, when such essential portions of state sovereignty are taken away, or prohibited to be exercised, it cannot be correctly asserted, that the constitution does not act upon the states. The language of the constitution is also imperative upon the states, as to the performance of many duties. It is imperative upon the state legislatures, to make laws prescribing the time, places and manner of holding elections for senators and representatives, and for electors of president and vice-president. And in these, as well as some other cases, congress have a right to revise, amend or supersede the laws which may be passed by state legislatures. When, therefore, the states are stripped of some of the highest attributes of sovereignty, and the same are given to the United States; when the legislatures of the states are, in some respects, under the control of congress, and in every case are, under the constitution, bound by the paramount authority of the United States; it is certainly difficult to support the argument, that the appellate power over the decisions of state courts is contrary to the genius of our institutions. . . .

Nor can such a right be deemed to impair the independence of state judges. It is assuming the very ground in controversy, to assert that they possess an absolute independence of the United States. In respect to the powers granted to the United States, they are not independent; they are expressly bound to obedience, by the letter of the constitution; and if they should unintentionally transcend their authority, or misconstrue the constitution, there is no more reason for giving their judgments an absolute and irresistible force, than for giving it to the acts of the other co-ordinate departments of state sovereignty . . . .

This is not all. A motive of another kind, perfectly compatible with the most sincere respect for state tribunals, might induce the grant of appellate power over the decisions. That motive is the importance, and even necessity of uniformity of decisions throughout the whole United States, upon all subjects within the purview of the constitution. Judges of equal learning and integrity, in different states, might differently interpret the statute, or a treaty of the United States, or even the constitution itself: if there were no revising authority to control these jarring and discordant judgments, and harmonize them into uniformity, the laws, the treaties and the constitution of the United States would be different, in different states, and might, perhaps, never have precisely the same construction, obligation or efficiency, in any two states. The public mischiefs that would attend such a state of things would be truly deplorable . . . .

On the whole, the court are of opinion, that the appellate power of the United States does extend to cases pending in the state courts; and that the 25th section of the judiciary act, which authorizes the exercise of this jurisdiction in the specified cases, by a writ of error, is supported by the letter and spirit of the constitution. We find no clause in that instrument which limits this power; and we dare not interpose a limitation, where the people have not been disposed to create one.

. . .

It is the opinion of the whole court, that the judgment of the court of appeals of Virginia, rendered on the mandate in this cause, be reversed, and the judgment of the district court, held at Winchester, be, and the same is hereby

Affirmed.

JOHNSON, J. . . . I acquiesce in their opinion, but not altogether in the reasoning or opinion of my brother who delivered it . . . .

Editors' Notes

(1) This is one of the few constitutional disputes for which John Marshall did not assign himself the task of writing the opinion of the Court. In this instance, he did not sit because he had become involved in the land speculation that revolved around the ownership of property once possessed by Loyalists during the Revolutionary War, whose title was at issue in this case.

(2) To avoid further conflict with Virginia's Court of Appeals, the Supreme Court sent its order directly to the state trial court in Winchester.

(3) Virginia's attack on § 25 was only one among many. See the two-part article by Charles Warren, "Legislative and Judicial Attacks on the Supreme Court of the United States—A History of the Twenty-Fifth Section of the Judiciary Act," 47 *Am.L.Rev.* 1; 47 ibid. 161 (1913).

(4) Story asserts that Congress was constitutionally obligated to create an entire system of federal courts. Does that conclusion follow from the plain words of Article III? Does it follow from the logic of federalism? See the discussion in Chapter 8, below. Canada and the Federal Republic of Germany, both federal systems, have depended primarily on the equivalent of state courts for the bulk of national civil and criminal jurisdiction. And it was not until after the Civil War that Congress conferred on federal courts anything approaching the full jurisdiction listed in Article III, and more recently—in the Emergency Price Control Act of 1942, for example—has specifically authorized enforcement of federal law, at least in civil cases, in state tribunals. See the discussion in Paul Bator, et al., eds., *Hart and Wechsler's The Federal Courts and the Federal System* (2d. ed.; Mineola, N.Y.: The Foundation Press, 1973), pp. 11–12, 309–322; Martin H. Redish, *Federal Jurisdiction* (Indianapolis: Bobbs-Merrill, 1980), pp. 21–24; and Henry J. Friendly, *Federal Jurisdiction* (New York: Columbia University Press, 1973), pp. 1–14.

"Do the courts of the States stand . . . in the relation of the inferior to the Supreme Court of the United States?"

A DISCOURSE ON THE CONSTITUTION AND GOVERNMENT OF THE UNITED STATES

John C. Calhoun.

Although he began his political career as an ardent nationalist, by 1828 Calhoun had become a sectionalist. As Vice President of the United States, U.S. Senator from South Carolina, Secretary of State, and elder statesman, he was the most systematic spokesman for nullification and then, following the iron road of his own logic, for secession as principles inherent in the American Constitution.

. . . Now, as there is nothing in the constitution which vests authority in the government of the United States, or any of its departments, to enforce its decision against that of the separate government of a State; and nothing in this clause [Art. III, Sec. 2, U.S. Con.] which makes the several States amenable to its process, it is manifest that there is nothing in it, which can possibly give the judicial power authority to enforce the decision of the government of the United States, against that of a separate State . . . .

It is, in the last place, contended,—that the Supreme Court of the United States has the right to decide on the constitutionality of all laws; and, in virtue of this, to decide, in the last resort, all questions involving a conflict between the constitution of the United States and laws and treaties made in pursuance thereof, on the one side, and the constitutions and laws of the several States on the other.

It is admitted, that the court has the right, in all questions of a judicial character which may come before it, where the laws and treaties of the United States, and the constitution and laws of a State are in conflict or brought in question, to decide which is, or is not consistent with the constitution of the United States. But it is denied that this power is peculiar to it; or that its decision, in the last resort, is binding on any but the parties to it, and its co-departments. So far from being peculiar to it, the right appertains, not only to the Supreme Court of the United States, but to all courts of the several States, superior and inferior. . . . Now, as the constitution of the United States is, within its sphere, supreme over all others appertaining to the system, it necessarily results, that where any law conflicts with it, it is the duty of the court, before which the question arises, to pronounce the constitution to be paramount. If it be the Supreme Court of the United States, its decision,—being that of the highest judicial tribunal, in the last resort, of the parties to the case or controversy,—is, of course, final as it respects them,—but only as it respects them. It results, that its decision is not binding as between the United States and the several States, as neither can make the other defendant in any controversy between them . . . .

[Calhoun moves to a discussion of Sec. 25 of the Judiciary Act of 1789.] The question is thus narrowed down to a single point;—Has

Congress the authority . . . to make a law providing for an appeal from the courts of the several States to the Supreme Court of the United States?

There is, on the face of the two clauses [the jurisdictional clauses of Art. III], nothing whatever to authorize the making of such a law. Neither of them names or refers, in the slightest manner to the States, or to the courts of the States; or gives the least authority, apparently, to legislate over or concerning either. The object of the former of these two clauses, is simply to extend the judicial power, so as to make it commensurate with the other powers of the government. . . . While the latter simply provides, in what cases the Supreme Court of the United States shall have original, and in what, appellate jurisdiction . . . .

Such being the plain meaning and intent of these clauses,—the question is;—How can Congress derive from them, authority to make a law providing for an appeal from the highest courts of the several States, in the cases specified in the 25th sect. of the Judiciary Act, to the Supreme Court of the United States?

To this question no answer can be given, without assuming that the State courts,—even the highest,—stand in the relation of inferior courts to the Supreme Court of the United States, wherever a question touching their authority comes before them. Without such an assumption, there is not, and cannot be a shadow of authority to warrant an appeal from the former to the latter. But does the fact sustain the assumption? Do the courts of the States stand, as to such questions, in the relation of the inferior to the Supreme Court of the United States? If so, it must be by some provision of the constitution of the United States. It cannot be a matter of course. How can it be reconciled with the admitted principle, that the federal government and those of the several States, are each supreme in their respective spheres? Each, it is admitted, is supreme, as it regards the other, in its proper sphere; and, of course, as has been shown, coequal and co-ordinate.

If this be true, then, the respective departments of each must be necessarily and equally so;—as the whole includes the parts. The State courts are the representatives of the reserved rights, vested in the governments of the several States, as far as it relates to the judicial power. Now, as these are reserved *against* the federal government,—as the very object and intent of the reservation, was to place them beyond the reach of its control,—how can the courts of the States be inferior to the Supreme Court of the United States; and, of course, subject to have their decisions re-examined and reversed by it, without, at the same time, subjecting the portion of the reserved rights of the governments of the several States, vested in it, to the control of the federal government? . . .

I have now shown that the 25th section of the judiciary act is unauthorized by the constitution; and that it rests on an assumption which would give to Congress the right to enforce, through the judiciary department, whatever measures it might think proper to adopt; and to put down all resistance by force. The effect of this is to make the government of the United States the sole judge . . . as to the extent of its powers, and to place the States and their separate governments and institutions at its mercy . . . .

"[N]o power is more clearly conferred by the Constitution and laws of the United States, than the power of this court to decide, ultimately and finally, all cases arising under such Constitution and laws. . . . "

ABLEMAN v. BOOTH
62 U.S. (21 How.) 506, 16 L.Ed. 169 (1859).

In the mid-1850s, a federal marshal arrested Sherman M. Booth, an abolitionist editor from Milwaukee, Wisconsin, and charged him with violating the Fugitive Slave Act by helping a slave to escape. Because there was no federal prison in the area, the marshal placed Booth in a local jail. The prisoner then petitioned the Wisconsin supreme court for habeas corpus.[1] That court granted the writ and declared the Fugitive Slave Act unconstitutional. The marshal obtained review in the U.S. Supreme Court. Before the justices heard the case, a federal trial court convicted Booth, sentenced him to a year in prison, and ordered him to pay a fine of $1,000. Again he sought habeas corpus from the Wisconsin supreme court, and again that court granted the writ, holding that the federal trial court's action was as unconstitutional as the statute on which the conviction was based. The local jailer freed Booth. The marshal asked the U.S. Supreme Court to review this second state decision as well. The justices consolidated the two appeals.

Mr. Chief Justice **TANEY** delivered the opinion of the court . . . .

If the judicial power exercised in this instance has been reserved to the States, no offence against the laws of the United States can be punished by their own courts, without the permission and according to the judgment of the courts of the State in which the party happens to be imprisoned; for, if the Supreme Court of Wisconsin possessed the power it has exercised . . . it necessarily follows that they must have the same judicial authority in relation to any other law of the United States. . . . And, moreover, if the power is possessed by the Supreme Court of the State of Wisconsin, it must belong equally to every other State in the Union, when the prisoner is within its territorial limits; and it is very certain that the State courts would not always agree in opinion; and it would often happen, that an act which was admitted to be an offence, and justly punished, in one State, would be regarded as innocent, and indeed as praiseworthy, in another. . . .

The judges of the Supreme Court of Wisconsin do not distinctly state from what source they suppose they have derived this judicial power. There can be no such thing as judicial authority, unless it is

---

1. An order to a jailer or other person having custody of a prisoner instructing him to bring that prisoner to court and show legal cause for holding him or her in custody.

conferred by a Government or sovereignty; and if the judges and courts of Wisconsin possess the jurisdiction they claim, they must derive it either from the United States or the State. It certainly has not been conferred on them by the United States; and it is equally clear that it was not in the power of the State to confer it . . . for no State can authorize one of its judges or courts to exercise judicial power . . . within the jurisdiction of another and independent Government. And although the State of Wisconsin is sovereign within its territorial limits to a certain extent, yet that sovereignty is limited and restricted by the Constitution of the United States. And the powers of the General Government, and of the State, although both exist and are exercised within the same territorial limits, are yet separate and distinct sovereignties, acting separately and independently of each other, within their respective spheres. And the sphere of action appropriate to the United States is as far beyond the reach of the judicial process issued by a State judge or a State court, as if the line of division was traced by landmarks and monuments visible to the eye . . . .

. . . The Constitution was not formed merely to guard the States against danger from foreign nations, but mainly to secure union and harmony at home . . . and to accomplish this purpose, it was felt by the people who adopted it, that it was necessary that many of the rights of sovereignty which the States then possessed should be ceded to the General Government; and that, in the sphere of action assigned to it, should be supreme, and strong enough to execute its own laws by its own tribunals, without interruption from a State or from State authorities . . . .

The language of the Constitution, by which this power is granted, is too plain to admit of doubt or to need comment. It declares that "this Constitution, and the laws of the United States which shall be passed in pursuance thereof, and all treaties made, or which shall be made, under the authority of the United States, shall be the supreme law of the land, and the judges in every State shall be bound thereby, anything in the Constitution or laws of any State to the contrary notwithstanding."

But the supremacy thus conferred on this Government could not peacefully be maintained, unless it was clothed with judicial power, equally paramount in authority to carry it into execution; for if left to the courts of justice of the several States, conflicting decisions would unavoidably take place, and the local tribunals could hardly be expected to be always free from the local influences of which we have spoken . . . .

Accordingly, it was conferred on the General Government, in clear, precise, and comprehensive terms. It is declared that its judicial power shall (among other subjects enumerated) extend to all cases in law and equity arising under the Constitution and laws of the United States, and that in such cases, as well as the others there enumerated, this court shall have appellate jurisdiction both as to law and fact, with such exceptions and under such regulations as Congress shall make. The appellate power, it will be observed, is conferred on this court in all cases or suits in which such a question shall arise. It is not confined to suits in the inferior courts of the United States, but extends to all cases where such a question arises, whether it be in a judicial tribunal of a State or of the United States. And it is manifest that this ultimate appellate power in a tribunal created by the Constitution itself was deemed essential to secure the independence and supremacy of the General Government in the sphere of action assigned to it; to make the Constitution and laws of the United States uniform, and the same in every State . . . .

This judicial power was justly regarded as indispensable, not merely to maintain the supremacy of the laws of the United States, but also to guard the States from any encroachment upon their reserved rights by the General Government. And as the Constitution is the fundamental and supreme law, if it appears that an act of Congress is not pursuant to it and within the limits of the power assigned to the Federal Government, it is the duty of the courts of the United States to declare it unconstitutional and void . . . . And as the final appellate power in all such questions is given to this court, controversies as to the respective powers of the United States and the States, instead of being determined by military and physical force are heard, investigated, and finally settled with the calmness and deliberation of judicial inquiry . . . .

. . . No State judge or court, after they are judicially informed that the party is imprisoned under the authority of the United States, has any right to interfere with him, or to require him to be brought before them. And if the authority of a State, in the form of judicial process or otherwise, should attempt to control the marshal or other authorized officer or agent of the United States, in any respect, in the custody of his prisoner, it would be his duty to resist it . . . . No judicial process . . . can have any lawful authority outside of the limits of the jurisdiction of the court or judge by whom it is issued; and an attempt to enforce it beyond these boundaries is nothing less than lawless violence.

Nor is there anything in this supremacy of the General Government, or the jurisdiction of its judicial tribunals, to awaken the jealousy or offend the natural and just pride of State sovereignty. Neither this Government, nor the powers of which we are speaking, were forced upon the States. The Constitution of the United States, with all the powers conferred by it on the General Government, and surrendered by the States, was the voluntary act of the people of the several States, deliberately done, for their own protection and safety against injustice from one another . . . .

. . . [N]o power is more clearly conferred by the Constitution and laws of the United States, than the power of this court to decide, ultimately and finally, all cases arising under such Constitution and laws; and for that purpose to bring here for revision, by writ of error, the judgment of a State court, where such questions have arisen, and the right claimed under them denied by the highest judicial tribunal in the State . . . .

The judgment of the Supreme Court of Wisconsin must therefore be reversed in each of the cases now before the court.

Editors' Notes

(1) The Wisconsin legislature adopted a resolution branding the U.S. Supreme Court's ruling "an act of undelegated power, and therefore without authority, void and of no force"; then repeated some of the language of the Second Kentucky Resolutions of 1799:

> That the government formed by the Constitution of the United States was not made the exclusive or final judge of the extent of the powers delegated to itself; but that as in all other cases of compact among parties having no common judge, each party has an equal right to judge for itself as well of infractions as the mode and measure of redress . . . .

Nevertheless, federal officers rearrested Booth in March, 1860, and he again sought habeas corpus from the state supreme court. This time, however, he did not succeed. One judge had to recuse himself because he had been the prisoner's attorney during early stages of the litigation, and the other two judges disagreed with each other about their authority to issue the writ. Booth was locked up in the federal building in Milwaukee. He was something of a popular hero who further embarrassed his jailers by refusing to pay the fine or to ask for a presidential pardon. An abolitionist mob provided the practical solution by freeing him. In 1861, the Wisconsin supreme court ruled that the U.S. district court had had jurisdiction to try Booth. Arnold v. Booth, (1861). For details, see Charles Warren, *The Supreme Court in U.S. History,* II, ch. 27, and Note, "Interposition vs. Judicial Power," 1 *Race Rels.L.Rep.* 465, 490–496 (1956).

(2) Wisconsin's resistance to the Fugitive Slave Act was not an isolated event. At least ten other northern and western states tried to suspend the statute's operation within their borders. See, Note, "Interposition vs. Judicial Power," 1 *Race Rels.L.Rep.* 465, 496 (1956); and for a more general treatment of the moral and constitutional problems of slavery, Robert M. Cover, *Justice Accused: Antislavery and the Judicial Process* (New Haven: Yale University Press, 1975).

"We pledge ourselves to use all lawful means to bring about a reversal of this decision . . . ."

NULLIFYING BROWN v. BOARD OF EDUCATION

In 1954, the Supreme Court in Brown v. Board of Education declared compulsory segregation in public schools to be a violation of the equal protection clause of the Fourteenth Amendment. The initial reaction of most southern public officials—and at that time all southern public officials were whites—was one of stunned disbelief. Then southern leaders mounted a massive counterattack that included "pupil placement" plans, efforts to outlaw the National Association for the Advancement of Colored People, closing public schools, outright physical violence, and, of course, nullification.

"We reaffirm our reliance on the Constitution as the fundamental law of the land."

A. THE SOUTHERN MANIFESTO: A DECLARATION OF CONSTITUTIONAL PRINCIPLES

(1956).*

The unwarranted decision of the Supreme Court in the public school cases is now bearing the fruit always produced when men substitute naked power for established law.

The Founding Fathers gave us a Constitution of checks and balances because they realized the inescapable lesson of history that no man or group of men can be safely entrusted with unlimited power. They framed this Constitution with its provisions for change by amendment in order to secure the fundamentals of government against the dangers of temporary popular passion or the personal predilections of public officeholders.

We regard the decision of the Supreme Court in the school cases as a clear abuse of judicial power. It climaxes a trend in the federal judiciary undertaking to legislate, in derogation of the authority of Congress, and to encroach upon the reserved rights of the States and the people.

The original Constitution does not mention education. Neither does the 14th amendment nor any other amendment. The debates preceding the submission of the 14th amendment clearly show that there was no intent that it should affect the system of education maintained by the States.

The very Congress which proposed the amendment subsequently provided for segregated schools in the District of Columbia.

When the amendment was adopted in 1868, there were 37 States of the Union. Every one of the 26 States that had any substantial racial differences among its people, either approved the operation of segregated schools already in existence or subsequently established such schools by action of the same law-making body which considered the 14th amendment . . . .

This interpretation [the "separate but equal" principle], restated time and again, became a part of the life of the people of many of the States and confirmed their habits, customs, traditions, and way of life. It is founded on elementary humanity and common sense, for parents should not be deprived by Government of the right to direct the lives and education of their own children.

Though there has been no constitutional amendment or act of Congress changing this established legal principle almost a century old,

---

* 102 *Congressional Record* 4460; 1 *Race Relations Law Reporter* 435 (1956). The declaration was signed by 19 Senators and 77 Representatives.

the Supreme Court of the United States, with no legal basis for such action, undertook to exercise their naked judicial power and substituted their personal political and social ideas for the established law of the land.

This unwarranted exercise of power by the Court, contrary to the Constitution, is creating chaos and confusion in the States principally affected. It is destroying the amicable relations between the white and Negro races that have been created through 90 years of patient effort by the good people of both races. It has planted hatred and suspicion where there has been heretofore friendship and understanding.

Without regard to the consent of the governed, outside agitators are threatening immediate and revolutionary changes in our public-school system. If done, this is certain to destroy the system of public education in some of the States.

With the gravest concern for the explosive and dangerous condition created by this decision and inflamed by outside meddlers:

We reaffirm our reliance on the Constitution as the fundamental law of the land.

We decry the Supreme Court's encroachments on rights reserved to the States and to the people, contrary to established law, and to the Constitution.

We commend the motives of those States which have declared the intention to resist forced integration by any lawful means.

We appeal to the States and people who are not directly affected by these decisions to consider the constitutional principles involved against the time when they too, on issues vital to them, may be the victims of judicial encroachment.

Even though we constitute a minority in the present Congress, we have full faith that a majority of the American people believe in the dual system of government which has enabled us to achieve our greatness and will in time demand that the reserved rights of the States and of the people be made secure against judicial usurpation.

We pledge ourselves to use all lawful means to bring about a reversal of this decision which is contrary to the Constitution and to prevent the use of force in its implementation.

In this trying period, as we all seek to right this wrong, we appeal to our people not to be provoked by the agitators and troublemakers invading our States and to scrupulously refrain from disorder and lawless acts.

"[A] question of contested power has arisen . . . ."

B. ALABAMA'S NULLIFICATION RESOLUTION *

Eight southern state legislatures—Alabama, Arkansas, Florida, Georgia, Louisiana, Mississippi, South Carolina, and Florida—formally "nullified" Brown v. Board of Education.

Whereas the Constitution of the United States was formed by the sanction of the several states, given by each in its sovereign capacity; and

Whereas the states being the parties to the constitutional compact, it follows of necessity that there can be no tribunal above their authority to decide, in the last resort, whether the compact made by them be violated; and, consequently, they must decide themselves in the last resort, such questions as may be of sufficient magnitude to require their interposition; and

Whereas a question of contested power has arisen: The Supreme Court of the United States asserts, for its part, that the states did, in fact, in 1868 upon the adoption of the Fourteenth Amendment, prohibit unto themselves the power to maintain racially separate public institutions; the State of Alabama, for its part, asserts that it and its sister states have never surrendered such right; and

Whereas this assertion upon the part of the Supreme Court of the United States, accompanied by threats of coercion and compulsion against the sovereign states of this Union, constitutes a deliberate, palpable, and dangerous attempt by the court to prohibit to the states certain rights and powers never surrendered by them; and

Whereas the question of contested power asserted in this resolution is not within the province of the court to determine, but that as in other cases in which one party to a compact asserts an infraction thereof, the judgment of all other equal parties to the compact must be sought to resolve the question; be it

Resolved by the legislature of Alabama, both houses thereof concurring:

That until the issue between the State of Alabama and the General Government is decided by the submission to the states, pursuant to Article V of the Constitution, of a suitable constitutional amendment that would declare, in plain and unequivocal language, that the states do surrender their power to maintain public schools and other public facilities on a basis of separation as to race, the Legislature of Alabama declares the decisions and orders of the Supreme Court of the United States relating to separation of races in the public schools are, as a matter of right, null, void, and of no effect; and the Legislature of Alabama declares to all men as a matter of right, this State is not bound to abide thereby; we declare, further, our firm intention to take all appropriate measures honorably and constitutionally available to

---

* This resolution became an Act on February 2, 1956, without approval of the Governor.
1 *Race Relations Law Reporter* 437 (1956).

us, to avoid this illegal encroachment upon our rights, and to urge upon our sister states their prompt and deliberate efforts to check further encroachment by the General Government, through judicial legislation, upon the reserved powers of all states . . . .

"No state . . . officer can war against the Constitution without violating his undertaking to support it."

COOPER v. AARON
358 U.S. 1, 78 S.Ct. 1401, 3 L.Ed.2d 5 (1958).

In 1955, after the Supreme Court's decision in Brown v. Board of Education declaring compulsory segregation in public education unconstitutional, Little Rock's school board drew up a plan for gradual desegregation of the city's schools. The National Association for the Advancement of Colored People sued to compel the board to follow a more rapid program, but the federal district court and the Court of Appeals for the Eighth Circuit approved the school board's timetable. Meanwhile, the Arkansas legislature joined with other southern legislatures in "nullifying" Brown and also adopted a bevy of statutes to avoid compliance with the ruling. Little Rock's school board, however, persisted in its plan; and when the first black children showed up at Central High School in September 1958, the Governor used the National Guard to bar their entry. After much legal maneuvering, mob violence, and federal military intervention, the black children were admitted to the school.

At the end of the year the school board asserted that Central High School had become so disrupted by tension and turmoil that education had become impossible. The board therefore asked the district court for permission to suspend desegregation for two and a half years, until popular feeling had calmed down. The district judge granted the request, but the court of appeals reversed his decision. The board sought and obtained certiorari from the Supreme Court.

Opinion of the Court by the Chief Justice [**WARREN**], Mr. Justice **BLACK**, Mr. Justice **FRANKFURTER**, Mr. Justice **DOUGLAS**, Mr. Justice **BURTON**, Mr. Justice **CLARK**, Mr. Justice **HARLAN**, Mr. Justice **BRENNAN**, and Mr. Justice **WHITTA-KER** . . . .

The constitutional rights of respondents are not to be sacrificed or yielded to the violence and disorder which have followed upon the actions of the Governor and Legislature. . . . Thus law and order are not here to be preserved by depriving the Negro children of their constitutional rights. The record before us clearly establishes that the growth of the Board's difficulties to a magnitude beyond its unaided power to control is the product of state action. Those difficulties, as counsel for the Board forthrightly conceded on the oral argument in this Court, can also be brought under control by state action.

The controlling legal principles are plain. The command of the Fourteenth Amendment is that no "State" shall deny to any person within its jurisdiction the equal protection of the law . . . . [T]he prohibitions of the Fourteenth Amendment extend to all action of the State denying equal protection of the laws; whatever the agency of the State taking the action, see Virginia v. Rives [1880]; Pennsylvania v. Board of Directors of City Trusts [1957]; Shelley v. Kraemer [1948], or whatever the guise in which it is taken . . . . In short, the constitutional rights of children not to be discriminated against in school admission on grounds of race or color declared by this Court in the Brown case can neither be nullified openly and directly by state legislators or state executive or judicial officers, nor nullified indirectly by them through evasive schemes for segregation whether attempted "ingeniously or ingenuously." Smith v. Texas [1940].

What has been said . . . is enough to dispose of the case. However, we should answer the premise of the actions of the Governor and Legislature that they are not bound by our holding in the Brown case. It is necessary only to recall some basic constitutional propositions which are settled doctrine.

Article 6 of the Constitution makes the Constitution the "supreme Law of the Land." In 1803, Chief Justice Marshall, speaking for a unanimous Court, referring to the Constitution as "the fundamental and paramount law of the nation," declared in the notable case of Marbury v. Madison that "It is emphatically the province and duty of the judicial department to say what the law is." This decision declared the basic principle that the federal judiciary is supreme in the exposition of the law of the Constitution, and that principle has ever since been respected by this Court and the Country as a permanent and indispensable feature of our constitutional system. It follows that the interpretation of the Fourteenth Amendment enunciated by this Court in the Brown Case is the supreme law of the land, and Art. 6 of the Constitution makes it of binding effect on the States "any Thing in the Constitution or Laws of any State to the Contrary notwithstanding." Every state legislator and executive and judicial officer is solemnly committed by oath taken pursuant to Art. 6, cl. 3 "to support this Constitution." Chief Justice Taney, speaking for a unanimous Court in 1859, said that this requirement reflected the framers' "anxiety to preserve it [the Constitution] in full force, in all its powers, and to guard against resistance to or evasion of its authority, on the part of a State . . . ." Ableman v. Booth [1859].

No state legislator or executive or judicial officer can war against the Constitution without violating his undertaking to support it. Chief Justice Marshall spoke for a unanimous Court in saying that: "If the legislatures of the several states may, at will, annul the judgments of the courts of the United States, and destroy the rights acquired under those judgments, the constitution itself becomes a solemn mockery . . . ." United States v. Peters [1809]. A Governor who asserts a power to nullify a federal court order is similarly restrained. If he had such power, said Chief Justice Hughes, in 1932, also for a unanimous Court, "it is manifest that the fiat of a state Governor, and not the

Constitution of the United States, would be the supreme law of the land; that the restrictions of the Federal Constitution upon the exercise of state power would be but impotent phrases . . . ."

It is, of course, quite true that the responsibility for public education is primarily the concern of the States, but it is equally true that such responsibilities, like all other state activity, must be exercised consistently with federal constitutional requirements . . . . The Constitution created a government dedicated to equal justice under law. The Fourteenth Amendment embodied and emphasized that ideal. State support of segregated schools through any arrangement, management, funds, or property cannot be squared with the Amendment's command that no State shall deny to any person within its jurisdiction the equal protection of the laws. The right of a student not to be segregated on racial grounds in schools so maintained is indeed so fundamental and pervasive that it is embraced in the concept of due process of law, Bolling v. Sharpe [1954]. The basic decision in Brown was unanimously reached by this Court only after the case had been briefed and twice argued and the issues had been given the most serious consideration. Since the first Brown opinion three new Justices have come to the Court. They are at one with the Justices still on the Court who participated in that basic decision as to its correctness, and that decision is now unanimously reaffirmed. The principles announced in that decision and the obedience of the States to them, according to the command of the Constitution, are indispensable for the protection of the freedoms guaranteed by our fundamental charter for all of us. Our constitutional ideal of equal justice under law is thus made a living truth.

Concurring opinion of Mr. Justice **FRANKFURTER**.

While unreservedly participating with my brethren in our joint opinion, I deem it appropriate also to deal individually with the great issue here at stake . . . .

> . . . The conception of a government by laws dominated the thoughts of those who founded this Nation and designed its Constitution, although they knew as well as the belittlers of the conception that laws have to be made, interpreted and enforced by men. To that end, they set apart a body of men, who were to be the depositories of law, who by their disciplined training and character and by withdrawal from the usual temptations of private interest may reasonably be expected to be 'as free, impartial, and independent as the lot of humanity will admit.' So strongly were the framers of the Constitution bent on securing a reign of law that they endowed the judicial office with extraordinary safeguards and prestige. No one, no matter how exalted his public office or how righteous his private motive, can be judge in his own case. That is what courts are for. United States v. United Mine Workers (concurring opinion) [1947].

The duty to abstain from resistance to "the supreme Law of the Land," U.S. Const. Art. 6, ¶ 2, as declared by the organ of our Government for ascertaining it, does not require immediate approval of it nor does it deny the right of dissent. Criticism need not be stilled. Active obstruction or defiance is barred. Our kind of society cannot endure if the controlling authority of the Law as derived from the Constitution is not to be the tribunal specially charged with the duty of ascertaining and declaring what is "the supreme Law of the Land." . . . Particularly is this so where the declaration of what "the supreme Law" commands on an underlying moral issue is not the dubious pronouncement of a gravely divided Court but is the unanimous conclusion of a long-matured deliberative process. The Constitution is not the formulation of the merely personal views of the members of this Court, nor can its authority be reduced to the claim that state officials are its controlling interpreters. Local customs, however hardened by time, are not decreed in heaven. Habits and feelings they engender may be counteracted and moderated. Experience attests that such local habits and feelings will yield, gradually though this be, to law and education. And educational influences are exerted not only by explicit teaching. They vigorously flow from the fruitful exercise of the responsibility of those charged with political official power and from the almost unconsciously transforming actualities of living under law . . . . .

IV

How to Interpret the Constitution

Earlier Parts of this book discussed the context of constitutional interpretation and questions of WHAT the Constitution is and WHO its authoritative interpreters are. This Part focuses on the query: HOW does one interpret the Constitution in a coherent and intellectually defensible manner? There is, as readers are by now painfully aware, no intelligent way to answer any of the questions around which this book is organized without becoming enmeshed in the others.

There is also no infallible way or set of ways to interpret the Constitution. The best that commentators, judges, and other public officials have been able to develop is an array of methods, each one flawed and each one dependent on a wider view of politics, indeed on a political theory, however inchoate or unconscious. As Chapter 2 pointed out and Chapter 8 will emphasize, how an interpreter views the political theory or mixture of theories underpinning the Constitution affects the methodological choices that he or she will make.

This Part of the book is by far the longest. It opens with Chapter 8, a lengthy essay that offers a scheme of interpretive methodology, arranging in a hierarchical fashion *approaches,* overarching views of the enterprise as a whole, *modes,* the ways in which interpreters having chosen certain *approaches* organize their tasks, and *techniques,* the more practical intellectual instruments interpreters apply. Choices among *approaches* affect choices among *modes;* and, at least for people who wish to act consistently, choices among *modes* then limit choices among *techniques.*

Although many of the illustrations will be familiar, most readers will find this chapter difficult because of its abstraction and its demands for self-conscious choice about processes of interpretation that all intelligent people use in much of our lives. We urge users to return to Chapter 8 as they read material in ensuing chapters and again when they have completed the book. At the end, this chapter may seem simple, no more—or less—than common sense. Some readers may even be able to construct their own, and perhaps better, plans of constitutional interpretation. But without some coherent, intellectually defensible, conceptual scheme to organize constitutional interpretation, the enterprise can easily degenerate into a mere matter of choosing the results one likes in particular controversies.

Chapters 9–17 flesh out Chapter 8 by organizing much of what is usually called constitutional law under several interpretive *modes.* These vary from structural analysis, to reinforcing representative democracy, to effecting fundamental rights. This organization, we think, shows that there is more coherence to constitutional interpretation than judges, commentators, or even students may believe.

A

GENERAL PROBLEMS

8

Approaches, Modes, and Techniques of Constitutional Interpretation

Anyone who has read this far must be impressed with the variety of ways in which judges, legislators, and presidents see problems of constitutional interpretation. They often seem to be disagreeing less on WHAT the Constitution means than on HOW to discover WHAT it means and WHO has responsibility for making that discovery. In short, method is as important in constitutional interpretation as in other disciplines.

This chapter sketches a three-tiered model under which some of the more widely used methodological schemes can fit. We label these tiers as *approaches to interpretation, modes of analysis,* and *analytical techniques. Approaches* refer to the most basic ways an interpreter perceives the Constitution; *modes* denote HOW a person utilizes those *approaches* in the enterprise of constitutional interpretation; and *techniques* signify specific interpretive tools. Choices among *approaches* affect what *modes* one can consistently employ; and choices among *modes* affect, though they do not precisely determine, an interpreter's choices among *techniques.*

Approaches and *modes* are abstractions from masses of judicial opinions and speeches by other public officials, not descriptions of what these people actually do or say they do in interpreting the Constitution. *Techniques,* however, are tools that interpreters habitually and consciously use.

I. APPROACHES TO INTERPRETATION

An *approach* refers, first, to an interpreter's understanding of the Constitution as consisting only of the text or as including but transcending the words of the document; second, to his or her viewing the Constitution as fixed or changing; and third, to an interpreter's vision of the Constitution as laying down only rules to be more or less rigidly followed or as reflecting an authoritative vision of a good society toward which the nation should aspire. Each of these three pairs represents a range of choice, not merely two sharply separated points. Together these *approaches* offer a framework, a basis for systematic and self-conscious interpretive methodology.

289

A. Textualism v. Transcendence

Analysis in Chapter 2 of constitutionalism and democracy and in Chapter 4 of WHAT the Constitution is provide the general outline of the problems here. We are again talking about WHAT the Constitution includes. At one end of the spectrum are those who emphasize the text. In the end, as in the beginning, is "the Word." At the other pole of the spectrum are those who see the Constitution as including not only the document plus certain practices within the wider political system and perhaps other documents, such as the Declaration of Independence, but also some combination of principles from democratic and constitutionalist theory.

The bulk of people who have written systematically about constitutional interpretation see it as including more than the document's words. But accepting this common view raises problems of WHAT else is included, HOW interpreters justify inclusion and exclusion, and HOW they should use extra-textual material in determining the Constitution's meaning.

B. A Fixed v. a Changing Constitution

Chapter 5 addressed the basic problem here. George Sutherland and Earl Warren represent views on continuity and change that are as different as we can find on the Supreme Court. In his dissent in the Minnesota Moratorium Case (1934; reprinted above, p. 136), Sutherland wrote: "A provision of the Constitution . . . does not admit of two distinctly opposite interpretations. It does not mean one thing at one time and an entirely different thing at another time." Warren, on the other hand, looked for the meaning of open-ended clauses like "cruel and unusual punishments" in "the evolving standards of decency that mark the progress of a maturing society." (See Trop v. Dulles [1958; reprinted above, p. 144].)

No authoritative interpreter, however, has publicly defended a view of the Constitution as being so open-ended that it may be given any shape that pleases. Conversely, one who believes in constitutional permanence need not opt for constitutional rigidity. The process of amendment, after all, allows change; and one might also concede that changes in circumstances impart fresh meanings to old words. "[W]hile the meaning of constitutional guaranties never varies," Sutherland added in the Minnesota Moratorium Case, "the scope of their application must expand or contract to meet new and different conditions which are constantly coming within the field of their operation."

C. The Constitution as Rules v. the Constitution as Vision

Here we confront differences among those who view the Constitution as a set of rules to be obeyed and those who believe the

Constitution also radiates aspirations that require interpreters to look beyond its rules toward larger goals, such as human dignity and autonomy.   The Constitution, Sotirios A. Barber[1] argues, is more than an attempt to cope with immediate problems; it is also an effort to move the nation toward certain values.   Interpreters who utilize this approach typically prefer some aspects of the document over others, even, perhaps, eventually to remove some constitutional compromises forced by "grinding necessity."

Marshall and Story spoke of "the spirit of the Constitution," and that term, as quaint as it sounds today,[2] captures much of what we are discussing.   Differences here focus on opposing concepts about whether it is proper for interpreters to consult that "spirit," and, if it is legitimate for them to do so, HOW to derive the message the spirit brings.   For those who see the Constitution primarily as a set of rules, interpretation is much like painting by the numbers; one colors areas with dyes indicated in the color chart.   For those who see the Constitution as committing the nation to a vision of a good—or at least, better—society, interpretation is a creative and difficult art. One needs a subtle "constitutional aesthetic" to say when creativity is necessary and HOW to use and apply it.[3]   Such interpretation requires discovering the Constitution's spirit, its underlying values, and then recomposing its aspirations; interpretation demands also faithful but imaginative adherence to that spirit, to the basic values that spawn its hopes for the good life.

In one sense at least, those who take an aspirational view of the Constitution claim to be more faithful to the text than those who see the Constitution as blueprint.   For aspirationalists take the Preamble's goals of promoting union, justice, tranquility, national defense, the general welfare, and liberty as independently authoritative textual grounding of certain constitutional values.   Those who see the Constitution as rules tend to look on the Preamble as a rhetorical flourish; they fasten onto the wording of the body of the document and its amendment as the valid source of constitutional values.

II. MODES OF ANALYSIS

An interpreter's basic perceptions of the Constitution—his or her *approach(es)* —shape the kind of analyses in which he or she will engage to determine constitutional meaning.   These interpretive *modes* will help in selecting and emphasizing the various *techniques* an interpreter will apply.

---

1. *On What the Constitution Means* (Baltimore, Md.: Johns Hopkins University Press, 1984).

2. But see the dis. op. of Justice O'Connor in Garcia v. San Antonio MTA (1985): "It is not enough [to be valid] that the 'end [of legislation] be legitimate'; the means chosen by Congress must not contravene the spirit of the Constitution."

3. For an important development of this concept, though in a different way from that implied here, see Lief H. Carter, *Contemporary Constitutional Lawmaking* (New York: Pergamon Press, 1985), chaps. 5–7.

A. Verbal Analysis

Here the familiar issue of plain words recurs. Because the American Constitution includes the document even if it is not limited to it, verbal analysis will always play a significant interpretive role. For interpreters who chose an *approach* restricting the Constitution to the text, defining the document's words and parsing its sentences are the critical, perhaps the final, steps in interpretation. For those who take a more capacious view of the Constitution's boundaries, verbal analysis will be the start but not necessarily the end of interpretation.

B. Historical Analysis

Most interpreters use, though seldom exclusively, some variant of historical analysis. Their choices among *approaches* restrict the ways in which they can, consistently at least, utilize this *mode.* Those who look on the Constitution as fixed in meaning are apt to believe that historical analysis will yield the correct answers to their problems. Those who see the Constitution as changing over time will be more interested in discovering patterns of development and adjustment. They will seek knowledge of the past to understand the present rather than simply to follow the past. They are more likely to see history as clarifying than as solving current problems, widening as often as narrowing alternatives.

C. Structural Analysis

Individual constitutional provisions may make little sense on their own or they may even conflict with one another. The First Amendment, for instance, forbids Congress both "to establish" a religion and to prohibit "the free exercise thereof." The two clauses "are cast in absolute terms, and either of which, if expanded to a logical extreme, would tend to clash with the other." [4] Exempting from compulsory military service those who object to war for religious reasons illustrates the difficulties. For Congress to force Quakers to fight would violate their free exercise of religion. Yet to exempt them is to give them preferred status because of their religious beliefs, and that may well constitute indirect establishment of a religion. (See the discussions of conscientious objection in Chapter 16, below, p. 1053.)

Theologians and literary critics who have long faced similar interpretive problems of opacity and conflict have recognized a "hermeneutic circle": One cannot understand the whole—of a document, a story, or other composition—without understanding the parts, but one cannot understand the parts without understanding the whole. Whether it takes the document or the "document plus" as its subject, constitutional interpretation also faces this dilemma.

---

4. Waltz v. Tax Commission (1970).

Constitutional commentators refer to interpretation that grasps the narrower horn of the hermeneutic dilemma as "clause-bound," tending to look at a particular constitutional segment as an isolated unit and to ignore connections, if any, with the larger entity. In contrast, structuralism breaks into the circle at the macro-level. As Madison put it in *Federalist* No. 40:

> There are two rules of construction, dictated by plain reason, as well as founded on legal axioms. The one is, that every part of the expression ought, if possible, be made to conspire to some common end. The other is, that where the several parts cannot be made to coincide, the less important should give way to the more important part; the means should be sacrificed to the end, rather than the end to the means.

More than a century and a half later, the Constitutional Court of West Germany stated more clearly the assumption "of inner unity" underlying Madison's argument and, more generally, structural analysis:

> A constitution has an inner unity, and the meaning of any one part is linked to that of other provisions. Taken as a unit, a constitution reflects certain overarching principles and fundamental decisions to which individual provisions are subordinate.[5]

We divide structuralism into several types, corresponding to various ways of visualizing WHAT the Constitution includes. First is textual structuralism, analysis that restricts itself to the document as amended and so could be quite attractive to textualists. Next is systemic structuralism, an analytic *mode* that considers constitutional interpretation as concerned not only with the document but also with the form and practices of the larger political system. Third is transcendent structuralism, which sees the Constitution as also including political theories that underpin the document and the system's practices. These kinds of structuralism are analytically distinct, but as we shall see interpreters sometimes run them together.

Poe v. Ullman (1961; reprinted above, p. 106) and Griswold v. Connecticut (1965; reprinted above, p. 113) provide variations on structuralist themes. Both cases confronted the Court with the question of the validity of a state's forbidding advising people about contraception. Dissenting in *Poe,* William O. Douglas wrote that the "notion of privacy is not drawn from the blue. It emanates from the totality of the constitutional scheme under which we live." John Marshall Harlan's dissent made a similar argument. The "liberty" protected by the due process clauses

> is not a series of isolated points pricked out in terms of the taking of property; the freedom of speech, press, and religion, the right to keep and bear arms; the freedom from unreasonable searches and seizures; and so on. It is a rational continuum which, broadly

---

5. The Southwest Case (1951; reprinted in Walter F. Murphy and Joseph Tanenhaus, eds., *Comparative Constitutional Law* [New York: St. Martin's, 1977], p. 208.)

speaking, includes a freedom from all substantial arbitrary imposition and purposeless restraints . . . .

In *Griswold* Douglas and Harlan mustered a majority. Writing
for the Court, Douglas began by looking at the document, but he did
not restrict analysis to any one clause. Instead, he examined the
interplay among the values he thought underlay the First, Third,
Fourth, Fifth, and Ninth Amendments. These clauses provided textual roots for partial rights to privacy in specific areas. Next he spoke
of these individual provisions as having "penumbras formed by emanations from those guarantees that give them life and substance."
Douglas then began to construct a general theory of privacy, and his
structural analysis, echoing his reference in *Poe* to "the totality of the
constitutional scheme," became transcendent in the sense of seeking
constitutional meaning from a theory of constitutionalism, outside the
document's four corners.

Of necessity, deciding distributions of powers among the branches of the federal government and between federal and state governments are all exercises in structuralism. Sometimes this analysis is
explicit—see the opinion of Chief Justice Chase in Texas v. White
(1869; reprinted below, p. 429)—sometimes it is implicit; sometimes
it is awkward and fumbling, with only blurred and fleeting images of
structure. Sometimes it reproduces, as does John Marshall's analysis
of federal-state relations in McCulloch v. Maryland (1819; reprinted
below, p. 413), a near-photograph of an interpreter's conception of
the system's structure. But seldom does that analysis restrict itself to
the exact words and phrases of the text. Indeed, it would be difficult
to do so in cases involving federalism because the document's words
on the issue are so few and so cryptic. It is only somewhat easier to
do so in disputes between branches of the national government
because the text, while more detailed in that respect, allocates powers
less by specific verbal directions than by intricately woven patterns of
sharing and dividing.

Among the greatest attractions of structural analysis is that it
makes intuitive sense to deal with a whole rather than with individual
pieces. It posits a coherence to constitutional interpretation. Its
drawbacks revolve around the fact that it is the interpreter who must
articulate the structure on which the Constitution, whatever it includes, hangs. But unless one sees that Constitution as consisting only
of clear, categorical commands, indeterminancy and an accompanying
need for reasoned elaboration attend all interpretive methodologies.

Because it is the interpreter who must articulate the structure,
different structuralists can view a problem quite differently. (See, for
example, the debates among the justices in National League of Cities
v. Usery [1976; reprinted below, p. 449] and Garcia v. San Antonio
MTA [1985; reprinted below, p. 461].) Difficulties are exacerbated
by the elasticity of structuralism, though it is no more malleable than
are supposedly "plain" words.

D. Doctrinal Analysis

Doctrinal analysis focuses on what previous interpreters have said the Constitution means, on its gloss as much or more than on its words. Here an interpreter seeks principles contained in or behind constitutional provisions and articulates them in the form of binding rules or precedents that are more detailed than the document's lean prose.

Inevitably, as the Constitution has been interpreted over the decades, some people, especially lawyers, have come to regard judicial decisions and practices of the other branches of government, such as judicial review and executive privilege, as carrying the same authoritative weight as the words of the document. And, often, when judges and commentators speak of constitutional interpretation they are actually talking about interpretation of judicially created doctrines such as "interstate commerce," "a wall of separation" or "one person, one vote."

Because doctrinal analysis deals with what later interpreters have said the Constitution means and because judges, other public officials, and commentators frequently adapt their interpretations to meet new circumstances (see the discussion of stare decisis, below, pp. 303–309), it is more congruent with a developmental *approach* to the Constitution's meaning than with an *approach* that sees the Constitution as unchanging except by formal amendment.

It is logically possible, however, to use a modified form of doctrinal analysis to support an *approach* that holds the Constitution to be permanent and to be contained solely in the text. To do so requires the interpreter to rely on an interpretation close in time to the adoption of the original Constitution or an amendment, on the supposition that contemporary interpreters had an understanding clearer than that of later generations about the provision's implications. In short, the interpreter seeks a doctrine that expounds an allegedly original and permanent meaning of the text.

E. Prudential Analysis

Whatever else it does, prudential analysis always pushes an interpreter to ask what wise public policy requires. It is concerned with effects of interpretations as well as with strategies to maximize the effects an interpreter wishes to occur or believes the Constitutions requires. One of its fundamental premises is that the Constitution is not a "suicide pact," [6] and thus to be valid any interpretation must allow the polity to survive and prosper.

The history of the Supreme Court's handling of racial segregation in public education from 1938 until 1954 provides an excellent

---

6. Kennedy v. Mendoza-Martinez (1963); see also Jackson's dis. op. in Terminello v. Chicago (1949). For a general discussion of such issues see, Walter F. Murphy, *Elements of Judicial Strategy* (Chicago: University of Chicago Press, 1964).

example of prudential interpretation. In 1896 Plessy v. Ferguson had announced the doctrine of "separate but equal": States could segregate by race if they provided equal facilities for each race. In reality, states made little effort to supply equal facilities, and judges often pretended not to notice. But by 1938, some justices understood that compulsory segregation grossly violated equal protection. At first, they had to persuade their brethren, and they did so by moving from case to case, undermining rather than directly attacking the old doctrine.

As a new majority coalesced, it too moved slowly, out of concern for whether white southerners would obey a decision invalidating segregation. Even in 1954 it took a great deal of persuasion and negotiation for Earl Warren to win a unanimous opinion. Most of the reluctant justices had practical rather than constitutional doubts. They were unsure the Court could make its decision stick in the face of anticipated southern resistance.[7]

Even then, the justices did not issue an order. They merely scheduled reargument, asking for advice on what sorts of decrees to issue. And, when in 1955 the Court finally disposed of the School Segregation Cases, it did so only with a decree requiring compliance "with all deliberate speed," a formula that allowed states to stall implementation for another decade until Congress passed new civil rights legislation.

Because prudence looks to the long run as well as the short, interpreters who apply this *mode* may sharply disagree with each other. Although it can be oriented toward a fixed view of the Constitution as supposedly conceived by the framers as well as toward adapting the Constitution to modern problems, interpreters who view the Constitution as set of textual commands fixed in meaning are likely to find the *mode* anathema. Justice Sutherland, dissenting in West Coast Hotel v. Parrish (1937; reprinted below, p. 987) against the Court's abandoning, under pressure from the President, the doctrine of "substantive due process"[8] in the economic sphere, claimed that a judge who allowed prudential considerations to affect his decision stood "forsworn." His duty, as he had said earlier in the Moratorium Case was to interpret the Constitution as it was written, regardless of the effects. If the people disapproved, they could amend the Constitution.

---

7. Richard Kluger, *Simple Justice* (New York: Knopf, 1976), pp. 678–699, has the basic story.

8. This doctrine, discussed in detail in Chapter 15, gained judicial acceptance from 1890 until 1937 where economic regulation was concerned. Its gist is that the prohibitions in the Fifth and Fourteenth amendments against government's taking "life, liberty, or property, without due process of law" impose substantive as well as procedural constraints. There are some forms of liberty that government may not take away, no matter what procedures it uses. John Hart Ely has responded: " 'substantive due process' is a contradiction in terms—sort of like 'green pastel redness' . . . . [A]nd 'procedural due process' is redundant." *Democracy and Distrust* (Cambridge, Mass.: Harvard University Press, 1980), p. 18. Although the Court no longer applies the doctrine to strike down regulations of private property, it continues to do so to protect other "fundamental rights." See, for example, the plurality opinion of Justice Powell in Moore v. City of East Cleveland (1977; reprinted below, p. 1145).

Given that most justices have had some experience in practical politics before going to the bench, and that presidents, legislators, and state officials face electorates, prudential considerations have seldom been totally absent from constitutional interpretation. At its best, the prudential *mode* may preserve the Constitution and the country by wisely construing—or by deciding not to construe—its provisions. At its worst, the prudential *mode* turns constitutional interpretation into mere expediency and so abandons any notion of the Constitution as a set of fundamental principles.

F. Purposive Analysis

Here we take up *modes* of interpretation closely related to an aspirational *approach*. Purposive analysis, sometimes called "teleological jurisprudence," asks WHAT the Constitution is and WHAT are its general aims, then uses the answers to organize interpretation. We shall discuss three specific examples of *modes* arising from these questions: (1) the doctrine of the clear mistake; (2) reinforcing representative democracy; and (3) giving effect to fundamental values.

1. *The Doctrine of the Clear Mistake.* Justice Felix Frankfurter referred to James Bradley Thayer as "our great master of constitutional law"[9] and called his article, "The Origin and Scope of the American Doctrine of Constitutional Law" (1893; reprinted below, p. 476), "the most important single essay" ever published in the field.[10] Thayer wrote just as the Court was beginning to etch laissez faire into the Constitution and to hold that "liberty of contract" was close to an absolute requirement for individual autonomy. (See Chapter 15, below.) Against this trend he argued for judicial restraint. Judges should hold acts of Congress or the President invalid only

> when those who have a right to make laws have not merely made a mistake, but have made a very clear one,—so clear that it is not open to question . . . .

In part, Thayer relied on democratic theory, but even more on a notion of separation of functions. It is the duty of Congress to legislate, that is, to weigh the costs and benefits of policies as well as their permissibility under the Constitution. The first set of those judgments judges must completely accept. The second set also falls outside the judicial realm *unless* the violation of the Constitution is so plain that no person could entertain rational doubts about the violation. The Constitution often admits of "different interpretations," and within a wide margin, courts should accord Congress "a free foot."

9. "A Note on Advisory Opinions," 37 *Harv.L.Rev.* 1002, 1004 (1924).

10. Quoted in A.T. Mason, W.M. Beaney, and D.G. Stephenson, Jr., eds., *American Constitutional Law* (7th ed.; Englewood Cliffs, N.J.: Prentice-Hall, 1983), p. 309.

Acceptance of Thayer's doctrine would simplify constitutional interpretation for judges. The burden of interpretation, as Justice Gibson argued in Eakin v. Raub (1825; reprinted above p. 221), would fall on the electorate and the officials they select. There is serious question whether a judge could follow Thayer without forsaking constitutionalism in the name of a particular arrangement—separation of institutions and functions—whose purpose supposedly is to protect constitutionalism.

2. *Reinforcing Representative Democracy.* This *mode* of organizing constitutional interpretation stresses the democratic element in the political system and prescribes a judicial role to support open political processes. In its early form, it was called the "doctrine of preferred freedoms" and originated in Justice Harlan Stone's footnote 4 in the Carolene Products Case (1938; reprinted below, p. 482). The sentence to which the footnote was appended said the usual duty of judges was to presume legislation constitutional. The footnote then listed three exceptional sets of circumstances in which judges might relax that presumption. In indirect and guarded language, paragraph 2 hinted at judicial responsibility for policing the political processes to ensure that all citizens could freely participate:

> It is unnecessary to consider now whether legislation which restricts those political processes which can ordinarily be expected to bring about a repeal of undesirable legislation, is to be subjected to more exacting judicial scrutiny . . . than are most other types of legislation.

Paragraph 3 raised a closely related question about democratic processes: "whether prejudices against discrete and insular minorities may be a special condition, which tends seriously to curtail the operation of those political processes ordinarily thought to be relied upon to protect minorities . . . ." Again Stone's circuitous language suggested special responsibility for judges to ensure that legislatures did not discriminate against the unrepresented.

Some judges and commentators—most recently John Hart Ely—believe that performing those two related functions pretty much exhausts the judicial role in constitutional interpretation. Ely contends that judges should usually invalidate only legislation that violates the document's provisions; but, like Stone, he would not have judges presume constitutional legislation that restricts processes of representative democracy or discriminates against minorities. For the most part, he argues, the Constitution delineates procedural rights and ways of getting policies enacted; it identifies very few substantive values. His "general theory," Ely says, "is one that bounds judicial review under the Constitution's open-ended provisions by insisting that it can appropriately concern itself only with questions of participation, and not with the substantive merits of the political choice under attack." [11]

---

11.   Supra note 8, p. 181.

But his theory strongly empowers the Court to act within the confines of this role.

Reinforcing representation prescribes wider scope for judicial power than does Thayer's doctrine of the clear mistake. At the same time, it offers a much narrower scope than do theories that stress the system's constitutionalism. Thus this method is open to attack as prescribing both too broad and too narrow a jurisprudence. Frankfurter thought it too broad. Although he several times claimed that he agreed with *Carolene Products,* he later sharply criticized Stone's basic point that the decree of judicial scrutiny of challenged legislation should vary according to the kind of legislation being challenged.

> There is no warrant in the constitutional basis of this Court's authority for attributing different roles to it depending upon the nature of the challenge to the legislation . . . . The right not to have one's property taken without just compensation has, so far as the scope of judicial power is concerned, the same constitutional dignity as the right to be protected against unreasonable searches and seizures, and the latter has no less claim than freedom of the press or freedom of speech or religious freedom.[12]

This argument has an element of truth. When read merely as a stringing together of specific clauses rather than as an organic whole, the document's "plain words" do not support such a special judicial role. To justify judges' reinforcing representation, one has to use a purposive *mode* based either in structural analysis, democratic theory, or constitutionalism.

Reinforcing representation is also vulnerable to attack as being too narrow. The broadened role it prescribes may in some aspects, such as concern for minorities, lessen constitutionalism's friction with democracy, but it may do so by depreciating constitutionalism. As Robert H. Jackson said in West Virginia v. Barnette, "The very purpose of a Bill of Rights was to withdraw certain subjects from the vicissitudes of political controversy, to place them beyond the reach of majorities and officials and to establish them as legal principles to be applied by the courts." (1943; reprinted below, p. 1027.)

3. *Giving Effect to Fundamental Values.* Other interpreters see constitutionalism as at least equal if not superior in rank to democracy. Following Madison in *Federalist* No. 10, they view the system as designed to defend substantive, fundamental values against governmental interference. This *mode* espouses a special role for the judiciary in protecting fundamental values. These may include, but are not limited to, protecting participation in the political processes and even-handed treatment of all citizens.

Just as emphasis on democratic theory has produced a range of theories, so can emphasis on fundamental values. It was the supposed centrality of rights of property and "liberty of contract" to individual autonomy that propelled the Court to curb governmental regulation of

---

12. West Virginia v. Barnette, dis. op. (1943; reprinted below, p. 1027).

the economy during the period 1890–1937. The basic value of individual autonomy has remained the same, but in more recent decades it has been privacy and personhood that has driven libertarian justices to strike down what they perceive as threats.

In Meyer v. Nebraska (1923; reprinted below, p. 1089), James C. McReynolds, a crusty advocate of laissez faire, put the notion of fundamental values in terms that the Court still quotes. He tied the *mode* to the word "liberty" in the Fifth and Fourteenth Amendments. That concept, he wrote,

> denotes not merely freedom from bodily restraint but also the right of any individual to contract, to engage in any of the common occupations of life, to acquire useful knowledge, to marry, establish a home and bring up children, to worship God according to the dictates of his own conscience, and generally to enjoy those privileges long recognized at common law as essential to the orderly pursuit of happiness by free men.

Fourteen years later, Justice Cardozo, a foe of laissez faire, also endorsed the notion of fundamental values. In Palko v. Connecticut (reprinted above, p. 94), he explained that some rights imbedded in the Bill of Rights were "so rooted in the traditions and conscience of our people as to be ranked as fundamental." The Fourteenth Amendment's due process clause "incorporated" those "fundamental" values, those that were "of the very essence of a scheme of ordered liberty," and so protected them against state as well as federal infringement.

Cardozo's notion of "fundamentality" was more elaborately tied to the document than McReynolds'. But a close textual tie, some argue, is not essential. The general theory of constitutionalism, as Chapter 2 showed, presumes the document floats in "an ocean of rights": If textual linkage is necessary, it is supplied by the Preamble's goals of justice, tranquility, and liberty; by the Bill of Rights, especially the Fifth, Eighth, and Ninth Amendments; and by the Thirteenth and Fourteenth Amendments.

Although one can argue that constitutionalism demands individual autonomy and respect for human dignity, a right to privacy, to be let alone, and that in "a constitution for a free people, there can be no doubt that the meaning of 'liberty' must be broad indeed," [13] no advocate of fundamental values has yet produced a calculus to demonstrate which listed rights are more or less important and which unlisted rights are so basic as to be accorded constitutional status. Harlan's efforts in Poe v. Ullman (1961; reprinted above p. 106) were heroic; but his message that American constitutional democracy was a synthesis of "the liberty of the individual" and "the demands of organized society," based on "what history teaches are the traditions from which it developed as well as the traditions from which it broke" was no more precise than his call for "judgment and restraint" in discovering that synthesis.

---

13. Board of Regents v. Roth (1972).

Absence of a mechanistic formula does not disturb all theorists of fundamental values. For such interpreters accent the polity's constitutionalism. The notion that judges (WHO interprets?), neither chosen by nor responsible to democratic processes, should exercise broad discretion is less discomforting to one who, in answer to the WHAT interrogative, emphasizes the system's constitutionalist component than to one who stresses its democratic elements.

Prof. Laurence H. Tribe maintains that reinforcing representation is only a particular kind of fundamental-values methodology, with fundamental values restricted to those of political participation and equal treatment.[14] In fact, fundamental values and preferred freedoms were closely connected historically. Stone had joined Cardozo's opinion in *Palko.* And, after all, the famous footnote in *Carolene Products* opens with a paragraph, written to placate Chief Justice Hughes, that spoke of a special judicial obligation to intervene when legislation "appears on its face to be within a specific prohibition of the Constitution." And a "specific prohibition" need not be limited to plain words. Hughes had earlier written that "[b]ehind the words of the constitutional provisions are postulates which limit and control."[15]

When regulations requiring children in public schools to salute the flag came before the Court, Stone did not consider it enough that processes for political change were open and that the regulations did not discriminate. (Minersville v. Gobitis [1940; reprinted below, p. 1017].) "The Constitution," he said, "expresses more than the conviction of the people that democratic processes must be preserved at all costs. It is also an expression of faith and a command that freedom of mind and spirit must be preserved . . . ."

Stone, though not Frankfurter in *Gobitis* or later Ely, thought reinforcing representation and protecting fundamental rights prescribe compatible judicial roles. But Stone did not explain when an interpreter should act more as the defender of constitutionalism, when more as the defender of representative democracy, and how to reconcile the two sets of roles without defeating one or the other purpose.

III. ANALYTICAL TECHNIQUES

At a lower level of abstraction are the conceptual tools that interpreters use to apply *approaches* and *modes* to specific problems. This section analyzes six of the most frequently employed *techniques:* Literalism, deductive inference, induction, intent of the framers, stare decisis, and balancing. Like all else in constitutional interpretation, these *techniques* are interrelated, and most interpreters will at some

---

14. "The Puzzling Persistence of Process-Based Constitutional Theories," 89 *Yale L.J.* 1063 (1980); reprinted as chap. 2 of his *Constitutional Choices* (Cambridge, Mass.: Harvard University Press, 1985).

15. Monaco v. Mississippi (1934).

time in his or her work employ all or most of them with varying degrees of emphasis.

A. Literalism

The most direct *technique* is literal interpretation. The Constitution, so literalists assert, consists only of the document and its amendments; and one can and should ascertain its meaning by reading its text. Insofar as "interpretation" is necessary, its task is limited to unscrambling pre-modern syntax and defining words that may, at first glance, seem unclear.

Earlier chapters have pointed out some of the limits of this *technique.* Many constitutional clauses are clear, specific, and emphatic. But language is, as Madison put it in *Federalist* No. 37, "a cloudy medium." Does government "establish" a church by giving textbooks to religious schools, or by busing children to and from those institutions, or by requiring a "nondenominational" prayer for children in public schools? What constitutes a denial of "equal protection of the laws"? Chapters 13–14 will show the labyrinth one has to travel to answer that question. And the Ninth Amendment's unenumerated rights forms a black hole that threatens to inhale all of literalism into its dense vortex.

The document also manifests glaring omissions. It does not mention such hallowed concepts as "the rule of law" or the presumption of innocence in criminal prosecutions. And while the Sixth Amendment guarantees trial by "an impartial jury," no clause mentions a right to trial before an impartial judge. Neither does the text refer to such practices as judicial review or executive privilege. As Chief Justice Marshall said in McCulloch v. Maryland (1819; reprinted below, p. 413):

> A constitution, to contain an accurate detail of all the subdivisions of which its great powers will admit, and all of the means by which they might be carried into execution, would partake of the prolixity of a legal code, and could scarcely be embraced by the human mind. It would, probably, never be understood by the public. Its nature, therefore, requires that only its great outlines should be marked, its important objects designated, and the minor ingredients which compose those objects be deduced form the nature of the objects themselves.

Thus, even professed literalists like Hugo L. Black have conceded the necessity of going beyond literalism. Deductive inference, inductive reasoning, and "intent of the framers" are the *techniques* most compatible with textualism.

B. Deductive Inference

"Deductive inference" from the text refers to what all intelligent people do when obliged to interpret a document: analyze its terms, then try to discern the premises of its arguments and the conclusions to which they lead. Some form of this *technique* is necessary to every *approach* and *mode*. One can see it employed in most judicial opinions—in fact, in almost every intellectual effort in all of life.

C. Inductive Reasoning

In a sense judges also induce theories into constitutional interpretation. That is, they construct the issues and materials associated with a case into a set of principles that have wider application. Typically this *technique* moves the issues and materials to a higher level of abstraction to secure a better grasp not only on a particular controversy but also on underlying constitutional values.

Even Justice Black worked out theories of the First Amendment as he applied it literally. In New York Times v. Sullivan (1964; reprinted below, p. 596), for instance, he argued that the Constitution's command against abridging freedom of the press was clear and binding not only because of its literal terms, but also because a free press was necessary to the kind of government established by the Constitution.

D. Intent of the Framers

When faced with broad, perplexing, or incomplete language, or even when trying to discern what structure holds the Constitution together, interpreters who approach the Constitution as permanent in meaning and limited to the text often try to discover what the framers of the document of 1787 or particular amendments intended their words to signify. "The whole aim of construction," Justice Sutherland asserted in the Moratorium Case, ". . . is to discover the meaning, to ascertain and give effect to the intent, of its framers and the people who adopted it."

There are, however, many difficulties with such a claim, even if one accepts the suppositions about WHAT the Constitution contains and how it changes. We put aside epistemological and ontological problems of reconstructing the minds of other human beings living in a different age and facing different problems.[16] Even were we somehow to solve these massive philosophical difficulties, practical problems would remain; and these become more serious as the "intent" sought refers to specific conceptions rather than broad, general purposes. It is quite different to argue, on the one hand, that the design of a constitution is to provide effective government to protect individual rights from private interference and also to limit government so that it cannot oppress its own citizens, and to argue, on the other hand, that: (a) those who drafted and/or ratified a certain

---

16. See espec. the work of Hans-Georg Gadamer, *Truth and Method* (New York: Crossroad, 1975); *Philosophical Hermeneutics*, David Linge, trans. and ed. (Berkeley, Cal.: University of California Press, 1976); *Reason in the Age of Science*, F.G. Lawrence, trans. (Cambridge, Mass.: MIT Press, 1981); and *Philosophical Apprenticeships*, R.R. Sullivan, trans. (Cambridge, Mass.: MIT Press, 1985).

constitutional clause meant only to authorize or outlaw a very particular set of actions; (b) we can know the specific thoughts the framers were thinking; and (c) what they meant to say rather than what they said in the document binds future generations.

1. *Difficulties of Recapturing the Past.* First, it is difficult to discern intentions of persons long dead. As Justice Jackson noted in his concurrence in the Steel Seizure Case (1952; reprinted below, p. 339):

> Just what our forefathers did envision, or would have envisioned had they foreseen modern conditions, must be divined from materials almost as enigmatic as the dreams Joseph was called upon to interpret for Pharaoh. A century and a half of partisan debate and scholarly speculation yields no net result but only supplies more or less apt quotations from respected sources on each side of any question. They largely cancel each other out.

The unyielding fact is that there were no stenographic records of the Convention. Madison and several others took notes during debates and edited them at night and after the convention. These notes, however, vary in detail and sometimes sketch incompatible pictures of particular aspects of the debates.

The Federalist Papers, written by John Jay, Madison, and Hamilton, are brilliant essays, but they provide scant evidence of what was in the framers' minds. The authors did not work in concert; each hastily composed his own essays,[17] as is evident in the fact that they sometimes contradicted themselves as well as each other.[18] Furthermore, Jay had not been a delegate to the Convention and so could have had only second-hand knowledge of what went on. Hamilton had been a delegate, but he had attended only about half the sessions and missed many of the most important debates. Only Madison could speak from full knowledge—though still subject to inevitable distortions of memory—and he (like Hamilton) took some positions in *The Federalist* that contradict those his notes report he took at the Convention. As Madison warned a friend, in reading the *Federalist* "it is fair to keep in mind that the authors might sometimes be influenced by the zeal of advocates." [19]

One might expect a more complete record for the Bill of Rights, proposed by the first Congress, but the situation is only marginally better. The early *Annals of Congress* do not contain a verbatim record of debates; and when the British burned Washington during the War

---

17. So Madison told Jefferson, August 10, 1788; Gaillard Hunt, ed., *The Writings of James Madison* (New York: Putnam's Sons, 1904), V, 246.

18. See the two-part article by Douglass Adair, "The Authorship of the Disputed Federalist Papers," 1 *Wm. & Mary Q.* 97, and 3 ibid. 235 (3rd ser., 1944); and Alpheus Thomas Mason, "*The Federalist*—A Split Personality," 57 *Am.Hist.Rev.* 625 (1952). More recently George W. Carey has disagreed with Adair and Mason: "Publius—a Split Personality?" 46 *Rev. of Pols.* 5 (1984).

19. To Edward Livingston, April 17, 1824; reprinted in *Letters and Other Writings of James Madison* (Philadelphia: Lippincott, 1865), III, 436.

of 1812, they destroyed other documents that might have been helpful in reconstructing history.

Documentary evidence of congressional speeches on amendments adopted since the Civil War is voluminous, but those torrents of words create as well as remove doubts. Not only did supporters and opponents dispute, but, like the authors of *The Federalist,* supporters sometimes disagreed with each other. Even the modern *Congressional Record* is misnamed. Some speeches printed there were never made; some actually made have been edited to include arguments, evidence, and witticisms absent from the originals. What the situation was for the Congresses that proposed the Fourteenth and Fifteenth amendments is difficult to say, but the grammatical purity of the *Congressional Globe* indicates some redaction.

In the face of incomplete and massaged data, conflicts among supporters as well as between friends and foes, Justice Frankfurter's observation takes on added power: In the final analysis, it is the amendment that Congress votes on, not the speeches.[20]

Difficulties multiply when one considers what the hundreds or even thousands of *ratifiers* and the people who chose them had in mind when they approved the original Constitution or its amendments,[21] for the ratifiers' consent was no less necessary than that of the Convention or Congress. Indeed, the ratifiers were the ultimate source of the Constitution's original authority.

There is another difficulty, one that forms a dilemma for those who believe in the binding power of what the framers of 1787–88 had in mind: They apparently believed that their specific intentions, as modern commentators use the term, should not be binding.[22] The weight of the historical evidence—and, for all the reasons just mentioned that evidence is not conclusive—indicates the framers wanted their purposes and the "intent of the document" as expressed in its own terms, including the Preamble, carried out. They did not, however, think of "intent" as including what individual framers had in mind. As Madison said about the notes he had taken at Philadelphia:

> As a guide in expounding and applying the provisions of the Constitution, the debates and incidental decisions of the Convention can have no authoritative character.[23]

Thus the dilemma: If one believes the "intent" of the framers is binding, one must not consider that form of intent as binding.

2. *Difficulties of Practical Application.* Assuming that an interpreter decided to ignore the framers' intent about their intent and an Archival Archangel suddenly produced a tape of debates supplemented by analyses reconciling arguments and counterarguments, could a

---

20. Adamson v. California, concur. op. (1947).

21. See William Anderson, "The Intention of the Framers," 49 *Am.Pol.Sci.Rev.* 340 (1955).

22. See H. Jefferson Powell, "The Original Understanding of Original Intent," 98 *Harv.L. Rev.* 885 (1985).

23. To Thomas Ritchie, September 15, 1821; in Madison's *Letters,* supra note 19, at p. 228.

nation, some critics ask, survive if the choice, each time it faced a crisis, were either to follow the specific intent of the framers, based on their knowledge of their world, or to amend the Constitution? Could a Constitution "endure for ages to come" if the powers to wage war and regulate commerce and rights to free speech, equal protection, or those left unenumerated had to mean exactly what white males of 1787 or 1868 had in mind? Under such conditions would the country survive if it had to wait to amend the Constitution before acting?

3. *Difficulties of Constitutional Theory.* A third set of difficulties pertain to constitutional theory. One such reservation follows Ronald Dworkin's distinction between "concepts" and "conceptions." (See his "Taking Rights Seriously," reprinted above p. 168.) By using broad language in the document, the framers asked the country to approve concepts, not narrow conceptions. Thus if their "intent" binds us, it is those concepts that have force.

Another variant of this difficulty revolves around the obligations of future generations to what the framers had in their minds rather than what they put into words. "What our forefathers said, they said. What they didn't say, they meant to leave to us, and what they said ambiguously, indefinitely, equivocally, or indistinctly, is in so far not said." [24]

One can also argue that the claim that "intent controls meaning" has no firmer textual basis in the constitutional document than it has in the framer's understanding of "intent." Basically, words, including words in a constitution, have meaning because they signify something that their audience understands. And each generation must re-understand those words as best it can—and that best will never be quite the same as the understanding of other generations with other problems and other cultures.

> Once written, a work leaves the control of its writer. The words of the Constitution, once they began their work of bringing a polity into force, lost their bond with the thoughts of the framers and established a bond with the political order. [25]

Anyone who rejects the *approach* of a rigidly fixed meaning for the Constitution must also reject the binding power of specific intentions of the framers. As Holmes said in Missouri v. Holland (1920; reprinted above, p. 132) "the words" of the Constitution

> called into life a being the development of which could not have been foreseen by the most gifted of its begetters . . . . The case before us must be considered in the light of our whole experience and not merely in that of what was said a hundred years ago.

---

24. Charles Curtis, *Lions Under the Throne* (Boston: Houghton Mifflin Co., 1947), pp. 7–8.

25. William F. Harris, II, "Bonding Word and Polity: The Logic of American Constitutionalism," 76 *Am.Pol.Sci.Rev.* 34, 44 (1982).

These objections relate to the binding power of specific meanings of individual clauses that framers may have had in their minds. They provide no argument against consulting either the framers' general purposes or their wisdom. Insofar as the United States remains a constitutional democracy, it still accepts the general purpose of the framers to establish and maintain such a polity. More specifically, many of those framers were politically astute, and sane people always consult wisdom. But a quest for wisdom is vastly different from a search for legally definitive answers.

E. Stare Decisis

Stare decisis is the feature that most clearly distinguishes the common law from other legal systems. Under this *technique*—literally, "the [previous] decision stands"—courts in medieval England, when few statutes regulated social conflict, proceeded inductively to formulate rules of law by trying to decide similar disputes similarly. Gradually, judges linked together their reasons for deciding these cases to formulate more general principles to handle future litigation.

Stare decisis is a means of reasoning by analogy; [26] it proceeds in three steps. First, a judge sees a similarity between the problems now presented and those of earlier cases. Second, he or she determines the rule of law used to settle earlier cases and, third, applies that rule to the dispute at hand. Eventually, a principle builds up for deciding similar problems. This *technique* of advancing case by case, slowly building or eroding rules of law rather than making law wholesale, makes incremental change an integral part of judicial decision making.

American judges have historically asserted authority to reverse themselves; but, even without overruling themselves, they have used stare decisis to change the law as well as to preserve the status quo. It is good form for courts to restrict or extend the reasoning behind earlier rulings. Even ignoring or misusing precedents is not an unknown judicial craft.

In the early decades of the nation, of course, there were few constitutional precedents to follow; but soon, as judges began to claim and exercise interpretive authority [WHO], reading judicial opinions became necessary to understand what the Constitution "really" meant. John Marshall, however, refused to punctuate opinions with references to previous decisions. He preferred a grander style of reasoning. He saw his task as elucidating the Constitution, not refining judicial doctrines. He saw the Constitution as expressing John Locke's political philosophy, and he construed its provisions accordingly.

Marshall's magisterial style has become the exception. Decisions of the Court and hence precedents waiting to be cited have multiplied. The sheer number of judicial decisions and various changes in doc-

---

26. The best analysis of stare decisis is in Edward H. Levi, *An Introduction to Legal Reasoning* (Chicago: University of Chicago Press, 1948), espec. chap. 1.

trine make it possible for judges to cite at least dicta [27] if not an actual holding to bolster a decision either way on virtually every dispute. Moreover, a citation can symbolize a whole jurisprudence. Thus the single word *Griswold* stands for the Court's acceptance in Griswold v. Connecticut (1965; reprinted above, p. 113) of constitutionally protected but unenumerated rights, such as that to privacy, and therewith a view of the Constitution as adaptable.

One must distinguish between a modern style in using precedents and stare decisis itself. Anticipated in theological treatises and aped in law reviews, that style cites, with near neurotic obsession, cases as authorities for almost any statement and heaps quotation upon quotation to show that the judge is true to the deposit of faith. The "string citation"—a listing of six or even a dozen cases that may be, though only tangentially, relevant—epitomizes the modern style. It communicates by deliberate redundancy, among the most venerable ways of teaching. The message is conveyed not only by the judge's words, but also by citations to earlier cases. The *technique* itself is part of the message: The Court is adhering to tradition.[28]

Stare decisis requires lower courts to follow higher courts, but higher courts may change their minds. And the Supreme Court often repeats that it is not rigidly bound by precedent in constitutional interpretation. The explanation is that, although Congress can rather easily correct judicial errors in statutory interpretation by passing a new statute, amending the Constitution is a long, awkward, and extraordinarily difficult process; thus judges should undo their own constitutional mistakes.

In fact, of course, a tribunal that frequently reversed itself could not expect others to respect its decisions. Not surprisingly, then, stare decisis is the normal guide even in the Supreme Court. Overrulings come, but they come infrequently. The justices tend to refuse to review cases that are covered by earlier rulings or, where a lower court has not followed those prior decisions, to reverse it summarily. When the Court takes a case, it is often because the issues are novel or because conflicting lines of precedent have developed. To meet these sorts of situations, the Court may expand or contract the principles justifying earlier decisions. And any change is eased by copious quotations from previous dicta now transformed, if only temporarily, into dogma.

Inflexibly followed, stare decisis could function as an instrument of permanence in constitutional interpretation. The costs of such consistency would, however, be high. The Supreme Court's first

---

27. Dicta—literally "words," in the singular, dictum—refer to statements in a judicial opinion not necessary to justify the decision. What are and are not dicta is often difficult even for the opinion writer to say. Indeed, it is the distinction that later courts make between the two that is crucial. See Levi, supra note 26, p. 2, and materials reprinted and literature cited in Walter F. Murphy and C. Herman Pritchett, eds., *Courts, Judges, and Politics* (4th ed.; New York: Random House, 1986), chap. 10.

28. See Martin Shapiro, "Toward a Theory of Stare Decisis," 1 *Jo. of Legal Studies* 125 (1972).

interpretation on a subject would be its last; if the Court were wrong, it would take a major conflict with Congress and/or the President, perhaps culminating in a constitutional amendment, to undo the damage. And, even if the Court's initial interpretation were "correct," much of the capacity of the Court to adapt its interpretations to changing problems would be lost, though interpreters who see the Constitution as fixed in meaning would view this loss as laudable.

In any event, stare decisis is more than the past's grip on the present. For issues thrashed over time and again, it can provide speedy solutions. It also facilitates incremental change. This dual role is important, but it is also limited. It offers little help in deciding whether to change or not change or whether to expand or contract a substantive doctrine. Most importantly, stare decisis' philosophy of incrementalism cautions judges to value continuity with old rules even while formulating new rules, and it provides a means of communicating fidelity to tradition even while adapting tradition.

F. Balancing

The symbol of justice in our society is a blindfolded goddess holding a set of scales in which she weighs litigants' claims. In the late middle ages, British courts of chancery were already speaking of their task as "balancing the equities." The analogy is pleasing, for it is characteristic of litigation that both parties have some right—and some wrong—on their side.

Modern use of balancing received great impetus during the early years of this century when Roscoe Pound, who was to become dean of the Harvard Law School, began to spread "sociological jurisprudence." Society, he argued, is composed of many interests, each pressing different and at times conflicting demands. "Law" is no more than the rules society devises to resolve those struggles. And those rules must be sufficiently malleable to develop as society's needs shift. "Law must be stable, and yet it cannot stand still." [29]

In this process, Pound saw judges as playing the crucial role. He wanted them to become "social engineers." Through study of history, economics, and sociology, they would discover the social interests vying for legal protection, "balance" those demands against each other, and create appropriate rules to reflect that weighing.

The metaphor of balancing—sometimes also appearing as "a weighing of interests"—has been widely used. A classic debate on this *technique* of constitutional interpretation came in Barenblatt v. United States (1958; reprinted below, p. 525). At issue was the authority of a congressional committee to compel a witness, who did not invoke the Fifth Amendment, to testify about earlier membership in the Communist party. Speaking for the Court, Justice Harlan pictured the clash as between the government's claim to protect the

---

29. *Interpretations of Legal History* (New York: Macmillan, 1923), p. 1.

country against subversion and Barenblatt's claim to free speech and association:

> Where First Amendment rights are asserted to bar governmental interrogation, resolution of the issue always involves a balancing by the courts of the competing private and public interests at stake in the particular circumstances shown . . . . We conclude that the balance between the individual and the governmental interests here at stake must be struck in favor of the latter, and that therefore the provisions of the First Amendment have not been offended.

In angry dissent, Hugo Black protested:

> I do not agree that laws directly abridging First Amendment free-doms can be justified by a congressional or a judicial balancing procedure . . . . To apply the Court's balancing test under such circumstances is to read the First Amendment to say
>
>> Congress shall pass no law abridging freedom of speech, press, assembly and petition, unless Congress and the Supreme Court reach the joint conclusion that on balance the interest of the Government in stifling these freedoms is greater than the interest of the people in having them exercised.

Black reasoned that the plain words of the Constitution ended the matter: "Congress shall make no law" abridging these freedoms, and "no law" meant "no law at all," not "no law unless on balance . . . ."

Judges have never explained precisely what it is they do when they "balance," nor do they distinguish among various kinds of balancing. Commentators have rushed into this intellectual void and have invented many categories under which to analyze judicial handi-work. One rather simple distinction may promote understanding: (1) Balancing as a means of interpreting a single constitutional clause; and (2) balancing as a means of resolving conflict between different parts of the Constitution.

In balancing as a means of interpreting a single constitutional clause, an element of the ad hoc, of an intuitive "feel" for particulars rather than an application of general rules, is especially evident. A court determines whether "the totality of the circumstances" triggers a constitutional protection or authorization. Some constitutional clauses invite such an interpretive *technique:* The Fourth Amendment forbids only "unreasonable" search and seizures, the Eighth Amendment only "excessive" bail or fines, and the Fifth Amendment requires "just compensation" for private property taken for public use. What is reasonable, just, or excessive, one might argue, can only be answered by assessing competing claims in light of peculiar factual circum-stances.

It is also tempting to use balancing to reconcile conflicts between different parts of the Constitution. As we have seen, the rights to free exercise of religion and to be free from an established religion may clash. The right to freedom of the press may collide with an accused's right to trial by an impartial jury. Balancing promises to maximize each value and to do so with less intellectual effort than structural analysis would require in its attempt to construct a larger theory that would harmonize or order the conflicting values.

These appeals are real. Balancing prescribes a role that judges have historically played; it finds reinforcing echoes in sociological jurisprudence; and it allows judges to temper the absolutes of legal rules with prudent regard for practical reality, even for justice. Balancing, Prof. Louis Henkin has written,[30] "provides bridges between the abstractions of principle and the life of facts. It bespeaks moderation and reasonableness, the Golden Mean." The real question, however, is whether for constitutional interpretation balancing is anything more than a metaphor.

It is easy to ridicule particular uses of balancing. Harlan's employment of the *technique* in *Barenblatt,* even a staunch advocate of balancing concedes, was a "sham."[31] Dean Pound had been careful to point out that there were different levels of interests, and that judges should be careful to compare them on the same plane. "If we put one as an individual interest and the other as a social interest we may decide the question . . . by our very way of putting it."[32] And, of course, it was precisely such a skewed balance that Harlan attempted in *Barenblatt.* As Black pointed out, if balancing were legitimate, what should have been balanced against Congress' authority to obtain information was not the right of a single person to privacy in his political associations, but, rather, the right of all citizens to make political choices, even mistakes, without fear of governmental reprisal.

A related, common misuse involves weighing of the marginal advantage of one interest against the total cost of another. In 1978, arguing against excluding evidence that had been illegally obtained, Chief Justice Burger proposed that the Court "balance the costs to society of losing perfectly competent evidence against the prospect of incrementally enhancing Fourth Amendment values."[33] What, of course, the Chief should have balanced against an incremental gain in deterring unlawful police conduct was the incremental cost to society of losing one particular piece of evidence, not the more general costs. Alternatively, he could have balanced the total advantage of the exclusionary rule in deterring police misconduct against the total social cost of losing probative evidence.

Misuse, of course, may be a more persuasive argument for proper use than for disuse. There are, however, more serious objections to balancing. First, it deeply involves judges in policy choices—precisely

---

30. "Infallibility under the Law: Constitutional Balancing," 78 *Colum.L.Rev.* 1022, 1047 (1978).

31. Dean Alfange, "The Balancing of Interests in Free Speech Cases: In Defense of an Abused Doctrine," 2 *Law in Transition Q.* 1, 24 (1965).

32. "A Survey of Social Interests," 57 *Harv.L.Rev.* 1, 2 (1943).

33. United States v. Ceccolini, concur. op. (1978).

the reason that Roscoe Pound advocated its use. In Dennis v. United States (1951; reprinted below, p. 510), Frankfurter asserted that demands of free speech and national security were "better served by candid and informed weighing of the competing interests . . . than by announcing dogmas too inflexible for the non-Euclidian problems to be solved." But, then he invoked the interrogative WHO:

> [W]ho is to balance the relevant factors and ascertain which is in the circumstances to prevail? . . . Primary responsibility for adjusting the interests which compete in the situation before us of necessity belongs to the Congress.

A second objection criticizes balancing as being little more than a ritual incantation that masks from judges as well as observers the true processes of interpretation. Judges do not explain either the nature of the scale on which they weigh competing interests, nor do they explain the relative weights they accord the items to be weighed.

This objection also applies to balancing as a means of reconciling conflicts among parts of the Constitution. If constitutional clauses are of equal importance, then it is difficult to see how "balancing" clauses against each other advances interpretation. If the clauses differ in importance, then the balancer must explain which are more important and why—and stick to those rankings when later problems arise.

Thus, critics argue, when one looks behind the metaphor one is usually left with an explanation that says no more than: "In this situation, the claims of Interest A outweigh the claims of Interest B." That sort of statement announces a decision, it does not provide a reasoned justification. Cardozo frankly conceded the point: "If you ask how he [the judge] is to know when one interest outweighs another, I can only answer that he must get his knowledge just as the legislator gets it, from experience and study and reflection; in brief, from life itself." [34] As Henkin comments, "balancing seems to emerge as an answer instead of a process, and the metaphor of balancing as the whole message." [35]

G. Moral and Political Philosophy

To some extent, all *approaches, modes,* and *techniques* are suffused with assumptions about moral and political philosophy. Many commentators [36] and some public officials are quite open and self-conscious in their use of moral and political philosophy, while others seem blithely unaware that they have been speaking philosophy all their interpretive lives, and yet others claim a duty and a capacity to reject

34. *The Nature of the Judicial Process* (New Haven: Yale University Press, 1921), p. 113.

35. Supra note 30, p. 1048.

36. See, for example, Milner Ball, *The Promise of American Law* (Athens, Ga.: University of Georgia Press, 1981); Barber, supra note 1; Alexander M. Bickel, *The Least Dangerous Branch* (Indianapolis, Ind.: Bobbs-Merrill, 1962), and *The Supreme Court and the Idea of Progress* (New York: Harper & Row, 1970); Ely, supra note 8; and Michael J. Perry, *The Constitution, the Courts, and Human Rights* (New Haven, Conn.: Yale University Press, 1982).

such influences.[37]   In any event, some interpreters believe that one must use such a *technique* —a tool of analysis—to rescue interpretation from personal preferences that might otherwise be imposed by the conflicts among precedents, the opacity of plain words, the mysteries of balancing, and the indeterminacies of structural analysis.

The way in which democratic and constitutionalist theory underpin the constitutional document and the entire political system channelize choices among specific moral and political philosophies, but it does not finely determine such selection.   Thus the particular means to reduce personal choice to a considerable extent depends on personal choice.   Yet, the question remains whether, in fact, an interpreter can avoid such choices and whether they will be more reasoned if made openly rather than subconsciously.

IV. CONCLUSIONS

This chapter has elaborated a three-tiered model of constitutional interpretation, *approaches, modes,* and *techniques.*   A choice at one level affects but does not absolutely determine choices at the lower level(s).   Thus an interpreter who took a textual *approach* to the Constitution and saw it as fixed in meaning could opt to use verbal and structural analyses as *modes* and literalism plus deductive inference as *techniques;* but he or she would find it logically difficult to choose a prudential *mode* or a purposive *mode* tied to a search for fundamental values, or to choose a version of the *technique* of stare decisis that focused on what judges rather than the text said or used that *technique* to effect change.

Each *approach, mode,* and *technique* offers only partial help, and our analyses have been critical, at times sharply so, in underlining flaws. There is no reason why an interpreter is restricted to a single choice at each of the three tiers.   Indeed, except perhaps for a complete literalist, it would be impossible to do so.   But even in their logically possible combinations these *approaches, modes,* and *techniques* do not promise success.   For in addition to parsimony of reasoning, internal consistency, and/or elegance of argument, any measure of success must also involve a capacity to convince a broad readership.   And such persuasion requires a coherent explanation and defense of (1) WHAT one basically believes the Constitution is; and (2) the validity of the methods one uses to interpret it (HOW).   Persuasion also demands (3) rigorous and consistent use of these methods.

APPENDIX

Informed readers undoubtedly noted that this chapter did not discuss several dichotomies widely applied in constitutional commentary: Strict v. Liberal Construction; Judicial Activism v. Self-Restraint;

---

37. See, for example, Robert H. Bork, "Neutral Principles and Some First Amendment Problems," 47 *Ind.L.J.* 2 (1971); "The Struggle Over the Role of the Court," *National Rev.* (Sept. 17, 1982), p. 1137; *Tradition and Morality in Constitutional Law* (Washington, D.C.: American Enterprise Institute, 1985), reprinted in part in Murphy and Pritchett, supra note 27.

Substance v. Procedure; and Interpretivism v. Non-Interpretivism. We think all four lead into blind analytic alleys.

A. Strict v. Liberal Construction

One cannot, with any consistency, strictly or liberally interpret a constitution without becoming mired in massive contradictions. How, for instance, does one "strictly" interpret the Ninth Amendment? Does a strict interpretation require that more or fewer rights be included in its protection? More generally, when one strictly interprets government's powers, one usually thereby also liberally interprets individual rights. Conversely, when one strictly interprets individual rights, one usually interprets governmental power broadly. An effort to interpret both powers and rights equally strictly would typically leave the interpreter in a gigantic muddle. One could attempt always to interpret rights broadly and powers strictly. Constitutionalism would certainly prescribe such a general course, but there is no authority in the text for doing so.

A similar sort of difficulty arises in conflicts between governmental agencies. Normally, construing the powers of one broadly means interpreting the powers of the other strictly, triggering the same logical dilemma as with rights, a dilemma that can be resolved only on the basis of a theory not expressed in the words of the document.

Further complicating matters is the fact that sometimes governmental powers and individual rights (or two sets of governmental powers) are not in a zero-sum relationship, as Cardozo's unpublished opinion in the Minnesota Moratorium Case (reprinted above, p. 136) pointed out. There are occasions when, as with federal enforcement of the Fourteenth Amendment, individual rights depend on government's exercising its powers or, as with the federal government's authority to conduct foreign relations, states' rights—even states' existence—may depend on federal power.

B. Judicial Activism v. Judicial Self-Restraint

Originally designed as an analytic tool,[38] this alternative is now more often a means of evaluating interpretations. One can share the belief that a constitutional democracy can no more tolerate judges' reading their purely personal values into the Constitution than it can tolerate tyrannical legislators or executives, and still find the dichomoty of very limited utility as an evaluative tool. Used in a principled fashion to limit judicial discretion, it posits that judges are obliged to defer to interpretations of Congress and/or the President and possibly state officials. In that sense, the dichotomy fits under the question of WHO shall interpret. It says nothing about HOW a judge should interpret the Constitution. And, because the constitutional document nowhere expresses a judicial duty of habitual defer-

---

38. Among the first to use the term was C. Herman Pritchett in his path-breaking work, *The Roosevelt Court* (New York: Macmillan, 1948).

ence to others, to argue for it requires elaboration of a theory, such as representative democracy.

Moreover, to the extent that the Constitution also rests on a theory of constitutionalism, on a notion of limitations on the power even of those who represent the people, it may require that judges actively oppose the choices of elected officials. Thus, used evaluatively, the dichotomy poses a dilemma: From different perspectives, judges may be activist either if they strike down legislation that, in their judgment, unconstitutionally expands powers or if they accept the validity of such legislation. In the first instance, they are activist vis-à-vis Congress, in the second activist vis-à-vis the Constitution.

As an analytic tool activism/restraint is also of small value. Few, if any, judges claim authority to read their personal views into the Constitution; but, in fact, all judges are at some time activists, at other times apostles of self-restraint. And they behave in this fashion because, so they argue and no doubt believe, the Constitution commands them to do so. Again one needs a complex and coherent theory of WHAT, WHO, and HOW to analyze as well as to evaluate treating different parts of the Constitution differently.

C. Substance v. Procedure

Should we read the constitutional document as primarily procedural—prescribing rules about how things are to be done—or primarily substantive—prescribing rules about what government is and is not to do? John Hart Ely presents an impressive theory of the Constitution as almost entirely procedural: The document is replete with commands about how officials are to be chosen and the processes they are to follow in creating public policy, but it contains very few rules about the content of public policy.[39] Substantive values often underlie procedural choices, like elections or public trials.[40]

This dichotomy is somewhat more helpful than the first two in that it makes some sense in analyzing parts of the written text. But the question quickly arises about the helpfulness of a dichotomy between process and substance. In the real world, the two are so interrelated that it is often difficult to distinguish them. The values behind both procedures and substance are usually closely related and may even merge.

D. Interpretivism v. Non-Interpretivism [41]

This dichotomy confounds the possibility of real insights in problems of constitutional interpretation. It defines "interpretivism" as an effort to find all constitutional meaning within the four corners

---

39. Supra note 8.

40. Laurence H. Tribe makes this point in his review of Ely, supra note 14.

41. For descriptions of this dichotomy, see: Thomas Grey, "Do We Have an Unwritten Constitution?" 27 *Stan.L.Rev.* 703 (1975); Ely, supra note 8, chap. 1; Michael J. Perry, *The Constitution, the Courts, and Human Rights* (New Haven, Conn.: Yale University Press, 1982), chap. 1.

of the document and "non-interpretivism" as allowing interpreters to move beyond the document and import values not there. The first difficulty is that interpretivism is impossible except for the simplest of issues on which there is unlikely to be disagreement to begin with. Plain words, as we saw, restrain our choices in constitutional interpretation, but they do not precisely determine them. Thus all interpretivists concede that one should look beyond the document, at least to what the framers and/or ratifiers intended to put within the four corners.[42] In effect this process would present another set of documents—records of speeches or writings of framers and ratifiers—whose words must also be collated, reconciled, interpreted, and applied.

Further, although some Realists of an earlier generation certainly thought that the power of text to constrain was small,[43] non-interpretivists do not claim authority to ignore or contradict the plain words, only to explain what they mean for the system as it has developed.

Thus what began as a clear dichotomy about the question HOW quickly dissolves. We are all interpretivists, we are all non-interpretivists. This supposed dichotomy befogs the real issues in constitutional interpretation, which relate precisely to the drawing—and justifications for the drawing—of lines between WHAT is and is not included in "the Constitution," WHO determines in an authoritative manner such issues for the polity, and HOW those authoritative interpreters make and justify their decisions.

SELECTED BIBLIOGRAPHY

Barber, Sotirios A. *On What the Constitution Means* (Baltimore: Johns Hopkins University Press, 1984).

Berger, Raoul. *Government by Judiciary* (Cambridge, Mass.: Harvard University Press, 1977).

Black, Charles L. *Structure and Relationship in Constitutional Law* (Baton Rouge, La.: Louisiana State University Press, 1969).

Black, Hugo L. *A Constitutional Faith* (New York: Knopf, 1969).

Bobbitt, Philip. *Constitutional Fate* (New York: Oxford University Press, 1982), espec. chaps. 1–7.

Brigham, John. *Constitutional Language* (Westport, Conn.: Greenwood Press, 1978).

Corwin, Edward S. "Constitution v. Constitutional Theory," 19 *Am. Pol.Sci.Rev.* 290 (1925); reprinted in Alpheus Thomas Mason and Gerald Garvey, eds., *American Constitutional History* (New York: Harper, 1964).

---

42. Thomas Grey asserts that interpretivism would sometimes authorize "[n]ormative inferences . . . from silences and omissions, from structures and relationships, as well as from explicit commands." Supra note 41 at 706 n. (1975). Given the open-ended nature of structural analysis and the far greater variety of plausible inferences from "silences and omissions," it is difficult to imagine what one could import into the Constitution via non-interpretivism that one could not through interpretivism.

43. See, for example, Charles P. Curtis, "The Role of Constitutional Text," in Edmond Cahn, ed., *Supreme Court and Supreme Law* (Bloomington, Ind.: Indiana University Press, 1954).

————. "The Constitution as Instrument and Symbol," 30 *Am.Pol. Sci.Rev.* 1071 (1936); reprinted in Richard Loss, ed., *Corwin on the Constitution* (Ithaca, N.Y.: Cornell University Press, 1981), vol. I.

Ducat, Craig R. *Modes of Constitutional Interpretation* (Minneapolis, Minn.: West Publishing Co., 1978).

Dworkin, Ronald. *Taking Rights Seriously* (Cambridge, Mass.: Harvard University Press, 1977).

————. *A Matter of Principle* (Cambridge, Mass.: Harvard University Press, 1985).

————. "The Forum of Principle," 56 *N.Y.U.L.Rev.* 469 (1981).

Ely, John Hart. *Democracy and Distrust* (Cambridge, Mass.: Harvard University Press, 1980).

Fleming, James E. "A Critique of John Hart Ely's Quest for the Ultimate Constitutional Interpretivism of Representative Democracy," 80 *Mich.L.Rev.* 634 (1982).

Harris, William F., II. "Bonding Word and Polity: The Logic of American Constitutionalism," 76 *Am.Pol.Sci.Rev.* 34 (1982).

Henkin, Louis. "Infallibility under the Law: Constitutional Balancing," 78 *Colum.L.Rev.* 1022 (1978).

Interpretation Symposium. 58 *So.Cal.L.Rev.* 1 (1985).

Mason, Alpheus Thomas. *Harlan Fiske Stone* (New York: Viking, 1956), espec. chaps. 19–22.

————. *The Supreme Court from Taft to Burger* (Baton Rouge, La.: Louisiana State University Press, 1979).

Mendelson, Wallace. "On the Meaning of the First Amendment: Absolutes in the Balance," 50 *Calif.L.Rev.* 729 (1963).

Miller, Arthur S. and Ronald F. Howell. "The Myth of Neutrality in Constitutional Adjudication," 27 *U.Chi.L.Rev.* 661 (1960).

Murphy, Walter F. "The Art of Constitutional Interpretation," in M. Judd Harmon, ed., *Essays on the Constitution of the United States* (Port Washington, N.Y.: Kennikat Press, 1978).

————. "Constitutional Interpretation: The Art of the Historian, Magician, or Statesman?" 87 *Yale L.J.* 1752 (1978).

————. "An Ordering of Constitutional Values," 53 *So.Cal.L.Rev.* 703 (1980).

————. "Constitutional Interpretation: Text, Values, and Processes," 9 *Revs. in Am.Hist.* 7 (1981).

Nimmer, Melville B. "The Right to Speak from *Times* to *Time*," 56 *Calif.L.Rev.* 935 (1968).

Powell, H. Jefferson. "The Original Understanding of Original Intent," 98 *Harv.L.Rev.* 885 (1985).

Powell, Thomas Reed. *Vagaries and Varieties in Constitutional Interpretation* (New York: Columbia University Press, 1956).

————. "The Logic and Rhetoric of Constitutional Law," 15 *Jo. of Phil., Psych., & Sc. Method* 654 (1918); reprinted in Robert G. McCloskey, ed., *Essays in Constitutional Law* (New York: Knopf, 1957).

Tribe, Laurence H. *Constitutional Choices* (Cambridge, Mass.: Harvard University Press, 1985).

Wechsler, Herbert. "Toward Neutral Principles of Constitutional Law," 73 *Harv.L.Rev.* 1 (1959).

B

STRUCTURALISM

Chapter 8 spoke in general terms about the nature of structural analysis, of its concern with the whole of the object to be interpreted, not merely of its discrete parts. In American constitution making overt use of structuralism began with the Philadelphia Convention, if not earlier. In the notes we have of the debates there, one can discern recurrent concern among the delegates about the wholeness of the new polity they were striving to create; and, on occasion, there was real resistance to the new document's spelling out details. Clearly at least some of the delegates wanted to construct a framework that was even more bare of details than the document that emerged.

Use of structural analysis in American constitutional interpretation began in the *Federalist.* Chapter 8 quoted Madison's argument in No. 40:

> There are two rules of construction, dictated by plain reason, as well as founded on legal axioms. The one is, that every part of the expression ought, if possible, be made to conspire to some common end. The other is, that where the several parts cannot be made to coincide, the less important should give way to the more important part; the means should be sacrificed to the end, rather than the end to the means.

When in Chisholm v. Georgia (1793) the Court faced its first important case testing the nature of federalism, it was appropriate that the justices looked not merely to specific clauses of the document, but also to the more general ideas that held the document—and the system—together. Perhaps the most significant of early uses of structuralism came in John Marshall's opinion for the Court in McCulloch v. Maryland (1819; reprinted below, p. 413).

The point is not that structuralism is the most ancient of *modes* of interpretation or that somehow it is "the best," but only that it has been with us from the beginning despite the fact that neither the framers nor early interpreters put that twentieth-century label on it. Still, we must keep in mind the difficulties that structuralism carries, most seriously the necessity for an interpreter to articulate the structure, either of the document, the larger political system, or the theories that surround and support both the document and the system.

This section illustrates structuralism in constitutional interpretation by taking up its two most obvious uses, settling problems of allocations of power among the branches of the national government (Chapter 9) and between the national and state governments (Chapter 10). One should keep in mind, however, that structural analysis need not be limited to such a narrow ambit. One can make a strong case that the structure of the document, system, and/or its underlying theories is one of representative democracy. Accepting such an argument would have broad implications for constitutional interpretation, quite like those that a purposive *mode* of representing representative democracy—developed in Chapters 11 and 12—explores.

One could make a similarly strong case for a constitutionalist structure to face the sorts of problems of fundamental rights that Chapters 15–17 address. Or one could, as we do throughout this book, argue that the system is one of constitutional democracy and organize most, if not all, of constitutional interpretation around structuralism. We have been more modest, but we think readers should be aware that the claims for the structuralist *mode* can be very broad.

SELECTED BIBLIOGRAPHY

Black, Charles L., Jr. *Structure and Relationship in Constitutional Law* (Baton Rouge, La.: Louisiana State University Press, 1969).

Bobbitt, Philip. *Constitutional Fate* (New York: Oxford University Press, 1982), chap. 6.

Brigham, John. *Constitutional Language* (Westport, Conn.: Greenwood Press, 1978).

Choper, Jesse H. *Judicial Review and the National Political Process* (Chicago: University of Chicago Press, 1980).

Ely, John Hart. *Democracy and Distrust* (Cambridge, Mass.: Harvard University Press, 1980).

Harris, William F. II. "Bonding Word and Polity," 76 *Am. Pol. Sci. Rev.* 34 (1982).

Tushnet, Mark V. "Legal Realism, Structural Review, and Prophecy," 8 *U. of Dayton L. Rev.* 809 (1983).

9

Structural Analysis: Sharing Power at the National Level

Relations among the three branches of the federal government and between the nation and the states seem tailor-made for structural analysis. But, despite early examples provided by Madison, Jefferson, Marshall, and Story and later by Jackson, Calhoun, and Lincoln, federal judges have seldom explicitly adopted this *mode* of analysis. Justice Harlan Stone's call, quoted in Chapter 8, for judges to read any particular provision of the Constitution "as a part of an organic whole" [1] does not resonate through the U.S. Reports. Even textual structuralism, which limits itself to the document, has only infrequently found a welcome in the Supreme Court.

Perhaps, however, we mistake the name for the reality. The term structuralism may be foreign to most of modern constitutional jurisprudence, but that *mode* of analysis is quite common. Sometimes it is disguised as literalism, deductive inference, or search for intent of the framers; but one can often find its ghost lurking in the shadows of judicial opinions. Indeed, one can make a strong case that it is impossible intelligently or even intelligibly to interpret relations among various branches of the national government or between state and national levels without having in mind a concept of the structure of the constitutional document as well as of the larger political system and political theories that inform its words and practices.

I. SHARED POWERS

As Chapter 2 indicated, some of the framers were quite conscious of the general framework of government they were establishing. Madison's grand strategy was to pit some economic, social and institutional interests against other economic, social, and institutional interests, to set power against power. *Federalist* No. 10, reprinted in Chapter 15 (p. 952) and No. 51, reprinted in this chapter (p. 328), clearly explain this design. Its function is not so much to separate *powers* but, as Richard E. Neudstadt put it, to separate *institutions* and require them to share powers.[2]

---

1. Wright v. United States, concur. op. (1938).

2. *Presidential Power* (New York: John Wiley, 1960), p. 33.

322

Chapter 3, pp. 48–52, provided detailed information about some of the ways in which these shared powers allow each of the three branches to check—and be checked by—the other two. The President is part of the legislative process; Congress, especially the Senate, participates in the executive process; both wield some judicial power; and judges, in interpreting the Constitution and the congressionalese of statutes, often of necessity legislate, just as in making sense of the bureaucratese of executive orders and applying laws to concrete cases their work sometimes merges with that of administrators.

Perhaps for our age the most difficult and consequential example of shared powers are those over war and foreign policy. Article I authorizes Congress "to declare war . . . to raise and support armies . . . to provide and maintain a navy . . . [and] to make rules for the government and regulation of the land and naval forces . . . ." Article II, however, makes the President commander-in-chief of the armed forces, authorizes him to conduct diplomacy, requires him to swear "to preserve, protect and defend the Constitution," and instructs him to "take care that the laws be faithfully executed." And Article VI confers on treaties the status of law, and treaties include agreements for mutual defense such as that of NATO.

These clauses, as Edward S. Corwin once remarked, form "an invitation to struggle for the privilege of directing American foreign policy." [3] And, of course, practical necessity seldom displays respect for constitutional texts. Presidents since George Washington have asserted constitutional authority to take military action to defend the United States without a declaration of war or other congressional approval. Individual legislators and occasionally Congress itself have contested this claim. The War Powers Act of 1973 (reprinted below, p. 351) represents one phase of this struggle between the executive and the legislature. Although sometimes judges have become involved—see, for example, Little v. Barreme (1804; reprinted below, p. 331); and the Prize Cases (1863; reprinted below, p. 334)—the Supreme Court has usually been sufficiently fortunate or wise to keep out of this dangerous field. [4]

In domestic politics, since the 1930s and the days of the New Deal, Congress has assumed a positive responsibility not merely to regulate the economy but also to keep it moving ahead and providing some measure of federal care for those whose lives the system disrupts. In considering legislation for such a complex world, Congress has seen its options as either setting broad policy goals and delegating large measures of discretionary authority to administrative officials or prescribing huge and intricately detailed codes. In the belief that they are institutionally ill-equipped to undertake the second task, legislators have typically opted for the first alternative.

---

3. *The President: Office and Powers* (4th rev. ed.; New York: New York University Press, 1957), p. 171.

4. See the Court's artful dodging of cases from the Vietnam War, especially Massachusetts v. Laird (1971) and Mora v. McNamara (1967), and later of the question of the validity of President Carter's abrogation of the defense treaty with Taiwan. Goldwater v. Carter (1979).

But delegation of discretion to say how and when a congressional policy comes into effect and filling in its details means that administrators, supposed subordinates of the President, are in effect legislating. To counter this threat to their own power, legislators have resorted to several tactics. Three have been especially important. The first, suggested by the Constitution's plain words, has been to exercise "administrative oversight"—a euphemism for intervening in the administration of laws, supposedly the President's task—through control of the budget. The second has been to increase the number of so-called independent regulatory commissions headed by people appointed in the regular fashion but serving for set terms and not responsible to the President.

The constitutionality of these first two devices was for a time uncertain. In the 1930s the Court on two occasions struck down statutes as so excessive in their delegation as to establish administrative agencies as miniature (and unelected) Congresses. Since then the justices have accepted the fiction that Congress determines general policy and only delegates authority to fill in the gaps.[5] Dicta in Myers v. United States (1926) queried just how "independent" of presidential control independent regulatory commissions were, but the Court cleared up that matter. Congress, the justices have said, can validly provide that commissioners of independent agencies shall serve for specific terms, rather than at the pleasure of the President.[6]

The third tactic has been to delegate broad legislative authority but to tie a string to the delegation through what is called the legislative veto. That is, the agency[7] to whom authority is delegated is required to lay its detailed plan before Congress; if Congress (sometimes the legislation will provide that if either house) disapproves, the regulations do not go into effect.

The benefits of allowing elected officials to regulate the work of appointed administrators is obvious; but the price is that the legislative veto shortcuts the White House. The President loses his opportunity to veto the change that Congress, in disapproving a set of regulations, may be effecting. The constitutional problems surrounding the legislative veto have not yet been resolved. INS v. Chadha (1983; reprinted below, p. 383) declared the practice unconstitutional. But since that time Congress has continued to use it, though often in a more subtle form, and another clash—and possible clarification or modification—seems likely.

---

5. See Justice White's dis. op. in *Chadha* (1983; reprinted below, p. 383). For a more general analysis, see Sotirios A. Barber, *The Constitution and the Delegation of Congressional Power* (Chicago: University of Chicago Press, 1975). Theodore W. Lowi has argued heatedly and eloquently that the pattern of congressional delegation constitutes an abdication of responsibility as well as a surrender of all hope of achieving coordinated and just public policies at the national level. *The End of Liberalism* (2nd ed.; New York: Norton, 1979).

6. Humphrey's Executor v. United States (1935); Wiener v. United States (1958).

7. We use the term "agency" here very broadly. Congress has even delegated law-making authority to the Supreme Court. See Eds.' Note (2) to INS v. Chadha (1983; reprinted below, p. 383).

Prof. Jesse H. Choper has made a long and powerful argument that the Court has no legitimate role to play as arbiter between Congress and the President or between the nation and the states. Each of these units has an array of political checks against the other. Judges, Choper reasons, should utilize their authority to protect individual citizens against government, in what would otherwise be an unequal struggle.[8] However one evaluates Choper's thesis, it is interesting that in the *Federalist*—see espec. No. 10, reprinted below, p. 95 and No. 51, reprinted below, p. 328,—Madison did not mention judicial review or even judges generally as elements in his grand design of pitting interests against interests at the national level. Only in *Federalist* No. 39 (reprinted below, p. 409) did he see judges as having an important role in maintaining the system's structure, and then only insofar as relations between the nation and the states are concerned.

II. INSTITUTIONAL INTEGRITY

These shared powers blur lines of authority among the three branches. None of them is completely autonomous. But each must retain a large degree of institutional integrity; otherwise one or two would dominate the other(s) and render sharing irrelevant as a limitation on governmental power. Making law, applying law, and interpreting law are difficult to distinguish at the edges; and thus it is often difficult to discern the exact character of particular action. Indeed, it may be partly legislative, partly executive, and partly judicial. Still, the system operates on the assumption that there is a core of authority that is legislative, a core that is executive, and yet a third that is judicial. For example, deciding an accused's guilt or innocence is a judicial issue,[9] determining in general what acts are crimes is a legislative matter,[10] just as making an arrest is executive. The constitutionally required sharing comes mostly at the edges rather than at the core.

Because these distinctions are neither "natural" nor linguistically required, but only roughly shaped by the document and long usage both before and since 1787, deciding what powers lie at the core of an institution's functions is a critical aspect of constitutional interpretation. For example, when would Congress' authority to make "exceptions" to the Supreme Court's appellate jurisdiction so trench on

---

8. *Judicial Review and the National Political Process* (Chicago: University of Chicago Press, 1980).

9. After listing the general powers of Congress, Art. I, § 9 provides: "No bill of attainder or ex post facto law shall be passed." Art. I, § 10 lays the same prohibitions against the states. A bill of attainder is a legislative act that convicts a person of crime and imposes punishment for that alleged deed. An ex post facto law has retroactive effect; it makes an act, legal when committed, a crime, or increases the punishment for an act committted in the past, or lowers the standards of proof for an act committed before passage of the bill.

10. United States v. Hudson & Goodwin (1812) held that there were no "common law crimes" against the United States; that is, only Congress could establish the criminal law, though, of course, judges might interpret what Congress had enacted.

judicial power as to destroy the Court's integrity as a separate institution of government? (See Ex parte McCardle [1869; reprinted below, p. 361] and the editors' notes.)

Here again various kinds of structural analysis come into play. What is likely to be determinative is the image an interpreter has of the Constitution's architectural scheme, as outlined in the document, perhaps also as it has been fleshed out by the operations of the larger political system, and perhaps as both the terms of the document and the system's development are explained by the political theories underpinning the Constitution. The cases reprinted here show the justices drawing—usually implicitly but sometimes explicitly—the structural lines that they see as outlining the respective powers of branches of the national government. Those cases also allow the justices to offer hints of their deeper visions of the American polity.

III. PLAN OF THIS CHAPTER

To illustrate the complexities of shared powers among separate and quasi-autonomous institutions, we have divided the cases and materials in this chapter into four sections. The first is general in nature and consists of Madison's effort in *Federalist* No. 51 to sketch an overall scheme. The second takes up one of the most troublesome of the shared powers, that to wage war. The third section addresses problems of preserving institutional integrity in a system of shared powers. The final section returns to problems of institutional interaction and confronts the nature of the power to appoint, to claim executive privilege, and to exercise the veto, legislative as well as executive.

SELECTED BIBLIOGRAPHY

Abraham, Henry J. *Justices and Presidents* (2d ed.; New York: Oxford University Press, 1985).

Arnold, R. Douglas. *Congress and the Bureaucracy* (New Haven, Conn.: Yale University Press, 1979).

Berger, Raoul. *Impeachment: The Constitutional Problems* (Cambridge, Mass.: Harvard University Press, 1973).

Bessette, Joseph M., and Jeffrey Tulis, eds. *The Presidency in the Constitutional Order* (Baton Rouge: Louisiana State University Press, 1981).

Corwin, Edward S. *The President: Office and Powers* 4th rev. ed. (New York: New York University Press, 1957).

Choper, Jesse H. *Judicial Review and the National Political Process* (Chicago: University of Chicago Press, 1980).

Fisher, Louis. *Presidential Spending Power* (Princeton: Princeton University Press, 1975).

————. *The Politics of Shared Power: Congress and the Executive* (Washington, D.C.: Congressional Quarterly Press, 1981).

_____. *Constitutional Conflicts Between Congress and the President* (Princeton, N.J.: Princeton University Press, 1985).

Gwyn, W.B. *The Meaning of Separation of Powers* (New Orleans: Tulane Studies in Political Science, 1965).

Harris, Joseph P. *Congressional Control of Administration* (Washington, D.C.: The Brookings Institution, 1964).

Henkin, Louis. *Foreign Affairs and the Constitution* (Mineola, N.Y.: Foundation Press, 1972).

Livingston, William S., Lawrence Dodd, and Richard L. Schott, eds., *The Presidency and the Congress: A Shifting Balance of Power?* (Austin: Lyndon Baines Johnson Library, 1979).

Maas, Arthur. *Muddy Waters: The Army Engineers and the Nation's Rivers* (Cambridge: Harvard University Press, 1951).

Murphy, Walter F. *Congress and the Court* (Chicago: University of Chicago Press, 1962).

Pritchett, C. Herman. *Congress versus the Supreme Court, 1957–1960* (Minneapolis: University of Minnesota Press, 1961).

Public Broadcasting System. "The War Powers: The President and Congress" (Videotape of seminar available from Media and Society Seminars, 204 Journalism, Columbia University, New York, N.Y. 10027).

Pyle, Christopher H., and Richard M. Pious, eds. *The President, Congress, and the Constitution* (New York: The Free Press, 1984).

Neudstadt, Richard E. *Presidential Power: The Politics of Leadership* (New York: John Wiley, 1960).

Schlesinger, Arthur M., Jr. *The Imperial Presidency* (New York: Popular Library, 1973).

Scigliano, Robert. *The Supreme Court and the Presidency* (New York: The Free Press, 1971).

Sofaer, Abraham D. *War, Foreign Affairs and Constitutional Power: The Origins* (Cambridge, Mass.; Ballinger, 1976).

Thomas, Ann Van Wynen, and A.J. Thomas. *The War-Making Powers of the President* (Dallas: Southern Methodist University Press, 1982).

Vile, M.J.C. *Constitutionalism and the Separation of Powers* (London: Oxford University Press, 1967).

I. A SYSTEM OF SHARED POWERS

"Ambition must be made to counteract ambition."

FEDERALIST NO. 51
James Madison (1788).

To what expedient, then, shall we finally resort, for maintaining in practice the necessary partition of power among the several departments as laid down in the Constitution? The only answer that can be given is that as all these exterior provisions are found to be inadequate the defect must be supplied, by so contriving the interior structure of the government as that its several constituent parts may, by their mutual relations, be the means of keeping each other in their proper places . . . . I will hazard a few general observations which may perhaps place it in a clearer light, and enable us to form a more correct judgment of the principles and structure of the government planned by the convention.

In order to lay a due foundation for that separate and distinct exercise of the different powers of government, which to a certain extent is admitted on all hands to be essential to the preservation of liberty, it is evident that each department should have a will of its own; and consequently should be so constituted that the members of each should have as little agency as possible in the appointment of the members of the others. Were this principle rigorously adhered to, it would require that all the appointments . . . should be drawn from the same fountain of authority, the people, through channels having no communication whatever with one another . . . . Some difficulties, however, and some additional expense would attend the execution of it. Some deviations, therefore, from the principle must be admitted. In the constitution of the judiciary department in particular, it might be inexpedient to insist rigorously on the principle: first, because peculiar qualifications being essential in the members, the primary consideration ought to be to select that mode of choice which best secures these qualifications; second, because the permanent tenure by which the appointments are held in that department must soon destroy all sense of dependence on the authority conferring them.

It is equally evident that the members of each department should be as little dependent as possible on those of the others for the emoluments annexed to their offices. Were the executive magistrate, or the judges, not independent of the legislature in this particular, their independence in every other would be merely nominal.

But the great security against a gradual concentration of the several powers in the same department consists in giving to those who administer each department the necessary constitutional means and personal motives to resist encroachments of the others. The provision for defense must in this, as in all other cases, be made commensurate to the danger of attack. Ambition must be made to counteract ambition. The interest of the man must be connected with the constitutional rights of the place. It may be a reflection on human nature that such devices should be necessary to control the abuses of government. But what is government itself but the greatest of all reflections on human nature? If men were angels, no government would be necessary. If angels were to govern men, neither external nor internal controls on government would be necessary. In framing a government which is to be administered by men over men, the great difficulty lies in this: you must first enable the government to control the governed; and in the next place oblige it to control itself. A dependence on the people is, no doubt, the primary control on the government; but experience has taught mankind the necessity of auxiliary precautions.

This policy of supplying, by opposite and rival interests, the defect of better motives, might be traced through the whole system of human affairs.   .   .   .   We see it particularly displayed in all the subordinate distributions of power, where the constant aim is to divide and arrange the several offices in such a manner as that each may be a check on the other—that the private interest of every individual may be a sentinel over the public rights.   .   .   .

But it is not possible to give to each department an equal power of self-defense. In republican government, the legislative authority necessarily predominates. The remedy for this inconveniency is to divide the legislature into different branches; and to render them, by different modes of election and different principles of action, as little connected with each other as the nature of their common functions and their common dependence on the society will admit. It may even be necessary to guard against dangerous encroachments by still further precautions. As the weight of the legislative authority requires that it should be thus divided, the weakness of the executive may require, on the other hand, that it should be fortified. An absolute negative on the legislature appears, at first view, to be the natural defense with which the executive magistrate should be armed. But perhaps it would be neither altogether safe nor alone sufficient .   .   .   .   May not this defect of an absolute negative be supplied by some qualified connection between this weaker department and the weaker branch of the stronger department, by which the latter may be led to support the constitutional rights of the former, without being too much detached from the rights of its own department?   .   .   .

There are, moreover, two considerations particularly applicable to the federal system of America, which place that system in a very interesting point of view.

First. In a single republic, all the power surrendered by the people is submitted to the administration of a single government; and the usurpations are guarded against by a division of the government into distinct and separate departments. In the compound republic of America, the power surrendered by the people is first divided between two distinct governments, and then the portion allotted to each subdivided among distinct and separate departments. Hence a double security arises to the rights of the people. The different governments will control each other, at the same time that each will be controlled by itself.

Second. It is of great importance in a republic not only to guard the society against the oppression of its rulers, but to guard one part of the society against the injustice of the other part. Different interests necessarily exist in different classes of citizens. If a majority be united by a common interest, the rights of the minority will be insecure. There are but two methods of providing against this evil: the one by creating a will in the community independent of the majority—that is, of the society itself; the other, by comprehending in the society so many separate descriptions of citizens as will render an unjust combination of a majority of the whole very improbable, if not impracticable. The first method prevails in all governments possessing an hereditary or self-appointed authority. This, at best, is but a precarious security; because a power independent of the society may as well espouse the unjust views of the major as the rightful interests of the minor party, and may possibly be turned against both parties. The second method will be exemplified in the federal republic of the United States. Whilst all authority in it will be derived from and dependent on the society, the society itself will be broken into so many parts, interests and classes of citizens, that the rights of individuals, or of the minority, will be in little danger from interested combinations of the majority. In a free government the security for civil rights must be the same as that for religious rights. It consists in the one case in the multiplicity of interests, and in the other in the multiplicity of sects. The degree of security in both cases will depend on the number of interests and sects; and this may be presumed to depend on the extent of country and number of people comprehended under the same government. . . . Justice is the end of government. It is the end of civil society. It ever has been and ever will be pursued until it be obtained, or until liberty be lost in the pursuit. In a society under the forms of which the stronger faction can readily unite and oppress the weaker, anarchy may as truly be said to reign as in a state of nature, where the weaker individual is not secured against the violence of the stronger; and as, in the latter state, even the stronger individuals are prompted, by the uncertainty of their condition, to submit to a government which may protect the weak as well as themselves; so, in the former state, will the more powerful factions or parties be gradually induced, by a like motive, to wish for a government which will protect all parties, the weaker as well as the more powerful. . . . In the extended republic of the United States, and among the great variety of interests, parties, and sects which it embraces, a coalition of a majority of the whole society could seldom take place on any other principles than those of justice and the general good; whilst there being thus less danger to a minor from the will of a major party, there must be less pretext, also, to provide for the security of the former, by introducing into the government a will not dependent on the latter, or, in other words, a will independent of the society itself. It is no less certain than it is important . . . that the larger the society, provided it lie within a practicable sphere, the more duly capable it will be of self-government. And happily for the *republican cause,* the practicable sphere may be carried to a very great extent by a judicious modification and mixture of the *federal principle.*

Publius

Editors' Note

For an analysis of the development of the general notion of playing off human frailties against each other as a principle of political and economic statesmanship, a notion connected to the case for capitalism, see Albert O. Hirschman, *The Passions and the Interests* (Princeton: Princeton University Press, 1977).

II. SHARING POWERS: THE POWER TO WAGE WAR

"[T]he legislature seem to have prescribed . . . the manner in which this law shall be carried into execution . . . ."

LITTLE v. BARREME (THE FLYING FISH)

6 U.S. (2 Cranch) 170, 2 L.Ed. 243 (1804).

During the Quasi-Naval War with France (1797–1800), Congress authorized the President to instruct captains of U.S. naval vessels to seize any American ship bound *to* a French port. The Secretary of the Navy ordered the seizure of American ships bound *to* or *from* a French port. In pursuance of that order, the frigate *Boston,* commanded by Captain Little, captured *The Flying Fish,* bound *from* the French West Indies, took her to an American port, and filed a libel (an action in maritime law to seize a ship) against her, alleging she was an American vessel. The district judge, whose limited jurisdiction included hearing such suits, held that the ship was actually Danish and disallowed the seizure; but he refused to award damages against Little because there had been probable cause to think *The Flying Fish* was American. The circuit court reversed, ruling that, because the ship was coming *from* not *to* a French port, she would not have been liable to seizure even if American. Little appealed to the U.S. Supreme Court.

MARSHALL, Chief Justice, now delivered the opinion of the Court

. . . .

It is by no means clear that the president of the United States, whose high duty it is to "take care that the laws be faithfully executed," and who is commander in chief of the armies and navies of the United States, might not, without any special authority for that purpose, in the then existing state of things, have empowered the officers commanding armed vessels of the United States, to seize and send into port for adjudication, American vessels which were forfeited by being engaged in this illicit commerce. But when it is observed . . . that the 5th section [of the statute] gives a special authority to seize on the high seas, and limits that authority to the seizure of vessels bound or sailing *to* a French port, the legislature seem to have prescribed that the manner in which this law shall be carried into execution, was to exclude a seizure of any vessel not bound *to* a French port. Of consequence, however strong the circumstances might be, which induced Captain Little to suspect *The Flying Fish* to be an American vessel, they could not excuse the detention of her, since he would not have been authorized to detain her had she been really American.

It was so obvious, that if only vessels sailing to a French port could be seized on the high seas, that the law would be very often evaded, that this act of congress appears to have received a different construction from the executive of the United States; a construction much better calculated to give it effect.

A copy of this act was transmitted by the secretary of the navy, to the captains of the armed vessels, who were ordered to consider the 5th section as a part of their instructions. The same letter contained the following clause:

> A proper discharge of the important duties enjoined on you, arising out of this act, will require the exercise of a sound and an impartial judgment. You are not only to do all that in you lies, to prevent all intercourse, whether direct or circuitous, between the ports of the United States and those of France or her dependencies, where the vessels are apparently as well as really American, and protected by American papers only, but you are to be vigilant that vessels of cargoes, really American, but covered by Danish or other foreign papers, and bound to or from French ports, do not escape you.

These orders, given by the executive, under the construction of the act of congress made by the department to which its execution was assigned, enjoin the seizure of American vessels sailing from a French port. Is the officer who obeys them liable for damages sustained by this misconstruction of the act, or will his orders excuse him? If his instructions afford him no protection, then the law must take its course, and he must pay such damages as are legally awarded against him; if they excuse an act, not otherwise excusable, it would then be necessary to inquire, whether this is a case in which the probable cause which existed to induce a suspicion that the vessel was American, would excuse the captor from damages when the vessel appeared in fact to be neutral.

I confess, the first bias of my mind was very strong in favour of the opinion, that though the instructions of the executive could not give a right, they might yet excuse from damages. I was much inclined to think, that a distinction ought to be taken between acts of civil and those of military officers; and between proceedings within the body of the country and those on the high seas. That implicit obedience which military men usually pay to the orders of their superiors, which indeed is indispensably necessary to every military system, appeared to me strongly to imply the principle that those orders, if not to perform a prohibited act, ought to justify the person whose general duty it is to obey them, and who is placed by the laws of his country in a situation which in general requires that he should obey them. I was strongly inclined to think that, where, in consequence of orders from the legitimate authority, a vessel is seized, with pure intention, the claim of the injured party for damages would be against that government from which the orders proceeded, and would be a proper subject for negotiation. But I have been convinced that I was mistaken, and I have receded from this first opinion. I acquiesce in that of my brethren, which is, that the instructions cannot change the nature of the transaction, or legalize an act which, without those instructions, would have been a plain trespass.

It becomes, therefore, unnecessary to inquire whether the probable cause afforded by the conduct of *The Flying Fish* to suspect her of being an American, would excuse Captain Little from damages for having seized and sent her into port, since, had she been an American, the seizure would have been unlawful?

Captain Little, then, must be answerable in damages to the owner of this neutral vessel, and as the account taken by order of the circuit court is not objectionable on its face, and has not been excepted to by counsel before the proper tribunal, this court can receive no objection to it.

There appears, then, to be no error in the judgment of the circuit court, and it must be affirmed with costs.

Editors' Notes

(1) On first reading, *The Flying Fish* seems perhaps important for international law in its holding that military and naval officers are liable for acting illegally, even when obeying direct orders of superiors. Otherwise, however, the case appears of little interest. But is there more here? What did this apparently trivial opinion of Marshall imply about the relations among Congress, the President, and the courts? Whose interpretation of a statute and more importantly of the Constitution's allocations of authority is to prevail?

(2) **Query:** What did Marshall imply about the President's power to wage war, even limited war, when Congress has laid down explicit terms? In the absence of any congressional directive? See Justice Clark's use of this ruling in his concur. op. in the Steel Seizure Case (1952; reprinted below, p. 339).

(3) Here Marshall skewered Jefferson almost as neatly as he had in *Marbury*. Not only did the Chief Justice claim judicial authority to determine the boundaries of authority between Congress and the President, but he had done so on a substantive issue on which Jefferson would have found it embarrassing to disagree publicly and assert a departmental theory of constitutional interpretation, for he had opposed the Quasi-War with France that John Adams and his Federalists had waged.

"Whether the President . . . has met with such armed
hostile resistance, and a civil war of such alarming proportions as will compel him to accord to them the character of belligerents, is a question to be decided *by him,* and
this Court must be governed by the decisions and acts of
the political department of the Government to which this
power was entrusted."

THE PRIZE CASES
67 U.S. (2 Black) 635, 17 L.Ed. 459 (1863).

In 1861, President Lincoln proclaimed a blockade of Southern ports, even
though Congress had not declared war. The Union navy seized and brought
to port as prizes several ships carrying goods to the South. The U.S. district
court condemned the vessels, and the owners appealed.

Mr. Justice **GRIER** delivered the opinion of the court . . . .

Let us enquire whether, at the time this blockade was instituted, a
state of war existed which would justify a resort to these means of
subduing the hostile force. . . .

By the Constitution, Congress alone has the power to declare a
national or foreign war. It cannot declare war against a State, or any
number of States, by virtue of any clause in the Constitution. The
Constitution confers on the President the whole Executive power. He
is bound to take care that the laws be faithfully executed. He is
Commander-in-chief of the Army and Navy of the United States, and of
the militia of the several States when called into the actual service of
the United States. He has no power to initiate or declare a war either
against a foreign nation or a domestic State. But by the Acts of
Congress of February 28th, 1795, and 3d of March, 1807, he is authorized to called out the militia and use the military and naval forces of the
United States in case of invasion by foreign nations, and to suppress
insurrection against the government of a State or of the United States.

If a war be made by invasion of a foreign nation, the President is
not only authorized but bound to resist force by force. He does not
initiate the war, but is bound to accept the challenge without waiting
for any special legislative authority. And whether the hostile party be
a foreign invader, or States organized in rebellion, it is none the less a
war, although the declaration of it be *"unilateral."* . . .

This greatest of civil wars . . . sprung forth suddenly from the
parent brain, a Minerva in the full panoply of *war.* The President was
bound to meet it in the shape it presented itself, without waiting for
Congress to baptize it with a name; and no name given to it by him or
them could change the fact.

It is not the less a civil war, . . . because it may be called an
"insurrection" by one side, and the insurgents be considered as rebels
or traitors. It is not necessary that the independence of the revolted
province or State be acknowledged in order to constitute it a party
belligerent in a war according to the law of nations. Foreign nations

acknowledge it as war by a declaration of neutrality. The condition of neutrality cannot exist unless there be two belligerent parties . . . .

As soon as the news of the attack on Fort Sumter, and the organization of a government by the seceding States, assuming to act as belligerents, could become known in Europe, . . . the Queen of England issued her proclamation of neutrality. . . . This was immediately followed by similar declarations or silent acquiescence by other nations . . . .

Whether the President in fulfilling his duties, as Commander-in-chief, in suppressing an insurrection, has met with such armed hostile resistance, and a civil war of such alarming proportions as will compel him to accord to them the character of belligerents, is a question to be decided *by him*, and this Court must be governed by the decisions and acts of the political department of the Government to which this power was entrusted. . . . The proclamation of blockade is itself official and conclusive evidence to the Court that a state of war existed which demanded and authorized a recourse to such a measure, under the circumstances peculiar to the case. . . .

If it were necessary to the technical existence of a war, that it should have a legislative sanction, we find it in almost every act passed at the extraordinary session of the Legislature of 1861, which was wholly employed in enacting laws to enable the Government to prosecute the war with vigor and efficiency. And finally, in 1861, we find Congress . . . in anticipation of such astute objections, passing an act "approving, legalizing, and making valid all the acts, proclamations, and orders of the President, &c., as if they had been *issued and done under the previous express authority* and direction of the Congress of the United States."

Without admitting that such an act was necessary under the circumstances, it is plain that if the President had in any manner assumed powers which it was necessary should have the authority or sanction of Congress, . . . this ratification has operated to perfectly cure the defect . . . .

The objection made to this act of ratification, that it is *ex post facto,* and therefore unconstitutional and void, might possibly have some weight on the trial of an indictment in a criminal Court. But precedents from that source cannot be received as authoritative in a tribunal administering public and international law.

. . . [T]herefore we are of the opinion that the President had a right, *jure belli,* to institute a blockade of ports in possession of the States in rebellion, which neutrals are bound to regard . . . .

Mr. Justice **NELSON,** dissenting. . . .

. . . [B]efore this insurrection against the established Government can be dealt with on the footing of a civil war, . . . it must be recognized or declared by the war-making power of the Government. . . . There is no difference in this respect between a civil or a public war. . . .

An idea seemed to be entertained that all that was necessary to constitute a war was organized hostility in the district of country in a state of rebellion. . . .

Now, in one sense, no doubt this is war, . . . but it is a statement simply of its existence in a material sense, and has no relevancy or weight when the question is what constitutes war in a legal sense, in the sense of the law of nations, and of the Constitution of the United States? For it must be a war in this sense to attach to it all the consequences that belong to belligerent rights. . . . [T]o constitute a civil war in the [legal] sense . . . it must be recognized or declared by the sovereign power of the State, and which sovereign power by our Constitution is lodged in the Congress of the United States—civil war, therefore, under our system of government, can exist only by an act of Congress, which requires the assent of two of the great departments of the Government, the Executive and Legislative. . . .

The Acts of 1795 and 1807 did not, and could not under the Constitution, confer on the President the power of declaring war against a State of this Union, or of deciding that war existed, and upon that ground authorize the capture and confiscation of the property of every citizen of the State whenever it was found on the waters. The laws of war, whether the war be civil or *inter gentes*, . . . convert every citizen of the hostile State into a public enemy, and treat him accordingly, whatever may have been his previous conduct. This great power over the business and property of the citizen is reserved to the legislative department by the express words of the Constitution. It cannot be delegated or surrendered to the Executive. Congress alone can determine whether war exists or should be declared; and until they have acted, no citizen of the State can be punished in his person or property, unless he has committed some offence against a law of Congress passed before the act was committed, which made it a crime, and defined the punishment. . . .

. . . I am compelled to the conclusion that no civil war existed between this Government and the States in insurrection till recognized by the Act of Congress 13th of July, 1861; . . . and, consequently, that the President had no power to set on foot a blockade under the law of nations, and that the capture of the vessel and cargo in this case, and in all cases before us in which the capture occurred before the 18th of July, 1861, for breach of blockade, or as enemies' property, are illegal and void, and that the decrees of condemnation should be reversed and the vessel and cargo restored.

Mr. Chief Justice **TANEY**, Mr. Justice **CATRON** and Mr. Justice **CLIFFORD**, concurred in the dissenting opinion of Mr. Justice **NELSON**.

Editors' Note

Because of the Dred Scott Case (1857), which ruled that a black person could not be a citizen of the United States, that slaves were mere property under the Constitution, and therefore that the Missouri Compromise of 1820, which had forbidden slavery in the territories north of latitude 36° 30′, deprived slaveowners of their property without due process of law, a large share of Republican politicians looked on the Supreme Court as pro-Southern. Two deaths and a resignation among the justices allowed Lincoln to change the orientation of the Court; but the closeness of the vote in the Prize Cases (5–4) helped persuade Congress to adopt a bill, already under consideration, to increase the number of the justices to ten and so allow Lincoln to increase what was perceived as a narrow Unionist majority.

"[T]he President alone has the power to speak or listen as a representative of the nation."

UNITED STATES v. CURTISS–WRIGHT EXPORT CORP.
299 U.S. 304, 57 S.Ct. 216, 81 L.Ed. 255 (1936).

In 1934 Congress adopted a Joint Resolution authorizing the President to prohibit the sale of arms and munitions to Bolivia and Paraguay, who were fighting over the Chaco, if he believed that such an embargo would contribution to peace. President Roosevelt immediately issued a proclamation forbidding arms shipments to either country. Shortly thereafter, the Department of Justice secured an indictment against Curtiss-Wright for selling machine guns to Bolivia. In the trial court, the corporation claimed that the President's proclamation had no legal force because Congress had unconstitutionally delegated legislative power to the executive. The district judge agreed and the government appealed directly to the Supreme Court.

Mr. Justice **SUTHERLAND** delivered the opinion of the Court. . . .

Whether, if the Joint Resolution had related solely to internal affairs it would be open to the challenge that it constituted an unlawful delegation of legislative power to the Executive, we find it unnecessary to determine. The whole aim of the resolution is to affect a situation entirely external to the United States, and falling within the category of foreign affairs. . . . [A]ssuming (but not deciding) that the challenged delegation, if it were confined to internal affairs, would be invalid, may it nevertheless be sustained on the ground that its exclusive aim is to afford a remedy for a hurtful condition within foreign territory?

It will contribute to the elucidation of the question if we first consider the differences between the powers of the Federal government in respect of foreign or external affairs and those in respect of domestic or internal affairs. . . .

The two classes of powers are different, both in respect of their origin and their nature. The broad statement that the Federal government can exercise no powers except those specifically enumerated in the Constitution, and such implied powers as are necessary and proper to carry into effect the enumerated powers, is categorically true only in respect of our internal affairs. In that field, the primary purpose of the Constitution was to carve from the general mass of legislative powers *then possessed by the states* such portions as it was thought desirable to vest in the Federal government, leaving those not included in the enumeration still in the states. That this doctrine applies only to powers which the states had, is self-evident. And since the states severally never possessed international powers, such powers could not have been carved from the mass of state powers but obviously were transmitted to the United States from some other source. . . .

The Union existed before the Constitution, which was ordained and established among other things to form "a more perfect Union." Prior to that event, it is clear that the Union, declared by the Articles of Confederation to be "perpetual," was the sole possessor of external sovereignty, and in the Union it remained without change save in so far as the Constitution in express terms qualified its exercise. . . .

It results that the investment of the Federal government with the powers of external sovereignty did not depend upon the affirmative grants of the Constitution. The powers to declare and wage war, to conclude peace, to make treaties, to maintain diplomatic relations with other sovereignties, if they had never been mentioned in the Constitution, would have vested in the Federal government as necessary concomitants of nationality. . . . As a member of the family of nations, the right and power of the United States in that field are equal to the right and power of the other members of the international family. Otherwise, the United States is not completely sovereign. . . . This the court [has] recognized, and [has] found the warrant for its conclusions not in the provisions of the Constitution, but in the law of nations.
. . .

Not only is the Federal power over external affairs in origin and essential character different from that over internal affairs, but participation in the exercise of the power is significantly limited. In this vast external realm, with its important, complicated, delicate and manifold problems, the President alone has the power to speak or listen as a representative of the nation. He *makes* treaties with the advice and consent of the Senate: but he alone negotiates . . . .

It is important to bear in mind that we are here dealing not alone with an authority vested in the President by an exertion of legislative power, but with such an authority plus the very delicate, plenary and exclusive power of the President as the sole organ of the Federal government in the field of international relations—a power which does not require as a basis for its exercise an act of Congress, but which, of course, like every other governmental power, must be exercised in subordination to the applicable provisions of the Constitution. It is quite apparent that if, in the maintenance of our international relations, embarrassment—perhaps serious embarrassment—is to be avoided and success for our aims achieved, congressional legislation which is to be made effective through negotiation and inquiry within the international field must often accord to the President a degree of discretion and freedom from statutory restriction which would not be admissible were domestic affairs alone involved. Moreover, he, not Congress, has the better opportunity of knowing the conditions which prevail in foreign countries, and especially is this true in time of war. He has his confidential sources of information. He has his agents in the form of diplomatic, consular and other officials. Secrecy in respect of information gathered by them may be highly necessary, and the premature disclosure of it productive of harmful results. . . .

This consideration, in connection with what we have already said on the subject, discloses the unwisdom of requiring Congress in this field of governmental power to lay down narrowly definite standards by which the President is to be governed. . . .

Reversed.

Mr. Justice **McREYNOLDS** [dissented].

Mr. Justice **STONE** took no part in the consideration or decision of this case.

———

"The Constitution is neither silent nor equivocal about who shall make the laws which the President is to execute"—Justice BLACK

"The actual art of governing under our Constitution does not and cannot conform to judicial definitions of the power of any of its branches based on isolated clauses or even single Articles torn from context."—Justice JACKSON

YOUNGSTOWN SHEET & TUBE CO. v. SAWYER

343 U.S. 579, 72 S.Ct. 863, 96 L.Ed. 1153 (1952).

In April, 1952, during the Korean War, after months of bargaining among the United Steel Workers, the steel industry, and the government, the union called a strike that would have shut down most of the country's steel production. Just a few hours before the strike was to begin, President Harry S Truman issued Executive Order 10340, directing Secretary of Commerce Charles Sawyer to seize the mills and operate them. "Seizure" consisted of sending telegrams to all the companies affected, telling them of the action taken and appointing the president of each firm as manager for the government. All assets and liabilities were to remain with the owners, although Sawyer's announced intention of reopening negotiations with the union might well have cost the companies future profits.

The day after the seizure, the President notified Congress of his action and said he would follow whatever course Congress prescribed. Congress took no action, but the steel companies, claiming they would suffer irreparable injury from the government's negotiating with the union, obtained an injunction against the seizure. The government won a stay of this order from the court of appeals and petitioned the Supreme Court for certiorari. The Court granted the writ, heard lengthy argument several days later, and handed down its decision a month after.

Mr. Justice **BLACK** delivered the opinion of the Court . . . .

The President's power, if any, to issue the order must stem either from an act of Congress or from the Constitution itself. There is no statute that expressly authorizes the President to take possession of property as he did here. Nor is there any act of Congress to which our attention has been directed from which such a power can fairly be implied. Indeed, we do not understand the Government to rely on statutory authorization for this seizure. There are two statutes which do authorize the President to take both personal and real property under certain conditions. However, the Government admits that . . . the President's order was not rooted in either . . . .

Moreover, the use of the seizure technique to solve labor disputes . . . was not only unauthorized by any congressional enactment; prior to this controversy, Congress had refused to adopt that method of settling labor disputes. When the Taft-Hartley Act was under consideration in 1947, Congress rejected an amendment which would have authorized such governmental seizures in cases of emergency . . . .

 . . . [T]he plan Congress adopted in that Act did not provide for seizure under any circumstances. Instead, the plan sought to bring about settlements by use of the customary devices of mediation, conciliation, investigation by boards of inquiry, and public reports. In some instances temporary injunctions were authorized to provide cooling-off periods. All this failing, the unions were left free to strike if the majority of the employees, by secret ballot, expressed a desire to do so.

It is clear that if the President had authority to issue the order he did, it must be found in some provisions of the Constitution. And it is not claimed that express constitutional language grants this power to the President. The contention is that presidential power should be implied from the aggregate of his powers under the Constitution. Particular reliance is placed on provisions in Art. II which say that "the executive Power shall be vested in a President . . . "; that "he shall take Care that the Laws be faithfully executed"; and that he "shall be Commander in Chief of the Army and Navy of the United States."

The order cannot properly be sustained as an exercise of the President's military power as Commander in Chief of the Armed Forces. The Government attempts to do so by citing a number of cases upholding broad powers in military commanders engaged in day-to-day fighting in a theater of war. Such cases need not concern us here. Even though "theater of war" be an expanding concept, we cannot with faithfulness to our constitutional system hold that the Commander in Chief of the Armed Forces has the ultimate power as such to take possession of private property in order to keep labor disputes from stopping production. This is a job for the Nation's lawmakers, not for its military authorities.

Nor can the seizure order be sustained because of the several constitutional provisions that grant executive power to the President. In the framework of our Constitution, the President's power to see that the laws are faithfully executed refutes the idea that he is to be a lawmaker. The Constitution limits his functions in the law-making process to the recommending of laws he thinks wise and the vetoing of laws he thinks bad. And the Constitution is neither silent nor equivocal about who shall make laws which the President is to execute. The first section of the first article says that "All legislative Powers herein granted shall be vested in a Congress of the United States . . . ."

The President's order does not direct that a congressional policy be executed in a manner prescribed by Congress—it directs that a presidential policy be executed in a manner prescribed by the President. The preamble of the order itself, like that of many statutes, sets out reasons why the President believes certain policies should be adopted, proclaims these policies as rules of conduct to be followed, and again, like a statute, authorizes a government official to promulgate additional rules and regulations consistent with the policy proclaimed and needed to carry that policy into execution. The power of Congress to adopt such public policies as those proclaimed by the order is beyond question. It can authorize the taking of private property for public use. It can make laws regulating the relationships between employers and employees, prescribing rules designed to settle labor disputes, and fixing wages and working conditions in certain fields of our economy. The Constitution did not subject this law-making power of Congress to presidential or military supervision or control.

It is said that other Presidents without congressional authority have taken possession of private business enterprises in order to settle labor disputes. But even if this be true, Congress has not thereby lost its exclusive constitutional authority to make laws necessary and proper to carry out the powers vested by the Constitution "in the Government of the United States, or any Department or Officer thereof."

The Founders of this Nation entrusted the lawmaking power to the Congress alone in both good and bad times. It would do no good to recall the historical events, the fears of power and the hopes for freedom that lay behind their choice. Such a review would but confirm our holding that this seizure order cannot stand.

The judgment of the District Court is

Affirmed.

Mr. Justice **FRANKFURTER** [concurring].

Although the considerations relevant to the legal enforcement of the principle of separation of powers seem to me more complicated and flexible than may appear from what Mr. Justice Black has written, I join his opinion because I thoroughly agree with the application of the principle to the circumstances of this case . . . .

. . . The Founders of this Nation were not imbued with the modern cynicism that the only thing that history teaches is that it teaches nothing. They acted on the conviction that the experience of man sheds a good deal of light on his nature . . . .

. . . For them the doctrine of separation of powers was not mere theory; it was a felt necessity . . . . These long-headed statesmen had no illusion that our people enjoyed biological or psychological immunities from the hazards of concentrated power. It is absurd to see a dictator in a representative product of the sturdy democratic traditions of the Mississippi Valley. The accretion of dangerous power does not come in a day. It does come, however slowly, from the generative force of unchecked disregard of the restrictions that fence in even the most disinterested assertion of authority.

The Framers, however, did not make the judiciary the overseer of our government. . . . Rigorous adherence to the narrow scope of the judicial function is especially demanded in controversies that arouse appeals to the Constitution. The attitude with which this Court must approach its duty when confronted with such issues is precisely the opposite of that normally manifested by the general public. So-called constitutional questions seem to exercise a mesmeric influence over the popular mind. This eagerness to settle—preferably forever—a specific problem on the basis of the broadest possible constitutional pronouncements may not unfairly be called one of our minor national traits . . . .

The path of duty for this Court, it bears repetition, lies in the opposite direction . . . .

So here our first inquiry must be not into the powers of the President, but into the powers of a District Judge to issue a temporary injunction in the circumstances of this case. Familiar as that remedy is, it remains an extraordinary remedy. To start with a consideration of the relation between the President's powers and those of Congress . . . . is to start at the wrong end. A plaintiff is not entitled to an injunction if money damages would fairly compensate him for any wrong he may have suffered. . . . . Again, a court of equity ought not to issue an injunction, even though a plaintiff otherwise makes out a case for it, if the plaintiff's right to an injunction is overborne by a commanding public interest against it. . . . . To deny inquiry into the President's power in a case like this, because of the damage to the public interest to be feared from upsetting its exercise by him, would in effect always preclude inquiry into challenged power, which presumably only avowed great public interest brings into action. And so, with the utmost unwillingness, with every desire to avoid judicial inquiry into the powers and duties of the other two branches of the government, I cannot escape consideration of the legality of Executive Order No. 10340.

The pole-star for constitutional adjudications is John Marshall's greatest judicial utterance that "it is a *constitution* we are expounding." M'Culloch v. Maryland [1819] That requires both a spacious view in applying an instrument of government "made for an undefined and expanding future," Hurtado v. California [1884], and as narrow a delimitation of the constitutional issues as the circumstances permit. Not the least characteristic of great statesmanship which the Framers manifested was the extent to which they did not attempt to bind the future. It is no less incumbent upon this Court to avoid putting fetters upon the future by needless pronouncements today

. . . .

The issue before us can be met, and therefore should be, without attempting to define the President's powers comprehensively . . . . The judiciary may . . . have to intervene in determining where authority lies as between the democratic forces in our scheme of government. But in doing so we should be wary and humble. Such is the teaching of this Court's role in the history of the country . . . .

The question before the Court comes in this setting. Congress has frequently—at least 16 times since 1916—specifically provided for executive seizure of production, transportation, communications, or storage facilities. In every case it has qualified this grant of power with limitations and safeguards. . . . The power to seize has uniformly been given only for a limited period or for a defined emergency, or has been repealed after a short period. Its exercise has been restricted to particular circumstances such as "time of war or when war is imminent," the needs of "public safety" or of "national security or defense," or "urgent and impending need."

Congress in 1947 was again called upon to consider whether governmental seizure should be used to avoid serious industrial shutdowns. Congress decided against conferring such power . . . .

It cannot be contended that the President would have had power to issue this order had Congress explicitly negated such authority in formal legislation. Congress has expressed its will to withhold this power from the President as though it had said so in so many words

. . . .

By the Labor Management Relations Act of 1947, Congress said to the President, "You may not seize. Please report to us and ask for seizure power if you think it is needed in a specific situation." . . .

No authority that has since been given to the President can by any fair process of statutory construction be deemed to withdraw the restriction or change the will of Congress as expressed by a body of enactments, culminating in the Labor Management Relations Act of 1947 . . . .

A scheme of government like ours no doubt at times feels the lack of power to act with complete, all-embracing, swiftly moving authority. No doubt a government with distributed authority, subject to be challenged in the courts of law, at least long enough to consider and adjudicate the challenge, labors under restrictions from which other governments are free. It has not been our tradition to envy such governments. In any event our government was designed to have such restrictions. The price was deemed not too high in view of the safe-guards which these restrictions afford . . . .

Mr. Justice **DOUGLAS,** concurring. . . .

Mr. Justice **JACKSON,** concurring in the judgment and opinion of the Court . . . .

A judge, like an executive adviser, may be surprised at the poverty of really useful and unambiguous authority applicable to concrete problems of executive power as they actually present themselves. Just what our forefathers did envision, or would have envisioned had they foreseen modern conditions, must be divined from materials almost as enigmatic as the dreams Joseph was called upon to interpret for Pharaoh. A century and a half of partisan debate and scholarly speculation yields no net result but only supplies more or less apt quotations from respected sources on each side of any question. They largely cancel each other. And court decisions are indecisive because of the judicial practice of dealing with the largest questions in the most narrow way.

The actual art of governing under our Constitution does not and cannot conform to judicial definitions of the power of any of its branches based on isolated clauses or even single Articles torn from context. While the Constitution diffuses power the better to secure liberty, it also contemplates that practice will integrate the dispersed powers into a workable government. It enjoins upon its branches separateness but interdependence, autonomy but reciprocity. Presidential powers are not fixed but fluctuate, depending upon their disjunction or conjunction with those of Congress. We may well begin by a somewhat oversimplified grouping of practical situations in which a President may doubt, or others may challenge, his powers, and by distinguishing roughly the legal consequences of this factor of relativity.

1. When the President acts pursuant to an express or implied authorization of Congress, his authority is at its maximum, for it includes all that he possesses in his own right plus all that Congress can delegate. . . . A seizure executed by the President pursuant to an Act of Congress would be supported by the strongest of presumptions . . . .

2. When the President acts in absence of either a congressional grant or denial of authority, he can only rely upon his own independent powers, but there is a zone of twilight in which he and Congress may have concurrent authority, or in which its distribution is uncertain. . . . In this area, any actual test of power is likely to depend on the imperatives of events and contemporary imponderables rather than on abstract theories of law.

3. When the President takes measures incompatible with the expressed or implied will of Congress, his power is at its lowest ebb, for then he can rely only upon his own constitutional powers minus any constitutional powers of Congress over the matter. Courts can sustain exclusive Presidential control in such a case only by disabling the Congress from acting upon the subject. Presidential claim to a power at once so conclusive and preclusive must be scrutinized with caution, for what is at stake is the equilibrium established by our constitutional system.

Into which of these classifications does this executive seizure of the steel industry fit? It is eliminated from the first by admission, for it is conceded that no congressional authorization exists for this seizure.
. . .

Can it then be defended under flexible texts available to the second category? It seems clearly eliminated from that class because Congress has not left seizure of private property an open field but has covered it by three statutory policies inconsistent with this seizure. . . .

This leaves the current seizure to be justified only by the severe tests under the third grouping, where it can be supported only by any remainder of executive power after subtraction of such powers as Congress may have over the subject. In short, we can sustain the President only by holding that seizure of such strike-bound industries is within his domain and beyond control by Congress . . . .

The Solicitor General seeks the power of seizure in three clauses of the Executive Article, the first reading, "The executive Power shall be vested in a President of the United States of America." Lest I be thought to exaggerate, I quote the interpretation which his brief puts upon it: "In our view, this clause constitutes a grant of all the executive powers of which the Government is capable." If that be true, it is difficult to see why the forefathers bothered to add several specific items, including some trifling ones.

. . . I cannot accept the view that this clause is a grant in bulk of all conceivable executive power but regard it as an allocation to the presidential office of the generic powers thereafter stated.

The clause on which the Government next relies is that "The President shall be Commander in Chief of the Army and Navy of the United States . . . ." . . . [T]his loose appellation is sometimes advanced as support for any presidential action, internal or external, involving use of force, the idea being that it vests power to do anything, anywhere, that can be done with an army or navy.

That seems to be the logic of an argument tendered at our bar— that the President having, on his own responsibility, sent American troops abroad derives from that act "affirmative power" to seize the means of producing a supply of steel for them. . . . [I]t is said he has invested himself with "war powers."

I cannot foresee all that it might entail if the Court should indorse this argument. Nothing in our Constitution is plainer than that declaration of a war is entrusted only to Congress. Of course, a state of war may in fact exist without a formal declaration. But no doctrine that the Court could promulgate would seem to me more sinister and alarming than that a President whose conduct of foreign affairs is so largely uncontrolled, and often even is unknown, can vastly enlarge his mastery over the internal affairs of the country by his own commitment of the Nation's armed forces to some foreign venture . . . .

There are indications that the Constitution did not contemplate that the title Commander-in-Chief *of the Army and Navy* will constitute him also Commander-in-Chief of the country, its industries and its inhabitants. He has no monopoly of "war powers," whatever they are. While Congress cannot deprive the President of the command of the army and navy, only Congress can provide him an army or navy to command . . . .

That military powers of the Commander-in-Chief were not to supersede representative government of internal affairs seems obvious from the Constitution and from elementary American history . . . .

We should not use this occasion to circumscribe, much less to contract, the lawful role of the President as Commander-in-Chief. I should indulge the widest latitude of interpretation to sustain his exclusive function to command the instruments of national force, at least when turned against the outside world for the security of our society. But, when it is turned inward, not because of rebellion but because of a lawful economic struggle between industry and labor, it should have no such indulgence. His command power is not such an absolute as might be implied from that office in a militaristic system but is subject to limitations consistent with a constitutional Republic whose law and policy-making branch is a representative Congress. The purpose of lodging dual titles in one man was to insure that the civilian would control the military, not to enable the military to subordinate the presidential office. No penance would ever expiate the sin against free government of holding that a President can escape control of executive powers by law through assuming his military role . . . .

The third clause in which the Solicitor General finds seizure powers is that "he shall take Care that the Laws be faithfully executed . . . ." That authority must be matched against words of the Fifth Amendment that "No person shall be . . . deprived of life, liberty or property, without due process of law . . . ." One gives a governmental authority that reaches so far as there is law, the other gives a private right that authority shall go no farther. These signify about all there is of the principle that ours is a government of laws, not of men, and that we submit ourselves to rulers only if under rules.

The Solicitor General lastly grounds support of the seizure upon nebulous, inherent powers never expressly granted but said to have accrued to the office from the customs and claims of preceding administrations. The plea is for a resulting power to deal with a crisis or an emergency according to the necessities of the case, the unarticulated assumption being that necessity knows no law. . . .

. . . [C]ontemporary foreign experience may be inconclusive as to the wisdom of lodging emergency powers somewhere in a modern government. But it suggests that emergency powers are consistent with free government only when their control is lodged elsewhere than in the Executive who exercises them. That is the safeguard that would be nullified by our adoption of the "inherent powers" formula. Nothing in my experience convinces me that such risks are warranted by any real necessity, although such powers would, of course, be an executive convenience.

In the practical working of our Government we already have evolved a technique within the framework of the Constitution by which normal executive powers may be considerably expanded to meet an emergency. Congress may and has granted extraordinary authorities which lie dormant in normal times but may be called into play by the Executive in war or upon proclamation of a national emergency.

. . .

. . . I have no illusion that any decision by this Court can keep power in the hands of Congress if it is not wise and timely in meeting its problems. A crisis that challenges the President equally, or perhaps primarily, challenges Congress. If not good law, there was worldly wisdom in the maxim attributed to Napoleon that "The tools belong to the man who can use them." We may say that power to legislate for emergencies belongs in the hands of Congress, but only Congress itself can prevent power from slipping through its fingers.

The essence of our free Government is "leave to live by no man's leave, underneath the law"—to be governed by those impersonal forces which we call law. Our Government is fashioned to fulfill this concept so far as humanly possible. The Executive, except for recommendation and veto, has no legislative power. The executive action we have here originates in the individual will of the President and represents an exercise of authority without law . . . . With all its defects, delays and inconveniences, men have discovered no technique for long preserving free government except that the Executive be under the law, and that the law be made by parliamentary deliberations.

Such institutions may be destined to pass away. But it is the duty of the Court to be last, not first, to give them up.

Mr. Justice **BURTON,** concurring in both the opinion and judgment of the Court . . . .

Mr. Justice **CLARK,** concurring in the judgment of the Court . . . .

One of this Court's first pronouncements upon the powers of the President under the Constitution was made by Chief Justice John Marshall some one hundred and fifty years ago. In Little v. Barreme [1804], he used this characteristically clear language in discussing the power of the President to instruct the seizure of the "Flying-Fish," a vessel bound from a French port:

It is by no means clear that the president of the United States whose high duty it is to "take care that the laws be faithfully executed," and who is commander in chief of the armies and navies of the United States, might not, without any special authority for that purpose, in the then existing state of things, have empowered the officers commanding the armed vessels of the United States, to seize and send into port for adjudication, American vessels which were forfeited by being engaged in this illicit commerce. But when it is observed that [an Act of Congress] gives a special authority to seize on the high seas, and limits that authority to the seizure of vessels bound or sailing *to* a French port, the legislature seem to have prescribed that the manner in which this law shall be carried into execution, was to exclude a seizure of any vessel *not* bound *to* a French port.

Accordingly, a unanimous Court held that the President's instructions had been issued without authority and that they could not "legalize an act which without those instructions would have been a plain trespass." I know of no subsequent holding of this Court to the contrary . . . .

I conclude that where Congress has laid down specific procedures to deal with the type of crisis confronting the President, he must follow those procedures in meeting the crisis; but that in the absence of such action by Congress, the President's independent power to act depends upon the gravity of the situation confronting the nation. I cannot sustain the seizure in question because here, as in Little v. Barreme, Congress had prescribed methods to be followed by the President in meeting the emergency at hand . . . .

Mr. Chief Justice **VINSON,** with whom Mr. Justice **REED** and Mr. Justice **MINTON** join, dissenting. . . .

Those who suggest that this is a case involving extraordinary powers should be mindful that these are extraordinary times. A world not yet recovered from the devastation of World War II has been forced to face the threat of another and more terrifying global conflict . . . .

. . . As an illustration of the magnitude of the over-all program, Congress has appropriated $130 billion for our own defense and for military assistance to our allies since the June, 1950, attack in Korea.

Even before Korea, steel production at levels above theoretical 100% capacity was not capable of supplying civilian needs alone. Since Korea, the tremendous military demand for steel has far exceeded the increases in productive capacity . . . .

The President has the duty to execute the foregoing legislative programs. Their successful execution depends upon continued production of steel and stabilized prices for steel . . . .

. . . The Union and the steel companies may well engage in a lengthy struggle. Plaintiff's counsel tells us that "sooner or later" the mills will operate again. That may satisfy the steel companies and, perhaps, the Union. But our soldiers and our allies will hardly be cheered with the assurance that the ammunition upon which their lives depend will be forthcoming—"sooner or later," or, in other words, "too little and too late."

Accordingly, if the President has any power under the Constitution to meet a critical situation in the absence of express statutory authorization, there is no basis whatever for criticizing the exercise of such power in this case.

The steel mills were seized for a public use . . . . Plaintiffs cannot complain that any provision in the Constitution prohibits the exercise of the power of eminent domain in this case. The Fifth Amendment provides: "nor shall private property be taken for public use, without just compensation." It is no bar to this seizure for, if the taking is not otherwise unlawful, plaintiffs are assured of receiving the required just compensation . . . .

Admitting that the Government could seize the mills, plaintiffs claim that the implied power of eminent domain can be exercised only under an Act of Congress . . . .

Under this view, the President is left powerless at the very moment when the need for action may be most pressing and when no one, other than he, is immediately capable of action . . . . [H]e is left powerless because a power not expressly given to Congress is nevertheless found to rest exclusively with Congress . . . .

. . . [I]n this case, we need only look to history and time-honored principles of constitutional law—principles that have been applied consistently by all branches of the Government throughout our history. It is those who assert the invalidity of the Executive Order who seek to amend the Constitution in this case.

A review of executive action demonstrates that our Presidents have on many occasions exhibited the leadership contemplated by the Framers when they made the President Commander in Chief, and imposed upon him the trust to "take Care that the Laws be faithfully executed." With or without explicit statutory authorization, Presidents have at such times dealt with national emergencies by acting promptly and resolutely to enforce legislative programs, at least to save those programs until Congress could act. Congress and the courts have responded to such executive initiative with consistent approval . . . .

[Vinson then cited a series of instances of seizure by Presidents Lincoln, Taft, and Franklin Roosevelt.]

Focusing now on the situation confronting the President on the night of April 8, 1952, we cannot but conclude that the President was performing his duty under the Constitution "to take Care that the Laws be faithfully executed"—a duty described by President Benjamin Harrison as "the central idea of the office."

The President reported to Congress the morning after the seizure that he acted because a work stoppage in steel production would immediately imperil the safety of the Nation by preventing execution of the legislative programs for procurement of military equipment . . . .

. . . The President's action served the same purpose as a judicial stay entered to maintain the status quo in order to preserve the jurisdiction of a court . . . .

Plaintiffs place their primary emphasis on the Labor Management Relations Act of 1947 . . . but do not contend that that Act contains any provision prohibiting seizure . . . .

The diversity of views expressed in the six opinions of the majority, the lack of reference to authoritative precedent, the repeated reliance upon prior dissenting opinions, the complete disregard of the uncontroverted facts showing the gravity of the emergency and the temporary nature of the taking all serve to demonstrate how far afield one must go to affirm the order of the District Court.

The broad executive power granted by Art. II to an officer on duty 365 days a year cannot, it is said, be invoked to avert disaster. Instead, the President must confine himself to sending a message to Congress recommending action. Under this messenger-boy concept of the Office, the President cannot even act to preserve legislative programs from destruction so that Congress will have something left to act upon . . . .

As the District Judge stated, this is no time for "timorous" judicial action. But neither is this a time for timorous executive action . . . . The President immediately informed Congress of his action and clearly stated his intention to abide by the legislative will. No basis for claims of arbitrary action, unlimited powers or dictatorial usurpation of congressional power appears from the facts of this case . . . .

Editors' Notes

(1) On the afternoon of the Court's decision, Truman ordered the mills returned to management. That same day the United Steel Workers began a strike that was to last more than seven weeks, aggravating an existing shortage of ammunition for troops in Korea. On the background and effects of the seizure, see: Grant McConnell, *The President Seizes the Steel Mills* (University: University of Alabama Case Program, 1960); Richard E. Neustadt, *Presidential Power* (New York: Wiley, 1960), chp. 2; Alan F. Westin, ed., *The Anatomy of a Constitutional Law Case* (New York: Macmillan, 1958). Truman claimed the ammunition shortage began after the strike—*Memoirs* (Garden City, N.Y.: Doubleday, 1955), II, chap. 29—but it had actually begun months before. For analyses of the justices' opinions, see Edward S. Corwin, "The Steel Seizure Case: A Judicial Brick Without Straw," 53 *Col.L.Rev.* 53 (1953); Paul G. Kauper, "The Steel Seizure Case," 51 *Mich.L.Rev.* 141 (1952); and C. Herman Pritchett, *Civil Liberties and the Vinson Court* (Chicago: University of Chicago Press, 1954), pp. 206–213.

(2) Compare the language of In re Neagle (1890), which grew out of feud between Justice Stephen Field and his former law partner David Terry, who had threatened to kill Field because the Justice had, while riding circuit, held that Mrs. Terry's divorce from her first husband was not valid and therefore she was not legally married to Terry. Some time later, Terry approached Field, riding circuit in California, and began what a marshal thought was an attack. The marshal then shot and killed Terry and was arrested by state officials.

The Department of Justice asked for a writ of habeas corpus under statutes that provided that federal officers should be tried in federal courts for acts committed while on duty. The case reached the Supreme Court; and the President's authority, in the absence of an act of Congress, to assign marshals for such protective duty was an important preliminary issue. The Court asked:

> Is this duty [of the President to "take care that the laws be faithfully executed"] limited to the enforcement of acts of Congress or of treaties of the United States, according to their *express terms,* or does it include the rights, duties and obligations growing out of the Constitution itself, our international relations, and the protection implied by the nature of the government under the Constitution?

The Court's answer was emphatically in favor of a broad scope for presidential power.

(3) **Query:** Compare Jackson's opinion with Black's in the Steel Case. To what extent does each implicitly use structural analysis? How do the structures they visualize differ? Or does the difference lie more in Black's use of textual structuralism and Jackson's of both textual and systemic structuralism? Is Frankfurter's opinion more or less broadly structuralist than Black's or Jackson's? Is Vinson's dissent also structural? If so, is it textualist, systemic, or transcendent?

"The constitutional powers of the President . . . to introduce United States Armed Forces into hostilities . . . are exercised only pursuant to (1) a declaration of war, (2) specific statutory authorization, or (3) a national emergency created by an attack upon the United States . . . ."

THE WAR POWERS RESOLUTION *

Joint Resolution Concerning the War Powers of Congress and the President

Resolved by the Senate and House of Representatives of the United States of America in Congress assembled, That:

SHORT TITLE

Section 1. This joint resolution may be cited as the "War Powers Resolution".

PURPOSE AND POLICY

Sec. 2. (a) It is the purpose of this joint resolution to fulfill the intent of the framers of the Constitution of the United States and insure that the collective judgment of both the Congress and the President will apply to the introduction of United States Armed Forces into hostilities, or into situations where imminent involvement in hostilities is clearly indicated by the circumstances, and to the continued use of such forces in hostilities or in such situations.

---

* H.J.Res. 542; Pub.L. 93–148 (1973); 87 Stat.555; 50 U.S.C. §§ 1541–1548. Passed over Presidential veto Nov. 7, 1973.

(b) Under article I, section 8, of the Constitution, it is specifically provided that the Congress shall have the power to make all laws necessary and proper for carrying into execution, not only its own powers but also all other powers vested by the Constitution in the Government of the United States, or in any department or officer thereof.

(c) The constitutional powers of the President as Commander-in-Chief to introduce United States Armed Forces into hostilities, or into situations where imminent involvement in hostilities is clearly indicated by the circumstances, are exercised only pursuant to (1) a declaration of war, (2) specific statutory authorization, or (3) a national emergency created by attack upon the United States, its territories or possessions, or its armed forces.

CONSULTATION

Sec. 3.　The President in every possible instance shall consult with Congress before introducing United States Armed Forces into hostilities or into situations where imminent involvement in hostilities is clearly indicated by the circumstances, and after every such introduction shall consult regularly with the Congress until United States Armed Forces are no longer engaged in hostilities or have been removed from such situations.

Sec. 4.　(a) In the absence of a declaration of war, in any case in which United States Armed Forces are introduced—

(1) into hostilities or into situations where imminent involvement in hostilities is clearly indicated by the circumstances;

(2) into the territory, airspace or waters of a foreign nation, while equipped for combat, except for deployments which relate solely to supply, replacement, repair, or training of such forces; or

(3) in numbers which substantially enlarge United States Armed Forces equipped for combat already located in a foreign nation;

the President shall submit within 48 hours to the Speaker of the House of Representatives and to the President pro tempore of the Senate a report, in writing, setting forth—

(A) the circumstances necessitating the introduction of United States Armed Forces;

(B) the constitutional and legislative authority under which such introduction took place; and

(C) the estimated scope and duration of the hostilities or involvement.

(b) The President shall provide such other information as the Congress may request in the fulfillment of its constitutional responsibilities with respect to committing the Nation to war and to the use of United States Armed Forces abroad.

(c) Whenever United States Armed Forces are introduced into hostilities or into any situation described in subsection (a) of this section, the President shall, so long as such armed forces continue to be engaged in such hostilities or situation, report to the Congress periodically on the status of such hostilities or situation as well as on the scope and duration of such hostilities or situation, but in no event shall he report to the Congress less often than once every six months.

CONGRESSIONAL ACTION

Sec. 5. (a) Each report submitted pursuant to section 4(a)(1) shall be transmitted to the Speaker of the House of Representatives and to the President pro tempore of the Senate on the same calendar day. Each report so transmitted shall be referred to the Committee on Foreign Affairs of the House of Representatives and to the Committee on Foreign Relations of the Senate for appropriate action. If, when the report is transmitted, the Congress has adjourned sine die or has adjourned for any period in excess of three calendar days, the Speaker of the House of Representatives and the President pro tempore of the Senate, if they deem it advisable (or if petitioned by at least 30 percent of the membership of their respective Houses) shall jointly request the President to convene Congress in order that it may consider the report and take appropriate action pursuant to this section.

(b) Within sixty calendar days after a report is submitted or is required to be submitted pursuant to section 4(a)(1), whichever is earlier, the President shall terminate any use of United States Armed Forces with respect to which such report was submitted (or required to be submitted), unless the Congress (1) has declared war or has enacted a specific authorization for such use of United States Armed Forces, (2) has extended by law such sixty-day period, or (3) is physically unable to meet as a result of an armed attack upon the United States. Such sixty-day period shall be extended for not more than an additional thirty days if the President determines and certifies to the Congress in writing that unavoidable military necessity respecting the safety of United States Armed Forces requires the continued use of such armed forces in the course of bringing about a prompt removal of such forces.

(c) Notwithstanding subsection (b), at any time that United States Armed Forces are engaged in hostilities outside the territory of the United States, its possessions and territories without a declaration of war or specific statutory authorization, such forces shall be removed by the President if the Congress so directs by concurrent resolution.*

. . . .

INTERPRETATION OF JOINT RESOLUTION

Sec. 8. (a) Authority to introduce United States Armed Forces into hostilities or into situations wherein involvement in hostilities is clearly indicated by the circumstances shall not be inferred—

(1) from any provision of law (whether or not in effect before the date of the enactment of this joint resolution), including any provision

---

* **Eds.' Note:** In 1983 Congress amended the act so as to replace "concurrent resolution" with "joint resolution." See Eds.' Note (5) below.

contained in any appropriation Act, unless such provision specifically authorizes the introduction of United States Armed Forces into hostilities or into such situations and states that it is intended to constitute specific statutory authorization within the meaning of this joint resolution; or

(2) from any treaty heretofore or hereafter ratified unless such treaty is implemented by legislation specifically authorizing the introduction of United States Armed Forces into hostilities or into such situations and stating that it is intended to constitute specific statutory authorization within the meaning of this joint resolution.

(b) Nothing in this joint resolution shall be construed to require any further specific statutory authorization to permit members of United States Armed Forces to participate jointly with members of the armed forces of one or more foreign countries in the headquarters operations of high-level military commands which were established prior to the date of enactment of this joint resolution and pursuant to the United Nations Charter or any treaty ratified by the United States prior to such date.

(c) For purposes of this joint resolution, the term "introduction of United States Armed Forces" includes the assignment of members of such armed forces to command, coordinate, participate in the movement of, or accompany the regular or irregular military forces of any foreign country or government when such military forces are engaged, or there exists an imminent threat that such forces will become engaged, in hostilities.

(d) Nothing in this joint resolution—

(1) is intended to alter the constitutional authority of the Congress or of the President, or the provisions of existing treaties; or

(2) shall be construed as granting any authority to the President with respect to the introduction of United States Armed Forces into hostilities or into situations wherein involvement in hostilities is clearly indicated by the circumstances which authority he would not have had in the absence of this joint resolution.

SEPARABILITY CLAUSE

Sec. 9.   If any provision of this joint resolution or the application thereof to any person or circumstance is held invalid, the remainder of the joint resolution and the application of such provision to any other person or circumstance shall not be affected thereby.

EFFECTIVE DATE

Sec. 10.   This joint resolution shall take effect on the date of its enactment.

Editors' Notes

(1) A Joint Resolution has the same force as a statute. It must be passed by both houses of Congress and (i) signed by the President; or (ii)

remain unsigned for ten days when Congress is in session; or (3) if the President vetoes it, as happened in this instance, be repassed by a two-thirds majority of each house.

(2) **Query**: To what extent can one argue that this joint resolution binds the President more than an ordinary statute because it is explicitly directed at him and only at him, whereas most statutes are general in their coverage? Insofar as this resolution is a congressional interpretation of the President's constitutional power does it bind him at all? What would Jefferson, Jackson, Lincoln, and Franklin Roosevelt say?

(3) **Query**: More narrowly, because § 2 is only a general statement of purpose and policy and does not require any action by the President, does it have any binding force? Is it no more than a statement of Congress' constitutional interpretation? How does its force differ, if at all, from that of §§ 3–4?

(4) **Query**: Six or seven times, President Ford placed American forces in combat or in situations likely to lead to combat; in none of these did he comply with the terms of the War Powers Resolution. President Carter engaged in one such operation, the abortive rescue effort of American diplomats in Iran. He did not have congressional authorization nor did he consult with Congress in advance; but he pulled the mission out before it engaged in hostile action. President Reagan did not follow the resolution's terms when he sent Marines into Lebanon in 1982 or when he invaded Grenada in 1983. In 1983, however, after Marines began taking heavy casualties in Lebanon, he largely complied with the provisions, though without conceding a constitutional obligation to do so. During the resolution's first dozen years, Presidents have ignored rather than defied it. But, suppose a President were to defy the resolution, what counteraction could Congress take? Is it likely that Congress would try to take its case to the Supreme Court? If that happened, is it likely the justices would hear and decide the case on its merits?

(5) Sec. 5(c) of the War Powers Resolution, authorizing Congress, by concurrent resolution, to direct the President to remove American forces from a theater of hostilities outside of the United States or its territories, contains a variant of the legislative veto. Concurrent resolutions are not submitted to the President for his approval or veto. INS v. Chadha (1983; reprinted below, p. 383) held the legislative veto unconstitutional because it removed this power of the President. To forestall challenge on that ground, Congress amended § 5(c) so as to replace "concurrent resolution" with "joint resolution," which, of course, is subject to a presidential veto. 97 Stat. 1062–63 (1983).

(6) For detailed analyses of the Resolution as well as its pre- and postnatal histories, see Robert Scigliano, "The War Powers Resolution and the War Powers," in Jeffrey M. Bessette and Jeffrey Tulis, eds., *The Presidency in the Constitutional Order* (Baton Rouge: Louisiana State University Press, 1981); and Christopher H. Pyle and Richard M. Pious, eds., *The President, Congress and the Constitution* (New York: The Free Press, 1984), chap. 3. See also: Graham T. Allison, "Making War," 40 *L. & Contemp. Probs.* 86 (1976); J. Terry Emerson, "War Powers Resolution Tested," 51 *Notre Dame Lawyer* 187 (1975); and Newell L. Highsmith, "Policing Executive Adventurism," 19 *Harv.J. of Legn.* 327 (1982).

III. INSTITUTIONAL INTEGRITY IN A SYSTEM OF SHARED POWERS

"The Congress is the legislative department of the government; the President is the executive department. Neither can be restrained in its actions by the judicial department; though the acts of both, when performed, are, in proper cases, subject to its cognizance."

MISSISSIPPI v. JOHNSON

71 U.S. (4 Wall.) 475, 18 L.Ed. 437 (1867).

The Chief Justice [**CHASE**] delivered the opinion of the Court.

A motion was made . . . in behalf of the State of Mississippi, for leave to file a bill in the name of the State, praying this court to perpetually enjoin and restrain Andrew Johnson, President of the United States . . . from executing, or in any manner carrying out, certain acts of Congress. . . .

The acts referred to are those of March 2d, and March 23d, 1867, commonly known as the Reconstruction Acts.

The Attorney-General objected to the leave asked for, upon the ground that no bill which makes a President a defendant, and seeks an injunction against him to restrain the performance of his duties as President, should be allowed to be filed in this court. . . .

The single point which requires consideration is this: Can the President be restrained from carrying into effect an act of Congress alleged to be unconstitutional?

It is assumed by the counsel for the State of Mississippi, that the President, in the execution of the Reconstruction Acts, is required to perform a mere ministerial duty. In this assumption there is, we think, a confounding of the terms ministerial and executive, which are by no means equivalent in import.

A ministerial duty, the performance of which may, in proper cases, be required of the head of a department, by judicial process, is one in respect to which nothing is left to discretion. It is a simple, definite duty, arising under conditions admitted or proved to exist, and imposed by law.

The case of Marbury v. Madison [1803] furnishes an illustration. A citizen had been nominated, confirmed, and appointed a justice of the peace for the District of Columbia, and his commission had been made out, signed, and sealed. Nothing remained to be done except delivery, and the duty of delivery was imposed by law on the Secretary of State. It was held that the performance of this duty might be enforced by mandamus issuing from a court having jurisdiction.

So, in the case of Kendall, Postmaster-General v. Stockton & Stokes [1838] an act of Congress had directed the Postmaster-General to credit Stockton & Stokes with such sums as the Solicitor of the Treasury should find due to them; and that officer refused to credit them with certain sums, so found due. It was held that the crediting of this money was a mere ministerial duty, the performance of which might be judicially enforced.

In each of these cases nothing was left to discretion. There was no room for the exercise of judgment. The law required the performance of a single specific act; and that performance, it was held, might be required by mandamus.

Very different is the duty of the President in the exercise of the power to see that the laws are faithfully executed, and among these laws the acts named in the bill. By the first of these acts he is required to assign generals to command in the several military districts, and to detail sufficient military force to enable such officers to discharge their duties under the law. By the supplementary act, other duties are imposed on the several commanding generals, and these duties must necessarily be performed under the supervision of the President as commander-in-chief. The duty thus imposed on the President is in no just sense ministerial. It is purely executive and political.

An attempt on the part of the judicial department of the government to enforce the performance of such duties by the President might be justly characterized, in the language of Chief Justice Marshall, as "an absurd and excessive extravagance."

It is true that in the instance before us the interposition of the court is not sought to enforce action by the Executive under constitutional legislation, but to restrain such action under legislation alleged to be unconstitutional. But we are unable to perceive that this circumstance takes the case out of the general principles which forbid judicial interference with the exercise of Executive discretion.

It was admitted in the argument that the application now made to us is without a precedent; and this is of much weight against it.

Had it been supposed at the bar that this court would, in any case, interpose, by injunction, to prevent the execution of an unconstitutional act of Congress, it can hardly be doubted that applications with that object would have been heretofore addressed to it.

Occasions have not been wanting. . . .

It will hardly be contended that Congress [the courts?] can interpose, in any case, to restrain the enactment of an unconstitutional law; and yet how can the right to judicial interposition to prevent such an enactment, when the purpose is evident and the execution of that purpose certain, be distinguished, in principle, from the right to such interposition against the execution of such a law by the President?

The Congress is the legislative department of the government; the President is the executive department. Neither can be restrained in its action by the judicial department; though the acts of both, when performed, are, in proper cases, subject to its cognizance.

The impropriety of such interference will be clearly seen upon consideration of its possible consequences.

Suppose the bill filed and the injunction prayed for allowed. If the President refuse obedience, it is needless to observe that the court is without power to enforce its process. If, on the other hand, the

President complies with the order of the court and refuses to execute the acts of Congress, is it not clear that a collision may occur between the executive and legislative departments of the government? May not the House of Representatives impeach the President for such refusal? And in that case could this court interfere, in behalf of the President, thus endangered by compliance with its mandate, and restrain by injunction the Senate of the United States from sitting as a court of impeachment? Would the strange spectacle be offered to the public wonder of an attempt by this court to arrest proceedings in that court?

These questions answer themselves. . . .

It has been suggested that the bill contains a prayer that, if the relief sought cannot be had against Andrew Johnson, as President, it may be granted against Andrew Johnson as a citizen of Tennessee. But it is plain that relief as against the execution of an act of Congress by Andrew Johnson, is relief against its execution by the President. A bill praying an injunction against the execution of an act of Congress by the incumbent of the presidential office cannot be received, whether it describes him as President or as a citizen of a State.

The motion for leave to file the bill is, therefore,

Denied.

Editors' Notes

(1) Within a few days, Georgia officials tried a different tack. They sued under the Court's original jurisdiction asking for an injunction against the Secretary of War, forbidding him to enforce the Reconstruction Acts. The Court dismissed the suits: "[T]he rights for the protection of which our authority is invoked, are the rights of sovereignty, of political jurisdiction, of government, of corporate existence as a State, with all its constitutional powers and privileges. No case of private rights or private property . . . is presented by the bill, in a judicial form, for the judgment of the court." Georgia v. Stanton (1867).

(2) The timing in these cases—the question of WHEN to interpret—was critical. *Mississippi* was argued in April and *Georgia* in May of 1867. Ex parte McCardle (1867; reprinted below, p. 361) had been argued in March, and Congress had removed the Court's appellate jurisdiction a few weeks later, just before these two cases were argued. Furthermore, the House had recently impeached President Johnson and his trial was scheduled to begin soon in the Senate. Thus there was no doubt that the Radical Republicans were firmly in control of Congress, were determined to curb the presidency, and were even more determined to maintain martial law in the South. The justices, as in *McCardle,* undoubtedly thought it wiser to avoid unnecessary conflict with such a Congress.

(3) For general discussions of constitutional interpretation during Reconstruction see: Michael Les Benedict, *A Compromise of Principle* (New York: Norton, 1974); Charles Fairman, *Reconstruction and Reunion, 1864–1888* (New York: Macmillan, 1971); Harold M. Hyman, *A More Perfect Union* (New

York: Knopf, 1973); and Stanley I. Kutler, *Judicial Power and Reconstruction Politics* (Chicago: University of Chicago Press, 1968).

" 'The Executive is as independent of either house of Congress as either house of Congress is independent of him . . . .' "

TRUMAN REFUSES TO OBEY A SUBPOENA *

In 1953, almost a year after Harry S Truman had left the presidency, the House Committee on Un-American Activities subpoenaed him to appear and testify. The committee was planning to question him about "subversives" who had been in the federal government during his administration, in particular about Harry Dexter White, an alleged Soviet spy. Mr. Truman responded in a letter to the committee's chairman.

Dear Sir:

I have your subpoena dated Nov. 9, 1953, directing my appearance before your committee on Friday, Nov. 13, in Washington. The subpoena does not state the matters upon which you seek my testimony, but I assume from the press stories that you seek to examine me with respect to matters which occurred during my tenure of the Presidency of the United States.

In spite of my personal willingness to cooperate with your committee, I feel constrained by my duty to the people of the United States to decline to comply with the subpoena.

In doing so, I am carrying out the provisions of the Constitution of the United States; and am following a long line of precedents, commencing with George Washington himself in 1796. Since his day, Presidents Jefferson, Monroe, Jackson, Tyler, Polk, Fillmore, Buchanan, Lincoln, Grant, Hayes, Cleveland, Theodore Roosevelt, Coolidge, Hoover and Franklin D. Roosevelt have declined to respond to subpoenas or demands for information of various kinds by Congress.

The underlying reason for this clearly established and universally recognized constitutional doctrine has been succinctly set forth by Charles Warren, one of our leading constitutional authorities, as follows:

> In this long series of contests by the Executive to maintain his constitutional integrity, one sees a legitimate conclusion from our theory of government. . . . Under our Constitution, each branch of the Government is designed to be a coordinate representative of the will of the people. . . . Defense by the Executive of his constitutional powers becomes in very truth, therefore, defense of popular rights— defense of power which the people granted to him.

It was in that sense that President Cleveland spoke of his duty to the people not to relinquish any of the powers of his great office. It was in that sense that President Buchanan stated the people have rights and prerogatives in the execution of his office by the President

---

* From the files of the House UnAmerican Activities Committee.

which every President is under a duty to see "shall never be violated in his person" but "passed to his successors unimpaired by the adoption of a dangerous precedent." In maintaining his rights against a trespassing Congress, the President defends not himself, but popular government; he represents not himself but the people.

President Jackson repelled an attempt by the Congress to break down the separation of powers in these words:

> For myself I shall repel all such attempts as an invasion of the principles of justice as well as of the Constitution, and I shall esteem it my sacred duty to the people of the United States to resist them as I would the establishment of a Spanish Inquisition.

I might commend to your reading the opinion of one of the committees of the House of Representatives in 1879, House Report 141, March 3, 1879, Forty-fifth Congress, Third Session, in which the House Judiciary Committee said the following:

> The Executive is as independent of either house of Congress as either house of Congress is independent of him, and they cannot call for the records of his actions, or the action of his officers against his consent, any more than he can call for any of the journals or records of the House or Senate.

It must be obvious to you that if the doctrine of separation of powers and the independence of the Presidency is to have any validity at all, it must be equally applicable to a President after his term of office has expired when he is sought to be examined with respect to any acts occurring while he is President.

The doctrine would be shattered, and the President, contrary to our fundamental theory of constitutional government, would become a mere arm of the Legislative Branch of the Government if he would feel during his term of office that his every act might be subject to official inquiry and possible distortion for political purposes.

If your intention, however, is to inquire into any acts as a private individual either before or after my Presidency and unrelated to any acts as President, I shall be happy to appear.

Yours Very Truly,
Harry S Truman

"I, too, shall adhere to this precedent."

NIXON REFUSES TO TESTIFY *

In February, 1977, Rep. Lester L. Wolff (Dem., N.Y.) invited former President Richard M. Nixon to testify before the Subcommittee on Asian and Pacific Affairs of the House Committee on International Relations on the question of obligations the United States might have undertaken in its cease-

---

* From the files of the House Subcommittee on Asian and Pacific Affairs.

fire agreement with North Vietnam to provide economic aid to that country. Nixon responded on May 14, 1977.

Dear Congressman Wolff:

As I am sure you are aware, your request of February 22 presents some fundamental and serious constitutional questions.

In 1953 a Committee of the House of Representatives sought to subpoena former President Truman to inquire about matters of which he had personal knowledge while he served as President. President Truman's response states what I believe is the correct constitutional guideline which a former President must follow . . . .

I, too, shall adhere to this precedent. However, because the issue of aid to the Hanoi Government is currently under consideration in the Congress, and without waiving the separation-of-powers principle, I want to be as helpful as I can in providing voluntarily my recollection of events surrounding the aid negotiation . . . . [Nixon then gave a detailed account of his remembrances and concluded that there was "no commitment of any kind, moral or legal, to provide aid to the Hanoi Government."]

"We are not at liberty to inquire into the motives of the legislature. We can only examine its power under the Constitution . . . ."

EX PARTE McCARDLE
74 U.S. (7 Wall.) 506, 19 L.Ed. 264 (1869).

As part of its plan of Reconstruction, the Radical Republicans in Congress pushed through statutes instituting martial law in the former Confederate states. In 1861, Chief Justice Roger Brooke Taney, riding circuit, had held unconstitutional Lincoln's use of military rule in Maryland during the early stages of the Civil War. Ex parte Merryman. (See below, Chapter 18.) Shortly after the war, in Ex parte Milligan (1866; reprinted below, p. 1190) the full Supreme Court declared unconstitutional that part of Lincoln's program, carried through without statutory authorization, using martial law in border states during the war. All nine justices agreed that the President, acting alone, had no such authority, and five went out of their way to say that even Congress could not have authorized trials of civilians by courts martial in areas where the dangers of war were not so severe as to make it impossible for regular civilian courts to operate.

Milligan thus threw a constitutional pall over military rule of the South, a policy the Radicals considered to be the heart of their program. The occasion for a test soon developed. The army arrested William McCardle, a bitter ex-Confederate colonel turned newspaper editor in Mississippi. He was charged with disturbing the peace and impeding Reconstruction by publishing editorials urging white people to boycott elections sponsored by the military government and threatening to publish the names of "the cowards, dogs and scoundrels" who did participate. While he was being held for trial by a court martial, he sought habeas corpus from a circuit court, and on losing appealed to the

Supreme Court. Ironically, he invoked not the Judiciary Act of 1789 but a statute Congress had enacted in 1867 to protect federal officers administering Reconstruction.

The Court set the case down for argument in early March, 1868. Chief counsel for McCardle was the noted former judge and sometime Reporter of the Supreme Court, Jeremiah S. Black, who had also successfully argued *Milligan.* His strategy "was nothing less than to free the Old South from the grasp of Congress,"[1] a plan that was evident to Radical leaders. To prevent the judicial axe from falling on their program, they looked to Article III, § 2 of the Constitution:

> In all other cases before mentioned, the supreme court shall have appellate jurisdiction, both as to law and fact, with such exceptions, and under such regulations as the Congress shall make.

Argument closed on March 9. By March 27, Congress had passed, President Johnson (though under impeachment and awaiting trial by the Senate) had vetoed, and Congress had repassed over his veto a bill repealing the act of 1867 that McCardle had used to get his case before the Court. Very much aware of the Radicals' mood, the justices delayed a decision while repeal was going through the legislative process. Justices Stephen Field and Robert Grier dissented. Grier's memorandum—never published in the official reports—was angry:

> By the postponement of the case we shall subject ourselves, whether justly or unjustly, to the imputation that we have evaded the performance of a duty imposed on us by the Constitution, and have waited for legislation to interpose to supersede our action and relieve us from our responsibility. I am not willing to be a partaker of the eulogy or opprobrium that may follow . . . .[2]

Jeremiah Black's comment was even more scathing: "The court stood still to be ravished and did not even hallo while the thing was getting done . . . ."[3]

The justices set reargument for the following term on the question whether the Court had jurisdiction to decide the case on its merits.

The Chief Justice [**CHASE**] delivered the opinion of the court.

The first question necessarily is that of jurisdiction; for, if the act of March, 1868, takes away the jurisdiction defined by the act of February, 1867, it is useless, if not improper, to enter into any discussion of other questions.

It is quite true, as was argued by the counsel for the petitioner, that the appellate jurisdiction of this court is not derived from acts of Congress. It is, strictly speaking, conferred by the Constitution. But it is conferred "with such exceptions and under such regulations as Congress shall make." . . .

The source of that jurisdiction, and the limitations of it by the Constitution and by statute, have been on several occasions subjects of

---

1. Charles Fairman, *Reconstruction and Reunion 1864–1888* (New York: Macmillan, 1971), I, 456.

2. Quoted in ibid., 474.

3. Ibid., 478.

consideration here. In the case of Durousseau v. The United States [1810], particularly, the whole matter was carefully examined, and the court held, that while "the appellate powers of this court are not given by the judicial act, but are given by the Constitution," they are, nevertheless, "limited and regulated by that act, and by such other acts as have been passed on the subject." The court said, further, that the judicial act was an exercise of the power given by the Constitution to Congress "of making exceptions to the appellate jurisdiction of the Supreme Court." "They have described affirmatively," said the court, "its jurisdiction, and this affirmative description has been understood to imply a negation of the exercise of such appellate power as is not comprehended within it."

The principle that the affirmation of appellate jurisdiction implies the negation of all such jurisdiction not affirmed having been thus established, it was an almost necessary consequence that acts of Congress, providing for the exercise of jurisdiction, should come to be spoken of as acts granting jurisdiction, and not as acts making exceptions to the constitutional grant of it.

The exception to appellate jurisdiction in the case before us, however, is not an inference from the affirmation of other appellate jurisdiction. . . . The provision of the act of 1867, affirming the appellate jurisdiction of this court in cases of *habeas corpus* is expressly repealed. It is hardly possible to imagine a plainer instance of positive exception.

We are not at liberty to inquire into the motives of the legislature. We can only examine into its power under the Constitution; and the power to make exceptions to the appellate jurisdiction of this court is given by express words.

What, then, is the effect of the repealing act upon the case before us? We cannot doubt as to this. Without jurisdiction the court cannot proceed at all in any cause. Jurisdiction is power to declare the law, and when it ceases to exist, the only function remaining to the court is that of announcing the fact and dismissing the cause. And this is not less clear upon authority than upon principle . . . .

It is quite clear, therefore, that this court cannot proceed to pronounce judgment in this case, for it has no longer jurisdiction of the appeal; and judicial duty is not less fitly performed by declining ungranted jurisdiction than in exercising firmly that which the Constitution and the laws confer.

Counsel seem to have supposed, if effect be given to the repealing act in question, that the whole appellate power of the court, in cases of *habeas corpus,* is denied. But this is an error. The act of 1868 does not except from that jurisdiction any cases but appeals from Circuit Courts under the act of 1867. It does not affect the jurisdiction which was previously exercised.

The appeal of the petitioner in this case must be

Dismissed for want of jurisdiction.

Editors' Notes

(1) One should read carefully the last substantive paragraph in the Chief Justice's opinion. Ex parte Yerger (1869) came up shortly after *McCardle;* there the Court ruled it had appellate jurisdiction because the litigant had invoked the Act of 1789, not the repealed statute of 1867.

(2) **Query**: Does *McCardle* imply that Congress could use its power to make exceptions to the justice's jurisdiction so as in effect to cripple the Court? Is there a constitutional difference between making an exception and abolishing an entire bloc of jurisdiction? Does the term "exceptions" imply a significant residuum? Prof. Henry M. Hart has argued: "[T]he exceptions must not be such as will destroy the essential role of the Supreme Court in the constitutional plan." ("The Power of Congress to Limit the Jurisdiction of Federal Courts," 66 *Harv.L.Rev.* 1362, 1365 [1953].) Invoking either a broad theory of constitutionalism or narrower structuralist view of the Constitution as requiring three branches of government that can effectively function, the Court might invalidate any drastic effort at jurisdictional surgery.

And some justices have hinted at just such a possibility. In *Yerger* Chief Justice Chase noted the circumstances in *McCardle* were "peculiar." Almost a century later, in a diversity case that splintered the Court into three factions, Justices Harlan, Brennan, and Stewart reasoned by analogy that, if Congress could make exceptions to the Supreme Court's jurisdiction, it could also do so to that of the Court of Claims. But they promptly added, "The authority is not, of course, unlimited." This disclaimer was not sufficient for Douglas and Black. They chided Harlan et al. for even citing *McCardle* with approval, noting, "There is a serious question whether the McCardle Case could command a majority view today." Glidden v. Zdanok (1962).

Perhaps *McCardle* stands for only two propositions: (1) In times of political crisis, the justices are not apt to take on the dominant branch of government—and with the President impeached, the Radicals in command of Congress, and the more extreme among them making threats about abolishing the Court, Congress in 1868–69 was the dominant branch and seemed determined to exploit its dominance; and (2) Even in a crisis, or perhaps especially in a crisis, the justices are willing to take—and suffer—great pains to retain control not only over HOW but also WHEN they will interpret the Constitution.

(3) For analyses that take a narrow view of the reach of congressional authority to control the Court's appellate jurisdiction, see in addition to Hart, cited above: Lawrence G. Sager, "Congressional Limitations on Congress' Authority to Regulate the Appellate Jurisdiction of the Federal Courts," 95 *Harv.L.Rev.* 17 (1981); and Gerald Gunther, "Congressional Power to Curtail Federal Court Jurisdiction," 36 *Stan.L.Rev.* 895 (1984). For analyses that take a broad view of congressional authority, see: Michael J. Perry, *The Constitution, the Courts, and Human Rights* (New Haven, Conn.: Yale University Press, 1982), pp. 129–145; and Herbert Wechsler, "The Court and the Constitution," 65 *Colum.L.Rev.* 1001 (1965). For an ingenious discussion of the problem of congressional control over the Court's appellate jurisdiction in the broader context of the structure of the national government, see Charles L. Black, "The Presidency and Congress," 32 *Wash. & Lee L.Rev.* 841 (1975);

(4) For the background of *McCardle,* see especially: Charles Fairman, *Reconstruction and Reunion 1864–1888* (New York: Macmillan, 1971), I, chap.

10; Harold M. Hyman, *A More Perfect Union* (New York: Knopf, 1973), chap. 27; and Stanley L. Kutler, *Judicial Power and Reconstruction Politics* (Chicago: University of Chicago Press, 1968).

(5) **Query:** To what extent can Congress frustrate judicial review by granting federal courts jurisdiction to enforce statutes but at the same time denying them authority to determine the constitutionality of those statutes? During World War II, the Emergency Price Control Act provided for criminal prosecutions in federal district courts but limited jurisdiction to hear attacks on the constitutionality of price control regulations to a special tribunal, the Emergency Court of Appeals, staffed by three federal judges serving during good behavior. The Supreme Court could review by certiorari. In Yakus v. United States (1944) the Court sustained this arrangement. The majority opinion, written by Chief Justice Stone, said:

> There is no constitutional requirement that that test [of constitutionality] be made in one tribunal rather than in another, so long as there is opportunity to be heard and for judicial review which satisfies the demands of due process, as is the case here.

Dissenting for himself and Justice Murphy, Rutledge protested:

> It is one thing for Congress to withhold jurisdiction. It is entirely another to confer it and direct that it be exercised in a manner inconsistent with constitutional requirements or . . . without regard to them. Once it is held that Congress can require the courts criminally to enforce unconstitutional laws or statutes . . . or to do so without regard to their validity, the way will have been found to circumvent the supreme law and, what is more, to make the courts parties to doing so. This Congress cannot do.

Rutledge continued:

> There are limits to the judicial power. Congress may impose others. And in some matters Congress or the President has final say under the Constitution. But whenever the judicial power is called into play, it is responsible directly to the fundamental law and no other authority can intervene to force or authorize the judicial body to disregard it. The problem therefore is not solely one of individual right or due process of law. It is equally one of the separation of the powers of government and of the constitutional integrity of the judicial process, more especially in criminal trials.

Yakus, like *McCardle,* was decided in the midst of crisis; and Stone's opinion, like Chase's, indicated the justices were well aware of the troubled times in which they were living. "The Constitution as a continuously operative charter of government does not," Stone wrote, "demand the impossible or the impracticable."

"I believe that the Senators are entitled to know how you feel . . . ."

HEARINGS ON THE NOMINATION OF WILLIAM J. BRENNAN, JR., TO BE AN ASSOCIATE JUSTICE OF THE U.S. SUPREME COURT *

In September 1956, during the middle of that year's presidential campaign, Justice Sherman Minton announced his retirement. As his successor, President Dwight D. Eisenhower chose William J. Brennan, Jr.; and because the Senate was not in session, the President, as the plain words of Article II, § 3 of the Constitution authorize, gave Brennan a recess appointment that would expire at the close of the next session of Congress. He immediately took his place on the Court and began participating in decision making. As soon as Congress reconvened in January 1957, the President sent Brennan's nomination to the Senate for its advice and consent on his appointment during "good behavior." The Committee on the Judiciary then conducted its hearings.

SENATOR JOSEPH MCCARTHY of Wisconsin. . . . On the basis of that part of his record that I am familiar with, I believe that Justice Brennan has demonstrated an underlying hostility to congressional attempts to expose the Communist conspiracy.

I can only conclude that his decisions on the Supreme Court are likely to harm our efforts to fight communism.

I shall, therefore, vote against his confirmation unless he is able to persuade me today that I am not in possession of the true facts with respect to his views.

I shall want to know if it is true that Justice Brennan, in his public speeches, has referred to congressional investigations of communism, for example, as "Salem witch hunts," and "inquisitions," and has accused congressional investigating committees of "barbarism."

I have evidence that he has done so . . . .

I would like to ask Mr. Brennan a few questions if I may . . . . Do you approve of congressional investigations and exposure of the Communist conspiracy set up?

Mr. BRENNAN. Not only do I approve, Senator, but personally I cannot think of a more vital function of the Congress than the investigatory function of its committees, and I can't think of a more important or vital objective of any committee investigation than that of rooting out subversives in Government.

Senator MCCARTHY. You, of course, I assume, will agree with me—and a number of the members of the committee—that communism is not merely a political way of life, it is a conspiracy designed to overthrow the United States Government.

Mr. BRENNAN. Will you forgive me an embarrassment, Senator. You appreciate that I am a sitting Justice of the Court. There are presently pending before the Court some cases in which I believe will have to be decided the question what is communism, at least in the

---

* *Hearings* before the Committee on the Judiciary, U.S. Senate, on the Nomination of William J. Brennan Jr. to be an Associate Justice of the U.S. Supreme Court, 85th Congress, 1st Session, pp. 5, 17–22, 34.

frame of reference in which those particular cases have come before the Court.

I know, too, that you appreciate that having taken an oath of office it is my obligation not to discuss any of those pending matters. With that qualification, whether under the label communism or any other label, any conspiracy to overthrow the Government of the United States is a conspiracy that I not only would do anything appropriate to aid suppressing, but a conspiracy which, of course, like every American, I abhor.

Senator McCARTHY. Mr. Brennan, I don't want to press you unnecessarily, but the question was simple. You have not been confirmed yet as a member of the Supreme Court. There will come before that Court a number of questions involving the all-important issue of whether or not communism is merely a political party or whether it represents a conspiracy to overthrow this Government.

I believe that the Senators are entitled to know how you feel about that and you won't be prejudicing then any cases by answering that question.

Mr. BRENNAN. Well, let me answer it, try to answer it, this way, Senator. Of course, my nomination is now before the Senate for consideration, nevertheless since October 16 I have in fact been sitting as a member of the Court. The oath I took, I took as unreservedly as I know you took your own, and as I know every Senator took his. And I know, too, that your oath imposes upon you the obligation to ask just such questions as these.

But I am in the position of having an oath of my own by which I have to guide my conduct and that oath obligates me not to discuss any matter presently pending before the Court . . . .

Senator McCARTHY. Mr. Brennan, we are asked to either vote to confirm or reject you. One of the things I have maintained is that you have adopted the gobbledegook that communism is merely a political party, it is not a conspiracy.

The Supreme Court has held that it is a conspiracy to overthrow the Government of this country. I am merely asking you a very simple question.

It doesn't relate to any lawsuit pending before the Supreme Court. Let me repeat it.

Do you consider communism merely as a political party or do you consider it as a conspiracy to overthrow this country?

Mr. BRENNAN. I can only answer, Senator, that believe me there are cases now pending in which the contention is made, at least in the frame of reference in which the case comes to the Court, that the definitions which have been given by the Congress to communism do not fit the particular circumstances . . . .

Senator McCARTHY. You know that the Congress has defined communism as a conspiracy. You are aware of that, aren't you?

Mr. BRENNAN. I know the Congress has enacted a definition, yes, sir.

Senator McCarthy. And I think it is important before we vote on your confirmation that we know whether you agree with that?

Mr. Brennan. You see, Senator, that is my difficulty, that I can't very well say more to you than that there are contending positions taken in given cases before us . . . .

Senator McCarthy . . . . This is all important, I would like to know whether or not the young man who is proposed for the Supreme Court feels that communism is a conspiracy or merely a political party. Now just so you won't be in the dark about my reason for asking that, the Daily Worker, all of the Communist-lip papers, and the Communist witnesses who have appeared before my committee, I assume the same is true of Senator Eastland's committee, have taken the position that it is merely a political party. I want to know whether you agree with that. That will affect your decision. It will affect my decision on how to vote on your confirmation. I hope it will affect the decision of other Senators.

Mr. Brennan. Senator, believe me I appreciate that what to one man is the path of duty may to another man be the path of folly, but I simply cannot venture any comment whatever that touches upon any matter pending before the Court.

Senator McCarthy. Mr. Brennan, I am not asking you to touch upon anything pending before the Court. I am asking you the general question:

Do you consider communism merely as a political party or do you consider it as a conspiracy to overthrow this country? . . .

Mr. Brennan. Senator, I cannot answer, I am sorry to say, beyond what I have . . . .

Senator O'Mahoney. Just let me clarify this. The Senator from Wisconsin has made it perfectly clear, as I understand it, that he is not asking the Justice to make any statement with respect to a pending case. Therefore, the oath of office that the Justice may have taken is not involved.

Senator McCarthy. Right.

Senator O'Mahoney. There is now pending before the Senate a resolution, sent here by the executive branch of the Government, by the President of the United States, who appeared before us in a joint session of Congress in which he asked Congress to pass a resolution authorizing him to employ the Armed Forces of the United States in the defense of any nation in the Middle East, undescribed though the Middle East was in the resolution, at the request of any nation there, which was being attacked by international communism.

Now the question I think that is in the mind of the Senator from Wisconsin is the question which I think has already been settled and on which you must have clear views. Do you believe that international communism is a conspiracy against the United States as well as against all other free nations?

Mr. Brennan. Yes, that question I answer definitely and affirmatively. I did not understand that was the question the Senator was asking me . . . .

Senator JENNER. May I interrupt right there? Does the Senator from Wyoming and does the Senator from Wisconsin draw a distinction between international communism and communism?

Senator O'MAHONEY. I don't.

Senator MCCARTHY. I don't draw a distinction.

Senator JENNER. I would like to know Mr. Justice Brennan's answer to that. Do you draw a distinction between international communism and communism?

Mr. BRENNAN. Let me put it this way, Senator. This is the difficulty. There are cases where, as I recall it, the particular issue is whether membership, what is membership, and whether if there is membership, does that come within the purview of the congressional statutes aimed at the conspiracy? I can't necessarily comment on those aspects because they are actual issues before the Court under the congressional legislation.

Senator JENNER. That is why it raises a question in my mind. In other words, if we have a Communist Party in the United States and the congressional committee has ascertained that it is hooked up with international communism, yet the domestic party might contend they are just national Communists, would that influence your thinking?

Mr. BRENNAN. Nothing would influence my thinking. All I am trying to get across is that I do have an obligation not to discuss any issues that are touched upon in cases before the Court.

Senator JENNER. I think in the question that Senator O'Mahoney placed—read the question, will you, please, Mr. Reporter, and the answer?

(Question and answer read.)

Senator JENNER. Delete the word "international" and just leave in the word "communism," what would be your answer?

Mr. BRENNAN. Of course, I accept the findings as they have been made by the Congress. The only thing I am trying to do, Senator, is to make certain that nothing I say touches upon the actual issues before us growing out of that legislation as applied in particular cases . . . .

Senator JENNER. My question, Mr. Chairman, was not based on cases pending. My question was in a similar vein.

In view of that would you answer the question?

Mr. BRENNAN. The answer is "Yes." I'm sorry to have confused the gentlemen.

The CHAIRMAN. Senator McCarthy, you may proceed.

Senator MCCARTHY. Let's see if we finally have the answer to this, Mr. Justice. You do agree that communism, striking the word "international" from it, communism does constitute a conspiracy against the United States—I am not talking about any case pending.

Mr. BRENNAN. Yes.

Senator MCCARTHY. Thank you . . . .

Senator O'MAHONEY. Mr. Chairman, let me address the question to the nominee, Associate Justice Brennan. I read it again from the statement filed with this committee under date of February 26, 1957, by Mr. Charles Smith.

> You are bound by your religion to follow the pronouncements of the Pope on all matters of faith and morals. There may be some controversies which involve matters of faith and morals and also matters of law and justice. But in matters of law and justice, you are bound by your oath to follow not papal decrees and doctrines, but the laws and precedents of this Nation. If you should be faced with such a mixed issue, would you be able to follow the requirements of your oath or would you be bound by your religious obligations?

Mr. BRENNAN. Senator, I think the oath that I took is the same one that you and all of the Congress, every member of the executive department up and down all levels of government take to support the Constitution and laws of the United States. I took that oath just as unreservedly as I know you did, and every member and everyone else of our faith in whatever office elected or appointive he may hold. And I say not that I recognize that there is any obligation superior to that, rather that there isn't any obligation of our faith superior to that. And my answer to the question is categorically that in everything I have ever done, in every office I have held in my life or that I shall ever do in the future, what shall control me is the oath that I took to support the Constitution and laws of the United States and so act upon the cases that come before me for decision that it is that oath and that alone which governs . . . .

Editors' Notes

(1) Soon after confirmation, Brennan joined in several rulings, most notably Watkins v. United States (1957), restricting the power of Congress to investigate, and others, especially Yates v. United States (1957; reprinted below, p. 519), curtailing congressional efforts to outlaw domestic communism.

(2) Eisenhower also had given recess appointments to Earl Warren as Chief Justice and Potter Stewart. In each instance, having to sit for some months before being confirmed caused embarrassment for the justices and at least some senators. See the staff study of the House Committee on the Judiciary, *Recess Appointment of Federal Judges*, 86th Cong., 1st Sess. (1959). In 1960, the Senate passed S.Res. 334, stating that it was the sense of the Senate that the President should not make recess appointments to the Supreme Court except to prevent or end a breakdown in the administration of the Court's business. The vote, 48–37, was strictly along party lines, not surprising considering that the Senate was controlled by the Democrats and Eisenhower was a Republican.

(3) In 1984, a panel of the Court of Appeals for the Ninth Circuit (courts of appeals normally sit in panels of three judges to review decisions of district courts) vacated a federal conviction resulting from a trial conducted by a judge who had a recess appointment. The court reasoned that a judge whose confirmation was pending would "scarcely be oblivious to the effect his decision may have on the vote of those officials," and Article III requires

federal judicial power be exercised only by judges who were truly independent, that is, serving during good behavior. Woodley v. United States. On rehearing, the full Court of Appeals, sitting en banc, reversed the panel and reinstated the conviction. United States v. Woodley (1985). Woodley did not seek certiorari from the Supreme Court.

(4) *Woodley* raises very important issues of constitutional interpretation. First, the panel's opinion questions the validity of decisions in which Brennan and Warren may have played significant roles before their confirmations—for Warren the School Segregation Cases (1954; reprinted below, p. 768) are the most obvious. Although he was confirmed before the decision was announced, he held a recess appointment during crucial stages of decision making. Second, although the panel's opinion in *Woodley* did not explicitly say so, it must be logically based on a conception of the Constitution as including a hierarchy of values. That is, the *panel* —though not the full Court of Appeals—held, in effect, that a specific clause authorizing the President to make recess appointments must give way to the higher value of an independent judiciary, even though the document does not explicitly state that value and does explicitly authorize recess appointments.

IV. INSTITUTIONAL INTERACTIONS IN A SYSTEM OF SHARED POWERS

" '[The Constitution] enjoins upon its branches separateness but interdependence, autonomy but reciprocity' "

BUCKLEY v. VALEO

424 U.S. 1, 96 S.Ct. 612, 46 L.Ed.2d 659 (1976).

In the Federal Election Campaign Act of 1974, Congress provided subsidies for and extensive regulations of presidential campaigning. To administer this complex statute, Congress established the Federal Election Commission, composed of eight members. The President would nominate two members, subject to confirmation by *both* the Senate and the House; the president pro tem of the Senate and the speaker of the House would each choose two members; and the remaining two, non-voting members, would be the secretary of the Senate and the clerk of the House of Representatives, serving ex officio.

(Portions of this case dealing with campaign practices and federal financing are reprinted in Chapter 12, at p. 677. Here we are concerned solely with the Court's handling of the challenge to the way in which the Commission was chosen.)

PER CURIAM . . . .

Appellants urge that since Congress has given the Commission wide-ranging rule-making and enforcement powers with respect to the substantive provisions of the Act, Congress is precluded under the principle of separation of powers from vesting in itself the authority to appoint those who will exercise such authority. Their argument is based on the language of Art. II, § 2, cl. 2, of the Constitution . . . . :

> [The President] shall nominate, and by and with the Advice and
> Consent of the Senate, shall appoint . . . all other Officers of the
> United States, whose Appointments are not herein otherwise provided
> for, and which shall be established by Law: but the Congress may by
> Law vest the Appointment of such inferior Officers, as they think
> proper, in the President alone, in the Courts of Law, or in the Heads of
> Departments.

Appellants' argument is that this provision is the exclusive method
by which those charged with executing the laws of the United States
may be chosen . . . . If the Legislature wishes the Commission to
exercise all of the conferred powers, then its members are in fact
"Officers of the United States" and must be appointed under the
Appointments Clause. But if Congress insists upon retaining the power
to appoint, then the members of the Commission may not discharge
those many functions of the Commission which can be performed only
by "Officers of the United States," as that term must be construed
within the doctrine of separation of powers.

Appellee Commission and amici in support of the Commission urge
that the Framers of the Constitution, while mindful of the need for
checks and balances among the three branches of the National Government, had no intention of denying to the Legislative Branch authority
to appoint its own officers. Congress, either under the Appointments
Clause or under its grants of substantive legislative authority and the
Necessary and Proper Clause in Art. I, is in their view empowered to
provide for the appointment to the Commission in the manner which it
did because the Commission is performing "appropriate legislative
functions." . . .

1. Separation of Powers . . .

James Madison, writing in the *Federalist* No. 47, defended the
work of the Framers against the charge that these three governmental
powers were not *entirely* separate from one another in the proposed
Constitution. He asserted that while there was some admixture, the
Constitution was nonetheless true to Montesquieu's well known maxim
that the legislative, executive, and judicial departments ought to be
separate and distinct. . . .

Yet it is also clear from the provisions of the Constitution itself,
and from the Federalist Papers, that the Constitution by no means
contemplates total separation of each of these three essential branches
of Government. The President is a participant in the lawmaking
process by virtue of his authority to veto bills enacted by Congress.
The Senate is a participant in the appointive process by virtue of its
authority to refuse to confirm persons nominated to office by the
President. The men who met in Philadelphia in the summer of 1787
were practical statesmen, experienced in politics, who viewed the principle of separation of powers as a vital check against tyranny. But they
likewise saw that a hermetic sealing off of the three branches of

Government from one another would preclude the establishment of a Nation capable of governing itself effectively. . . .

. . . Mr. Justice Jackson, concurring in the opinion and the judgment of the Court in Youngstown Sheet & Tube Co. v. Sawyer (1952), succinctly characterized this understanding:

> While the Constitution diffuses power the better to secure liberty, it also contemplates that practice will integrate the dispersed powers into a workable government. It enjoins upon its branches separateness but interdependence, autonomy but reciprocity.

The Framers regarded the checks and balances that they had built into the tripartite Federal Government as a self-executing safeguard against the encroachment or aggrandizement of one branch at the expense of the other . . . .

This Court has not hesitated to enforce the principle of separation of powers embodied in the Constitution when its application has proved necessary for the decisions of cases or controversies properly before it. The Court has held that executive or administrative duties of a nonjudicial nature may not be imposed on judges holding office under Art. III of the Constitution. United States v. Ferreira (1852); Hayburn's Case (1792). The Court has held that the President may not execute and exercise legislative authority belonging only to Congress. *Youngstown.*

. . .

More closely in point to the facts of the present case is this Court's decision in Springer v. Philippine Islands (1928), where the Court held that the legislature of the Philippine Islands could not provide for legislative appointment to executive agencies.

2. The Appointments Clause

The principle of separation of powers was not simply an abstract generalization in the minds of the Framers: it was woven into the document that they drafted . . . . Article I, § 1, declares: "All legislative Powers herein granted shall be vested in a Congress of the United States." Article II, § 1, vests the executive power "in a President of the United States of America," and Art. III, § 1, declares that "The judicial Power of the United States, shall be vested in one supreme Court, and in such inferior Courts as the Congress may from time to time ordain and establish." The further concern of the Framers of the Constitution with maintenance of the separation of powers is found in the so-called "Ineligibility" and "Incompatibility" Clauses contained in Art. I, § 6:

> No Senator or Representative shall, during the Time for which he was elected, be appointed to any civil Office under the Authority of the United States, which shall have been created, or the Emoluments whereof shall have been encreased during such time; and no Person holding any Office under the United States, shall be a Member of either House during his Continuance in Office.

It is in the context of these cognate provisions of the document that we must examine the language of Art. II, § 2, cl. 2, which appellants contend provides the only authorization for appointment of those to whom substantial executive or administrative authority is given by statute . . . .

The Appointments Clause could, of course, be read as merely dealing with etiquette or protocol in describing "Officers of the United States," but the drafters had a less frivolous purpose in mind. . . .

We think that the term "Officers of the United States" as used in Art. II, defined to include "all persons who can be said to hold an office under the government" in United States v. Germaine [1879], is a term intended to have substantive meaning. We think its fair import is that any appointee exercising significant authority pursuant to the laws of the United States is an Officer of the United States, and must, therefore, be appointed in the manner prescribed by § 2, cl. 2, of that Article.

If "all persons who can be said to hold an office under the government about to be established under the Constitution were intended to be included within one or the other of these modes of appointment," *Germaine*, it is difficult to see how the members of the Commission may escape inclusion. If a Postmaster first class, Myers v. United States (1926), and the clerk of a district court, Ex parte Hennen (1839), are inferior officers of the United States within the meaning of the Appointments Clause, as they are, surely the Commissioners before us are at the very least such "inferior Officers" within the meaning of that Clause.

Although two members of the Commission are initially selected by the President, his nominations are subject to confirmation not merely by the Senate, but by the House of Representatives as well. The remaining four voting members of the Commission are appointed by the President pro tempore of the Senate and by the Speaker of the House. While the second part of the Clause authorizes Congress to vest the appointment of the officers described in that part in "the Courts of Law, or in the Heads of Departments," neither the Speaker of the House nor the President pro tempore of the Senate comes within this language.

The phrase "Heads of Departments," used as it is in conjunction with the phrase "Courts of Law," suggests that the Departments referred to are themselves in the Executive Branch or at least have some connection with that branch. While the Clause expressly authorizes Congress to vest the appointment of certain officers in the "Courts of Law," the absence of similar language to include Congress must mean that neither Congress nor its officers were included within the language "Heads of Departments" in this part of cl. 2.

Thus with respect to four of the six voting members of the Commission, neither the President, the head of any department, nor the Judiciary has any voice in their selection.

The Appointments Clause specifies the method of appointment only for "Officers of the United States" whose appointment is not "otherwise provided for" in the Constitution. But there is no provision of the Constitution remotely providing any alternative means for the selection of the members of the Commission or for anybody like them. . . .

Appellee Commission and amici contend somewhat obliquely that because the Framers had no intention of relegating Congress to a position below that of the coequal Judicial and Executive Branches of the National Government, the Appointments Clause must somehow be read to include Congress or its officers as among those in whom the appointment power may be vested. But the debates of the Constitutional Convention, and the Federalist Papers, are replete with expressions of fear that the Legislative Branch of the National Government will aggrandize itself at the expense of the other two branches. The debates during the Convention, and the evolution of the draft version of the Constitution, seem to us to lend considerable support to our reading of the language of the Appointments Clause itself . . . .

Appellee Commission and amici urge that because of what they conceive to be the extraordinary authority reposed in Congress to regulate elections, this case stands on a different footing than if Congress had exercised its legislative authority in another field. There is, of course, no doubt that Congress has express authority to regulate congressional elections, by virtue of the power conferred in Art. I, § 4. This Court has also held that it has very broad authority to prevent corruption in national Presidential elections. Burroughs v. United States (1934). But Congress has plenary authority in all areas in which it has substantive legislative jurisdiction, M'Culloch v. Maryland (1819), so long as the exercise of that authority does not offend some other constitutional restriction. We see no reason to believe that the authority of Congress over federal election practices is of such a wholly different nature from the other grants of authority to Congress that it may be employed in such a manner as to offend well-established constitutional restrictions stemming from the separation of powers.

The position that because Congress has been given explicit and plenary authority to regulate a field of activity, it must therefore have the power to appoint those who are to administer the regulatory statute is both novel and contrary to the language of the Appointments Clause. Unless their selection is elsewhere provided for, all officers of the United States are to be appointed in accordance with the Clause. Principal officers are selected by the President with the advice and consent of the Senate. Inferior officers Congress may allow to be appointed by the President alone, by the heads of departments, or by the Judiciary. No class or type of officer is excluded because of its special functions. The President appoints judicial as well as executive officers. Neither has it been disputed—and apparently it is not now disputed—that the Clause controls the appointment of the members of a typical administrative agency even though its functions, as this Court recognized in Humphrey's Executor v. United States (1935), may be "predominantly quasi-judicial and quasi-legislative" rather than executive. The Court in that case carefully emphasized that although the members of such agencies were to be independent of the Executive in their day-to-day operations, the Executive was not excluded from selecting them. . . .

The trilogy of cases from this Court dealing with the constitutional authority of Congress to circumscribe the President's power to *remove* officers of the United States is entirely consistent with this conclusion. In *Myers*, the Court held that Congress could not by statute divest the President of the power to remove an officer in the Executive Branch whom he was initially authorized to appoint. In explaining its reasoning in that case, the Court said:

> The vesting of the executive power in the President was essentially a grant of the power to execute the laws. But the President alone and unaided could not execute the laws. He must execute them by the assistance of subordinates . . . . As he is charged specifically to take care that they be faithfully executed, the reasonable implication, even in the absence of express words, was that as part of his executive power he should select those who were to act for him under his direction in the execution of the laws. . . .
>
> . . .

In the later case of *Humphrey's Executor,* where it was held that Congress could circumscribe the President's power to remove members of independent regulatory agencies, the Court was careful to note that it was dealing with an agency intended to be independent of executive authority *"except in its selection."* (emphasis in original). Wiener v. United States (1958), which applied the holding in *Humphrey's Executor* to a member of the War Claims Commission, did not question in any respect that members of independent agencies are not independent of the Executive with respect to their appointments . . . .

Editors' Notes

(1) **Query:** Does the logic of *Buckley* require that the President nominate various administrative officials of Congress such as the sergeant at arms of each house? If so, what happens to the institutional integrity of Congress? Do cl. 5, § 2 and cl. 5 of § 3 of Art. I, authorizing the House to choose a speaker and the Senate a president pro tem and each to select "their officers," come into play? In context, do the words "other officers" imply administrative officials who do not fall into Art. II's category of "all other officers of the United States"? What sort of response would a structuralist offer?

(2) By the time of this decision, the Electoral Commission had been sitting for almost two years and had made many decisions and issued a number of regulations. Despite holding that the members of the Commission would have to be chosen according to the literal terms of Art. II, § 2, cl. 2 of the Constitution, the Court refused to invalidate the Commission's previous work and stayed for thirty days its order against future actions by the Commission as then constituted, so that Congress would have time to amend the statute to

provide for new appointments by the President with the advice of the Senate. Congress quickly adopted such an amendment.

"[W]e must weigh the importance of the general privilege of confidentiality of presidential communications . . . against the inroads of such a privilege on the fair administration of criminal justice."

UNITED STATES v. NIXON

418 U.S. 683, 94 S.Ct. 3090, 41 L.Ed.2d 1039 (1974).

This case, dealing with a President's claim to executive privilege pitted against criminal defendants' claims to need tapes in his possession to defend themselves at a criminal trial, is reprinted above at p. 234.

" 'I deem it an imperative duty to maintain the supremacy of that sacred instrument (the Constitution) and the immunities of the Department entrusted to my care.' "

A PRESIDENTIAL LEGAL OPINION *

Robert H. Jackson.

. . . [It] is extraordinary for the President to render a legal opinion to the Attorney General. The occasion for this unusual procedure was a provision of the Lend-Lease Act which the President thought constitutionally objectionable but politically necessary. It reads:

> After June 30, 1943, or after the passage of a concurrent resolution of the two Houses before June 30, 1943, which declares that the powers conferred by or pursuant to subsection (a) are no longer necessary to promote the defense of the United States, neither the President nor the head of any department or agency shall exercise any of the powers conferred by or pursuant to subsection (a).

The Bill drafted by joint efforts of several executive departments and proposed by the President contained no such provision. I do not recall . . . whether during the congressional consideration the President personally agreed to it. Mr. [Edward R.] Stettinius mentions it, however, as an amendment that administration forces in Congress accepted as not damaging to the essential principles of the Bill and designed to meet criticism from the opposition that the Bill gave too much power to the Executive. As thus passed, the President approved it on March 11, 1941. Two days later Senator Murdock, who had argued in debate that the provision was unconstitutional, wrote to the President recounting objections to the provision. The President dis-

---

* 66 *Harvard Law Review* 1353–1361 (1953). Reprinted with permission of the Harvard Law Review Association.

Robert H. Jackson was an Associate Justice of the United States Supreme Court (1941–54); he had served as Attorney General before going to the Court.

cussed with me his concern about it and later sent me the following note:

The White House
March 17, 1941

Memorandum for the Attorney General:

I should like to file with the Attorney General an official memorandum placing me on record in regard to that provision of the Lend-Lease Bill which seeks to repeal legislation by concurrent resolution of the two houses of Congress.

Would you try your hand at drafting such a memorandum? I should say in it, of course, that the emergency was so great that I signed the bill in spite of a clearly unconstitutional provision contained in it.

I enclose letter from Senator Murdock, together with marked passages relating to the debate and relating to legislative rules and precedents.

F.D.R.

This reached me the day before I was to leave Washington as a guest of the President, who, weary from the Lend-Lease battle, had arranged a fishing trip to the Bahamas. I passed the memorandum and letter to Alexander Holtzoff, Special Assistant to the Attorney General, to formulate the statement requested.

While we were at sea, Congress passed the bill making appropriations to carry Lend-Lease into execution. . . .

This event brought about renewed discussion of the obnoxious clause of the Lend-Lease Act. It did no immediate harm . . . . I really regarded the question as interesting but rather academic.

But the President feared the long-range effect of the precedent. Obviously it was a device to evade the veto which the Constitution gave to the President. It enabled a bare majority of a quorum in each of the two Houses to terminate his powers. But for the provision, they could not be cut off before the fixed date of expiration except by passing a repealing Act, which would be subject to veto. He could thus preserve his powers, unless two-thirds of each House voted to override his veto. The scheme of the Act . . . took this powerful weapon away from the Executive. And the President was impressed by the question which Senator Murdock asked in the debates: "could we not attach the same clause, or a similar clause, to every piece of legislation which leaves the Congress, and by so doing destroy the veto power of the President?" It was a stratagem, as the President pointed out, never useful to the administration but only useful to increase the leverage of the opposition.

But was it unconstitutional? That was a different question . . . . The question on which my doubts were not fully satisfied never bothered the President in the least. It seemed to me to depend on whether the provision was to be considered as a reservation or limitation by which the granted power would expire or terminate on the contingency of a concurrent resolution or was to be regarded as authorizing a repeal by concurrent resolution. Senator Connally, in support of the President on the Lend-Lease Bill, had argued:

> If we may terminate this bill by its terms on June 30, 1943, then we may terminate it upon any other happening or any other event which may transpire in the future.
>
> The reason for that is that it is in the act itself; it is a limitation upon the length of time and the length of operation of the act itself, and in no sense a repeal or modification of an existing act. The provision is written in the heart of the measure that the bill shall not last longer than June 30, 1943, and, prior to that date, it shall not last beyond any time after the Congress shall pass a concurrent resolution.
>
> . . . [T]he Supreme Court of the United States has held that Congress in enacting legislation has the right to hinge its operation either upon some antecedent event or upon some subsequent event, and that upon the happening of that event, such as a proclamation by the President, if that is provided in the law, the act shall either terminate or shall become operative, as the case may be, as provided in the legislation.

The President, however, invariably referred to the offending procedure as a repeal. His reasoning was that so well put on the floor by Senator Murdock:

> When you bring the measure back to the Congress and invoke the legislative will to terminate legislation, in my opinion you violate the Constitution, unless you follow the procedure set forth in the Constitution.

Then why should the President not say so, publicly and at once, by a press release, a speech, or in answer to a question planted at press conference? . . . The reason was political. His views, strangely enough, were those used by the opponents of the Lend-Lease Bill, some of whom were his consistent political enemies, to justify their opposition to the Bill. They argued that the device for recalling their grant of power was unconstitutional and therefore illusory. His loyal supporters, on the other hand, had argued that the provision was valid and therefore effective as a check on any runaway executive action. For the President to make public his views at that time would confirm and delight his opposition and let down his friends. It might seriously alienate some of his congressional support at a time when he would need to call on it frequently. It would also strengthen fear in the country that he was seeking to increase his personal power.

Why, then, not drop the matter entirely? He had to reckon on the possibility, even if remote, of an attempt to invoke the provision. If he then challenged its constitutionality, he would be confronted with his own signature to the Act he was contesting. Therefore, he wanted a record that his constitutional scruples did not arise only after the shoe began to pinch, and, so far as possible, to excuse his approval and counteract its effect. He did not want the precedent created by his yielding to ripen into a custom which would impair the powers which properly appertained to his great office. Only a statement of his own could do that. . . .

Returning to Washington on April 1, I received from Mr. Holtzoff the memorandum he had prepared. He, like the President, assumed— what seemed the debatable point—that concurrent resolutions under the provision would be the same as repealing legislation. But it stated faithfully the President's position, and that was what mattered and what was requested. I forwarded it to the President on April 3. Without further discussion with me and without change, he signed it on the date it bears. It reads:

THE WHITE HOUSE
WASHINGTON
April 7, 1941

MEMORANDUM FOR THE ATTORNEY GENERAL

On March 11, 1941, I attached my approval to the bill (H.R.1776) entitled "An Act to Promote the Defense of the United States." The bill was an outstanding measure which sought to meet a momentous emergency of great magnitude in world affairs. In view of this impelling consideration, I felt constrained to sign the measure, in spite of the fact that it contained a provision which, in my opinion, is clearly unconstitutional. I have reference to the clause of Section 3(c) of the Act, providing that after the passage of a concurrent resolution by the two Houses before June 30, 1943, which declares that the powers conferred by or pursuant to subsection (a) are no longer necessary to promote the defense of the United States, neither the President nor the head of any Department or agency shall exercise any of the powers conferred by or pursuant to subsection (a), with certain specified exceptions. In effect, this provision is an attempt by Congress to authorize a repeal by means of a concurrent resolution of the two Houses, of certain provisions of an Act of Congress.

The Constitution of the United States, Article I, Section 7, prescribes the mode in which laws shall be enacted. It provides that "Every bill which shall have passed the House of Representatives and the Senate, shall, before it become a law, be presented to the President of the United States; if he approves he shall sign it, but if not he shall return it, with his objections to that House in which it shall have originated." It is thereupon provided that if after reconsideration two-thirds of each House shall agree to pass the bill, it shall become law. The Constitution contains no provision whereby the Congress may legislate by concurrent resolution without the approval of the President. The only instance in which a bill may become law without the approval of the President is when the President vetoes a bill and it is then repassed by two-thirds vote in each House.

It is too clear for argument that action repealing an existing Act itself constitutes an Act of Congress and, therefore, is subject to the foregoing requirements. A repeal of existing provisions of law, in whole or in part, therefore, may not be accomplished by a concurrent resolution of the two Houses.

In order that I may be on record as indicating my opinion that the foregoing provision of the so-called Lend-Lease Act is unconstitutional, and in order that my approval of the bill, due to the existing exigencies of the world situation, may not be construed as a tacit acquiescence in any contrary view, I am requesting you to place this memorandum in the official files of the Department of Justice. I am desirous of having this done for the further reason that I should not wish my action in approving the bill which includes this invalid clause, to be used as a precedent for any future legislation comprising provisions of a similar nature.

In conclusion, I may refer to the following pertinent remarks of President Andrew Jackson: "I deem it an imperative duty to maintain the supremacy of that sacred instrument (the Constitution) and the immunities of the Department entrusted to my care."

/s/ Franklin D. Roosevelt

The following note, however, accompanied the return of the opinion to me:

THE WHITE HOUSE
WASHINGTON

April 7, 1941.

MEMORANDUM FOR

THE ATTORNEY GENERAL.

Dear Mr. Attorney General

    I enclose herewith the formal memorandum placing me on record in regard to the unconstitutionality of that provision of Section 3 (c) of the Lend-Lease Act, Public No. 11, 77th Congress, which authorizes repeal by a concurrent resolution of the Congress.

    I think that this formal memorandum from me to you should be published some day as an official document, and I leave the method thereof to your discretion.

             Franklin D. Roosevelt
                F. D. R.

[D7644]

It evidently was dictated by the President and, after the custom of those days, his initials were typed at its end. These he had crossed out and had signed the same initials in longhand. Then he struck those out and signed his full name. Also, he penned in the salutation . . . .

"Explicit and unambiguous provisions of the Constitution prescribe and define the respective functions of the Congress and the President in the legislative process."

IMMIGRATION AND NATURALIZATION SERVICE v. CHADHA

462 U.S. 919, 103 S.Ct. 2764, 77 L.Ed.2d 317 (1983).

Jagdish Rai Chadha came to the United States in 1966 on a student visa, which expired in 1972. The Immigration and Naturalization Service (INS) began proceedings to deport him. After hearings, the attorney general recommended Chadha not be deported and his status changed to permanent resident alien. Under § 244(c)(2) of the Immigration and Nationality Act, either house of Congress could veto such recommendations:

[I]f [within a specified time after the attorney general's recommendation] . . . either the Senate or the House of Representatives passes a resolution stating . . . that it does not favor the suspension of such deportation, the Attorney General shall deport such alien . . . . If . . . neither the Senate nor the House of Representatives shall pass such a resolution, the Attorney General shall cancel deportation proceedings.

In 1975, within the time allowed by the Act, the House voted to reject the attorney general's recommendation and to deport Chadha and five other aliens. Chadha exhausted his administrative remedies by contesting (and losing) the order within INS and appealed to the U.S. Court of Appeals for the Ninth Circuit. That court invited the Senate and House to intervene as *amici curiae,* then ruled that the House had violated the concept of separation of powers. INS appealed to the Supreme Court.

Chief Justice **BURGER** delivered the opinion of the Court . . . .

I . . .

Political Question

. . . It is argued that Congress' Article I power "To establish an uniform Rule of Naturalization," combined with the Necessary and Proper Clause, grants it unreviewable authority over the regulation of aliens. The plenary authority of Congress over aliens under Art. I, § 8, cl. 4 is not open to question, but what is challenged here is whether Congress has chosen a constitutionally permissible means of implementing that power. As we made clear in Buckley v. Valeo (1976); "Congress has plenary authority in all cases in which it has substantive legislative jurisdiction, M'Culloch v. Maryland (1819), so long as the exercise of that authority does not offend some other constitutional restriction."

. . . As identified in Baker v. Carr (1962), a political question may arise when any one of the following circumstances is present:

a textually demonstrable constitutional commitment of the issue to a coordinate political department; or a lack of judicially discoverable and manageable standards for resolving it; or the impossibility of deciding without an initial policy determination of a kind clearly for nonjudicial discretion; or the impossibility of a court's undertaking independent resolution without expressing lack of the respect due coordinate branches of government; or an unusual need for unquestioning adherence to a political decision already made; or the potentiality of embarrassment from multifarious pronouncements by various departments on one question.

Congress apparently directs its assertion of nonjusticiability to the first of the *Baker* factors by asserting that Chadha's claim is "an assault on the legislative authority to enact Section 244(c)(2)." But if this turns the question into a political question virtually every challenge to the constitutionality of a statute would be a political question. Chadha indeed argues that one House of Congress cannot constitutionally veto the Attorney General's decision to allow him to remain in this country. No policy underlying the political question doctrine suggests that Congress or the Executive, or both acting in concert and in compliance with Art. I, can decide the constitutionality of a statute; that is a decision for the courts.[1]

Other *Baker* factors are likewise inapplicable to this case . . . . Art. I provides the "judicially discoverable and manageable standards" of *Baker* for resolving the question presented by this case. . . . and . . . there is no possibility of "multifarious pronouncements" on this question.

It is correct that this controversy may, in a sense, be termed "political." But the presence of constitutional issues with significant political overtones does not automatically invoke the political question doctrine. . . . Resolution of litigation challenging the constitutional authority of one of the three branches cannot be evaded by courts because the issues have political implications in the sense urged by Congress. Marbury v. Madison (1803), was also a "political" case, involving as it did claims under a judicial commission alleged to have been duly signed by the President but not delivered. But "courts cannot reject as 'no law suit' a bona fide controversy as to whether some action denominated 'political' exceeds constitutional authority." *Baker.* . . .

---

1. The suggestion is made that § 244(c)(2) is somehow immunized from constitutional scrutiny because the Act containing § 244(c)(2) was passed by Congress and approved by the President. Marbury v. Madison (1803), resolved that question. The assent of the Executive to a bill which contains a provision contrary to the Constitution does not shield it from judicial review. See Smith v. Maryland (1979); National League of Cities v. Usery (1976); Buckley v. Valeo (1976); Myers v. United States (1926). In any event, eleven Presidents, from Mr. Wilson through Mr. Reagan, who have been presented with this issue have gone on record at some point to challenge Congressional vetoes as unconstitutional . . . . Furthermore, it is not uncommon for Presidents to approve legislation containing parts which are objectionable on constitutional grounds . . . . [Footnote by the Court.]

III

A

. . . We begin, of course, with the presumption that the challenged statute is valid. Its wisdom is not the concern of the courts . . . .

By the same token, the fact that a given law or procedure is efficient, convenient, and useful in facilitating functions of government, standing alone, will not save it if it is contrary to the Constitution. Convenience and efficiency are not the primary objectives—or the hallmarks—of democratic government and our inquiry is sharpened rather than blunted by the fact that Congressional veto provisions are appearing with increasing frequency in statutes which delegate authority to executive and independent agencies. . . .

Justice White undertakes to make a case for the proposition that the one-House veto is a useful "political invention," and we need not challenge that assertion. . . . But policy arguments supporting even useful "political inventions" are subject to the demands of the Constitution . . . .

Explicit and unambiguous provisions of the Constitution prescribe and define the respective functions of the Congress and of the Executive in the legislative process. . . . Art. I provides:

> All legislative Powers herein granted shall be vested in a Congress of the United States, which shall consist of a Senate *and* a House of Representatives.

> Every Bill which shall have passed the House of Representatives *and* the Senate, *shall,* before it become a Law, be presented to the President of the United States; . . . .

> *Every* Order, Resolution, or Vote to which the Concurrence of the Senate and House of Representatives may be necessary (except on a question of Adjournment) *shall be* presented to the President of the United States; and before the Same shall take Effect, *shall be* approved by him, or being disapproved by him, *shall be* repassed by two thirds of the Senate and House of Representatives, according to the Rules and Limitations prescribed in the Case of a Bill. (Emphasis added).

These provisions of Art. I are integral parts of the constitutional design for the separation of powers. . . . Just as we relied on the textual provision of Art. II, § 2, cl. 2, to vindicate the principle of separation of powers in *Buckley,* we find that the purposes underlying the Presentment Clauses and the bicameral requirement guide our resolution of the important question presented in this case. The very structure of the articles delegating and separating powers under Arts. I, II, and III exemplify the concept of separation of powers and we now turn to Art. I.

B

The Presentment Clauses

The records of the Constitutional Convention reveal that the requirement that all legislation be presented to the President before becoming law was uniformly accepted by the Framers. Presentment to the President and the Presidential veto were considered so imperative that the draftsmen took special pains to assure that these requirements could not be circumvented. During the final debate on Art. I, § 7, cl. 2, James Madison expressed concern that it might easily be evaded by the simple expedient of calling a proposed law a "resolution" or "vote" rather than a "bill." As a consequence, Art. I, § 7, cl. 3, was added.

The decision to provide the President with a limited and qualified power to nullify proposed legislation by veto was based on the profound conviction of the Framers that the powers conferred on Congress were the powers to be most carefully circumscribed. It is beyond doubt that lawmaking was a power to be shared by both Houses and the President

. . . .

The President's role in the lawmaking process also reflects the Framers' careful efforts to check whatever propensity a particular Congress might have to enact oppressive, improvident, or ill-considered measures. The President's veto role in the legislative process was described later during public debate on ratification:

> It establishes a salutary check upon the legislative body, calculated to guard the community against the effects of faction, precipitancy, or of any impulse unfriendly to the public good which may happen to influence a majority of that body . . . . The primary inducement to conferring the power in question upon the Executive is to enable him to defend himself; the secondary one is to increase the chances in favor of the community against the passing of bad laws through haste, inadvertence, or design. *The Federalist* No. 73.

The Court also has observed that the Presentment Clauses serve the important purpose of assuring that a "national" perspective is grafted on the legislative process:

> The President is a representative of the people just as the members of the Senate and of the House are, and it may be, at some times, on some subjects, that the President elected by all the people is rather more representative of them all than are the members of either body of the Legislature whose constituencies are local and not countrywide . . . . Myers v. United States (1926).

C

Bicameralism

The bicameral requirement of Art. I, §§ 1, 7 was of scarcely less concern to the Framers than was the Presidential veto and indeed the two concepts are interdependent. By providing that no law could take effect without the concurrence of the prescribed majority of the Members of both Houses, the Framers reemphasized their belief . . . that legislation should not be enacted unless it has been carefully and fully considered by the Nation's elected officials. In the Constitutional Convention debates on the need for a bicameral legislature, James Wilson, later to become a Justice of this Court, commented:

> Despotism comes on mankind in different shapes. Sometimes in an Executive, sometimes in a military, one. Is there danger of a Legislative despotism? Theory & practice both proclaim it. If the Legislative authority be not restrained, there can be neither liberty nor stability; and it can only be restrained by dividing it within itself, into distinct and independent branches. In a single house there is no check, but the inadequate one, of the virtue & good sense of those who compose it.
> . . . .

. . . The President's participation in the legislative process was to protect the Executive Branch from Congress and to protect the whole people from improvident laws. The division of the Congress into two distinctive bodies assures that the legislative power would be exercised only after opportunity for full study and debate in separate settings. The President's unilateral veto power, in turn, was limited by the power of two thirds of both Houses of Congress to overrule a veto thereby precluding final arbitrary action of one person. It emerges clearly that the prescription for legislative action in Art. I, §§ 1, 7 represents the Framers' decision that the legislative power of the Federal government be exercised in accord with a single, finely wrought and exhaustively considered, procedure.

IV . . .

Although not "hermetically" sealed from one another, *Buckley*, the powers delegated to the three Branches are functionally identifiable. When any Branch acts, it is presumptively exercising the power the Constitution has delegated to it. See Hampton & Co. v. United States (1928). . . .

Beginning with this presumption, we must nevertheless establish that the challenged action under § 244(c)(2) is of the kind to which the procedural requirements of Art. I, § 7 apply . . . .

. . . Whether actions taken by either House are, in law and fact, an exercise of legislative power depends not on their form but upon "whether they contain matter which is properly to be regarded as legislative in its character and effect."

Examination of the action taken here by one House pursuant to § 244(c)(2) reveals that it was essentially legislative . . . . The one-House veto operated in this case to overrule the Attorney General and mandate Chadha's deportation; absent the House action, Chadha would remain in the United States. Congress has *acted* and its action has altered Chadha's status.

The legislative character of the one-House veto in this case is confirmed by the character of the Congressional action it supplants. . . . Without the challenged provision in § 244(c)(2), this [deportation] could have been achieved, if at all, only by legislation requiring deportation. Similarly, a veto by one House of Congress under § 244(c) (2) cannot be justified as an attempt at amending the standards set out in § 244(a)(1), or as a repeal of § 244 as applied to Chadha. Amendment and repeal of statutes, no less than enactment, must conform with Art. I.

. . . [W]hen the Framers intended to authorize either House of Congress to act alone and outside of its prescribed bicameral legislative role, they narrowly and precisely defined the procedure for such action. There are but four provisions in the Constitution, explicit and unambiguous, by which one House may act alone with the unreviewable force of law, not subject to the President's veto:

(a) The House of Representatives alone was given the power to initiate impeachments. Art. I, § 2, cl. 6;

(b) The Senate alone was given the power to conduct trials following impeachment on charges initiated by the House and to convict following trial. Art. I, § 3, cl. 5;

(c) The Senate alone was given final unreviewable power to approve or to disapprove presidential appointments. Art. II, § 2, cl. 2;

(d) The Senate alone was given unreviewable power to ratify treaties negotiated by the President. Art. II, § 2, cl. 2.

Clearly, when the Draftsmen sought to confer special powers on one House, independent of the other House, or of the President, they did so in explicit, unambiguous terms . . . .[2] These exceptions are narrow, explicit, and separately justified; none of them authorize the action challenged here. On the contrary, they provide further support for the conclusion that Congressional authority is not to be implied and for the conclusion that the veto provided for in § 244(c)(2) is not authorized by the constitutional design of the powers of the Legislative Branch . . . .

Affirmed.

Justice **POWELL** concurring in the judgment . . . .

The Framers perceived that "[t]he accumulation of all powers legislative, executive and judiciary in the same hands, whether of one, a few or many, and whether hereditary, self appointed, or elective, may justly be pronounced the very definition of tyranny." The *Federalist* No. 47. Theirs was not a baseless fear. Under British rule, the

---

2. An exception from the Presentment Clauses was ratified in Hollingsworth v. Virginia (1798). There the Court held presidential approval was unnecessary for a proposed constitutional amendment which had passed both Houses of Congress by the requisite two-thirds majority.

One might also include another "exception" to the rule that Congressional action having the force of law be subject to the bicameral requirement and the Presentment Clauses. Each House has the power to act alone in determining specified internal matters. Art. I, § 7, cl. 2, 3, and § 5, cl. 2. However, this "exception" only empowers Congress to bind itself and is noteworthy only insofar as it further indicates the Framers' intent that Congress not act in any legally binding manner outside a closely circumscribed legislative arena, except in specific and enumerated instances . . . . [Footnote by the Court.]

colonies suffered the abuses of unchecked executive power that were attributed, at least popularly, to an hereditary monarchy. . . . During the Confederation, the States reacted by removing power from the executive and placing it in the hands of elected legislators. But many legislators proved to be little better than the Crown . . . .

One abuse that was prevalent during the Confederation was the exercise of judicial power by the state legislatures. The Framers were well acquainted with the danger of subjecting the determination of the rights of one person to the "tyranny of shifting majorities." . . .

It was to prevent the recurrence of such abuses that the Framers vested the executive, legislative, and judicial powers in separate branches. Their concern that a legislature should not be able unilaterally to impose a substantial deprivation on one person was expressed not only in this general allocation of power, but also in more specific provisions, such as the Bill of Attainder Clause, Art. I, § 9, cl. 3. As the Court recognized in United States v. Brown (1965), "the Bill of Attainder Clause was intended not as a narrow, technical . . . prohibition, but rather as an implementation of the separation of powers, a general safeguard against legislative exercise of the judicial function, or more simply—trial by legislature." This Clause, and the separation of powers doctrine generally, reflect the Framer's concern that trial by a legislature lacks the safeguards necessary to prevent the abuse of power.

The Constitution does not establish three branches with precisely defined boundaries. Rather, as Justice Jackson wrote, "[w]hile the Constitution diffuses power the better to secure liberty, it also contemplates that practice will integrate the dispersed powers into a workable government. It enjoins upon its branches separateness but interdependence, autonomy but reciprocity." Youngstown Sheet & Tube Co. v. Sawyer (1952) (concurring opinion). The Court thus has been mindful that the boundaries between each branch should be fixed "according to common sense and the inherent necessities of the governmental coordination." J.W. Hampton, Jr. & Co. v. United States (1928). But where one branch has impaired or sought to assume a power central to another branch, the Court has not hesitated to enforce the doctrine. See *Buckley.*

Functionally, the doctrine may be violated in two ways. One branch may interfere impermissibly with the other's performance of its constitutionally assigned function. See Nixon v. Administrator of General Services (1977); United States v. Nixon (1974). Alternatively, the doctrine may be violated when one branch assumes a function that more properly is entrusted to another. See *Youngstown*; Springer v. Philippine Islands (1928). This case presents the latter situation
. . . . .

On its face, the House's action appears clearly adjudicatory. The House did not enact a general rule; rather it made its own determination that six specific persons did not comply with certain statutory criteria. It thus undertook the type of decision that traditionally has been left to other branches. . . . Where, as here, Congress has exercised a power "that cannot possibly be regarded as merely in aid of the legislative function of Congress," *Buckley*, the decisions of this Court have held that Congress impermissibly assumed a function that the Constitution entrusted to another branch, see id.; cf. *Springer*.

The impropriety of the House's assumption of this function is confirmed by the fact that its action raises the very danger the Framers sought to avoid—the exercise of unchecked power. In deciding whether Chadha deserves to be deported, Congress is not subject to any internal constraints that prevent it from arbitrarily depriving him of the right to remain in this country. Unlike the judiciary or an administrative agency, Congress is not bound by established substantive rules. Nor is it subject to the procedural safeguards, such as the right to counsel and a hearing before an impartial tribunal, that are present when a court or an agency adjudicates individual rights. The only effective constraint on Congress' power is political, but Congress is most accountable politically when it prescribes rules of general applicability. When it decides rights of specific persons, those rights are subject to "the tyranny of a shifting majority."

Chief Justice Marshall observed: "It is the peculiar province of the legislature to prescribe general rules for the government of society; the application of those rules would seem to be the duty of other departments." Fletcher v. Peck (1810). In my view, when Congress undertook to apply its rules to Chadha, it exceeded the scope of its constitutionally prescribed authority. I would not reach the broader question whether legislative vetoes are invalid under the Presentment Clauses.

Justice **WHITE,** dissenting . . . .

structuralism   I . . .

The prominence of the legislative veto mechanism in our contemporary political system and its importance to Congress can hardly be overstated. It has become a central means by which Congress secures the accountability of executive and independent agencies. Without the legislative veto, Congress is faced with a Hobson's choice: either to refrain from delegating the necessary authority, leaving itself with a hopeless task of writing laws with the requisite specificity to cover endless special circumstances across the entire policy landscape, or in the alternative, to abdicate its lawmaking function to the executive branch and independent agencies. . . . Accordingly, over the past five decades, the legislative veto has been placed in nearly 200 statutes.

. . .

. . . [T]he legislative veto is more than "efficient, convenient, and useful." It is an important if not indispensable political invention that allows the President and Congress to resolve major constitutional and policy differences, assures the accountability of independent regulatory agencies, and preserves Congress' control over lawmaking. Perhaps there are other means of accommodation and accountability, but the increasing reliance of Congress upon the legislative veto suggests that the alternatives to which Congress must now turn are not entirely satisfactory.

The history of the legislative veto also makes clear that it has not been a sword with which Congress has struck out to aggrandize itself at the expense of the other branches—the concerns of Madison and Hamilton. Rather, the veto has been a means of defense, a reservation of ultimate authority necessary if Congress is to fulfill its designated role under Article I as the nation's lawmaker. While the President has often objected to particular legislative vetoes, generally those left in the hands of congressional committees, the Executive has more often agreed to legislative review as the price for a broad delegation of authority. To be sure, the President may have preferred unrestricted power, but that could be precisely why Congress thought it essential to retain a check on the exercise of delegated authority.

II

For all these reasons, the apparent sweep of the Court's decision today is regretable. The Court's Article I analysis appears to invalidate all legislative vetoes irrespective of form or subject. . . . Courts should always be wary of striking statutes as unconstitutional; to strike an entire class of statutes based on consideration of a somewhat atypical and more-readily indictable exemplar of the class is irresponsible. It was for cases such as this one that Justice Brandeis wrote:

> . . . The Court will not "formulate a rule of constitutional law broader than is required by the precise facts to which it is to be applied." Ashwander v. Tennessee Valley Authority (1936) (concurring opinion). . . .

If the legislative veto were as plainly unconstitutional as the Court strives to suggest, its broad ruling today would be more comprehensible. But, the constitutionality of the legislative veto is anything but clear-cut. The issue divides scholars, courts, attorneys general, and the two other branches of the National Government. If the veto devices so flagrantly disregarded the requirements of Article I as the Court today suggests, I find it incomprehensible that Congress, whose members are bound by oath to uphold the Constitution, would have placed these mechanisms in nearly 200 separate laws over a period of 50 years.

. . . The Constitution does not directly authorize or prohibit the legislative veto. Thus, our task should be to determine whether the legislative veto is consistent with the purposes of Art. I and the principles of Separation of Powers which are reflected in that Article and throughout the Constitution. We should not find the lack of a specific constitutional authorization for the legislative veto surprising, and I would not infer disapproval of the mechanism from its absence. From the summer of 1787 to the present the government of the United States has become an endeavor far beyond the contemplation of the Framers. . . . But the wisdom of the Framers was to anticipate that the nation would grow and new problems of governance would require different solutions. . . .

. . . In my view, neither Article I of the Constitution nor the doctrine of separation of powers is violated by this mechanism by which our elected representatives preserve their voice in the governance of the nation.

III . . .

. . . There is no question that a bill does not become a law until it is approved by both the House and the Senate, and presented to the President. . . . I agree with the Court that the President's qualified veto power is a critical element in the distribution of powers under the Constitution. . . . I also agree that the bicameral approval required by Art. I, §§ 1, 7 "was of scarcely less concern to the Framers than was the Presidential veto," and that the need to divide and disperse legislative power figures significantly in our scheme of Government. . . .

It does not, however, answer the constitutional question before us. The power to exercise a legislative veto is not the power to write new law without bicameral approval or presidential consideration. The veto must be authorized by statute and may only negative what an Executive department or independent agency has proposed. On its face, the legislative veto no more allows one House of Congress to make law than does the presidential veto confer such power upon the President . . . .

. . . The Court's holding today that all legislative-type action must be enacted through the lawmaking process ignores that legislative authority is routinely delegated to the Executive branch, to the independent regulatory agencies, and to private individuals and groups . . . .

This Court's decisions sanctioning such delegations make clear that Article I does not require all action with the effect of legislation to be passed as a law.

Theoretically, agencies and officials were asked only to "fill up the details," and the rule was that "Congress cannot delegate any part of its legislative power except under a limitation of a prescribed standard." United States v. Chicago, Milwaukee R. Co. (1931). . . . In practice, however, restrictions on the scope of the power that could be delegated diminished and all but disappeared. In only two instances did the Court find an unconstitutional delegation. Panama Refining Co. v. Ryan (1935); Schechter Poultry Corp. v. United States (1935). In other cases, the "intelligible principle" through which agencies have attained enormous control over the economic affairs of the country was held to include such formulations as "just and reasonable," Tagg Bros. & Moorhead v. United States (1930), "public interest," New York Central Securities Corp. v. United States (1932), "public convenience, interest, or necessity," Federal Radio Comm. v. Nelson Bros. Bond & Mortgage Co. (1933), and "unfair methods of competition." FTC v. Gratz (1920).

. . . [T]hese cases establish that by virtue of congressional delegation, legislative power can be exercised by independent agencies and Executive departments without the passage of new legislation . . . .

If Congress may delegate lawmaking power to independent and executive agencies, it is most difficult to understand Article I as forbidding Congress from also reserving a check on legislative power for itself. Absent the veto, the agencies receiving delegations of legislative or quasi-legislative power may issue regulations having the force of law without bicameral approval and without the President's signature. . . .

Nor are there strict limits on the agents that may receive such delegations of legislative authority so that it might be said that the legislature can delegate authority to others but not to itself. While most authority to issue rules and regulations is given to the executive branch and the independent regulatory agencies, statutory delegations to private persons have also passed this Court's scrutiny. . . . Currin v. Wallace (1939) . . . United States v. Rock Royal Co-operative (1939) . . . . Assuming *Currin* and *Rock Royal Co-operative* remain sound law, the Court's decision today suggests that Congress may place a "veto" power over suspensions of deportation in private hands or in the hands of an independent agency, but is forbidden from reserving such authority for itself. . . .

More fundamentally . . . the Court concedes that certain administrative agency action, such as rulemaking, "may resemble lawmaking" and recognizes that "[t]his Court has referred to agency activity as being 'quasi-legislative' in character." . . . Such rules and adjudications by the agencies meet the Court's own definition of legislative action for they "alter[ ] the legal rights, duties, and relations of persons . . . outside the legislative branch," and involve "determinations of policy." Under the Court's analysis, the Executive Branch and the independent agencies may make rules with the effect of law while Congress, in whom the Framers confided the legislative power, Art. I, § 1, may not exercise a veto which precludes such rules from having operative force. . . .

The Court also takes no account of perhaps the most relevant consideration: However resolutions of disapproval under § 244(c)(2) are formally characterized, in reality, a departure from the status quo occurs only upon the concurrence of opinion among the House, Senate, and President. Reservations of legislative authority to be exercised by Congress should be upheld if the exercise of such reserved authority is consistent with the distribution of and limits upon legislative power that Article I provides. . . .

The central concern of the presentation and bicameralism requirements of Article I is that when a departure from the legal status quo is undertaken, it is done with the approval of the President and both Houses of Congress—or, in the event of a presidential veto, a two-thirds majority in both Houses. This interest is fully satisfied by the operation of § 244(c)(2) . . . .

IV

. . . . It is true that the purpose of separating the authority of government is to prevent unnecessary and dangerous concentration of power in one branch. For that reason, the Framers saw fit to divide and balance the powers of government so that each branch would be checked by the others. . . .

But the history of the separation of powers doctrine is also a history of accommodation and practicality. Apprehensions of an overly powerful branch have not led to undue prophylactic measures that handicap the effective working of the national government as a whole. The Constitution does not contemplate total separation of the three branches of Government. *Buckley* . . . .

Our decisions reflect this judgment. . . . The separation of powers doctrine has heretofore led to the invalidation of government action only when the challenged action violated some express provision in the Constitution. . . .

This is the teaching of Nixon v. Administrator of Gen. Servs. (1977), which . . . set forth a framework for evaluating such claims:

> [I]n determining whether the Act disrupts the proper balance between the coordinate branches, the proper inquiry focuses on the extent to which it prevents the Executive Branch from accomplishing its constitutionally assigned functions. United States v. Nixon (1974). Only where the potential for disruption is present must we then determine whether that impact is justified by an overriding need to promote objectives within the constitutional authority of Congress.

Section 244(c)(2) survives this test. The legislative veto provision does not "prevent the Executive Branch from accomplishing its constitutionally assigned functions." First, it is clear that the Executive Branch has no "constitutionally assigned" function of suspending the deportation of aliens. " 'Over no conceivable subject is the legislative power of Congress more complete than it is over' the admission of aliens." Kleindiest v. Mandel (1972). Nor can it be said that the inherent function of the Executive Branch in executing the law is involved. . . . Here, § 244 grants the executive only a qualified suspension authority and it is only that authority which the President is constitutionally authorized to execute.

Moreover, the Court believes that the legislative veto we consider today is best characterized as an exercise of legislative or quasi-legislative authority. Under this characterization, the practice does not, even on the surface, constitute an infringement of executive or judicial prerogative. The Attorney General's suspension of deportation is equivalent to a proposal for legislation. . . . So understood, congressional review does not undermine . . . the "weight and dignity" that attends the decisions of the Executive Branch.

Nor does § 244 infringe on the judicial power, as Justice Powell would hold. Section 244 makes clear that Congress has reserved its own judgment as part of the statutory process. Congressional action does not substitute for judicial review of the Attorney General's decisions. The Act provides for judicial review of the refusal of the Attorney General to suspend a deportation and to transmit a recommendation to Congress. INS v. Wang (1981) (per curiam). But the courts have not been given the authority to review whether an alien should be given permanent status; review is limited to whether the Attorney General has properly applied the statutory standards for essentially denying the alien a recommendation that his deportable status be changed by the Congress . . . .

I do not suggest that all legislative vetoes are necessarily consistent with separation of powers principles. A legislative check on an inherently executive function, for example that of initiating prosecutions, poses an entirely different question. But the legislative veto device here—and in many other settings—is far from an instance of legislative tyranny over the Executive. It is a necessary check on the unavoidably expanding power of the agencies, both executive and independent, as they engage in exercising authority delegated by Congress.

Justice **REHNQUIST**, with whom Justice **WHITE** joins, dissenting

. . . .

Editors' Notes

(1) **Query:** Compare the opinions of Burger and White across several of the dimensions of constitutional interpretation discussed in Chapter 8. Which takes the more static and which the more developmental view of the Constitution? Which looks for constitutional meaning mainly in the text and original intent and which looks more to the operations of the larger system? In what senses do both use structural analyses?

(2) Ironically, *Chadha* questions its own legitimacy. Indeed, it casts a shadow over the validity of all federal judicial proceedings. The case went through the federal judicial system under procedural rules that, though they had the force of law, had been insulated from a presidential veto. Congress has authorized the Supreme Court (in fact special committees of the Judicial Conference of the United States) to draft rules for bankruptcy as well as for civil, criminal, and appellate procedure for all federal courts. If not disapproved by Congress within 90 days, these rules take on the force of law and repeal all conflicting federal statutes. (The statute authorizing the Court to set the rules of civil procedure is found at 28 U.S.C. § 2072; for criminal procedure, at 18 U.S.C. §§ 3771–3772.) Justices Black and Douglas several times objected to this process not only because of the Court's role as mere conduit for the Judicial Conference but also because: "The Constitution, as we read it, provides that all laws shall be enacted by the House, the Senate, and the President, not by the mere failure of Congress to reject proposals of an outside agency . . . ." 374 U.S. 865–866 (1963). Justice Frankfurter objected because he thought that by promulgating rules the Court was prejudging issues that might come before it. 323 U.S. 821 (1944).

(3) As Chapter 6 pointed out, *Chadha* is one of the few instances in which the Court has explicitly claimed supremacy over Congress and the President in constitutional interpretation.

(4) In a series of summary per curiam decisions on July 6, 1983, the Court reaffirmed *Chadha*. Justice White filed a dissent in U.S. House of Representatives v. FTC, which cites and explains the various rulings and rechallenges *Chadha*. Whatever the long-range effects of *Chadha* will be, its doctrine about the legislative veto may not long stand unmodified, or at least it may have only limited practical effect. As Louis Fisher, a noted authority on relations among the three branches of government, put it: "Are they [provisions for legislative vetoes] unconstitutional? By the Court's definition they are. Will this change the behavior between [congressional] committees and [executive] agencies? Probably not." "Legislative Vetoes, Phoenix Style," *Extensions* (Spring, 1984); reprinted in Walter F. Murphy and C. Herman Pritchett, eds., *Courts, Judges, and Politics* (4th ed.; New York: Random House, 1986). In the first year after *Chadha* Congress included a legislative veto in 53 bills and the President signed them all into law, though with disclaimers similar to that of FDR about the Lend-Lease Act. More subtly, chairmen of various congressional committees and subcommittees have been working out informal legislative vetoes with agency heads, while the leadership has been carrying out involuted procedures under the formal rules of each house and also substituting joint resolutions for the one-house veto. The net effect may be to weaken rather than strengthen executive power. See Fisher, "Constitutional Interpretation by Members of Congress," 63 *N.C.L.Rev.* 707 (1985), and his "Judicial Misjudgments about the Lawmaking Process," 45 *Pub.Admin.Rev.* 705 (1985).

(5) Among the authorities who had supported the constitutionality of the legislative veto was Edward S. Corwin, *The Presidency: Office and Powers* (4th rev. ed.; New York: New York University Press, 1957), pp. 129–130; for an extended defense of the legislative veto, written long before *Chadha,* see Murray Dry, "The Congressional Veto and the Constitutional Separation of Powers," in Joseph M. Bessette and Jeffrey Tulis, eds., *The Presidency in the Constitutional Order* (Baton Rouge: Louisiana State University Press, 1981).

(6) For a general study of the legislative veto, see Barbara Hinkson Craig, *The Legislative Veto* (Boulder, Colo.: Westview Press, 1983). For intensive surveys of congressional, judicial, and scholarly reactions to *Chadha,* see Louis Fisher, "One year after *INS v. Chadha,*" Library of Congress, Congressional Research Service, mimeo'd, 1984; and his other writings cited in Eds.' Note (4). See also: U.S. House of Representatives, Committee on Rules, *Hearings: Legislative Veto after Chadha,* 98th Cong., 2d sess. (1984); Stephen Breyer, "The Legislative Veto after *Chadha,*" 72 *Geo.L.J.* 785 (1984); Donald E. Elliott, "INS v. Chadha," 1983 *Sup.Ct.Rev.* 125; Elliott H. Levitas and Stanley M. Brand, "Congressional Review of Executive and Agency after *Chadha:* 'The Son of Legislative Veto' Lives On," 72 *Geo.L.J.* 801 (1984); Peter L. Strauss, "Was There a Baby in the Bathwater?" 1983 *Duke L.J.* 789; Strauss, "The Place of Agencies in Government," 84 *Col.L.Rev.* 573 (1984); Laurence H. Tribe, "The Legislative Veto Decision," 21 *Harv.J. on Leg'n* 1 (1984); and Note, "Severability of Legislative Veto Provisions," 97 *Harv.L.Rev.* 1184 (1984).

10

Sharing Powers: The Nature of the Union

The concept of federalism shares at least one trait with that of separation of powers: Its popularity far exceeds its precision. At very least, however, a federal system requires that political power be shared between, on the one hand, a central government and, on the other, local governments. It differs from a unitary system in that local governments possess authority independent of the will of the central government. It differs from a confederation in that, first, the central government does not need the consent of local units to act within its orbit of authority and, second, it can operate directly on citizens rather than only indirectly through local governments.

But these distinctions are quite modern. There were no exact models of federalism for the framers to follow. Indeed, as the peculiar phrasing of Madison's essay in *Federalist* No. 39 (reprinted below, p. 409) shows, the very term "federalism" did not then exist in its current meaning. It is a creation not only of the Convention but of decades of constitutional development.

Much of the debate at Philadelphia focused on the structure that the new government would take. Madison initially joined Edmund Randolph in sponsoring the Virginia Plan, which would have come close to reducing the states to administrative subdivisions of the nation. But even the unhappy experiences under the Articles of Confederation had not convinced a majority of the delegates that such a centralization of power was justified. Here, as in their broader political perspective, the framers distrusted all concentrations of power.

The principal reasons for opposing ratification were fear of the strength of the new national government and its undemocratic character. The opponents, the Anti-Federalists, were defeated because people like Madison and Hamilton convinced their fellow citizens that the new "compound republic"[1] was not a threat to their liberties. But the Anti-Federalists did not roll over and die. They continued— and their successors still continue—to struggle to maximize local autonomy within the constitutional framework.

---

1. Madison, *Federalist,* No. 51.

I. STRUCTURALISM

The plain words of the constitutional document provide only limited guidance about distributions of power between state and nation. Article VI contains the clearest clause:

> This Constitution, and the laws of the United States which shall be made in pursuance thereof; and all treaties made, or which shall be made, under the authority of the United States, shall be the supreme law of the land; and the judges in every state shall be bound thereby, any thing in the Constitution or laws of any state to the contrary notwithstanding.

But to say the Constitution is supreme tells nothing about how the Constitution distributes power. The critical questions here are WHAT to define as the "Constitution," HOW to interpret substantive clauses of the document as well as any other elements of the "Constitution," and WHO interprets the "Constitution."

Several sections of the document offer somewhat different clues about distributions of power. The Tenth Amendment provides the strongest textual support for a deep residuum of state authority:

> The powers not delegated to the United States by the Constitution, nor prohibited by it to the States, are reserved to the States respectively, or to the people.

That amendment, however, was at best only a partial victory for opponents of a muscular national government, and many of them looked on it as a defeat. Several times they had tried to repeat the words of the Articles of Confederation by inserting "expressly" before "delegated." Each time they were voted down and so failed to repudiate the notion of implied national powers contained in the "sweeping clause" of Article I, which delegates to Congress authority "to make all laws which shall be necessary and proper for carrying into execution the foregoing [specifically listed] powers, and all other powers vested by this Constitution in the Government of the United States, or in any Department or officer thereof."

Thus, on the one hand, the constitutional document confers on the national government certain powers that are specifically enumerated, if not defined, as well as certain implied powers that are neither enumerated nor defined. On the other hand, it leaves "to the states respectively, or to the people," all other powers. Those declarations are not particularly helpful except as read in a larger context.

A. Textual Structuralism

And it is in insisting on reading the larger context that structuralism makes its peculiar mark on constitutional interpretation. Textual structuralism would require examination of all relevant clauses of the document. The Preamble lists "to form a more perfect Union" as the

Constitution's very first objective. The body of the document, as originally written, also: (i) denies to each level of government some powers, such as authority to enact bills of attainder or ex post facto laws (Art. I, §§ 9–10); (ii) specifically strikes at some of the state abuses of power by forbidding states to issue paper money, impair the obligations of contracts, or tax exports (Art. I, § 10); (iii) less directly attacks other abuses by expressly delegating (Art. I, § 8) to Congress authority to regulate "commerce with foreign nations, and among the several states, and with the Indian tribes," as well as to "establish . . . uniform laws on the subject of bankruptcies throughout the United States"; and (iv) fleshes out national power by a long list (Art. I, § 8) of specific things the new government can do.

In addition, Art. IV requires the federal government to guarantee each state "a republican form of government" and to protect all states against invasion and insurrection. That same article guarantees the territorial integrity of each state, and establishes a network of relations among the states, including obligations to return fugitive criminals and persons "held to service or labor"—an opaque euphemism for slaves—and to accord "full faith and credit" to each other's public acts. Art. V further protects federalism by providing that no state can be deprived of its equal representation in the Senate, even by constitutional amendment, without its consent. Art. I also guarantees to each state at least one member of the House of Representatives.

Groping for recognition of national citizenship, Art. IV also says that "citizens of each state shall be entitled to all privileges and immunities of citizens in the several states," but does not even hint at what these "privileges and immunities" might include. Art. I echoes the notion of national citizenship by empowering Congress to enact "an uniform rule of naturalization."

An imaginative textual structuralist would also be concerned with what the document does not contain. While it includes a process for admitting new states and federal guarantees for the territorial and political integrity of all states, it has no provision for a state to secede from the Union. Thus Chief Justice Waite could say in Texas v. White (1869; reprinted below, p. 429): "The Constitution, in all its provisions, looks to an indestructible Union, composed of indestructible States."

The Bill of Rights, so people apparently assumed at the time and the Supreme Court unanimously held in Barron v. Baltimore (1833), imposed restrictions solely on the federal government. Here, the Court and the country put aside literalism as an interpretive mode, for the words of amendments 2–9 are general and make no mention of the *federal* as opposed to state government.

Adoption of the Eleventh Amendment, denying federal courts authority to hear "any suit in law or equity, commenced or prosecuted against one of the United States by citizens of another state, or by citizens or subjects of a foreign state," increased the states' freedom from national control. In Hans v. Louisiana (1890), the Court expanded that freedom by once again refusing to interpret the document's words as meaning precisely what they said. The justices held that the amendment also forbade federal courts to hear suits against a state begun by that state's own citizens.[2]

The Fourteenth, that "great centralizing Amendment,"[3] pulls in the opposite direction. Although, its early interpretations (see the Slaughter-Houses Cases [1873; reprinted below, p. 435]) denied that the amendment effected a fundamental change in the structure of American federalism, it has over time nationalized not only most of the Bill of Rights (see Eds.' Notes to Palko v. Connecticut [1937; reprinted above p. 94]) but also the very concept of American citizenship as itself a fundamental right that neither state or national government can take away. (See Trop v. Dulles [1958; reprinted above, p. 144] and the cases discussed in the Eds.' Notes to that ruling.) Moreover, national citizenship carries with it a bundle of other rights, substantive as well as procedural. In sum, as Chapters 11–17 will show, the Fourteenth Amendment has provided textual grounding for a jurisprudence that protects rights against all levels of government, much as Justice Chase argued in Calder v. Bull (1798; reprinted above, p. 86) that "the nature of our free republican government" did.

B. Systemic and Transcendent Structuralism

These constitutional provisions lay down general principles and so prevent many kinds of disputes from arising, but even taken together they leave many important problems unresolved. What does congressional authority to regulate commerce include? How far does it reach into matters that, on their face, seem local? What does "necessary and proper" include, only powers that are absolutely essential or those that are merely convenient? In either instance, what are the "powers not delegated to the United States"? When can federal judges substitute their judgments about the Constitution's nature, scope, and content for those of state officials?

To solve these sorts of difficulties every constitutional interpreter has seen in or perhaps even brought to his or her reading of the document a larger concept of the structure of the federal system. As John Marshall explained in McCulloch v. Maryland (1819; reprinted below, p. 413), when the Court sustained congressional authority to charter a national bank:

> There is no express provision for the case, but the claim has been
> sustained on a principle which so entirely pervades the constitution,
> is so intermixed with the materials which compose it, so interwoven

---

2. *Hans'* reading of the constitutional text is strained, and recently four justices have attacked the validity of its interpretation. See Atascadero State Hospital v. Scanlon (1985) and Green v. Mansour (1985).

3. Justice Jackson for the Court in Fay v. New York (1947).

with its web, so blended with its texture, as to be incapable of being
separated from it, without rending it into shreds.

To the justices, that "principle" may have been one that "entirely
pervades the constitution," but Thomas Jefferson could not find it
there. The Constitution, he complained, had become "a mere thing
of wax in the hands of the judiciary, which they may twist and shape
into any form they please." [4] And even Marshall's admiring biogra-
pher thought that in *McCulloch* the Chief Justice had proceeded with
"sublime audacity." [5] During the following summer, Marshall spent
much of his time writing a series of newspaper articles under the pen
name "A Friend of the Constitution," [6] replying to articles by Virginia
judges (also published under pen names), not only castigating *McCulloch* for having "rendered the Constitution the sport of legal ingenuity," [7] but also furiously attacking its conception of federalism.

This bitter debate underlines both the necessity and the illusive-
ness of structural arguments, for, no less than Marshall—and no less
than modern justices in National League of Cities v. Usery (1976;
reprinted below, p. 449) and Garcia v. San Antonio MTA (1985;
reprinted below, p. 461)—the jurists from Virginia envisioned an
architectural scheme of American federalism whose outlines the constitutional document only roughly sketches. That vision differed from
Marshall's, but it was no more closely connected to the document's
text than was his; indeed, probably less so.

II. THEORIES OF AMERICAN FEDERALISM

A. National Supremacy

By holding that a citizen of one state could sue another state in a
federal court, Chisholm v. Georgia (1793) in effect ruled that the
national government was, within certain fields, superior to the states.
The Eleventh Amendment reversed the specific holding about federal
jurisdiction, but not about federal supremacy. And through most of
John Marshall's tenure as Chief Justice (1801–1835), the Court did
not retreat from that basic doctrine. Fletcher v. Peck (1810; reprinted below, p. 956) was the first instance [8] in which the justices declared
a state statute unconstitutional and Martin v. Hunter's Lessee (1816;

---

4. To Spencer Roane, September 6, 1819, in Andrew A. Lipscomb, ed., *The Writings of
Thomas Jefferson* (Washington: The Thomas Jefferson Memorial Association, 1903), XV, 213. It
is worth noting, in light of the discussion of Who shall interpret in Chapters 6 and 7, that
Jefferson was criticizing Marshall for *not* declaring an act of Congress unconstitutional. Was
Jefferson being inconsistent with his departmental theory of interpretation?

5. Albert J. Beveridge, *The Life of John Marshall* (Boston: Houghton Mifflin Co., 1919), IV,
302.

6. See Gerald Gunther, ed., *John Marshall's Defense of McCulloch v. Maryland* (Stanford, Cal.:
Stanford University Press, 1969).

7. Quoted in Charles Warren, *The Supreme Court in United States History* (Rev. ed.; Boston:
Little, Brown & Co., 1926), I, 557.

8. In effect, Ware v. Hylton (1796) invalidated a Virginia statute as conflicting with Jay's
Treaty, though the justices did not specifically hold the state statute unconstitutional.

reprinted above, p. 266) reaffirmed earlier pronouncements that federal judges were superior to state jurists in constitutional interpretation.

McCulloch v. Maryland offered a classic structuralist justification for national supremacy. First, Marshall argued that the federal government is not the creature of the state governments. Rather, like the Constitution itself, it "proceeds directly from the people; is 'ordained and established' in the name of the people . . . . The government of the Union, then . . . is, emphatically and truly, a government of the people." (Madison in *Federalist* No. 39 [reprinted below, p. 409] had offered a somewhat less nationalistic explanation of the Constitution's source; but he was trying to persuade people to accept a greater degree of centralized power than in their existing system.) Second, Marshall joined this "fact" of the people as the source of national authority to the supremacy clause to reason that:

> If any one proposition could command the universal consent of mankind, we might expect it would be this—that the government of the Union, though limited in its powers, is supreme within its sphere of action. This would seem to result necessarily from its nature. It is the government of all; its powers are delegated by all; it represents all, and acts for all.

Third, he went on to construe the "sweeping clause" broadly and to interpret "necessary and proper" to mean "appropriate." Thus he concluded that Congress not only had authority to incorporate a bank but also that "the states have no power, by taxation or otherwise, to retard, impede, burden, or in any manner control the operation of constitutional laws enacted by Congress . . . ."

B. "Dual Federalism"

Judicial opinions may point toward solutions of pressing problems of public policy; but, even when as cleverly reasoned as John Marshall's, seldom by themselves alone do they fully and finally resolve those problems. Among the difficulties that *McCulloch* did not have to face was that of state regulation of matters that apparently fell within the ambit of federal control but over which Congress had not acted. And for ensuing generations, state regulation of commerce has provided a frequent battleground.

Marshall dodged this issue in Gibbons v. Ogden (1824), involving the authority of New York to regulate commerce between itself and New Jersey; he found an obscure federal licensing statute that enabled him to point to a congressional exercise of its power. In his final years, as he was losing control of his Court to new justices more concerned to protect state interests, he ignored the federal licensing act to sustain state control over navigable waters [9]—in effect, giving up a little to preserve as much national supremacy as he could.

---

9. Willson v. Blackbird Creek Marsh Co. (1829).

Marshall's successor as Chief Justice, Roger Brooke Taney, had a much less nationalistic view of federalism. Whereas Marshall saw the nation as supreme, within its sphere, over the states and the Court as an agent of national supremacy, Taney and a majority of his colleagues tended to see state and nation as almost co-equal sovereigns. As Edward S. Corwin said, "the Court under Taney sometimes talked as if it regarded all the reserved powers of the States as limiting national power . . . ." [10] The Court became, if anything, more important politically, because it operated as umpire between these two almost equals. When, however, states challenged federal *judicial* authority, Taney and his brethren could speak as nationalistically as Marshall, as the Court's opinion in Ableman v. Booth (1859; reprinted above, p. 274) illustrates.

Near the end of the nineteenth century, when the justices became persuaded that the Constitution required economic laissez-faire, they turned to dual federalism as a weapon against federal regulation of the economy. There was a great deal of irony here, for Taney had largely developed his doctrine to allow state governments to regulate commercial affairs in the absence of congressional action. From 1890 until 1937, however, the justices often used dual federalism to strike down federal regulation on grounds that it somehow interfered with powers reserved to the states. When, for example, the federal government tried to break up a monopoly that controlled 97 per cent of sugar refining,[11] the Court held it irrelevant that the business was involved in commerce on a national scale. Manufacturing was local and therefore under state authority; that authority limited the power of Congress to "regulate commerce . . . among the several States." (At the same time, the Court was using other weapons to invalidate state social and economic legislation—see the discussion in Chapter 15.)

It was necessary for the justices to play games with stare decisis by either ignoring or misstating Marshall's jurisprudence; it was also useful, if not essential, to sin against textualism. To justify striking down a congressional effort to ban goods made by child labor from being shipped in interstate commerce, the Court not only took a narrow view of the "sweeping clause," it also read the Tenth Amendment so expansively as to include the word expressly, which the states righters had been unable to put in. As Justice Day wrote for the Court:

> In interpreting the Constitution it must never be forgotten that the Nation is made up of States to which are entrusted the powers of local government. And to them and to the people the powers not

---

10. "Introduction to the 1953 Edition," reprinted in Lester S. Jayson et al., eds., *The Constitution of the United States of America: Analysis and Interpretation* (Washington, D.C.: Government Printing Office, 1973), p. xix.

11. United States v. E.C. Knight (1895).

expressly delegated to the National Government are reserved.[12] [Italics added.]

Thus the justices could strike down federal efforts to regulate economic affairs as invading state authority under the Tenth Amendment and state efforts to regulate the same matters as violating due process.

C. A Return to John Marshall and National Supremacy

As we have seen, Roosevelt's landslide victory in the election of 1936 and his threat to pack the Court tipped the minds of the justices enough to end their affair with liassez-faire. In the spring of 1937, the old justices began expanding their views about the reach of the commerce clause.[13] In 1941, Justice Stone quoted Marshall in Gibbons v. Ogden to hold for the Court that the "power of Congress over interstate commerce 'is complete in itself, may be exercised to its utmost extent, and acknowledges no limitations other than are prescribed in the Constitution.'" The Tenth Amendment, Stone continued,

> states but a truism that all is retained which has not been surrendered. There is nothing in the history of its adoption to suggest that it was more than declaratory of the relationship between the national and state government as it had been established by the Constitution before the amendment or that its purpose was other than to allay fears that the new national government might seek to exercise powers not granted, and that the states might not be able to exercise fully their reserved powers.[14]

Wickard v. Filburn (1942) showed just how far the President, Congress, and the Court were willing to go. There the justices sustained a fine against a farmer for planting 11 more acres of wheat than the quota set by the Secretary of Agriculture. That Farmer Filburn intended to use the wheat for his own consumption was of no import, because if he ate his own wheat he would not buy bread or flour and so might still affect the national market.

During the decades that followed, the principal questions the justices asked about national regulation of commerce were those of statutory interpretation. They treated as settled Congress' constitutional authority to regulate almost any commercial activity it wanted. It was under this broad view of the commerce power that the Court sustained provisions of the Civil Rights Act of 1964 outlawing segregation in most hotels, restaurants, and similar facilities.[15]

Federal regulations touching on state as contrasted with private activity have generated more lasting problems. Taxation has been

---

12. Hammer v. Dagenhart (1918).

13. See espec. NLRB v. Jones & Laughlin (1937); NLRB v. Fruehauf Trailor Co. (1937); NLRB v. Friedman-Harry Marks Clothing Co. (1937).

14. United States v. Darby Lumber Co. (1941).

15. See espec. Heart of Atlanta Motel v. United States (1964).

SHARING POWERS: THE NATURE OF THE UNION

peculiarly vexsome. As part of dual federalism, the Court, beginning with Collector v. Day (1871), extrapolated from *McCulloch*'s insistence on the immunity of federal instrumentalities from state taxation, to the immunity of state instrumentalities from federal taxation.[16] These immunities did not reach "normal" commercial activities, such as selling liquor, in which states might become involved, but they did include salaries of governmental employees or income from selling to either level of government goods, such as motorcycles for police, needed to carry out its official work.

Coming shortly after the constitutional revolution of 1937, Helvering v. Gerhart (1939) was the crucial case in undoing this aspect of dual federalism, but many problems remain. First, differentiating between "normal" commercial activities and essential state operations, though easy at the core, is sometimes difficult at the edges.[17] Second, even general regulations not related to taxation, such as those setting minimum wage and hours, when applied to state employees, can have a significant impact on a state's expenditures and so on its public policies. It was to these sorts of puzzles that the Court has recently returned in cases like National League of Cities v. Usury (1976; reprinted below, p. 449) and Garcia v. San Antonio MTA (1985; reprinted below, p. 461). *National League of Cities* transmitted strong hints that dual federalism was beginning a new incarnation, then *Garcia* performed a quick burial; but the dissenters predicted a rapid resurrection.

III. PROTECTING FEDERALISM: A TASK FOR JUDGES OR LEGISLATORS?

"Federalism," a noted English scholar has claimed, "means legalism—the predominance of the judiciary in the Constitution."[18] This aspect of limited powers returns us directly to the question Chapters 6 and 7 addressed: WHO shall interpret? Certainly American judges usually dominate in safeguarding the federal nature of the system.

Nevertheless the propriety of that role and even its efficacy are open to dispute. Political scientists like Morton Grodzins[19] and Daniel J. Elazar[20] have claimed that the strongest protection for the states comes not from judges but from the way federalism permeates all American political structures, formal and informal. Political parties, like most interest groups, are federal in their organization. Senators and representatives are elected from individual states, not from the nation as a whole. And while they take oaths as national

16. These rulings, at least those coming after 1913, ignored the plain words of the Sixteenth Amendment: "The Congress shall have power to lay and collect taxes on incomes, from whatever source derived . . . ."

17. See the way in which the Court splintered in New York v. United States (1946).

18. A.V. Dicey, *Introduction to the Study of the Law of the Constitution* (6th ed.; London: Macmillan, 1902), pp. 170–171.

19. *The American System,* ed. Daniel J. Elazar, (Chicago: Rand, McNally, 1966).

20. *American Federalism* (3rd. ed.; New York: Harper & Row, 1984).

officials, they cannot afford to run roughshod over the wishes—and bases of power—of those on whom they depend for reelection. Indeed, a typical criticism of Congress is that it behaves more as a collection of ambassadors from the states than a body of national officers.[21]

The President's constituency is national, but to get anything done he has to win Congress' consent; and, even within the executive branch, he must operate through sets of bureaucracies that often display deeper loyalty to senators and representatives on budgetary subcommittees (and those legislators' concerns for local interests) than to a temporary tenant of the White House. Furthermore, to save money, create jobs for constituents, and ease the appearance of a threat to state authority, Congress often provides that state and local officials will share in administering federal laws.

At the start, the *Federalist* had stressed the federal structure of the national government (see espec. No. 39, reprinted below p. 409, and Nos. 32–33, 44–46, 82, 84), and John Marshall had integrated such an analysis into his opinion in *McCulloch:* A state tax on a national instrumentality was far more dangerous than a national tax on a state instrumentality, the Chief Justice reasoned, because only the citizens of a single state were represented in any state legislature and thus part of the people would be taxing the whole people. Congress, however, included representatives from all the states, and thus a general national tax was a tax on all voted on by all.

Differences about the relative importance of the judiciary in protecting federalism have sharply divided constitutional interpreters. Marshall, as we have seen, looked principally to the political processes, Taney to the courts. A majority of the justices have usually been willing, and sometimes anxious, to mark the boundaries between state and federal power, but some have been reluctant. Hugo Black, for instance, did not want the Court to decide when state regulation of commerce trespassed on congressional power. It was to Congress, he argued, that the Constitution delegated the power to regulate commerce. And Congress was quite able of exercising that authority. Judges should restrict themselves to construing congressional action: "A century and a half of constitutional history and government admonishes this Court to leave that choice to the elected representatives of the people themselves, where it properly belongs both on democratic principles and the requirements of efficient government."[22]

---

21. For a study linking congressional behavior with a felt necessity for reelection, see David R. Mayhew, *Congress: The Electoral Connection* (New Haven: Yale University Press, 1974).

22. Dissenting in Southern Pacific Co. v. Arizona (1945); see also his dissent in Hood v. DuMond (1949). In both these cases Justice Jackson joined the majority, but he apparently also accepted the primacy of political processes as protectors as federalism. As he wrote for the Court in Wickard v. Filburn (1942): Marshall in Gibbons v. Ogden (1824) had "made emphatic the embracing and penetrating nature of [the commerce power] by warning that effective restraints on its exercise must proceed from political rather than from judicial processes."

National League of Cities and *Garcia* continue this debate. As Justice Blackmun said for the Court in the latter case, "the principal means chosen by the Framers to ensure the role of the States in the federal system lies in the structure of the Federal Government itself." After reasoning echoing Grodzins and Elazar, Blackmun concluded:

> [T]he Framers chose to rely on a federal system in which special restraints on federal power over the States inhered principally in the workings of the National Government itself, rather than in discrete limitations on the objects of federal authority. State sovereign interests, then, are more properly protected by procedural safeguards inherent in the structure of the federal system than by judicially created limitations on federal power.

Some scholars have generalized even more broadly from this sort of argument. Jesse H. Choper, for example, would have judges surrender the role of federal arbiter. Both state and national governments, he asserts, can readily defend their interests in the political processes.[23] Courts should conserve their time, energy, and power, he maintains, to protect individual rights, for private citizens seldom have the political strength to stand up against governmental officials. So restricting judges' constitutional concerns might well accord with strategic notions of economy of force and concentration of power, but Hugo Black was unusual among the justices in being anxious to give up such an important role. As Justice William O. Douglas once noted—and with some historic justification: "We sit as a court of law functioning primarily as a referee in the federal system."[24]

IV. THE CONTINUING STRUGGLE

In the period through the Civil War, differences about the nature of the Union posed the most serious danger to the survival of the American Republic. The threat of atomic war now heavily overshadows all problems of constitutional construction; but even among domestic difficulties, federalism does not seem especially serious and certainly not dramatic. It was replaced as *the* central constitutional question a generation after the Civil War by questions created by the rise of American capitalism: How can the polity accommodate individual liberty in an age of increasing interdependence? That problem is still with us, though the specific issues are now raised by other "fundamental rights" such as those to privacy and equal treatment by government.

One should recognize that questions of federalism typically revolve around specific issues of public policy such as the legitimacy of a national bank or the validity of governmental regulation of economic affairs. It is also clear that questions of federalism are also questions

---

23. *Judicial Review and the National Political Process* (Chicago: University of Chicago Press, 1980). Choper also makes, as Chapter 9 indicated, a similar argument against judges' setting boundaries of power between Congress and the President.

24. Walker v. Birmingham, dis. op. (1967).

of power: Who shall govern, state or national officials? Or in some areas, neither? In this context, especially when so many of recent abuses of civil liberties have come from local rather than national majorities, it is easy to forget that the basic purpose of federalism is the same as that of separating institutions at the national level: to protect individual liberty by diffusing political power.

SELECTED BIBLIOGRAPHY

Barber, Sotirios A. *On What the Constitution Means* (Baltimore: The Johns Hopkins University Press, 1984), chap. 4.

Berns, Walter. "The Meaning of the 10th Amendment," in Robert A. Goldwin, ed., *A Nation of States* (Chicago: Rand, McNally, 1974).

Black, Charles L. *Structure and Relationship in American Constitutional Law* (Baton Rouge: Louisiana State University Press, 1969).

Choper, Jesse H. *Judicial Review and the National Political Process* (Chicago: University of Chicago Press, 1980).

Corwin, Edward S., "The Passing of Dual Federalism," 36 *Va.L.Rev.* 1 (1950).

Diamond, Martin. "What the Framers Meant by Federalism," in Robert A. Goldwin, ed., *A Nation of States* (Chicago: Rand, McNally, 1974).

Duchachek, Ivo D. *Comparative Federalism* (New York: Holt, Rinehart & Winston, 1970).

Elazar, Daniel J. *American Federalism* (3rd ed.; New York: Harper & Row, 1984).

Freund, Paul. "A Supreme Court in a Federation," 53 *Colum.L.Rev.* 597 (1953).

————. "Umpiring the Federal System," in Arthur W. MacMahon, ed. *Federalism Mature and Emergent* (New York: Doubleday, 1955).

Grodzins, Morton. *The American System,* ed. Daniel J. Elazar. (Chicago: Rand, McNally, 1966).

Harris, William F., II. "Bonding Word and Polity," 76 *Am.Pol Sci. Rev.* 34 (1982).

Howard, A.E. Dick. "The Supreme Court and Federalism," in *The Courts: Pendulum of Federalism* (Washington, D.C.: The Roscoe Pound-American Trial Lawyers Ass'n, 1979).

Lofgren, Charles A. "The Origins of the Tenth Amendment," in Ronald K.L. Collins, ed., *Constitutional Government in America* (Durham, N.C.: Carolina Academic Press, 1980).

MacMahon, Arthur W., ed. *Federalism Mature and Emergent* (New York: Doubleday, 1955).

McWhinney, Edward. *Comparative Federalism* (Toronto: University of Toronto Press, 1962).

Mason, Alpheus Thomas, ed. *The States Rights Debate: Anti-Federalism and the Constitution* (2nd ed.; Englewood Cliffs, N.J.: Prentice-Hall, 1972).

Pritchett, C. Herman. *Constitutional Law of the Federal System* (Englewood Cliffs, N.J.: Prentice-Hall, 1984), chaps. 4–5, 11–13.

Riker, William H. *Federalism: Origin, Operation, Significance* (Boston: Little, Brown, 1964).

Storing, Herbert J. *What the Anti-Federalists Were For* (Chicago: University of Chicago Press, 1981).

"The proposed Constitution . . . is, in strictness, neither a national nor a federal Constitution, but a composition of both."

FEDERALIST NO. 39

James Madison (1788).

. . . The first question that offers itself is whether the general form and aspect of the government be strictly republican. It is evident that no other form would be reconcilable with the genius of the people of America; with the fundamental principles of the Revolution; or with that honorable determination which animates every votary of freedom to rest all our political experiments on the capacity of mankind for self-government. . . .

If we resort for a criterion to the different principles on which different forms of government are established, we may define a republic to be . . . a government which derives all its powers directly or indirectly from the great body of the people, and is administered by persons holding their offices during pleasure for a limited period, or during good behavior. It is *essential* to such a government that it be derived from the great body of the society, not from an inconsiderable proportion or a favored class of it . . . . It is *sufficient* for such a government that the persons administering it be appointed, either directly or indirectly, by the people; and that they hold their appointments by either of the tenures just specified . . . .

On comparing the Constitution planned by the convention with the standard here fixed, we perceived at once that it is, in the most rigid sense, conformable to it. The House of Representatives . . . is elected immediately by the great body of the people. The Senate . . . derives its appointment indirectly from the people. The President is indirectly derived from the choice of the people, according to the example in most of the States. Even the judges, with all other officers of the Union, will, as in the several States, be the choice, though a remote choice, of the people themselves. The duration of the appointments is equally conformable to the republican standard and to the model of State constitutions. . . .

Could any further proof be required of the republican complexion of this system, the most decisive one might be found in its absolute prohibition of titles of nobility, both under the federal and the State governments; and in its express guaranty of the republican form to each of the latter.

"But it was not sufficient," say the adversaries of the proposed Constitution, "for the convention to adhere to the republican form. They ought with equal care to have preserved the *federal* * form, which regards the Union as a *Confederacy* of sovereign states; instead of which they have framed a *national* government, which regards the Union as a *consolidation* of the States." And it is asked by what authority this bold and radical innovation was undertaken? . . .

. . . [I]t will be necessary . . . first, to ascertain the real character of the government in question; secondly, to inquire how far the convention were authorized to propose such a government; and thirdly, how far the duty they owed to their country could supply any defect of regular authority.

First.—In order to ascertain the real character of the government, it may be considered in relation to the foundation on which it is to be established; to the sources from which its ordinary powers are to be drawn; to the operation of those powers; to the extent of them; and to the authority by which future changes in the government are to be introduced.

On examining the first relation, it appears, on one hand, that the Constitution is to be founded on the assent and ratification of the people of America, given by deputies elected for the special purpose; but, on the other, that this assent and ratification is to be given by the people, not as individuals composing one entire nation, but as composing the distinct and independent States to which they respectively belong. It is to be the assent and ratification of the several States, derived from the supreme authority in each State—the authority of the people themselves. The act, therefore, establishing the Constitution will not be a *national* but a *federal* act.

* **Eds.' Note:** Madison uses the term "federal" to refer to an arrangement closer to what modern analysts would call a confederation, that is, a union of sovereign states with a weak central government that operates only vis-á-vis the states and not directly on citizens of those states. Today we refer to the mixed system Madison describes here as "federal" and make a three-fold distinction among a confederation, a federal system, and a unitary system in which the central government is supreme in all spheres and local governments are merely its creatures. Each individual American state has a unitary system: Local governments exist at the sufferance of the state government, at least in formal terms, though the actual power of some local officials may be such as to make them more influential than many state officials.

That it will be a federal and not a national act . . . is obvious from this single consideration: that it is to result neither from the decision of a *majority* of the people of the Union, nor from that of a *majority* of the States. It must result from the *unanimous* assent of the several States that are parties to it, differing no otherwise from their ordinary assent than in its being expressed, not by the legislative authority, but by that of the people themselves. Were the people regarded in this transaction as forming one nation, the will of the majority of the whole people of the United States would bind the minority . . . . Each State, in ratifying the Constitution, is considered as a sovereign body independent of all others, and only to be bound by its own voluntary act. In this relation, then, the new Constitution will, if established, be a *federal* and not a *national* constitution.

The next relation is to the sources from which the ordinary powers of government are to be derived. The House of Representatives will derive its powers from the people of America; and the people will be represented in the same proportion and on the same principle as they are in the legislature of a particular State. So far the government is *national,* not *federal.* The Senate, on the other hand, will derive its powers from the States as political and coequal societies; and these will be represented on the principle of equality in the Senate, as they now are in the existing Congress. So far the government is *federal,* not *national.* The executive power will be derived from a very compound source. The immediate election of the President is to be made by the States in their political characters. The votes allotted to them are in a compound ratio, which considers them partly as distinct and coequal societies, partly as unequal members of the same society. The eventual election again, is to be made by that branch of the legislature * which consists of the national representatives; but in this particular act they are to be thrown into the form of individual delegations from so many distinct and co-equal bodies politic. From this aspect of the government it appears to be of a mixed character, presenting at least as many *federal* as *national* features.

. . . [As to] the *operation of the government* . . . the Constitution . . . falls under the *national* not the *federal* character; though perhaps not so completely as has been understood. In several cases, and particularly in the trial of controversies to which States may be parties, they must be viewed and proceeded against in their collective and political capacities only. But the operation of the government on the people in their individual capacities, in its ordinary and most essential proceedings, will, in the sense of its opponents, on the whole, designate it, in this relation, a *national* government.

But if the government be national with regard to the *operation* of its powers, it changes its aspect again when we contemplate it in relation to the extent of its powers. The idea of a national government

---

* **Eds.' Note:** This comment is one of several hints that the framers thought the Electoral College would usually nominate candidates for the presidency and the House would make the final choice.

involves in it not only an authority over the individual citizens, but an indefinite supremacy over all persons and things, so far as they are objects of lawful government. Among a people consolidated into one nation, this supremacy is completely vested in the national legislature. Among communities united for particular purposes, it is vested partly in the general and partly in the municipal legislatures. In the former case, all local authorities are subordinate to the supreme; and may be controlled, directed, or abolished by it at pleasure. In the latter, the local or municipal authorities form distinct and independent portions of the supremacy, no more subject, within their respective spheres, to the general authority than the general authority is subject to them, within its own sphere. In this relation, then, the proposed government cannot be deemed a *national* one; since its jurisdiction extends to certain enumerated objects only, and leaves to the several States a residuary and inviolable sovereignty over all other objects. It is true that in controversies relating to the boundary between the two jurisdictions, the tribunal which is ultimately to decide is to be established under the general government. But this does not change the principle of the case. The decision is to be impartially made, according to the rules of the Constitution; and all the usual and most effectual precautions are taken to secure this impartiality. Some such tribunal is clearly essential to prevent an appeal to the sword and a dissolution of the compact; and that it ought to be established under the general rather than under the local governments, or, to speak more properly, that it could be safely established under the first alone, is a position not likely to be combated.

If we try the Constitution by its last relation to the authority by which amendments are to be made, we find it neither wholly *national* nor wholly *federal*. . . . In requiring more than a majority, and particularly in computing the proportion by *States,* not by *citizens,* it departs from the national and advances towards the *federal* character; in rendering the concurrence of less than the whole number of States sufficient, it loses again the *federal* and partakes of the *national* character.

The proposed Constitution, therefore . . . is, in strictness, neither a national nor a federal Constitution, but a composition of both. In its foundation it is federal, not national; in the sources from which the ordinary powers of the government are drawn, it is partly federal and partly national; in the operation of these powers, it is national, not federal; in the extent of them, again, it is federal, not national; and, finally in the authoritative mode of introducing amendments, it is neither wholly federal nor wholly national.

Publius.

"It is a mistake, that the constitution was not designed to operate upon the states, in their corporate capacities."

MARTIN v. HUNTER'S LESSEE

14 U.S. (1 Wheat.) 304, 4 L.Ed. 97 (1816).

This case, upholding the supremacy of a national treaty over a state law and of constitutional interpretations by federal over those of state judges, is reprinted above at p. 266.

"[T]he government of the Union, though limited in its powers, is supreme within its sphere of action."

McCULLOCH v. MARYLAND

17 U.S. (4 Wheat.) 316, 4 L.Ed. 579 (1819).

In 1811, during James Madison's first administration, the Jeffersonians allowed the Bank of the United States, originally chartered in 1791 at the urging of the arch-Federalist, Alexander Hamilton, to die. But, in 1816, national fiscal difficulties following the War of 1812 persuaded the Jeffersonians to recharter the Bank, which quickly became an aggressive financial institution successful in attracting much of the business of competing state banks. Local banks sought relief from their own legislatures, and many states, including Maryland, began to tax the national bank. Maryland required banks not chartered by its legislature to issue notes only on special stamped paper which the state would supply at an annual fee of $15,000 plus an additional charge for each note. James McCulloch, cashier of the Baltimore branch of the Bank of the United States, took time out from his systematic looting of the bank's resources to refuse to pay the tax. Maryland then obtained a judgment for the taxes from the Baltimore County court, and the state's Court of Appeals sustained the ruling. McCulloch sought a writ of error from the U.S. Supreme Court.

MARSHALL, Ch. J., delivered the opinion of the court:

In the case now to be determined, the defendant, a sovereign state, denies the obligation of a law enacted by the legislature of the Union, and the plaintiff, on his part, contests the validity of an act which has been passed by the legislature of that state. The constitution of our country, in its most interesting and vital parts, is to be considered; the conflicting powers of the government of the Union and of its members, as marked in that constitution, are to be discussed; and an opinion given, which may essentially influence the great operations of the government. No tribunal can approach such a question without a deep sense of its importance, and of the awful responsibility involved in its decision. But it must be decided peacefully, or remain a source of hostile legislation, perhaps of hostility of a still more serious nature; and if it is to be so decided, by this tribunal alone can the decision be made. On the Supreme Court of the United States has the constitution of our country devolved this important duty.

The first question made in the cause is, has Congress power to incorporate a bank?

It . . . can scarcely be considered as an open question, entirely unprejudiced by the former proceedings of the nation respecting it. The principle now contested was introduced at a very early period of our history, has been recognized by many successive legislatures, and has been acted upon by the judicial department, in cases of peculiar delicacy, as a law of undoubted obligation.

appeal to history

It will not be denied that a bold and daring usurpation might be resisted, after an acquiescence still longer and more complete than this. But it is conceived that a doubtful question, one on which human reason may pause, and the human judgment be suspended, in the decision of which the great principles of liberty are not concerned, but the respective powers of those who are equally the representatives of the people, are to be adjusted; if not put at rest by the practice of the government, ought to receive a considerable impression from that practice. An exposition of the constitution, deliberately established by legislative acts, on the faith of which an immense property has been advanced, ought not to be lightly disregarded.

The power now contested was exercised by the first Congress elected under the present constitution.

The bill for incorporating the bank of the United States did not steal upon an unsuspecting legislature, and pass unobserved. Its principle was completely understood, and was opposed with equal zeal and ability. . . . The original act was permitted to expire; but a short experience of the embarrassments to which the refusal to revive it exposed the government, convinced those who were most prejudiced against the measure of its necessity and induced the passage of the present law. It would require no ordinary share of intrepidity to assert that a measure adopted under these circumstances was a bold and plain usurpation, to which the constitution gave no countenance.

These observations belong to the cause; but they are not made under the impression that, were the question entirely new, the law would be found irreconcilable with the constitution.

In discussing this question, the counsel for the state of Maryland have deemed it of some importance in the construction of the constitution, to consider that instrument not as emanating from the people, but as the act of sovereign and independent states. The powers of the general government, it has been said, are delegated by the states, who alone are truly sovereign; and must be exercised in subordination to the states, who alone possess supreme dominion.

It would be difficult to sustain this proposition. The convention which framed the constitution was indeed elected by the state legislatures. But the instrument, when it came from their hands, was a mere proposal, without obligation, or pretensions to it. It was reported to the then existing Congress of the United States, with a request that it might "be submitted to a convention of delegates, chosen in each state by the people thereof, under the recommendation of its legislature, for their assent and ratification." This mode of proceeding was adopted; and by the convention, by Congress, and by the state legislatures, the instrument was submitted to the people. They acted upon it in the only manner in which they can act safely, effectively, and wisely, on such a subject, by assembling in convention. It is true, they assembled in their several states—and where else should they have assembled? No political dreamer was ever wild enough to think of breaking down the lines which separate the states, and of compounding the American people into one common mass. Of consequence, when they act, they act in their states. But the measures they adopt do not, on that account, cease to be the measures of the people themselves, or become the measures of the state governments.

From these conventions the constitution derives its whole authority. The government proceeds directly from the people; is "ordained and established" in the name of the people . . . . The assent of the states, in their sovereign capacity, is implied in calling a convention, and thus submitting that instrument to the people. But the people were at perfect liberty to accept or reject it; and their act was final. It required not the affirmance, and could not be negatived, by the state governments. The constitution, when thus adopted, was of complete obligation, and bound the state sovereignties.

It has been said that the people had already surrendered all their powers to the state sovereignties, and had nothing more to give. But, surely, the question whether they may resume and modify the powers granted to government does not remain to be settled in this country . . . . To the formation of a league, such as was the confederation, the state sovereignties were certainly competent. But when, "in order to form a more perfect union," it was deemed necessary to change this alliance into an effective government, possessing great and sovereign powers, and acting directly on the people, the necessity of referring it to the people, and of deriving its powers directly from them, was felt and acknowledged by all.

The government of the Union, then (whatever may be the influence of this fact on the case), is, emphatically, and truly, a government of the people. In form and in substance it emanates from them. Its powers are granted by them, and are to be exercised directly on them, and for their benefit.

This government is acknowledged by all to be one of enumerated powers. . . . But the question respecting the extent of the powers actually granted, is perpetually arising, and will probably continue to arise, as long as our system shall exist.

In discussing these questions, the conflicting powers of the general and state governments must be brought into view, and the supremacy of their respective laws, when they are in opposition, must be settled.

If any one proposition could command the universal assent of mankind, we might expect it would be this—that the government of the Union, though limited in its powers, is supreme within its sphere of action. This would seem to result necessarily from its nature. It is the government of all; its powers are delegated by all; it represents all, and acts for all. Though any one state may be willing to control its operations, no state is willing to allow others to control them. The nation, on those subjects on which it can act, must necessarily bind its component parts. But this question is not left to mere reason; the people have, in express terms, decided it by saying, "this constitution, and the laws of the United States, which shall be made in pursuance thereof," "shall be the supreme law of the land," and by requiring that the members of the state legislatures, and the officers of the executive and judicial departments of the states shall take the oath of fidelity to it.

The government of the United States, then, though limited in its powers, is supreme; and its laws, when made in pursuance of the constitution, form the supreme law of the land, "anything in the constitution or laws of any state to the contrary notwithstanding."

Among the enumerated powers, we do not find that of establishing a bank or creating a corporation. But there is no phrase in the instrument which, like the articles of confederation, excludes incidental or implied powers; and which requires that everything granted shall be expressly and minutely described. Even the 10th amendment, which was framed for the purpose of quieting the excessive jealousies which had been excited, omits the word "expressly," and declares only that the powers "not delegated to the United States, nor prohibited to the states, are reserved to the states or to the people;" thus leaving the question, whether the particular power which may become the subject of contest has been delegated to the one government, or prohibited to the other, to depend on a fair construction of the whole instrument. The men who drew and adopted this amendment had experienced the embarrassments resulting from the insertion of this word in the articles of confederation, and probably omitted it to avoid those embarrassments. A constitution, to contain an accurate detail of all the subdivisions of which its great powers will admit, and of all the means by which they may be carried into execution, would partake of a prolixity of a legal code, and could scarcely be embraced by the human mind. It would probably never be understood by the public. Its nature, therefore, requires, that only its great outlines should be marked, its important objects designated, and the minor ingredients which compose those objects be deduced from the nature of the objects themselves. That this idea was entertained by the framers of the American constitution, is not only to be inferred from the nature of the instrument, but from the language. Why else were some of the limitations, found in the ninth section of the 1st article, introduced? It is also, in some degree, warranted by their having omitted to use any restrictive term which might prevent its receiving a fair and just interpretation. In considering this question, then, we must never forget that it is *a constitution* we are expounding.

Although, among the enumerated powers of government, we do not find the word "bank" or "incorporation," we find the great powers to lay and collect taxes; to borrow money; to regulate commerce; to declare and conduct a war; and to raise and support armies and navies. The sword and the purse, all the external relations, and no inconsiderable portion of the industry of the nation, are entrusted to its government. It can never be pretended that these vast powers draw after them others of inferior importance, merely because they are inferior. . . . But it may with great reason be contended, that a government, entrusted with such ample powers, on the due execution of which the happiness and prosperity of the nation so vitally depends, must also be entrusted with ample means for their execution. The power being given, it is the interest of the nation to facilitate its execution. It can never be their interest, and cannot be presumed to have been their intention, to clog and embarrass its execution by withholding the most appropriate means. Throughout this vast republic, from the St. Croix to the Gulf of Mexico, from the Atlantic to the Pacific, revenue is to be collected and expended, armies are to be marched and supported. . . . Is that construction of the constitution to be preferred which would render these operations difficult, hazardous, and expensive? Can we adopt that construction (unless the words imperiously require it) which would impute to the framers of that instrument, when granting these powers for the public good, the intention of impeding their exercise by withholding a choice of means? If, indeed, such be the mandate of the constitution, we have only to obey; but that instrument does not profess to enumerate the means by which the powers it confers may be executed; nor does it prohibit the creation of a corporation, if the existence of such a being be essential to the beneficial exercise of those powers. It is, then, the subject of fair inquiry, how far such means may be employed. It is not denied that the powers given to the government imply the ordinary means of execution. . . . But it is denied that the government has its choice of means; or, that it may employ the most convenient means, if, to employ them, it be necessary to erect a corporation.

On what foundation does this argument rest? On this alone: The power of creating a corporation, is one appertaining to sovereignty, and is not expressly conferred on Congress. This is true. But all legislative powers appertain to sovereignty . . . .

The government which has a right to do an act, and has imposed on it the duty of performing that act, must, according to the dictates of reason, be allowed to select the means; and those who contend that it may not select any appropriate means, that one particular mode of effecting the object is excepted, take upon themselves the burden of establishing that exception . . . .

. . . The power of creating a corporation, though appertaining to sovereignty, is not, like the power of making war, or levying taxes, or of regulating commerce, a great substantive and independent power, which cannot be implied as incidental to other powers, or used as a means of executing them. It is never the end for which other powers are exercised, but a means by which other objects are accomplished

. . . . No sufficient reason is, therefore, perceived, why it may not
pass as incidental to those powers which are expressly given, if it be a
direct mode of executing them.

But the constitution of the United States has not left the right of
Congress to employ the necessary means for the execution of the
powers conferred on the government to general reasoning. To its
enumeration of powers is added that of making "all laws which shall be
necessary and proper, for carrying into execution the foregoing powers,
and all other powers vested by this constitution, in the government of
the United States, or in any department thereof."

The counsel for the State of Maryland have urged . . . that this
clause, though in terms a grant of power, is not so in effect; but is
really restrictive of the general right, which might otherwise be implied, of selecting means for executing the enumerated powers.

In support of this proposition, they have found it necessary to
contend, that this clause was inserted for the purpose of conferring on
Congress the power of making laws . . . .

. . . [W]ould it have entered into the mind of a single member of
the convention that an express power to make laws was necessary to
enable the legislature to make them? That a legislature, endowed with
legislative powers, can legislate, is a proposition too self-evident to have
been questioned.

But the argument on which most reliance is placed, is drawn from
the peculiar language of this clause. Congress is not empowered by it
to make all laws, which may have relation to the powers conferred on
the government, but such only as may be "*necessary and proper*" for
carrying them into execution. The word "*necessary*" is considered as
controlling the whole sentence, and as limiting the right to pass laws
for the execution of the granted powers, to such as are indispensable,
and without which the power would be nugatory. That it excludes the
choice of means, and leaves to Congress, in each case, that only which is
most direct and simple.

Is it true that this is the sense in which the word "necessary" is
always used? Does it always import an absolute physical necessity, so
strong that one thing, to which another may be termed necessary,
cannot exist without that other? We think it does not. If reference be
had to its use, in the common affairs of the world, or in approved
authors, we find that it frequently imports no more than that one thing
is convenient, or useful, or essential to another. To employ the means
necessary to an end, is generally understood as employing any means
calculated to produce the end, and not as being confined to those single
means, without which the end would be entirely unattainable. Such is
the character of human language, that no word conveys to the mind, in
all situations, one single definite idea; and nothing is more common
than to use words in a figurative sense. Almost all compositions
contain words, which, taken in their rigorous sense, would convey a
meaning different from that which is obviously intended. It is essential
to just construction, that many words which import something exces-

sive should be understood in a more mitigated sense—in that sense which common usage justifies. The word "necessary" is of this description. It has not a fixed character peculiar to itself. It admits of all degrees of comparison . . . . A thing may be necessary, very necessary, absolutely or indispensably necessary. To no mind would the same idea be conveyed by these several phrases . . . . It is, we think, impossible to compare the sentence which prohibits a state from laying "imposts or duties on imports or exports, except what may be *absolutely* necessary for executing its inspection laws," [Art. I, § 10] with that which authorizes Congress "to make all laws which shall be necessary and proper for carrying into execution" the powers of the general government, without feeling a conviction that the convention understood itself to change materially the meaning of the word "necessary," by prefixing the word "absolutely." This word, then, like others, is used in various senses; and, in its construction, the subject, the context, the intention of the person using them, are all to be taken into view.

Let this be done in the case under consideration. The subject is the execution of those great powers on which the welfare of a nation essentially depends. It must have been the intention of those who gave these powers, to insure, as far as human prudence could insure, their beneficial execution. This could not be done by confining the choice of means to such narrow limits as not to leave it in the power of Congress to adopt any which might be appropriate, and which were conducive to the end. This provision is made in a constitution intended to endure for ages to come, and, consequently, to be adapted to the various *crises* of human affairs. To have prescribed the means by which government should, in all future time, execute its powers, would have been to change, entirely, the character of the instrument, and give it the properties of a legal code. It would have been an unwise attempt to provide, by immutable rules, for exigencies which, if foreseen at all, must have been seen dimly, and which can be best provided for as they occur. To have declared that the best means shall not be used, but those alone without which the power given would be nugatory, would have been to deprive the legislature of the capacity to avail itself of experience, to exercise its reason, and to accommodate its legislation to circumstances. If we apply this principle of construction to any of the powers of the government, we shall find it so pernicious in its operation that we shall be compelled to discard it . . . .

In ascertaining the sense in which the word "necessary" is used in this clause of the constitution, we may derive some aid from that with which it is associated. Congress shall have power "to make all laws which shall be necessary and proper to carry into execution" the powers of the government. If the word "necessary" was used in that strict and rigorous sense for which the counsel for the state of Maryland contend, it would be an extraordinary departure from the usual course of the human mind, as exhibited in composition, to add a word, the only possible effect of which is to qualify that strict and rigorous meaning; to present to the mind the idea of some choice of means of legislation not straightened and compressed within the narrow limits for which gentlemen contend.

But the argument which most conclusively demonstrates the error of the construction contended for by the counsel for the state of Maryland, is founded on the intention of the convention, as manifested in the whole clause. To waste time and argument in proving that without it Congress might carry its powers into execution, would be not much less idle than to hold a lighted taper to the sun. As little can it be required to prove, that in the absence of this clause, Congress would have some choice of means. That it might employ those which, in its judgment, would most advantageously effect the object to be accomplished. That any means adapted to the end, any means which tended directly to the execution of the constitutional powers of the government, were in themselves constitutional. This clause, as construed by the state of Maryland, would abridge, and almost annihilate this useful and necessary right of the legislature to select its means. That this could not be intended, is, we should think, had it not been already controverted, too apparent for controversy. We think so for the following reasons:

1st. The clause is placed among the powers of Congress, not among the limitations on those powers.

2d. Its terms purport to enlarge, not to diminish the powers vested in the government. It purports to be an additional power, not a restriction on those already granted. No reason has been, or can be assigned for thus concealing an intention to narrow the discretion of the national legislature under words which purport to enlarge it . . . . If, then, their intention had been, by this clause, to restrain the free use of means which might otherwise have been implied, that intention would have been inserted in another place, and would have been expressed in terms resembling these. "In carrying into execution the foregoing powers, and all others," & c., "no laws shall be passed but such as are necessary and proper." . . .

We admit, as all must admit, that the powers of the government are limited, and that its limits are not to be transcended. But we think the sound construction of the constitution must allow to the national legislature that discretion, with respect to the means by which the powers it confers are to be carried into execution, which will enable that body to perform the high duties assigned to it, in the manner most beneficial to the people. Let the end be legitimate, let it be within the scope of the constitution, and all means which are appropriate, which are plainly adapted to that end, which are not prohibited, but consist with the letter and spirit of the constitution, are constitutional.

That a corporation must be considered as a means not less usual, not of higher dignity, not more requiring a particular specification than other means, has been sufficiently proved . . . .

. . . Should Congress, in the execution of its powers, adopt measures which are prohibited by the constitution; or should Congress, under the pretext of executing its powers pass laws for the accomplishment of objects not intrusted to the government, it would become the painful duty of this tribunal, should a case requiring such a decision come before it, to say that such an act was not the law of the land. But where the law is not prohibited, and is really calculated to effect any of the objects entrusted to the government, to undertake here to inquire into the degree of its necessity, would be to pass the line which circumscribes the judicial department, and to tread on legislative ground. This court disclaims all pretensions to such a power . . . .

It being the opinion of the court that the act incorporating the bank is constitutional, and that the power of establishing a branch in the state of Maryland might be properly exercised by the bank itself, we proceed to inquire:

2. Whether the state of Maryland may, without violating the constitution, tax that branch?

That the power of taxation is one of vital importance; that it is retained by the states; that it is not abridged by the grant of a similar power to the government of the Union; that it is to be concurrently exercised by the two governments: are truths which have never been denied. But, such is the paramount character of the constitution that its capacity to withdraw any subject from the action of even this power, is admitted. The states are expressly forbidden to lay any duties on imports or exports, except what may be absolutely necessary for executing their inspection laws. If the obligation of this prohibition must be conceded . . . .the same paramount character would seem to restrain . . . .a state from such other exercise of this power, as is in its nature incompatible with, and repugnant to, the constitutional laws of the Union. A law, absolutely repugnant to another, as entirely repeals that other as if express terms of repeal were used.

On this ground the counsel for the bank place its claim to be exempted from the power of a state to tax its operations. There is no express provision for the case, but the claim has been sustained on a principle which so entirely pervades the constitution, is so intermixed with the materials which compose it, so interwoven with its web, so blended with its texture, as to be incapable of being separated from it without rending it into shreds.

This great principle is, that the constitution and the laws made in pursuance thereof are supreme; that they control the constitution and laws of the respective states, and cannot be controlled by them. From this, which may be almost termed an axiom, other propositions are deduced as corollaries . . . . These are, 1st. That a power to create implies a power to preserve. 2d. That a power to destroy if wielded by a different hand, is hostile to, and incompatible with these powers to create and to preserve. 3d. That where this repugnancy exists, that authority which is supreme must control, not yield to that over which it is supreme . . . .

That the power of taxing it by the states may be exercised so as to destroy it, is too obvious to be denied. But taxation is said to be an absolute power, which acknowledges no other limits than those expressly prescribed in the constitution, and like sovereign power of every other description, is trusted to the discretion of those who use it. But the very terms of this argument admit that the sovereignty of the state, in the article of taxation itself, is subordinate to, and may be controlled by the constitution of the United States. How far it has been controlled by that instrument must be a question of construction. In making this construction, no principle not declared can be admissible, which would defeat the legitimate operations of a supreme government. It is of the very essence of supremacy to remove all obstacles to its action within its own sphere, and so to modify every power vested in subordinate governments as to exempt its own operations from their own influence. This effect need not be stated in terms. It is so involved in the declaration of supremacy, so necessarily implied in it, that the expression of it could not make it more certain. We must, therefore, keep it in view while construing the constitution . . . .

. . . . It is admitted that the power of taxing the people and their property is essential to the very existence of government, and may be legitimately exercised on the objects to which it is applicable, to the utmost extent to which the government may chose to carry it. The only security against the abuse of this power is found in the structure of the government itself. In imposing a tax the legislature acts upon its constituents. This is in general a sufficient security against erroneous and oppressive taxation.

The people of a state, therefore, give to their government a right of taxing themselves and their property, and as the exigencies of government cannot be limited, they prescribe no limits to the exercise of this right, resting confidently on the interest of the legislator, and on the influence of the constituents over their representative, to guard them against its abuse. But the means employed by the government of the Union have no such security, nor is the right of a state to tax them sustained by the same theory. Those means are not given by the people of a particular state, not given by the constituents of the legislature, which claim the right to tax them, but by the people of all the states. They are given by all, for the benefit of all—and upon theory, should be subjected to that government only which belongs to all . . . .

If we measure the power of taxation residing in a state, by the extent of sovereignty which the people of a single state possess, and can confer on its government, we have an intelligible standard, applicable to every case to which the power may be applied. We have a principle which leaves the power of taxing the people and property of a state unimpaired; which leaves to a state the command of all its resources, and which places beyond its reach, all those powers which are conferred by the people of the United States on the government of the Union, and all those means which are given for the purpose of carrying those powers into execution. We have a principle which is safe for the states, and safe for the Union. . . . We are not driven to the perplexing inquiry, so unfit for the judicial department, what degree of taxation is the legitimate use, and what degree may amount to the abuse of the power. The attempt to use it on the means employed by the government of the Union, in pursuance of the constitution, is itself an abuse, because it is the usurpation of a power which the people of a single state cannot give . . . .

That the power to tax involves the power to destroy; that the power to destroy may defeat and render useless the power to create; that there is a plain repugnance, in conferring on one government a power to control the constitutional measures of another, which other, with respect to those very measures, is declared to be supreme over that which exerts the control, are propositions not to be denied. But all inconsistencies are to be reconciled by the magic of the word *confidence.* Taxation, it is said, does not necessarily and unavoidably destroy. To carry to the excess of destruction would be an abuse, to presume which, would banish that confidence which is essential to all government.

But is this a case of confidence? Would the people of any one state trust those of another with a power to control the most insignificant operations of their state government? We know they would not. Why, then, should we suppose that the people of any one state should be willing to trust those of another with a power to control the operations of a government to which they have confided the most important and most valuable interests? In the legislature of the Union alone, are all represented. The legislature of the Union alone, therefore, can be trusted by the people with the power of controlling measures which concern all, in the confidence that it will not be abused. This, then, is not a case of confidence, and we must consider it as it really is.

If we apply the principle for which the state of Maryland contends, to the constitution generally, we shall find it capable of changing totally the character of that instrument. We shall find it capable of arresting all the measures of the government, and of prostrating it at the foot of the states. The American people have declared their constitution, and the laws made in pursuance thereof, to be supreme; but this principle would transfer the supremacy, in fact, to the states.

If the states may tax one instrument, employed by the government in the execution of its powers, they may tax any and every other instrument. They may tax the mail; they may tax the mint; they may tax patent-rights; they may tax the papers of the custom-house; they may tax judicial process; they may tax all the means employed by the government, to an excess which would defeat all the ends of government. This was not intended by the American people. They did not design to make their government dependent on the states.

In the course of the argument, *The Federalist* has been quoted; and the opinions expressed by the authors of that work have been justly supposed to be entitled to great respect in expounding the constitution. No tribute can be paid to them which exceeds their merit; but in

Framer's Intent
insight   not solution

applying their opinions to the cases which may arise in the progress of our government, a right to judge of their correctness must be retained; and, to understand the argument, we must examine the proposition it maintains, and the objections against which it is directed. . . .

The objections to the constitution which are noticed in these numbers, were to the undefined power of the government to tax, not to the incidental privilege of exempting its own measures from state taxation . . . .

It has also been insisted, that, as the power of taxation in the general and state governments is acknowledged to be concurrent, every argument which would sustain the right of the general government to tax banks chartered by the states, will equally sustain the right of the states to tax banks chartered by the general government.

But the two cases are not on the same reason. The people of all the states have created the general government, and have conferred upon it the general power of taxation. The people of all the states, and the states themselves, are represented in Congress, and, by their representatives, exercise this power. When they tax the chartered institutions of the states, they tax their constituents; and these taxes must be uniform. But, when a state taxes the operations of the government of the United States, it acts upon institutions created, not by their own constituents, but by people over whom they claim no control. It acts upon the measures of a government created by others as well as themselves, for the benefit of others in common with themselves. The difference is that which always exists, and always must exist, between the action of the whole on a part, and the action of a part on the whole—between the laws of a government declared to be supreme, and those of a government which, when in opposition to those laws, is not supreme.

But if the full application of this argument could be admitted, it might bring into question the right of Congress to tax the state banks, and could not prove the right of the states to tax the Bank of the United States. . . .

We are unanimously of opinion that the law passed by the legislature of Maryland, imposing a tax on the Bank of the United States, is unconstitutional and void.

This opinion does not deprive the states of any resources which they originally possessed. It does not extend to a tax paid by the real property of the bank, in common with the other real property within the state, nor to a tax imposed on the interest which the citizens of Maryland may hold in this institution, in common with other property of the same description throughout the state. But this is a tax on the operations of the bank, and is, consequently, a tax on the operation of an instrument employed by the government of the Union to carry its powers into execution. Such a tax must be unconstitutional.

Editors' Notes

(1) **Query:** How does Marshall view the architectural scheme of the constitutional system? Is there a basic unity between the *modes* of his analysis regarding congressional power to incorporate a bank and state power to tax that corporation?

(2) Compare Marshall's view of the structure of American federalism with that of Madison in *Federalist* No. 39, reprinted above, p. 409. To what extent does Madison agree with Marshall's claim that the national government (and so the Constitution) "proceeds directly from the people; is 'ordained and established' in the name of the people"?

(3) "[W]e must never forget that it is *a constitution* we are expounding" is probably the most often quoted passage in American constitutional law. As Justice Frankfurter remarked: "It bears repeating because it is, I believe, the single most important utterance in the literature of constitutional law—most important because most comprehensive and comprehending." What is "most comprehensive and comprehending" about it? Presumably proponents of alternative concepts of the Constitution discussed in Chapters 4 and 5 would contend that they never forget that it is *a constitution* they are expounding, but they would disagree about the nature of the Constitution to be expounded. What is Marshall's conception of the Constitution? How does it fit with the various views discussed in Chapters 4 and 5? Would his meaning have been expressed more aptly had he written: "[W]e must never forget WHAT the Constitution is that we are expounding"?

(4) Consider the structure of Marshall's reasoning in *McCulloch*. He first establishes a point by "general reasoning" and inferences from the nature and structure of the Constitution; only then does he utilize the "plain words" of specific passages to buttress his argument. What does this method of proceeding imply about the nature of the Constitution and the proper *approaches/modes/techniques* of constitutional interpretation?

(5) As the headnote to this case indicated, the Bank was an explosive issue in the politics of the time. In that context, the justices feared Maryland's court of appeals would not obey their ruling. Thus, rather than merely reversing the state court, the justices entered an unusual decree:

> . . . It is, therefore, Adjudged and Ordered, that the said judgment of the said Court of Appeals of the State of Maryland in this case be, and the same hereby is, reversed and annulled. And this Court, proceeding to render such judgment as the said Court of Appeals should have rendered; it is further Adjudged and Ordered, that the judgment of the said Baltimore County Court be reversed and annulled, and that judgment be entered in the said Baltimore County Court for the said James W. McCulloch.

(6) That judgment ended this particular piece of litigation, but the basic issue returned to the Court. See especially Osborn v. Bank of the U.S. (1824), when Ohio used physical force to extract a similar tax. The Court held such action unconstitutional. The battle against the Bank continued until Andrew Jackson's veto of the Bank bill in 1832 spelled the death of the BUS as an important national institution. His references in the veto message (reprinted above, p. 225) to a decision of the Supreme Court are, of course, to *McCulloch*. The best account of the war against the bank is Bray Hammond,

Banks and Politics in America from the Revolution to the Civil War (Princeton, N.J.: Princeton University Press, 1957).

(7) After the Civil War, Marshall's dicta regarding federal authority to tax state instrumentalities underwent a rollercoaster history. Beginning with Collector v. Day (1871), the Court handed down a long series of rulings setting up walls of reciprocal tax immunity. As part of its doctrine of "dual federalism," the Court held that states were entitled to the same protection against federal taxation as the United States was against states. How does dual federalism conflict with Marshall's view of the structure of the Union? Holmes protested against dual federalism as well as against Marshall's claim that the power to tax necessarily involves the power to destroy. As he dissented in Panhandle Oil Co. v. Knox (1928):

> In those days [Marshall's] it was not recognized as it is today that most of the distinctions of the law are distinctions of degree. If the States had any power it was assumed that they had all power, and that the necessary alternative was to deny it altogether. . . . The power to tax is not the power to destroy while this Court sits.

Assuming Holmes is correct on this point, would that undermine Marshall's argument? To what extent does Marshall base his reasoning on the assumption that the most important restraint on the taxing power is that of the ballot box?

(8) In the 1930s, the Court retreated from dual federalism in its general constitutional jurisprudence as well as in the specific field of intergovernmental tax immunity and returned pretty much to Marshall's conclusions if not his reasoning. See especially Graves v. New York ex rel. O'Keefe (1939). New York v. United States (1946) reraised the issue in the next decade and showed how divided the justices were over the principles to apply to this phase of federal relations. For an excellent account of the rise and fall of reciprocal tax immunity through the end of World War II, see Samuel J. Konefsky, *Chief Justice Stone and the* World *Supreme Court* (New York: Macmillan, 1946). Although the opposing pair of 5–4 decisions in National League of Cities v. Usery (1976; reprinted below, p. 449) and Garcia v. San Antonio MTA (1985; reprinted below, p. 461) demonstrate that problems of state-federal relations are hardly fully resolved, it is likely that the Court would sustain a federal tax that reached any state activity except one that is uniquely capable of being performed by a state, for example, collecting taxes or operating a legislature. Conversely, the Court would probably sustain any clear congressional decision to exempt federal activity from state taxation. For a recent summary of the law, see C. Herman Pritchett, *Constitutional Law of the Federal System* (Englewood Cliffs, N.J.: Prentice-Hall, 1984), chap. 11.

"The people of these United States constitute one nation."

CRANDALL v. NEVADA

73 U.S. (6 Wall.) 35, 18 L.Ed. 744 (1868).

In 1865, three years before adoption of the Fourteenth Amendment, Nevada levied a tax of one dollar on every person leaving the state by public conveyance and required the transporting company to collect the tax and turn it over to the state treasury. Later, Nevada officials arrested Crandall, an agent for the Pioneer Stage Co. at Carson City, for refusing to collect the tax. In his defense, he asserted that the levy was unconstitutional. After losing in state courts, he obtained a writ of error from the U.S. Supreme Court.

Mr. Justice **MILLER** delivered the opinion of the court . . . .

The people of these United States constitute one nation. They have a government in which all of them are deeply interested. This government has necessarily a capital established by law, where its principal operations are conducted. Here sits its legislature, composed of Senators and Representatives, from the states and from the people of the states. Here resides the President, directing through thousands of agents, the execution of the laws over all this vast country. Here is the seat of the supreme judicial power of the nation, to which all its citizens have a right to resort to claim justice at its hands. Here are the great Executive Departments, administering the offices of the mails, of the public lands, of the collection and distribution of the public revenues, and of our foreign relations. These are all established and conducted under the admitted powers of the Federal government. That government has a right to call to this point any or all of its citizens to aid in its service, as members of the Congress, of the courts, of the Executive Departments, and to fill all its other offices; and this right cannot be made to depend upon the pleasure of a state over whose territory they must pass to reach the point where these services must be rendered. The government also, has its offices of secondary importance in all other parts of the country. On the seacoasts and on the rivers it has its ports of entry. In the interior it has its land offices, its revenue offices, and its sub-treasuries. In all these it demands the services of its citizens, and is entitled to bring them to those points from all quarters of the nation, and no power can exist in a state to obstruct this right that would not enable it to defeat the purposes for which the government was established.

The Federal power has a right to declare and prosecute wars and, as a necessary incident, to raise and transport troops through and over the territory of any state of the Union.

If this right is dependent in any sense, however limited, upon the pleasure of a state, the government itself may be overthrown by an obstruction to its exercise. Much the largest part of the transportation of troops during the late Rebellion was by railroads, and largely through states whose people were hostile to the Union. If the tax levied by Nevada on railroad passengers had been the law of Tennessee, enlarged to meet the wishes of her people, the Treasury of the United States could not have paid the tax necessary to enable its armies to pass through her territory.

But if the government has these rights on her own account, the citizen also has correlative rights. He has the right to come to the seat of government to assert any claim he may have upon that government, or to transact any business he may have with it. To seek its protection, to share its offices, to engage in administering its functions, he has a right to free access to its sea-ports, through which all the operations of foreign trade and commerce are conducted, to the sub-treasuries, the land offices, the revenue offices, and the court of justice in the several states, and this right is in its nature independent of the will of any state over whose soil he must pass in the exercise of it.

The views here advanced are neither novel nor unsupported by authority. The question of the taxing power of the states, as its exercise has affected the functions of the Federal government, has been repeatedly considered by this court, and the right of the states in this mode to impede or embarrass the constitutional operations of that government, or the rights which its citizens hold under it, has been uniformly denied.

The leading case of this class is that of McCulloch v. Maryland [1819]. . . .

It is not possible to condense the conclusive argument of Chief Justice Marshall in that case, and it is too familiar to justify its reproduction here; but an extract or two, in which the results of his reasoning are stated, will serve to show its applicability to the case before us. "That the power of taxing the bank by the states," he says, "may be exercised so as to destroy it, is too obvious to be denied. But taxation is said to be an absolute power which acknowledges no other limits than those prescribed by the Constitution; and, like sovereign power of any description, is trusted to the discretion of those who use it. But the very terms of this argument admit that the sovereignty of the state in the article of taxation is subordinate to, and may be controlled by, the Constitution of the United States." . . .

It will be observed that it was not the extent of the tax in that case which was complained of, but the right to levy any tax of that character. So in the case before us, it may be said that a tax of one dollar for passing through the state of Nevada, by stage coach, or by railroad, cannot sensibly affect any function of the government, or deprive a citizen of any valuable right. But if the state can tax a railroad passenger one dollar, it can tax him $1,000. If one state can do this, so can every other state. And thus one or more states covering the only practicable routes of travel from the east to the west, or from the north to the south, may totally prevent or seriously burden all transportation of passengers from one part of the country to the other . . . .

In The Passenger Cases [1849] . . . . Justice Grier, with whom Justice Catron concurred, makes this one of the four propositions on which they held the [state] tax [on immigrants coming into the United States] void in those cases. Judge Wayne expresses his assent to Judge Grier's views; and perhaps this ground received the concurrence of more of the members of the court who constituted the majority than any other. But the principles here laid down may be found more clearly stated in the dissenting opinion of the Chief Justice in those cases, and with more direct pertinency to the case now before us than anywhere else. After expressing his views fully in favor of the validity of the tax, which he said had exclusive reference to foreigners, so far as those cases were concerned, he proceeds to say, for the purpose of preventing misapprehension, that so far as the tax affected American citizens, it could not in his opinion be maintained. He then adds: "Living as we do under a common government, charged with the great concerns of the whole Union, every citizen of the United States, from the most remote states or territories, is entitled to free access, not only to the principal departments established at Washington, but also to its judicial tribunals and public offices in every state in the Union. . . . For all the great purposes for which the Federal government was formed we are one people, with one common country. We are all citizens of the United States, and as members of the same community must have the right to pass and repass through every part of it without interruption, as freely as in our own states. And a tax imposed by a state, for entering its territory or harbors, is inconsistent with the rights which belong to citizens of other states as members of the Union, and with the objects which that Union was intended to attain. Such a power in the states could produce nothing but discord and mutual irritation, and they very clearly do not possess it."

Although these remarks are found in a dissenting opinion, they do not relate to the matter on which the dissent was founded. They accord with the inferences which we have already drawn from the Constitution itself, and from the decision of this court in exposition of that instrument.

Those principles, as we have already stated them in this opinion, must govern the present case.

The judgment of the Supreme Court of the State of Nevada is, therefore, reversed, and the case remanded to that court, with directions to discharge the plaintiff in error from custody.

Mr. Justice **CLIFFORD**. . . .

. . . I hold that the act of the state legislature is inconsistent with the power conferred upon Congress to regulate commerce among the several states, and I think the judgment of the court should have been placed exclusively upon that ground. . . .

The Chief Justice [**CHASE**] also dissents, and concurs in the views I have expressed.

"The Constitution, in all its provisions, looks to an indestructible Union, composed of indestructible States."

TEXAS v. WHITE
74 U.S. (7 Wall.) 700, 19 L.Ed. 227 (1869).

As an indemnification for adjustments in Texas's boundary, Congress in 1851 gave that state 5,000 U.S. bonds, with a face value of $1,000 each, redeemable in gold in 1865. During the last months of the Civil War, the

Texas Military Board turned over some of these bonds to George W. White and John Chiles in exchange for a promise to deliver supplies needed for the war. The arrangement smacked of fraud, for the Confederacy was crumbling and the agreement called for White and Childs, if they could not deliver the supplies, to return not the gold U.S. bonds but an equivalent amount in almost worthless state bonds.

Not surprisingly White and Chiles did not deliver the supplies; instead, shortly after the war, they produced the worthless Confederate paper in an effort to discharge their obligation. The provisional governor—an official appointed by the President of the United States until a convention could draft a new state constitution—refused to accept the "paper" and branded the agreement as a swindle. In February, 1867, Texas filed an original suit in the U.S. Supreme Court—Article III of the Constitution allows a state to invoke the Court's original jurisdiction—asking for an order that White and Chiles return the U.S. bonds.

During the leisurely course of litigation—the Court would decide the case almost two years to the day after it was filed—Congress had enacted much more stringent policies of Reconstruction than Presidents Lincoln and Johnson had followed. The new legislation denied the former Confederate states representation in Congress and removed their elected civil state governments. In their place, Congress established military officers as rulers. Thus the Court confronted a series of questions: What was Texas's constitutional status during the Civil War? What was its status immediately after the war when the suits were filed? And, assuming that the Court would rule that secession was unconstitutional and so Texas had always remained a member of the Union, what was its status now, when it had no senators or congressmen and was under military rule? Was it still a state in the Constitution's sense of that term? If so, was it not entitled to representation in Congress and were its people not entitled, as Article IV of the Constitution ordered the federal government to guarantee them, to a "republican" not a military form of government? In sum, if Texas were still a state in the constitutional sense, then were not the policies of Radical Reconstruction unconstitutional?

The answers to these questions were all the more difficult and delicate because of the belligerent mood of Congress. Not only were the Radicals determined to exact retribution from the South for the bloody Civil War, but they were also determined to run the federal government. They had impeached and tried Andrew Johnson during the time the case had been on the Court's docket; and, in an effort to prevent the justices from declaring part of Reconstruction unconstitutional, Congress had also removed part of the Court's appellate jurisdiction; see the discussion of Ex parte McCardle (1869), in Chapter 9 at pp. 361–363.

We reprint here only those parts of the opinions dealing with questions relating to Texas's statehood—and so to the structure of the American constitutional system.

The Chief Justice [**CHASE**] delivered the opinion of the Court . . . .

. . . . It is not to be questioned that this court has original jurisdiction of suits by States against citizens of other States, or that the States entitled to invoke this jurisdiction must be States of the Union. But it is equally clear that no such jurisdiction has been conferred upon this court of suits by any other political communities than such States . . . .

If, therefore, it is true that the State of Texas was not at the time of filing this bill, or is not now, one of the United States, we have no jurisdiction of this suit . . . .

In the Constitution the term "state" most frequently expresses the combined idea . . . of people, territory, and government. A state, in the ordinary sense of the Constitution, is a political community of free citizens, occupying a territory of defined boundaries, and organized under a government sanctioned and limited by a written constitution, and established by the consent of the governed. It is the union of such states, under a common constitution, which forms the distinct and greater political unit, which that Constitution designates as the United States, and makes of the people and states which compose it one people and one country . . . .

Did Texas, in consequence of these acts [of seceding, joining the Confederacy, and warring against the United States], cease to be a State? Or, if not, did the State cease to be a member of the Union? . . .

The Union of the States never was a purely artificial and arbitrary relation. It began among the colonies and grew out of common origin, mutual sympathies, kindred principles, similar interests, and geographical relations. It was confirmed and strengthened by the necessities of war, and received definite form, and character, and sanction from the Articles of Confederation. By these the Union was solemnly declared to "be perpetual." And when these Articles were found to be inadequate to the exigencies of the country, the Constitution was ordained "to form a more perfect Union." It is difficult to convey the idea of indissoluble unity more clearly than by these words. What can be indissoluble if a perpetual Union, made more perfect, is not?

But the perpetuity and indissolubility of the Union, by no means implies the loss of distinct and individual existence, or of the right of self-government by the States. Under the Articles of Confederation each State retained its sovereignty, freedom, and independence, and every power, jurisdiction, and right not expressly delegated to the United States. Under the Constitution, though the powers of the States were much restricted, still, all powers not delegated to the United States, nor prohibited to the States, are reserved to the States respectively, or to the people . . . . Not only, therefore, can there be no loss of separate and independent autonomy to the States, through their union under the Constitution, but it may be not unreasonably said that the preservation of the States, and the maintenance of their governments, are as much within the design and care of the Constitution as the preservation of the Union and the maintenance of the National government. The Constitution, in all its provisions, looks to an indestructible Union, composed of indestructible States.

When, therefore, Texas became one of the United States, she entered into an indissoluble relation. All the obligations of perpetual union, and all the guaranties of republican government in the Union, attached at once to the State. The act which consummated her admission into the Union was something more than a compact; it was the incorporation of a new member into the political body. And it was final. The union between Texas and the other States was as complete, as perpetual, and as indissoluble as the union between the original States. There was no place for reconsideration, or revocation, except through revolution, or through consent of the States.

Considered therefore as transactions under the Constitution, the ordinance of secession, adopted by the convention and ratified by a majority of the citizens of Texas, and all the acts of her legislature intended to give effect to that ordinance, were absolutely null. . . .

Our conclusion therefore is, that Texas continued to be a State, and a State of the Union, notwithstanding the transactions to which we have referred. And this conclusion, in our judgment, is not in conflict with any act or declaration of any department of the National government, but entirely in accordance with the whole series of such acts and declarations since the first outbreak of the rebellion.

But in order to the exercise, by a State, of the right to sue in this court, there needs to be a State government, competent to represent the State in its relations with the National government, so far at least as the institution and prosecution of a suit is concerned.

And it is by no means a logical conclusion, from the premises which we have endeavored to establish, that the governmental relations of Texas to the Union remained uñaltered. Obligations often remain unimpaired, while relations are greatly changed. . . .

. . . No one has been bold enough to contend that, while Texas was controlled by a government hostile to the United States, and in affiliation with a hostile confederation, waging war upon the United States, senators chosen by her legislature, or representatives elected by her citizens, were entitled to seats in Congress; or that any suit, instituted in her name, could be entertained in this court. All admit that, during this condition of civil war, the rights of the State as a member, and of her people as citizens of the Union, were suspended. The government and the citizens of the State, refusing to recognize their constitutional obligations, assumed the character of enemies, and incurred the consequences of rebellion.

These new relations imposed new duties upon the United States. The first was that of suppressing the rebellion. The next was that of re-establishing the broken relations of the State with the Union. . . .

The authority for the performance of the first had been found in the power to suppress insurrection and carry on war; for the performance of the second, authority was derived from the obligation of the United States to guarantee to every State in the Union a republican form of government. . . .

There being no government in Texas in constitutional relations with the Union, it became the duty of the United States to provide for the restoration of such a government. . . .

In the exercise of the power conferred [on the United States] by the guaranty clause, as in the exercise of every other constitutional power, a discretion in the choice of means is necessarily allowed. It is essential only that the means must be necessary and proper for carrying into execution the power conferred, through the restoration of the State to its constitutional relations . . . and that no acts be done, and no authority exerted, which is [sic] either prohibited or unsanctioned by the Constitution.

It is not important to review, at length, the measures which have been taken . . . by the executive and legislative departments of the National government. . . .

. . . . The power exercised by the President was supposed, doubtless, to be derived from his constitutional functions, as commander-in-chief; and, so long as the war continued, it cannot be denied that he might institute temporary government within insurgent districts, occupied by the National forces, or take measures, in any State, for the restoration of State government faithful to the Union, employing, however, in such efforts, only such means and agents as were authorized by constitutional laws.

But, the power to carry into effect the clause of guaranty is primarily a legislative power, and resides in Congress [Luther v. Borden (1849)]. . . .

The action of the President must, therefore, be considered as provisional, and, in that light, it seems to have been regarded by Congress. . . . [Congress] proceeded, after long deliberation, to adopt various measures for reorganization and restoration. These measures were embodied in proposed amendments to the Constitution, and in the acts known as the Reconstruction Acts, which have been so far carried into effect, that a majority of the States which were engaged in the rebellion have been restored to their constitutional relations, under forms of government, adjudged to be republican by Congress, through the admission of their "Senators and Representatives into the councils of the Union." . . .

. . . . We do not inquire here into the constitutionality of this legislation so far as it relates to military authority, or to the paramount authority of Congress. It suffices to say, that the terms of the acts necessarily imply recognition of actually existing governments; and that in point of fact, the governments thus recognized, in some important respects, still exist.

What has thus been said generally describes, with sufficient accuracy, the situation of Texas. A provisional governor of the State was appointed by the President in 1865; in 1866 a governor was elected by the people under the constitution of that year; at a subsequent date a governor was appointed by the commander of the district. Each of the three exercised executive functions and actually represented the State in the executive department.

In the case before us each has given his sanction to the prosecution of the suit, and we find no difficulty . . . in holding that the sanction thus given sufficiently warranted the action of the solicitor and counsel in behalf of the State. The necessary conclusion is that the suit was instituted and is prosecuted by competent authority.

The question of jurisdiction being thus disposed of, we proceed to the consideration of the merits. . . . [The Court held that Texas was entitled to recover the bonds.]

Mr. Justice **GRIER**, dissenting. . . .

The original jurisdiction of this court can be invoked only by one of the United States. . . .

Is Texas one of these United States? . . .

This is to be decided as *a political fact,* not as a *legal fiction.* This court is bound to know and notice the public history of the nation.

If I regard the truth of history for the last eight years, I cannot discover the State of Texas as one of these United States. . . .

Is Texas a State, now represented by members chosen by the people of that State and received on the floor of Congress? Has she two senators to represent her as a State in the Senate of the United States? Has her voice been heard in the late election of President? Is she not now held and governed as a conquered province by military force? The act of Congress of March 2d, 1867, declares Texas to be a "rebel State," and provides for its government until a legal and republican State government could be legally established. It constituted Louisiana and Texas the fifth military district, and made it subject, not to the civil authority, but to the "military authorities of the United States."

It is true that no organized rebellion now exists there, and the courts of the United States now exercise jurisdiction over the people of that province. But this is no test of the State's being in the Union; Dacotah [sic] is no State, and yet the courts of the United States administer justice there as they do in Texas. The Indian tribes, who are governed by military force, cannot claim to be States of the Union. Wherein does the condition of Texas differ from theirs? . . .

. . . I am not disposed to join in any essay to prove Texas to be a State of the Union, when Congress have decided that she is not. It is a question of fact, I repeat, and of fact only. *Politically,* Texas is not *a State in this Union.* Whether rightfully out of it or not is a question not before the court. . . .

[Mr. Justice **SWAYNE** and Mr. Justice **MILLER** concurred with Mr. Justice **GRIER**]

"[W]e do not see in those amendments any purpose to destroy the main features of the general system."—Justice **MILLER**

"The privileges and immunities designated are those *which of right belong to the citizens of all free governments.*"—Justice **FIELD**

"Fairly construed these amendments may be said to rise to the dignity of a new Magna Charta."—Justice **SWAYNE**

SLAUGHTER–HOUSE CASES
83 U.S. (16 Wall.) 36, 21 L.Ed. 394 (1873).

Congress proposed the Fourteenth Amendment in 1866, and slightly more than two years later the Secretary of State certified that the necessary twenty-eight of the then thirty-seven states had ratified it. That process, however, had been very difficult and controversial. Many states had refused to assent because their officials believed the amendment would radically change the federal structure of the political system. Indeed, the final five state legislatures agreed only under coercion. They were members of the former Confederacy, and the Reconstruction Congress had made ratification a condition for their "readmission" into the Union. Even then ratification was immediately possible only because the Secretary of State refused to accept notices from the legislatures of New Jersey, Ohio, and Oregon revoking their earlier ratifications. (The Supreme Court heard no challenge to the validity of the Fourteenth Amendment, but decades later ruled in Coleman v. Miller [1939] that when an amendment became part of the Constitution was a political not a justiciable question.)

Very quickly, however, the Court was presented with questions about the new amendment's scope. In 1869, the Crescent City Live-Stock Landing and Slaughter-House Co. bribed officials of New Orleans and the carpetbag legislature of Louisiana to grant the company a twenty-five year monopoly to operate meat-slaughtering facilities for New Orleans. Several hundred butchers joined together in the Butchers Benevolent Association and hired John A. Campbell, who at the outbreak of the Civil War had resigned his seat on the U.S. Supreme Court and returned to Alabama, to direct their attack on the monopoly. The "foreign" character of the state legislature and its ties to "Radical Reconstruction" stirred up glowing embers of hatred both among ex-Confederates and staunch Unionists.

In an ironic twist, Campbell invoked the Fourteenth Amendment to attack state authority in the name of nationally protected rights of the individual. He lost in state courts but obtained a writ of error from his former colleagues.

Mr. Justice **MILLER** . . . delivered the opinion of the court . . . .

The plaintiffs in error . . . allege that the statute is a violation of the Constitution of the United States in . . . :

That it creates involuntary servitude . . . ;

That it abridges the privileges and immunities of citizens of the United States;

That it denies to the plaintiffs the equal protection of the laws; and,

That it deprives them of their property without due process of law . . . .

This court is thus called upon for the first time to give construction to these articles.

We do not conceal from ourselves the great responsibility which this duty devolves upon us. No questions so far-reaching and pervading in their consequences, so profoundly interesting to the people of this country, and so important in their bearing upon the relations of the United States, and of the several States to each other and to the citizens of the States and the United States, have been before this court during the official life of any of its present members. We have given every opportunity for a full hearing at the bar; we have discussed it freely and compared views among ourselves; we have taken ample time for careful deliberation . . . .

The most cursory glance at these articles [Thirteenth, Fourteenth, and Fifteenth Amendments] discloses a unity of purpose, when taken in connection with the history of the times, which cannot fail to have an important bearing on any question of doubt concerning their true meaning. Nor can such doubts, when any reasonably exist, be safely and rationally solved without a reference to that history; for in it is found the occasion and the necessity for recurring again to the great source of power in this country, the people of the States, for additional guarantees of human rights; additional powers to the Federal government; additional restraints upon those of the States. Fortunately that history is fresh within the memory of us all, and its leading features . . . free from doubt . . . .

. . . . [I]n the light of this recapitulation of events [the Civil War and Reconstruction], almost too recent to be called history . . . and on the most casual examination of the language of these amendments, no one can fail to be impressed with the one pervading purpose found in them all . . . . ; . . . . the freedom of the slave race, the security and firm establishment of that freedom, and the protection of the newly-made freeman and citizen from the oppression of those who had formerly exercised unlimited dominion over him. It is true that only the fifteenth amendment, in terms, mentions the negro by speaking of his color and his slavery. But it is just as true that each of the other articles was addressed to the grievances of that race . . . .

We do not say that no one else but the negro can share in this protection. Both the language and the spirit of these articles are to have their fair and just weight in any question of construction . . . . But what we do say . . . . is, that in any fair and just construction of any section or phrase of these amendments, it is necessary to look to the purpose which we have said was the pervading spirit of them all, the evil they were intended to remedy, and the process of continued addition to the Constitution, until that purpose was supposed to be accomplished, as far as constitutional law can accomplish it.

The first section of the fourteenth article . . . opens with a definition of citizenship—not only citizenship of the United States, but citizenship of the States. No such definition was previously found in the Constitution . . . . But it had been held by this court, in the celebrated Dred Scott case, only a few years before the outbreak of the civil war, that a man of African descent, whether a slave or not, was not and could not be a citizen of a State or of the United States. This decision, while it met the condemnation of some of the ablest statesmen and constitutional lawyers of the country, had never been overruled . . . .

To remove this difficulty primarily, and to establish a clear and comprehensive definition of citizenship . . . the first clause of the first section was framed.

"All persons born or naturalized in the United States, and subject to the jurisdiction thereof, are citizens of the United States and of the State wherein they reside."

. . . It declares that persons may be citizens of the United States without regard to their citizenship of a particular State, and it over-turns the Dred Scott decision by making all persons born within the United States and subject to its jurisdiction citizens of the United States. That its main purpose was to establish the citizenship of the negro can admit of no doubt . . . .

It is quite clear, then, that there is a citizenship of the United States, and a citizenship of a State, which are distinct from each other, and which depend upon different characteristics or circumstances in the individual . . . .

. . . The argument, however, in favor of the plaintiffs [in error] rests wholly on the assumption that the citizenship is the same, and the privileges and immunities guaranteed by the clause are the same.

The language is, "No State shall make or enforce any law which shall abridge the privileges or immunities of citizens of *the United States*." It is a little remarkable, if this clause was intended as a protection to the citizen of a State against the legislative power of his own State, that the word citizen of the State should be left out when it is so carefully used, and used in contradistinction to citizens of the United States, in the very sentence which precedes it. It is too clear for argument that the change in phraseology was adopted understandingly and with a purpose.

Of the privileges and immunities of the citizen of the United States, and of the privileges and immunities of the citizen of the State . . . it is only the former which are placed by this clause under the protection of the Federal Constitution . . . .

In the Constitution of the United States . . . the corresponding provision is found in section two of the fourth article, in the following words: "The citizens of each State shall be entitled to all the privileges and immunities of citizens of the several States."

There can be but little question that the purpose of both these provisions is the same, and that the privileges and immunities intended are the same in each . . . .

Fortunately we are not without judicial construction of this clause of the Constitution. The first and the leading case on the subject is that of Corfield v. Coryell [1823], decided by Mr. Justice Washington in the Circuit Court . . . .

"The inquiry," he says, "is, what are the privileges and immunities of citizens of the several States? We feel no hesitation in confining these expressions to those privileges and immunities which are fundamental; which belong of right to the citizens of all free governments, and which have at all times been enjoyed by citizens of the several States which compose this Union . . . . What these fundamental principles are, it would be more tedious than difficult to enumerate. They may all, however, be comprehended under the following general heads: protection by the government, with the right to acquire and possess property of every kind, and to pursue and obtain happiness and safety, subject, nevertheless, to such restraints as the government may prescribe for the general good of the whole."

This definition . . . is adopted in the main by this court in Ward v. The State of Maryland [1871] . . . .

In . . . Paul v. Virginia [1869], the [U.S. Supreme] court, in expounding this clause of the Constitution, says that "the privileges and immunities secured to citizens of each State in the several States . . . are those privileges and immunities which are common to the citizens in the latter States under their constitution and laws by virtue of their being citizens."

The constitutional provision there alluded to did not create those rights, which it called privileges and immunities of citizens of the States. . . . Nor did it profess to control the power of the State governments over the rights of its own citizens.

Its sole purpose was to declare to the several States, that whatever those rights, as you grant or establish them to your own citizens, or as you limit or qualify, or impose restrictions on their exercise, the same, neither more nor less, shall be the measure of the rights of citizens of other States within your jurisdiction.

. . . [U]p to the adoption of the recent amendments, no claim or pretense was set up that those rights depended on the Federal government for their existence or protection, beyond the very few express limitations which the Federal Constitution imposed upon the States— such, for instance, as the prohibition against *ex post facto* laws, bills of attainder, and laws impairing the obligation of contracts. But with the exception of these and a few other restrictions, the entire domain of the privileges and immunities of citizens of the States . . . lay within the constitutional and legislative power of the States . . . . Was it the purpose of the fourteenth amendment, by the simple declaration that no State should make or enforce any law which shall abridge the privileges and immunities of citizens of the United States, to transfer the security and protection of all the civil rights which we have mentioned, from the States to the Federal government? And where it is declared that Congress shall have the power to enforce that article, was it intended to bring within the power of Congress the entire domain of civil rights heretofore belonging exclusively to the States?

All this and more must follow, if the proposition of the plaintiffs be sound. For not only are these rights subject to the control of Congress whenever in its discretion any of them are supposed to be abridged by State legislation, but that body may also pass laws in advance, limiting and restricting the exercise of legislative power by the States, in their most ordinary and usual function, as in its judgment it may think proper on all such subjects. And still further, such a construction . . . would constitute this court a perpetual censor upon all legislation of the States, on the civil rights of their own citizens . . . . The argument, we admit, is not always the most conclusive which is drawn from the consequences urged against the adoption of a particular construction of an instrument. But when, as in the case before us, these consequences are so serious, so far-reaching and pervading, so great a departure from the structure and spirit of our institutions when the effect is to fetter and degrade the State governments by subjecting them to the control of Congress, in the exercise of powers heretofore universally conceded to them of the most ordinary and fundamental character; when in fact it radically changes the whole theory of the relations of the State and Federal governments to each other and of both these governments to the people; the argument has a force that is irresistible, in the absence of language which expresses such a purpose too clearly to admit of doubt.

We are convinced that no such results were intended by the Congress which proposed these amendments, nor by the legislatures of the States which ratified them.

Having shown that the privileges and immunities relied on in the argument are those which belong to citizens of the States as such, and that they are left to the State governments for security and protection . . . we may hold ourselves excused from defining the privileges and immunities of citizens of the United States which no State can abridge, until some case involving those privileges may make it necessary to do so.

But lest it should be said that no such privileges and immunities are to be found if those we have been considering are excluded, we venture to suggest some which owe their existence to the Federal government, its National character, its Constitution, or its laws.

One of these is well described in the case of Crandall v. Nevada [1868] . . .[,] the right of the citizens of this great country, protected by implied guarantees of its Constitution, "to come to the seat of government to assert any claim he may have upon that government, to transact any business he may have with it, to seek its protection, to share its offices, to engage in administering its functions. He has the right of free access to its seaports . . . to the sub-treasuries, land offices, and courts of justice in the several States." And ". . . for all the great purposes for which the Federal government was established, we are one people, with one common country, we are all citizens of the United States;". . . .

Another privilege of a citizen of the United States is to demand the care and protection of the Federal government over his life, liberty, and property when on the high seas or within the jurisdiction of a foreign government . . . . The right to peaceably assemble and petition for redress of grievances, the privilege of the writ of *habeas corpus,* are rights of the citizen guaranteed by the Federal Constitution. The right to use the navigable waters of the United States, however they may penetrate the territory of the several States, all rights secured to our citizens by treaties with foreign nations, are dependent upon citizenship of the United States, and not citizenship of a State. One of these privileges is conferred by the very article under consideration. It is that a citizen of the United States can, of his own volition, become a citizen of any State of the Union by a *bona fide* residence therein, with the same rights as other citizens of that State. To these may be added the rights secured by the thirteenth and fifteenth articles of amendment, and by the other clause of the fourteenth, next to be considered.

But it is useless to pursue this branch of the inquiry, since we are of opinion that the rights claimed by these plaintiffs in error, if they have any existence, are not privileges and immunities of citizens of the United States . . . .

The argument has not been much pressed in these cases that the defendant's charter deprives the plaintiffs [in error] of their property without due process of law, or that it denies them the equal protection of the law. The first of these paragraphs has been in the Constitution since the adoption of the fifth amendment, as a restraint upon the Federal power . . . .

We are not without judicial interpretation . . . of the meaning of this clause. And it is sufficient to say that under no construction of that provision that we have ever seen, or that we deem admissible, can the restraint imposed by . . . Louisiana . . . be held to be a deprivation of property within the meaning of that provision.

"Nor shall any State deny to any person within its jurisdiction the equal protection of the laws."

In the light of the history of these amendments, and the pervading purpose of them . . . it is not difficult to give a meaning to this clause. The existence of laws in the States where the newly emancipated negroes resided, which discriminated with gross injustice and hardship against them as a class, was the evil to be remedied . . . .

If, however, the States did not conform their laws to its requirements, then by the fifth section of the article of amendment Congress was authorized to enforce it by suitable legislation. We doubt very much whether any action of a State not directed by way of discrimination against the negroes as a class, or on account of their race, will ever be held to come within the purview of this provision. It is so clearly a provision for that race and that emergency, that a strong case would be necessary for its application to any other. But as it is a State that is to be dealt with, and not alone the validity of its laws, we may safely leave that matter until Congress shall have exercised its power, or some case of State oppression, by denial of equal justice in its courts, shall have claimed a decision at our hands. . . .

The adoption of the first eleven amendments to the Constitution so soon after the original instrument was accepted, shows a prevailing sense of danger at that time from the Federal power. And it cannot be denied that such jealousy continued to exist with many patriotic men until the breaking out of the late civil war. It was then discovered that the true danger of the perpetuity of the Union was in the capacity of the State organizations to combine and concentrate all the powers of the State, and of contiguous States, for a determined resistance to the General Government.

Unquestionably this has given great force to the argument, and added largely to the number, of those who believe in the necessity of a strong National government.

But, however pervading this sentiment, and however it may have contributed to the adoption of the amendments we have been considering, we do not see in those amendments any purpose to destroy the main features of the general system. Under the pressure of all the excited feeling growing out of the war, our statesmen have still believed that the existence of the States with powers for domestic and local government, including the regulation of civil rights—the rights of person and of property—was essential to the perfect working of our complex form of government, though they may have thought proper to impose additional limitations on the States, and to confer additional power on that of the Nation.

But whatever fluctuations may be seen in the history of public opinion on this subject during the period of our national existence, we think it will be found that this court, so far as its functions require, has always held with a steady and even hand the balance between State and Federal power, and we trust that such may continue to be the history of its relation to that subject so long as it shall have duties to perform which demand of it a construction of the Constitution, or any of its parts. . . .

Affirmed.

Mr. Justice **FIELD**, dissenting . . . .

The first clause of the fourteenth amendment . . . recognizes in express terms, if it does not create, citizens of the United States, and it makes their citizenship dependent upon the place of their birth, or the fact of their adoption, and not upon the constitution or laws of any State or the condition of their ancestry. A citizen of a State is now only a citizen of the United States residing in that State. The fundamental rights, privileges, and immunities now belong to him as a citizen of the United States, and are not dependent upon his citizenship of any State . . . .

The amendment does not attempt to confer any new privileges or immunities upon citizens, or to enumerate or define those already existing. It assumes that there are such privileges and immunities which belong of right to citizens as such, and ordains that they shall not be abridged by State legislation. If this inhibition has no reference to privileges and immunities of this character but only refers . . . to such privileges and immunities as were before its adoption specially designated in the Constitution or necessarily implied as belonging to citizens of the United States, it was a vain and idle enactment, which accomplished nothing, and most unnecessarily excited Congress and the people on its passage. The supremacy of the Constitution and the laws of the United States always controlled any State legislation of that character. But if the amendment refers to the natural and inalienable rights which belong to all citizens, the inhibition has a profound significance and consequence.

What then are the privileges and immunities which are secured against abridgment by State legislation?

In the first section of the Civil Rights Act Congress has given its interpretation to these terms, or at least has stated some of the rights which, in its judgment, these terms include . . . the right "to make and enforce contracts, to sue, be parties and give evidence, to inherit, purchase, lease, sell, hold, and convey real and personal property, and to full and equal benefit of all laws and proceedings for the security of person and property." That act, it is true, was passed before the fourteenth amendment, but the amendment was adopted . . . to obviate objections to legislation of similar character, extending the protection of the National government over the common rights of all citizens of the United States. Accordingly, after its ratification, Congress re-enacted the act under the belief that whatever doubts may have previously existed of its validity, they were removed by the amendment . . . .

[Field then recited the same history of the term "privileges and immunities" as had Miller and also quoted the same passage from Corfield v. Coryell (1823).] . . . The privileges and immunities designated are those *which of right belong to the citizens of all free governments.* Clearly among these must be placed the right to pursue a lawful employment in a lawful manner without other restraint than such as equally affects all persons. In the discussions in Congress upon the passage of the Civil Rights Act repeated reference was made to this language of Mr. Justice Washington . . . .

What the clause in question [in Art. 4] did for the protection of citizens of one State against hostile and discriminating legislation of other States, the fourteenth amendment does for the protection of every citizen of the United States against hostile and discriminating legislation against him in favor of others, whether they reside in the same or different States. If under the fourth article of the Constitution equality of privileges and immunities is secured between citizens of different States, under the fourteenth amendment the same equality is secured between citizens of the United States.

It will not be pretended that under the fourth article of the Constitution any State could create a monopoly in any known trade or manufacture in favor of her own citizens, or any portion of them, which would exclude an equal participation in the trade or manufacture monopolized by citizens of other States . . . .

Now, what the clause in question does for the protection of citizens of one State against the creation of monopolies in favor of citizens of other States, the fourteenth amendment does for the protection of every citizen of the United States against the creation of any monopoly whatsoever. The privileges and immunities of citizens of the United States, of every one of them, is secured against abridgment in any form by any State. The fourteenth amendment places them under the guardianship of the National authority. All monopolies in any known trade or manufacture are an invasion of these privileges, for they encroach upon the liberty of citizens to acquire property and pursue happiness, and were held void at common law . . . .

In all these cases there is a recognition of the equality of right among citizens in the pursuit of the ordinary avocations of life, and a declaration that all grants of exclusive privilege . . . are against common right, and void.

. . . And when the Colonies separated from the mother country no privilege was more fundamentally recognized or more completely incorporated into the fundamental law of the country than that every free subject . . . was entitled to pursue his happiness by following any of the known established trades and occupations . . . subject only to such restraints as equally affected all others. The immortal document which proclaimed the independence of the country declared as self-evident truths that the Creator had endowed all men "with certain inalienable rights, and that among these are life, liberty, and the pursuit of happiness; and that to secure these rights governments are instituted among men." . . .

This equality of right . . . is the distinguishing privilege of citizens of the United States . . . . The State may prescribe such regulations as will promote the public health, secure the good order and advance the general prosperity of society, but when once prescribed, the pursuit or calling must be free to be followed by every citizen who is within the conditions designated, and will conform to the regulations. This is the fundamental idea upon which our institutions rest, and unless adhered to in the legislation of the country our government will be a republic only in name. The fourteenth amendment . . . makes it essential to the validity of the legislation of every State that this equality of right should be respected . . . . [G]rants of exclusive privilege, such as is made by the act in question, are opposed to the whole theory of free government, and it requires no aid from any bill of rights to render them void. That only is a free government, in the American sense of the term, under which the inalienable right of every citizen to pursue his happiness is unrestrained, except by just, equal, and impartial laws.

I am authorized by the Chief Justice [**CHASE**], Mr. Justice **SWAYNE**, and Mr. Justice **BRADLEY** to state that they concur with me in this dissenting opinion.

Mr. Justice **BRADLEY**, also dissenting: . . . .

. . . A citizen of the United States has a perfect constitutional right to go to and reside in any State he chooses, and to claim citizenship therein, and an equality of rights with every other citizen; and the whole power of the nation is pledged to sustain him in that right. . . . Citizenship of the United States ought to be, and, according to the Constitution, is, a sure and undoubted title to equal rights in any and every State in this Union, subject to such regulations as the legislature may rightfully prescribe. If a man be denied full equality before the law, he is denied one of the essential rights of citizenship as a citizen of the United States.

Every citizen, then, being primarily a citizen of the United States, and, secondarily, a citizen of the State where he resides, what, in general, are the privileges and immunities of a citizen of the United States? Is the right, liberty, or privilege of choosing any lawful employment one of them? . . .

This seems to me to be the essential question before us . . . . And, in my judgment, the right of any citizen to follow whatever lawful employment he chooses to adopt (submitting himself to all lawful regulations) is one of his most valuable rights, and one which the legislature of a State cannot invade, whether restrained by its own constitution or not.

The right of a State to regulate the conduct of its citizens is undoubtedly a very broad and extensive one. . . . But there are certain fundamental rights which this right of regulation cannot infringe. It may prescribe the manner of their exercise, but it cannot subvert the rights themselves. I speak now of the rights of citizens of any free government . . . . In this free country, the people of which inherited certain traditional rights and privileges from their ancestors, citizenship means something. It has certain privileges and immunities attached to it which the government, whether restricted by express or implied limitations, cannot take away or impair. . . . And these privileges and immunities attach as well to citizenship of the United States as to citizenship of the States.

The people of this country brought with them to its shores the rights of Englishmen; the rights which had been wrested from English sovereigns at various periods of the nation's history . . . .

. . . [P]ersonal rights . . . were claimed by the very first Congress of the Colonies, assembled in 1774, as the undoubted inheritance of the people of this country; and the Declaration of Independence, which was the first political act of the American people in their independent sovereign capacity, lays the foundation of our National existence upon this broad proposition: "That all men are created equal; that they are endowed by their Creator with certain inalienable rights; that among these are life, liberty, and the pursuit of happiness." Here again we have the great threefold division of the rights of free-men, asserted as the rights of man. Rights to life, liberty, and the pursuit of happiness are equivalent to the rights of life, liberty, and property. These are the fundamental rights which can only be taken away by due process of law, and which can only be interfered with, or the enjoyment of which can only be modified, by lawful regulations necessary or proper for the mutual good of all; and these rights, I contend, belong to the citizens of every free government.

For the preservation, exercise, and enjoyment of these rights the individual citizen, as a necessity, must be left free to adopt such calling, profession, or trade as may seem to him most conducive to that end. Without this right he cannot be a freeman. This right to choose one's calling is an essential part of that liberty which it is the object of government to protect; and a calling, when chosen, is a man's property and right. Liberty and property are not protected where these rights are arbitrarily assailed.

. . . [C]itizenship is not an empty name, but . . . , in this country at least, it has connected with it certain incidental rights, privileges, and immunities of the greatest importance. And to say that these rights and immunities attach only to State citizenship, and not to citizenship of the United States, appears to me to evince a very narrow and insufficient estimate of constitutional history and the rights of men, not to say the rights of the American people. . . .

[Justice Bradley here also quotes *Corfield.*]

But we are not bound to resort to implication, or to the constitutional history of England, to find an authoritative declaration of some of the most important privileges and immunities of citizens of the United States. It is in the Constitution itself. The Constitution, it is true, as it stood prior to the recent amendments, specifies, in terms, only a few of the personal privileges and immunities of citizens, but they are very comprehensive in their character. The States were merely prohibited from passing bills of attainder, *ex post facto* laws, laws impairing the obligation of contracts, and perhaps one or two more. But others of the greatest consequence were enumerated, although they were only secured, in express terms, from invasion by the Federal government; such as the right of *habeas corpus,* the right of trial by jury, of free exercise of religious worship, the right of free speech and a free press, the right peaceably to assemble for the discussion of public measures, the right to be secure against unreasonable searches and seizures, and above all, and including almost all the rest, the right of *not being deprived of life, liberty, or property, without due process of law.* These, and still others are specified in the original

Constitution, or in the early amendments of it, as among the privileges and immunities of citizens of the United States, or, what is still stronger for the force of the argument, the rights of all persons, whether citizens or not.

But even if the Constitution were silent, the fundamental privileges and immunities of citizens, as such, would be no less real and no less inviolable than they now are. It was not necessary to say in words that the citizens of the United States should have and exercise all the privileges of citizens; the privilege of buying, selling, and enjoying property; the privilege of engaging in any lawful employment for a livelihood; the privilege of resorting to the laws for redress of injuries, and the like. Their very citizenship conferred these privileges, if they did not possess them before. And these privileges they would enjoy whether they were citizens of any State or not . . . .

The granting of monopolies, or exclusive privileges to individuals or corporations, is an invasion of the right of others to choose a lawful calling, and an infringement of personal liberty . . . .

Lastly: Can the Federal courts administer relief to citizens of the United States whose privileges and immunities have been abridged by a State? Of this I entertain no doubt. Prior to the fourteenth amendment this could not be done, except in a few instances, for the want of the requisite authority . . . .

. . . . In my judgment, it was the intention of the people of this country in adopting that amendment to provide National security against violation by the States of the fundamental rights of the citizen . . . . .

In my view, a law which prohibits a large class of citizens from adopting a lawful employment, or from following a lawful employment previously adopted, does deprive them of liberty as well as property, without due process of law. Their right of choice is a portion of their liberty; their occupation is their property. Such a law also deprives those citizens of the equal protection of the laws . . . .

The constitutional question is distinctly raised in these cases; the constitutional right is expressly claimed . . . . Our jurisdiction and our duty are plain and imperative.

It is futile to argue that none but persons of the African race are intended to be benefited by this amendment. They may have been the primary cause of the amendment, but its language is general, embracing all citizens, and I think it was purposely so expressed.

The mischief to be remedied was not merely slavery and its incidents and consequences; but that spirit of insubordination and disloyalty to the National government which had troubled the country for so many years in some of the States, and that intolerance of free speech and free discussion which often rendered life and property insecure, and led to much unequal legislation. The amendment was an attempt to give voice to the strong National yearning for that time and that condition of things, in which American citizenship should be a sure guaranty of safety, and in which every citizen of the United States might stand erect on every portion of its soil, in the full enjoyment of every right and privilege belonging to a freeman, without fear of violence or molestation.

But great fears are expressed that this construction of the amendment will lead to enactments by Congress interfering with the internal affairs of the States, and establishing therein civil and criminal codes of law for the government of the citizens, and thus abolishing the State governments in everything but name; or else, that it will lead the Federal courts to draw to their cognizance the supervision of State tribunals on every subject of judicial inquiry, on the plea of ascertaining whether the privileges and immunities of citizens have not been abridged.

In my judgment no such practical inconveniences would arise. Very little, if any, legislation on the part of Congress would be required to carry the amendment into effect. Like the prohibition against passing a law impairing the obligation of a contract, it would execute itself. The point would be regularly raised, in a suit at law, and settled by final reference to the Federal court. As the privileges and immunities protected are only those fundamental ones which belong to every citizen, they would soon become so far defined as to cause but a slight accumulation of business in the Federal courts. Besides, the recognized existence of the law would prevent its frequent violation. But even if the business of the National courts should be increased, Congress could easily supply the remedy by increasing their number and efficiency. The great question is, What is the true construction of the amendment? When once we find that, we shall find the means of giving it effect
. . . .

Mr. Justice **SWAYNE**, dissenting. . . .

The first eleven amendments to the Constitution were intended to be checks and limitations upon the government which that instrument called into existence. They had their origin in a spirit of jealousy on the part of the States, which existed when the Constitution was adopted. . . .

. . . [The Thirteenth, Fourteenth, and Fifteenth] amendments are a new departure, and mark an important epoch in the constitutional history of the country. They trench directly upon the power of the State, and deeply affect those bodies. They are, in this respect, at the opposite pole from the first eleven.

Fairly construed these amendments may be said to rise to the dignity of a new Magna Charta . . . .

The first section of the fourteenth amendment is alone involved in the consideration of these cases. No searching analysis is necessary to eliminate its meaning. Its language is intelligible and direct. Nothing can be more transparent. Every word employed has an established signification. There is no room for construction. There is nothing to construe. Elaboration may obscure, but cannot make clearer, the intent and purpose sought to be carried out . . . .

These amendments are all consequences of the late civil war. The prejudices and apprehension as to the central government which prevailed when the Constitution was adopted were dispelled by the light of experience. The public mind became satisfied that there was less danger of tyranny in the head than of anarchy and tyranny in the members. The provisions of this section are all eminently conservative in their character. They are a bulwark of defence, and can never be made an engine of oppression. The language employed is unqualified in its scope. There is no exception in its terms, and there can be properly none in their application. By the language "citizens of the United States" was meant *all* such citizens; and by "any person" was meant *all* persons within the jurisdiction of the State. No distinction is intimated on account of race or color. This court has no authority to interpolate a limitation that is neither expressed nor implied. Our duty is to execute the law, not to make it. The protection provided was not intended to be confined to those of any particular race or class, but to embrace equally all races, classes, and conditions of men. It is objected that the power conferred is novel and large. The answer is that the novelty was known and the measure deliberately adopted. The power is beneficent in its nature, and cannot be abused. It is such as should exist in every well-ordered system of polity. Where could it be more appropriately lodged than in the hands to which it is confided? It is necessary to enable the government of the nation to secure to every one within its jurisdiction the rights and privileges enumerated, which, according to the plainest considerations of reason and justice and the fundamental principles of the social compact, all are entitled to enjoy. Without such authority any government claiming to be national is glaringly defective. The construction adopted by the majority of my brethren is, in my judgment, much too narrow. It defeats, by a limitation not anticipated, the intent of those by whom the instrument was framed and of those by whom it was adopted. To the extent of that limitation it turns, as it were, what was meant for bread into a stone. By the Constitution, as it stood before the war, ample protection was given against oppression by the Union, but little was given against wrong and oppression by the States. That want was intended to be supplied by this amendment. Against the former this court has been called upon more than once to interpose. Authority of the same amplitude was intended to be conferred as to the latter. But this arm of our jurisdiction is, in these cases, stricken down by the judgment just given. Nowhere, than in this court, ought the will of the nation, as thus expressed, to be more liberally construed or more cordially executed . . . .

Editors' Notes

(1) **Query**: All the opinions here accept the notion that before the Fourteenth Amendment there were few federal constitutional restraints on the states. Marshall certainly so held in Barron v. Baltimore (1833) when he ruled

that the Bill of Rights does not apply to the states; but what about his opinion in Fletcher v. Peck (1810; reprinted below p. 956) and Chase's in Calder v. Bull (1798; reprinted above, p. 86)?

(2) According to Justice Miller, what was the effect of the Fourteenth Amendment on the structure of American federalism? Bradley? Swayne? Did Field need the Fourteenth Amendment to justify his conclusions?

(3) As far as "privileges or immunities" are concerned, *Slaughter-House* still stands, though it would have been more logical for the Court to have read the Bill of Rights into the Fourteenth Amendment through that clause than through due process. One objection to "privileges or immunities" as such a vehicle is that it only prohibits states from abridging the "privileges or immunities of citizens of the United States," apparently leaving open the possibility of denying such rights to aliens and to corporations who, while legal persons, are not citizens. But, as John Hart Ely points out, the ban is not against denying citizens their privileges or immunities but against denying such rights; thus grammatically the clause could protect aliens as well as corporations. *Democracy and Distrust* (Cambridge: Harvard University Press, 1980), p. 25.

(4) The Court has done little to expand the scope of the Thirteenth Amendment. It has, however, completely gutted *Slaughter-House*'s interpretation of the equal protection and due process clauses. Indeed, the argument is strong that Swayne's description of the Fourteenth Amendment as "a new Magna Charta" has become a reality.

"[W]hen we are dealing with words that also are a constituent act, like the Constitution of the United States, we must realize that they have called into life a being the development of which could not have been foreseen completely by the most gifted of its begetters."

MISSOURI v. HOLLAND
252 U.S. 416, 40 S.Ct. 382, 64 L.Ed. 641 (1920).

This case, sustaining the constitutionality of a treaty against a challenge from a state that it was invalid because of "some invisible radiation from the general terms of the Tenth Amendment," is reprinted above at p. 132.

"Congress may not exercise that power [over commerce] so as to force directly upon the States its choices as to how essential decisions regarding the conduct of integral governmental functions are to be made."

NATIONAL LEAGUE OF CITIES v. USERY
426 U.S. 833, 96 S.Ct. 2465, 49 L.Ed.2d 245 (1976).

In 1974 Congress amended the Fair Labor Standards Act so as to bring within its minimum wage and maximum hours coverage almost all public employees in the states and cities. Individual cities, states, the National League of Cities, and the National Governors' Conference brought suit in a special three-judge federal district court to enjoin the secretary of labor from enforcing the amendments to the FLSA, claiming they violated the Tenth Amendment. The district court dismissed the suit, and plaintiffs appealed directly to the U.S. Supreme Court, as allowed when the original suit is heard by a three-judge district court.

Mr. Justice **REHNQUIST** delivered the opinion of the Court . . . . .

II

It is established beyond peradventure that the Commerce Clause of Art I of the Constitution is a grant of plenary authority to Congress. That authority is, in the words of Mr. Chief Justice Marshall in Gibbons v. Ogden (1824), "the power to regulate; that is, to prescribe the rule by which commerce is to be governed." When considering the validity of asserted applications of this power to wholly private activity, the Court has made it clear that

> [e]ven activity that is purely intrastate in character may be regulated
> by Congress, where the activity, combined with like conduct by others
> similarly situated, affects commerce among the States or with foreign
> nations. Fry v. United States (1975).

Congressional power over areas of private endeavor, even when its exercise may pre-empt express state law determinations contrary to the result which has commended itself to the collective wisdom of Congress, has been held to be limited only by the requirement that "the means chosen by [Congress] must be reasonably adapted to the end permitted by the Constitution." Heart of Atlanta Motel v. United States (1964).

Appellants in no way challenge these decisions establishing the breadth of authority granted Congress under the commerce power. Their contention . . . is that when Congress seeks to regulate directly the activities of States as public employers, it transgresses an affirmative limitation on the exercise of its power akin to other commerce power affirmative limitations contained in the Constitution. Congressional enactments which may be fully within the grant of legislative authority contained in the Commerce Clause may nonetheless be invalid because found to offend against the right to trial by jury contained in the Sixth Amendment . . . or the Due Process Clause of the Fifth Amendment. Appellants' essential contention is that the 1974 amendments to the Act, while undoubtedly within the scope of the Commerce Clause, encounter a similar constitutional barrier because they are to be applied directly to the States and subdivisions of States as employers.

This Court has never doubted that there are limits upon the power of Congress to override state sovereignty, even when exercising its otherwise plenary powers to tax or to regulate commerce . . . . In [Maryland v.] Wirtz [1968], for example, the Court took care to assure the appellants that it had "ample power to prevent . . . 'the utter destruction of the State as a sovereign political entity.'" In *Fry*, the

Court recognized that an express declaration of this limitation is found in the Tenth Amendment:

> While the Tenth Amendment has been characterized as a "truism," stating merely that "all is retained which has not been surrendered," United States v. Darby (1941), it is not without significance. The Amendment expressly declares the constitutional policy that Congress may not exercise power in a fashion that impairs the States' integrity or their ability to function effectively in a federal system.

In New York v. United States (1946), Mr. Chief Justice Stone, speaking for four Members of an eight-Member Court in rejecting the proposition that Congress could impose taxes on the States so long as it did so in a non-discriminatory manner, observed:

> A State may, like a private individual, own real property and receive income. But in view of our former decisions we could hardly say that a general nondiscriminatory real estate tax (apportioned), or an income tax laid upon citizens and States alike could be constitutionally applied to the State's capitol, its State-house, its public school houses, public parks, or its revenues from taxes or school lands, even though all real property and all income of the citizen is taxed. . . .

The expressions in these more recent cases trace back to earlier decisions of this Court recognizing the essential role of the States in our federal system of government. Mr. Chief Justice Chase, ... [i]n Texas v. White (1869), declared that "[t]he Constitution, in all its provisions, looks to an indestructible Union, composed of indestructible States." In Lane County v. Oregon (1869), his opinion for the Court said:

> Both the States and the United States existed before the Constitution . . . . [I]n many articles of the Constitution the necessary existence of the States, and, within their proper spheres, the independent authority of the States, is distinctly recognized. . . .

Appellee Secretary argues that the cases in which this Court has upheld sweeping exercises of authority by Congress, even though those exercises pre-empted state regulation of the private sector, have already curtailed the sovereignty of the States quite as much as the 1974 amendments to the Fair Labor Standards Act. We do not agree. It is one thing to recognize the authority of Congress to enact laws regulating individual businesses necessarily subject to the dual sovereignty of the government of the Nation and of the State in which they reside. It is quite another to uphold a similar exercise of congressional authority directed, not to private citizens, but to the States as States. We have repeatedly recognized that there are attributes of sovereignty attaching to every state government which may not be impaired by Congress, not because Congress may lack an affirmative grant of legislative authority to reach the matter, but because the Constitution prohibits it from exercising the authority in that manner. . . .

One undoubted attribute of state sovereignty is the States' power to determine the wages which shall be paid to those whom they employ in order to carry out their governmental functions, what hours those persons will work, and what compensation will be provided where these employees may be called upon to work overtime. The question we must resolve here, then, is whether these determinations are " 'functions essential to separate and independent existence.'" Coyle v. Oklahoma (1911), quoting from *Lane County*, so that Congress may not abrogate the States' otherwise plenary authority to make them.

In their complaint appellants advanced estimates of substantial costs which will be imposed upon them by the 1974 amendments. . . .

Judged solely in terms of increased costs in dollars, these allegations show a significant impact on the functioning of the governmental bodies involved. The Metropolitan Government of Nashville and Davidson County, Tenn., for example, asserted that the Act will increase its costs of providing essential police and fire protection, without any increase in service or in current salary levels, by $938,000 per year . . . . The State of California . . . estimated that application of the Act to its employment practices will necessitate an increase in its budget of between $8 million and $16 million.

Increased costs are not, of course, the only adverse effects which compliance with the Act will visit upon state and local governments, and in turn upon the citizens who depend upon those governments . . . . [F]or example, California asserted that it could not comply with the overtime costs (approximately $750,000 per year) which the Act required to be paid to California Highway Patrol cadets during their academy training program. California reported that it had thus been forced to reduce its academy training program from 2,080 hours to only 960 hours, a compromise undoubtedly of substantial importance to those whose safety and welfare may depend upon the preparedness of the California Highway Patrol.

This type of forced relinquishment of important governmental activities is further reflected in the complaint's allegation that the city of Inglewood, Cal. has been forced to curtail its affirmative action program for providing employment opportunities for men and women interested in a career in law enforcement . . . .

Quite apart from the substantial costs imposed upon the States and their political subdivisions, the Act displaces state policies regarding the manner in which they will structure delivery of those governmental services which their citizens require. The Act, speaking directly to the States qua States, requires that they shall pay all but an extremely limited minority of their employees the minimum wage rates currently chosen by Congress. It may well be that as a matter of economic policy it would be desirable that States, just as private employers, comply with these minimum wage requirements. But it cannot be gainsaid that the federal requirement directly supplants the considered policy choices of the States' elected officials and administrators as to how they wish to structure pay scales in state employment. . . . The only "discretion" left to them under the Act is either to attempt to increase their revenue to meet the additional financial burden imposed upon them by paying congressionally prescribed wages to their existing complement of employees, or to reduce that complement to a number which can be paid the federal minimum wage without increasing revenue.

This dilemma presented by the minimum wage restrictions may seem not immediately different from that faced by private employers, who have long been covered by the Act . . . . The difference, however, is that a State is not merely a factor in the "shifting economic arrangements" of the private sector of the economy, Kovacs v. Cooper (1949) (Frankfurter, J., concurring), but is itself a coordinate element in the system established by the Framers for governing our Federal Union . . . .

Our examination of the effect of the 1974 amendments . . . satisfies us that both the minimum wage and the maximum hour provisions will impermissibly interfere with the integral governmental functions of these bodies . . . . [T]heir application will . . . significantly alter or displace the States' abilities to structure employer-employee relationships in such areas as fire prevention, police protection, sanitation, public health, and parks and recreation. These activities are typical of those performed by state and local governments in discharging their dual functions of administering the public law and furnishing public services. Indeed, it is functions such as these which governments are created to provide, services such as these which the States have traditionally afforded their citizens. If Congress may withdraw from the States the authority to make those fundamental employment decisions upon which their systems for performance of these functions must rest, we think there would be little left of the States' " 'separate and independent existence.' " Coyle. Thus, even if appellants may have overestimated the effect which the Act will have upon their current levels and patterns of governmental activity, the dispositive factor is that Congress has attempted to exercise its Commerce Clause authority to prescribe minimum wages and maximum hours to be paid by the States in their capacities as sovereign governments. In so doing, Congress has sought to wield its power in a fashion that would impair the States' "ability to function effectively in a federal system." Fry. This exercise of congressional authority does not comport with the federal system of government embodied in the Constitution. We hold that insofar as the challenged amendments operate to directly displace the States' freedom to structure integral operations in areas of traditional governmental functions, they are not within the authority granted Congress by Art I, § 8, cl. 3.

III

One final matter requires our attention. Appellee has vigorously urged that we cannot, consistently with the Court's decisions in Wirtz and Fry rule against him here. . . .

We think our holding today quite consistent with *Fry*. The enactment at issue there was occasioned by an extremely serious problem which endangered the well-being of all the component parts of our federal system and which only collective action by the National Government might forestall. The means selected were carefully drafted so as not to interfere with the States' freedom beyond a very limited, specific period of time. The effect of the across-the-board freeze authorized by that Act, moreover, displaced no state choices as to how governmental operations should be structured, nor did it force the States to remake such choices themselves. Instead, it merely required that the wage scales and employment relationships which the States themselves had chosen be maintained during the period of the emergency. Finally, the Economic Stabilization Act operated to reduce the pressures upon state budgets rather than increase them. These factors distinguish the statute in *Fry* from the provisions at issue here. The limits imposed upon the commerce power when Congress seeks to apply it to the States are not so inflexible as to preclude temporary enactments tailored to combat a national emergency. . . .

With respect to the Court's decision in *Wirtz*, we reach a different conclusion. . . . There are undoubtedly factual distinctions between the two situations, but in view of the conclusions expressed earlier in this opinion we do not believe the reasoning in *Wirtz* may any longer be regarded as authoritative.

Wirtz relied heavily on the Court's decision in United States v. California (1936). The opinion quotes the following language from that case:

> "[We] look to the activities in which the states have traditionally engaged as marking the boundary of the restriction upon the federal taxing power. But there is no such limitation upon the plenary power to regulate commerce. The state can no more deny the power if its exercise has been authorized by Congress than can an individual."

But we have reaffirmed today that the States as States stand on a quite different footing from an individual or a corporation when challenging the exercise of Congress' power to regulate commerce. We think the dicta from United States v. California, simply wrong. Congress may not exercise that power so as to force directly upon the States its choices as to how essential decisions regarding the conduct of integral governmental functions are to be made. We agree that such assertions of power, if unchecked, would indeed, as Mr. Justice Douglas cautioned in his dissent in *Wirtz*, allow "the National Government [to] devour the essentials of state sovereignty," . . . and would therefore transgress the bounds of the authority granted Congress under the Commerce Clause. While there are obvious differences between the schools and hospitals involved in *Wirtz*, and the fire and police departments affected here, each provides an integral portion of those governmental services which the States and their political subdivisions have traditionally afforded their citizens. We are therefore persuaded that *Wirtz* must be overruled.

Reversed.

Mr. Justice **BLACKMUN**, concurring.

. . . Although I am not untroubled by certain possible implications of the Court's opinion . . . I do not read the opinion so despairingly as does my Brother Brennan. In my view, the result with respect to the statute under challenge here is necessarily correct. I may misinterpret the Court's opinion, but it seems to me that it adopts a balancing approach, and does not outlaw federal power in areas such as environmental protection, where the federal interest is demonstrably greater and where state facility compliance with federal standards would be essential. With this understanding on my part of the Court's opinion, I join it.

Mr. Justice **BRENNAN**, with whom Mr. Justice **WHITE** and Mr. Justice **MARSHALL** join, dissenting.

The Court concedes that Congress enacted the 1974 amendments pursuant to its exclusive power under Art I, § 8, cl 3, of the Constitution "[t]o regulate Commerce . . . among the several States." It must therefore be surprising that my Brethren should choose this bicentennial year of our independence to repudiate principles governing judicial interpretation of our Constitution settled since the time of Mr. Chief Justice John Marshall, discarding his postulate that the Constitution contemplates that restraints upon exercise by Congress of its plenary commerce power lie in the political process and not in the judicial process. For 152 years ago Mr. Chief Justice Marshall enunciated that principle to which, until today, his successors on this Court have been faithful.

> [T]he power over commerce . . . is vested in Congress as absolutely as it would be in a single government. . . . *The wisdom and the discretion of Congress, their identity with the people, and the influence which their constituents possess at elections, are . . . the sole restraints on which they have relied, to secure them from its abuse. They are the restraints on which the people must often rely solely, in all representative governments.* Gibbons v. Ogden (1824) [emphasis added].

Only 34 years ago, Wickard v. Filburn (1942) reaffirmed that "[a]t the beginning Chief Justice Marshall . . . made emphatic the embracing and penetrating nature of [Congress' commerce] power by warning that effective restraints on its exercise must proceed from political rather than from judicial processes."

My Brethren do not successfully obscure today's patent usurpation of the role reserved for the political process by their purported discovery in the Constitution of a restraint derived from sovereignty of the States on Congress' exercise of the commerce power. Mr. Chief Justice Marshall recognized that limitations "prescribed in the constitution,"

Gibbons v. Ogden, restrain Congress' exercise of the power . . . .
Thus laws within the commerce power may not infringe individual
liberties protected by the First Amendment, . . . the Fifth Amendment, . . . or the Sixth Amendment . . . . But there is no
restraint based on state sovereignty requiring or permitting judicial
enforcement anywhere expressed in the Constitution; our decisions
over the last century and a half have explicitly rejected the existence of
any such restraint on the commerce power. . . .

My Brethren thus have today manufactured an abstraction without
substance, founded neither in the words of the Constitution nor on
precedent. An abstraction having such profoundly pernicious consequences is not made less so by characterizing the 1974 amendments as
legislation directed against the "States qua States." . . . [M]y Brethren make no claim that the 1974 amendments are not regulations of
"commerce"; rather they overrule *Wirtz* in disagreement with historic
principles that United States v. California reaffirmed . . . . [M]y
Brethren are also repudiating the long line of our precedents holding
that a judicial finding that Congress has not unreasonably regulated a
subject matter of "commerce" brings to an end the judicial role. "Let
the end be legitimate, let it be within the scope of the constitution, and
all means which are appropriate, which are plainly adapted to that end,
which are not prohibited, but consist with the letter and spirit of the
constitution, are constitutional." M'Culloch v. Maryland [1819].

The reliance of my Brethren upon the Tenth Amendment as "an
express declaration of [a state sovereignty] limitation," . . . not only
suggests that they overrule governing decisions of this Court that
address this question but must astound scholars of the Constitution.
For not only early decisions, *Gibbons*, *M'Culloch*, and Martin v. Hunter's Lessee (1816), hold that nothing in the Tenth Amendment constitutes a limitation on congressional exercise of powers delegated by the
Constitution to Congress. Rather, as the Tenth Amendment's significance was more recently summarized:

> The amendment states but a truism that all is retained which has not
> been surrendered. There is *nothing in the history of its adoption to
> suggest that it was more than declaratory of the relationship between
> the national and state governments as it had been established by the
> Constitution before the amendment* . . . . United States v. Darby
> [emphasis added].

My Brethren purport to find support for their novel state-sovereignty doctrine in the concurring opinion of Mr. Chief Justice Stone in
New York v. United States (1946). That reliance is plainly misplaced,
. . . [for] the Chief Justice was addressing not the question of a state
sovereignty restraint upon the exercise of the commerce power, but
rather the principle of implied immunity of the States and Federal
Government from taxation by the other . . . .

In contrast, the apposite decision that Term to the question whether the Constitution implies a state sovereignty restraint upon congres-

sional exercise of the commerce power is Case v. Bowles (1946) . . . .
The Court . . . in an opinion joined by Mr. Chief Justice Stone,
reason[ed]:

> [T]he [State's] argument is that the extent of that power as applied to
> state functions depends on whether these are "essential" to the state
> government. The use of the same criterion in measuring the constitu-
> tional power of Congress to tax has proved to be unworkable, and we
> reject it as a guide in the field here involved. Cf. United States v.
> California . . . .

. . . Even more significant for our purposes is . . . . United States v.
California. . . . [which] directly presented the question whether any
state sovereignty restraint precluded application of the Federal Safety
Appliance Act to a state-owned and -operated railroad. . . . Mr.
Justice Stone rejected the contention in an opinion for a unanimous
Court. His rationale is a complete refutation of today's holding:

> . . . The sovereign power of the states is necessarily diminished to
> the extent of the grants of power to the federal government in the
> Constitution . . . .
> The analogy of the constitutional immunity of state instrumentali-
> ties from federal taxation . . . is not illuminating. That immunity is
> implied from the nature of our federal system and the relationship
> within it of state and national governments, and is equally a restric-
> tion on taxation by either of the instrumentalities of the other. Its
> nature requires that it be so construed as to allow to each government
> reasonable scope for its taxing power . . . which would be unduly
> curtailed if either by extending its activities could withdraw from the
> taxing power of the other subjects of taxation traditionally within it.
> . . . Hence we look to the activities in which the states have
> traditionally engaged as marking the boundary of the restriction upon
> the federal taxing power. *But there is no such limitation upon the
> plenary power to regulate commerce. The state can no more deny the
> power if its exercise has been authorized by Congress than can an
> individual.* . . . [Emphasis added].

Today's repudiation of this unbroken line of precedents that firmly
reject my Brethren's ill-conceived abstraction can only be regarded as a
transparent cover for invalidating a congressional judgment with which
they disagree. The only analysis even remotely resembling that adopted today is found in a line of opinions dealing with the Commerce
Clause and the Tenth Amendment that ultimately provoked a constitutional crisis for the Court in the 1930's. E.g. Carter v. Carter Coal Co.
(1936); United States v. Butler (1936); Hammer v. Dagenhart . . .
(1918). We tend to forget that the Court invalidated legislation during
the Great Depression, not solely under the Due Process Clause, but also
and primarily under the Commerce Clause and the Tenth Amendment.
It may have been the eventual abandonment of that overly restrictive
construction of the commerce power that spelled defeat for the Court-
packing plan, and preserved the integrity of this institution, . . . see,

e.g. United States v. Darby (1941); NLRB v. Jones & Laughlin Steel Corp. (1937), but my Brethren today are transparently trying to cut back on that recognition of the scope of the commerce power. My Brethren's approach to this case is not far different from the dissenting opinions in the cases that averted the crisis.

That no precedent justifies today's result is particularly clear from the awkward extension of the doctrine of state immunity from federal taxation—an immunity conclusively distinguished by Mr. Justice Stone in *California,* and an immunity that is "narrowly limited" because "the people of all the states have created the national government and are represented in Congress," Helvering v. Gerhardt (1938) (Stone, J.)—to fashion a judicially enforceable restraint on Congress' exercise of the commerce power that the Court has time and again rejected as having no place in our constitutional jurisprudence. "[W]here [Congress] keeps within its sphere and violates no express constitutional limitation it has been the rule of this Court, going back almost to the founding days of the Republic, not to interfere." Katzenbach v. McClung (1964). . . . The 1974 amendments are . . . an entirely legitimate exercise of the commerce power, not in the slightest restrained by any doctrine of state sovereignty cognizable in this Court . . . . [S]ince *Wirtz* is overruled, the Fair Labor Standards Act is invalidated in its application to all state employees "in [any areas] that the States have regarded as integral parts of their governmental activities." This standard is a meaningless limitation on the Court's state-sovereignty doctrine, and thus today's holding goes beyond even what the States of Washington and California urged in *Case* and *California*, and by its logic would overrule those cases . . . . I cannot recall another instance in the Court's history when the reasoning of so many decisions covering so long a span of time has been discarded in such a roughshod manner. That this is done without any justification not already often advanced and consistently rejected, clearly renders today's decision an ipse dixit reflecting nothing but displeasure with a congressional judgment.

My Brethren's treatment of *Fry* further illustrates the paucity of legal reasoning or principle justifying today's result. Although the Economic Stabilization Act "displace[d] the States' freedom," . . . the result in *Fry* is not disturbed since the interference was temporary and only a national program enforced by the Federal Government could have alleviated the country's economic crisis. Thus, although my Brethren by fiat strike down the 1974 amendments without analysis of countervailing national considerations, *Fry* by contrary logic remains undisturbed because, on balance, countervailing national considerations override the interference with the State's freedom. Moreover, it is sophistry to say the Economic Stabilization Act "displaced no state choices," . . . but that the 1974 amendments do . . . . It is absurd to suggest that there is a constitutionally significant distinction between curbs against increasing wages and curbs against paying wages lower than the federal minimum . . . .

Certainly the paradigm of sovereign action—action qua State—is in the enactment and enforcement of state laws. Is it possible that my Brethren are signaling abandonment of the heretofore unchallenged principle that Congress "can, if it chooses, entirely displace the States to the full extent of the far-reaching Commerce Clause"? Bethlehem Steel Co. v. New York State Board (1947) (opinion of Frankfurter, J.) [T]he ouster of state laws obviously curtails or prohibits the States' prerogatives to make policy choices respecting subjects clearly of greater significance to the "State qua State" than the minimum wage paid to state employees . . . .

My Brethren do more than turn aside longstanding constitutional jurisprudence that emphatically rejects today's conclusion. More alarming is the startling restructuring of our federal system, and the role they create therein for the federal judiciary. This Court is simply not at liberty to erect a mirror of its own conception of a desirable governmental structure. If the 1974 amendments have any "vice," . . . my Brother Stevens is surely right that it represents "merely . . . a policy issue which has been firmly resolved by the branches of government having power to decide such questions." It bears repeating "that effective restraints on . . . exercise [of the commerce power] must proceed from political rather than from judicial processes." *Wickard.*

It is unacceptable that the judicial process should be thought superior to the political process in this area. Under the Constitution the Judiciary has no role to play beyond finding that Congress has not made an unreasonable legislative judgment respecting what is "commerce." . . .

Judicial restraint in this area merely recognizes that the political branches of our Government are structured to protect the interests of the States, as well as the Nation as a whole, and that the States are fully able to protect their own interests in the premises. Congress is constituted of representatives in both the Senate and House elected from the States. The *Federalist* No. 45 . . . . Decisions upon the extent of federal intervention under the Commerce Clause into the affairs of the States are in that sense decisions of the States themselves. Judicial redistribution of powers granted the National Government by the terms of the Constitution violates the fundamental tenet of our federalism that the extent of federal intervention into the States' affairs in the exercise of delegated powers shall be determined by the States' exercise of political power through their representatives in Congress. See Wechsler, The Political Safeguards of Federalism: The Role of the States in the Composition and Selection of the National Government, 54 Col.L.Rev. 543 (1954). There is no reason whatever to suppose that in enacting the 1974 amendments Congress, even if it might extensively obliterate state sovereignty by fully exercising its plenary power respecting commerce, had any purpose to do so. Surely the presumption must be to the contrary. Any realistic assessment of our federal political system, dominated as it is by representatives of the people *elected from the States,* yields the conclusion that it is highly unlikely that those representatives will ever be motivated to disregard totally the concerns of these States. The *Federalist* No. 46 . . . .

My Brethren's disregard for precedents recognizing these long-settled constitutional principles is painfully obvious in their cavalier treatment of *Wirtz.* Without even a passing reference to the doctrine of stare decisis, *Wirtz*—regarded as controlling only last Term, *Fry* . . . —is by exercise of raw judicial power overruled.

No effort is made to distinguish the FLSA amendments sustained in *Wirtz* from the 1974 amendments. We are told at the outset that "the 'far-reaching implications' of *Wirtz* should be overruled," . . . ; later it is said that the "reasoning in *Wirtz*" is no longer "authoritative." My Brethren then merely restate their essential-function test and say that *Wirtz* must "therefore" be overruled. There is no analysis whether *Wirtz* reached the correct result, apart from any flaws in reasoning, even though we are told that "there are obvious differences" between this case and *Wirtz.* Are state and federal interests being silently balanced, as in the discussion of *Fry*? The best I can make of it is that the 1966 FLSA amendments are struck down and *Wirtz* is overruled on the basis of the conceptually unworkable essential-function test; and that the test is unworkable is demonstrated by my Brethren's inability to articulate any meaningful distinctions among state-operated railroads, . . . state-operated schools and hospitals, and state-operated police and fire departments.

We are left then with a catastrophic judicial body blow at Congress' power under the Commerce Clause. Even if Congress may nevertheless accomplish its objectives—for example, by conditioning grants of federal funds upon compliance with federal minimum wage and overtime standards, cf. Oklahoma v. CSC (1947)—there is an ominous portent of disruption of our constitutional structure implicit in today's mischievous decision. I dissent.

Mr. Justice **STEVENS**, dissenting.

The Court holds that the Federal Government may not interfere with a sovereign State's inherent right to pay a substandard wage to the janitor at the state capitol. The principle on which the holding rests is difficult to perceive.

The Federal Government may, I believe, require the State to act impartially when it hires or fires the janitor, to withhold taxes from his paycheck, to observe safety regulations when he is performing his job, to forbid him from burning too much soft coal in the capitol furnace, from dumping untreated refuse in an adjacent waterway, from overloading a state-owned garbage truck, or from driving either the truck or the governor's limousine over 55 miles an hour. Even though these and many other activities of the capitol janitor are activities of the State qua State, I have no doubt that they are subject to federal regulation.

I agree that it is unwise for the Federal Government to exercise its power in the ways described in the Court's opinion . . . .

My disagreement with the wisdom of this legislation may not, of course, affect my judgment with respect to its validity. On this issue there is no dissent from the proposition that the Federal Government's power over the labor market is adequate to embrace these employees. Since I am unable to identify a limitation on that federal power that would not also invalidate federal regulation of state activities that I consider unquestionably permissible, I am persuaded that this statute is valid . . . .

Editors' Notes

(1) **Query:** With the vote 5–4, Blackmun's joining Rehnquist's opinion was essential to its becoming the opinion of the Court rather than merely expressing the views of four justices. To what extent was Blackmun's interpretation of Rehnquist's opinion justified? In effect, was Blackmun publicly serving notice that he would not endorse a return to dual federalism? Compare his opinion for the Court in Garcia v. San Antonio MTA (1985), the very next case we reprint.

(2) Brennan's assertion that *National League of Cities* would "astound scholars of the Constitution" turned out to be accurate. See espec.: Sotirios A. Barber, "National League of Cities v. Usery: New Meaning for the Tenth Amendment," 1976 *Sup.Ct.Rev.* 161; Karen Flax, "In the Wake of National League of Cities v. Usery: A Derelict Makes Waves," 34 *So.Car.L.Rev.* 649 (1983); Charles A. Lofgren, "National League of Cities v. Usery: Dual Federalism Reborn," 4 *Claremont Jo. of Pub. Affrs.* 19 (1977); Frank I. Michelman, "States' Rights and States' Roles: The Permutations of 'Sovereignty' in *National League of Cities v. Usery*," 86 *Yale L.J.* 1165 (1977); C. Herman Pritchett, *Constitutional Law of the Federal System* (Englewood Cliffs, N.J.: Prentice-Hall, 1983), pp. 234–235; Laurence H. Tribe, "Unravelling *National League of Cities*," 90 *Harv.L Rev.* 1065 (1977).

"[T]he principal means . . . to ensure the role of States in the federal system is the structure of the Federal Government itself."

GARCIA v. SAN ANTONIO METROPOLITAN TRANSIT AUTHORITY

—— U.S. ——, 105 S.Ct. 1005, 83 L.Ed.2d 1016 (1985).

It became clear from Blackmun's vote in Equal Employment Opportunity Commission v. Wyoming (1983), in which he joined the four dissenters in *National League of Cities* to erode that ruling, that the ambivalence he had expressed in 1976 had not abated in the intervening seven years. Thus the stage was set for a new constitutional battle when the U.S. Department of Labor claimed that the San Antonio Metropolitan Transit Authority (SAMTA), a county-owned agency operating a system of mass transit, had to abide by the

Fair Labor Standards Act as amended in 1974. SAMTA filed suit against the Department of Labor, claiming, on the basis of *National League of Cities* constitutional immunity from the Act and won in the lower courts. The Department of Labor appealed to the Supreme Court.

Justice **BLACKMUN** delivered the opinion of the Court . . . .

We revisit . . . an issue raised in National League of Cities v. Usery (1976). In that litigation, this Court, by a sharply divided vote, ruled that the Commerce Clause does not empower Congress to enforce the minimum-wage and overtime provisions of the Fair Labor Standards Act (FLSA) against the States "in areas of traditional governmental functions." Although *National League of Cities* supplied some examples of "traditional governmental functions," it did not offer a general explanation of how a "traditional" function is to be distinguished from a "nontraditional" one. Since then, federal and state courts have struggled with the task, thus imposed, of identifying a traditional function for purposes of state immunity under the Commerce Clause . . . .

Our examination of this "function" standard applied in these and other cases over the last eight years now persuades us that the attempt to draw the boundaries of state regulatory immunity in terms of "traditional governmental function" is not only unworkable but is inconsistent with established principles of federalism and, indeed, with those very federalism principles on which *National League of Cities* purported to rest. That case, accordingly, is overruled . . . .

II

Appellees have not argued that SAMTA is immune from regulation under the FLSA on the ground that it is a local transit system engaged in intrastate commercial activity. In a practical sense, SAMTA's operations might well be characterized as "local." Nonetheless, it long has been settled that Congress' authority under the Commerce Clause extends to intrastate economic activities that affect interstate commerce. See, e.g., Hodel v. Virginia Surface Mining & Recl. Assn. (1981); Heart of Atlanta Motel, Inc. v. United States, (1964); Wickard v. Filburn (1942); United States v. Darby (1941). Were SAMTA a privately owned and operated enterprise, it could not credibly argue that Congress exceeded the bounds of its Commerce Clause powers in prescribing minimum wages and overtime rates for SAMTA's employees. Any constitutional exemption from the requirements of the FLSA therefore must rest on SAMTA's status as a governmental entity rather than on the "local" nature of its operations.

The prerequisites for governmental immunity under *National League of Cities* were summarized by this Court in *Hodel*. Under that summary, four conditions must be satisfied before a state activity may be deemed immune from a particular federal regulation under the Commerce Clause. First, it is said that the federal statute at issue must regulate "the 'States as States.'" Second, the statute must "address matters that are indisputably 'attribute[s] of state sovereignty.' " Third, state compliance with the federal obligation must "directly impair [the States'] ability 'to structure integral operations in areas of traditional governmental functions.' " Finally, the relation of state and federal interests must not be such that "the nature of the federal interest . . . justifies state submission."

The controversy in the present cases has focused on the third *Hodel* requirement—that the challenged federal statute trench on "traditional governmental functions." The District Court voiced a common concern: "Despite the abundance of adjectives, identifying which particular state functions are immune remains difficult." Just how troublesome the task has been is revealed by the results reached in other federal cases. Thus, courts have held that regulating ambulance services, licensing automobile drivers, operating a municipal airport, performing solid waste disposal, and operating a highway authority are functions *protected* under *National League of Cities*. At the same time, courts have held that issuance of industrial development bonds, regulation of intrastate natural gas sales, regulation of traffic on public roads, regulation of air transportation, operation of a telephone system, leasing and sale of natural gas, operation of a mental health facility, and provision of in-house domestic serves for the handicapped are *not* entitled to immunity. We find it difficult, if not impossible, to identify an organizing principle that places each of the cases in the first group on one side of a line and each of the cases in the second group on the other side. The constitutional distinction between licensing drivers and regulating traffic, for example, or between operating a highway authority and operating a mental health facility, is elusive at best.

Thus far, this Court itself has made little headway in defining the scope of the governmental functions deemed protected under *National League of Cities*. In that case the Court set forth examples of protected and unprotected functions, but provided no explanation of how those examples were identified. The only other case in which the Court has had occasion to address the problem is [Transportation Union v.] Long Island [1982]. We there observed: "The determination of whether a federal law impairs a state's authority with respect to 'areas of traditional [state] functions' may at times be a difficult one." The accuracy of that statement is demonstrated by this Court's own difficulties in *Long Island* in developing a workable standard for "traditional governmental functions." . . .

. . . Neither do any of the alternative standards that might be employed to distinguish between protected and unprotected governmental functions appear manageable. We rejected the possibility of making immunity turn on a purely historical standard of "tradition" in *Long Island*, and properly so. The most obvious defect of a historical approach to state immunity is that it prevents a court from accommodating changes in the historical functions of States, changes that have resulted in a number of once-private functions like education being assumed by the States and their subdivisions. . . . .

A nonhistorical standard for selecting immune governmental functions is likely to be just as unworkable as is a historical standard. The goal of identifying "uniquely" governmental functions, for example, has been rejected by the Court in the field of government tort liability in part because the notion of a "uniquely" governmental function is unmanageable. See Indian Towing Co. v. United States (1955); see also Lafayette v. Louisiana Power & Light Co. (1978) (dissenting opinion) . . . .

We believe, however, that there is a more fundamental problem at work here, a problem that explains why the Court was never able to provide a basis for the governmental/proprietary distinction in the intergovernmental tax immunity cases and why an attempt to draw similar distinctions with respect to federal regulatory authority under *National League of Cities* is unlikely to succeed . . . . The problem is that neither the governmental/proprietary distinction nor any other that purports to separate out important governmental functions can be faithful to the role of federalism in a democratic society. The essence of our federal system is that within the realm of authority left open to them under the Constitution, the States must be equally free to engage in any activity that their citizens choose for the common weal, no matter how unorthodox or unnecessary anyone else—including the judiciary—deems state involvement to be. Any rule of state immunity that looks to the "traditional," "integral," or "necessary" nature of governmental functions inevitably invites an unelected federal judiciary to make decisions about which state policies it favors and which ones it dislikes . . . .

We therefore now reject, as unsound in principle and unworkable in practice, a rule of state immunity from federal regulation that turns on a judicial appraisal of whether a particular governmental function is "integral" or "traditional." Any such rule leads to inconsistent results at the same time that it disserves principles of democratic self-governance, and it breeds inconsistency precisely because it is divorced from those principles. . . .

III

The central theme of *National League of Cities* was that the States occupy a special position in our constitutional system and that the scope of Congress' authority under the Commerce Clause must reflect that position. Of course, the Commerce Clause by its specific language does not provide any special limitation on Congress' actions with respect to the States. See EEOC v. Wyoming (1983) (concurring opinion). It is equally true, however, that the text of the Constitution provides the beginning rather than the final answer to every inquiry into questions of federalism, for "[b]ehind the words of the constitutional provisions are postulates which limit and control." Monaco v. Mississippi (1934). *National League of Cities* reflected the general conviction that the Constitution precludes "the National Government [from] devour[ing] the essentials of state sovereignty." Maryland v.

Wirtz [1968] (dissenting opinion). In order to be faithful to the underlying federal premises of the Constitution, courts must look for the "postulates which limit and control."

What has proved problematic is not the perception that the Constitution's federal structure imposes limitations on the Commerce Clause, but rather the nature and content of those limitations . . . .

We doubt that courts ultimately can identify principled constitutional limitations on the scope of Congress' Commerce Clause powers over the States merely by relying on *a priori* definitions of state sovereignty. In part, this is because of the elusiveness of objective criteria for "fundamental" elements of state sovereignty, a problem we have witnessed in the search for "traditional governmental functions." There is, however, a more fundamental reason: the sovereignty of the States is limited by the Constitution itself. A variety of sovereign powers, for example, are withdrawn from the States by Article I, § 10. Section 8 of the same Article works an equally sharp contraction of state sovereignty by authorizing Congress to exercise a wide range of legislative powers and (in conjunction with the Supremacy Clause of Article VI) to displace contrary state legislation. By providing for final review of questions of federal law in this Court, Article III curtails the sovereign power of the States' judiciaries to make authoritative determinations of law. Finally, the developed application, through the Fourteenth Amendment, of the greater part of the Bill of Rights to the States limits the sovereign authority that States otherwise would possess to legislate with respect to their citizens and to conduct their own affairs.

The States unquestionably do "retai[n] a significant measure of sovereign authority." EEOC v. Wyoming (Powell, J., dissenting). They do so, however, only to the extent that the Constitution has not divested them of their original powers and transferred those powers to the Federal Government. In the words of James Madison to the Members of the First Congress: "Interference with the power of the States was no constitutional criterion of the power of Congress. If the power was not given, Congress could not exercise it; if given, they might exercise it, although it should interfere with the laws, or even the Constitution of the States." . . .

As a result, to say that the Constitution assumes the continued role of the States is to say little about the nature of that role . . . .

When we look for the States' "residuary and inviolable sovereignty," the *Federalist* No. 39 (J. Madison), in the shape of the constitutional scheme rather than in predetermined notions of sovereign power, a different measure of state sovereignty emerges. Apart from the limitation on federal authority inherent in the delegated nature of Congress' Article I powers, the principal means chosen by the Framers to ensure the role of the States in the federal system lies in the structure of the Federal Government itself. It is no novelty to observe that the composition of the Federal Government was designed in large part to protect the States from overreaching by Congress. The Framers thus gave the

States a role in the selection both of the Executive and the Legislative Branches of the Federal Government. The States were vested with indirect influence over the House of Representatives and the Presidency by their control of electoral qualifications and their role in presidential elections. U.S. Const., Art. I, § 2, and Art. II, § 1. They were given more direct influence in the Senate, where each State received equal representation and each Senator was to be selected by the legislature of his State. Art. I, § 3. The significance attached to the States' equal representation in the Senate is underscored by the prohibition of any constitutional amendment divesting a State of equal representation without the State's consent. Art. V . . . .

. . . In short, the Framers chose to rely on a federal system in which special restraints on federal power over the States inhered principally in the workings of the National Government itself, rather than in discrete limitations on the objects of federal authority. State sovereign interests, then, are more properly protected by procedural safeguards inherent in the structure of the federal system than by judicially created limitations on federal power.

The effectiveness of the federal political process in preserving the States' interests is apparent even today in the course of federal legislation. On the one hand, the States have been able to direct a substantial proportion of federal revenues into their own treasuries in the form of general and program-specific grants in aid. The federal role in assisting state and local governments is a longstanding one; Congress provided federal land grants to finance state governments from the beginning of the Republic, and direct cash grants were awarded as early as 1887 under the Hatch Act. In the past quarter-century alone, federal grants to States and localities have grown from $7 billion to $96 billion. As a result, federal grants now account for about one-fifth of state and local government expenditures . . . . [A]t the same time that the States have exercised their influence to obtain federal support, they have been able to exempt themselves from a wide variety of obligations imposed by Congress under the Commerce Clause. For example, the Federal Power Act, the National Labor Relations Act, the Labor-Management Reporting and Disclosure Act, the Occupational Safety and Health Act, the Employee Retirement Insurance Security Act, and the Sherman Act all contain express or implied exemptions for States and their subdivisions. The fact that some federal statutes such as the FLSA extend general obligations to the States cannot obscure the extent to which the political position of the States in the federal system has served to minimize the burdens that the States bear under the Commerce Clause.

We realize that changes in the structure of the Federal Government have taken place since 1789, not the least of which has been the substitution of popular election of Senators by the adoption of the Seventeenth Amendment in 1913, and that these changes may work to alter the influence of the States in the federal political process. Nonetheless . . . we are convinced that the fundamental limitation that the constitutional scheme imposes òn the Commerce Clause to protect the "States as States" is one of process rather than one of result. Any substantive restraint on the exercise of Commerce Clause powers must find its justification in the procedural nature of this basic limitation, and it must be tailored to compensate for possible failings in the national political process rather than to dictate a "sacred province of state autonomy." EEOC v. Wyoming.

Insofar as the present cases are concerned, then, we need go no further than to state that we perceive nothing in the overtime and minimum-wage requirements of the FLSA, as applied to SAMTA, that is destructive of state sovereignty or violative of any constitutional provision . . . .

IV . . .

Though the separate concurrence [of Justice Blackmun] providing the fifth vote in *National League of Cities* was "not untroubled by certain possible implications" of the decision, the Court in that case attempted to articulate affirmative limits on the Commerce Clause power in terms of core governmental functions and fundamental attributes of state sovereignty. But the model of democratic decisionmaking the Court there identified underestimated, in our view, the solicitude of the national political process for the continued vitality of the States. Attempts by other courts since then to draw guidance from this model have proved it both impracticable and doctrinally barren. In sum, in *National League of Cities* the Court tried to repair what did not need repair.

We do not lightly overrule recent precedent. We have not hesitated, however, when it has become apparent that a prior decision has departed from a proper understanding of congressional power under the Commerce Clause. See United States v. Darby (1941). Due respect for the reach of congressional power within the federal system mandates that we do so now.

National League of Cities v. Usery is overruled. The judgment of the District Court is reversed, and these cases are remanded to that court for further proceedings consistent with this opinion.

It is so ordered.

Justice **POWELL**, with whom the Chief Justice [**BURGER**], Justice **REHNQUIST**, and Justice **O'CONNOR** join, dissenting . . . .

There are, of course, numerous examples over the history of this Court in which prior decisions have been reconsidered and overruled. There have been few cases, however, in which the principle of *stare decisis* and the rationale of recent decisions were ignored as abruptly as we now witness. The reasoning of the Court in *National League of Cities,* and the principle applied there, have been reiterated consistently over the past eight years. Since its decision in 1976, *National League of Cities* has been cited and quoted in opinions joined by every member of the present Court. Hodel v. Virginia Surface Mining &

Recl. Assn. (1981); United Transportation Union v. Long Island R. Co. (1982); FERC v. Mississippi (1982). Less than three years ago, in *Long Island R. Co.,* a unanimous Court reaffirmed the principles of *National League of Cities* but found them inapplicable to the regulation of a railroad heavily engaged in interstate commerce . . . .

The Court in that case recognized that the test "may at times be a difficult one," but it was considered in that unanimous decision as settled constitutional doctrine . . . .

Although the doctrine is not rigidly applied to constitutional questions, "any departure from the doctrine of *stare decisis* demands special justification." Arizona v. Rumsey (1984). See also Oregon v. Kennedy (1982) (Stevens, J., concurring). In the present case, the five Justices who compose the majority today participated in *National League of Cities* and the cases reaffirming it. The stability of judicial decision, and with it respect for the authority of this Court, are not served by the precipitous overruling of multiple precedents that we witness in this case.

Whatever effect the Court's decision may have in weakening the application of *stare decisis,* it is likely to be less important than what the Court has done to the Constitution itself. A unique feature of the United States is the *federal* system of government guaranteed by the Constitution and implicit in the very name of our country. Despite some genuflecting in [the] Court's opinion to the concept of federalism, today's decision effectively reduces the Tenth Amendment to meaningless rhetoric when Congress acts pursuant to the Commerce Clause . . . .

To leave no doubt about its intention, the Court renounces its decision in *National League of Cities* because it "inevitably invites an unelected federal judiciary to make decisions about which state policies its favors and which ones it dislikes." In other words, the extent to which the States may exercise their authority, when Congress purports to act under the Commerce Clause, henceforth is to be determined from time to time by political decisions made by members of the federal government, decisions the Court says will not be subject to judicial review. I note that it does not seem to have occurred to the Court that *it* —an unelected majority of five Justices—today rejects almost 200 years of the understanding of the constitutional status of federalism. In doing so, there is only a single passing reference to the Tenth Amendment. Nor is so much as a dictum of any court cited in support of the view that the role of the States in the federal system may depend upon the grace of elected federal officials, rather than on the Constitution as interpreted by this Court . . . .

The Court apparently thinks that the States' success at obtaining federal funds for various projects and exemptions from the obligations of some federal statutes is indicative of the "effectiveness of the federal political process in preserving the States' interests . . . ." But such political success is not relevant to the question whether the political *processes* are the proper means of enforcing constitutional limitations.

The fact that Congress generally does not transgress constitutional limits on its power to reach State activities does not make judicial review any less necessary to rectify the cases in which it does do so. The States' role in our system of government is a matter of constitutional law, not of legislative grace. "The powers not delegated to the United States by the Constitution, nor prohibited by it to the States, are reserved to the States, respectively, or to the people." U.S. Const., Amend. 10.

More troubling than the logical infirmities in the Court's reasoning is the result of its holding, i.e., that federal political officials, invoking the Commerce Clause, are the sole judges of the limits of their own power. This result is inconsistent with the fundamental principles of our constitutional system. See, e.g., The *Federalist* No. 78 (Hamilton). At least since Marbury v. Madison [1803] it has been the settled province of the federal judiciary "to say what the law is" with respect to the constitutionality of acts of Congress. In rejecting the role of the judiciary in protecting the States from federal overreaching, the Court's opinion offers no explanation for ignoring the teaching of the most famous case in our history. . . .

. . . [T]he Court today propounds a view of federalism that pays only lip service to the role of the States. . . . [I]t fails to recognize the broad, yet specific areas of sovereignty that the Framers intended the States to retain. Indeed, the Court barely acknowledges that the Tenth Amendment exists. . . . The Court recasts this language to say that the States retain their sovereign powers "only to the extent that the Constitution has not divested them of their original powers and transferred those powers to the Federal Government." This rephrasing is not a distinction without a difference; rather, it reflects the Court's unprecedented view that Congress is free under the Commerce Clause to assume a State's traditional sovereign power, and to do so without judicial review of its action. Indeed, the Court's view of federalism appears to relegate the States to precisely the trivial role that opponents of the Constitution feared they would occupy . . . .

Justice **REHNQUIST**, dissenting . . . .

I join both Justice Powell's and Justice O'Connor's thoughtful dissents . . . . I do not think it incumbent on those of us in dissent to spell out further the fine points of a principle that will, I am confident, in time again command the support of a majority of this Court.

Justice **O'CONNOR**, with whom Justice **POWELL** and Justice **REHNQUIST** join, dissenting.

The Court today surveys the battle scene of federalism and sounds a retreat. Like Justice Powell, I would prefer to hold the field and, at the very least, render a little aid to the wounded. I join Justice Powell's opinion. I also write separately to note my fundamental disagreement with the majority's views of federalism and the duty of this Court . . . .

It has been difficult for this Court to craft the bright lines defining the scope of state autonomy protected by *National League of Cities.* Such difficulty is to be expected whenever constitutional concerns as important as federalism and the effectiveness of the commerce power come into conflict. Regardless of the difficulty, it is and will remain the duty of this Court to reconcile these concerns in the final instance. That the Court shuns this task today by appealing to the "essence of federalism" can provide scant comfort to those who believe our federal system requires something more than a unitary, centralized government. I would not shirk the duty acknowledged by *National League of Cities* and its progeny, and I share Justice Rehnquist's belief that this Court will in time again assume its constitutional responsibility . . . .

Editors' Notes

(1) **Query**: In his concurrence in *National League of Cities,* Justice Blackmun said that the majority opinion had used a balancing test and that he joined with that understanding. To what extent did the majority in *National League of Cities* in fact use a balancing test? To what extent did Blackmun in *Garcia?*

(2) Powell takes Blackmun to task for his interpretation of the Constitution as mainly providing structural protections for states in the composition of the national government. But does Powell himself use a structuralist argument? If so, how does it differ from Blackmun's?

(3) One should note carefully Rehnquist and O'Connor's predictions that *Garcia* 's emphasis on political rather than judicial protections for states would be short lived. The majority was narrow, 5–4, as it was in *National League of Cities.* The Carter administration had begun the appeal in *Garcia,* and Reagan had asked the Court only to distinguish, not to overrule *National League of Cities.*

(4) In July, 1985, the Senate Committee on Labor and Human Resources began holding hearings on proposals to amend the Fair Labor Standards Act to exclude state employees. At the same time, the Department of Labor announced it would not begin active enforcement of the FLSA against the states until October 15, giving states more than six months to comply with *Garcia.*

C

KEEPING POLITICAL PROCESSES OPEN

Chapter 2 discussed the competing political theories of constitutionalism and democracy that underpin the American system of constitutional democracy. Chapter 8 elaborated several "purposive" *modes* of constitutional interpretation. Among those were the "doctrine of the clear mistake" and "reinforcing representative democracy." While the two differ in significant ways, both are products of democratic theory and would rather tightly confine judicial interpretation of the Constitution.

The "doctrine of the clear mistake" was most clearly stated by Prof. James Bradley Thayer of the Harvard Law School in 1893, just as the Supreme Court was beginning to etch the economics of laissez faire into the Constitution. Earlier that year, Justice David Brewer had told the New York State Bar Association that the country faced grave dangers from "the black flag of anarchism, flaunting destruction to property," and "the red flag of socialism, inviting a redistribution of property." Identifying the labor movement and governmental regulation as immediate perils, he saw "the multitudes—the majority" as ready to ransack rights to own property and engage in business. His solution was straightforward: "strengthen the judiciary."

> I am firmly persuaded that the salvation of the Nation, the permanence of government of and by the people, rests upon the independence and vigor of the judiciary, to stay the waves of popular feeling, to restrain the greedy hand of the many from filching from the few that which they have honestly acquired . . . .[1]

In contrast, Thayer argued that judges should leave policy making to the officials whom the people had elected to Congress and uphold the constitutionality of *federal* statutes except when their conflict with the Constitution was clear beyond a reasonable doubt. (We reprint his article at p. 476.)

"Reinforcing representative democracy" entails a broader, though still limited, set of roles for courts. In general, as with "the clear mistake," judges should presume that statutes are valid and place the burden of proving otherwise on the challenger. (Because their concern is with democracy at all levels, proponents of "reinforcing"

---

1. "The Movement of Coercion," 16 *Procs. of the N.Y.St.Bar Ass'n* 37 (1893).

typically presume the validity of state as well as federal law.) Justice Harlan Fiske Stone initially put the elements of this *mode* of constitutional interpretation into a coherent, if not yet complete, form in footnote 4 to his opinion for the Court in United States v. Carolene Products (1938; reprinted below, p. 482). Later judges and commentators,[2] including Louis Lusky, who as Stone's clerk drafted the earliest version of the footnote,[3] have expanded and reinterpreted the model that Stone sketched.

The timing of the footnote is important. For much of the previous fifty years, a majority of the justices had been following Brewer rather than Thayer and had read their economic views into and out of the Constitution so as to thwart both state and federal efforts to cope with the problems of industrial and finance capitalism. The Great Depression that enveloped the country in 1929 and the Court's war against Roosevelt's New Deal had left laissez faire—and the nation—in shambles. By 1938, the Court had retreated, saying it would presume economic regulation to be constitutional. This withdrawal caused much heart-wrenching among the justices (see George Sutherland's powerful dissent in West Coast Hotel v. Parrish (1937; reprinted below, p. 987), and raised fundamental questions about the future of constitutional interpretations by judges. If they were to presume economic regulation constitutional, why not all regulation? On what principles could they draw lines?

Judges faced other problems, both practical and intellectual. In Europe, totalitarianism had become a widespread and established fact. With varying amounts of murderous violence, Mussolini, Stalin, and Hitler each suppressed political dissent. In addition, the obscenity of Nazism's racism was becoming increasingly plain. These developments helped sharpen some Americans' awareness of their own country's intolerance toward dissent and the ugly racism that belied ideals of equality. The justices had already been acting more boldly in upholding First-Amendment freedoms and had taken a few tentative steps toward questioning the validity of governmentally imposed segregation. A year before *Carolene Products,* Palko v. Connecticut (reprinted above, p. 94) had held that the Constitution contained a hierarchy of values and that the First Amendment was near the apex of that scale.

In this context, Stone (and his clerk Louis Lusky)[4] outlined what people at the time called "the preferred position," what more recent

---

2. See, for example: Alpheus Thomas Mason, *The Supreme Court from Taft to Burger* (Baton Rouge, La.: Louisiana State University Press, 1979), and John Hart Ely, *Democracy and Distrust* (Cambridge, Mass.: Harvard University Press, 1980). Although a political philosopher rather than a constitutional "commentator," Michael Walzer has expounded a theory quite similar to Ely's: "Philosophy and Democracy," 9 *Pol. Theory* 379 (1981).

3. See Lusky's own discussion, several decades later: *By What Right?* (Charlottesville, Va.: Michie Co., 1975).

4. The footnote's genesis is described by Alpheus Thomas Mason: *Security Through Freedom* (Ithaca, N.Y.: Cornell University Press, 1955), and *Harlan Fiske Stone* (New York: Viking, 1956), espec. chap. 31. Stone always denied his ideas were novel; he got them, he said, from Holmes and Brandeis. Lusky, too, has modestly minimized his own very important role.

commentators have subtly changed and rechristened "reinforcing representative democracy." The gist of the argument is that the American political system is basically one of a representative democracy in which the various conditions listed in Chapter 2 obtain. The people are entitled to rule themselves by being able to choose their government after full and open debate and through an electoral process in which each citizen can participate. The Constitution (usually construed to include only the document plus a version of democratic theory) does prescribe some specific limitations on governmental choice; but, as with "the clear mistake," judges should allow the people's elected representatives—and therefore the people—latitude in interpreting that Constitution. It is the fact that laws are made by the people's duly elected representatives and do not violate the plain words of the constitutional document that gives such laws validity, not their conformity to values—other than those of democracy—judges hold.

But in several kinds of situations, so the rationale goes, judges should change the presumption of constitutionality. (Some proponents say "relax it," others "drop it," and still others "reverse it.") The presumption does not hold: first, when legislation restricts rights to free political communication and open political processes; and, second, when legislation singles out for disadvantage minorities who lack political power. At the urging of Chief Justice Hughes, Stone added a third exception (placed first in his footnote) which some commentators, including Lusky, would like to discount heavily: when legislation impinges on a right of an individual citizen listed in the constitutional document.

Carolene Products has become the centerpiece of latter-day constitutional interpretation. A half century later, judges and commentators are still wrangling over the validity, utility, and implications of the jurisprudence that Stone and Lusky so tantilizingly suggested. We organize much of the rest of the book around its contents. Section D, Chapters 13 and 14, discusses the second exception and many of the complexities of "equal protection of the laws"; Section E, Chapters 15–17, takes up the third exception and the difficulties of defining and distinguishing among constitutional rights. This section focuses on a few of the more obvious problems of an open political system, particularly freedom of speech and press and the rights to join with others to influence political decisions and, of course, to vote, to have one's vote counted, and counted equally.

It should be clear that, although Chapters 13 and 14 center on constitutional interpretation as influenced by democratic theory, the political theory of constitutionalism is not indifferent to the issues involved. For it, too, is concerned about freedom of communication not only as an aspect of the right of all citizens to participate in their government but also as part of the self-expression that is vital to the individual's full development.

SELECTED BIBLIOGRAPHY

Anastaplo, George. *The Constitutionalist* (Dallas: Southern Methodist University Press, 1971).

Barber, Sotirios A. *On What the Constitution Means* (Baltimore, Md.: Johns Hopkins University Press, 1984).

Black, Hugo L. *A Constitutional Faith* (New York: Knopf, 1969).

Choper, Jesse H. *Judicial Review and the National Political Process* (Chicago: University of Chicago Press, 1980).

Douglas, William O. *We, the Judges* (New York: Doubleday, 1955), espec. chap. 9.

Elliott, Ward. E.Y. *The Rise of Guardian Democracy* (Cambridge, Mass.: Harvard University Press, 1974).

Ely, John Hart. *Democracy and Distrust* (Cambridge, Mass.: Harvard University Press, 1980).

Emerson, Thomas I. *Toward a General Theory of the First Amendment* (New York: Random House, 1963).

Gabin, Sanford B. *Judicial Review and the Reasonable Doubt Test* (Port Washington, N.Y.: Kennikat Press, 1980).

Levy, Leonard W. *Legacy of Suppression* (Cambridge: The Belknap Press of Harvard University Press, 1960).

_____. "On the Origins of the Free Press Clause," 32 *UCLA L.Rev.* 177 (1984).

_____. "The *Legacy* Reexamined," 37 *Stan.L.Rev.* 767 (1985).

Lusky, Louis. *By What Right?* (Charlottesville, Va.: Michie Co., 1975).

Mason, Alpheus Thomas. *Security Through Freedom* (Ithaca, N.Y.: Cornell University Press, 1955).

_____. *Harlan Fiske Stone* (New York: Viking, 1956), espec. chap. 31.

_____. *The Supreme Court from Taft to Burger* (Baton Rouge, La.: Louisiana State University Press, 1979).

Meiklejohn, Alexander. *Free Speech and Its Relation to Self-Government* (New York: Harpers, 1948).

Paletz, David L., and William F. Harris, II. "Four-Letter Threats to Authority," 37 *J. of Pols.* 955 (1975).

Schwartz, Bernard. *Super Chief: Earl Warren and his Supreme Court* (New York: New York University Press, 1983).

Symposium. "Judicial Review versus Democracy," 42 *Ohio St.L.J.* (1981).

Tribe, Laurence H. "The Puzzling Persistence of Process-Based Constitutional Theories," 89 *Yale L.J.* 1063 (1980); reprinted as chap. 2 in his *Constitutional Choices* (Cambridge, Mass.: Harvard University Press, 1985).

"[W]hatever choice is rational is constitutional."

THE ORIGIN AND SCOPE OF THE AMERICAN DOCTRINE OF CONSTITUTIONAL LAW *

James Bradley Thayer (1893).

II

When at last this power of the judiciary was everywhere established, and added to the other bulwarks of our written constitutions, how was the power to be conceived of? Strictly as a judicial one . . . . Therefore, since the power now in question was a purely judicial one, in the first place, there were many cases where it had no operation. In the case of purely political acts and of the exercise of more discretion, it mattered not that other departments were violating the constitution, the judiciary could not interfere; on the contrary, they must accept and enforce their acts . . . .

Again, where the power of the judiciary did have place, its whole scope was this; namely, to determine, for the mere purpose of deciding a litigated question properly submitted to the court, whether a particular disputed exercise of power was forbidden by the constitution. In doing this the court was so to discharge its office as not to deprive another department of any of its proper power, or to limit it in the proper range of its discretion. Not merely, then, do these questions, when presenting themselves in the courts for judicial action, call for a peculiarly large method in the treatment of them, but especially they require an allowance to be made by the judges for the vast and not definable range of legislative power and choice, for that wide margin of considerations which address themselves only to the practical judgment of a legislative body. Within that margin, as among all these legislative considerations, the constitutional law-makers must be allowed a free foot. In so far as legislative choice, ranging here unfettered, may select one form of action or another, the judges must not interfere, since *their* question is a naked judicial one.

Moreover, such is the nature of this particular judicial question that the preliminary determination by the legislature is a fact of very great importance, since the constitutions expressly intrust to the legislature this determination; they cannot act without making it. Furthermore, the constitutions not merely intrust to the legislatures a preliminary determination of the question, but they contemplate that this determination may be the final one; for they secure no revision of it. It is only as litigation may spring up, and as the course of it may happen to raise the point of constitutionality, that any question for the courts can regularly emerge. It may be, then, that the mere legislative decision will accomplish results throughout the country of the profoundest importance before any judicial question can arise or be decided,—as in the case of the first and second charters of the United

---

* 7 *Harvard Law Review* 129 (1893).
Thayer was Professor at the Harvard Law School.

States Bank, and of the legal tender laws of thirty years ago and later
. . . .

It is plain that where a power so momentous as this primary authority to interpret is given, the actual determinations of the body to whom it is intrusted are entitled to a corresponding respect; and this not on mere grounds of courtesy or conventional respect, but on very solid and significant grounds of policy and law. The judiciary may well reflect that if they had been regarded by the people as the chief protection against legislative violation of the constitution, they would not have been allowed merely this incidental and postponed control. They would have been let in, as it was sometimes endeavored in the conventions to let them in, to a revision of the laws before they began to operate. As the opportunity of the judges to check and correct unconstitutional Acts is so limited, it may help us to understand why the extent of their control, when they do have the opportunity, should also be narrow.

It was, then, all along true, and it was foreseen, that much which is harmful and unconstitutional may take effect without any capacity in the courts to prevent it, since their whole power is a judicial one. Their interference was but one of many safeguards, and its scope was narrow.

The rigor of this limitation upon judicial action is sometimes freely recognized, yet in a perverted way which really operates to extend the judicial function beyond its just bounds. The court's duty, we are told, is the mere and simple office of construing two writings and comparing one with another, as two contracts or two statutes are construed and compared when they are said to conflict; of declaring the true meaning of each, and, if they are opposed to each other, of carrying into effect the constitution as being of superior obligation,—an ordinary and humble judicial duty, as the courts sometimes describe it. This way of putting it easily results in the wrong kind of disregard of legislative considerations; not merely in refusing to let them directly operate as grounds of judgment, but in refusing to consider them at all. Instead of taking them into account and allowing for them as furnishing possible grounds of legislative action, there takes place a pedantic and academic treatment of the texts of the constitution and the laws. And so we miss that combination of a lawyer's rigor with a statesman's breadth of view which should be found in dealing with this class of questions in constitutional law. Of this petty method we have many specimens; they are found only too easily to-day in the volumes of our current reports.

In order, however, to avoid falling into these narrow and literal methods, in order to prevent the courts from forgetting, as Marshall said, that "it is a constitution we are expounding," these literal precepts about the nature of the judicial task have been accompanied by a rule of administration which has tended, in competent hands, to give matters a very different complexion.

III

Let us observe the course which the courts, in point of fact, have taken, in administering this interesting jurisdiction.

They began by resting it upon the very simple ground that the legislature had only a delegated and limited authority under the constitutions; that these restraints, in order to be operative, must be regarded as so much law; and, as being law, that they must be interpreted and applied by the court. This was put as a mere matter of course. The reasoning was simple and narrow. Such was Hamilton's method in the *Federalist* [No. 78] . . . .

But these simple precepts were supplemented by a very significant rule of administration,—one which corrected their operation, and brought into play large considerations not adverted to in the reasoning so far mentioned. In 1811, Chief Justice Tilghman, of Pennsylvania, while asserting the power of the court to hold laws unconstitutional, but declining to exercise it in a particular case, stated this rule as follows:—

> For weighty reasons, it has been assumed as a principle in consti-
> tutional construction by the Supreme Court of the United States, by
> this court, and every other court of reputation in the United States,
> that an Act of the legislature is not to be declared void unless the
> violation of the constitution is so manifest as to leave no room for
> reasonable doubt.

When did this rule of administration begin? Very early. We observe that it is referred to as thoroughly established in 1811. . . .

IV

. . . [T]he rule in question is something more than a mere form of language, a mere expression of courtesy and deference. It means far more than that. The courts have perceived with more or less distinct-ness that this exercise of the judicial function does in truth go far beyond the simple business which judges sometimes describe. If their duty were in truth merely and nakedly to ascertain the meaning of the text of the constitution and of the impeached Act of the legislature, and to determine, as an academic question, whether in the court's judgment the two were in conflict, it would, to be sure, be an elevated and important office, one dealing with great matters, involving large public considerations, but yet a function far simpler than it really is. Having ascertained all this, yet there remains a question—the really momen-tous question—whether, after all, the court can disregard the Act. It cannot do this as a mere matter of course,—merely because it is concluded that upon a just and true construction the law is unconstitu-tional. That is precisely the significance of the rule of administration that the courts lay down. It can only disregard the Act when those who have the right to make laws have not merely made a mistake, but have made a very clear one,—so clear that it is not open to rational question. That is the standard of duty to which the courts bring legislative Acts; that is the test which they apply,—not merely their own judgment as to constitutionality, but their conclusion as to what judgment is permissible to another department which the constitution has charged with the duty of making it. This rule recognizes that, having regard to the great, complex, ever-unfolding exigencies of government, much which will seem unconstitutional to one man, or body of men, may reasonably not seem so to another; that the constitution often admits of different interpretations; that there is often a range of choice and judgment; that in such cases the constitution does not impose upon the legislature any one specific opinion, but leaves open this range of choice; and that whatever choice is rational is constitutional. This is the principle which the rule that I have been illustrating affirms and supports . . . .

It must indeed be studiously remembered, in judicially applying such a test as this of what a legislature may reasonably think, that virtue, sense, and competent knowledge are always to be attributed to that body. The conduct of public affairs must always go forward upon conventions and assumptions of that sort. "It is a *postulate*," said Mr. Justice Gibson, "in the theory of our government . . . that the people are wise, virtuous, and competent to manage their own affairs." "It would be indecent in the extreme," said Marshall, C.J., "upon a private contract between two individuals to enter into an inquiry respecting the corruption of the sovereign power of a State." And so in a court's revision of legislative acts, as in its revision of a jury's acts, it will always assume a duly instructed body; and the question is not merely what persons may rationally do who are such as we often see, in point of fact, in our legislative bodies, persons untaught it may be, indocile, thoughtless, reckless, incompetent,—but what those other persons, competent, well-instructed, sagacious, attentive, intent only on public ends, fit to represent a self-governing people, such as our theory of government assumes to be carrying on our public affairs,—what such persons may reasonably think or do, what is the permissible view for them . . . . The reasonable doubt, then, of which our judges speak is that reasonable doubt which lingers in the mind of a competent and duly instructed person who has carefully applied his faculties to the question. The rationally permissible opinion of which we have been talking is the opinion reasonably allowable to such a person as this.

It may be suggested that this is not the way in which the judges in fact put the matter; e.g., that Marshall, in McCulloch *v.* Maryland, seeks to establish the court's own opinion of the constitutionality of the legislation establishing the United States Bank. But in recognizing that this is very often true, we must remember that where the court is sustaining an Act, and finds it to be constitutional in its own opinion, it is fit that this should be said, and that such a declaration is all that the case calls for; it disposes of the matter. But it is not always true; there are many cases where the judges sustain an Act because they are in doubt about it; where they are not giving their own opinion that it is constitutional, but are merely leaving untouched a determination of the legislature; as in the case where a Massachusetts judge concurred in the opinion of his brethren that a legislative Act was "competent for the legislature to pass, and was not unconstitutional," "upon the single ground that the Act is not so clearly unconstitutional, its invalidity so free from reasonable doubt, as to make it the duty of the judicial department, in view of the vast interests involved in the result, to declare it void." The constant declaration of the judges that the question for them is not one of the mere and simple preponderance of reasons for or against, but of what is very plain and clear, clear beyond a reasonable doubt,—this declaration is really a steady announcement that their decisions in support of the constitutionality of legislation do not, as of course, import their own opinion of the true construction of the constitution, and that the strict meaning of their words, when they hold an Act constitutional, is merely this,—not unconstitutional beyond a reasonable doubt . . . .

It all comes back, I think, to this. The rule under discussion has in it an implied recognition that the judicial duty now in question touches the region of political administration, and is qualified by the necessities and proprieties of administration. If our doctrine of constitutional law—which finds itself, as we have seen, in the shape of a narrowly stated substantive principle, with a rule of administration enlarging the otherwise too restricted substantive rule—admits now of a juster and simpler conception, that is a very familiar situation in the development of law. What really took place in adopting our theory of constitutional law was this: we introduced for the first time into the conduct of government through its great departments a judicial sanction, as among these departments,—not full and complete, but partial. The judges were allowed, indirectly and in a degree, the power to revise the action of other departments and to pronounce it null. In simple truth, while this is a mere judicial function, it involves, owing to the subject-matter with which it deals, taking a part, a secondary part, in the political conduct of government. If that be so, then the judges must apply methods and principles that befit their task. In such a work there can be no permanent or fitting *modus vivendi* between the different departments unless each is sure of the full co-operation of the others, so long as its own action conforms to any reasonable and fairly permissible view of its constitutional power. The ultimate arbiter of what is rational and permissible is indeed always the courts, so far as litigated cases bring the question before them. This leaves to our courts a great and stately jurisdiction. It will only imperil the whole of it if it is sought to give them more. They must not step into the shoes of the law-maker, or be unmindful of the hint that is found in the sagacious remark of an English bishop nearly two centuries ago, quoted lately from Mr. Justice Holmes:—

> Whoever hath an absolute authority to interpret any written or spoken laws, it is he who is truly the lawgiver, to all intents and purposes, and not the person who first wrote or spoke them.

V . . .

. . . [There are also] questions arising out of the existence of our double system, with two written constitutions, and two governments, one of which, within its sphere, is of higher authority than the other. The relation to the States of the paramount government as a whole, and its duty in all questions involving the powers of the general government to maintain that power as against the States in its fulness, seem to fix also the duty of each of its departments; namely, that of maintaining this paramount authority in its true and just proportions, to be determined by itself. If a State legislature passes a law which is impeached in the due course of litigation before the national courts, as being in conflict with the supreme law of the land, those courts may have to ask themselves a question different from that which would be applicable if the enactments were those of a co-ordinate department. When the question relates to what is admitted not to belong to the national power, then whoever construes a State constitution, whether the State or national judiciary, must allow to that legislature the full range of rational construction. But when the question is whether State action be or be not conformable to the paramount constitution, the supreme law of the land, we have a different matter in hand. Fundamentally, it involves the allotment of power between the two governments,—where the line is to be drawn. True, the judiciary is still debating whether a legislature has transgressed its limit; but the departments are not co-ordinate, and the limit is at a different point. The judiciary now speaks as representing a paramount constitution and government, whose duty it is, in all its departments, to allow to that constitution nothing less than its just and true interpretation; and having fixed this, to guard it against any inroads from without . . . .

[VI]

. . . It has been often remarked that private rights are more respected by the legislatures of some countries which have no written constitution, than by ours. No doubt our doctrine of constitutional law has had a tendency to drive out questions of justice and right, and to fill the mind of legislators with thoughts of mere legality, of what the constitution allows. And moreover, even in the matter of legality, they have felt little responsibility; if we are wrong, they say, the courts will correct it. If what I have been saying is true, the safe and permanent road towards reform is that of impressing upon our people a far stronger sense than they have of the great range of possible harm and evil that our system leaves open, and must leave open, to the legislatures, and of the clear limits of judicial power; so that responsibility may be brought sharply home where it belongs. The checking and cutting down of legislative power, by numerous detailed prohibitions in the constitution, cannot be accomplished without making the government petty and incompetent . . . . Under no system can the power of courts go far to save a people from ruin; our chief protection lies elsewhere. If this should be true, it is of the greatest public importance to put the matter in its true light.

Editors' Query

Thayer's doctrine of deference rests on the principle of maintaining a close connection between "the people" and their elected representatives. How would his doctrine logically change if the representative connection were to weaken or even break, perhaps because of the representatives themselves or the electoral system? Would Thayer's principle then require judicial intervention?

———

"It is unnecessary to consider now whether legislation which restricts those political processes which can ordinarily be expected to bring about repeal of undesirable legislation, is to be subjected to more exacting judicial scrutiny . . . ."

UNITED STATES v. CAROLENE PRODUCTS CO.
304 U.S. 144, 58 S.Ct. 778, 82 L.Ed. 1234 (1938).

The Filled Milk Act of 1923 forbade shipment in interstate commerce of skimmed milk compounded with fat or oils obtained from products other than milk and made to look like milk. A federal grand jury indicted the Carolene Products Co. for shipping such a product, Milnut. At the trial, the company demurred to the indictment. (In effect, a demurrer says even if the facts alleged by the other side are true, so what? They do not add up to a violation of a valid statute.) This tactic was, of course, a means of attacking the constitutionality of the Filled Milk Act. The trial judge sustained the demurrer, and the United States appealed. (There had been no trial so there was no issue of double jeopardy.)

This case was argued on April 6, 1938, almost exactly a year after the famous "switch in time that saved nine"—the Supreme Court's acceptance of the legitimacy of a greater governmental role in economic life and a concomitantly broader view of the reach of congressional power under the commerce clause. Thus, it was reasonably clear what would be the response of a majority of the justices to the basic substantive question in the case regarding congressional authority to regulate commerce. Two justices, Cardozo and Reed, did not participate, and only one, McReynolds, had strong enough objections to the statute's constitutionality to dissent from the decision of the majority—though Justice Butler must have had serious reservations.

As it turned out, the only thorny issue revolved around the fact that the case was a criminal prosecution: Could the defendant introduce evidence that the legislative findings supporting the statute were erroneous or at least described a set of circumstances that were sufficiently different from the company's as to make the law, even if generally valid, unconstitutional as applied specifically to this case? (See, below, the section of the opinion of the Court marked *Third.*)

After the conference on April 9, Chief Justice Hughes assigned the task of writing the opinion of the Court to Justice Harlan Fiske Stone. Stone, nominated by Calvin Coolidge in 1925, had quickly become a judicial ally of Holmes and Brandeis and later of Justice Cardozo. During the Court's war with the New Deal, Stone had often voted and written to sustain governmental power and to urge his brethren to distinguish between the commands of the Constitution and their personal values.

At the time of *Carolene Products,* constitutional jurisprudence was in a state of flux if not chaos. The justices had just repudiated their former role of protectors of the individual's formal—as opposed, sometimes, to real—economic autonomy and in doing so had returned to an even older doctrine, that of presuming acts of Congress and the states to be constitutional. In retrospect, the Court's casting off form for reality does not appear as so momentous a change in a general policy of protecting constitutionalism's value of individual autonomy. At the time, however, the future was not so clearly charted. Up until this period, the Court had on some occasions protected other aspects of individual liberty than private property and "freedom of contract" against government, but overall its record was spotty if not spotted.

On the one hand, Stone thought the country was well rid of judges as makers of economic policy. On the other hand, he was deeply troubled by other aspects of civil liberty. He tried to spend his summers traveling. In Europe he had witnessed the evils of Nazism and in the United States seen too much evidence of religious and racial hatred. He wanted to take the opportunity to create a new jurisprudence, one that would leave economic policy making to democratically elected officials while still not placing other civil liberties, especially those of small minorities, completely in the hands of representatives of the majority.

Stone's solution was to plant the seeds of a new jurisprudence in a footnote to this otherwise unremarkable case. It was a tactic he liked to employ, one that took advantage of his more conservative colleagues' reverence for stare decisis. He often operated, a law clerk remarked, "like a squirrel storing nuts to be pulled out at some later time. And there was mischief as well as godliness in his delight when his ruse was undetected and the chestnuts safely stored away."

We shall reprint excerpts from the text of the opinion, indicate where Stone placed what became the most doctrinally important footnote in the Court's history, and then discuss separately the genesis of that critical appendage.

Mr. Justice **STONE** delivered the opinion of the Court . . . .

First. The power to regulate commerce is the power "to prescribe the rule by which commerce is to be governed," Gibbons v. Ogden [1824], and extends to the prohibition of shipments in such commerce, Reid v. Colorado [1902]; Lottery Case (Champion v. Ames) [1903]. The power "is complete in itself, may be exercised to its utmost extent and acknowledges no limitations other than are prescribed by the Constitution." *Gibbons.* Hence Congress is free to exclude from interstate commerce articles whose use in the states for which they are destined it may reasonably conceive to be injurious to the public health, morals or welfare, *Reid*; Lottery Case; Hipolite Egg Co. v. United States [1911];

Hoke v. United States [1913], or which contravene the policy of the state of their destination. Kentucky Whip & Collar Co. v. Illinois C.R. Co. [1937]. Such a regulation is not a forbidden invasion of state power either because its motive or its consequence is to restrict the use of articles of commerce within the states of destination, and is not prohibited unless by the Due Process Clause of the Fifth Amendment . . . .

Second. The prohibition of shipment of appellee's product in interstate commerce does not infringe the Fifth Amendment. Twenty years ago this Court, in Hebe Co. v. Shaw [1919], held that a state law which forbids the manufacture and sale of a product assumed to be wholesome and nutritive, made of condensed skimmed milk, compounded with coconut oil, is not forbidden by the Fourteenth Amendment. The power of the legislature to secure a minimum of particular nutritive elements in a widely used article of food and to protect the public from fraudulent substitutions, was not doubted; and the Court thought that there was ample scope for the legislative judgment that prohibition of the offending article was an appropriate means of preventing injury to the public.

We see no persuasive reason for departing from that ruling here, where the Fifth Amendment is concerned; and since none is suggested, we might rest decision wholly on the presumption of constitutionality. But affirmative evidence also sustains the statute. In twenty years evidence has steadily accumulated of the danger to the public health from the general consumption of foods which have been stripped of elements essential to the maintenance of health. The Filled Milk Act was adopted by Congress after committee hearings, in the course of which eminent scientists and health experts testified. An extensive investigation was made of the commerce in milk compounds in which vegetable oils have been substituted for natural milk fat, and of the effect upon the public health of the use of such compounds as a food substitute for milk. The conclusions drawn from evidence presented at the hearings were embodied in reports of the House Committee on Agriculture and the Senate Committee on Agriculture and Forestry. Both committees concluded, as the statute itself declares, that the use of filled milk as a substitute for pure milk is generally injurious to health and facilitates fraud on the public . . . .

There is nothing in the Constitution which compels a legislature, either national or state, to ignore such evidence, nor need it disregard the other evidence which amply supports the conclusions of the Congressional committees that the danger is greatly enhanced where an inferior product, like appellee's, is indistinguishable from a valuable food of almost universal use, thus making fraudulent distribution easy and protection of the consumer difficult . . . .

Appellee raises no valid objection to the present statute by arguing that its prohibition has not been extended to oleomargarine or other butter substitutes in which vegetable fats or oils are substituted for butter fat. The Fifth Amendment has no equal protection clause, and even that of the Fourteenth, applicable only to the states, does not compel their legislatures to prohibit all like evils, or none. A legislature may hit at an abuse which it has found, even though it has failed to strike at another. Central Lumber Co. v. South Dakota [1912].

Third. We may assume for present purposes that no pronouncement of a legislature can forestall attack upon the constitutionality of the prohibition which it enacts by applying opprobrious epithets to the prohibited act, and that a statute would deny due process which precluded the disproof in judicial proceedings of all facts which would show or tend to show that a statute depriving the suitor of life, liberty or property had a rational basis.

But such we think is not the purpose or construction of the statutory characterization of filled milk as injurious to health and as a fraud upon the public. There is no need to consider it here as more than a declaration of the legislative findings deemed to support and justify the action taken as a constitutional exertion of the legislative power, aiding informed judicial review, as to the reports of legislative committees, by revealing the rationale of the legislation. Even in the absence of such aids the existence of facts supporting the legislative judgment is to be presumed, for regulatory legislation affecting ordinary commercial transactions is not to be pronounced unconstitutional unless in the light of the facts made known or generally assumed it is of such a character as to preclude the assumption that it rests upon some rational basis within the knowledge and experience of the legislators.[4] The present statutory findings affect appellee no more than the reports of the Congressional committees; and since in the absence of the statutory findings they would be presumed, their incorporation in the statute is no more prejudicial than surplusage.

Where the existence of a rational basis for legislation whose constitutionality is attacked depends upon facts beyond the sphere of judicial notice, such facts may properly be made the subject of judicial inquiry, Borden's Farm Products Co. v. Baldwin [1934], and the constitutionality of a statute predicated upon the existence of a particular state of facts may be challenged by showing to the court that those facts have ceased to exist. Chastleton Corp. v. Sinclair [1924]. Similarly we recognize that the constitutionality of a statute, valid on its face, may be assailed by proof of facts tending to show that the statute as applied to a particular article is without support in reason because the article, although within the prohibited class, is so different from others of the class as to be without the reason for the prohibition, Railroad Retirement Bd. v. Alton R. Co. [1935]; see Whitney v. California [1927] . . . . But by their very nature such inquiries, where the legislative judgment is drawn in question, must be restricted to the issue whether any state of facts either known or which could reasonably be assumed affords support for it. Here the demurrer challenges the validity of the

---

4. Eds.' Note: It was at this point that Stone inserted the historic footnote. We reprint it in its original and final draft, together with correspondence between Stone and Chief Justice Hughes, after the concurrence of Justice Butler.

statute on its face and it is evident from all the considerations presented to Congress, and those of which we may take judicial notice, that the
question is at least debatable whether commerce in filled milk should
be left unregulated, or in some measure restricted, or wholly prohibited. As that decision was for Congress, neither the finding of a court
arrived at by weighing the evidence, nor the verdict of a jury can be
substituted for it. Price v. Illinois [1915]; South Carolina State Highway Dept. v. Barnwell Bros. [1938] . . . .

The prohibition of shipment in interstate commerce of appellee's
product, as described in the indictment, is a constitutional exercise of
the power to regulate interstate commerce . . . .

Reversed.

Mr. Justice **BLACK** concurs in the result and in all of the opinion
except the part marked "Third."

Mr. Justice **McREYNOLDS** thinks that the judgment should be affirmed.

Mr. Justice **CARDOZO** and Mr. Justice **REED** took no part in the
consideration or decision of this case.

Mr. Justice **BUTLER**

I concur in the result . . . .

Stone turned to his law clerk, Louis Lusky, who was later to become a
distinguished professor of law at Columbia University, to draft the footnote,
accepting what Lusky wrote almost without change. (Lusky later explained
some of the philosophy behind the footnote in "Minority Rights and the Public
Interest," 52 *Yale L.J.* 1 [1942], and in *By What Right?* [Charlottesville, Va.:
The Michie Co., 1975]. He has always been very modest about his own role
in this drama.)

As circulated, that note was appended to the murky sentence: "Even in
the absence of such aids [extensive legislative findings of facts] the existence
of facts supporting the legislative judgment is to be presumed, for regulatory
legislation affecting ordinary commercial transactions is not to be pronounced
unconstitutional unless in the light of the facts made known or generally
assumed it is of such a character as to preclude the assumption that it rests
upon some rational basis within the knowledge and experience of the legislator."

As Stone initially circulated the opinion among the justices for their
comments, the footnote read:

[4] Different considerations may apply, and one attacking the constitutionality of a statute may be thought to bear a lighter burden, when
the legislation aims at restricting the corrective political processes
which can ordinarily be expected to bring about repeal of undesirable
legislation. So, statutory interferences with political organizations,
Stromberg v. California [1931]; Fiske v. Kansas [1927]; Whitney v.
California [1927]; Herndon v. Lowry [1937]; and see Holmes, J., in

Gitlow v. New York [1925], and with the dissemination of information, Near v. Minnesota [1931]; Grosjean v. American Press Co. [1936]; Lovell v. Griffin [1938], have been subjected to a more exacting judicial test than have been other types of statutes. Like considerations may be relevant in comparable situations, as when the right to vote, cf. Nixon v. Condon [1932], or peaceably to assemble is involved, or when a statute is directed at particular religions, Pierce v. Society of Sisters [1925], at a national, Meyer v. Nebraska [1923]; Bartels v. Iowa [1923]; Farrington v. Tokushige [1927], or at racial minorities. Nixon v. Herndon [1927]; Nixon v. Condon. Prejudice against discrete and insular minorities may be a special condition in such situations, which tends seriously to curtail the operation of those political processes normally to be relied on to protect minorities, and which may call for a correspondingly more searching judicial scrutiny. Compare McCulloch v. Maryland [1819]; South Carolina v. Barnwell Bros. [1938], n. 2, and cases cited.[1]

Chief Justice Hughes, who had a sharper eye than most of the brethren, read footnote four with care. Some of its implications displeased him. As he wrote Stone:

Supreme Court of the United States
Washington, D.C.
April 18, 1938.

No. 640.—*United States v. Carolene Products Co.*
Dear Justice Stone:

I am somewhat disturbed by your Note 4 on page 6. Is it true that "different considerations" apply in the instances you mention? Are the "considerations" different or does the difference lie not in the *test* but in the nature of the right invoked? When we say that a statute is invalid on its face, do we not mean that, in relation to the right invoked against it, the legislative action raises no presumption in its favor and has no rational support? Thus, in dealing with freedom of speech and of the press, as in the recent Lovell case, the legislative action putting the press broadly under license and censorship is directly opposed to the constitutional guaranty and for that reason has no presumption to support it. Of course, the test, whether there is a rational basis, must always have regard to the particular matter to which the test is applied and in that sense there may be different considerations in different cases. In that view the distinction between the two forms of statement may be only a verbal one, but may not the

---

1. **Eds.' Note:** Note 2 in *Barnwell* was another of Stone's doctrinal plants, that one specifically related to the reach of state authority over commerce, but it did put forth as one reason for close judicial oversight the absence of political control by the voters of one state over what the legislature of another state might do. In this respect, Stone's argument paralleled that of Chief Justice Marshall in McCulloch v. Maryland (1819; reprinted above, p. 413.)

phrasing of your note lead to some misunderstanding and bring us in the future into an unnecessary controversy over forms of expresson?

Faithfully,

Mr. Justice Stone.

The vote at conference had been 6–1 to reverse the district court and to sustain the statute, but Justice Black expressed concern that the third section of Stone's opinion allowed dangerous judicial intrusions into the legislative domain, while Justice Butler thought that section dangerously curtailed judicial power. Stone was trying to keep the two justices in his camp, though their conflicting views made it impossible to satisfy both. Knowing he had little chance with Butler, who was still smarting under the Court's withdrawal in 1937, Stone concentrated on winning Black over. They differed, but on the margins of doctrine rather than at the core—or at least so they both then thought. Black, on the other hand, was a very stubborn man, as Stone knew. Furthermore, Stone had little intellectual respect for his new colleague, whom he thought to be unlearned and precipitate rather than scholarly and judicious in striving for goals they both desired. In the end, despite Stone's efforts at reconciliation, Black refused to join in the third part of the opinion.

When he received Hughes' note, Stone could not yet be sure that he would lose both Butler and Black. But he did know that if neither joined his opinion, he would not have a majority of the full Court, though he would have a majority of the seven sitting justices, and so technically could speak for "the Court." If, however, Hughes also went his own way, Stone would speak for only three justices (himself, Brandeis and Roberts), not for the Court as an institution. And what he hoped would be the seeds of a new constitutional jurisprudence would be denied the soil in which they could best grow. Thus keeping the Chief Justice in the fold was a practical necessity. It was also a practical possibility, despite ideological differences between the Chief and Stone, for Hughes, like his predecessor William Howard Taft, always tried to avoid writing dissenting or concurring opinions. He thought it was his role as chief justice to lead the Court, not to criticize it.

Within a day of receiving the Chief's letter, Stone had reworked footnote 4. He replied to Hughes:

April 19, 1938

Dear Chief Justice:

I am recirculating my opinion in No. 640, United States v. Carolene Products Company, with some changes in the body of the opinion at pages 6 and 7. In view of your letter I have also revised the note on page 6.

You are quite right in saying that the specific prohibitions of the first ten amendments and the same prohibitions when adopted by the

Fourteenth Amendment leave no opportunity for presumption of constitutionality where statutes on their face violate the prohibition. There are, however, possible restraints on liberty and political rights which do not fall within those specific prohibitions and are forbidden only by the general words of the due process clause of the Fourteenth Amendment. I wish to avoid the possibility of having what I have written in the body of the opinion about the presumption of constitutionality in the ordinary run of due process cases applied as a matter of course to these other more exceptional cases. For that reason it seemed to me desirable to file a caveat in the note, without, however, committing the Court to any proposition contained in it. The notion that the Court should be more alert to protect constitutional rights in those cases where there is danger that the ordinary political processes for the correction of undesirable legislation may not operate has been announced for the Court by many judges, notably Chief Justice Marshall in McCulloch v. Maryland, with reference to taxation of governmental instrumentalities, and Justices Bradley, Field and Miller in state taxation or regulation affecting interstate commerce—cases collected in Note 2 in South Carolina v. Barnwell Bros., Inc., No. 161 this term.

I hope you will find the note acceptable in its present form, but if not I shall be glad if you will let me know.

Yours faithfully,

The Chief Justice.

To placate the Chief Justice, Stone inserted a reference to Hughes's opinion in DeJonge v. Oregon (1937) and, more importantly, added a fresh opening paragraph to the footnote. Stone also divided the older part of the footnote into two paragraphs so that now he addressed three separate problems—and in his usual indirect manner. The Chief found the new version acceptable and joined Stone's opinion, which thus became the opinion of the Court, though representing the views of only four of the seven justices who heard *Carolene Products.* As it appears in the U.S. Reports, the three paragraphs of footnote four read:

⁴ There may be narrower scope for operation of the presumption of constitutionality when legislation appears on its face to be within a specific prohibition of the Constitution, such as those of the first ten amendments, which are deemed equally specific when held to be embraced within the Fourteenth. See Stromberg v. California [1931]; Lovell v. Griffin [1938].

It is unnecessary to consider now whether legislation which restricts those political processes which can ordinarily be expected to bring about repeal of undesirable legislation, is to be subjected to more exacting judicial scrutiny under the general prohibitions of the Fourteenth Amendment than are most other types of legislation. On restrictions upon the right to vote, see Nixon v. Herndon [1927]; Nixon v. Condon [1932]; on restraints upon the dissemination of information, see Near v. Minnesota [1931]; Grosjean v. American Press Co. [1936]; Lovell v. Griffin [1938]; on interferences with political organizations, see Stromberg v. California [1931]; Fiske v. Kansas [1927]; Whitney v. California [1927]; Herndon v. Lowry [1937]; and see Holmes, J., in Gitlow v. New York [1925]; as to peaceable assembly, see De Jonge v. Oregon [1937].

Nor need we inquire whether similar considerations enter into the review of statutes directed at particular religious, Pierce v. Society of Sisters [1925], or national, Meyer v. Nebraska [1923]; Bartels v. Iowa [1923]; Farrington v. Tokushige [1927], or racial minorities, Nixon v. Herndon [1927]; Nixon v. Condon [1932]; whether prejudices against discrete and insular minorities may be a special condition, which tends seriously to curtail the operation of those political processes ordinarily thought to be relied upon to protect minorities, and which may call for a correspondingly more searching judicial inquiry. Compare McCulloch v. Maryland [1819]; South Carolina State Highway Department v. Barnwell [1938], note 2, and cases cited.

Editors' Note

THE HISTORY OF FOOTNOTE FOUR

As the Introductory Essay to this Section indicates, much of American constitutional interpretation from 1938 until the present unfolds in the history of footnote 4. The so-called "preferred freedoms" doctrine and its variant "reinforcing representative democracy," which accord a special place to the rights to vote and to communicate political ideas, owe much of their force to the rationale behind paragraph 2. What we term "modern" equal protection and its levels (or "tiers") of judicial scrutiny of challenged legislation stem from paragraph 3 of that footnote. And, the notion of fundamental rights, though articulated as early as Justice Chase in Calder v. Bull (1798; reprinted above, p. 86), finds support in paragraph 1, as does the Court's insistence on strict governmental observance of the procedural guarantees of the Bill of Rights in criminal prosecutions.

That importance, however, does not imply that the principles behind the footnote may not conflict with each other. Nor does it mean that the justices have uniformly carried out the logic of Stone's jurisprudence. Even he nodded at times. In Colegrove v. Green (1946), one of the last cases he heard, he argued in conference that Illinois' gerrymandering congressional districts so grossly as to make some in downstate contain one-eighth the population of others in Chicago did not present an issue that the justices should decide. "It isn't court business," Justice Murphy recorded Stone as saying. Somehow Stone forgot the justification for the Court's protecting fair and open political processes that paragraph 2 encapsulated.

Still, Stone made ready disciples among some of the new men who came to the Court. Black, Douglas, Murphy, Rutledge, and, for a time, Frankfurter and Jackson found the footnote to foreshadow a new and welcome jurisprudence. Indeed, Black, Douglas, Murphy, and Rutledge wanted to extend paragraph 2 to the point of presuming unconstitutional any legislation that restricted rights to speak, write, or vote.[1] It was not, however, until the period of the Warren Court (1953–69) that Stone's seeds would come to full flower.[2]

During Stone's tenure, the opposition to his approach came principally from the four justices, Sutherland, Van Devanter, McReynolds, and Butler, who objected to judicial deference in general rather than to his rubrics for relaxing deference. (See West Coast Hotel v. Parrish [1937; reprinted below, p. 987].) The leader of the opposition that would develop after the Four Horsemen left the bench was Felix Frankfurter.

In 1938, however, Frankfurter's opposition lay in the distant future. Indeed, while still a professor at the Harvard Law School, he congratulated Stone on footnote 4.:

> You, yourself, wrote an admirable opinion in the milk case, and I was especially excited by your note 4. I have just finished a series of lectures to the laity on The Court and Mr. Justice Holmes, in which I've tried to reconcile his latitudinarian attitude toward constitutionality in cases other than civil liberties, to use a loose phrase, with his attitude in civil liberties cases. That bit in these lectures, when they are published, may interest you. Your note is extremely suggestive and opens up new territory.[3]

Frankfurter's letter must have comforted Stone, for he thought he was articulating what was latent in earlier opinions of Holmes and Brandeis. As far as paragraph 2 was concerned, this modesty was probably accurate. The two older justices had, after some hesitation, come to see freedom of speech and press as a central value in the political system, one that the Court should be alert to protect.[4]

It is far more difficult, however, to find much of either Holmes or Brandeis in paragraph 3. Holmes in particular tended to denigrate arguments based on equal protection. (See, for example, his opinion for the Court in Buck v. Bell [1927; reprinted below, p. 1105], dismissing appeals to equal protection as "the usual last resort of constitutional arguments.") And Brandeis' views on deference to legislative judgment often led to similar results.[5]

In any event, Frankfurter had written that Holmes believed the Court should be wary of deferring to legislative judgment when a statute restricted freedom of speech or press. And, during his early years on the Court,

---

1. See the debates in Thomas v. Collins (1946) and Kovacs v. Cooper (1949); many of the cases are analyzed in C. Herman Pritchett: *The Roosevelt Court* (New York: Macmillan, 1948), chaps. 5, 7, 9, & 10; and *Civil Liberties and the Vinson Court* (Chicago: University of Chicago Press, 1954), pp. 32–36.

2. See Alpheus Thomas Mason, *The Supreme Court from Taft to Burger* (Baton Rouge, La.: Louisiana State University Press, (1979), chaps. 4–7; John Hart Ely, *Democracy and Distrust* (Cambridge, Mass.: Harvard University Press, 1980), chap. 2; Walter F. Murphy, "Deeds under a Doctrine," 59 *Am.Pol.Sci.Rev.* 64 (1965).

3. Frankfurter to Stone, April 27, 1938; the Stone Papers, the Library of Congress. We are indebted to Claire Laporte of the Princeton Class of 1982 for providing this letter.

4. Compare their views in Schenck v. United States (1919) and its companion cases with those in Abrams v. United States (1919), Gitlow v. New York (1925), and, most especially, Whitney v. California (1927; reprinted below, p. 503).

5. See his dissent for himself and Holmes in Royster Guano Co. v. Virginia (1920).

Frankfurter himself took such a position. During debate on the First Flag Salute Case (1940; reprinted below, p. 1017), he tried to persuade Stone to join his opinion:

> I am aware of the important distinction which you skillfully adumbrated in your footnote 4 (particularly the second paragraph of it) . . . . I agree with that distinction; I regard it as basic. [The complete text of this letter is reprinted below, p. 1019.]

And, eight months later, Frankfurter wrote for the Court in AFL v. Swing (1941) that judges should protect freedom of discussion "with a jealous eye." He cited footnote 4 as one of three authorities for that role.

Soon, however, Frankfurter began to withdraw his endorsement of footnote 4, whether for personal or jurisprudential reasons.[6] More and more often, he dissociated himself from Stone as well as Black, Douglas, Murphy, and later Rutledge when they gave preference to claims to freedom of political expression. In 1943, dissenting in the Second Flag Salute Case (reprinted below, p. 1027), Frankfurter repudiated his earlier view of a hierarchy among constitutional values:

> The Constitution does not give us greater veto power when dealing with one phase of "liberty" than with another . . . . Judicial restraint is equally necessary whenever an exercise of political or legislative power is challenged. There is no warrant in the constitutional basis of this Court's authority for attributing different roles to it depending upon the nature of the challenge to the legislation. Our power does not vary according to the particular provision of the Bill of Rights which is invoked. The right not to have one's property taken without just compensation has, so far as the scope of judicial power is concerned, the same constitutional dignity as the right to be protected against unreasonable searches and seizures, and the latter has no less claim than freedom of the press or freedom of speech or religious freedom.

In 1949, concurring in Kovacs v. Cooper, he attacked the fruits of Carolene Products as "mischievous" and added: "A footnote hardly seems to be an appropriate way of announcing a new constitutional doctrine." He then went to considerable lengths to show that Stone's note had neither contained anything original nor implied that legislation touching the First Amendment was presumptively invalid.

In 1951 Frankfurter returned to the offensive: "It has been suggested, with the casualness of a footnote, that such legislation is not presumptively valid."[7] All legislation, he reasserted, carried presumptive validity.

Carrying the fight to a more personal level, he was determined to undermine Stone's reputation as a jurist. Thus Frankfurter was gleeful when in 1955 he read in Alpheus Thomas Mason's Security Through Freedom that not only had Louis Lusky drafted footnote 4 but that Stone often allowed his clerks such authority. "I have good grounds," Frankfurter wrote to a friend at Harvard, "for believing that Lusky wrote the heart of that footnote, but it never occurred to me that it was 'a striking example of Justice Stone's custom'

---

6. For a fascinating inquiry into Frankfurter's psyche, see Harry N. Hirsch, The Enigma of Felix Frankfurter (New York: Basic Books, 1981).

7. Dennis v. United States, concur. op. (1951).

. . . . In light of this disclosure by Mason, I should think my phrase 'the casualness of a footnote' . . . is a model of moderation." [8]

Neither Stone's death nor that of Frankfurter, Murphy, Rutledge, Black, Douglas, and the other members of the Roosevelt Court ended disputes over the meaning of footnote 4 and its centrality for constitutional interpretation. In 1973, for instance, Justice Rehnquist repeated several of Frankfurter's objections and added some of his own.[9] But Rehnquist spoke in dissent; and the majority, though citing footnote 4, ignored critiques of *Carolene Products*.

That treatment has been typical of the Court's behavior. Not since Kovacs v. Cooper in 1949 have the justices engaged in a full scale debate of *Carolene Products*. Nevertheless, footnote 4 continues to be the hinge on which much of modern constitutional argument turns. A great deal of recent academic controversy revolves around that note; [10] and, among the justices, one can hear its creak in such opinions as Landmark Communications v. Virginia (1978), where Chief Justice Burger said for the Court that "[d]eference to a legislative finding cannot limit judicial inquiry when First Amendment rights are at stake"; or in Harris v. McRae (1980), where Justice Stewart wrote for the majority that "[i]t is well settled that . . . if a law 'impinges upon a fundamental right explicitly or implicitly secured by the Constitution [it] is presumptively unconstitutional.' "

Douglas, Murphy, Rutledge, and the young Justice Black would have rejoiced at these words. Frankfurter would have been appalled, as might the elder Black. And Stone himself might not have been altogether pleased at his apparent triumph. Undoubtedly, he meant to move the Court beyond *Carolene Products'* cautious words. But his penchant for indirection and his fear that judges might again, as they had in the 1930s, overreach their authority led him to be wary of presuming legislation unconstitutional.

---

8. Frankfurter to Paul Freund, October 24, 1955; the Frankfurter Papers, the Library of Congress.

9. Sugarman v. McDougall.

10. For example: Bruce A. Ackerman, "Beyond *Carolene Products*," 98 *Harv.L.Rev.* 713 (1985); Louis Lusky, *By What Right?* (Charlottesville, Va.: Michie, 1975); Walter F. Murphy, "The Art of Constitutional Interpretation," in M. Judd Harmon, ed., *Essays on the Constitution of the United States* (Port Washington, N.Y.: Kennikat Press, 1978); and Mason, *supra* note 2. Ely's *Democracy and Distrust* drew the most attention; for analyses, see: Paul Brest, "The Fundamental Rights Controversy," 90 *Yale L.J.* 1063 (1981); James E. Fleming, "A Critique of John Hart Ely's Quest for the Ultimate Constitutional Interpretivism of Representative Democracy," 80 *Mich.L.Rev.* 634 (1982); Sanford V. Levinson, "Judicial Review and the Problem of the Comprehensible Constitution," 59 *Tex.L.Rev.* 395 (1981); Walter F. Murphy, "Constitutional Interpretation," 9 *Revs. in Am.Hist.* 7 (1981); Symposium, "Judicial Review versus Democracy," 42 *Ohio State L.J.* 1 (1981); and Laurence H. Tribe, "The Puzzling Persistence of Process-Based Constitutional Theories," 89 *Yale L.J.* 1063 (1980); reprinted as chap. 2 in his *Constitutional Choices* (Cambridge, Mass.: Harvard University Press, 1985).

11

Freedom of Political Communication

The U.S. Reports are studded with eloquent panegyrics to freedom of political communication. As Hugo Black said in 1941:

> . . . I view the guaranties of the First Amendment as the foundation upon which our governmental structure rests . . . . Freedom to speak and write about public questions is as important to the life of our government as the heart is to the human body. In fact, this privilege is the heart of our government. If that heart be weakened, the result is debilitation; if it be stilled, the result is death.[1]

But inspired rhetoric does not solve fundamental political problems. This chapter will examine, as part of the larger question of how to interpret the Constitution, the way in which American public officials have approached troublesome issues of freedom of communication.

I. COMMUNICATION AND CONSTITUTIONAL INTERPRETATION

A. From Democratic Theory to Literal Interpretation

The core of democratic theory is formed around free political communication. It is, as Justice Holmes said, "more than self-expression, it is the essence of self-government."[2] If the people are to choose their leaders and influence those leaders' selections of policies, citizens must have an opportunity to learn about candidates and their proposals for public policy. Only then can choice be intelligent and free. Two distinct, equally important, and functionally interlocking rights are involved: that of every citizen to participate in self-government by trying to win support for his or her politically relevant ideas; and that of potential listeners to hear and be informed so that they may decide how best—in *their* judgments—to allocate their political resources.

Like democratic theory, constitutionalism also highly values freedom of communication. A constitutionalist would argue that, insofar as government censors a person's ideas, it denies him or her both full

---

1. Milkwagon Drivers Union v. Meadowmoor Dairies, dis. op. (1941).
2. Abrams v. United States, dis. op. (1919).

494

participation in self-government and the liberty of free development of personality. A government that determines what thoughts its people may express degrades those people, treats them as children rather than as free citizens whose dignity and liberty it is government's purpose to defend and foster. Indeed, constitutionalism would move a step further than democratic theory and include all ideas, not merely those that might have clear political relevance.

Structuralists—textual, systemic, and transcendental—might make similar arguments. (Cf. Brennan's concur. op. in Richmond Newspapers v. Virginia [1980; reprinted below, p. 587.]) The organization of the constitutional document, the operations of the system, and the architectural scheme prescribed by the two political theories that underpin the Constitution all point toward the critical nature of free political communication.

Even the most stolid textualist who believes that constitutional interpretation should be limited to the words of the document should logically agree about the centrality of the First Amendment's guarantees of freedom of speech, press, assembly, and petition. For, unlike many other parts of the Bill of Rights, the First Amendment is cast in absolute terms. The Fourth Amendment, for example, forbids only "unreasonable" searches and seizures and the Fifth does not forbid all takings of "life, liberty, or property" but only such takings "without due process of law." In contrast, the First Amendment reads: "Congress shall make no law . . . abridging the freedom of speech, or of the press; or the right of the people peaceably to assemble to petition the Government for a redress of grievances." "My view is," the Supreme Court's great literalist wrote,

> without exception, without any ifs, buts, or whereases, that freedom of speech means the government shall not do anything to people, or, in the words of Magna Carta, move against people either for the views they have or the views they express or the words they speak or write . . . . I simply believe that 'Congress shall make no law' means Congress shall make no law.[3]

B. The Interplay of Other Values

If democratic theorists, constitutionalists, structuralists, and literalists are unanimous that free communication of political ideas is an imperative for the American polity, it would seem that any problems that arise would be only of marginal significance and thus easily resolved. In fact, however, freedom of communication is among the most troubled areas of constitutional interpretation. In part the cause lies in the failure of judges as well as legislators and executives to articulate clearly and apply consistently a coherent theory of what it is they are doing. But part of the difficulty also lies in the complicated interplay of different sets of values in political life and therefore in constitutional interpretation.

---

3. Hugo L. Black, *A Constitutional Faith* (New York: Knopf, 1969), p. 45.

In the abstract, there is agreement that government lacks authority either to deny people the information they need to formulate political judgments or to express those judgments so as to influence their fellow citizens and the course of public policy. In particular situations, however, most people are willing to grant exceptions, for there are other values at work than those of open political processes or free self expression. First, the line between what is politically relevant and what is not—a line that a constitutionalist would not draw—is fuzzy. What, for instance, is the relationship between sexual mores and political values? After all, views about sexual freedom may well be related to more general views about society and the rules by which it should be governed.

In some situations the political element may be apparent, but it may occur alongside other values. Cohen v. California (1971; reprinted below, p. 564) addresses a situation in which a young man phrased his political message in obscene terms that offended many people.

Furthermore, there may be limits to how far a democratic theorist would push the concept of politically relevant communication or a constitutionalist the concept of free communication as necessary to the expression of one's individuality. Few, for example, would concede that a group of Mafiosi who were conspiring to bribe a senator were protected in their plotting because their speech was related to public policy or because it was necessary to voice the evil within their personalities.

Even speech or writing filled with obvious political content that does not involve what people ordinarily think of as crime might cause difficulties. How far can one go in the rough and tumble of political debate to assail the character of an opponent? Do the rights of some citizens to decent reputations automatically yield to the rights of other citizens to voice their political views as forcefully as they can? On the other hand, if those arguing for or against particular candidates and policies have to stop to analyze complex laws of defamation, can debate be truly free and open? Here some versions of constitutional and democratic theories might offer quite different responses. New York Times v. Sullivan (1964; reprinted below, p. 596) and Time v. Firestone (1976; reprinted below, p. 606) take up those sorts of problems.

If debate is to be open, need contestants have equal access to privately owned, monopolistic, and very expensive mass media of communications? Chapter 12 explores some of the paradoxes of money and democratic politics; Miami Herald v. Tornillo (1974; reprinted there), examines the problem as it is affected by government's ordering the media to provide equal time or space.

Perhaps the most intractable difficulties concern national security. Not many people acknowledge that the public's right to information includes access to the codes used to program the Air Force's nuclear tipped missiles or the Navy's defense against Soviet submarines. Yet without some detailed and accurate information it is impossible to make informed judgments about the adequacy of defense policy— certainly a primary concern to all citizens. And who, without actually knowing all the details of classified information, can distinguish between protecting vital military secrets and hiding information that might embarrass officials? During the Vietnam War, for instance, the last to learn about American bombings of Cambodia were the American voters. The Pentagon Papers Case (1971; reprinted below, p. 576) presented some of these issues.

Constitutional interpretation is further complicated by the fact that absolutely free political communication raises difficulties for democratic theory. The nub of democracy is that, after full debate and free elections, the people's chosen representatives shall govern, subject only to such restraints as the people have put on themselves and their representatives. But what about threats to harm or even kill a public official? (See Gooding v. Wilson [1972; reprinted below, p. 539], and Watts v. United States [1969; reprinted below, p. 549].) Or speech that urges people to resort to violence to stop minorities from exercising their rights as full citizens? (See Brandenburg v. Ohio [1969], reprinted below at p. 544.) Or speech and writing that try to identify U.S. intelligence agents in foreign countries and so expose them to assassination? (See Watts v. United States [1969] and Haig v. Agee [1981], reprinted at pp. 549 and 533.) All these means threaten to negate democratic processes as well as the rule of law.

Even more basic are questions about the legitimacy of efforts to organize a group to use violence to destroy a democratic political system. Such efforts present the age-old problem of sedition; and protecting democracy against internal subversion raises difficulties similar to those of protecting military secrets. On an even wider scale than assassination or illegal action against minorities, sedition emphatically tries to overturn democratic procedures.

On the other hand, it is both easy and tempting for those in office to label opponents as seditionists. It was, after all, a charge levelled not only against communists, socialists, pacifists, union organizers, career diplomats who thought in the late 1940s that the United States should recognize Red China, opponents of racial segregation, critics of the FBI, foes of the war in Vietnam, enemies of Richard Nixon, and, more recently, advocates of a nuclear freeze, but also Thomas Jefferson, whose democracy was too radical for many Federalists. And, although he himself escaped legal action under the Sedition Act of 1798, many of his followers were victims of prosecutions under that statute. It was out of these experiences that Jefferson urged in his first inaugural address:

> [L]et us reflect that, having banished from our land that religious intolerance under which mankind has so long bled and suffered, we have gained little if we countenance a political intolerance as despotic, as wicked, and capable of as bitter and bloody persecutions . . . . If there be any among us who would wish to dissolve

this Union or to change its republican form, let them stand undisturbed as monuments of the safety with which error of opinion may
be tolerated where reason is free to combat it.[4]

In 1937, speaking for the Court in De Jonge v. Oregon, Charles
Evans Hughes echoed Jefferson's message:

> The greater the importance of safeguarding the community
> from incitements to overthrow of our institutions by force and
> violence, the more imperative is the need to preserve inviolate the
> constitutional rights of free speech, free press and free assembly in
> order to maintain the opportunity for free political discussion, to the
> end that government may be responsive to the will of the people
> and that changes, if desired, may be obtained by peaceful means.
> Therein lies the security of the Republic, the very foundation of
> constitutional government.

Where charges of sedition or subversion have been made, the
Supreme Court has only intermittently given close attention either to
Jefferson's specific words or to the democratic theory on which they
were based.[5] As a result, it has awkwardly grappled with such
conundra, as shown by Dennis v. United States (1951), Yates v.
United States (1957), and Barenblatt v. United States (1959) (all
reprinted below). In these as in other cases, the justices have left
themselves vulnerable to attack for their failure either to state coherent constitutionalist theories or to protect democratic processes. One
should keep in mind, however, that if legislators or executives had
more clearly thought through the theoretical and practical difficulties
of punishing communication of political ideas, judges would probably
not have faced such constitutional dilemmas.

II. PRINCIPLES OF INTERPRETATION

Although Stone's distinctions in *Carolene Products* have formed a
pivot around which modern constitutional interpretation revolves,
there has been wide disagreement about the legitimacy as well as the
meaning of those distinctions. Some justices have ignored them;
others like Felix Frankfurter came to think them fundamentally wrong;
others, like Black and Douglas and later Potter Stewart[6] extended
Stone's suggestions; others, like Chief Justice Warren Burger,[7] would

---

4. Andrew A. Lipscomb, ed., *The Writings of Thomas Jefferson* (Washington: The Thomas
Jefferson Memorial Association, 1903), III, 318–319.

5. Note also the Court's ducking the issue of whether illegal federal surveillance of radical
groups exerted such a "chilling effect" on freedom of political communication as to violate the
First Amendment: Laird v. Tatum (1972).

6. See, for example, his opinion for the Court in Harris v. McRae (1980), quoting his
plurality opinion in Mobile v. Bolden (1980): "It is well settled that . . . if a law 'impinges
upon a fundamental right explicitly or implicitly secured by the Constitution [it] is presumptively
unconstitutional.' "

7. See Burger's plurality opinion in Fullilove v. Klutznick (1980; reprinted below, p. 816)
quoting his opinion for the Court in Columbia Broadcasting v. Democratic National Committee
(1973) that the Court accords " 'great weight to the decisions of Congress' even though the

restrict them; and even Stone himself at times seemed unsure about where his jurisprudence led.[8]

Before World War I, there were almost no judicial interpretations of the First Amendment. Even the Sedition Act of 1798, a federal statute, did not generate a challenge that reached the Supreme Court. And it was not until 1925 in Gitlow v. New York that the Court held the Fourteenth Amendment protected free speech against state action.

Between World War I and *Carolene Products,* the Court usually applied one of two standards to test legislation challenged under the First Amendment's free speech or press clauses. The first was the so-called "clear and present danger" rule. As enunciated by Holmes in cases growing out of opposition to World War I, the rule would sustain regulations of communication if what was spoken or written posed a "clear and present danger" to some important interest that government could protect.[9] In this test's first applications, the Court used it to justify sending people to jail for arguing that the draft was unconstitutional and that the United States should not intervene in the Russian civil war.[10] Later, Holmes and Brandeis tried to refine "clear and present danger" to protect rather than threaten free speech. As Brandeis explained in Whitney v. California (1927; reprinted below, p. 503):

> [N]o danger flowing from speech can be deemed clear and present, unless the incidence of evil apprehended is so imminent that it may befall before there is opportunity for full discussion. If there be time to expose through discussion the falsehood and fallacies . . . the remedy to be applied is more speech, not enforced silence. Only an emergency can justify repression . . . .
>
> Moreover, even imminent danger cannot justify resort to prohibition of these functions essential to effective democracy, unless the evil apprehended is relatively serious . . . . The fact that speech is likely to result in some violence or in destruction of property is not enough to justify its suppression. There must be the probability of serious injury to the State.

For some decades, "clear and present danger" managed to coexist with Stone's concept of "preferred freedoms." And, in the 1930s and 1940s, the Court occasionally used the test as Holmes and Brandeis wished; but by the early 1950s both those who were terrified by the specter of domestic communism and those who, like Justice Douglas, dismissed communist agitators as "miserable merchants of unwanted ideas" agreed that "clear and present danger" was not a useful rule to

---

legislation implicate[s] constitutional rights guaranteed by the First Amendment." See also Burger's opinion for the Court in Landmark Communications v. Virginia (1978), discussed above in "A Note on the History of Footnote Four," p. 493.

8. Stone voted in Colegrove v. Green (1946) that legislative malapportionment did not present a justiciable issue. See the discussion above in "A Note on the History of Footnote Four," p. 490.

9. Schenck v. United States (1919).

10. Abrams v. United States (1919) and Debs v. United States (1919).

interpret the First Amendment.   The former thought it was too restrictive of governmental power, the latter found it too restrictive of freedom of speech.   The test reappeared in Brandenburg v. Ohio (1969; reprinted below, p. 544), only to vanish again.

The second rule bears the label "bad tendency."   It was never so clearly articulated as "clear and present danger," but Justice Sanford summarized it for the Court in *Whitney:*

> a State in the exercise of it police power may punish those who abuse this freedom [of expression] by utterances inimical to the public welfare, tending to incite to crime, disturb the public peace, or endanger the foundations of organized government and threaten its overthrow by unlawful means . . . .

By the early 1930s, the Court had quietly dropped this test.

Since *Carolene Products,* the Court has occasionally used various forms of the *technique* of balancing to test the constitutionality of legislation under the First Amendment.   Barenblatt v. United States (1959; reprinted below, p. 525) offers the starkest example.   Felix Frankfurter joined the majority in *Barenblatt;* but eight years earlier, although he had seen balancing as the critical *technique* of constitutional interpretation, he had argued that in a democracy the legislature must strike that balance, not the judiciary:

> Courts are not representative bodies.   They are not designed to be a good reflex of a democratic society. . . . Primary responsibility for adjusting the interests that compete . . . of necessity belongs to the Congress. [Dennis v. United States, concur. op. (1951; reprinted below, p. 510).]

Judges, Frankfurter maintained, should only ensure that the "balance" that the legislature set falls within reasonable limits, not whether it is "correct" or the "best" of possible alternatives.

At first glance, the simplest solution appears to be Black's literalism.   But as Chapters 1 and 8 pointed out, literal interpretation suffers from severe problems, and Black's own record reflects some of those difficulties.   He excluded from constitutional protection direct action as well as such "symbolic" acts of communication as picketing,[11] wearing armbands in a public school,[12] or burning a draft card [13] or an American flag.[14]   He also wanted to sustain convictions of demonstrators for parading in an orderly fashion outside a courtroom.   "Justice cannot be rightly administered," he explained, "nor are the lives and safety of prisoners secure, when throngs of people clamor against the processes of justice outside the courthouse or jailhouse door." [15]

---

11. Milk Wagon Drivers Union v. Meadowmoor Dairies, dis. op. (1941); Giboney v. Empire Storage (1949).

12. Tinker v. Des Moines, dis. op. (1969).

13. United States v. O'Brien (1968).

14. Street v. New York, dis. op. (1969).

15. Cox v. Louisiana, dis. op. (1965).

These distinctions may make practical sense but they are not products of literal interpretation. Furthermore, any distinction between political words and action is thin. Not only is the usual purpose of words to cause deeds—words are "the triggers of action," Judge Learned Hand once wrote [16]—but verbal persuasion is typically interlaced with symbols. The flag, the log cabin, the fiery cross, the swastika, "Watergate," "Wall Street," and "star wars" all express politically laden values.

In any event, although Black was frequently on the winning side in cases involving freedom of communication, he was never able to persuade a majority of his colleagues to accept literalness, even his modified version, as more than a starting point for constitutional interpretation.

There is no magic key here. No particular *approach, mode,* or *technique* of interpretation, or combination of them, will program an interpreter so that "correct" constitutional answers will appear on mental screens. Yet some offer more help than others. A structural *mode* as well as the purposive *mode* of reinforcing representative democracy, explained in detail in Chapter 8, provide means of conceiving problems of freedom of political communication and participation in a systematic, comprehensive fashion. Neither *mode* promises infallibility or guarantees wisdom; but each, in quite closely related ways, provides a perspective, an opportunity to see such problems as a whole and their relations to an entire constitutional order, rather than as discrete problems to be met on an ad hoc basis. Even Hugo Black's literalism was heavily flavored with democratic theory. "Our First Amendment," he summed up, "was a bold effort . . . to establish a country with no legal restrictions of any kind upon the subjects people could investigate, discuss and deny." [17]

SELECTED BIBLIOGRAPHY

Amdur, Robert. "Scanlon on Freedom of Expression," 9 *Phil. & Pub. Affairs* 287 (1980).

Anastaplo, George. *The Constitutionalist* (Dallas: Southern Methodist University Press, 1971).

Barber, Sotirios A. *On What the Constitution Means* (Baltimore: John Hopkins University Press, 1984).

Black, Hugo L. *A Constitutional Faith* (New York: Knopf, 1969).

Choper, Jesse H. *Judicial Review and the National Political Process* (Chicago: University of Chicago Press, 1980).

Ely, John Hart. *Democracy and Distrust* (Cambridge: Harvard University Press, 1980).

Emerson, Thomas I. *Toward a General Theory of the First Amendment* (New York: Random House, 1963).

---

16. Masses Publishing Co. v. Patten (1917).

17. "The Bill of Rights," 35 *N.Y.U. L. Rev.* 865 (1960).

Levy, Leonard W. *Legacy of Suppression* (Cambridge: The Belknap Press of Harvard University Press, 1960). (Note Levy's modifications of his views reported in the article by Hynes, listed above.)

————. "The *Legacy* Reexamined," 37 *Stan. L. Rev.* 767 (1985).

Lusky, Louis. *By What Right?* (Charlottesville, Va.: Michie Co., 1975).

Mason, Alpheus T. *The Supreme Court from Taft to Burger* (Baton Rouge: Louisiana State University Press, 1979).

Meiklejohn, Alexander. *Free Speech and Its Relation to Self-Government* (New York: Harpers, 1948).

Miller, J.C. *Crisis in Freedom: The Alien and Sedition Acts* (Boston: Little, Brown, 1951).

Murphy, Paul L. *World War I and the Origins of Civil Liberties in the United States* (New York: Norton, 1979).

O'Brien, David M. *The Public's Right to Know* (New York: Praeger, 1981).

Pool, Ithiel de Sola. *Technologies of Freedom* (Cambridge: The Belknap Press of Harvard University Press, 1983).

Pritchett, C. Herman. *Constitutional Civil Liberties* (Englewood Cliffs, N.J.: Prentice-Hall, 1984), espec. Chaps. 2–5.

Rabban, David M. "The First Amendment in its Forgotten Years," 90 *Yale L.J.* 514 (1981).

Scanlon, T.M. "A Theory of Freedom of Expression," 2 *Phil. & Pub. Affairs* 204 (1972).

————. "Freedom of Expression and Categories of Expression," 40 *U.Pitts.L.Rev.* 519 (1979).

Schwartz, Bernard. *Super Chief: Earl Warren and his Supreme Court* (New York: New York University Press, 1983).

Smith, James Morton. *Freedom's Fetters: The Alien and Sedition Laws and American Civil Liberties* (Ithaca, N.Y.: Cornell University Press, 1956).

Symposium. "Judicial Review versus Democracy," 42 *Ohio St.L.J.* (1981).

Tribe, Laurence H. "The Puzzling Persistence of Process-Based Constitutional Theories," 89 *Yale L.J.* 1063 (1980); reprinted as chap. 2 in his *Constitutional Choices* (Cambridge, Mass.: Harvard University Press, 1985).

I. ADVOCACY OR INCITEMENT TO VIOLENT POLITICAL CHANGE

"[A] State in the exercise of its police power may punish those who abuse this freedom by utterances inimical to the public welfare, tending to incite to crime, disturb the public peace, or endanger the foundations of organized government and threaten its overthrow by unlawful means. . . ."—Justice SANFORD

"If there be time to expose through discussion the falsehood and fallacies, to avert the evil by the process of education, the remedy to be applied is more speech, not enforced silence."—Justice BRANDEIS

WHITNEY v. CALIFORNIA
274 U.S. 357, 47 S.Ct. 641, 71 L.Ed. 1095 (1927).

In 1919 Anita Whitney attended a convention in Oakland, Cal., held to organize a state branch of the Communist Labor party, which had links to the Communist International in Moscow. The national party's program called for "a unified revolutionary working class movement in America" to reorganize society and bring about a communist commonwealth. During the convention she signed a proposal urging the value of political action and electoral activity. The resolution did not pass; instead, the convention adopted the national party's program. Whitney stayed at the convention and remained an active member of the party. She was later convicted under California's Criminal Syndicalism Act, which made it a felony to organize or join a group advocating, aiding, or abetting acts of violence to achieve political or industrial change. She obtained a writ of error from the U.S. Supreme Court after state appellate courts affirmed her conviction.

Mr. Justice **SANFORD** delivered the opinion of the Court . . . .

1. While it is not denied that the evidence warranted the jury in finding that the defendant became a member of and assisted in organizing the Communist Labor Party of California, and that this was organized to advocate, teach, aid or abet criminal syndicalism as defined by the Act, it is urged that the Act, as here construed and applied, deprived the defendant of her liberty without due process of law in that it has made her action in attending the Oakland convention unlawful by reason of "a subsequent event brought about against her will, by the agency of others," with no showing of a specific intent on her part to join in the forbidden purpose of the association, and merely because, by reason of a lack of "prophetic" understanding she failed to foresee the quality that others would give to the convention. The argument is, in effect, that the character of the state organization could not be forecast when she attended the convention; that she had no purpose of helping to create an instrument of terrorism and violence; that she "took part in formulating and presenting to the convention a resolution which, if adopted, would have committed the new organization to a legitimate

policy of political reform by the use of the ballot"; that it was not until after the majority of the convention turned out to be "contrary-minded, and other less temperate policies prevailed" that the convention could have taken on the character of criminal syndicalism; and that as this was done over her protest, her mere presence in the convention, however violent the opinions expressed therein, could not thereby become a crime. This contention, while advanced in the form of a constitutional objection to the Act, is in effect nothing more than an effort to review the weight of the evidence for the purpose of showing that the defendant did not join and assist in organizing the Communist Labor Party of California with a knowledge of its unlawful character and purpose. This question, which is foreclosed by the verdict of the jury—sustained by the Court of Appeal over the specific objection that it was not supported by the evidence—is one of fact merely which is not open to review in this Court, involving as it does no constitutional question whatever. And we may add that the argument entirely disregards the facts: that the defendant had previously taken out a membership card in the National Party, that the resolution which she supported did not advocate the use of the ballot to the exclusion of violent and unlawful means of bringing about the desired changes in industrial and political conditions; and that, after the constitution of the California Party had been adopted, and this resolution had been voted down and the National Program accepted, she not only remained in the convention, without protest, until its close, but subsequently manifested her acquiescence by attending as an alternate member of the State Executive Committee and continuing as a member of the Communist Labor Party.

2. It is clear that the Syndicalism Act is not repugnant to the due process clause by reason of vagueness and uncertainty of definition . . . .

The Act, plainly, meets the essential requirement of due process that a penal statute be "sufficiently explicit to inform those who are subject to it, what conduct on their part will render them liable to its penalties," and be couched in terms that are not "so vague that men of common intelligence must necessarily guess at its meaning and differ as to its application." . . . So, as applied here, the Syndicalism Act required of the defendant no "prophetic" understanding of its meaning . . . .

3. Neither is the Syndicalism Act repugnant to the equal protection clause, on the ground that, as its penalties are confined to those who advocate a resort to violent and unlawful methods as a means of changing industrial and political conditions, it arbitrarily discriminates between such persons and those who may advocate a resort to these methods as a means of maintaining such conditions.

It is settled by repeated decisions of this Court that the equal protection clause does not take from a State the power to classify in the adoption of police laws, but admits of the exercise of a wide scope of discretion, and avoids what is done only when it is without any reasonable basis and therefore is purely arbitrary; and that one who assails the classification must carry the burden of showing that it does not rest upon any reasonable basis, but is essentially arbitrary . . . .

4. Nor is the Syndicalism Act as applied in this case repugnant to the due process clause as a restraint of the rights of free speech, assembly, and association.

That the freedom of speech which is secured by the Constitution does not confer an absolute right to speak, without responsibility, whatever one may choose, or an unrestricted and unbridled license giving immunity for every possible use of language and preventing the punishment of those who abuse this freedom; and that a State in the exercise of its police power may punish those who abuse this freedom by utterances inimical to the public welfare, tending to incite to crime, disturb the public peace, or endanger the foundations of organized government and threaten its overthrow by unlawful means, is not open to question. Gitlow v. New York [1925].

By enacting the provisions of the Syndicalism Act the State has declared, through its legislative body, that to knowingly be or become a member of or assist in organizing an association to advocate, teach or aid and abet the commission of crimes or unlawful acts of force, violence or terrorism as a means of accomplishing industrial or political changes, involves such danger to the public peace and the security of the State, that these acts should be penalized in the exercise of its police power. That determination must be given great weight. Every presumption is to be indulged in favor of the validity of the statute, . . . and it may not be declared unconstitutional unless it is an arbitrary or unreasonable attempt to exercise the authority vested in the State in the public interest. . . .

The essence of the offense denounced by the Act is the combining with others in an association for the accomplishment of the desired ends through the advocacy and use of criminal and unlawful methods. It partakes of the nature of a criminal conspiracy. That such united and joint action involves even greater danger to the public peace and security than the isolated utterances and acts of individuals, is clear. We cannot hold that, as here applied, the Act is an unreasonable or arbitrary exercise of the police power of the State, unwarrantably infringing any right of free speech, assembly or association, or that those persons are protected from punishment by the due process clause who abuse such rights by joining and furthering an organization thus menacing the peace and welfare of the State . . . .

Affirmed.

Mr. Justice **BRANDEIS** [joined by Justice **HOLMES**], concurring

. . . .

[Under this California statute,] [t]he mere act of assisting in forming a society for teaching syndicalism, of becoming a member of it, or of
assembling with others for that purpose is given the dynamic quality of
crime. There is guilt although the society may not contemplate immediate promulgation of the doctrine. Thus the accused is to be punished,
not for contempt, incitement or conspiracy, but for a step in preparation, which, if it threatens the public order at all, does so only remotely.
The novelty in the prohibition introduced is that the statute aims, not
at the practice of criminal syndicalism, nor even directly at the preaching of it, but at association with those who propose to preach it.

Despite arguments to the contrary which had seemed to me persuasive, it is settled that the due process clause of the Fourteenth Amendment applies to matters of substantive law as well as to matters of
procedure. Thus all fundamental rights comprised within the term
liberty are protected by the Federal Constitution from invasion by the
States. The right of free speech, the right to teach and the right of
assembly are, of course, fundamental rights. See Meyer v. Nebraska
[1923]; Pierce v. Society of Sisters [1925]; Gitlow v. New York [1925];
Farrington v. Tokushige [1927]. These may not be denied or abridged.
But, although the rights of free speech and assembly are fundamental,
they are not in their nature absolute. Their exercise is subject to
restriction, if the particular restriction proposed is required in order to
protect the State from destruction or from serious injury, political,
economic or moral. That the necessity which is essential to a valid
restriction does not exist unless speech would produce, or is intended to
produce, a clear and imminent danger of some substantive evil which
the State constitutionally may seek to prevent has been settled. See
Schenck v. United States [1919].

It is said to be the function of the legislature to determine whether
at a particular time and under the particular circumstances the formation of, or assembly with, a society organized to advocate criminal
syndicalism constitutes a clear and present danger of substantive evil;
and that by enacting the law here in question the legislature of
California determined that question in the affirmative . . . . The
legislature must obviously decide, in the first instance, whether a
danger exists which calls for a particular protective measure. But
where a statute is valid only in case certain conditions exist, the
enactment of the statute cannot alone establish the facts which are
essential to its validity. Prohibitory legislation has repeatedly been
held invalid, because unnecessary, where the denial of liberty involved
was that of engaging in a particular business. The power of the courts
to strike down an offending law is no less when the interests involved
are not property rights, but the fundamental personal rights of free
speech and assembly.

This Court has not yet fixed the standard by which to determine
when a danger shall be deemed clear; how remote the danger may be
and yet be deemed present; and what degree of evil shall be deemed
sufficiently substantial to justify resort to abridgement of free speech

and assembly as the means of protection. To reach sound conclusions on these matters, we must bear in mind why a State is, ordinarily, denied the power to prohibit dissemination of social, economic and political doctrine which a vast majority of its citizens believes to be false and fraught with evil consequence.

Those who won our independence believed that the final end of the State was to make men free to develop their faculties; and that in its government the deliberative forces should prevail over the arbitrary. They valued liberty both as an end and as a means. They believed liberty to be the secret of happiness and courage to be the secret of liberty. They believed that freedom to think as you will and to speak as you think are means indispensable to the discovery and spread of political truth; that without free speech and assembly discussion would be futile; that with them, discussion affords ordinarily adequate protection against the dissemination of noxious doctrine; that the greatest menace to freedom is an inert people; that public discussion is a political duty; and that this should be a fundamental principle of the American government.[1] They recognized the risks to which all human institutions are subject. But they knew that order cannot be secured merely through fear of punishment for its infraction; that it is hazardous to discourage thought, hope and imagination; that fear breeds repression; that repression breeds hate; that hate menaces stable government; that the path of safety lies in the opportunity to discuss freely supposed grievances and proposed remedies; and that the fitting remedy for evil counsels is good ones. Believing in the power of reason as applied through public discussion, they eschewed silence coerced by law—the argument of force in its worst form. Recognizing the occasional tyrannies of governing majorities, they amended the Constitution so that free speech and assembly should be guaranteed.

Fear of serious injury cannot alone justify suppression of free speech and assembly. Men feared witches and burnt women. It is the function of speech to free men from the bondage of irrational fears. To justify suppression of free speech there must be reasonable ground to fear that serious evil will result if free speech is practiced. There must be reasonable ground to believe that the danger apprehended is imminent. There must be reasonable ground to believe that the evil to be prevented is a serious one. Every denunciation of existing law tends in some measure to increase the probability that there will be violation of it. Condonation of a breach enhances the probability. Expressions of approval add to the probability. Propagation of the criminal state of mind by teaching syndicalism increases it. Advocacy of law-breaking heightens it still further. But even advocacy of violation, however reprehensible morally, is not a justification for denying free speech where the advocacy falls short of incitement and there is nothing to indicate that the advocacy would be immediately acted on. The wide

---

1. Compare Thomas Jefferson . . . . : "If there be any among us who would wish to dissolve this union or change its republican form, let them stand undisturbed as monuments of the safety with which error of opinion may be tolerated where reason is left free to combat it." [Footnote by Justice Brandeis].

difference between advocacy and incitement, between preparation and attempt, between assembling and conspiracy, must be borne in mind. In order to support a finding of clear and present danger it must be shown either that immediate serious violence was to be expected or was advocated, or that the past conduct furnished reason to believe that such advocacy was then contemplated.

Those who won our independence by revolution were not cowards. They did not fear political change. They did not exalt order at the cost of liberty. To courageous, self-reliant men, with confidence in the power of free and fearless reasoning applied through the processes of popular government, no danger flowing from speech can be deemed clear and present, unless the incidence of the evil apprehended is so imminent that it may befall before there is opportunity for full discussion. If there be time to expose through discussion the falsehood and fallacies, to avert the evil by the processes of education, the remedy to be applied is more speech, not enforced silence. Only an emergency can justify repression. Such must be the rule if authority is to be reconciled with freedom. Such, in my opinion, is the command of the Constitution. It is therefore always open to Americans to challenge a law abridging free speech and assembly by showing that there was no emergency justifying it.

Moreover, even imminent danger cannot justify resort to prohibition of these functions essential to effective democracy, unless the evil apprehended is relatively serious. Prohibition of free speech and assembly is a measure so stringent that it would be inappropriate as the means for averting a relatively trivial harm to society. A police measure may be unconstitutional merely because the remedy, although effective as means of protection, is unduly harsh or oppressive . . . . The fact that speech is likely to result in some violence or in destruction of property is not enough to justify its suppression. There must be the probability of serious injury to the State. Among free men, the deterrents ordinarily to be applied to prevent crime are education and punishment for violations of the law, not abridgment of the rights of free speech and assembly . . . .

Whether in 1919, when Miss Whitney did the things complained of, there was in California such clear and present danger of serious evil, might have been made the important issue in the case. She might have required that the issue be determined either by the court or the jury. She claimed below that the statute as applied to her violated the Federal Constitution; but she did not claim that it was void because there was no clear and present danger of serious evil, nor did she request that the existence of these conditions of a valid measure thus restricting the rights of free speech and assembly be passed upon by the court or a jury. On the other hand, there was evidence on which the court or jury might have found that such danger existed. I am unable to assent to the suggestion in the opinion of the Court that assembling with a political party, formed to advocate the desirability of a proletarian revolution by mass action at some date necessarily far in the future, is not a right within the protection of the Fourteenth Amendment. In the present case, however, there was other testimony which tended to establish the existence of a conspiracy, on the part of members of the International Workers of the World, to commit present serious crimes; and likewise to show that such a conspiracy would be furthered by the activity of the society of which Miss Whitney was a member. Under these circumstances the judgment of the state court cannot be disturbed . . . .

Editors' Notes

(1) In Dennis v. United States (1951; reprinted below, p. 510) Chief Justice Vinson remarked in his plurality opinion: "Although no case subsequent to *Whitney* and Gitlow [v. New York (1925)] has expressly overruled the majority opinions in those cases, there can be no doubt that subsequent opinions have inclined toward the Holmes-Brandeis rationale." *Gitlow* had also applied the "bad tendency" test; in addition, however, it had held for the first time that the Fourteenth Amendment protected against state infringement on freedom of speech. See Eds.' Notes to Palko v. Connecticut (1937), above, at p. 94. In 1969, Brandenburg v. Ohio (reprinted below, p. 544), explicitly overruled *Whitney*.

(2) How accurate is Brandeis' claim that the founders were avid advocates of free speech? Not only did the Sedition Act of 1798 (1 Stat. 596) punish attempting violent overthrow of the government, it also made it a felony for any person to:

> write, print, utter, or publish or . . . cause or procure to be written, printed, uttered or published, or . . . knowingly and willingly assist or aid in writing, printing, uttering or publishing any false, scandalous and malicious writing or writings against the government of the United States, or either house of the Congress of the United States, or the President of the United States, with intent to defame the said government, or either house of the said Congress, or the said President, or to bring them, or either of them, into contempt or disrepute . . . .

And prosecutors as well as judges took a broad view of what the Act forbade. David Brown's offense was not untypical. He called the Federalists who controlled Congress and the presidency "a tyrannic association of five hundred out of five millions" who reaped "all the benefits of public property and live upon the ruins of the rest of the community." For this crime, Justice Chase— Supreme Court justices in those days "rode circuit" and presided at trials— carried out his belief that "[t]here is nothing we should dread more than the licentiousness of the press," and sentenced Brown to pay a fine of $450 and to serve 18 months in prison. See John C. Miller, *Crisis in Freedom: The Alien and Sedition Acts* (Boston: Little, Brown, 1951), pp. 114–119.

According to Leonard Levy, Madison's and Jefferson's principal constitutional reason for opposing this statute was that it interfered with state authority, not that it violated the First Amendment. Only well into the course of the debate did the Jeffersonians begin to formulate a theory of free speech and press as we would recognize them. See Levy, *Legacy of Suppression* (Cambridge: The Belknap Press of Harvard University Press, 1960), as well as his later modification of his views in "The *Legacy* Reexamined," 37 Stan.L. Rev. 767 (1985).

(3) Even conceding that Brandeis' history might be wrong, to what extent was he correct in his statement of the theory that the First Amendment necessarily implies?

(4) To what extent can one discern in Brandeis' opinion in *Whitney* the roots of ¶ 2 of *Carolene Products'* footnote and so the modern mode of reinforcing representative democracy?

" 'In each case [courts] must ask whether the gravity of "evil," discounted by its improbability, justifies such invasion of free speech as is necessary to avoid the danger.' "—Chief Justice VINSON

"It is not for us to decide how we would adjust the clash of interests which this case presents . . ."—Justice FRANKFURTER

"The First Amendment makes confidence in the common sense of our people and in their maturity of judgment the great postulate of our democracy."—Justice DOUGLAS

DENNIS v. UNITED STATES
341 U.S. 494, 71 S.Ct. 857, 95 L.Ed. 1137 (1951).

In 1949 a federal district court convicted eleven leaders of the Communist party for violating §§ 2 and 3 of the Smith Act. Sec. 2 makes it a crime "to knowingly and willfully advocate, abet, advise, or teach the duty, necessity, desirability, or propriety of overthrowing or destroying any government in the United States by force or violence, or by assassination of any officer of such government"; or, with intent to cause such overthrow, to publish or display written material advocating violent overthrow of government; or to organize or help organize a group to carry out such aims. Sec. 3 makes it a crime to attempt any of the actions specified in § 2. The Court of Appeals for the Second Circuit sustained the convictions, and Dennis et al. sought certiorari from the Supreme Court, claiming, among other things, that the Act breached the First Amendment's protection of freedom of speech and association, was so indefinite in its terms as to offend against the Fifth Amendment's requirements of due process, and that there was insufficient evidence that they had violated the statute's terms. The Court granted certiorari, but limited to whether the Smith Act abridged freedom of speech or association or was "void for vagueness."

Mr. Chief Justice **VINSON** announced the judgment of the Court and an opinion in which Mr. Justice **REED,** Mr. Justice **BURTON** and Mr. Justice **MINTON** join . . . .

II

The obvious purpose of the statute is to protect existing Government, not from change by peaceable, lawful and constitutional means, but from change by violence, revolution and terrorism. That it is within the *power* of the Congress to protect the Government of the United States from armed rebellion is a proposition which requires little discussion. Whatever theoretical merit there may be to the argument that there is a "right" to rebellion against dictatorial governments is without force where the existing structure of the government provides for peaceful and orderly change. We reject any principle of governmental helplessness in the face of preparation for revolution, which principle . . . carried to its logical conclusion must lead to anarchy . . . . The question with which we are concerned here is not whether Congress has such *power*, but whether the *means* which it has employed conflict with the First and Fifth Amendments to the Constitution.

One of the bases for the contention that the means which Congress has employed are invalid takes the form of an attack on the face of the statute on the grounds that by its terms, it prohibits academic discussion of the merits of Marxism-Leninism, that it stifles ideas and is contrary to all concepts of a free speech and a free press . . . .

The very language of the Smith Act negates the interpretation which petitioners would have us impose on that Act. It is directed at advocacy, not discussion. Thus, the trial judge properly charged the jury that they could not convict if they found that petitioners did "no more than pursue peaceful studies and discussions or teaching and advocacy in the realm of ideas." . . . Such a charge is in strict accord with the statutory language, and illustrates the meaning to be placed on those words . . . . Congress was concerned with the very kind of activity in which the evidence showed these petitioners engaged.

III . . .

No important case involving free speech was decided by this Court prior to Schenck v. United States (1919). The question the Court faced was whether the evidence was sufficient to sustain the conviction. Writing for a unanimous Court, Justice Holmes stated that the "question in every case is whether the words used are used in such circumstances and are of such a nature as to create a clear and present danger that they will bring about the substantive evils that Congress has a right to prevent." . . .

In several later cases involving convictions under the Criminal Espionage Act, the nub of the evidence the Court held sufficient to meet the "clear and present danger" test . . . was . . . : Frohwerk v. United States (1919)—publication of twelve newspaper articles attacking the war; Debs v. United States (1919)—one speech attacking United States' participation in the war; Abrams v. United States (1920)—circulation of copies of two different socialist circulars attacking the war; Schaefer v. United States (1920)—publication of a German-language newspaper with allegedly false articles, critical of capitalism and the war; Pierce v. United States (1920)—circulation of copies of a four-page pamphlet written by a clergyman, attacking the purposes of the war and United States' participation therein . . . .

The rule we deduce from these cases is that where an offense is specified by a statute in nonspeech or nonpress terms, a conviction relying upon speech or press as evidence of violation may be sustained only when the speech or publication created a "clear and present danger" of attempting or accomplishing the prohibited crime, e.g., interference with enlistment . . . .

The next important case before the Court in which free speech was the crux of the conflict was Gitlow v. New York (1925). There New York had made it a crime to "advocate . . . the necessity or propriety of overthrowing . . . the government by force . . . ." The evidence of violation of the statute was that the defendant had published a Manifesto attacking the Government and capitalism. The convictions were sustained, Justices Holmes and Brandeis dissenting. The majority refused to apply the "clear and present danger" test to the specific utterance . . . . Justices Holmes and Brandeis refused to accept this approach. [I]n Whitney v. California (1927) . . . the Court was confronted with a conviction under the California Criminal Syndicalist statute. The Court sustained the conviction, Justices Brandeis and Holmes concurring in the result. In their concurrence they repeated that even though the legislature had designated certain speech as criminal, this could not prevent the defendant from showing that there was no danger that the substantive evil would be brought about.

Although no case subsequent to *Whitney* and *Gitlow* has expressly overruled the majority opinions in those cases, there is little doubt that subsequent opinions have inclined toward the Holmes-Brandeis rationale. . . . American Communications Asso. v. Douds [1950] suggested that neither Justice Holmes nor Justice Brandeis ever envisioned that a shorthand phrase should be crystallized into a rigid rule to be applied inflexibly without regard to the circumstances of each case. Speech is not an absolute, above and beyond control by the legislature when its judgment, subject to review here, is that certain kinds of speech are so undesirable as to warrant criminal sanction. Nothing is more certain in modern society than the principle that there are no absolutes, that a name, a phrase, a standard has meaning only when associated with the considerations which gave birth to the nomenclature. . . . To those who would paralyze our Government in the face of impending threat by encasing it in a semantic strait jacket we must reply that all concepts are relative.

In this case we are squarely presented with the application of the "clear and present danger" test, and must decide what that phrase imports. We first note that many of the cases in which this Court has reversed convictions by use of this or similar tests have been based on the fact that the interest which the States was attempting to protect was itself too insubstantial to warrant restriction of speech. . . . Overthrow of the Government by force and violence is certainly a substantial enough interest for the Government to limit speech. Indeed this is the ultimate value of any society, for if a society cannot protect its very structure from armed internal attack, it must follow that no subordinate value can be protected . . . .

Obviously, the words cannot mean that before the Government may act, it must wait until the *putsch* is about to be executed, the plans have been laid and the signal is awaited. If Government is aware that a group aiming at its overthrow is attempting to indoctrinate its members and to commit them to a course whereby they will strike when the leaders feel the circumstances permit, action by the Government is required . . . . Certainly an attempt to overthrow the Government by force, even though doomed from the outset because of inadequate numbers or power of the revolutionists, is a sufficient evil for Congress to prevent. The damage which such attempts create both physically and politically to a nation makes it impossible to measure the validity in terms of the probability of success, or the immediacy of a successful attempt. In the instant case the trial judge charged the jury that they could not convict unless they found that petitioners intended to overthrow the Government "as speedily as circumstances would permit." This does not mean, and could not properly mean, that they would not strike until there was certainty of success. What was meant was that the revolutionists would strike when they thought the time was ripe. We must therefore reject the contention that success or probability of success is the criterion.

The situation with which Justices Holmes and Brandeis were concerned in *Gitlow* was a comparatively isolated event, bearing little relation in their minds to any substantial threat to the safety of the community . . . . They were not confronted with any situation comparable to the instant one—the development of an apparatus designed and dedicated to the overthrow of the Government in the context of world crisis after crisis.

Chief Judge Learned Hand, writing for the majority below, interpreted the phrase as follows: "In each case [courts] must ask whether the gravity of the 'evil,' discounted by its improbability, justifies such invasion of free speech as is necessary to avoid the danger." We adopt this statement of the rule . . . .

The formation by petitioners of such a highly organized conspiracy, with rigidly disciplined members subject to call when the leaders, these petitioners, felt that the time had come for action, coupled with the inflammable nature of world conditions, similar uprisings in other countries, and the touch-and-go nature of our relations with countries with whom petitioners were in the very least ideologically attuned, convince us that their convictions were justified on this score. And this analysis disposes of the contention that a conspiracy to advocate, as distinguished from the advocacy itself, cannot be constitutionally restrained, because it comprises only the preparation. It is the existence of the conspiracy which creates the danger . . . . If the ingredients of the reaction are present, we cannot bind the Government to wait until the catalyst is added . . . .

Affirmed.

Mr. Justice **CLARK** took no part in the consideration or decision of this case.

Mr. Justice **FRANKFURTER** concurring in affirmance of the judgment . . . .

The demands of free speech in a democratic society as well as the interest in national security are better served by candid and informed weighing of the competing interests, within the confines of the judicial process, than by announcing dogmas too inflexible for the non-Euclidian problems to be solved.

But how are competing interests to be assessed? Since they are not subject to quantitative ascertainment, the issue necessarily resolves itself into asking who is to make the adjustment?—who is to balance the relevant factors and ascertain which interest is in the circumstances to prevail? Full responsibility for the choice cannot be given to the courts. Courts are not representative bodies. They are not designed to be a good reflex of a democratic society. Their judgment is best informed, and therefore most dependable, within narrow limits. Their essential quality is detachment, founded on independence. History teaches that the independence of the judiciary is jeopardized when courts become embroiled in the passions of the day and assume primary responsibility in choosing between competing political, economic and social pressures.

Primary responsibility for adjusting the interests which compete in the situation before us of necessity belongs to the Congress . . . . We are to set aside the judgment of those whose duty it is to legislate only if there is no reasonable basis for it. Sinking Fund Cases [1879]; Mugler v. Kansas [1887]; United States v. Carolene Products [1938]. We are to determine whether a statute is sufficiently definite to meet the constitutional requirements of due process, and whether it respects the safeguards against undue concentration of authority secured by separation of power. United States v. Cohen Grocery [1921]. We must assure fairness of procedure. And, of course, the proceedings in a particular case before us must have the warrant of substantial proof. Beyond these powers we must not go . . . . Above all we must remember that this Court's power of judicial review is not "an exercise of the powers of a super-legislature." . . .

Some members of the Court—and at times a majority—have done more. They have suggested that our function in reviewing statutes restricting freedom of expression differs sharply from our normal duty in sitting in judgment on legislation. . . . It has been suggested, with the casualness of a footnote, that such legislation is not presumptively valid, see *Carolene Products* and it has been weightily reiterated that freedom of speech has a "preferred position" among constitutional safeguards. Kovacs v. Cooper [1949].

Free speech cases are not an exception to the principle that we are not legislators, that direct policy-making is not our province. How best to reconcile competing interests is the business of legislatures, and the balance they strike is a judgment not to be displaced by ours, but to be respected unless outside the pale of fair judgment . . . .

On the one hand is the interest in security. The Communist Party was not designed by these defendants as an ordinary political party . . . .

In 1947 . . . at least 60,000 members were enrolled in the Party. Evidence was introduced in this case that the membership was organized in small units, linked by an intricate chain of command, and protected by elaborate precautions designed to prevent disclosure of individual identity. There are no reliable data tracing acts of sabotage or espionage directly to these defendants. But a Canadian Royal Commission appointed in 1946 to investigate espionage reported that it was "overwhelmingly established" that "the Communist movement was the principal base within which the espionage network was recruited." The most notorious spy * in recent history was led into the service of the Soviet Union through Communist indoctrination. Evidence supports the conclusion that members of the Party seek and occupy positions of importance in political and labor organizations. Congress was not barred by the Constitution from believing that indifference to such experience would be an exercise not of freedom but of irresponsibility.

On the other hand is the interest in free speech. The right to exert all governmental powers in aid of maintaining our institutions and resisting their physical overthrow does not include intolerance of opinions and speech that cannot do harm although opposed and perhaps alien to dominant, traditional opinion. The treatment of its minorities, especially their legal position, is among the most searching tests of the level of civilization attained by a society. It is better for those who have almost unlimited power of government in their hands to err on the side of freedom. We have enjoyed so much freedom for so long that we are perhaps in danger of forgetting how much blood it cost to establish the Bill of Rights . . . .

. . . Suppressing advocates of overthrow inevitably will also silence critics who do not advocate overthrow but fear that their criticism may be so construed . . . . It is a sobering fact that in sustaining the conviction before us we can hardly escape restriction on the interchange of ideas.

. . . Freedom of expression is the well-spring of our civilization— the civilization we seek to maintain and further by recognizing the right of Congress to put some limitation upon expression. Such are the paradoxes of life . . . .

It is not for us to decide how we would adjust the clash of interests which this case presents were the primary responsibility for reconciling it ours. Congress has determined that the danger created by advocacy of overthrow justifies the ensuing restriction on freedom of speech. The determination was made after due deliberation, and the serious-

---

* **Eds.' Note:** Frankfurter was referring to Dr. Klaus Fuchs, convicted in England of giving atomic secrets to the Soviet Union in the late 1940s.

ness of the congressional purpose is attested by the volume of legislation passed to effectuate the same ends.

Can we then say that the judgment Congress exercised was denied it by the Constitution? Can we establish a constitutional doctrine which forbids the elected representatives of the people to make this choice? Can we hold that the First Amendment deprives Congress of what it deemed necessary for the Government's protection?

To make validity of legislation depend on judicial reading of events still in the womb of time—a forecast, that is, of the outcome of forces at best appreciated only with knowledge of the topmost secrets of nations—is to charge the judiciary with duties beyond its equipment . . . .

Civil liberties draw at best only limited strength from legal guaranties. Preoccupation by our people with the constitutionality, instead of with the wisdom, of legislation or of executive action is preoccupation with a false value. . . . Focusing attention on constitutionality tends to make constitutionality synonymous with wisdom. When legislation touches freedom of thought and freedom of speech, such a tendency is a formidable enemy of the free spirit. Much that should be rejected as illiberal, because repressive and envenoming, may well be not unconstitutional. The ultimate reliance for the deepest needs of civilization must be found outside their vindication in courts of law; apart from all else, judges, howsoever they may conscientiously seek to discipline themselves against it, unconsciously are too apt to be moved by the deep undercurrents of public feeling. A persistent, positive translation of the liberating faith into the feelings and thoughts and actions of men and women is the real protection against attempts to strait-jacket the human mind. Such temptations will have their way, if fear and hatred are not exorcised. The mark of a truly civilized man is confidence in the strength and security derived from the inquiring mind . . . . Without open minds there can be no open society. And if society be not open the spirit of man is mutilated and becomes enslaved . . . .

Mr. Justice **JACKSON**, concurring . . . .

This prosecution is the latest of never-ending, because never successful, quests for some legal formula that will secure an existing order against revolutionary radicalism. It requires us to reappraise, in the light of our own times and conditions, constitutional doctrines devised under other circumstances to strike a balance between authority and liberty . . . .

The highest degree of constitutional protection is due to the individual acting without conspiracy. But even an individual cannot claim that the Constitution protects him in advocating or teaching overthrow of government by force or violence. I should suppose no one would doubt that Congress has power to make such attempted overthrow a crime. But the contention is that one has the constitutional right to work up a public desire and a will to do what it is a crime to attempt. I think direct incitement by speech or writing can be made a crime, and I think there can be a conviction without also proving that the odds favored its success by 99 to 1, or some other extremely high ratio . . . .

Mr. Justice **BLACK,** dissenting . . . .

At the outset I want to emphasize what the crime involved in this case is, and what it is not. These petitioners were not charged with an attempt to overthrow the Government. They were not charged with overt acts of any kind designed to overthrow the Government. They were not even charged with saying anything or writing anything designed to overthrow the Government. The charge was that they agreed to assemble and to talk and publish certain ideas at a later date: The indictment is that they conspired to organize the Communist Party and to use speech or newspapers and other publications in the future to teach and advocate the forcible overthrow of the Government. No matter how it is worded, this is a virulent form of prior censorship of speech and press, which I believe the First Amendment forbids . . . .

So long as this Court exercises the power of judicial review . . . I cannot agree that the First Amendment permits us to sustain laws suppressing freedom of speech and press on the basis of Congress' or our own notions of mere "reasonableness." Such a doctrine waters down the First Amendment so that it amounts to little more than an admonition to Congress. The Amendment as so construed is not likely to protect any but those "safe" or orthodox views which rarely need its protection . . . .

Public opinion being what it now is, few will protest the conviction of these Communist petitioners. There is hope, however, that in calmer times, when present pressures, passions and fears subside, this or some later Court will restore the First Amendment liberties to the high preferred place where they belong in a free society.

Mr. Justice **DOUGLAS,** dissenting.

If this were a case where those who claimed protection under the First Amendment were teaching the techniques of sabotage, the assassination of the President, the filching of documents from public files, the planting of bombs, the art of street warfare, and the like, I would have no doubts. The freedom to speak is not absolute; the teaching of methods of terror and other seditious conduct should be beyond the pale along with obscenity and immorality. This case was argued as if those were the facts. . . .

So far as the present record is concerned, what petitioners did was to organize people to teach and themselves teach the Marxist-Leninist doctrine contained chiefly in four books: *Foundations of Leninism* by Stalin (1924), *The Communist Manifesto* by Marx and Engels (1848), *State and Revolution* by Lenin (1917), *History of the Communist Party of the Soviet Union* (B) (1939) . . . .

How it can be said that there is a clear and present danger that this advocacy will succeed is, therefore, a mystery. Some nations less resilient than the United States, where illiteracy is high and where democratic traditions are only budding, might have to take drastic steps and jail these men for merely speaking their creed. But in America they are miserable merchants of unwanted ideas. . . . The fact that their ideas are abhorrent does not make them powerful . . . .

The First Amendment provides that "Congress shall make no law . . . abridging the freedom of speech." The Constitution provides no exception. This does not mean, however, that the Nation need hold its hand until it is in such weakened condition that there is no time to protect itself from incitement to revolution. Seditious conduct can always be punished. But the command of the First Amendment is so clear that we should not allow Congress to call a halt to free speech except in the extreme case of peril from the speech itself. The First Amendment makes confidence in the common sense of our people and in their maturity of judgment the great postulate of our democracy. . . . The First Amendment reflects the philosophy of Jefferson "that it is time enough for the rightful purposes of civil government for its officers to interfere when principles break out into overt acts against peace and good order." The political censor has no place in our public debates . . . .

Editors' Notes

(1) **Query:** Is it possible to elaborate opposing theories of democracy from opinions on both sides of *Dennis?* What would these (opposing?) theories look like?

(2) What effects on freedom of speech and association would Jackson's views about conspiracy have?

(3) Vinson cited American Communications Assn v. Douds (1950), which had sustained the Taft-Hartley Act's requirement that labor union officials swear not only that they were not members of the Communist party but also that they did not *believe* in its doctrines. Congress repealed this section in 1959; and in 1965, reviewing an earlier conviction for perjury under the old section, the Court in effect reversed *Douds,* holding the requirement of the oath constituted a bill of attainder. United States v. Brown.

(4) For a perceptive analysis of *Dennis,* see: C. Herman Pritchett, *Civil Liberties and the Vinson Court* (Chicago: University of Chicago Press, 1954), pp. 71–79.

"The distinction between advocacy of abstract doctrine and advocacy directed at promoting unlawful action is one that has been consistently recognized in the opinions of this Court . . . ."

YATES v. UNITED STATES

354 U.S. 298, 77 S.Ct. 1064, 1 L.Ed.2d 1356 (1957).

Shortly after *Dennis,* the Department of Justice obtained indictments under the Smith Act against fourteen lower echelon leaders of the Communist party. The specific charges and evidence were quite similar to those lodged in *Dennis,* and some of the defendants had also been among the accused in that earlier case. The jury convicted, the court of appeals affirmed, and the Supreme Court granted certiorari.

Mr. Justice **HARLAN** delivered the opinion of the Court . . . .

[The first part of the opinion dealt with the meaning of the word "organize" in the Smith Act. Harlan concluded that it meant only the initial founding of a group. Thus, because the Smith Act was subject to a three-year statute of limitations, the Communist party had been "organized" in 1945 (it was disbanded during World War II), and the indictments had not been obtained until 1951, petitioners could not be tried for violating that section of the act.]

II. INSTRUCTIONS TO THE JURY

Petitioners contend that the instructions to the jury were fatally defective in that the trial court refused to charge that, in order to convict, the jury must find that the advocacy which the defendants conspired to promote was a kind calculated to "incite" persons to action for the forcible overthrow of the Government. It is argued that advocacy of forcible overthrow as mere *abstract doctrine* is within the free speech protection of the First Amendment; that the Smith Act, consistently with that constitutional provision, must be taken as proscribing only the sort of advocacy which incites to illegal *action*

. . . .

There can be no doubt from the record that in so instructing the jury the court regarded as immaterial, and intended to withdraw from the jury's consideration, any issue as to the character of the advocacy in terms of its capacity to stir listeners to forcible action . . . .

We are thus faced with the question whether the Smith Act prohibits advocacy and teaching of forcible overthrow as an abstract principle, divorced from any effort to instigate action to that end, so long as such advocacy or teaching is engaged in with evil intent. We hold that it does not.

The distinction between advocacy of abstract doctrine and advocacy directed at promoting unlawful action is one that has been consistently recognized in the opinions of this Court, beginning with Fox v. Washington [1915] and Schenck v. United States [1919]. This distinction was heavily underscored in Gitlow v. New York [1925] . . . .

We need not, however, decide the issue before us in terms of constitutional compulsion, for our first duty is to construe this statute. In doing so we should not assume that Congress chose to disregard a constitutional danger zone so clearly marked, or that it used the words "advocate" and "teach" in their ordinary dictionary meanings when they had already been construed as terms of art carrying a special and limited connotation. . . . Cf. United States v. Carolene Products [1938]. The legislative history of the Smith Act and related bills shows beyond all question that Congress was aware of the distinction between the advocacy or teaching of abstract doctrine and the advocacy or teaching of action, and that it did not intend to disregard it. The statute was aimed at the advocacy and teaching of concrete action for the forcible overthrow of the Government, and not of principles divorced from action.

The Government's reliance on this Court's decision in Dennis v. United States (1951) is misplaced. The jury instructions which were refused here were given there, and were referred to by this Court as requiring "the jury to find the facts *essential* to establish the substantive crime." . . . It is true that at one point in the late Chief Justice's opinion it is stated that the Smith Act "is directed at advocacy, not discussion," . . . but it is clear that the reference was to advocacy of action, not ideas, for in the very next sentence the opinion emphasizes that the jury was properly instructed that there could be no conviction for "advocacy in the realm of ideas." The two concurring opinions in that case likewise emphasize the distinction with which we are concerned . . . .

. . . The essence of the *Dennis* holding was that indoctrination of a group in preparation for future violent action, as well as exhortation to immediate action, by advocacy found to be directed to "action for the accomplishment" of forcible overthrow, to violence "as a rule or principle of action," and employing "language of incitement," is not constitutionally protected when the group is of sufficient size and cohesiveness, is sufficiently oriented toward action, and other circumstances are such as reasonably to justify apprehension that action will occur . . . .

In light of the foregoing we are unable to regard the District Court's charge upon this aspect of the case as adequate. The jury was never told that the Smith Act does not denounce advocacy in the sense of preaching abstractly the forcible overthrow of the Government . . . . The essential distinction is that those to whom the advocacy is addressed must be urged to *do* something, now or in the future, rather than merely to *believe* in something . . . .

III. THE EVIDENCE

The determinations already made require a reversal of these convictions. Nevertheless, in the exercise of our power . . . to "direct the entry of such appropriate judgment . . . as may be just under the circumstances," we have conceived it to be our duty to scrutinize this lengthy record with care, in order to determine whether the way should be left open for a new trial of all or some of these petitioners . . . .

. . . . [W]hen it comes to Party advocacy or teaching in the sense of a call to forcible action at some future time we cannot but regard this record as strikingly deficient. At best this voluminous record shows but a half dozen or so scattered incidents which even under the loosest standards could be deemed to show such advocacy. Most of these were not connected with any of the petitioners, or occurred many years before the period covered by the indictment. We are unable to regard this sporadic showing as sufficient to justify viewing the Communist Party as the nexus between these petitioners and the conspiracy charged. We need scarcely say that however much one may abhor even the abstract preaching of forcible overthrow of government, or believe that forcible overthrow is the ultimate purpose to which the Communist Party is dedicated, it is upon the evidence in the record that the petitioners must be judged in this case . . . .

[The Court then found the evidence too insubstantial to permit the retrial of five of the defendants and so directed an acquittal. The Court found the evidence against the other nine to be sufficiently weighty to allow the government to seek a retrial if it wished.]

Mr. Justice **BURTON,** concurring in the result.

I agree with the result reached by the Court and with the opinion of the Court except as to its interpretation of the term "organize" as used in the Smith Act . . . .

Mr. Justice **BRENNAN** and Mr. Justice **WHITTAKER** took no part in the consideration or decision of this case.

Mr. Justice **BLACK,** with whom Mr. Justice **DOUGLAS** joins, concurring in part and dissenting in part.

I

. . . . In my judgment the statutory provisions on which these prosecutions are based abridge freedom of speech, press and assembly . . . .

II

Since the Court proceeds on the assumption that the statutory provisions involved are valid, however, I feel free to express my views about the issues it considers.

First.—I agree with Part I of the Court's opinion that deals with the statutory term, "organize". . . .

Second.—I also agree with the Court insofar as it holds that the trial judge erred in instructing that persons could be punished under the Smith Act for teaching and advocating forceful overthrow as an abstract principle. But on the other hand, I cannot agree that the instruction which the Court indicates it might approve is constitutionally permissible. . . . I believe that the First Amendment forbids Congress to punish people for talking about public affairs, whether or not such discussion incites to action, legal or illegal. . . .

Third.—I also agree with the Court that [five of the] petitioners . . . should be ordered acquitted . . . I think the same action should also be taken as to the remaining nine. . . .

III

In essence, petitioners were tried upon the charge that they believe in and want to foist upon this country . . . a despicable form of authoritarian government in which voices criticizing the existing order are summarily silenced. I fear that the present type of prosecutions are more in line with the philosophy of authoritarian government than with that expressed by our First Amendment.

Doubtlessly, dictators have to stamp out causes and beliefs which they deem subversive to their evil regimes. But governmental suppression of causes and beliefs seems to me to be the very antithesis of what our Constitution stands for. . . . The First Amendment provides the only kind of security system that can preserve a free government—one that leaves the way wide open for people to favor, discuss, advocate or incite causes and doctrines however obnoxious and antagonistic such views may be to the rest of us.

Mr. Justice **CLARK** dissenting. . . .

The petitioners . . . were engaged in this conspiracy with the defendants in *Dennis.* . . .

The conspiracy includes the same group of defendants as in the Dennis case though petitioners here occupied a lower echelon in the party hierarchy. They, nevertheless, served in the same army and were engaged in the same mission. The convictions here were based upon evidence closely paralleling that adduced in *Dennis* . . . .

I would affirm the convictions. However, the Court has freed five of the convicted petitioners and ordered new trials for the remaining nine. As to the five, it says that the evidence is "clearly insufficient." I agree with the Court of Appeals, the District Court, and the jury that the evidence showed guilt beyond a reasonable doubt. . . . In any event, this Court should not acquit anyone here. In its long history I find no case in which an acquittal has been ordered by this Court solely on the *facts.* It is somewhat late to start in now usurping the function of the jury. . . .

I cannot agree that half of the indictment against the remaining nine petitioners should be quashed as barred by the statute of limitations. I agree with my Brother Burton that the Court has incorrectly interpreted the term "organize" as used in the Smith Act. . . . This construction frustrates the purpose of the Congress for the Act was passed in 1940 primarily to curb the growing strength and activity of the Party. Under such an interpretation all prosecution would have been barred at the very time of the adoption of the Act for the Party was formed in 1919. If the Congress had been concerned with the initial establishment of the Party it would not have used the words "helps or attempts," nor the phrase "group, or assembly of persons." It was concerned with the new Communist fronts, cells, schools, and other groups, as well as assemblies of persons, which were being created nearly every day under the aegis of the Party to carry on its purposes. . . . The decision today prevents for all time any prosecution of Party members under this subparagraph of the Act.

. . . I have studied the section of the opinion concerning the instructions and frankly its "artillery of words" leaves me confused as to why the majority concludes that the charge as given was insufficient. I thought that *Dennis* merely held that a charge was sufficient where it requires a finding that "the Party advocates the theory that there is a duty and necessity to overthrow the Government by force and violence . . . not as a prophetic insight or as a bit of . . . speculation, but as a program for winning adherents and as a policy to be translated into action" as soon as the circumstances permit. . . . I notice, however, that to the majority

> The essence of the *Dennis* holding was that indoctrination of a group in preparation for future violent action, as well as exhortation to immediate action, by advocacy found to be directed to "action for the accomplishment" of forcible overthrow, to violence "as a rule or principle of action," and employing "language of incitement," . . . is not constitutionally protected when the group is of sufficient size and cohesiveness, is sufficiently oriented toward action, and other circumstances are such as reasonably to justify apprehension that action will occur.

I have read this statement over and over but do not seem to grasp its meaning for I see no resemblances between it and what the respected Chief Justice wrote in *Dennis,* nor do I find any such theory in the concurring opinions. As I see it, the trial judge charged in essence all that was required under the *Dennis* opinions. . . .

Editors' Notes

(1) **Query:** To what extent does Harlan's distinction between "advocacy of abstract doctrine" and "advocacy directed at unlawful action" conform to the plain words or even general sense of the Smith Act? To what extent does that distinction make sense in the real world? Can one powerfully advocate a belief without understanding that, insofar as the argument is convincing, it will incite others to act on that belief? Would an interpreter who took seriously "reinforcing representative democracy" as an interpretive mode find that reading Harlan's distinction into the Smith Act preserved the statute's constitutionality?

(2) Note the narrowness of Harlan's opinion. He manages to encapsulate, perhaps even disguise, critical constitutional questions about protection of democratic processes within statutory interpretation.

(3) Why the shift between *Dennis* and *Yates?* Changes among the justices had some effect. John Marshall Harlan, II, had replaced Robert H. Jackson; and Earl Warren, whose chief justiceship was to become synonymous with civil liberty, had succeeded Fred Vinson. Two other members of the majority in *Dennis,* Sherman Minton and Stanley Reed, had retired, though their replacements, William J. Brennan, Jr., and Charles E. Whittaker did not sit in *Yates.* Thus only two of the six members of the majority in *Dennis,* Harold Burton and Felix Frankfurter, were still on the Court when *Yates* was decided. Both of the dissenters, Black and Douglas, were still sitting. Frankfurter switched sides, at least to the extent of joining Harlan's "constitutional interpretation as statutory interpretation." Burton also switched, though he had reservations. Tom Clark, who had been attorney general when *Dennis* began, had taken no part in that ruling, though his dissent in *Yates* indicates how he would have voted. Brennan, of course, became closely allied with the views of Warren, Douglas, and Black about the First Amendment.

There may have been other reasons for change. In 1951, the anti-Communist hysteria fanned by Richard Nixon and Joseph McCarthy was near its peak. Six years later, the mood of the country had sobered. It is unlikely that judges were unaffected by either sets of sentiments. As Justice Benjamin Cardozo once observed: "The great tides and currents which engulf the rest of men do not turn aside in their course and pass the judges by." *The Nature of the Judicial Process* (New Haven, Conn.: Yale University Press, 1921), p. 168.

(4) When the justices met in conference after *Yates* was argued, the vote was four (Reed, Burton, Minton, and Clark) to affirm the convictions, three to reverse (Warren, Black, and Douglas), and two justices (Frankfurter and Harlan) "passed." Warren suggested postponing a final vote for a few weeks. During that interval Minton retired and Frankfurter and Harlan joined Warren et al. to make the vote 5–3 to reverse. Warren assigned the task of writing the opinion of the Court to Harlan, hoping that because of his middle position he might persuade some of the dissenters to join him. By the time the decision was announced, Reed had also retired, leaving the final vote 5–2. We recite this history because it helps explain some other rulings, notably Barenblatt v. United States (1959; reprinted below, p. 525), in which Harlan and Frankfurter apparently flipflopped. The point is that they were never firm members of the liberal bloc of the Warren Court (at that time Warren, Black, and Douglas, and when Minton retired Brennan, and some years later Goldberg then Fortas and Marshall). See the analysis in Bernard Schwartz, *Super Chief* (New York: New York University Press, 1983), pp. 232–234.

(5) After *Yates,* the Department of Justice dropped all prosecutions under the Smith Act that involved charges of advocacy, did not retry any of the nine defendants not acquitted by the Supreme Court, and through March, 1986 had not again used these clauses. The reactions to *Yates* varied. Communists were delighted: "We rejoice. Victory is, indeed, sweet," *The People's World* crowed. Conservatives wept. "The boys in the Kremlin," the *Chicago Tribune* lamented, "may wonder why they need a 5th column in the United States so long as the Supreme Court is determined to be so helpful." Reaction in Congress took the form of a massive attack on the Court. For details, see C. Herman Pritchett, *Congress versus the Supreme Court* (Minneapolis: University of Minnesota Press, 1961), and Walter F. Murphy, *Congress and the Court*

(Chicago: University of Chicago Press, 1962). After several legislative battles, Congress amended the Smith Act to define "organize" to include the day-to-day operations of maintaining a group.

> **"Where First Amendment rights are asserted to bar governmental interrogation resolution of the issue always involves a balancing by the courts of the competing private and public interests at stake . . . ."—Justice HARLAN**

> **"This is closely akin to the notion that neither the First Amendment nor any other provision of the Bill of Rights should be enforced unless the Court believes it is *reasonable* to do so."—Justice BLACK**

BARENBLATT v. UNITED STATES
360 U.S. 109, 79 S.Ct. 1081, 3 L.Ed.2d 1115 (1960).

Rule XI of the House of Representatives authorized the Committee on Un-American Activities to investigate propaganda that was "un-American" or attacked the "principle of the form of government guaranteed by our Constitution." Investigating supposed communist influence in education, the committee called as a witness Lloyd Barenblatt, who had been a graduate student and teaching assistant at the University of Michigan and later an instructor at Vassar and had been identified by another witness as having been a communist while at Michigan. He refused to answer questions, claiming that the committee was abridging his rights under the First, Ninth, and Tenth Amendments, conducting a legislative trial, and subjecting him to a bill of attainder. He was cited for contempt of Congress and convicted in a district court; the court of appeals affirmed.

Meanwhile, the Supreme Court decided Watkins v. United States (1957). That decision reversed another conviction for contempt of Congress on narrow grounds: The committee had not clearly informed Watkins of the relevance of its questions to a valid legislative purpose. Warren's opinion for the Court, however, had gone out of its way to castigate congressional investigations that tried to expose and punish people for their political views. In and outside of Congress, *Watkins* was viewed as a warning that the Court was going to protect the First Amendment against congressional campaigns for political orthodoxy. And, when Barenblatt petitioned for certiorari, the Court granted the writ and remanded the case to the court of appeals for reconsideration in light of *Watkins.*

The court of appeals reaffirmed its decision and Barenblatt again sought and obtained certiorari. In the interim between *Watkins* and *Barenblatt,* another set of events occurred. Southern Democrats and conservative Republicans had joined together in a multi-pronged attack on the Supreme Court for its decisions in *Watkins,* the School Segregation Cases, *Yates,* and several other rulings that had protected alleged subversives in government as well as the rights of the criminally accused. Due to the work of a coalition of liberal Democrats and Republicans and to Lyndon Johnson's adroitness as majority leader of the Senate and his ambition to become President, all but one of the attacks failed, although several came very close to passage—close enough to constitute a warning to the Court of congressional power.

Mr. Justice **HARLAN** delivered the opinion of the Court.

Once more the Court is required to resolve the conflicting constitutional claims of congressional power and of an individual's right to resist its exercise . . . .

. . . In the present case congressional efforts to learn the extent of a nationwide, indeed world wide, problem have brought one of its investigating committees into the field of education. Of course, broadly viewed, inquiries cannot be made into the teaching that is pursued in any of our educational institutions. When academic teaching-freedom and its corollary learning-freedom, so essential to the well-being of the Nation, are claimed, this Court will always be on the alert against intrusion by Congress into this constitutionally protected domain. But this does not mean that the Congress is precluded from interrogating a witness merely because he is a teacher. An educational institution is not a constitutional sanctuary from inquiry into matters that may otherwise be within the constitutional legislative domain merely for the reason that inquiry is made of someone within its walls . . . .

Our function, at this point, is purely one of constitutional adjudication in the particular case and upon the particular record before us, not to pass judgment upon the general wisdom or efficacy of the activities of this Committee in a vexing and complicated field.

The precise constitutional issue confronting us is whether the Subcommittee's inquiry into petitioner's past or present membership in the Communist Party transgressed the provisions of the First Amendment, which of course reach and limit congressional investigations. Watkins [v. United States (1957)].

The Court's past cases establish sure guides to decision. Undeniably, the First Amendment in some circumstances protects an individual from being compelled to disclose his associational relationships. However, the protections of the First Amendment, unlike a proper claim of the privilege against self-incrimination under the Fifth Amendment, do not afford a witness the right to resist inquiry in all circumstances. Where First Amendment rights are asserted to bar governmental interrogation resolution of the issue always involves a balancing by the courts of the competing private and public interests at stake in the particular circumstances shown. These principles were recognized in the Watkins Case, where, in speaking of the First Amendment in relation to congressional inquiries, we said: "It is manifest that despite the adverse effects which follow upon compelled disclosure of private matters, not all such inquiries are barred . . . . The critical element is the existence of, and the weight to be ascribed to, the interest of the Congress in demanding disclosures from an unwilling witness." More recently in National Association for Advancement of Colored People v. State of Alabama [1958] we applied the same principles in judging state action claimed to infringe rights of association assured by the Due Process Clause of the Fourteenth Amendment, and stated that the " 'subordinating interest of the State must be compelling' " in order to overcome the individual constitutional rights at stake. See Sweezy v. New Hampshire, concur. op. [1957]. In light of these principles we now consider petitioner's First Amendment claims.

The first question is whether this investigation was related to a valid legislative purpose, for Congress may not constitutionally require an individual to disclose his political relationships or other private affairs except in relation to such a purpose. See *Watkins.*

That Congress has wide power to legislate in the field of Communist activity in this Country, and to conduct appropriate investigations in aid thereof, is hardly debatable. The existence of such power has never been questioned by this Court, and it is sufficient to say, without particularization, that Congress has enacted or considered in this field a wide range of legislative measures, not a few of which have stemmed from recommendations of the very Committee whose actions have been drawn in question here. In the last analysis this power rests on the right of self-preservation, "the ultimate value of any society." Dennis v. United States [1951]. Justification for its exercise in turn rests on the long and widely accepted view that the tenets of the Communist Party include the ultimate overthrow of the Government of the United States by force and violence, a view which has been given formal expression by the Congress.

On these premises, this Court in its constitutional adjudications has consistently refused to view the Communist Party as an ordinary political party, and has upheld federal legislation aimed at the Communist problem which in a different context would certainly have raised constitutional issues of the gravest character. On the same premises this Court has upheld under the Fourteenth Amendment state legislation requiring those occupying or seeking public office to disclaim knowing membership in any organization advocating overthrow of the Government by force and violence, which legislation none can avoid seeing was aimed at membership in the Communist Party. Similarly, in other areas, this Court has recognized the close nexus between the Communist Party and violent overthrow of government . . . . To suggest that because the Communist Party may also sponsor peaceable political reforms the constitutional issues before us should now be judged as if that Party were just an ordinary political party from the standpoint of national security, is to ask this Court to blind itself to world affairs which have determined the whole course of our national policy since the close of World War II . . . and to the vast burdens which these conditions have entailed for the entire Nation.

We think that investigatory power in this domain is not to be denied Congress solely because the field of education is involved. . . .

Nor can we accept the further contention that this investigation should not be deemed to have been in furtherance of a legislative purpose because the true objective of the Committee and of the Congress was purely "exposure." So long as Congress acts in pursuance of its constitutional power, the Judiciary lacks authority to intervene on the basis of the motives which spurred the exercise of that power. Arizona v. California [1931].

"It is, of course, true," as was said in McCray v. United States [1904], "that if there be no authority in the judiciary to restrain a lawful exercise of power by another department of the government, where a wrong motive or purpose has impelled to the exertion of the power, that abuses of a power conferred may be temporarily effectual. The remedy for this, however, lies, not in the abuse by the judicial authority of its functions, but in the people, upon whom, after all, under our institutions, reliance must be placed for the correction of abuses committed in the exercise of a lawful power."

Finally, the record is barren of other factors which in themselves might sometimes lead to the conclusion that the individual interests at stake were not subordinate to those of the state. There is no indication in this record that the Subcommittee was attempting to pillory witnesses. Nor did petitioner's appearance as a witness follow from indiscriminate dragnet procedures, lacking in probable cause for belief that he possessed information which might be helpful to the Subcommittee. And the relevancy of the questions put to him by the Subcommittee is not open to doubt.

We conclude that the balance between the individual and the governmental interests here at stake must be struck in favor of the latter, and that therefore the provisions of the First Amendment have not been offended.

We hold that petitioner's conviction for contempt of Congress discloses no infirmity, and that the judgment of the Court of Appeals must be affirmed.

Mr. Justice **BLACK,** with whom The Chief Justice **[WARREN]** and
    Mr. Justice **DOUGLAS** concur, dissenting . . . .

II

The First Amendment says in no equivocal language that Congress shall pass no law abridging freedom of speech, press, assembly or petition. The activities of this Committee, authorized by Congress, do precisely that, through exposure, obloquy and public scorn. See *Watkins* . . . . The Court does not really deny this fact but relies on a combination of three reasons for permitting the infringement: (A) The notion that despite the First Amendment's command Congress can abridge speech and association if this Court decides that the governmental interest in abridging speech is greater than an individual's interest in exercising that freedom, (B) the Government's right to "preserve itself," (C) the fact that the Committee is only after Communists or suspected Communists in this investigation.

(A) I do not agree that laws directly abridging First Amendment freedoms can be justified by a congressional or judicial balancing process. There are, of course, cases suggesting that a law which primarily regulates conduct but which might also indirectly affect speech can be upheld if the effect on speech is minor in relation to the need for control of the conduct. With these cases I agree. Typical of them are Cantwell v. Connecticut [1940] and Schneider v. Irvington [1939]. Both of these involved the right of a city to control its streets. In *Cantwell,* a man had been convicted of breach of the peace for playing a phonograph on the street. He defended on the ground that he was disseminating religious views and could not, therefore, be stopped. We upheld his defense, but in so doing we pointed out that the city did have substantial power over conduct on the streets even where this power might to some extent affect speech. A State, we said, might "by general and non-discriminatory legislation regulate the times, the places, and the manner of soliciting upon its streets, and holding meetings thereon." . . . But even such laws governing conduct, we emphasized, must be tested, though only by a balancing process, if they indirectly affect ideas. On one side of the balance, we pointed out, is the interest of the United States in seeing that its fundamental law protecting freedom of communication is not abridged; on the other the obvious interest of the State to regulate conduct within its boundaries. In *Cantwell* we held that the need to control the streets could not justify the restriction made on speech. We stressed the fact that where a man had a right to be on a street, "he had a right peacefully to impart his views to others." . . . Similar views were expressed in *Schneider,* which concerned ordinances prohibiting the distribution of handbills to prevent littering. . . . But we did not in *Schneider,* any more than in *Cantwell,* even remotely suggest that a law directly aimed at curtailing speech and political persuasion could be saved through a balancing process. Neither these cases, nor any others, can be read as allowing legislative bodies to pass laws abridging freedom of speech, press and association merely because of hostility to views peacefully expressed in a place where the speaker had a right to be. Rule XI, on its face and as here applied, since it attempts inquiry into beliefs, not action—ideas and associations, not conduct—does just that.

To apply the Court's balancing test under such circumstances is to read the First Amendment to say

> Congress shall pass no law abridging freedom of speech, press, assembly and petition, unless Congress and the Supreme Court reach the joint conclusion that on balance the interest of the Government in stifling these freedoms is greater than the interest of the people in having them exercised.

This is closely akin to the notion that neither the First Amendment nor any other provision of the Bill of Rights should be enforced unless the Court believes it is *reasonable* to do so. Not only does this violate the genius of our *written* Constitution, but it runs expressly counter to the injunction to Court and Congress made by Madison when he introduced the Bill of Rights.

> If they [the first ten amendments] are incorporated into the Constitu-
> tion, independent tribunals of justice will consider themselves in a
> peculiar manner the guardians of those rights; they will be an impene-
> trable bulwark against *every* assumption of power in the Legislative or
> Executive: they will be naturally led to resist *every* encroachment
> upon rights expressly stipulated for in the Constitution by the declara-
> tion of rights.

Unless we return to this view of our judicial function, unless we once
again accept the notion that the Bill of Rights means what it says and
that this Court must enforce that meaning, I am of the opinion that our
great charter of liberty will be more honored in the breach than in the
observance.

But even assuming what I cannot assume, that some balancing is
proper in this case, I feel that the Court after stating the test ignores it
completely.   At most it balances the right of the Government to
preserve itself, against Barenblatt's right to refrain from revealing
Communist affiliations. Such a balance, however, mistakes the factors
to be weighed. In the first place, it completely leaves out the real
interest in Barenblatt's silence, the interest of the people as a whole in
being able to join organizations, advocate causes and make political
"mistakes" without later being subjected to governmental penalties for
having dared to think for themselves. It is this right, the right to err
politically, which keeps us strong as a Nation. For no number of laws
against communism can have as much effect as the personal conviction
which comes from having heard its arguments and rejected them, or
from having once accepted its tenets and later recognized their worth-
lessness. Instead, the obloquy which results from investigations such
as this not only stifles "mistakes" but prevents all but the most
courageous from hazarding any views which might at some later time
become disfavored. This result, whose importance cannot be overestimated, is doubly crucial when it affects the universities, on which we
must largely rely for the experimentation and development of new
ideas essential to our country's welfare. It is these interests of society,
rather that Barenblatt's own right to silence, which I think the Court
should put on the balance against the demands of the Government, if
any balancing process is to be tolerated. Instead they are not mentioned, while on the other side the demands of the Government are
vastly overstated and called "self-preservation." It is admitted that
this Committee can only seek information for the purpose of suggesting
laws, and that Congress' power to make laws in the realm of speech and
association is quite limited, even on the Court's test. Its interest in
making such laws in the field of education, primarily a state function,
is clearly narrower still. Yet the Court styles this attenuated interest
self-preservation and allows it to overcome the need our country has to
let us all think, speak, and associate politically as we like and without
fear of reprisal. Such a result reduces "balancing" to a mere play on
words and is completely inconsistent with the rules this Court has
previously given for applying a "balancing test," where it is proper:
"[T]he courts should be *astute* to examine the *effect* of the challenged

legislation. Mere *legislative preferences or beliefs* . . . may well support regulation directed at other personal activities, but be insufficient to justify such as diminishes the exercise of rights so vital to the maintenance of democratic institutions." *Schneider.* (Italics supplied.)

(B) Moreover, I cannot agree with the Court's notion that First Amendment freedoms must be abridged in order to "preserve" our country. That notion rests on the unarticulated premise that this Nation's security hangs upon its power to punish people because of what they think, speak or write about, or because of those with whom they associate for political purposes. The Government, in its brief, virtually admits this position when it speaks of the "communication of unlawful ideas." I challenge this premise, and deny that ideas can be proscribed under our Constitution. I agree that despotic governments cannot exist without stifling the voice of opposition to their oppressive practices. The First Amendment means to me, however, that the only constitutional way our Government can preserve itself is to leave its people the fullest possible freedom to praise, criticize or discuss, as they see fit, all governmental policies and to suggest, if they desire, that even its most fundamental postulates are bad and should be changed; "Therein lies the security of the Republic, the very foundation of constitutional government." [De Jonge v. Oregon (1937).] . . .

(C) The Court implies, however, that the ordinary rules and requirements of the Constitution do not apply because the Committee is merely after Communists and they do not constitute a political party but only a criminal gang. . . . Of course it has always been recognized that members of the Party who, either individually or in combination, commit acts in violation of valid laws can be prosecuted. But the Party as a whole and innocent members of it could not be attainted merely because it had some illegal aims and because some of its members were lawbreakers. . . .

. . . [N]o matter how often or how quickly we repeat the claim that the Communist Party is not a political party, we cannot outlaw it, as a group, without endangering the liberty of all of us. The reason is not hard to find, for mixed among those aims of communism which are illegal are perfectly normal political and social goals. . . .

. . . History should teach us then, that in times of high emotional excitement minority parties and groups which advocate extremely unpopular social or governmental innovations will always be typed as criminal gangs and attempts will always be made to drive them out. It was knowledge of this fact, and of its great dangers, that caused the Founders of our land to enact the First Amendment as a guarantee that neither Congress nor the people would do anything to hinder or destroy the capacity of individuals and groups to seek converts and votes for any cause, however radical or unpalatable their principles might seem under the accepted notions of the time. . . .

III

Finally, I think Barenblatt's conviction violates the Constitution because the chief aim, purpose and practice of the House Un-American

Activities Committee, as disclosed by its many reports, is to try witnesses and punish them because they are or have been Communists or
because they refuse to admit or deny Communist affiliations.   The
punishment imposed is generally punishment by humiliation and public shame.   There is nothing strange or novel about this kind of
punishment.   It is in fact one of the oldest forms of governmental
punishment known to mankind; branding, the pillory, ostracism and
subjection to public hatred being but a few examples of it. . . .

   . . . [E]ven assuming that the Federal Government can compel
witnesses to testify as to Communist affiliations in order to subject
them to ridicule and social and economic retaliation, I cannot agree
that this is a legislative function.   Such publicity is clearly punishment,
and the Constitution allows only one way in which people can be
convicted and punished. . . .

   . . . [T]he Constitution proscribes *all* bills of attainder by State or
Nation . . . .   It does this because the Founders believed that
punishment was too serious a matter to be entrusted to any group other
than an independent judiciary and a jury of twelve men acting on
previously passed, unambiguous laws, with all the procedural safeguards they put in the Constitution as essential to a fair trial. . . .

Mr. Justice **BRENNAN,** dissenting. . . .

Editors' Notes

   (1) **Query**: Is *Barenblatt's* general attitude toward the First Amendment
closer to that of *Dennis* or *Yates* ?   Does *Barenblatt* accord a "preferred
position" to the First Amendment?   How can it be squared with a judicial
mission of "reinforcing representative democracy"?

   (2) See the discussion of balancing as a *technique* of constitutional
interpretation in Chapter 8, at pp. 309–312.   The person most responsible for
the resurgence of "balancing" in judicial decision making, Dean Roscoe
Pound, had warned that there were different levels of interests or rights.   At
times he had distinguished among individual, social, and public interests and at
other times only between individual and social.   Pound cautioned judges to
place whatever interests were to be balanced on the same plane, just as Black
insisted in his dissent.   "If we put one as an individual interest and the other
as a social interest," Pound wrote, "we may decide the question . . . by our
very way of putting it."   "A Survey of Social Interests," 57 *Harv.L.Rev.* 1, 2
(1943).

   (3) There were six members of the majority in *Watkins* : Warren, Black,
Douglas, Brennan, Frankfurter, and Harlan.   Clark dissented, and Burton and
Whittaker did not participate.   In *Barenblatt,* the first four dissented, while
Harlan and Frankfurter joined Clark, Whittaker, and Potter Stewart, who had
replaced Burton in 1958.   When considering the influence of the congressional
attacks during 1957–58 on the Court, it is worth recalling that Frankfurter was
the justice who spoke most often of the judiciary's duty to defer to Congress.
See, for example, his concur. op. in *Dennis,* above, p. 510.

(4) It is also important to know that Frankfurter had had serious reservations about Warren's opinion in *Watkins.* The draft that Warren had first circulated within the Court put heavy stress on the First Amendment. Frankfurter tried to rewrite that opinion. "Don't begin with First Amendment," he urged the Chief Justice. "Begin with due process and stay with it." ("Due process" here referred to the committee's obligation to inform the witness of the relevance of its questions to a valid legislative purpose.) Warren accepted most of Frankfurter's suggestions, but his final opinion still placed heavy emphasis on the First Amendment. "*Watkins,*" Frankfurter protested, "is not a First Amendment case." And he warned that legislators were apt to react angrily to *Watkins,* a prediction that proved to be a gross understatement. See Walter F. Murphy, *Congress and the Court* (Chicago: University of Chicago Press, 1962), chaps. 5–11. When Barenblatt petitioned for certiorari, asking the Court to review his conviction, Frankfurter and Harlan both voted to deny. They said they thought that the committee, unlike in *Watkins,* had informed the witness of the relevance of its questions. As senior justice in the majority, Frankfurter assigned to Harlan the task of writing the opinion of the Court, perhaps in part for the same reason that Warren had assigned Harlan that job in *Yates.* For an analysis based on papers of the justices, from which these quotations are taken, see Bernard Schwartz, *Super Chief* (New York: New York University Press, 1983), pp. 234–239, 326.

(5) It is curious, given Frankfurter's and Harlan's desire for a ruling restricted to the question of the committee's informing the witness of the relevance of its questions, that Harlan's opinion in *Barenblatt* so directly addressed the First Amendment. How can one account for that fact? What principles might justify pigeon-holing a case under one clause of the constitutional document and attempting to insulate a problem from the implications of other clauses of the document—or other aspects of the Constitution more broadly conceived?

(6) For a history of the House Un-American Activities Committee, see Robert K. Carr, *The House Un-American Activities Committee* (Ithaca, N.Y.: Cornell University Press, 1952).

"The mere fact that Agee is also engaged in criticism of the Government does not render his conduct beyond the reach of the law."

HAIG v. AGEE

453 U.S. 280, 101 S.Ct. 2766, 69 L.Ed.2d 640 (1981).

In 1974, Philip Agee, who for some years had been an agent for the CIA, announced in London he was launching a "campaign" to "fight the United States CIA wherever it is operating" and his intent "to expose CIA officers and agents and take the measures necessary to drive them out of the countries where they are operating." He then went to various countries, recruited collaborators, trained them in techniques of clandestine operations, and repeatedly identified persons whom he claimed were working for the CIA. In 1979 the Secretary of State revoked Agee's passport. Agee brought suit through an attorney (he himself remained in West Germany after having been expelled from Britain) in a federal district court to enjoin the Secretary from carrying out the revocation. He admitted the facts as alleged by the Secretary but claimed that revocation of his passport violated his rights to criticize the government and to travel freely. The district court issued the injunction and the court of appeals affirmed. The Secretary of State sought and obtained certiorari.

[Much of the discussion within the Supreme Court concerned the authority over passports that Congress had delegated to the executive. We reprint only those portions of the opinions dealing with the constitutional issues.]

Chief Justice **BURGER** delivered the opinion of the Court. . . .

III

Agee also attacks the Secretary's action on three constitutional grounds: first, that the revocation of his passport impermissibly burdens his freedom to travel; second, that the action was intended to penalize his exercise of free speech and deter his criticism of Government policies and practices; and third, that failure to accord him a prerevocation hearing violated his Fifth Amendment right to procedural due process.

In light of the express language of the passport regulations, which permits their application only in cases involving likelihood of "serious damage" to national security or foreign policy, these claims are without merit.

Revocation of a passport undeniably curtails travel, but the freedom to travel abroad with a "letter of introduction" in the form of a passport issued by the sovereign is subordinate to national security and foreign policy considerations; as such, it is subject to reasonable governmental regulation. The Court has made it plain that the *freedom* to travel outside the United States must be distinguished from the *right* to travel within the United States. This was underscored in Califano v. Aznavorian (1978):

> Aznavorian urges that the freedom of international travel is basically equivalent to the constitutional right to interstate travel recognized by this Court for over 100 years. Edwards v. California [1941]; Twining v. New Jersey [1908]; Williams v. Fears [1900]; Crandall v. Nevada [1868]; Passenger Cases [1849] (Taney, C.J., dissenting). But this Court has often pointed out the crucial difference between the freedom to travel internationally and the right of interstate travel.
>
> "The constitutional right of interstate travel is virtually unqualified. United States v. Guest (1966); Griffin v. Breckenridge (1971). By contrast the 'right' of international travel has been considered to be no more than an aspect of the 'liberty' protected by the Due Process Clause of the Fifth Amendment. As such this 'right,' the Court has held, can be regulated within the bounds of due process." [Citations omitted.] Califano v. Torres [1978].

It is "obvious and unarguable" that no governmental interest is more compelling than the security of the Nation. Aptheker v. Secretary of State [1964]. Protection of the foreign policy of the United States is a governmental interest of great importance, since foreign policy and national security considerations cannot neatly be compartmentalized.

Measures to protect the secrecy of our Government's foreign intelligence operations plainly serve these interests. Thus, in Snepp v. United States (1980), we held that "[t]he Government has a compelling interest in protecting both the secrecy of information important to our national security and the appearance of confidentiality so essential to the effective operation of our foreign intelligence service." The Court in United States v. Curtiss-Wright Export Corp. [1936] properly emphasized:

> [The President] has his confidential sources of information. He has his agents in the form of diplomatic, consular and other officials. Secrecy in respect of information gathered by them may be highly necessary, and the premature disclosure of it productive of harmful results.

Not only has Agee jeopardized the security of the United States, but he has also endangered the interests of countries other than the United States—thereby creating serious problems for American foreign relations and foreign policy. Restricting Agee's foreign travel, although perhaps not certain to prevent all of Agee's harmful activities, is the only avenue open to the Government to limit these activities.

Assuming, arguendo, that First Amendment protections reach beyond our national boundaries, Agee's First Amendment claim has no foundation. The revocation of Agee's passport rests in part on the content of his speech: specifically, his repeated disclosures of intelligence operations and names of intelligence personnel. Long ago, however, this Court recognized that "[n]o one would question but that a government might prevent actual obstruction to its recruiting service or the publication of the sailing dates of transports or the number and location of troops." Near v. Minnesota (1931), citing Z. Chafee, *Freedom of Speech* 10 (1920). Agee's disclosures, among other things, have the declared purpose of obstructing intelligence operations and the recruiting of intelligence personnel. They are clearly not protected by the Constitution. The mere fact that Agee is also engaged in criticism of the Government does not render his conduct beyond the reach of the law.

To the extent the revocation of his passport operates to inhibit Agee, "it is an inhibition of *action*," rather than of speech. Zemel [v. Rusk (1965)] (emphasis supplied). Agee is as free to criticize the United States Government as he was when he held a passport—always subject, of course, to express limits on certain rights by virtue of his contract with the Government. See *Snepp* . . . .

On this record, the Government is not required to hold a prerevocation hearing. In Cole v. Young [1956], we held that federal employees who hold "sensitive" positions "where they could bring about any discernible adverse effects on the Nation's security" may be suspended without a presuspension hearing. For the same reasons, when there is a substantial likelihood of "serious damage" to national security or foreign policy as a result of a passport holder's activities in foreign countries, the Government may take action to ensure that the holder may not exploit the sponsorship of his travels by the United States. "[W]hile the Constitution protects against invasions of individual rights, it is not a suicide pact." Kennedy v. Mendoza-Martinez (1963). The Constitution's due process guarantees call for no more than what has been accorded here: a statement of reasons and an opportunity for a prompt postrevocation hearing. . . .

Reversed and remanded.

Justice **BLACKMUN,** concurring . . . .

Justice **BRENNAN,** with whom Justice **MARSHALL** joins, dissenting . . . .

I suspect that this case is a prime example of the adage that "bad facts make bad law." Philip Agee is hardly a model representative of our Nation. And the Executive Branch has attempted to use one of the only means at its disposal, revocation of a passport, to stop respondent's damaging statements. But just as the Constitution protects both popular and unpopular speech, it likewise protects both popular and unpopular travelers. And it is important to remember that this decision applies not only to Philip Agee, whose activities could be perceived as harming the national security, but also to other citizens who may merely disagree with Government foreign policy and express their views . . . .

Editors' Notes

(1) In 1978 Frank W. Snepp, III, a former CIA agent, published *Decent Interval* (New York: Random House), a critical analysis of earlier American policy in Vietnam. He had not submitted the manuscript to the Agency for review as his contract of employment had required. On the other hand, the government conceded the book contained no classified information that had not already been published elsewhere. Six justices, without hearing oral argument or having briefs on the merits, treated the case solely as a matter of breach of contract and ordered Snepp to give the government all royalties the book earned. Snepp v. United States (1980). Stevens, joined by Brennan and Marshall, dissented. Perhaps the reason the Court missed the basic issue of free criticism of public policy was that *Snepp* came up just after publication of Bob Woodward and Scott Armstrong, *The Brethren* (New York: Simon & Schuster, 1979), which purported to be an inside history of the Burger Court and had been heavily based on gossip (some of it true) provided by young law clerks who had, without doubt, betrayed their justices' trust.

(2) CIA v. Sims (1985) held that Congress had given the CIA very broad exemption from the obligation to disclose information under the Freedom of Information Act.

II. THREATS OF VIOLENCE AGAINST INDIVIDUALS OR GROUPS

"[T]he right of free speech is not absolute at all times and under all circumstances."

CHAPLINSKY v. NEW HAMPSHIRE
315 U.S. 568, 62 S.Ct. 766, 86 L.Ed. 1031 (1942).

Walter Chaplinsky, a Jehovah's Witness, was distributing literature and talking to people on the streets of a small town in New Hampshire on a Saturday afternoon. When local citizens complained to the town marshal about Chaplinsky's calling all religion "a racket," the marshal replied that Chaplinsky had a lawful right to do what he was doing, but also warned Chaplinsky that the crowd was getting restless. Later, after an incident near a busy intersection, a traffic policeman took Chaplinsky into custody. The marshal, having heard a riot had started, came on the scene and repeated his warning to Chaplinsky. The marshal claimed that Chaplinsky then replied, "You are a God damned racketeer" and "a damned Fascist." Chaplinsky admitted using such terms, except for the name of God, but he also insisted that he had first asked the marshal for protection against those who wanted to stop him from speaking and that the marshal had then cursed him. It was only after that, Chaplinsky said, he had used the words in question.

Chaplinsky was tried and convicted under a state statute which made it a crime to "address any offensive, derisive or annoying word to any other person who is lawfully in any street or public place," or to "call him by any offensive or derisive name," or to "make any noise or exclamation in his presence and hearing with intent to deride, offend or annoy him, or to prevent him from pursuing his lawful business or occupation." The state courts sustained the conviction, and Chaplinsky appealed to the U.S. Supreme Court.

Mr. Justice **MURPHY** delivered the opinion of the Court . . . .

It is now clear that "Freedom of speech and freedom of the press, which are protected by the First Amendment from infringement by Congress, are among the fundamental personal rights and liberties which are protected by the Fourteenth Amendment from invasion by state action." Lovell v. Griffin [1938]. Freedom of worship is similarly sheltered. Cantwell v. Connecticut [1940].

Appellant assails the statute as a violation of all three freedoms, speech, press, and worship, but only an attack on the basis of free speech is warranted. The spoken, not the written, word is involved. And we cannot conceive that cursing a public officer is the exercise of religion in any sense of the term. But even if the activities of the appellant which preceded the incident could be viewed as religious in character, and therefore entitled to the protection of the Fourteenth

Amendment, they would not cloak him with immunity from the legal consequences for concomitant acts committed in violation of a valid criminal statute . . . .

Allowing the broadest scope to the language and purpose of the Fourteenth Amendment, it is well understood that the right of free speech is not absolute at all times and under all circumstances. There are certain well-defined and narrowly limited classes of speech, the prevention and punishment of which have never been thought to raise any Constitutional problem. These include the lewd and obscene, the profane, the libelous, and the insulting or "fighting" words—those which by their very utterance inflict injury or tend to incite an immediate breach of the peace. It has been well observed that such utterances are no essential part of any exposition of ideas, and are of such slight social value as a step to truth that any benefit that may be derived from them is clearly outweighed by the social interest in order and morality. "Resort to epithets or personal abuse is not in any proper sense communication of information or opinion safeguarded by the Constitution, and its punishment as a criminal act would raise no question under that instrument." *Cantwell.*

The state statute here challenged comes to us authoritatively construed by the highest court of New Hampshire . . . .

On the authority of its earlier decisions, the state court declared that the statute's purpose was to preserve the public peace, no words being "forbidden except such as have a direct tendency to cause acts of violence by the persons to whom, individually, the remark is addressed." It was further said:

> The word "offensive" is not to be defined in terms of what a particular addressee thinks. . . . The test is what men of common intelligence would understand would be words likely to cause an average addressee to fight. . . . The English language has a number of words and expressions which by general consent are "fighting words" when said without a disarming smile. . . . Such words, as ordinary men know, are likely to cause a fight. So are threatening, profane or obscene revilings. Derisive and annoying words can be taken as coming within the purview of the statute as heretofore interpreted only when they have this characteristic of plainly tending to excite the addressee to a breach of the peace. . . . The statute, as construed, does no more than prohibit the face-to-face words plainly likely to cause a breach of the peace by the addressee, words whose speaking constitute a breach of the peace by the speaker—including "classical fighting words," words in current use less "classical" but equally likely to cause violence, and other disorderly words, including profanity, obscenity and threats.

We are unable to say that the limited scope of the statute as thus construed contravenes the Constitutional right of free expression. It is a statute narrowly drawn and limited to define and punish specific conduct lying within the domain of state power, the use in a public place of words likely to cause a breach of the peace. Cf. *Cantwell;*

Thornhill v. Alabama [1940] . . . . A statute punishing verbal acts, carefully drawn so as not unduly to impair liberty of expression, is not too vague for a criminal law. Cf. Fox v. Washington [1915].

Nor can we say that the application of the statute to the facts disclosed by the record substantially or unreasonably impinges upon the privilege of free speech. Argument is unnecessary to demonstrate that the applications "damned racketeer" and "damned Fascist" are epithets likely to provoke the average person to retaliation, and thereby cause a breach of the peace . . . .

Affirmed.

"[T]he statute must be carefully drawn or be authoritatively construed to punish only unprotected speech and not be susceptible of application to protected expression."

GOODING v. WILSON

405 U.S. 518, 92 S.Ct. 1103, 31 L.Ed.2d 408 (1972).

Johnny C. Wilson, while involved in a protest against the war in Vietnam, had made such remarks to a police office as: "White son of a bitch, I'll kill you," and "You son of a bitch, I'll choke you to death." He was convicted under § 26–6303 of the Georgia Code, which made it a crime "without provocation, [to] use to or of another, and in his presence . . . opprobrious words or abusive language, tending to cause a breach of the peace . . . ." The state supreme court sustained the conviction and Wilson brought habeas corpus proceedings in a federal district court. The district judge held the statute unconstitutionally vague, the court of appeals affirmed, and Georgia appealed to the Supreme Court.

Mr. Justice **BRENNAN** delivered the opinion of the Court . . . .

Section 26–6303 punishes only spoken words. It can therefore withstand appellee's attack upon its facial constitutionality only if, as authoritatively construed by the Georgia courts, it is not susceptible of application to speech, although vulgar or offensive, that is protected by the First and Fourteenth Amendments, Cohen v. California (1971); Terminiello v. Chicago (1949). Only the Georgia courts can supply the requisite construction, since of course "we lack jurisdiction authoritatively to construe state legislation." United States v. Thirty-seven Photographs (1971). It matters not that the words appellee used might have been constitutionally prohibited under a narrowly and precisely drawn statute. At least when statutes regulate or proscribe speech and when no readily apparent construction suggests itself as a vehicle for rehabilitating the statutes in a single prosecution," Dombrowski v. Pfister (1965), the transcendent value to all society of constitutionally protected expression is deemed to justify allowing "attacks on overly broad statutes with no requirement that the person making the attack demonstrate that his own conduct could not be regulated by a statute drawn with the requisite narrow specificity," id.; see also Baggett v.

Bullit (1964); Coates v. Cincinnati (1971) (White, J., dissenting); United States v. Raines (1960); NAACP v. Button (1963). This is deemed necessary because persons whose expression is constitutionally protected may well refrain from exercising their rights for fear of criminal sanctions provided by a statute susceptible of application to protected expression . . . .

The constitutional guarantees of freedom of speech forbid the States to punish the use of words or language not within "narrowly limited classes of speech." Chaplinsky v. New Hampshire (1942). Even as to such a class, however, because "the line between speech unconditionally guaranteed and speech which may legitimately be regulated, suppressed, or punished is finely drawn," Speiser v. Randall (1958), "[i]n every case the power to regulate must be so exercised as not, in attaining a permissible end, unduly to infringe the protected freedom," Cantwell v. Connecticut (1940). In other words, the statute must be carefully drawn or be authoritatively construed to punish only unprotected speech and not be susceptible of application to protected expression. "Because First Amendment freedoms need breathing space to survive, government may regulate in the area only with narrow specificity." NAACP v. Button.

Appellant does not challenge these principles but contends that the Georgia statute is narrowly drawn to apply only to a constitutionally unprotected class of words—"fighting" words—"those which by their very utterance inflict injury or tend to incite an immediate breach of the peace." *Chaplinsky.*

[The Court then distinguished *Chaplinsky* on grounds that the New Hampshire supreme court had narrowly interpreted the statute applied there to punish only "fighting words."]

. . . . Our decisions since *Chaplinsky* have continued to recognize state power constitutionally to punish "fighting" words under carefully drawn statutes not also susceptible of application to protected expression, *Cohen*; Bachellar v. Maryland (1970); see Street v. New York (1969). We reaffirm that proposition today.

Appellant argues that the Georgia appellate courts have by construction limited the proscription of § 26–6303 to "fighting" words, as the New Hampshire Supreme Court limited the New Hampshire statute. Neither the District Court nor the Court of Appeals so read the Georgia decisions. On the contrary, the District Court expressly stated, "Thus, in the decisions brought to this Court's attention, no meaningful attempt has been made to limit or properly define these terms." The District Judge and one member of the unanimous Court of Appeals panel were Georgia practitioners before they ascended the bench. Their views of Georgia law necessarily are persuasive with us. We have, however made our own examination of the Georgia cases, both those cited and others discovered in research. That examination brings us to the conclusion, in agreement with the courts below . . . .

[The Court then detailed earlier interpretations of the statute by Georgia's courts.]

We conclude that "[t]he separation of legitimate from illegitimate speech calls for more sensitive tools than [Georgia] has supplied." *Speiser.* The most recent decision of the Georgia Supreme Court, in rejecting appellee's attack on the constitutionality of § 26–6303, stated that the statute "conveys a definite meaning as to the conduct forbidden, measured by common understanding and practice." Because earlier appellate decisions applied § 26–6303 to utterances where there was no likelihood that the person addressed would make an immediate violent response, it is clear that the standard allowing juries to determine guilt "measured by common understanding and practice" does not limit the application of § 26–6303 to "fighting" words defined by *Chaplinsky.* Rather, that broad standard effectively "licenses the jury to create its own standard in each case." Herndon v. Lowry (1937). Accordingly, we agree with the conclusion of the District Court, "[t]he fault of the statute is that it leaves wide open the standard of responsibility, so that it is easily susceptible to improper application." . . .

Affirmed.

Mr. Justice **POWELL** and Mr. Justice **REHNQUIST** took no part in the consideration or decision of this case.

Mr. Chief Justice **BURGER,** dissenting.

I fully join in Mr. Justice Blackmun's dissent against the bizarre result reached by the Court. It is not merely odd, it is nothing less than remarkable that the court can find a state statute void on its face, not because of its language—which is the traditional test—but because of the way courts of that State have applied the statute in a few isolated cases, decided as long ago as 1905 and generally long before this Court's decision in *Chaplinsky.* Even if all of those cases had been decided yesterday, they do nothing to demonstrate that the narrow language of the Georgia statute has any significant potential for sweeping application to suppress or deter important protected speech . . . .

Mr. Justice **BLACKMUN,** with whom The Chief Justice [**BURGER**] joins, dissenting.

It seems strange, indeed, that in this day a man may say to a police officer, who is attempting to restore access to a public building, "White son of a bitch, I'll kill you" and "You son of a bitch, I'll choke you to death," and say to an accompanying officer, "You son of a bitch, if you ever put your hands on me again, I'll cut you all to pieces," and yet constitutionally cannot be prosecuted and convicted under a state statute that makes it a misdemeanor to "use to or of another, and in his presence . . . opprobrious words or abusive language, tending to cause a breach of the peace. . . . " This, however, is precisely what the Court pronounces as the law today.

The Supreme Court of Georgia, when the conviction was appealed, unanimously held the other way. Surely any adult who can read—and I do not exclude this appellee-defendant from that category—should reasonably expect no other conclusion. The words of Georgia Code § 26–6303 are clear. They are also concise. They are not, in my view, overbroad or incapable of being understood. Except perhaps for the "big" word "opprobrious"—and no point is made of its bigness—any Georgia schoolboy would expect that this defendant's fighting and provocative words to the officers were covered by § 26–6303. Common sense permits no other conclusion. This is demonstrated by the fact that the appellee, and this Court, attack the statute, not as it applies to the appellee, but as it conceivably might apply to others who might utter other words.

The Court reaches its result by saying that the Georgia statute has been interpreted by the State's courts so as to be applicable in practice to otherwise constitutionally protected speech. It follows, says the Court, that the statute is overbroad and therefore is facially unconstitutional and to be struck down in its entirety . . . .

The Court would justify its conclusion by unearthing a 66-year-old decision, of the Supreme Court of Georgia, and two intermediate appellate court cases over 55 years old, broadly applying the statute in those less permissive days, and by additional reference to (a) a 1956 Georgia intermediate court decision, which, were it the first and only Georgia case, would surely not support today's decision, and (b) another intermediate appellate court decision, relating, not to § 26–6303, but to another statute.

This Court appears to have developed its overbreadth rationale in the years since these early Georgia cases. The State's statute, therefore, is condemned because the State's courts have not had an opportunity to adjust to this Court's modern theories of overbreadth . . . .

I cannot join the Court in placing weight upon the fact that Judge Smith of the United States District Court had been a Georgia practitioner and that Judge Morgan of the Court of Appeals had also practiced in that State. After all, each of these Georgia federal judges is bound by this Court's self-imposed straitjacket of the overbreadth approach . . . .

For me, *Chaplinsky*, was good law when it was decided and deserves to remain as good law now. A unanimous Court, including among its members Chief Justice Stone and Justices Black, Reed, Douglas, and Murphy, obviously thought it was good law. But I feel that by decisions such as this one and, indeed, *Cohen*, the Court, despite its protestations to the contrary, is merely paying lip service to *Chaplinsky*. As the appellee states in a footnote to his brief, "Although there is no doubt that the state can punish 'fighting words' this appears to be about all that is left of the decision in *Chaplinsky*." If this is what the overbreadth doctrine means, and if this is what it produces, it urgently needs re-examination. The Court has painted itself into a corner from which it, and the States, can extricate themselves only with difficulty.

Editors' Notes

(1) As part of the restrictions of federalism, a long line of cases has held that national courts lack authority to interpret state statutes. They are to apply those statutes either according to their plain words or as interpreted by state judges. If the plain words are ambiguous and there is no state judicial interpretation of the statute, federal judges are supposed to apply the doctrine of "equitable abstention" and retain jurisdiction of the case while allowing the litigants to seek an authoritative interpretation from state tribunals. See, for example, Harrison v. NAACP (1959) and NAACP v. Button (1963; reprinted below, p. 723).

(2) The doctrine of "overbreadth" is a negative way of saying that a statute that affects communication of ideas must be narrowly phrased (or construed by the courts) so as to have a minimal effect on speech or writing as contrasted with deeds. In effect, "overbreadth" has become a judicial test for constitutionality. Judges, as C. Herman Pritchett has put it, look at the statute "on its face," not as it has been applied in a particular case. The Court has been willing to relax the usual rule of standing that one may assert only one's own rights. "The parties and the facts in the case become almost irrelevant. The statute itself is on trial." (*Constitutional Civil Liberties* [Englewood Cliffs, N.J.: Prentice-Hall, 1984], p. 32.) This process, Justice Black pointed out in Younger v. Harris (1971), is to some extent "fundamentally at odds with the function of federal courts in our constitutional plan. The power and duty of the judiciary to declare laws unconstitutional are in the final analysis derived from its responsibility for resolving concrete disputes brought before courts for decision . . . ." The Court's rationale for this relaxation is that freedom of communication is critically important and, because of the "chilling effect" of broadly sweeping statutes, litigants are unlikely to assert their First Amendment rights so that the statutes may be properly challenged. As one would expect from *Younger* and from the dissents in *Gooding,* the doctrine of overbreadth remains controversial among the justices as well as among commentators.

For discussion see Laurence H. Tribe, *American Constitutional Law* (Mineola, N.Y.: Foundation Press, 1978), pp. 710–716; and Ernest H. Schopler, "Annotation: The Supreme Court's Views as to Overbreadth of Legislation in Connection with First Amendment Rights," 45 L.Ed.2d 725 (1976).

(3) **Query:** To what extent does the doctrine of overbreadth allow the Court to avoid difficult questions regarding the nature and reach of freedom of communication, and to what extent does it represent an effort to make concrete the implications of democratic theory for constitutional interpretation?

(4) For other cases relating to obscene language and the First Amendment, see Cohen v. California (1971; reprinted below, p. 564) and discussion in the Eds.' Notes to that ruling.

"[T]he constitutional guarantees of free speech and free press do not permit a State to forbid or proscribe advocacy of the use of force or of law violation except where such advocacy is directed to inciting or producing imminent lawless action and is likely to incite or produce such action."—The COURT

"I see no place in the regime of the First Amendment for any 'clear and present danger' test, whether strict and tight as some would make it, or free-wheeling as the Court in *Dennis* rephrased it."—Justice DOUGLAS

BRANDENBURG v. OHIO
395 U.S. 444, 89 S.Ct. 1827, 23 L.Ed.2d 430 (1969).

Ohio's Criminal Syndicalism Act makes it a crime to "advocate . . . the duty, necessity, or propriety of crime, sabotage, violence, or unlawful methods of terrorism as a means of accomplishing industrial or political reform" or to "voluntarily assemble with any society, group, or assemblage of persons to teach or advocate the doctrines of political syndicalism." Clarence Brandenburg, a leader of the Ku Klux Klan, was convicted under this statute for organizing Klan meetings and arranging for their filming and broadcasting. All of the participants were hooded, but only some were armed. Included in the speeches were such remarks as, "Personally, I believe the nigger should be returned to Africa, the Jew to Israel," and:

We're not a revengent organization, but if our President, our Congress, our Supreme Court continues to suppress the white, Caucasian race, it's possible that there might have to be some revengeance taken.

The Ohio appellate courts sustained the conviction and Brandenburg appealed to the U.S. Supreme Court.

PER CURIAM . . . .

The Ohio Criminal Syndicalism Statute was enacted in 1919. From 1917 to 1920, identical or quite similar laws were adopted by 20 States and two territories. In 1927, this Court sustained the constitutionality of California's Criminal Syndicalism Act, the text of which is quite similar to that of the laws of Ohio. Whitney v. California. The Court upheld the statute on the ground that, without more, "advocating" violent means to effect political and economic change involves such danger to the security of the State that the State may outlaw it. Cf. Fiske v. Kansas (1927). But *Whitney* has been thoroughly discredited by later decisions. See Dennis v. United States [1951]. These later decisions have fashioned the principle that the constitutional guarantees of free speech and free press do not permit a State to forbid or proscribe advocacy of the use of force or of law violation except where such advocacy is directed to inciting or producing imminent lawless action and is likely to incite or produce such action. As we said in Noto v. United States (1961), "the mere abstract teaching . . . of the moral propriety or even moral necessity for a resort to force and violence, is not the same as preparing a group for violent action and steeling it to such action." See also Herndon v. Lowry (1937); Bond v. Floyd (1966). A statute which fails to draw this distinction impermissibly intrudes upon the freedoms guaranteed by the First and Fourteenth Amendments. It sweeps within its condemnation speech which our Constitution has immunized from governmental control. Cf. Yates v. United States (1957); De Jonge v. Oregon (1937); Stromberg v. California (1931).

Measured by this test, Ohio's Criminal Syndicalism Act cannot be sustained. The Act punishes persons who "advocate or teach the duty, necessity, or propriety" of violence "as a means of accomplishing industrial or political reform"; or who publish or circulate or display any book or paper containing such advocacy; or who "justify" the commission of violent acts "with intent to exemplify, spread or advocate the propriety of the doctrines of criminal syndicalism"; or who "voluntarily assemble" with a group formed "to teach or advocate the doctrines of criminal syndicalism." Neither the indictment nor the trial judge's instructions to the jury in any way refined the statute's bald definition of the crime in terms of mere advocacy not distinguished from incitement to imminent lawless action.

. . . Such a statute falls within the condemnation of the First and Fourteenth Amendments. The contrary teaching of *Whitney* cannot be supported, and that decision is therefore overruled.

Reversed.

Mr. Justice **BLACK,** concurring.

I agree with the views expressed by Mr. Justice Douglas in his concurring opinion in this case that the "clear and present danger" doctrine should have no place in the interpretation of the First Amendment. I join the Court's opinion, which, as I understand it, simply cites Dennis v. United States (1951), but does not indicate any agreement on the Court's part with the "clear and present danger" doctrine on which Dennis purported to rely.

Mr. Justice **DOUGLAS,** concurring . . . .

. . .

The "clear and present danger" test was adumbrated by Mr. Justice Holmes in a case arising during World War I—a war "declared" by the Congress, not by the Chief Executive. The case was Schenck v. United States [1919], where the defendant was charged with attempts to cause insubordination in the military and obstruction of enlistment. The pamphlets that were distributed urged resistance to the draft, denounced conscription, and impugned the motives of those backing the war effort. The First Amendment was tendered as a defense. Mr. Justice Holmes in rejecting that defense said:

The question in every case is whether the words used are used in such circumstances and are of such a nature as to create a clear and present

danger that they will bring about the substantive evils that Congress
has a right to prevent. It is a question of proximity and degree.

Frohwerk v. United States [1919], also authored by Mr. Justice
Holmes, involved prosecution and punishment for publication of articles very critical of the war effort in World War I. *Schenck* was
referred to as a conviction for obstructing security "by words of persuasion." And the conviction in *Frohwerk* was sustained because "the
circulation of the paper was in quarters where a little breath would be
enough to kindle a flame."

Debs v. United States [1919], was the third of the trilogy of the
1918 Term. Debs was convicted of speaking in opposition to the war
where his "opposition was so expressed that its natural and intended
effect would be to obstruct recruiting."

> If that was intended and if, in all the circumstances, that would be its
> probable effect, it would not be protected by reason of its being part of
> a general program and expressions of a general and conscientious
> belief.

In the 1919 Term, the Court applied the *Schenck* doctrine to affirm
the convictions of other dissidents in World War I. Abrams v. United
States [1919] was one instance. Mr. Justice Holmes, with whom Mr.
Justice Brandeis concurred, dissented. While adhering to *Schenck*, he
did not think that on the facts a case for overriding the First Amendment had been made out:

> It is only the present danger of immediate evil or an intent to bring it
> about that warrants Congress in setting a limit to the expression of
> opinion where private rights are not concerned. Congress certainly
> cannot forbid all effort to change the mind of the country.

Another instance was Schaefer v. United States [1920], in which
Mr. Justice Brandeis, joined by Mr. Justice Holmes, dissented. A third
was Pierce v. United States [1920], in which again Mr. Justice Brandeis,
joined by Mr. Justice Holmes, dissented.

Those, then, were the World War I cases that put the gloss of
"clear and present danger" on the First Amendment. Whether the war
power—the greatest leveler of them all—is adequate to sustain that
doctrine is debatable. The dissents in *Abrams, Schaefer,* and *Pierce*
show how easily "clear and present danger" is manipulated to crush
what Brandeis called "[t]he fundamental right of free men to strive for
better conditions through new legislation and new institutions" by
argument and discourse (*Pierce*) even in time of war. Though I doubt
if the "clear and present danger" test is congenial to the First Amendment in time of a declared war, I am certain it is not reconcilable with
the First Amendment in days of peace.

The Court quite properly overrules *Whitney,* which involved advocacy of ideas which the majority of the Court deemed unsound and
dangerous.

Mr. Justice Holmes, though never formally abandoning the "clear and present danger" test, moved closer to the First Amendment ideal when he said in dissent in Gitlow v. New York [1925]:

> Every idea is an indictment. It offers itself for belief and if believed it is acted on unless some other belief outweighs it or some failure of energy stifles the movement at its birth. The only difference between the expression of an opinion and an incitement in the narrower sense is the speaker's enthusiasm for the result. Eloquence may set fire to reason. But whatever may be thought of the redundant discourse before us it had no chance of starting a present conflagration. If in the long run the beliefs expressed in proletarian dictatorship are destined to be accepted by the dominant forces of the community, the only meaning of free speech is that they should be given their chance and have their way.

We have never been faithful to the philosophy of that dissent.

The Court in Herndon v. Lowry [1937] overturned a conviction for exercising First Amendment rights to incite insurrection because of lack of evidence of incitement. In Bridges v. California [1941], we approved the "clear and present danger" test in an elaborate dictum that tightened it and confined it to a narrow category. But in *Dennis* we opened wide the door, distorting the "clear and present danger" test beyond recognition . . . .

Out of the "clear and present danger" test came other offspring. Advocacy and teaching of forcible overthrow of government as an abstract principle is immune from prosecution. Yates v. United States [1957]. But an "active" member, who has a guilty knowledge and intent of the aim to overthrow the Government by violence, Noto v. United States [1961], may be prosecuted. Scales v. United States [1961]. And the power to investigate, backed by the powerful sanction of contempt, includes the power to determine which of the two categories fits the particular witness. Barenblatt v. United States [1959]. And so the investigator roams at will through all of the beliefs of the witness, ransacking his conscience and his innermost thoughts . . . .

My own view is quite different. I see no place in the regime of the First Amendment for any "clear and present danger" test, whether strict and tight as some would make it, or free-wheeling as the Court in *Dennis* rephrased it.

When one reads the opinions closely and sees when and how the "clear and present danger" test has been applied, great misgivings are aroused. First, the threats were often loud but always puny and made serious only by judges so wedded to the status quo that critical analysis made them nervous. Second, the test was so twisted and perverted in *Dennis* as to make the trial of those teachers of Marxism an all-out political trial which was part and parcel of the cold war that has eroded substantial parts of the First Amendment.

Action is often a method of expression and within the protection of the First Amendment.

Suppose one tears up his own copy of the Constitution in eloquent protest to a decision of this Court. May he be indicted? . . .

Last Term the Court held in United States v. O'Brien [1968] that a registrant under Selective Service who burned his draft card in protest of the war in Vietnam could be prosecuted. The First Amendment was tendered as a defense and rejected, the Court saying:

> The issuance of certificates indicating the registration and eligibility classification of individuals is a legitimate and substantial administrative aid in the functioning of this system. And legislation to insure the continuing availability of issued certificates serves a legitimate and substantial purpose in the system's administration.

But O'Brien was not prosecuted for not having his draft card available when asked for by a federal agent. He was indicted, tried, and convicted for burning the card. And this Court's affirmance of that conviction was not, with all respect, consistent with the First Amendment.

The act of praying often involves body posture and movement as well as utterances. It is nonetheless protected by the Free Exercise Clause. Picketing, as we have said on numerous occasions, is "free speech plus." See Bakery Drivers Local v. Wohl (Douglas, J., concurring) [1942]; Giboney v. Empire Storage [1949]; Hughes v. Superior Court [1950]; Labor Bd. v. Fruit Packers (Black, J., concurring and Harlan, J., dissenting) [1964]; Cox v. Louisiana (op. of Black, J.) [1965]; Food Employees v. Logan Plaza (Douglas, J., concurring) [1968]. That means it can be regulated when it comes to the "plus" or "action" side of the protest. It can be regulated as to the number of pickets and the place and hours, because traffic and other community problems would otherwise suffer.

But none of these considerations are implicated in the symbolic protest of the Vietnam war in the burning of a draft card.

One's beliefs have long been thought to be sanctuaries which government could not invade. *Barenblatt* is one example of the ease with which that sanctuary can be violated. The lines drawn by the Court between the criminal act of being an "active" Communist and the innocent act of being a nominal or inactive Communist mark the difference only between deep and abiding belief and casual or uncertain belief. But I think that all matters of belief are beyond the reach of subpoenas or the probings of investigators. That is why the invasions of privacy made by investigating committees were notoriously unconstitutional. That is the deep-seated fault in the infamous loyalty-security hearings which, since 1947 when President Truman launched them, have processed 20,000,000 men and women. Those hearings were primarily concerned with one's thoughts, ideas, beliefs, and convictions. They were the most blatant violations of the First Amendment we have ever known.

The line between what is permissible and not subject to control and what may be made impermissible and subject to regulation is the line between ideas and overt acts.

The example usually given by those who would punish speech is the case of one who falsely shouts fire in a crowded theatre.

This is, however, a classic case where speech is brigaded with action. See Speiser v. Randall (Douglas, J., concurring [1958]). They are indeed inseparable and a prosecution can be launched for the overt acts actually caused. Apart from rare instances of that kind, speech is, I think, immune from prosecution. Certainly there is no constitutional line between advocacy of abstract ideas as in *Yates* and advocacy of political action as in *Scales*. The quality of advocacy turns on the depth of the conviction; and government has no power to invade that sanctuary of belief and conscience.

Editors' Query

How would a constitutionalist respond to Holmes's dissenting statement in *Gitlow*, quoted in Douglas' concurrence: "If in the long run the beliefs expressed in proletarian dictatorship are destined to be accepted by the dominant forces of the community, the only meaning of free speech is that they should be given their chance and have their way." Is constitutionalism neutral as to results? Is democratic theory quite so neutral as Holmes? Would constitutionalist theory set limits to political communication different from those of democratic theory? How?

"What is a threat must be distinguished from what is constitutionally protected speech."

WATTS v. UNITED STATES

394 U.S. 705, 89 S.Ct. 1399, 22 L.Ed.2d 664 (1969).

In 1966, as a political rally near the Washington Monument was breaking up, Robert Watts, an 18-year-old, got into a discussion with a small group. One of the other participants suggested that Watts should get some more education before expressing his views. Watts allegedly responded:

They holler at us to get an education. And now I have already received my draft classification as 1–A and I have got to report for my physical this Monday coming. I am not going. If they ever make me carry a rifle the first man I want to get my sights on is L[yndon]. B. J[ohnson] . . . . They are not going to make me kill any of my black brothers.

Watts was arrested, tried, and convicted for violating the federal statute forbidding the making of

any threat to take the life of or to inflict bodily harm upon the President of the United States, the President-elect, the Vice President, or other officer next in the order of success to the office of President of the United States, or the Vice President-elect . . . .

The court of appeals affirmed and Watts petitioned for certiorari.

PER CURIAM . . . .

Certainly the statute under which petitioner was convicted is constitutional on its face. The Nation undoubtedly has a valid, even an overwhelming, interest in protecting the safety of its Chief Executive and in allowing him to perform his duties without interference from threats of physical violence. Nevertheless, a statute such as this one, which makes criminal a form of pure speech, must be interpreted with the commands of the First Amendment clearly in mind. What is a threat must be distinguished from what is constitutionally protected speech . . . .

We do not believe that the kind of political hyperbole indulged in by petitioner fits within that statutory term. For we must interpret the language Congress chose "against the background of a profound national commitment to the principle that debate on public issues should be uninhibited, robust, and wide-open, and that it may well include vehement, caustic, and sometimes unpleasantly sharp attacks on government and public officials." New York Times Co. v. Sullivan (1964). The language of the political arena, like the language used in labor disputes, see Linn v. United Plant Guard Workers of America (1966), is often vituperative, abusive, and inexact. We agree with petitioner that his only offense here was "a kind of very crude offensive method of stating a political opposition to the President." Taken in context, and regarding the expressly conditional nature of the statement and the reaction of the listeners, we do not see how it could be interpreted otherwise . . . .

Mr. Justice **STEWART** would deny the petition for certiorari.

Mr. Justice **WHITE** dissents.

Mr. Justice **DOUGLAS** concurring . . . .

Mr. Justice **FORTAS,** with whom Mr. Justice **HARLAN** joins, dissenting.

The Court holds, without hearing, that this statute is constitutional and that it is here wrongly applied. Neither of these rulings should be made without hearing, even if we assume that they are correct . . . .

Editors' Note

For an analysis of this statute, see the annotation "Validity and Construction of Federal Statute (18 U.S.C. § 871) Punishing Threats Against the President," 22 L.Ed.2d 988 (1970).

III. SYMBOLIC SPEECH

"We cannot accept the view that an apparently limitless variety of conduct can be labeled 'speech' whenever the person engaging in the conduct intends thereby to express an idea."

UNITED STATES v. O'BRIEN

391 U.S. 367, 88 S.Ct. 1673, 20 L.Ed.2d 672 (1968).

David O'Brien and three companions, protesting against the war in Vietnam, burned their draft cards on the steps of the South Boston Courthouse before a large crowd, some of whose members began attacking the protestors. FBI agents took the protestors to safety, informed them of their rights, and arrested them for violating the 1965 amendment to the Universal Military Training and Service Act of 1948. This amendment provides criminal punishment for anyone who "knowingly destroys, [or] knowingly mutilates" a draft card. O'Brien was convicted in the district court, but the Court of Appeals for the first circuit reversed, holding the 1965 amendment violated the First Amendment. The Department of Justice sought and obtained certiorari.

Mr. Chief Justice **WARREN** delivered the opinion of the Court

. . . .

II

O'Brien first argues that the 1965 Amendment is unconstitutional as applied to him because his act of burning his registration certificate was protected "symbolic speech" within the First Amendment. His argument is that the freedom of expression which the First Amendment guarantees includes all modes of "communication of ideas by conduct," and that his conduct is within this definition because he did it in "demonstration against the war and against the draft."

We cannot accept the view that an apparently limitless variety of conduct can be labeled "speech" whenever the person engaging in the conduct intends thereby to express an idea. However, even on the assumption that the alleged communicative element in O'Brien's conduct is sufficient to bring into play the First Amendment, it does not necessarily follow that the destruction of a registration certificate is constitutionally protected activity. This Court has held that when "speech" and "nonspeech" elements are combined in the same course of conduct, a sufficiently important governmental interest in regulating the nonspeech element can justify incidental limitations on First Amendment freedoms. To characterize the quality of the governmental interest which must appear, the Court has employed a variety of descriptive terms: compelling;[1] substantial;[2] subordinating;[3] paramount;[4] cogent;[5] strong.[6] Whatever imprecision inheres in these

1. NAACP v. Button (1963); see also Sherbert v. Verner (1963). [Footnote by the Court.]

2. NAACP v. Button; NAACP v. Alabama (1958). [Footnote by the Court.]

3. Bates v. Little Rock (1960). [Footnote by the Court.]

4. Thomas v. Collins (1946); see also *Sherbert*. [Footnote by the Court.]

terms, we think it clear that a government regulation is sufficiently justified if it is within the constitutional power of the Government; if it furthers an important or substantial governmental interest; if the governmental interest is unrelated to the suppression of free expression; and if the incidental restriction on alleged First Amendment freedoms is no greater than is essential to the furtherance of that interest. We find that the 1965 Amendment to § 12(b)(3) of the Universal Military Training and Service Act meets all of these requirements, and consequently that O'Brien can be constitutionally convicted for violating it.

The constitutional power of Congress to raise and support armies and to make all laws necessary and proper to that end is broad and sweeping. Lichter v. United States (1948); Selective Draft Law Cases [1918].

The power of Congress to classify and conscript manpower for military service is "beyond question." *Lichter;* Selective Draft Law Cases. Pursuant to this power, Congress may establish a system of registration for individuals liable for training and service, and may require such individuals within reason to cooperate in the registration system. The issuance of certificates indicating the registration and eligibility classification of individuals is a legitimate and substantial administrative aid in the functioning of this system. And legislation to insure the continuing availability of issued certificates serves a legitimate and substantial purpose in the system's administration.

O'Brien . . . essentially adopts the position that such certificates are so many pieces of paper designed to notify registrants of their registration or classification, to be retained or tossed in the wastebasket according to the convenience or taste of the registrant . . . .

. . . We agree that the registration certificate contains much information of which the registrant needs no notification. This circumstance, however, does not lead to the conclusion that the certificate serves no purposes but that, like the classification certificate, it serves purposes in addition to initial notification. Many of these purposes would be defeated by the certificates' destruction or mutilation. Among these are:

1. The registration certificate serves as proof that the individual described thereon has registered for the draft . . . . [A]vailability of the certificates for such display relieves the Selective Service System of the administrative burden it would otherwise have in verifying the registration and classification of all suspected delinquents. Further, since both certificates are in the nature of "receipts" attesting that the registrant has done what the law requires, it is in the interest of the just and efficient administration of the system that they be continually available, in the event, for example, of a mix-up in the registrant's file. Additionally, in a time of national crisis, reasonable availability to each

---

5. *Bates.* [Footnote by the Court.]

6. *Sherbert.* [Footnote by the Court.]

registrant of the two small cards assures a rapid and uncomplicated means for determining his fitness for immediate induction . . . .

2. The information supplied on the certificates facilitates communication between registrants and local boards, simplifying the system and benefiting all concerned . . . .

3. Both certificates carry continual reminders that the registrant must notify his local board of any change of address, and other specified changes in his status . . . .

4. The regulatory scheme involving Selective Service certificates includes clearly valid prohibitions against the alteration, forgery, or similar deceptive misuse of certificates. The destruction or mutilation of certificates obviously increases the difficulty of detecting and tracing abuses such as these. Further, a mutilated certificate might itself be used for deceptive purposes . . . .

We think it apparent that the continuing availability to each registrant of his Selective Service certificates substantially furthers the smooth and proper functioning of the system that Congress has established to raise armies. We think it also apparent that the Nation has a vital interest in having a system for raising armies that functions with maximum efficiency and is capable of easily and quickly responding to continually changing circumstances. For these reasons, the Government has a substantial interest in assuring the continuing availability of issued Selective Service certificates.

It is equally clear that the 1965 Amendment specifically protects this substantial governmental interest. We perceive no alternative means that would more precisely and narrowly assure the continuing availability of issued Selective Service certificates than a law which prohibits their wilful mutilation or destruction. Compare Sherbert v. Verner (1963), and the cases cited therein. The 1965 Amendment prohibits such conduct and does nothing more. . . . When O'Brien deliberately rendered unavailable his registration certificate, he wilfully frustrated this governmental interest. For this noncommunicative impact of his conduct, and for nothing else, he was convicted.

The case at bar is therefore unlike one where the alleged governmental interest in regulating conduct arises in some measure because the communication allegedly integral to the conduct is itself thought to be harmful. In Stromberg v. California (1931), for example, this Court struck down a statutory phrase which punished people who expressed their "opposition to organized government" by displaying "any flag, badge, banner, or device." Since the statute there was aimed at suppressing communication it could not be sustained as a regulation of noncommunicative conduct. . . .

III

O'Brien finally argues that the 1965 Amendment is unconstitutional as enacted because what he calls the "purpose" of Congress was "to suppress freedom of speech." We reject this argument because under

settled principles the purpose of Congress, as O'Brien uses that term, is
not a basis for declaring this legislation unconstitutional.

It is a familiar principle of constitutional law that this Court will
not strike down an otherwise constitutional statute on the basis of an
alleged illicit legislative motive. As the Court long ago stated:

> The decisions of this court from the beginning lend no support
> whatever to the assumption that the judiciary may restrain the exer-
> cise of lawful power on the assumption that a wrongful purpose or
> motive has caused the power to be exerted. McCray v. United States
> (1904).

This fundamental principle of constitutional adjudication was reaffirmed and the many cases were collected by Mr. Justice Brandeis for
the Court in Arizona v. California (1931).

Inquiries into congressional motives or purposes are a hazardous
matter. When the issue is simply the interpretation of legislation, the
Court will look to statements by legislators for guidance as to the
purpose of the legislature,[7] because the benefit to sound decisionmaking in this circumstance is thought sufficient to risk the possibility
of misreading Congress' purpose. It is entirely a different matter when
we are asked to void a statute that is, under well-settled criteria,
constitutional on its face, on the basis of what fewer than a handful of
Congressmen said about it. What motivates one legislator to make a
speech about a statute is not necessarily what motivates scores of
others to enact it, and the stakes are sufficiently high for us to eschew
guesswork. We decline to void essentially on the ground that it is
unwise legislation which Congress had the undoubted power to enact
and which could be reenacted in its exact form if the same or another
legislator made a "wiser" speech about it.

O'Brien's position, and to some extent that of the court below, rest
upon a misunderstanding of Grosjean v. American Press Co. (1936), and
Gomillion v. Lightfoot (1960). These cases stand, not for the proposition that legislative motive is a proper basis for declaring a statute
unconstitutional, but that the inevitable effect of a statute on its face

---

7. The Court may make the same assumption in a very limited and well-defined class
of cases where the very nature of the constitutional question requires an inquiry into
legislative purpose. The principal class of cases is readily apparent—those in which
statutes have been challenged as bills of attainder. This Court's decisions have defined a
bill of attainder as a legislative Act which inflicts punishment on named individuals or
members of an easily ascertainable group without a judicial trial. In determining
whether a particular statute is a bill of attainder, the analysis necessarily requires an
inquiry into whether the three definitional elements—specificity in identification, punishment, and lack of a judicial trial—are contained in the statute. The inquiry into whether
the challenged statute contains the necessary element of punishment has on occasion led
the Court to examine the legislative motive in enacting the statute. See, e.g., United
States v. Lovett (1946). Two other decisions not involving a bill of attainder analysis
contain an inquiry into legislative purpose or motive of the type that O'Brien suggests we
engage in in this case. Kennedy v. Mendoza-Martinez (1963); Trop v. Dulles (1958). The
inquiry into legislative purpose or motive in *Kennedy* and *Trop,* however, was for the
same limited purpose as in the bill of attainder decisions—i.e., to determine whether the
statutes under review were punitive in nature. We face no such inquiry in this case.
. . . [Footnote by the Court.]

may render it unconstitutional. Thus, in *Grosjean* the Court, having concluded that the right of publications to be free from certain kinds of taxes was a freedom of the press protected by the First Amendment, struck down a statute which on its face did nothing other than impose just such a tax. Similarly, in *Gomillion,* the Court sustained a complaint which, if true, established that the "inevitable effect" of the redrawing of municipal boundaries was to deprive the petitioners of their right to vote for no reason other than that they were Negro. In these cases, the purpose of the legislation was irrelevant, because the inevitable effect—the "necessary scope and operation," *McCray* (1904)—abridged constitutional rights. The statute attacked in the instant case has no such inevitable unconstitutional effect, since the destruction of Selective Service certificates is in no respect inevitably or necessarily expressive. Accordingly, the statute itself is constitutional. . . .

. . . Accordingly, we vacate the judgment of the Court of Appeals and reinstate the judgment of the District Court . .   .   .

Mr. Justice **MARSHALL** took no part in the consideration or decision of these cases.

Mr. Justice **HARLAN,** concurring.

The crux of the Court's opinion, which I join, is of course its general statement that "a government regulation is sufficiently justified if it is within the constitutional power of the Government; if it furthers an important or substantial governmental interest; if the governmental interest is unrelated to the suppression of free expression; and if the incidental restriction on alleged First Amendment freedoms is no greater than is essential to the furtherance of that interest."

I wish to make explicit my understanding that this passage does not foreclose consideration of First Amendment claims in those rare instances when an "incidental" restriction upon expression, imposed by a regulation which furthers an "important or substantial" governmental interest and satisfies the Court's other criteria, in practice has the effect of entirely preventing a "speaker" from reaching a significant audience with whom he could not otherwise lawfully communicate. This is not such a case, since O'Brien manifestly could have conveyed his message in many ways other than by burning his draft card.

Mr. Justice **DOUGLAS,** dissenting.

The Court states that the constitutional power of Congress to raise and support armies is "broad and sweeping" and that Congress' power "to classify and conscript manpower for military service is 'beyond question.'" This is undoubtedly true in times when, by declaration of Congress, the Nation is in a state of war. The underlying and basic problem in this case, however, is whether conscription is permissible in the absence of a declaration of war. That question has not been briefed nor was it presented in oral argument; but it is, I submit, a question upon which the litigants and the country are entitled to a ruling. I have discussed in Holmes v. United States [1968] the nature of the legal issue and it will be seen from my dissenting opinion in that case that this Court has never ruled on the question. It is time that we made a ruling. This case should be put down for reargument and heard with Holmes v. United States and with Hart v. United States, in which the Court today denies certiorari . . . .

Editors' Notes

(1) When *O'Brien* was first discussed at conference, the justices unanimously agreed to reverse the court of appeals. Warren's first circulated draft placed much nonverbal communication outside the Constitution's protection: "[A]n act unrelated to the employment of language or other inherently expressive symbols is not speech within the First Amendment if as a matter of fact the act has an immediate and harmful impact not completely apart from any impact arising by virtue of the claimed communication itself." (Quoted in Bernard Schwartz, *Super Chief* [New York: New York University Press, 1983], p. 684; we depend on Schwartz's account for what transpired within the Court.) This approach pleased Hugo Black, but it disturbed some of the other justices, particularly Harlan and Brennan. The former circulated a concurrence critical of the Chief's draft and the latter, a close friend of Warren, tried to persuade the Chief that O'Brien had raised valid First Amendment issues, but that the government's interest in regulating such conduct was compelling, an approach like that which Brennan had taken in NAACP v. Button (1963; reprinted below, p. 723).

(2) **Query:** Given Earl Warren's avid defense of democratic theory (for instance, his opinion for the Court in Reynolds v. Sims [1964; reprinted below, p. ___]), how does one account for the approach to the First Amendment he took in his draft opinion in *O'Brien*? In his opinion as published?

(3) Street v. New York (1969) presented somewhat similar issues. On hearing of the murder of James Meredith, the black civil rights leader, Sidney Street, a young black man, burned an American flag and told a crowd, "If they did that to Meredith, we don't need an American flag." He was convicted under a state statute making it a misdemeanor "publicly [to] mutilate, deface, defile, or defy, trample upon or cast contempt upon, either by words or act," an American flag. Justice Harlan, who had dissented in Tinker v. Des Moines (1969; reprinted as the next case, p. 557), which had upheld symbolic speech by school children, wrote the opinion of the Court reversing Street's conviction because either his speech or his burning the flag or both might have provided the basis for his conviction, and his speech was constitutionally protected. Warren, Black, White and Fortas dissented. Fortas, author of the Court's opinion in *Tinker,* had initially joined the majority, but had later changed his mind. See Schwartz, *Super Chief,* pp. 732–734.

Smith v. Goguen (1974) reversed the conviction of a man who wore a small cloth version of the American flag on the seat of his jeans and held that a Massachusetts statute that punished anyone who "treats contemptuously" the American flag was "void for vagueness," that is, the statute's terms were so unclear as to give no warning about the kind of conduct outlawed.

(4) The Court has not been nearly so consistent in closing its eyes to legislative motivation as Warren's opinion would lead one to believe. See, for example, Washington v. Davis (1976), espec. the concur. op. of Stevens, criticizing the Court's use of this sort of search and Paul Brest, "Palmer v. Thompson: An Approach to the Problem of Unconstitutional Legislative Motivation," 1971 *Sup.Ct.Rev.* 95. Some commentators, most notably John Hart Ely, believe that the Court should look for legislative motivation in constitutional interpretation. See his "Legislative and Administrative Motivation in Constitutional Law," 79 *Yale L.J.* 1205 (1970), critiquing *O'Brien;* and *Democracy and Distrust* (Cambridge: Harvard University Press, 1981), espec. pp. 136–148. Ely, however, argues that "the inquiry's most important ingredient by far must be the actual terms of the law or provision in issue, read in light of its foreseeable effects and a healthy dose of common sense, and not, though it can help occasionally, its legislative history." (*Democracy and Distrust*, p. 130.)

Perhaps the root of the difficulty here lies in the failure of judges and commentators to distinguish among *motivation,* the factors working on and within a person to cause him or her to act in a particular way, *intent,* what one immediately has in mind to accomplish, and *purpose,* the larger object one tries to attain by a certain action. The first, *motivation,* probably lies beyond the competence of judges or even psychiatrists to discover in a group the size of legislature. The second and third are difficult to distinguish because in some respects *intent* may be a shorter ranged form of *purpose.* But if it is correct to assume that legislators, like reasonable people, mean to accomplish the results that logically follow from their actions, *purpose* can often be seen, as Ely says, in what a legislature does.

"[F]ree speech is not a right that is given only to be so circumscribed that it exists in principle but not in fact."

TINKER v. DES MOINES SCHOOL DISTRICT

393 U.S. 503, 89 S.Ct. 733, 21 L.Ed.2d 731 (1969).

A small group of teen-aged students in Des Moines planned to wear black armbands to classes to protest the war in Vietnam. Hearing about the plan, school principals decided to forbid wearing armbands and to suspend students who disobeyed the order. Several students defied the principals' edict and were suspended. Their families sought an injunction from a U.S. district court forbidding the principals and the school district to discipline the children for their symbolic protest. The parents lost in the district court. That decision was affirmed by an equally divided court of appeals. The parents sought and obtained certiorari from the Supreme Court.

Mr. Justice **FORTAS** delivered the opinion of the Court . . . .

I

The District Court recognized that the wearing of an armband for the purpose of expressing certain views is the type of symbolic act that is within the Free Speech Clause of the First Amendment. See West Virginia v. Barnette (1943); Stromberg v. California (1931). Cf. Thornhill v. Alabama, (1940); Edwards v. South Carolina (1963); Brown v. Louisiana (1966). As we shall discuss, the wearing of armbands in the circumstances of this case was entirely divorced from actually or potentially disruptive conduct by those participating in it. It was closely akin to "pure speech" which, we have repeatedly held, is entitled to comprehensive protection under the First Amendment. Cf. Cox v. Louisiana (1965); Adderly v. Florida (1966).

First Amendment rights, applied in light of the special characteristics of the school environment, are available to teachers and students. It can hardly be argued that either students or teachers shed their constitutional rights to freedom of speech or expression at the schoolhouse gate. This has been the unmistakable holding of this Court for almost 50 years. In Meyer v. Nebraska (1923), and Bartels v. Iowa (1923), this Court, in opinions by Mr. Justice McReynolds, held that the Due Process Clause of the Fourteenth Amendment prevents States from forbidding the teaching of a foreign language to young students. Statutes to this effect, the Court held, unconstitutionally interfere with the liberty of teacher, student, and parent. See also Pierce v. Society of Sisters (1925); *Barnette*; Wieman v. Updegraff (1952) (concurring opinion); Sweezy v. New Hampshire (1957); Shelton v. Tucker (1960); Keyishian v. Board of Regents (1967); Epperson v. Arkansas (1968).

In *Barnette*, this Court held that under the First Amendment, the student in public school may not be compelled to salute the flag. Speaking through Mr. Justice Jackson, the Court said:

> The Fourteenth Amendment . . . protects the citizen against the State itself and all of its creatures—Boards of Education not excepted. These have, of course, important, delicate, and highly discretionary functions, but none that they may not perform within the limits of the Bill of Rights. That they are educating the young for citizenship is reason for scrupulous protection of Constitutional freedoms of the individual, if we are not to strangle the free mind at its source and teach youth to discount important principles of our government as mere platitudes.

On the other hand, the Court has repeatedly emphasized the need for affirming the comprehensive authority of the States and of school officials, consistent with fundamental constitutional safeguards, to prescribe and control conduct in the schools. See *Epperson, Meyer.* Our problem lies in the area where students in the exercise of First Amendment rights collide with the rules of the school authorities.

II

The problem posed by the present case does not relate to regulation of the length of skirts or the type of clothing, to hair style, or deportment. It does not concern aggressive, disruptive action or even group demonstrations. Our problem involves direct, primary First Amendment rights akin to "pure speech."

The school officials banned and sought to punish petitioners for a silent, passive expression of opinion, unaccompanied by any disorder or disturbance on the part of petitioners. There is here no evidence whatever of petitioners' interference, actual or nascent, with the schools' work or of collision with the rights of other students to be secure and to be let alone. Accordingly, this case does not concern speech or action that intrudes upon the work of the schools or the rights of other students . . . .

The District Court concluded that the action of the school authorities was reasonable because it was based upon their fear of a disturbance from the wearing of the armbands. But, in our system, undifferentiated fear or apprehension of disturbance is not enough to overcome the right to freedom of expression. Any departure from absolute regimentation may cause trouble. Any variation from the majority's opinion may inspire fear. Any word spoken, in class, in the lunchroom, or on the campus, that deviates from the views of another person may start an argument or cause a disturbance. But our Constitution says we must take this risk, Terminiello v. Chicago (1949); and our history says that it is this sort of hazardous freedom—this kind of openness—that is the basis of our national strength and of the independence and vigor of Americans who grow up and live in this relatively permissive, often disputatious, society.

In order for the State in the person of school officials to justify prohibition of a particular expression of opinion, it must be able to show that its action was caused by something more than a mere desire to avoid the discomfort and unpleasantness that always accompany an unpopular viewpoint. Certainly where there is no finding and no showing that engaging in the forbidden conduct would "materially and substantially interfere with the requirements of appropriate discipline in the operation of the school," the prohibition cannot be sustained.

In the present case, the District Court made no such finding, and our independent examination of the record fails to yield evidence that the school authorities had reason to anticipate that the wearing of the armbands would substantially interfere with the work of the school or impinge upon the rights of other students. . . .

On the contrary, the action of the school authorities appears to have been based upon an urgent wish to avoid the controversy which might result from the expression, even by the silent symbol of armbands, of opposition to this Nation's part in the conflagration in Vietnam. . . .

It is also relevant that the school authorities did not purport to prohibit the wearing of all symbols of political or controversial significance. The record shows that students in some of the schools wore buttons relating to national political campaigns, and some even wore the Iron Cross, traditionally a symbol of Nazism. The order prohibiting the wearing of armbands did not extend to these. Instead, a particular symbol—black armbands worn to exhibit opposition to this Nation's involvement in Vietnam—was singled out for prohibition. Clearly, the prohibition of expression of one particular opinion, at least without evidence that it is necessary to avoid material and substantial interference with schoolwork or discipline, is not constitutionally permissible.

In our system, state-operated schools may not be enclaves of totalitarianism. School officials do not possess absolute authority over their students. Students in school as well as out of school are "persons" under our Constitution. They are possessed of fundamental rights which the State must respect, just as they themselves must respect their obligations to the State. . . .

Under our Constitution, free speech is not a right that is given only to be so circumscribed that it exists in principle but not in fact. Freedom of expression would not truly exist if the right could be exercised only in an area that a benevolent government has provided as a safe haven for crackpots. The Constitution says that Congress (and the States) may not abridge the right to free speech. This provision means what it says. . . .

Reversed and remanded.

Mr. Justice **STEWART,** concurring . . . .

Mr. Justice **WHITE,** concurring.

While I join the Court's opinion, I deem it appropriate to note . . . that the Court continues to recognize a distinction between communicating by words and communicating by acts or conduct which sufficiently impinges on some valid state interest . . . .

Mr. Justice **BLACK,** dissenting . . . .

. . . First, the Court concludes that the wearing of armbands is "symbolic speech" which is "akin to 'pure speech'" and therefore protected by the First and Fourteenth Amendments. Secondly, the Court decides that the public schools are an appropriate place to exercise "symbolic speech" as long as normal school functions are not "unreasonably" disrupted. Finally, the Court arrogates to itself, rather than to the State's elected officials charged with running the schools, the decision as to which school disciplinary regulations are "reasonable."

Assuming that the Court is correct in holding that the conduct of wearing armbands for the purpose of conveying political ideas is protected by the First Amendment, cf., e.g., Giboney v. Empire Storage (1949), the crucial remaining questions are whether students and teachers may use the schools at their whim as a platform for the exercise of free speech—"symbolic" or "pure"—and whether the courts will allocate to themselves the function of deciding how the pupils' school day will be spent. While I have always believed that under the First and Fourteenth Amendments neither the State nor the Federal Government has any authority to regulate or censor the content of speech, I have never believed that any person has a right to give speeches or engage in demonstrations where he pleases and when he pleases. This Court has already rejected such a notion. In Cox v. Louisiana (1965), for example, the Court clearly stated that the rights of free speech and assembly "do not mean that everyone with opinions or beliefs to express may address a group at any public place and at any time."

While the record does not show that any of these armband students shouted, used profane language, or were violent in any manner, detailed testimony by some of them shows their armbands caused comments, warnings by other students, the poking of fun at them, and a warning by an older football player that other, nonprotesting students had better let them alone. There is also evidence that a teacher of mathematics had his lesson period practically "wrecked" chiefly by disputes with Mary Beth Tinker, who wore her armband for her "demonstration."

Even a casual reading of the record shows that this armband did divert students' minds from their regular lessons, and that talk, comments, etc., made John Tinker "self-conscious" in attending school with his armband. . . . [T]he armbands did exactly what the elected school officials and principals foresaw they would, that is, took the students' minds off their classwork and diverted them to thoughts about the highly emotional subject of the Vietnam war. . . .

The United States District Court refused to hold that the state school order violated the First and Fourteenth Amendments. Holding that the protest was akin to speech, which is protected by the First and Fourteenth Amendments, that court held that the school order was "reasonable" and hence constitutional. . . . Two cases upon which the Court today heavily relies for striking down this school order used this test of reasonableness, Meyer v. Nebraska (1923), and Bartels v. Iowa (1923) . . . . This constitutional test of reasonableness prevailed in this Court for a season. It was this test that brought on President Franklin Roosevelt's well-known Court fight. His proposed legislation did not pass, but the fight left the "reasonableness" constitutional test dead on the battlefield, so much so that this Court in Ferguson v. Skrupa, after a thorough review of the old cases, was able to conclude in 1963:

> There was a time when the Due Process Clause was used by this Court to strike down laws which were thought unreasonable, that is, unwise or incompatible with some particular economic or social philosophy.
>
>   . . .
>
> The doctrine that prevailed in *Lochner, Coppage, Adkins, Burns,* and like cases—that due process authorizes courts to hold laws unconstitutional when they believe the legislature has acted unwisely—has long since been discarded.

The *Ferguson* case totally repudiated the old reasonableness-due process test, the doctrine that judges have the power to hold laws unconstitutional upon the belief of judges that they "shock the conscience" or that they are "unreasonable," "arbitrary," "irrational," "contrary to fundamental 'decency,'" or some other such flexible term without precise boundaries. I have many times expressed my opposition to that concept on the ground that it gives judges power to strike down any law they do not like. If the majority of the Court today, by agreeing to the opinion of my Brother Fortas, is resurrecting that old reasonableness-due process test, I think the constitutional change should be plainly, unequivocally, and forthrightly stated for the benefit of the bench and bar . . . . Other cases cited by the Court do not, as implied, follow the McReynolds reasonableness doctrine. West Virginia v. Barnette, clearly reject[ed] the "reasonableness" test . . . . Neither Thornhill v. Alabama; Stromberg v. California; Edwards v. South Carolina; nor Brown v. Louisiana related to schoolchildren at all, and none of these cases embraced Mr. Justice McReynolds' reasonableness test; and *Thornhill, Edwards,* and *Brown* relied on the vagueness of state statutes under scrutiny to hold them unconstitutional. . . .

I deny, therefore, that it has been the "unmistakable holding of this Court for almost 50 years" that "students" and "teachers" take with them into the "schoolhouse gate" constitutional rights to "freedom of speech or expression." Even *Meyer* did not hold that. . . . The truth is that a teacher of kindergarten, grammar school, or high school pupils no more carries into a school with him a complete right to freedom of speech and expression than an anti-Catholic or anti-Semite carries with him a complete freedom of speech and religion into a Catholic church or Jewish synagogue. Nor does a person carry with him into the United States Senate or House, or into the Supreme Court, or any other court, a complete constitutional right to go into those places contrary to their rules and speak his mind on any subject he pleases. It is a myth to say that any person has a constitutional right to say what he pleases, where he pleases, and when he pleases. Our Court has decided precisely the opposite. See, e.g., Cox v. Louisiana . . . . .

. . . This case, therefore, wholly without constitutional reasons in my judgment, subjects all the public schools in the country to the whims and caprices of their loudest-mouthed, but maybe not their brightest, students. I, for one, am not fully persuaded that school pupils are wise enough, even with this Court's expert help from Washington, to run the 23,390 public school systems in our 50 States. I wish, therefore, wholly to disclaim any purpose on my part to hold that the Federal Constitution compels the teachers, parents, and elected school officials to surrender control of the American public school system to public school students. I dissent.

Mr. Justice **HARLAN**, dissenting.

I certainly agree that state public school authorities in the discharge of their responsibilities are not wholly exempt from the requirements of the Fourteenth Amendment respecting the freedoms of expression and association. At the same time I am reluctant to believe that there is any disagreement between the majority and myself on the proposition that school officials should be accorded the widest authority in maintaining discipline and good order in their institutions. To translate that proposition into a workable constitutional rule, I would, in cases like this, cast upon those complaining the burden of showing that a particular school measure was motivated by other than legitimate school concerns—for example, a desire to prohibit the expression of an unpopular point of view, while permitting expression of the dominant opinion.

Finding nothing in this record which impugns the good faith of respondents in promulgating the armband regulation, I would affirm the judgment below.

Editors' Notes

Clark v. Community for Creative Non-Violence (1984) sustained a District of Columbia ordinance that banned sleeping in public parks. A group advocating increased public assistance for the homeless had claimed they were exercising their rights to engage in symbolic speech by camping out in parks around the White House. For the majority, Justice White wrote that, even if sleeping in a park overnight was "expressive conduct to some extent protected by the First Amendment," it was subject to reasonable governmental regulation. He then applied the rule of Cantwell v. Connecticut (1940; reprinted below, p. 1014) that government could regulate "the time, place, and manner" of public demonstrations as long as its administration was neutral as to content of the message the demonstrators wished to convey. Here, White found, regulation "narrowly focuses on the Government's substantial interest in maintaining the parks in the heart of our capital in an attractive and intact condition, readily available to the millions of people who wish to see and enjoy them."

"The constitutional right of free expression . . . is designed and intended to remove governmental restraints from the arena of public discussion, putting the decision as to what views shall be voiced largely in the hands of each of us, in the hope that use of such freedom will ultimately produce a more capable citizenry and more perfect polity and in the belief that no other approach would comport with the premise of individual dignity and choice upon which our political system rests."

COHEN v. CALIFORNIA
403 U.S. 15, 91 S.Ct. 1780, 29 L.Ed.2d 284 (1971).

Paul Robert Cohen was sentenced to 30 days imprisonment for violating a state law against disturbing "the peace or quiet of any neighborhood or person." To protest the draft and the war in Vietnam, he had gone to a state courthouse, wearing a jacket bearing the slogan, "Fuck the draft." There was no evidence that he had spoken any words in the courthouse prior to his arrest. An appellate court sustained the conviction, the California supreme court refused review, and Cohen appealed to the U.S. Supreme Court.

Mr. Justice **HARLAN** delivered the opinion of the Court.

This case may seem at first blush too inconsequential to find its way into our books, but the issue it presents is of no small constitutional significance . . . .

I . . .

The conviction quite clearly rests upon the asserted offensiveness of the *words* Cohen used to convey his message to the public. The only "conduct" which the State sought to punish is the fact of communication. Thus, we deal here with a conviction resting solely upon "speech," not upon any separately identifiable conduct which allegedly was intended by Cohen to be perceived by others as expressive of particular views but which, on its face, does not necessarily convey any message and hence arguably could be regulated without effectively repressing Cohen's ability to express himself. Cf. United States v. O'Brien (1968). Further, the State certainly lacks power to punish Cohen for the underlying content of the message the inscription conveyed. At least so long as there is no showing of an intent to incite disobedience to or disruption of the draft, Cohen could not, consistently with the First and Fourteenth Amendments, be punished for asserting the evident position on the inutility or immorality of the draft his jacket reflected. Yates v. United States (1957).

Appellant's conviction, then, rests squarely upon his exercise of the "freedom of speech" protected from arbitrary governmental interference by the Constitution and can be justified, if at all, only as a valid regulation of the manner in which he exercised that freedom, not as a permissible prohibition on the substantive message it conveys. This does not end the inquiry, of course, for the First and Fourteenth Amendments have never been thought to give absolute protection to every individual to speak whenever or wherever he pleases, or to use any form of address in any circumstances that he chooses. In this vein, too, however, we think it important to note that several issues typically associated with such problems are not presented here.

In the first place, Cohen was tried under a statute applicable throughout the entire State. Any attempt to support this conviction on the ground that the statute seeks to preserve an appropriately decorous atmosphere in the courthouse where Cohen was arrested must fail in the absence of any language in the statute that would have put appellant on notice that certain kinds of otherwise permissible speech or conduct would nevertheless, under California law, not be tolerated in certain places . . . .

In the second place . . . this case cannot be said to fall within those relatively few categories of instances where prior decisions have established the power of government to deal more comprehensively with certain forms of individual expression simply upon a showing that such a form was employed. This is not, for example, an obscenity case. Whatever else may be necessary to give rise to the States' broader power to prohibit obscene expression, such expression must be, in some significant way, erotic. Roth v. United States (1957). It cannot plausibly be maintained that this vulgar allusion to the Selective Service System would conjure up such psychic stimulation in anyone likely to be confronted with Cohen's crudely defaced jacket.

This Court has also held that the States are free to ban the simple use, without a demonstration of additional justifying circumstances, of so-called "fighting words," those personally abusive epithets which, when addressed to the ordinary citizen, are, as a matter of common knowledge, inherently likely to provoke violent reaction. Chaplinsky v. New Hampshire (1942). While the four-letter word displayed by Cohen in relation to the draft is not uncommonly employed in a personally provocative fashion, in this instance it was clearly not "directed to the person of the hearer." Cantwell v. Connecticut (1940). No individual actually or likely to be present could reasonably have regarded the words on appellant's jacket as a direct personal insult. Nor do we have here an instance of the exercise of the State's police power to prevent a speaker from intentionally provoking a given group to hostile reaction. Cf. Feiner v. New York (1951). There is . . . no showing that anyone who saw Cohen was in fact violently aroused or that appellant intended such a result.

Finally . . . much has been made of the claim that Cohen's distasteful mode of expression was thrust upon unwilling or unsuspecting viewers, and that the State might therefore legitimately act as it did in order to protect the sensitive from otherwise unavoidable exposure to appellant's crude form of protest. Of course, the mere presumed presence of unwitting listeners or viewers does not serve automatically to justify curtailing all speech capable of giving offense. While this Court has recognized that government may properly act in many situations to prohibit intrusion into the privacy of the home of unwelcome views and ideas which cannot be totally banned from the public dialogue, e.g., Rowan v. Post Office Dept. (1970), we have at the same time consistently stressed that "we are often 'captives' outside the sanctuary of the home and subject to objectionable speech." Ibid. The ability of government, consonant with the Constitution, to shut off discourse solely to protect others from hearing it is, in other words, dependent upon a showing that substantial privacy interests are being invaded in an essentially intolerable manner. Any broader view of this authority would effectively empower a majority to silence dissidents simply as a matter of personal predilections.

In this regard, persons confronted with Cohen's jacket were in a quite different posture than, say, those subjected to the raucous emissions of sound trucks blaring outside their residences. Those in the Los Angeles courthouse could effectively avoid further bombardment of their sensibilities simply by averting their eyes. And, while it may be that one has a more substantial claim to a recognizable privacy interest when walking through a courthouse corridor than, for example, strolling through Central Park, surely it is nothing like the interest in being free from unwanted expression in the confines of one's own home . . . . .

II

Against this background, the issue flushed by this case stands out in bold relief. It is whether California can excise, as "offensive conduct," one particular scurrilous epithet from the public discourse, either upon the theory of the court below that its use is inherently likely to cause violent reaction or upon a more general assertion that the States, acting as guardians of public morality, may properly remove this offensive word from the public vocabulary.

The rationale of the California court is plainly untenable. At most it reflects an "undifferentiated fear or apprehension of disturbance [which] is not enough to overcome the right to freedom of expression." Tinker v. Des Moines Indep. Community School Dist. (1969). We have been shown no evidence that substantial numbers of citizens are standing ready to strike out physically at whoever may assault their sensibilities with execrations like that uttered by Cohen. There may be some persons about with such lawless and violent proclivities, but that is an insufficient base upon which to erect, consistently with constitutional values, a governmental power to force persons who wish to ventilate their dissident views into avoiding particular forms of expression. The argument amounts to little more than the self-defeating proposition that to avoid physical censorship of one who has not sought to provoke such a response by a hypothetical coterie of the violent and lawless, the States may more appropriately effectuate that censorship themselves.

Admittedly, it is not so obvious that the First and Fourteenth Amendments must be taken to disable the States from punishing public utterance of this unseemly expletive in order to maintain what they regard as a suitable level of discourse within the body politic. We think, however, that examination and reflection will reveal the short-comings of a contrary viewpoint.

. . . [W]e cannot overemphasize that, in our judgment, most situations where the State has a justifiable interest in regulating speech will fall within one or more of the various established exceptions, discussed above but not applicable here, to the usual rule that governmental bodies may not prescribe the form or content of individual expression. Equally important to our conclusion is the constitutional backdrop against which our decision must be made. The constitutional right of free expression is powerful medicine in a society as diverse and populous as ours. It is designed and intended to remove governmental restraints from the arena of public discussion, putting the decision as to what views shall be voiced largely into the hands of each of us, in the hope that use of such freedom will ultimately produce a more capable citizenry and more perfect polity and in the belief that no other approach would comport with the premise of individual dignity and choice upon which our political system rests. See Whitney v. California (1927) (Brandeis, J., concurring).

To many, the immediate consequence of this freedom may often appear to be only verbal tumult, discord, and even offensive utterance. These are, however, within established limits, in truth necessary side effects of the broader enduring values which the process of open debate permits us to achieve. That the air may at times seem filled with verbal cacophony is, in this sense not a sign of weakness but of strength. We cannot lose sight of the fact that, in what otherwise might seem a trifling and annoying instance of individual distasteful abuse of a privilege, these fundamental societal values are truly implicated. That is why "[w]holly neutral futilities . . . come under the protection of free speech as fully as do Keats' poems or Donne's sermons," Winters v. New York (1948) (Frankfurter, J., dissenting), and why "so long as the means are peaceful, the communication need not meet standards of acceptability," Organization for a Better Austin v. Keefe (1971).

Against this perception of the constitutional policies involved, we discern certain more particularized considerations that peculiarly call for reversal of this conviction. First, the principle contended for by the State seems inherently boundless. How is one to distinguish this from any other offensive word? Surely the State has no right to cleanse public debate to the point where it is grammatically palatable to the most squeamish among us. Yet no readily ascertainable general principle exists for stopping short of that result were we to affirm the judgment below. For, while the particular four-letter word being litigated here is perhaps more distasteful than most others of its genre, it is nevertheless often true that one man's vulgarity is another's lyric. Indeed, we think it is largely because governmental officials cannot make principled distinctions in this area that the Constitution leaves matters of taste and style so largely to the individual.

Additionally, we cannot overlook the fact, because it is well illustrated by the episode involved here, that much linguistic expression serves a dual communicative function: it conveys not only ideas capable of relatively precise, detached explication, but otherwise inexpressible emotions as well. In fact, words are often chosen as much for their emotive as their cognitive force. We cannot sanction the view that the Constitution, while solicitous of the cognitive content of individual speech, has little or no regard for that emotive function which, practically speaking, may often be the more important element of the overall message sought to be communicated. Indeed, as Mr. Justice Frankfurter has said, "[o]ne of the prerogatives of American citizenship is the right to criticize public men and measures—and that means not only informed and responsible criticism but the freedom to speak foolishly and without moderation." Baumgartner v. United States (1944).

Finally . . . we cannot indulge the facile assumption that one can forbid particular words without also running a substantial risk of suppressing ideas in the process. Indeed, governments might soon seize upon the censorship of particular words as a convenient guise for banning the expression of unpopular views. We have been able, as noted above, to discern little social benefit that might result from running the risk of opening the door to such grave results.

It is, in sum, our judgment that, absent a more particularized and compelling reason for its actions, the State may not, consistently with the First and Fourteenth Amendments, make the simple public display here involved of this single four-letter expletive a criminal offense. Because that is the only arguably sustainable rationale for the conviction here at issue, the judgment below must be

Reversed.

Mr. Justice **BLACKMUN,** with whom the Chief Justice [**BURGER**] and Mr. Justice **BLACK** join.

I dissent . . . .

1. Cohen's absurd and immature behavior was mainly conduct and little speech. . . . Further, the case appears to me to be well within the sphere of Chaplinsky v. New Hampshire (1942) . . . . As a consequence, this Court's agonizing First Amendment values seems misplaced and unnecessary.

2. I am not at all certain that the California Court of Appeal's construction of [the state statute] is now the authoritative California construction . . . .

Mr. Justice **WHITE** concurs in paragraph 2 of Mr. Justice **BLACK-MUN's** dissenting opinion.

Editors' Notes

(1) **Query**: Most of the cases involving freedom of communication that we have read so far ostensibly relate to politically relevant communications and thus to democratic theory. To what extent was Harlan invoking constitutionalism when he wrote that no other approach than absence of governmental restraint on free expression "would comport with the premise of individual dignity and choice upon which our political system rests"? Do *Cohen* in particular and the other cases in general point to conflicts between the demands of constitutionalism and democracy when freedom of communication is concerned?

(2) For a discussion of *Cohen*, see David L. Paletz and William F. Harris, II, "Four-Letter Threats to Authority," 37 *Jo. of Pols.* 955 (1975).

(3) The strongest dissent against the principles enunciated in *Cohen* came a year later, after Lewis F. Powell had replaced Hugo Black and William Rehnquist had taken John Marshall Harlan II's place. The Court remanded three cases—Rosenfeld v. New Jersey (1972), Lewis v. New Orleans (1972), and Brown v. Oklahoma (1972)—to lower courts for reconsideration in light of *Cohen* and Gooding v. Wilson (1972; reprinted above, p. 539). Powell, joined by Burger and Blackmun, dissented, noting that Rosenfeld had spoken before an audience of about 150 people, including about 40 children and 25 women, and had used "the adjective 'M_____ F_____' on four occasions, to describe the teachers, the school board, the town and his own country." He had been convicted under a state statute making it disorderly conduct to utter indecent language in a public place. Powell added:

> The preservation of the right to free and robust speech is accorded high priority in our society and under the Constitution. Yet, there are other significant values. One of the hallmarks of a civilized society is the level and quality of discourse. We have witnessed in recent years a disquieting deterioration in the standards of taste and civility in speech. For the increasing number of persons who derive satisfaction from vocabularies dependent upon filth and obscenities, there are abundant opportunities to gratify their debased tastes. But our free society must be flexible enough to tolerate even such a debasement provided it occurs without subjecting unwilling audiences to the type of verbal nuisance committed in this case. The shock and sense of affront, and sometimes the injury to mind and spirit, can be as great from words as from some physical attacks . . . .

Chief Justice Burger—joined by Blackmun and Rehnquist—was more foreboding:

> The important underlying aspect of these cases goes really to the function of law in preserving ordered liberty. Civilized people refrain from "taking the law into their own hands" because of a belief that the government, as their agent, will take care of the problem in an organized, orderly way with as nearly a uniform response as human skills can manage. History is replete with evidence of what happens when the law cannot or does not provide a collective response for conduct so widely regarded as impermissible and intolerable.
>
> It is barely a century since men in parts of this country carried guns constantly because the law did not afford protection. In that setting, the words used in these cases, if directed toward such an

armed civilian, could well have led to death or serious bodily injury.
When we undermine the general belief that the law will give protection against fighting words and profane and abusive language such as
the utterances involved in these cases, we take steps to return to the
law of the jungle . . . .

IV. POLITICAL CENSORSHIP

" '[T]o the press alone, chequered as it is with abuses, the
world is indebted for all the triumphs which have been
gained by reason and humanity over error and oppression; . . . to the same beneficent source the United
States owes much of the lights which conducted them to
the ranks of a free and independent nation . . . .' "

NEAR v. MINNESOTA
283 U.S. 697, 51 S.Ct. 625, 75 L.Ed. 1357 (1931).

In a series of articles published during Prohibition for the alleged purpose
of pushing reform in Minneapolis' government, *The Saturday Press* vilified,
among others, the mayor, the police chief, and the city's two largest newspapers for taking orders from "Jew Gangsters."   One article asserted that
"Practically every vendor of vile hooch, every owner of a moonshine still, every
snake-faced gangster and embryonic yegg in the Twin Cities is a JEW," and
urged Jews to "rid themselves of the odium and stigma the RODENTS OF
THEIR OWN RACE HAVE BROUGHT UPON THEM."   The local prosecuting
attorney invoked a state statute that provided for abatement by injunction, as a
public nuisance, of a "malicious, scandalous and defamatory newspaper,
magazine or other periodical," and obtained an order against the publisher,
J.M. Near, barring future issues of the paper.   The state supreme court upheld
the injunction and the statute on which it was based.   Near appealed to the
U.S. Supreme Court.

Mr. Chief Justice **HUGHES** delivered the opinion of the Court . . . .

This statute . . . is unusual, if not unique, and raises questions of
grave importance transcending the local interests involved in the
particular action. It is no longer open to doubt that the liberty of the
press and of speech is within the liberty safeguarded by the due process
clause of the 14th Amendment from invasion by state action. . . .
Gitlow v. New York [1925]; Whitney v. California [1927]; Stromberg v.
California [1931]. In maintaining this guaranty, the authority of the
State to enact laws to promote the health, safety, morals and general
welfare of its people is necessarily admitted. The limits of this sovereign power must always be determined with appropriate regard to the
particular subject of its exercise . . . .   [T]his court has held that
the power of the state stops short of interference with what are deemed
to be certain indispensable requirements of the liberty assured . . . .
[Like liberty of contract,] [l]iberty of speech and of the press is also not
an absolute right, and the state may punish its abuse . . . .   Liberty,

in each of its phases, has its history and connotation and, in the present instance, the inquiry is as to the historic conception of the liberty of the press and whether the statute under review violates the essential attributes of that liberty . . . .

. . . [I]n passing upon constitutional questions the court has regard to substance and not to mere matters of form, and . . . in accordance with familiar principles, the statute must be tested by its operation and effect . . . .

If we cut through mere details of procedure, the operation and effect of the statute in substance is that public authorities may bring the owner or publisher of a newspaper or periodical before a judge upon a charge of conducting a business of publishing scandalous and defamatory matter—in particular that the matter consists of charges against public officers of official dereliction—and unless the owner or publisher is able and disposed to bring competent evidence to satisfy the judge that the charges are true and are published with good motives and for justifiable ends, his newspaper or periodical is suppressed and further publication is made punishable as a contempt. This is of the essence of censorship.

The question is whether a statute authorizing such proceedings in restraint of publication is consistent with the conception of the liberty of the press as historically conceived and guaranteed. In determining the extent of the constitutional protection, it has been generally, if not universally, considered that it is the chief purpose of the guaranty to prevent previous restraints upon publication. The struggle in England, directed against the legislative power of the licenser, resulted in renunciation of the censorship of the press. . . . The distinction was early pointed out between the extent of the freedom with respect to censorship under our constitutional system and that enjoyed in England. Here, as Madison said, "The great and essential rights of the people are secured against legislative as well as against executive ambition. They are secured, not by laws paramount to prerogative, but by constitutions paramount to laws. This security of the freedom of the press requires that it should be exempt not only from previous restraint by the executive, as in Great Britain, but from legislative restraint also."

. . . The preliminary freedom extends as well to the false as to the true; the subsequent punishment may extend as well to the true as to the false. This was the law of criminal libel apart from statute in most cases, if not in all. . . .

. . . [I]t is recognized that punishment for the abuse of the liberty accorded to the press is essential to the protection of the public, and that the common law rules that subject the libeler to responsibility for the public offense, as well as for the private injury, are not abolished by the protection extended in our constitutions. The law of criminal libel rests upon that secure foundation. There is also the conceded authority of courts to punish for contempt when publications directly tend to prevent the proper discharge of judicial functions. Patterson v. Colorado [1907]. In the present case, we have no occasion to inquire as to the permissible scope of subsequent punishment. For whatever wrong the appellant has committed or may commit, by his publications, the state appropriately affords both public and private redress by its libel laws . . . . [T]he statute in question does not deal with punishments; it provides for no punishment, except in case of contempt for violation of the court's order, but for suppression and injunction, that is, for restraint upon publication.

The objection has also been made that the principle as to immunity from previous restraint is stated too broadly, if every such restraint is deemed to be prohibited. That is undoubtedly true; the protection even as to previous restraint is not absolutely unlimited. But the limitation has been recognized only in exceptional cases. "When a nation is at war many things that might be said in time of peace are such a hindrance to its effort that their utterance will not be endured so long as men fight and that no court could regard them as protected by any constitutional right." Schenck v. United States [1919]. No one would question but that a government might prevent actual obstruction to its recruiting service or the publication of the sailing dates of transports or the number and location of troops. On similar grounds, the primary requirements of decency may be enforced against obscene publications. The security of the community life may be protected against incitements to acts of violence and the overthrow by force of orderly government. The constitutional guaranty of free speech does not "protect a man from an injunction against uttering words that may have all the effect of force." Gompers v. Bucks Stove & Range Co. [1911]; Schenck. These limitations are not applicable here . . . .

The exceptional nature of its limitations places in a strong light the general conception that liberty of the press, historically considered and taken up by the Federal Constitution, has meant, principally, although not exclusively, immunity from previous restraints or censorship. The conception of the liberty of the press in this country had broadened with the exigencies of the colonial period and with the efforts to secure freedom from oppressive administration. That liberty was especially cherished for the immunity it afforded from previous restraint of the publication of censure of public officers and charges of official miscon-duct . . . .

. . . Madison, who was the leading spirit in the preparation of the 1st Amendment of the Federal Constitution, thus described the practice and sentiment which led to the guaranties of liberty of the press in state constitutions:

> In every state, probably, in the Union, the press has exerted a
> freedom in canvassing the merits and measures of public men of every
> description which has not been confined to the strict limits of the
> common law. On this footing the freedom of the press has stood; on
> this footing it yet stands . . . . Some degree of abuse is inseparable
> from the proper use of everything, and in no instance is this more true
> than in that of the press. It has accordingly been decided by the
> practice of the states, that it is better to leave a few of its noxious

branches to their luxuriant growth, than, by pruning them away, to injure the vigour of those yielding the proper fruits. And can the wisdom of this policy be doubted by any who reflect that to the press alone, chequered as it is with abuses, the world is indebted for all the triumphs which have been gained by reason and humanity over error and oppression; who reflect that to the same beneficent source the United States owe much of the lights which conducted them to the ranks of a free and independent nation, and which have improved their political system into a shape so auspicious to their happiness? Had "Sedition Acts," forbidding every publication that might bring the constituted agents into contempt or disrepute, or that might excite the hatred of the people against the authors of unjust or pernicious measures, been uniformly enforced against the press, might not the United States have been languishing at this day under the infirmities of a sickly Confederation? Might they not, possibly, be miserable colonies, groaning under a foreign yoke?

The fact that for approximately one hundred and fifty years there has been almost an entire absence of attempts to impose previous restraints upon publications relating to the malfeasance of public officers is significant of the deep-seated conviction that such restraints would violate constitutional right . . . .

The importance of this immunity has not lessened. While reckless assaults upon public men, and efforts to bring obloquy upon those who are endeavoring faithfully to discharge official duties, exert a baleful influence and deserve the severest condemnation in public opinion, it cannot be said that this abuse is greater, and it is believed to be less, than that which characterized the period in which our institutions took shape. Meanwhile, the administration of government has become more complex, the opportunities for malfeasance and corruption have multiplied, crime has grown to most serious proportions, and the danger of its protection by unfaithful officials and of the impairment of the fundamental security of life and property by criminal alliances and official neglect, emphasizes the primary need of a vigilant and courageous press, especially in great cities. The fact that the liberty of the press may be abused by miscreant purveyors of scandal does not make any the less necessary the immunity of the press from previous restraint in dealing with official misconduct. Subsequent punishment for such abuses as may exist is the appropriate remedy, consistent with constitutional privilege . . . .

For these reasons we hold the statute, so far as it authorized the proceedings in this action under clause (b) of section one, to be an infringement of the liberty of the press guaranteed by the 14th Amendment. We should add that this decision rests upon the operation and effect of the statute, without regard to the question of the truth of the charges contained in the particular periodical. . . .

Mr. Justice **BUTLER,** dissenting:

The decision of the court in this case declares Minnesota and every other state powerless to restrain by injunction the business of publishing and circulating among the people malicious, scandalous and defamatory periodicals that in due course of judicial procedure has been adjudged to be a public nuisance. It gives to freedom of the press a meaning and a scope not heretofore recognized and construes "liberty" in the due process clause of the 14th Amendment to put upon the states a Federal restriction that is without precedent . . . .

It is of the greatest importance that the states shall be untrammeled and free to employ all just and appropriate measures to prevent abuses of the liberty of the press.

In his work on the Constitution, . . . Justice Story [said] . . . :

> That this amendment was intended to secure to every citizen an absolute right to speak, or write, or print whatever he might please, without any responsibility, public or private, therefor, is a supposition too wild to be indulged by any rational man. This would be to allow to every citizen a right to destroy at his pleasure the reputation, the peace, the property, and even the personal safety of every other citizen. . . . Civil society could not go on under such circumstances. Men would then be obliged to resort to private vengeance to make up for the deficiencies of the law . . . . It is plain, then, that the language of this amendment imports no more than that every man shall have a right to speak, write, and print his opinions upon any subject whatsoever, without any prior restraint, so always that he does not injure any other person in his rights, person, property, or reputation; and so always that he does not thereby disturb the public peace, or attempt to subvert the government. . . .

. . . His statement concerned the definite declaration of the 1st Amendment. It is not suggested that the freedom of press included in the liberty protected by the 14th Amendment, which was adopted after Story's definition, is greater than that protected against congressional action.

The Minnesota statute does not operate as a *previous* restraint on publication within the proper meaning of that phrase. It does not authorize administrative control in advance such as was formerly exercised by the licensers and censors but prescribes a remedy to be enforced by a suit in equity. In this case there was previous publication made in the course of the business of regularly producing malicious, scandalous and defamatory periodicals. The business and publications unquestionably constitute an abuse of the right of free press. . . . The restraint authorized is only in respect of continuing to do what has been duly adjudged to constitute a nuisance . . . .

. . . As that resulting from lewd publications constitutionally may be enjoined it is hard to understand why the one resulting from a regular business of malicious defamation may not.

It is well known, as found by the state supreme court, that existing libel laws are inadequate effectively to suppress evils resulting from the kind of business and publications that are shown in this case. The doctrine that measures such as the one before us are invalid because they operate as previous restraints to infringe freedom of press exposes the peace and good order of every community and the business and private affairs of every individual to the constant and protracted false and malicious assaults of any insolvent publisher who may have purpose and sufficient capacity to contrive and put into effect a scheme or program for oppression, blackmail or extortion. . . .

Mr. Justice **VAN DEVANTER,** Mr. Justice **McREYNOLDS,** and Mr. Justice **SUTHERLAND,** concur in this opinion.

Editors' Notes

(1) **Query**: How useful for constitutional interpretation in this case is a literal (textual) approach? What sort of approach did Hughes use? Butler?

(2) *Near* was the first case in which the Court held that the Fourteenth Amendment "incorporated" the First Amendment's protection of freedom of the press. Perhaps it is the fact that this was a maiden venture that made Hughes' opinion so cautious, so careful to point out limitations on freedom of the press rather than to explain its breadth. As the notes below indicate, the Court has since reduced many of the limitations that Hughes mentioned.

(3) **Query:** Did Butler's dissent attack incorporating freedom of press into the Fourteenth Amendment or Hughes's notion of what freedom of the press includes? Is there a coherent theory that would accord standards of "civility" the weight Butler assigns them? Would it be more constitutionalist or democratic in nature—or would it be neither?

(4) **Query:** What was the relevance of Near's victims' having been mostly public officials? Did Hughes not strongly indicate that private citizens and perhaps even public officials might have used normal libel laws to secure monetary damages from Near? The Court has since drastically restricted the availability of libel as a remedy for "public figures"; see New York Times v. Sullivan (1964; reprinted below, p. 596), Time v. Firestone (1976; reprinted below, p. 606), and cases discussed in the notes to those decisions.

(5) Hughes mentioned "criminal libel" as a remedy available to Near's victims. What was involved was a regular criminal prosecution, brought by a district attorney or similar official, with the crime defined as defaming another person by written words. The justification was that libel in some sense constituted a breach of the peace, analogous to a physical attack. That sort of action has largely dropped out of usage in the United States, though it formed part of the basis for the Sedition Act of 1798. In any event, were a criminal libel action to be brought, it would be subject to at least the same restrictions as a private action in libel. See Garrison v. Louisiana (1964).

(6) Hughes spoke of "the conceded authority of courts to punish for contempt when publications directly tend to prevent the proper discharge of judicial functions." The principle that judges have such authority to punish newspapers is still valid, but the Supreme Court has so limited it that it is difficult to imagine its being legitimately exercised in the real world. C. Herman Pritchett analyzes the cases: *Constitutional Civil Liberties* (Englewood Cliffs, N.J.: Prentice-Hall, 1984), pp. 73–75.

(7) Hughes also said that Minnesota's statute was unusual if not unique, implying widespread legal support for freedom of communication. Such

nostalgia may have been misplaced. See David M. Rabban, "The First Amendment in its Forgotten Years," 90 *Yale L.J.* 514 (1981), who argues that there was much litigation involving claims to freedom of speech and press during the early twentieth century and that the "overwhelming majority of pre[World War I] decisions in all jurisdictions rejected free speech claims . . . . No court was more unsympathetic to freedom of expression than the Supreme Court . . . ."

" 'Any system of prior restraints of expression comes to this Court bearing a heavy presumption against its constitutional validity.' "

THE PENTAGON PAPERS CASE (NEW YORK TIMES v. UNITED STATES)

403 U.S. 713, 91 S.Ct. 2140, 29 L.Ed.2d 822 (1971).

In 1971, the *New York Times* and the *Washington Post* obtained stolen copies of classified documents that formed an internal governmental study, *History of U.S. Decision-Making Process on Viet Nam Policy,* popularly called *The Pentagon Papers.* After some delay, the two newspapers began publishing the documents. The Department of Justice sought injunctions from federal district courts in New York and the District of Columbia against further publication. The court in New York refused the request, but later that same day the Court of Appeals for the Second Circuit sent the case back to the district court for further hearings and granted a temporary injunction. In Washington, the district court also refused to issue the injunction, but there the Court of Appeals for the District of Columbia sustained the refusal. Both sides petitioned for certiorari on an expedited basis. The Court granted the petition but issued an order restraining publication until after its decision on the merits. Four days after oral argument, the Court announced its judgment.

PER CURIAM. . . .

"Any system of prior restraints of expression comes to this Court bearing a heavy presumption against its constitutional validity." Bantam Books, Inc. v. Sullivan (1963); see also Near v. Minnesota (1931). The Government "thus carries a heavy burden of showing justification for the imposition of such a restraint." Organization for a Better Austin v. Keefe (1971). The District Court for the Southern District of New York in the *New York Times* case and the District Court for the District of Columbia and the Court of Appeals for the District of Columbia Circuit in the *Washington Post* case held that the Government had not met that burden. We agree . . . .

Mr. Justice **BLACK**, with whom Mr. Justice **DOUGLAS** joins, concurring . . . .

Our Government was launched in 1789 with the adoption of the Constitution. The Bill of Rights, including the First Amendment, followed in 1791. Now, for the first time in the 182 years since the founding of the Republic, the federal courts are asked to hold that the

First Amendment does not mean what it says, but rather means that the Government can halt the publication of current news of vital importance to the people of this country.

In seeking injunctions against these newspapers and in its presentation to the Court, the Executive Branch seems to have forgotten the essential purpose and history of the First Amendment. . . . The Bill of Rights changed the original Constitution into a new charter under which no branch of government could abridge the people's freedoms of press, speech, religion, and assembly. Yet the Solicitor General argues and some members of the Court appear to agree that the general powers of the Government adopted in the original Constitution should be interpreted to limit and restrict the specific and emphatic guarantees of the Bill of Rights adopted later. I can imagine no greater perversion of history. Madison and the other Framers of the First Amendment, able men that they were, wrote in language they earnestly believed could never be misunderstood: "Congress shall make no law . . . abridging the freedom . . . of the press . . . ." Both the history and language of the First Amendment support the view that the press must be left free to publish news, whatever the source, without censorship, injunctions, or prior restraints.

In the First Amendment the Founding Fathers gave the free press the protection it must have to fulfill its essential role in our democracy. The press was to serve the governed, not the governors. The Government's power to censor the press was abolished so that the press would remain forever free to censure the Government. The press was protected so that it could bare the secrets of government and inform the people. Only a free and unrestrained press can effectively expose deception in government. And paramount among the responsibilities of a free press is the duty to prevent any part of the government from deceiving the people and sending them off to distant lands to die of foreign fevers and foreign shot and shell . . . .

The Government's case here is based on premises entirely different from those that guided the Framers of the First Amendment. The Solicitor General has carefully and emphatically stated:

> Now, Mr. Justice [Black], your construction of . . . [the First Amendment] is well known, and I certainly respect it. You say that no law means no law, and that should be obvious. I can only say, Mr. Justice, that to me it is equally obvious that "no law" does not mean "no law", and I would seek to persuade the Court that that is true. . . . [T]here are other parts of the Constitution that grant powers and responsibilities to the Executive, and . . . the First Amendment was not intended to make it impossible for the Executive to function or to protect the security of the United States.

And the Government argues in its brief that in spite of the First Amendment, "[t]he authority of the Executive Department to protect the nation against publication of information whose disclosure would endanger the national security stems from two interrelated sources:

the constitutional power of the President over the conduct of foreign affairs and his authority as Commander-in-Chief." . . .[1]

. . . To find that the President has "inherent power" to halt the publication of news by resort to the courts would wipe out the First Amendment and destroy the fundamental liberty and security of the very people the Government hopes to make "secure." . . .

The word "security" is a broad, vague generality whose contours should not be invoked to abrogate the fundamental law embodied in the First Amendment. . . . The guarding of military and diplomatic secrets at the expense of informed representative government provides no real security for our Republic. The Framers of the First Amendment . . . sought to give this new society strength and security by providing that freedom of speech, press, religion, and assembly should not be abridged. . . .

Mr. Justice **DOUGLAS**, with whom Mr. Justice **BLACK** joins, concurring . . . .

It should be noted at the outset that the First Amendment provides that "Congress shall make no law . . . abridging the freedom of speech, or of the press." That leaves, in my view, no room for governmental restraint on the press.

There is, moreover, no statute barring the publication by the press of the material which the *Times* and the *Post* seek to use . . . .

So any power that the Government possesses must come from its "inherent power."

The power to wage war is "the power to wage war successfully." See Hirabayashi v. United States [1943]. But the war power stems from a declaration of war. The Constitution by Art. I, § 8, gives Congress, not the President, power "[t]o declare War." Nowhere are presidential wars authorized. We need not decide therefore what leveling effect the war power of Congress might have.

These disclosures may have a serious impact. But that is no basis for sanctioning a previous restraint on the press . . . .

The Government says that it has inherent powers to go into court and obtain an injunction to protect the national interest, which in this case is alleged to be national security.

Near v. Minnesota [1931] repudiated that expansive doctrine in no uncertain terms.

The dominant purpose of the First Amendment was to prohibit the widespread practice of governmental suppression of embarrassing information. . . . A debate of large proportions goes on in the Nation

---

1. Compare the views of the Solicitor General with those of James Madison, the author of the First Amendment. When speaking of the Bill of Rights in the House of Representatives, Madison said: "If they [the first ten amendments] are incorporated into the Constitution, independent tribunals of justice will consider themselves in a peculiar manner the guardians of those rights; they will be an impenetrable bulwark against every assumption of power in the Legislative or Executive; they will be naturally led to resist every encroachment upon rights expressly stipulated for in the Constitution by the declaration of rights" . . . . [Footnote by Justice Black.]

over our posture in Vietnam. That debate antedated the disclosure of
the contents of the present documents. The latter are highly relevant
to the debate in progress.

Secrecy in government is fundamentally anti-democratic, perpetuating bureaucratic errors. Open debate and discussion of public issues
are vital to our national health. On public questions there should be
"uninhibited, robust, and wide-open" debate. New York Times Co. v.
Sullivan [1964] . . . .

Mr. Justice **BRENNAN,** concurring . . . .

The error that has pervaded these cases from the outset was the
granting of any injunctive relief whatsoever, interim or otherwise. The
entire thrust of the Government's claim throughout these cases has
been that publication of the material sought to be enjoined "could," or
"might," or "may" prejudice the national interest in various ways. But
the First Amendment tolerates absolutely no prior judicial restraints of
the press predicated upon surmise or conjecture that untoward consequences may result. Our cases, it is true, have indicated that there is a
single, extremely narrow class of cases in which the First Amendment's
ban on prior judicial restraint may be overridden. Our cases have thus
far indicated that such cases may arise only when the Nation "is at
war," Schenck v. United States (1919), during which times "[n]o one
would question but that a government might prevent actual obstruction
to its recruiting service or the publication of the sailing dates of
transports or the number and location of troops." Near v. Minnesota
(1931). Even if the present world situation were assumed to be tantamount to a time of war, or if the power of presently available armaments would justify even in peacetime the suppression of information
that would set in motion a nuclear holocaust, in neither of these actions
has the Government presented or even alleged that publication of items
from or based upon the material at issue would cause the happening of
an event of that nature . . . .

Mr. Justice **STEWART,** with whom Mr. Justice **WHITE** joins, concurring.

In the governmental structure created by our Constitution, the
Executive is endowed with enormous power in the two related areas of
national defense and international relations. This power, largely unchecked by the Legislative and Judicial branches, has been pressed to
the very hilt since the advent of the nuclear missile age. For better or
for worse, the simple fact is that a President of the United States
possesses vastly greater constitutional independence in these two vital
areas of power than does, say, a prime minister of a country with a
parliamentary form of government.

In the absence of the governmental checks and balances present in
other areas of our national life, the only effective restraint upon
executive policy and power in the areas of national defense and international affairs may lie in an enlightened citizenry—in an informed and

critical public opinion which alone can here protect the values of democratic government. For this reason, it is perhaps here that a press that is alert, aware, and free most vitally serves the basic purpose of the First Amendment. For without an informed and free press there cannot be an enlightened people.

Yet it is elementary that the successful conduct of international diplomacy and the maintenance of an effective national defense require both confidentiality and secrecy. Other nations can hardly deal with this Nation in an atmosphere of mutual trust unless they can be assured that their confidences will be kept. And within our own executive departments, the development of considered and intelligent international policies would be impossible if those charged with their formulation could not communicate with each other freely, frankly, and in confidence. In the area of basic national defense the frequent need for absolute secrecy is, of course, self-evident.

I think there can be but one answer to this dilemma, if dilemma it be. The responsibility must be where the power is. If the Constitution gives the Executive a large degree of unshared power in the conduct of foreign affairs and the maintenance of our national defense, then under the Constitution the Executive must have the largely unshared duty to determine and preserve the degree of internal security necessary to exercise that power successfully. It is an awesome responsibility, requiring judgment and wisdom of a high order. I should suppose that moral, political, and practical considerations would dictate that a very first principle of that wisdom would be an insistence upon avoiding secrecy for its own sake. For when everything is classified, then nothing is classified, and the system becomes one to be disregarded by the cynical or the careless, and to be manipulated by those intent on self-protection or self-promotion. . . . But . . . it is the constitutional duty of the Executive—as a matter of sovereign prerogative and not as a matter of law as the courts know law—through the promulgation and enforcement of executive regulations, to protect the confidentiality necessary to carry out its responsibilities in the fields of international relations and national defense.

This is not to say that Congress and the courts have no role to play. Undoubtedly Congress has the power to enact specific and appropriate criminal laws to protect government property and preserve government secrets . . . . And if a criminal prosecution is instituted, it will be the responsibility of the courts to decide the applicability of the criminal law under which the charge is brought. Moreover, if Congress should pass a specific law authorizing civil proceedings in this field, the courts would likewise have the duty to decide the constitutionality of such a law as well as its applicability to the facts proved.

But in the cases before us we are asked neither to construe specific regulations nor to apply specific laws. We are asked, instead, to perform a function that the Constitution gave to the Executive, not the Judiciary. We are asked, quite simply, to prevent the publication by two newspapers of material that the Executive Branch insists should not, in the national interest, be published. I am convinced that the Executive is correct with respect to some of the documents involved. But I cannot say that disclosure of any of them will surely result in direct, immediate, and irreparable damage to our Nation or its people. That being so, there can under the First Amendment be but one judicial resolution of the issues before us. . . .

Mr. Justice **WHITE,** with whom Mr. Justice **STEWART** joins, concurring.

I concur in today's judgments, but only because of the concededly extraordinary protection against prior restraints enjoyed by the press under our constitutional system. I do not say that in no circumstances would the First Amendment permit an injunction against publishing information about government plans or operations. Nor, after examining the materials the Government characterizes as the most sensitive and destructive, can I deny that revelation of these documents will do substantial damage to public interests. Indeed, I am confident that their disclosure will have that result. But I nevertheless agree that the United States has not satisfied the very heavy burden that it must meet to warrant an injunction against publication in these cases, at least in the absence of express and appropriately limited congressional authorization for prior restraints in circumstances such as these . . . .

. . . To sustain the Government in these cases would start the courts down a long and hazardous road that I am not willing to travel, at least without congressional guidance and direction . . . .

. . . [T]erminating the ban on publication of the relatively few sensitive documents the Government now seeks to suppress does not mean that the law either requires or invites newspapers or others to publish them or that they will be immune from criminal action if they do. Prior restraints require an unusually heavy justification under the First Amendment; but failure by the Government to justify prior restraints does not measure its constitutional entitlement to a conviction for criminal publication. That the Government mistakenly chose to proceed by injunction does not mean that it could not successfully proceed in another way. . . .

. . . I am not, of course, saying that either of these newspapers has yet committed a crime or that either would commit a crime if it published all the material now in its possession . . . .

Mr. Justice **MARSHALL**, concurring.

. . . The issue is whether this Court or the Congress has the power to make law . . . .

The problem here is whether in these particular cases the Executive Branch has authority to invoke the equity jurisdiction of the courts to protect what it believes to be the national interest . . . . The Government argues that in addition to the inherent power of any government to protect itself, the President's power to conduct foreign affairs and his position as Commander in Chief give him authority to impose censorship on the press to protect his ability to deal effectively with foreign nations and to conduct the military affairs of the country. Of course, it is beyond cavil that the President has broad powers by virtue of his primary responsibility for the conduct of our foreign affairs and his position as Commander in Chief . . . . And in some situations it may be that under whatever inherent powers the Government may have, as well as the implicit authority derived from the President's mandate to conduct foreign affairs and to act as Commander in Chief, there is a basis for the invocation of the equity jurisdiction of this Court as an aid to prevent the publication of material damaging to "national security," however that term may be defined.

It would, however, be utterly inconsistent with the concept of separation of powers for this Court to use its power of contempt to prevent behavior that Congress has specifically declined to prohibit . . . . The Constitution provides that Congress shall make laws, the President execute laws, and courts interpret laws. Youngstown Sheet & Tube Co. v. Sawyer (1952). It did not provide for government by injunction in which the courts and the Executive Branch can "make law" without regard to the action of Congress. It may be more convenient for the Executive Branch if it need only convince a judge to prohibit conduct rather than ask the Congress to pass a law, and it may be more convenient to enforce a contempt order than to seek a criminal conviction in a jury trial. Moreover, it may be considered politically wise to get a court to share the responsibility for arresting those who the Executive Branch has probable cause to believe are violating the law. But convenience and political considerations of the moment do not justify a basic departure from the principles of our system of government.

In these cases we are not faced with a situation where Congress has failed to provide the Executive with broad power to protect the Nation from disclosure of damaging state secrets. Congress has on several occasions given extensive consideration to the problem of protecting the military and strategic secrets of the United States. This consideration has resulted in the enactment of statutes making it a crime to receive, disclose, communicate, withhold, and publish certain documents, photographs, instruments, appliances, and information. . . .

. . . Congress has specifically rejected passing legislation that would have clearly given the President the power he seeks here and made the current activity of the newspapers unlawful. When Congress specifically declines to make conduct unlawful it is not for this Court to redecide those issues—to overrule Congress. See *Youngstown Sheet & Tube Co.*

The Executive Branch has not gone to Congress and requested that the decision to provide such power be reconsidered. Instead the Executive Branch comes to this Court and asks that it be granted the power Congress refused to give . . . .

Mr. Chief Justice **BURGER**, dissenting.

So clear are the constitutional limitations on prior restraint against expression, that . . . we have had little occasion to be concerned with cases involving prior restraints against news reporting on matters of public interest. There is, therefore, little variation among the members of the Court in terms of resistance to prior restraints against publication. Adherence to this basic constitutional principle, however, does not make these cases simple. In these cases, the imperative of a free and unfettered press comes into collision with another imperative, the effective functioning of a complex modern government and specifically the effective exercise of certain constitutional powers of the Executive. Only those who view the First Amendment as an absolute in all circumstances—a view I respect, but reject—can find such cases as these to be simple or easy . . . .

Why are we in this posture, in which only those judges to whom the First Amendment is absolute and permits of no restraint in any circumstances or for any reason, are really in a position to act?

I suggest we are in this posture because these cases have been conducted in unseemly haste . . . . The prompt setting of these cases reflects our universal abhorrence of prior restraint. But prompt judicial action does not mean unjudicial haste.

Here, moreover, the frenetic haste is due in large part to the manner in which the *Times* proceeded from the date it obtained the purloined documents. It seems reasonably clear now that the haste precluded reasonable and deliberate judicial treatment of these cases and was not warranted. The precipitate action of this Court aborting trials not yet completed is not the kind of judicial conduct that ought to attend the disposition of a great issue.

The newspapers make a derivative claim under the First Amendment; they denominate this right as the public "right to know"; by implication, the *Times* asserts a sole trusteeship of that right by virtue of its journalistic "scoop." The right is asserted as an absolute. Of course, the First Amendment right itself is not an absolute . . . .[1] An issue of this importance should be tried and heard in a judicial atmosphere conducive to thoughtful, reflective deliberation, especially when haste, in terms of hours, is unwarranted in light of the long period the *Times,* by its own choice, deferred publication.

It is not disputed that the *Times* has had unauthorized possession of the documents for three to four months, during which it has had its expert analysts studying them, presumably digesting them and preparing the material for publication. During all of this time, the *Times,*

---

1. . . . . [T]he *Times* conducted its analysis of the 47 volumes of Government documents over a period of several months and did so with a degree of security that a government might envy. Such security was essential, of course, to protect the enterprise from others. Meanwhile the *Times* has copyrighted its material and there were strong intimations in the oral argument that the *Times* contemplated enjoining its use by any other publisher in violation of its copyright. Paradoxically this would afford it a protection, analogous to prior restraint, against all others—a protection the *Times* denies the Government of the United States. [Footnote by Chief Justice Burger.]

presumably in its capacity as trustee of the public's "right to know," has held up publication for purposes it considered proper and thus public knowledge was delayed. No doubt this was for a good reason; the analysis of 7,000 pages of complex material drawn from a vastly greater volume of material would inevitably take time and the writing of good news stories takes time. But why should the United States Government, from whom this information was illegally acquired by someone, along with all the counsel, trial judges, and appellate judges be placed under needless pressure? After these months of deferral, the alleged "right to know" has somehow and suddenly become a right that must be vindicated instanter . . . .

The consequences of all this melancholy series of events is that we literally do not know what we are acting on. . . .

I would affirm the Court of Appeals for the Second Circuit and allow the District Court to complete the trial aborted by our grant of certiorari, meanwhile preserving the status quo in the *Post* case. I would direct that the District Court on remand give priority to the *Times* case to the exclusion of all other business of that court but I would not set arbitrary deadlines. . . .

Mr. Justice **HARLAN**, with whom The Chief Justice [**BURGER**] and
    Mr. Justice **BLACKMUN** join, dissenting. . . .

    . . . With all respect, I consider that the Court has been almost irresponsibly feverish in dealing with these cases. . . .

This frenzied train of events took place in the name of the presumption against prior restraints created by the First Amendment. Due regard for the extraordinarily important and difficult questions involved in these litigations should have led the Court to shun such a precipitate timetable. . . .

Forced as I am to reach the merits of these cases, I dissent from the opinion and judgments of the Court. . . .

    . . . It is plain to me that the scope of the judicial function in passing upon the activities of the Executive Branch of the Government in the field of foreign affairs is very narrowly restricted. This view is, I think, dictated by the concept of separation of powers upon which our constitutional system rests.

In a speech on the floor of the House of Representatives, Chief Justice John Marshall, then a member of that body, stated: "The President is the sole organ of the nation in its external relations, and its sole representative with foreign nations." . . .

From this constitutional primacy in the field of foreign affairs, it seems to me that certain conclusions necessarily follow. . . .

The power to evaluate the "pernicious influence" of premature disclosure is not, however, lodged in the Executive alone. I agree that, in performance of its duty to protect the values of the First Amendment against political pressures, the judiciary must review the initial Executive determination to the point of satisfying itself that the subject matter of the dispute does lie within the proper compass of the

President's foreign relations power. Constitutional considerations forbid "a complete abandonment of judicial control." . . . Moreover, the judiciary may properly insist that the determination that disclosure of the subject matter would irreparably impair the national security be made by the head of the Executive Department concerned—here the Secretary of State or the Secretary of Defense—after actual personal consideration by that officer. This safeguard is required in the analogous area of executive claims of privilege for secrets of state. . . .

But in my judgment the judiciary may not properly go beyond these two inquiries and redetermine for itself the probable impact of disclosure on the national security. . . .

Even if there is some room for the judiciary to override the executive determination, it is plain that the scope of review must be exceedingly narrow. . . .

Pending further hearings in each case conducted under the appropriate ground rules, I would continue the restraints on publication. I cannot believe that the doctrine prohibiting prior restraints reaches to the point of preventing courts from maintaining the status quo long enough to act responsibly in matters of such national importance as those involved here.

Mr. Justice **BLACKMUN**, dissenting.

The country would be none the worse off were the cases tried quickly, to be sure, but in the customary and properly deliberative manner. The most recent of the material, it is said, dates no later than 1968, already about three years ago, and the *Times* itself took three months to formulate its plan of procedure and, thus, deprived its public for that period.

The First Amendment, after all, is only one part of an entire Constitution. Article II of the great document vests in the Executive Branch primary power over the conduct of foreign affairs and places in that branch the responsibility for the Nation's safety. Each provision of the Constitution is important, and I cannot subscribe to a doctrine of unlimited absolutism for the First Amendment at the cost of downgrading other provisions. First Amendment absolutism has never commanded a majority of this Court. See, for example, Near v. Minnesota (1931), and Schenck v. United States (1919). What is needed here is a weighing, upon properly developed standards, of the broad right of the press to print and of the very narrow right of the Government to prevent. Such standards are not yet developed. The parties here are in disagreement as to what those standards should be. But even the newspapers concede that there are situations where restraint is in order and is constitutional. . . .

It may well be that if these cases were allowed to develop as they should be developed, and to be tried as lawyers should try them and as courts should hear them, free of pressure and panic and sensationalism, other light would be shed on the situation and contrary considerations, for me, might prevail. But that is not the present posture of the litigation.

The Court, however, decides the cases today the other way. I therefore add one final comment.

I strongly urge, and sincerely hope, that these two newspapers will be fully aware of their ultimate responsibilities to the United States of America. . . . I hope that damage has not already been done. If, however, damage has been done, and if, with the Court's action today, these newspapers proceed to publish the critical documents and there results therefrom "the death of soldiers, the destruction of alliances, the greatly increased difficulty of negotiation with our enemies, the inability of our diplomats to negotiate," to which list I might add the factors of prolongation of the war and of further delay in the freeing of United States prisoners, then the Nation's people will know where the responsibility for these sad consequences rests.

Editors' Notes

(1) **Query**: Compare the various opinions here as they relate to divisions of power within the national government with those in the Steel Seizure Case (1952; reprinted above, p. 339) and INS v. Chadha (1983; reprinted above, p. 383). Does any opinion have the sophistication of Jackson's opinion in the Steel Seizure Case? What interpretive standards should one apply to distinguish levels of sophistication?

(2) Does Black's literalism force him into a logical contradiction? In other cases, he would have limited constitutional rights to those explicitly listed in the constitutional document; see espec. his dis. op. in the Birth Control Case, Griswold v. Connecticut (1963; reprinted above p. 113). But what right does the First Amendment establish against either judicial or executive interference with freedom of the press or, more generally, of expression? The First Amendment says "Congress shall make no law," not "Government shall not interfere with. . . ." Douglas also used a literal approach in *Pentagon Papers* (unlike in *Griswold*); but, as a constitutionalist, he demanded that government put its finger on a constitutional clause that authorizes interference with freedom of the press.

(3) C. Herman Pritchett writes that "the Court's opinions [in *Pentagon Papers*] do not add up to a sound defense of freedom of the press. It would appear that at least four members of the Court, and possibly five, believed that the newspapers could be criminally punished for their action." *Constitutional Civil Liberties* (Englewood Cliffs, N.J.: Prentice-Hall, 1984), p. 65. Assuming that Pritchett is correct about the views of the four (or five) justices, does their belief in newspaper's criminal liability for publishing stolen, classified documents threaten freedom of the press? Do the plain words of the constitutional document answer this question? Where would democratic theory lead? Constitutionalism? Do any of the doctrines the Court has developed help formulate a response?

(4) The United States has no "Official Secrets Act" as do most countries; thus, when the Department of Justice indicted Daniel Ellsberg for passing the documents to the *Times*, it had to charge him in very general terms. The prosecution foundered when it became known that, under orders from Nixon's White House, the government had engaged in assorted crimes, including

breaking into the office of Ellsberg's psychiatrist to try to obtain information that might embarrass him. No criminal action was ever brought against the *Times* or other newspapers.

(5) Less than a month after the Court's decision, the version of the papers as printed in the *New York Times* was published as a paperback book, *The Pentagon Papers* (New York: Bantam Books, 1971), under the supervision of James L. Greenfield, based on investigative reporting by Neil Sheehan. As it turned out, there was much embarrassing information about the way in which presidents from Eisenhower to Johnson had bungled American relations with and in IndoChina, but no great military secrets were involved.

(6) For analyses of the Court's ruling and its various opinions, see in addition to Pritchett cited in note (3), above: Louis Henkin, "The Right to Know and the Duty to Withhold," 120 *U.Pa.L.Rev.* 271 (1971); David M. O'Brien, *The Public's Right to Know* (New York: Praeger, 1981), pp. 155–165; Martin Shapiro, *The Pentagon Papers and the Courts* (San Francisco: Chandler, 1972); Sanford J. Ungar, *The Papers and the Papers* (New York: Dutton, 1972).

(7) In 1979, the magazine *The Progressive* proposed to publish an article, "The H-Bomb Secret," which many people erroneously thought would be a do-it-yourself manual. The Department of Justice obtained a preliminary injunction against publication, but withdrew its case when it became apparent that the article, written by a non-expert, simply brought together previously published material.

(8) Prior restraint is more common in the United States than the firmness of the Court's language here and in *Near* (1931; reprinted above, p. 570) would lead one to expect. For a discussion, see Pritchett, supra note (3), espec. pp. 67–72.

(9) See Snepp v. United States (1980) and CIA v. Sims (1985), discussed above in Eds.' Notes (1) and (2) to Haig v. Agee (1981; reprinted above p. 533).

"[T]he First Amendment . . . has a *structural* role to play in . . . our Republican system of self-government."

RICHMOND NEWSPAPERS, INC. v. VIRGINIA

448 U.S. 555, 100 S.Ct. 2814, 65 L.Ed.2d 973 (1980).

In 1976 a state circuit court in Richmond, Va., convicted a man named Stevenson of second-degree murder. The Virginia supreme court reversed, and the second and third trials ended in mistrials. In 1978, just before the fourth trial got underway, defense counsel asked the presiding judge to close the courtroom to spectators and journalists so that jurors would not read inaccurate news summaries of testimony they had heard or speculation about evidence that the judge had excluded. The prosecution offered no objection and the judge, who had presided over two of the previous trials, so ordered, citing his authority under the Virginia Code, which allowed for excluding persons in order to ensure a fair trial, "provided that the right of the accused to a public trial shall not be violated." Later that day, Richmond Newspapers, Inc., objected to being barred from the courtroom. After a hearing on the closure, from which reporters were also barred, the judge reaffirmed his order.

When Stevenson's trial resumed the next day, the judge in the absence of the jury granted a defense motion to strike the prosecution's evidence and found Stevenson not guilty. The state supreme court dismissed an appeal of the closure order, and Richmond Newspapers, Inc., obtained certiorari from the U.S. Supreme Court.

Mr. Chief Justice **BURGER** announced the judgment of the Court and delivered an opinion in which Mr. Justice **WHITE** and Mr. Justice **STEVENS** joined. . . .

II . . .

A

The origins of the proceeding which has become the modern criminal trial in Anglo-American justice can be traced back beyond reliable historical records. . . . What is significant for present purposes is that throughout its evolution, the trial has been open to all who cared to observe.

In the days before the Norman Conquest, cases in England were generally brought before moots, such as the local court of the hundred or the county court, which were attended by the freemen of the community. Somewhat like modern jury duty, attendance at these early meetings was compulsory on the part of the freemen, who were called upon to render judgment.

With the gradual evolution of the jury system in the years after the Norman Conquest . . . , the duty of all freemen to attend trials to render judgment was relaxed, but there is no indication that criminal trials did not remain public. . . .

From these early times, although great changes in courts and procedure took place, one thing remained constant: the public character of the trial at which guilt or innocence was decided. . . .

We have found nothing to suggest that the presumptive openness of the trial, which English courts were later to call "one of the essential qualities of a court of justice," Daubney v. Cooper (1829), was not also an attribute of the judicial systems of colonial America. In Virginia, for example, such records as there are of early criminal trials indicate that they were open. . . .

In some instances, the openness of trials was explicitly recognized as part of the fundamental law of the colony. . . .

B

. . . [T]he historical evidence demonstrates conclusively that at the time when our organic laws were adopted, criminal trials both here and in England had long been presumptively open. This is no quirk of history; rather, it has long been recognized as an indispensable attribute of an Anglo-American trial. . . .

. . . The early history of open trials in part reflects the widespread acknowledgement, long before there were behavioral scientists, that public trials had significant community therapeutic value. Even without such experts to frame the concept in words, people sensed from experience and observation that, especially in the administration of criminal justice, the means used to achieve justice must have the support derived from public acceptance of both the process and its results.

When a shocking crime occurs, a community reaction of outrage and public protest often follows . . . . Thereafter the open processes of justice serve an important prophylactic purpose, providing an outlet for community concern, hostility, and emotion. Without an awareness that society's responses to criminal conduct are underway, natural human reactions of outrage and protest are frustrated and may manifest themselves in some form of vengeful "self-help," as indeed they did regularly in the activities of vigilante "committees" on our frontiers . . . .

Civilized societies withdraw both from the victim and the vigilante the enforcement of criminal laws, but they cannot erase from people's consciousness the fundamental, natural yearning to see justice done— or even the urge for retribution. The crucial prophylactic aspects of the administration of justice cannot function in the dark; no community catharsis can occur if justice is "done in a corner [or] in any covert manner." It is not enough to say that results alone will satiate the natural community desire for "satisfaction." . . . To work effectively, it is important that society's criminal process "satisfy the appearance of justice," Offutt v. United States (1954), and the appearance of justice can best be provided by allowing people to observe it . . . .

C

From this unbroken, uncontradicted history, supported by reasons as valid today as in centuries past, we are bound to conclude that a presumption of openness inheres in the very nature of a criminal trial under our system of justice. . . .

Despite the history of criminal trials being presumptively open since long before the Constitution, the State presses its contention that neither the Constitution nor the Bill of Rights contains any provision which by its terms guarantees to the public the right to attend criminal trials. Standing alone, this is correct, but there remains the question whether, absent an explicit provision, the Constitution affords protection against exclusion of the public from criminal trials.

III

A

The First Amendment, in conjunction with the Fourteenth, prohibits governments from "abridging the freedom of speech, or of the press; or the right of the people peaceably to assemble, and to petition the Government for a redress of grievances." These expressly guaranteed freedoms share a common core purpose of assuring freedom of communication on matters relating to the functioning of government. Plainly it would be difficult to single out any aspect of government of higher concern and importance to the people than the manner in which criminal trials are conducted; as we have shown, recognition of this pervades the centuries-old history of open trials and the opinions of this Court.

The Bill of Rights was enacted against the backdrop of the long history of trials being presumptively open . . . . In guaranteeing freedoms such as those of speech and press, the First Amendment can be read as protecting the right of everyone to attend trials so as to give meaning to those explicit guarantees. "[T]he First Amendment goes beyond protection of the press and the self-expression of individuals to prohibit government from limiting the stock of information from which members of the public may draw." First National Bank of Boston v. Bellotti (1978). Free speech carries with it some freedom to listen. "In a variety of contexts this Court has referred to a First Amendment right to 'receive information and ideas.'" Kleindienst v. Mandel (1972). What this means in the context of trials is that the First Amendment guarantees of speech and press, standing alone, prohibit government from summarily closing courtroom doors which had long been open to the public at the time that amendment was adopted. "For the First Amendment does not speak equivocally . . . . It must be taken as a command of the broadest scope that explicit language, read in the context of a liberty-loving society, will allow." Bridges v. California (1941).

. . . The explicit, guaranteed rights to speak and to publish concerning what takes place at a trial would lose much meaning if access to observe the trial could, as it was here, be foreclosed arbitrarily.

B

The right of access to places traditionally open to the public, as criminal trials have long been, may be seen as assured by the amalgam of the First Amendment guarantees of speech and press; and their affinity to the right of assembly is not without relevance . . . .[1]

---

1. When the First Congress was debating the Bill of Rights, it was contended that there was no need separately to assert the right of assembly because it was subsumed in freedom of speech. Mr. Sedgwick of Massachusetts argued that inclusion of "assembly" among the enumerated rights would tend to make the Congress "appear trifling in the eyes of their constituents . . . . If people freely converse together, they must assemble for that purpose; it is a self-evident, unalienable right which the people possess; it is certainly a thing that never would be called in question . . . ."

. . . Since the right existed independent of any written guarantee, Sedgwick went on to argue that if it were the drafting committee's purpose to protect all inherent rights of the people by listing them, "they might have gone into a very lengthy enumeration of rights," but this was unnecessary, he said, "in a Government where none of them were intended to be infringed." . . .

Mr. Page of Virginia responded, however, that at times "such rights have been opposed," and that "people have . . . been prevented from assembling together on their lawful occasions":

[T]herefore it is well to guard against such stretches of authority, by inserting the privilege in the declaration of rights. If the people could be deprived of the power of assembly under any pretext whatsoever, they might be deprived of every other privilege contained in the clause. Ibid. The motion to strike "assembly" was defeated
. . . .

[Footnote by the Chief Justice.]

"The right of peaceable assembly is a right cognate to those of free speech and free press and is equally fundamental." DeJonge v. Oregon (1937). People assemble in public places not only to speak or to take action, but also to listen, observe, and learn; indeed, they may "assembl[e] for any lawful purpose," Hague v. C.I.O. (1939) (opinion of Stone, J.). Subject to the traditional time, place, and manner restrictions, see, e.g. Cox v. New Hampshire (1941); see also Cox v. Louisiana (1965), streets, sidewalks, and parks are places traditionally open, where First Amendment rights may be exercised . . . . [A] trial courtroom also is a public place where the people generally—and representatives of the media—have a right to be present, and where their presence historically has been thought to enhance the integrity and quality of what takes place . . . .

C

The State argues that the Constitution nowhere spells out a guarantee for the right of the public to attend trials, and that accordingly no such right is protected. The possibility that such a contention could be made did not escape the notice of the Constitution's draftsmen; they were concerned that some important rights might be thought disparaged because not specifically guaranteed. It was even argued that because of this danger no Bill of Rights should be adopted. See, e.g., A. Hamilton, *The Federalist* no. 84. In a letter to Thomas Jefferson in October of 1788, James Madison explained why he, although "in favor of a bill of rights," had "not viewed it in an important light" up to that time: "I conceive that in a certain degree . . . the rights in question are reserved by the manner in which the federal powers are granted." He went on to state "there is great reason to fear that a positive declaration of some of the most essential rights could not be obtained in the requisite latitude."

But arguments such as the State makes have not precluded recognition of important rights not enumerated. Notwithstanding the appropriate caution against reading into the Constitution rights not explicitly defined, the Court has acknowledged that certain unarticulated rights are implicit in enumerated guarantees. For example, the rights of association and of privacy, the right to be presumed innocent and the right to be judged by a standard of proof beyond a reasonable doubt in a criminal trial, as well as the right to travel, appear nowhere in the Constitution or Bill of Rights. Yet these important but unarticulated rights have nonetheless been found to share constitutional protection in common with explicit guarantees. The concerns expressed by Madison and others have thus been resolved; fundamental rights, even though not expressly guaranteed, have been recognized by the Court as indispensable to the enjoyment of rights explicitly defined.

We hold that the right to attend criminal trials is implicit in the guarantees of the First Amendment; without the freedom to attend such trials, which people have exercised for centuries, important as-

pects of freedom of speech and "of the press could be eviscerated."
Branzburg [v. Hayes (1972)] . . . .

D

. . . Absent an overriding interest articulated in findings [of a
particular set of circumstances], the trial of a criminal case must be
open to the public.[2]

Reversed.

Mr. Justice **POWELL** took no part in the consideration or decision in
this case.

Mr. Justice **WHITE,** concurring . . . .

Mr. Justice **STEVENS,** concurring . . . .

Mr. Justice **BRENNAN,** with whom Mr. Justice **MARSHALL** joins,
concurring in the judgment . . . .

I . . .

The Court's approach in right of access cases simply reflects the
special nature of a claim of First Amendment right to gather information. Customarily, First Amendment guarantees are interposed to
protect communication between speaker and listener. When so employed against prior restraints, free speech protections are almost
insurmountable. See Nebraska Press Assn. v. Stuart (1976); New York
Times Co. v. United States (1971). See generally Brennan, Address, 32
Rutgers L.Rev. 173, 176 (1979). But the First Amendment embodies
more than a commitment to free expression and communicative interchange for their own sakes; it has a *structural* role to play in
securing and fostering our republican system of self-government. See
United States v. Carolene Prods. Co. (1938); Grosjean v. American
Press Co. (1936); Stromberg v. California (1931); Ely, *Democracy and
Distrust* 93–94 (1980); Emerson, *The System of Freedom of Expression* 7
(1970); Meiklejohn, *Free Speech and Its Relation to Self-Government*
(1948). Implicit in this structural role is not only "the principle that
debate on public issues should be uninhibited, robust, and wide-open,"
New York Times [v. Sullivan (1964)], but the antecedent assumption
that valuable public debate—as well as other civic behavior—must be
informed. The structural model links the First Amendment to that
process of communication necessary for a democracy to survive, and

---

2. We have no occasion here to define the circumstances in which all or parts of a
criminal trial may be closed to the public . . . , but our holding today does not mean
that the First Amendment rights of the public and representatives of the press are
absolute . . . . [A] trial judge, in the interest of the fair administration of justice,
[may] impose reasonable limitations on access to a trial . . . . [Footnote by the Chief
Justice.]

thus entails solicitude not only for communication itself, but for the indispensable conditions of meaningful communication.[1]

However, because "the stretch of this protection is theoretically endless," . . . it must be invoked with discrimination and temperance. For so far as the participating citizen's need for information is concerned, "[t]here are few restrictions on action which could not be clothed by ingenious argument in the garb of decreased data flow." Zemel v. Rusk (1965). An assertion of the prerogative to gather information must accordingly be assayed by considering the information sought and the opposing interests invaded.

This judicial task is as much a matter of sensitivity to practical necessities as it is of abstract reasoning. But at least two helpful principles may be sketched. First, the case for a right of access has special force when drawn from an enduring and vital tradition of public entree to particular proceedings or information. Such a tradition commands respect in part because the Constitution carries the gloss of history. More importantly, a tradition of accessibility implies the favorable judgment of experience. Second, the value of access must be measured in specifics. Analysis is not advanced by rhetorical statements that all information bears upon public issues; what is crucial in individual cases is whether access to a particular government process is important in terms of that very process . . . .

II

"This nation's accepted practice of guaranteeing a public trial to an accused has its roots in our English common law heritage." In re Oliver (1948) . . . .

This Court too has persistently defended the public character of the trial process. *Oliver* established that the Due Process Clause of the Fourteenth Amendment forbids closed criminal trials . . . . Even more significantly for our present purpose, *Oliver* recognized that open trials are bulwarks of our free and democratic government: public access to court proceedings is one of the numerous "checks and balances" of our system, because "contemporaneous review in the forum of public opinion is an effective restraint on possible abuse of judicial power."

Tradition, contemporaneous state practice, and this Court's own decisions manifest a common understanding that "[a] trial is a public event. What transpires in the court room is public property." Craig v. Harney (1947).

III

Publicity serves to advance several of the particular purposes of the trial (and, indeed, the judicial) process. Open trials play a fundamental

---

1. The technique of deriving specific rights from the structure of our constitutional government, or from other explicit rights, is not novel. The right of suffrage has been inferred from the nature of "a free and democratic society" and from its importance as a "preservative of other basic civil and political rights . . . ." Reynolds v. Sims (1964). [Footnote by Justice Brennan.]

role in furthering the efforts of our judicial system to assure the criminal defendant a fair and accurate adjudication of guilt or innocence. But, as a feature of our governing system of justice, the trial process serves other, broadly political, interests, and public access advances these objectives as well. To that extent, trial access possesses specific structural significance.

The trial is a means of meeting "the notion, deeply rooted in the common law, that 'justice must satisfy the appearance of justice.'" Levine v. United States (1960). For a civilization founded upon principles of ordered liberty to survive and flourish, its members must share the conviction that they are governed equitably. It also mandates a system of justice that demonstrates the fairness of the law to our citizens. One major function of the trial, hedged with procedural protections and conducted with conspicuous respect for the rule of law, is to make that demonstration.

Secrecy is profoundly inimical to this demonstrative purpose of the trial process. . . .

But the trial is more than a demonstrably just method of adjudicating disputes and protecting rights. It plays a pivotal role in the entire judicial process, and, by extension, in our form of government. Under our system, judges are not mere umpires, but, in their own sphere, lawmakers—a coordinate branch of *government.* While individual cases turn upon the controversies between parties, or involve particular prosecutions, court rulings impose official and practical consequences upon members of society at large. Moreover, judges bear responsibility for the vitally important task of construing and securing constitutional rights. Thus, so far as the trial is the mechanism for judicial factfinding, as well as the initial forum for legal decisionmaking, it is a genuine governmental proceeding.

It follows that the conduct of the trial is preeminently a matter of public interest . . . .

More importantly, public access to trials acts as an important check, akin in purpose to the other checks and balances that infuse our system of government. "The knowledge that every criminal trial is subject to contemporaneous review in the forum of public opinion is an effective restraint on possible abuse of judicial power," *Oliver* . . . .

IV

. . . What countervailing interests might be sufficiently compelling to reverse this presumption of openness need not concern us now, for the statute at stake here authorizes trial closures at the unfettered discretion of the judge and parties . . . .

Mr. Justice **STEWART,** concurring in the judgment . . . .

Mr. Justice **BLACKMUN,** concurring in the judgment . . . .

. . . I remain convinced that the right to a public trial is to be found where the Constitution explicitly placed it—in the Sixth Amendment.

The Court, however, has eschewed the Sixth Amendment route. The plurality turns to other possible constitutional sources and invokes a veritable potpourri of them—the speech clause of the First Amendment, the press clause, the assembly clause, the Ninth Amendment, and a cluster of penumbral guarantees recognized in past decisions. This course is troublesome, but it is the route that has been selected and, at least for now, we must live with it. . . .

Having said all this, and with the Sixth Amendment set to one side in this case, I am driven to conclude, as a secondary position, that the First Amendment must provide some measure of protection for public access to the trial . . . .

Mr. Justice **REHNQUIST,** dissenting.

In the Gilbert & Sullivan operetta *Iolanthe,* the Lord Chancellor recites:

> The Law is the true embodiment
> of everything that's excellent,
> It has no kind of fault or flaw,
> And I, my lords, embody the law.

It is difficult not to derive more than a little of this flavor from the various opinions supporting the judgment in this case . . . .

. . . I do not believe that either the First or Sixth Amendments, as made applicable to the States by the Fourteenth, require that a State's reasons for denying public access to a trial, where both the prosecuting attorney and the defendant have consented to an order of closure approved by the judge, are subject to any additional constitutional review at our hands. And I most certainly do not believe that the Ninth Amendment confers upon us any such power to review orders of state trial judges closing trials in such situations.

We have at present 50 state judicial systems and one federal judicial system in the United States, and our authority to reverse a decision by the highest court of the State is limited to only those occasions when the state decision violates some provision of the United States Constitution. And that authority should be exercised with a full sense that the judges whose decisions we review are making the same effort as we to uphold the Constitution. As said by Mr. Justice Jackson, concurring in the result in Brown v. Allen [1953], "we are not final because we are infallible, but we are infallible only because we are final."

The proper administration of justice in any nation is bound to be a matter of the highest concern to all thinking citizens. But to gradually rein in, as this Court has done over the past generation, all of the ultimate decisionmaking power over how justice shall be administered, not merely in the federal system but in each of the 50 States, is a task that no Court consisting of nine persons, however gifted, is equal to. Nor is it desirable that such authority be exercised by such a tiny numerical fragment of the 220 million people who compose the population of this country. In the same concurrence just quoted, Mr. Justice Jackson accurately observed that "[t]he generalities of the Fourteenth Amendment are so indeterminate as to what state actions are forbidden that this Court has found it a ready instrument, in one field or another, to magnify federal, and incidentally its own, authority over the states."

. . . Nothing in the reasoning of Chief Justice Marshall in Marbury v. Madison (1803) requires that this Court through ever broadening use of the Supremacy Clause smother a healthy pluralism which would ordinarily exist in a national government embracing 50 States.

The issue here is not whether the "right" to freedom of the press conferred by the First Amendment to the Constitution overrides the defendant's "right" to a fair trial conferred by other amendments to the Constitution; it is instead whether any provision in the Constitution may fairly be read to prohibit what the trial judge in the Virginia state court system did in this case. Being unable to find any such prohibition in the First, Sixth, Ninth, or any other Amendments to the United States Constitution, or in the Constitution itself, I dissent.

Editors' Queries

(1) To what extent did Burger and Brennan disagree in this case?
(2) Is Brennan's merger of structural analysis with an argument from democratic theory successful?

V. RIGHT TO REPUTATION VERSUS FREEDOM OF COMMUNICATION

"The constitutional guarantees require . . . . a federal rule that prohibits a public official from recovering damages for a defamatory falsehood relating to his official conduct unless he proves that the statement was made with 'actual malice'—that is, with knowledge that it was false or with reckless disregard of whether it was false or not."

NEW YORK TIMES v. SULLIVAN
376 U.S. 254, 84 S.Ct. 710, 11 L.Ed.2d 686 (1964).

In 1960, when the Civil Rights Movement in the South was gaining momentum, the *New York Times* printed an advertisement, "Heed Their Rising Voices," which sought financial support and described the brutal reaction of police in Montgomery, Ala., and Orangeburg, S.C., to peaceful protests by black students seeking to affirm "human dignity" protected by the Constitution. Peaceful efforts at reform, the advertisement claimed, were "being met by an unprecedented wave of terror by those who would deny and negate that document . . . " L.B. Sullivan, a city commissioner of Montgomery, whose work included supervision of police, sued the *Times* and four persons whose names had appeared (without their permission) as sponsoring the advertisement. The *Times* conceded that the ad was inaccurate in some of its details, but noted that it had not named any individual as responsible for the violence. The jury awarded damages of $500,000. The Alabama supreme court affirmed, holding the advertisement was libelous *per se* and not privileged under the First and Fourteenth amendments. By the time the *Times* had sought and obtained certiorari and presented oral argument, eleven other suits by local officials, asking for $5.6 million, were pending against it.

Mr. Justice **BRENNAN** delivered the opinion of the Court.

We are required in this case to determine for the first time the extent to which the constitutional protections for speech and press limit a State's power to award damages in a libel action brought by a public official against critics of his official conduct. . . .

I

We may dispose at the outset of two grounds asserted to insulate the judgment of the Alabama courts from constitutional scrutiny. The first is the proposition relied on by the State Supreme Court—that "The Fourteenth Amendment is directed against State action and not private action." That proposition has no application to this case. Although this is a civil lawsuit between private parties, the Alabama courts have applied a state rule of law which petitioners claim to impose invalid restrictions on their constitutional freedoms of speech and press.
. . .

The second contention is that the constitutional guarantees of freedom of speech and of the press are inapplicable here, at least so far as the *Times* is concerned, because the allegedly libelous statements were published as part of a paid, "commercial" advertisement . . . .

The publication here . . . communicated information, expressed opinion, recited grievances, protested claimed abuses, and sought financial support on behalf of a movement whose existence and objectives are matters of the highest public interest and concern. . . . That the *Times* was paid for publishing the advertisement is as immaterial in this connection as is the fact that newspapers and books are sold.
. . . Any other conclusion would discourage newspapers from carrying "editorial advertisements" of this type, and so might shut off an important outlet for the promulgation of information and ideas by persons who do not themselves have access to publishing facilities—who wish to exercise their freedom of speech even though they are not members of the press . . . .

II . . .

Respondent relies heavily, as did the Alabama courts, on statements of this Court to the effect that the Constitution does not protect libelous publications. Those statements do not foreclose our inquiry

here. None of the cases sustained the use of libel laws to impose
sanctions upon expression critical of the official conduct of public
officials . . . .

. . . Like insurrection, contempt, advocacy of unlawful acts,
breach of the peace, obscenity, solicitation of legal business, and the
various other formulae for the repression of expression that have been
challenged in this Court, libel can claim no talismanic immunity from
constitutional limitations. It must be measured by standards that
satisfy the First Amendment.

The general proposition that freedom of expression upon public
questions is secured by the First Amendment has long been settled by
our decisions. The constitutional safeguard, we have said, "was fashioned to assure unfettered interchange of ideas for the bringing about
of political and social changes desired by the people." Roth v. United
States [1957]. "The maintenance of the opportunity for free political
discussion to the end that government may be responsive to the will of
the people and that changes may be obtained by lawful means, an
opportunity essential to the security of the Republic, is a fundamental
principle of our constitutional system." Stromberg v. California [1931].
"[I]t is a prized American privilege to speak one's mind, although not
always with perfect good taste, on all public institutions," Bridges v.
California [1941], and this opportunity is to be afforded for "vigorous
advocacy" no less than "abstract discussion." N.A.A.C.P. v. Button
[1963] . . . .

Thus we consider this case against the background of a profound
national commitment to the principle that debate on public issues
should be uninhibited, robust, and wide-open, and that it may well
include vehement, caustic, and sometimes unpleasantly sharp attacks
on government and public officials. The present advertisement, as an
expression of grievance and protest on one of the major public issues of
our time, would seem clearly to qualify for the constitutional protection. The question is whether it forfeits that protection by the falsity
of some of its factual statements and by its alleged defamation of
respondent.

Authoritative interpretations of the First Amendment guarantees
have consistently refused to recognize an exception for any test of
truth—whether administered by judges, juries, or administrative officials—and especially one that puts the burden of proving truth on the
speaker. Cf. Speiser v. Randall [1958]. The constitutional protection
does not turn upon "the truth, popularity, or social utility of the ideas
and beliefs which are offered." *Button* . . . . As Madison said,
"Some degree of abuse is inseparable from the proper use of every
thing; and in no instance is this more true than in that of the press."
. . .

Injury to official reputation affords no more warrant for repressing
speech that would otherwise be free than does factual error. Where
judicial officers are involved, this Court has held that concern for the

dignity and reputation of the courts does not justify the punishment as criminal contempt of criticism of the judge or his decision. *Bridges* . . . . This is true even though the utterance contains "half-truths" and "misinformation." Pennekamp v. Florida [1946]. Such repression can be justified, if at all, only by a clear and present danger of the obstruction of justice. . . . If judges are to be treated as "men of fortitude, able to thrive in a hardy climate," Craig v. Harney [1947], surely the same must be true of other government officials, such as elected city commissioners. Criticism of their official conduct does not lose its constitutional protection merely because it is effective criticism and hence diminishes their official reputations.

If neither factual error nor defamatory content suffices to remove the constitutional shield from criticism of official conduct, the combination of the two elements is no less inadequate. This is the lesson to be drawn from the great controversy over the Sedition Act of 1798, . . . which first crystallized a national awareness of the central meaning of the First Amendment . . . .

Madison prepared the Report [Of the Virginia legislature against the Alien and Sedition laws, discussed above, Chapter 7, at pp. 263–264—Eds.] in support of the protest. His premise was that the Constitution created a form of government under which "The people, not the government, possess the absolute sovereignty." The structure of the government dispersed power in reflection of the people's distrust of concentrated power, and of power itself at all levels. . . . Earlier, in a debate in the House of Representatives, Madison had said: "If we advert to the nature of Republican Government, we shall find that the censorial power is in the people over the Government, and not in the Government over the people." . . . The right of free public discussion of the stewardship of public officials was thus, in Madison's view, a fundamental principle of the American form of government . . . .

The state rule of law is not saved by its allowance of the defense of truth. . . . Allowance of the defense of truth, with the burden of proving it on the defendant, does not mean that only false speech will be deterred . . . . Under such a rule, would-be critics of official conduct may be deterred from voicing their criticism, even though it is believed to be true and even though it is in fact true, because of doubt whether it can be proved in court or fear of the expense of having to do so. They tend to make only statements which "steer far wider of the unlawful zone." *Speiser.* The rule thus dampens the vigor and limits the variety of public debate. It is inconsistent with the First and Fourteenth Amendments.

The constitutional guarantees require, we think, a federal rule that prohibits a public official from recovering damages for a defamatory falsehood relating to his official conduct unless he proves that the statement was made with "actual malice"—that is, with knowledge that it was false or with reckless disregard of whether it was false or not. . . .

Such a privilege for criticism of official conduct is appropriately analogous to the protection accorded a public official when *he* is sued for libel by a private citizen . . . . The reason for the official privilege is said to be that the threat of damage suits would otherwise "inhibit the fearless, vigorous, and effective administration of policies of government" and "dampen the ardor of all but the most resolute, or the most irresponsible, in the unflinching discharge of their duties." Barr v. Matteo [1959]. Analogous considerations support the privilege for the citizen-critic of government. It is as much his duty to criticize as it is the official's duty to administer . . . . It would give public servants an unjustified preference over the public they serve, if critics of official conduct did not have a fair equivalent of the immunity granted to the officials themselves.

We conclude that such a privilege is required by the First and Fourteenth Amendments.

III

We hold today that the Constitution delimits a State's power to award damages for libel in actions brought by public officials against critics of their official conduct. Since this is such an action, the rule requiring proof of actual malice is applicable. . . .

Since respondent may seek a new trial, we deem that considerations of effective judicial administration require us to review the evidence in the present record to determine whether it could constitutionally support a judgment for respondent. This Court's duty is not limited to the elaboration of constitutional principles; we must also in proper cases review the evidence to make certain that those principles have been constitutionally applied. This is such a case, particularly since the question is one of alleged trespass across "the line between speech unconditionally guaranteed and speech which may legitimately be regulated." *Speiser.* . . . In cases where that line must be drawn, the rule is that we "examine for ourselves the statements in issue and the circumstances under which they were made to see . . . whether they are of a character which the principles of the First Amendment, as adopted by the Due Process Clause of the Fourteenth Amendment, protect." *Pennekamp.* . . .

Applying these standards, we consider that the proof presented to show actual malice lacks the convincing clarity which the constitutional standard demands, and hence that it would not constitutionally sustain the judgment for respondent under the proper rule of law. The case of the individual petitioners requires little discussion. Even assuming that they could constitutionally be found to have authorized the use of their names on the advertisement, there was no evidence whatever that they were aware of any erroneous statements or were in any way reckless in that regard . . . .

As to the *Times,* we similarly conclude that the facts do not support a finding of actual malice . . . . We think the evidence against the *Times* supports at most a finding of negligence in failing to discover the misstatements, and is constitutionally insufficient to show the recklessness that is required for a finding of actual malice . . . .

We also think the evidence was constitutionally defective in another respect: it was incapable of supporting the jury's finding that the allegedly libelous statements were made "of and concerning" respondent . . . .

There was no reference to respondent in the advertisement, either by name or official position . . . . Although the statements may be taken as referring to the police, they did not on their face make even an oblique reference to respondent as an individual.

. . . For good reason, "no court of last resort in this country has ever held, or even suggested, that prosecutions for libel on government have any place in the American system of jurisprudence." City of Chicago v. Tribune Co. (1923 [Supreme Court of Illinois]). The present proposition would sidestep this obstacle by transmuting criticism of government, however impersonal it may seem on its face, into personal criticism, and hence potential libel, of the officials of whom the government is composed. There is no legal alchemy by which a State may thus create the cause of action that would otherwise be denied . . . . Raising as it does the possibility that a good-faith critic of government will be penalized for his criticism, the proposition relied on by the Alabama courts strikes at the very center of the constitutionally protected area of free expression. . . .

Reversed and remanded.

Mr. Justice **BLACK,** with whom Mr. Justice **DOUGLAS** joins, concurring.

. . . I base my vote to reverse on the belief that the First and Fourteenth Amendments not merely "delimit" a State's power to award damages to "public officials against critics of their official conduct" but completely prohibit a State from exercising such a power. The Court goes on to hold that a State can subject such critics to damages if "actual malice" can be proved against them. "Malice," even as defined by the Court, is an elusive, abstract concept, hard to prove and hard to disprove. The requirement that malice be proved provides at best an evanescent protection for the right critically to discuss public affairs and certainly does not measure up to the sturdy safeguard embodied in the First Amendment . . . .

In my opinion the Federal Constitution has dealt with this deadly danger to the press in the only way possible without leaving the free press open to destruction—by granting the press an absolute immunity for criticism of the way public officials do their public duty. . . . Stopgap measures like those the Court adopts are in my judgment not enough. This record certainly does not indicate that any different verdict would have been rendered here whatever the Court had charged the jury about "malice," "truth," "good motives," "justifiable ends," or any other legal formulas which in theory would protect the press. Nor does the record indicate that any of these legalistic words would have caused the courts below to set aside or to reduce the half-million-dollar verdict in any amount . . . .

We would, I think, more faithfully interpret the First Amendment by holding that at the very least it leaves the people and the press free to criticize officials and discuss public affairs with impunity . . . . While our Court has held that some kinds of speech and writings, such as "obscenity," Roth v. United States [1957], and "fighting words," Chaplinsky v. New Hampshire [1942], are not expression within the protection of the First Amendment, freedom to discuss public affairs and public officials is unquestionably, as the Court today holds, the kind of speech the First Amendment was primarily designed to keep within the area of free discussion. To punish the exercise of this right to discuss public affairs or to penalize it through libel judgments is to abridge or shut off discussion of the very kind most needed. This Nation, I suspect, can live in peace without libel suits based on public discussions of public affairs and public officials. But I doubt that a country can live in freedom where its people can be made to suffer physically or financially for criticizing their government, its actions, or its officials. "For a representative democracy ceases to exist the moment that the public functionaries are by any means absolved from their responsibility to their constituents; and this happens whenever the constituent can be restrained in any manner from speaking, writing, or publishing his opinions upon any public measure, or upon the conduct of those who may advise or execute it." [1] An unconditional right to say what one pleases about public affairs is what I consider to be the minimum guarantee of the First Amendment . . . .

Mr. Justice **GOLDBERG** with whom Mr. Justice **DOUGLAS** joins, concurring in the result . . . .

In my view, the First and Fourteenth Amendments to the Constitution afford to the citizen and to the press an absolute, unconditional privilege to criticize official conduct despite the harm which may flow from excesses and abuses. . . . The right should not depend upon a probing by the jury of the motivation of the citizen or press. The theory of our Constitution is that every citizen may speak his mind and every newspaper express its view on matters of public concern and may not be barred from speaking or publishing because those in control of government think that what is said or written is unwise, unfair, false, or malicious . . . .

. . . It may be urged that deliberately and maliciously false statements have no conceivable value as free speech. That argument, however, is not responsive to the real issue presented by this case, which is whether that freedom of speech which all agree is constitutionally protected can be effectively safeguarded by a rule allowing the imposition of liability upon a jury's evaluation of the speaker's state of

---

1. 1 Tucker, *Blackstone's Commentaries* (1803), 297.

mind. If individual citizens may be held liable in damages for strong words, which a jury finds false and maliciously motivated, there can be little doubt that public debate and advocacy will be constrained. And if newspapers, publishing advertisements dealing with public issues, thereby risk liability, there can also be little doubt that the ability of minority groups to secure publication of their views on public affairs and to seek support for their causes will be greatly diminished . . . .

This is not to say that the Constitution protects defamatory statements directed against the private conduct of a public official or private citizen. Freedom of press and of speech insures that government will respond to the will of the people and that changes may be obtained by peaceful means. Purely private defamation has little to do with the political ends of a self-governing society. The imposition of liability for private defamation does not abridge the freedom of public speech or any other freedom protected by the First Amendment . . . .

The conclusion that the Constitution affords the citizen and the press an absolute privilege for criticism of official conduct does not leave the public official without defenses against unsubstantiated opinions or deliberate misstatements. "Under our system of government, counterargument and education are the weapons available to expose these matters, not abridgment . . . of free speech . . . ." Wood v. Georgia [1962]. The public official certainly has equal if not greater access than most private citizens to media of communication. In any event, despite the possibility that some excesses and abuses may go unremedied, we must recognize that "the people of this nation have ordained in the light of history, that, in spite of the probability of excesses and abuses, [certain] liberties are, in the long view, essential to enlightened opinion and right conduct on the part of the citizens of a democracy." Cantwell v. Connecticut [1940]. As Mr. Justice Brandeis correctly observed, "sunlight is the most powerful of all disinfectants."
. . . .

Editors' Notes

(1) The Court's reexamination here of the trial record of a state court, especially where the state supreme court has affirmed the trial court's findings, is unusual, but it is not unprecedented. See, for example, Fiske v. Kansas (1927). Rule 52(a) of the Federal Rules of Civil Procedure establishes a similar policy for review of cases from federal courts:

> Findings of fact shall not be set aside [on appellate review] unless
> clearly erroneous, and due regard shall be given to the opportunity of
> the trial court to judge the credibility of the witnesses.

Bose Corp. v. Consumers Union (1984), which began in a federal court, modified Rule 52(a), where the First Amendment is involved, and elevated the modification into "a rule of federal constitutional law" that would be applicable to review of state decisions as well. As Justice Stevens wrote for the majority:

The requirement of independent appellate review reiterated in New York Times v. Sullivan is a rule of federal constitutional law. It emerged from the exigency of deciding concrete cases; it is law in its purest form under our common law heritage. It reflects a deeply held conviction that judges—and particularly members of this Court—must exercise such review in order to preserve the precious liberties established and ordained by the Constitution. The question whether the evidence in the record in a defamation case is of the convincing clarity required to strip the utterance of First Amendment protection is not merely a question for the trier of fact. Judges, as expositors of the Constitution, must independently decide whether the evidence in the record is sufficient to cross the constitutional threshold that bars the entry of any judgment that is not supported by clear and convincing proof of "actual malice."

(2) Brennan's opinion in *New York Times* differs from Black's and also Goldberg's. Which has the firmest basis in the "plain words" of the document? In the document's structure? In democratic theory? What about constitutionalism? How much more protective of the reputation of a public official would constitutionalism be than democratic theory?

(3) But how far would a democratic theorist want to push Black, Douglas, and Goldberg's reasoning or even Brennan's in *New York Times?* Could some of those opinions work to keep decent people out of politics? Justice Fortas, for example, vainly protested in St. Amant v. Thompson (1968) against the Court's reversing a judgment for damages secured by a public official against a man who, on a television program, falsely accused him of being a criminal:

> The First Amendment does not require that we license shotgun attacks on public officials in virtually unlimited open-season. The occupation of public officeholder does not forfeit one's membership in the human race.

It has been possible, however, for at least a few public officials to win judgments for libel under *New York Times.* Senator Barry Goldwater did so against *Fact Magazine,* which during the presidential campaign of 1964 pictured him as having a dangerously paranoid personality. The Supreme Court denied certiorari, over dissents from Black and Douglas. Ginzburg v. Goldwater (1970).

(4) *New York Times* concerned public officials, not private citizens, and Brennan's opinion of the Court was silent about whether its special protection of the press when writing about public officials applied to suits brought by private citizens. Black, on the other hand, would have outlawed all suits for libel. He did not say that in *New York Times,* but two years earlier, in a public interview, he had made his position quite clear:

> I have no doubt that the provision [First Amendment], as written and adopted, intended that there should be no libel or defamation law in the United States under the United States Government, just absolutely none so far as I am concerned . . . .
>
> My belief is that the First Amendment was made applicable to the states by the Fourteenth. I do not hesitate, so far as my own view is concerned, as to what should be and what I hope will sometime be

the constitutional doctrine that just as it was not intended to authorize damage suits for mere words as distinguished from conduct as far as the Federal Government is concerned, the same rule should apply to the states. ["Justice Black and First Amendment 'Absolutes': A Public Interview," 37 *N.Y.U.L.Rev.* 549, 557–558 (1962); The interview is also reprinted in Irving Dilliard, ed., *One Man's Stand for Freedom* (New York: Knopf, 1971), pp. 467ff.]

The justices soon had to face the question of the reach of *New York Times.* The Court soon constructed a middle category of people, whom it labeled "public figures," a vague term that included those who, while not public officials or candidates for public office, were newsworthy because of their occupations, such as a retired general who had vocally supported many political causes (Associated Press v. Walker [1967]), or a football coach at a large university (Curtis Publishing Co. v. Butts [1967]), or labor and management officials engaged in collective bargaining (Letter Carriers v. Austin [1974]), or, of course, a candidate for public office (Monitor Patriot Co. v. Roy [1971]).

Black (joined by Douglas) would have written into law the absolute immunity of the press, as he had said in the interview (Rosenbloom v. Metromedia [1971]). Brennan would have extended the requirement of "actual malice" to suits by private citizens if the allegedly libelous statements concerned matters of public interest (*Rosenbloom*); but the eight justices in that case split five different ways, with no majority opinion.

Three years after *Rosenbloom,* the Court held, 5–4, that *New York Times'* requirement of a showing of "actual malice" did not apply when the plaintiff was a private citizen. Gertz v. Welsh (1974). *Gertz* also held, however, that (1) while states had wide latitude to set their own standards in defamation suits between private citizens and news media, they could not make the media liable for damages without a showing that the media were at fault; (2) Even private citizens could not recover "punitive"—as contrasted with "actual"— damages in the absence of a finding of "actual malice." In addition, *Gertz* offered a somewhat more precise definition of a "public figure":

> For the most part those who attain this status have assumed roles of especial prominence in the affairs of society. Some occupy positions of such persuasive power and influence that they are deemed public figures for all purposes. More commonly, those classed as public figures have thrust themselves to the forefront of particular public controversies in order to influence the resolution of the issues involved.

For further discussion of who is a public figure, see Time v. Firestone (1976; reprinted as the next case, p. 606).

(5) The Court has only begun to settle the difficult problem of what evidence is sufficient to show "actual malice." Herbert v. Lando (1979) allowed a public figure who alleged he had been libeled by a producer on a television program and later in a magazine article to question the producer about such matters as his decisions to include and exclude evidence and his opinions about the veracity of some of his witnesses. After the Supreme Court's ruling, the Court of Appeals for the Second Circuit ultimately dismissed Herbert's suit against CBS and *The Atlantic Monthly*, holding that nine specific statements lacked any evidence of actual malice. The court refused to allow the complaint to go forward on the basis that the two remaining inaccurate but incidental statements were also not actionable as defamation. In 1985

General William Westmoreland's suit against the Columbia Broadcasting System for allegedly damaging his reputation in a televised program was settled out of court in CBS's favor before the conclusion of an extended trial. The General claimed that CBS so selected evidence, edited the film, and coached hostile witnesses as to have shown reckless disregard for the truth or falsity of its claim that he had misled the President about the strength of North Vietnam forces in South Vietnam.

(6) For general discussions of *New York Times* and the cases since, see: Annotation, "Progeny of New York Times v. Sullivan in the Supreme Court," 61 L.Ed.2d 975 (1980); Harry Kalven, The *New York Times* Case," 1964 *Sup.Ct. Rev.* 191; Melville B. Nimmer, "The Right to Speak from *Times* to *Time*," 56 *Calif.L.Rev.* 935 (1968); and C. Herman Pritchett, *Constitutional Civil Liberties* (Englewood Cliffs, N.J.: Prentice-Hall, 1984), pp. 101–108.

"[E]recting the *New York Times* barrier against all plaintiffs seeking to recover for injuries for defamatory falsehoods published in what are alleged to be reports of judicial proceedings would effect substantial depreciation of the individual's interest in protection from such harm, without any convincing assurance that such a sacrifice is required under the First Amendment."

TIME, INC. v. FIRESTONE
424 U.S. 448, 96 S.Ct. 958, 47 L.Ed.2d 154 (1976).

In 1966, Mary Alice Firestone asked a Florida court to grant her separate maintenance from her husband, Russell A. Firestone, Jr., scion of one of the nation's wealthiest families. He filed a counterclaim for divorce, charging her with extreme mental cruelty and adultery. The court granted the divorce, assigning an alimony of $3,000 a month and saying in an opaque opinion, "it is the conclusion and finding of the court that neither party is domesticated . . . ." *Time Magazine* received information about the divorce from several sources, including the Associated Press. After some checking, the editors ran the following story in the "Milestones" section of the magazine:

> DIVORCED: By Russell A. Firestone, Jr., 41, heir to the tire fortune: Mary Alice Sullivan Firestone, 32, his third wife; a one time Palm Beach schoolteacher; on grounds of extreme cruelty and adultery. . . . The 17-month intermittent trial produced enough testimony of extramarital adventures on both sides, the judge said, "to make Dr. Freud's hair curl."

After *Time* refused to print a retraction, Mary Alice Firestone sued for libel in a Florida court and won a judgment of $100,000, sustained on appeal by the state supreme court. *Time* sought and obtained certiorari from the U.S. Supreme Court.

Mr. Justice **REHNQUIST** delivered the opinion of the Court . . . .

II

Petitioner initially contends that it cannot be liable for publishing any falsehood defaming respondent unless it is established that the publication was made "with actual malice," as that term is defined in New York Times Co. v. Sullivan (1964). Petitioner advances two arguments . . . : that respondent is a "public figure" within this Court's decisions extending *New York Times* to defamation suits brought by such individuals, see, e.g., Curtis Publishing Co. v. Butts (1967); and that the *Time* item constituted a report of a judicial proceeding, a class of subject matter which petitioner claims deserves the protection of the "actual malice" standard even if the story is proved to be defamatorily false or inaccurate. We reject both arguments.

In Gertz v. Robert Welch, Inc. (1974), we have recently further defined the meaning of "public figure" for the purposes of the First and Fourteenth Amendments:

> For the most part those who attain this status have assumed roles of especial prominence in the affairs of society. Some occupy positions of such persuasive power and influence that they are deemed public figures for all purposes. More commonly, those classed as public figures have thrust themselves to the forefront of particular public controversies in order to influence the resolution of the issues involved.

Respondent did not assume any role of especial prominence in the affairs of society, other than perhaps Palm Beach society, and she did not thrust herself to the forefront of any particular public controversy in order to influence the resolution of the issues involved in it.

Petitioner contends that because the Firestone divorce was characterized by the Florida Supreme Court as a "cause célèbre," it must have been a public controversy and respondent must be considered a public figure. But in so doing petitioner seeks to equate "public controversy" with all controversies of interest to the public. Were we to accept this reasoning, we would reinstate the doctrine advanced in the plurality opinion in Rosenbloom v. Metromedia, Inc. (1971), which concluded that the *New York Times* privilege should be extended to falsehoods defamatory of private persons whenever the statements concern matters of general or public interest. In *Gertz*, however, the Court repudiated this position, stating that "extension of the *New York Times* test proposed by the *Rosenbloom* plurality would abridge [a] legitimate state interest to a degree that we find unacceptable."

Dissolution of a marriage through judicial proceedings is not the sort of "public controversy" referred to in *Gertz*, even though the marital difficulties may be of interest to some portion of the reading public. Nor did respondent freely choose to publicize issues as to the propriety of her married life. She was compelled to go to court by the State in order to obtain legal release from the bonds of matrimony. We have said that in such an instance "resort to the judicial process . . . is no more voluntary in a realistic sense than that of the defendant called upon to defend his interests in court." Boddie v. Connecticut (1971) . . . . She assumed no "special prominence in the resolution of public questions". *Gertz*. We hold respondent was not a "public figure" for the purpose of determining the constitutional protection afforded petitioner's report of the factual and legal basis for her divorce.

For similar reasons we likewise reject petitioner's claim for automatic extension of the *New York Times* privilege to all reports of judicial proceedings. It is argued that information concerning proceedings in our Nation's courts have such importance to all citizens as to justify extending special First Amendment protection to the press when reporting on such events. We have recently accepted a significantly more confined version of this argument by holding that the Constitution precludes States from imposing civil liability based upon the publication of truthful information contained in official court records open to public inspection. Cox Broadcasting Corp. v. Cohn (1975).

Petitioner would have us extend the reasoning of *Cox Broadcasting* to safeguard even inaccurate and false statements, at least where "actual malice" has not been established. But its argument proves too much. It may be that all reports of judicial proceedings contain some informational value implicating the First Amendment, but recognizing this is little different from labeling all judicial proceedings matters of "public or general interest". . . . Whatever their general validity, use of such subject-matter classifications to determine the extent of constitutional protection afforded defamatory falsehoods may too often result in an improper balance between the competing interests in this area. . . . By confining inquiry to whether a plaintiff is a public officer or a public figure . . . we sought a more appropriate accommodation between the public's interest in an uninhibited press and its equally compelling need for judicial redress of libelous utterances. Cf. Chaplinsky v. New Hampshire (1942).

Presumptively erecting the *New York Times* barrier against all plaintiffs seeking to recover for injuries from defamatory falsehoods published in what are alleged to be reports of judicial proceedings would effect substantial depreciation of the individual's interest in protection from such harm, without any convincing assurance that such a sacrifice is required under the First Amendment. And in some instances such an undiscriminating approach might achieve results directly at odds with the constitutional balance intended. . . .

It may be argued that there is still room for application of the *New York Times* protections to more narrowly focused reports of what actually transpires in the courtroom. But even so narrowed, the suggested privilege is simply too broad. Imposing upon the law of private defamation the rather drastic limitations worked by *New York Times* cannot be justified by generalized references to the public interest in reports of judicial proceedings. The details of many, if not most, courtroom battles would add almost nothing toward advancing the uninhibited debate on public issues thought to provide principal support for the decision in *New York Times*. And while participants in some litigation may be legitimate "public figures," either generally or for the limited purpose of that litigation, the majority will more likely resemble respondent, drawn into a public forum largely against their will in order to attempt to obtain the only redress available to them or to defend themselves against actions brought by the State or by others. There appears little reason why these individuals should substantially forfeit that degree of protection which the law of defamation would otherwise afford them simply by virtue of their being drawn into a courtroom. The public interest in accurate reports of judicial proceedings is substantially protected by *Cox Broadcasting.* As to inaccurate and defamatory reports of facts, matters deserving no First Amendment protection . . . we think *Gertz* provides an adequate safeguard for the constitutionally protected interests of the press and affords it a tolerable margin for error by requiring some type of fault.

III

Petitioner has urged . . . that it could not be held liable for publication of the "Milestones" item because its report of respondent's divorce was factually correct. . . . But this issue was submitted to the jury . . . . By returning a verdict for respondent the jury necessarily found that the identity of meaning which petitioner claims does not exist even for laymen. The Supreme Court of Florida upheld this finding on appeal . . . . Because demonstration that an article was true would seem to preclude finding the publisher at fault . . . we have examined the predicate for petitioner's contention. We believe the Florida courts properly could have found the "Milestones" item to be false.

For petitioner's report to have been accurate, the divorce granted Russell Firestone must have been based on a finding by the divorce court that his wife had committed extreme cruelty toward him *and* that she had been guilty of adultery. This is indisputably what petitioner reported in its "Milestones" item, but it is equally indisputable that these were not the facts. Russell Firestone alleged in his counterclaim that respondent had been guilty of adultery, but the divorce court never made any such finding. Its judgment . . . did not specify that the basis for the judgment was either of the two grounds alleged in the counterclaim. The Supreme Court of Florida on appeal concluded that the ground actually relied upon by the divorce court was "lack of domestication of the parties" . . . . Petitioner may well argue that the meaning of the trial court's decree was unclear, but this does not license it to choose from among several conceivable interpretations the one most damaging to respondent . . . . We believe there is ample support for the jury's conclusion, affirmed by the Supreme Court of Florida . . . .

IV

Gertz established, however, that not only must there be evidence to support an award of compensatory damages, there must also be evidence of some fault on the part of a defendant charged with publishing defamatory material. No question of fault was submitted to the jury in this case because under Florida law the only findings required for determination of liability were whether the article was defamatory, whether it was true and whether the defamation, if any, caused respondent harm.

The failure to submit the question of fault to the jury does not, of itself establish noncompliance with the constitutional requirements established in *Gertz*, however. Nothing in the Constitution requires that assessment of fault in a civil case tried in a state court be made by a jury, nor is there any prohibition against such a finding being made in the first instance by an appellate, rather than a trial, court . . . . If we were satisfied that one of the Florida courts which considered this case had supportably ascertained petitioner was at fault, we would be required to affirm the judgment below.

But the only alternative source of such a finding, given that the issue was not submitted to the jury, is the opinion of the Supreme Court of Florida. That opinion appears to proceed generally on the assumption that a showing of fault was not required . . . .

In the absence of a finding in some element of the state court system that there was fault, we are not inclined to canvass the record to make such a determination . . . . Accordingly, the judgment of the Supreme Court of Florida is vacated and the case remanded for further proceedings not inconsistent with this opinion.

So Ordered.

Mr. Justice **STEVENS** took no part in the consideration or decision of this case.

Mr. Justice **POWELL,** with whom Mr. Justice **STEWART** joins, concurring.

A clear majority of the Court adheres to the principles of *Gertz* . . . . But it is evident from the variety of views expressed that perceptions differ as to the proper application of such principles to this bizarre case. In order to avoid the appearance of fragmentation of the Court on the basic principles involved, I join the opinion of the Court. I add this concurrence to state my reaction to the record . . . .

In *Gertz* we held that "so long as they do not impose liability without fault, the States may define for themselves the appropriate standard of liability for a publisher or broadcaster of defamatory falsehood injurious to a private individual." Thus, while a State may elect to hold a publisher to a lesser duty of care, there is no First Amendment constraint against allowing recovery upon proof of negligence. The applicability of such a fault standard was expressly limited to circumstances where, as here, "the substance of the defamatory statement 'makes substantial danger to reputation apparent.'" By requiring a showing of fault the Court in *Gertz* sought to shield the press and broadcast media from a rule of strict liability that could lead to intolerable self-censorship and at the same time recognize the legitimate state interest in compensating private individuals for wrongful injury from defamatory falsehoods.

In one paragraph near the end of its opinion, the Supreme Court of Florida cited *Gertz* in concluding that *Time* was guilty of "journalistic negligence." But . . . it is not evident . . . that any type of fault standard was in fact applied . . . . [T]he ultimate question here is . . . : did *Time* exercise the reasonably prudent care that a State may constitutionally demand of a publisher or broadcaster prior to a publication whose content reveals its defamatory potential?

The answer to this question depends upon a careful consideration of all the relevant evidence concerning *Time's* actions prior to the publication of the "Milestones" article . . . .

. . . My point in writing is to emphasize that, against the background of a notorious divorce case and a decree that invited misunderstanding, there *was* substantial evidence supportive of *Time's* defense that it was not guilty of actionable negligence. At the very least the jury or court assessing liability in this case should have weighed these factors and this evidence before reaching a judgment. There is no indication in the record before us that this was done in accordance with *Gertz.*

Mr. Justice **BRENNAN,** dissenting . . . .

I

In a series of cases beginning with *New York Times*, this Court has held that the laws of libel and defamation, no less than other legal modes of restraint on the freedoms of speech and press, are subject to constitutional scrutiny under the First Amendment. The Court has emphasized that the central meaning of the free expression guarantee is that the body politic of this Nation shall be entitled to the communications necessary for self-governance, and that to place restraints on the exercise of expression is to deny the instrumental means required in order that the citizenry exercise that ultimate sovereignty reposed in its collective judgment by the constitution. Accordingly, we have held that laws governing harm incurred by individuals through defamation or invasion of privacy, although directed to the worthy objective of ensuring the "essential dignity and worth of every human being" necessary to a civilized society, Rosenblatt v. Baer (1966) (Stewart, J., concurring), must be measured and limited by constitutional constraints assuring the maintenance and well-being of the system of free expression. Although "calculated falsehood" is no part of the expression protected by the central meaning of the First Amendment, Garrison v. Louisiana (1964), error and misstatement is recognized as inevitable in any scheme of truly free expression and debate . . . . Therefore, in order to avoid the self-censorship that would necessarily accompany strict or simple fault liability for erroneous statements, rules governing liability for injury to reputation are required to allow an adequate margin for error—protecting some misstatements so that the "freedoms of expression . . . have the 'breathing space' that they 'need . . . to survive.'" *New York Times.* "To insure the ascertainment and publication of the truth about public affairs, it is essential that the First Amendment protect some erroneous publications as well as true ones." St. Amant v. Thompson (1968). For this reason, *New York Times* held that liability for defamation of a public official may not be imposed in the absence of proof of actual malice on the part of the person making the erroneous statement.

Identical considerations led the Court last Term in *Cox Broadcasting,* to hold that the First Amendment commands an absolute privilege to truthfully report the contents of public records reflecting the subject matter of judicial proceedings. Recognizing the possibility of injury to legitimate privacy interests of persons affected by such proceedings, the Court was nevertheless constrained in light of the strong First Amendment values involved to conclude that no liability whatever could be imposed by the State for reports damaging to those concerns . . . .

> Public records by their very nature are of interest to those concerned with the administration of government, and a public benefit is performed by the reporting of the true contents of the records by the media. The freedom of the press to publish that information appears to us to be of critical importance to our type of government in which the citizenry is the final judge of the proper conduct of public business. . . .

II

It is true, of course, that the Court in *Gertz* cut back on the scope of application of the *New York Times* privilege as it had evolved through the plurality opinion in *Rosenbloom.* *Rosenbloom* had held the *New York Times* privilege applicable to "all discussion and communication involving matters of public or general concern, without regard to whether the persons involved are famous or anonymous." But in light of the Court's perception of an altered balance between the conflicting values at stake where the person defamed is in some sense a "private individual" *Gertz* held First Amendment interests adequately protected in such circumstances so long as defamation liability is restricted to a requirement of "fault" and proof of "actual injury" resulting from the claimed defamation. However, the extension of the relaxed standard of *Gertz* to news reporting of events transpiring in and decisions arising out of public judicial proceedings is unwarranted by the terms of *Gertz* itself, is contrary to other well-established precedents of this Court and, most importantly, savages the cherished values encased in the First Amendment . . . .

At stake in the present case is the ability of the press to report to the citizenry the events transpiring in the Nation's judicial systems. There is simply no meaningful or constitutionally adequate way to report such events without reference to those persons and transactions that form the subject matter in controversy. . . . The Court has recognized that with regard to the judiciary, no less than other areas of government, the press performs an indispensable role by "subjecting the . . . judicial processes to extensive public scrutiny and criticism."

Sheppard v. Maxwell (1966). And it is critical that the judicial processes be open to such scrutiny and criticism, for, as the Court has noted in the specific context of labor disputes, the more acute public controversies are, "the more likely it is that in some aspect they get into court." Bridges v. California (1941). Indeed, slight reflection is needed to observe the insistent and complex interaction between controversial judicial proceedings and popular impressions thereof and fundamental legal and political changes in the Nation throughout the 200 years of evolution of our political system. With the judiciary as with all other aspects of government, the First Amendment guarantees to the people of this Nation that they shall retain the necessary means of control over their institutions that might in the alternative grow remote, insensitive, and finally acquisitive of those attributes of sovereignty not delegated by the Constitution.

Also no less true than in other areas of government, error in reporting and debate concerning the judicial process is inevitable. Indeed, in view of the complexities of that process and its unfamiliarity to the laymen who report it, the probability of inadvertent error may be substantially greater . . . .

Mr. Justice **WHITE**, dissenting . . . .

Mr. Justice **MARSHALL**, dissenting . . . .

Editors' Notes

(1) **Query:** Rehnquist asserted that "labeling all judicial proceedings [as] matters of 'public or general interest' . . . may too often result in an improper balance between competing interests in this area." Did Rehnquist himself use balancing as a technique of constitutional interpretation? Did Brennan in his dissent here or in his opinion for the Court in *New York Times*? How would one describe the *approaches, modes,* and *techniques* of the two justices in these cases? (For an argument that Brennan used a particular form of balancing in *New York Times,* see Melville B. Nimmer, "The Right to Speak from *Times* to *Time*," 56 *Calif.L.Rev.* 935 (1968).

(2) **Query:** To return to a perennial question: Would constitutionalism offer a different response to Time v. Firestone from that which democratic theory would put forth?

(3) The Court's apparent emphasis on Mrs. Firestone's right to reputation made its ruling three weeks later in Paul v. Davis (1976; reprinted below, p. 1161) all the more puzzling. In an opinion also written by Rehnquist, the Court held, by the same 5–3 division as in *Time,* with Stevens again taking no part, that there was no right to a good name protected by the federal Constitution. As Brennan pointed out in his dissent:

> It is strange that the Court should hold that the interest in one's good name and reputation is not embraced within the concept of "liberty" or "property" under the Fourteenth Amendment, and yet hold that the

same interest, when recognized under state law, is sufficient to overcome the specific protections of the First Amendment.

Is it possible to construct a coherent theory of constitutional interpretation that would simultaneously produce Time v. Firestone and Paul v. Davis?

12

Political Participation

Problems of freedom of political communication are intricate and fascinating in their own right, so much so that they may distract attention from the fundamental problem: HOW should the Constitution be interpreted? This bloc of chapters is focusing on one particular answer to the question of HOW: That judges have a very limited part to play in interpretation, one restricted to keeping the political processes open, reinforcing representative democracy so that popularly chosen officials can decide most of the substantive issues of public policy, even those involving constitutional interpretation.

Chapter Two discussed six minimal institutional conditions necessary for representative democracy: (1) Popular election for limited terms of the most important policy makers to governmental offices that allow a majority to govern; (2) Universal adult suffrage; (3) Electoral districts of approximately equal population that are not skewed to give disproportionate advantages to particular political parties or interests; (4) Free entry of citizens as candidates for electoral office; (5) Freedom of political communication so that citizens can be as informed as they wish to be about issues and candidates competing for public office; and, closely related to several of these, (6) Freedom to associate with other people to try to convince them of the rightness of one's views and/or to join with others of similar views to influence campaigns (to electioneer) and officeholders (to lobby).

The problems raised by freedom of communication are inseparable from the difficulties involved in achieving the other freedoms essential to representative democracy. One cannot effectively campaign, join with others, lobby, or even vote intelligently if government controls what can and cannot be communicated. Most basically, if government controls all or even a large share of politically relevant information, elections themselves become charades. But, as the complexity of the cases in Chapter 11 demonstrated, freedom of political communication raises a host of difficulties, theoretical and practical, for constitutional interpretation.

And, even more so than with political communication, no regulation at all of the rights of political participation might well produce anarchy. A chaos of bribery, fraudulent voting, frivolous candidacies, and criminal conspiracies might flourish in the name of free political participation. At very least, government must protect the rights to participate from interference by other private citizens, lest violence determine electoral results.

Federalism and racial hatred have complicated the situation in the United States, but after some initial hesitation,[1] the Court sustained the efforts of Reconstruction Congresses to protect black voters from violence. As the justices unanimously held in Ex parte Yarborough (1884), affirming the conviction of a group of whites for beating up a black man who was trying to vote:

> If [the federal] government is anything more than a mere aggregation of delegated agents of other States and governments . . . it must have the power to protect the elections on which its existence depends from open violence and insidious corruption.

The history of state, mostly but not exclusively southern, efforts to keep blacks from voting is long and sordid. Southern influence in the Senate forced proponents of civil rights to wage their counter-campaign in the federal courts. Although blacks suffered significant defeats,[2] they finally succeeded in persuading the Supreme Court to invalidate the white primary,[3] which had, until the end of World War II, been the principal "legal" means of violating the Constitution. It was not, however, until the School Segregation Cases (1954; reprinted below, p. 768) helped trigger the Civil Rights Movement that Congress finally enacted a comprehensive statute, the Voting Rights Act of 1965 (amended in 1970, 1975, and 1982), to protect against both subtle and not-so-subtle forms of fraud that for much of a century had kept blacks (and often poor whites) from voting.[4] South Carolina v. Katzenbach (1965) and its progeny[5] sustained the main provisions of the law.

Protecting citizens against violence and fraud in the electoral processes are, as Ex parte Yarborough held, obvious governmental duties. But what else must or even can government do to protect or even enhance rights to political participation?

I. TO WHAT EXTENT DOES THE CONSTITUTION INCLUDE DEMOCRATIC THEORY?

The reach of participatory rights and the degree to which they are protected by the Constitution are problematic. It takes a broad leap over logic, history, and current practice to claim that the Constitution

---

1. See, for example, United States v. Reese (1876), and United States v. Cruikshank (1876).

2. For example: Williams v. Mississippi (1890), Giles v. Harris (1903), and Grovey v. Townsend (1935).

3. Smith v. Allwright (1944), Terry v. Adams (1953).

4. See C. Herman Pritchett, *Constitutional Civil Liberties* (Englewood Cliffs, N.J.: Prentice-Hall, 1984), pp. 342–346 for summaries of the Act of 1965 and its amendments. See also Howard Ball, Dale Crane, and Thomas P. Lasuth, *Compromised Compliance: Implementation of the 1965 Voting Rights Act* (Westport, Conn.: Greenwood Press, 1982).

5. See especially: United States v. Mississippi (1965); Katzenbach v. Morgan (1966; reprinted above, p. 239), Oregon v. Mitchell (1970), Mobile v. Bolden (1980), and Rome v. United States (1980). See also Alexander Bickel, "The Voting Rights Cases," 1966 *Sup.Ct.Rev.* 79.

fully incorporates democratic theory. Its coexistence in tension with constitutionalism raises a set of limitations at the theoretical level. Moreover, not only were the framers wary of democracy, but one can also find a continuing ambivalence in the persistence of such patently nonmajoritarian institutions as a Senate equally representing each state regardless of population, an electoral college skewed to overrepresent less populous states, and an appointed judiciary.

Even the simple act of voting poses problems. Article I provides that those eligible to vote for the most numerous house of their state legislature are eligible to vote for candidates for the House of Representatives; and the Seventeenth Amendment, ratified in 1913, set the same standards for senatorial elections. All the document's other provisions, however, are negative: The Fifteenth forbids discrimination against potential voters on account of race, the Nineteenth on account of sex, the Twenty-sixth on account of age for those over eighteen, and the Twenty-fourth, which applies only to senatorial, congressional, and presidential elections, on account of failure to pay a tax.[6] Thus a strictly literal interpretation of the Constitution would produce the same result today as the Court's ruling in 1875 that "the Constitution of the United States does not confer the right of suffrage on any one. . . ."[7]

A theory of representative democracy may also demand electoral districts of equal population, but the constitutional document itself says nothing directly about such a requirement. For those who like to delve into the intent of the framers, both the Founding Fathers and those who proposed and ratified the Fourteenth and Fifteenth Amendments were intimately familiar with gerrymandering. Indeed, Elbridge Gerry, for whom the American practice of deliberately drawing unfair electoral lines was named, was himself a member of the Philadelphia Convention. Moreover, the framers of the Fourteenth Amendment apparently did not think that the equal protection clause applied to suffrage, for they quickly proposed the Fifteenth Amendment, which forbids discrimination among prospective voters, but only on the basis of race or previous condition of servitude; it does not mention other factors, such as maldistricting.

A structuralist might argue, as would many democratic theorists, that the architectural scheme of the document as well as of the historical development of the political system require "one person, one vote."[8] But the advent of that rule in American constitutional

6. Harper v. Virginia (1967; reprinted above, p. 151) went further, holding that the equal protection clause forbids making the right to vote depend on the payment of any tax, and so applies to elections of state as well as federal officers.

7. Minor v. Happersett (1875), sustaining a state constitutional provision limiting the suffrage to males. The Nineteenth Amendment, adopted in 1920, formally changed the constitutional rule, although by that time most states allowed women to vote.

8. Like structuralists, democratic theorists have to confront the harsh fact that weighting votes equally may exclude minorities from having effective representation in governmental institutions chosen by popular election. United Jewish Organizations v. Carey (1977) and Doe v. Bolton (1980) presented this problem to the Court, but the majority brushed it aside in both instances. Interpreters who endorse majoritarian theories of democracy rely on either "virtual" representa-

law is quite recent. (See Baker v. Carr [1962; reprinted below, p. 624] and Reynolds v. Sims [1964: reprinted below, p. 632].) And Warren's opinion for the Court in *Reynolds,* like Douglas' in Gray v. Sanders (1963)—which first set out the rule of "one person, one vote"—had much deeper roots in contemporary forms of democratic theory than in the text of the constitutional document or the history of the political system.

Thus to a considerable extent, the Court in this century has leaped across logic, history, and practice to read much, though not all, of democratic theory into the Constitution. Stone's footnote four in *Carolene Products* (1938; reprinted above, p. 482) was by no means the first decision to stress the importance of the political process in protecting all constitutional rights, but it established a landmark for the judiciary's special task of keeping the political processes open. And Warren's opinion in *Reynolds* highlighted the linkage between constitutional interpretation and democratic theory: "The right to vote freely for the candidate of one's choice is of the essence of a democratic society, and any restrictions on that right strike at the heart of representative government." In dissent, Harlan eloquently protested that the Court was applying a particular version of democratic theory, not a doctrine found in the explicit terms of the constitutional document or in the system's accepted practices. And he challenged imposition of the rule by unelected judges as itself anti-democratic.

In sum, Warren and Harlan disagreed fundamentally about the Court's function, about whether it should interpret the Constitution so as to articulate specific standards to "reinforce representative democracy." They also differed profoundly on the interpretation of democratic theory, illustrating that even agreement about the Constitution's democratic character does not automatically eliminate interpretive uncertainty. Ironically, Hugo Black, the great literalist, was on Warren's side, not Harlan's; but, as we have suggested, Black laced his literalism with political theory.[9]

II. PRACTICAL PROBLEMS

A. Voting: Problems of Districting, Literacy, and Residence

Interpreters who accept "reinforcing representative democracy" as well as the substantive doctrine of "one person, one vote" face many practical problems. First, the mobility of the American people makes it impossible to draw electoral lines that encompass equal populations or, given the diversity of the country, that do not somehow give an advantage to particular interests or parties. How much

---

tion to take care of such minorities or existence within the community of cross-cutting cleavages that can make, as coalitions form and reform as issues change, the political power of even small groups significant. See the discussion in Chapter 2, above, pp. 25–26.

9. Black even wrote the opinion of the Court in Wesberry v. Sanders (1964), which applied the principle of "one person, one vote" to congressional districting.

deviation from the norm is permissible? The Warren Court seemed to be moving to near mathematical uniformity,[10] but more recently the justices have been less strict, allowing variations in districts that reach as high as sixteen per cent,[11] but not those that reached twenty per cent.[12] Gerrymandering presents judges with even thornier problems, and so far the Court has warily entered this particular corner of the "political thicket" of apportionment.[13]

Second, does the Constitution, even if liberally suffused with democratic theory, allow government to condition voting on literacy in English? The document is utterly silent on the point, except insofar as the equal protection clause may be involved. The argument in favor of the limitation is that it makes voting, which has an impact on all citizens' lives not merely that of the voter, an informed act. There are two arguments against: (1) Literacy is not a legitimate basis on which to distinguish among citizens; and (2) literacy tests lend themselves to discriminatory administration. Recent constitutional debate has centered more on the second than the first point.

Around the turn of the century, the Court upheld such tests, even though it was obvious that southern states were unfairly administering them to exclude blacks.[14] In 1959, the Court unanimously reiterated this view, holding that it was not unreasonable for North Carolina to conclude that only those who could read were likely to be politically informed.[15] Congress later concluded that state officials were often using literacy tests so as to deny some citizens equal protection and, interpreting the Constitution for itself, forbade states to refuse the ballot to anyone who had completed six years of education in the United States *or* Puerto Rico. This provision provoked a furious debate within the Court about WHO was the authoritative interpreter of the Constitution, but Katzenbach v. Morgan (1966; reprinted above, p. 239) upheld the validity of the clause. In 1970 Congress suspended for five years all literacy tests as prerequisites to voting—sustained by Oregon v. Mitchell (1970)—and five years later made the suspension permanent.[16]

A third difficulty involves residency and registration. If government had no such regulations, nothing would prevent people from voting two or more times in the same election, a rather common

10. Swann v. Adams (1967), Kirkpatrick v. Preisler (1969).

11. Mahan v. Howell (1973).

12. Chapman v. Meier (1975).

13. See, for example: Wright v. Rockefeller (1964), United Jewish Organizations v. Carey (1977), and Karcher v. Daggett (1983). Only in the last did the Court strike down a state plan (New Jersey's) that constructed electoral districts of approximately equal population in such a way as to give distinct advantages to certain individuals and interests.

14. Giles v. Harris (1903); Guinn v. United States (1915). See also Williams v. Mississippi (1890).

15. Lassiter v. Northampton (1959). The Court, however, became much more cynical about requirements that prospective voters show registrars they "understood" or could "interpret" the state or national constitutions. *Giles* and *Williams,* cited in note 13, sustained such tests, but Louisiana v. United States (1965) struck them down.

16. 42 U.S.C. §§ 1973b(e)(2).

occurrence in large cities before enactment of laws requiring registration of voters. But demanding long periods of residence may deprive citizens of equal protection. How long is too long? Dunn v. Blumstein (1972) held that Tennessee's requirement of one year's residence to vote in state elections infringed both the right to vote and to travel freely. Thirty days residence, the Court noted, was the period Congress set in the Voting Rights Act of 1970 for eligibility to vote in presidential elections, and that "appears to be an ample period of time for the State to complete whatever administrative tasks are necessary to prevent fraud—and a year, or three months, too much." But then Marston v. Lewis (1973) and Burns v. Fortson (1973) sustained state claims that fifty days were necessary to complete accurate voting lists.

While these cases differ in detail, they do agree on two points: (1) To protect against fraud, states may require a minimum period of residency; and (2) "minimum" is measured in weeks, not months, lest it interfere with the rights to vote and to move one's residence freely within the country.

B. The Right to Associate

At first glance, the right to associate seems free of such difficulties. It is fundamental to representative democracy, and the First Amendment specifically recognizes "the right of the people peaceably to assemble, and to petition the government for a redress of grievances." But rights to assemble and petition may be more limited than a general right to associate. Do these rights encompass association for all political purposes? Do they include a right of communists to form a political party that would preach the propriety and necessity of forcefully overthrowing the Constitution? (See Barenblatt v. United States [1959; reprinted above p. 525]; Scales v. United States [1961; reprinted below p. 652] and Aptheker v. Secretary of State [1964; reprinted below, p. 657].) Do these rights allow small, unpopular groups who advocate peaceful change to keep their membership secret lest supporters be subject to community pressures? (See NAACP v. Alabama [1958; reprinted below, p. 646]). Can the Ku Klux Klan assert such a right to secrecy? (See New York v. Zimmerman [1928; reprinted below p. 643].)

C. Money and Politics: Contributing and Spending

Money poses special dangers for democratic politics. The costs of political campaigning are astronomical. Does the right to participate in political campaigns allow wealthy individuals or groups to *contribute* as much money as they wish to particular candidates? Does the right to campaign freely allow wealthy candidates, individuals, or groups to *spend* however much money it takes to blanket the mass media of communications to try to influence voters? For government to limit the amount of money one may contribute or spend certainly limits the capacity of candidates and their partisans to communicate freely. On the other hand, does representative democracy have a "compelling interest" in making certain that elections are held rather than bought? The Court wrestled with these issues in Buckley v. Valeo (1976; reprinted below, p. 677), and First National Bank v. Bellotti (1978; reprinted below, p. 690).

D. Money and Politics: Access to the Mass Media

Closely related to questions about campaign expenditures is the issue of access to mass media of communications. To operate a radio or television station and perhaps even more so a newspaper of any size requires huge amounts of capital. Because of such costs and the finite number of radio frequencies and TV channels available, control over these media is typically monopolistic and so gives the owners immense advantages in reaching the public with their opinions. Can government constitutionally require the holders of such monopolies to accord equal time to their political opponents? (See Miami Herald v. Tornillo [1974; reprinted below, p. 714].)

E. Lobbying

Lobbying raises similar issues. It is a right closely connected to those of free political communication—who better to communicate ideas to than one who holds power? And, human nature being what it is, lobbying is much more likely to be effective when the lobbyist has something besides sweet reason to offer. His votes and those of his associates are, of course, at stake; but what about money, perhaps contributions to campaign chests? The line between lobbying— essential we would *now* [17] all agree to representative democracy—and bribery can be fine indeed. Where can one legitimately draw it? To what extent can government regulate such activities? The Court tried hard to avoid this cluster of issues in United States v. Harriss (1954; reprinted below, p. 718.)

If there is a right to lobby legislators and executives, is there a penumbral right of individuals and groups to "lobby" judges in the sense of sponsoring lawsuits to bring the power of the court to bear to protect particular interests? After all, constitutional interpretation makes a substantial difference not only in the general ways the polity operates but also in the specific policies it pursues. One need only watch the flurry of political activity that precedes and accompanies the selection of judges to realize how widespread is an understanding of the importance of judicial decisions on public policy.

And organizational support is often available to help—in fact, sometimes to seek out and encourage—litigants to use the courts to achieve goals of public policy. Some groups like the NAACP, the

---

17. See, however, Trist v. Child (1874), which, in effect, held lobbying to be against public morals and voided a contract by which a client agreed to pay a lobbyist. The case is discussed in a note to United States v. Harriss (1954; reprinted below, at p. 718).

National Association of Manufacturers, and the AFL–CIO stand ready to support litigants who share their interests, just as the American Civil Liberties Union often assists in cases begun by others that raise important questions of constitutional rights.

For people who have no hope of achieving influence in the legislative process, courts may stand as the only havens against private or governmental oppression. (See the third paragraph of *Carolene Products* footnote 4; reprinted above, p. 482.) For individuals acting on their own to go to court to protect their rights seems natural. But does the situation change when people, who have used their right to associate to form organizations, bring their collective resources, financial and otherwise, to bear in the judicial process? The Court first fully confronted the issues of judicial lobbying in NAACP v. Button (1963; reprinted below, p. 723).

III. REINFORCING REPRESENTATIVE DEMOCRACY AND REDUCING JUDICIAL DISCRETION

No less than for freedom of communication, defining the existence and extent of other rights essential to democracy poses difficult problems for constitutional interpretation. Because of the document's silence, one must first read a version or versions of democratic theory into the Constitution to deduce from that instrument many basic participatory rights such as "one person, one vote." When compared to constitutionalism's defense of an active role for judges in protecting such fundamental substantive values as those to property and privacy (see Chapters 15–17), "reinforcing representative democracy" may seek less judicial discretion and judicial policy making. But this doctrine by no means eliminates either.

Indeed, this answer to the question of HOW to interpret the Constitution is grounded on the legitimacy of judges' making three great and related interpretive decisions that are not commanded by the plain words of the document: (1) That the Constitution is based on, or incorporates in its structure, a theory of representative democracy; (2) that judges therefore have a special obligation to insure that the political processes are open, so that the electorate has in fact the opportunity to choose public officials to represent their views on public policy; and (3) that judges must thereafter defer on most other issues, including many of substantive constitutional interpretation, to the judgment of such freely chosen officials.

The first decision responds to the WHAT interrogative, the second and third to WHO. Constitutionalists might accept the first and second decisions as correct, though incomplete, but they would consider the third an abdication of constitutional responsibility.

SELECTED BIBLIOGRAPHY

Abernathy, Glenn. *The Right of Assembly and Association* (Columbia, S.C.: University of South Carolina Press, 1961).

Bathe, David H. "Annotation: Supreme Court's Views Regarding First Amendment Guaranties of Speech or of the Press as Applied to Electoral or Referendum Process," 71 L.Ed.2d 1000 (1983).

Elliott, Ward E.Y. *The Rise of Guardian Democracy: The Supreme Court's Role in Voting Rights Disputes, 1845–1969* (Cambridge, Mass.: Harvard University Press, 1974).

Fellman, David. "Constitutional Rights of Association," 1961 *Sup.Ct. Rev.* 74.

Horn, Robert A. *Groups and the Constitution* (Stanford, Cal.: Stanford University Press, 1956.)

Kramer, Donald T. "Annotation: The Supreme Court and the First Amendment Right of Association," 33 L.Ed.2d 865 (1973).

Murphy, Walter F., and C. Herman Pritchett, eds., *Courts, Judges, and Politics* (4th ed; New York: Random House, 1986), Chap. 5.

Note. "Developments in the Law—Class Actions," 89 *Harv.L.Rev.* 1319 (1976).

Pateman, Carole. *Participation and Democratic Theory* (Cambridge: Cambridge University Press, 1970).

Pritchett, C. Herman. *Constitutional Civil Liberties* (Englewood Cliffs, N.J.: Prentice-Hall, 1984), Chap. 6.

Still, Jonathan W. "Political Equality and Election Systems," 91 *Ethics* 375 (1981).

Tribe, Laurence H. *American Constitutional Law* (Mineola, N.Y.: The Foundation Press, 1978), §§ 12–23, 13–28.

Vose, Clement E. "Litigation as a Form of Pressure Group Activity," 319 *The Annals* 20 (1958).

_____. "The National Consumers League and the Brandeis Brief," 1 *Midw. J. of Pol.Sci.* 267 (1957).

_____. *Caucasians Only: The Supreme Court, the NAACP and the Restrictive Covenant Cases* (Berkeley, Cal.: University of California Press, 1959).

Wright, J. Skelly. "Politics and the Constitution: Is Money Speech?" 85 *Yale L.J.* 1001 (1976).

I. THE RIGHT TO VOTE AND HAVE ONE'S VOTE COUNTED EQUALLY

"[T]he mere fact that the suit seeks protection of a political right does not mean it presents a political question."

BAKER v. CARR

369 U.S. 186, 82 S.Ct. 691, 7 L.Ed.2d 663 (1962).

The Supreme Court squarely confronted the issue of malapportionment of legislative districts in Colegrove v. Green (1946). The rural, Republican legislature of Illinois had declined for many decades to reapportion the state, thus maintaining district lines that did not reflect the great shift in population from the farms to urban areas. Three professors from the Chicago area sued in a federal district court, claiming that this system of gerrymandering-by-default of congressional districts, resulting as it did in some districts in and around Chicago having nine times the population of those in rural regions, was unconstitutional.

The district court dismissed the suit and the professors appealed. One would have expected that, when the case reached the Supreme Court, Chief Justice Stone as author of footnote four of *Carolene Products* would have invoked the second paragraph of that footnote and asserted a special judicial role to protect a right of citizens to have their votes counted equally. He, however, wanted no part of this controversy and told the conference "This isn't court business." According to Frank Murphy's notes of that discussion Justice Black was equally wary: "I don't want to get involved in control of elections in state and nation. I don't think [the] courts had power to make them [states] act." Apparently, only William O. Douglas spoke out for reversing the district court. (Murphy's notes indicate that he voted with Douglas, but Justice Burton's notes record Murphy as passing when his turn came.)

Stone died before the decision in *Colegrove* was announced and Justice Jackson did not participate—he was at Nurnberg serving as the chief Allied prosecutor at the war crimes trials of Nazi leaders. In the meantime, Douglas had persuaded Black, and Murphy, if he had wavered at the conference, also joined Black and Douglas. The switches, Stone's death, and Jackson's nonparticipation left a peculiar situation. There were three votes to affirm (Frankfurter, Reed, and Burton) on grounds that redistricting presented a political not a justiciable question. There were three votes to reverse (Black, Douglas, and Murphy) on grounds that redistricting presented a justiciable issue. The seventh vote, that of Justice Wiley Rutledge, was to affirm. He pretty much agreed with Douglas et al. that the issue was justiciable, but thought that it was so close to the election of 1946 that the courts would do more harm than good if they intervened at this time. (Rutledge may also have had tactical reasons for his stance; see Eds.' Note (5) that follows this case.)

Because of the power and eloquence of Frankfurter's separate opinion, most commentators assumed that the Court had treated districting as a political question and would continue to do so. And, indeed, the Court later dismissed several other challenges to malapportioned systems. Then in 1960 Gomillion v. Lightfoot struck down, as a violation of the Fifteenth Amendment ban against denials of the vote on the basis of race, Alabama's efforts to redraw the electoral districts in Tuskegee so as to exclude most black residents. Many observers construed *Gomillion,* especially since Frankfurter had written the opinion of the Court, as signalling a reversal of *Colegrove* and quickly new attacks on maldistricting began. The first to reach the Supreme Court came from Tennessee, which had not redrawn the lines for state legislative districts since 1901.

When the justices met in conference after oral argument, they were again equally divided, with one justice badly torn between the two sides. Black and Douglas had remained adamant over the years. They were now joined by Brennan and even Warren, who as governor had presided over what he admitted was the most malapportioned state in the country and had opposed reapportionment for what he frankly conceded were reasons of political expediency. Frankfurter had also not changed his mind. For him *Gomillion* was different from *Colegrove* because *Gomillion* involved racial discrimination, a violation of the Fifteenth Amendment. Harlan agreed, as to some extent did Tom Clark. Justice Charles Whittaker was not sure that *Colegrove* had been correctly decided but he did not want to see it overturned by a closely divided Court. Potter Stewart saw much reason in both positions and did not vote. The Court ordered reargument for the fall of 1961.

Reargument left eight of the justices unchanged, but Potter Stewart tentatively voted with Douglas et al. Thus the initial, if not very firm, decision was 5–4; but, Stewart would agree only that legislative districting presented a justiciable rather than a political question. He was not yet sure what sort of remedy a court could provide, so there could be no opinion on the merits, only directions to the district court, which had dismissed the suit, to hear it.

Black and Douglas talked to Warren and suggested that he not assign the opinion to himself or to either of them. All three had taken public stands on the issue and none was especially diplomatic. Assigning the opinion to Stewart might keep him in the fold, but his differences with the other four on reapportionment were real, and he and Douglas had sharp disagreements about judicial style. On the other hand, Brennan, as both a master at negotiation and a good friend of Stewart, was ideal. Warren agreed. The opinion went through almost twenty drafts, as Brennan patiently wrote and rewrote to meet the fresh objections that occurred to Stewart and counter the strong pressure that Frankfurter and Harlan were putting on Stewart to join them.

Shortly before the decision was to be announced, Whittaker retired because of ill health, leaving the vote 5–3. Then, after initially being pleased with Frankfurter's dissent, Clark began to have doubts. Eventually, he switched sides, leaving the vote at 6–2. Clark, like Warren, Black, Douglas, and Brennan himself, wanted to decide the case on the merits and hold that Tennessee's apportionment denied urban citizens equal protection of the laws. Five votes for that sort of decision were there; but at such a late stage Stewart might well have asked that the case be argued once again, and it would be difficult to oppose him. The new majority contented themselves with the thought that once the Court held that maldistricting presented a justiciable issue, there would be ample opportunity to speak to the merits.

Mr. Justice **BRENNAN** delivered the opinion of the Court. . . .

IV

Justiciability

In holding that the subject matter of this suit was not justiciable, the District Court relied on Colegrove v. Green [1946] and subsequent *per curiam* cases. We understand the District Court to have read the cited cases as compelling the conclusion that since the appellants sought to have a legislative apportionment held unconstitutional, their suit presented a "political question" and was therefore nonjusticiable. We hold that this challenge to an apportionment presents no nonjusticiable "political question. . . ."

Of course the mere fact that the suit seeks protection of a political right does not mean it presents a political question. Such an objection "is little more than a play upon words." Nixon v. Herndon [1927]. Rather, it is argued that apportionment cases, whatever the actual wording of the complaint, can involve no federal constitutional right except one resting on the guaranty of a republican form of government, and that complaints based on that clause have been held to present political questions which are nonjusticiable.

We hold that the claim pleaded here neither rests upon nor implicates the Guaranty Clause and that its justiciability is therefore not foreclosed by our decisions of cases involving that clause. . . .

Our discussion . . . requires review of a number of political question cases, in order to expose the attributes of the doctrine— attributes which, in various settings, diverge, combine, appear, and disappear in seeming disorderliness. . . . That review reveals that in the Guaranty Clause cases and in the other "political question" cases, it is the relationship between the judiciary and the coordinate branches of the Federal Government, and not the federal judiciary's relationship to the States, which gives rise to the "political question."

We have said that "in determining whether a question falls within [the political question] category, appropriateness under our system of government of attributing finality to the action of the political departments and also the lack of satisfactory criteria for a judicial determination are dominant considerations." Coleman v. Miller [1939]. The nonjusticiability of a political question is primarily a function of the separation of powers. Much confusion results from the capacity of the "political question" label to obscure the need for case-by-case inquiry. Deciding whether a matter has in any measure been committed by the Constitution to another branch of government, or whether the action of that branch exceeds whatever authority has been committed, is itself a delicate exercise in constitutional interpretation, and is a responsibility of this Court as ultimate interpreter of the Constitution. To demonstrate this requires no less than to analyze representative cases and to infer from them the analytical threads that make up the political question doctrine. We shall then show that none of those threads catches this case.

Foreign relations. There are sweeping statements to the effect that all questions touching foreign relations are political questions. Not only does resolution of such issues frequently turn on standards that defy judicial application, or involve the exercise of a discretion demonstrably committed to the executive or legislature; but many such questions uniquely demand single-voiced statement of the Government's views. Yet it is error to suppose that every case or controversy which touches foreign relations lies beyond judicial cognizance. Our cases in this field seem invariably to show a discriminating analysis of the particular question posed, in terms of the history of its management by the political branches, of its susceptibility to judicial handling in the light of its nature and posture in the specific case, and of the possible consequences of judicial action. . . .

Dates of duration of hostilities. Though it has been stated broadly that "the power which declared the necessity is the power to declare its cessation, and what the cessation requires," Commercial Trust Co. v. Miller [1923], here too analysis reveals isolable reasons for the presence of political questions, underlying this Court's refusal to review the political departments' determination of when or whether a war has ended. Dominant is the need for finality in the political determination.
. . .

Validity of enactments. In *Coleman* this Court held that the questions of how long a proposed amendment to the Federal Constitution remained open to ratification, and what effect a prior rejection had on a subsequent ratification, were committed to congressional resolution and involved criteria of decision that necessarily escaped the judicial grasp. . . .

The status of Indian tribes. This Court's deference to the political departments in determining whether Indians are recognized as a tribe, while it reflects familiar attributes of political questions . . . also has a unique element in that "the relation of the Indians to the United States is marked by peculiar and cardinal distinctions which exist no where else. . . ." Cherokee Nation v. Georgia [1831]. . . .

It is apparent that several formulations which vary slightly according to the settings in which the questions arise may describe a political question, although each has one or more elements which identifies it as essentially a function of the separation of powers. Prominent on the surface of any case held to involve a political question is found a textually demonstrable constitutional commitment of the issue to a coordinate political department; or a lack of judicially discoverable and manageable standards for resolving it; or the impossibility of deciding without an initial policy determination of a kind clearly for nonjudicial discretion; or the impossibility of a court's undertaking independent resolution without expressing lack of the respect due coordinate branches of government; or an unusual need for unquestioning adherence to a political decision already made; or the potentiality of embarrassment from multifarious pronouncements by various departments on one question.

Unless one of these formulations is inextricable from the case at bar, there should be no dismissal for nonjusticiability on the ground of a political question's presence. The doctrine of which we treat is one of "political questions," not one of "political cases." The courts cannot reject as "no law suit" a bona fide controversy as to whether some action denominated "political" exceeds constitutional authority. . . .

But it is argued that this case shares the characteristics of decisions that constitute a category not yet considered, cases concerning the Constitution's guaranty, in Art. IV, § 4, of a republican form of government. A conclusion as to whether the case at bar does present a political question cannot be confidently reached until we have considered those cases with special care. We shall discover that Guaranty Clause claims involve those elements which define a "political question," and for that reason and no other, they are nonjusticiable. In particular, we shall discover that the nonjusticiability of such claims has nothing to do with their touching upon matters of state governmental organization. . . .

[The opinion then reviewed at length Luther v. Borden (1849) and other cases involving the "republican form of government" issue.]

We come, finally to the ultimate inquiry whether our precedents as to what constitutes a nonjusticiable "political question" bring the case before us under the umbrella of that doctrine. A natural beginning is to note whether any of the common characteristics which we have been able to identify and label descriptively are present. We find none: The question here is the consistency of state action with the Federal Constitution. We have no question decided, or to be decided, by a political branch of government coequal with this Court. Nor do we risk embarrassment of our government abroad, or grave disturbance at home if we take issue with Tennessee as to the constitutionality of her action here challenged. Nor need the appellants, in order to succeed in this action, ask the Court to enter upon policy determinations for which judicially manageable standards are lacking. Judicial standards under the Equal Protection Clause are well developed and familiar, and it has been open to courts since the enactment of the Fourteenth Amendment to determine, if on the particular facts they must, that a discrimination reflects *no* policy, but simply arbitrary and capricious action. . . .

Reversed and remanded.

Mr. Justice **WHITTAKER** did not participate in the decision of this case.

Mr. Justice **DOUGLAS,** concurring. . . .

Mr. Justice **CLARK,** concurring. . . .

Mr. Justice **STEWART,** concurring. . . .

Mr. Justice **FRANKFURTER,** with whom Mr. Justice **HARLAN** joins, dissenting. . . .

We were soothingly told at the bar of this Court that we need not worry about the kind of remedy a court could effectively fashion once the abstract constitutional right to have courts pass on a state-wide system of electoral districting is recognized as a matter of judicial rhetoric, because legislatures would heed the Court's admonition. This is not only a euphoric hope. It implies a sorry confession of judicial impotence in place of a frank acknowledgement that there is not under our Constitution a judicial remedy for every political mischief. . . . In this situation as in others of like nature, appeal for relief does not belong here. Appeal must be to an informed, civically militant electorate. In a democratic society like ours, relief must come through an aroused popular conscience that sears the conscience of the people's representatives. . . .

In sustaining appellants' claim . . . this Court's uniform course of decision over the years is overruled or disregarded. . . .

The *Colegrove* doctrine . . . represents long judicial thought and experience. From its earliest opinions this Court has consistently recognized a class of controversies which do not lend themselves to judicial standards and judicial remedies. . . .

1. The cases concerning war or foreign affairs, for example, are usually explained by the necessity of the country's speaking with one voice in such matters. While this concern alone undoubtedly accounts for many of the decisions, others do not fit the pattern. . . . A controlling factor in such cases is that, decision respecting these kinds of complex matters of policy being traditionally committed not to courts but to the political agencies of government for determination by criteria of political expediency, there exists no standard ascertainable by settled judicial experience or process by reference to which a political decision affecting the question at issue between the parties can be judged. . . .

2. The Court has been particularly unwilling to intervene in matters concerning the structure and organization of the political institutions of the States. The abstention from judicial entry into such areas has been greater even than that which marks the Court's ordinary approach to issues of state power challenged under broad federal guarantees. . . .

3. The cases involving Negro disfranchisement are no exception to the principle. . . . For here the controlling command of Supreme Law is plain and unequivocal. An end of discrimination against the Negro was the compelling motive of the Civil War Amendments. . . .

4. The Court has refused to exercise its jurisdiction to pass on "abstract questions of political power, of sovereignty, of government." Massachusetts v. Mellon [1923]. . . . The crux of the matter is that courts are not fit instruments of decision where what is essentially at stake is the composition of those large contests of policy traditionally

fought out in non-judicial forums, by which governments and the actions of governments are made and unmade. . . .

5. The influence of these converging considerations—the caution not to undertake decision where standards meet for judicial judgment are lacking, the reluctance to interfere with matters of state government in the absence of an unquestionable and effectively enforceable mandate, the unwillingness to make courts arbiters of the broad issues of political organization historically committed to other institutions and for whose adjustment the judicial process is ill-adapted—has been decisive of the settled line of cases, reaching back more than a century, which holds that Art. IV, § 4, of the Constitution, guaranteeing to the States "a Republican Form of Government," is not enforceable through the courts. . . .

The present case involves all of the elements that have made the Guarantee Clause cases non-justiciable. It is, in effect a Guarantee Clause claim masquerading under a different label. But it cannot make the case more fit for judicial action that appellants invoke the Fourteenth Amendment rather than Art. IV, § 4, where, in fact, the gist of their complaint is the same. . . .

Here appellants attack "the State as a State. . . ." Their complaint is that the basis of representation of the Tennessee Legislature hurts them. They assert that "a minority now rules in Tennessee," that the apportionment statute results in a "distortion of the constitutional system," that the General Assembly is no longer "a body representative of the people of the State of Tennessee," all "contrary to the basic principle of representative government. . . ." Accepting appellants' own formulation of the issue, one can know this handsaw from a hawk. Such a claim would be non-justiciable not merely under Art. IV, § 4, but under any clause of the Constitution, by virtue of the very fact that a federal court is not a forum for political debate. . . .

But appellants, of course, do not rest on this claim *simpliciter*. In invoking the Equal Protection Clause, they assert that the distortion of representative government complained of is produced by systematic discrimination against them, by way of "a debasement of their votes. . . ."

. . . Appellants invoke the right to vote and to have their votes counted. But they are permitted to vote and their votes are counted. They go to the polls, they cast their ballots, they send their representatives to the state councils. Their complaint is simply that the representatives are not sufficiently numerous or powerful—in short, that Tennessee has adopted a basis of representation with which they are dissatisfied. . . . What is actually asked of the Court in this case is to choose among competing bases of representation—ultimately, really, among competing theories of political philosophy—in order to establish an appropriate frame of government for the State of Tennessee and thereby for all the States of the Union.

. . . This is not a case in which a State has, through a device however oblique and sophisticated, denied Negroes or Jews or redheaded persons a vote, or given them only a third or a sixth of a vote. That was Gomillion v. Lightfoot [1961]. . . . What Tennessee illustrates is an old and still widespread method of representation—representation by local geographical division, only in part respective of population—in preference to others, others, forsooth, more appealing. Appellants contest this choice and seek to make this Court the arbiter of the disagreement. They would make the Equal Protection Clause the charter of adjudication, asserting that the equality which it guarantees comports, if not the assurance of equal weight to every voter's vote, at least the basic conception that representation ought to be proportionate to population, a standard by reference to which the reasonableness of apportionment plans may be judged.

To find such a political conception legally enforceable in the broad and unspecific guarantee of equal protection is to rewrite the Constitution. . . .

Dissenting opinion of Mr. Justice **HARLAN,** whom Mr. Justice **FRANKFURTER** joins. . . .

Editors' Notes:

(1) **Query:** In his *Memoirs* (New York: Doubleday, 1977), p. 306, Earl Warren said that not the School Segregation Cases (1954) but Baker v. Carr "was the most important case of my tenure on the Court." Why would he say that?

(2) **Query:** Who was more faithful to democratic theory, Brennan or Frankfurter? Why? Who was the more faithful to the text of the constitutional document?

(3) The expectation that the Court would receive more cases involving reapportionment was, of course, quickly fulfilled. See the discussion in and notes to Reynolds v. Sims (1964; reprinted as the next case, p. 632). Stewart's differences with Black, Douglas, Warren, and Brennan would become more clear. "One, person, one vote" was not his notion of what the Fourteenth Amendment commanded. Clark, too, despite his wanting to get to the merits in *Baker* and invalidate Tennessee's apportionment, was not taken with that formula. He and Stewart preferred a more flexible judicial approach that would invalidate districting plans only when they appeared "irrational" or systematically frustrated the will of the majority. See their separate opinion in *Reynolds.*

(4) **Query:** It is in *Baker,* that Brennan made the claim for the Court "as the ultimate interpreter of the Constitution." Does that claim appear so acceptable now as it did when we first encountered it in Chapter 6?

(5) The long headnote to this case comes partially from Bernard Schwartz, *Super Chief* (New York: New York University Press, 1983), pp. 410–428 and partially from interviews, one very shortly after *Baker* came down, with two justices who participated in the case. Schwartz apparently believes that in *Colegrove,* Rutledge did not join Black, Douglas, and Murphy because if he had the case would have been put over for reargument during the next term. Jackson would have returned from Nurnberg and Fred Vinson, Stone's succes-

sor, would have voted as Stone had and Frankfurter's views would have carried a 5–4 majority instead of being those of only three justices. There are two problems with this explanation: First, Murphy and Burton record Rutledge as agreeing with Frankfurter at the first conference, while Stone was still alive, that districting presented a political question ("I don't think it is [a] judicial controversy," Murphy records him as saying, and Burton's docket book notes that Rutledge voted to dismiss the appeal because it was "political.") Second, had Rutledge changed his vote after Stone's death, Black, Douglas, and Murphy would have had a fourth vote and would have won in *Colegrove* since only seven justices participated in the case.

"[R]epresentative government is in essence self-government . . . and each and every citizen has an inalienable right to full and effective participation in the political processes of his State's legislative bodies."

REYNOLDS v. SIMS
377 U.S. 533, 84 S.Ct. 1362, 12 L.Ed.2d 506 (1964).

Following Baker v. Carr, the Court was quickly presented with opportunities to decide the substantive constitutional issues presented by maldistricting. Gray v. Sanders (1963) invalidated Georgia's "county unit" system, under which votes of residents of rural counties counted more than those in urban areas. There the Court first announced the doctrine of "one person, one vote." Wesberry v. Sanders (1964) applied the rule to congressional districting as well. Shortly after, the Court faced fourteen cases challenging other aspects of legislative districting. In *Reynolds,* a group of private citizens challenged Alabama's apportionment of seats in the state legislature. That apportionment had not changed since the census of 1900. According to the 1960 census, population in districts for the lower house ranged from 6,700 to 104,000, and for the senate from 15,000 to 634,000. The U.S. district court rejected several state proposals for redistricting because they still included wide disparities in population and ordered state officials to carry out the court's own plan for reapportionment. For different reasons, both the private citizens and the state appealed to the U.S. Supreme Court.

Mr. Chief Justice **WARREN** delivered the opinion of the Court. . . . .

II

Undeniably the Constitution of the United States protects the right of all qualified citizens to vote, in state as well as in federal elections. A consistent line of decisions by this Court in cases involving attempts to deny or restrict the right of suffrage has made this indelibly clear. . . . . And history has seen a continuing expansion of the scope of the right of suffrage in this country. The right to vote freely for the candidate of one's choice is of the essence of a democratic society, and any restrictions on that right strike at the heart of representative government. And the right of suffrage can be denied by a debasement or dilution of the weight of a citizen's vote just as effectively as by wholly prohibiting the free exercise of the franchise. . . .

III

A predominant consideration in determining whether a State's legislative apportionment scheme constitutes an invidious discrimination violative of rights asserted under the Equal Protection Clause is that the rights allegedly impaired are individual and personal in nature. . . . Like Skinner v. Oklahoma [1942], such a case "touches a sensitive and important area of human rights," and "involves one of the basic civil rights of man," presenting questions of alleged "invidious discriminations . . . against groups or types of individuals in violation of the constitutional guaranty of just and equal laws." Undoubtedly, the right of suffrage is a fundamental matter in a free and democratic society. Especially since the right to exercise the franchise in a free and unimpaired manner is preservative of other basic civil and political rights, any alleged infringement of the right of citizens to vote must be carefully and meticulously scrutinized. . . . [I]n Yick Wo v. Hopkins [1886] the Court referred to "the political franchise of voting" as "a fundamental political right, because preservative of all rights."

Legislators represent people, not trees or acres. Legislators are elected by voters, not farms or cities or economic interests. As long as ours is a representative form of government, and our legislatures are those instruments of government elected directly by and directly representative of the people, the right to elect legislators in a free and unimpaired fashion is a bedrock of our political system. . . . Weighting the votes of citizens differently, by any method or means, merely because of where they happen to reside, hardly seems justifiable. One must be ever aware that the Constitution forbids "sophisticated as well as simple-minded modes of discrimination." Lane v. Wilson [1939]. . . .

State legislatures are, historically, the fountainhead of representative government in this country. . . . But representative government is in essence self-government through the medium of elected representatives of the people, and each and every citizen has an inalienable right to full and effective participation in the political processes of his State's legislative bodies. Most citizens can achieve this participation only as qualified voters through the election of legislators to represent them. Full and effective participation by all citizens in state government requires, therefore, that each citizen have an equally effective voice in the election of members of his state legislature. Modern and viable state government needs, and the Constitution demands, no less.

Logically, in a society ostensibly grounded on representative government, it would seem reasonable that a majority of the people of a State could elect a majority of that State's legislators. To conclude differently, and to sanction minority control of state legislative bodies, would appear to deny majority rights in a way that far surpasses any

possible denial of minority rights that might otherwise be thought to
result. Since legislatures are responsible for enacting laws by which all
citizens are to be governed, they should be bodies which are collectively
responsive to the popular will. And the concept of equal protection has
been traditionally viewed as requiring the uniform treatment of persons standing in the same relation to the governmental action questioned or challenged. With respect to the allocation of legislative representation, all voters, as citizens of a State, stand in the same relation
regardless of where they live. Any suggested criteria for the differentiation of citizens are insufficient to justify any discrimination, as to the
weight of their votes, unless relevant to the permissible purposes of
legislative apportionment. Since the achieving of fair and effective
representation for all citizens is concededly the basic aim of legislative
apportionment, we conclude that the Equal Protection Clause guarantees the opportunity for equal participation by all voters in the election
of state legislators. Diluting the weight of votes because of place of
residence impairs basic constitutional rights under the Fourteenth
Amendment just as much as invidious discriminations based upon
factors such as race. Brown v. Board of Education [1954], or economic
status, Griffin v. Illinois [1956], Douglas v. California [1963]. Our
constitutional system amply provides for the protection of minorities by
means other than giving them majority control of state legislatures.
. . .

We are told that the matter of apportioning representation in a
state legislature is a complex and many faceted one. We are advised
that States can rationally consider factors other than population in
apportioning legislative representation. We are admonished not to
restrict the power of the States to impose differing views as to political
philosophy on their citizens. We are cautioned about the dangers of
entering into political thickets and mathematical quagmires. Our
answer is this: a denial of constitutionally protected rights demands
judicial protection; our oath and our office require no less of us. . . .

To the extent that a citizen's right to vote is debased, he is that
much less a citizen. The fact that an individual lives here or there is
not a legitimate reason for overweighting or diluting the efficacy of his
vote. . . . Representation schemes once fair and equitable become
archaic and outdated. But the basic principle of representative government remains, and must remain, unchanged—the weight of a citizen's
vote cannot be made to depend on where he lives. . . . A citizen, a
qualified voter, is no more nor no less so because he lives in the city or
on the farm. This is the clear and strong command of our Constitution's Equal Protection Clause. This is an essential part of the concept
of a government of laws and not men. This is at the heart of Lincoln's
vision of "government of the people, by the people, [and] for the
people." The Equal Protection Clause demands no less than substantially equal state legislative representation for all citizens, of all places
as well as of all races.

IV

We hold that, as a basic constitutional standard, the Equal Protection Clause requires that the seats in both houses of a bicameral state legislature must be apportioned on a population basis. Simply stated, an individual's right to vote for state legislators is unconstitutionally impaired when its weight is in a substantial fashion diluted when compared with votes of citizens living in other parts of the State. . . .

V

. . . [We] find the federal analogy inapposite and irrelevant to state legislative districting schemes. Attempted reliance on the federal analogy appears often to be little more than an after-the-fact rationalization offered in defense of maladjusted state apportionment arrangements. . . .

The system of representation in the two Houses of the Federal Congress is one ingrained in our Constitution, as part of the law of the land. It is one conceived out of compromise and concession indispensable to the establishment of our federal republic. Arising from unique historical circumstances, it is based on the consideration that in establishing our type of federalism a group of formerly independent States bound themselves together under one national government. . . .

Political subdivisions of States—counties, cities, or whatever—never were and never have been considered as sovereign entities. Rather, they have been traditionally regarded as subordinate governmental instrumentalities created by the State to assist in the carrying out of state governmental functions. . . . The relationship of the States to the Federal Government could hardly be less analogous. . . .

. . . The right of a citizen to equal representation and to have his vote weighted equally with those of all other citizens in the election of members of one house of a bicameral state legislature would amount to little if States could effectively submerge the equal-population principle in the apportionment of seats in the other house. . . .

We do not believe that the concept of bicameralism is rendered anachronistic and meaningless when the predominant basis of representation in the two state legislative bodies is required to be the same—population. A prime reason for bicameralism, modernly considered, is to insure mature and deliberate consideration of, and to prevent precipitate action on, proposed legislative measures. Simply because the controlling criterion for apportioning representation is required to be the same in both houses does not mean that there will be no differences in the composition and complexion of the two bodies. Different constituencies can be represented in the two houses. One body could be composed of single-member districts while the other could have at least some multimember districts. The length of terms of the legislators in the separate bodies could differ. The numerical size of the two bodies could be made to differ, even significantly, and the geographical size of districts from which legislators are elected could also be made to differ.

And apportionment in one house could be arranged so as to balance off minor inequities in the representation of certain areas in the other house. . . .

VI

. . . [T]he Equal Protection Clause requires that a State make an honest and good faith effort to construct districts, in both houses of its legislature, as nearly of equal population as is practicable. We realize that it is a practical impossibility to arrange legislative districts so that each one has an identical number of residents, or citizens, or voters. Mathematical exactness or precision is hardly a workable constitutional requirement. . . .

A State may legitimately desire to maintain the integrity of various political subdivisions, insofar as possible, and provide for compact districts of contiguous territory in designing a legislative apportionment scheme. Valid considerations may underlie such aims. Indiscriminate districting, without any regard for political subdivision or natural or historical boundary lines, may be little more than an open invitation to partisan gerrymandering. . . .

. . . So long as the divergences from a strict population standard are based on legitimate considerations incident to the effectuation of a rational state policy, some deviations from the equal-population principle are constitutionally permissible. . . . But neither history alone, nor economic or other sorts of group interests, are permissible factors in attempting to justify disparities from population-based representation. Citizens, not history or economic interests, cast votes. Considerations of area alone provide an insufficient justification for deviations from the equal-population principle. Again, people, not land or trees or pastures, vote. Modern developments and improvements in transportation and communications make rather hollow, in the mid-1960's, most claims that deviations from population-based representation can validly be based solely on geographical considerations. . . .

A consideration that appears to be of more substance in justifying some deviations from population-based representation in state legislatures is that of insuring some voice to political subdivisions, as political subdivisions. . . . In many States much of the legislature's activity involves the enactment of so-called local legislation, directed only to the concerns of particular political subdivisions. And a State may legitimately desire to construct districts along political subdivision lines to deter the possibilities of gerrymandering. However . . . if even as a result of a clearly rational state policy of according some legislative representation to political subdivisions, population is submerged as the controlling consideration in the apportionment of seats in the particular legislative body, then the right of all of the State's citizens to cast an effective and adequately weighted vote would be unconstitutionally impaired.

VII

One of the arguments frequently offered as a basis for upholding a State's legislative apportionment arrangement, despite substantial disparities from a population basis in either or both houses, is grounded on congressional approval, incident to admitting States into the Union, of state apportionment plans containing deviations from the equal-population principle. Proponents of this argument contend that congressional approval of such schemes, despite their disparities from population-based representation, indicates that such arrangements are plainly sufficient as establishing a "republican form of government." As we stated in Baker [v. Carr (1962)], some questions raised under the Guaranty Clause are nonjusticiable, where "political" in nature and where there is a clear absence of judicially manageable standards. Nevertheless, it is not inconsistent with this view to hold that, despite congressional approval of state legislative apportionment plans at the time of admission into the Union, even though deviating from the equal-population principle here enunciated, the Equal Protection Clause can and does require more. And an apportionment scheme in which both houses are based on population can hardly be considered as failing to satisfy the Guaranty Clause requirement. Congress presumably does not assume, in admitting States into the Union, to pass on all constitutional questions relating to the character of state governmental organization. In any event, congressional approval, however well-considered, could hardly validate an unconstitutional state legislative apportionment. Congress simply lacks the constitutional power to insulate States from attack with respect to alleged deprivations of individual constitutional rights. . . .

[Affirmed.]

Mr. Justice **HARLAN,** dissenting. . . .

. . . Whatever may be thought of this holding as a piece of political ideology—and even on that score the political history and practices of this country from its earliest beginnings leave wide room for debate (see the dissenting opinion of Frankfurter, J., in *Baker*)—I think it demonstrable that the Fourteenth Amendment does not impose this political tenet on the States or authorize this Court to do so.

. . . Stripped of aphorisms, the Court's argument boils down to the assertion that appellees' right to vote has been invidiously "debased" or "diluted" by systems of apportionment which entitle them to vote for fewer legislators than other voters, an assertation which is tied to the Equal Protection Clause only by the constitutionally frail tautology that "equal" means "equal."

Had the Court paused to probe more deeply into the matter, it would have found that the Equal Protection Clause was never intended to inhibit the States in choosing any democratic method they pleased for the apportionment of their legislatures. This is shown by the language of the Fourteenth Amendment taken as a whole, by the understanding of those who proposed and ratified it, and by the political practices of the States at the time the Amendment was adopted. It is confirmed by numerous state and congressional actions since the adoption of the Fourteenth Amendment, and by the common understanding of the Amendment as evidenced by subsequent constitutional amendments and decisions of this Court before *Baker* made an abrupt break with the past in 1962. . . .

     . . . Since it can . . . be shown beyond doubt that state legislative apportionments . . . are wholly free of constitutional limitations, save such as may be imposed by the Republican Form of Government Clause (Const. Art. IV, § 4), the Court's action now bringing them within the purview of the Fourteenth Amendment amounts to nothing less than an exercise of the amending power by this Court.

So far as the Federal Constitution is concerned, the complaints in these cases should all have been dismissed below for failure to state a cause of action, because what has been alleged or proved shows no violation of any constitutional right. . . .

I

[Harlan then examined in great detail the history of the adoption of the Fourteenth Amendment and concluded:]

The facts recited above show beyond any possible doubt:

(1) that Congress, with full awareness of and attention to the possibility that the States would not afford full equality in voting rights to all their citizens, nevertheless deliberately chose not to interfere with the States' plenary power in this regard when it proposed the Fourteenth Amendment;

(2) that Congress did not include in the Fourteenth Amendment restrictions on the States' power to control voting rights because it believed that if such restrictions were included, the Amendment would not be adopted; and

(3) that at least a substantial majority, if not all, of the States which ratified the Fourteenth Amendment did not consider that in so doing, they were accepting limitations on their freedom, never before questioned, to regulate voting rights as they chose. . . .

II

The Court's elaboration of its new "constitutional" doctrine indicates how far—and how unwisely—it has strayed from the appropriate bounds of its authority. The consequence of today's decision is that in all but the handful of States which may already satisfy the new requirements the local District Court or, it may be, the state courts, are given blanket authority and the constitutional duty to supervise apportionment of the State Legislatures. It is difficult to imagine a more intolerable and inappropriate interference by the judiciary with the independent legislatures of the States. . . .

Although the Court—necessarily, as I believe—provides only generalities in elaboration of its main thesis, its opinion nevertheless fully demonstrates how far removed these problems are from fields of judicial competence. Recognizing that "indiscriminate districting" is an invitation to "partisan gerrymandering," the Court nevertheless excludes virtually every basis for the formation of electoral districts other than "indiscriminate districting." . . . : (1) history; (2) "economic or other sorts of group interests"; (3) area; (4) geographical considerations; (5) a desire "to insure effective representation for sparsely settled areas"; (6) "availability of access of citizens to their representatives"; (7) theories of bicameralism (except those approved by the Court); (8) occupation; (9) "an attempt to balance urban and rural power"; (10) the preference of a majority of voters in the State.

So far as presently appears, the *only* factor which a State may consider, apart from numbers, is political subdivisions. But even "a clearly rational state policy" recognizing this factor is unconstitutional if "population is submerged as the controlling consideration. . . ."

I know of no principle of logic or practical or theoretical politics, still less any constitutional principle, which establishes all or any of these exclusions. . . . So far as the Court says anything at all on this score, it says only that "legislators represent people, not trees or acres"; that "citizens, not history or economic interests, cast votes"; that "people, not land or trees or pastures, vote." All this may be conceded. But it is surely equally obvious, and, in the context of elections, more meaningful to note that people are not ciphers and that legislators can represent their electors only by speaking for their interests—economic, social, political—many of which do reflect the place where the electors live. The Court does not establish, or indeed even attempt to make a case for the proposition that conflicting interests within a State can only be adjusted by disregarding them when voters are grouped for purposes of representation.

CONCLUSION

. . . What is done today deepens my conviction that judicial entry into this realm is profoundly ill-advised and constitutionally impermissible. . . . I believe that the vitality of our political system, on which in the last analysis all else depends, is weakened by reliance on the judiciary for political reform; in time a complacent body politic may result.

These decisions also cut deeply into the fabric of our federalism. What must follow from them may eventually appear to be the product of state legislatures. Nevertheless, no thinking person can fail to recognize that the aftermath of these cases, however desirable it may be thought in itself, will have been achieved at the cost of a radical alteration in the relationship between the States and the Federal Government, more particularly the Federal Judiciary. Only one who has an overbearing impatience with the federal system and its political processes will believe that that cost was not too high or was inevitable.

Finally, these decisions give support to a current mistaken view of the Constitution and the constitutional function of this Court. This view, in a nutshell, is that every major social ill in this country can find its cure in some constitutional "principle," and that this Court should "take the lead" in promoting reform when other branches of government fail to act. The Constitution is not a panacea for every blot upon the public welfare, nor should this Court, ordained as a judicial body, be thought of as a general haven for reform movements. The Constitution is an instrument of government, fundamental to which is the premise that in a diffusion of governmental authority lies the greatest promise that this Nation will realize liberty for all its citizens. This Court, limited in function in accordance with that premise, does not serve its high purpose when it exceeds its authority, even to satisfy justified impatience with the slow workings of the political process. For when, in the name of constitutional interpretation, the Court *adds* something to the Constitution that was deliberately excluded from it, the Court in reality substitutes its view of what should be so for the amending process. . . .

Mr. Justice **STEWART**, whom Mr. Justice **CLARK** joins, dissenting.*
. . .

I

What the Court has done is to convert a particular political philosophy into a constitutional rule, binding upon each of the 50 States. . . . My own understanding of the various theories of representative government is that no one theory has ever commanded unanimous assent among political scientists, historians, or others who have considered the problem. But even if it were thought that the rule announced today by the Court is, as a matter of political theory, the most desirable general rule which can be devised as a basis for the make-up of the representative assembly of a typical State, I could not join in the fabrication of a constitutional mandate which imports and forever freezes one theory of political thought into our Constitution, and forever denies to every State any opportunity for enlightened and progressive innovation in the design of its democratic institutions.
. . .

Representative government is a process of accommodating group interests through democratic institutional arrangements. . . . Appropriate legislative apportionment, therefore, should ideally be designed to insure effective representation in the State's legislature, in cooperation with other organs of political power, of the various groups and interests making up the electorate.
. . . [L]egislators do not represent faceless numbers. They represent . . . people with identifiable needs and interests . . . which can often be related to the geographical areas in which these people

---

* **Eds.' Note:** Justices Stewart and Clark concurred in the result in *Reynolds,* but dissented in companion cases, WMCA v. Lomenzo and Lucas v. Colorado (1964).

live. The very fact of geographic districting, the constitutional validity of which the Court does not question, carries with it an acceptance of the idea of legislative representation of regional needs and interests. Yet if geographical residence is irrelevant, as the Court suggests, and the goal is solely that of equally "weighted" votes, I do not understand why the Court's constitutional rule does not require the abolition of districts and the holding of all elections at large.

The fact is, of course, that population factors must often to some degree be subordinated in devising a legislative apportionment plan which is to achieve the important goal of ensuring a fair, effective, and balanced representation of the regional, social, and economic interests within a State. And the further fact is that throughout our history the apportionments of State Legislatures have reflected the strongly felt American tradition that the public interest is composed of many diverse interests, and that in the long run it can better be expressed by a medley of component voices than by the majority's monolithic command. What constitutes a rational plan reasonably designed to achieve this objective will vary from State to State, since each State is unique, in terms of topography, geography, demography, history, heterogeneity and concentration of population, variety of social and economic interests, and in the operation and interrelation of its political institutions. But so long as a State's apportionment plan reasonably achieves, in the light of the State's own characteristics, effective and balanced representation of all substantial interests, without sacrificing the principle of effective majority rule, that plan cannot be considered irrational.

. . . .

. . . . I think that the Equal Protection Clause demands but two basic attributes of any plan of state legislative apportionment. First, ... in the light of the State's own characteristics and needs, the plan must be a rational one. Secondly, ... the plan must be such as not to permit the systematic frustration of the will of a majority of the electorate of the State. I think it is apparent that any plan of legislative apportionment which could be shown to reflect no policy, but simply arbitrary and capricious action or inaction, and that any plan which could be shown systematically to prevent ultimate effective majority rule, would be invalid under accepted Equal Protection Clause standards. But, beyond this, I think there is nothing in the Federal Constitution to prevent a State from choosing any electoral legislative structure it thinks best suited to the interests, temper, and customs of its people. . . .

Editors' Notes

(1) **Query:** What are the fundamental differences between Warren and Harlan? Where do Stewart and Clark fit into this debate?

(2) Warren said in *Reynolds* that the Court was not requiring mathematical exactness, but several rulings during the next few years came close to demanding such equality. More recent decisions have taken a somewhat

looser attitude, though the Court did invalidate a districting scheme that contained variations in population of 20 per cent. See the discussion and cases cited in the Introduction to this Chapter, above, p. 619.

(3) With sophisticated computer programming, it is not difficult to give particular office holders, parties, or interests, great advantages in drawing electoral boundaries of districts that have approximately equal populations. In Gomillion v. Lightfoot (1960), a case that preceded Baker v. Carr and involved an effort by officials of Tuskegee, Alabama, to draw very intricate lines to minimize black voting power, the justices boldly faced up to this sort of gerrymandering. (See Bernard Taper, *Gomillion versus Lightfoot* [New York: McGraw-Hill, 1962]; and Jo Desha Lucas, "Dragon in the Thicket," 1961 *Sup. Ct.Rev.* 194.) But only once between *Gomillion* and the end of 1985 has the Court coped with this problem. See Karcher v. Daggett (1983), discussed in the Introduction to this Chapter, above, p. 619.

(4) **Query:** Does "one person, one vote" apply to all kinds of elections? Kramer v. Union Free School District (1969) struck down a New York statute limiting the right to vote in school district elections to certain kinds of taxpayers or parents of children attending public schools. See also Cipriano v. Houma (1969) and Phoenix v. Kolodzieski (1970) for much the same reasoning and results.

Then in 1973 the Court executed a significant shift in Salyer Land Co. v. Tulare Lake Basin Water Storage District, which sustained a state law limiting the right to vote for directors of a water district to landowners. Laurence H. Tribe believed that "*Salyer* plainly rests on the most problematic of foundations and should be treated as a narrowly limited exception to a powerful general principle that interest-based restrictions [on the right to vote] are constitutionally disfavored." *American Constitutional Law* (Mineola, N.Y.: The Foundation Press, 1978), p. 765. Certainly the tone of *Kramer* suggested Tribe's conclusions. But three years after he wrote, Ball v. James (1981) upheld an Arizona law limiting eligibility to vote for directors of a water district facility to those who own land and apportioning voting power among landowners according to how much land they have. What do these rulings do to the notion of open political processes and to the Court's having a special role to insure that openness?

"[W]ealth or fee paying has . . . no relation to voting qualifications; the right to vote is too precious, too fundamental to be so burdened or conditioned."

HARPER v. VIRGINIA STATE BOARD OF ELECTIONS
383 U.S. 663, 86 S.Ct. 1079, 16 L.Ed.2d 169 (1966).

This case, invalidating as a denial of equal protection Virginia's requirement that voters in state elections pay a tax of $1.50, is reprinted above at p. 151.

Editors' Notes

(1) **Query:** Douglas said at the opening of his opinion that "the right to vote in federal elections is conferred by Art. I, § 2 of the Constitution." In what way, if any, can one accept that statement as correct?

(2) **Query:** To what extent did Douglas' reasoning in *Harper* and Warren's in *Reynolds* (1964; reprinted above, p. 632) depend on structural analyses of the Constitution? To the degree either justice used a form of structural analyses, was it mainly of the document? Or did it extend to the political system? Beyond to the logic of the political theory(ies) on which the Constitution is based? (See the discussion of structuralism as a *mode* of interpretation in Chapter 8, pp. 292–294.)

"At-large voting schemes and multimember districts tend to minimize the voting strength of minority groups. . . . [But] this Court has repeatedly held that they are not unconstitutional per se."

ROGERS v. LODGE

458 U.S. 613, 102 S.Ct. 3272, 73 L.Ed.2d 1012 (1982).

This case affirmed lower court decisions that the political system of a Georgia county that elected its governing board from the county as a whole, without division into geographic subunits, violated the equal protection clause. The justices debated the proper standards to apply when faced with a policy— here an electoral system—that produced an adverse impact on a racial minority. The opinions are reprinted below, at p. 792.

II. THE RIGHT TO ASSOCIATE

"[L]iberty in this regard, like most other personal rights, must yield to the rightful exertion of the police power."

NEW YORK EX REL. BRYANT v. ZIMMERMAN

278 U.S. 63, 49 S.Ct. 61, 73 L.Ed. 184 (1928).

With certain exceptions for labor unions and benevolent associations, New York required every incorporated and unincorporated society of more than twenty members that imposed an oath as a condition of membership to file with the secretary of state a copy of its constitution, by-laws, and oath, as well as an annual list of officers and members. Any person who became or remained a member of an association that failed to comply with the registration provisions committed a misdemeanor. The Ku Klux Klan did not register, and George W. Bryant, a Klansman from Buffalo, was convicted and sent to jail. Later he sought habeas corpus from a state judge, alleging that he had been prosecuted under an unconstitutional statute. He lost at all three levels of state courts and obtained a writ of error from the U.S. Supreme Court.

Mr. Justice **VAN DEVANTER** delivered the opinion of the Court.
. . .

The relator's contention under the due process clause is that the statute deprives him of liberty in that it prevents him from exercising his right of membership in the association. But his liberty in this regard, like most other personal rights, must yield to the rightful exertion of the police power. There can be no doubt that under that power the State may prescribe and apply to associations having an oath-bound membership any reasonable regulation calculated to confine their purposes and activities within limits which are consistent with the rights of others and the public welfare. The requirement . . . that each association shall file with the secretary of state a sworn copy of its constitution, oath of membership, etc., with a list of members and officers is such a regulation. It proceeds on the two-fold theory that the State within whose territory and under whose protection the association exists is entitled to be informed of its nature and purpose, of whom it is composed and by whom its activities are conducted, and that requiring this information to be supplied for the public files will operate as an effective or substantial deterrent from violations of public and private right to which the association might be tempted if such a disclosure were not required. The requirement is not arbitrary or oppressive, but reasonable and likely to be of real effect. Of course, power to require the disclosure includes authority to prevent individual members of an association which has failed to comply from attending meetings or retaining membership with knowledge of its default. We conclude that the due process clause is not violated.

The main contention made under the equal protection clause is that the statute discriminates against the Knights of the Ku Klux Klan and other associations in that it excepts from its requirements several associations having oath-bound membership, such as labor unions, the Masonic fraternity, the Independent Order of Odd Fellows, the Grand Army of the Republic and the Knights of Columbus. . . .

The courts below . . . reached the conclusion that the classification was justified by a difference between the two classes of associations shown by experience, and that the difference consisted (a) in a manifest tendency on the part of one class to make the secrecy surrounding its purposes and membership a cloak for acts and conduct inimical to personal rights and public welfare, and (b) in the absence of such a tendency on the part of the other class. In pointing out this difference one of the courts said of the Ku Klux Klan, the principal association in the included class: "It is a matter of common knowledge that this organization functions largely at night, its members disguised by hoods and gowns and doing things calculated to strike terror into the minds of the people"; and later said of the other class: "These organizations and their purposes are well known, many of them having been in existence for many years. Many of them are oath-bound and secret. But we hear no complaints against them regarding violation of the peace or interfering with the rights of others." . . .

We assume that the legislature had before it such information as was readily available, including the published report of a hearing before a committee of the House of Representatives of the 57th Congress relating to the formation, purposes and activities of the Ku Klux Klan. If so, it was advised—putting aside controverted evidence—that the order was a revival of the Ku Klux Klan of an earlier time with additional features borrowed from the Know Nothing and the A.P.A. orders of other periods; that its membership was limited to native born, gentile, protestant whites; that in part of its constitution and printed creed it proclaimed the widest freedom for all and full adherence to the Constitution of the United States, in another exacted of its members an oath to shield and preserve "white supremacy," and in still another declared any person actively opposing its principles to be "a dangerous ingredient in the body politic of our country and an enemy to the weal of our national commonwealth"; that it was conducting a crusade against Catholics, Jews and Negroes and stimulating hurtful religious and race prejudices; that it was striving for political power and assuming a sort of guardianship over the administration of local, state and national affairs; and that at times it was taking into its own hands the punishment of what some of its members conceived to be crimes.

We think it plain that the action of the courts below in holding that there was a real and substantial basis for the distinction made between the two sets of associations or orders was right and should not be disturbed. . . .

Judgment affirmed.

Separate opinion of Mr. Justice **McREYNOLDS.**

. . . I think we have no jurisdiction of this writ of error and that it should be dismissed. . . .

Editors' Notes:

(1) The date of this case is 1928. Only three years earlier, Gitlow v. New York had for the first time held that the Fourteenth Amendment applied the First Amendment to the states. Despite the freshness of *Gitlow,* Van Devanter's opinion took a general liberty of association for granted, though his view of what that liberty encompasses may seem a bit narrow. The meaning and scope of a constitutional right to associate become more central—and controversial—in later cases reprinted in this chapter.

(2) Ex rel. (*ex relatione*) refers to a procedure under which a suit is brought in the name of the government but "on the relation" or "on the information" of and on behalf of another party. Here New York procedure required Bryant's suit to be begun in the name of the state against Zimmerman, who was the chief of police in Buffalo.

"It is beyond debate that freedom to engage in association for the advancement of beliefs and ideas is an inseparable aspect of the 'liberty' assured by the Due Process Clause of the Fourteenth Amendment. . . ."

NAACP v. ALABAMA

357 U.S. 449, 78 S.Ct. 1163, 2 L.Ed.2d 1488 (1958).

Following the National Association for the Advancement of Colored People's famous victory in the School Segregation Cases (1954), ten southern states began a concerted counter-attack, branding the organization as, among other things, a communist-inspired group. (See, for example, the two-volume pamphlet issued by the Georgia Education Commission, *Communism and the NAACP.*) These states convened legislative investigations, began court actions to produce membership lists and prosecutions for allegedly "fomenting" litigation and failing to register under Anti-Ku Klux Klan laws, similar to that upheld in New York ex rel. Bryant v. Zimmerman (1928; reprinted above, p. 643). A Louisiana statute threatened with dismissal any public school teacher who was found "advocating or in any manner performing any act toward bringing about integration of the races within the public school system," and Georgia would have punished such advocacy or action by revoking the teacher's license "forever."

Alabama's attack was the first to reach the U.S. Supreme Court. (See also NAACP v. Button [1963; reprinted below, p. 723].) The attorney general brought suit in a state circuit court seeking an injunction to forbid the NAACP to carry on activities in the state because it had failed to register as required by law. In 1956, before hearing evidence on the merits of the case, the trial judge issued a temporary injunction and also ordered the Association to produce its records and membership lists. The NAACP gave all the records requested except the names of rank-and-file members, who, it said, would be subjected to great harassment in communities hostile to desegregation. (During the proceedings, the judge won re-election on a platform that promised he would drive the NAACP out of the state; after the election he refused to disqualify himself from presiding at the rest of the trial.)

When the Association did not comply with the order regarding membership lists, the judge held it in contempt and fined it $100,000. The Alabama supreme court twice refused to review the ruling, and the NAACP obtained certiorari from the U.S. Supreme Court.

Mr. Justice **HARLAN** delivered the opinion of the Court. . . .

II

The Association both urges that it is constitutionally entitled to resist official inquiry into its membership lists, and that it may assert, on behalf of its members, a right personal to them to be protected from compelled disclosure by the State of their affiliation with the Association as revealed by the membership lists. We think that petitioner argues more appropriately the rights of its members, and that its nexus with them is sufficient to permit that it act as their representative before this Court. In so concluding, we reject respondent's argument that the Association lacks standing to assert here constitutional rights pertaining to the members, who are not of course parties to the litigation.

To limit the breadth of issues which must be dealt with in particular litigation, this Court has generally insisted that parties rely only on constitutional rights which are personal to themselves. Tileston v. Ullman [1943]. This rule is related to the broader doctrine that constitutional adjudication should where possible be avoided. See Ashwander v. Tennessee Valley Authority (concurring opinion) [1938]. The principle is not disrespected where constitutional rights of persons who are not immediately before the Court could not be effectively vindicated except through an appropriate representative before the Court. See Barrows v. Jackson [1951]; Joint Anti-Fascist Refugee Committee v. McGrath (concurring opinion) [1951].

If petitioner's rank-and-file members are constitutionally entitled to withhold their connection with the Association despite the production order, it is manifest that this right is properly assertable by the Association. To require that it be claimed by the members themselves would result in nullification of the right at the very moment of its assertion. Petitioner is the appropriate party to assert these rights, because it and its members are in every practical sense identical. . . . Cf. Pierce v. Society of Sisters [1925].

III

We thus reach petitioner's claim that the production order in the state litigation trespasses upon fundamental freedoms protected by the Due Process Clause of the Fourteenth Amendment. Petitioner argues that in view of the facts and circumstances shown in the record, the effect of compelled disclosure of the membership lists will be to abridge the rights of its rank-and-file members to engage in lawful association in support of their common beliefs. . . .

Effective advocacy of both public and private points of view, particularly controversial ones, is undeniably enhanced by group association, as this Court has more than once recognized by remarking upon the close nexus between the freedoms of speech and assembly. De Jonge v. Oregon [1937]; Thomas v. Collins [1945]. It is beyond debate that freedom to engage in association for the advancement of beliefs and ideas is an inseparable aspect of the "liberty" assured by the Due Process Clause of the Fourteenth Amendment, which embraces freedom of speech. See Gitlow v. New York [1925]; Palko v. Connecticut [1937]; Cantwell v. Connecticut [1940]; Staub v. Baxley [1958]. Of course, it is immaterial whether the beliefs sought to be advanced by association pertain to political, economic, religious or cultural matters, and state action which may have the effect of curtailing the freedom to associate is subject to the closest scrutiny.

The fact that Alabama, so far as is relevant to the validity of the contempt judgment presently under review, has taken no direct action, to restrict the right of petitioner's members to associate freely, does not end inquiry into the effect of the production order. In the domain of these indispensable liberties, whether of speech, press, or association, the decisions of this Court recognize that abridgement of such rights, even though unintended, may inevitably follow from varied forms of governmental action. . . . Similar recognition of possible unconstitutional intimidation of the free exercise of the right to advocate underlay this Court's narrow construction of the authority of a congressional committee investigating lobbying and of an Act regulating lobbying, although in neither case was there an effort to suppress speech. United States v. Rumely [1953]; United States v. Harriss [1954]. The governmental action challenged may appear to be totally unrelated to protected liberties. Statutes imposing taxes upon rather than prohibiting particular activity have been struck down when perceived to have the consequence of unduly curtailing the liberty of freedom of press assured under the Fourteenth Amendment. Grosjean v. American Press Co. [1936]; Murdock v. Pennsylvania [1943].

It is hardly a novel perception that compelled disclosure of affiliation with groups engaged in advocacy may constitute as effective a restraint on freedom of association as the forms of governmental action in the cases above were thought likely to produce upon the particular constitutional rights there involved. This Court has recognized the vital relationship between freedom to associate and privacy in one's associations. When referring to the varied forms of governmental action which might interfere with freedom of assembly, it said in American Communications Asso. v. Douds [1950]: "A requirement that adherents of particular religious faiths or political parties wear identifying arm-bands, for example, is obviously of this nature." Compelled disclosure of membership in an organization engaged in advocacy of particular beliefs is of the same order. Inviolability of privacy in group association may in many circumstances be indispensable to preservation of freedom of association, particularly where a group espouses dissident beliefs.

We think that the production order . . . must be regarded as entailing the likelihood of a substantial restraint upon the exercise by petitioner's members of their right to freedom of association. Petitioner has made an uncontroverted showing that on past occasions revelation of the identity of its rank-and-file members has exposed these members to economic reprisal, loss of employment, threat of physical coercion, and other manifestations of public hostility. Under these circumstances, we think it apparent that compelled disclosure of petitioner's Alabama membership is likely to affect adversely the ability of petitioner and its members to pursue their collective effort to foster beliefs which they admittedly have the right to advocate, in that it may induce members to withdraw from the Association and dissuade others from joining it because of fear of exposure of their beliefs shown through their associations and of the consequences of this exposure.

It is not sufficient to answer, as the State does here, that whatever repressive effect compulsory disclosure of names of petitioner's members may have upon participation by Alabama citizens in petitioner's activities follows not from *state* action but from *private* community pressures. The crucial factor is the interplay of governmental and private action, for it is only after the initial exertion of state power represented by the production order that private action takes hold.

We turn to the final question whether Alabama has demonstrated an interest in obtaining the disclosures it seeks from petitioner which is sufficient to justify the deterrent effect which we have concluded these disclosures may well have on the free exercise by petitioner's members of their constitutionally protected right of association.

Such a ". . . subordinating interest of the State must be compelling," Sweezy v. New Hampshire (concurring opinion) [1957]. It is not of moment that the State has here acted solely through its judicial branch, for whether legislative or judicial, it is still the application of state power which we are asked to scrutinize.

It is important to bear in mind that petitioner asserts no right to absolute immunity from state investigation, and no right to disregard Alabama's laws. . . . Petitioner has not objected to divulging the identity of its members who are employed by or hold official positions with it. It has urged the rights solely of its ordinary rank-and-file members. . . .

Whether there was "justification" in this instance turns solely on the substantiality of Alabama's interest in obtaining the membership lists. . . . The issues in the litigation commenced by Alabama . . . were whether the character of petitioner and its activities in Alabama had been such as to make petitioner subject to the registration statute, and whether the extent of petitioner's activities without qualifying suggested its permanent ouster from the State. Without intimating the slightest view upon the merits of these issues, we are unable to perceive that the disclosure of the names of petitioner's rank-and-file members has a substantial bearing on either of them. As matters stand in the state court, petitioner (1) has admitted its presence and conduct of activities in Alabama since 1918; (2) has offered to comply in all respects with the state qualification statute, although preserving its contention that the statute does not apply to it; and (3) has apparently complied satisfactorily with the production order, except for the membership lists, by furnishing the Attorney General with varied business records, its charter and statement of purposes, the names of all of its directors and officers, and with the total number of its Alabama members and the amount of their dues. These last items would not on this record appear subject to constitutional challenge and have been furnished, but whatever interest the State may have in obtaining names of ordinary members has not been shown to be sufficient to overcome petitioner's constitutional objections to the production order.

From what has already been said, we think it apparent that New York ex rel. Bryant v. Zimmerman [1928] cannot be relied on in support of the State's position, for that case involved markedly different considerations in terms of the interest of the State in obtaining disclosure. . . . The decision was based on the particular character of the Klan's activities, involving acts of unlawful intimidation and violence, which the Court assumed was before the state legislature when it enacted the statute, and of which the Court itself took judicial notice. Furthermore, the situation before us is significantly different from that in *Bryant,* because the organization there had made no effort to comply with any of the requirements of New York's statute but rather had refused to furnish the State with *any* information as to its local activities.

We hold that the immunity from state scrutiny of membership lists which the Association claims on behalf of its members is here so related to the right of the members to pursue their lawful private interests privately and to associate freely with others in so doing as to come within the protection of the Fourteenth Amendment. And we conclude that Alabama has fallen short of showing a controlling justification for the deterrent effect on the free enjoyment of the right to associate which disclosure of membership lists is likely to have. Accordingly, the judgment of civil contempt and the $100,000 fine which resulted from petitioner's refusal to comply with the production order in this respect must fall. . . .

Reversed.

Editors' Notes

(1) For the background to this and similar cases, see Walter F. Murphy, "The South Counterattacks: The Anti-NAACP Laws," 12 *West.Pol.Q.* 371 (1959).

(2) The Supreme Court "remanded" the case "for proceedings not inconsistent with this opinion." The case then went back to Alabama's supreme court. Twice the NAACP moved that that court direct the trial judge to proceed in accordance with the U.S. Supreme Court's ruling. In 1959, however, the Alabama supreme court held that the U.S. Supreme Court had acted on a "mistaken premise" and therefore reaffirmed the trial judge's adjudication of contempt. The NAACP returned to the U.S. Supreme Court and won a second, but limited victory. It had sought a mandamus—a direct order to the court below in place of the usual diplomatic formula regarding "proceedings not inconsistent with" the Court's opinion—but the justices contented themselves with reversing the Alabama supreme court and noting: "[T]he Alabama Supreme Court is foreclosed from reexamining the grounds of our disposition. . . . We assume that the State Supreme Court, thus advised, will not fail to proceed promptly with the disposition of the matters left open under our mandate. . . ." NAACP v. Alabama (1959).

The assumption was unwarranted. The NAACP was unable to obtain a hearing in the Alabama supreme court for more than a year, during which time the injunction against it remained in force. The Association then began an action in a U.S. district court to obtain a federal injunction against the operation of the state injunction. The district court dismissed, and the Court of Appeals for the Fifth Circuit affirmed, holding that the doctrine of "equitable abstention" required that the issues be settled in state courts. The NAACP again obtained review in the U.S. Supreme Court. In October, 1961, the justices directed the court of appeals to instruct the district judge to hold hearings unless "within a reasonable time, no later than January 2, 1962," the state courts had proceeded. NAACP v. Gallion (1961).

In December, 1961, five years after the state trial court had issued its "temporary" injunction, that court held its first hearings on the merits of the case. Shortly after, the trial court made its injunction permanent. Alabama's supreme court affirmed, and in 1964 the case came to the U.S. Supreme Court for the fourth time.

The justices still spoke softly, but this time they brandished their big stick:

The judgment below must be reversed. . . . [W]e are asked to formulate a decree for entry in the state courts which will insure the Association's right to conduct activities in Alabama without further delay. While such a course undoubtedly lies within this Court's power, Martin v. Hunter's Lesseee [1816], we prefer to follow our usual practice and remand the case to the Supreme Court of Alabama for further proceedings not inconsistent with this opinion. Such proceedings should include the prompt entry of a decree . . . vacating in all respects the permanent injunction . . . and permitting the Association to take all steps necessary to qualify it to do business in Alabama. Should we unhappily be mistaken in our belief that the Supreme Court of Alabama will promptly implement this decision, leave is given the Association to apply to this Court for further appropriate relief. NAACP v. Alabama (1964).

Six weeks later, Lyndon Johnson signed into law the Civil Rights Act of 1964, which for the first time put federal executive and legislative power unmistakably behind the concept of racial justice that the U.S. Supreme Court had found in the Constitution. Shortly thereafter, the Alabama judges dissolved the injunction.

———

"Where First Amendment rights are asserted to bar governmental interrogation resolution of the issue always involves a balancing by the courts of the competing private and public interests at stake. . . ."—Justice HARLAN

"This is closely akin to the notion that neither the First Amendment nor any other provision of the Bill of Rights should be enforced unless the Court believes it is *reasonable* to do so."—Justice BLACK

BARENBLATT v. UNITED STATES

360 U.S. 109, 79 S.Ct. 1081, 3 L.Ed.2d 1115 (1960).

This case, involving a clash between Barenblatt's right under the First Amendment to be silent about his political associations and a claim by a congressional committee to be able to obtain answers from him about his participation in the Communist party, is reprinted above at p. 525.

"Any thought that due process puts beyond the reach of the criminal law all individual associational relationships, unless accompanied by the commission of specific acts of criminality, is dispelled by familiar concepts of the law of conspiracy. . . ."

SCALES v. UNITED STATES
367 U.S. 203, 81 S.Ct. 1469, 6 L.Ed.2d 782 (1961).

Junius Irving Scales, former chairman of the Communist party in North and South Carolina, was convicted under the clause of the Smith Act making it a crime to be a member of an organization that advocated violent overthrow of a government in the United States. The court of appeals upheld the conviction, and the Supreme Court granted certiorari.

Mr. Justice **HARLAN** delivered the opinion of the Court. . . .

II. CONSTITUTIONAL CHALLENGE

. . . . The jury was instructed that in order to convict it must find that within the three-year limitations period (1) the Communist Party advocated the violent overthrow of the Government, in the sense of present "advocacy of action" to accomplish that end as soon as circumstances were propitious; and (2) petitioner was an "active" member of the Party, and not merely "a nominal, passive, inactive or purely technical" member, with knowledge of the Party's illegal advocacy and a specific intent to bring about violent overthrow "as speedily as circumstances would permit."

The constitutional attack upon the membership clause, as thus construed, is that the statute offends (1) the Fifth Amendment, in that it impermissibly imputes guilt to an individual merely on the basis of his associations and sympathies . . . and (2) the First Amendment, in that it infringes on free political expression and association. Subsidiarily, it is argued that the statute cannot be interpreted as including a requirement of a specific intent to accomplish violent overthrow, or as requiring that membership in a proscribed organization must be "active" membership, in the absence of both or either of which it is said the statute becomes a fortiori unconstitutional. It is further contended that even if the adjective "active" may properly be implied as a qualification upon the term "member," petitioner's conviction would nonetheless be unconstitutional, because so construed that statute would be impermissibly vague under the Fifth and Sixth Amendments, and so applied would in any event infringe the Sixth Amendment, in that the indictment charged only that Scales was a "member," not an "active" member, of the Communist Party.

1. Statutory Construction. . . .

The only two elements of the crime . . . about which there is controversy are . . . "specific intent" and "active" membership. As to the former, this Court held in Dennis v. United States [1951] that even though the "advocacy" and "organizing" provisions of the Smith Act . . . did not expressly contain such a specific intent element, such a requirement was fairly to be implied. We think that the reasoning of *Dennis* applies equally to the membership clause. . . .

We find hardly greater difficulty in interpreting the membership clause to reach only "active" members. We decline to attribute to Congress a purpose to punish nominal membership . . . not merely because of the close constitutional questions that such a purpose would raise . . . but also for two other reasons: It is not to be lightly inferred that Congress intended to visit upon mere passive members the heavy penalties imposed by the Smith Act. Nor can we assume that it was Congress' purpose to allow the quality of the punishable membership to be measured solely by the varying standards of that relationship as subjectively viewed by different organizations. It is more reasonable to believe that Congress contemplated an objective standard fixed by the law itself. . . . Petitioner's particular constitutional objections to this construction are misconceived. The indictment was not defective in failing to charge that Scales was an "active" member of the Party, for that factor was not in itself a discrete element of the crime, but an inherent quality of the membership element. . . . Nor do we think that the objection on the score of vagueness is a tenable one. The distinction between "active" and "nominal" membership is well understood in common parlance. . . .

We find no substance in the further suggestion that petitioner could not . . . anticipate a construction of the statute that included within its elements activity and specific intent, and hence that he was not duly warned of what the statute made criminal. It is, of course, clear that the lower courts' construction was narrower, not broader, than the one for which petitioner argues . . . and that therefore, according to petitioner's own construction, his actions were forbidden by the statute. . . .

2. Fifth Amendment

In our jurisprudence guilt is personal, and when the imposition of punishment on a status or on conduct can only be justified by reference to the relationship of that status or conduct to other concededly criminal activity . . . that relationship must be sufficiently substantial to satisfy the concept of personal guilt in order to withstand attack under the Due Process Clause of the Fifth Amendment. . . .

Any thought that due process puts beyond the reach of the criminal law all individual associational relationships, unless accompanied by the commission of specific acts of criminality, is dispelled by familiar concepts of the law of conspiracy. . . .

What must be met, then, is the argument that membership, even when accompanied by the elements of knowledge and specific intent, affords an insufficient quantum of participation in the organization's alleged criminal activity. . . . It must indeed be recognized that a person who merely becomes a member of an illegal organization, by that "act" alone need be doing nothing more than signifying his assent to its purposes and activities on one hand, and providing, on the other, only the sort of moral encouragement which comes from the knowledge that others believe in what the organization is doing. . . .

In an area of the criminal law which this Court has indicated more than once demands its watchful scrutiny (see *Dennis;* Yates [v. United States (1957)]; and see also Noto v. United States [1961]), these factors have weight and must be found to be overborne in a total constitutional assessment of the statute. We think, however, they are duly met when the statute is found to reach only "active" members having also a guilty knowledge and intent. . . .

3. First Amendment

Little remains to be said concerning the claim that the statute infringes First Amendment freedoms. It was settled in *Dennis* that the advocacy with which we are here concerned is not constitutionally protected speech, and it was further established that a combination to promote such advocacy, albeit under the aegis of what purports to be a political party, is not such association as is protected by the First Amendment. We can discern no reason why membership, when it constitutes a purposeful form of complicity in a group engaging in this same forbidden advocacy, should receive any greater degree of protection from the guarantees of that Amendment. . . .

Affirmed.

Mr. Justice **BLACK**, dissenting.

. . . My reasons for dissenting . . . are primarily those set out by Mr. Justice Brennan—that § 4(f) of the Subversive Activities Control Act * bars prosecution under the membership clause of the Smith Act— and Mr. Justice Douglas. . . .

There are, however, two additional points that I think should also be mentioned.

. . . [T]he Court has practically rewritten the statute . . . by treating the requirements of "activity" and "specific intent" as implicit in words that plainly do not include them. . . . It seems clear to me that neither petitioner nor anyone else could ever have guessed that this law would be held to mean what this Court now holds it does mean. . . . [P]etitioner has been convicted under a law that is, at best, unconstitutionally vague and, at worst, ex post facto. . . .

Secondly, I think it is important to point out the manner in which this case re-emphasizes the freedom-destroying nature of the "balancing

---

* **Eds.' Note:** Specifying that neither membership nor holding office in any "Communist controlled" organization would, of itself, constitute a federal crime.

test" presently in use by the Court to justify its refusal to apply specific constitutional protections of the Bill of Rights. In some of the recent cases . . . the Court has suggested that it was justified in the application of this "test" because no direct abridgment of First Amendment freedoms was involved, the abridgment in each of these cases being, in the Court's opinion, nothing more than "an incident of the informed exercise of a valid governmental function." A possible implication of that suggestion was that if the Court were confronted with what it would call a direct abridgment of speech, it would not apply the "balancing test" but would enforce the protections of the First Amendment according to its own terms. This case causes me to doubt that such an implication is justified. . . .

Mr. Justice DOUGLAS, dissenting.

When we allow petitioner to be sentenced to prison for six years for being a "member" of the Communist Party, we make a sharp break with traditional concepts of First Amendment rights and make serious Mark Twain's lighthearted comment that "It is by the goodness of God that in our country we have those three unspeakably precious things: freedom of speech, freedom of conscience, and the prudence never to practice either of them."

Even the Alien and Sedition Laws—shameful reminders of an early chapter in intolerance—never went so far as we go today. . . .

We legalize today guilt by association, sending a man to prison when he committed no unlawful act. Today's break with tradition is a serious one. It borrows from the totalitarian philosophy. . . .

The case is not saved by showing that petitioner was an active member. None of the activity constitutes a crime. . . . Scales was the Chairman of the North and South Carolina Districts of the Communist Party. He recruited new members into the Party, and promoted the advanced education of selected young Party members in the theory of communism to be undertaken at secret schools. He was a director of one such school. He explained the principles of the Party to an FBI agent who posed as someone interested in joining the Party, and furnished him literature, including articles which criticized in vivid language the American "aggression" in Korea and described American "atrocities" committed on Korean citizens. He once remarked that the Party was setting up underground means of communication, and in 1951 he himself "went underground." At the school of which Scales was director, students were told (by someone else) that one of the Party's weaknesses was in failing to place people in key industrial positions. One witness told of a meeting arranged by Scales at which the staff of the school urged him to remain in his position in an industrial plant rather than return to college. In Scales' presence students at the school were once shown how to kill a person with a pencil, a device which, it was said, might come in handy on a picket line. Other evidence showed Scales to have made several statements or distributed literature containing implicating passages. Among them were comments to the effect that the Party line was that the Negroes in the South and the working classes should be used to foment a violent revolution; that a Communist government could not be voted into power in this country . . .; that force was the only way to achieve the revolution . . .; that the revolution would come within a generation; that it would be easier in the United States than in Russia to effectuate the revolution because of assistance and advice from Russian Communists. . . .

Not one single illegal act is charged to petitioner. That is why the essence of the crime covered by the indictment is merely belief. . . .

Mr. Justice **BRENNAN,** with whom the Chief Justice [**WARREN**] and Mr. Justice **DOUGLAS** join, dissenting. . . .

Editors' Notes

(1) **Query:** Harlan relied more heavily on *Dennis* than on *Yates,* even though he wrote the opinion for the Court in *Yates* and there was no opinion for the Court in *Dennis.* How does one explain that emphasis? How can one distinguish between *Scales* and NAACP v. Alabama (1958; reprinted above, p. 646), in which Harlan also wrote the opinion of the Court?

(2) **Query:** Where did the right to associate stand after *Scales?* The answer to that question is complicated by a series of other decisions. Noto v. United States (1961), decided the same day as *Scales* and by the same 5-judge majority again speaking through Harlan, reversed the conviction of another communist under the Smith Act's membership clause on grounds that the evidence at the trial had been insufficient to prove that the Communist party had advocated direct action to overthrow the government by force. Also on the same day, Communist Party v. Subversive Activities Control Board (SACB) (1961) upheld, again 5–4, the constitutionality of a requirement of the Internal Security Act of 1950 that groups held by the SACB to be "communist controlled" register with the attorney general and give, among other items, the names and addresses of all members.

When the Communist party refused to register, the attorney general tried to enforce another section of the 1950 act that required, under such circumstances, all individual members to register. Albertson v. SACB (1965) unanimously held that section of the law unconstitutional. The effects of the Smith Act as upheld by *Scales,* the Court reasoned, made compulsory registration equivalent to compulsory self-incrimination. Aptheker v. Secretary of State (1964; reprinted below, p. 657) invalidated the section of the Internal Security Act of 1950 that refused passports to American citizens who belonged to a communist organization, and United States v. Robel (1967) struck down the section that made it a crime for a member of such an organization to hold a job in a defense industry once the SACB had ordered the organization to register. In 1973 the Nixon administration allowed the SACB to die by declining to ask Congress to appropriate funds to keep it in existence.

(3) By the time the Court decided *Scales* in 1961, he had broken with the party. Thus a reformed communist was the only person in prison in the United

States for being a communist. President Kennedy pardoned Scales at Christmas, 1962.

"Since freedom of association is itself guaranteed in the First Amendment, restrictions imposed upon the right to travel cannot be dismissed by asserting that the right to travel could be fully exercised if the individual would first yield up his membership in a given association."

APTHEKER v. SECRETARY OF STATE
378 U.S. 500, 84 S.Ct. 1659, 12 L.Ed.2d 992 (1964).

Sec. 6 of the Subversives Activities Control Act of 1950 provides that, when the Subversives Activities Control Board requires a communist organization to register:

> [I]t shall be unlawful for any member of such organization, with knowledge or notice that such organization is so registered or that such order has become final—
>
> (1) to make application for a passport, or the renewal of a passport, to be issued or renewed by or under the authority of the United States; or
>
> (2) to use or attempt to use any such passport.

In 1962, after the Subversives Activities Control Board ordered the Communist party to register, the State Department revoked the passports of Herbert Aptheker and other officers of the party. After obtaining an administrative hearing that affirmed the revocation, Aptheker et al. sued in a special three-judge district court for an injunction against the revocation. They lost and appealed to the U.S. Supreme Court.

Mr. Justice **GOLDBERG** delivered the opinion of the Court. . . .

I

In 1958 in Kent v. Dulles, this Court declared that the right to travel abroad is "an important aspect of the citizen's 'liberty' " guaranteed in the Due Process Clause of the Fifth Amendment. The Court stated that:

> The right to travel is a part of the 'liberty' of which the citizen cannot be deprived without due process of law under the Fifth Amendment. . . . Freedom of movement across frontiers in either direction, and inside frontiers as well, was a part of our heritage. Travel abroad, like travel within the country, . . . may be as close to the heart of the individual as the choice of what he eats, or wears, or reads. Freedom of movement is basic in our scheme of values. . . .

. . . The denial of a passport, given existing domestic and foreign laws, is a severe restriction upon, and in effect a prohibition against, world-wide foreign travel. . . . The restrictive effect of the legislation cannot be gainsaid by emphasizing, as the Government seems to do, that a member of a registering organization could recapture his freedom to travel by simply in good faith abandoning his membership in the organization. Since freedom of association is itself guaranteed in the First Amendment, restrictions imposed upon the right to travel cannot be dismissed by asserting that the right to travel could be fully exercised if the individual would first yield up his membership in a given association. . . .

. . . It is a familiar and basic principle, recently reaffirmed in NAACP v. Alabama [1958], that "a governmental purpose to control or prevent activities constitutionally subject to state regulation may not be achieved by means which sweep unnecessarily broadly and thereby invade the area of protected freedoms." See, e.g., NAACP v. Button [1963]; Louisiana ex rel. Gremillion v. NAACP [1961]; Shelton v. Tucker [1960]; Schware v. Board [1957]; Martin v. Struthers [1943]; Cantwell v. Connecticut [1940]; Schneider v. State [1939]. . . .

This principle requires that we consider the congressional purpose underlying § 6 of the Control Act. The Government emphasizes that the legislation in question flows, as the statute itself declares, from the congressional desire to protect our national security. That Congress under the Constitution has power to safeguard our Nation's security is obvious and unarguable. Cf. Kennedy v. Mendoza-Martinez [1963]. As we said in *Mendoza-Martinez*, "while the Constitution protects against invasions of individual rights, it is not a suicide pact." At the same time the Constitution requires that the powers of government "must be so exercised as not, in attaining a permissible end, unduly to infringe" a constitutionally protected freedom. *Cantwell.*

Section 6 provides that any member of a Communist organization which has registered or has been ordered to register commits a crime if he attempts to use or obtain a United States passport. The section applies to members who act "with knowledge or notice" that the organization is under a final registration order. "Notice" is specifically defined in § 13(k). That section provides that publication in the Federal Register of the fact of registration or of issuance of a final registration order "shall constitute notice to all members of such organization that such order has become final." Thus the terms of § 6 apply whether or not the member actually knows or believes that he is associated with what is deemed to be a "Communist-action" or a "Communist-front" organization. The section also applies whether or not one knows or believes that he is associated with an organization operating to further aims of the world Communist movement and "to establish a Communist totalitarian dictatorship in the countries throughout the world. . . ." . . . The provision therefore sweeps within its prohibition both knowing and unknowing members. . . . In Wieman v. Updegraff [1952], the Court held that the due process guarantee of the Constitution was violated when a State, in an attempt to bar disloyal individuals from its employ, excluded persons solely on the basis of organizational memberships without regard to their knowledge concerning the organizations to which they had belonged. The Court concluded that: "Indiscriminate classification of innocent with knowing activity must fall as an assertion of arbitrary power."

Section 6 also renders irrelevant the member's degree of activity in the organization and his commitment to its purpose. These factors, like knowledge, would bear on the likelihood that travel by such a person would be attended by the type of activity which Congress sought to control. As the Court has elsewhere noted, "men in adhering to a political party or other organization notoriously do not subscribe unqualifiedly to all of its platforms or asserted principles. Cf. Schneiderman v. United States [1943].

. . . The prohibition of § 6 applies regardless of the purposes for which an individual wishes to travel. Under the statute it is a crime for a notified member of a registered organization to apply for a passport to travel abroad to visit a sick relative, to receive medical treatment, or for any other wholly innocent purpose. In determining whether there has been an abridgment of the Fifth Amendment's guarantee of liberty, this Court must recognize the danger of punishing a member of a Communist organization "for his adherence to lawful and constitutionally protected purposes, because of other and unprotected purposes which he does not necessarily share." Noto v. United States [1961]; Scales v. United States [1961]. . . .

In determining the constitutionality of § 6, it is also important to consider that Congress has within its power "less drastic" means of achieving the congressional objective of safeguarding our national security. Shelton v. Tucker. . . .

In our view the foregoing considerations compel the conclusion that § 6 of the Control Act is unconstitutional on its face. The section, judged by its plain import and by the substantive evil which Congress sought to control, sweeps too widely and too indiscriminately across the liberty guaranteed in the Fifth Amendment. The prohibition against travel is supported only by a tenuous relationship between the bare fact of organizational membership and the activity Congress sought to proscribe. . . . The section therefore is patently not a regulation "narrowly drawn to prevent the supposed evil," cf. *Cantwell,* yet here, as elsewhere, precision must be the touchstone of legislation so affecting basic freedoms, NAACP v. Button. . . .

Reversed and remanded.

Mr. Justice **BLACK,** concurring. . . .

. . . I think the whole Act including § 6, is not a valid law, that it sets up a comprehensive statutory plan which violates the Federal Constitution because (1) it constitutes a "Bill of Attainder," which Art. I § 9, of the Constitution forbids Congress to pass; (2) it penalizes and punishes appellants and restricts their liberty on legislative and administrative fact-findings that they are subversives, and in effect traitors to their country, without giving them the benefit of a trial according to due process, which requires a trial by jury before an independent judge, after an indictment, and in accordance with all the other procedural protections of the Fourth, Fifth, and Sixth Amendments; and (3) it denies appellants the freedom of speech, press, and association which the First Amendment guarantees. . . .

Mr. Justice **DOUGLAS**, concurring. . . .

We noted in Kent v. Dulles [1958] that "freedom of movement," both internally and abroad, is "deeply ingrained" in our history. I would not suppose that a Communist, any more than an indigent, could be barred from traveling interstate. I think that a Communist, the same as anyone else, has this right. Being a Communist certainly is not a crime; and while traveling may increase the likelihood of illegal events happening, so does being alive. . . .

Freedom of movement, at home and abroad, is important for job and business opportunities—for cultural, political, and social activities—for all the commingling which gregarious man enjoys. Those with the right of free movement use it at times for mischievous purposes. But that is true of many liberties we enjoy. We nevertheless place our faith in them, and against restraint, knowing that the risk of abusing liberty so as to give rise to punishable conduct is part of the price we pay for this free society.

Freedom of movement is kin to the right of assembly and to the right of association. These rights may not be abridged, De Jonge v. Oregon [1937]; NAACP v. Alabama [1958], only illegal conduct being within the purview of crime in the constitutional sense.

War may be the occasion for serious curtailment of liberty. Absent war, I see no way to keep a citizen from traveling within or without the country, unless there is power to detain him. Ex parte Endo [1944]. . . .

Mr. Justice **CLARK**, whom Mr. Justice **HARLAN** joins and whom Mr. Justice **WHITE** joins in part, dissenting. . . .

II

. . . While the right to travel abroad is a part of the liberty protected by the Fifth Amendment, the Due Process Clause does not prohibit reasonable regulation of life, liberty or property. Here the restriction is reasonably related to the national security. As we said in Barenblatt v. United States (1959):

> That Congress has wide power to legislate in the field of Communist activity in this Country, and to conduct appropriate investigations in aid thereof, is hardly debatable. The existence of such power has never been questioned by this Court. . . . In the last analysis this power rests on the right of self-preservation, "the ultimate value of any society," Dennis v. United States [1951].

The right to travel is not absolute. Congress had ample evidence that use of passports by Americans belonging to the world Communist movement is a threat to our national security. . . . The Congress had before it evidence that such use of passports by Communist Party members: enabled the leaders of the world Communist movement in the Soviet Union to give orders to their comrades in the United States and to exchange vital secrets as well; facilitated the training of American Communist leaders by experts in sabotage and the like in Moscow; gave closer central control to the world Communist movement; and, of utmost importance, provided world Communist leaders with passports for Soviet secret agents to use in the United States for espionage purposes. This evidence afforded the Congress a rational basis upon which to place the denial of passports to members of the Communist Party in the United States. The denial is reasonably related to the national security. The degree of restraint upon travel is outweighed by the dangers to our very existence.

The remedy adopted by the Congress is reasonably tailored to accomplish the purpose. It may be true that not every member of the Party would endanger our national security by traveling abroad, but which Communist Party member is worthy of trust? Since the Party is a secret, conspiratorial organization subject to rigid discipline by Moscow, the Congress merely determined that it was not wise to take the risk which foreign travel by Communists entailed. . . .

Mr. Justice **WHITE** joins in Section I of this dissent and for the reasons stated therein would affirm the judgment.

Editors' Notes

(1) **Query:** What combination of *approaches, modes,* and *techniques* of constitutional interpretation does Goldberg use? How did his usage(s) compare with that/those of Clark? Of Black? Douglas?

(2) Compare the result, the reasoning, and the methods of constitutional interpretation used here with those in Trop v. Dulles (1958; reprinted above, p. 144) and Haig v. Agee (1981; reprinted above, p. 533), which also involved revocation or denial of passports.

(3) United States v. Robel (1967) invalidated that portion of the Internal Security Act of 1950 that forbade members of a communist controlled organization "to engage in any employment in any defense facility."

(4) **Query:** For some reason, the Court, when discussing a right to travel, seldom mentions Crandall v. Nevada (1868; reprinted above, p. 426), even though it would seem to be directly in point. To what extent might this omission be due to the justices' reluctance to engage in *overt* structural analysis?

**"The right to associate for expressive purposes is not
. . . absolute. Infringements on that right may be justified by regulations adopted to serve compelling state
interests, unrelated to the expression of ideas, that cannot
be achieved through means significantly less restrictive
of associational freedoms."**

ROBERTS v. UNITED STATES JAYCEES
468 U.S. 609, 104 S.Ct. 3244, 82 L.Ed.2d 462 (1984).

The United States Jaycees, or Junior Chamber of Commerce, is a national
organization whose objectives are "to inculcate . . . a spirit of genuine
Americanism and civic interest . . . and to provide [members] with opportunity for personal development and achievement and an avenue for intelligent
participation . . . in the affairs of their community, state and nation. . . ."
Before this case, membership was limited to males between the ages of 18
and 35.

In 1974 and 1975, two local chapters in Minnesota began admitting
women and were sanctioned by the national association and threatened with
expulsion. Several of the women members then filed charges of discrimination with the state Department of Human Rights. While those proceedings
were in progress, the national organization sued in a federal district court
alleging that the Minnesota Human Rights Act was unconstitutional. The
district judge certified to the state supreme court the question whether the Act
covered the Jaycees, and that tribunal ruled it did. After full trial, the district
court sustained the statute, but the Court of Appeals for the Eighth Circuit
reversed. The state then appealed to the U.S. Supreme Court.

Justice **BRENNAN** delivered the opinion of the Court. . . .

II

Our decisions have referred to constitutionally protected "freedom
of association" in two distinct senses. In one line of decisions, the
Court has concluded that choices to enter into and maintain certain
intimate human relationships must be secured against undue intrusion
by the State because of the role of such relationships in safeguarding
the individual freedom that is central to our constitutional scheme. In
this respect, freedom of association receives protection as a fundamental element of personal liberty. In another set of decisions, the Court
has recognized a right to associate for the purpose of engaging in those
activities protected by the First Amendment—speech, assembly, petition for the redress of grievances, and the exercise of religion. The
Constitution guarantees freedom of association of this kind as an
indispensable means of preserving other individual liberties.

The intrinsic and instrumental features of constitutionally protected association may, of course, coincide. In particular, when the State
interferes with individuals' selection of those with whom they wish to
join in a common endeavor, freedom of association in both of its forms
may be implicated. The Jaycees contend that this is such a case. Still,
the nature and degree of constitutional protection afforded freedom of

association may vary depending on the extent to which one or the other aspect of the constitutionally protected liberty is at stake in a given case. We therefore find it useful to consider separately the effect of applying the Minnesota statute to the Jaycees on what could be called its members' freedom of intimate association and their freedom of expressive association.

A

The Court has long recognized that, because the Bill of Rights is designed to secure individual liberty, it must afford the formation and preservation of certain kinds of highly personal relationships a substantial measure of sanctuary from unjustified interference by the State. E.g., Pierce v. Society of Sisters (1925); Meyer v. Nebraska (1923). Without precisely identifying every consideration that may underlie this type of constitutional protection, we have noted that certain kinds of personal bonds have played a critical role in the culture and traditions of the Nation by cultivating and transmitting shared ideals and beliefs; they thereby foster diversity and act as critical buffers between the individual and the power of the State. See, e.g., Zablocki v. Redhail (1978); Moore v. East Cleveland (1977) (plurality opinion); Wisconsin v. Yoder (1973); Griswold v. Connecticut (1965); *Pierce*. See also Gilmore v. Montgomery (1974); NAACP v. Alabama (1958); Poe v. Ullman (1961) (Harlan, J., dissenting). Moreover, the constitutional shelter afforded such relationships reflects the realization that individuals draw much of their emotional enrichment from close ties with others. Protecting these relationships from unwarranted state interference therefore safeguards the ability independently to define one's identity that is central to any concept of liberty.

The personal affiliations that exemplify these considerations, and that therefore suggest some relevant limitations on the relationships that might be entitled to this sort of constitutional protection, are those that attend the creation and sustenance of a family—marriage, e.g., Zablocki; childbirth, e.g., Carey [v. Population Services (1977)]; the raising and education of children, e.g., Smith v. Organization of Foster Families; and cohabitation with one's relatives, e.g., *Moore*. Family relationships, by their nature, involve deep attachments and commitments to the necessarily few other individuals with whom one shares not only a special community of thoughts, experiences, and beliefs but also distinctively personal aspects of one's life. Among other things, therefore, they are distinguished by such attributes as relative smallness, a high degree of selectivity in decisions to begin and maintain the affiliation, and seclusion from others in critical aspects of the relationship. As a general matter, only relationships with these sorts of qualities are likely to reflect the considerations that have led to an understanding of freedom of association as an intrinsic element of personal liberty. Conversely, an association lacking these qualities— such as a large business enterprise—seems remote from the concerns giving rise to this constitutional protection. Accordingly, the Constitu-

tion undoubtedly imposes constraints on the State's power to control
the selection of one's spouse that would not apply to regulations
affecting the choice of one's fellow employees.

Between these poles, of course, lies a broad range of human
relationships that may make greater or lesser claims to constitutional
protection from particular incursions by the State. Determining the
limits of state authority over an individual's freedom to enter into a
particular association therefore unavoidably entails a careful assessment of where that relationship's objective characteristics locate it on a
spectrum from the most intimate to the most attenuated of personal
attachments. See generally Runyon v. McCrary (1976) (Powell, J.,
concurring). We need not mark the potentially significant points on
this terrain with any precision. We note only that factors that may be
relevant include size, purpose, policies, selectivity, congeniality, and
other characteristics that in a particular case may be pertinent. In
this case, however, several features of the Jaycees clearly place the
organization outside of the category of relationships worthy of this kind
of constitutional protection.

The undisputed facts reveal that the local chapters of the Jaycees
are large and basically unselective groups. . . . [T]he Minneapolis
chapter had approximately 430 members, while the St. Paul chapter
had about 400. Apart from age and sex, neither the national organization nor the local chapters employs any criteria for judging applicants
for membership, and new members are routinely recruited and admitted with no inquiry into their backgrounds. In fact, a local officer
testified that he could recall no instance in which an applicant had
been denied membership on any basis other than age or sex. . . .
Furthermore, despite their inability to vote, hold office, or receive
certain awards, women affiliated with the Jaycees attend various meetings, participate in selected projects, and engage in many of the
organization's social functions. . . .

. . . Accordingly, we conclude that the Jaycees chapters lack the
distinctive characteristics that might afford constitutional protection to
the decision of its members to exclude women. . . .

B

An individual's freedom to speak, to worship, and to petition the
Government for the redress of grievances could not be vigorously
protected from interference by the State unless a correlative freedom to
engage in group effort toward those ends were not also guaranteed.
See, e.g., Rent Control Coalition for Fair Housing v. Berkeley (1981).
According protection to collective effort on behalf of shared goals is
especially important in preserving political and cultural diversity and
in shielding dissident expression from suppression by the majority.
See, e.g. Gilmore; Griswold; NAACP v. Button (1963); NAACP v.
Alabama. Consequently, we have long understood as implicit in the
right to engage in activities protected by the First Amendment a
corresponding right to associate with others in pursuit of a wide variety

of political, social, economic, educational, religious, and cultural ends. See, e.g., NAACP v. Claiborne Hardware Co. (1982); Larson v. Valente (1982); In re Primus (1978); Abood v. Detroit Board of Education (1977). In view of the various protected activities in which the Jaycees engage, that right is plainly implicated in this case.

. . . There can be no clearer example of an intrusion into the internal structure or affairs of an association than a regulation that forces the group to accept members it does not desire. Such a regulation may impair the ability of the original members to express only those views that brought them together. Freedom of association therefore plainly presupposes a freedom not to associate.

The right to associate for expressive purposes is not, however, absolute. Infringements on that right may be justified by regulations adopted to serve compelling state interests, unrelated to the suppression of ideas, that cannot be achieved through means significantly less restrictive of associational freedoms. E.g., Brown v. Socialist Workers (1982); Democratic Party v. Wisconsin (1981); Buckley v. Valeo (1976); Cousins v. Wigoda (1975); American Party v. White (1974); NAACP v. Button; Shelton v. Tucker (1960). We are persuaded that Minnesota's compelling interest in eradicating discrimination against its female citizens justifies the impact that application of the statute to the Jaycees may have on the male members' associational freedoms.

On its face, the Minnesota Act does not aim at the suppression of speech, does not distinguish between prohibited and permitted activity on the basis of viewpoint, and does not license enforcement authorities to administer the statute on the basis of such constitutionally impermissible criteria. Nor do the Jaycees contend that the Act has been applied in this case for the purpose of hampering the organization's ability to express its views. Instead, as the Minnesota Supreme Court explained, the Act reflects the State's strong historical commitment to eliminating discrimination and assuring its citizens equal access to publicly available goods and services. That goal, which is unrelated to the suppression of expression, plainly serves compelling state interests of the highest order.

The Minnesota Human Rights Act at issue here is an example of public accommodations laws that were adopted by some States beginning a decade before enactment of their federal counterpart, the Civil Rights Act of 1875. Indeed, when this Court invalidated that federal statute in the Civil Rights Cases (1883), it emphasized the fact that state laws imposed a variety of equal access obligations on public accommodations. . . . These laws provided the primary means for protecting the civil rights of historically disadvantaged groups until the Federal Government reentered the field in 1957. . . . In 1973, the Minnesota legislature added discrimination on the basis of sex to the types of conduct prohibited by the statute.

By prohibiting gender discrimination in places of public accommodation, the Minnesota Act protects the State's citizenry from a number of serious social and personal harms. In the context of reviewing state actions under the Equal Protection Clause, this Court has frequently noted that discrimination based on archaic and overbroad assumptions about the relative needs and capacities of the sexes forces individuals to labor under stereotypical notions that often bear no relationship to their actual abilities. It thereby both deprives persons of their individual dignity and denies society the benefits of wide participation in political, economic, and cultural life. See, e.g., Heckler v. Mathews (1984); Mississippi University for Women v. Hogan (1982); Frontiero v. Richardson (1973) (plurality opinion). . . . Thus, in upholding Title II of the Civil Rights Act of 1964, which forbids race discrimination in public accommodations, we emphasized that its "fundamental object . . . was to vindicate 'the deprivation of personal dignity that surely accompanies denials of equal access to public establishments.'" Heart of Atlanta Motel v. United States (1964). That stigmatizing injury, and the denial of equal opportunities that accompanies it, is surely felt as strongly by persons suffering discrimination on the basis of their sex as by those treated differently because of their race. . . .

In applying the Act to the Jaycees, the State has advanced those interests through the least restrictive means of achieving its ends. Indeed, the Jaycees have failed to demonstrate that the Act imposes any serious burdens on the male members' freedom of expressive association. See Hishon v. King & Spalding (1984) (law firm "has not shown how its ability to fulfill [protected] function[s] would be inhibited by a requirement that it consider [a woman lawyer] for partnership on her merits"); see also *Buckley*. To be sure, as the Court of Appeals noted, a "not insubstantial part" of the Jaycees' activities constitutes protected expression on political, economic, cultural, and social affairs. . . . There is, however, no basis in the record for concluding that admission of women as full voting members will impede the organization's ability to engage in these protected activities or to disseminate its preferred views. The Act requires no change in the Jaycees' creed of promoting the interests of young men, and it imposes no restrictions on the organization's ability to exclude individuals with ideologies or philosophies different from those of its existing members. Cf. Democratic Party v. Wisconsin (recognizing the right of political parties to "protect themselves 'from intrusion by those with adverse political principles'"). Moreover, the Jaycees already invite women to share the group's views and philosophy and to participate in much of its training and community activities. Accordingly, any claim that admission of women as full voting members will impair a symbolic message conveyed by the very fact that women are not permitted to vote is attenuated at best.

While acknowledging that "the specific content of most of the resolutions adopted over the years by the Jaycees has nothing to do with sex," the Court of Appeals nonetheless entertained the hypothesis that women members might have a different view or agenda with respect to these matters so that, if they are allowed to vote, "some change in the Jaycees' philosophical cast can reasonably be expected."

It is similarly arguable that, insofar as the Jaycees is organized to promote the views of young men whatever those views happen to be, admission of women as voting members will change the message communicated by the group's speech because of the gender-based assumptions of the audience. Neither supposition, however, is supported by the record. In claiming that women might have a different attitude about such issues as the federal budget, school prayer, voting rights, and foreign relations, or that the organization's public positions would have a different effect if the group were not "a purely young men's association," the Jaycees rely solely on unsupported generalizations.
. . . [W]e have repeatedly condemned legal decisionmaking that relies uncritically on such assumptions. See, e.g., Palmore v. Sidoti (1984); Heckler v. Mathews. In the absence of a showing far more substantial than that attempted by the Jaycees, we decline to indulge in the sexual stereotyping that underlies appellee's contention that, by allowing women to vote, application of the Minnesota Act will change the content or impact of the organization's speech.

In any event, even if enforcement of the Act causes some incidental abridgement of the Jaycees' protected speech, that effect is no greater than is necessary to accomplish the State's legitimate purposes. . . . [A]cts of invidious discrimination in the distribution of publicly available goods, services, and other advantages cause unique evils that government has a compelling interest to prevent—wholly apart from the point of view such conduct may transmit. Accordingly, like violence or other types of potentially expressive activities that produce special harms distinct from their communicative impact, such practices are entitled to no constitutional protection. Runyon v. McCrary (1976). In prohibiting such practices, the Minnesota Act therefore "responds precisely to the substantive problem which legitimately concerns" the State and abridges no more speech or associational freedom than is necessary to accomplish that purpose. See City Council v. Taxpayers for Vincent (1984). . . .

Reversed.

Justice **REHNQUIST** concurs in the judgment.

The Chief Justice [**BURGER**] and Justice **BLACKMUN** took no part in the decision of this case.

Justice **O'CONNOR**, concurring in part and concurring in the judgment.

I join Parts I and III of the Court's opinion. . . . With respect to Part II–A of the Court's opinion, I agree . . . that the Jaycees cannot claim a right of association deriving from this Court's cases concerning "marriage, procreation, contraception, family relationships, and child rearing and education." Paul v. Davis (1976). . . . Whatever the precise scope of the rights recognized in such cases, they do not encompass associational rights of a 295,000-member organization whose activities are not "private" in any meaningful sense of that term.

I part company with the Court over its First Amendment analysis in Part II–B of its opinion. I agree with the Court that application of the Minnesota law to the Jaycees does not contravene the First Amendment, but I reach that conclusion for reasons distinct from those offered by the Court. . . .

I

The Court analyzes Minnesota's attempt to regulate the Jaycees' membership using a test that I find both over-protective of activities undeserving of constitutional shelter and under-protective of important First Amendment concerns. The Court declares that the Jaycees' right of association depends on the organization's making a "substantial" showing that the admission of unwelcome members "will change the message communicated by the group's speech." I am not sure what showing the Court thinks would satisfy its requirement of proof of a membership-message connection, but whatever it means, the focus on such a connection is objectionable.

Imposing such a requirement, especially in the context of the balancing-of-interests test articulated by the Court, raises the possibility that certain commercial associations, by engaging occasionally in certain kinds of expressive activities, might improperly gain protection for discrimination. The Court's focus raises other problems as well. How are we to analyze the First Amendment associational claims of an organization that invokes its right, settled by the Court in NAACP v. Alabama (1958), to protect the privacy of its membership? And would the Court's analysis of this case be different if, for example, the Jaycees membership had a steady history of opposing public issues thought (by the Court) to be favored by women? It might seem easy to conclude, in the latter case, that the admission of women to the Jaycees' ranks would affect the content of the organization's message, but I do not believe that should change the outcome of this case. Whether an association is or is not constitutionally protected in the selection of its membership should not depend on what the association says or why its members say it.

The Court's readiness to inquire into the connection between membership and message reveals a more fundamental flaw in its analysis. The Court pursues this inquiry as part of its mechanical application of a "compelling interest" test, under which the Court weighs the interests of the State of Minnesota in ending gender discrimination against the Jaycees' First Amendment right of association. The Court entirely neglects to establish at the threshold that the Jaycees is an association whose activities or purposes should engage the strong protections that the First Amendment extends to expressive associations.

On the one hand, an association engaged exclusively in protected expression enjoys First Amendment protection of both the content of its message and the choice of its members. Protection of the message itself is judged by the same standards as protection of speech by an individual. Protection of the association's right to define its membership derives from the recognition that the formation of an expressive association is the creation of a voice, and the selection of members is the definition of that voice. . . . A ban on specific group voices on public affairs violates the most basic guarantee of the First Amendment—that citizens, not the government, control the content of public discussion.

On the other hand, there is only minimal constitutional protection of the freedom of *commercial* association. There are, of course, some constitutional protections of commercial speech—speech intended and used to promote a commercial transaction with the speaker. But the State is free to impose any rational regulation on the commercial transaction itself. The Constitution does not guarantee a right to choose employees, customers, suppliers, or those with whom one engages in simple commercial transactions, without restraint from the State. A shopkeeper has no constitutional right to deal only with persons of one sex.

The dichotomy between rights of commercial association and rights of expressive association is also found in the more limited constitutional protections accorded an association's recruitment and solicitation activities and other dealings with its members and the public. . . . Thus, after careful scrutiny, we have upheld regulations on matters such as the financial dealings between an association and its members, see *Buckley*, disclosure of membership lists to the State, see NAACP v. Alabama; *Shelton*, access to the ballot, time limits on registering before elections, and similar matters, see, e.g., Rosario v. Rockefeller (1973); Dunn v. Blumstein (1972); Williams v. Rhodes (1968). See also Heffron v. International Society for Krishna Consciousness, Inc. (1981). By contrast, an organization engaged in commercial activity enjoys only minimal constitutional protection of its recruitment, training, and solicitation activities. While the Court has acknowledged a First Amendment right to engage in non-deceptive commercial advertising, governmental regulation of the commercial recruitment of new members, stockholders, customers, or employees is valid if rationally related to the government's ends.

Many associations cannot readily be described as purely expressive or purely commercial. No association is likely ever to be exclusively engaged in expressive activities. . . . The standard for deciding just how much of an association's involvement in commercial activity is enough to suspend the association's First Amendment right to control its membership cannot, therefore, be articulated with simple precision. . . . The standard must nevertheless give substance to the ideal of complete protection for purely expressive association, even while it readily permits state regulation of commercial affairs.

In my view, an association should be characterized as commercial, and therefore subject to rationally related state regulation of its membership and other associational activities, when, and only when, the association's activities are not predominantly of the type protected by the First Amendment. It is only when the association is predominantly engaged in protected expression that state regulation of its membership will necessarily affect, change, dilute, or silence one collective voice that would otherwise be heard. An association must choose its market. Once it enters the marketplace of commerce in any substantial degree it loses the complete control over its membership that it would otherwise enjoy if it confined its affairs to the marketplace of ideas.

Determining whether an association's activity is predominantly protected expression will often be difficult, if only because a broad range of activities can be expressive. It is easy enough to identify expressive words or conduct that are strident, contentious, or divisive, but protected expression may also take the form of quiet persuasion, inculcation of traditional values, instruction of the young, and community service. Cf. *Pierce; Meyer.* The purposes of an association, and the purposes of its members in adhering to it, are doubtless relevant in determining whether the association is primarily engaged in protected expression. . . . A group boycott or refusal to deal for political purposes may be speech, NAACP v. Claiborne Hardware Co., though a similar boycott for purposes of maintaining a cartel is not. Even the training of outdoor survival skills or participation in community service might become expressive when the activity is intended to develop good morals, reverence, patriotism, and a desire for self-improvement.

The considerations that may enter into the determination of when a particular association of persons is predominantly engaged in expression are therefore fluid and somewhat uncertain. But the Court has recognized the need to draw similar lines in the past. Two examples, both addressed in cases decided this Term, stand out.

The first concerns claims of First Amendment protection made by lawyers. On the one hand, some lawyering activity is undoubtedly protected by the First Amendment. . . . *Primus;* see NAACP v. Button. On the other hand, ordinary law practice for commercial ends has never been given special First Amendment protection. . . . We emphasized this point only this Term in *Hishon,* where we readily rejected a large commercial law firm's claim to First Amendment protection for alleged gender-based discriminatory partnership decisions for associates of the firm. . . . As a commercial enterprise, the law firm could claim no First Amendment immunity from employment discrimination laws, and that result would not have been altered by a showing that the firm engaged even in a substantial amount of activity entitled to First Amendment protection.

We have adopted a similar analysis in our cases concerning association with a labor union. A State is free to impose rational regulation of the membership of a labor union representing "the general *business* needs of employees." Railway Mail Assn. v. Corsi (1945) (emphasis added). The State may not, on the other hand, compel association with a union engaged in ideological activities. *Abood.* . . . We applied this distinction in Ellis v. Railway Clerks (1984), decided this Term.

Again, the constitutional inquiry is not qualified by any analysis of governmental interests and does not turn on an individual's ability to establish disagreement with the particular views promulgated by the union. It is enough if the individual simply expresses unwillingness to be associated with the union's ideological activities.

In summary, this Court's case law recognizes radically different constitutional protections for expressive and non-expressive associations. . . . The proper approach to analysis of First Amendment claims of associational freedom is, therefore, to distinguish non-expressive from expressive associations and to recognize that the former lack the full constitutional protections possessed by the latter.

II

Minnesota's attempt to regulate the membership of the Jaycees chapters operating in that State presents a relatively easy case for application of the expressive-commercial dichotomy. . . .

. . . Notwithstanding its protected expressive activities, the Jaycees . . . is, first and foremost, an organization that, at both the national and local levels, promotes and practices the art of solicitation and management. The organization claims that the training it offers its members gives them an advantage in business, and business firms do indeed sometimes pay the dues of individual memberships for their employees. . . .

Recruitment and selling are commercial activities, even when conducted for training rather than for profit. The "not insubstantial" volume of protected Jaycees activity found by the Court of Appeals is simply not enough to preclude state regulation of the Jaycees' commercial activities. The State of Minnesota has a legitimate interest in ensuring nondiscriminatory access to the commercial opportunity presented by membership in the Jaycees. . . .

Editors' Notes

(1) **Query:** Do constitutionalist and democratic theories make different demands in this case?

(2) **Query:** Justice O'Connor said that Brennan's opinion for the Court used balancing as a *technique* of constitutional interpretation? Was she correct? What interpretive *mode* (*s*) and/or *techniques* did she use, a version of the two-tiered test (rational-basis v. strict scrutiny) or something quite different?

(3) For other cases dealing with classification by sex, see Chapter 14.

III. MONEY AND POLITICS: THE RIGHT TO CAMPAIGN AND TO RUN FOR PUBLIC OFFICE

"[T]he government has an interest in regulating the conduct and 'the speech of its employees that differ[s] significantly from those it possesses in connection with the regulation of the speech of the citizenry in general. . . .' "

CIVIL SERVICE COMMISSION v. NATIONAL ASSOCIATION OF LETTER CARRIERS
413 U.S. 548, 93 S.Ct. 2880, 37 L.Ed.2d 796 (1973).

Sec. 9a of the Hatch Act provides:

An employee in an Executive Agency or an individual employed by the government of the District of Columbia may not—

(1) use his official authority or influence for the purpose of interfering with or affecting the result of an election; or

(2) take an active part in political management or in political campaigns.

In 1947 United Public Workers v. Mitchell sustained the constitutionality of § 9a and the myriad of regulations the Civil Service Commission had issued under it. Over the next twenty-five years, however, the Supreme Court became more sensitive of and concerned to protect rights of political association and participation; and the National Association of Letter Carriers, several local Democratic and Republican committees, and six individual federal employees filed suit in a federal district court rechallenging the constitutionality of § 9a. The special three-judge district court that heard the case agreed that constitutional doctrine had changed since *Mitchell* and invalidated § 9a. The Civil Service Commission appealed directly to the Supreme Court, the normal procedure when a special three-judge district court has made the initial decision.

Mr. Justice **WHITE** delivered the opinion of the Court. . . .

II . . .

We unhesitatingly reaffirm the *Mitchell* holding that Congress had, and has, the power to prevent Mr. Poole and others like him from holding a party office, working at the polls and acting as party paymaster for other party workers. . . .

. . . Our judgment is that neither the First Amendment nor any other provision of the Constitution invalidates a law barring this kind of partisan political conduct by federal employees.

A

Such decision on our part would no more than confirm the judgment of history, a judgment made by this country over the last century that it is in the best interest of the country, indeed essential, that federal service should depend upon meritorious performance rather than political service, and that the political influence of federal employees on others and on the electoral process should be limited. . . .

[The Court then recited a long chronicle of concern from Jefferson to recent times of involvement by federal employees in partisan politics.]

B

. . . The restrictions so far imposed on federal employees are not aimed at particular parties, groups or points of view, but apply equally to all partisan activities of the type described. They discriminate against no racial, ethnic or religious minorities. Nor do they seek to control political opinions or beliefs, or to interfere with or influence anyone's vote at the polls.

But as the Court held in Pickering v. Board of Education (1968), the government has an interest in regulating the conduct and "the speech of its employees that differ[s] significantly from those it possesses in connection with regulation of the speech of the citizenry in general. The problem in any case is to arrive at a balance between the interest of the [employee], as a citizen, in commenting upon matters of public concern and the interest of the [government], as an employer, in promoting the efficiency of the public services it performs through its employees." Although Congress is free to strike a different balance than it has, if it so chooses, we think the balance it has so far struck is sustainable by the obviously important interests sought to be served by the limitations on partisan political activities now contained in the Hatch Act.

It seems fundamental in the first place that employees in the Executive Branch of the Government, or those working for any of its agencies, should administer the law in accordance with the will of Congress, rather than in accordance with their own or the will of· a political party. . . . A major thesis of the Hatch Act is that to serve this great end of Government—the impartial execution of the laws—it is essential that federal employees not, for example, take formal positions in political parties, not undertake to play substantial roles in partisan political campaigns and not run for office on partisan political tickets. Forbidding activities like these will reduce the hazards to fair and effective government.

There is another consideration in this judgment: it is not only important that the Government and its employees in fact avoid practicing political justice, but it is also critical that they appear to the public to be avoiding it if confidence in the system of representative Government is not to be eroded to a disastrous extent.

Another major concern of the restriction against partisan activities by federal employees was perhaps the immediate occasion for enactment of the Hatch Act in 1939. That was the conviction that the rapidly expanding Government work force should not be employed to build a powerful, invincible and perhaps corrupt political machine.
. . . .

A related concern . . . was to further serve the goal that employment and advancement in the Government service not depend on
political performance, and at the same time to make sure that Government employees would be free from pressure and from express or tacit
invitation to vote in a certain way or perform political chores in order
to curry favor with their superiors rather than to act out their own
beliefs. . . .

Neither the right to associate nor the right to participate in
political activities is absolute in any event. See, e.g., Rosario v. Rockefeller (1973); Dunn v. Blumstein (1972); Bullock v. Carter (1972);
Jenness v. Fortson (1971); Williams v. Rhodes (1968). Nor are the
management, financing and conduct of political campaigns wholly free
from governmental regulation. We agree with the basic holding of
Mitchell that plainly identifiable acts of political management and
political campaigning may constitutionally be prohibited on the part of
federal employees. . . .

III

But however constitutional the proscription of identifiable partisan
conduct in understandable language may be, the District Court's judgment was that [Sec. 9(a)] was both unconstitutionally vague and fatally
overbroad. Appellees make the same contentions here, but we cannot
agree that the section is unconstitutional on its face for either reason.
. . .

For the foregoing reasons, the judgment of the District Court is
reversed.

So ordered.

Mr. Justice **DOUGLAS,** with whom Mr. Justice **BRENNAN** and Mr.
Justice **MARSHALL** concur, dissenting. . . .

There is no [statutory] definition of what "an active part . . . in
political campaigns" means. The Act incorporates over 3,000 rulings of
the Civil Service Commission between 1886 and 1940 and many hundreds of rulings since 1940. But even with that gloss on the Act, the
critical phrases lack precision. In 1971 the Commission published a
three-volume work entitled *Political Activities Reporter* which contain
over 800 of its decisions since the enactment of the Hatch Act. . . .

The chilling effect of these vague and generalized prohibitions is so
obvious as not to need elaboration. That effect would not be material
to the issue of constitutionality if only the normal contours of the police
power were involved. On the run of social and economic matters the
"rational basis" standard which *Mitchell* applied would suffice. But
what may have been unclear to some in *Mitchell* should by now be
abundantly clear to all. We deal here with a First Amendment right to
speak, to propose, to publish, to petition Government, to assemble.
Time and place are obvious limitations. Thus no one could object if
employees were barred from using office time to engage in outside
activities whether political or otherwise. But it is of no concern of

Government what an employee does in his or her spare time . . . unless what he or she does impairs efficiency or other facets of the merits of his job. Some things, some activities do affect or may be thought to affect the employee's job performance. But his political creed, like his religion, is irrelevant. . . . If Government employment were only a "privilege," then all sorts of conditions might be attached. But it is now settled that Government employment may not be denied or penalized "on a basis that infringes his constitutionally protected interest—especially his interest in freedom of speech." See Perry v. Sindermann [1972]. . . .

Free discussion of governmental affairs is basic in our constitutional system. Sweezy v. New Hampshire [1957]; Mills v. Alabama [1966]; Monitor Patriot Co. v. Roy [1971]. Laws that trench on that area must be narrowly and precisely drawn to deal with precise ends. Overbreadth in the area of the First Amendment has a peculiar evil, the evil of creating chilling effects which deter the exercise of those freedoms. Dombrowski v. Pfister [1965]. . . .

The present Act cannot be appropriately narrowed to meet the need for narrowly drawn language not embracing First Amendment speech or writing without substantial revision. That rewriting cannot be done by the Commission because Congress refused to delegate to it authority to regulate First Amendment rights. . . .

Is a letter a permissible "expression" of views or a prohibited "solicitation?" The Solicitor General says it is a "permissible" expression; but the Commission ruled otherwise. For an employee who does not have the Solicitor General as counsel great consequences flow from an innocent decision. She may lose her job. Therefore the most prudent thing is to do nothing. Thus is self-imposed censorship imposed on many nervous people who live on narrow economic margins.

I would strike this provision of the law down as unconstitutional so that a new start may be made on this old problem that confuses and restricts nearly 5 million federal, state, and local public employees today that live under the present Act.

Editors' Notes

(1) Pickering v. Board of Education (1968), on which Justice White relied, invalidated the firing of a public school teacher for openly criticizing the board of education's allocation of money between athletics and academics. Marshall, for the Court, held that Pickering's comments were about "a matter of legitimate public concern" and so were protected by the First and Fourteenth amendments. The reasoning, however, was not clear. At one point Marshall identified the proper constitutional test as that which White quoted:

The problem in any case is to find a balance between the interests of the [employee], as a citizen, in commenting upon matters of public concern and the interest of the State, as employer, in promoting the efficiency of the public services it performs through its employees.

But, toward the end of his opinion, Marshall added:

> In sum, we hold that, in a case such as this, absent proof of false statements knowingly or recklessly made by him, a teacher's exercise of his right to speak on issue of public importance may not furnish the basis for his dismissal from public employment.

(2) Regardless of what Marshall meant, White used *Pickering* to bolster "balancing" as a *technique* of constitutional interpretation. Was there more to White's reasoning? To the degree he relied on balancing, what interests did he identify here as pitted against each other? How can one generalize from the relative weights he attached to these interests to similar sorts of factual situations that may arise under the First Amendment? In sum, can one find guiding principles in his opinion? What about Douglas' opinion? What *approaches/modes/techniques* did he use? How much more (or less) useful is Douglas' opinion in pointing toward general rules?

(3) Connick v. Myers (1983) sustained a district attorney's firing of one of his assistant attorneys for what he alleged was insubordination in circulating a questionnaire to fellow staff members regarding some of the office's internal policies. The assistant alleged that her discharge violated her rights under the First and Fourteenth amendments. White wrote for the Court again: "For at least 15 years, it has been settled that a state cannot condition public employment on a basis that infringes the employee's constitutionally protected interest in freedom of expression." Once more he quoted *Pickering*'s balancing test and concluded that the balance was against the employee. In so doing, White explicitly refused to lay down a general standard by which to judge future cases of this sort.

(4) In March, 1976, prodded by unions representing federal employees, Congress passed HR 8617, which would have substantially amended the Hatch Act. The bill would have retained existing prohibitions against: any federal employee's using his or her official authority to influence another person's vote, a senior official's eliciting or trying to prevent a contribution to a political fund from a junior employee, and any political solicitations by federal employees within federal buildings or while in uniform. The bill would also have kept most of the Hatch Act's restrictions on political activities by members of the Internal Revenue Service, the Department of Justice, and the Central Intelligence Agency. On the other hand, HR 8617 would have allowed all other federal employees to exercise their full political rights of participation. President Ford vetoed the bill, and its supporters in Congress lacked the necessary two-thirds majority to override his action.

———

"The First Amendment denies government the power to determine that spending to promote one's political views is wasteful, excessive or unwise."

BUCKLEY v. VALEO

424 U.S. 1, 96 S.Ct. 612, 46 L.Ed.2d 659 (1976).

As a result of the scandals incipient in the high cost of running for public office and the frequent necessity for candidates to rely on financial contributions from a few large donors, and particularly as a result of the scandals during Richard Nixon's presidency when he and his aides pressured many businessmen for gifts of money (and in turn were pressured by those donors for special governmental treatment), Congress in 1974 extensively amended the Federal Election Campaign Act. In its new form, that statute:

1. Limits to $1,000 contributions by individuals to any candidate for federal office and to $25,000 contributions by any committee;
2. Forbids individuals or groups acting independently of a candidate for federal office to spend more than $1,000 to aid that candidate;
3. Requires candidates for federal office to report for the public record contributions beyond a certain amount;
4. Provides for public funding of presidential campaigns;
5. Establishes a Federal Election Commission to oversee administration of the act's provisions.

A wide array of political figures quickly filed suit in a federal district court, attacking the constitutionality of various provisions. Among the litigants were former Senator Eugene McCarthy, a noted liberal, and James Buckley, the ultra-conservative senator from New York. In an unusual procedure, the district judge "certified" the questions (sent them) to the Court of Appeals for the Second Circuit. That tribunal upheld the statute, and the challengers appealed to the Supreme Court.

PER CURIAM. . . .

I. CONTRIBUTION AND EXPENDITURE LIMITATIONS . . .

A. General Principles

The Act's contribution and expenditure limitations operate in an area of the most fundamental First Amendment activities. Discussion of public issues and debate on the qualifications of candidates are integral to the operation of the system of government established by our Constitution. The First Amendment affords the broadest protection to such political expression in order "to assure [the] unfettered interchange of ideas for the bringing about of political and social changes desired by the people." Roth v. United States (1957). . . .

The First Amendment protects political association as well as political expression. The constitutional right of association explicated in NAACP v. Alabama (1958) stemmed from the Court's recognition that "[e]ffective advocacy of both public and private points of view, particularly controversial ones, is undeniably enhanced by group association." Subsequent decisions have made clear that the First and Fourteenth Amendments guarantee " 'freedom to associate with others for the common advancement of political beliefs and ideas,' " a freedom that encompasses " '[t]he right to associate with the political party of one's choice.' " Kusper v. Pontikes (1973). . . .

Appellees contend that what the Act regulates is conduct, and that its effect on speech and association is incidental at most. Appellants respond that contributions and expenditures are at the very core of political speech, and that the Act's limitations thus constitute restraints on First Amendment liberty that are both gross and direct. . . .

The expenditure of money simply cannot be equated with such conduct as destruction of a draft card. Some forms of communication made possible by the giving and spending of money involve speech alone, some involve conduct primarily, and some involve a combination of the two. Yet this Court has never suggested that the dependence of a communication on the expenditure of money operates itself to introduce a nonspeech element or to reduce the exacting scrutiny required by the First Amendment. . . .

Even if the categorization of the expenditure of money as conduct were accepted, the limitations challenged here would not meet the [United States v.] O'Brien [1968] test because the governmental interests advanced in support of the Act involve "suppressing communication." The interests served by the Act include restricting the voices of people and interest groups who have money to spend and reducing the overall scope of federal election campaigns. Although the Act does not focus on the ideas . . . it is aimed in part at equalizing the relative ability of all voters to affect electoral outcomes by placing a ceiling on expenditures for political expression by citizens and groups. . . . [I]t is beyond dispute that the interest in regulating the alleged "conduct" of giving or spending money "arises in some measure because the communication allegedly integral to the conduct is itself thought to be harmful." *O'Brien.*

Nor can the Act's contribution and expenditure limitations be sustained, as some of the parties suggest, by reference to the constitutional principles reflected [by cases that permit governmental limitations that are reasonable regulations of time, place, and manner of expression]. . . . The critical difference between this case and those time, place and manner cases is that the present Act's contribution and expenditure limitations impose direct quantity restrictions on political communication and association by persons, groups, candidates, and political parties in addition to any reasonable time, place, and manner regulations otherwise imposed.

A restriction on the amount of money a person or group can spend on political communication during a campaign necessarily reduces the quantity of expression by restricting the number of issues discussed, the depth of their exploration, and the size of the audience reached. This is because virtually every means of communicating ideas in today's mass society requires the expenditure of money. . . .

The expenditure limitations contained in the Act represent substantial rather than merely theoretical restraints on the quantity and diversity of political speech. The $1,000 ceiling on spending "relative to a clearly identified candidate," . . . would appear to exclude all citizens and groups except candidates, political parties, and the institutional press from any significant use of the most effective modes of communication. . . .

By contrast with a limitation upon expenditures for political expression, a limitation upon the amount that any one person or group may contribute to a candidate or political committee entails only a marginal restriction upon the contributor's ability to engage in free communication. A contribution serves as a general expression of support for the candidate and his views, but does not communicate the underlying basis for the support. The quantity of communication by the contributor does not increase perceptibly with the size of the contribution, since the expression rests solely on the undifferentiated symbolic act of contributing. At most, the size of the contribution provides a very rough index of the intensity of the contributor's support for the candidate. A limitation on the amount of money a person may give to a candidate or campaign organization thus involves little direct restraint on his political communication, for it permits the symbolic expression of support evidenced by a contribution but does not in any way infringe the contributor's freedom to discuss candidates and issues. While contributions may result in political expression if spent by a candidate or an association to present views to the voters, the transformation of contributions into political debate involves speech by someone other than the contributor. . . .

The Act's contribution and expenditure limitations also impinge on protected associational freedoms. Making a contribution, like joining a political party, serves to affiliate a person with a candidate. In addition, it enables like-minded persons to pool their resources in furtherance of common political goals. The Act's contribution ceilings thus limit one important means of associating with a candidate or committee, but leave the contributor free to become a member of any political association and to assist personally in the association's efforts on behalf of candidates. And the Act's contribution limitations permit associations and candidates to aggregate large sums of money to promote effective advocacy. By contrast, the Act's $1,000 limitation on independent expenditures "relative to a clearly identified candidate" precludes most associations from effectively amplifying the voice of their adherents, the original basis for the recognition of First Amendment protection of the freedom of association. . . .

In sum, although the Act's contribution and expenditure limitations both implicate fundamental First Amendment interests, its expenditure ceilings impose significantly more severe restrictions on protect-

ed freedoms of political expression and association than do its
limitations on financial contributions. . . .

B. Contribution Limitations . . .

Appellants contend that the $1,000 contribution ceiling unjustifi-
ably burdens First Amendment freedoms, employs overbroad dollar
limits, and discriminates against candidates opposing incumbent office
holders and against minor-party candidates in violation of the Fifth
Amendment. We address each of these claims of invalidity in turn.
. . . [Noting that close scrutiny is in order when government limits
freedom to associate, the Court nevertheless recognized that a sufficiently important state concern might permit some curtailment.]

Appellees argue that the Act's restrictions on large campaign
contributions are justified by three governmental interests. According
to the parties and *amici,* the primary interest served by the limitations
and, indeed, by the Act as a whole, is the prevention of corruption and
the appearance of corruption spawned by the real or imagined coercive
influence of large financial contributions on candidates' positions and
on their actions if elected to office. Two "ancillary" interests underlying the Act are also allegedly furthered by the $1,000 limits on
contributions. First, the limits serve to mute the voices of affluent
persons and groups in the election process and thereby to equalize the
relative ability of all citizens to affect the outcome of elections. Second,
it is argued, the ceilings may to some extent act as a brake on the
skyrocketing cost of political campaigns and thereby serve to open the
political system more widely to candidates without access to sources of
large amounts of money.

It is unnecessary to look beyond the Act's primary purpose—to
limit the actuality and appearance of corruption resulting from large
individual financial contributions—in order to find a constitutionally
sufficient justification for the $1,000 contribution limitation. Under a
system of private financing of elections, a candidate lacking immense
personal or family wealth must depend on financial contributions from
others to provide the resources necessary to conduct a successful
campaign. The increasing importance of the communications media
and sophisticated mass-mailing and polling operations to effective
campaigning make the raising of large sums of money an ever more
essential ingredient of an effective candidacy. To the extent that large
contributions are given to secure a political *quid pro quo* from current
and potential office holders, the integrity of our system of representative democracy is undermined. Although the scope of such pernicious
practices can never be reliably ascertained, the deeply disturbing examples surfacing after the 1972 election demonstrate that the problem is
not an illusory one.

Of almost equal concern as the danger of actual *quid pro quo*
arrangements is the impact of the appearance of corruption stemming
from public awareness of the opportunities for abuse inherent in a
regime of large individual financial contributions. . . .

Appellants contend that the contribution limitations must be invalidated because bribery laws and narrowly drawn disclosure requirements constitute a less restrictive means of dealing with "proven and suspected *quid pro quo* arrangements." But laws making criminal the giving and taking of bribes deal with only the most blatant and specific attempts of those with money to influence governmental action. And while disclosure requirements serve the many salutary purposes discussed elsewhere in this opinion, Congress was surely entitled to conclude that disclosure was only a partial measure, and that contribution ceilings were a necessary legislative concomitant to deal with the reality or appearance of corruption. . . .

The Act's $1,000 contribution limitation focuses precisely on the problem of large campaign contributions—the narrow aspect of political association where the actuality and potential for corruption have been identified—while leaving persons free to engage in independent political expression, to associate actively through volunteering their services, and to assist to a limited but nonetheless substantial extent in supporting candidates and committees with financial resources. Significantly, the Act's contribution limitations in themselves do not undermine to any material degree the potential for robust and effective discussion of candidates and campaign issues by individual citizens, associations, the institutional press, candidates, and political parties.

We find that, under the rigorous standard of review established by our prior decisions, the weighty interests served by restricting the size of financial contributions to political candidates are sufficient to justify the limited effect upon First Amendment freedoms caused by the $1,000 contribution ceiling. . . .

Appellants' first overbreadth challenge to the contribution ceilings rests on the proposition that most large contributors do not seek improper influence over a candidate's position or an office holder's action. Although the truth of that proposition may be assumed, it does not undercut the validity of the $1,000 contribution limitation. Not only is it difficult to isolate suspect contributions but, more importantly, Congress was justified in concluding that the interest in safeguarding against the appearance of impropriety requires that the opportunity for abuse inherent in the process of raising large monetary contributions be eliminated.

A second, related overbreadth claim is that the $1,000 restriction is unrealistically low. . . . While the contribution limitation provisions might well have been structured to take account of the graduated expenditure limitations for congressional and Presidential campaigns, Congress's failure to engage in such fine tuning does not invalidate the legislation. . . . Such distinctions in degree become significant only when they can be said to amount to differences in kind.

Apart from these First Amendment concerns, appellants argue that the contribution limitations work such an invidious discrimination between incumbents and challengers that the statutory provisions must be declared unconstitutional on their face. . . . [I]t is important at the outset to note that the Act applies the same limitations on contributions to all candidates regardless of their present occupations, ideological views, or party affiliations. Absent record evidence of invidious discrimination against challengers as a class, a court should generally be hesitant to invalidate legislation which on its face imposes even-handed restrictions.

There is no such evidence to support the claim that the contribution limitations in themselves discriminate against major-party challengers to incumbents. Challengers can and often do defeat incumbents in federal elections. . . . The charge of discrimination against minor-party and independent candidates is more troubling, but the record provides no basis for concluding that the Act invidiously disadvantages such candidates. As noted above, the Act on its face treats all candidates equally. . . . And the restriction would appear to benefit minor-party and independent candidates relative to their major-party opponents because major-party candidates receive far more money in large contributions. Although there is some force to appellants' response that minor-party candidates are primarily concerned with their ability to amass the resources necessary to reach the electorate rather than with their funding position relative to their major-party opponents, the record is virtually devoid of support for the claim that the $1,000 contribution limitation will have a serious effect on the initiation and scope of minor-party and independent candidacies. Moreover, any attempt to exclude minor parties and independents en masse from the Act's contribution limitations overlooks the fact that minor-party candidates may win elective office or have a substantial impact on the outcome of an election.

. . . [W]e conclude that the impact of the Act's $1,000 contribution limitation on major-party challengers and on minor-party candidates does not render the provision unconstitutional on its face. . . .

C. Expenditure Limitations . . .

. . . [On the question of the $1,000 limitation on expenditures for a candidate, the Court after considering the vagueness of the language of that section of the law (Section 608(e)(1), turned to the First Amendment aspects of that question.]

We find that the governmental interest in preventing corruption and the appearance of corruption is inadequate to justify § 608(e)(1)'s ceiling on independent expenditures. First, assuming, *arguendo,* that large independent expenditures pose the same dangers of actual or apparent *quid pro quo* arrangements as do large contributions, § 608(e)(1) does not provide an answer that sufficiently relates to the elimination of those dangers. Unlike the contribution limitations' total ban on the giving of large amounts of money to candidates, § 608(e)(1) prevents only some large expenditures. So long as persons and groups eschew expenditures that in express terms advocate the election or defeat of a clearly identified candidate, they are free to spend as much as they want to promote the candidate and his views. The exacting interpretation of the statutory language necessary to avoid unconstitutional vagueness thus undermines the limitation's effectiveness as a loophole-closing provision by facilitating circumvention by those seeking to exert improper influence upon a candidate or officeholder. It would naively underestimate the ingenuity and resourcefulness of persons and groups desiring to buy influence to believe that they would have much difficulty devising expenditures that skirted the restriction on express advocacy of election or defeat but nevertheless benefited the candidate's campaign. Yet no substantial societal interest would be served by a loophole-closing provision designed to check corruption that permitted unscrupulous persons and organizations to expend unlimited sums of money in order to obtain improper influence over candidates for elective office. . . .

Second, quite apart from the shortcomings of § 608(e)(1) in preventing any abuses generated by large independent expenditures, the independent advocacy restricted by the provision does not presently appear to pose dangers of real or apparent corruption comparable to those identified with large campaign contributions. . . .

While the independent expenditure ceiling thus fails to serve any substantial governmental interest in stemming the reality or appearance of corruption in the electoral process, it heavily burdens core First Amendment expression. For the First Amendment right to " 'speak one's mind . . . on all public institutions' " includes the right to engage in " 'vigorous advocacy' no less than 'abstract discussion.' " New York Times Co. v. Sullivan [1964]. Advocacy of the election or defeat of candidates for federal office is no less entitled to protection under the First Amendment than the discussion of political policy generally or advocacy of the passage or defeat of legislation.

It is argued, however, that the ancillary governmental interest in equalizing the relative ability of individuals and groups to influence the outcome of elections serves to justify the limitation on express advocacy of the election or defeat of candidates imposed by § 608(e)(1)'s expenditure ceiling. But the concept that government may restrict the speech of some elements of our society in order to enhance the relative voice of others is wholly foreign to the First Amendment, which was designed "to secure 'the widest possible dissemination of information from diverse and antagonistic sources,' " and " 'to assure unfettered interchange of ideas for the bringing about of political and social changes desired by the people.' " *New York Times.* . . . The First Amendment's protection against governmental abridgment of free expression cannot properly be made to depend on a person's financial ability to engage in public discussion. . . .

For the reasons stated, we conclude that § 608(e)(1)'s independent expenditure limitation is unconstitutional under the First Amendment. . . .

[The law also limits expenditures by a candidate from his own or his family's funds.]

These ceilings vary from $50,000 for Presidential or Vice Presidential candidates to $35,000 for senatorial candidates, and $25,000 for most candidates for the House of Representatives. . . . The candidate, no less than any other person, has a First Amendment right to engage in the discussion of public issues and vigorously and tirelessly to advocate his own election and the election of other candidates. Indeed, it is of particular importance that candidates have the unfettered opportunity to make their views known so that the electorate may intelligently evaluate the candidates' personal qualities and their positions on vital public issues before choosing among them on election day. . . . Section 608(a)'s ceiling on personal expenditures by a candidate in furtherance of his own candidacy thus clearly and directly interferes with constitutionally protected freedoms.

The primary governmental interest served by the Act—the prevention of actual and apparent corruption of the political process—does not support the limitation on the candidate's expenditure of his own personal funds. . . . Indeed, the use of personal funds reduces the candidate's dependence on outside contributions and thereby counteracts the coercive pressures and attendant risks of abuse to which the Act's contribution limitations are directed.

The ancillary interest in equalizing the relative financial resources of candidates competing for elective office, therefore, provides the sole relevant rationale for § 608(a)'s expenditure ceiling. That interest is clearly not sufficient to justify the provision's infringement of fundamental First Amendment rights. First, the limitation may fail to promote financial equality among candidates. . . . Second, and more fundamentally, the First Amendment simply cannot tolerate § 608(a)'s restriction upon the freedom of a candidate to speak without legislative limit on behalf of his own candidacy. We therefore hold that § 608(a)'s restriction on a candidate's personal expenditures is unconstitutional. . . .

[The law also places an upper limit on the amount that may be spent in seeking election to federal offices. Presidential candidates may spend no more than $10 million to win nomination and no more than $20 million for the general election. Senatorial candidates' limits are set by the size of the voting age population, and Representatives are held to $70,000. (The figures are periodically adjusted for inflation.)]

No governmental interest that has been suggested is sufficient to justify the restriction on the quantity of political expression imposed by § 608(c)'s campaign expenditure limitations. . . . The interest in alleviating the corrupting influence of large contributions is served by the Act's contribution limitations and disclosure provisions rather than by § 608(c)'s campaign expenditure ceilings. . . . There is no indication that the substantial criminal penalties for violating the contribution ceilings combined with the political repercussion of such violations will be insufficient to police the contribution provisions. Extensive reporting, auditing, and disclosure requirements applicable to both contributions and expenditures by political campaigns are designed to facilitate the detection of illegal contributions. . . .

The interest in equalizing the financial resources of candidates competing for federal office is no more convincing a justification for restricting the scope of federal election campaigns. Given the limitation on the size of outside contributions, the financial resources available to a candidate's campaign, like the number of volunteers recruited, will normally vary with the size and intensity of the candidate's support. There is nothing invidious, improper, or unhealthy in permitting such funds to be spent to carry the candidate's message to the electorate. Moreover, the equalization of permissible campaign expenditures might serve not to equalize the opportunities of all candidates, but to handicap a candidate who lacked substantial name recognition or exposure of his views before the start of the campaign.

Campaign expenditure ceilings appear to be designed primarily to serve the governmental interests in reducing the allegedly skyrocketing costs of political campaigns. . . . [Appellees stressed that since 1952 campaign costs have gone up by 300 per cent and the price index by 57 per cent; appellants, however, argued that campaign costs have not exceeded the increases in general advertising or gross national product.] In any event, the mere growth in the cost of federal election campaigns in and of itself provides no basis for governmental restrictions on the quantity of campaign spending and the resulting limitation on the scope of federal campaigns. The First Amendment denies government the power to determine that spending to promote one's political views is wasteful, excessive, or unwise. In the free society ordained by our Constitution it is not the government, but the people— individually as citizens and candidates and collectively as associations and political committees—who must retain control over the quantity and range of debate on public issues in a political campaign.

For these reasons we hold that § 608(c) is constitutionally invalid. . . .

II. REPORTING AND DISCLOSURE REQUIREMENTS . . .

The governmental interests sought to be vindicated by the disclosure requirements . . . fall into three categories. First, disclosure provides the electorate with information "as to where political campaign money comes from and how it is spent by the candidate" in order to aid the voters in evaluating those who seek federal office. It allows voters to place each candidate in the political spectrum more precisely than is often possible solely on the basis of party labels and campaign speeches. The sources of a candidate's financial support also alert the voter to the interests to which a candidate is most likely to be responsive and thus facilitate predictions of future performance in office.

Second, disclosure requirements deter actual corruption and avoid the appearance of corruption by exposing large contributions and expenditures to the light of publicity. This exposure may discourage those who would use money for improper purposes either before or after the election. A public armed with information about a candidate's most generous supporters is better able to detect any post-election special favors that may be given in return. . . . Congress in enacting these requirements . . . may have been mindful of Mr. Justice Brandeis' advice:

> Publicity is justly commended as a remedy for social and industrial diseases. Sunlight is said to be the best of disinfectants; electric light the most efficient policeman.

Third, and not least significant, recordkeeping, reporting, and disclosure requirements are an essential means of gathering the data necessary to detect violations of the contribution limitations described above.

The disclosure requirements, as a general matter, directly serve substantial governmental interests. In determining whether these interests are sufficient to justify the requirements we must look to the extent of the burden that they place on individual rights.

It is undoubtedly true that public disclosure of contributions to candidates and political parties will deter some individuals who otherwise might contribute. In some instances, disclosure may even expose contributors to harassment or retaliation. These are not insignificant burdens on individual rights, and they must be weighted carefully against the interests which Congress has sought to promote by this legislation. . . .

[Appellants argued that disclosure could have an adverse effect on small or new parties because potential donors might fear harassment.]

There could well be a case, similar to those before the Court in [NAACP v.] Alabama and Bates [v. Little Rock (1960)], where the threat to the exercise of First Amendment rights is so serious and the state interest furthered by disclosure so insubstantial that the Act's requirements cannot be constitutionally applied. But no appellant in this case has tendered record evidence of the sort proffered in [NAACP v.] Alabama. . . .

We recognize that unduly strict requirements of proof could impose a heavy burden. . . . The evidence proffered need only show a reasonable probability that the compelled disclosure of a party's contributors' names will subject them to threats, harassment, or reprisals from either Government officials or private parties. . . .

In summary, we find no constitutional infirmities in the recordkeeping, reporting, and disclosure provisions of the act.

III. PUBLIC FINANCING OF PRESIDENTIAL ELECTION CAMPAIGNS . . .

Section 9006 establishes a Presidential Election Campaign Fund . . . financed from general revenues in the aggregate amount designated by individual taxpayers under § 6096, who on their income tax returns may authorize payment to the Fund of one dollar of their tax liability in the case of an individual return or two dollars in the case of a joint return.

[Appellants argued that these provisions favor the two established parties to the detriment of smaller, new parties, or independents because the size of the subsidy for existing minor parties is a function of the size of its vote at the *last* presidential election and because, while existing parties would receive their subsidies at the start of presidential campaigns, new parties and independents would receive theirs only after the election, according to the percentage of popular votes they won. The Court disagreed, saying the two major parties *are* different from minor parties and independents and that affording equal access to campaign funds for every small group that wanted to run a candidate for President would open "a raid on the United States Treasury."]

Mr. Chief Justice **BURGER**, concurring in part and dissenting in part.

. . . I dissent from those parts of the Court's holding sustaining the statutory provisions (a) for disclosure of small contributions, (b) for limitations on contributions, and (c) for public financing of Presidential campaigns. In my view, the Act's disclosure scheme is impermissibly broad and violative of the First Amendment as it relates to reporting contributions in excess of $10 and $100. The contribution limitations infringe on First Amendment liberties and suffer from the same infirmities that the Court correctly sees in the expenditure ceilings. The system for public financing of Presidential campaigns is, in my judgment, an impermissible intrusion by the Government into the traditionally private political process.

More broadly, the Court's result does violence to the intent of Congress in this comprehensive scheme of campaign finance. By dissecting the Act bit by bit, and casting off vital parts, the Court fails to recognize that the whole of this Act is greater than the sum of its parts. Congress intended to regulate all aspects of federal campaign finances, but what remains after today's holding leaves no more than a shadow of what Congress contemplated. I question whether the residue leaves a workable program. . . .

Mr. Justice **WHITE**, concurring in part and dissenting in part. . . .

Mr. Justice **MARSHALL**, concurring in part and dissenting in part. . . .

The concern that candidacy for public office not become, or appear to become, the exclusive province of the wealthy assumes heightened significance when one considers the impact of § 608(b), which the Court today upholds. That provision prohibits contributions from individuals and groups to candidates in excess of $1,000, and contributions from political committees in excess of $5,000. While the limitations on contributions are neutral in the sense that all candidates are foreclosed from accepting large contributions, there can be no question that large contributions generally mean more to the candidate without a substantial personal fortune to spend on his campaign. Large contributions are the less wealthy candidate's only hope of countering the wealthy candidate's immediate access to substantial sums of money. With that option removed, the less wealthy candidate is without the means to match the large initial expenditures of money of which the wealthy candidate is capable. In short, the limitations on contributions put a premium on a candidate's personal wealth.

In view of § 608(b)'s limitations on contributions, then, [the section of the Act that permits unlimited expenditures of the candidate's own money or that of his family] emerges not simply as a device to reduce the natural advantage of the wealthy candidate, but as a provision providing some symmetry to a regulatory scheme that otherwise enhances the natural advantage of the wealthy. Regardless of whether the goal of equalizing access would justify a legislative limit on personal candidate expenditures standing by itself, I think it clear that that goal justifies § 608(a)'s limits when they are considered in conjunction with the remainder of the Act. I therefore respectfully dissent from the Court's invalidation of § 608(a). . . .

Mr. Justice **BLACKMUN,** concurring in part and dissenting in part.

. . .

Mr. Justice **REHNQUIST,** concurring in part and dissenting in part.

. . .

I concur in Parts I, II, and IV of the Court's opinion. I concur in so much of Part III . . . as holds that the public funding of the cost of a Presidential election campaign is a permissible exercise of congressional authority under the power to tax and spend granted by Art. I [of the Constitution], but I dissent from [that section of Part III], which holds that certain aspects of the statutory treatment of minor parties and independent candidates are constitutionally valid. . . .

I would hold that, as to general election financing, Congress has not merely treated the two major parties differently from minor parties and independents, but has discriminated in favor of the former in such a way as to run afoul of the Fifth and First Amendments to the Constitution.

Editors' Notes

(1) That portion of the opinion holding unconstitutional the way in which members of Federal Election Commission were appointed is reprinted above, p. 371.

(2) As it did in passing in several other opinions we have read, the Court applied a constitutional test here:

[S]ignificant encroachments on First Amendment rights . . . cannot be justified by a mere showing of some legitimate governmental interest. Since [NAACP v.] Alabama we have required that the

> *subordinating* interests of the State must survive *exacting scrutiny.* We have also insisted that there be a "relevant correlation" or "substantial relation" between the governmental interest and the [infringement of a First Amendment right]. [Italics supplied.]

The Court's wording of the test varies. Usually it uses "strict scrutiny" rather than "exacting scrutiny." The phrase originated in Stone's footnote 4 in *Carolene Products* (1938; reprinted above, p. 482), where he used the terms "more exacting judicial scrutiny" and "more searching judicial inquiry." (Douglas' opinion for the Court in Skinner v. Oklahoma [1942; reprinted below, p. 868] first used the term "strict scrutiny.") The Court has more fully developed this notion of judges' strictly scrutinizing legislation that touches on certain kinds of rights in cases that, like *Skinner,* involve equal protection of the laws; see below, Chapters 13 and 14. But it has often applied the doctrine in rulings involving such "fundamental" rights as those protected by the First Amendment or included under a right to privacy; see below, Chapter 17.

As *Buckley* indicates, when the Court applies "strict scrutiny," it does not presume the challenged legislation is constitutional. Rather quite the opposite. As the Court held in Harris v. McRae (1980): "if a law 'impinges upon a fundamental right explicitly or implictly secured by the Constitution [it] is presumptively unconstitutional.'" The Court throws the burden onto the government to prove that there is (1) a "compelling" or "subordinating" public interest at stake that should take precedence over the individual right; (2) a close connection between the challenged policy and protection of that "compelling interest"; and usually (3) no way the government can protect that "compelling interest" by means that intrude less severely on the particular fundamental right. As one would guess, the government (state or federal) seldom wins when it faces this test.

(3) Is "strict scrutiny" merely a more sophisticated balancing test? If so, does it meet the criticisms that are usually directed at "balancing" as a *technique* of constitutional interpretation. (See Chapter 8, above, at pp. 309–312.)

(4) *Buckley* denied minor parties a blanket exemption from disclosing names of contributors but hinted at a sympathetic hearing if there were a claim of harassment because of such disclosure. See above, p. 686. Brown v. Socialist Workers Party (1982) fulfilled that promise by holding unconstitutional Ohio's requirements of disclosure of contributors, as applied to the Socialist Workers party, a small group devoted to "the abolition of capitalism," which had been the target of dozens of burglaries by the FBI during the 1960s. For a five-judge majority, Marshall wrote: "In Buckley v. Valeo (1976), this Court held that the First Amendment prohibits the government from compelling disclosures by a minor party that can show a 'reasonable probability' that the compelled disclosures will subject those identified to 'threats, harassment, or reprisals.'" Is this a fair reading of *Buckley* at p. 686? See the discussion of stare decisis as a technique of constitutional interpretation, Chapter 8, above, pp. 307–309.

(5) FEC v. National Conservation Political Action Committee (1985) invalidated § 9012(f) of the 1974 Act as a violation of the First Amendment. That section forbade political action committees to spend more than $1,000 to assist a presidential candidate who had accepted federal campaign subsidies. Speaking for five members of the Court, Rehnquist relied heavily on *Buckley:*

"[A]llowing the presentation of views while forbidding the expenditure of more than $1,000 to present them [in a presidential campaign] is much like allowing a speaker in a public hall to express his views while denying him use of an amplifying system." Stevens concurred in part and dissented in part. Brennan, White, and Marshall dissented. White commented: "The First Amendment protects the right to speak, not the right to spend"; and he, along with Brennan and Marshall, thought that governmental interests in preventing electoral fraud justified whatever intrusion the section made on freedom of communication.

(6) For commentary on *Buckley*, see: Laurence H. Tribe, *American Constitutional Law* (Mineola, N.Y.: Foundation Press, 1978), pp. 798–811; Daniel D. Polsby, "Buckley v. Valeo," 1976 *Sup.Ct.Rev.* 1; Marlene A. Nicholson, "Buckley v. Valeo," 1977 *Wisc.L.Rev.* 323 (1976); J. Skelly Wright, "Politics and the Constitution," 85 *Yale L.J.* 1001 (1976); and Comment, "Buckley v. Valeo," 76 *Colum.L.Rev.* 852 (1976).

"[T]he press does not have a monopoly on either the First Amendment or the ability to enlighten."

FIRST NATIONAL BANK OF BOSTON v. BELLOTTI
435 U.S. 765, 98 S.Ct. 1407, 55 L.Ed.2d 707 (1978).

Chapter 55, § 8 of the Massachusetts General Laws forbade certain kinds of corporations, including banks, trusts, insurance companies, and public power firms, to contribute to candidates for public office or to campaigns for or against public referenda. In 1976, two banks and three other corporations covered by § 8 announced they were going to spend money to publicize their opposition to a proposal for a graduated income tax, scheduled for a referendum that year. The state attorney general warned the corporations that he would proceed against them under § 8 if they carried out their plan. The corporations then sued in a state court to have the statute declared unconstitutional as a violation of the First Amendment. The Supreme Judicial Court of Massachusetts, however, sustained § 8, and the corporations appealed to the U.S. Supreme Court.

Mr. Justice **POWELL** delivered the opinion of the Court. . . .

III

The court below framed the principal question in this case as whether and to what extent corporations have First Amendment rights. We believe that the court posed the wrong question. The Constitution often protects interests broader than those of the party seeking their vindication. The First Amendment, in particular, serves significant societal interests. The proper question therefore is not whether corporations "have" First Amendment rights and, if so, whether they are coextensive with those of natural persons. Instead, the question must be whether § 8 abridges expression that the First Amendment was meant to protect. We hold that it does.

A

The speech proposed by appellants is at the heart of the First Amendment's protection. . . . In appellants' view, the enactment of a graduated personal income tax, as proposed to be authorized by constitutional amendment, would have a seriously adverse effect on the economy of the State. The importance of the referendum issue to the people and government of Massachusetts is not disputed. Its merits, however, are the subject of sharp disagreement.

As the Court said in Mills v. Alabama (1966), "there is practically universal agreement that a major purpose of [the First] Amendment was to protect the free discussion of governmental affairs." If the speakers here were not corporations, no one would suggest that the State could silence their proposed speech. It is the type of speech indispensable to decisionmaking in a democracy, and this is no less true because the speech comes from a corporation rather than an individual. The inherent worth of the speech in terms of its capacity for informing the public does not depend upon the identity of its source, whether corporation, association, union, or individual. . . .

. . . The question in this case, simply put, is whether the corporate identity of the speaker deprives this proposed speech of what otherwise would be its clear entitlement to protection. We turn now to that question.

B

The court below . . . concluded that a corporation's First Amendment rights must derive from its property rights under the Fourteenth.

This is an artificial mode of analysis, untenable under decisions of this Court. . . . Freedom of speech and the other freedoms encompassed by the First Amendment always have been viewed as fundamental components of the liberty safeguarded by the Due Process Clause, see Gitlow v. New York (1925); NAACP v. Alabama (1958); Stromberg v. California (1931); DeJonge v. Oregon (1937); Warren, The New "Liberty" Under the Fourteenth Amendment, 39 Harv.L.Rev. 431 (1926), and the Court has not identified a separate source for the right when it has been asserted by corporations. . . .

The press cases emphasize the special and constitutionally recognized role of that institution in informing and educating the public, offering criticism, and providing a forum for discussion and debate. Mills. But the press does not have a monopoly on either the First Amendment or the ability to enlighten. Cf. Buckley v. Valeo [1976]; Red Lion Broadcasting Co. v. FCC (1969); New York Times Co. v. Sullivan (1964); Associated Press v. United States (1945). Similarly, the Court's decisions involving corporations in the business of communication or entertainment are based not only on the role of the First Amendment in fostering individual self-expression but also on its role in affording the public access to discussion, debate, and the dissemina-

tion of information and ideas.[1] See *Red Lion;* Stanley v. Georgia
(1969); Time, Inc. v. Hill (1967). Even decisions seemingly based
exclusively on the individual's right to express himself acknowledge
that the expression may contribute to society's edification. Winters v.
New York (1948).

Nor do our recent commercial speech cases lend support to appellee's business interest theory. They illustrate that the First Amendment goes beyond protection of the press and the self-expression of
individuals to prohibit government from limiting the stock of information from which members of the public may draw. A commercial
advertisement is constitutionally protected not so much because it
pertains to the seller's business as because it furthers the societal
interest in the "free flow of commercial information." Virginia State
Bd. of Pharmacy v. Virginia Citizens Consumer Council (1976); see
Linmark Associates, Inc. v. Willingboro [1977]. . . .

In the realm of protected speech, the legislature is constitutionally
disqualified from dictating the subjects about which persons may speak
and the speakers who may address a public issue. Police Dept. of
Chicago v. Mosley (1972). If a legislature may direct business corporations to "stick to business," it also may limit other corporations—
religious, charitable, or civic—to their respective "business" when addressing the public. Such power in government to channel the expression of views is unacceptable under the First Amendment. Especially
where, as here, the legislature's suppression of speech suggests an
attempt to give one side of a debatable public question an advantage in
expressing its views to the people, the First Amendment is plainly
offended. Yet the State contends that its action is necessitated by
governmental interests of the highest order. We next consider these
asserted interests.

IV

The constitutionality of § 8's prohibition of the "exposition of
ideas" by corporations turns on whether it can survive the exacting
scrutiny necessitated by a state-imposed restriction of freedom of
speech. Especially where, as here, a prohibition is directed at speech
itself, and the speech is intimately related to the process of governing,
"the State may prevail only upon showing a subordinating interest
which is compelling," Bates v. Little Rock (1960), "and the burden is on
the government to show the existence of such an interest." Elrod v.
Burns (1976). Even then, the State must employ means "closely drawn
to avoid unnecessary abridgment. . . ." *Buckley.*

The Supreme Judicial Court did not subject § 8 to "the critical
scrutiny demanded under accepted First Amendment and equal protec-

---

1. The suggestion in Mr. Justice White's dissent that the First Amendment affords
less protection to ideas that are not the product of "individual choice" would seem to
apply to newspaper editorials and every other form of speech created under the auspices
of a corporate body. No decision of this Court lends support to such a restrictive notion.
[Footnote by the Court.]

tion principles," *Buckley,* because of its view that the First Amendment does not apply to appellants' proposed speech. . . .

A

Preserving the integrity of the electoral process, preventing corruption, and "sustain[ing] the active, alert responsibility of the individual citizen in a democracy for the wise conduct of government" are interests of the highest importance. *Buckley;* United States v. Automobile Workers (1957); Burroughs v. United States (1934). Preservation of the individual citizen's confidence in government is equally important. *Buckley;* CSC v. Letter Carriers (1973).

Appellee advances a number of arguments in support of his view that these interests are endangered by corporate participation in discussion of a referendum issue. They hinge upon the assumption that such participation would exert an undue influence on the outcome of a referendum vote, and—in the end—destroy the confidence of the people in the democratic process and the integrity of government. According to appellee, corporations are wealthy and powerful and their views may drown out other points of view. If appellee's arguments were supported by record or legislative findings that corporate advocacy threatened imminently to undermine democratic processes, thereby denigrating rather than serving First Amendment interests, these arguments would merit our consideration. Cf. *Red Lion.* But there has been no showing that the relative voice of corporations has been overwhelming or even significant in influencing referenda in Massachusetts, or that there has been any threat to the confidence of the citizenry in government.

Nor are appellee's arguments inherently persuasive or supported by the precedents of this Court. Referenda are held on issues, not candidates for public office. The risk of corruption perceived in cases involving candidate elections simply is not present in a popular vote on a public issue. To be sure, corporate advertising may influence the outcome of the vote; this would be its purpose. But the fact that advocacy may persuade the electorate is hardly a reason to suppress it: The Constitution "protects expression which is eloquent no less than that which is unconvincing." Kingsley Int'l Pictures Corp. v. Regents [1959]. . . . Moreover, the people in our democracy are entrusted with the responsibility for judging and evaluating the relative merits of conflicting arguments. They may consider, in making their judgment, the source and credibility of the advocate. But if there be any danger that the people cannot evaluate the information and arguments advanced by appellants, it is a danger contemplated by the Framers of the First Amendment. . . .

B

Finally, appellee argues that § 8 protects corporate shareholders, an interest that is both legitimate and traditionally within the province of state law. The statute is said to serve this interest by preventing the use of corporate resources in furtherance of views with which some shareholders may disagree. This purpose is belied, however, by the provisions of the statute, which are both underinclusive and overinclusive.

The underinclusiveness of the statute is self-evident. Corporate expenditures with respect to a referendum are prohibited, while corporate activity with respect to the passage or defeat of legislation is permitted,. . . . Nor does § 8 prohibit a corporation from expressing its views, by the expenditure of corporate funds, on any public issue until it becomes the subject of a referendum, though the displeasure of disapproving shareholders is unlikely to be any less. . . .

Nor is the fact that § 8 is limited to banks and business corporations without relevance. Excluded from its provisions and criminal sanctions are entities or organized groups in which numbers of persons may hold an interest or membership, and which often have resources comparable to those of large corporations. Minorities in such groups or entities may have interests with respect to institutional speech quite comparable to those of minority shareholders in a corporation. . . .

The overinclusiveness of the statute is demonstrated by the fact that § 8 would prohibit a corporation from supporting or opposing a referendum proposal even if its shareholders unanimously authorized the contribution or expenditure. . . .

[*Reversed.*]

Mr. Chief Justice **BURGER** concurring. . . .

Mr. Justice **WHITE,** with whom Mr. Justice **BRENNAN** and Mr. Justice **MARSHALL** join, dissenting. . . .

I

There is now little doubt that corporate communications come within the scope of the First Amendment. This, however, is merely the starting point of analysis, because an examination of the First Amendment values that corporate expression furthers and the threat to the functioning of a free society it is capable of posing reveals that it is not fungible with communications emanating from individuals and is subject to restrictions which individual expression is not. Indeed, what some have considered to be the principal function of the First Amendment, the use of communication as a means of self-expression, self-realization, and self-fulfillment, is not at all furthered by corporate speech. It is clear that the communications of profitmaking corporations are not "an integral part of the development of ideas, of mental exploration and of the affirmation of self." They do not represent a manifestation of individual freedom or choice. Undoubtedly, as this Court has recognized, see NAACP v. Button (1963), there are some corporations formed for the express purpose of advancing certain ideological causes shared by all their members or, as in the case of the press, of disseminating information and ideas. Under such circumstances, association in a corporate form may be viewed as merely a means of achieving effective self-expression. But this is hardly the case generally with corporations operated for the purpose of making profits. Shareholders in such entities do not share a common set of political or social views, and they certainly have not invested their money for the purpose of advancing political or social causes or in an enterprise engaged in the business of disseminating news and opinion. In fact . . . the government has a strong interest in assuring that investment decisions are not predicated upon agreement or disagreement with the activities of corporations in the political arena.

. . . [T]here is no basis whatsoever for concluding that these views are expressive of the heterogeneous beliefs of their shareholders whose convictions on many political issues are undoubtedly shaped by considerations other than a desire to endorse any electoral or ideological cause which would tend to increase the value of a particular corporate investment. This is particularly true where, as in this case . . . [the managers] have not been able to demonstrate that the issue involved has any material connection with the corporate business. Thus when a profitmaking corporation contributes to a political candidate this does not further the self-expression or self-fulfillment of its shareholders in the way that expenditures from them as individuals would.

The self-expression of the communicator is not the only value encompassed by the First Amendment. One of its functions, often referred to as the right to hear or receive information, is to protect the interchange of ideas. Any communication of ideas, and consequently any expenditure of funds which makes the communication of ideas possible, it can be argued, furthers the purposes of the First Amendment. This proposition does not establish, however, that the right of the general public to receive communications financed by means of corporate expenditures is of the same dimension as that to hear other forms of expression. In the first place . . . corporate expenditures designed to further political causes lack the connection with individual self-expression. . . . Ideas which are not a product of individual choice are entitled to less First Amendment protection. Secondly, the restriction of corporate speech concerned with political matters impinges much less severely upon the availability of ideas to the general public than do restrictions upon individual speech. Even the complete curtailment of corporate communications concerning political or ideological questions not integral to day-to-day business functions would leave individuals, including corporate shareholders, employees, and customers, free to communicate their thoughts. . . .

I recognize that there may be certain communications undertaken by corporations which could not be restricted without impinging seriously upon the right to receive information. In the absence of advertising and similar promotional activities, for example, the ability of consumers to obtain information relating to products manufactured by corporations would be significantly impeded. There is also a need for employees, customers, and shareholders of corporations to be able to receive communications about matters relating to the functioning of

corporations. . . . None of these considerations, however, are implicated by a prohibition upon corporate expenditures relating to referenda concerning questions of general public concern having no connection
with corporate business affairs.

It bears emphasis here that the Massachusetts statute forbids the
expenditure of corporate funds in connection with referenda but in no
way forbids the board of directors of a corporation from formulating
and making public what it represents as the views of the corporation
even though the subject addressed has no material effect whatsoever on
the business of the corporation. These views could be publicized at the
individual expense of the officers, directors, stockholders, or anyone
else interested in circulating the corporate view on matters irrelevant
to its business.

The governmental interest in regulating corporate political communications, especially those relating to electoral matters, also raises
considerations which differ significantly from those governing the regulation of individual speech. Corporations are artificial entities created
by law for the purpose of furthering certain economic goals. In order
to facilitate the achievement of such ends, special rules relating to such
matters as limited liability, perpetual life, and the accumulation, distribution, and taxation of assets are normally applied to them. States
have provided corporations with such attributes in order to increase
their economic viability and thus strengthen the economy generally. It
has long been recognized, however, that the special status of corporations has placed them in a position to control vast amounts of economic
power which may, if not regulated, dominate not only the economy but
also the very heart of our democracy, the electoral process. . . .
[T]he interest of Massachusetts and the many other States which have
restricted corporate political activity is . . . preventing institutions
which have been permitted to amass wealth as a result of special
advantages extended by the State for certain economic purposes from
using that wealth to acquire an unfair advantage in the political
process. . . . The State need not permit its own creation to consume it. . . .

This Nation has for many years recognized the need for measures
designed to prevent corporate domination of the political process. The
Corrupt Practices Act, first enacted in 1907, has consistently barred
corporate contributions in connection with federal elections. This
Court has repeatedly recognized that one of the principal purposes of
this prohibition is "to avoid the deleterious influences on federal
elections resulting from the use of money by those who exercise control
over large aggregations of capital." *Automobile Workers.* See Pipefit-
ters v. United States (1972); United States v. CIO [1948]. Although this
Court has never adjudicated the constitutionality of the Act, there is no
suggestion in its cases construing it, that this purpose is in any sense
illegitimate or deserving of other than the utmost respect. . . .

II

There is an additional overriding interest related to the prevention of corporate domination . . . .: assuring that shareholders are not compelled to support and financially further beliefs with which they disagree where, as is the case here, the issue involved does not materially affect the business, property, or other affairs of the corporation. The State has not interfered with the prerogatives of corporate management to communicate about matters that have material impact on the business affairs entrusted to them. . . . But Massachusetts *has* chosen to forbid corporate management from spending corporate funds in referenda elections absent some demonstrable effect of the issue on the economic life of the company. In short, corporate management may not use corporate monies to promote what does not further corporate affairs but what in the last analysis are the purely personal views of the management, individually or as a group.

This is not only a policy which a State may adopt consistent with the First Amendment but one which protects the very freedoms that this Court has held to be guaranteed by the First Amendment. In Board of Education v. Barnette (1943), the Court struck down a West Virginia statute which compelled children enrolled in public school to salute the flag and pledge allegiance to it on the ground that the First Amendment prohibits public authorities from requiring an individual to express support for or agreement with a cause with which he disagrees or concerning which he prefers to remain silent. . . . Last Term, in Abood v. Detroit Board of Education (1977), we confronted these constitutional questions and held that a State may not, even indirectly, require an individual to contribute to the support of an ideological cause he may oppose as a condition of employment. . . .

. . . The interest which the State wishes to protect here is identical to that which the Court has previously held to be protected by the First Amendment: the right to adhere to one's own beliefs and to refuse to support the dissemination of the personal and political views of others, regardless of how large a majority they may compose. . . .

Mr. Justice **REHNQUIST**, dissenting.

This Court decided at an early date, with neither argument nor discussion, that a business corporation is a "person" entitled to the protection of the Equal Protection Clause of the Fourteenth Amendment. Santa Clara County v. Southern Pacific R. Co. (1886). Likewise, it soon became accepted that the property of a corporation was protected under the Due Process Clause of that same Amendment. See, e.g., Smyth v. Ames (1898). Nevertheless, we concluded soon thereafter that the liberty protected by that Amendment "is the liberty of natural, not artificial persons." Northwestern Nat. Life Ins. Co. v. Riggs (1906). Before today, our only considered and explicit departures from that holding have been that a corporation engaged in the business of publishing or broadcasting enjoys the same liberty of the press as is enjoyed by natural persons, Grosjean v. American Press Co. (1936), and that a nonprofit membership corporation organized for the purpose of "achieving . . . equality of treatment by all government, federal, state and local, for the members of the Negro community" enjoys certain liberties of political expression.   NAACP v. Button (1963). . . .

. . . The appellants herein either were created by the Commonwealth or were admitted into the Commonwealth only for the limited purposes described in their charters and regulated by state law.   Since it cannot be disputed that the mere creation of a corporation does not invest it with all the liberties enjoyed by natural persons, United States v. White (1944) (corporations do not enjoy the privilege against self-incrimination), our inquiry must seek to determine which constitutional protections are "incidental to its very existence."   . . .

. . . A State grants to a business corporation the blessings of potentially perpetual life and limited liability to enhance its efficiency as an economic entity.   It might reasonably be concluded that those properties, so beneficial in the economic sphere, pose special dangers in the political sphere.   . . .

I can see no basis for concluding that the liberty of a corporation to engage in political activity with regard to matters having no material effect on its business is necessarily incidental to the purposes for which the Commonwealth permitted these corporations to be organized or admitted within its boundaries.   . . .

It is true, as the Court points out, that recent decisions of this Court have emphasized the interest of the public in receiving the information offered by the speaker seeking protection.   The free flow of information is in no way diminished by the Commonwealth's decision to permit the operation of business corporations with limited rights of political expression.   All natural persons, who owe their existence to a higher sovereign than the Commonwealth, remain as free as before to engage in political activity.   Cf. Maher v. Roe (1977).   . . .

Editors' Notes

(1) **Query**: The opinions here claim three purposes lie behind the First Amendment's protection of freedom of communication: (i) The public's right to be informed so it can make wise political choices (Powell, White, and Rehnquist); (ii) individual "self-expression, self-realization, and self-fulfillment" (White); and, (iii) implicit in all three opinions, the personal right to influence the political processes (perhaps "self-expression" rather than "self-realization" or self-fulfillment).   Which of these pertain to democratic theory, which to constitutionalism?

(2) **Query**: To what extent can it be said that each of these opinions represents an example of "reinforcing representative democracy"?   If more than one opinion does, does that fact say anything about the utility of this particular purposive mode of constitutional interpretation?   Do other modes promise more precision here?   Should we seek precision in this area?

(3) Note again the Court's use of "strict scrutiny" or "critical scrutiny" at p. 692.

(4) For analyses of *First National Bank,* see: Charles R. O'Kelley, "The Constitutional Rights of Corporations Revisited," 67 *Geo.L.J.* 1347 (1979); Thomas R. Kiley, "PACing the Burger Court: The Corporate Right to Speak and the Public Right to Hear after First National Bank of Boston v. Bellottti," 22 *Am.L.Rev.* 427 (1980); and Comment, "The Corporation and the Constitution," 90 *Yale L.J.* 1883 (1981).

"No body politic worthy of being called a democracy entrusts the selection of leaders to a process of auction or barter. . . . But a candidate's promise to confer some ultimate benefit on the voter, qua taxpayer, citizen, or member of the general public, does not lie beyond the pale of First Amendment protection."

BROWN v. HARTLAGE

456 U.S. 45, 102 S.Ct. 1523, 71 L.Ed.2d 732 (1982).

Sec. 121.055 of the Revised Statutes of Kentucky reads:

No candidate for nomination or election to any state, county, city or district office shall expend, pay, promise, loan or become pecuniarily liable in any way for money or other thing of value, either directly or indirectly, to any person in consideration of the vote or financial or moral support of that person.

In Sparks v. Boggs (1960) the Kentucky Court of Appeals interpreted § 121.055 to outlaw a pledge made by a candidate to serve in office at a reduced salary. In 1979, running for county commissioner against an incumbent, Earl Hartlage, Carl Brown attacked the "outrageous salaries" paid to commissioners and promised that if elected he would immediately reduce the commissioners' compensation. Upon learning of Sparks v. Boggs, Brown issued a statement formally withdrawing his pledge to reduce salaries. He won the election anyway, but Hartlage filed suit in a state court, asking the judge to void election because Brown had engaged in a corrupt practice in violation of § 121.055.

Hartlage lost in the trial court; but the court of appeals reversed on the basis of *Sparks,* and Kentucky's supreme court refused to hear the case. Brown then sought and obtained certiorari from the U.S. Supreme Court.

Justice **BRENNAN** delivered the opinion of the Court. . . .

II

We begin our analysis of § 121.055 by acknowledging that the States have a legitimate interest in preserving the integrity of their electoral processes. Just as a State may take steps to ensure that its governing political institutions and officials properly discharge public responsibilities and maintain public trust and confidence, a State has a legitimate interest in upholding the integrity of the electoral process itself. But when a State seeks to uphold that interest by restricting speech, the limitations on state authority imposed by the First Amendment are manifestly implicated.

At the core of the First Amendment are certain basic conceptions about the manner in which political discussion in a representative democracy should proceed. As we noted in Mills v. Alabama (1966):

> Whatever differences may exist about interpretations of the First Amendment, there is practically universal agreement that a major purpose of that Amendment was to protect the free discussion of governmental affairs. This of course includes discussions of candidates, structures and forms of government, the manner in which government is operated or should be operated, and all such matters relating to political processes.

The free exchange of ideas provides special vitality to the process traditionally at the heart of American constitutional democracy—the political campaign. "[I]f it be conceded that the First Amendment was 'fashioned to assure the unfettered interchange of ideas for the bringing about of political and social changes desired by the people,' then it can hardly be doubted that the constitutional guarantee has its fullest and most urgent application precisely to the conduct of campaigns for political office." Monitor Patriot Co. v. Roy (1971). The political candidate does not lose the protection of the First Amendment when he declares himself for public office. Quite to the contrary. . . .

When a State seeks to restrict directly the offer of ideas by a candidate to the voters, the First Amendment surely requires that the restriction be demonstrably supported not only by a legitimate state interest, but a compelling one, and that the restriction operate without unnecessarily circumscribing protected expression.

III

On its face, § 121.055 prohibits a candidate from offering material benefits to voters in consideration for their votes, and, conversely, prohibits candidates from accepting payments in consideration for the manner in which they serve their public function. Sparks v. Boggs (1960) placed a not entirely obvious gloss on that provision with respect to candidate utterances concerning the salaries of the office for which they were running, by barring the candidate from promising to reduce his salary when that salary was already "fixed by law." We thus consider the constitutionality of § 121.055 with respect to the proscription evident on the face of the statute, and in light of the more particularized concerns suggested by the Sparks gloss. We discern three bases upon which the application of the statute to Brown's promise might conceivably be justified: first, as a prohibition on buying votes; second, as facilitating the candidacy of persons lacking independent wealth; and third, as an application of the State's interests and prerogatives with respect to factual misstatements. We consider these possible justifications in turn.

A

The first sentence of § 121.055 prohibits a political candidate from giving, or promising to give, anything of value to a voter in exchange for his vote or support. In many of its possible applications, this provision would appear to present little constitutional difficulty, for a State may surely prohibit a candidate from buying votes. No body politic worthy of being called a democracy entrusts the selection of leaders to a process of auction or barter. . . . Although agreements to engage in illegal conduct undoubtedly possess some element of association, the State may ban such illegal agreements without trenching on any right of association protected by the First Amendment. The fact that such an agreement necessarily takes the form of words does not confer upon it, or upon the underlying conduct, the constitutional immunities that the First Amendment extends to speech. . . . See Hoffman Estates v. Flipside, Hoffman Estates, Inc. (1982); Central Hudson Gas & Electric Corp. v. Public Service Comm'n (1980); Pittsburgh Press Co. v. Human Relations Comm'n (1973).

It is thus plain that *some* kinds of promises made by a candidate to voters, and *some* kinds of promises elicited by voters from candidates, may be declared illegal without constitutional difficulty. But it is equally plain that there are constitutional limits on the State's power to prohibit candidates from making promises in the course of an election campaign. Some promises are universally acknowledged as legitimate, indeed "indispensable to decision-making in a democracy," First National Bank of Boston v. Bellotti (1978); and the "maintenance of the opportunity for free political discussion to the end that government may be responsive to the will of the people and that changes may be obtained by lawful means . . . is a fundamental principle of our constitutional system." Stromberg v. California (1931). Candidate commitments enhance the accountability of government officials to the people whom they represent, and assist the voters in predicting the effect of their vote. The fact that some voters may find their self-interest reflected in a candidate's commitment does not place that commitment beyond the reach of the First Amendment. We have never insisted that the franchise be exercised without taint of individual benefit; indeed, our tradition of political pluralism is partly predicated on the expectation that voters will pursue their individual good through the political process, and that the summation of these individual pursuits will further the collective welfare. So long as the hoped-for personal benefit is to be achieved through the normal processes of government, and not through some private arrangement, it has always been, and remains, a reputable basis upon which to cast one's ballot.

It remains to determine the standards by which we might distinguish between those "private arrangements" that are inconsistent with democratic government, and those candidate assurances that promote the representative foundation of our political system. . . .

It is clear that the statements of petitioner Brown in the course of the August 15 press conference were very different in character from the corrupting agreements and solicitations historically recognized as unprotected by the First Amendment. Notably, Brown's commitment to serve at a reduced salary was made openly, subject to the comment and criticism of his political opponent and to the scrutiny of the voters. We think the fact that the statement was made in full view of the electorate offers a strong indication that the statement contained nothing fundamentally at odds with our shared political ethic.

.   .   . [T]here is no *constitutional* basis upon which Brown's pledge to reduce his salary might be equated with a candidate's promise to pay voters for their support from his own pocketbook. Although upon election Brown would undoubtedly have had a valid claim to the salary that had been "fixed by law," Brown did not offer the voters a payment from his personal funds. His was a declaration of intention to exercise the fiscal powers of government office within what he believed (albeit erroneously) to be the recognized framework of office. At least to outward appearances, the commitment was fully in accord with our basic understanding of legitimate activity by a government body. Before any implicit monetary benefit to the individual taxpayer might have been realized, public officials—among them, of course, Brown himself—would have had to approve that benefit in accordance with the good faith exercise of their public duties. .   .   .

In addition .   .   . it is impossible to discern in Brown's generalized commitment any invitation to enter into an agreement that might place the statement outside the realm of unequivocal protection that the Constitution affords to political speech. Not only was the source of the promised benefit the public fisc, but that benefit was to extend beyond those voters who cast their ballots for Brown, to all taxpayers and citizens. .   .   .

In sum, Brown did not offer some private payment or donation in exchange for voter support. .   .   . Like a promise to lower taxes, to increase efficiency in government, or indeed to increase taxes in order to provide some group with a desired public benefit or public service, Brown's promise to reduce his salary cannot be deemed beyond the reach of the First Amendment, or considered as inviting the kind of corrupt arrangement the appearance of which a State may have a compelling interest in avoiding. See Buckley v. Valeo [1976].

A State may insist that candidates seeking the approval of the electorate work within the framework of our democratic institutions, and base their appeal on assertions of fitness for office and statements respecting the means by which they intend to further the public welfare. But a candidate's promise to confer some ultimate benefit on the voter, qua taxpayer, citizen, or member of the general public, does not lie beyond the pale of First Amendment protection.

B

Sparks relied in part on the interest a State may have in ensuring that the willingness of some persons to serve in public office without remuneration does not make gratuitous service the sine qua non of plausible candidacy. The State might legitimately fear that such emphasis on free public service might result in persons of independent wealth but less ability being chosen over those who, though better qualified, could not afford to serve at a reduced salary. But if § 121.055 was designed to further this interest, it chooses a means unacceptable under the First Amendment. In barring certain public statements with respect to this issue, the State ban runs directly contrary to the fundamental premises underlying the First Amendment as the guardian of our democracy. That Amendment embodies our trust in the free exchange of ideas as the means by which the people are to choose between good ideas and bad, and between candidates for political office. The State's fear that voters might make an ill-advised choice does not provide the State with a compelling justification for limiting speech. It is simply not the function of government to "select which issues are worth discussing or debating," Police Department of Chicago v. Mosley (1972), in the course of a political campaign.

C . . .

. . . Kentucky has provided that a candidate for public office forfeits his electoral victory if he errs in announcing that he will, if elected, serve at a reduced salary. . . . The chilling effect of such absolute accountability for factual misstatements in the course of political debate is incompatible with the atmosphere of free discussion contemplated by the First Amendment in the context of political campaigns. See *Monitor Patriot*; Ocala Star-Banner Co. v. Damron (1971). Although the state interest in protecting the political process from distortions caused by untrue and inaccurate speech is somewhat different from the state interest in protecting individuals from defamatory falsehoods, the principles underlying the First Amendment remain paramount. Whenever compatible with the underlying interests at stake, under the regime of that Amendment "we depend for . . . correction not on the conscience of judges and juries but on the competition of other ideas." Gertz v. Robert Welch, Inc. [1974]. In a political campaign, a candidate's factual blunder is unlikely to escape the notice of, and correction by, the erring candidate's political opponent. The preferred First Amendment remedy of "more speech, not enforced silence," Whitney v. California (Brandeis, J., concurring) [1927], thus has special force. There has been no showing in this case that petitioner made the disputed statement other than in good faith and without knowledge of its falsity, or that he made the statement with reckless disregard whether it was false or not. Moreover, petitioner retracted the statement promptly after discovering that it might have been false. Under these circumstances, nullifying petitioner's election victory was inconsistent with the atmosphere of robust political debate protected by the First Amendment. . . .

[*Reversed.*]

The Chief Justice [**BURGER**] concurs in the judgment.

Justice **REHNQUIST**, concurring in the result. . . .

Editors' Notes

(1) **Query:** At p. 701 Brennan began to discuss "the standards by which we might distinguish between 'those private arrangements' that are inconsistent with democratic government, and those candidate assurances that promote the representative foundation of our political system." What were those standards? Cf. Madison in *Federalist* No. 10, reprinted below, p. 952.

(2) Why would inconsistency with principles of democratic government raise a constitutional question?

(3) If voting is a constitutional right of the individual citizen, why can he or she not sell his or her vote or exchange it for something else of value? In what *constitutionally* significant way does selling one's vote differ from voting for a candidate whom the voters knows will reward him or her with public office or some other benefit, such as a tax reduction for people in a particular income bracket or welfare payments for others?

(4) Notice that the U.S. Supreme Court takes § 121.055 as it has been interpreted by the courts of Kentucky. The Supreme Court could not, as it did in the case of a federal statute in *Yates* (1957; reprinted above, p. 519) or United States v. Harriss (1954; reprinted below p. 718), interpret a state statute so as to avoid constitutional questions.

"A State's claim that it is enhancing the ability of its citizenry to make wise decisions by restricting the flow of information to them must be viewed with some skepticism."

ANDERSON v. CELEBREZZE

460 U.S. 780, 103 S.Ct. 1564, 75 L.Ed.2d 547 (1983).

Ohio required independent candidates for the presidency to file a statement and nominating petition signed by 5,000 qualified voters 75 days before the primary election (229 days before the general election). In 1980, John Anderson did not file the necessary papers until May, two months after the deadline but some weeks before the state primary elections and well before the national nominating conventions had met. Ohio officials denied him a place on the ballot, and he filed suit in a U.S. district court. The judge ordered the state to place Anderson's name on the ballot, but the Court of Appeals for the 6th Circuit reversed. Noting that the courts of appeals for the 1st and 4th circuits had sustained orders against enforcement of similar laws in Maine and Maryland, the Supreme Court granted certiorari.

Justice **STEVENS** delivered the opinion of the Court. . . .

I

. . . . "[T]he rights of voters and the rights of candidates do not lend themselves to neat separation; laws that affect candidates always have at least some theoretical, correlative effect on voters." Bullock v. Carter (1972). Our primary concern is with the tendency of ballot access restrictions "to limit the field of candidates from which voters might choose." Therefore, "[i]n approaching candidate restrictions, it is essential to examine in a realistic light the extent and nature of their impact on voters."

The impact of candidate eligibility requirements on voters implicates basic constitutional rights.[1] Writing for a unanimous Court in NAACP v. Alabama (1958), Justice Harlan stated that it "is beyond debate that freedom to engage in association for the advancement of beliefs and ideas is an inseparable aspect of the 'liberty' assured by the Due Process Clause of the Fourteenth Amendment, which embraces freedom of speech." In our first review of Ohio's electoral scheme, Williams v. Rhodes (1968), this Court explained the interwoven strands of "liberty" affected by ballot access restrictions:

> [T]he state laws place burdens on two different, although overlapping, kinds of rights—the right of individuals to associate for the advancement of political beliefs, and the right of qualified voters, regardless of their political persuasion, to cast their votes effectively. Both of these rights, of course, rank among our most precious freedoms.

As we have repeatedly recognized, voters can assert their preferences only through candidates or parties or both. . . . The right to vote is "heavily burdened" if that vote may be cast only for major-party candidates at a time when other parties or other candidates are "clamoring for a place on the ballot." *Williams.* The exclusion of candidates also burdens voters' freedom of association, because an election campaign is an effective platform for the expression of views on the issues of the day, and a candidate serves as a rallying-point for like-minded citizens.

Although these rights of voters are fundamental, not all restrictions imposed by the States on candidates' eligibility for the ballot impose constitutionally-suspect burdens on voters' rights to associate or to choose among candidates. We have recognized that, "as a practical matter, there must be a substantial regulation of elections if they are to be fair and honest and if some sort of order, rather than chaos, is to accompany the democratic processes." Storer v. Brown (1974). To achieve these necessary objectives, States have enacted comprehensive and sometimes complex election codes. Each provision of these schemes, whether it governs the registration and qualifications of voters, the selection and eligibility of candidates, or the voting process itself, inevitably affects . . . the individual's right to vote and his right to associate with others for political ends. Nevertheless, the state's important regulatory interests are generally sufficient to justify reasonable, nondiscriminatory restrictions.

---

1. In this case, we base our conclusions directly on the First and Fourteenth Amendments and do not engage in a separate Equal Protection Clause analysis. We rely, however, on the analysis in a number of our prior election cases resting on the Equal Protection Clause of the Fourteenth Amendment. These cases, applying the "fundamental rights" strand of equal protection analysis, have identified the First and Fourteenth Amendment rights implicated by restrictions on the eligibility of voters and candidates, and have considered the degree to which the State's restrictions further legitimate state interests. [Footnote by the Court.]

Constitutional challenges to specific provisions of a State's election laws therefore cannot be resolved by any "litmus-paper test" that will separate valid from invalid restrictions. *Storer.* Instead, a court must resolve such a challenge by an analytical process that parallels its work in ordinary litigation. It must first consider the character and magnitude of the asserted injury to the rights protected by the First and Fourteenth Amendments. . . . It then must identify and evaluate the precise interests put forward by the State as justifications for the burden imposed by its rule. In passing judgment, the Court must not only determine the legitimacy and strength of each of those interests; it also must consider the extent to which those interests make it necessary to burden the plaintiff's rights. Only after weighing all these factors is the reviewing court in a position to decide whether the challenged provision is unconstitutional. . . .

II

An early filing deadline may have a substantial impact on independent-minded voters. In election campaigns, particularly those which are national in scope, the candidates and the issues simply do not remain static over time. . . . Such developments will certainly affect the strategies of candidates who have already entered the race; they may also create opportunities for new candidacies. Yet Ohio's filing deadline prevents persons who wish to be independent candidates from entering the significant political arena established in the State by a Presidential election campaign—and creating new political coalitions of Ohio voters—at any time after mid-to-late March. At this point developments in campaigns for the major-party nominations have only begun, and the major parties will not adopt their nominees and platforms for another five months. . . .

[The statute] also burdens the signature-gathering efforts of independents who decide to run in time to meet the deadline. When the primary campaigns are far in the future and the election itself is even more remote, the obstacles facing an independent candidate's organizing efforts are compounded. Volunteers are more difficult to recruit and retain, media publicity and campaign contributions are more difficult to secure, and voters are less interested in the campaign.

. . . [I]t is especially difficult for the State to justify a restriction that limits political participation by an identifiable political group whose members share a particular viewpoint, associational preference, or economic status. "Our ballot access cases . . . focus on the degree to which the challenged restrictions operate as a mechanism to exclude certain classes of candidates from the electoral process. The inquiry is whether the challenged restriction unfairly or unnecessarily burdens 'the availability of political opportunity.' " Clements v. Fashing (1982) (plurality opinion), quoting Lubin v. Panish (1974).[2]

---

2. In addition, because the interests of minor parties and independent candidates are not well represented in state legislatures, the risk that the First Amendment rights of those groups will be ignored in legislative decisionmaking may warrant more careful judicial scrutiny. [S]ee generally United States v. Carolene Products Co. (1938); J. Ely,

A burden that falls unequally on new or small political parties or on independent candidates impinges, by its very nature, on associational choices protected by the First Amendment. It discriminates against those candidates and—of particular importance—against those voters whose political preferences lie outside the existing political parties. By limiting the opportunities of independent-minded voters to associate in the electoral arena to enhance their political effectiveness as a group, such restrictions threaten to reduce diversity and competition in the marketplace of ideas. In short, the primary values protected by the First Amendment—"a profound national commitment to the principle that debate on public issues should be uninhibited, robust, and wide-open," New York Times Co. v. Sullivan (1964)—are served when election campaigns are not monopolized by the existing political parties.

Furthermore, in the context of a Presidential election, state-imposed restrictions implicate a uniquely important national interest. For the President and the Vice President of the United States are the only elected officials who represent all the voters in the Nation. Moreover, the impact of the votes cast in each State is affected by the votes cast for the various candidates in other States. Thus in a Presidential election a State's enforcement of more stringent ballot access requirements, including filing deadlines, has an impact beyond its own borders. Similarly, the State has a less important interest in regulating Presidential elections than statewide or local elections, because the outcome of the former will be largely determined by voters beyond the State's boundaries. . . . The Ohio filing deadline challenged in this case does more than burden the associational rights of independent voters and candidates. It places a significant state-imposed restriction on a nationwide electoral process.

III

The State identifies three separate interests that it seeks to further by its early filing deadline for independent Presidential candidates. . . .

Voter Education

There can be no question about the legitimacy of the State's interest in fostering informed and educated expressions of the popular will in a general election. Moreover, the Court of Appeals correctly identified that interest as one of the concerns that motivated the Framers' decision not to provide for direct popular election of the President. We are persuaded, however, that the State's important and legitimate interest in voter education does not justify the specific restriction on participation in a Presidential election that is at issue in this case.

The passage of time since the Constitutional Convention in 1787 has brought about two changes that are relevant to the reasonableness of Ohio's statutory requirement that independents formally declare

---

Democracy and Distrust: A Theory of Judicial Review 73–88 (1980). [Footnote by the Court.]

their candidacy at least seven months in advance of a general election. First . . . today even trivial details about national candidates are instantaneously communicated nationwide in both verbal and visual form. Second . . . today the vast majority of the electorate not only is literate but is informed on a day-to-day basis about events and issues that affect election choices. . . . [I]t is somewhat unrealistic to suggest that it takes more than seven months to inform the electorate about the qualifications of a particular candidate simply because he lacks a partisan label.

Our cases reflect a greater faith in the ability of individual voters to inform themselves about campaign issues. . . .

It is also by no means self-evident that the interest in voter education is served at all by a requirement that independent candidates must declare their candidacy before the end of March. . . . Had the requirement been enforced in Ohio, petitioner Anderson might well have determined that it would be futile for him to allocate any of his time and money to campaigning in that State. The Ohio electorate might thereby have been denied whatever benefits his participation in local debates could have contributed to an understanding of the issues. A State's claim that it is enhancing the ability of its citizenry to make wise decisions by restricting the flow of information to them must be viewed with some skepticism. As we observed in another First Amendment context, it is often true "that the best means to that end is to open the channels of communication rather than to close them." Virginia Pharmacy Board v. Virginia Consumer Council (1976).

Equal Treatment

We also find no merit in the State's claim that the early filing deadline serves the interest of treating all candidates alike. . . .

The consequences of failing to meet the statutory deadline are entirely different for party primary participants and independents. The name of the nominees of the Democratic and Republican parties will appear on the Ohio ballot in November even if they did not decide to run until after Ohio's March deadline had passed, but the independent is simply denied a position on the ballot if he waits too long.[3] Thus, under Ohio's scheme, the major parties may include all events preceding their national conventions in the calculus that produces their respective nominees and campaign platforms, but the independent's judgment must be based on a history that ends in March. . . .

Political Stability

. . . The State's brief explains that the State has a substantial interest in protecting the two major political parties from "damaging intraparty feuding." . . .

---

3. It is true, of course, that Ohio permits "write-in" votes for independents. We have previously noted that this opportunity is not an adequate substitute for having the candidate's name appear on the printed ballot. . . . [Citing Lubin v. Panish (1974).] [Footnote by the Court.]

Ohio's asserted interest in political stability amounts to a desire to protect existing political parties from competition. . . .

In *Williams* we squarely held that protecting the Republican and Democratic parties from external competition cannot justify the virtual exclusion of other political aspirants from the political arena. Addressing Ohio's claim that it "may validly promote a two-party system in order to encourage compromise and political stability," we wrote:

> The fact is, however, that the Ohio system does not merely favor a 'two-party system'; it favors two particular parties—the Republicans and the Democrats—and in effect tends to give them a complete monopoly. There is, of course, no reason why two parties should retain a permanent monopoly on the right to have people vote for or against them. Competition in ideas and governmental policies is at the core of our electoral process and of the First Amendment freedoms.

. . .

. . . [*Storer*] recognized the legitimacy of the State's interest in preventing "splintered parties and unrestrained factionalism." But we did not suggest that a political party could invoke the powers of the State to assure monolithic control over its own members and supporters. Political competition that draws resources away from the major parties cannot, for that reason alone, be condemned as "unrestrained factionalism." . . . Moreover, we pointed out that the policy "involves no discrimination against independents."

Ohio's challenged restriction is substantially different from the California provisions upheld in *Storer*. . . . [T]he early filing deadline does discriminate against independents. And the deadline is neither a "sore loser" provision nor a disaffiliation statute. Furthermore, it is important to recognize that *Storer* upheld the State's interest in avoiding political fragmentation in the context of elections wholly within the boundaries of California. The State's interest in regulating a nationwide Presidential election is not nearly as strong; no State could singlehandedly assure "political stability" in the Presidential context. The Ohio deadline does not serve any state interest in "maintaining the integrity of the various routes to the ballot" for the Presidency, because Ohio's Presidential preference primary does not serve to narrow the field for the general election. A major party candidate who loses the Ohio primary, or who does not even run in Ohio, may nonetheless appear on the November general election ballot as the party's nominee. In addition, the national scope of the competition for delegates at the Presidential nominating conventions assures that "intraparty feuding" will continue until August. . . .

IV

. . . Under any realistic appraisal, the "extent and nature" of the burdens Ohio has placed on the voters' freedom of choice and freedom of association, in an election of nationwide importance, unquestionably outweigh the State's minimal interest in imposing a March deadline.

Reversed.

Justice **REHNQUIST**, with whom Justice **WHITE**, Justice **POWELL**, and Justice **O'CONNOR** join, dissenting.

Article II of the Constitution provides that "[e]ach State shall appoint, in such Manner as the Legislature thereof may direct, a Number of Electors" who shall select the President of the United States. This provision, one of few in the Constitution that grants an express plenary power to the States, conveys "the broadest power of determination" and "[i]t recognizes that [in the election of a President] the people act through their representatives in the legislature, and *leaves it to the legislature exclusively to define the method of effecting the object."* McPherson v. Blacker (1892) (emphasis added). . . .

. . . [T]he Constitution does not require that a State allow any particular Presidential candidate to be on its ballot, and so long as the Ohio ballot access laws are rational and allow nonparty candidates reasonable access to the general election ballot,[1] this Court should not interfere with Ohio's exercise of its Article II, § 1, cl 2 power. . . .

Anderson makes no claim, and thus has offered no evidence to show, that the early filing deadline impeded his "signature-gathering efforts." That alone should be enough to prevent the Court from finding that the deadline has such an impact. A statute "is not to be upset upon hypothetical and unreal possibilities, if it would be good upon the facts as they are." Pullman Co. v. Knott (1914). What information the record does contain on this point leads to a contrary conclusion. The record shows that in 1980 five independent candidates submitted nominating petitions with the necessary 5,000 signatures by the March 20 deadline and thus qualified for the general election ballot in Ohio. . . .

The Court's intimation that the Ohio filing deadline infringes on a nonparty candidate who makes the decision to run for President after the March deadline is similarly without support in the record. . . . Anderson was not such a candidate. Anderson formally announced his candidacy for the Presidency on June 8, 1979—over nine months before Ohio's March 20 deadline. . . .

Finally, there is nothing in the record to indicate that this is a case where "independent-minded voters" are prevented from rallying behind a candidate selected later in the election year so as to guaranty "major parties" a monopoly on the election process. Like-minded voters who do not want to participate in an existing political party are at complete liberty to form a new political party. . . . It is true that Ohio provides this benefit only where a group of voters acts with some foresight and shows a degree of support among the electorate, but this case presents no challenge to these requirements.

---

1. Anderson would not have been totally excluded from participating in the general election since Ohio allows for "write-in" candidacies. The Court suggests, however, that this is of no relevance because a write-in procedure "is not an adequate substitute for having the candidate's appear on the printed ballot." [Footnote 3, above.] Until today the Court had not squarely so held and in fact in earlier decisions the Court had treated the availability of write-in candidacies as quite relevant. See *Storer.* [Footnote by Justice Rehnquist.]

. . . [T]he effect of the Ohio filing deadline is quite easily summarized: it requires that a candidate, who has already decided to run for President, decide by March 20 which route his candidacy will take. . . . Anderson . . . submitted in a timely fashion his nominating petition for Ohio's Republican Primary. Then, realizing that he had no chance for the Republican nomination, Anderson sought to change the form of this candidacy. The Ohio filing deadline prevented him from making this change. Quite clearly, rather than prohibiting him from seeking the Presidency, the filing deadline only prevented Anderson from having two shots at it in the same election year.

Thus, Ohio's filing deadline does not create a restriction "denying the franchise to citizens." Likewise, Ohio's filing deadline does not create a restriction that makes it "virtually impossible" for new-party candidates or nonparty candidates to qualify for the ballot, such as those addressed in *Williams, Bullock*, and *Lubin*. Yet in deciding this case, we are not without guidance from prior decisions by this Court.

In *Storer,* the Court was faced with a California statute prohibiting an independent candidate from affiliating with a political party for 12 months preceding the primary election. This required a prospective candidate to decide on the form of his candidacy at a date some eight months earlier than Ohio requires. In upholding, in the face of a First Amendment challenge, this disaffiliation statute and a statute preventing candidates who had lost a primary from running as independents, the Court determined that the laws were "expressive of a general state policy aimed at maintaining the integrity of various routes to the ballot," and that the statutes furthered "the State's interest," described by the Court as "compelling," "in the stability of its political system."
. . . .

> . . . *It appears obvious to us that the one-year disaffiliation provision furthers the State's interest in the stability of its political system. We also consider that interest as not only permissible, but compelling and as outweighing the interest the candidate and his supporters may have in making a late rather than early decision to seek independent ballot status.* . . .

The similarities between the effect of the Ohio filing deadline and the California disaffiliation statute are obvious.

Refusing to own up to the conflict its opinion creates with *Storer,* the Court tries to distinguish it, saying that it "did not suggest that a political party could invoke the powers of the State to assure monolithic control over its own members and supporters." The Court asserts that the Ohio filing deadline is more like the statutory scheme in *Williams,* which were designed to protect " 'two particular parties—the Republicans and the Democrats—and in effect tends to give them a complete monopoly.' " . . . But this simply is not the case. The Ohio filing deadline in no way makes it "virtually impossible" . . . for new parties or nonparty candidates to secure a position on the general election ballot. It does require early decisions. But once a decision is made, there is no claim that the additional requirements for new parties and nonparty candidates are too burdensome. In fact, past experience has shown otherwise. What the Ohio filing deadline prevents is a candidate such as Anderson from seeking a party nomination and then, finding that he is rejected by the party, bolting from the party to form an independent candidacy. This is precisely the same behavior that California sought to prevent by the disaffiliation statute this Court upheld in *Storer*. . . .

The Court further notes that "*Storer* upheld the State's interest in avoiding political fragmentation in the context of elections wholly within the boundaries of California. The State's interest in regulating a nationwide Presidential election is not nearly as strong." . . . The Court's characterization of the election simply is incorrect. The Ohio general election in 1980, among other things, was for the appointment of Ohio's representatives to the Electoral College. The Court . . . fails to come to grips with this fact. While Ohio may have a lesser interest in who is ultimately selected by the Electoral College, its interest in who is supported by its own Presidential electors must be at least as strong as its interest in electing other representatives. . . .

The Court suggests that *Storer* is not controlling since in that case the Court held that the California disaffiliation statute was not discriminatory because party candidates were prohibited from affiliating with another political party for the 12 months preceding the primary election. The Court says that Ohio's filing deadline does discriminate against nonparty candidates. But merely saying it is so does not make it so. . . .

The point the Court misses is that in cases like this and *Storer*, we have never required that States meet some kind of "narrowly tailored" standard in order to pass constitutional muster. In reviewing election laws like Ohio's filing deadline, we have said before that a court's job is to ensure that the State "in no way freezes the status quo, but implicitly recognizes the potential fluidity of American political life." *Jenness v. Fortson* (1971). If it does not freeze the status quo, then the State's laws will be upheld if they are "tied to a particularized legitimate purpose, and [are] in no sense invidious or arbitrary." *Rosario v. Rockefeller* (1973). The Court tries to avoid the rules set forth in some of these cases, saying that such rules were "applicable only to party primaries" and that "this case involves restrictions on access to the general election ballot." The fallacy in this reasoning is quite apparent: one cannot restrict access to the primary ballot without also restricting access to the general election ballot. . . .

The Ohio filing deadline easily meets the test described above. [T]he interest of the "stability of its political system," *Storer*, . . . alone is sufficient to support Ohio ballot access laws. . . . But this is not the only interest furthered by Ohio's laws.

Ohio maintains that requiring an early declaration of candidacy gives its voters a better opportunity to take a careful look at the candidates and see how they withstand the close scrutiny of a political campaign. . . . But the Court finds that "the State's important and legitimate interest in voter education does not justify the specific restriction on participation in a Presidential election that is at issue in this case." . . .

I cannot agree with the suggestion that the early deadline reflects a lack of "faith" in the voters. That Ohio wants to give its voters as much time as possible to gather information on the potential candidates would seem to lead to the contrary conclusion. There is nothing improper about wanting as much time as possible in which to evaluate all available information when making an important decision. Besides, the Court's assertion that it does not take seven months to inform the electorate is difficult to explain in light of the fact that Anderson allowed himself some 19 months to complete this task; and we are all well aware that Anderson's decision to make an early go of it is not atypical. . . .

Editors' Notes

(1) As the debate between Stevens and Rehnquist indicates, the Court's reasoning in earlier cases involving restrictions on access to the ballot had not been doctrinally consistent. See especially Clements v. Fashing (1982), which sustained a Texas law forbidding state judges and certain other officials to run for the state legislature. Rehnquist wrote the principal opinion, but it commanded five votes on only some of the issues. Stevens voted with Rehnquist to uphold the statute but for different reasons.

(2) In *Anderson,* Stevens prescribed the proper decisional strategy as that of "weighing" the various interests at stake: The Court

> must first consider the character and magnitude of the asserted injury to the rights protected by the First and Fourteenth Amendments. . . . It must then identify and evaluate the precise interests put forward by the State. . . . [T]he Court must not only determine the legitimacy and strength of each of those interests; it must also consider the extent to which those interests make it necessary to burden the plaintiff's rights.

Query: Did Stevens' opinion carry out these steps? How does this sort of test differ from "strict scrutiny" used in Buckley v. Valeo (1976; reprinted above, p. 371) and explained in the notes to that case? To what degree is Stevens merely "balancing"?

IV. MONEY AND POLITICS: ACCESS TO
THE MASS MEDIA

"A responsible press is an undoubtedly desirable goal, but press responsibility is not mandated by the Constitution. . . ."

MIAMI HERALD PUBLISHING CO. v. TORNILLO
418 U.S. 241, 94 S.Ct. 2831, 41 L.Ed.2d 730 (1974).

A Florida statute required a newspaper to print, at no cost, with equal space and in as prominent a position and typeface as the original story or editorial, any response that political candidates may make to the paper's charges concerning his or her official conduct or personal character. In 1972, the *Miami Herald* published two editorials critical of the candidacy of Pat Tornillo, Jr., for the state house of representatives. The *Herald* refused Tornillo's request to print his rebuttal. He then sued in a state court, but the trial judge held the statute violated the First Amendment. Florida's supreme court reversed, reasoning that the right-of-reply statute enhanced rather than abridged the rights to freedom of communication protected by the First Amendment. The *Herald* appealed to the U.S. Supreme Court.

Mr. Chief Justice **BURGER** delivered the opinion of the Court. . . .

III

A . . .

Appellant contends the statute is void on its face because it purports to regulate the content of a newspaper in violation of the First Amendment. Alternatively it is urged that the statute is void for vagueness since no editor could know exactly what words would call the statute into operation. It is also contended that the statute fails to distinguish between critical comment which is and which is not defamatory.

B

The appellee and supporting advocates of an enforceable right of access to the press vigorously argue that government has an obligation to ensure that a wide variety of views reach the public. . . . It is urged that at the time the First Amendment to the Constitution was enacted in 1791 as part of our Bill of Rights the press was broadly representative of the people it was serving. While many of the newspapers were intensely partisan and narrow in their views, the press collectively presented a broad range of opinions to readers. Entry into publishing was inexpensive; pamphlets and books provided meaningful alternatives to the organized press for the expression of unpopular ideas and often treated events and expressed views not covered by conventional newspapers. A true marketplace of ideas existed in which there was relatively easy access to the channels of communication.

Access advocates submit that although newspapers of the present are superficially similar to those of 1791 the press of today is in reality very different from that known in the early years of our national existence. In the past half century a communications revolution has seen the introduction of radio and television into our lives, the promise of a global community through the use of communications satellites, and the spectre of a "wired" nation by means of an expanding cable television network with two-way capabilities. The printed press, it is said, has not escaped the effects of this revolution. Newspapers have become big business and there are far fewer of them to serve a larger literate population. Chains of newspapers, national newspapers, national wire and news services, and one-newspaper towns, are the dominant features of a press that has become noncompetitive and enormously powerful and influential in its capacity to manipulate popular opinion and change the course of events. Major metropolitan newspapers have collaborated to establish news services national in scope. Such national news organizations provide syndicated "interpretive reporting" as well as syndicated features and commentary, all of which can serve as part of the new school of "advocacy journalism."

The elimination of competing newspapers in most of our large cities, and the concentration of control of media that results from the only newspaper's being owned by the same interests which own a television station and a radio station, are important components of this trend toward concentration of control of outlets to inform the public.

The result of these vast changes has been to place in a few hands the power to inform the American people and shape public opinion. Much of the editorial opinion and commentary that is printed is that of syndicated columnists distributed nationwide and, as a result, we are told, on national and world issues there tends to be a homogeneity of editorial opinion, commentary, and interpretive analysis. The abuses of bias and manipulative reportage are, likewise, said to be the result of the vast accumulations of unreviewable power in the modern media empires. In effect, it is claimed, the public has lost any ability to respond or to contribute in a meaningful way to the debate on issues. The monopoly of the means of communication allows for little or no critical analysis of the media except in professional journals of very limited readership. . . .

Proponents of enforced access to the press take comfort from language in several of this Court's decisions which suggests that the First Amendment acts as a sword as well as a shield, that it imposes obligations on the owners of the press in addition to protecting the press from government regulation. In Associated Press v. United States (1945), the Court, in rejecting the argument that the press is immune from the antitrust laws by virtue of the First Amendment, stated:

> The First Amendment, far from providing an argument against application of the Sherman Act, here provides powerful reasons to the contrary. That Amendment rests on the assumption that the widest

possible dissemination of information from diverse and antagonistic sources is essential to the welfare of the public, that a free press is a condition of a free society. Surely a command that the government itself shall not impede the free flow of ideas does not afford non-governmental combinations a refuge if they impose restraints upon that constitutionally guaranteed freedom. Freedom to publish means freedom for all and not for some. Freedom to publish is guaranteed by the Constitution, but freedom to combine to keep others from publishing is not. Freedom of the press from governmental interference under the First Amendment does not sanction repression of that freedom by private interests. . . .

Access advocates note that Mr. Justice Douglas a decade ago expressed his deep concern regarding the effects of newspaper monopolies:

Where one paper has a monopoly in an area, it seldom presents two sides of an issue. It too often hammers away on one ideological or political line using its monopoly position not to educate people, not to promote debate, but to inculcate in its readers one philosophy, one attitude—and to make money." "The newspapers that give a variety of views and news that is not slanted or contrived are few indeed. And the problem promises to get worse. . . .

IV . . .

The Court foresaw the problems relating to government-enforced access as early as its decision in Associated Press v. United States. There it carefully contrasted the private "compulsion to print" called for by the Association's bylaws with the provisions of the District Court decree against appellants which "does not compel AP or its members to permit publication of anything which their 'reason' tells them should not be published." . . . .

. . . . [T]he Court has expressed sensitivity as to whether a restriction or requirement constituted the compulsion exerted by government on a newspaper to print that which it would not otherwise print. The clear implication has been that any such a compulsion to publish that which " 'reason' tells them should not be published" is unconstitutional. A responsible press is an undoubtedly desirable goal, but press responsibility is not mandated by the Constitution and like many other virtues it cannot be legislated.

Appellee's argument that the Florida statute does not amount to a restriction of appellant's right to speak because "the statute in question here has not prevented the *Miami Herald* from saying anything it wished" begs the core question. . . . The Florida statute operates as a command in the same sense as a statute or regulation forbidding appellant to publish specified matter. Governmental restraint on publishing need not fall into familiar or traditional patterns to be subject to constitutional limitations on governmental powers. Grosjean v. American Press Co. (1936). The Florida statute exacts a penalty on the basis of the content of a newspaper. The first phase of the penalty resulting from the compelled printing of a reply is exacted in terms of the cost in printing and composing time and materials and in taking up space that could be devoted to other material the newspaper may have preferred to print. . . .

Faced with the penalties that would accrue to any newspaper that published news or commentary arguably within the reach of the right-of-access statute, editors might well conclude that the safe course is to avoid controversy. Therefore, under the operation of the Florida statute, political and electoral coverage would be blunted or reduced. Government-enforced right of access inescapably "dampens the vigor and limits the variety of public debate," New York Times Co. v. Sullivan (1964). . . .

Even if a newspaper would face no additional costs to comply with a compulsory access law and would not be forced to forgo publication of news or opinion by the inclusion of a reply, the Florida statute fails to clear the barriers of the First Amendment because of its intrusion into the function of editors. A newspaper is more than a passive receptacle or conduit for news, comment, and advertising. The choice of material to go into a newspaper, and the decisions made as to limitations on the size and content of the paper, and treatment of public issues and public officials—whether fair or unfair—constitute the exercise of editorial control and judgment. It has yet to be demonstrated how governmental regulation of this crucial process can be exercised consistent with First Amendment guarantees of a free press as they have evolved to this time. . . .

Reversed.

Mr. Justice **BRENNAN,** with whom Mr. Justice **REHNQUIST** joins, concurring. . . .

Mr. Justice **WHITE,** concurring.

. . . According to our accepted jurisprudence, the First Amendment erects a virtually insurmountable barrier between government and the print media so far as government tampering, in advance of publication, with news and editorial content is concerned. New York Times Co. v. United States (1971). A newspaper or magazine is not a public utility subject to "reasonable" governmental regulation in matters affecting the exercise of journalistic judgment as to what shall be printed. Cf. Mills v. Alabama (1966). We have learned, and continue to learn, from what we view as the unhappy experiences of other nations where government has been allowed to meddle in the internal editorial affairs of newspapers. Regardless of how beneficent-sounding the purposes of controlling the press might be, we prefer "the power of reason as applied through public discussion" and remain intensely skeptical about those measures that would allow government to insinuate itself into the editorial rooms of this Nation's press. . . .

Editors' Notes

(1) **Query:** Of what help are "the plain words" of the First Amendment in settling such problems as these? What interests could an interpreter intelligently "balance" here? What would be their relative weights in such a balancing process? Does a structural analysis offer assistance in these cases? To what extent is *Miami Herald* congruent with the demands of democratic theory? Does constitutionalism have anything important to add?

(2) **Query:** Red Lion Broadcasting Co. v. Federal Communications Commission (1969) sustained the FCC's "fairness doctrine," which requires radio and television stations to allow time for response by people personally attacked in broadcasts or by political candidates whose opponents a station may have endorsed. Conceding that the First Amendment was relevant to broadcasting and noting that there were far more people seeking licenses to broadcast than there were frequencies available, the Court held: "It does not violate the First Amendment to treat licensees given the privilege of using scarce radio frequencies as proxies for the entire community, obligated to give suitable time and attention to matters of great public concern." How can one reconcile *Red Lion* and *Miami Herald*? Which would be financially more difficult to start, a new radio station or a daily newspaper? Is the answer to that question relevant to constitutional interpretation?

V. THE RIGHT TO LOBBY GOVERNMENTAL OFFICIALS

"[T]he voice of the people may all too easily be drowned out by the voice of special interest groups seeking favored treatment while masquerading as proponents of the public weal."

UNITED STATES v. HARRISS
347 U.S. 612, 74 S.Ct. 808, 98 L.Ed. 989 (1954).

Section 305 of the Federal Regulation of Lobbying Act requires "every person receiving any contributions or expending any money" to influence passage or defeat of congressional legislation to file the name and address of each person who makes a contribution of $500 or more or to whom $10 or more is paid as well as the total of all contributions and expenditures. Section 308 requires "any person who shall engage himself for pay or for any consideration" to influence congressional legislation to register under oath and give the name of employers or clients by whom he is or is to be paid, a full accounting of expenses and expenditures, the legislation with which he is concerned, and citations to any material which he has "caused to be published."

A group of lobbyists were charged with failing to register and to report expenditures. The district judge dismissed the charges on the grounds that the statute was an unconstitutional abridgment of First Amendment freedoms of speech, assembly, and petition. The government appealed.

Mr. Chief Justice **WARREN** delivered the opinion of the Court. . . .

I

The constitutional requirement of definiteness is violated by a criminal statute that fails to give a person of ordinary intelligence fair notice that his contemplated conduct is forbidden by the statute. The underlying principle is that no man shall be held criminally responsible for conduct which he could not reasonably understand to be proscribed.

On the other hand, if the general class of offenses to which the statute is directed is plainly within its terms, the statute will not be struck down as vague even though marginal cases could be put where doubts might arise. United States v. Petrillo [1947]. And if this general class of offenses can be made constitutionally definite by a reasonable construction of the statute, this Court is under a duty to give the statute that construction. . . .

. . . The key section of the Lobbying Act is § 307, entitled "Persons to Whom Applicable". . . .

> The provisions of this title shall apply to any person (except a political committee as defined in the Federal Corrupt Practices Act, and duly organized State or local committees of a political party), who by himself, or through any agent or employee or other persons in any manner whatsoever, directly or indirectly, solicits, collects, or receives money or any other thing of value to be used principally to aid, or the principal purpose of which person is to aid, in the accomplishment of any of the following purposes:
>
> (a) The passage or defeat of any legislation by the Congress of the United States.
>
> (b) To influence, directly or indirectly, the passage or defeat of any legislation by the Congress of the United States.

This section modifies the substantive provisions of the Act, including § 305 and § 308. In other words, unless a "person" falls within the category established by § 307, the disclosure requirements of § 305 and § 308 are inapplicable. Thus coverage under the Act is limited to those persons (except for the specified political committees) who solicit, collect, or receive contributions of money or other thing of value, and then only if the principal purpose of either the persons or the contributions is to aid in the accomplishment of the aims set forth in § 307(a) and (b). In any event, the solicitation, collection, or receipt of money or other thing of value is a prerequisite to coverage under the Act.

The Government urges a much broader construction—namely, that under § 305 a person must report his expenditures to influence legislation even though he does not solicit, collect, or receive contributions as provided in § 307. Such a construction, we believe, would do violence to the title and language of § 307 as well as its legislative history. If the construction urged by the Government is to become law, that is for Congress to accomplish by further legislation.

We now turn to the alleged vagueness of the purposes set forth in § 307(a) and (b). As in United States v. Rumely [1953] which involved the interpretation of similar language, we believe this language should be construed to refer only to " 'lobbying in its commonly accepted sense' "—to direct communication with members of Congress on pending or proposed federal legislation. The legislative history of the Act makes clear that, at the very least, Congress sought disclosure of such direct pressures, exerted by the lobbyist[s] themselves or through their hirelings or through an artificially stimulated letter campaign. It is likewise clear that Congress would have intended the Act to operate on this narrower basis, even if a broader application to organizations seeking to propagandize the general public were not permissible.

There remains for our consideration the meaning of "the principal purpose" and "to be used principally to aid." The legislative history of the Act indicates that the term "principal" was adopted merely to exclude from the scope of § 307 those contributions and persons having only an "incidental" purpose of influencing legislation. Conversely, the "principal purpose" requirement does not exclude a contribution which in substantial part is to be used to influence legislation through direct communication with Congress or a person whose activities in substantial part are directed to influencing legislation through direct communication with Congress. If it were otherwise—if an organization, for example, were exempted because lobbying was only one of its main activities—the Act would in large measure be reduced to a mere exhortation against abuse of the legislative process. In construing the Act narrowly to avoid constitutional doubts, we must also avoid a construction that would seriously impair the effectiveness of the Act in coping with the problem it was designed to alleviate.

To summarize, therefore, there are three prerequisites to coverage under § 307: (1) the "person" must have solicited, collected, or received contributions; (2) one of the main purposes of such "person," or one of the main purposes of such contributions, must have been to influence the passage or defeat of legislation by Congress; (3) the intended method of accomplishing this purpose must have been through direct communication with members of Congress. And since § 307 modifies the substantive provisions of the Act, our construction of § 307 will of necessity also narrow the scope of § 305 and § 308. . . . Thus § 305 is limited to those persons who are covered by § 307; and when so covered, they must report all contributions and expenditures having the purpose of attempting to influence legislation through direct communication with Congress. Similarly, § 308 is limited to those persons (with the stated exceptions) who are covered by § 307 and who, in addition, engage themselves for pay or for any other valuable consideration for the purpose of attempting to influence legislation through direct communication with Congress. Construed in this way, the Lobbying Act meets the constitutional requirement of definiteness.

II

Thus construed, §§ 305 and 308 also do not violate the freedoms guaranteed by the First Amendment—freedom to speak, publish, and petition the Government.

Present-day legislative complexities are such that individual members of Congress cannot be expected to explore the myriad pressures to which they are regularly subjected. Yet full realization of the American ideal of government by elected representatives depends to no small extent on their ability to properly evaluate such pressures. Otherwise the voice of the people may all too easily be drowned out by the voice of special interest groups seeking favored treatment while masquerading as proponents of the public weal. This is the evil which the Lobbying Act was designed to help prevent.

Toward that end, Congress has not sought to prohibit these pressures. It has merely provided for a modicum of information from those who for hire attempt to influence legislation or who collect or spend funds for that purpose. It wants only to know who is being hired, who is putting up the money and how much. It acted in the same spirit and for a similar purpose in passing the Federal Corrupt Practices Act—to maintain the integrity of the basic governmental process. See Burroughs & Cannon v. United States [1934]. . . .

Reversed.

Mr. Justice **CLARK** took no part in the consideration or decision of this case.

Mr. Justice **DOUGLAS** with whom Mr. Justice **BLACK** concurs, dissenting. . . .

Mr. Justice **JACKSON,** dissenting. . . .

The clearest feature of this case is that it begins with an Act so mischievously vague that the Government charged with its enforcement does not understand it, for some of its important assumptions are rejected by the Court's interpretation. The clearest feature of the Court's decision is that it leaves the country under an Act which is not much like any Act passed by Congress. . . .

The Act passed by Congress would appear to apply to all persons who (1) solicit or receive funds for the purpose of lobbying, (2) receive and expend funds for the purpose of lobbying, or (3) merely expend funds for the purpose of lobbying. The Court at least eliminates this last category from coverage of the Act, though I should suppose that more serious evils affecting the public interest are to be found in the way lobbyists spend their money than in the ways they obtain it. . . .

Also, Congress enacted a statute to reach the raising and spending of funds for the purpose of influencing congressional action *directly or indirectly.* The Court entirely deletes "indirectly" and narrows "directly" to mean "direct communication with members of Congress." These two constructions leave the Act touching only a part of the practices Congress deemed sinister.

Finally, as if to compensate for its deletions from the Act, the Court expands the phrase "the principal purpose" so that it now refers to any contribution which "in substantial part" is used to influence legislation.

I agree, of course, that we should make liberal interpretations to save legislative Acts, including penal statutes which punish conduct traditionally recognized as morally "wrong." Whoever kidnaps, steals, kills, or commits similar acts of violence upon another is bound to know that he is inviting retribution by society, and many of the statutes which define these long-established crimes are traditionally and perhaps necessarily vague. But we are dealing with a novel offense that has no established bounds and no such moral basis. The criminality of the conduct dealt with here depends entirely upon a purpose to influence legislation. . . .

The First Amendment forbids Congress to abridge the right of the people "to petition the Government for a redress of grievances." If this right is to have an interpretation consistent with that given to other First Amendment rights, it confers a large immunity upon activities of persons, organizations, groups and classes to obtain what they think is due them from government. Of course, their conflicting claims and propaganda are confusing, annoying and at times, no doubt, deceiving and corrupting. But we may not forget that our constitutional system is to allow the greatest freedom of access to Congress, so that the people may press for their selfish interests, with Congress acting as arbiter of their demands and conflicts.

In matters of this nature, it does not seem wise to leave the scope of a criminal Act, close to impinging on the right of petition, dependent upon judicial construction for its limitations. Judicial construction, constitutional or statutory, always is subject to hazards of judicial reconstruction. One may rely on today's narrow interpretation only at his peril, for some later Court may expand the Act to include, in accordance with its terms, what today the Court excludes. . . . The *ex post facto* provision of our Constitution has not been held to protect the citizen against a retroactive change in decisional law. . . . As long as this statute stands on the books, its vagueness will be a contingent threat to activities which the Court today rules out, the contingency being a change of views by the Court as hereafter constituted. . . .

Editors' Notes

(1) **Query:** In this case Warren engaged in the same sort of avoidance as did Harlan in Yates v. United States (1957; reprinted above, p. 519) by concealing constitutional interpretation under the guise of statutory interpretation. Why?

(2) "Void for vagueness," often mentioned by the Court in passing, refers to the doctrine that the elementary fairness encompassed in the basic notion of due process of law requires a statute to be sufficiently clear that its terms and its scope may be understood. Thus, for example, the Court could strike

down a New Jersey statute that made it a crime to be a "gangster," Lanzetta v. New Jersey (1939), and a New York law forbidding the showing of "sacrilegious" motion pictures, Burstyn v. Wilson (1952). Obviously, the doctrine is related to that of "overbreadth"; see the discussion of that concept in the editors' notes to Gooding v. Wilson (1972; reprinted above, p. 539). See Anthony Amsterdam, "The Void-for-Vagueness Doctrine," 109 *U.Pa.L. Rev.* 67 (1960).

(3) Here and even more so in NAACP v. Button (1963), reprinted next, the Court was very solicitous of a right to lobby, though conscious of the possibility of its misuse. Indeed, the justices practically assumed without discussion that such a right is protected by the First Amendment. It had not always been so. Trist v. Child (1874) invalidated a contract under which Nicholas Trist agreed to give L.M. Child a share of what Child could persuade Congress to pay Trist for his negotiating the Treaty of Guadelupe Hidalgo with Mexico (1848). The Court treated lobbying, even as here where there was no evidence of any effort at bribery, with great moral disdain, noting that:

> If the instances were numerous, open, and tolerated, they would be regarded as measuring the decay of public morals and the degeneracy of the times. . . . If the agent is truthful, and conceals nothing, all is well. If he uses nefarious means with success, the spring-head and the stream of legislation are polluted. To legalize the traffic of such service, would open a door at which fraud and falsehood would not fail to enter and make themselves felt at every accessible point.

"We need not, in order to find constitutional protection for the kind of cooperative, organizational activity disclosed by this record . . . subsume such activity under a narrow, literal conception of freedom of speech, petition or assembly."

NAACP v. BUTTON

371 U.S. 415, 83 S.Ct. 328, 9 L.Ed.2d 405 (1963).

As part of its program of "massive resistance" to thwart implementation of the School Segregation Cases (1954), Virginia joined the southern attack on the NAACP (see the headnote to NAACP v. Alabama, above, p. 646), enacting in 1956 a bevy of laws to curb the organization's capacity "to litigate by day and to think about litigation by night." Given the NAACP's frequent tactic of urging its members to file law suits—under the rules of standing an individual litigant is almost always necessary—and even asking people at meetings to sign blank forms authorizing the Association to file suits in their names, were statutes regulating the practice of law and redefining the old crimes of barratry ("habitual stirring up of quarrels"), champerty (assisting another to start or continue a law suit), and maintenance ("officious intermeddling" in a law suit by encouraging another to sue, usually by paying money to the potential litigant).

The NAACP attacked the constitutionality of five of these statutes in a federal district court, which struck down three but under the doctrine of equitable abstention refused to rule on the others until they had been interpreted by state courts. Virginia appealed to the U.S. Supreme Court, which held that the district court should have applied equitable abstention to all five. Harrison v. NAACP (1959).

The NAACP went into state courts to repeat its challenge to four of the five acts. State judges declared two of the statutes inapplicable to the Association's activities and another unconstitutional. The NAACP then obtained certiorari to contest the other statute, chapter 33 of the Acts of the Assembly, 1956 Extra Session. That chapter banned in very general terms "improper solicitation of any legal or professional business."

Mr. Justice **BRENNAN** delivered the opinion of the Court. . . .

II

Petitioner challenges the decision of the Supreme Court of Appeals on many grounds. But we reach only one: that Chapter 33 as construed and applied abridges the freedoms of the First Amendment, protected against state action by the Fourteenth. More specifically, petitioner claims that the chapter infringes the right of the NAACP and its members and lawyers to associate for the purpose of assisting persons who seek legal redress for infringements of their constitutionally guaranteed and other rights. We think petitioner may assert this right on its own behalf, because, though a corporation, it is directly engaged in those activities, claimed to be constitutionally protected, which the statute would curtail. Cf. Grosjean v. American Press Co. [1936]. We also think petitioner has standing to assert the corresponding rights of its members. See National Asso. for Advancement of Colored People v. Alabama [1958]; Bates v. Little Rock [1960]; Louisiana ex rel. Gremillion v. National Asso. for Advancement of Colored People [1961].

We reverse the judgment of the Virginia Supreme Court of Appeals. We hold that the activities of the NAACP, its affiliates and legal staff shown on this record are modes of expression and association protected by the First and Fourteenth Amendments which Virginia may not prohibit, under its power to regulate the legal profession, as improper solicitation of legal business violative of Chapter 33 and the Canons of Professional Ethics.

A

We meet at the outset the contention that "solicitation" is wholly outside the area of freedoms protected by the First Amendment. To this contention there are two answers. The first is that a state cannot foreclose the exercise of constitutional rights by mere labels. The second is that abstract discussion is not the only species of communication which the Constitution protects; the First Amendment also protects vigorous advocacy, certainly of lawful ends, against governmental intrusion. Thomas v. Collins [1945]; Herndon v. Lowry [1937]. In the context of NAACP objectives, litigation is not a technique of resolving private differences; it is a means for achieving the lawful objectives of equality of treatment by all government, federal, state and local, for the members of the Negro community in this country. It is thus a form of political expression. Groups which find themselves unable to achieve their objectives through the ballot frequently turn to the courts. Just as it was true of the opponents of New Deal legislation during the 1930's, for example, no less is it true of the Negro minority today. And under the conditions of modern government, litigation may well be the sole practicable avenue open to a minority to petition for redress of grievances.

We need not, in order to find constitutional protection for the kind of cooperative, organizational activity disclosed by this record, whereby Negroes seek through lawful means to achieve legitimate political ends, subsume such activity under a narrow, literal conception of freedom of speech, petition or assembly. For there is no longer any doubt that the First and Fourteenth Amendments protect certain forms of orderly group activity. Thus we have affirmed the right "to engage in association for the advancement of beliefs and ideas." National Asso. for Advancement of Colored People v. Alabama. We have deemed privileged, under certain circumstances, the efforts of a union official to organize workers. *Thomas.* . . . And we have refused to countenance compelled disclosure of a person's political associations. . . .

The NAACP is not a conventional political party; but the litigation it assists, while serving to vindicate the legal rights of members of the American Negro community, at the same time and perhaps more importantly, makes possible the distinctive contribution of a minority group to the ideas and beliefs of our society. For such a group, association for litigation may be the most effective form of political association.

B

Our concern is with the impact of enforcement of Chapter 33 upon First Amendment freedoms. . . . For us, the words of Virginia's highest court are the words of the statute. Hebert v. Louisiana [1926].
. . . .

. . . If the line drawn by the decree between the permitted and prohibited activities of the NAACP, its members and lawyers is an ambiguous one, we will not presume that the statute curtails constitutionally protected activity as little as possible. For standards of permissible statutory vagueness are strict in the area of free expression. See Smith v. California [1959]; Winters v. New York [1948]; Herndon v. Lowry [1937]; Stromberg v. California [1931]; United States v. CIO, (Rutledge, J., concurring) [1948]. Furthermore, the instant decree may be invalid if it prohibits privileged exercises of First Amendment rights whether or not the record discloses that the petitioner has engaged in privileged conduct. For in appraising a statute's inhibitory effect upon such rights, this Court has not hesitated to take into account possible applications of the statute in other factual contexts besides that at bar. Thornhill v. Alabama [1940]; *Winters.* . . . These freedoms are delicate and vulnerable, as well as supremely precious in our society.

The threat of sanctions may deter their exercise almost as potently as the actual application of sanctions. Cf. *Smith*; Speiser v. Randall [1958]. Because First Amendment freedoms need breathing space to survive, government may regulate in the area only with narrow specificity. Cantwell v. Connecticut [1940].

We read the decree of the Virginia Supreme Court of Appeals in the instant case as proscribing any arrangement by which prospective litigants are advised to seek the assistance of particular attorneys. No narrower reading is plausible. . . .

. . . It is enough that a vague and broad statute lends itself to selective enforcement against unpopular causes. We cannot close our eyes to the fact that the militant Negro civil rights movement has engendered the intense resentment and opposition of the politically dominant white community of Virginia; litigation assisted by the NAACP has been bitterly fought. In such circumstances, a statute broadly curtailing group activity leading to litigation may easily become a weapon of oppression, however evenhanded its terms appear. Its mere existence could well freeze out of existence all such activity on behalf of the civil rights of Negro citizens. . . .

. . . If there is an internal tension between proscription and protection in the statute, we cannot assume that, in its subsequent enforcement, ambiguities will be resolved in favor of adequate protection of First Amendment rights. Broad prophylactic rules in the area of free expression are suspect. See e.g., Near v. Minnesota [1931]. Precision of regulation must be the touchstone in an area so closely touching our most precious freedoms.

C

The second contention is that Virginia has a subordinating interest in the regulation of the legal profession . . . which justifies limiting petitioner's First Amendment rights. . . . However, the State's attempt to equate the activities of the NAACP and its lawyers with common-law barratry, maintenance and champerty, and to outlaw them accordingly, cannot obscure the serious encroachment worked by Chapter 33 upon protected freedoms of expression. The decisions of this Court have consistently held that only a compelling state interest in the regulation of a subject within the State's constitutional power to regulate can justify limiting First Amendment freedoms. . . . For a State may not, under the guise of prohibiting professional misconduct, ignore constitutional rights. See Schware v. Board of Bar Examiners [1957]; Konigsberg v. State Bar [1957]. In National Asso. for Advancement of Colored People v. Alabama, we said, "In the domain of these indispensable liberties, whether of speech, press, or association, the decisions of this Court recognize that abridgment of such rights, even though unintended, may inevitably follow from varied forms of governmental action." Later, in *Bates*, we said, "[w]here there is a significant encroachment upon personal liberty, the State may prevail only upon showing a subordinating interest which is compelling." . . .

However valid may be Virginia's interest in regulating the traditionally illegal practices of barratry, maintenance and champerty, that interest does not justify the prohibition of the NAACP activities disclosed by this record. Malicious intent was of the essence of the common-law offenses of fomenting or stirring up litigation. And whatever may be or may have been true of suits against government in other countries, the exercise in our own, as in this case, of First Amendment rights to enforce constitutional rights through litigation, as a matter of law, cannot be deemed malicious. . . .

Mr. Justice **WHITE,** concurring in part and dissenting in part. . . .

If we had before us, which we do not, a narrowly drawn statute proscribing only the actual day-to-day management and dictation of the tactics, strategy and conduct of litigation by a lay entity such as the NAACP, the issue would be considerably different, at least for me; for in my opinion neither the practice of law by such an organization nor its management of the litigation of its member or others is constitutionally protected. Both practices are well within the regulatory power of the State. In this regard I agree with my Brother Harlan.

It is not at all clear to me, however, that the opinion of the majority would not also strike down such a narrowly drawn statute. To the extent that it would, I am in disagreement. . . .

Mr. Justice **HARLAN,** whom Mr. Justice **CLARK** and Mr. Justice **STEWART** join, dissenting. . . .

II

Freedom of expression embraces more than the right of an individual to speak his mind. It includes also his right to advocate and his right to join with his fellows in an effort to make that advocacy effective. Thomas v. Collins [1945]; National Asso. for Advancement of Colored People v. Alabama [1958]; Bates v. Little Rock [1960]. And just as it includes the right jointly to petition the legislature for redress of grievances, so it must include the right to join together for purposes of obtaining judicial redress. . . . Litigation is often the desirable and orderly way of resolving disputes of broad public significance, and of obtaining vindication of fundamental rights. This is particularly so in the sensitive area of racial relationships.

But to declare that litigation is a form of conduct that may be associated with political expression does not resolve this case. Neither the First Amendment nor the Fourteenth constitutes an absolute bar to government regulation in the fields of free expression and association. This Court has repeatedly held that certain forms of speech are outside the scope of the protection of those Amendments, and that, in addition, "general regulatory statutes, not intended to control the content of speech but incidentally limiting its unfettered exercise," are permissible "when they have been found justified by subordinating valid governmental interests." The problem in each such case is to weigh the legitimate interest of the State against the effect of the regulation on individual rights. . . .

. . . [T]he basic rights in issue are those of the petitioner's members to associate, to discuss, and to advocate. Absent the gravest danger to the community, these rights must remain free from frontal attack or suppression, and the state court has recognized this. . . . But litigation, whether or not associated with the attempt to vindicate constitutional rights, is *conduct:* it is speech *plus.* Although the State surely may not broadly prohibit individuals with a common interest from joining together to petition a court for redress of their grievances, it is equally certain that the State may impose reasonable regulations limiting the permissible form of litigation and the manner of legal representation within its borders. . . .

So here, the question is whether the particular regulation of conduct concerning litigation has a reasonable relation to the further-ance of a proper state interest, and whether that interest outweighs any foreseeable harm to the furtherance of protected freedoms.

III

The interest which Virginia has here asserted is that of maintain-ing high professional standards among those who practice law within its borders. This Court has consistently recognized the broad range of judgments that a State may properly make in regulating any profes-sion. But the regulation of professional standards for members of the bar comes to us with even deeper roots in history and policy, since courts for centuries have possessed disciplinary powers incident to the administration of justice. See Cohen v. Hurley [1961]; Konigsberg v. California [1957]; Martin v. Walton [1961].

The regulation before us has its origins in the long-standing com-mon-law prohibitions of champerty, barratry, and maintenance, the closely related prohibitions in the Canons of Ethics against solicitation and intervention by a law intermediary, and statutory provisions for-bidding the unauthorized practice of law. . . .

First, with regard to the claimed absence of the pecuniary element, it cannot well be suggested that the attorneys here are donating their services, since they are in fact compensated for their work. Nor can it tenably be argued that petitioner's litigating activities fall into the accepted category of aid to indigent litigants. . . .

. . . [A]voidance of improper pecuniary gain is not the only relevant factor in determining standards of professional conduct. Run-ning perhaps even deeper is the desire of the profession, of courts, and of legislatures to prevent any interference with the uniquely personal relationship between lawyer and client and to maintain untrammeled by outside influences the responsibility which the lawyer owes to the courts he serves.

When an attorney is employed by an association or corporation to represent individual litigants, two problems arise, whether or not the association is organized for profit and no matter how unimpeachable its motives. The lawyer becomes subject to the control of a body that is not itself a litigant and that, unlike the lawyers it employs, is not subject to strict professional discipline as an officer of the court. In addition, the lawyer necessarily finds himself with a divided allegiance—to his employer and to his client—which may prevent full compliance with his basic professional obligations. . . .

Second, it is claimed that the interests of petitioner and its members are sufficiently identical to eliminate any "serious danger" of "professionally reprehensible conflicts of interest." . . .

. . . [I]t may be in the interests of the Association in every case to make a frontal attack on segregation, to press for an immediate breaking down of racial barriers, and to sacrifice minor points that may win a given case for the major points that may win other cases too. But in a particular litigation, it is not impossible that after authorizing action in his behalf, a Negro parent, concerned that a continued frontal attack could result in schools closed for years, might prefer to wait with his fellows a longer time for good-faith efforts by the local school board than is permitted by the centrally determined policy of the NAACP. Or he might see a greater prospect of success through discussions with local school authorities than through the litigation deemed necessary by the Association. The parent, of course, is free to withdraw his authorization, but is his lawyer, retained and paid by petitioner and subject to its directions on matters of policy, able to advise the parent with that undivided allegiance that is the hallmark of the attorney-client relation? I am afraid not. . . .

Third, it is said that the practices involved here must stand on a different footing because the litigation that petitioner supports concerns the vindication of constitutionally guaranteed rights. . . .

. . . The true question is whether the State has taken action which unreasonably obstructs the assertion of federal rights. Here, it cannot be said that the underlying state policy is inevitably inconsistent with federal interests. The State has sought to prohibit the solicitation and sponsoring of litigation by those who have no standing to initiate that litigation themselves and who are not simply coming to the assistance of indigent litigants. Thus the state policy is not unrelated to the federal rules of standing. . . .

The impact of such a prohibition on the rights of petitioner and its members to free expression and association cannot well be deemed so great as to require that it be struck down in the face of this substantial state interest. The important function of organizations like petitioner in vindicating constitutional rights is not of course to be minimized, but that function is not, in my opinion, substantially impaired by this statute. Of cardinal importance, this regulatory enactment as construed does not in any way suppress assembly, or advocacy of litigation in general or in particular. Moreover, contrary to the majority's suggestion, it does not, in my view, prevent petitioner from recommending the services of attorneys who are not subject to its directions and control. . . .

IV

The Court's remaining line of reasoning is that Chapter 33 as construed . . . must be struck down on the score of vagueness and ambiguity. I think that this "vagueness" concept has no proper place in this case and only serves to obscure rather than illuminate the true questions presented. . . .

Editors' Notes

(1) **Query:** To what degree does Brennan's opinion for the Court exemplify "reinforcing representative democracy"? Can democratic theory with logical consistency advocate preferential constitutional protection to groups' lobbying for substantive rights before courts staffed by appointed officials serving for what amounts to life tenure? How can one draw a valid and practical distinction between groups' (or individuals') rights to lobby in the courts for procedural as contrasted with substantive rights? To what extent do the difficulties here, assuming there are difficulties, find their roots in ¶ 2 of footnote 4 of Stone's opinion in *Carolene Products* (1938; reprinted above, p. 482)?

(2) Brennan's opinion alluded to southern states' resistance to the School Segregation Cases (1954), and the defiance publicly voiced by southern officials, including those of Virginia, must have moved the justices to read with suspicion supposedly neutral statutes.

(3) **Query:** Brennan did not mention that in most of the states of the Old Confederacy it was extraordinarily difficult if not impossible for blacks to vote. (The Voting Rights Act of 1965 was still two years in the future.) Thus, if Chapter 33 was, as its authors boasted and not as the Virginia judges claimed, an effort to keep the NAACP from litigating and if Virginia continued to be successful in barring blacks from the polls, what other avenues for social change were open to southern blacks? In sum, was Harlan's opinion either naive or was he simply saying, like Locke, that blacks could only "appeal to heaven," that is, resort to revolution, to effect social change? Is it helpful for him to call for "balancing"?

(4) For an analysis of *Button,* see: Walter F. Murphy and Robert F. Birkby, "Interest Group Conflict in the Judicial Arena: The First Amendment and Group Access to the Court," 42 *Tex.L.Rev* 1018 (1964). For a general approach to interest groups in the courts, see: Clement E. Vose, "Litigation as a Form of Pressure Group Activity," 319 *The Annals* 20 (1958); and for a detailed study of the NAACP's tactics, his *Caucasians Only* (Berkeley: University of California Press, 1959). For an analysis of the problems of attorney-client relationships in litigation designed to change public policy, see Derrick Bell, "Serving Two Masters: Integration Ideals and Client Interests in School Desegregation Litigation," 85 *Yale L.J.* 470 (1976).

(5) Brotherhood of Railroad Trainmen v. Virginia (1964), United Mine Workers v. Illinois State Bar (1967), and United Transportation Union v. State

Bar of Michigan (1971) applied to economic organizations *Button*'s inclusion of a right under the First Amendment of groups to utilize the courts. Despite the fears White expressed in his separate opinion in *Button,* he joined the majority in the first two of these cases and dissented only in part in the third. Harlan did not change his stance, though he, too, dissented only in part in the Michigan case.

D

TREATING EQUALS EQUALLY

In this Section we confront the problem of HOW to interpret the Constitution in yet another context, that created by the constitutional command of equal protection of the laws.

In silent but dramatic contrast to the ringing proclamation of the Declaration of Independence that "all men are created equal," neither the original constitutional document nor the Bill of Rights explicitly guarantees citizens equal treatment by state or federal government. The closest the original document came was in Article I's denial of federal and state authority to "grant any title of nobility" and Article IV's mandate that "citizens of each State shall be entitled to all privileges and immunities of citizens of the several States." There was no effort to define or even to list the "privileges and immunities of citizens of the several States"; [1] and, if Dred Scott v. Sanford (1857) were correct in its historical analysis, neither was there any expectation that blacks would become citizens.

One might stretch the imagination and argue that the Fifth Amendment's banning the federal government's [2] taking "life, liberty, or property, without due process of law" also imposed a requirement of equal protection. Due process, so the argument would run—and did so run in Bolling v. Sharpe (1954; reprinted below, p. 772)— includes notions of fairness, and fairness includes some idea of equal treatment; thus, "due process" includes an "equal protection component."

The most obvious reason for the absence of explicit guarantees of equal treatment by government was, of course, the existence of slavery. Victory in the Civil War made possible the end of this cause of the problem. The Thirteenth Amendment struck a massive blow for equality as well as for liberty when it declared: "Neither slavery nor involuntary servitude, except as a punishment for crime whereof

---

1. For an early attempt to define these terms see Corfield v. Coryell (Justice Bushrod Washington, riding circuit, 1823); see also The Slaughter-House Cases (1873; reprinted above, p. 435) and the discussion in C. Herman Pritchett, *Constitutional Law of the Federal System* (Englewood Cliffs, N.J.: Prentice Hall, 1984), pp. 83–86.

2. The plain words of the Fifth Amendment, written in the passive voice, do not limit its terms to the federal government, but the Court so ruled in Barron v. Baltimore (1833). See the discussion above in the Ed.'s Note on the application of the Bill of Rights to the States, following Palko v. Connecticut (1937; reprinted above, p. 94).

the party shall have been duly convicted, shall exist within the United States, or any place subject to their jurisdiction." The Fourteenth added the document's only explicit general [3] guarantee of equal treatment: "nor shall any state . . . deny to any person within its jurisdiction the equal protection of the laws." These terms are sweeping but they are also Delphic. One immediately encounters problems of defining "state," "person," and "equal protection."

A. State Action

The Supreme Court has construed the phrase "nor shall any state" as excluding constitutional protection against unequal treatment by fellow citizens. The Civil Rights Cases (1883) struck down a federal statute that forbade private citizens to discriminate on account of race in public accommodations. The government argued that § 5 of the amendment, empowering Congress to enforce its terms, authorized the statute. The Court, however, insisted on a literal and clause-bound interpretation and held: "Individual invasion of individual rights is not the subject-matter of the amendment."

But it is painfully obvious that the heavy hand of the state can be felt even where the state is apparently absent. In recent decades judges have been more sensitive to this fact, and the Civil Rights Cases have been partially, if obliquely, overruled.[4] Nevertheless, Congress, the presidency, and the Court continue to hold the view that, for the Fourteenth Amendment to come into play, there must be a palpable connection between the state and the private individual or group doing the discriminating. Judges have tended more to solve specific problems presented by particular cases than to offer general guidelines to determine when state action is or is not present. One thing, however, seems clear: A state may not escape the Fourteenth Amendment by allowing private citizens or corporations to perform

---

3. The Fifteenth Amendment in forbidding discrimination against the right to vote because of race or previous condition of servitude, the Nineteenth because of sex, the Twenty-Sixth because of age for those over eighteen, and the Twenty-fourth in elections for federal officials because of failure to pay any tax, all affect equality but in more particular ways.

4. See espec. Heart of Atlanta Motel v. United States (1964), and Katzenbach v. McClung (1964), sustaining the Civil Rights Act of 1964, which was even broader in its protection of civil rights than the act of 1875 that *Civil Rights* invalidated. In *Heart of Atlanta* and *Katzenbach,* the Court based its decisions on congressional authority to regulate "commerce among the several states." The justices distinguished *Civil Rights* because there the Court had not considered the reach of the commerce clause. Concurring, Justice Douglas bluntly said that he would have preferred to have based the ruling on § 5 of the Fourteenth Amendment and so would have expressly overruled *Civil Rights.* In any event, the Court's finding in *Katzenbach* that the commerce clause allowed Congress to regulate the affairs of a small barbeque restaurant, when coupled with the Court's equally imperial view of the commerce clause in other cases—see espec. Wickard v. Filburn (1942; discussed above, p. 404)—leaves little that Congress cannot regulate. Nevertheless, it is important to realize that these cases validate *congressional* protection of civil rights; they do not require either the states or Congress to protect individual rights against discrimination by other private citizens or, in the absence of explicit congressional authorization, federal courts to do so either.

such public functions as elections [5] and possibly education.[6] Beyond that point, one confronts "a wilderness of single instances." [7]

The specific limitation of "state action" has been punctured in another way. In many early cases, the justices had noted that the equal protection clause did not bind the federal government, only the states. But in Hirabayashi v. United States (1943), upholding the curfew against Japanese-Americans, Chief Justice Stone's majority opinion acknowledged some federal obligation to govern even-handedly and vaguely hinted that had the equal protection clause applied to the federal government, the Court might have decided in favor of the Nisei.

The justices continued to think about the problem, and eleven years later the school segregation case from the District of Columbia, Bolling v. Sharpe (1954; reprinted below, p. 772), ruled that the due process clause of the Fifth Amendment included a concept of equal treatment in its general requirement of fair treatment. But Chief Justice Warren was careful to say that "we do not imply that the two [equal protection and due process] are interchangeable phrases."

Gradually, however, the Court began to merge the concepts and in 1975 Weinberger v. Wiesenfeld asserted that the "Court's approach to Fifth Amendment equal protection claims has always been precisely the same as to equal protection claims under the Fourteenth Amendment." [8] Thus we witness not only an erasure of decades of decisions but also a reverse twist on the incorporation doctrine (see above, p. 98): Instead of deciding that the Fourteenth Amendment incorporated part of the Bill of Rights, the Court ruled that the Bill of Rights incorporated part of the Fourteenth Amendment. On its face, this reasoning is strange—John Hart Ely called it "gibberish both syntactically and historically" [9]—but it makes sense if one uses structural analysis or if one considers how much a political theory of constitutionalism permeates the notion of "the Constitution."

---

5. This is the teaching of the later white primary cases, espec. Terry v. Adams (1953).

6. See, for example, Griffin v. Prince Edward County (1964); Walter F. Murphy, "Public Education with Private Funds?" 20 *J. of Pols.* 635 (1958). For more recent studies of the developing concept of "state action," see: Robert J. Glennon, Jr., and John E. Nowak, "A Functional Analysis of the Fourteenth 'State Action' Requirement," 1976 *Sup.Ct.Rev.* 221; L.F. Goldstein, "The Death and Transfiguration of the State Action Doctrine," 4 *Hast.Con.L.Q.* 1 (1977); Jesse Choper, "Thoughts on State Action," 1979 *Wash.U.L.Q.* 775.

7. For a discussion of the cases on this point, see C. Herman Pritchett, *Constitutional Civil Liberties* (Englewood Cliff, N.J.: Prentice-Hall, 1984), pp. 275–279.

8. Later the Court has conceded, however, that there are some differences. Hampton v. Mow Sun Wong (1976) noted that "the two protections are not always coextensive. Not only does the language of the two Amendments differ, but more importantly, there may be overriding national interests which justify selective federal legislation that would be unacceptable for an individual State." Justice Brennan, the author of the Court's opinion in *Weinberger,* was apparently troubled by these sentences and filed a brief concurring opinion.

9. *Democracy and Distrust* (Cambridge, Mass.: Harvard University Press, 1980), p. 32.

B. Who is Included Under "Person"?

"Person" also presents difficult issues of definition. Does the word refer only to humans or does it include corporations? Without hearing argument on the point, the Court in Santa Clara County v. Southern Pacific (1886) held that a corporation was a "person" for purposes of the Fourteenth Amendment. And so, despite an occasional protest, the matter stands today.

A more open and emotionally charged issue is whether a fetus is a "person" entitled not merely to due process and equal protection but to any constitutionally cognizable claim of protection and respect by government. Roe v. Wade (1973) held that a fetus was not a person under the Fourteenth Amendment; but, as a continuing debate over various right-to-life measures (see, for example, the material reprinted above at pp. 247–254) shows, the issue is still very much alive.

Also of great importance is the question whether "person" basically pertains to an individual as an individual or as a member of a group. The latter interpretation sees the amendment's purpose as protecting disadvantaged groups—some, like blacks, rather easily identifiable; others, like the poor, quite amorphous. The distinction between an individual or group basis for equal protection is hardly sharp, for each of us suffers injury as an individual, yet none of us can live except as a member of a group—in most cases several groups.[10]

Still, there are differences. For example, an "affirmative action" plan that would try to repair past damage by giving some degree of preference to members of groups who previously suffered from official discrimination needs a constitutional base that recognizes a wider degree of group disadvantage as well as of group liability than a purely individualized concept of "person" would allow. The latter would not necessarily oppose affirmative action, but it would limit the benefits of such programs to individuals who could show that discrimination had injured them personally and not simply their group generally.

The plain words of the equal protection clause, taken alone, seem to favor an individualized meaning; but, one might argue, the purpose behind those words requires a broader concept. Part of the difficulty the justices have had in resolving problems of affirmative action (see espec. Regents v. Bakke [1978; reprinted below, p. 804] and Fullilove v. Klutznick [1980; reprinted below, p. 816]) might be due to their refusal to face up to these two views of the reach of the amendment and to choose between them.

---

10. For a debate on this issue, which indicates how much the two approaches have in common as well as how much they differ, see: Owen M. Fiss, "Groups and the Equal Protection Clause," 5 *Phil. & Pub. Affrs.* 107 (1976); and Paul Brest, "In Defense of the Anti-Discrimination Principle," 90 *Harv.L.Rev.* 1 (1976). See also Vernon Van Dyke, "Justice as Fairness: For Groups?" 69 *Am.Pol.Sci.Rev.* 607 (1975).

C. What Does "Equal Protection" Mean?

As a practical matter, the equal protection clause cannot forbid states to make distinctions, or the clause would be self-destructive. "Sometimes," as the Court observed in Jenness v. Fortson (1971), "the grossest discrimination can lie in treating things that are different as though they were exactly alike. . . ." A law that exacted the same amount of taxes from a poor as from a rich person or required universal military service without exempting the physically disabled would merely emphasize existing inequality. Statutes that allowed the blind as well as the sighted to drive automobiles or anyone at all to perform surgery, dispense drugs, teach in public schools, or serve as a law enforcement official would be absurd.

"The Equal Protection Clause is itself a classic paradox," Justice Rehnquist has said:

> It creates a requirement of equal treatment to be applied to the process of legislation—legislation whose very purpose is to draw lines in such a way that different people are treated differently. The problem presented is one of sorting the legislative distinctions which are acceptable from those which involve invidiously unequal treatment. . . . [E]qual protection does not mean that all persons must be treated alike. Rather, its general principle is that persons similarly situated should be treated similarly.[11]

But even that statement of high principle, Rehnquist conceded, does little to settle specific cases. "For the crux of the problem is *whether persons are similarly situated* for purposes of the state action at issue." Complicating analysis is the severe temptation of human beings to see themselves as differently situated, to place their own interests ahead of others', and, consequently, for those who have or can influence political power to use government for self-advancement. In effect, though seldom in name, we all tend to make self-serving distinctions and to rationalize them as being objectively valid and socially necessary.

Moreover, a degree of discrimination based on wealth may be inevitable in a technological society. Many occupations that we might all agree should require governmental regulation regarding admission—medicine or law, for instance—also are among the most lucrative and prestigious. In addition, these sorts of professions usually require long and expensive graduate training. Thus educational requirements confer advantages on people who have or whose families have large monetary resources.

Entry into less well-paying and less prestigious but still important occupations, such as police and clerical service, usually demands lower though real levels of reading and writing abilities obtainable through a *good* high school education, along with cultural skills generally associated with white, middle-class society. These requirements may effectively bar most members of certain minorities who tend not to have

---

11. Trimble v. Gordon, dis. op. (1973).

had the opportunity to obtain or take advantage of good secondary educations and to whose subculture such white, middle-class skills are alien. (See Washington v. Davis [1976; reprinted below, p. 787].)

Thus constitutional interpretation is left with a knotty problem: On the one hand, classification is essential in a complex world. On the other, we all tend to see distinctions that benefit us as "necessary," and even treatment that is in fact based on "objective" criteria may confer advantages closely correlated with wealth, status, and ethnic background. By what standards can constitutional interpreters distinguish between useful, perhaps necessary, distinctions and those that violate equal protection of the laws?

One looks to the usual sources of constitutional meaning. As is typically true, "intent of the framers" is illusive. The larger purpose behind the equal protection clause, most historians agree, was to help the newly freed slaves by, on the one hand, outlawing the harsh "black codes" that white southern governments had enacted to keep former slaves "in their place" and, on the other, by legitimizing the sort of federal protection of black civil rights embodied in the Civil Rights Act of 1866. But the words of the amendment include more than blacks; they reach "any person." As the Court noted in Strauder v. West Virginia (1880; reprinted below, p. 753), the amendment "speaks in general terms, and these are as comprehensive as possible."

As is also typically the case, stare decisis provides not one but several answers, and they are difficult to reconcile. The opinions reprinted in Chapters 13 and 14 display some coherent threads of reasoning, but one would have to be very naive to think that the development of constitutional doctrine here has followed in a smooth line of deductions from previous cases.

Practice also supplies more than one answer, and some of them form an unhappy portrait of discrimination that in design and effect ensured the continued inequality of blacks, orientals, women, and other politically weak minorities. Indeed, it has been the contradiction between the practices and ideals of the political system that has forced judges, legislators, and executive officials to interpret and reinterpret the Fourteenth Amendment. These difficulties indicate once again the need for "rules of recognition" to distinguish between constitution-building practices and those that threaten to destroy constitutional values.

Structural analysis might help here. Looking at the structure of the document might provide more light than does examination of isolated clauses. In 1964 Justice Arthur Goldberg claimed that "the idea of equality pervades the document." [12] He conceded—as he had to—the absence of a specific equal protection clause, but he argued that: (1) Article IV constrained both levels of government by guaranteeing to each state a republican form of government and so denied the ancient distinction between king and vassal; (2) Equality "was

---

12. "Equality and Governmental Action," 39 *N.Y.U.L.Rev.* 205, 206 (1964).

encompassed within the concept of liberty"; and (3) The document was framed against a background in which many state constitutions guaranteed equal protection and the objective of the Mayflower Compact, "the framing of 'just & equall lawes,' " was a living ideal.

To this list one could add the clauses, already mentioned, forbidding titles of nobility and imposing on the federal government, at least, the requirement of moving against a person's life, liberty, or property only with "due process of law." This sort of analysis makes a plausible, though not overwhelming, case for Goldberg's thesis.

Adding the structure of the political system to what is to be analyzed blurs the picture for the reasons noted in the discussion of practices. The theories that underlie the document and the system offer some hope, for democratic theory and constitutionalism to some extent reinforce each other here. Both postulate the equal worth and dignity of each human being. Still, there are important differences in the argument of the two theories.

Democracy requires equal access to the ballot box and the legal right to communicate freely with fellow citizens and public officials. Its logic, however, does not impose any requirements about the substantive content of the policy produced by officials chosen under a system of free elections, so long as that policy does not restrict the openness of the political processes. Laws that seriously disadvantage particular individuals or groups, but still leave the avenues of change open, are perfectly valid. The people at the next election can judge whether they wish to choose new officials and new policies. For democratic theory, it is the *process* that legitimates public policy, not the substance of that policy.

Constitutionalism, on the other hand, asserts that the value of equality of citizenship takes precedence over any procedural blessing given by the people or their representatives. What Ronald Dworkin calls a "right to equal concern and respect"[13] trumps the majority's authority to disadvantage individuals or groups so as to deny them dignity.

But the gap between democratic and constitutionalist theory may be narrower than their differing logics imply. Democratic theorists, many of whom prefer to pass over the fact that their theory offers no assurance for equal protection beyond equal participation,[14] would probably argue that legislation so gross in its discriminatory effects as to stigmatize minorities would imperil equal political access by destroying the capacity of the stigmatized to communicate persuasively

---

13. *Taking Rights Seriously* (Cambridge: Harvard University Press, 1977), p. 180.

14. See, for example, Ely, supra note 9, and Michael Walzer, "Philosophy and Democracy," 9 *Pol. Theory* 379 (1981). Walzer, would "accept" two limitations, borrowed from Rousseau, on the power of the people in a representative democracy: Their representatives would have to legislate generally and the people can never surrender their sovereignty. One can, of course, accept whatever limitations one wants; but, looking only at the first limitation, it is difficult to see either: (1) Why one who believes in the legitimizing authority of process should logically impose constraints on the substantive decisions that process produces; or (2) How one could accept the first limitation without establishing some sort of referee outside (and above?) the people and their representatives to determine when legislation was not general.

with other citizens. Thus these theorists would to some extent agree
with the conclusions, though not the reasoning, of constitutionalists
about the necessity of equality.

In practice, then, the two theories would unite where a legislative
distinction imposed a stigma. But there is no substantive policy short
of stigma that democratic theory would forbid. Constitutionalism's
limits on classifications would be tighter. Stigma merely marks an
outer limit of a denial of dignity. More positively, constitutionalism
requires that the substance of public policy be even-handed. "Fairness," like "justice," is an elusive concept, but constitutionalism is
comfortable with both. The Court applied undiluted constitutionalist
theory in Hampton v. Mow Sun Wong (1976):

> The federal sovereign, like the States, must govern impartially.
> The concept of equal justice under law is served by the Fifth
> Amendment's guarantee of due process, as well as by the Equal
> Protection Clause of the Fourteenth Amendment.

We can say that accepting constitutionalism as one of the theoretical bases of the Constitution buttresses not only Goldberg's claim that
"the idea of equality permeates the document," but also the Court's
decision in Bolling v. Sharpe and later cases that the federal government is also bound to accord equal protection. Further, we can say
that constitutionalism requires an interpretation of the equal protection clause that is sensitive to those adversely affected by legislative
classifications. What we cannot say on the basis of this sort of abstract
analysis is precisely how generous interpreters should be or exactly
what doctrines they should apply.

Nevertheless, it is important to understand that, through its heavy
emphasis on equal dignity and worth, constitutionalism infuses the
equal protection clause with a generous meaning. In so doing, it
gives judges broader authority to look behind the face of legislative
distinctions than does democratic theory. The introductory essays and
the cases reprinted in the next two chapters try to convey some notion
of the way in which the Supreme Court and indirectly Congress have
tried, however stumblingly, to formulate more specific standards
within this general framework.

We once again caution users of this book, in reading the cases in
these chapters, not to become lost in the twists and turns of development of legal doctrines. This Part of the book focuses on HOW to
interpret the Constitution, and inevitably WHAT interpreters see the
Constitution as including will affect their decisions, just as will visions
they have of the society to which the Constitution is pointing.

To an interpreter who views "the Constitution" as no more than
the document, "equal protection of the laws" may mean only that a
legislature must offer a reason for its classification that does not offend
the document's specific terms. To an interpreter with a broader view
of "the Constitution," the equal protection and due process clauses
may serve two much broader functions. First, they may operate as the
document's references to a political theory that demands not only that

government accord equal dignity and respect in its dealings with all persons within its jurisdiction, but also that the laws it enacts to control relations among private citizens reflect a similar imperative. Second and related, those clauses may manifest a vision of a society in which citizens enjoy freedom from governmental and societal prejudice based on such irrelevant factors as race, ethnicity, sex, or wealth, and are judged by the ways in which they use their talents.

The differences between these interpreters may lie not only in their conceptions of WHAT the Constitution includes and the visions of the society to which it points, but also in differing answers to the question of WHO interprets which aspects of the Constitution. We are studying mainly judicial action, and, as we have frequently seen, a judge may well conclude that his or her role is peripheral to that of elected public officials in some facets of constitutional interpretation. Thus we once again find it necessary to keep the larger process of constitutional interpretation in focus as we try to grasp the convoluted doctrines that judges have created to cope with discrete—and fascinating—problems. In every important piece of constitutional interpretation, the cords of WHAT, WHO, and HOW braid together.

SELECTED BIBLIOGRAPHY

Baer, Judith A. *Equality under the Constitution* (Ithaca, N.Y.: Cornell University Press, 1984).

Ball, Milner S. *The Promise of American Law* (Athens, Ga.: University of Georgia Press, 1981).

Bickel, Alexander M. "The Original Understanding and the Segregation Decision," 69 *Harv.L.Rev.* 1 (1955).

Brest, Paul. "In Defense of the Anti-Discrimination Principle," 90 *Harv.L.Rev.* 1 (1976).

Dworkin, Ronald. "What is Equality?" 10 *Phil. & Pub. Affrs.* 185 (1981); 10 ibid. 283 (1981) (2 parts).

Fiss, Owen M. "Groups and the Equal Protection Clause," 5 *Phil. & Pub. Affrs.* 107 (1976).

Green, Philip. *The Pursuit of Inequality* (New York: Pantheon, 1981).

Gunther, Gerald, "In Search of Evolving Doctrine on a Changing Court," 86 *Harv.L.Rev.* 1 (1972).

Harris, Robert J. *The Quest for Equality* (Baton Rouge, La.: Louisiana State University Press, 1960).

Hartz, Louis. *The Liberal Tradition in America* (New York: Harcourt, Brace, 1955).

Karst, Kenneth L. "Equal Citizenship under the Fourteenth Amendment," 91 *Harv.L.Rev.* 1 (1977).

Pennock, J. Roland, and John W. Chapman, eds. *Equality* (New York: Lieber-Alberton, 1967).

Perry, Michael J. "Modern Equal Protection: A Conceptualization and an Appraisal," 79 *Colum.L.Rev.* 1023 (1979).

Pole, J.R. *The Pursuit of Equality in American History* (Berkeley: University of California Press, 1978).

Pritchett, C. Herman. *Constitutional Civil Liberties* (Englewood Cliffs, N.J.: Prentice-Hall, 1984), chaps. 10, 12.

Ryan, William. *Equality* (New York: Pantheon, 1981).

Sandalow, Terrence. "Judicial Protection of Minorities," 75 *Mich.L. Rev.* 1162 (1977).

Sartori, Giovanni. *Democratic Theory* (New York: Praeger, 1965), chaps. 13–15.

tenBroek, Jacobus. *Equal Under Law:* (New York: Macmillan, 1965). (Originally published in 1951 under the title, *The Antislavery Origins of the Fourteenth Amendment.*)

Tribe, Laurence H. *American Constitutional Law* (Mineola, N.Y.: Foundation Press, 1978), chap. 17.

Tussman, Joseph, and Jacobus tenBroek, "The Equal Protection of the Laws," 37 *Calif.L.Rev.* 341 (1949).

Van Dyke, Vernon. "Justice as Fairness: For Groups?" 69 *Am.Pol. Sci.Rev.* 607 (1975).

Williams, Bernard A.O. "The Idea of Equality," in H.A. Bedau, ed., *Justice and Equality* (Englewood Cliffs, N.J.: Prentice-Hall, 1971).

Wright, J. Skelly. "Judicial Review and the Equal Protection Clause," 15 *Harv.Civ.Rights-Civ.Libs.L.Rev.* 1 (1980).

13

The Problems of Equal Protection, I

The Slaughter-House Cases (1873; reprinted above, p. 435) provided the first important opportunity for judicial interpretation of the Fourteenth Amendment, but the justices gave the equal protection clause short shrift. For the majority, Justice Miller found it inapplicable to the butchers' plight, and the dissenters were much more concerned with due process and privileges or immunities. But if *Slaughter-House* augured for a limited scope for equal protection generally, it suggested great promise for blacks. It "is not difficult," Miller wrote,

> to give a meaning to this clause. The existence of laws in the States where the newly emancipated negroes resided, which discriminated with gross injustice and hardship against them as a class, was the evil to be remedied.

I. FROM *SLAUGHTER-HOUSE* TO *CAROLENE PRODUCTS*

A. Race Relations

In this regard, *Slaughter-House* echoed Railroad Co. v. Brown (1873), which interpreted a congressional act granting a franchise to the Washington and Alexandria Railroad to operate in the District of Columbia. One of the conditions of the franchise was that no person should be excluded because of race. The railroad allowed anyone who could pay to travel, but it ran separate cars for whites and blacks. In this initial test of "separate but equal," the Court was curt: "This is an ingenious attempt to evade a compliance with the obvious meaning of the requirement." Segregation was "discrimination," the justices unanimously held.

A few other early cases picked up on *Slaughter-House*'s promise. Strauder v. Virginia (1880; reprinted below, p. 753) said that the Fourteenth Amendment secured for blacks "exemption from legal discriminations, implying inferiority in civil society. . . ." And Yick Wo v. Hopkins (1886; reprinted below, p. 756) indicated a judicial willingness to look at reality as well as legal rules. There the justices struck down a San Francisco ordinance that supposedly regulated all laundries but had in fact been administered to harass those operated by Chinese. "Though the law itself be fair on its face and impartial in its appearance," the Court said,

> yet, if it is applied and administered with an evil eye and an unequal hand, so as practically to make unjust and illegal discriminations between persons in similar circumstances, material to their rights, the denial of equal justice is still within the prohibition of the Constitution.

But these decisions were islands in a sea of judicial indifference to the rights of persons who were not white males.[1] To resolve the disputed Hayes-Tilden election, the Compromise of 1877 allowed the Republicans to retain the White House in exchange for an end to Reconstruction rule in the South, a promise of new capital to develop the area, and the transfer of responsibility for protecting black civil rights from federal to southern state officials, who, of course, would be white. The eminent historian C. Vann Woodward[2] sees the Civil Rights Cases (1883) as a judicial ratification of that compromise in its denial of federal authority to protect blacks against private discrimination in public accommodations. And it is worth noting that Justice Joseph P. Bradley, who wrote the majority opinion in the Civil Rights Cases, had been the "neutral" member of the special commission that resolved the Hayes-Tilden deadlock. He had cast his vote for Hayes in each contested election.

More indicative of the Court's attitude than *Railroad Co.* and *Yick Wo* were cases like Hall v. DeCuir (1876), which invalidated as burdening interstate commerce a state statute that forbade transportation companies to segregate passengers by race, and Louisville, New Orleans & Texas Rr. v. Mississippi (1890), which, despite the commerce clause and despite *Hall,* sustained a state statute requiring segregation in transportation.[3]

Plessy v. Ferguson (1896) was the landmark ruling that repudiated *Slaughter-House*'s promise by fully validating "separate but equal." By a 7–1 vote the justices upheld a newer Louisiana statute mandating segregation in transportation. The Fourteenth Amendment, the majority wrote, "could not have been intended to abolish distinctions based upon color, or to enforce social, as distinguished from political equality, or a commingling of the two races upon terms unsatisfactory to either." The principal criterion the Court applied to test segregation's validity was its "reasonableness," and that test was easily met:

> In determining the question of reasonableness [the State] is at liberty to act with reference to the established usages, customs and

---

1. See, for instance, the Court's sustaining in Bradwell v. Illinois (1873) a state law that did not allow women to practice law, and in Minor v. Happersett (1875) a state law denying women the right to vote.

2. *The Strange Career of Jim Crow* (2d ed.; New York: Oxford University Press, 1966); *Reunion and Reaction* (Garden City, N.Y.: Doubleday, 1951); *Origins of the New South* (Baton Rouge, La.: Louisiana State University Press, 1951).

3. For an analysis of the cases see Derrick A. Bell, Jr., *Race, Racism and American Law* (2d ed.; Boston: Little, Brown, 1980), chap. 4.

traditions of the people, and with a view to the promotion of their comfort, and the preservation of the public peace and good order.

Just as in the Civil Rights Cases, so in *Plessy,* Justice John Marshall Harlan, I, dissented. Although a former slave holder and sometime opponent of the adoption of both the Thirteenth and Fourteenth amendments—he said he had fought to save the Union, not to lose his slaves—he argued: "Our Constitution is color-blind, and neither knows nor tolerates classes among citizens."

Harlan's prediction in *Plessy* that "the judgment this day rendered will, in time, prove to be quite as pernicious as the decision made by this tribunal in the *Dred Scott* case" was prophetic. *Plessy*'s rationale, soon applied to other areas of social life,[4] legitimized Jim Crow and ensured that the vestiges of slavery would continue to plague Americans through the next century. Only several decades after *Plessy* did the Court begin to show interest in protecting black civil rights, and even then the judicial record hardly demonstrated sensitivity toward people suffering "legal discriminations, implying inferiority in civil society."[5] Notwithstanding the Civil War and the Civil War amendments to the Constitution, blacks for all practical purposes remained second-class citizens. They still "had no rights," as Chief Justice Taney had put it in *Dred Scott* (1857).

In the late 1920s and early 1930s, the justices looked skeptically at the white primary,[6] but in 1935 Grovey v. Townsend held that it was constitutional for a political party, even in a one-party southern state, to restrict voting in primaries to whites, as long as state law did not require such a restriction. (Smith v. Allwright reversed this decision in 1944.)

B. Economic Regulation

Without a doubt, racism colored the way the justices, like most white Americans, viewed the separate and unequal world of blacks. But there was also a general judicial indifference to equal protection. During an age when judges were crusading for "substantive due process" to guard property rights against governmental regulation, equality was simply not a value that the legal system was championing. Justice Holmes was not far from the judicial norm when he sneered in Buck v. Bell (1927; reprinted below, p. 1105) that an appeal to equal protection was "the usual last resort in constitutional arguments."

---

4. For education, see: Cumming v. Board (1899); Berea College v. Kentucky (1908); and Gong Lum v. Rice (1927).

5. McCabe v. Atchison, Topeka & Santa Fe (1914) conceded the right of blacks travelling interstate to accommodations that were in fact equal even though separate, but held the plaintiffs had no standing to sue. Buchanan v. Warley (1917) and its companion cases struck a blow for equality by invalidating state statutes requiring segregated housing. At issue was not only equal protection, but also the right to own and dispose of private property, a right to which the Court from 1890 to 1937 usually gave a preferred position. Guinn v. United States (1915) held unconstitutional a state statute that imposed strict restrictions on the right to vote but granted exceptions to all those whose ancestors had been eligible to vote in 1866, i.e., whites.

6. Nixon v. Herndon (1927); Nixon v. Condon (1932).

The Court was quite content to allow government broad leeway, in economic as well as racial relations, to establish classifications. As in *Plessy,* the rule was that of reasonableness. "If the selection or classification is neither capricious nor arbitrary, and rests upon some reasonable consideration of difference or policy, there is no denial of equal protection of the laws." [7] Lindsley v. Natural Carbonic Gas Co. (1911) spelled out these components in some detail:

1. The equal protection clause . . . does not take from the State the power to classify in the adoption of police laws, but admits of the exercise of a wide scope of discretion . . . and avoids what is done only when it is without any reasonable basis and therefore is purely arbitrary.
2. A classification having some reasonable basis does not offend against that clause merely because it is not made with mathematical nicety or because in practice it results in some inequality.
3. When the classification in such a law is called into question, if any state of facts reasonably can be conceived that would sustain it, the existence of that state of facts at the time the law was enacted must be assumed.
4. One who assails the classification in such a law must carry the burden of showing that it does not rest upon any reasonable basis, but is essentially arbitrary.

C. Caste in America and the Shadow of Nazism

The 1930s brought not only the New Deal but the beginnings of a change in judicial and popular attitudes. As the evils of Nazism and its persecution of Jews became more apparent, it grew increasingly difficult to justify America's own caste society, harshly silhouetted by frequent lynchings (at least 75 between 1930 and 1936) and kangaroo courts. In Scottsboro, Alabama, for instance, seven young blacks had been accused of raping two white women. The evidence that the crimes had actually occurred was flimsy, but the police did not feel it necessary to conduct any sort of investigation beyond taking the complaint of the "victims." The defendants were divided into three groups and each trial was completed in less than a day, a pace made easier by the court's dispensing with such niceties as a right to counsel. The jury, from which blacks had been excluded, did its part, almost instantly finding all defendants guilty and imposing the death penalty.

Twice, in 1932 and 1935, the cases reached the U.S. Supreme Court; twice the justices reversed the convictions, establishing for the first time indigents' right to court-appointed counsel in state cases, though only under limited circumstances,[8] and reaffirming the right to be tried by a jury from which members of one's race had not been systematically excluded.[9] Nevertheless, as in NAACP v. Alabama

---

7. Brown-Forman Co. v. Kentucky (1910).

8. Powell v. Alabama (1932).

9. Norris v. Alabama (1935).

(1958; reprinted above, p. 646), the state drove ahead and reconvicted four of the seven.

In 1936, a case from Mississippi presented the justices with a shocking example of brutality against blacks.[10] There a deputy sheriff, accompanied by friends, arrested three black men for murder. They hanged one from a tree, lowering him periodically to ask if he would confess. When this tactic failed, they tied him to the tree and whipped him. When this tactic also failed, they released this suspect but later rearrested him. After additional hours of torture, the man confessed when promised that if he did so the beatings would stop. The other two accused were also tortured, though somewhat less cruelly, until they, too, agreed to confess.

At the trial, the rope scars were still plainly visible on the throat of the first black defendant, but all three were convicted and sentenced to death after a proceeding that rivaled Scottsboro's in swiftness and was as unencumbered by defense counsel. Mississippi's supreme court found the case to be disgraceful but said the Fifth Amendment's protection against self-incrimination did not bind the states, as, indeed, Twining v. New Jersey (1908) had held. The U.S. Supreme Court reversed without overruling *Twining*, holding, inter alia, that use of torture violated due process and so voided a confession.

These sorts of cases must have brought home to the justices what at some level of consciousness they already knew, that the caste system was unspeakably cruel to blacks, the American Untouchables. Moreover, there was no hope for change through the political processes. Blacks in the South, where more than three-quarters of them then lived, were disenfranchised, and southern senators were able to filibuster to death every serious proposal by northern liberals to enact new civil rights laws. That same legislative influence and the ability to deliver the electoral votes of "the solid South" to the Democratic party's presidential candidate meant that the Department of Justice was not about to enforce existing federal statutes protecting civil rights. Thus there were only two avenues of political change: the courts or violence.[11]

Blacks were not alone in their plight. On the West Coast, orientals were subjected to legal and social discrimination, in the Southwest Mexican-Americans, and Indians wherever they found themselves. In no part of the country were women the equals of men where law and economics were concerned. Anti-Semitism and anti-Catholicism suffused much of American social life, though they were no legal barriers against these minorities. It was, rather, the Jehovah's Witnesses who dramatized the prevalence of religious bigotry. Not only were the Witnesses subjected to legal harassment by being

---

10. Brown v. Mississippi (1936).

11. The Communist party made concerted but unsuccessful efforts to persuade blacks that revolution was the only solution. See Wilson Record, *The Negro and the Communist Party* (Chapel Hill: University of North Carolina Press, 1951). For a reversal of a conviction of a Communist organizer in Georgia, see Herndon v. Lowry (1937), decided a year before *Carolene Products.*

arrested for distributing religious pamphlets without a license to sell—
something no policeman would have dared ask of white Protestants—
but they were also often subjected to physical beatings plus tarrings
and featherings. As a tiny group, the Witnesses had no hope of
wielding influence in the electoral processes, but the courts were open
to them. And in the 1930s a trickle of their cases began to reach the
Supreme Court.[12]

II. *CAROLENE PRODUCTS*

Thus, after 1937 the justices were conducting their search for a
new jurisprudence in a context that boded ill for the ideals of
constitutionalism and democracy. Mean spirited religious and racial
intolerance seemed triumphant, and the Court's ability to do anything
was severely constrained. It had just lost its war against the New
Deal and had halted its efforts to write laissez-faire economics into the
Constitution. This crushing defeat made it tempting to abandon
constitutionalism, presume all legislation constitutional, and let the
people rely on the political checks of democratic processes. On the
other hand, the plight of minorities pointed to the dangers of such a
course. The political processes were often choked and even where
open offered little chance for unpopular groups. For Justice Harlan
Fiske Stone, who travelled frequently around Europe, the similarities
to Nazi Germany must have been painfully striking.

It was to cope with these difficulties that Stone formulated
footnote 4 in *Carolene Products* (1938; reprinted above, p. 482). Its
third paragraph dealt with the problem of equal protection:

> Nor need we inquire whether similar considerations [regarding the
> Court's presuming a statute constitutional] enter into the review of
> statutes directed at particular religious, or national, or racial minori-
> ties: whether prejudices against discrete and insular minorities may
> be a special condition, which tends seriously to curtail the operation
> of those political processes ordinarily to be relied upon to protect
> minorities, and which may call for a correspondingly more searching
> judicial inquiry.

To some extent, Stone was prescribing a new jurisprudence; to
some extent he was also providing a general explanation of what the
justices were beginning to do, even though they themselves—and
even Stone—may have only been vaguely aware of what theories they
were weaving. Very rapidly, some of his prescription became part of
a description. Eight months after *Carolene Products,* the Court
launched the first of what would be many attacks against Jim Crow,
holding unconstitutional Missouri's plan to provide legal education for
blacks by paying their tuition to law schools out of state.[13]

As we have seen, several of the justices whom Roosevelt nominated—Black, Douglas, Murphy, and Rutledge in particular, to a

---

12. For an account of the Witnesses' use of the courts, see David R. Manwaring, *Render unto
Caesar* (Chicago: University of Chicago Press, 1962).

13. Missouri ex rel. Gaines v. Canada (1938).

lesser extent Jackson, and, for a time, even Frankfurter—were or soon became adherents of Stone's message in *Carolene Products.* Much of their work centered around paragraph two and its emphasis on the necessity of open political processes; thus they gave a "preferred position" to the First Amendment. But no less doggedly and with greater harmony they worked first to undermine and then to end the legal life of segregation. Brown v. Board (1954) came as the climax to a long campaign that played out the common law's usage of stare decisis, gradually expanding exceptions to a doctrine— here "separate but equal"—until there was nothing left of it but a shell.[14]

A. The Limited Scope of "Deferential Scrutiny"

In cases challenging economic regulation, the Court continued— and still continues—to follow the rules laid down in *Lindsley* (1911), what has been called "deferential scrutiny." Reasonableness is the test; the Court presumes the existence of the facts to support the legislature's judgment; and the burden of proof rests on the challenger. (See the cases reprinted below, Williamson v. Lee Optical [1955; at p. 763] and New Orleans v. Dukes [1976; at p. 765].)

B. The Development and Expansion of "Strict Scrutiny"

During the period after 1938, however, the Court began to develop a different standard for other kinds of problems involving equal protection. The volatility of American race relations made the justices reluctant to spell out clearly their new jurisprudence, but where classification by race was concerned, they relaxed the presumption of constitutionality. In *Carolene Products* Stone had suggested a "more searching judicial inquiry" (¶ 3) or "more exacting judicial scrutiny" (¶ 2). In Skinner v. Oklahoma (1942), Justice Douglas penned what would eventually become the Court's term of art, "strict scrutiny."

Skinner, however, had no overt racial content. Ironically, it was Hirabayashi v. United States (1943) and Korematsu v. United States (1944), sustaining first a curfew on and then the imprisonment of Japanese-Americans, that prefigured much of the new libertarian doctrine. In *Hirabayashi* Stone said:

> Distinctions between citizens solely because of their ancestry are by their very nature odious to a free people whose institutions are founded upon the doctrine of equality. For that reason, legislative classification or discrimination based on race alone has often been held to be a denial of equal protection.

---

14. See, for example: *Transportation:* Mitchell v. United States (1941); Morgan v. Virginia (1946); Bob-Lo Excursion Co. v. Michigan (1948); Henderson v. United States (1950); *Education:* Sipuel v. Bd. of Regents (1948); Fisher v. Hurst (1948); Sweatt v. Painter (1950); McLaurin v. Bd. of Regents (1950).

Stone cited three cases to support his last sentence, none of which had quite held classification by race was, alone, enough to deny equal protection, but all of which pointed in that direction. Thus the Chief Justice was, as in *Carolene Products,* reshaping constitutional law as he was describing it.

Hugo Black, speaking for the Court in *Korematsu,* penned two more seminal phrases. First, he said "rigid scrutiny"—a variation on "strict scrutiny"—was the standard to be applied to classifications involving racial minorities. Second, he explicitly used a concept to which Stone had alluded in both *Carolene Products* and *Hirabayashi,* "suspect classification":

> [A]ll legal restrictions which curtail the civil rights of a single racial group are immediately suspect. That it not to say that all such restrictions are unconstitutional. It is to say that courts must subject them to more rigid scrutiny.

The School Segregation Cases (1954) removed much of the necessity for diplomatic veiling of the Court's new jurisprudence in equal protection; perhaps those decisions also made it clearer to the justices themselves precisely what they were doing. In any event, over the next few decades the justices developed the notions of strict scrutiny and suspect classification and then melded them with a concept of "fundamental rights" to create a nest of tests to assess the constitutionality of statutes challenged as denying equal protection.

The essence of these tests is that where neither a "suspect classification" nor a "fundamental right" is involved, the Court applies rules of "deferential scrutiny," that is, it asks only for a reasonable relation between the legislation and some valid goal and presumes the existence of facts to support the legislature's judgment. Where, however, either a "suspect classification" or a "fundamental right" is involved, the Court invokes "strict scrutiny."

From time to time the justices have used slightly different phrases to describe this "upper tier-test," but essentially it means that the burden of proof shifts from the challenger to the government to show that: (1) a "compelling" governmental interest is at stake; (2) the connection (or fit) between the challenged governmental action and that compelling governmental interest is very close (on occasion the Court has said the connection must be "necessary"[15]); and (3) government could not secure that compelling interest by a different classification or by a lesser infringement on a fundamental right—by "less drastic means," was the way Shelton v. Tucker (1960) put it.

The Court's use of these very different sets of standards has been called a "two-tiered" approach. But, as we shall see in Chapter 16 (espec. San Antonio v. Rodriguez [1973; reprinted below, p. 858]), there is serious question whether the Court has not in fact used a sliding scale rather than two points. Further complicating analysis, the justices in 1976[16] found a middle tier for reviewing classifications that

---

15. Shapiro v. Thompson (1969; reprinted below, p. 873.)

16. Craig v. Boren (1976; reprinted below, p. 844).

were neither so suspicious as to trigger strict scrutiny nor so harmless as to allow deferential scrutiny.

We have passed over the questions of what makes a classification "suspect," what makes a right "fundamental," and what makes a governmental interest "compelling." Chapter 14 takes up those points, though with no claim to resolving them any more satisfactorily than the justices have. Here we note only that race has become *the* suspect classification. Its use usually carries not a halo of reasonableness but a mark of invidiousness. As Justice Stewart wrote for the Court in 1979:

> Certain classifications . . . in themselves supply a reason to infer antipathy. Race is the paradigm. A racial classification, regardless of the purported motivation, is presumptively invalid and can be upheld only upon extraordinary justification.[17]

Since *Brown,* the Court has sometimes strained mightily for consistency here, as the cases involving affirmative action show. (See espec. Bd. of Regents v. Bakke [1978; reprinted below, p. 804]; and Fullilove v. Klutznick [1980; reprinted below, p. 816].) Morton v. Mancari (1974) validated the preference, mandated by statute, the Bureau of Indian Affairs gives to members of "federally recognized" tribes, holding that this preference was not racial because it was limited to particular Indians. It was designed, the justices said, to further self-government of the tribes and was similar in effect to the requirement that senators be inhabitants of the states from which they are elected. "Here, the preference is reasonably and directly related to a legitimate, nonracially based goal. This is the principal characteristic that generally is absent from proscribed forms of racial discrimination."

III. THE ORGANIZATION OF THE CASES

Section A of this chapter focuses on the background of equal protection, the early promises and then the bitter reality. Section B examines several modern applications of deferential scrutiny, showing how part of the early jurisprudence is still operating. Then Sections C and D take up the development of the notion of suspect classifications, restricted here to race and ethnicity, and leaving for Chapter 16 the expansion of that concept. Finally, Section E addresses affirmative action, which poses one of the most difficult problems not only of public policy but also of constitutional interpretation. Dissenting in the *Bakke* Case, Justice Blackmun put the problem as a dilemma: "In order to get beyond racism, we must first take account of race.

---

17. Personnel Administrator v. Feeney. The matter, however, is not always so simple, as the next paragraph indicates. See also the concur. op. of Black, Harlan, and Stewart in Lee v. Washington (1968), where the Court had unanimously struck down segregation in Alabama's prisons: "[P]rison authorities have the right, acting in good faith and in particularized circumstances, to take into account racial tensions in maintaining security, discipline, and good order in prisons and jails."

. . . And in order to treat some people equally, we must treat them differently."

SELECTED BIBLIOGRAPHY

Bell, Derrick A., Jr. *Race, Racism and American Law* (2d ed.; Boston: Little, Brown, 1980).

Bickel, Alexander M. "The Original Understanding and the Segregation Decision," 69 *Harv.L.Rev.* 1 (1955).

Brest, Paul. "In Defense of the Anti-Discrimination Principle," 90 *Harv.L.Rev.* 1 (1976).

Chang, David. "The Bus Stops Here: Defining the Constitutional Right of Equal Educational Opportunity and an Appropriate Remedial Process," 63 *Bost.U.L.Rev.* 1 (1983).

Cohen, Marshall, Thomas Nagel and Thomas Scanlon, eds. *Equality and Preferential Treatment* (Princeton: Princeton University Press, 1977).

Dworkin, Ronald. *A Matter of Principle* (Cambridge, Mass.: Harvard University Press, 1985), chaps. 14–16.

Ely, John Hart. *Democracy and Distrust* (Cambridge, Mass.: Harvard University Press, 1980), espec. chaps. 4–6.

Fiss, Owen M. "Groups and the Equal Protection Clause," 5 *Phil. & Pub.Affrs.* 107 (1976).

Goldman, Alan H. *Justice and Reverse Discrimination* (Princeton, N.J.: Princeton University Press, 1979).

Graglia, Lino A. *Disaster by Decree: The Supreme Court's Decisions on Race and the Schools* (Ithaca, N.Y.: Cornell University Press, 1976).

Gunther, Gerald, "In Search of Evolving Doctrine on a Changing Court," 86 *Harv.L.Rev.* 1 (1972).

Harris, Robert J. *The Quest for Equality* (Baton Rouge, La.: Louisiana State University Press, 1960).

Kirp, David L., *Just Schools: The Idea of Racial Equality in American Education* (Berkeley, Cal.: University of California Press, 1982).

Kluger, Richard. *Simple Justice: The History of Brown v. Board of Education and Black America's Struggle for Equality* (New York: Knopf, 1976).

Mason, Alpheus Thomas. *Harlan Fiske Stone* (New York: Viking, 1956), espec. chaps. 19–22.

Orfield, Gary. *Must We Bus?* (Washington, D.C.: The Brookings Institution, 1978).

Pennock, J. Roland, and John W. Chapman, eds. *Equality* (New York: Lieber-Alberton, 1967).

Pritchett, C. Herman. *Constitutional Civil Liberties* (Englewood Cliffs, N.J.: Prentice-Hall, 1984), chaps. 10, 12.

Sowell, Thomas. *Markets and Minorities* (New York: Basic Books, 1981).

————. *Ethnic America* (New York: Basic Books, 1981).

Tribe, Laurence H. *American Constitutional Law* (Mineola, N.Y.: Foundation Press, 1978), chap. 17.

————. *Constitutional Choices* (Cambridge, Mass.: Harvard University Press, 1985), chaps. 14–16.

Wilkinson, J. Harvie, III. *From Brown to Bakke* (New York: Oxford University Press, 1979).

Wright, J. Skelly. "Judicial Review and the Equal Protection Clause," 15 *Harv.Civ.Rights-Civ.Libs.L.Rev.* 1 (1980).

I. HISTORICAL BACKGROUND: THE PROMISE AND THE REALITY

"The very fact that colored people are singled out and expressly denied by a statute all right to participate in the administration of the law, as jurors because of their color, though they are citizens, and may be in other respects fully qualified, is practically a brand upon them, affixed by law."

STRAUDER v. WEST VIRGINIA

100 U.S. (10 Otto) 303, 25 L.Ed. 664 (1880).

A West Virginia grand jury indicted Strauder, a black man, for murder; and a petit (trial) jury convicted him of that crime. State law forbade blacks to serve on either kind of jury, and Strauder's counsel unsuccessfully contended at the trial and on appeal within the state judicial system that this exclusion denied his client equal protection of the laws. The U.S. Supreme Court granted a writ of error.

Mr. Justice **STRONG** delivered the opinion of the Court. . . .

. . . [The controlling question] is not whether a colored man . . . has a right to a grand or a petit jury composed in whole or in part of persons of his own race or color; but it is whether . . . all persons of his race or color may be excluded by law, solely because of their race or color, so that by no possibility can any colored man sit upon the jury.

The questions are important, for they demand a construction of the recent amendments of the Constitution. . . . The Fourteenth

Amendment . . . is one of a series of constitutional provisions having a common purpose; namely, securing to a race recently emancipated . . . all the civil rights that the superior race enjoy. The true spirit and meaning of the amendments, as we said in the Slaughter-House Cases [1873], cannot be understood without keeping in view the history of the times when they were adopted, and the general objects they plainly sought to accomplish. . . . [I]t required little knowledge of human nature to anticipate that those who had long been regarded as an inferior and subject race would, when suddenly raised to the rank of citizenship, be looked upon with jelousy and positive dislike, and that State Laws might be enacted or enforced to perpetuate the distinctions that had before existed. Discriminations against them had been habitual. It was well known that in some States laws making such discriminations then existed, and others might well be expected. The colored race, as a race, was abject and ignorant, and in that condition was unfitted to command the respect of those who had superior intelligence. Their training had left them mere children, and as such they needed the protection which a wise government extends to those who are unable to protect themselves. They especially needed protection against unfriendly action in the States where they were resident. It was in view of these considerations the Fourteenth Amendment was framed and adopted. It was designed to assure to the colored race the enjoyment of all the civil rights that under the law are enjoyed by white persons, and to give to that race the protection of the general government, in that enjoyment, whenever it should be denied by the States. It not only gave citizenship and the privileges of citizenship to persons of color, but it denied to any State the power to withhold from them the equal protection of the laws, and authorized Congress to enforce its provisions by appropriate legislation. To quote . . . *Slaughter-House:* "No one can fail to be impressed with the one pervading purpose found in all the amendments, lying at the foundation of each, and without which none of them would have been suggested—. . . the freedom of the slave race, the security and firm establishment of that freedom, and the protection of the newly made freeman and citizen from the oppressions of those who had formerly exercised unlimited dominion over them." . . . "We doubt very much whether any action of a State, not directed by way of discrimination against the negroes, as a class, will ever be held to come within the purview of this provision."

If this is the spirit and meaning of the amendment, whether it means more or not, it is to be construed liberally, to carry out the purposes of its framers. . . . [It declares] that the law in the States shall be the same for the black as for the white; that all persons, whether colored or white, shall stand equal before the laws of the States, and, in regard to the colored race, for whose protection the amendment was primarily designed, that no discrimination shall be made against them by law because of their color[.] The words of the amendment, it is true, are prohibitory, but they contain a necessary implication of a positive immunity, or right, most valuable to the colored race—. . . exemption from legal discriminations, implying inferiority in civil society, lessening the security of their enjoyment of the rights which others enjoy, and discriminations which are steps towards reducing them to the condition of a subject race.

That the West Virginia statute respecting juries . . . is such a discrimination ought not to be doubted. Nor would it be if the persons excluded by it were white men. If in those States where the colored people constitute a majority of the entire population a law should be enacted excluding all white men from jury service . . . no one would be heard to claim that it would not be a denial to white men of the equal protection of the laws. Nor if a law should be passed excluding all naturalized Celtic Irishmen, would there be any doubt of its inconsistency with the spirit of the amendment. The very fact that colored people are singled out and expressly denied by a statute all right to participate in the administration of the law, as jurors, because of their color, though they are citizens, and may be in other respects fully qualified, is practically a brand upon them, affixed by the law; an assertion of their inferiority, and a stimulant to that race prejudice which is an impediment to securing to individuals of the race that equal justice which the law aims to secure to all others.

The right to a trial by jury is guaranteed to every citizen of West Virginia by the Constitution of that State. . . . The very idea of a jury is a body of men composed of the peers or equals of the person whose rights it is selected or summoned to determine; that is, of his neighbors, fellows, associates, persons having the same legal status in society as that which he holds. . . . [P]rejudices often exist against particular classes in the community, which . . . operate in some cases to deny to persons of those classes the full enjoyment of that protection which others enjoy. . . . The framers of the constitutional amendment must have known full well the existence of such prejudice and its likelihood to continue against the manumitted slaves and their race, and that knowledge was doubtless a motive that led to the amendment. By their manumission and citizenship the colored race became entitled to the equal protection of the laws of the States in which they resided; and the apprehension that . . . there might be discrimination against them, was the inducement to bestow upon the national government the power to enforce the provision that no State shall deny to them the equal protection of the laws. . . . It is not easy to comprehend how it can be said that while every white man is entitled to a trial by a jury . . . selected without discrimination against his color, and a negro is not, the latter is equally protected by the law with the former. . . .

We do not say that, within the limits from which it is not excluded by the amendment, a State may not prescribe the qualifications of its jurors, and in so doing make discriminations. It may confine the selection to males, to freeholders, to citizens, to persons within certain ages, or to persons having educational qualifications. We do not believe the Fourteenth Amendment was ever intended to prohibit this.

Looking at its history, it is clear it had no such purpose. Its aim was against discrimination because of race or color. . . . [I]ts design was to protect an emancipated race, and to strike down all possible legal discriminations against those who belong to it. "In giving construction to any of these articles [amendments], it is necessary to keep the main purpose steadily in view." "It is so clearly a provision for that race and that emergency, that a strong case would be necessary for its application to any other." [*Slaughter-House.*] We are not now called upon to affirm or deny that it had other purposes.

The Fourteenth Amendment makes no attempt to enumerate the rights it designed to protect. It speaks in general terms, and those are as comprehensive as possible. Its language is prohibitory; but every prohibition implies the existence of rights and immunities, prominent among which is an immunity from inequality of legal protection, either for life, liberty, or property. Any State action that denies this immunity to a colored man is in conflict with the Constitution. . . .

[*Reversed.*]

Mr. Justice **FIELD.**

I dissent . . . and Mr. Justice **CLIFFORD** concurs with me.

————

"Though the law itself be fair on its face and impartial in appearance, yet, if it is applied and administered by public authority with an evil eye and an unequal hand, so as practically to make unjust and illegal discriminations between persons in similar circumstances, material to their rights, the denial of equal justice is still within the prohibition of the Constitution."

YICK WO v. HOPKINS
118 U.S. 356, 6 S.Ct. 1064, 30 L.Ed. 220 (1886).

An ordinance of San Francisco County required special permission to operate a laundry in a building constructed of materials other than brick or stone. Of the approximately 320 laundries in the city, only ten were not made of wood. With only one exception, the county granted all applications for special permission filed by Caucasians, but denied all 200 submitted by Chinese. Yick Wo and 150 other Chinese aliens continued to operate their laundries and were convicted under the ordinance. The state supreme court affirmed the convictions, and Yick Wo and another Chinese obtained a writ of error from the U.S. Supreme Court.

Mr. Justice **MATTHEWS** delivered the opinion of the Court. . . .

The rights of the petitioners . . . are not less because they are aliens and subjects of the Emperor of China. . . .

The Fourteenth Amendment to the Constitution is not confined to the protection of citizens. It says: "Nor shall any State deprive any person of life, liberty, or property without due process of law; nor deny to any person within its jurisdiction the equal protection of the laws." These provisions are universal in their application, to all persons within the territorial jurisdiction, without regard to any differences of race, of color, or of nationality; and the equal protection of the laws is a pledge of the protection of equal laws. . . . [Petitioners contend that the ordinances] are void on their face, as being within the prohibitions of the Fourteenth Amendment; and, in the alternative, if not so, that they are void by reason of their administration, operating unequally, so as to punish in the present petitioners what is permitted to others as lawful, without any distinction of circumstances—an unjust and illegal discrimination, it is claimed, which, though not made expressly by the ordinances is made possible by them.

When we consider the nature and the theory of our institutions of government, the principles upon which they are supposed to rest, and review the history of their development, we are constrained to conclude that they do not mean to leave room for the play and action of purely personal and arbitrary power. Sovereignty itself is, of course, not subject to law, for it is the author and source of law; but in our system, while sovereign powers are delegated to the agencies of government, sovereignty itself remains with the people, by whom and for whom all government exists and acts. And the law is the definition and limitation of power. It is, indeed, quite true, that there must always be lodged somewhere, and in some person or body, the authority of final decision; and in many cases of mere administration the responsibility is purely political, no appeal lying except to the ultimate tribunal of the public judgment, exercised either in the pressure of opinion or by means of the suffrage. But the fundamental rights to life, liberty, and the pursuit of happiness . . . are secured by those maxims of constitutional law which are the monuments showing the victorious progress of the race in securing to men the blessings of civilization under the reign of just and equal laws, so that, in the famous language of the Massachusetts Bill of Rights, the government of the commonwealth "may be a government of laws and not of men." For, the very idea that one man may be compelled to hold his life, or the means of living, or any material right essential to the enjoyment of life, at the mere will of another, seems to be intolerable in any country where freedom prevails, as being the essence of slavery itself.

There are many illustrations that might be given of this truth, which would make manifest that it was self-evident in the light of our system of jurisprudence. The case of the political franchise of voting is one. Though not regarded strictly as a natural right, but as a privilege merely conceded by society according to its will, under certain conditions, nevertheless it is regarded as a fundamental political right, because preservative of all rights. . . .

. . . In the present cases we are not obliged to reason from the probable to the actual. . . . For the cases present the ordinances in actual operation. . . . Though the law itself be fair on its face and impartial in appearance, yet, if it is applied and administered by public authority with an evil eye and an unequal hand, so as practically to make unjust and illegal discriminations between persons in similar circumstances, material to their rights, the denial of equal justice is still within the prohibition of the Constitution. . . .

The present cases, as shown by the facts disclosed in the record, are within this class. It appears that both petitioners have complied with every requisite, deemed by the law or by the public officers charged with its administration, necessary for the protection of neighboring property from fire, or as a precaution against injury to the public health. No reason whatever, except the will of the supervisors, is assigned why they should not be permitted to carry on, in the accustomed manner, their harmless and useful occupation, on which they depend for a livelihood. And while this consent of the supervisors is withheld from them and from two hundred others who have also petitioned, all of whom happen to be Chinese subjects, eighty others, not Chinese subjects, are permitted to carry on the same business under similar conditions. The fact of this discrimination is admitted. No reason for it is shown, and the conclusion cannot be resisted, that no reason for it exists except hostility to the race and nationality to which the petitioners belong, and which in the eye of the law is not justified. The discrimination is, therefore, illegal, and the public administration which enforces it is a denial of the equal protection of the laws and a violation of the Fourteenth Amendment of the Constitution. The imprisonment of the petitioners is, therefore, illegal, and they must be discharged.

[*Reversed.*]

"Laws permitting, and even requiring, [racial] separation in places where they are liable to be brought into contact do not necessarily imply the inferiority of either race to the other."

PLESSY v. FERGUSON

163 U.S. 537, 16 S.Ct. 1138, 41 L.Ed. 256 (1896).

In 1890 the Louisiana legislature enacted a law requiring railroads to provide "equal but separate" accommodations for "white" and "colored" passengers. Homer Plessy, who was seven-eighths Caucasian and one-eighth black, was arrested and convicted for refusing to comply with a conductor's order to sit in a coach assigned to colored people. The state supreme court rejected Plessy's claims that the law violated the Thirteenth and Fourteenth amendments, but he obtained a writ of error from the U.S. Supreme Court.

Mr. Justice **BROWN** delivered the opinion of the Court. . . .

1. That [the act] does not conflict with the Thirteenth Amendment, which abolished slavery and involuntary servitude, except as a punishment for crime, is too clear for argument. Slavery implies involuntary servitude—a state of bondage; the ownership of mankind as a chattel, or at least the control of the labor and services of one man for the benefit of another, and the absence of a legal right to the disposal of his own person, property and services. . . .

A statute which implies merely a legal distinction between the white and colored races—a distinction which is founded in the color of the two races, and which must always exist so long as white men are distinguished from the other race by color—has no tendency to destroy the legal equality of the two races, or reestablish a state of involuntary servitude. Indeed, we do not understand that the Thirteenth Amendment is strenuously relied upon by the plaintiff in error in this connection.

2. . . . The object of the [Fourteenth] Amendment was undoubtedly to enforce the absolute equality of the two races before the law, but in the nature of things it could not have been intended to abolish distinctions based upon color, or to enforce social, as distinguished from political equality, or a commingling of the two races upon terms unsatisfactory to either. Laws permitting, and even requiring, their separation in places where they are liable to be brought into contact do not necessarily imply the inferiority of either race to the other and have been generally, if not universally, recognized as within the competency of the state legislatures in the exercise of their police power. The most common instance of this is connected with the establishment of separate schools for white and colored children, which has been held to be a valid exercise of the legislative power even by courts of States where the political rights of the colored race have been longest and most earnestly enforced.

One of the earliest of these cases is that of Roberts v. Boston [1849], in which the Supreme Judicial Court of Massachusetts held that the general school committee of Boston had power to make provision for the instruction of colored children in separate schools established exclusively for them, and to prohibit their attendance upon the other schools. "The great principle," said Chief Justice Shaw. . . .

> is that by the constitution and laws of Massachusetts, all persons without distinction of age, sex, birth or color, origin or condition, are equal before the law. . . . But, when this great principle comes to be applied to the actual and various conditions of persons in society, it will not warrant the assertion, that men and women are legally clothed with the same civil and political powers, and that children and adults are legally to have the same functions and be subject to the same treatment; but only that the rights of all, as they are settled and regulated by law, are equally entitled to the paternal consideration and protections of the law for their maintenance and security.

It was held that the powers of the committee extended to the establish-ment of separate schools for children of different ages, sexes, and colors.
. . . Similar laws have been enacted by Congress under its general power of legislation over the District of Columbia, as well as by the legislatures of many of the States, and have been generally, if not uniformly, sustained by the courts.

Laws forbidding the intermarriage of the two races may be said in a technical sense to interfere with the freedom of contract, and yet have been universally recognized as within the police power of the State.

The distinction between laws interfering with the political equality of the negro and those requiring the separation of the two races in schools, theatres and railway carriages has been frequently drawn by this court.   Strauder v. West Virginia [1880]. . . .

. . . [W]e think the enforced separation of the races, as applied to the internal commerce of the State, neither abridges the privileges or immunities of the colored man, deprives him of his property without due process of law, nor denies him the equal protection of the laws, within the meaning of the Fourteenth Amendment. . . .

It is claimed by the plaintiff in error that, in any mixed communi-ty, the reputation of belonging to the dominant race, in this instance the white race, is *property,* in the same sense that a right of action, or of inheritance, is property. Conceding this to be so, for the purposes of this case, we are unable to see how this statute deprives him of, or in any way affects his right to, such property. If he be a white man and assigned to a colored coach, he may have his action for damages against the company for being deprived of his so called property. Upon the other hand, if he be a colored man and be so assigned, he has been deprived of no property, since he is not lawfully entitled to the reputa-tion of being a white man.

. . . [I]t is also suggested . . . that the same argument that will justify the state legislature in requiring railways to provide separate accommodations for the two races will also authorize them to require separate cars to be provided for people whose hair is of a certain color, or who are aliens, or who belong to certain nationalities, or to enact laws requiring colored people to walk upon one side of the street, and white people upon the other, or requiring white men's houses to be painted white, and colored men's black, or their vehicles or business signs to be of different colors, upon the theory that one side of the street is as good as the other, or that a house or vehicle of one color is as good as one of another color. The reply to all this is that every exercise of the police power must be reasonable, and extend only to such laws as are enacted in good faith for the promotion for the public good, and not for the annoyance or oppression of a particular class. Yick Wo v. Hopkins [1886]. . . .

So far, then, as a conflict with the Fourteenth Amendment is concerned, the case reduces itself to the question whether the statute of Louisiana is a reasonable regulation, and with respect to this there must necessarily be a large discretion on the part of the legislature. In determining the question of reasonableness it is at liberty to act with reference to the established usages, customs and traditions of the people, and with a view to the promotion of their comfort, and the preservation of the public peace and good order. Gauged by this standard, we cannot say that a law which authorizes or even requires the separation of the two races in public conveyances is unreasonable, or more obnoxious to the Fourteenth Amendment than the acts of Congress requiring separate schools for colored children in the District of Columbia, the constitutionality of which does not seem to have been questioned, or the corresponding acts of state legislatures.

We consider the underlying fallacy of the plaintiff's argument to consist in the assumption that the enforced separation of the two races stamps the colored race with a badge of inferiority. If this be so, it is not by reason of anything found in the act, but solely because the colored race chooses to put that construction upon it. The argument necessarily assumes that if, as has been more than once the case, and is not unlikely to be so again, the colored race should become the dominant power in the state legislature, and should enact a law in precisely similar terms, it would thereby relegate the white race to an inferior position. We imagine that the white race, at least, would not acquiesce in this assumption. The argument also assumes that social prejudices may be overcome by legislation, and that equal rights cannot be secured to the negro except by an enforced commingling of the two races. We cannot accept this proposition. If the two races are to meet upon terms of social equality, it must be the result of natural affinities, a mutual appreciation of each other's merits and a voluntary consent of individuals. . . . Legislation is powerless to eradicate racial instincts or to abolish distinctions based upon physical differences, and the attempt to do so can only result in accentuating the difficulties of the present situation. If the civil and political rights of both races be equal one cannot be inferior to the other civilly or politically. If one race be inferior to the other socially, the Constitution of the United States cannot put them upon the same plane. . . .

Affirmed.

Mr. Justice **HARLAN** dissenting. . . .

The white race deems itself to be the dominant race in this country. And so it is, in prestige, in achievements, in education, in wealth and in power. So, I doubt not, it will continue to be for all time, if it remains true to its great heritage and holds fast to the principles of constitutional liberty. But in view of the Constitution, in the eye of the law, there is in this country no superior, dominant, ruling class of citizens. There is no caste here. Our Constitution is color-blind, and neither knows nor tolerates classes among citizens. In respect of civil rights, all citizens are equal before the law. The humblest is the peer of the most powerful. The law regards man as man, and takes no account of his surroundings or of his color when his civil rights as guaranteed by the supreme law of the land are involved. It is, therefore, to be regretted that this high tribunal, the final expositor of the fundamental law of the land, has reached the conclusion that it is competent for a State to regulate the enjoyment by citizens of their civil rights solely upon the basis of race.

In my opinion, the judgment this day rendered will, in time, prove to be quite as pernicious as the decision made by this tribunal in the *Dred Scott* case [1857]. . . . [It] will not only stimulate aggressions, more or less brutal and irritating, upon the admitted rights of colored citizens, but will encourage the belief that it is possible, by means of state enactments, to defeat the beneficent purposes which the people of the United States had in view when they adopted the recent amendments of the Constitution. . . . The destinies of the two races, in this country, are indissolubly linked together, and the interests of both require that the common government of all shall not permit the seeds of race hate to be planted under the sanction of law. What can more certainly arouse race hate, what more certainly create and perpetuate a feeling of distrust between these races, than state enactments, which, in fact, proceed on the ground that colored citizens are so inferior and degraded that they cannot be allowed to sit in public coaches occupied by white citizens? That, as all will admit, is the real meaning of such legislation as was enacted in Louisiana.

The sure guarantee of the peace and security of each race is the clear, distinct, unconditional recognition by our governments, National and State, of every right that inheres in civil freedom, and of the equality before the law of all citizens of the United States without regard to race. State enactments regulating the enjoyment of civil rights, upon the basis of race, and cunningly devised to defeat legitimate results of the war, under the pretence of recognizing equality of rights, can have no other result than to render permanent peace impossible, and to keep alive a conflict of races, the continuance of which must do harm to all concerned. This question is not met by the suggestion that social equality cannot exist between the white and black races in this country . . . ; for social equality no more exists between two races when travelling in a passenger coach or a public highway than when members of the same races sit by each other in a street car or in the jury box, or stand or sit with each other in a political assembly, or when they use in common the streets of a city or town. . . .

The arbitrary separation of citizens, on the basis of race, while they are on a public highway, is a badge of servitude wholly inconsistent with the civil freedom and the equality before the law established by the Constitution. It cannot be justified upon any legal grounds.

. . . We boast of the freedom enjoyed by our people above all other peoples. But it is difficult to reconcile that boast with a state of the law which, practically, puts the brand of servitude and degradation upon a large class of our fellow-citizens, our equals before the law. The thin disguise of "equal" accommodations for passengers in railroad coaches will not mislead any one, nor atone for the wrong this day done. . . .

I am of opinion that the statute of Louisiana is inconsistent with the personal liberty of citizens, white and black, in that State, and hostile to both the spirit and letter of the Constitution of the United States. If laws of like character should be enacted in the several States of the Union, the effect would be in the highest degree mischievous. Slavery, as an institution tolerated by law would, it is true, have disappeared from our country, but there would remain a power in the States, by sinister legislation, to interfere with the full enjoyment of the blessings of freedom; to regulate civil rights, common to all citizens, upon the basis of race; and to place in a condition of legal inferiority a large body of American citizens, now constituting a part of the political community called the People of the United States, for whom, and by whom through representatives, our government is administered. Such a system is inconsistent with the guarantee given by the Constitution to each State of a republican form of government, and may be stricken down by Congressional action, or by the courts in the discharge of their solemn duty to maintain the supreme law of the land, anything in the constitution or laws of any State to the contrary notwithstanding. . . .

Mr. Justice **BREWER** did not hear the argument or participate in the decision of this case.

II. DEFERENTIAL SCRUTINY

"[R]eform may take one step at a time, addressing itself to the phase of the problem which seems most acute to the legislative mind."

WILLIAMSON v. LEE OPTICAL CO.
348 U.S. 483, 75 S.Ct. 461, 99 L.Ed. 563 (1955).

Oklahoma's legislature enacted a complex statute regulating visual care. Its effect was to reduce drastically the scope of optician's lawful activities and correspondingly to increase those phases of visual care that could be performed only by ophthalmologists or optometrists. Lee Optical Co. sued in a federal district court, claiming that, by taking away their business, the statute deprived them of their property without due process and denied them equal protection of the laws. The district court declared the statute unconstitutional, and Oklahoma appealed to the Supreme Court.

Mr. Justice **DOUGLAS** delivered the opinion of the Court. . . .

. . . First, [the District Court] held invalid under the Due Process Clause of the Fourteenth Amendment the portions of § 2 which make it unlawful for any person not a licensed optometrist or ophthalmologist to fit lenses to a face or to duplicate or replace into frames lenses or

other optical appliances, except upon written prescriptive authority of
an Oklahoma licensed ophthalmologist or optometrist.

An ophthalmologist is a duly licensed physician who specializes in
the care of the eyes. An optometrist examines eyes for refractive error,
recognizes (but does not treat) diseases of the eye, and fills prescriptions
for eyeglasses. The optician is an artisan qualified to grind lenses, fill
prescriptions, and fit frames.

The effect of § 2 is to forbid the optician from fitting or duplicating
lenses without a prescription from an ophthalmologist or optometrist.
In practical effect, it means that no optician can fit old glasses into new
frames or supply a lens, whether it be a new lens or one to duplicate a
lost or broken lens, without a prescription. The District Court conceded that it was in the competence of the police power of a State to
regulate the examination of the eyes. But it rebelled at the notion that
a State could require a prescription from an optometrist or ophthalmologist "to take old lenses and place them in new frames and then fit the
completed spectacles to the *face* of the eyeglass wearer." . . . The
Court found that through mechanical devices and ordinary skills the
optician could take a broken lens or a fragment thereof, measure its
power, and reduce it to prescriptive terms. The court held that
"Although on this precise issue of duplication, the legislature in the
instant regulation was dealing with a matter of public interest, the
particular means chosen are neither reasonably necessary nor reasonably related to the end sought to be achieved." It was, accordingly, the
opinion of the court that this provision of the law violated the Due
Process Clause by arbitrarily interfering with the optician's right to do
business. . . .

The Oklahoma law may exact a needless, wasteful requirement in
many cases. But it is for the legislature, not the courts, to balance the
advantages and disadvantages of the new requirement. It appears that
in many cases the optician can easily supply the new frames or new
lenses without reference to the old written prescription. It also appears that many written prescriptions contain no directive data in
regard to fitting spectacles to the face. But in some cases the directions
contained in the prescription are essential, if the glasses are to be fitted
so as to correct the particular defects of vision or alleviate the eye
condition. The legislature might have concluded that the frequency of
occasions when a prescription is necessary was sufficient to justify this
regulation of the fitting of eyeglasses. Likewise, when it is necessary to
duplicate a lense, a written prescription may or may not be necessary.
But the legislature might have concluded that one was needed often
enough to require one in every case. Or the legislature may have
concluded that eye examinations were so critical, not only for correction of vision but also for detection of latent ailments or diseases, that
every change in frames and every duplication of a lens should be
accompanied by a prescription from a medical expert. To be sure, the
present law does not require a new examination of the eyes every time
the frames are changed or the lenses duplicated. For if the old

prescription is on file with the optician, he can go ahead and make the new fitting or duplicate the lenses. But the law need not be in every respect logically consistent with its aims to be constitutional. It is enough that there is an evil at hand for correction, and that it might be thought that the particular legislative measure was a rational way to correct it.

The day is gone when this Court uses the Due Process Clause of the Fourteenth Amendment to strike down state laws, regulatory of business and industrial conditions, because they may be unwise, improvident, or out of harmony with a particular school of thought. See West Coast Hotel Co. v. Parrish [1937].

Secondly, the District Court held that it violated the Equal Protection Clause of the Fourteenth Amendment to subject opticians to this regulatory system and to exempt, as § 3 of the Act does, all sellers of ready-to-wear glasses. The problem of legislative classification is a perennial one, admitting of no doctrinaire definition. Evils in the same field may be of different dimensions and proportions, requiring different remedies. Or so the legislature may think. Or the reform may take one step at a time, addressing itself to the phase of the problem which seems most acute to the legislative mind. The legislature may select one phase of one field and apply a remedy there, neglecting the others. The prohibition of the Equal Protection Clause goes no further than the invidious discrimination. We cannot say that that point has been reached here. For all this record shows, the ready-to-wear branch of this business may not loom large in Oklahoma or may present problems of regulation distinct from the other branch. . . .

[Reversed.]

Mr. Justice **HARLAN** took no part in the consideration or decision of these cases.

―――――

"[I]n the local economic sphere, it is only the invidious discrimination, the wholly arbitrary act, which cannot stand consistently with the Fourteenth Amendment."

NEW ORLEANS v. DUKES
472 U.S. 297, 96 S.Ct. 2513, 49 L.Ed.2d 511 (1976).

In 1972 New Orleans amended its ordinances to forbid "pushcart vendors" within the old French Quarter of the city, the Vieux Carré. The amendment, however, contained a "grandfather clause": Any pushcart peddler who had been in business for eight or more years could continue to operate in the Vieux Carré. Nancy Dukes, who had operated a pushcart there for only two years, sued in a federal district court, claiming the amendment denied her equal protection. She lost, but the Court of Appeals for the Fifth Circuit reversed. New Orleans then appealed to the U.S. Supreme Court.

PER CURIAM. . . .

II

The record makes abundantly clear that the amended ordinance, including the "grandfather provision," is solely an economic regulation aimed at enhancing the vital role of the French Quarter's tourist-oriented charm in the economy of New Orleans.

When local economic regulation is challenged solely as violating the Equal Protection Clause, this Court consistently defers to legislative determinations as to the desirability of particular statutory discriminations. Unless a classification trammels fundamental personal rights or is drawn upon inherently suspect distinctions such as race, religion, or alienage, our decisions presume the constitutionality of the statutory discriminations and require only that the classification challenged be rationally related to a legitimate state interest. States are accorded wide latitude in the regulation of their local economies under their police powers, and rational distinctions may be made with substantially less than mathematical exactitude. . . . [I]n the local economic sphere, it is only the invidious discrimination, the wholly arbitrary act, which cannot stand consistently with the Fourteenth Amendment. See, e.g., Ferguson v. Skrupa (1963).

The Court of Appeals held in this case, however, that the "grandfather provision" failed even the rationality test. We disagree. The city's classification rationally furthers the purpose which the Court of Appeals recognized the city had identified as its objective in enacting the provision, that is, as a means "to preserve the appearance and custom valued by the Quarter's residents and attractive to tourists." The legitimacy of that objective is obvious. The City Council plainly could further that objective by making the reasoned judgment that street peddlers and hawkers tend to interfere with the charm and beauty of a historic area and disturb tourists and disrupt their enjoyment of that charm and beauty, and that such vendors in the Vieux Carré, the heart of the city's tourist industry, might thus have a deleterious effect on the economy of the city. They therefore determined that to ensure the economic vitality of that area, such businesses should be substantially curtailed in the Vieux Carré, if not totally banned.

It is suggested that the "grandfather provision," allowing the continued operation of some vendors was a totally arbitrary and irrational method of achieving the city's purpose. But rather than proceeding by the immediate and absolute abolition of all pushcart food vendors, the city could rationally choose initially to eliminate vendors of more recent vintage. This gradual approach to the problem is not constitutionally impermissible. The governing constitutional principle was stated in Katzenbach v. Morgan [1966]:

> [W]e are guided by the familiar principles that a "statute is not invalid under the Constitution because it might have gone farther than it did," Roschen v. Ward [1929], that a legislature need not "strike at all evils at the same time," Semler v. Dental Examiners [1935], and that "reform may take one step at a time, addressing itself to the phase of

the problem which seems most acute to the legislative mind," Williamson v. Lee Optical Co. [1955].

The city could reasonably decide that newer businesses were less likely
to have built up substantial reliance interests in continued operation in
the Vieux Carré and that the two vendors who qualified under the
"grandfather clause"—both of whom had operated in the area for over
20 years rather than only eight—had themselves become part of the
distinctive character and charm that distinguishes the Vieux Carré.
We cannot say that these judgments so lack rationality that they
constitute a constitutionally impermissible denial of equal protection.

Nevertheless, relying on Morey v. Doud (1957), as its "chief guide,"
the Court of Appeals held that . . . the "grandfather clause" . . .
could not stand because "the hypothesis that a present eight year
veteran of the pushcart hot dog market in the Vieux Carré will
continue to operate in a manner more consistent with the traditions of
the Quarter than would any other operator is without foundation."
. . . Morey was the only case in the last half century to invalidate a
wholly economic regulation solely on equal protection grounds. Morey
is, as appellee and the Court of Appeals properly recognized, essentially
indistinguishable from this case, but the decision so far departs from
proper equal protection analysis in cases of exclusively economic regulation that it should be, and it is, overruled.

[Reversed.]

Mr. Justice **MARSHALL** concurs in the judgment.

Mr. Justice **STEVENS** took no part in the consideration or decision of
this case.

Editors' Notes

(1) Perhaps one of the problems with the Court's use of terms such as
"rationality" or "rational basis test" is that the justices use "rational" in a
loose, common-sensical way, not in the more technical sense that social
scientists would employ that word. See, for example, Sidney Verba, "Assumptions of Rationality and Non-Rationality in Models of the International System,"
14 *World Pols.* 93 (1961). For analyses of the Court's use of rationality, see:
Scott Bice, "Rationality Analysis in Constitutional Law," 65 *Minn.L.Rev.* 1
(1980); Hans A. Linde, "Due Process of Lawmaking," 55 *Neb.L.Rev.* 197
(1976); and Frank I. Michelman, "Political Markets and Community Self-
Determination," 53 *Ind.L.J.* 145 (1978).

(2) **Query:** Is there any way the state can lose if the Court applies the
sort of deferential scrutiny it did in these cases? (See the discussion of
Lindsley v. Natural Carbonic Gas Co. [1911] in the Introductory Essay to this
Chapter.) What happens then to the promise of equal protection of the laws?
Does it vanish or does deferential judicial scrutiny merely turn from the
question of HOW to interpret to WHO interprets, with the Court's offering the

answer that this aspect of constitutional interpretation falls almost completely under the jurisdiction of legislators and administrators?

III. THE BEGINNING OF SUSPECT CLASSIFICATIONS: RACE AND ETHNICITY

"Separate educational facilities are inherently unequal."

BROWN v. BOARD OF EDUCATION OF TOPEKA, I
347 U.S. 483, 74 S.Ct. 686, 98 L.Ed. 873 (1954).

From its founding in 1909, the National Association for the Advancement of Colored People fought to bring a measure of racial justice to the United States and, more specifically, to overturn Plessy v. Ferguson (1896). The group had only mixed success, but in 1938 its operations became more effective when a young black lawyer named Thurgood Marshall became director of the NAACP's Legal Defense and Educational Fund. He converted what had been a series of scattered skirmishes into a centrally directed campaign that carefully selected plaintiffs and targets for law suits and coordinated legal arguments and tactics with sympathetic organizations like the American Civil Liberties Union.

Over the next dozen years, Marshall won every case he got before the U.S. Supreme Court as he pursued a strategy of gradually undermining the constitutional bases of racial segregation. In 1950 Sweatt v. Painter signalled that the climax of the judicial phase of the campaign was near. There the Court held that Texas's creation of a separate law school for blacks did not accord equal protection. The state could provide tangible, physical facilities that were separate, but it could not provide equality in such intangibles as prestige and alumni. If the justices were serious about the importance of intangibles, then all public school segregation was doomed, for no one pretended that black schools were equal to white on that score, and few pretended that they were often physically equal either. Many southern states began crash programs, allocating dozens of millions of dollars to improve the quality of black schools, but the move came too late. In 1951, the NAACP, in the name of black children, sponsored litigation in Kansas, Delaware, South Carolina, Virginia, and the District of Columbia directly challenging the concept of "separate but equal."

The supreme court of Delaware ordered black children admitted to all-white schools but intimated that they might be resegregated when the state completed its program to equalize physical facilities. In the other cases, federal courts reaffirmed Plessy, and the NAACP appealed to the Supreme Court.

When the cases were first heard during the 1952 term, the justices divided 5–4 and concluded that it would invite disaster to decide such a crucial and volatile issue when the Court was so closely divided. They set the cases down for reargument during the 1953 term. Shortly before the new term began, Chief Justice Fred M. Vinson died and Eisenhower gave a recess appointment to Earl Warren to become the new chief. Under Warren's smooth diplomacy, the Court eventually reached a unanimous decision. The last potential dissenter, Stanley Reed, gave in at the end, saying that if the decision were to be effective it would have to be unanimous, and that he loved the Court more than he treasured his personal views.

Mr. Chief Justice **WARREN** delivered the opinion of the Court. . . .

The plaintiffs contend that segregated public schools are not "equal" and cannot be made "equal," and that hence they are deprived of the equal protection of the laws. Because of the obvious importance of the question presented, the Court took jurisdiction. Argument was heard in the 1952 Term, and reargument was heard this Term on certain questions propounded by the Court.

Reargument was largely devoted to the circumstances surrounding the adoption of the Fourteenth Amendment in 1868. It covered exhaustively consideration of the Amendment in Congress, ratification by the states, then existing practices in racial segregation, and the views of proponents and opponents of the Amendment. This discussion and our own investigation convince us that, although these sources cast some light, it is not enough to resolve the problem with which we are faced. At best, they are inconclusive. The most avid proponents of the post-War Amendments undoubtedly intended them to remove all legal distinctions among "all persons born or naturalized in the United States." Their opponents, just as certainly, were antagonistic to both the letter and the spirit of the Amendments and wished them to have the most limited effect. What others in Congress and the state legislatures had in mind cannot be determined with any degree of certainty.

An additional reason for the inconclusive nature of the Amendment's history, with respect to segregated schools, is the status of public education at that time. In the South, the movement toward free common schools, supported by general taxation, had not yet taken hold. Education of white children was largely in the hands of private groups. Education of Negroes was almost nonexistent, and practically all of the race were illiterate. In fact, any education of Negroes was forbidden by law in some states. Today, in contrast, many Negroes have achieved outstanding success in the arts and sciences as well as in the business and professional world. It is true that public school education at the time of the Amendment had advanced further in the North, but the effect of the Amendment on Northern States was generally ignored in the congressional debates. Even in the North, the conditions of public education did not approximate those existing today. The curriculum was usually rudimentary; ungraded schools were common in rural areas; the school term was but three months a year in many states; and compulsory school attendance was virtually unknown. As a consequence, it is not surprising that there should be so little in the history of the Fourteenth Amendment relating to its intended effect on public education.

In the first cases in this Court construing the Fourteenth Amendment, decided shortly after its adoption, the Court interpreted it as proscribing all state-imposed discriminations against the Negro race. The doctrine of "separate but equal" did not make its appearance in this Court until 1896 in the case of Plessy v. Ferguson, involving not education but transportation. American courts have since labored with the doctrine for over half a century. In this Court, there have been six cases involving the "separate but equal" doctrine in the field of public education. In Cumming v. County Board of Education [1899] and Gong Lum v. Rice [1927], the validity of the doctrine itself was not challenged. In more recent cases, all on the graduate school level, inequality was found in that specific benefits enjoyed by white students were denied to Negro students of the same educational qualifications. Missouri ex rel. Gaines v. Canada [1938]; Sipuel v. University of Oklahoma [1948]; Sweatt v. Painter [1950]; McLaurin v. Oklahoma State Regents [1950]. In none of these cases was it necessary to reexamine the doctrine to grant relief to the Negro plaintiff. And in *Sweatt*, the Court expressly reserved decision on the question whether *Plessy* should be held inapplicable to public education.

In the instant cases, that question is directly presented. Here, unlike *Sweatt*, there are findings below that the Negro and white schools involved have been equalized, or are being equalized, with respect to buildings, curricula, qualifications and salaries of teachers, and other "tangible" factors. Our decision, therefore, cannot turn on merely a comparison of these tangible factors in the Negro and white schools involved in each of the cases. We must look instead to the effect of segregation itself on public education.

In approaching this problem, we cannot turn the clock back to 1868 when the Amendment was adopted, or even to 1896 when *Plessy* was written. We must consider public education in the light of its full development and its present place in American life throughout the Nation. Only in this way can it be determined if segregation in public schools deprives these plaintiffs of the equal protection of the laws.

Today, education is perhaps the most important function of state and local governments. Compulsory school attendance laws and the great expenditures for education both demonstrate our recognition of the importance of education to our democratic society. It is required in the performance of our most basic public responsibilities, even service in the armed forces. It is the very foundation of good citizenship. Today it is a principal instrument in awakening the child to cultural values, in preparing him for later professional training, and in helping him to adjust normally to his environment. In these days, it is doubtful that any child may reasonably be expected to succeed in life if he is denied the opportunity of an education. Such an opportunity, where the state has undertaken to provide it, is a right which must be made available to all on equal terms.

We come then to the question presented: Does segregation of children in public schools solely on the basis of race, even though the physical facilities and other "tangible" factors may be equal, deprive the children of the minority group of equal educational opportunities? We believe that it does.

In *Sweatt*, in finding that a segregated law school for Negroes could not provide them equal educational opportunities, this Court relied in large part on "those qualities which are incapable of objective measurement but which make for greatness in a law school." In *McLaurin*, the

Court, in requiring that a Negro admitted to a white graduate school be treated like all other students, again resorted to intangible considerations: ". . . his ability to study, to engage in discussions and exchange views with other students, and, in general, to learn his profession." Such considerations apply with added force to children in grade and high schools. To separate them from others of similar age and qualifications solely because of their race generates a feeling of inferiority as to their status in the community that may affect their hearts and minds in a way unlikely ever to be undone. The effect of this separation on their educational opportunities was well stated by a finding in the Kansas case by a court which nevertheless felt compelled to rule against the Negro plaintiffs:

> Segregation of white and colored children in public schools has a detrimental effect upon the colored children. The impact is greater when it has the sanction of the law; for the policy of separating the races is usually interpreted as denoting the inferiority of the negro group. A sense of inferiority affects the motivation of a child to learn. Segregation with the sanction of law, therefore, has a tendency to [retard] the educational and mental development of Negro children and to deprive them of some of the benefits they would receive in a racial[ly] integrated school system.

Whatever may have been the extent of psychological knowledge at the time of *Plessy*, this finding is amply supported by modern authority.[1] Any language in *Plessy* contrary to this finding is rejected.

We conclude that in the field of public education the doctrine of "separate but equal" has no place. Separate educational facilities are inherently unequal. Therefore, we hold that the plaintiffs and others similarly situated for whom the actions have been brought are, by reason of the segregation complained of, deprived of the equal protection of the laws guaranteed by the Fourteenth Amendment. This disposition makes unnecessary any discussion whether such segregation also violates the Due Process Clause of the Fourteenth Amendment.

Because these are class actions, because of the wide applicability of this decision, and because of the great variety of local conditions, the formulation of decrees in these cases presents problems of considerable complexity. On reargument, the consideration of appropriate relief was necessarily subordinated to the primary question—the constitutionality of segregation in public education. We have now announced that such segregation is a denial of the equal protection of the laws. In order that we may have the full assistance of the parties in formulating decrees, the cases will be restored to the docket, and the parties are

---

1. K.B. Clark, *Effect of Prejudice and Discrimination on Personality Development* (Midcentury White House Conference on Children and Youth, 1950); Witmer and Kotinsky, *Personality in the Making* (1952), ch VI; Deutscher and Chein, "The Psychological Effects of Enforced Segregation: A Survey of Social Science Opinion," 26 *J.Psychol.* 259 (1948); Chein, "What are the Psychological Effects of Segregation Under Conditions of Equal Facilities?" 3 *Int.J.Opinion and Attitude Res.* 229 (1949); Brameld, "Educational Costs," in *Discrimination and National Welfare* (MacIver, ed, 1949), 44–48; Frazier, *The Negro in the United States* (1949), 674–681. And see generally Myrdal, *An American Dilemma* (1944). [This footnote was numbered 11 by the Court—Eds.]

requested to present further argument on Questions 4 and 5 previously propounded by the Court for the reargument this Term. . . .

It is so ordered.

Editors' Notes

(1) The questions set for reargument dealing with the form the decree implementing the decision should take are reprinted in footnote 1 to *Brown*, II, below at p. 774.

(2) For a superb study of the origin and development of these cases in local communities, lower courts, and within the U.S. Supreme Court, see Richard Kluger, *Simple Justice* (New York: Knopf, 1976). See also Bernard Schwartz, *Super Chief* (New York: New York University Press, 1983), chap. 3; and William O. Douglas, *The Court Years, 1939–1975* (New York: Random House, 1980), chap. 5.

"[T]he concepts of equal protection and due process, both stemming from the American ideal of fairness, are not mutually exclusive. . . . [D]iscrimination may be so unjustifiable as to be violative of due process."

BOLLING v. SHARPE

347 U.S. 497, 74 S.Ct. 693, 98 L.Ed. 884 (1954).

This is a companion case from the District of Columbia to the four suits from the states decided under *Brown*, I.

Mr. Chief Justice **WARREN** delivered the opinion of the Court. . . .

We have this day held that the Equal Protection Clause of the Fourteenth Amendment prohibits the states from maintaining racially segregated public schools. The legal problem in the District of Columbia is somewhat different, however. The Fifth Amendment, which is applicable in the District of Columbia, does not contain an equal protection clause as does the Fourteenth Amendment which applies only to the states. But the concepts of equal protection and due process, both stemming from our American ideal of fairness, are not mutually exclusive. The "equal protection of the laws" is a more explicit safeguard of prohibited unfairness than "due process of law," and, therefore, we do not imply that the two are always interchangeable phrases. But, as this Court has recognized, discrimination may be so unjustifiable as to be violative of due process.

Classifications based solely upon race must be scrutinized with particular care, since they are contrary to our traditions and hence constitutionally suspect. [Korematsu v. United States (1944); Hirabayashi v. United States (1943).] As long ago as 1896, this Court declared the principle "that the Constitution of the United States, in its present form, forbids, so far as civil and political rights are concerned, discrimination by the General Government, or by the States, against any citizen because of his race." [Gibson v. Mississippi (1896).] And in Buchanan v. Warley [1917], the Court held that a statute which limited the right of a property owner to convey his property to a person of another race was, as an unreasonable discrimination, a denial of due process of law.

Although the Court has not assumed to define "liberty" with any great precision, that term is not confined to mere freedom from bodily restraint. Liberty under law extends to the full range of conduct which the individual is free to pursue, and it cannot be restricted except for a proper governmental objective. Segregation in public education is not reasonably related to any proper governmental objective, and thus it imposes on Negro children of the District of Columbia a burden that constitutes an arbitrary deprivation of their liberty in violation of the Due Process Clause.

In view of our decision that the Constitution prohibits the states from maintaining racially segregated public schools, it would be unthinkable that the same Constitution would impose a lesser duty on the Federal Government. We hold that racial segregation in the public schools of the District of Columbia is a denial of the due process of law guaranteed by the Fifth Amendment to the Constitution. . . .

It is so ordered.

Editors' Notes

(1) This case marked a significant change in equal protection beyond reaffirming *Brown,* I's holding. In a process that would take several decades to ripen, the Court in *Bolling* began to read the equal protection clause into the Bill of Rights. See Weinberger v. Wiesenfeld (1975): "[T]he Court's approach to Fifth Amendment equal protection has always been precisely the same as to equal protection claims under the Fourteenth Amendment." A year later, however, a majority in Hampton v. Mow Sun Wong (1976) admitted there were some differences: "[T]he two protections are not always coextensive. Not only does the language of the two Amendments differ, but more importantly, there may be overriding national interests which justify selective federal legislation that would be unacceptable for an individual State."

(2) The irony of the Court's citing *Hirabayashi* and *Korematsu* to strike down racial discrimination is marvelous but frequently repeated, as the discussion of *Korematsu* in Chapter 3 pointed out. See also the Court's similar use of these cases in Loving v. Virginia (1966; reprinted below, p. 777).

"... with all deliberate speed. ...."

BROWN v. BOARD OF EDUCATION OF TOPEKA, II
349 U.S. 294, 75 S.Ct. 753, 99 L.Ed. 1083 (1955).

Mr. Chief Justice **WARREN** delivered the opinion of the Court. . . .

These cases were decided on May 17, 1954. The opinions of that date, declaring the fundamental principle that racial discrimination in public education is unconstitutional, are incorporated herein by reference. All provisions of federal, state, or local law requiring or permitting such discrimination must yield to this principle. There remains for consideration the manner in which relief is to be accorded.

Because these cases arose under different local conditions and their disposition will involve a variety of local problems, we requested further argument on the question of relief.[1] In view of the nationwide importance of the decision, we invited the Attorney General of the United States and the Attorneys General of all states requiring or permitting racial discrimination in public education to present their views on that question. The parties, the United States, and the States of Florida, North Carolina, Arkansas, Oklahoma, Maryland, and Texas filed briefs and participated in the oral argument.

These presentations were informative and helpful to the Court in its consideration of the complexities arising from the transition to a system of public education freed of racial discrimination. The presentations also demonstrated that substantial steps to eliminate racial discrimination in public schools have already been taken, not only in some of the communities in which these cases arose, but in some of the states appearing as amici curiae, and in other states as well. . . .

Full implementation of these constitutional principles may require solution of varied local school problems. School authorities have the primary responsibility for elucidating, assessing, and solving these

---

1. Further argument was requested on the following questions previously propounded by the Court:

4. Assuming it is decided that segregation in public schools violates the Fourteenth Amendment

(a) would a decree necessarily follow providing that, within the limits set by normal geographic school districting, Negro children should forthwith be admitted to schools of their choice, or

(b) may this Court, in the exercise of its equity powers, permit an effective gradual adjustment to be brought about from existing segregated systems to a system not based on color distinctions?

5. On the assumption on which questions 4(a) and (b) are based, and assuming further that this Court will exercise its equity powers to the end described in question 4 (b),

(a) should this Court formulate detailed decrees in these cases;

(b) if so, what specific issues should the decrees reach;

(c) should this Court appoint a special master to hear evidence with a view to recommending specific terms for such decrees;

(d) should this Court remand to the courts of first instance with directions to frame decrees in these cases, and if so what general directions should the decrees of this Court include and what procedures should the courts of first instance follow in arriving at the specific terms of more detailed decrees? [Footnote by the Court.]

problems; courts will have to consider whether the action of school authorities constitutes good faith implementation of the governing constitutional principles. Because of their proximity to local conditions and the possible need for further hearings, the courts which originally heard these cases can best perform this judicial appraisal. Accordingly, we believe it appropriate to remand the cases to those courts.

In fashioning and effectuating the decrees, the courts will be guided by equitable principles. Traditionally, equity has been characterized by a practical flexibility in shaping its remedies and by a facility for adjusting and reconciling public and private needs. These cases call for the exercise of these traditional attributes of equity power. At stake is the personal interest of the plaintiffs in admission to public schools as soon as practicable on a nondiscriminatory basis. To effectuate this interest may call for elimination of a variety of obstacles in making the transition to school systems operated in accordance with the constitutional principles set forth in our May 17, 1954, decision. Courts of equity may properly take into account the public interest in the elimination of such obstacles in a systematic and effective manner. But it should go without saying that the vitality of these constitutional principles cannot be allowed to yield simply because of disagreement with them.

While giving weight to these public and private considerations, the courts will require that the defendants make a prompt and reasonable start toward full compliance with our May 17, 1954, ruling. Once such a start has been made, the courts may find that additional time is necessary to carry out the ruling in an effective manner. The burden rests upon the defendants to establish that such time is necessary in the public interest and is consistent with good faith compliance at the earliest practicable date. To that end, the courts may consider problems related to administration, arising from the physical condition of the school plant, the school transportation system, personnel, revision of school districts and attendance areas into compact units to achieve a system of determining admission to the public schools on a nonracial basis, and revision of local laws and regulations which may be necessary in solving the foregoing problems. They will also consider the adequacy of any plans the defendants may propose to meet these problems and to effectuate a transition to a racially nondiscriminatory school system. During this period of transition, the courts will retain jurisdiction of these cases.

The judgments below, except that in the Delaware case, are accordingly reversed and the cases are remanded to the District Courts to take such proceedings and enter such orders and decrees consistent with this opinion as are necessary and proper to admit to public schools on a racially nondiscriminatory basis with all deliberate speed the parties to these cases. The judgment in the Delaware case—ordering the immediate admission of the plaintiffs to schools previously attended only by white children—is affirmed on the basis of the principles stated in our May 17, 1954, opinion, but the case is remanded to the Supreme

Court of Delaware for such further proceedings as that Court may deem necessary in light of this opinion.

It is so ordered.

Editors' Notes

(1) Southern reactions to the School Segregation Cases tended to be defiantly hostile. "Massive Resistance" was one response—avoiding the impact of the decisions by simple foot-dragging; using "pupil placement plans" that somehow kept blacks in segregated schools and "freedom of choice" schemes that, in effect, allowed whites to choose not to go to integrated schools; invoking the police power to justify maintaining segregation to preserve public peace; claiming immunity from suit under the Eleventh Amendment; threatening to close (and in Prince Edward County, Va., where one of the original suits had begun, actually closing) public schools; and counterattacking against the NAACP (see NAACP v. Alabama [1958; reprinted above, p. 646]; and NAACP v. Button [1963; reprinted above, p. 723]). Some state legislatures tried to reopen the question of WHO interprets for the federal system by "nullifying" *Brown* (see Alabama's resolution, reprinted above, p. 280). Most dangerous, of course, were frequent outbreaks of violence that threatened the safety of young blacks (as well as white civil rights workers) who dared to assert what the Court had said were their constitutional rights.

During much of the next decade, the justices avoided as much as they could further discussion of the issue of segregation. Their strategy was to affirm in terse per curiam orders lower court decisions striking down segregation and similarly reverse those sustaining segregation. The most notable exception was Cooper v. Aaron (1958; reprinted above, p. 281), when the Governor of Arkansas called out troops to prevent enforcement of a federal district court's order to desegregate. In several other cases raising the issue of state laws outlawing racially mixed marriages, the justices evaded the issue. See the discussion in the headnote to Loving v. Virginia (1967; reprinted below, p. 777).

In the ten years after *Brown, II,* there was some desegregation in the border states but almost none whatsoever in the South. Then Congress enacted the Civil Rights Act of 1964 (78 Stat. 241), which, in addition to making refusal to serve blacks on an equal basis in accommodations affecting "commerce among the several states," cut off federal grants to states that did not desegregate public schools. Segregated public schools remain a reality; but, once southern state officials realized that the 1964 act meant what it said, defiance changed to compliance, though initially begrudging. Armed with presidential and congressional support, the justices in 1968 discarded their diplomacy and spoke imperatively. In Green v. New Kent County, they unanimously said: "This deliberate perpetuation of the unconstitutional dual system can only have compounded the harm of such a system. . . . The burden on the school board today is to come forward with a plan that promises realistically to work, and promises realistically to work *now.*" During most of the last decade and a half, the difficulties of desegregating public schools have differed little from region to region—which is to say that there are as many problems outside as within the South, not that the problems have vanished.

(2) In its per curiam orders the Court invalidated state-mandated segregation in recreational facilities—Muir v. Louisville (1954); Baltimore v. Dawson (1954); Holmes v. Atlanta (1955); and New Orleans v. Detiege (1955)—and in local transportation—Gayle v. Browder (1956), a case growing out of the sit-in that helped turn Dr. Martin Luther King, Jr.s' Southern Christian Leadership Conference into a national civil rights movement.

(3) For an analysis of the aftermath of *Brown,* see Stephen L. Wasby, A.A. D'Amato, and R. Metrailer, *Desegregation from Brown to Alexander* (Carbondale, Ill.: Southern Illinois University Press, 1977); Richard Kluger, *Simple Justice* (New York: Knopf, 1975), chap. 27; Jack W. Peltason, *58 Lonely Men: Southern Federal Judges and School Desegregation* (New York: Harcourt, Brace & World, 1961); and Jack Bass, *Unlikely Heroes* (New York: Simon & Schuster, 1981).

"At the very least, the Equal Protection Clause demands that racial classifications, especially suspect in criminal classifications, be subjected to 'the most rigid scrutiny".

. . .

LOVING v. VIRGINIA
388 U.S. 1, 87 S.Ct. 1817, 18 L.Ed.2d 1010 (1967).

In 1883 Pace v. Alabama sustained a statute punishing fornication between a white person and a Negro and imposing a greater penalty than for the same act committed by persons of the same race. This statute was typical of laws in most southern states which, to protect the "purity of the white race," forbade interracial marriage or other forms of sexual intercourse. As southern officials were quick to point out, the logic of the School Segregation Cases threatened the validity of these statutes. "Racial mongrelization" turned into a white southern bugaboo in the fight against desegregation. "Let them in the schools today and tomorrow they'll be marrying your daughters," became a rallying cry.

Recognizing the power of this white fear, the justices were loath to let logic dominate prudence. Shortly after *Brown,* I, they denied certiorari to a black woman whom Alabama had sentenced to prison for marrying a white man. (Jackson v. Alabama [1954].)

A case from Virginia provided a second opportunity, which the justices also cautiously declined. Using the state's anti-miscegenation statute as the basis of decision, Virginia had annulled a marriage between a white woman and a man of Chinese extraction; the husband claimed he had been denied equal protection and appealed—that is, took his case to the U.S. Supreme Court as a matter of right. (See the discussion in Appendix A, below, of the supposed differences between an appeal and a petition for certiorari.) Justice Frankfurter urged his colleagues not to decide such a volatile issue so soon after the School Segregation cases. He stressed "the Court's responsibility in not thwarting or seriously handicapping the enforcement of its decision in the segregation cases." (Quoted in Bernard Schwartz, *Super Chief* [New York: New York University Press, 1983], p. 159.) The justices temporized by remanding the case to the state courts asking for clarifications of the record. Naim v. Naim (1955).

The Virginia supreme court of appeals curtly responded that the record was adequate for decision; there was no procedure for the sort of clarification the Supreme Court had asked for; and the original decision was correct anyway. Faced with this public rebuke, the justices backed away and dismissed the appeal on grounds that the lack of a clarified record "leaves the case devoid of a properly presented federal question." (Naim v. Naim [1956].) One angry law clerk who demanded an explanation from his justice was told, "One bombshell at a time is enough." Earl Warren, who along with Black had opposed the remand in *Naim,* was more pungent: "That's what happens when you turn your ass to the grandstand!" (Quoted in Schwartz, p. 162.)

But issues of interracial sex and marriage would return to the Court, as the justices knew. In McLaughlin v. Florida (1964), the justices took a small step toward invalidating anti-miscegenation laws, but once more they proceeded cautiously. They reversed a conviction for interracial cohabitation and the statute on which it was based, but only because the state had not shown "some overriding statutory purpose requiring the proscription of the specified conduct when engaged in between a white person and a Negro, but not otherwise." Stewart and Douglas preferred a flat statement that all such statutes were unconstitutional.

Three years after *McLaughlin* and the Civil Rights Act of 1964, Virginia provided yet another opportunity. Richard Loving, a white man, and Mildred Jeter, a black woman, both residents of Virginia, were married in the District of Columbia. When they returned to Virginia, they were convicted for violating the state statute making racial intermarriage a crime. Virginia's Supreme Court of Appeals upheld the conviction and the constitutionality of the statute. The Lovings then appealed to the U.S. Supreme Court.

Mr. Chief Justice **WARREN** delivered the opinion of the Court. . . .

This case presents a constitutional question never addressed by this Court: whether a statutory scheme adopted by the State of Virginia to prevent marriages between persons solely on the basis of racial classifications violates the Equal Protection and Due Process Clauses of the Fourteenth Amendment. . . .

I

In upholding the constitutionality of these provisions, the Supreme Court of Appeals of Virginia referred to its 1955 decision in Naim v. Naim as stating the reasons supporting the validity of these laws. In *Naim,* the state court concluded that the State's legitimate purposes were "to preserve the racial integrity of its citizens," and to prevent "the corruption of blood," "a mongrel breed of citizens, and "the obliteration of racial pride," obviously an endorsement of the doctrine of White Supremacy. The court also reasoned that marriage has traditionally been subject to state regulation without federal intervention, and, consequently, the regulation of marriage should be left to exclusive state control by the Tenth Amendment.

While the state court is no doubt correct in asserting that marriage is a social relation subject to the State's police power, the State does not contend . . . that its powers to regulate marriage are unlimited notwithstanding the commands of the Fourteenth Amendment. Nor could it do so in light of Meyer v. Nebraska (1923) and Skinner v. Oklahoma (1942). Instead, the State argues that the meaning of the Equal Protection Clause, as illuminated by the statements of the Framers, is only that state penal laws containing an interracial element as part of the definition of the offense must apply equally to whites and Negroes in the sense that members of each race are punished to the same degree. Thus, the State contends that, because its miscegenation statutes punish equally both the white and the Negro participants in an interracial marriage, these statutes, despite their reliance on racial classifications, do not constitute an invidious discrimination based upon race. The second argument . . . is that, if the Equal Protection Clause does not outlaw miscegenation statutes because of their reliance on racial classifications, the question of constitutionality would thus become whether there was any rational basis for a State to treat interracial marriages differently from other marriages. On this question, the State argues, the scientific evidence is substantially in doubt and, consequently, this Court should defer to the wisdom of the state legislature in adopting its policy of discouraging interracial marriages.

Because we reject the notion that the mere "equal application" of a statute containing racial classifications is enough to remove the classifications from the Fourteenth Amendment's proscription of all invidious racial discriminations, we do not accept the State's contention that these statutes should be upheld if there is any possible basis for concluding that they serve a rational purpose. The mere fact of equal application does not mean that our analysis of these statutes should follow the approach we have taken in cases involving no racial discrimination where the Equal Protection Clause has been arrayed against a statute discriminating between the kinds of advertising which may be displayed on trucks in New York City, Railway Express Agency, Inc. v. New York (1949). . . . In cases involving distinctions not drawn according to race, the Court has merely asked whether there is any rational foundation for the discriminations, and has deferred to the wisdom of the state legislatures. In the case at bar, however, we deal with statutes containing racial classifications, and the fact of equal application does not immunize the statute from the very heavy burden of justification which the Fourteenth Amendment has traditionally required of state statutes drawn according to race.

The State argues that statements in the Thirty-ninth Congress about the time of the passage of the Fourteenth Amendment indicate that the Framers did not intend the Amendment to make unconstitutional state miscegenation laws. Many of the statements alluded to by the State concern the debates over the Freedman's Bureau Bill . . . and the Civil Rights Act of 1866. . . . While these statements have

some relevance to the intention of Congress in submitting the Fourteenth Amendment, . . . they pertained to the passage of specific
statutes and not to the broader, organic purpose of a constitutional
amendment. As for the various statements directly concerning the
Fourteenth Amendment, we have said in connection with a related
problem, that although these historical sources "cast some light" they
are not sufficient to resolve the problem; "[a]t best, they are inconclusive. . . . " Brown v. Board of Education (1954). See also Strauder
v. West Virginia (1880). We have rejected the proposition that the
debates in the Thirty-ninth Congress or in the state legislatures which
ratified the Fourteenth Amendment supported the theory advanced by
the State, that the requirement of equal protection of the laws is
satisfied by penal laws defining offenses based on racial classifications
so long as white and Negro participants in the offense were similarly
punished. McLaughlin v. Florida (1964).

The State finds support for its "equal application" theory in the
decision of the Court in Pace v. Alabama (1883). In that case, the Court
upheld a conviction under an Alabama statute forbidding adultery or
fornication between a white person and a Negro which imposed a
greater penalty than that of a statute proscribing similar conduct by
members of the same race. The Court reasoned that the statute could
not be said to discriminate against Negroes because the punishment for
each participant in the offense was the same. However, as recently as
the 1964 Term, in rejecting the reasoning of that case, we stated "*Pace*
represents a limited view of the Equal Protection Clause which has not
withstood analysis in the subsequent decisions of this Court." *Mc-
Laughlin*. . . . As we there demonstrated, the Equal Protection
Clause requires the consideration of whether the classifications drawn
by any statute constitute an arbitrary and invidious discrimination.
The clear and central purpose of the Fourteenth Amendment was to
eliminate all official state sources of invidious racial discrimination in
the States. Slaughter-House Cases (1873); *Strauder*; Shelley v. Kraemer (1948).

There can be no question but that Virginia's miscegenation statutes rest solely upon distinctions drawn according to race. . . .
Over the years, this Court has consistently repudiated "[d]istinctions
between citizens solely because of their ancestry" as being "odious to a
free people whose institutions are founded upon the doctrine of equality." Hirabayashi v. United States (1943). At the very least, the Equal
Protection Clause demands that racial classifications, especially suspect
in criminal statutes, be subjected to the "most rigid scrutiny," Korematsu v. United States (1944), and, if they are ever to be upheld, they must
be shown to be necessary to the accomplishment of some permissible
state objective, independent of the racial discrimination which it was
the object of the Fourteenth Amendment to eliminate. Indeed, two
members of this Court have already stated that they "cannot conceive
of a valid legislative purpose . . . which makes the color of a person's

skin the test of whether his conduct is a criminal offense." *McLaughlin* (Stewart, J., joined by Douglas, J., concurring).

There is patently no legitimate overriding purpose independent of invidious racial discrimination which justifies this classification. The fact that Virginia prohibits only interracial marriages involving white persons demonstrates that the racial classifications must stand on their own justification, as measures designed to maintain White Supremacy. We have consistently denied the constitutionality of measures which restrict the rights of citizens on account of race. There can be no doubt that restricting the freedom to marry solely because of racial classifications violates the central meaning of the Equal Protection Clause.

II

These statutes also deprive the Lovings of liberty without due process of law in violation of the Due Process Clause of the Fourteenth Amendment. The freedom to marry has long been recognized as one of the vital personal rights essential to the orderly pursuit of happiness by free men.

Marriage is one of the "basic civil rights of man," fundamental to our very existence and survival. *Skinner.* To deny this fundamental freedom on so unsupportable a basis as the racial classifications embodied in these statutes, classifications so directly subversive of the principle of equality at the heart of the Fourteenth Amendment, is surely to deprive all the State's citizens of liberty without due process of law. The Fourteenth Amendment requires that the freedom of choice to marry not be restricted by invidious racial discriminations. Under our Constitution, the freedom to marry, or not marry, a person of another race resides with the individual and cannot be infringed by the State.

. . .

[*Reversed.*]

Mr. Justice **STEWART**, concurring. . . .

Editors' Note

(1) **Query**: Warren offered two bases for the Court's decision the statute: (i) used a suspect classification that could not withstand strict scrutiny and (ii) impinged on a fundamental right. Why this violation of Occam's razor?

———

"[L]egal restrictions which curtail the civil rights of a single racial group are immediately suspect. . . . [C]ourts must subject them to the most rigid scrutiny."

KOREMATSU v. UNITED STATES

323 U.S. 214, 65 S.Ct. 193, 89 L.Ed. 194 (1944).

This case, sustaining the imprisonment of American citizens of Japanese ancestry during World War II, is reprinted below, at p. 1197.

"The Fourteenth Amendment is not directed solely against discrimination due to a 'two-class theory'—that is, based upon differences between 'white' and Negro."

HERNANDEZ v. TEXAS

347 U.S. 475, 74 S.Ct. 667, 98 L.Ed. 866 (1954).

Pete Hernandez, an American citizen of Mexican descent, was indicted for murder by a grand jury in Jackson County, Texas, convicted by a petit jury, and sentenced to life imprisonment. Prior to and at the trial, his counsel objected to both juries because Mexican-Americans had been systematically excluded from service on them. The judge denied these motions, the state supreme court affirmed, and the U.S. Supreme Court granted certiorari.

Mr. Chief Justice **WARREN** delivered the opinion of the Court. . . .

In numerous decisions, this Court has held that it is a denial of the equal protection of the laws to try a defendant of a particular race or color under an indictment issued by a grand jury, or before a petit jury, from which all persons of his race or color have, solely because of that race or color, been excluded by the State, whether acting through its legislature, its courts, or its executive or administrative officers. Although the Court has had little occasion to rule on the question directly, it has been recognized since Strauder v. West Virginia [1880] that the exclusion of a class of persons from jury service on grounds other than race or color may also deprive a defendant who is a member of that class of the constitutional guarantee of equal protection of the laws. The State of Texas would have us hold that there are only two classes—white and Negro—within the contemplation of the Fourteenth Amendment. The decisions of this Court do not support that view. And, except where the question presented involves the exclusion of persons of Mexican descent from juries, Texas courts have taken a broader view of the scope of the equal protection clause.

Throughout our history differences in race and color have defined easily identifiable groups which have at times required the aid of the courts in securing equal treatment under the laws. But community prejudices are not static, and from time to time other differences from the community norm may define other groups which need the same protection. Whether such a group exists within a community is a question of fact. When the existence of a distinct class is demonstrated, and it is further shown that the laws, as written or as applied, single out that class for different treatment not based on some reasonable classification, the guarantees of the Constitution have been violated. The Fourteenth Amendment is not directed solely against discrimination due to a "two-class theory"—that is, based upon differences between "white" and Negro.

. . . The exclusion of otherwise eligible persons from jury service solely because of their ancestry or national origin is discrimination prohibited by the Fourteenth Amendment. The Texas statute makes no such discrimination, but the petitioner alleges that those administering the law do.

The petitioner's initial burden in substantiating his charge of group discrimination was to prove that persons of Mexican descent constitute a separate class in Jackson County, distinct from "whites." One method by which this may be demonstrated is by showing the attitude of the community. Here the testimony of responsible officials and citizens contained the admission that residents of the community distinguished between "white" and "Mexican." The participation of persons of Mexican descent in business and community groups was shown to be slight. Until very recent times, children of Mexican descent were required to attend a segregated school for the first four grades. At least one restaurant in town prominently displayed a sign announcing "No Mexicans Served." On the courthouse grounds at the time of the hearing, there were two men's toilets, one unmarked, and the other marked "Colored Men" and "Hombres Aqui" ("Men Here"). No substantial evidence was offered to rebut the logical inference to be drawn from these facts, and it must be concluded that petitioner succeeded in his proof.

Having established the existence of a class, petitioner was then charged with the burden of proving discrimination. To do so, he relied on the pattern of proof established by Norris v. Alabama [1935]. In that case, proof that Negroes constituted a substantial segment of the population of the jurisdiction, that some Negroes were qualified to serve as jurors, and that none had been called for jury service over an extended period of time, was held to constitute prima facie proof of the systematic exclusion of Negroes from jury service. This holding, sometimes called the "rule of exclusion," has been applied in other cases, and it is available in supplying proof of discrimination against any delineated class.

The petitioner established that 14% of the population of Jackson County were persons with Mexican or Latin American surnames, and that 11% of the males over 21 bore such names. The County Tax Assessor testified that 6 or 7 percent of the freeholders on the tax rolls of the County were persons of Mexican descent. The State of Texas stipulated that "for the last twenty-five years there is no record of any person with a Mexican or Latin American name having served on a jury commission, grand jury or petit jury in Jackson County." The parties also stipulated that "there are some male persons of Mexican or Latin American descent in Jackson County who, by virtue of being citizens, householders, or freeholders, and having all other legal prerequisites to jury service, are eligible to serve as members of a jury commission, grand jury and/or petit jury."

The petitioner met the burden of proof imposed in Norris v. Alabama [1935]. To rebut the strong prima facie case of the denial of the equal protection of the laws guaranteed by the Constitution thus established, the State offered the testimony of five jury commissioners that they had not discriminated against persons of Mexican or Latin American descent in selecting jurors. They stated that their only objective had been to select those whom they thought were best qualified. This testimony is not enough to overcome the petitioner's case. . . .

Circumstances or chance may well dictate that no persons in a certain class will serve on a particular jury or during some particular period. But it taxes our credulity to say that mere chance resulted in there being no members of this class among the over six thousand jurors called in the past 25 years. The result bespeaks discrimination, whether or not it was a conscious decision on the part of any individual jury commissioner. The judgment of conviction must be reversed.

To say that this decision revives the rejected contention that the Fourteenth Amendment requires proportional representation of all the component ethnic groups of the community on every jury ignores the facts. The petitioner did not seek proportional representation, nor did he claim a right to have persons of Mexican descent sit on the particular juries which he faced. His only claim is the right to be indicted and tried by juries from which all members of his class are not systematically excluded—juries selected from among all qualified persons regardless of national origin or descent. To this much, he is entitled by the Constitution.

Reversed.

Editors' Notes

(1) Castaneda v. Partida (1977) added an interesting twist. Partida had been convicted of rape; later he sought habeas corpus from a federal district court, claiming that Mexican-Americans had been excluded from the grand jury. He offered statistics to show that, although the county had a population 79 per cent Mexican-American, over the past eleven years only 39 per cent of the grand jurors had had Spanish surnames. The district court refused habeas corpus, in part because the judge thought it unlikely that a governing majority would discriminate against itself. Partida appealed and won in the court of appeals, and Texas obtained review on cert. The Supreme Court, however, held for Partida. For the majority, Justice Blackmun said: "Because of the many facets of human motivation, it would be unwise to presume as a matter of law that human beings of one definable group will not discriminate against members of their group."

(2) **Query**: To what extent does Blackmun's statement in *Partida* undercut arguments for affirmative action? He was aware of the application of his statement and added in a footnote: "This is not a case where a majority is

practicing benevolent discrimination in favor of a traditionally disfavored minority, although that situation illustrates that motivations not immediately obvious might enter into discrimination against 'one's own kind.' " Does this addition change the answer to the query at the beginning of this note?

IV. HOW TO END RACIAL INEQUALITY: COPING WITH INACTION

THE IMPLEMENTATION OF *BROWN*

As we have seen, southern resistance to *Brown* was bitter, and evasions produced a generation of litigation. Judicial decisions and the Civil Rights Act of 1964 eventually stripped away most of the legal fig leaves cloaking a "separate but equal" way of life; but de facto segregation remains a glaring problem not only in the South but in every part of the country. Judges, administrators, and interest groups like the NAACP that work to end caste in our society have all relearned the hard lesson that it is much easier to pronounce constitutional principles than to transform them into working public policy.

Passage of the 1964 Act brought federal administrators into these difficulties, but judges still get more than their fair share of such burdens. Swann v. Charlotte-Mecklenburg (1971) sustained a lower court's requirement that a southern city take positive steps to end segregation. Speaking for the Supreme Court, Chief Justice Burger held that, if a school district had a history of deliberately segregating students by race, there was a presumption that still existing segregation was the result of that previous policy. For Charlotte, N.C. the justices approved a system of busing students across neighborhoods to achieve integration.

The yellow school bus soon became a major instrument of desegregation and to many white (and some black) parents a symbol of oppression. As a result of private action and official inaction, in most urban areas, housing is segregated—in some cities, isolated—by race. Thus schools cannot be integrated without sweeping changes in traditional practices of assigning children to the nearest schools. To right this constitutional wrong, Burger said in *Swann,* "[d]esegregation plans cannot be limited to the walk-in school. . . ."

The Court has confronted a bevy of responses to problems of implementation, most of them arising outside the South.[1] Although the justices have not retreated from the principles behind *Brown,* at times they have evidenced deeper concern for other values. In Milliken v. Bradley (1974), for instance, a five-judge majority reversed a federal district judge's decision ordering a desegregation plan that involved school districts in the entire metropolitan area of Detroit. Detroit's board of education had been the only defendant, and only the city had been shown to have been guilty of housing, employment, and educational policies that had produced segregated schools. An equitable remedy should be commensurate with the violation of rights, the majority reasoned. Therefore surrounding communities should not have to atone for

---

1. See, for example, Wright v. Emporia (Virginia) (1972); Keyes v. School District No. 1 (Colorado) (1973); Milliken v. Bradley (Michigan) (1972); and Columbus v. Penick (Ohio) (1979).

Detroit's sins. "No single tradition in public education," Chief Justice Burger wrote, "is more deeply rooted than local control over the operation of the schools. . . ."

The four dissenters pointed out that: (1) in Detroit proper more than 75 per cent of children were black, making real desegregation physically impossible if the order were confined to the city limits; (2) state authorities had in various ways cooperated with real estate agents and home owners to restrict blacks to the city's inner core, helping create existing problems; (3) under Michigan's law, school districts were *state,* not local, agencies; and (4) under the Fourteenth Amendment, a city or a school board has no status of its own other than as a state agency; thus the order need not, as a matter of constitutional law, be restricted to the city. "Today's holding, I fear," Thurgood Marshall charged, "is more a reflection of a perceived public mood that we have gone far enough in enforcing the Constitution's guarantee of equal justice than it is the product of neutral principles of law."

On occasion the Court has closely followed *Milliken,*[2] but Columbus v. Penick (1979) may be more typical of the justices' attitudes.[3] There the Court upheld a federal judge's order for desegregation of the entire school system Columbus, Ohio. For the majority, Justice White said that *"Brown* and Green [v. New Kent County (1968)] imposed an affirmative duty to desegregate." The district judge had found and the Supreme Court agreed that there had been purposeful efforts to segregate by city officials.

In assessing remedies to implement *Brown,* the justices have relied heavily on doctrinal analysis as a *mode* and the *technique* of stare decisis to inch that doctrinal analysis forward—or backward or sideways. They have tended to immerse themselves in the wealth of factual material that surrounds each case, to proceed along lines analogous to what anthropologists call "thick description." The doctrine the Court has been applying to implement *Brown* is that the Fourteenth Amendment outlaws *purposeful,* but only *purposeful,* segregation, whether accomplished by governmental action or inaction. Finding purpose in positive governmental action is often extraordinarily difficult; discovering it in governmental inaction produces difficulties akin to those of finding the framers' original intent, as the next two cases reprinted here, Washington v. Davis (1976) and Rogers v. Lodge (1982) demonstrate.

---

2. Dayton v. Brinkman (1977).

3. See, for example, Washington v. Seattle (1982); Delaware v. Evans (1983); and Metropolitan County Board v. Kelley (1983). On the other hand, Crawford v. Board (1983) upheld a California referendum forbidding state judges to reassign pupils or require busing unless a federal court "would be permitted under federal decisional law" to use such means to remedy a violation of the Fourteenth Amendment.

"[W]e have difficulty understanding how a law establishing a racially neutral qualification for employment is nevertheless racially discriminatory . . . simply because a greater proportion of Negroes fails to qualify than members of other racial or ethnic groups."

WASHINGTON v. DAVIS

426 U.S. 229, 96 S.Ct. 2040, 48 L.Ed.2d 597 (1976).

In 1971 Griggs v. Duke Power Co. interpreted Title VII of the Civil Rights Act of 1964, aimed at banning racial discrimination in employment in businesses involved in "commerce among the several states." The Duke Power Co., which had previously limited its most desirable jobs to whites, set up educational achievements and high scores on intelligence tests as prerequisites for those jobs. Few blacks qualified and a group of them claimed the "prerequisites" were discriminatory. The Court agreed, holding that the "prerequisites" were not related to the actual jobs.

At about the same time, several blacks filed suit in the District of Columbia, attacking the constitutionality under the Fifth Amendment as well as the legality under civil rights statutes of the hiring practices for police in the District. To be accepted for the police training program, an applicant had to receive a grade of at least 40 out of 80 on "Test 21," an examination used throughout the federal civil service to gauge verbal ability, reading, and comprehension. Plaintiffs claimed that Test 21 excluded a far larger proportion of blacks than whites and bore no relationship to job performance and asked for a summary judgment on the constitutional issue. The district court found the test was a valid instrument, but the court of appeals reversed. The District of Columbia sought and obtained certiorari.

Mr. Justice **WHITE** delivered the opinion of the Court. . . .

The central purpose of the Equal Protection Clause of the Fourteenth Amendment is the prevention of official conduct discriminating on the basis of race. It is also true that the Due Process Clause of the Fifth Amendment contains an equal protection component prohibiting the United States from invidiously discriminating between individuals or groups. Bolling v. Sharpe (1954). But our cases have not embraced the proposition that a law or other official act, without regard to whether it reflects a racially discriminatory purpose, is unconstitutional *solely* because it has a racially disproportionate impact. . . .

The school desegregation cases have also adhered to the basic equal protection principle that the invidious quality of a law claimed to be racially discriminatory must ultimately be traced to a racially discriminatory purpose. . . . The essential element of de jure segregation is "a current condition of segregation resulting from intentional state action." Keyes v. School Dist. No. 1 (1973). "The differentiating factor between de jure segregation and so-called de facto segregation . . . is *purpose* or *intent* to segregate." . . .

This is not to say that the necessary discriminatory racial purpose must be express or appear on the face of the statute, or that a law's disproportionate impact is irrelevant. . . . A statute, otherwise

neutral on its face, must not be applied so as invidiously to discriminate
on the basis of race. Yick Wo v. Hopkins (1886). It is also clear from
the cases dealing with racial discrimination in the selection of juries
that the systematic exclusion of Negroes is itself such an "unequal
application of the law . . . as to show intentional discrimination."
Akins v. Texas [1945]. . . .

Necessarily, an invidious discriminatory purpose may often be
inferred from the totality of the relevant facts, including the fact, if it is
true, that the law bears more heavily on one race than another. It is
also not infrequently true that the discriminatory impact . . . may
for all practical purposes demonstrate unconstitutionality because in
various circumstances the discrimination is difficult to explain on
nonracial grounds. Nevertheless, we have not held that a law, neutral
on its face and serving ends otherwise within the power of government
to pursue, is invalid under the Equal Protection Clause simply because
it may affect a greater proportion of one race than of another. Disproportionate impact is not irrelevant, but it is not the sole touchstone of
an invidious racial discrimination forbidden by the Constitution.
Standing alone, it does not trigger the rule, McLaughlin v. Florida
(1964), that racial classifications are to be subjected to the strictest
scrutiny and are justifiable only by the weightiest of considerations.

There are some indications to the contrary in our cases. In Palmer
v. Thompson (1971), . . . [t]he opinion warned against grounding
decision on legislative purpose or motivation, thereby lending support
for the proposition that the operative effect of the law rather than its
purpose is the paramount factor. But the holding of the case was that
the legitimate purposes of the ordinance—to preserve peace and avoid
deficits—were not open to impeachment by evidence that the council-
men were actually motivated by racial considerations. Whatever dicta
the opinion may contain, the decision did not involve, much less
invalidate, a statute or ordinance having neutral purposes but disproportionate racial consequences.

Wright v. Council of City of Emporia (1972) also indicates that in
proper circumstances, the racial impact of a law, rather than its
discriminatory purpose, is the critical factor. . . .

That neither *Palmer* nor *Wright* was understood to have changed the
prevailing rule is apparent from *Keyes,* where the principal issue in
litigation was whether and to what extent there had been purposeful
discrimination resulting in a partially or wholly segregated school system.
Nor did other later cases indicate that either *Palmer* or *Wright* had
worked a fundamental change in equal protection law. . . .

As an initial matter, we have difficulty understanding how a law
establishing a racially neutral qualification for employment is nevertheless racially discriminatory and denies "any person . . . equal
protection of the laws" simply because a greater proportion of Negroes
fails to qualify than members of other racial or ethnic groups. Had
respondents, along with all others who had failed Test 21, whether
white or black, brought an action claiming that the test denied each of
them equal protection of the laws as compared with those who had

passed with high enough scores to qualify them as police recruits, it is most unlikely that their challenge would have been sustained. Test 21, which is administered generally to prospective Government employees, concededly seeks to ascertain whether those who take it have acquired a particular level of verbal skill; and it is untenable that the Constitution prevents the Government from seeking modestly to upgrade the communicative abilities of its employees rather than to be satisfied with some lower level of competence, particularly where the job requires special ability to communicate orally and in writing. Respondents, as Negroes, could no more successfully claim that the test denied them equal protection than could white applicants who also failed. The conclusion would not be different in the face of proof that more Negroes than whites had been disqualified by Test 21. That other Negroes also failed to score well would, alone, not demonstrate that respondents individually were being denied equal protection of the laws by the application of an otherwise valid qualifying test being administered to prospective police recruits.

Nor on the facts of the case before us would the disproportionate impact of Test 21 warrant the conclusion that it is a purposeful device to discriminate against Negroes. . . . [T]he test is neutral on its face and rationally may be said to serve a purpose the Government is constitutionally empowered to pursue. . . . [W]e think the District Court correctly held that the affirmative efforts of the Metropolitan Police Department to recruit black officers, the changing racial composition of the recruit classes and of the force in general, and the relationship of the test to the training program negated any inference that the Department discriminated on the basis of race or that "a police officer qualifies on the color of his skin rather than ability."

Under Title VII [of the Civil Rights Act of 1964], Congress provided that when hiring and promotion practices disqualifying substantially disproportionate numbers of blacks are challenged, discriminatory purpose need not be proved, and that it is an insufficient response to demonstrate some rational basis for the challenged practices. It is necessary, in addition, that they be "validated" in terms of job performance in any one of several ways, perhaps by ascertaining the minimum skill, ability or potential necessary for the position at issue and determining whether the qualifying tests are appropriate for the selection of qualified applicants for the job in question. However this process proceeds, it involves a more probing judicial review of, and less deference to, the seemingly reasonable acts of administrators and executives than is appropriate under the Constitution where special racial impact, without discriminatory purpose, is claimed. We are not disposed to adopt this more rigorous standard for the purposes of applying the Fifth and the Fourteenth Amendments in cases such as this.

A rule that a statute designed to serve neutral ends is nevertheless invalid, absent compelling justification, if in practice it benefits or burdens one race more than another would be far-reaching and would raise serious questions about, and perhaps invalidate, a whole range of tax, welfare, public service, regulatory, and licensing statutes that may

be more burdensome to the poor and to the average black than to the
more affluent white. . . .

[Reversed.]

Mr. Justice **STEWART** [concurs].

Mr. Justice **STEVENS** concurring. . . .

The requirement of purposeful discrimination is a common thread
running through the cases summarized [by the Court.]. . . . Although it may be proper to use the same language to describe the
constitutional claim in each of these contexts, the burden of proving a
prima facie case may well involve differing evidentiary considerations.
The extent of deference that one pays to the trial court's determination
of the factual issue, and indeed, the extent to which one characterizes
the intent issue as a question of fact or a question of law, will vary in
different contexts.

Frequently the most probative evidence of intent will be objective
evidence of what actually happened rather than evidence describing the
subjective state of mind of the actor. For normally the actor is
presumed to have intended the natural consequences of his deeds. This
is particularly true in the case of governmental action which is frequently the product of compromise, of collective decisionmaking, and of
mixed motivation. It is unrealistic, on the one hand, to require the
victim of alleged discrimination to uncover the actual subjective intent
of the decisionmaker or, conversely, to invalidate otherwise legitimate
action simply because an improper motive affected the deliberation of a
participant in the decisional process. A law conscripting clerics should
not be invalidated because an atheist voted for it.

My point in making this observation is to suggest that the line
between discriminatory purpose and discriminatory impact is not nearly as bright, and perhaps not quite as critical, as the reader of the
Court's opinion might assume. I agree, of course, that a constitutional
issue does not arise every time some disproportionate impact is shown.
On the other hand, when the disproportion is as dramatic as in
Gomillion v. Lightfoot [1960] or _Yick Wo_, it really does not matter
whether the standard is phrased in terms of purpose or effect. Therefore, although I accept the statement of the general rule in the Court's
opinion, I am not yet prepared to indicate how that standard should be
applied in the many cases which have formulated the governing standard in different language.

My agreement with . . . the Court's opinion rests on a ground
narrower than the Court describes. I do not rely at all on the evidence
of good-faith efforts to recruit black police officers. In my judgment,
neither those efforts nor the subjective good faith of the District
administration, would save Test 21 if it were otherwise invalid.

There are two reasons why I am convinced that the challenge to
Test 21 is insufficient. First, the test serves the neutral and legitimate

purpose of requiring all applicants to meet a uniform minimum standard of literacy. Reading ability is manifestly relevant to the police function, there is no evidence that the required passing grade was set at an arbitrarily high level, and there is sufficient disparity among high schools and high school graduates to justify the use of a separate uniform test. Second, the same test is used throughout the federal service. The applicants for employment in the District of Columbia Police Department represent such a small fraction of the total number of persons who have taken the test that their experience is of minimal probative value in assessing the neutrality of the test itself. That evidence, without more, is not sufficient to overcome the presumption that a test which is this widely used by the Federal Government is in fact neutral in its effect as well as its "purpose" as that term is used in constitutional adjudication. . . .

Mr. Justice **BRENNAN**, with whom Mr. Justice **MARSHALL** joins, dissenting [on statutory grounds]. . . .

Editors' Notes

(1) Village of Arlington Heights v. Metropolitan Housing Development Corp. (1977) held that a real estate developer who had been denied a zoning permit to build integrated low and moderate cost housing in a suburb of Chicago had failed to show the denial was caused by a racially discriminatory purpose. " 'Disproportionate impact is not irrelevant, but it is not the sole touchstone of an invidious racial discrimination,' " Justice Powell said for the majority, quoting from Washington v. Davis. "Proof of racially discriminatory intent or purpose is required to show a violation of the Equal Protection Clause." But, he added, "*Davis* does not require a plaintiff to prove that the challenged action rested solely on racially discriminatory purposes. Rarely can it be said that a legislature or administrative body operating under a broad mandate made a decision motivated solely by a single concern, or even that a particular purpose was the 'dominant' or 'primary' one." Powell then offered a summary sketch of some of the factors at which a court should look to determine whether "racially discriminatory intent existed":

> Determining whether invidious discriminatory purpose was a motivating factor demands a sensitive inquiry into such circumstantial and direct evidence of intent as may be available. The impact of the official action—whether it "bears more heavily on one race than another," Washington v. Davis [1976]—may provide an important starting point. Sometimes a clear pattern, unexplainable on grounds other than race, emerges from the effect of the state action even when the governing legislation appears neutral on its face. Yick Wo v. Hopkins (1886); Guinn v. United States (1915); Lane v. Wilson (1939); Gomillion v. Lightfoot (1960). The evidentiary inquiry is then relatively easy. But such cases are rare. Absent a pattern as stark as that in *Gomillion* or *Yick Wo*, impact alone is not determinative, and the Court must look to other evidence.

The historical background of the decision is one evidentiary source, particularly if it reveals a series of official actions taken for invidious purposes. See Lane v. Wilson [1939]; Griffin v. School Board [1964]; Schnell v. Davis (1949); cf. Keyes v. School Dist. No. 1, Denver, Colo. [1973]. The specific sequence of events leading up to the challenged decision also may shed some light on the decisionmaker's purposes. Reitman v. Mulkey (1967); Grosjean v. American Press Co. (1936). For example, if the property involved here always had been zoned R–5 but suddenly was changed to R–3 when the town learned of MHDC's plans to erect integrated housing, we would have a far different case. Departures from the normal procedural sequence also might afford evidence that improper purposes are playing a role. Substantive departures too may be relevant, particularly if the factors usually considered important by the decisionmaker strongly favor a decision contrary to the one reached.

The legislative or administrative history may be highly relevant, especially where there are contemporary statements by members of the decisionmaking body, minutes of its meetings, or reports. In some extraordinary instances the members might be called to the stand at trial to testify concerning the purpose of the official action, although even then such testimony frequently will be barred by privilege. See Tenney v. Brandhove (1951); United States v. Nixon (1974); 8 J. Wigmore, Evidence § 2371 (McNaughton rev. ed. 1961).

(2) White in *Davis* and Powell in *Arlington Heights* seem to equate "purpose" and "intent" and at times even "motive" with the other two. Would it improve doctrinal analysis to distinguish among these three concepts?

(3) For an analysis of *Davis*, see Barbara Lerner, "Washington v. Davis: Quantity, Quality, and Equality in Employment Testing," 1976 *Sup.Ct.Rev.* 263.

"Purposeful racial discrimination invokes the strictest scrutiny of adverse differential treatment. Absent such purpose, differential impact is subject only to the test of rationality."

ROGERS v. LODGE

458 U.S. 613, 102 S.Ct. 3272, 73 L.Ed.2d 1012 (1982).

Eight black citizens of Burke County, Georgia, filed a class action in a federal district court, claiming that the county's political system denied their constitutional rights under the First, Thirteenth, Fourteenth, and Fifteenth amendments, as well as their statutory rights under federal civil rights laws. The county chose the five members of its governing board by at-large elections, that is, there were no subdivisions of the county. Each candidate had to win a county-wide election. No black had ever been selected. The district judge found for the plaintiffs and ordered that the county be divided into five geographic areas, each of which would be the electoral district for a commissioner. The court of appeals affirmed, and the county appealed.

Mr. Justice **WHITE** delivered the opinion of the Court. . . .

II

At-large voting schemes and multimember districts tend to minimize the voting strength of minority groups by permitting the political majority to elect *all* representatives of the district. A distinct minority, whether it be a racial, ethnic, economic, or political group, may be unable to elect any representatives in an at-large election, yet may be able to elect several representatives if the political unit is divided into single-member districts. The minority's voting power in a multimember district is particularly diluted when bloc voting occurs and ballots are cast along strict majority-minority lines. While multimember districts have been challenged for "their winner-take-all aspects, their tendency to submerge minorities and to over-represent the winning party," Whitcomb v. Chavis (1971), this Court has repeatedly held that they are not unconstitutional per se. Mobile v. Bolden [1980]; White v. Regester (1973); *Whitcomb*. The Court has recognized, however, that multimember districts violate the Fourteenth Amendment if "conceived or operated as purposeful devices to further racial . . . discrimination" by minimizing, cancelling out or diluting the voting strength of racial elements in the voting population. *Whitcomb*. Cases charging that multimember districts unconstitutionally dilute the voting strength of racial minorities are thus subject to the standard of proof generally applicable to Equal Protection Clause cases. Washington v. Davis (1976) and Village of Arlington Heights v. Metropolitan Housing Development Corp. (1977) made it clear that in order for the Equal Protection Clause to be violated, "the invidious quality of a law claimed to be racially discriminatory must ultimately be traced to a racially discriminatory purpose." . . .[1]

Arlington Heights and *Davis* both rejected the notion that a law is invalid under the Equal Protection Clause simply because it may affect a greater proportion of one race than another. However, both cases recognized that discriminatory intent need not be proven by direct evidence. . . . Thus determining the existence of a discriminatory purpose "demands a sensitive inquiry into such circumstantial and direct evidence of intent as may be available." *Arlington Heights*.

In *Mobile* the Court was called upon to apply these principles to the at-large election system in Mobile, Alabama. . . .

Justice Stewart, writing for himself and three other Justices, noted that to prevail . . . plaintiffs had to prove the system was "conceived or operated as [a] purposeful devic[e] to further racial . . . discrimination." Such a requirement "is simply one aspect of the basic principle that only if there is purposeful discrimination can there be a violation of the Equal Protection Clause of the Fourteenth Amendment". . . . Another Justice agreed with the standard of proof recognized by the plurality. (White, J., dissenting).

---

1. Purposeful racial discrimination invokes the strictest scrutiny of adverse differential treatment. Absent such purpose, differential impact is subject only to the test of rationality. *Davis*. [Footnote by the Court.]

The plurality went on to conclude that the District Court had failed to comply with this standard. . . . Finally, the plurality concluded that the evidence upon which the lower courts had relied was "insufficient to prove an unconstitutionally discriminatory purpose in the present case." Justice Stevens rejected the intentional discrimination standard but concluded that the proof failed to satisfy the legal standard that in his view was the applicable rule. He therefore concurred in the judgment of reversal. Four other Justices, however, thought the evidence sufficient to satisfy the purposeful discrimination standard. One of them, Justice Blackmun, nevertheless concurred in the Court's judgment because he believed an erroneous remedy had been imposed. . . .

. . . First, and fundamentally, we are unconvinced that the District Court in this case applied the wrong legal standard. Not only was the District Court's decision rendered a considerable time after *Davis* and *Arlington Heights,* but the trial judge also had the benefit of Nevett v. Sides (1978), where the Court of Appeals for the Fifth Circuit assessed the impact of *Davis* and *Arlington Heights* and held that "a showing of racially motivated discrimination is a necessary element in an equal protection voting dilution claim. . . ." The court stated that "[t]he ultimate issue in a case alleging unconstitutional dilution of the votes of a racial group is whether the districting plan under attack exists because it was intended to diminish or dilute the political efficacy of that group." The Court of Appeals also explained that although the evidentiary factors outlined in Zimmer [v. McKeithen (1973)] were important considerations in arriving at the ultimate conclusion of discriminatory intent, the plaintiff is not limited to those factors. . . .

The District Court referred to *Nevett* and demonstrated its understanding of the controlling standard. . . . The District Court then proceeded to deal with what it considered to be the relevant proof and concluded that the at-large scheme of electing commissioners, "although racially neutral when adopted, is being *maintained* for invidious purposes." That system "while neutral in origin . . . has been subverted to invidious purposes." . . .

III

A

We are also unconvinced that we should disturb the District Court's finding that the at-large system in Burke County was being maintained for the invidious purpose of diluting the voting strength of the black population. . . .

B

The District Court found that blacks have always made up a substantial majority of the population in Burke County, but that they are a distinct minority of the registered voters. There was also overwhelming evidence of bloc voting along racial lines. Hence, although there had been black candidates, no black had ever been elected to the Burke County commission. These facts bear heavily on the issue of purposeful discrimination. Voting along racial lines allows those elected to ignore black interests without fear of political consequences, and without bloc voting the minority candidates would not lose elections solely because of their race. . . .

Under our cases, however, such facts are insufficient in themselves to prove purposeful discrimination absent other evidence such as proof that blacks have less opportunity to participate in the political processes and to elect candidates of their choice. United Jewish Organizations v. Carey (1977); *White; Whitcomb.* See also *Mobile.* Both the District Court and the Court of Appeals thought the supporting proof in this case was sufficient to support an inference of intentional discrimination. The supporting evidence was organized primarily around the factors which *Nevett* had deemed relevant to the issue of intentional discrimination. . . .

The District Court began by determining the impact of past discrimination on the ability of blacks to participate effectively in the political process. Past discrimination was found to contribute to low black voter registration because prior to the Voting Rights Act of 1965, blacks had been denied access to the political process by means such as literacy tests, poll taxes, and white primaries. The result was that "Black suffrage in Burke County was virtually non-existent." Black voter registration in Burke County has increased following the Voting Rights Act to the point that some 38 per cent of blacks eligible to vote are registered to do so. On that basis the District Court inferred that "past discrimination has had an adverse effect on black voter registration which lingers to this date." Past discrimination against blacks in education also had the same effect. Not only did Burke County schools discriminate against blacks as recently as 1969, but some schools still remain essentially segregated and blacks as a group have completed less formal education than whites.

The District Court found further evidence of exclusion from the political process. Past discrimination had prevented blacks from effectively participating in Democratic Party affairs and in primary elections. . . . There were also property ownership requirements that made it difficult for blacks to serve as chief registrar in the county. There had been discrimination in the selection of grand jurors, the hiring of county employees, and in the appointments to boards and committees which oversee the county government. The District Court thus concluded that historical discrimination had restricted the present opportunity of blacks effectively to participate in the political process. Evidence of historical discrimination is relevant to drawing an inference of purposeful discrimination. . . .

Extensive evidence was cited by the District Court to support its finding that elected officials of Burke County have been unresponsive and insensitive to the needs of the black community, which increases the likelihood that the political process was not equally open to blacks.

This evidence ranged from the effects of past discrimination which still haunt the county courthouse to the infrequent appointment of blacks to county boards and committees; the overtly discriminatory pattern of paving county roads; the reluctance of the county to remedy black complaints, which forced blacks to take legal action to obtain school and grand jury desegregation; and the role played by the County Commissioners in the incorporation of an all-white private school to which they donated public funds for the purchase of band uniforms.

The District Court also considered the depressed socio-economic status of Burke County blacks. It found that proportionately more blacks than whites have incomes below the poverty level. Nearly 53 per cent of all black families living in Burke County had incomes equal to or less than three-fourths of a poverty-level income. Not only have blacks completed less formal education than whites, but the education they have received "was qualitatively inferior to a marked degree." Blacks tend to receive less pay than whites, even for similar work, and they tend to be employed in menial jobs more often than whites. Seventy-three per cent of houses occupied by blacks lacked all or some plumbing facilities; only 16 per cent of white-occupied houses suffered the same deficiency. The District Court concluded that the depressed socio-economic status of blacks results in part from "the lingering effects of past discrimination."

Although finding that the state policy behind the at-large electoral system in Burke County was "neutral in origin," the District Court concluded that the policy "has been subverted to invidious purposes." . . .

The trial court considered, in addition, several factors which this Court has indicated enhance the tendency of multimember districts to minimize the voting strength of racial minorities. See *Whitcomb*. It found that the sheer geographic size of the county, which is nearly two-thirds the size of Rhode Island, "has made it more difficult for Blacks to get to polling places or to campaign for office." . . . The majority vote requirement was found "to submerge the will of the minority" and thus "deny the minority's access to the system." The court also found the requirement that candidates run for specific seats enhances [appelle's] lack of access because it prevents a cohesive political group from concentrating on a single candidate. Because Burke County has no residency requirement, "[a]ll candidates could reside in Waynesboro, or in 'lilly-white' neighborhoods. To that extent, the denial of access becomes enhanced."

. . . . As in *White*, the District Court's findings were "sufficient to sustain [its] judgment . . . and, on this record, we have no reason to disturb them."

IV

We also find no reason to overturn the relief ordered by the District Court. . . .

[*Affirmed.*]

Justice **POWELL**, with whom Justice **REHNQUIST** joins, dissenting.

.   .   .

II

The Court's decision today relies heavily on the capacity of the federal district courts—essentially free from any standards propounded by this Court—to determine whether at-large voting systems are "being maintained for the invidious purpose of diluting the voting strength of the black population." Federal courts thus are invited to engage in deeply subjective inquiries into the motivations of local officials in structuring local governments. Inquiries of this kind not only can be "unseemly," see Karst, The Costs of Motive-Centered Inquiry, 15 *San Diego Law Rev.* 1163, 1164 (1978); they intrude the federal courts— with only the vaguest constitutional direction—into an area of intensely local and political concern.   .   .   .

.   .   .

A   .   .   .

.   .   . In the absence of compelling reasons of both law and fact, the federal judiciary is unwarranted in undertaking to restructure state political systems. This is inherently a political area, where the identification of a seeming violation does not necessarily suggest an enforceable judicial remedy—or at least none short of a system of quotas or group representation. Any such system, of course, would be antithetical to the principles of our democracy.

B

.   .   . "The central purpose of the Equal Protection Clause of the Fourteenth Amendment is the prevention of official conduct discriminating on the basis of race." *Davis.* Because I am unwilling to abandon this central principle in cases of this kind, I cannot join Justice Stevens's opinion.

Nonetheless, I do agree with him that what he calls "objective" factors should be the focus of inquiry in vote-dilution cases. Unlike the considerations on which the lower courts relied in this case and in *Mobile,* the factors identified by Justice Stevens as "objective" in fact are direct, reliable, and unambiguous indices of discriminatory *intent.* If we held, as I think we should, that the district courts must place primary reliance on these factors to establish discriminatory intent, we would prevent federal court inquiries into the *subjective* thought processes of local officials—at least until enough objective evidence had been presented to warrant discovery into subjective motivations in this complex, politically charged area. By prescribing such a rule we would hold federal courts to a standard that was judicially manageable. And we would remain faithful to the central protective purpose of the Equal Protection Clause.

In the absence of proof of discrimination by reliance on the kind of objective factors identified by Justice Stevens, I would hold that the factors cited by the Court of Appeals are too attenuated as a matter of law to support an inference of discriminatory intent. I would reverse its judgment on that basis.

Justice **STEVENS,** dissenting.

. . . The record in this case amply supports the conclusion that the governing officials of Burke County have repeatedly denied black citizens rights guaranteed by the Fourteenth and Fifteenth Amendments to the Federal Constitution. No one could legitimately question the validity of remedial measures, whether legislative or judicial, designed to prohibit discriminatory conduct by public officials and to guarantee that black citizens are effectively afforded the rights to register and to vote. . . .

Nor, in my opinion, could there be any doubt about the constitutionality of an amendment to the Voting Rights Act that would require Burke County and other covered jurisdictions to abandon specific kinds of at-large voting schemes that perpetuate the effects of past discrimination. . . .

The Court's decision today, however, is not based on either its own conception of sound policy or any statutory command. The decision rests entirely on the Court's interpretation of the requirements of the Federal Constitution. Despite my sympathetic appraisal of the Court's laudable goals, I am unable to agree with its approach to the constitutional issue that is presented. In my opinion, this case raises questions that encompass more than the immediate plight of disadvantaged black citizens. I believe the Court errs by holding the structure of the local governmental unit unconstitutional without identifying an acceptable, judicially-manageable standard for adjudicating cases of this kind.

I

The Court's entry into the business of electoral reapportionment in 1962 was preceded by a lengthy and scholarly debate over the role the judiciary legitimately could play in what Justice Frankfurter described in Colegrove v. Green [1946] as a "political thicket." . . .

In 1962, the Court changed course. . . . [I]t held that the political question doctrine did not foreclose judicial review. Baker v. Carr. That decision represents one of the great landmarks in the history of this Court's jurisprudence.

Two aspects of the Court's opinion in *Baker* are of special relevance to the case the Court decides today. First, the Court's scholarly review of the political question doctrine focused on the dominant importance of satisfactory standards for judicial determination. Second, the Court's articulation of the relevant constitutional standard made no reference to subjective intent. The host of cases that have arisen in the wake of *Baker* have shared these two characteristics. They have formulated, refined, and applied a judicially manageable standard that has become known as the one-person, one-vote rule; they have attached no significance to the subjective intent of the decisionmakers who adopted or maintained the official rule under attack. . . .

. . . [The Court] starts from the premise that Burke County's at-large method of electing its five county commissioners is, on its face, unobjectionable. The otherwise valid system is unconstitutional, however, because it makes it more difficult for the minority to elect commissioners and because the majority that is now in power has maintained the system for that very reason. Two factors are apparently of critical importance: (1) the intent of the majority to maintain control; and (2) the racial character of the minority.

I am troubled by each aspect of the Court's analysis. . . . Assuming, however, that the system is otherwise valid, I do not believe that the subjective intent of the persons who adopted the system in 1911, or the intent of those who have since declined to change it, can determine its constitutionality. Even if the intent of the political majority were the controlling constitutional consideration, I could not agree that the only political groups that are entitled to protection under the Court's rule are those defined by racial characteristics. . . . .

III

Ever since I joined the Court, I have been concerned about the Court's emphasis on subjective intent as a criterion for constitutional adjudication. Although that criterion is often regarded as a restraint on the exercise of judicial power, it may in fact provide judges with a tool for exercising power that otherwise would be confined to the legislature. My principal concern with the subjective intent standard, however, is unrelated to the quantum of power it confers upon the judiciary. It is based on the quality of that power. For in the long run constitutional adjudication that is premised on a case-by-case appraisal of the subjective intent of local decisionmakers cannot possibly satisfy the requirement of impartial administration of the law that is embodied in the Equal Protection Clause of the Fourteenth Amendment.

The facts of this case illustrate the ephemeral character of a constitutional standard that focuses on subjective intent. When the suit was filed in 1976, approximately 58 percent of the population of Burke County was black and approximately 42 percent was white. Because black citizens had been denied access to the political process—through means that have since been outlawed by the Voting Rights Act of 1965—and because there had been insufficient time to enable the registration of black voters to overcome the history of past injustice, the majority of registered voters in the county were white. The at-large electoral system therefore served, as a result of the presence of bloc voting, to maintain white control of the local government. Whether it would have continued to do so would have depended on a mix of at least three different factors—the continuing increase in voter registration among blacks, the continuing exodus of black residents from the county, and the extent to which racial bloc voting continued to dominate local politics.

If those elected officials in control of the political machinery had formed the judgment that these factors created a likelihood that a bloc of black voters was about to achieve sufficient strength to elect an entirely new administration, they might have decided to abandon the at-large system and substitute five single-member districts with the boundary lines drawn to provide a white majority in three districts and a black majority in only two. Under the Court's intent standard, such a change presumably would violate the Fourteenth Amendment. It is ironic that the remedy ordered by the District Court fits that pattern precisely.[1]

If votes continue to be cast on a racial basis, the judicial remedy virtually guarantees that whites will continue to control a majority of seats on the county board. It is at least possible that white control of the political machinery has been frozen by judicial decree at a time when increased black voter registration might have led to a complete change of administration. Since the federal judge's intent was unquestionably benign rather than individuous—and, unlike that of state officials, is presumably not subject in any event to the Court's standard—that result has been accomplished without violating the Federal Constitution.

In the future, it is not inconceivable that the white officials who are likely to remain in power under the District Court's plan will desire to perpetuate that system and to continue to control a majority of seats on the county commission. Under this Court's standard, if some of those officials harbor such an intent for an "invidious" reason, the District Court's plan will itself become unconstitutional. It is not clear whether the invidious intent would have to be shared by all three white commissioners, by merely a majority of two, or by simply one if he were influential. It is not clear whether the issue would be affected by the intent of the two black commissioners, who might fear that a return to an at-large system would undermine the certainty of two black seats.
. . . In sum, as long as racial consciousness exists in Burke County, its governmental structure is subject to attack. . . .
    . . . [T]he question becomes whether the system was *maintained* for a discriminatory purpose. Whose intentions control? Obviously not the voters, although they may be most responsible for the attitudes and actions of local government. Assuming that it is the intentions of the "state actors" that is critical, how will their mental processes be discovered? Must a specific proposal for change be defeated? What if

---

1. The following table shows a breakdown of the population of the districts in the plan selected by the District Court as to race and voting age:

District	Voting Age Population	Black Voting Age Population (%)	White Voting Age Population (%)
1	2,048	1,482 (72.4)	556 (27.6)
2	2,029	1,407 (69.3)	622 (30.7)
3	2,115	978 (46.2)	1,137 (53.8)
4	2,112	947 (44.6)	1,175 (55.4)
5	2,217	803 (36.2)	1,414 (63.8)

[Footnote by Justice Stevens.]

different motives are held by different legislators or, indeed, by a single official? Is a selfish desire to stay in office sufficient to justify a failure to change a governmental system?

The Court avoids these problems by failing to answer the very question that its standard asks. Presumably, according to the Court's analysis, the Burke County governmental structure is unconstitutional because it was maintained at some point for an invidious purpose. Yet the Court scarcely identifies the manner in which changes to a county governmental structure are made. There is no reference to any unsuccessful attempt to replace the at-large system with single-member districts. It is incongruous that subjective intent is identified as the constitutional standard and yet the persons who allegedly harbored an improper intent are never identified or mentioned. . . .

. . . I am not convinced, however, that the Constitution affords a right—and this is the *only* right the Court finds applicable in this case—to have every official decision made without the influence of considerations that are in some way "discriminatory." Is the failure of a state legislature to ratify the Equal Rights Amendment invalid if a federal judge concludes that a majority of the legislators harbored stereotypical views of the proper role of women in society? Is the establishment of a memorial for Jews slaughtered in World War II unconstitutional if civic leaders believe that their cause is more meritorious than that of victimized Palestinian refugees? Is the failure to adopt a state holiday for Martin Luther King, Jr. invalid if it is proved that state legislators believed that he does not deserve to be commemorated? Is the refusal to provide medicaid funding for abortions unconstitutional if officials intend to discriminate against women who would abort a fetus?

A rule that would invalidate all governmental action motivated by racial, ethnic or political considerations is too broad. Moreover, in my opinion the Court is incorrect in assuming that the intent of elected officials is invidious when they are motivated by a desire to retain control of the local political machinery. For such an intent is surely characteristic of politicians throughout the country. . . .

[A] device that serves no purpose other than to exclude minority groups from effective political participation is unlawful under objective standards. But if a political majority's intent to maintain control of a legitimate local government is sufficient to invalidate any electoral device that makes it more difficult for a minority group to elect candidates—regardless of the nature of the interest that gives the minority group cohesion—the Court is not just entering a "political thicket"; it is entering a vast wonderland of judicial review of political activity.

The obvious response to this suggestion is that this case involves a racial group and that governmental decisions that disadvantage such a group must be subject to special scrutiny under the Fourteenth Amendment. I therefore must consider whether the Court's holding can legitimately be confined to political groups that are identified by racial characteristics.

IV . . .

Groups of every character may associate together to achieve legitimate common goals. If they voluntarily identify themselves by a common interest in a specific issue, by a common ethnic heritage, by a common religious belief, or by their race, that characteristic assumes significance as the bond that gives the group cohesion and political strength. When referring to different kinds of political groups, this Court has consistently indicated that . . . the Equal Protection Clause does not make some groups of citizens more equal than others. See Zobel v. Williams [1982] (Brennan, J., concurring). Thus, the Court has considered challenges to discrimination based on "differences of color, race, nativity, religious opinions [or] political affiliations," American Sugar Refining Co. v. Louisiana [1900], to redistricting plans that serve "to further racial or economic discrimination," *Whitcomb*, to biases "tending to favor particular political interests or geographic areas." Abate v. Mundt [1971]. Indeed, in its opinion today the Court recognizes that the practical impact of the electoral system at issue applies equally to any "distinct minority, whether it be a racial, ethnic, economic, or political group."

A constitutional standard that gave special protection to political groups identified by racial characteristics would be inconsistent with the basic tenet of the Equal Protection Clause. Those groups are no more or less able to pursue their interests in the political arena than are groups defined by other characteristics. Nor can it be said that racial alliances are so unrelated to political action that any electoral decision that is influenced by racial consciousness—as opposed to other forms of political consciousness—is inherently irrational. For it is the very political power of a racial or ethnic group that creates a danger that an entrenched majority will take action contrary to the group's political interests. . . . It would be unrealistic to distinguish racial groups from other political groups on the ground that race is an irrelevant factor in the political process.

Racial consciousness and racial association are not desirable features of our political system. We all look forward to the day when race is an irrelevant factor in the political process. In my opinion, however, that goal will best be achieved by eliminating the vestiges of discrimination that motivate disadvantaged racial and ethnic groups to vote as indentifiable units. Whenever identifiable groups in our society are disadvantaged, they will share common political interests and tend to vote as a "bloc." In this respect, racial groups are like other political groups. A permanent constitutional rule that treated them differently would, in my opinion, itself tend to perpetuate race as a feature distinct from all others; a trait that makes persons different in the eyes of the law. . . .

My conviction that all minority groups are equally entitled to constitutional protection against the misuse of the majority's political power does not mean that I would abandon judicial review of such action. . . . [A] gerrymander as grotesque as the boundaries condemned in Gomillion v. Lightfoot [1960] is intolerable whether it fences out black voters, Republican voters, or Irish-Catholic voters. But if the standard the Court applies today extends to all types of minority groups, it is either so broad that virtually every political device is vulnerable or it is so undefined that federal judges can pick and choose almost at will among those that will be upheld and those that will be condemned.

There are valid reasons for concluding that certain minority groups—such as the black voters in Burke County, Georgia—should be given special protection from political oppression by the dominant majority. But those are reasons that justify the application of a legislative policy choice rather than a constitutional principle that cannot be confined to special circumstances or to a temporary period in our history. Any suggestion that political groups in which black leadership predominates are in need of a permanent constitutional shield against the tactics of their political opponents underestimates the resourcefulness, the wisdom, and the demonstrated capacity of such leaders. . . .

Editors' Notes

(1) **Query:** Dissenting in *Mobile* (1980), Justice Marshall protested that the plurality had failed "to distinguish two distinct lines of equal protection decisions: those involving suspect classifications and those involving fundamental rights." Where the former were involved, "a showing of discriminatory purpose is necessary to impose strict scrutiny of facially neutral classifications having a racially discriminatory impact." On the other hand, "if a classification 'impinges upon a fundamental right explicitly or implicitly protected by the Constitution . . . strict judicial scrutiny' is required, regardless of whether the infringement was intentional." And, Marshall closed his logical noose, the Court had often held that the right to a vote, an undiluted vote, equal to that of every other citizen, was a fundamental right. Thus search for discriminatory purpose in voting cases was irrelevant. In *Rogers,* however, Marshall joined the majority in its quest for discriminatory purpose. Why?

(2) In addition to the article by Kenneth L. Karst, "The Costs of Motive-Centered Inquiry," 15 *San Diego L.Rev.* 1163 (1978), cited by Justice Powell, see also John Hart Ely, "The Centrality and Limits of Motivation Analysis," 15 *ibid.* 1155 (1978); these articles were part of a symposium on legislative motivation published in that volume. See also earlier works: Paul Brest, "Palmer v. Thompson: An Approach to the Problem of Unconstitutional Motive," 1971 *Sup.Ct.Rev.* 95; John Hart Ely, "Legislative and Administrative Motivation in Constitutional Law," 79 *Yale L.J.* 1205 (1970), and chap. 6 of his *Democracy and Distrust* (Cambridge, Mass.: Harvard University Press, 1980); Michael J. Perry, "The Disproportionate Impact Theory of Racial Discrimina-

tion," 125 *U.Pa.L.Rev.* 540 (1977); and Laurence H. Tribe, *American Constitutional Law* (Mineola, N.Y.: Foundation Press, 1978), pp. 1028–1032.

V. HOW TO END RACIAL INEQUALITY: AFFIRMATIVE ACTION

"The guarantees of equal protection cannot mean one thing when applied to one individual and something else when applied to a person of another color."—Justice POWELL

"[W]e cannot . . . let color blindness become myopia which masks the reality that many 'created equal' have been treated within our lifetimes as inferior both by law and their fellow citizens."—Justices BRENNAN, WHITE, MARSHALL, and BLACKMUN

REGENTS OF THE UNIVERSITY OF CALIFORNIA v. BAKKE
438 U.S. 265, 98 S.Ct. 2733, 57 L.Ed.2d 750 (1978).

Affirmative action seemed headed for its first major judicial test of constitutionality when Defunis v. Odegaard reached the Supreme Court during its 1973 term. Marco DeFunis, a white male, had been denied admission to the law school at the University of Washington, while 36 of the 37 black, Chicano, Indian, and Filipino applicants who were accepted had lower scores on the Law School Admission Test and lower college grades. DeFunis sued in a state court, claiming a denial of equal protection. The trial court ordered the University to admit him, but the state supreme court reversed, although not until he was in his second year. DeFunis then petitioned the U.S. Supreme Court for certiorari and obtained a stay from Justice Douglas, sitting as a circuit judge, of the state supreme court's order, pending the U.S. Supreme Court's decision. By the time oral argument was completed, DeFunis was in the middle of his third year, and the law school announced that, regardless of the Court's ruling, he would be allowed to graduate. The Supreme Court then held the case to be moot.

The issue would quickly return, however. As part of its plan for "affirmative action," the Medical School of the University of California at Davis established a special admissions program for members of minority groups, allotting to them 16 of the 100 places in each entering class. In 1973 and 1974, the school denied admission to Allan Bakke, a white male, even though, according to the supposed standards for acceptance, he scored well above most candidates admitted under the special program. (The mean College Grade Point Average of those admitted in 1974 under the special program was 2.62; Bakke's was 3.51 on a scale in which A = 4, B = 3, C = 2, D = 1, and F = 0. On the national Medical College Admission Test, Bakke scored in the ninety-sixth percentile on verbal aptitude and in the ninety-seventh on scientific aptitude; the average scores of those admitted under the special program were at the thirty-fourth and thirty-seventh percentiles. Moreover, at least one person so admitted had had a C− average in college and scored in the lower third of the country on both verbal and scientific aptitude.)

After his second rejection, Bakke filed suit in a state court, which held Davis's "affirmative action" plan unconstitutional because it was based on race.

The court, however, refused to order Bakke's admission on grounds that he had not proved that he would have been admitted in the absence of the special program. Both Bakke and Davis appealed parts of the judgment. California's Supreme Court ruled that the "affirmative action" plan violated both the Fourteenth Amendment and Title VI of the Civil Rights Act of 1964. (The most relevant section, 601, reads: "No person in the United States shall, on the ground of race, color, or national origin, be excluded from participation in, be denied the benefits of, or be subjected to discrimination under any program or activity receiving Federal financial assistance." The Medical School at Davis was receiving federal financial aid.) The court ordered Bakke admitted. Davis then sought and obtained certiorari from the U.S. Supreme Court.

The Justices could not agree on an opinion for the Court. Four (Brennan, White, Marshall, and Blackmun) thought the "affirmative action" plan constitutional and legal under Title VI and voted to deny Bakke admission. Four (Burger, Stewart, Rehnquist, and Stevens) believed that Title VI outlawed Davis's plan and voted for Bakke's admission. This even division made the role of the ninth Justice, Lewis F. Powell, decisive.

Mr. Justice **POWELL** announced the judgment of the Court. . . .

. . . . I believe that so much of the judgment of the California court as holds petitioner's special admissions program unlawful and directs that respondent be admitted to the Medical School must be affirmed. For the reasons expressed in a separate opinion, my Brothers The Chief Justice [Burger], Mr. Justice Stewart, Mr. Justice Rehnquist, and Mr. Justice Stevens concur in this judgment. . . .

I also conclude . . . that the portion of the court's judgment enjoining petitioner from according any consideration to race in its admissions process must be reversed. For reasons expressed in separate opinions, my Brothers Mr. Justice Brennan, Mr. Justice White, Mr. Justice Marshall, and Mr. Justice Blackmun concur in this judgment. . . .

II

[Justice Powell analyzed the wording and legislative history of Title VI of the Civil Rights Act of 1964 and concluded that it proscribed "only those racial classifications that would violate the Equal Protection Clause or the Fifth Amendment." Thus he moved to the basic constitutional question: Did California's plan of affirmative action deny Bakke equal protection?]

III

A . . .

. . . . [T]he parties fight a sharp preliminary action over the proper characterization of the special admissions program. Petitioner prefers to view it as establishing a "goal" of minority representation. . . . Respondent . . . labels it a racial quota.

This semantic distinction is beside the point: the special admissions program is undeniably a classification based on race and ethnic background. To the extent that there existed a pool of at least minimally qualified minority applicants to fill the 16 special admissions seats, white applicants could compete only for 84 seats in the entering class, rather than the 100 open to minority applicants. Whether this limitation is described as a quota or a goal, it is a line drawn on the basis of race and ethnic status.

The guarantees of the Fourteenth Amendment extend to persons. Its language is explicit: "No state shall . . . deny to any person within its jurisdiction the equal protection of the laws." It is settled beyond question that the "rights created by the first section of the Fourteenth Amendment are, by its terms, guaranteed to the individual. . . . ." The guarantee of equal protection cannot mean one thing when applied to one individual and something else when applied to a person of another color. If both are not accorded the same protection, then it is not equal.

Nevertheless, petitioner argues that the court below erred in applying strict scrutiny to the special admissions programs because white males . . . are not a "discrete and insular minority" requiring extraordinary protection from the majoritarian political process. [United States v.] Carolene Products Co. (1938). This rationale, however, has never been invoked in our decisions as a prerequisite to subjecting racial or ethnic distinctions to strict scrutiny. Nor has this Court held that discreteness and insularity constitute necessary preconditions to a holding that a particular classification is invidious. . . . These characteristics may be relevant in deciding whether or not to add new types of classifications to the list of "suspect" categories or whether a particular classification survives close examination. Racial and ethnic classifications, however, are subject to stringent examination without regard to these additional characteristics. [Korematsu v. United States (1944).]

B . . .

Although many of the Framers of the Fourteenth Amendment conceived of its primary function as bridging the vast distance between members of the Negro race and the white "majority" the Amendment itself was framed in universal terms, without reference to color, ethnic origin, or condition of prior servitude. As this Court recently remarked . . . "the 39th Congress was intent upon establishing in federal law a broader principle than would have been necessary to meet the particular and immediate plight of the newly freed Negro slaves." McDonald v. Santa Fe Trail Transp. Co. (1976). . . .

Over the past 30 years, this Court has embarked upon the crucial mission of interpreting the Equal Protection Clause with the view of assuring to all persons "the protection of equal laws." Yick Wo [v. Hopkins (1886)] in a Nation confronting a legacy of slavery and racial discrimination. . . . Because the landmark decisions in this area arose in response to the continued exclusion of Negroes from the mainstream of American society, they could be characterized as involving discrimination by the "majority" white race against the Negro

minority. But they need not be read as depending upon that characterization for their results. It suffices to say that "[o]ver the years, this
Court consistently repudiated '[d]istinctions between citizens solely because of their ancestry' as being 'odious to a free people whose institutions are founded upon the doctrine of equality.'" Hirabayashi v.
United States (1943).

Petitioner urges us to adopt for the first time a more restrictive
view of the Equal Protection Clause and hold that discrimination
against members of the white "majority" cannot be suspect if its
purpose can be characterized as "benign." The clock of our liberties,
however, cannot be turned back to 1868. [Brown v. Board of Education
(1954)] It is far too late to argue that the guarantee of equal protection
to *all* persons permits the recognition of special wards entitled to a
degree of protection greater than that accorded others. . . .

Once the artificial line of a "two-class theory" of the Fourteenth
Amendment is put aside, the difficulties entailed in varying the level of
judicial review according to a perceived "preferred" status of a particular racial or ethnic minority are intractable. The concepts of "majority" and "minority" necessarily reflect temporary arrangements and
political judgments. . . . [T]he white "majority" itself is composed
of various minority groups, most of which can lay claim to a history of
prior discrimination. . . . There is no principled basis for deciding
which groups would merit "heightened judicial solicitude" and which
would not. . . .

Moreover, there are serious problems of justice connected with the
idea of preference itself. First, it may not always be clear that a so-
called preference is in fact benign. Courts may be asked to validate
burdens imposed upon individual members of particular groups in order
to advance the group's general interest. . . . Nothing in the Constitution supports the notion that individuals may be asked to suffer
otherwise impermissible burdens in order to enhance the societal standing of their ethnic groups. Second, preferential programs may only
reinforce common stereotypes holding that certain groups are unable to
achieve success without special protection. . . . Third, there is a
measure of inequity in forcing innocent persons . . . to bear the
burdens of redressing grievances not of their making.

By hitching the meaning of the Equal Protection Clause to these
transitory considerations, we would be holding, as a constitutional
principle, that judicial scrutiny of classifications touching on racial and
ethnic background may vary with the ebb and flow of political forces.
Disparate constitutional tolerance of such classifications well may serve
to exacerbate racial and ethnic antagonisms rather than alleviate
them. . . . Also, the mutability of a constitutional principle, based
upon shifting political and social judgments, undermines the chances
for consistent application of the Constitution from one generation to the
next, a critical feature of its coherent interpretation. . . . In expounding the Constitution, the Court's role is to discern "principles
sufficiently absolute to give them roots throughout the community and

continuity over significant periods of time, and to lift them above the level of the pragmatic political judgments. . . ."

If it is the individual who is entitled to judicial protection . . . rather than the individual only because of his membership in a particular group, then constitutional standards may be applied consistently. Political judgments regarding the necessity for the particular classification may be weighed in the constitutional balance . . . but the standard of justification will remain constant. This is as it should be, since those political judgments are the product of rough compromise struck by contending groups within the democratic process. When they touch upon an individual's race or ethnic background, he is entitled to a judicial determination that the burden he is asked to bear on that basis is precisely tailored to serve a compelling governmental interest. . . .

IV

We have held that in "order to justify the use of a suspect classification, a State must show that its purpose or interest is both constitutionally permissible and substantial, and that its use of the classification is 'necessary . . . to the accomplishment' of its purpose or the safeguarding of its interest." In re Griffiths (1973); Loving v. Virginia (1967). . . .

A

If petitioner's purpose is to assure within its student body some specified percentage of a particular group merely because of its race or ethnic origin, such a preferential purpose must be rejected . . . as facially invalid. Preferring members of any one group for no reason other than race or ethnic origin is discrimination for its own sake. This the Constitution forbids. E.g., *Loving, Brown.*

B

The State certainly has a legitimate and substantial interest in ameliorating, or eliminating . . . the disabling effects of identified discrimination. . . .

We have never approved a classification that aids persons perceived as members of relatively victimized groups at the expense of other innocent individuals in the absence of judicial, legislative, or administrative findings of constitutional or statutory violations. . . . After such findings . . . the governmental interest in preferring members of the injured groups at the expense of others is substantial, since the legal rights of the victims must be vindicated. . . . Without such findings of constitutional or statutory violations, it cannot be said that the government has any greater interest in helping one individual than in refraining from harming another. Thus, the government has no compelling justification for inflicting such harm.

Petitioner does not purport to have made, and is in no position to make such findings. . . . Lacking this capability, petitioner has not carried its burden of justification on this issue.

Hence, the purpose of helping certain groups whom the faculty of the Davis Medical School perceived as victims of "societal discrimination" does not justify a classification that imposes disadvantages upon persons . . . who bear no responsibility for whatever harm the beneficiaries of the special admissions program are thought to have suffered. . . .

C

Petitioner identifies, as another purpose of its program, improving the delivery of health care services to communities currently underserved. It may be assumed that in some situations a State's interest in facilitating the health care of its citizens is sufficiently compelling to support the use of a suspect classification. But there is virtually no evidence in the record indicating that petitioner's special admissions program is either needed or geared to promote that goal. . . .

D

The fourth goal asserted by petitioner is the attainment of a diverse student body. This clearly is a constitutionally permissible goal for an institution of higher education. Academic freedom, though not a specifically enumerated constitutional right, long has been viewed as a special concern of the First Amendment. The freedom of a university to make its own judgments as to education includes the selection of its student body. . . .

Thus, in arguing that its universities must be accorded the right to select those students who will contribute the most to the "robust exchange of ideas," petitioner invokes a countervailing constitutional interest, that of the First Amendment. In this light, petitioner must be viewed as seeking to achieve a goal that is of paramount importance in the fulfillment of its mission.

It may be argued that there is greater force to these views at the undergraduate level than in a medical school where the training is centered primarily on professional competency. But even at the graduate level, our tradition and experience lend support to the view that the contribution of diversity is substantial. . . . Physicians serve a heterogeneous population. An otherwise qualified medical student with a particular background—whether it be ethnic, geographic, culturally advantaged or disadvantaged—may bring to a professional school of medicine experiences, outlooks and ideas that enrich the training of its student body and better equip its graduates to render with understanding their vital service to humanity.

Ethnic diversity, however, is only one element in a range of factors a university properly may consider in attaining the goal of a heterogeneous student body. Although a university must have wide discretion in making the sensitive judgments as to who should be admitted, constitutional limitations protecting individual rights may not be disregarded. . . . [T]he question remains whether the program's racial classification is necessary to promote this interest. . . .

V

A

It may be assumed that the reservation of a specified number of seats in each class for individuals from the preferred ethnic groups would contribute to the attainment of considerable ethnic diversity in the student body.   But petitioner's argument that this is the only effective means of serving the interest of diversity is seriously flawed. In a most fundamental sense the argument misconceives the nature of the state interest. . . .   It is not an interest in simple ethnic diversity. . . .   The diversity that furthers a compelling state interest encompasses a far broader array of qualifications and characteristics of which racial or ethnic origin is but a single though important element.   Petitioner's special admissions program, focused solely on ethnic diversity, would hinder rather than further attainment of genuine diversity.

The experience of other university admissions programs which take race into account in achieving the educational diversity valued by the First Amendment, demonstrates that the assignment of a fixed number of places to a minority group is not a necessary means toward that end. An illuminating example is found in the Harvard College program:

> In recent years Harvard College has expanded the concept of diversity to include students from disadvantaged economic, racial and ethnic groups. . . .
>
> In practice, this new definition of diversity has meant that race has been a factor in some admission decisions.   When the Committee on Admissions reviews the large middle group of applicants who are "admissible" . . .   the race of an applicant may tip the balance in his favor just as [may] geographic origin. . . .   A farm boy from Idaho can bring something . . .   that a Bostonian cannot offer.   Similarly, a black student can usually bring something that a white person cannot offer. . . .
>
>   . . . [T]he Committee has not set target-quotas for the number of blacks, or of musicians, football players, physicists or Californians. . . . [Rather] in choosing among thousands of applicants who are not only "admissible" academically but have other strong qualities, the Committee, with a number of criteria in mind, pays some attention to distribution among many types and categories of students. . . .

In such an admissions program, race or ethnic background may be deemed a "plus" in a particular applicant's file, yet it does not insulate the individual from comparison with all other candidates for the available seats.   The file of a particular black applicant may be examined for his potential contribution to diversity without the factor of race being decisive when compared, for example, with that of an applicant identified as an Italian-American if the latter is thought to exhibit qualities more likely to promote beneficial educational pluralism.   Such qualities could include exceptional personal talents, unique work or service experience, leadership potential, maturity, demonstrated compassion, a history of overcoming disadvantage, ability to communicate with the poor, or other qualifications deemed important. . . .

This kind of program treats each applicant as an individual in the admissions process. The applicant who loses out on the last available seat to another candidate receiving a "plus" on the basis of ethnic background will not have been foreclosed from all consideration for that seat simply because he was not the right color or had the wrong surname. It would mean only that his combined qualifications, which may have included similar nonobjective factors, did not outweigh those of the other applicant. His qualifications would have been weighed fairly and competitively, and he would have no basis to complain of unequal treatment. . . .

It has been suggested that an admissions program which considers race only as one factor is simply a subtle and more sophisticated—but no less effective—means of according racial preference than the Davis program. A facial intent to discriminate, however, is evident in petitioner's preference program and not denied in this case. No such facial infirmity exists in an admissions program where race or ethnic background is simply one element—to be weighed fairly against other elements—in the selection process. . . .

B . . .

. . . [W]hen a State's distribution of benefits or imposition of burdens hinges on the color of a person's skin or ancestry, that individual is entitled to a demonstration that the challenged classification is necessary to promote a substantial state interest. Petitioner has failed to carry this burden. . . .

[Affirmed in part and reversed in part.]

Opinion of Mr. Justice **BRENNAN**, Mr. Justice **WHITE**, Mr. Justice **MARSHALL**, and Mr. Justice **BLACKMUN**, concurring in the judgment in part and dissenting. . . .

I . . .

The Fourteenth Amendment, the embodiment in the Constitution of our abiding belief in human equality, has been the law of our land for only slightly more than half its 200 years. And for half of that half, the Equal Protection Clause of the Amendment was largely moribund. . . . Worse than desuetude, the Clause was early turned against those whom it was intended to set free, condemning them to a "separate but equal" status before the law, a status always separate but seldom equal. Not until 1954 was this odious doctrine interred by our decision in Brown v. Board of Education and its progeny, which proclaimed that separate schools and public facilities of all sorts were inherently unequal and forbidden under our Constitution. Even then inequality was not eliminated with "all deliberate speed." . . . [O]fficially sanctioned discrimination is not a thing of the past.

Against this background, claims that law must be "colorblind" or that the datum of race is no longer relevant to public policy must be seen as aspiration rather than as description of reality. This is not to denigrate aspiration; for reality rebukes us that race has too often been used by those who would stigmatize and oppress minorities. Yet we cannot—and . . . need not under our Constitution or Title VI . . .—let color blindness become myopia which masks the reality that many "created equal" have been treated within our lifetimes as inferior both by the law and by their fellow citizens.

II

[The four Justices then examined the text and legislative history of the Civil Rights Act of 1964 and concluded that the statute did not outlaw affirmative action plans such as that of Davis.]

III

A

The assertion of human equality is closely associated with the proposition that differences in color or creed, birth or status, are neither significant nor relevant to the way in which persons should be treated. Nonetheless, the position . . . summed up by the shorthand phrase "[o]ur Constitution is color-blind," Plessy v. Ferguson (1896) (Harlan, J., dissenting), has never been adopted by this Court as the proper meaning of the Equal Protection Clause. Indeed, we have expressly rejected this proposition on a number of occasions.

Our cases have always implied that an "overriding statutory purpose" could be found that would justify racial classifications. . . .

We conclude, therefore, that racial classifications are not *per se* invalid under the Fourteenth Amendment. Accordingly, we turn to the problem of articulating what our role should be in reviewing state action that expressly classifies by race, e.g. *Loving, Korematsu*.

B . . .

Unquestionably we have held that a government practice or statute which restricts "fundamental rights" or which contains "suspect classifications" is to be subjected to "strict scrutiny" and can be justified only if it furthers a compelling government purpose and, even then, only if no less restrictive alternative is available. . . . But no fundamental right is involved here. . . . Nor do whites as a class have any of the "traditional indicia of suspectness: the class is not saddled with such disabilities, or subjected to such a history of purposeful unequal treatment, or relegated to such a position of political powerlessness as to command extraordinary protection from the majoritarian political process." [San Antonio v. Rodriguez (1973).] See *Carolene Products* n. 4.

. . .

. . . Nor . . . [do] the University's purposes contravene the cardinal principle that racial classifications that stigmatize—because they are drawn on the presumption that one race is inferior to another or because they put the weight of government behind racial hatred and separatism—are invalid without more. . . .

On the other hand . . . this case . . . should [not] be analyzed by applying the very loose rational-basis standard of review that is the very least that is always applied in equal protection cases. . . . [A] number of considerations . . . lead us to conclude that racial classifications designed to further remedial purposes " 'must serve important governmental objectives and must be substantially related to achievement of those objectives.' " Craig v. Boren (1976).

First, race, like, "gender-based classifications too often [has] been inexcusably utilized to stereotype and stigmatize politically powerless segments of society." . . .

Second, race, like gender and illegitimacy . . . is an immutable characteristic which its possessors are powerless to escape or set aside. While a classification is not *per se* invalid because it divides classes on the basis of an immutable characteristic . . . it is nevertheless true that such divisions are contrary to our deep belief that "legal burdens should bear some relationship to individual responsibility or wrongdoing" . . . and that advancement sanctioned, sponsored, or approved by the State should ideally be based on individual merit or achievement. . . .

In sum, because of the significant risk that racial classifications established for ostensibly benign purposes can be misused . . . to justify such a classification an important and articulated purpose for its use must be shown. In addition, any statute must be stricken that stigmatizes any group or that singles out those least well represented in the political process to bear the brunt of a benign program. Thus our review under the Fourteenth Amendment should be . . . strict and searching. . . .

IV

Davis's articulated purpose of remedying the effects of past societal discrimination is, under our cases, sufficiently important to justify the use of race-conscious admissions programs where there is a sound basis for concluding that minority underrepresentation is substantial and chronic, and that the handicap of past discrimination is impeding access of minorities to the medical school. . . .

B

Properly construed, therefore, our prior cases unequivocally show that a state government may adopt race-conscious programs if the purpose of such programs is to remove the disparate racial impact its actions might otherwise have and if there is reason to believe that the disparate impact is itself the product of past discrimination, whether its own or that of society at large. There is no question that Davis's program is valid under this test. . . .

Davis clearly could conclude that the serious and persistent underrepresentation of minorities in medicine . . . is the result of handicaps under which minority applicants labor as a consequence of a background of deliberate, purposeful discrimination against minorities in education and in society generally, as well as in the medical profession. From the inception of our national life, Negroes have been subjected to unique legal disabilities impairing access to equal educational opportunity. . . . The generation of minority students applying to Davis Medical School since it opened in 1968 . . . clearly have been victims of this discrimination. Judicial decrees recognizing discrimination in public education in California testify to the fact of widespread discrimination suffered by California-born minority applicants; many minority group members living in California, moreover, were born and reared in school districts in southern States segregated by law. . . . [T]he conclusion is inescapable that applicants to medical school must be few indeed who endured the effects of *de jure* segregation, the resistance to *Brown*, or the equally debilitating pervasive discrimination fostered by our long history of official discrimination . . . and yet come to the starting line with an education equal to whites.

. . . [T]he Department of Health, Education, and Welfare, the expert agency charged by Congress with promulgating regulations enforcing Title VI of the Civil Rights Act of 1964 . . . has also reached the conclusion that race may be taken into account in situations where a failure to do so would limit participation by minorities in federally funded programs. . . .

C

The second prong of our test—whether the Davis program stigmatizes any discrete group or individual and whether race is reasonably used in light of the program's objectives—is clearly satisfied by the Davis program.

It is not even claimed that Davis's program in any way operates to stigmatize or single out any discrete and insular, or even any identifiable, nonminority group. Nor will harm comparable to that imposed upon racial minorities by exclusion or separation on grounds of race be the likely result of the program. . . .

Nor was Bakke in any sense stamped as inferior by the Medical School's rejection of him. . . . Unlike discrimination against racial minorities, the use of racial preferences for remedial purposes does not inflict a pervasive injury upon individual whites in the sense that wherever they go or whatever they do there is a significant likelihood that they will be treated as second-class citizens because of their color.
. . . .

D

We disagree with the lower courts' conclusion that the Davis program's use of race was unreasonable in light of its objectives. . . . [T]here are no practical means by which it could achieve its ends in the foreseeable future without the use of race-conscious measures. . . .

E

Finally, Davis's special admissions program cannot be said to violate the Constitution simply because it has set aside a predetermined number of places for qualified minority applicants rather than using minority status as a positive factor to be considered in evaluating applications of disadvantaged minority applicants. For purposes of constitutional adjudication, there is no difference between the two approaches. In any admissions program which accords special consideration to disadvantaged racial minorities, a determination of the degree of preference to be given is unavoidable, and any given preference that results in the exclusion of a white candidate is no more or no less constitutionally acceptable than a program such as that at Davis. . . .

Separate opinion of Mr. Justice **WHITE**. . . .

[Justice White contended that Title VI of the Civil Rights Act of 1964 did not provide for enforcement by private action, and that consequently the courts had no jurisdiction in Bakke's case.]

Mr. Justice **MARSHALL**. . . .

Mr. Justice **BLACKMUN**. . . .

I suspect that it would be impossible to arrange an affirmative action program in a racially neutral way and have it successful. To ask that this be so is to demand the impossible. In order to get beyond racism, we must first take account of race. There is no other way. And in order to treat some persons equally, we must treat them differently. We cannot—we dare not—let the Equal Protection Clause perpetuate racial supremacy. . . .

Mr. Justice **STEVENS**, with whom The Chief Justice [**BURGER**], Mr. Justice **STEWART**, and Mr. Justice **REHNQUIST** join, concurring in part and dissenting in part. . . .

. . . Our settled practice . . . is to avoid the decision of a constitutional issue if a case can be fairly decided on a statutory ground. . . . The more important the issue, the more force there is to this doctrine. In this case, we are presented with a constitutional question of undoubted and unusual importance. Since, however, a dispositive statutory claim was raised at the very inception of this case, and squarely decided in the portion of the trial court judgment affirmed by the California Supreme Court, it is our plain duty to confront it. Only if petitioner should prevail on the statutory issue would it be necessary to decide whether the University's admissions program violated the Equal Protection Clause of the Fourteenth Amendment.

Section 601 of the Civil Rights Act of 1964 provides:

No person in the United States shall, on the ground of race, color, or national origin, be excluded from participation in, be denied the

benefits of, or be subjected to discrimination under any program or
activity receiving Federal financial assistance.

The University, through its special admissions policy, excluded
Bakke from participation in its program of medical education because
of his race. The University also acknowledges that it was, and still is,
receiving federal financial assistance. The plain language of the statute therefore requires affirmance of the judgment below. A different
result cannot be justified unless that language misstates the actual
intent of the Congress that enacted the statute or the statute is not
enforceable in a private action. Neither conclusion is warranted.
. . .

Editors' Notes

(1) **Query:** To what degree is the division of Justice Powell from Brennan,
White, Marshall, and Blackmun the result of a difference on the question
whether the equal protection clause pertains to individuals or to groups? See
the discussion on this general point in the Introductory Essay to this Section, at
p. 736.

(2) **Query:** Justice Brennan's opinion made much of the claim that
affirmative action does not "stigmatize" whites. To what extent is "stigma"
relevant to the plain words of the Fourteenth Amendment? To the structure of
the document? To the structure of the larger political system? To the political
theories that underlie the document and the political system?

(3) Brennan's opinion also alluded to a different level of scrutiny and so
to a different test that the Court created to consider challenges to classifications based on sex; he explained and applied the test for the Court in Craig
v. Boren (1976; reprinted below, p. 844). Essentially it requires that the
classification "serve important governmental [not compelling] objectives and
must be substantially related [not closely related or necessary] to achievement of those objectives." Brennan would apply that test to plans for
affirmative action.

"[I]n no organ of government . . . does there repose a
more comprehensive remedial power than in the Congress, expressly charged by the Constitution with competence and authority to enforce equal protection guarantees."

FULLILOVE v. KLUTZNICK
448 U.S. 448, 100 S.Ct. 2758, 65 L.Ed.2d 902 (1980).

In § 103(f)(2) of the Public Works Employment Act of 1977, Congress
provided that:

Except to the extent that the Secretary [of Commerce] determines
otherwise, no grant shall be made under this Act for any local public
works project unless the applicant gives satisfactory assurance to the

Secretary that at least ten per centum of the amount of each grant shall be expended for minority business enterprises. For the purposes of this paragraph, the term "minority business enterprise" (MBE) means a business at least 50 per centum of which is owned by minority group members or, in the case of a publicly owned business, at least 51 per centum of the stock of which is owned by minority group members. For the purposes of the preceding sentence, minority group members are citizens of the United States who are Negroes, Spanish-speaking, Orientals, Eskimos, and Aleuts.

Later that year several contracting and subcontracting firms filed suit in a federal district court, asking for an injunction against the Secretary of Commerce as well as city and state officials in New York who accepted grants under § 103(f)(2). The contractors claimed that the section, on its face, violated the equal protection clause and the "equal protection component" of the Fifth Amendment. Both the district court and the court of appeals upheld the constitutionality of § 103(f)(2). The contractors obtained certiorari from the Supreme Court.

Mr. Chief Justice **BURGER** announced the judgment of the Court and delivered an opinion in which Mr. Justice **WHITE** and Mr. Justice **POWELL** joined. . . .

III

When we are required to pass on the constitutionality of an Act of Congress, we assume "the gravest and most delicate duty that this Court is called on to perform." Blodgett v. Holden (1927) (opinion of Holmes, J.). A program that employs racial or ethnic criteria, even in a remedial context, calls for close examination; yet we are bound to approach our task with appropriate deference to the Congress, a co-equal branch charged by the Constitution with the power to "provide for the . . . general Welfare of the United States" and "to enforce by appropriate legislation" the equal protection guarantees of the Fourteenth Amendment. In Columbia Broadcasting System, Inc. v. Democratic National Committee (1973), we accorded "great weight to the decisions of Congress" even though the legislation implicated fundamental constitutional rights guaranteed by the First Amendment. The rule is not different when a congressional program raises equal protection concerns.

Here we pass, not on a choice made by a single judge or a school board but on a considered decision of the Congress and the President. However, in no sense does that render it immune from judicial scrutiny and it "is not to say we 'defer' to the judgment of the Congress . . . on a constitutional question," or that we would hesitate to invoke the Constitution should we determine that Congress has overstepped the bounds of its constitutional power. *Columbia Broadcasting*. . . .

Our analysis proceeds in two steps. At the outset, we must inquire whether the *objectives* of this legislation are within the power of Congress. If so, we must go on to decide whether the limited use of racial and ethnic criteria, in the context presented, is a constitutionally permissible *means* for achieving the congressional objectives and does not violate the equal protection component of the Due Process Clause of the Fifth Amendment.

A

1

In enacting the MBE provision, it is clear that Congress employed an amalgam of its specifically delegated powers. The Act, by its very nature, is primarily an exercise of the Spending Power. . . . This Court has recognized that the power to "provide for the . . . general Welfare" is an independent grant of legislative authority, distinct from other broad congressional powers. Buckley v. Valeo (1976); United States v. Butler (1936). Congress has frequently employed the Spending Power to further broad policy objectives by conditioning receipt of federal monies upon compliance by the recipient with federal statutory and administrative directives. This Court has repeatedly upheld against constitutional challenge the use of this technique to induce governments and private parties to cooperate voluntarily with federal policy. . . .

The MBE program is structured within this familiar legislative pattern. . . .

. . . The reach of the Spending Power, within its sphere, is at least as broad as the regulatory powers of Congress. If, pursuant to its regulatory powers, Congress could have achieved the objectives of the MBE program, then it may do so under the Spending Power. And we have no difficulty perceiving a basis for accomplishing the objectives of the MBE program through the Commerce Power . . . and through the power to enforce the equal protection guarantees of the Fourteenth Amendment. . . .

2

We turn first to the Commerce Power. . . . Had Congress chosen to do so, it could have drawn on the Commerce Clause to regulate the practices of prime contractors on federally funded public works projects. Katzenbach v. McClung (1964); Heart of Atlanta Motel v. United States [1964]. The legislative history of the MBE provision shows that there was a rational basis for Congress to conclude that the subcontracting practices of prime contractors could perpetuate the prevailing impaired access by minority businesses to public contracting opportunities, and that this inequity has an effect on interstate commerce. Thus Congress could take necessary and proper action to remedy the situation. . . .

. . . Insofar as the MBE program pertains to the actions of private prime contractors, the Congress could [also] have achieved its objectives under the Commerce Clause. We conclude that in this respect the objectives of the MBE provision are within the scope of the Spending Power.

3

In certain contexts, there are limitations on the reach of the Commerce Power to regulate the actions of state and local governments. National League of Cities v. Usery (1976). To avoid such complications, we look to § 5 of the Fourteenth Amendment for the power to regulate the procurement practices of state and local grantees of federal funds. A review of our cases persuades us that the objectives of the MBE program are within the power of Congress under § 5 "to enforce by appropriate legislation" the equal protection guarantees of the Fourteenth Amendment.

In Katzenbach v. Morgan (1966), we equated the scope of this authority with the broad powers expressed in the Necessary and Proper Clause. "Correctly viewed, § 5 is a positive grant of legislative power authorizing Congress to exercise its discretion in determining whether and what legislation is needed to secure the guarantees of the Fourteenth Amendment." . . .

. . . Congress reasonably determined that the prospective elimination of [discriminatory] barriers to minority firm access to public contracting opportunities generated by the 1977 Act was appropriate to ensure that those businesses were not denied equal opportunity to participate in federal grants to state and local governments, which is one aspect of the equal protection of the laws. Insofar as the MBE program pertains to the actions of state and local grantees, Congress could have achieved its objectives by use of its power under § 5 of the Fourteenth Amendment. We conclude that in this respect the objectives of the MBE provision are within the scope of the Spending Power. . . .

B

We now turn to the question whether, as a means to accomplish these plainly constitutional objectives, Congress may use racial and ethnic criteria, in this limited way, as a condition attached to a federal grant. We are mindful that "[i]n no matter should we pay more deference to the opinion of Congress than in its choice of instrumentalities to perform a function that is within its power," National Mutual Insurance Co. v. Tidewater Transfer Co. (1949) (opinion of Jackson, J.). However, . . . [w]e recognize [that the equal protection component of the Due Process Clause of the Fifth Amendment requires] careful judicial evaluation to assure that any congressional program that employs racial or ethnic criteria to accomplish the objective of remedying the present effects of past discrimination is narrowly tailored to the achievement of that goal. . . .

1

As a threshold matter, we reject the contention that in the remedial context the Congress must act in a wholly "color-blind" fashion. . . . [I]n Board of Education v. Swann (1971), we . . . held that "[j]ust as the race of students must be considered in determining whether a constitutional violation has occurred, so also must race be considered in formulating a remedy." . . .

When we have discussed the remedial powers of a federal court, we have been alert to the limitation that "[t]he power of the federal courts to restructure the operation of local and state governmental entities 'is not plenary. . . .' [A] federal court is required to tailor 'the scope of the remedy' to fit the nature and extent of the . . . violation." Dayton Board of Education v. Brinkman [I] (1977) (quoting Milliken v. Bradley (1974), and Swann v. Charlotte-Mecklenburg Board of Education [1971]. Here we deal, . . . not with the limited remedial powers of a federal court, . . . but with the broad remedial powers of Congress. It is fundamental that in no organ of government, state or federal, does there repose a more comprehensive remedial power than in the Congress, expressly charged by the Constitution with competence and authority to enforce equal protection guarantees. Congress not only may induce voluntary action to assure compliance with existing federal statutory or constitutional antidiscrimination provisions, but also, where Congress has authority to declare certain conduct unlawful, it may, as here, authorize and induce state action to avoid such conduct.

2

A more specific challenge to the MBE program is the charge that it impermissibly deprives nonminority businesses of access to at least some portion of the government contracting opportunities generated by the Act. . . .
. . . [A]lthough we may assume that the complaining parties are innocent of any discriminatory conduct, it was within congressional power to act on the assumption that in the past some nonminority businesses may have reaped competitive benefit over the years from the virtual exclusion of minority firms from these contracting opportunities.

3

Another challenge to the validity of the MBE program is the assertion that it is underinclusive—that it limits its benefit to specified minority groups rather than extending its remedial objectives to all businesses whose access to government contracting is impaired by the effects of disadvantage or discrimination. Such an extension would, of course, be appropriate for Congress to provide; it is not a function for the courts.

Even in this context, the well-established concept that a legislature may take one step at a time to remedy only part of a broader problem is not without relevance. See Dandridge v. Williams (1970); Williamson v. Lee Optical (1955). . . .

The Congress has not sought to give select minority groups a preferred standing in the construction industry, but has embarked on a remedial program to place them on a more equitable footing with respect to public contracting opportunities. There has been no showing in this case that Congress has inadvertently effected an invidious discrimination by excluding from coverage an identifiable minority group that has been the victim of a degree of disadvantage and discrimination equal to or greater than that suffered by the groups encompassed by the MBE program. . . .

4

It is also contended that the MBE program is overinclusive—that it bestows a benefit on businesses identified by racial or ethnic criteria which cannot be justified on the basis of competitive criteria or as a remedy for the present effects of identified prior discrimination. It is conceivable that a particular application of the program may have this effect; however, the peculiarities of specific applications are not before us in this case. . . .

IV

Congress, after due consideration, perceived a pressing need to move forward with new approaches in the continuing effort to achieve the goal of equality of economic opportunity. In this effort, Congress has necessary latitude to try new techniques such as the limited use of racial and ethnic criteria to accomplish remedial objectives. . . . That the program may press the outer limits of congressional authority affords no basis for striking it down. . . .

In a different context . . . Mr. Justice Brandeis had this to say:

> To stay experimentation in things social and economic is a grave responsibility. Denial of the right to experiment may be fraught with serious consequences to the Nation. New State Ice Co. v. Liebmann (1932) (dissenting opinion).

Any preference based on racial or ethnic criteria must necessarily receive a most searching examination to make sure that it does not conflict with constitutional guarantees. This case is one which requires; and which has received, that kind of examination. This opinion does not adopt, either expressly or implicitly, the formulas of analysis articulated in such cases as University of California Regents v. Bakke (1978). However, our analysis demonstrates that the MBE provision would survive judicial review under either "test" articulated in the several *Bakke* opinions. The MBE provision . . . does not violate the Constitution.

Affirmed.

Mr. Justice **POWELL,** concurring.

Although I would place greater emphasis than The Chief Justice on the need to articulate judicial standards of review in conventional terms, . . . I join [his] opinion and write separately to apply the analysis set forth by my opinion in *Bakke.*

. . . . Section 103(f)(2) employs a racial classification that is constitutionally prohibited unless it is a necessary means of advancing a compelling governmental interest. . . .

. . . In my view, the effect of the set-aside is limited and so widely dispersed that its use is consistent with fundamental fairness.

. . . [T]he set-aside is a reasonably necessary means of furthering the compelling governmental interest in redressing the discrimination that affects minority contractors. Any marginal unfairness to innocent nonminority contractors is not sufficiently significant—or sufficiently identifiable—to outweigh the governmental interest served by § 103(f)(2). When Congress acts to remedy identified discrimination, it may exercise discretion in choosing a remedy that is reasonably necessary to accomplish its purpose. Whatever the exact breadth of that discretion, I believe that it encompasses the selection of the set-aside in this case. . . .

Distinguishing the rights of all citizens to be free from racial classifications from the rights of some citizens to be made whole is a perplexing, but necessary, judicial task. When we first confronted such an issue in *Bakke*, I concluded that the Regents of the University of California were not competent to make, and had not made, findings sufficient to uphold the use of the race-conscious remedy they adopted. . . . [U]se of racial classifications, which are fundamentally at odds with the ideals of a democratic society implicit in the Due Process and Equal Protection Clauses, cannot be imposed simply to serve transient social or political goals, however worthy they may be. But the issue here turns on the scope of congressional power, and Congress has been given a unique constitutional role in the enforcement of the post-Civil War Amendments. In this case, where Congress determined that minority contractors were victims of purposeful discrimination and where Congress chose a reasonably necessary means to effectuate its purpose, I find no constitutional reason to invalidate § 103(f)(2).

Mr. Justice **MARSHALL**, with whom Mr. Justice **BRENNAN**, and Mr. Justice **BLACKMUN** join, concurring in judgment.

My resolution of the constitutional issue in this case is governed by the separate opinion I coauthored in *Bakke*. In my view, the 10% minority set-aside provision . . . passes constitutional muster under the standard announced in that opinion. . . .

Mr. Justice **STEWART**, with whom Mr. Justice **REHNQUIST** joins, dissenting. . . .

"Our Constitution is color-blind, and neither knows nor tolerates classes among citizens. . . . The law regards man as man, and takes no account of his surroundings or of his color. . . ." Those words were written by a Member of this Court 84 years ago. Plessy v Ferguson [1896] (Harlan, J., dissenting). [Mr. Justice Harlan's] colleagues disagreed with him, and held that a statute that required the separation of people on the basis of their race was constitutionally valid because it was a "reasonable" exercise of legislative power and had been "enacted in good faith for the promotion [of] the public good. . . ." Today, the Court upholds a statute that accords a preference to citizens who are "Negroes, Spanish-speaking, Orientals, Indians, Eskimos, and Aleuts," for much the same reasons. I think today's decision is wrong for the same reason that *Plessy* was wrong. . . .

The equal protection standard of the Constitution has one clear and central meaning—it absolutely prohibits invidious discrimination by government. . . . Under our Constitution, any official action that treats a person differently on account of his race or ethnic origin is inherently suspect and presumptively invalid. Bolling v. Sharpe [1954]; Korematsu v. United States [1944]. . . .

. . . In short, racial discrimination is by definition invidious discrimination.

The rule cannot be any different when the persons injured by a racially biased law are not members of a racial minority. The guarantee of equal protection is "universal in [its] application, to all persons . . . without regard to any differences of race, of color, or of nationality." Yick Wo v. Hopkins [1886]. . . . From the perspective of a person detrimentally affected by a racially discriminatory law, the arbitrariness and unfairness is entirely the same, whatever his skin color and whatever the law's purpose, be it purportedly "for the promotion of the public good" or otherwise. . . .

. . . [The Court's] self-evident truisms [about Congress's powers to spend, to regulate commerce, and to enforce § 5 of the Fourteenth Amendment] do not begin to answer the question before us in this case. For in the exercise of its powers, Congress must obey the Constitution just as the legislatures of all the States must. . . . If a law is unconstitutional, it is no less unconstitutional just because it is a product of the Congress of the United States. . . .

Mr. Justice **STEVENS**, dissenting. . . .

Our historic aversion to titles of nobility is only one aspect of our commitment to the proposition that the sovereign has a fundamental duty to govern impartially. When government accords different treatment to different persons, there must be a reason for the difference. Because racial characteristics so seldom provide a relevant basis for disparate treatment, and because classifications based on race are potentially so harmful to the entire body politic, it is especially important that the reasons for any such classification be clearly identified and unquestionably legitimate. . . .

. . . I assume that the wrong committed against the Negro class is both so serious and so pervasive that it would constitutionally justify an appropriate classwide recovery. . . . But that serious classwide wrong cannot in itself justify the particular classification Congress has made in this Act. Racial classifications are simply too pernicious to permit any but the most exact connection between justification and classification. Quite obviously, the history of discrimination against black citizens in America cannot justify a grant of privileges to Eskimos or Indians.

Even if we assume that each of the six racial subclasses has suffered its own special injury at some time in our history, surely it does not necessarily follow that each of those subclasses suffered harm of identical magnitude. . . . There is no reason to assume, and nothing in the legislative history suggests, much less demonstrates, that each of these subclasses is equally entitled to reparations from the United States Government.

At best, the statutory preference is a somewhat perverse form of reparation for the members of the injured classes. For those who are the most disadvantaged within each class are the least likely to receive any benefit from the special privilege even though they are the persons most likely still to be suffering the consequences of the past wrong. A random distribution to a favored few is a poor form of compensation for an injury shared by many.

. . . [If the history of discrimination against Negroes] can justify such a random distribution of benefits on racial lines . . ., it will serve not merely as a basis for remedial legislation, but rather as a permanent source of justification for grants of special privileges. For if there is no duty to attempt either to measure the recovery by the wrong or to distribute that recovery within the injured class in an evenhanded way, our history will adequately support a legislative preference for almost any ethnic, religious, or racial group with the political strength to negotiate "a piece of the action" for its members.

Although I do not dispute the validity of the assumption that each of the subclasses identified in the Act has suffered a severe wrong at some time in the past, I cannot accept this slapdash statute as a legitimate method of providing classwide relief. . . .

III

The legislative history of the Act discloses that there is a group of legislators in Congress identified as the "Black Caucus" and that members of that group argued that if the Federal Government was going to provide $4,000,000,000 of new public contract business, their constituents were entitled to "a piece of the action." . . .

The legislators' interest in providing their constituents with favored access to benefits distributed by the Federal Government is, in my opinion, a plainly impermissible justification for this racial classification.

IV

The interest in facilitating and encouraging the participation by minority business enterprises in the economy is unquestionably legitimate. Any barrier to such entry and growth . . . should be vigorously and thoroughly removed. . . . This statute, however, is not designed to remove any barriers to entry. Nor does its sparse legislative history detail any insuperable or even significant obstacles to entry into the competitive market. . . .

This Act has a character that is fundamentally different from a carefully drafted remedial measure like the Voting Rights Act of 1965.

. . . Whereas the enactment of the Voting Rights Act was preceded by exhaustive hearings and debates concerning discriminatory denial of access to the electoral process, and became effective in specific States only after specific findings were made, this statute authorizes an automatic nationwide preference for all members of a diverse racial class regardless of their possible interest in the particular geographic areas where the public contracts are to be performed. . . .

A comparable approach in the electoral context would support a rule requiring that at least 10% of the candidates elected to the legislature be members of specified racial minorities. Surely that would be an effective way of ensuring black citizens the representation that has long been their due. Quite obviously, however, such a measure would merely create the kind of inequality that an impartial sovereign cannot tolerate. Yet that is precisely the kind of "remedy" that this Act authorizes. In both political and economic contexts, we have a legitimate interest in seeing that those who were disadvantaged in the past may succeed in the future. But neither an election nor a market can be equally accessible to all if race provides a basis for placing a special value on votes or dollars. . . .

V

A judge's opinion that a statute reflects a profoundly unwise policy determination is an insufficient reason for concluding that it is unconstitutional. Congress has broad power to spend money to provide for the "general Welfare of the United States," to "regulate Commerce among the several States," to enforce the Civil War Amendments, and to discriminate between aliens and citizens. But the exercise of these broad powers is subject to the constraints imposed by the Due Process Clause of the Fifth Amendment. That Clause has both substantive and procedural components; it performs the office of both the Due Process and Equal Protection Clauses of the Fourteenth Amendment in requiring that the federal sovereign act impartially.

Unlike Mr. Justice Stewart and Mr. Justice Rehnquist, however, I am not convinced that the [Due Process] Clause contains an absolute prohibition against any statutory classification based on race. I am nonetheless persuaded that it does impose a special obligation to scrutinize any governmental decisionmaking process that draws nationwide distinctions between citizens on the basis of their race and incidentally also discriminates against noncitizens in the preferred racial classes. For just as procedural safeguards are necessary to guarantee impartial decisionmaking in the judicial process, so can they play a vital part in preserving the impartial character of the legislative process. . . .

Although it is traditional for judges to accord the same presumption of regularity to the legislative process no matter how obvious it may be that a busy Congress has acted precipitately, I see no reason why the character of their procedures may not be considered relevant to the decision whether the legislative product has caused a deprivation of liberty or property without due process of law. Whenever Congress creates a classification that would be subject to strict scrutiny under the Equal Protection Clause of the Fourteenth Amendment if it had been fashioned by a state legislature, it seems to me that judicial review should include a consideration of the procedural character of the decisionmaking process. A holding that the classification was not adequately preceded by a consideration of less drastic alternatives or adequately explained by a statement of legislative purpose would be far less intrusive than a final determination that the substance of the decision is not "narrowly tailored to the achievement of that goal." . . .

In all events, rather than take the substantive position expressed in Mr. Justice Stewart's dissenting opinion, I would hold this statute unconstitutional on a narrower ground. It cannot fairly be characterized as a "narrowly tailored" racial classification because it simply raises too many serious questions that Congress failed to answer or even to address in a responsible way. The risk that habitual attitudes toward classes of persons, rather than analysis of the relevant characteristics of the class, will serve as a basis for a legislative classification is present when benefits are distributed as well as when burdens are imposed. In the past, traditional attitudes too often provided the only explanation for discrimination against women, aliens, illegitimates, and black citizens. Today there is a danger that awareness of past injustice will lead to automatic acceptance of new classifications that are not in fact justified by attributes characteristic of the class as a whole.

When Congress creates a special preference, or a special disability, for a class of persons, it should identify the characteristic that justifies the special treatment. When the classification is defined in racial terms, I believe that such particular identification is imperative.

In this case, only two conceivable bases for differentiating the preferred classes from society as a whole have occurred to me: (1) that they were the victims of unfair treatment in the past and (2) that they are less able to compete in the future. Although the first of these factors would justify an appropriate remedy for past wrongs, . . . this statute is not such a remedial measure. The second factor is simply not true. Nothing in the record of this case, the legislative history of the Act, or experience that we may notice judicially provides any support for such a proposition. It is up to Congress to demonstrate that its unique statutory preference is justified by a relevant characteristic that is shared by the members of the preferred class. In my opinion, because it has failed to make that demonstration, it has also failed to discharge its duty to govern impartially embodied in the Fifth Amendment. . . .

Editors' Notes

(1) **Query:** Does Burger actually subject § 103(f)(2) to strict scrutiny?

(2) **Query:** To what extent does Powell rely on balancing as a *technique* of constitutional interpretation here? To what extent is his approach in *Fullilove* consistent with that which he took in *Bakke?*

(3) In Firefighters v. Stotts (1984), the Court interpreted Title VII of the Civil Rights Act of 1964, outlawing racial discrimination in employment, as protecting "bona fide" seniority programs and thus allowing a city, faced with budgetary cutbacks, to lay off workers according to length of service even though that standard meant that a disproportionate share of blacks, as the last hired, would be the first fired. The majority did not consider it important that the city involved, Memphis, had been hiring blacks under an affirmative action plan approved by the local federal district court and that the discharges under the seniority system would undermine that plan.

(4) Among the better studies of affirmative action are: Henry J. Abraham, "Some Post-*Bakke* and *Weber* Reflections on 'Reverse Discrimination,' " 14 *Uni. of Richmond L.Rev.* 373 (1980); Marshall Cohen, Thomas Nagel and Thomas Scanlon, eds., *Equality and Preferential Treatment* (Princeton: Princeton University Press, 1977); Joel Dreyfuss and Charles Lawrence, III, *The Bakke Case* (New York: Harcourt, Brace, Jovanovitch, 1979); Terry Eastland and William J. Bennett, *Counting by Race* (New York: Basic Books, 1979); John Hart Ely, "The Constitutionality of Reverse Discrimination," 41 *U.Chi.L.Rev.* 723 (1974); Alan H. Goldman, *Justice and Reverse Discrimination* (Princeton: Princeton University Press, 1979); Allan P. Sindler, *Bakke, DeFunis, and Minority Admissions* (New York: Longman, 1978); Laurence H. Tribe, *American Constitutional Law* (Mineola, N.Y.: Foundation Press, 1978), pp. 1032–1052; J. Harvie Wilkinson, III, *From Brown* to *Bakke* (New York: Oxford University Press, 1979).

14

The Problems of Equal Protection, II

As part of a broader analysis of the question of HOW to interpret the Constitution, Chapter 13 focused on substantive problems of equal protection arising out of race. Left open was a host of other problems. First, in discussing the "two-tiered" model of strict and deferential scrutiny, we did not explore the reach of the notions of "suspect classification," "suspect class," "compelling" governmental interest, or "fundamental right." Second, Chapter 13 alluded to but did not address a possible expansion of the "tiers" in analysis from two to three or even to a scale with many gradations. Also untouched was the most basic question: Is a two-, three-, or multi-tiered model especially useful in interpreting the Constitution?

The introductory essay and the cases that follow take up those kinds of issues. We repeat the earlier caution against allowing a necessary understanding of the Court's byzantine doctrines to distract from the basic interrogatives of WHAT, WHO, and HOW.

I. THE TWO-TIERED MODEL

At the outset, one should keep in mind a distinction that many interpreters forget. There is an important conceptual difference between "suspect classifications" and "suspect classes." Members of the Supreme Court tend to use the terms interchangeably and so confuse their own as well as others' analyses. To discover a suspect class—in Stone's terms, a "discrete and insular" minority—an interpreter must look to the social history surrounding particular groups in this country. A "suspect classification" is one, like race or religion, whose very nature presumptively offends constitutional standards—though that definition tells us little about what or where to find a full statement of those standards. Because this essay is designed to introduce readers to the Court's work, we shall only occasionally allude to this distinction, but we think it is an important component of HOW to interpret the Constitution.

A. What Classes/Classifications Are Suspect?

There is neither an historical nor a logical reason why Stone's reference in *Carolene Products* to "discrete and insular minorities" should include only racial or ethnic groups. This open-endedness is both a strength and a weakness of the jurisprudence that he planted. Its strength lies in its generality, its potential application to a whole genre of minorities legally disadvantaged by a hostile or insensitive majority. At the same time, the price of that generality is indefiniteness. "It would hardly take extraordinary ingenuity," Justice Rehnquist once protested, "for a lawyer to find 'insular and discrete' minorities at every turn in the road." [1]

Who qualifies as a "discrete and insular" minority? Who other than blacks and perhaps Indians can demand the special judicial protection of "strict scrutiny"? Justice Powell, speaking for the Court in San Antonio v. Rodriguez (1973; reprinted below, p. 858), tried to answer the question. A suspect class, he said, is one that has been

> saddled with such disabilities, or subjected to such a history of purposeful unequal treatment, or relegated to such a position of political powerlessness as to command extraordinary protection from the majoritarian political processes.

Powell's effort was honest; but, like Brennan's in Cleburne v. Cleburne Living Center (1985; reprinted below, p. 916), it suffers from indeterminancy. How much "purposeful unequal treatment" must a group have experienced "to command" special judicial protection? How ancient (or recent) does the history of unequal treatment have to be? More broadly, is any group, in fact, now in a condition of "political powerlessness"? Before the Thirteenth Amendment, slaves obviously were; blacks in the South before the Voting Rights Act of 1965 were; women before they got the vote very likely were. The real issue, however, is seldom one of having power or being powerless. Power is rarely a dichotomous variable.

Except perhaps for the very sick or elderly who cannot take part in politics, Indians on reservations, and illegal aliens, few *adults* are politically powerless. Even a minority as historically despised and oppressed as homosexuals has recently won significant political victories, including electing a mayor of a major metropolis. The plain fact is that most adult citizens have *some* political power: They can speak out, vote, lobby, and, as important, use the courts to affect and perhaps even effect public policy, as NAACP v. Button (1963; reprinted above, p. 723) noted. Even aliens, including illegals, often have this last option, and they, too, can influence public policy as Plyler v. Doe (1982; reprinted below, p. 907) shows.

Focusing on "suspect classes" frames the central question as: How little power does it take for a group to require special protection? To that query, the Court has made no more generalized response than Powell's in *San Antonio* or Brennan's in *Cleburne,* though individual justices have offered more detailed answers. (See the separate opinions of Stevens and Marshall in *Cleburne.*) Focusing on "suspect classifications" poses as a basic question of HOW to inter-

---

1. Sugarman v. Dougall, dis. op. (1973).

pret: "What standards of classification does the Constitution outlaw or
at least require government to bear a heavy burden to justify?"

Specifically, the Court has had to face claims from a wide range of
groups. Illegitimate children, the poor, aliens, the aging, women,
homosexuals, the physically and mentally handicapped have all
claimed special status.[2] The Court has often ignored such claims by
deciding cases on other grounds or by denying certiorari.[3] *Cleburne,*
however, squarely addressed not only particular problems of the
retarded but also some of the fundamental difficulties about "suspect
classes" and tiers of analysis.

Illegitimate children seem to fit perfectly Powell's definition of a
"suspect class." First, they are now and have historically been
"saddled with" legal "disabilities" on their rights to inherit property
from their fathers and to sue if their fathers have been wrongfully or
accidentally killed. Second, that unequal treatment is purposeful:
Statutes and judicial decisions make no effort to disguise an effort to
discriminate against illegitimate in favor of legitimate children.
Third, as children and therefore ineligible to vote, they are about as
close to being politically powerless as any group in our society.
Fourth, to add one of Stone's criteria, their treatment is the result of a
prejudice, to whose existence there is no more eloquent testimony
than the connotation of the word "bastard." Yet the Court has
consistently refused to recognize illegitimacy as a suspect classification;
and it has been Louis F. Powell who has written many of these
opinions.[4]

The aged have suffered even sharper defeats in the courts, though
they have fared better in Congress.[5] Massachusetts v. Murgia (1976),

---

2. See Judith A. Baer, *Equality under the Fourteenth Amendment* (Ithaca, N.Y.: Cornell
University Press, 1983), espec. chaps. 7–9; Comment, "Mental Illness: A Suspect Classifica-
tion?" 83 *Yale L.J.* 1237 (1974); M.P. and R. Borgdoff, "A History of Unequal Treatment:
The Qualifications of Handicapped Persons as a 'Suspect Class' Under the Equal Protection
Clause," 15 *Santa Clara Lawyer* 855 (1975). E. Carrington Boggan, et al., *The Rights of Gay
People* (New York: Avon, 1975). Much of the recent litigation on the rights of the handicapped
has focused on interpretation of the Rehabilitation Act of 1973. See John E. Finn, "Implied
Rights of Action Under the Rehabilitation Act of 1973," 68 *Geo.L.J.* 1229 (1980).

3. The Court did, however, grant certiorari in Bowers v. Hardwick (1986), after having
denied it in Longstaff v. INS (1984). In *Longstaff* lower courts had sustained congressional
legislation barring immigration of homosexuals, psychopaths, mental defectives, and certain
felons. When he entered the United States nineteen years earlier, Longstaff had not acknowledged he was gay, and that fact came out when he applied for citizenship. See also denial of
certiorari in New York v. Uplinger (1984), in which state courts had reaffirmed their earlier
ruling that New York's sodomy law was unconstitutional. (The Supreme Court had also denied
certiorari in that earlier case, New York v. Onofre [1981].)

4. See the discussion of the cases in C. Herman Pritchett, *Constitutional Civil Liberties*
(Englewood Cliffs, N.J.: Prentice-Hall, 1984), pp. 329–330. Pritchett's use of the term
"quagmire" to describe the situation into which the Court has gotten itself is charitable. The
justices, one might contend, have been struggling with their consciences to find some sort of
middle classification into which to put illegitimacy or to use a version of a "rational basis" test
stronger than deferential scrutiny. See the discussion below in Part III of this essay and Powell's
opinion in Weber v. Aetna Casualty Co. (1972), quoted in note 33, below, and Blackmun's
comment in Mathews v. Lucas (1976), quoted at p. 838, below.

5. See the Age Discrimination in Employment Act of 1967, as amended in 1978; 29 U.S.C.
§ 621ff. In essence, the statute forbids employers to discriminate against employees between
the ages of 40 and 70 because of age. The Act makes certain exceptions for managerial

for example, refused to look on the aged as a suspect class. At issue was a law requiring uniformed state police to retire at 50. Repeating Powell's definition, the majority, blithely mixing *class* and *classification,* added:

> The class subject to the compulsory retirement . . . consists of uniformed state police officers over the age of 50. [The statute] cannot be said to discriminate only against the elderly. Rather, it draws the line at a certain age in middle life. But even old age does not define a "discrete and insular" group, United States v. Carolene Products (1938), in need of "extraordinary protection from the majoritarian political process." Instead, it marks a stage that each of us will reach if we live out our normal span. Even if the statute could be said to impose a penalty upon a class defined as the aged, it would not impose a distinction sufficiently akin to those classifications that have have found suspect to call for strict scrutiny.

Three years later, using much the same reasoning, Vance v. Bradley sustained compulsory retirement for foreign service officers at age 60.

With other claims, the Court has not always been consistent in its responses. For a time it seemed that the poor had succeeded in establishing wealth as a suspect *classification.* [6] Certainly Justice Harlan thought so, and he opposed that course of decisions. See his dissent in Shapiro v. Thompson (1969; reprinted above, p. 873). That same year, Chief Justice Warren remarked in his opinion for the Court in McDonald v. Board of Election Commissioners that "a careful examination on our part is especially warranted where lines are drawn on the basis of wealth or race, Harper v. Virginia [1966], two factors which would independently render a classification suspect and thereby demand a more exacting judicial scrutiny." But *San Antonio* swept away that apparent victory.

Aliens seemingly won special status for themselves. "Aliens as a class," the Court said in Graham v. Richardson (1971), "are a prime example of a 'discrete and insular' minority (see United States v. Carolene Products Co. [1938]) for whom such heightened judicial solicitude is appropriate." The Court later reaffirmed this condition,[7] but then hedged, sustaining exclusions of aliens from police forces and public school teaching.[8] Speaking through Thurgood Marshall in

---

personnel. The Age Discrimination Act of 1975, 42 U.S.C. § 6101ff, forbids discrimination on the basis of age in programs receiving federal funds.

6. As, for example, eight justices said in Roberts v. LaVallee (1967): "Our decisions for more than a decade now have made it clear that differences in access to the instruments needed to vindicate legal rights, when based upon the financial situation of the defendant, are repugnant to the Constitution." See also: Griffin v. Illinois (1955); Douglas v. California (1963); Harper v. Virginia (1966; reprinted above, p. 151); Swenson v. Bosler (1967); Shapiro v. Thompson (1969; reprinted below, p. 873); and Boddie v. Connecticut (1971).

7. Sugarman v. Dougall (1973); In re Griffiths (1973); Examining Bd. v. Flores (1976); Nyquist v. Mauclet (1977).

8. See Foley v. Connelie (1978) and Cabell v. Chavez-Salido (1982), sustaining state regulations requiring certain kinds of police officers to be citizens, and Ambach v. Norwick (1979), upholding a state law limiting teaching in public schools to citizens. In *Cabell,* Blackmun, the author of *Graham* and several other opinions holding alienage a suspect classification, dissented: "[T]oday's decision rewrites the Court's precedents, ignores history,

Bernal v. Fainter (1984), a majority of eight justices seems to have found a rationale to explain its meanderings:

> As a general matter, a State law that discriminates on the basis of alienage can be sustained only if it can withstand strict judicial scrutiny. . . . [T]o withstand strict scrutiny the law must advance a compelling State interest by the least restrictive means available. . . . We have, however, developed a narrow exception to the rule that discrimination based on alienage triggers strict scrutiny. This exception has been labelled the "political function" exception and applies to laws that exclude aliens from positions [like police and public school teaching] intimately related to the process of democratic self-government.

In *Bernal* the Court held that the office of notary public did not qualify for the "political function" exception, thus joining professions such as law and engineering that had also failed.[9]

In sum, there is no short answer to the question of what other *classifications* than those based on race or ethnicity are suspect or *classes* other than racial and ethnic minorities and aliens are entitled to special judicial protection. Justice Rehnquist, who is fundamentally opposed to the jurisprudence behind the *Carolene Products* footnote, has waged a long battle [10] against including any category other than race, with a begrudging acceptance of national origin, and has, for the time being, nearly won that phase of his campaign.

Several times the justices have said that excluding from certain benefits people who recently arrived in the state is an "invidious" classification,[11] but it is not evident, in light of the Court's insistence in these and other rulings that the right to travel interstate, or at least to "migrate" to establish a new residence, is "fundamental," how much those decisions to invoke strict scrutiny turned on the existence of a suspect *class* or *classification* and how much on a fundamental right. And alienage, as we have seen, is suspect only under some circumstances, pointing toward degrees of suspicion with which a majority of the justices view different classifications, as Thurgood Marshall claimed in his dissent in *San Antonio*. We take up that point under Part II of this introductory essay and in several of the cases reprinted below—especially *San Antonio* (at p. 858), Craig v. Boren (1976; at p. 844), and *Cleburne* (1985; at p. 916).

---

defies common sense, and reinstates the deadening mantle of state parochialism in public employment." For a general discussion that predates some of these cases, see David Carlinger, *The Rights of Aliens* (New York: Avon, 1977).

9. In re Griffiths (1973) (law); Examining Bd. v. Flores (1976) (civil engineering).

10. See espec. his dissents in *Sugarman*, supra note 7, and Trimble v. Gordon (1977).

11. Shapiro v. Thompson (1969; reprinted below, p. 873); Dunn v. Blumstein (1972); and Memorial Hospital v. Maricopa County (1974).

B. What Constitutes a "Compelling" Governmental Interest?

The Court has offered no general criteria. We have a long list of claims that the justices have rejected and a short list of those they have accepted. Neither, however, pretends to be exhaustive. Among those rejected have been administrative convenience,[12] having the names of the rank-and-file members of an organization to facilitate an investigation of the association,[13] keeping the races "pure," [14] high professional standards for lawyers,[15] filling lower civil service positions with people knowledgeable of and loyal to American traditions,[16] maintenance of state ownership of fish in offshore waters,[17] and distributing limited state funds available for welfare only to long-term residents [18] and citizens.[19]

Among those sustained as "compelling" have been a federal interest in national security,[20] a federal [21] interest in maintaining the integrity and the appearance of integrity of the electoral processes, and a strong suggestion from three concurring justices of such a state interest in preserving discipline in its prisons.[22] This second list is brief because, when the Court has found that government has used a suspect classification or infringed a fundamental right, the decision to hold the regulation unconstitutional has been almost automatic.

C. What is a "Fundamental" Right?

The whole issue of what rights are "fundamental," how that status should be determined, and who should make the decisions is the subject of the cases and materials in Section E of this Part of the book. As one would suspect, the questions are difficult and the debate bitter, if not always intellectually acute. (See espec. the opinions reprinted below in *San Antonio* [p. 858], Shapiro v. Thompson [p. 873], and Moore v. East Cleveland [p. 1145].) These sorts of inquiries may be logically distinct from considerations of equality; but, because of the Court's use and development of strict scrutiny, they have become entangled with problems of equal protection.

---

12. Frontiero v. Richardson (1973; reprinted below, p. 840).

13. NAACP v. Alabama (1958; reprinted above, p. 646).

14. Loving v. Virginia (1967; reprinted below, p. 777).

15. Examining Bd. v. Flores (1976).

16. Sugarman v. Dougall (1973).

17. Takahashi v. Fish & Game Commn. (1948).

18. Shapiro v. Thompson (1969) reprinted below, p. 873; Memorial Hospital v. Maricopa County (1974).

19. Graham v. Richardson (1971).

20. Korematsu v. United States (1944; reprinted below, p. 1197).

21. Buckley v. Valeo (1976; reprinted above, p. 371).

22. Lee v. Washington (1968).

Here we would note only that, influenced either by democratic theory or constitutionalism (and sometimes by both), the Court has decided that certain rights are fundamental. As Chapter Two pointed out, democratic theory stresses the primacy of rights of political expression and participation (see espec. New York Times v. Sullivan [1964; reprinted above, p. 596] and Buckley v. Valeo [1976; reprinted above, p. 371]). Constitutionalism emphasizes others relating to individual autonomy and dignity. And, true to constitutionalism's spirit, the justices have not required that fundamental rights be listed in the document. Thus the Court has applied the label not only to privacy (see Griswold v. Connecticut [1963; reprinted above, p. 113]), but also to such rights as those to marry,[23] to travel,[24] to a presumption of innocence when accused of crime,[25] and a requirement that in criminal trials government prove guilt beyond a reasonable doubt.[26]

II. IS THE COURT ACTUALLY USING A TWO-TIERED TEST?

A. Continua versus Two Tiers

Dissenting in *San Antonio,* Justice Marshall spelled out his oft-stated argument that the Court had not used and should not use a simple two-tiered model. Rather, he claimed, the test had been—and rightfully so—much less rigid and much more sophisticated, involving several continua or sliding scales along which the justices measure the amount of suspicion that they throw on a classification, the degree of fundamentality of the individual's right, and the nature of the government's interest.

Although in recent years a majority has rejected Marshall's reasoning, in Dunn v. Blumstein (1972) he wrote an opinion for the Court that pretty much used the sorts of spectra that he advocated in *San Antonio.* *Dunn* involved a challenge to a Tennessee law requiring a year's residency within the state as a prerequisite to voting for state officials. After noting that the right to travel interstate was fundamental, Marshall said for the Court:

[D]urational residency laws must be measured by a strict equal protection test: they are unconstitutional unless a State can demonstrate that such laws are *"necessary* to promote a *compelling* governmental interest." Shapiro v. Thompson [1969] (first emphasis added); Kramer v. Union Free School District [1969].

---

23. *Loving,* supra note 14.

24. United States v. Guest (1966); *Shapiro* (1969); Memorial Hospital v. Maricopa County (1974). For an attack on the notion of a fundamental right to travel, see Rehnquist's dissent in *Memorial Hospital.*

25. In re Winship (1970; reprinted below, p. 1101).

26. Jackson v. Virginia (1979); see also Sandstrom v. Montana (1979).

So far his opinion was unexceptional. But he continued:

> Thus phrased, the constitutional question may sound like a mathe-
> matical formula. But legal "tests" do not have the precision of
> mathematical formulas. The key words emphasize a *matter of degree:*
> that a heavy burden of justification is on the State, and that the
> statute will be closely scrutinized in light of its asserted purposes.
> [Italics supplied.]

Marshall's analysis moved Justice White in Vlandis v. Kline
(1973) to remark that "it is clear that we employ not just one, or two,
but as my Brother Marshall has so ably demonstrated, a 'spectrum of
standards.' " Justice Stevens' concurrence in *Cleburne* (below, p. 916)
expresses at least some agreement with Marshall. The Court's treatment of illegitimate children supports this argument, as do the more
recent cases concerning aliens. In both areas, the Court has applied
something stronger than deferential scrutiny, but weaker than strict
scrutiny. But White in *Vlandis* and Stevens in *Cleburne* spoke only for
himself, and the Court continues to reject use of a continuum instead
of tiers.

B. Discovery of a Middle Ground: A Three-Tiered Test

As is often true in life, sex has provoked a methodological crisis
in constitutional interpretation. Classifications by gender have been
commonplace in American legal history and have become a target of
the women's movement. Four members of the Court—Brennan,
Douglas, White, and Marshall—would have held such classifications
suspect (Frontiero v. Richardson [1973; reprinted below, p. 840]),
but were unable to pick up the necessary fifth vote. A few years later,
however, Craig v. Boren (1976; reprinted below, p. 844) presented
the occasion for compromise. Six justices—Brennan, White, Marshall,
Blackmun, Powell, and Stevens—agreed that if sexual classifications
were not quite suspect neither were they entitled to the sorts of
presumption that socio-economic legislation merited.

In effect, *Craig* made gender a "somewhat suspicious" category,
and the Court created a new test, somewhere between strict and
deferential scrutiny:

> [C]lassifications by gender must serve important [not compelling or
> merely legitimate] governmental objectives and must be substantial-
> ly related [not closely related or necessary to nor merely rationally
> related] to achievement of those objectives.

Whether other classifications or not-so-fundamental rights will
also find a niche in this middle tier remains to be seen.[27] It is possible

---

27. One can make a strong case that the Court, speaking through Powell, used a middle tier
in treating illegitimacy in Weber v. Aetna Casualty (1972) and Trimble v. Gordon (1977). Lalli
v. Lalli (1978) and Parham v. Hughes (1979) cut back on *Weber* and *Trimble,* but there was no
opinion for the Court in either case, and the issues in *Parham* were complicated by the presence
of a classification by gender. Still, concurring in *Lalli,* Justice Blackmun said that *Trimble* had
become "a derelict." One can also make a case that, taken together, these decisions evidence a
new and stronger kind of test that insists on a "rational basis" for classifications. See, below Part
III of this introductory essay and *Plyler* as well as *Cleburne.*

that the Court will some day announce that all along it has been using the sorts of continua that Marshall described. It is also possible that the Court will retreat from the middle tier, as, indeed, it did to some extent for a short time in Rostker v. Goldberg (1981) when it sustained male-only registration for a military draft. It is further possible that the justices, as they continue to cope with the problem of HOW to interpret, will shed their tiers and adopt a test (or set of tests) that differs in kind from both strict and deferential scrutiny.

III. A TEST WITHOUT TIERS?

Students exposed to essays on equal protection are typically confused and frustrated. Reading the cases will probably decrease confusion but at the cost of increasing frustration. It may be of some comfort to know that many judges and commentators [28] share that frustration. One of the more fundamental criticisms is based on a concern that in using a two-, three- or multi-tiered model, the justices are engaged in little more than a form of "balancing" that both exacerbates all the problems of this *technique* discussed in Chapter 8, at pp. 309–312, and masks them even from the judges.

The justices have become restive under their own doctrine. One detects three levels of criticism. First is an unhappiness with the way the Court applies the tests in particular cases, exemplified by Justice Potter Stewart's protest in one instance that he found the majority's use of suspect categories as "little short of fantasy." [29] Second, and at a deeper level, Marshall claims that the two-tiered model (and his objections hold almost as well for a three-tier model) misstates what the Court has actually been doing and is also much too rigid. Marshall, as we have seen, would modify the model to fit along a more finely graded scale.

Third, and much more radical in his critique as well as his solution, is William H. Rehnquist. He has recognized that in its current doctrine the Court is simultaneously dealing with the interrogatives WHO and HOW. These tiered tests, he has said, are mere smoke screens to hide judicial policy making: "whenever the Court feels that a societal group is 'discrete and insular,' it has the constitutional mandate to prohibit legislation that somehow treats the group differently from some other group." Rehnquist would leave this sort of policy making to elected officials and replace all tiered models with a simpler one that would look only for a "rational" connection

---

28. See, for example: Richard H. Seeburger, "The Muddle of the Middle Tier," 48 *Mo.L. Rev.* 587 (1983); Steven G. Calabresi, "A Madisonian Interpretation of the Equal Protection Doctrine," 91 *Yale L.J.* 1403 (1982); Cass Sunstein, "Public Values, Private Interests, and the Equal Protection Clause," 1982 *Sup.Ct.Rev.* 127; Jeffrey H. Blattner, "The Supreme Court's 'Intermediate' Equal Protection Decisions," 8 *Hastings Con.L.J.* 777 (1981); Michael J. Perry, "Modern Equal Protection: A Conceptualization and Appraisal," 79 *Colum.L.Rev.* 1023 (1979). J. Harvie Wilkinson, III, "The Supreme Court, the Equal Protection Clause, and the Three Faces of Constitutional Equality," 61 *Va.L.Rev.* 945 (1975); John E. Nowak, "Realigning the Standards of Review under the Equal Protection Guarantee," 62 *Geo.L.J.* 1071 (1974).

29. Zablocki v. Redhail, concur. op. (1978).

between a legitimate governmental end and a particular statutory classification. Race, he would add, is inherently irrational under the plain purpose of the Fourteenth Amendment.

Justice John Paul Stevens has frequently disagreed with Rehnquist on the Constitution's response to problems of equal protection, but he too has expressed serious reservations about the dominant models. "There is," he wrote in *Craig*, "only one Equal Protection Clause," implying a single standard for all kinds of cases. Implicit in Stevens' criticism is either a rational-basis model or a version of Marshall's. (See his concur. op. in *Cleburne,* below, p. 916.) [30]

Along these lines—and some years before Stevens came to the Court—Professor Gerald Gunther suggested [31] a model of equal protection that he called an "expanded reasonable means inquiry" or "rationality review 'with bite' ":

> Stated most simply, it would have the Court take seriously a constitutional requirement that has never been formally abandoned: that legislative means must substantially further legislative ends. . . . Putting consistent new bite into the old equal protection would mean that the Court would be less willing to supply justifying rationales by exercising its imagination. . . . Moreover, it would have the Justices gauge the question of reasonableness of questionable means on the basis of materials that are offered to the Court, rather than resorting to rationalizations created by perfunctory judicial hypothesizing.

Gunther's model has great attraction, though it would complicate judges' work by requiring them to examine evidence and arguments to a far greater extent than they need do under the existing tests, which tend to yield near-automatic answers.

Still, major problems would remain.[32] Gunther says that his model "would concern itself solely with means, not ends." That limitation might appeal to a democratic theorist, but it raises grave difficulties for constitutionalism. If a court could look only at means, not ends, what could it do except say amen to a statute whose end was to keep some minority "in its place" and did so very effectively by denying that group access to certain goods, services, or opportunities? Gunther immediately qualified his model to allow the Court to return to a form of strict scrutiny under such circumstances: "[W]hen classifications such as race or interests such as speech are involved,

---

30. See also Railroad Retirement Bd. v. Fritz (1980), where speaking through Rehnquist, the Court applied traditional "deferential scrutiny" to uphold classificatory changes in the statute regarding retirement benefits of railroad employees. Concurring, Justice Stevens conceded that what was at issue was socio-economic regulation; but, he added: "When Congress deprives a small class of persons of vested rights that are protected—and, indeed, even enhanced—for others who are in a similar though not identical position, I believe the Constitution requires something more than merely a 'conceivable' or a 'plausible' explanation for the unequal treatment."

31. "In Search of Evolving Doctrine on a Changing Court," 86 *Harv.L.Rev.* 1 (1972). Gunther is apparently still willing to defend his model, see the 11th ed. of his *Constitutional Law—Cases and Materials* (Mineola, N.Y.: Foundation Press, 1985), pp. 604–605.

32. For a skeptical appraisal of Gunther's model, see Hans Linde, "Due Process of Lawmaking," 55 *Neb.L.Rev.* 197 (1976).

tighter reins on the legislature would remain appropriate." That concession, necessary as it may be to satisfy the demands of constitutionalism, revives all the problems of strict scrutiny.

We may be on the cusp of judicial change toward Gunther's model. Plyler v. Doe (1982; reprinted below, p. 907) and *Cleburne* show a majority of the justices applying a test of rationality that, as Justice Blackmun put it in an earlier illegitimacy case, "is not a toothless one." [33] It bears little resemblance to the Court's use of rationality in Williamson v. Lee Optical (1955; reprinted above, p. 763). *Plyler* used a standard of rationality, but it threw the burden on the state to prove the rational connection between its goals and the exclusion of the children of illegal aliens from public schools.[34]

Whether *Plyler* and *Cleburne* are turning points or merely more twists in an old road remains to be seen. But one must ask to what extent the sort of jurisprudence that Stone was fostering in *Carolene Products* is viable without some variation of strict scrutiny. Indeed does constitutionalism itself demand some version of this test? Could these demands be met by a rational basis model that proceded along the kind of spectrum that Marshall suggested, requiring more and more convincing arguments by government to justify classifications or restrictions of the sort previously covered by strict scrutiny? How would such a test differ from strict scrutiny?

IV. THE SCOPE AND PERMANENCE OF CONSTITUTIONAL MEANING

Through the smoke that covers the Court's backing and filling across tangled masses of models and counter-models of equal protection, two obvious facts stand out. First, constitutional interpretation in this area has moved far from the document's text. Neither the older models, the now dominant model, or any of the more seriously proposed changes sinks its roots very deeply into the words of the Fourteenth or Fifth amendments. Some are grounded in a mystical belief in "the intent of the framers," others in rather unsystematic analyses of political theory, and still others in free choices among a wide range of alternatives presented by previous decisions; but none makes the black letter of the text more than the starting point of responding to the question of HOW to interpret.

Second, in trying to cope with the HOW interrogative where equal protection is involved, the Court—no doubt unintentionally—

---

33. Mathews v. Lucas (1979). Compare Justice Powell's comment, speaking for the Court in Weber v. Aetna Casualty (1972), a challenge to a Louisiana statute that allowed illegitimate children to share in workmen's compensation benefits only to the extent that the maximum amount allowable had not been claimed by the parent's legitimate children: "The Louisiana Supreme Court emphasized strongly the State's interest in protecting 'legitimate family relationships'. . . . . We do not question the importance of that interest; what we do question is how the challenged statute will promote it."

34. This change, if it is a change, has not arrived unheralded. See, for instance, *Mathews* and *Weber*, note 33 above, and Railroad Retirement Bd. v. Fritz (1980), espec. Stevens' concur. op., discussed above in note 30.

has thrown considerable light on the discussions in Chapter 5 of constitutional change. Whether the Constitution should or should not be permanent, over the last century the meaning of "equal protection of the laws" has several times changed and done so in politically as well as jurisprudentially consequential ways. Moreover, that process of change is continuing.

SELECTED BIBLIOGRAPHY

Baer, Judith A. *Equality Under the Fourteenth Amendment* (Ithaca, N.Y.: Cornell University Press, 1983).

Comment. "Mental Illness: A Suspect Classification?" 83 *Yale L.J.* 1237 (1974).

Gunther, Gerald. "In Search of Evolving Doctrine on a Changing Court," 86 *Harv.L.Rev.* 1 (1972).

Karst, Kenneth L. "Equal Citizenship under the Fourteenth Amendment," 91 *Harv.L.Rev.* 1 (1977).

Michelman, Frank I. "On Protecting the Poor Through the Fourteenth Amendment," 83 *Harv.L.Rev.* 7 (1969).

Per-Lee, Daniel A. "Annotation: Validity, under Equal Protection Clause of the Fourteenth Amendment, of Gender-Based Classifications Arising by Operation of State Law," 60 L.Ed.2d 1188 (1980).

Porter, Mary Cornelia. "Androgeny and the Supreme Court," 1 *Women & Pols.* 23 (1981).

Pritchett, C. Herman. *Constitutional Civil Liberties* (Englewood Cliffs, N.J.: Prentice-Hall, 1984), chaps. 10, 12.

Tribe, Laurence H. *American Constitutional Law* (Mineola, N.Y.: Foundation Press, 1978), chap. 16.

I. SUSPECT CLASSIFICATIONS: SEX?

"[C]lassifications based upon sex, like classifications based upon race, alienage, or national origin, are inherently suspect, and must therefore be subjected to strict judicial scrutiny."—Justice BRENNAN

"It is unnecessary for the Court in this case to characterize sex as a suspect classification, with all the far-reaching implications of such a holding."—Justice POWELL

FRONTIERO v. RICHARDSON
411 U.S. 677, 93 S.Ct. 1764, 36 L.Ed.2d 583 (1973).

Under military regulations a serviceman's wife automatically counted as his dependent for the purposes of increased housing allowances and medical benefits. A servicewoman's husband, in contrast, counted as a dependent only if the servicewoman proved that he was in fact dependent on her for half his support. Lt. Sharon Frontiero brought suit in a federal district court, contending that these regulations unconstitutionally discriminated against her and other servicewomen. The district court sustained the regulations, and she appealed to the Supreme Court.

Mr. Justice **BRENNAN** announced the judgment of the Court and delivered an opinion in which Mr. Justice **DOUGLAS**, Mr. Justice **WHITE**, and Mr. Justice **MARSHALL** join. . . .

. . . [T]he question for decision is whether this difference in treatment constitutes an unconstitutional discrimination against servicewomen in violation of the Due Process Clause of the Fifth Amendment.[1] . . .

II

At the outset, appellants contend that classifications based upon sex, like classifications based upon race, alienage, and national origin, are inherently suspect and must therefore be subjected to close judicial scrutiny. We agree and, indeed, find at least implicit support for such an approach in our unanimous decision only last Term in Reed v. Reed (1971). . . .

The Court noted [in *Reed*] that the [statute challenged there] "provides that different treatment be accorded to the applicants on the basis of their sex; it thus establishes a classification subject to scrutiny under the Equal Protection Clause." Under "traditional" equal protection analysis, a legislative classification must be sustained unless it is "patently arbitrary" and bears no rational relationship to a legitimate governmental interest. McGowan v. Maryland (1961); Dandridge v. Williams (1970).

. . . [In *Reed,*] the Court implicitly rejected appellee's apparently rational explanation of the statutory scheme, and concluded that, by ignoring the individual qualifications of particular applicants, the chal-

---

1. "[W]hile the Fifth Amendment contains no equal protection clause, it does forbid discrimination that is 'so unjustifiable as to be violative of due process.' " Schneider v. Rusk (1964); See Shapiro v. Thompson (1969); Bolling v. Sharpe (1954). [Footnote by Justice Brennan.]

lenged statute provided "dissimilar treatment for men and women who are . . . similarly situated." The Court therefore held that, even though the State's interest in achieving administrative efficiency "is not without some legitimacy," "[t]o give a mandatory preference to members of either sex over members of the other, merely to accomplish the elimination of hearings on the merits, is to make the very kind of arbitrary legislative choice forbidden by the [Constitution]. . . ." This departure from "traditional" rational-basis analysis with respect to sex-based classifications is clearly justified.

There can be no doubt that our Nation has had a long and unfortunate history of sex discrimination. Traditionally, such discrimination was rationalized by an attitude of "romantic paternalism" which, in practical effect, put women, not on a pedestal, but in a cage. Indeed, this paternalistic attitude became so firmly rooted in our national consciousness that, 100 years ago, a distinguished Member of this Court was able to proclaim:

> Man is, or should be, woman's protector and defender. The natural and proper timidity and delicacy which belongs to the female sex evidently unfits it for many of the occupations of civil life. The constitution of the family organization, which is founded in the divine ordinance, as well as in the nature of things, indicates the domestic sphere as that which properly belongs to the domain and functions of womanhood. The harmony, not to say identity, of interests and views which belong, or should belong, to the family institution is repugnant to the idea of a woman adopting a distinct and independent career from that of her husband. . . .
>
> . . . The paramount destiny and mission of woman are to fulfil the noble and benign offices of wife and mother. This is the law of the Creator. Bradwell v. Illinois (1873) (Bradley, J., concurring).

As a result of notions such as these, our statute books gradually became laden with gross, stereotyped distinctions between the sexes and, indeed, throughout much of the 19th century the position of women in our society was, in many respects, comparable to that of blacks under the pre-Civil War slave codes. Neither slaves nor women could hold office, serve on juries, or bring suit in their own names, and married women traditionally were denied the legal capacity to hold or convey property or to serve as legal guardians of their own children. And although blacks were guaranteed the right to vote in 1870, women were denied even that right—which is itself "preservative of other basic civil and political rights" [Reynolds v. Sims (1964)]—until adoption of the Nineteenth Amendment half a century later.

It is true, of course, that the position of women in America has improved markedly in recent decades. Nevertheless, it can hardly be doubted that, in part because of the high visibility of the sex characteristic, women still face pervasive, although at times more subtle, discrimination in our educational institutions, in the job market and, perhaps most conspicuously, in the political arena.

Moreover, since sex, like race and national origin, is an immutable characteristic determined solely by the accident of birth, the imposition of special disabilities upon the members of a particular sex because of their sex would seem to violate "the basic concept of our system that legal burdens should bear some relationship to individual responsibility. . . ." Weber v. Aetna Casualty & Surety Co. (1972). And what differentiates sex from such nonsuspect statutes as intelligence or physical disability, and aligns it with the recognized suspect criteria, is that the sex characteristic frequently bears no relation to ability to perform or contribute to society. As a result statutory distinctions between the sexes often have the effect of invidiously relegating the entire class of females to inferior legal status without regard to the actual capabilities of its individual members.

We might also note that, over the past decade, Congress has itself manifested an increasing sensitivity to sex-based classifications. In Title VII of the Civil Rights Act of 1964, for example, Congress expressly declared that no employer, labor union, or other organization subject to the provisions of the Act shall discriminate against any individual on the basis of "race, color, religion, sex, or national origin." Similarly, the Equal Pay Act of 1963 provides that no employer covered by the Act "shall discriminate . . . between employees on the basis of sex." *   And § 1 of the Equal Rights Amendment, passed by Congress on March 22, 1972, and submitted to the legislatures of the States for ratification, declares that "[e]quality of rights under the law shall not be denied or abridged by the United States or by any State on account of sex." Thus, Congress itself has concluded that classifications based upon sex are inherently invidious, and this conclusion of a coequal branch of Government is not without significance to the question presently under consideration. Cf. Oregon v. Mitchell (1970) (opinion of Brennan, White, and Marshall, JJ.); Katzenbach v. Morgan (1966).

With these considerations in mind, we can only conclude that classifications based upon sex, like classifications based upon race, alienage, or national origin, are inherently suspect, and must therefore be subjected to strict judicial scrutiny. Applying the analysis mandated by that stricter standard of review, it is clear that the statutory scheme now before us is constitutionally invalid.

III

The sole basis of the classification established in the challenged statutes is the sex of the individuals involved. . . .

Moreover, the Government concedes that the differential treatment accorded men and women under these statutes serves no purpose other than mere "administrative convenience." In essence, the Government maintains that, as an empirical matter, wives in our society frequently are dependent upon their husbands, while husbands rarely are dependent upon their wives. Thus, the Government argues that Congress might reasonably have concluded that it would be both cheaper and easier simply conclusively to presume that wives of male members are financially dependent upon their husbands, while burdening female members with the task of establishing dependency in fact.

The Government offers no concrete evidence, however, tending to support its view that such differential treatment in fact saves the

---

* **Eds.' Note:** The proposed amendment was not ratified by three-quarters of the states.

Government any money. In order to satisfy the demands of strict judicial scrutiny, the Government must demonstrate, for example, that it is actually cheaper to grant increased benefits with respect to *all* male members, than it is to determine which male members are in fact entitled to such benefits and to grant increased benefits only to those members whose wives actually meet the dependency requirement. Here, however, there is substantial evidence that, if put to the test, many of the wives of male members would fail to qualify for benefits. And in light of the fact that the dependency determination with respect to the husbands of female members is presently made solely on the basis of affidavits, rather than through the more costly hearing process, the Government's explanation of the statutory scheme is, to say the least, questionable.

In any case, our prior decisions make clear that, although efficacious administration of governmental programs is not without some importance, "the Constitution recognizes higher values than speed and efficiency." Stanley v. Illinois (1972). And when we enter the realm of "strict judicial scrutiny," there can be no doubt that "administrative convenience" is not a shibboleth, the mere recitation of which dictates constitutionality. See Shapiro v. Thompson (1969). On the contrary, any statutory scheme which draws a sharp line between the sexes, *solely* for the purpose of achieving administrative convenience, necessarily commands "dissimilar treatment for men and women who are . . . similarly situated," and therefore involves the "very kind of arbitrary legislative choice forbidden by the [Constitution]. . . ." *Reed.* We therefore conclude that, by according differential treatment to male and female members of the uniformed services for the sole purpose of achieving administrative convenience, the challenged statutes violate the Due Process Clause of the Fifth Amendment insofar as they require a female member to prove the dependency of her husband.

Reversed.

Mr. Justice **STEWART** concurs in the judgment. . . .

Mr. Justice **REHNQUIST** dissents. . . .

Mr. Justice **POWELL**, with whom The Chief Justice [**BURGER**] and Mr. Justice **BLACKMUN** join, concurring in the judgment.

I agree that the challenged statutes constitute an unconstitutional discrimination against service-women in violation of the Due Process Clause of the Fifth Amendment, but I cannot join the opinion of Mr. Justice Brennan, which would hold that all classifications based upon sex, "like classifications based upon race, alienage, and national origin," are "inherently suspect and must therefore be subjected to close judicial scrutiny." It is unnecessary for the Court in this case to characterize sex as a suspect classification, with all of the far-reaching implications of such a holding. *Reed*, which abundantly supports our decision today, did not add sex to the narrowly limited group of classifications which are inherently suspect. In my view, we can and should decide this case on the authority of *Reed* and reserve for the future any expansion of its rationale.

There is another, and I find compelling, reason for deferring a general categorizing of sex classifications as invoking the strictest test of judicial scrutiny. The Equal Rights Amendment, which if adopted will resolve the substance of this precise question, has been approved by the Congress and submitted for ratification by the States. If this Amendment is duly adopted, it will represent the will of the people accomplished in the manner prescribed by the Constitution. By acting prematurely and unnecessarily, as I view it, the Court has assumed a decisional responsibility at the very time when state legislatures, functioning within the traditional democratic process, are debating the proposed Amendment. It seems to me that this reaching out to pre-empt by judicial action a major political decision which is currently in process of resolution does not reflect appropriate respect for duly prescribed legislative processes.

There are times when this Court, under our system, cannot avoid a constitutional decision on issues which normally should be resolved by the elected representatives of the people. But democratic institutions are weakened, and confidence in the restraint of the Court is impaired, when we appear unnecessarily to decide sensitive issues of broad social and political importance at the very time they are under consideration within the prescribed constitutional processes.

"[C]lassifications by gender must serve important governmental objectives and must be substantially related to achievement of those objectives."

CRAIG v. BOREN
429 U.S. 190, 97 S.Ct. 451, 50 L.Ed.2d 397 (1976).

Title 37, §§ 241 and 245 of the Oklahoma code forbade the sale of 3.2 per cent beer to males under 21 and to females under 18. Craig, a male between 18 and 21, sued in a federal district court, alleging that §§ 241 and 245 invidiously discriminated against males 18–20 years of age. The district court sustained the constitutionality of the provisions, and Craig appealed to the Supreme Court.

Mr. Justice **BRENNAN** delivered the opinion of the Court. . . .

. . . Reed [v. Reed (1971)] emphasized that statutory classifications that distinguish between males and females are "subject to scrutiny under the Equal Protection Clause." To withstand constitutional challenge, previous cases establish that classifications by gender must serve important governmental objectives and must be substantially related to achievement of those objectives . . . [*Reed* and subsequent cases] have rejected administrative ease and convenience as sufficiently important objectives to justify gender-based classifications.

See, e.g., Stanley v. Illinois (1972); Frontiero v. Richardson (1973).
. . .

Reed has also provided the underpinning for decisions that have invalidated statutes employing gender as an inaccurate proxy for other more germane bases of classification. Hence, "archaic and overbroad" generalizations, Schlesinger v. Ballard [1975], concerning the financial position of servicewomen, *Frontiero,* and working women, Weinberger v. Wiesenfeld (1975), could not justify use of a gender line in determining eligibility for certain governmental entitlements. Similarly, increasingly outdated misconceptions concerning the role of females in the home rather than in the "marketplace and world of ideas" were rejected as loose-fitting characterizations incapable of supporting state statutory schemes that were premised upon their accuracy. Stanton v. Stanton [1975]. In light of the weak congruence between gender and the characteristic or trait that gender purported to represent, it was necessary that the legislatures choose either to realign their substantive laws in a gender-neutral fashion, or to adopt procedures for identifying those instances where the sex-centered generalization actually comported with fact.

. . . We turn then to the question whether, under *Reed,* the difference between males and females with respect to the purchase of 3.2% beer warrants the differential in age drawn by the Oklahoma statute. We conclude that it does not.

We accept for purposes of discussion the District Court's identification of the objective underlying §§ 241 and 245 as the enhancement of traffic safety. Clearly, the protection of public health and safety represents an important function of state and local governments. However, appellees' statistics in our view cannot support the conclusion that the gender-based distinction closely serves to achieve that objective and therefore the distinction cannot under *Reed* withstand equal protection challenge.

The appellees introduced a variety of statistical surveys. First, an analysis of arrest statistics for 1973 demonstrated that 18–20-year-old male arrests for "driving under the influence" and "drunkenness" substantially exceeded female arrests for that same age period. Similarly, youths aged 17–21 were found to be overrepresented among those killed or injured in traffic accidents, with males again numerically exceeding females in this regard. Third, a random roadside survey in Oklahoma City revealed that young males were more inclined to drive and drink beer than were their female counterparts. Fourth, Federal Bureau of Investigation nationwide statistics exhibited a notable increase in arrests for "driving under the influence." Finally, statistical evidence gathered in other jurisdictions . . . was offered to corroborate Oklahoma's experience by indicating the pervasiveness of youthful participation in motor vehicle accidents following the imbibing of alcohol. . . .

Even were this statistical evidence accepted as accurate, it nevertheless offers only a weak answer to the equal protection question presented here. The most focused and relevant of the statistical surveys, arrests of 18–20-years-olds for alcohol-related driving offenses, exemplifies the ultimate unpersuasiveness of this evidentiary record. Viewed in terms of the correlation between sex and the actual activity that Oklahoma seeks to regulate—driving while under the influence of alcohol—the statistics broadly establish that .18% of females and 2% of males in that age group were arrested for that offense. While such a disparity is not trivial in a statistical sense, it hardly can form the basis for employment of a gender line as a classifying device. Certainly if maleness is to serve as a proxy for drinking and driving, a correlation [sic] of 2% must be considered an unduly tenuous "fit." Indeed, prior cases have consistently rejected the use of sex as a decision-making factor even though the statutes in question certainly rested on far more predictive empirical relationships than this.

Moreover, the statistics exhibit a variety of other shortcomings that seriously impugn their value to equal protection analysis. Setting aside the obvious methodological problems, the surveys do not adequately justify the salient features of Oklahoma's gender-based traffic-safety law. None purports to measure the use and dangerousness of 3.2% beer as opposed to alcohol generally, a detail that is of particular importance since, in light of its low alcohol level, Oklahoma apparently considers the 3.2% beverage to be "nonintoxicating." Moreover, many of the studies, while graphically documenting the unfortunate increase in driving while under the influence of alcohol, make no effort to relate their findings to age-sex differentials as involved here. Indeed, the only survey that explicitly centered its attention upon young drivers and their use of beer—albeit apparently not of the diluted 3.2% variety—reached results that hardly can be viewed as impressive in justifying either a gender or age classification.

There is no reason to belabor this line of analysis. It is unrealistic to expect either members of the judiciary or state officials to be well versed in the rigors of experimental or statistical technique. But this merely illustrates that proving broad sociological propositions by statistics is a dubious business, and one that inevitably is in tension with the normative philosophy that underlies the Equal Protection Clause. Suffice to say that the showing offered by the appellees does not satisfy us that sex represents a legitimate, accurate proxy for the regulation of drinking and driving. In fact, when it is further recognized that Oklahoma's statute prohibits only the selling of 3.2% beer to young males and not their drinking the beverage once acquired (even after purchase by their 18–20-year-old female companions), the relationship between gender and traffic safety becomes far too tenuous to satisfy *Reed*'s requirement that the gender-based difference be substantially related to achievement of the statutory objective. . . .

We conclude that the gender-based differential . . . constitutes a denial of the equal protection of the laws to males aged 18–20. . . .

[*Reversed.*]

Mr. Justice **POWELL,** concurring.

I join the opinion of the Court . . . [a]lthough I do have reservations as to some of the discussion concerning the appropriate standard for equal protection analysis. . . .

. . . I agree that *Reed* is the most relevant precedent. But I find it unnecessary, in deciding this case, to read that decision as broadly as some of the Court's language may imply. *Reed* and subsequent cases involving gender-based classifications make clear that the Court subjects such classifications to a more critical examination than is normally applied when "fundamental" constitutional rights and "suspect classes" are not present.[1]

Mr. Justice **STEVENS,** concurring.

There is only one Equal Protection Clause. It requires every State to govern impartially. It does not direct the courts to apply one standard of review in some cases and a different standard in other cases. Whatever criticism may be leveled at a judicial opinion implying that there are at least three such standards applies with the same force to a double standard.

I am inclined to believe that what has become known as the two-tiered analysis of equal protection claims does not describe a completely logical method of deciding cases, but rather is a method the Court has employed to explain decisions that actually apply a single standard in a reasonably consistent fashion. I also suspect that a careful explanation of the reasons motivating particular decisions may contribute more to an identification of that standard than an attempt to articulate it in all-encompassing terms. It may therefore be appropriate for me to state the principal reasons which persuaded me to join the Court's opinion.

In this case, the classification is objectionable because it is based on an accident of birth, because it is a mere remnant of the now almost universally rejected tradition of discriminating against males in this age bracket, and because, to the extent it reflects any physical difference between males and females, it is actually perverse. The question then is whether the traffic safety justification put forward by the State is sufficient to make an otherwise offensive classification acceptable.

---

1. As is evident from our opinions, the Court has had difficulty in agreeing upon a standard of equal protection analysis that can be applied consistently to the wide variety of legislative classifications. There are valid reasons for dissatisfaction with the "two-tier" approach that has been prominent in the Court's decisions in the past decade. Although viewed by many as a result-oriented substitute for more critical analysis, that approach—with its narrowly limited "upper-tier"—now has substantial precedential support. As has been true of *Reed* and its progeny, our decision today will be viewed by some as a "middle-tier" approach. While I would not endorse that characterization and would not welcome a further subdividing of equal protection analysis, candor compels the recognition that the relatively deferential "rational basis" standard of review normally applied takes on a sharper focus when we address a gender-based classification. So much is clear from our recent cases. For thoughtful discussions of equal protection analysis, see, e.g., Gunther, The Supreme Court, 1971 Term—Foreword in Search of Evolving Doctrine on a Changing Court: A Model for A Newer Equal Protection, 86 *Harv.L.Rev.* 1 (1972); Wilkinson, The Supreme Court, the Equal Protection Clause and the Three Faces of Constitutional Equality, 61 *Va.L.Rev.* 945 (1975). [Footnote by Justice Powell.]

The classification is not totally irrational. For the evidence does indicate that there are more males than females in this age bracket who drive and also more who drink. Nevertheless, there are several reasons why I regard the justification as unacceptable. It is difficult to believe that the statute was actually intended to cope with the problem of traffic safety, since it has only a minimal effect on access to a not very intoxicating beverage and does not prohibit its consumption. Moreover, the empirical data .   . . accentuate the unfairness of treating all 18–20-year-old males as inferior to their female counterparts. The legislation imposes a restraint on 100% of the males in the class allegedly because about 2% of them have probably violated one or more laws relating to the consumption of alcoholic beverages. It is unlikely that this law will have a significant deterrent effect either on that 2% or on the law-abiding 98%. But even assuming some such slight benefit, it does not seem to me that an insult to all of the young men of the State can be justified by visiting the sins of the 2% on the 98%.

Mr. Justice **BLACKMUN,** concurring in part. .   .   .

Mr. Justice **STEWART,** concurring in the judgment. .   .   .

The disparity created by these Oklahoma statutes amounts to total irrationality. For the statistics upon which the State now relies .   .   . wholly fail to prove or even suggest that 3.2% beer is somehow more deleterious when it comes into the hands of a male aged 18–20 than of a female of like age. The disparate statutory treatment of the sexes here, without even a colorably valid justification or explanation, thus amounts to invidious discrimination. See *Reed.*

Mr. Chief Justice **BURGER,** dissenting. .   .   .

I am in general agreement with Mr. Justice Rehnquist's dissent, but even at the risk of compounding the obvious confusion created by those voting to reverse the District Court, I will add a few words.
.   .   . Though today's decision does not go so far as to make gender-based classifications "suspect," it makes gender a disfavored classification. Without an independent constitutional basis supporting the right asserted or disfavoring the classification adopted, I can justify no substantive constitutional protection other than the normal McGowan v. Maryland [1961] protection afforded by the Equal Protection Clause.
The means employed by the Oklahoma Legislature to achieve the objectives sought may not be agreeable to some judges, but since eight Members of the Court think the means not irrational, I see no basis for striking down the statute as violative of the Constitution simply because we find it unwise, unneeded, or possibly even a bit foolish.
.   .   .

Mr. Justice **REHNQUIST**, dissenting.

The Court's disposition of this case is objectionable on two grounds. First is its conclusion that *men* challenging a gender-based statute which treats them less favorably than women may invoke a more stringent standard of judicial review than pertains to most other types of classifications. Second is the Court's enunciation of this standard, without citation to any source, as being that "classifications by gender must serve *important* governmental objectives and must be *substantially* related to achievement of those objectives" (Emphasis added). The only redeeming feature of the Court's opinion, to my mind, is that it apparently signals a retreat by those who joined the plurality opinion in *Frontiero* from their view that sex is a "suspect" classification for purposes of equal protection analysis. I think the Oklahoma statute challenged here need pass only the "rational basis" equal protection analysis expounded in cases such as *McGowan* and Williamson v. Lee Optical Co. (1955), and I believe that it is constitutional under that analysis.

I . . .

. . . . [T]he Court's application here of an elevated or "intermediate" level scrutiny, like that invoked in cases dealing with discrimination against females, raises the question of why the statute here should be treated any differently from countless legislative classifications unrelated to sex which have been upheld under a minimum rationality standard.

Most obviously unavailable to support any kind of special scrutiny in this case, is a history or pattern of past discrimination, such as was relied on by the plurality in *Frontiero* to support its invocation of strict scrutiny. There is no suggestion in the Court's opinion that males in this age group are in any way peculiarly disadvantaged, subject to systematic discriminatory treatment, or otherwise in need of special solicitude from the courts. . . .

It is true that a number of our opinions contain broadly phrased dicta implying that the same test should be applied to all classifications based on sex, whether affecting females or males. E.g., *Frontiero; Reed.*

However, before today, no decision of this Court has applied an elevated level of scrutiny to invalidate a statutory discrimination harmful to males, except where the statute impaired an important personal interest protected by the Constitution. There being no such interest here, and there being no plausible argument that this is a discrimination against females, the Court's reliance on our previous sex-discrimination cases is ill-founded. It treats gender classification as a talisman which—without regard to the rights involved or the persons affected—calls into effect a heavier burden of judicial review.

The Court's conclusion that a law which treats males less favorably than females "must serve important governmental objectives and must be substantially related to achievement of those objectives" apparently comes out of thin air. The Equal Protection Clause contains no such language, and none of our previous cases adopt that standard. I would think we have had enough difficulty with the two standards of review which our cases have recognized—the norm of "rational basis," and the "compelling state interest" required where a "suspect classification" is involved—so as to counsel weightily against the insertion of still another "standard" between those two. How is this Court to divine what objectives are important? How is it to determine whether a particular law is "substantially" related to the achievement of such objective, rather than related in some other way to its achievement? Both of the phrases used are so diaphanous and elastic as to invite subjective judicial preferences or prejudices relating to particular types of legislation, masquerading as judgments whether such legislation is directed at "important" objectives or, whether the relationship to those objectives is "substantial" enough.

I would have thought that if this Court were to leave anything to decision by popularly elected branches of the Government, where no constitutional claim other than that of equal protection is invoked, it would be the decision as to what governmental objectives to be achieved by law are "important," and which are not. As for the second part of the Court's new test, the Judicial Branch is probably in no worse position than the Legislative or Executive Branches to determine if there is *any* rational relationship between a classification and the purpose which it might be thought to serve. But the introduction of the adverb "substantially" requires courts to make subjective judgments as to operational effects, for which neither their expertise nor their access to data fits them. And even if we manage to avoid both confusion and the mirroring of our own preferences in the development of this new doctrine, the thousands of judges in other courts who must interpret the Equal Protection Clause may not be so fortunate.

II

The applicable rational-basis test is one which

> permits the States a wide scope of discretion in enacting laws which affect some groups of citizens differently than others. The constitutional safeguard is offended only if the classification rests on grounds wholly irrelevant to the achievement of the State's objective. State legislatures are presumed to have acted within their constitutional power despite the fact that, in practice, their laws result in some inequality. A statutory discrimination will not be set aside if any state of facts reasonably may be conceived to justify it. *McGowan.*

Our decisions indicate that application of the Equal Protection Clause in a context not justifying an elevated level of scrutiny does not demand "mathematical nicety" or the elimination of all inequality. Those cases recognize that the practical problems of government may require rough accommodations of interests, and hold that such accommodations should be respected unless no reasonable basis can be found to support them. Dandridge v. Williams [1970]. Whether the same ends might have been better or more precisely served by a different approach is no part of the judicial inquiry under the traditional minimum rationality approach. . . .

The Court's criticism of the statistics relied on by the District Court conveys the impression that a legislature in enacting a new law is to be subjected to the judicial equivalent of a doctoral examination in statistics. Legislatures are not held to any rules of evidence such as those which may govern courts or other administrative bodies, and are entitled to draw factual conclusions on the basis of the determination of probable cause which an arrest by a police officer normally represents. In this situation, they could reasonably infer that the incidence of drunk driving is a good deal higher than the incidence of arrest. . . .

Quite apart from [the] alleged methodological deficiencies in the statistical evidence, the Court appears to hold that that evidence, on its face, fails to support the distinction drawn in the statute. The Court notes that only 2% of males (as against .18% of females) in the age group were arrested for drunk driving, and that this very low figure establishes "an unduly tenuous 'fit' " between maleness and drunk driving in the 18–20-year-old group. On this point the Court misconceives the nature of the equal protection inquiry.

The rationality of a statutory classification for equal protection purposes does not depend upon the statistical "fit" between the class and the trait sought to be singled out. It turns on whether there may be a sufficiently higher incidence of the trait within the included class than in the excluded class to justify different treatment. Therefore the present equal protection challenge to this gender-based discrimination poses only the question whether the incidence of drunk driving among young men is sufficiently greater than among young women to justify differential treatment. Notwithstanding the Court's critique of the statistical evidence, that evidence suggests clear differences between the drinking and driving habits of young men and women. Those differences are grounds enough for the State reasonably to conclude that young males pose by far the greater drunk-driving hazard. . . . The gender-based difference in treatment in this case is therefore not irrational. . . .

"Although the test for determining the validity of gender-based classification is straightforward, it must be applied free of fixed notions concerning the roles and abilities of males and females."

MISSISSIPPI UNIVERSITY FOR WOMEN v. HOGAN
458 U.S. 718, 102 S.Ct. 3331, 73 L.Ed.2d 1090 (1982).

In Craig v. Boren, the justices seemed to have reached a compromise—heightened but not strict scrutiny for classifications by sex. In 1981, however, two opinions written by Justice Rehnquist raised serious questions about how long that compromise would hold. The first, Michael M. v. Superior Court, found no sexual discrimination in a conviction of a 17½ year-old male for statutory rape of a 16½ year-old female. For four of the five justices in the majority, Rehnquist wrote:

> [W]e do not apply so-called "strict scrutiny" to [gender-based] classifications. Our cases have held, however, that the traditional minimal rationality test takes on a somewhat "sharper focus" when gender-based classifications are challenged. See Craig v. Boren (1976) (Powell, J., concurring).

Conceding that the purpose of punishing males for intercourse with females under 18 but not females for intercourse with males under 18 was "somewhat less than clear," Rehnquist accepted the state's argument that it was to prevent pregnancies among teen-agers and that this was a "strong interest."

In the second case, Rostker v. Goldberg, Rehnquist wrote for the Court, upholding by a 6–3 vote the Military Selective Service Act, which requires only males to register for the draft. The majority found Congress' restricting compulsory service to males to be reasonable. The opinion, full of deference toward congressional power to raise armies and wage war, finessed the question of requiring any standard stricter than a rational basis. Some observers, however, discounted Rostker's signifying change because it involved congressional powers that the Court had traditionally been reluctant to question. Michael M. was more difficult to discount, though Rehnquist had made a slight bow toward a form of heightened scrutiny.

Mississippi University for Women, a state institution in Columbus, Miss., provided a new test of the compromise's vitality. From its founding, MUW had limited enrollment to women. Joe Hogan, a male nurse resident in Columbus, applied for admission to the School of Nursing to obtain a bachelor's degree in his field. Solely on the basis of his sex, MUW denied him admission to a degree-granting program, though he was allowed to audit classes. He sued for an injunction in a federal district court, lost, and won on appeal. Mississippi then sought and obtained certiorari.

Justice **O'CONNOR** delivered the opinion of the Court.

This case presents the narrow issue of whether a state statute that excludes males from enrolling in a state-supported professional nursing school violates the Equal Protection Clause of the Fourteenth Amendment. . . .

II

We begin our analysis aided by several firmly-established principles. Because the challenged policy expressly discriminates among applicants on the basis of gender, it is subject to scrutiny under the Equal Protection Clause of the Fourteenth Amendment. Reed v. Reed (1971). That this statute discriminates against males rather than against females does not exempt it from scrutiny or reduce the standard of review. Caban v. Mohammed (1979); Orr v. Orr (1979). Our decisions also establish that the party seeking to uphold a statute that classifies individuals on the basis of their gender must carry the burden of showing an "exceedingly persuasive justification" for the classification. Kirchberg v. Feenstra (1981); Personnel Administrator of Massachusetts v. Feeney (1979). The burden is met only by showing at least that the classification serves "important governmental objectives and that the discriminatory means employed" are "substantially related to the achievement of those objectives." Wengler v. Druggists Mutual Insurance Co. (1980).

Although the test for determining the validity of a gender-based classification is straightforward, it must be applied free of fixed notions concerning the roles and abilities of males and females. Care must be taken in ascertaining whether the statutory objective itself reflects archaic and stereotypic notions. Thus, if the statutory objective is to exclude or "protect" members of one gender because they are presumed to suffer from an inherent handicap or to be innately inferior, the objective itself is illegitimate. See Frontiero v. Richardson (1973) (plurality opinion).

If the State's objective is legitimate and important, we next determine whether the requisite direct, substantial relationship between objective and means is present. The purpose of requiring that close relationship is to assure that the validity of a classification is determined through reasoned analysis rather than through the mechanical application of traditional, often inaccurate, assumptions about the proper roles of men and women. . . .

III

A

The State's primary justification for maintaining the single-sex admissions policy of MUW's School of Nursing is that it compensates for discrimination against women and, therefore, constitutes educational affirmative action. As applied to the School of Nursing, we find the State's argument unpersuasive.

In limited circumstances, a gender-based classification favoring one sex can be justified if it intentionally and directly assists members of the sex that is disproportionately burdened. See Schlesinger v. Ballard (1975). However, we consistently have emphasized that "the mere recitation of a benign, compensatory purpose is not an automatic shield which protects against any inquiry into the actual purposes underlying a statutory scheme." Weinberger v. Wiesenfeld (1975). The same searching analysis must be made, regardless of whether the State's objective is to eliminate family controversy, Reed, to achieve administrative efficiency, Frontiero, or to balance the burdens borne by males and females.

It is readily apparent that a State can evoke a compensatory purpose to justify an otherwise discriminatory classification only if members of the gender benefited by the classification actually suffer a disadvantage related to the classification. We considered such a situation in Califano v. Webster (1977), which involved a challenge to a statutory classification that allowed women to eliminate more low-earning years than men for purposes of computing Social Security retirement benefits. Although the effect of the classification was to allow women higher monthly benefits than were available to men with the same earning history, we upheld the statutory scheme, noting that it took into account that women "as such have been unfairly hindered from earning as much as men" and "work[ed] directly to remedy" the resulting ecomonic disparity.

A similar pattern of discrimination against women influenced our decision in *Schlesinger*. There, we considered a federal statute that granted female Naval officers a 13-year tenure of commissioned service before mandatory discharge, but accorded male officers only a nine-year tenure. We recognized that, because women were barred from combat duty, they had had fewer opportunities for promotion than had their male counterparts. By allowing women an additional four years to reach a particular rank before subjecting them to mandatory discharge, the statute directly compensated for other statutory barriers to advancement.

In sharp contrast, Mississippi has made no showing that women lacked opportunities to obtain training in the field of nursing or to attain positions of leadership in that field when the MUW School of Nursing opened its door or that women currently are deprived of such opportunities. In fact, in 1970, the year before the School of Nursing's first class enrolled, women earned 94 percent of the nursing baccalaureate degrees conferred in Mississippi and 98.6 percent of the degrees earned nationwide. That year was not an aberration; one decade earlier, women had earned all the nursing degrees conferred in Mississippi and 98.9 percent of the degrees conferred nationwide. As one would expect, the labor force reflects the same predominance of women in nursing. . . .

Rather than compensate for discriminatory barriers faced by women, MUW's policy of excluding males from admission to the School of Nursing tends to perpetuate the stereotyped view of nursing as an exclusively woman's job. . . . Thus, we conclude that, although the State recited a "benign, compensatory purpose," it failed to establish that the alleged objective is the actual purpose underlying the discriminatory classification.

The policy is invalid also because it fails the second part of the equal protection test, for the State has made no showing that the gender-based classification is substantially and directly related to its proposed compensatory objective. To the contrary, MUW's policy of permitting men to attend classes as auditors fatally undermines its claim that women, at least those in the School of Nursing, are adversely affected by the presence of men. . . .

. . . .

[*Affirmed.*]

Chief Justice **BURGER,** dissenting.

I agree generally with Justice Powell's dissenting opinion. I write separately, however, to emphasize that the Court's holding today is limited to the context of a professional nursing school. Since the

Court's opinion relies heavily on its finding that women have traditionally dominated the nursing profession, it suggests that a State might
well be justified in maintaining, for example, the option of an all-
women's business school or liberal arts program.

Justice **BLACKMUN**, dissenting. . . .

I have come to suspect that it is easy to go too far with rigid rules
in this area of claimed sex discrimination, and to lose—indeed destroy—values that mean much to some people by forbidding the State
from offering them a choice while not depriving others of an alternate
choice. Justice Powell in his separate opinion advances this theme
well.

While the Court purports to write narrowly, declaring that it does
not decide the same issue with respect to "separate but equal" undergraduate institutions for females and males, or with respect to units of
MUW other than its School of Nursing, there is inevitable spillover
from the Court's ruling today. That ruling, it seems to me, places in
constitutional jeopardy any state-supported educational institution that
confines its student body in any area to members of one sex, even
though the State elsewhere provides an equivalent program to the
complaining applicant. The Court's reasoning does not stop with the
School of Nursing of the Mississippi University for Women.

I hope that we do not lose all values that some think are worth-
while (and are not based on differences of race or religion) and relegate
ourselves to needless conformity. The ringing words of the Equal
Protection Clause of the Fourteenth Amendment—what Justice Powell
aptly describes as its "liberating spirit,"—do not demand that price.

Justice **POWELL**, with whom Justice **REHNQUIST** joins, dissenting.

The Court's opinion bows deeply to conformity. Left without
honor—indeed, held unconstitutional—is an element of diversity that
has characterized much of American education and enriched much of
American life. The Court in effect holds today that no State now may
provide even a single institution of higher learning open only to women
students. It gives no heed to the efforts of the State of Mississippi to
provide abundant opportunities for young men and young women to
attend coeducational institutions, and none to the preferences of the
more than 40,000 young women who over the years have evidenced
their approval of an all-women's college by choosing Mississippi University for Women (MUW) over seven coeducational universities within the
State. The Court decides today that the Equal Protection Clause
makes it unlawful for the State to provide women with a traditionally
popular and respected choice of educational environment. It does so in
a case instituted by one man, who represents no class, and whose
primary concern is personal convenience.

It is undisputed that women enjoy complete equality of opportunity
in Mississippi's public system of higher education. Of the State's eight
universities and 16 junior colleges, all except MUW are coeducational.

At least two other Mississippi universities would have provided respondent with the nursing curriculum that he wishes to pursue. . . .

I

Coeducation, historically, is a novel educational theory. From grade school through high school, college, and graduate and professional training, much of the nation's population during much of our history has been educated in sexually segregated classrooms. At the college level, for instance, until recently some of the most prestigious colleges and universities—including most of the Ivy League—had long histories of single-sex education. As Harvard, Yale, and Princeton remained all-male colleges well into the second half of this century, the "Seven Sister" institutions established a parallel standard of excellence for women's colleges. . . .

The sexual segregation of students has been a reflection of, rather than an imposition upon, the preference of those subject to the policy. It cannot be disputed, for example, that the highly qualified women attending the leading women's colleges could have earned admission to virtually any college of their choice. Women attending such colleges have chosen to be there, usually expressing a preference for the special benefits of single-sex institutions. Similar decisions were made by the colleges that elected to remain open to women only.

The arguable benefits of single-sex colleges also continue to be recognized by students of higher education. . . .

II

The issue in this case is whether a State transgresses the Constitution when—within the context of a public system that offers a diverse range of campuses, curricula, and educational alternatives—it seeks to accommodate the legitimate personal preferences of those desiring the advantages of an all-women's college. In my view, the Court errs seriously by assuming—without argument or discussion—that the equal protection standard generally applicable to sex discrimination is appropriate here. That standard was designed to free women from "archaic and overbroad generalizations. . . ." *Schlesinger*. In no previous case have we applied it to invalidate state efforts to *expand* women's choices. Nor are there prior sex discrimination decisions by this Court in which a male plaintiff, as in this case, had the choice of an equal benefit.

The cases cited by the Court therefore do not control the issue now before us. In most of them women were given no opportunity for the same benefit as men. Cases involving male plaintiffs are equally inapplicable. . . .

By applying heightened equal protection analysis to this case, the Court frustrates the liberating spirit of the Equal Protection Clause. It forbids the States from providing women with an opportunity to choose the type of university they prefer. And yet it is these women whom the Court regards as the *victims* of an illegal, stereotyped perception of the role of women in our society. The Court reasons this way in a case in which no woman has complained, and the only complainant is a man who advances no claims on behalf of anyone else. His claim, it should be recalled, is not that he is being denied a substantive educational opportunity, or even the right to attend an all-male or a coeducational college. It is *only* that the colleges open to him are located at inconvenient distances.

III . . .

In sum, the practice of voluntarily chosen single-sex education is an honored tradition in our country. . . . Mississippi's accommodation of such student choices is legitimate because it is completely consensual and is important because it permits students to decide for themselves the type of college education they think will benefit them most. Finally, Mississippi's policy is substantially related to its long-respected objective.

IV

A distinctive feature of America's tradition has been respect for diversity. This has been characteristic of the peoples from numerous lands who have built our country. It is the essence of our democratic system. At stake in this case as I see it is the preservation of a small aspect of this diversity. But that aspect is by no means insignificant, given our heritage of available choice between single-sex and coeducational institutions of higher learning. The Court answers that there is discrimination—not just that which may be tolerable, as for example between those candidates for admission able to contribute most to an educational institution and those able to contribute less—but discrimination of constitutional dimension. But, having found "discrimination," the Court finds it difficult to identify the victims. It hardly can claim that women are discriminated against. A constitutional case is held to exist solely because one man found it inconvenient to travel to any of the other institutions made available to him by the State of Mississippi. In essence he insists that he has a right to attend a college in his home community. This simply is not a sex discrimination case. The Equal Protection Clause was never intended to be applied to this kind of case.

Editors' Note

Query: Does *MUW* lay to rest doubts about the continuing vitality of some form of heightened or intermediate scrutiny for sex-based classifications that *Rostker* and *Michael M.* raised?

———

II. SUSPECT CLASSIFICATIONS: WEALTH?

"[W]here wealth is involved, the Equal Protection Clause does not require absolute equality or precisely equal advantages. . . . [And it] is not the province of this Court to create substantive constitutional rights in the name of guaranteeing equal protection of the laws."

SAN ANTONIO SCHOOL DISTRICT v. RODRIGUEZ
411 U.S. 1, 93 S.Ct. 1278, 36 L.Ed.2d 16 (1973).

In a program similar to that of almost all states, Texas's Minimum Foundation School Program provides basic financial support for public schools; each district supplements those funds through local property taxes. Because the amount and value of taxable property varies from district to district, the amount of money available to finance public schools also widely varies. For example, the expenditure in Edgewood Independent School District, a poor and heavily Mexican-American area in urban San Antonio, was $356 per pupil in 1967–68, about 60 per cent of the $594 per pupil that Alamo Heights, a residential "Anglo" district, spent. Parents of students in Edgewood brought a class action in a federal district court, claiming that Texas, in offering them an education unequal to that it offered students in other districts, denied them equal protection. Relying on cases like Harper v. Virginia (1966; reprinted above, p. 151), the district court held that wealth was a suspect classification, education was a fundamental interest, the rules of strict scrutiny applied, and the unequal financing plan was unconstitutional. Texas appealed to the Supreme Court.

Mr. Justice **POWELL** delivered the opinion of the Court. . . .

I . . .

. . . We must decide, first, whether the Texas system of financing public education operates to the disadvantage of some suspect class or impinges upon a fundamental right explicitly or implicitly protected by the Constitution, thereby requiring strict judicial scrutiny. . . . If not, the Texas scheme must still be examined to determine whether it rationally furthers some legitimate, articulated state purpose and therefore does not constitute an invidious discrimination in violation of the Equal Protection Clause of the Fourteenth Amendment.

II . . .

. . . [W]e find neither the suspect-classification nor the fundamental-interest analysis persuasive.

A

The wealth discrimination discovered by the District Court in this case and by several other courts that have recently struck down school financing laws in other States is quite unlike any of the forms of wealth discrimination heretofore reviewed by this Court. . . . [T]he courts in these cases have virtually assumed their findings of a suspect classification through a simplistic process of analysis: since, under the traditional systems of financing public schools, some poorer people receive less expensive educations than other more affluent people, these systems discriminate on the basis of wealth. This approach largely ignores the hard threshold questions, including whether it makes a difference for purposes of consideration under the Constitution that the class of disadvantaged "poor" cannot be identified or defined in customary equal protection terms, and whether the relative—rather than absolute—nature of the asserted deprivation is of significant consequence. . . .

. . . The individuals, or groups of individuals, who constituted the class discriminated against in our prior cases shared two distinguishing characteristics: . . . they were completely unable to pay for some desired benefit, and as a consequence, they sustained an absolute deprivation of a meaningful opportunity to enjoy that benefit. . . .

Only appellees' first possible basis for describing the class disadvantaged by the Texas school-financing system—discrimination against a class of definably "poor" persons—might arguably meet the criteria established in these prior cases. Even a cursory examination, however, demonstrates that neither of the two distinguishing characteristics of wealth classifications can be found here. First, . . . appellees have made no effort to demonstrate that it operates to the peculiar disadvantage of any class fairly definable as indigent, or as composed of persons whose incomes are beneath any designated poverty level. Indeed . . . there is no basis on the record in this case for assuming that the poorest people . . . are concentrated in the poorest districts.

Second, . . . lack of personal resources has not occasioned an absolute deprivation of the desired benefit. The argument here is not that the children in districts having relatively low assessable property values are receiving no public education; rather, it is that they are receiving a poorer quality education than that available to children in districts having more assessable wealth. . . . [A] sufficient answer . . . is that, at least where wealth is involved, the Equal Protection Clause does not require absolute equality or precisely equal advantages. Nor, indeed, in view of the infinite variables affecting the educational process, can any system assure equal quality of education except in the most relative sense. Texas asserts that . . . [b]y providing 12 years of free public school education, and by assuring teachers, books, transportation and operating funds, [it] has endeavored to "guarantee, for the welfare of the state as a whole, that all people shall have at least an adequate program of education. . . ." No proof was offered at trial persuasively discrediting or refuting the State's assertion. . . .

. . . [A]ppellees and the District Court may have embraced a second [approach,] which might be characterized as a theory of relative or comparative discrimination based on family income. Appellees sought to prove that a direct correlation exists between the wealth of families within each district and the expenditures therein for education. . . .

The principal evidence adduced in support of this comparative discrimination claim is an affidavit submitted by Professor Joele S. Berke of Syracuse University's Educational Finance Policy Institute. . . .

Professor Berke's affidavit is based on a survey of approximately 10% of the school districts in Texas. His findings . . . show only that the wealthiest few districts in the sample have the highest median family incomes and spend the most on education, and that the several poorest districts have the lowest family incomes and devote the least amount of money to education. For the remainder of the districts—96 districts comprising almost 90% of the sample—the correlation is inverted, i.e., the districts that spend next to the most money on education are populated by families having next to the lowest median family incomes while the districts spending the least have the highest median family incomes. It is evident that . . . no factual basis exists upon which to found a claim of comparative wealth discrimination.

This brings us, then, to the third way in which the classification scheme might be defined—*district* wealth discrimination. . . . [T]he disadvantaged class might be viewed as encompassing every child in every district except the district that has the most assessable wealth and spends the most education. Alternatively, the class might be defined more restrictively to include children in districts with assessable property which falls below the statewide average, or median, or below some other artificially defined level.

However described, it is clear that appellees' suit asks this Court to extend its most exacting scrutiny to review a system that allegedly discriminates against a large, diverse, and amorphous class, unified only by the common factor of residence in districts that happen to have less taxable wealth than other districts. The system of alleged discrimination and the class it defines have none of the traditional indicia of suspectness: the class is not saddled with such disabilities, or subjected to such a history of purposeful unequal treatment, or relegated to such a position of political powerlessness as to command extraordinary protection from the majoritarian political process.

We thus conclude that the Texas system does not operate to the peculiar disadvantage of any suspect class. But [recognizing] that this Court has never heretofore held that wealth discrimination alone provides an adequate basis for invoking strict scrutiny, appellees . . . also assert that the State's system impermissibly interferes with the exercise of a "fundamental" right [to education] and that accordingly the prior decisions of this Court require the application of the strict standard of judicial review. . . .

B

In Brown v. Board of Education (1954) a unanimous Court recognized that "education is perhaps the most important function of state and local governments." . . .

Nothing this Court holds today in any way detracts from our historic dedication to public education. . . . But the importance of a service performed by the State does not determine whether it must be regarded as fundamental for purposes of examination under the Equal Protection Clause. . . .

The lesson of [prior] cases . . . is plain. It is not the province of this Court to create substantive constitutional rights in the name of guaranteeing equal protection of the laws. Thus the key to discovering whether education is "fundamental" is not to be found in comparisons of the relative societal significance of education as opposed to subsistence [Dandridge v. Williams (1970)] or housing [Lindsey v. Normet (1972)]. Nor is it to be found by weighing whether education is as important as the right to travel [Shapiro v. Thompson (1969)]. Rather, the answer lies in assessing whether there is a right to education explicitly or implicitly guaranteed by the Constitution. Skinner v. Oklahoma (1942).

Education, of course, is not among the rights afforded explicit protection under our Federal Constitution. Nor do we find any basis for saying it is implicitly so protected. . . . It is appellees' contention, however, that education is distinguishable from other services and benefits provided by the State because it bears a peculiarly close relationship to other rights and liberties accorded protection under the Constitution. Specifically, they insist that education is itself a fundamental personal right because it is essential to the effective exercise of First Amendment freedoms and to intelligent utilization of the right to vote. In asserting a nexus between speech and education, appellees urge that the right to speak is meaningless unless the speaker is capable of articulating his thoughts intelligently and persuasively. . . . Likewise, they argue that the corollary right to receive information becomes little more than a hollow privilege when the recipient has not been taught to read, assimilate, and utilize available knowledge.

A similar line of reasoning is pursued with respect to the right to vote. . . .

We need not dispute any of these propositions. The Court has long afforded zealous protection against unjustifiable governmental interference with the individual's rights to speak and to vote. Yet we have never presumed to possess either the ability or the authority to guarantee to the citizenry the most *effective* speech or the most *informed* electoral choice. That these may be desirable goals of a system of freedom of expression and of a representative form of government is not to be doubted. . . . But they are not values to be implemented by judicial intrusion into otherwise legitimate state activities.

Even if it were conceded that some identifiable quantum of education is a constitutionally protected prerequisite to the meaningful exercise of either right, we have no indication that the present levels of educational expenditure in Texas provide an education that . . . fails to provide each child with an opportunity to acquire the basic minimal skills necessary. . . .

Furthermore, the logical limitations on appellees' nexus theory are difficult to perceive. How, for instance, is education to be distinguished from the significant personal interests in the basics of decent food and shelter? Empirical examination might well buttress an assumption that the ill-fed, ill-clothed, and ill-housed are among the most ineffective participants in the political process, and that they derive the least enjoyment from the benefits of the First Amendment. If so, appellees' thesis would cast serious doubt on the authority of *Dandridge* and *Lindsey*. . . .

C . . .

. . . [We] lack both the expertise and the familiarity with local problems so necessary to the making of wise decisions with respect to the raising and disposition of public revenues. . . . [T]his case also involves the most persistent and difficult questions of educational policy, another area in which this Court's lack of specialized knowledge and experience counsels against premature interference with the informed judgments made at the state and local levels. . . .

It must be remembered, also, that every claim arising under the Equal Protection Clause has implications for the relationship between national and state power under our federal system. Questions of federalism are always inherent in the process of determining whether a State's laws are to be accorded the traditional presumption of constitutionality, or are to be subjected instead to rigorous judicial scrutiny. . . . [I]t would be difficult to imagine a case having a greater potential impact on our federal system than the one now before us, in which we are urged to abrogate systems of financing public education presently in existence in virtually every State.

The foregoing considerations buttress our conclusion that Texas' system of public school finance is an inappropriate candidate for strict judicial scrutiny. These same considerations are relevant to the determination whether that system, with its conceded imperfections, nevertheless bears some rational relationship to a legitimate state purpose. . . .

III . . .

Appellees do not question the propriety of Texas' dedication to local control of education. To the contrary, they attack the school-financing system precisely because, in their view, it does not provide the same level of local control and fiscal flexibility in all districts. . . . While it is no doubt true that reliance on local property taxation for school revenues provides less freedom of choice with respect to expenditures for some districts than for others, the existence of "some inequality" in the manner in which the State's rationale is achieved is not alone a sufficient basis for striking down the entire system. McGowan v. Maryland (1961). It may not be condemned simply because it imperfectly effectuates the State's goals. *Dandridge.* Nor must the financing system fail because . . . other methods of satisfying the State's interest, which occasion "less drastic" disparities in expenditures, might be conceived. Only where state action impinges on the exercise of fundamental constitutional rights or liberties must it be found to have chosen the least restrictive alternative. . . .

Appellees further urge that the Texas system is unconstitutionally arbitrary because it allows the availability of local taxable resources to turn on "happenstance." . . . But any scheme of local taxation . . . . requires the establishment of jurisdictional boundaries that are inevitably arbitrary. It is equally inevitable that some localities are going to be blessed with more taxable assets than others. . . .

Moreover, if local taxation for local expenditure is an unconstitutional method of providing for education then it may be an equally impermissible means of providing other necessary services customarily financed largely from local property taxes, including local police and fire protection, public health and hospitals, and public utility facilities of various kinds. We perceive no justification for such a severe denigration of local property taxation and control as would follow from appellees' contentions. . . .

In sum, . . . we cannot say that such disparities [among districts] are the product of a system that is so irrational as to be invidiously discriminatory. . . . The Texas plan is not the result of hurried, ill-conceived legislation [or] of purposeful discrimination against any group or class. On the contrary, it is rooted in decades of experience in Texas and elsewhere, and in major part is the product of responsible studies by qualified people. . . . We are unwilling to assume for ourselves a level of wisdom superior to that of legislators, scholars, and educational authorities in 49 States, especially where the alternatives proposed are only recently conceived and nowhere yet tested. The constitutional standard under the Equal Protection Clause is whether the challenged state action rationally furthers a legitimate state purpose or interest. We hold that the Texas plan abundantly satisfies this standard. . . .

Reversed.

Mr. Justice **STEWART**, concurring. . . .

Mr. Justice **BRENNAN**, dissenting. . . .

Mr. Justice **WHITE**, with whom Mr. Justice **DOUGLAS** and Mr. Justice **BRENNAN** join, dissenting. . . .

Mr. Justice **MARSHALL**, with whom Mr. Justice **DOUGLAS** concurs, dissenting. . . .

. . . [A]ppellants and the majority may believe that the Equal Protection Clause cannot be offended by substantially unequal state treatment of persons who are similarly situated so long as the State provides everyone with some unspecified amount of education which evidently is "enough." The basis for such a novel view is far from clear. It is, of course, true that the Constitution does not require precise equality in the treatment of all persons. . . . But this Court has never suggested that because some "adequate" level of benefits is provided to all, discrimination in the provision of services is therefore constitutionally excusable. The Equal Protection Clause is not addressed to the minimal sufficiency but rather to the unjustifiable inequalities of state action. It mandates nothing less than that "all

persons similarly circumstanced shall be treated alike." F.S. Royster
Guano Co. v. Virginia (1920).

. . . I cannot accept [the majority's] emasculation of the Equal
Protection Clause. . . .

. . . The Court apparently seeks to establish today that equal
protection cases fall into one of two neat categories which dictate the
appropriate standard of review—strict scrutiny or mere rationality.
But this Court's decisions . . . defy such easy categorization. A
principled reading of what this Court has done reveals that it has
applied a spectrum of standards in reviewing discrimination allegedly
violative of the Equal Protection Clause. This spectrum clearly comprehends variations in the degree of care with which the Court will
scrutinize particular classifications, depending, I believe, on the constitutional and societal importance of the interest adversely affected and
the recognized invidiousness of the basis upon which the particular
classification is drawn. I find in fact that many of the Court's recent
decisions embody the very sort of reasoned approach to equal protection
analysis for which I previously argued. . . . *Dandridge* (dissenting
opinion).

I therefore cannot accept the majority's labored efforts to demonstrate that fundamental interests, which call for strict scrutiny of the
challenged classification, encompass only established rights which we
are somehow bound to recognize from the text of the Constitution itself.
To be sure, some interests which the Court has deemed to be fundamental for purposes of equal protection analysis are themselves constitutionally protected rights. . . . *Shapiro*. But it will not do to
suggest that the "answer" to whether an interest is fundamental for
purposes of equal protection analysis is *always* determined by whether
that interest "is a right . . . explicitly or implicitly guaranteed by the
Constitution."

I would like to know where the Constitution guarantees the right
to procreate, *Skinner*, or the right to vote in state elections, e.g.,
Reynolds v. Sims (1964), or the right to an appeal from a criminal
conviction, e.g., Griffin v. Illinois (1956). These are instances in which,
due to the importance of the interests at stake, the Court has displayed
a strong concern with the existence of discriminatory state treatment.
But the Court has never said or indicated that these are interests which
independently enjoy full-blown constitutional protection. . . .

The majority is, of course, correct when it suggests that the process
of determining which interests are fundamental is a difficult one. But
I do not . . . accept the view that the process need necessarily
degenerate into an unprincipled, subjective "picking-and-choosing" between various interests or that it must involve this Court in creating
"substantive constitutional rights in the name of guaranteeing equal
protection of the laws." Although not all fundamental interests are
constitutionally guaranteed, the determination of which interests are
fundamental should be firmly rooted in the text of the Constitution.
The task in every case should be to determine the extent to which

constitutionally guaranteed rights are dependent on interests not mentioned in the Constitution. As the nexus between the specific constitutional guarantee and the nonconstitutional interest draws closer, the nonconstitutional interest becomes more fundamental and the degree of judicial scrutiny applied when the interest is infringed on a discriminatory basis must be adjusted accordingly. Thus, it cannot be denied that interests such as procreation, the exercise of the state franchise, and access to criminal appellate processes are not fully guaranteed to the citizen by our Constitution. But these interests have nonetheless been afforded special judicial consideration in the face of discrimination because they are, to some extent, interrelated with constitutional guarantees. . . . Only if we closely protect the related interests from state discrimination do we ultimately ensure the integrity of the constitutional guarantee itself. . . . [See, e.g., Eisenstadt v. Baird (1972); Reed v. Reed (1971); and Weber v. Aetna Casualty & Surety Co. (1972)].

. . . In the context of economic interests, we find that discriminatory state action is almost always sustained, for such interests are generally far removed from constitutional guarantees. . . . But the situation differs markedly when discrimination against important individual interests with constitutional implications and against particularly disadvantaged or powerless classes is involved. . . . .

. . . [I]f the discrimination inherent in the Texas scheme is scrutinized with the care demanded by the interest and classification present in this case, the unconstitutionality of that scheme is unmistakable.

. . . It is true that this Court has never deemed the provision of free public education to be required by the Constitution. . . . Nevertheless, the fundamental importance of education is amply indicated by the prior decisions of this Court, by the unique status accorded public education by our society, and by the close relationship between education and some of our most basic constitutional values. . . .

Education directly affects the ability of a child to exercise his First Amendment interests, both as a source and as a receiver of information and ideas. . . .

Of particular importance is the relationship between education and the political process. . . . Education may instill the interest and provide the tools necessary for political discourse and debate. Indeed, it has frequently been suggested that education is the dominant factor affecting political consciousness and participation. . . . [O]f most immediate and direct concern must be the demonstrated effect of education on the exercise of the franchise by the electorate. . . . Data from the Presidential Election of 1968 clearly demonstrates a direct relationship between participation in the electoral process and level of educational attainment. . . .

While ultimately disputing little of this, the majority seeks refuge in the fact that the Court has "never presumed to possess either the ability or the authority to guarantee to the citizenry the most *effective* speech or the most *informed* electoral choice." . . . This serves only to blur what is in fact at stake. . . . Appellees do not now seek the best education Texas might provide. They do seek, however, an end to state discrimination resulting from the unequal distribution of taxable district property wealth. . . . As this Court held in *Brown*, the opportunity of education, "where the state has undertaken to provide it, is a right which must be made available to all on equal terms." The factors just considered . . . compel us to recognize the fundamentality of education and to scrutinize with appropriate care the bases for state discrimination affecting equality of educational opportunity in Texas' school districts—a conclusion which is only strengthened when we consider the character of the classification in this case. . . .

As the Court points out, . . . no previous decision has deemed the presence of just a wealth classification to be sufficient basis to call forth rigorous judicial scrutiny of allegedly discriminatory state action. [This] may be explainable on a number of grounds. The "poor" may not be seen as politically powerless as certain discrete and insular minority groups. Personal poverty may entail much the same social stigma as historically attached to certain racial or ethnic groups. But personal poverty is not a permanent disability; its shackles may be escaped. Perhaps most importantly, though, personal wealth may not necessarily share the general irrelevance as a basis for legislative action that race or nationality is recognized to have. While the "poor" have frequently been a legally disadvantaged group, it cannot be ignored that social legislation must frequently take cognizance of the economic status of our citizens. Thus, we have generally gauged the invidiousness of wealth classifications with an awareness of the importance of the interests being affected and the relevance of personal wealth to those interests. See Harper v. Virginia Bd. of Elections [1966].

When evaluated with these considerations in mind, it seems to me that discrimination on the basis of group wealth in this case likewise calls for careful judicial scrutiny. First, . . . while local district wealth may serve other interests, it bears no relationship whatsoever to the [important] interest of Texas school children in the educational opportunity afforded them by the State of Texas. . . . Discrimination on the basis of group wealth may not, to be sure, reflect the social stigma frequently attached to personal poverty. Nevertheless, insofar as group wealth discrimination involves wealth over which the disadvantaged individual has no significant control, it represents in fact a more serious basis of discrimination than does personal wealth. . . . Cf. *Weber*.

The disability of the disadvantaged class in this case extends as well into the political processes upon which we ordinarily rely as adequate for the protection and promotion of all interests. Here legislative reallocation of the State's property wealth must be sought in the face of inevitable opposition from significantly advantaged districts that have a strong vested interest in the preservation of the status quo, a problem not completely dissimilar to that faced by underrepresented districts prior to the Court's intervention in the process of reapportionment, see Baker v. Carr (1962).

Nor can we ignore the extent to which, in contrast to our prior decisions, the State is responsible for the wealth discrimination in this instance. . . . The means for financing public education in Texas are selected and specified by the State. . . .

. . . [Therefore,] both the nature of the interest and the classification dictate close judicial scrutiny of the purposes which Texas seeks to serve with its present educational financing scheme and of the means it has selected to serve that purpose.

The only justification offered by appellants . . . is local educational control. . . .

In Texas, [however,] statewide laws regulate in fact the most minute details of local public education. . . .

Moreover, even if we accept Texas' general dedication to local control in educational matters, it is difficult to find any evidence of such dedication with respect to fiscal matters. . . . In fact [fiscal policy] is largely determined by the amount of taxable property located in the district—a factor over which local voters can exercise no control. . . .

In my judgment, . . . the State has selected means wholly inappropriate to secure its purported interest in assuring its school districts local fiscal control. . . .

Editors' Notes

(1) **Query:** Armed with the benefit of having already read later cases on "semi-suspect" classifications, especially Craig v. Boren (1976; reprinted above, at p. 844), and Mississippi University for Women v. Hogan (1982; reprinted above, at p. 851), which justice, Powell or Marshall, do you think offered the more accurate explanation of how the Court *does* treat various classifications? How the Court *should* treat different kinds of classifications? To what extent did Powell change his mind in *Craig*? One should reconsider this question after reading Cleburne v. Cleburne Living Center (1985; reprinted below, p. 916).

(2) Prior to *San Antonio,* the question of wealth as a nonsuspect classification was not nearly so clear as either Justice Powell claimed or Marshall conceded. See the discussion in the Introductory Essay, above, at p. 831. In addition, California's supreme court invalidated, as a denial of equal protection, a financing plan similar to Texas's, Serrano v. Priest (1971); as did Michigan's supreme court, Milliken v. Green (1972); and, on state grounds, New Jersey's, Robinson v. Cahill (1973). Later, the Michigan Supreme Court granted a rehearing and vacated its earlier judgment, Milliken v. Green (1973), because of *San Antonio.* In Harris v. McRae (1980; reprinted below, p. 898), the U.S. Supreme Court reaffirmed that wealth is not a suspect classification. Later, by dismissing, "for want of a substantial federal question," appeals from decisions in New York sustaining the constitutionality of that state's unequal financing of

education—Bd. of Edn. of Rochester v. Nyquist (1983), and Bd. of Edn., Levittown v. Nyquist (1983), the Court avoided reopening the constitutional issue.

(3) Among the more interesting analyses of the problems of wealth and equal protection are: Judith Areen and Leonard Ross, "The Rodriguez Case," 1976 *Sup.Ct.Rev.* 33; Frank I. Michelman, "On Protecting the Poor through the Fourteenth Amendment," 83 *Harv.L.Rev.* 7 (1969); C. Herman Pritchett, *Constitutional Civil Liberties* (Englewood Cliffs, N.J.: Prentice-Hall, 1984), pp. 322–324; Laurence H. Tribe, *American Constitutional Law* (Mineola, N.Y.: Foundation Press, 1978), chap. 16; and Ralph K. Winter, Jr., "Poverty, Economic Equality, and the Equal Protection Clause," 1972 *Sup.Ct.Rev.* 51.

(4) We suggest that, as you read the cases on equal protection and fundamental rights, taken up in detail in the next section of this chapter, you keep in mind the debate in *San Antonio* between Justices Powell and Marshall on (a) whether such rights can be divided into two neat categories, parallel to suspect and nonsuspect classifications; and (b) how to identify rights to which judges should give (degrees of?) special protection.

"[I]t simply does not follow that a woman's freedom of choice [to have an abortion] carries with it a constitutional entitlement to the financial resources to avail herself of the full range of protected choices."

HARRIS v. McRAE

448 U.S. 297, 100 S.Ct. 2671, 65 L.Ed.2d 784 (1980).

This decision, upholding a provision in an appropriation bill forbidding use of federal funds to finance abortions unless the pregnancy was caused by rape or was endangering the life of the mother, is reprinted below, at p. 898.

III. STRICT SCRUTINY AND FUNDAMENTAL RIGHTS

"We are dealing here with legislation which involves one of the basic civil rights of man. . . . [S]trict scrutiny of the classification which a state makes in sterilization law is essential, lest . . . invidious discriminations are made against groups or types of individuals in violation of the constitutional guaranty of just and equal laws."

SKINNER v. OKLAHOMA

316 U.S. 535, 62 S.Ct. 1110, 86 L.Ed. 1655 (1942).

In 1935 Oklahoma adopted a statute requiring sterilization of "habitual criminals"—persons convicted two or more times for some felonies involving moral turpitude. The act allowed notice to the defendant, an opportunity to be heard, and the right to trial by jury; but the only issue triable was whether the defendant "may be rendered sexually sterile without detriment to his or her general health." The statute excepted certain "white collar" crimes from its coverage: "offenses arising out of the violation of the prohibitory laws [Oklahoma was a "dry" state then], revenue acts, embezzlement, or political offenses, shall not be considered to come or be considered within the terms of this Act." Buck v. Bell (1927; reprinted below, p. 1105) provided some constitutional support. There the Supreme Court had rejected challenges based on fundamental rights and equal protection and had upheld compulsory sterilization of mental defectives.

In 1926, Jack Skinner was convicted in Oklahoma of stealing chickens and in 1929 and 1934 of robbery with firearms. Because each of these felonies involved moral turpitude, the state began proceedings to order his sterilization. Skinner challenged the substance and process of the statute as unconstitutional. After losing in state courts, he sought and obtained certiorari from the U.S. Supreme Court. The case troubled the justices and they took it up off and on at conference for more than a month. Stone was particularly ill at ease and suggested reargument. He was convinced the statute was unconstitutional but he was not quite sure how to get around the presumption of constitutionality, though he did not think it should apply where, as here, the legislature did not know what it was doing. He was also troubled by *Buck,* though he had voted with the majority in that case. After the final vote, the Court was unanimous in holding the act unconstitutional, though the justices differed in their reasoning. Perhaps as an indication of his own indecision and his dislike of using the equal protection clause in such a case, Stone assigned the task of writing the opinion of the Court to William O. Douglas.

Mr. Justice **DOUGLAS** delivered the opinion of the Court. . . .

This case touches a sensitive and important area of human rights. Oklahoma deprives certain individuals of a right which is basic to the perpetuation of a race—the right to have offspring. . . .

Several objections to the constitutionality of the Act have been pressed upon us. It is urged that the Act cannot be sustained as an exercise of the police power in view of the state of scientific authorities respecting inheritability of criminal traits. It is argued that due process is lacking because under this Act, unlike the act upheld in Buck v. Bell [1927], the defendant is given no opportunity to be heard on the issue as to whether he is the probable potential parent of socially undesirable offspring. . . . We pass those points without intimating an opinion on them, for there is a feature of the Act which clearly condemns it. That is its failure to meet the requirements of the equal protection clause of the Fourteenth Amendment.

We do not stop to point out all of the inequalities in this Act. A few examples will suffice. In Oklahoma grand larceny is a felony. Larceny is grand larceny when the property taken exceeds $20 in value. Embezzlement is punishable "in the manner prescribed for feloniously stealing property of the value of that embezzled." Hence he who embezzles property worth more than $20 is guilty of a felony. A clerk who appropriates over $20 from his employer's till and a stranger who steals the same amount are thus both guilty of felonies. If the latter repeats his act and is convicted three times, he may be sterilized. But the clerk is not subject to the pains and penalties of the Act no matter how large his embezzlements nor how frequent his convictions. A person who enters a chicken coop and steals chickens commits a felony; and he may be sterilized if he is thrice convicted. If, however, he is a bailee of the property and fraudulently appropriates it, he is an embezzler. Hence no matter how habitual his proclivities for embezzlement are and no matter how often his conviction, he may not be sterilized. . . .

It was stated in *Buck* that the claim that state legislation violates the equal protection clause of the Fourteenth Amendment is "the usual last resort of constitutional arguments." Under our constitutional system the States in determining the reach and scope of particular legislation need not provide "abstract symmetry." They may mark and set apart the classes and types of problems according to the needs and as dictated or suggested by experience. It was in that connection that Mr. Justice Holmes, speaking for the Court in Bain Peanut Co. v. Pinson [1931], stated, "We must remember that the machinery of government would not work if it were not allowed a little play in its joints." . . . Thus, if we had here only a question as to a State's classification of crimes, such as embezzlement or larceny, no substantial federal question would be raised. . . .

But the instant legislation runs afoul of the equal protection clause, though we give Oklahoma that large deference which the rule of the foregoing cases requires. We are dealing here with legislation which involves one of the basic civil rights of man. Marriage and procreation are fundamental to the very existence and survival of the race. The power to sterilize, if exercised, may have subtle, far-reaching and devastating effects. In evil or reckless hands it can cause races or types which are inimical to the dominant group to wither and disappear. There is no redemption for the individual whom the law touches. Any experiment which the State conducts is to his irreparable injury. He is forever deprived of a basic liberty. We mention these matters not to reexamine the scope of the police power of the States. We advert to them merely in emphasis of our view that strict scrutiny of the classification which a state makes in a sterilization law is essential, lest unwittingly or otherwise, invidious discriminations are made against groups or types of individuals in violation of the constitutional guaranty of just and equal laws. The guaranty of "equal protection of the laws is a pledge of the protection of equal laws." Yick Wo v. Hopkins [1886]. When the law lays an unequal hand on those who have committed intrinsically the same quality of offense and sterilizes one and not the other, it has made as invidious a discrimination as if it had selected a particular race or nationality for oppressive treatment. Sterilization of those who have thrice committed grand larceny with immunity for those who are embezzlers is a clear, pointed, unmistakable discrimination. Oklahoma makes no attempt to say that he who commits larceny by trespass or trick or fraud has biologically inheritable traits which he who commits embezzlement lacks. . . . Only when it comes to sterilization are the pains and penalties of the law different. The equal protection clause would indeed be a formula of empty words if such conspicuous artificial lines could be drawn. In *Buck,* the Virginia [sterilization] statute was upheld though it applied only to feeble-minded persons in institutions of the State. But it was pointed out that "so far as the operations enable those who otherwise must be kept confined to be returned to the world, and thus open the asylum to others, the equality aimed at will be more nearly reached." Here there is no such saving feature. Embezzlers are forever free. Those who steal or take in other ways are not. . . .

Reversed.

Mr. Chief Justice **STONE** concurring:

I concur in the result, but I am not persuaded that we are aided in reaching it by recourse to the equal protection clause.

If Oklahoma may resort generally to the sterilization of criminals on the assumption that their propensities are transmissible to future generations by inheritance, I seriously doubt that the equal protection clause requires it to apply the measure to all criminals in the first instance, or to none.

Moreover, if we must presume that the legislature knows—what science has been unable to ascertain—that the criminal tendencies of any class of habitual offenders are transmissible regardless of the varying mental characteristics of its individuals, I should suppose that we must likewise presume that the legislature, in its wisdom, knows that the criminal tendencies of some classes of offenders are more likely to be transmitted than those of others. And so I think the real question we have to consider is not one of equal protection, but whether the wholesale condemnation of a class to such an invasion of personal liberty, without opportunity to any individual to show that his is not the type of case which would justify resort to it, satisfies the demands of due process.

There are limits to the extent to which the presumption of constitutionality can be pressed, especially where the liberty of the person is concerned (see United States v. Carolene Products Co., note 4 [1938]) and where the presumption is resorted to only to dispense with a procedure which the ordinary dictates of prudence would seem to demand for the protection of the individual from arbitrary action. Although petitioner here was given a hearing to ascertain whether sterilization would be detrimental to his health, he was given none to discover whether his criminal tendencies are of an inheritable type. Undoubtedly a state may, after appropriate inquiry, constitutionally interfere with the personal liberty of the individual to prevent the transmission by inheritance of his socially injurious tendencies. *Buck.* But until now we have not been called upon to say that it may do so without giving him a hearing and opportunity to challenge the existence as to him of the only facts which could justify so drastic a measure.

Science has found and the law has recognized that there are certain types of mental deficiency associated with delinquency which are inheritable. But the State does not contend—nor can there be any pretense—that either common knowledge or experience, or scientific investigation, has given assurance that the criminal tendencies of any class of habitual offenders are universally or even generally inheritable. In such circumstances, inquiry whether such is the fact in the case of any particular individual cannot rightly be dispensed with. Whether the procedure by which a statute carries its mandate into execution satisfies due process is a matter of judicial cognizance. A law which condemns, without hearing, all the individuals of a class to so harsh a measure as the present because some or even many merit condemnation, is lacking in the first principles of due process. And so, while the state may protect itself from the demonstrably inheritable tendencies of the individual which are injurious to society, the most elementary notions of due process would seem to require it to take appropriate steps to safeguard the liberty of the individual by affording him, before he is condemned to an irreparable injury in his person, some opportunity to show that he is without such inheritable tendencies. The state is called on to sacrifice no permissible end when it is required to reach its objective by a reasonable and just procedure adequate to safeguard rights of the individual which concededly the Constitution protects.

Mr. Justice **JACKSON** concurring:

I join the Chief Justice in holding that the hearings provided are too limited in the context of the present Act to afford due process of law. I also agree with the opinion of Mr. Justice Douglas that the scheme of classification set forth in the Act denies equal protection of the law. I disagree with the opinion of each in so far as it rejects or minimizes the grounds taken by the other. . . .

There are limits to the extent to which a legislatively represented majority may conduct biological experiments at the expense of the dignity and personality and natural powers of a minority—even those who have been guilty of what the majority define as crimes. But this Act falls down before reaching this problem, which I mention only to avoid the implication that such a question may not exist because not discussed. On it I would also reserve judgment.

Editors' Notes

(1) This is the first time that the Court used the term "strict scrutiny" in a case involving equal protection. (Cf. Stone's term in *Carolene Products* footnote 4, "more exacting judicial scrutiny.")

(2) It is interesting that the Court chose to use equal protection as the grounds for decision rather than carrying through on Douglas' forthright statement that marriage and procreation were fundamental rights and holding the state law invalid on those grounds. Perhaps so soon after the Old Court's

use of "substantive due process"—1937 was only five years past when *Skinner* came down—it would have been untimely if not impolitic for the young justices to reinvoke that concept. Discussing *Skinner* twenty years later, Douglas said that he had thought from the beginning that the case should be decided on equal-protection grounds. Stone and Roberts, the only two people from 1937 among the sitting justices, were both unhappy with the use of equal protection, but Roberts agreed not to go public with his doubts. "Murphy and Black and Frankfurter, Reed and I," Douglas recalled, "were very clear on the equal-protection point from the beginning." "Transcriptions of Conversations between Justice William O. Douglas and Prof. Walter F. Murphy," (Recorded 1961–93; Mudd Library, Princeton University), pp. 158–160.

(3) Douglas also reported that he did not want *Skinner* to disturb Buck v. Bell (1927). See the notes to that case, below at pp. 1106–1108.

(4) Can paragraphs 2 and 3 of Stone's *Carolene Products* theory justify the outcome in *Skinner*? Can paragraph 1? Did the Court need a broader based, or more carefully articulated, theory to sustain *Skinner*? To what extent did Jackson's concurrence point toward such a theory?

"The Fourteenth Amendment requires that the freedom of choice to marry not be restricted by invidious racial discriminations."

LOVING v. VIRGINIA

388 U.S. 1, 87 S.Ct. 1817, 18 L.Ed.2d 1010 (1967).

This decision, striking down Virginia's statute forbidding racial intermarriage, is reprinted above, at p. 777.

"[A]ny classification which serves to penalize the exercise of [a fundamental] right, unless shown to be necessary to promote a *compelling* governmental interest, is unconstitutional."

SHAPIRO v. THOMPSON

394 U.S. 618, 89 S.Ct. 1322, 22 L.Ed.2d 600 (1969).

Connecticut, Pennsylvania, and the District of Columbia denied welfare benefits to people who had not resided in the jurisdiction for at least one year. Poor people in all three jurisdictions filed suits in federal district courts, and each court held the denial to violate equal protection. The states and the District appealed to the Supreme Court.

Mr. Justice **BRENNAN** delivered the opinion of the Court. . . .

II

. . . [T]he effect of the waiting-period requirement in each case is to create two classes of needy resident families indistinguishable from each other except that one is composed of residents who have resided a year or more, and the second of residents who have resided less than a year, in the jurisdiction. On the basis of this sole difference the first class is granted and the second class is denied welfare aid upon which may depend the ability of the families to obtain the very means to subsist—food, shelter, and other necessities of life. . . . [A]ppellees' central contention is that the statutory prohibition of benefits to residents of less than a year creates a classification which constitutes an invidious discrimination denying them equal protection of the laws. We agree. The interests which appellants assert are promoted by the classification either may not constitutionally be promoted by government or are not compelling governmental interests.

III

Primarily, appellants justify the waiting-period requirement as a protective device to preserve the fiscal integrity of state public assistance programs. It is asserted that people who require welfare assistance during their first year of residence in a State are likely to become continuing burdens on state welfare programs. Therefore, the argument runs, if such people can be deterred from entering the jurisdiction by denying them welfare benefits during the first year, state programs to assist long-time residents will not be impaired by a substantial influx of indigent newcomers. . . .

We do not doubt that the one-year waiting-period device is well suited to discourage the influx of poor families in need of assistance.

This Court long ago recognized that the nature of our Federal Union and our constitutional concepts of personal liberty unite to require that all citizens be free to travel throughout the length and breadth of our land uninhibited by statutes, rules, or regulations which unreasonably burden or restrict this movement. That proposition was early stated by Chief Justice Taney in the Passenger Cases (1849):

> For all the great purposes for which the Federal government was formed, we are one people, with one common country. We are all citizens of the United States; and, as members of the same community, must have the right to pass and repass through every part of it without interruption, as freely as in our own States.

We have no occasion to ascribe the source of this right to travel interstate to a particular constitutional provision.[1] It suffices that, as Mr. Justice Stewart said for the Court in United States v. Guest (1966):

> The constitutional right to travel from one State to another . . . occupies a position fundamental to the concept of our Federal Union.

---

1. In Corfield v. Coryell (1825) [Washington, J., on circuit], Paul v. Virginia (1869), and Ward v. Maryland (1871), the right to travel interstate was grounded upon the Privileges and Immunities Clause of Art. IV, § 2. See also Slaughter-House Cases (1873); Twining v. New Jersey (1908). In Edwards v. California (1941) (Douglas and Jackson, JJ., concurring), and Twining v. New Jersey reliance was placed on the Privileges and Immunities Clause of the Fourteenth Amendment. See also Crandall v. Nevada (1868). In *Edwards* and the *Passenger Cases* a commerce clause approach was employed. See also Kent v. Dulles (1958); Aptheker v. Secretary of State (1964); Zemel v. Rusk (1965), where the freedom of Americans to travel outside the country was grounded upon the Due Process Clause of the Fifth Amendment. [Footnote by the Court.]

It is a right that has been firmly established and repeatedly recognized.
. . .

Thus, the purpose of deterring the in-migration of indigents cannot serve as justification for the classification created by the one-year waiting period, since that purpose is constitutionally impermissible. If a law has "no other purpose . . . than to chill the assertion of constitutional rights by penalizing those who choose to exercise them, then it [is] patently unconstitutional." United States v. Jackson (1968).

Alternatively, appellants argue that . . . the challenged classification may be justified as a permissible state attempt to discourage those indigents who would enter the State solely to obtain larger benefits. We observe first that none of the statutes before us is tailored to serve that objective. Rather, the class of barred newcomers is all-inclusive, lumping the great majority who come to the State for other purposes with those who come for the sole purpose of collecting higher benefits. In actual operation, therefore, the three statutes enact what in effect are nonrebuttable presumptions that every applicant for assistance in his first year of residence came to the jurisdiction solely to obtain higher benefits. Nothing whatever in any of these records supplies any basis in fact for such a presumption.

More fundamentally, a State may no more try to fence out those indigents who seek higher welfare benefits than it may try to fence out indigents generally. . . .

Appellants argue further that the challenged classification may be sustained as an attempt to distinguish between new and old residents on the basis of the contribution they have made to the community through the payment of taxes. . . . Appellants' reasoning would logically permit the State to bar new residents from schools, parks, and libraries or deprive them of police and fire protection. Indeed it would permit the State to apportion all benefits and services according to the past tax contributions of its citizens. The Equal Protection Clause prohibits such an apportionment of state services.

We recognize that a State has a valid interest in preserving the fiscal integrity of its programs. It may legitimately attempt to limit its expenditures, whether for public assistance, public education, or any other program. But a State may not accomplish such a purpose by invidious distinctions between classes of its citizens. It could not, for example, reduce expenditures for education by barring indigent children from its schools. . . .

IV

Appellants next advance as justification certain administrative and related governmental objectives allegedly served by the waiting-period requirement. They argue that the requirement (1) facilitates the planning of the welfare budget; (2) provides an objective test of residency; (3) minimizes the opportunity for recipients fraudulently to receive payments from more than one jurisdiction; and (4) encourages early entry of new residents into the labor force.

At the outset, we reject appellants' argument that a mere showing of a rational relationship between the waiting period and these four admittedly permissible state objectives will suffice to justify the classification. See Lindsley v. Natural Carbonic Gas Co. (1911); McGowan v. Maryland (1961). . . . [I]n moving from State to State or to the District of Columbia appellees were exercising a constitutional right, and any classification which serves to penalize the exercise of that right, unless shown to be necessary to promote a *compelling* governmental interest, is unconstitutional. Cf. Skinner v. Oklahoma (1942); Korematsu v. United States (1944).

The argument that the waiting-period requirement facilitates budget predictability is wholly unfounded. The records in all three cases are utterly devoid of evidence that either State or the District of Columbia in fact uses the one-year requirement as a means to predict the number of people who will require assistance in the budget year. . . . [T]he claim . . . is plainly belied by the fact that the requirement is not also imposed on applicants who are long-term residents, the group that receives the bulk of welfare payments. . . .

The argument that the waiting period serves as an administratively efficient rule of thumb for determining residency similarly will not withstand scrutiny. The residence requirement and the one-year waiting-period requirement are distinct and independent prerequisites for assistance under these three statutes, and the facts relevant to the determination of each are directly examined by the welfare authorities. . . .

Similarly, there is no need for a State to use the one-year waiting period as a safeguard against fraudulent receipt of benefits; for less drastic means are available, and are employed, to minimize that hazard. Of course, a State has a valid interest in preventing fraud by any applicant, whether a newcomer or a long-time resident. It is not denied, however, that the investigations now conducted entail inquiries into facts relevant to that subject. . . .

Pennsylvania suggests that the one-year waiting period is justified as a means of encouraging new residents to join the labor force promptly. But this logic would also require a similar waiting period for long-term residents of the State. A state purpose to encourage employment provides no rational basis for imposing a one-year waiting-period restriction on new residents only.

We conclude therefore that appellants in these cases do not use and have no need to use the one-year requirement for the governmental purposes suggested. Thus, even under traditional equal protection tests a classification of welfare applicants according to whether they have lived in the State for one year would seem irrational and unconstitutional. But, of course, the traditional criteria do not apply in these cases. Since the classification here touches on the fundamental right of interstate movement, its constitutionality must be judged by the stricter standard of whether it promotes a *compelling* state interest. Under this standard, the waiting-period requirement clearly violates the Equal Protection Clause.[2]

V

Connecticut and Pennsylvania argue, however, that the constitutional challenge to the waiting-period requirements must fail because Congress expressly approved the imposition of the requirement by the States as part of the jointly funded AFDC program. . . .

On its face, the statute does not approve, much less prescribe, a one-year requirement. It merely directs the Secretary of Health, Education, and Welfare not to disapprove plans submitted by the States because they include such a requirement. . . .

But even if we were to assume, arguendo, that Congress did approve the imposition of a one-year waiting period, . . . [t]he provision . . . would be unconstitutional. Congress may not authorize the States to violate the Equal Protection Clause. . . .

Affirmed.

Mr. Justice **STEWART**, concurring.

In joining the opinion of the Court, I add a word in response to the dissent of my Brother Harlan. . . .

The Court today does *not* "pick out particular human activities, characterize them as 'fundamental,' and give them added protection. . . ." To the contrary, the Court simply recognizes, as it must, an established constitutional right, and gives to that right no less protection than the Constitution itself demands.

"The constitutional right to travel from one State to another . . . has been firmly established and repeatedly recognized." United States v. Guest [1966]. This constitutional right . . . is *not* a mere conditional liberty subject to regulation and control under conventional due process or equal protection standards. . . . *Guest.* . . . Like the right of association, NAACP v. Alabama [1958], it is a virtually unconditional personal right, guaranteed by the Constitution to us all.

It follows, as the Court says, that "the purpose of deterring the inmigration of indigents . . . is constitutionally impermissible." And it further follows . . . that any *other* purposes offered in support of a law that so clearly impinges upon the constitutional right of interstate travel must be shown to reflect a *compelling* governmental interest. . . . As Mr. Justice Harlan wrote for the Court more than a decade ago, "[T]o justify the deterrent effect . . . on the free exercise . . . of their constitutionally protected right . . . a '. . . subordinating interest of the State must be compelling.'" NAACP v. Alabama. . . .

---

2. We imply no view of the validity of waiting-period *or* residence requirements determining eligibility to vote, eligibility for tuition-free education, to obtain a license to practice a profession, to hunt or fish, and so forth. Such requirements may promote compelling state interests on the one hand, or, on the other, may not be penalties upon the exercise of the constitutional right of interstate travel. [Footnote by the Court.]

The Court today, therefore, is not "contriving new constitutional principles." It is deciding these cases under the aegis of established constitutional law.

Mr. Chief Justice **WARREN**, with whom Mr. Justice **BLACK** joins, dissenting. . . .

II

Congress has imposed a residence requirement in the District of Columbia and authorized the States to impose similar requirements. The issue before us must therefore be framed in terms of whether Congress may create minimal residence requirements, not whether the States, acting alone, may do so. . . . Appellees insist that . . . Congress, even under its "plenary" power to control interstate commerce, is constitutionally prohibited from imposing residence requirements. . . .

Congress, pursuant to its commerce power, has enacted a variety of restrictions upon interstate travel. . . . Although these restrictions operate as a limitation upon free interstate movement of persons, their constitutionality appears well settled. . . .

Most of our [right-to-travel] cases fall into two categories: those in which *state*-imposed restrictions were involved, see, e.g., *Edwards; Crandall*, and those concerning congressional decisions to remove impediments to interstate movement, see, e.g., *Guest*. Since the focus of our inquiry must be whether Congress would exceed permissible bounds by imposing residence requirements, neither group of cases offers controlling principles.

In only three cases have we been confronted with an assertion that Congress has impermissibly burdened the right to travel. *Kent* did invalidate a burden on the right to travel; however, the restriction was voided on the nonconstitutional basis that Congress did not intend to give the Secretary of State power to create the restriction at issue. *Zemel*, on the other hand, sustained a flat prohibition of travel to certain designated areas and rejected an attack that Congress could not constitutionally impose this restriction. *Aptheker* is the only case in which this Court invalidated on a constitutional basis a congressionally imposed restriction. *Aptheker* also involved a flat prohibition but in combination with a claim that the congressional restriction compelled a potential traveler to choose between his right to travel and his First Amendment right of freedom of association. . . . *Aptheker* thus contains two characteristics distinguishing it from the appeals now before the Court: a combined infringement of two constitutionally protected rights and a flat prohibition upon travel. Residence requirements do not create a flat prohibition, for potential welfare recipients may move from State to State and establish residence wherever they please. Nor is any claim made by appellees that residence requirements compel them to choose between the right to travel and another constitutional right.

Zemel, the most recent of the three cases, provides a framework for analysis. The core inquiry is "the extent of the governmental restriction imposed" and the "extent of the necessity for the restriction". . . . As already noted, travel itself is not prohibited. Any burden inheres solely in the fact that a potential welfare recipient might take into consideration the loss of welfare benefits for a limited period of time if he changes his residence. Not only is this burden of uncertain degree, but appellees themselves assert there is evidence that few welfare recipients have in fact been deterred by residence requirements. . . .

The insubstantiality of the restriction imposed by residence requirements must then be evaluated in light of the possible congressional reasons for such requirements. See, e.g., *McGowan.* Our cases require only that Congress have a rational basis for finding that a chosen regulatory scheme is necessary to the furtherance of interstate commerce. See, e.g., Katzenbach v. McClung (1964); Wickard v. Filburn (1942). Certainly, a congressional finding that residence requirements allowed each State to concentrate its resources upon new and increased programs of rehabilitation ultimately resulting in an enhanced flow of commerce as the economic condition of welfare recipients progressively improved is rational and would justify imposition of residence requirements under the Commerce Clause. . . .

. . . Since the congressional decision is rational and the restriction on travel insubstantial, I conclude that residence requirements can be imposed by Congress as an exercise of its power to control interstate commerce consistent with the constitutionally guaranteed right to travel. . . .

The Court's decision reveals only the top of the iceberg. Lurking beneath are the multitude of situations in which States have imposed residence requirements including eligibility to vote, to engage in certain professions or occupations or to attend a state-supported university. Although the Court takes pains to avoid acknowledging the ramifications of its decision, its implications cannot be ignored. I dissent.

Mr. Justice **HARLAN,** dissenting. . . .

II

. . . [T]he Court has applied an equal protection doctrine of relatively recent vintage: the rule that statutory classifications which either are based upon certain "suspect" criteria or affect "fundamental rights" will be held to deny equal protection unless justified by a "compelling" governmental interest. . . .

The "compelling interest" doctrine, which today is articulated more explicitly than ever before, constitutes an increasingly significant exception to the long-established rule that a statute does not deny equal protection if it is rationally related to a legitimate governmental objective. The "compelling interest" doctrine has two branches. The branch which requires that classifications based upon "suspect" criteria be supported by a compelling interest apparently had its genesis in case[s] involving racial classifications, which have, at least since *Korematsu*, been regarded as inherently "suspect." The criterion of "wealth" apparently was added to the list of "suspects" as an alternative justification for the rationale in Harper v. Virginia Bd. of Elections (1966). . . . The criterion of political allegiance may have been added in Williams v. Rhodes (1968). Today the list apparently has been further enlarged to include classifications based upon recent interstate movement, and perhaps those based upon the exercise of *any* constitutional right. . . .

I think that this branch of the "compelling interest" doctrine is sound when applied to racial classifications, for historically the Equal Protection Clause was largely a product of the desire to eradicate legal distinctions founded upon race. However, I believe that the more recent extensions have been unwise. For the reasons stated in my dissenting opinion in *Harper*, I do not consider wealth a "suspect" statutory criterion. And when, as in *Williams* and the present case, a classification is based upon the exercise of rights guaranteed against state infringement by the Federal Constitution, then there is no need for any resort to the Equal Protection Clause; in such instances, this Court may properly and straightforwardly invalidate any undue burden upon those rights under the Fourteenth Amendment's Due Process Clause.

The second branch of the "compelling interest" principle is even more troublesome. For it has been held that a statutory classification is subject to the "compelling interest" test if the result of the classification may be to affect a "fundamental right," regardless of the basis of the classification. This rule was foreshadowed in *Skinner,* in which an Oklahoma statute providing for compulsory sterilization of "habitual criminals" was held subject to "strict scrutiny" mainly because it affected "one of the basic civil rights." After a long hiatus, the principle re-emerged in Reynolds v. Sims (1964), in which state apportionment statutes were subjected to an unusually stringent test because "any alleged infringement of the right of citizens to vote must be carefully and meticulously scrutinized." . . . This branch of the doctrine was also an alternate ground in *Harper* and apparently was a basis of the holding in *Williams.* It has reappeared today in the Court's cryptic suggestion that the "compelling interest" test is applicable merely because the result of the classification may be to deny the appellees "food, shelter, and other necessities of life," as well as in the Court's statement that "[s]ince the classification here touches on the fundamental right of interstate movement, its constitutionality must be judged by the stricter standard of whether it promotes a *compelling* state interest."

I think this branch of the "compelling interest" doctrine particularly unfortunate and unnecessary. It is unfortunate because it creates an exception which threatens to swallow the standard equal protection rule. Virtually every state statute affects important rights. This

Court has repeatedly held, for example, that the traditional equal protection standard is applicable to statutory classifications affecting such fundamental matters as the right to pursue a particular occupation, the right to receive greater or smaller wages or to work more or less hours, and the right to inherit property. Rights such as these are in principle indistinguishable from those involved here, and to extend the "compelling interest" rule to all cases in which such rights are affected would go far toward making this Court a "super-legislature." This branch of the doctrine is also unnecessary. When the right affected is one assured by the Federal Constitution, any infringement can be dealt with under the Due Process Clause. But when a statute affects only matters not mentioned in the Federal Constitution and is not arbitrary or irrational, I must reiterate that I know of nothing which entitles this Court to pick out particular human activities, characterize them as "fundamental," and give them added protection under an unusually stringent equal protection test. . . .

. . . If the issue is regarded purely as one of equal protection, then, for the reasons just set forth, this nonracial classification should be judged by ordinary equal protection standards. . . . In light of [the] undeniable relation of residence requirements to valid legislative aims, it cannot be said that the requirements are "arbitrary" or "lacking in rational justification." . . .

III

The next issue, which I think requires fuller analysis than that deemed necessary by the Court under its equal protection rationale, is whether a one-year welfare residence requirement amounts to an undue burden upon the right of interstate travel [and thus a denial of due process].

[The decisive question is] whether the governmental interests served by residence requirements outweigh the burden imposed upon the right to travel. In my view, a number of considerations militate in favor of constitutionality. First, . . . four separate, legitimate governmental interests are furthered by residence requirements. Second, the impact of the requirements upon the freedom of individuals to travel interstate is indirect and, according to evidence put forward by the appellees themselves, insubstantial. Third, these are not cases in which a State or States, acting alone, have attempted to interfere with the right of citizens to travel, but one in which the States have acted within the terms of a limited authorization by the National Government, and in which Congress itself has laid down a like rule for the District of Columbia. Fourth, the legislatures which enacted these statutes have been fully exposed to the arguments of the appellees as to why these residence requirements are unwise, and have rejected them. This is not, therefore, an instance in which legislatures have acted without mature deliberation.

Fifth, and of longer-range importance, the field of welfare assistance is one in which there is a widely recognized need for fresh solutions and consequently for experimentation. Invalidation of welfare residence requirements might have the unfortunate consequence of discouraging the Federal and State Governments from establishing unusually generous welfare programs in particular areas on an experimental basis, because of fears that the program would cause an influx of persons seeking higher welfare payments. Sixth and finally, a strong presumption of constitutionality attaches to statutes of the types now before us. Congressional enactments come to this Court with an extremely heavy presumption of validity. A similar presumption of constitutionality attaches to state statutes, particularly when, as here, a State has acted upon a specific authorization from Congress. . . .

Taking all of these competing considerations into account, I believe that the balance definitely favors constitutionality. . . .

. . . Today's decision, it seems to me, reflects to an unusual degree the current notion that this Court possesses a peculiar wisdom all its own whose capacity to lead this Nation out of its present troubles is contained only by the limits of judicial ingenuity in contriving new constitutional principles to meet each problem as it arises. For anyone who, like myself, believes that it is an essential function of this Court to maintain the constitutional divisions between state and federal authority and among the three branches of the Federal Government, today's decision is a step in the wrong direction. This resurgence of the expansive view of "equal protection" carries the seeds of more judicial interference with the state and federal legislative process, much more indeed than does the judicial application of "due process" according to traditional concepts (see my dissenting opinion in Duncan v. Louisiana (1968)), about which some members of this Court have expressed fears as to its potentialities for setting us judges "at large." I consider it particularly unfortunate that this judicial roadblock to the powers of Congress in this field should occur at the very threshold of the current discussions regarding the "federalizing" of these aspects of welfare relief.

Editors' Notes

(1) **Query:** Compare Harlan's dissenting remarks here, "The criterion of wealth was apparently added to the list of 'suspects' as an alternative justification for the rationale in Harper v. Virginia Board of Elections" [1966; reprinted above, p. 151], with the Court's claim in San Antonio that it had never held wealth to be a suspect classification. And contrast's Brennan's remark about "food, shelter, and other necessities of life." Was he intimating the existence of a fundamental constitutional right to the means of subsistence?

(2) The Court's handling of residency requirements has produced a jumbled mass of individual decisions: Starns v. Malkerson (1971) summarily upheld Minnesota's requirement that college students reside in the state for one year before being eligible for reduced tuition available to state residents. Vlandis v. Kline (1973) struck down Connecticut's classifying as ineligible for reduced tuition at state colleges anyone who had a "legal address" out of

state during the previous year. The majority opinion stressed that it was not the residency requirement that was invalid, but the statute's "irrebuttable presumption" that anyone who had had a legal address out of state was a non-resident. (See the Annotation by Ernest H. Schopler, "Validity under Federal Constitution of State Residency Requirements Relevant to Charging Tuition and Other Fees by Colleges and Universities," 37 L.Ed.2d 1056 [1974].)

Dunn v. Blumstein (1972) invalidated a year's residency requirement for voting in state elections, as a violation of equal protection—the classification penalized the fundamental right to travel. Marston v. Lewis (1973) and Burns v. Fortson (1973) upheld fifty-day requirements.

Memorial Hospital v. Maricopa County (1974) struck down, 8–1, Arizona's limiting non-emergency, free medical care to people who had resided in a county for more than a year. Marshall's opinion for the Court tried to make some sense of the residency cases. He conceded that even "a bona fide residence requirement would burden the right to travel," but claimed that Shapiro "was concerned only with the right to migrate 'with intent to settle and abide' or, as the Court put it, 'to migrate, resettle, find a new job, and start a new life.' " What Shapiro outlawed, Marshall said, were only efforts to use waiting periods as penalties for exercising the right to travel.

Sosna v. Iowa (1975) sustained a state residency requirement of one-year to obtain a divorce. Rehnquist wrote the opinion of the Court and distinguished cases like Shapiro as pitting administrative and budgetary interests against constitutional rights. Divorce was a matter of a different order; its effects could concern only the state and one litigant. Both spouses are involved, and a final decree often involves provisions for support and custody of children. Martinez v. Bynum (1983) sustained a Texas statute that denied children living apart from their parents free attendance at public schools if they were in the school district "for the primary purpose of attending the free public schools." For the majority, Powell wrote that a

> bona fide residence requirement, appropriately defined and uniformly applied, furthers the substantial [note he did not say "compelling"] state interest in assuring that services provided for its residents are enjoyed only by its residents. Such a requirement with respect to attendance in free public schools does not violate the Equal Protection Clause. It does not burden or penalize the constitutional right of interstate travel, for any person is free to move to a State and to establish residence there. A bona fide residence requirement simply requires that the person *does* establish residence before demanding the services that are restricted to residents.

To what extent did the regulations invalidated in Shapiro simply require that indigents establish residence before claiming welfare benefits? Perhaps a variation on Marshall's "explanation" of Shapiro in Memorial Hospital expresses what the Court has been trying to get at: States may not apply residency requirements to poor and sick people who are not likely to be able to establish residency without some form of public assistance; for less urgent services, such as free public education, and for political participation, it may set up "reasonable" residency requirements to distinguish between transients and members of the community. In any event, Marshall was displeased with the decision in Martinez: "The majority's approach reflects a misinterpretation of the Texas statute, a misunderstanding of the concept of residence, and a misapplication of this Court's past decisions concerning the constitutionality of residence requirements."

(3) Problems of the right to travel, residency requirements, and state benefits reserved to state citizens raise the question of the meaning of national citizenship under the opening clause of the Fourteenth Amendment ("All persons born or naturalized in the United States . . . are citizens of the United States and of the State wherein they reside") and Article IV, § 2 ("The citizens of each State shall be entitled to all privileges and immunities of citizens in the several States"). For discussions, see: C. Herman Pritchett, *Constitutional Law of the Federal System* (Englewood Cliffs, N.J.: Prentice-Hall, 1984), pp. 83–86; and Laurence H. Tribe, *American Constitutional Law* (Mineola, N.Y.: Foundation Press, 1978), §§ 6–32 to 6–33.

(4) *Shapiro* concerned only the right to travel within the United States. For more recent decisions on foreign travel, see Haig v. Agee (1981; reprinted above, p. 533), upholding revocation of a citizen's passport for reasons of national security, and Regan v. Wald (1984) sustaining the Treasury Department's authority under the Trading with the Enemy Act to ban travel to Cuba.

"In the area of economics and social welfare, a State does not violate the Equal Protection Clause merely because the classifications made by its laws are imperfect."

DANDRIDGE v. WILLIAMS
397 U.S. 471, 90 S.Ct. 1153, 25 L.Ed.2d 491 (1970).

Under the joint federal-state program of Aid to Families with Dependent Children (AFDC), Maryland provided a sliding scale of payments to poor families. The exact amount depended on the number of children in the family and an administrative determination of the help the family needed to achieve a minimum standard of living. In no case, however, could the welfare payment exceed $250 a month. Ms. Linda Williams and others sued in a federal district court, attacking the regulations setting a maximum to the grant as violating the basic federal statute and denying members of large families equal protection. The district court agreed on both issues and Maryland appealed to the Supreme Court.

Mr. Justice **STEWART** delivered the opinion of the Court. . . .

I

[Stewart concluded that Maryland's policy did not conflict with federal statutory provisions.]

II

Although a State may adopt a maximum grant system in allocating its funds available for AFDC payments without violating the [federal] Act, it may not, of course, impose a regime of invidious discrimination in violation of the Equal Protection Clause. . . . The regulations can be clearly justified, Maryland argues, in terms of legitimate state interests in encouraging gainful employment, in maintaining an equitable balance in economic status between welfare families and those supported by a wage-earner, in providing incentives for family planning, and in allocating available public funds in such a way as fully to meet the needs of the largest possible number of families. . . . The District Court, while apparently recognizing the validity of at least some of these state concerns, nonetheless held that the regulation "is invalid on its face for overreaching"—that it violates the Equal Protection Clause "[b]ecause it cuts too broad a swath on an indiscriminate basis as applied to the entire group of AFDC eligibles to which it purports to apply. . . ."

If this were a case involving government action claimed to violate the First Amendment guarantee of free speech, a finding of "overreaching" would be significant and might be crucial. For when otherwise valid governmental regulation sweeps so broadly as to impinge upon activity protected by the First Amendment, its very overbreadth may make it unconstitutional. See, e.g., Shelton v. Tucker [1960]. But . . . here we deal with state regulation in the social and economic field, not affecting freedoms guaranteed by the Bill of Rights, and claimed to violate the Fourteenth Amendment only because the regulation results in some disparity in grants of welfare payments to the largest AFDC families.[1] For this Court to approve the invalidation of state economic or social regulation as "overreaching" would be far too reminiscent of an era when the Court thought the Fourteenth Amendment gave it power to strike down state laws "because they may be unwise, improvident, or out of harmony with a particular school of thought." Williamson v. Lee Optical Co. [1955]. That era long ago passed into history. Ferguson v. Skrupa [1963].

In the area of economics and social welfare, a State does not violate the Equal Protection Clause merely because the classifications made by its laws are imperfect. If the classification has some "reasonable basis," it does not offend the Constitution simply because the classification "is not made with mathematical nicety or because in practice it results in some inequality." Lindsley v. Natural Carbonic Gas Co. [1911]. . . . "A statutory discrimination will not be set aside if any state of facts reasonably may be conceived to justify it." McGowan v. Maryland [1961].

To be sure, the cases . . . enunciating this fundamental standard . . . have in the main involved state regulation of business or industry. The administration of public welfare assistance, by contrast, involves the most basic economic needs of impoverished human beings. We recognize the dramatically real factual difference between the cited cases and this one, but we can find no basis for applying a different constitutional standard. . . .

---

1. Cf. Shapiro v. Thompson [1969], where, by contrast, the Court found state interference with the constitutionally protected freedom of interstate travel. [Footnote by the Court.]

Under this long-established meaning of the Equal Protection Clause, it is clear that the Maryland maximum grant regulation is constitutionally valid. We need not explore all the reasons that the State advances in justification of the regulation. It is enough that a solid foundation for the regulation can be found in the State's legitimate interest in encouraging employment and in avoiding discrimination between welfare families and the families of the working poor. By combining a limit on the recipient's grant with permission to retain money earned, without reduction in the amount of the grant, Maryland provides an incentive to seek gainful employment. And by keying the maximum family AFDC grants to the minimum wage a steadily employed head of a household receives, the State maintains some semblance of an equitable balance between families on welfare and those supported by an employed breadwinner.

It is true that in some AFDC families there may be no person who is employable. It is also true that with respect to AFDC families whose determined standard of need is below the regulatory maximum, and who therefore receive grants equal to the determined standard, the employment incentive is absent. But the Equal Protection Clause does not require that a State must choose between attacking every aspect of a problem or not attacking the problem at all. It is enough that the State's action be rationally based and free from invidious discrimination. The regulation before us meets that test.

We do not decide today that the Maryland regulation is wise, that it best fulfills the relevant social and economic objectives that Maryland might ideally espouse, or that a more just and humane system could not be devised. . . . [T]he intractable economic, social, and even philosophical problems presented by public welfare assistance programs are not the business of this Court. The Constitution may impose certain procedural safeguards upon systems of welfare administration, Goldberg v. Kelly [1970]. But [it] does not empower this Court to second-guess state officials charged with the difficult responsibility of allocating limited public welfare funds among the myriad of potential recipients. . . .

[Reversed.]

Mr. Justice **BLACK,** with whom the Chief Justice [**BURGER**] joins, concurring. . . .

Mr. Justice **HARLAN,** concurring. . . .

As I stated in dissent in *Shapiro,* I find no solid basis for the doctrine . . . that certain statutory classifications will be held to deny equal protection unless justified by a "compelling" governmental interest, while others will pass muster if they meet traditional equal protection standards. . . .

It is on this basis, and not because this case involves only interests in "the area of economics and social welfare," that I join the Court's constitutional holding.

Mr. Justice **DOUGLAS,** dissenting. .   .   .

On the basis of the inconsistency of the Maryland maximum grant regulation with the [federal statute], I would affirm the judgment below.

Mr. Justice **MARSHALL,** whom Mr. Justice **BRENNAN** joins, dissenting.

For the reason stated by Mr. Justice Douglas .   .   . I believe that the Court has erroneously concluded that Maryland's maximum grant regulation is consistent with the federal statute. .   .   .

More important in the long run .   .   . is the Court's emasculation of the Equal Protection Clause as a constitutional principle applicable to the area of social welfare administration. .   .   .

The Court recognizes .   .   . that this case involves "the most basic economic needs of impoverished human beings," and that there is therefore a "dramatically real factual difference" between the instant case and those decisions upon which the Court relies. [This] acknowledgment .   .   . is a candid recognition that the Court's decision today is wholly without precedent. .   .   .

The Maryland AFDC program in its basic structure operates uniformly with regard to all needy children by taking into account the basic subsistence needs of all eligible individuals in the formulation of the standards of need for families of various sizes. However, superimposed upon this uniform system is the maximum grant regulation, the operative effect of which is to create two classes of needy children and two classes of eligible families: those small families and their members who receive payments to cover their subsistence needs and those large families who do not. .   .   .

.   .   . [A]s a general principle, individuals should not be afforded different treatment by the State unless there is a relevant distinction between them. .   .   . Consequently, the State may not, in the provision of important services or the distribution of governmental payments, supply benefits to some individuals while denying them to others who are similarly situated. See, e.g., Griffin v. County School Board of Prince Edward County (1964).

In the instant case, the only distinction between those children with respect to whom assistance is granted and those children who are denied such assistance is the size of the family into which the child permits himself to be born. The class of individuals with respect to whom payments are actually made (the first four or five eligible dependent children in a family), is grossly underinclusive in terms of the class that the AFDC program was designed to assist, namely, *all* needy dependent children. Such underinclusiveness .   .   . [compels] the State to come forward with a persuasive justification for the classification.

The Court never undertakes to inquire for such a justification; rather it avoids the task by focusing upon the abstract dichotomy

between two different approaches to equal protection problems that
have been utilized by this Court.

Under the so-called "traditional test," a classification is said to be
permissible . . . unless it is "without any reasonable basis." On the
other hand, if the classification affects a "fundamental right," then the
state interest in perpetuating the classification must be "compelling" in
order to be sustained.

This case simply defies easy characterization in terms of one or the
other of these "tests." The cases relied on by the Court, in which a
"mere rationality" test was actually used are most accurately described
as involving the application of equal protection reasoning to the regulation of business interests. The extremes to which the Court has gone in
dreaming up rational bases for state regulation in that area may in
many instances be ascribed to a healthy revulsion from the Court's
earlier excesses in using the Constitution to protect interests that have
more than enough power to protect themselves in the legislative halls.
This case, involving the literally vital interests of a powerless minority—poor families without breadwinners—is far removed from the area
of business regulation, as the Court concedes. Why then is the standard used in those cases imposed here? We are told no more than that
this case falls in "the area of economics and social welfare." . . .

In my view, equal protection analysis of this case is not appreciably
advanced by the a priori definition of a "right," fundamental or
otherwise. Rather, concentration must be placed upon the character of
the classification in question, the relative importance to individuals in
the class discriminated against of the governmental benefits that they
do not receive, and the asserted state interests in support of the
classification. As we said only recently, "In determining whether or
not a state law violates the Equal Protection Clause, we must consider
the facts and circumstances behind the law, the interests which the
State claims to be protecting, and the interests of those who are
disadvantaged by the classification." Kramer v. Union School District
(1969), quoting Williams v. Rhodes (1968).[1]

It is the individual interests here at stake that, as the Court
concedes, most clearly distinguished this case from the "business regulation" equal protection cases. AFDC support to needy dependent
children provides the stuff that sustains those children's lives: food,
clothing, shelter. And this Court has already recognized several times
that when a benefit, even a "gratuitous" benefit, is necessary to sustain
life, stricter constitutional standards, both procedural and substantive,[2]
are applied to the deprivation of that benefit.

---

1. This is esentially what this Court has done in applying equal protection concepts in
numerous cases, though the various aspects of the approach appear with a greater or
lesser degree of clarity in particular cases. See, e.g., McLaughlin v. Florida [1964];
Carrington v. Rash (1965); Douglas v. California (1963); Skinner v. Oklahoma [1942].
. . . . [Footnote by Justice Marshall.]

2. Compare Shapiro v. Thompson [1969] striking down one-year residency requirement
for welfare eligibility as violation of equal protection, and noting that the benefits in
question are "the very means to subsist—food, shelter, and other necessities of life," with
Kirk v. Board of Regents [Cal. Supreme Ct, 1969], appeal dismissed [by U.S. Supreme Ct,

Nor is the distinction upon which the deprivation is here based—the distinction between large and small families—one that readily commends itself as a basis for determining which children are to have support approximating subsistence and which are not. Indeed, governmental discrimination between children on the basis of a factor over which they have no control—the number of their brothers and sisters—bears some resemblance to the classification between legitimate and illegitimate children which we condemmed as a violation of the Equal Protection Clause in Levy v. Louisiana (1968).

The asserted state interests in the maintenance of the maximum grant regulation, on the other hand, are hardly clear. In the early stages of this litigation, the State attempted to rationalize [the regulation] on the theory that it was merely a device to conserve state funds.

. . .

. . . [T]he State apparently [has] abandoned reliance on the fiscal justification. In its place, there have now appeared several different rationales. . . . Maryland has urged that the maximum grant regulation serves to maintain a rough equality between [minimum] wage earning families and AFDC families, thereby increasing the political support for—or perhaps reducing the opposition to—the AFDC program. It is questionable whether the Court really relies on this ground. . . . The only question presented here is whether, having once undertaken such a program, the State may arbitrarily select from among the concededly eligible those to whom it will provide benefits. And it is too late to argue that political expediency will sustain discrimination not otherwise supportable. Cf. Cooper v. Aaron (1958).

Vital to the employment-incentive basis found by the Court to sustain the regulation is, of course, the supposition that an appreciable number of AFDC recipients are in fact employable. . . . The District Court found that of Maryland's more than 32,000 AFDC families, only about 116 could be classified as having employable members.

. . .

[Moreover,] to the extent there is a legitimate state interest in encouraging heads of AFDC households to find employment, application of the maximum grant regulation is also grossly *underinclusive* because it singles out and affects only large families. . . . There is simply no indication whatever that heads of large families, as opposed to heads of small families, are particularly prone to refuse to seek or to maintain employment. . . .

"for want of a substantial federal question"] (1970), [in which the state supreme court upheld a] one-year residency requirement for tuition-free graduate education at state university, and distinguish[ed] *Shapiro* on the ground that it "involved the immediate and pressing need for preservation of life and health of persons unable to live without public assistance, and their dependent children."

These cases . . . suggest that whether or not there is a constitutional "right" to subsistence . . . deprivations of benefits necessary for subsistence will receive closer constitutional scrutiny, under both the Due Process and Equal Protection Clauses, than will deprivations of less essential forms of government entitlements. [Footnote by Justice Marshall. See Eds.' Note 2 to *Shapiro,* above, at p. 873.]

. . . Were this a case of pure business regulation, . . . I do not believe that the regulation [could] be sustained even under the Court's "reasonableness" test.

. . . [I]t cannot suffice merely to invoke the spectre of the past and to recite from *Lindsley* and *Williamson* to decide the case. Appellees are not a gas company or an optical dispenser; they are needy dependent children and families who are discriminated against by the State. The basis of that discrimination—the classification of individuals into large and small families—is too arbitrary and too unconnected to the asserted rationale, the impact on those discriminated against— the denial of even a subsistence existence—too great, and the supposed interests served too contrived and attenuated to meet the requirements of the Constitution. . . .

Editors' Note

(1) Compare the spectrum or continuum for classifications and rights that Marshall's dissent here suggests with the fuller statement of that position he articulates in his dissent in *San Antonio* (1973; reprinted above, p. 858).

(2) **Query:** Does Stewart's opinion for the Court try to identify a "fundamental right" or a "suspect classification" that might trigger strict scrutiny? What fundamental right might be involved?

(3) Lindsey v. Normet (1972) refused to find constitutional protection for a right to decent housing. For the Court, Justice White, echoing Harlan's dissent in *Shapiro,* wrote: "[T]he Constitution does not provide judicial remedies for every social and economic ill. . . . Absent constitutional mandate, the assurance of adequate housing and the definition of landlord-tenant relationships are legislative, not judicial, functions. . . ."

(4) In *Dandridge* Stewart referred to procedural safeguards surrounding governmental welfare programs. The leading case is probably still Goldberg v. Kelly (1970), which ruled that before a state could terminate welfare payments it had to accord the person affected a hearing. For a discussion of later cases, see Laurence H. Tribe, *American Constitutional Law* (Mineola, N.Y.: Foundation Press, 1978), chap. 10.

"When a statutory classification significantly interferes with the exercise of a fundamental right, it cannot be upheld unless it is supported by sufficiently important state interests and is closely tailored to effectuate only those interests."

ZABLOCKI v. REDHAIL
434 U.S. 374, 98 S.Ct. 673, 54 L.Ed.2d 618 (1978).

Wisconsin Statutes, §§ 245.10(1), (4), (5) (1973), provided that no one "having minor issue not in his custody and which he is under obligation to support by any court order or judgment" could remarry without obtaining the permission of a court, which could not grant permission unless the petitioner showed that he had met his obligations to support the offspring covered by the order and that such children were not likely to become "public charges." Invoking these provisions, Thomas Zablocki, a county clerk, denied Roger Redhail a marriage license. Redhail, who was unable to meet the statutory conditions, then filed suit in a U.S. district court. That court held that the law denied equal protection, and Wisconsin appealed to the U.S. Supreme Court.

Mr. Justice **MARSHALL** delivered the opinion of the Court. . . .

II

In evaluating §§ 245.10(1), (4), (5) under the Equal Protection Clause, "we must first determine what burden of justification the classification created thereby must meet, by looking to the nature of the classification and the individual interests affected." Memorial Hospital v. Maricopa County (1974). Since our past decisions make clear that the right to marry is of fundamental importance, and since the classification at issue here significantly interferes with the exercise of that right, we believe that "critical examination" of the state interests advanced in support of the classification is required. Massachusetts Board of Retirement v. Murgia (1976).

The leading decision of this Court on the right to marry is Loving v. Virginia (1967). In that case, an interracial couple who had been convicted of violating Virginia's miscegenation laws challenged the statutory scheme on both equal protection and due process grounds. The Court's opinion could have rested solely on the ground that the statutes discriminated on the basis of race in violation of the Equal Protection Clause. But the Court went on to hold that the laws arbitrarily deprived the couple of a fundamental liberty protected by the Due Process Clause, the freedom to marry. The Court's language on the latter point bears repeating:

> The freedom to marry has long been recognized as one of the vital personal rights essential to the orderly pursuit of happiness by free men.
>
> Marriage is one of the "basic civil rights of man," fundamental to our very existence and survival. Quoting Skinner v. Oklahoma (1942).

Although *Loving* arose in the context of racial discrimination, prior and subsequent decisions of this Court confirm that the right to marry is of fundamental importance for all individuals. Long ago, in Maynard v. Hill (1888), the Court characterized marriage as "the most important relation in life," and as "the foundation of the family and of society, without which there would be neither civilization nor progress." In Meyer v. Nebraska (1923), the Court recognized that the right "to marry, establish a home and bring up children" is a central part of the liberty protected by the Due Process Clause, and in *Skinner*, marriage was described as "fundamental to the very existence and survival of the race."

More recent decisions have established that the right to marry is part of the fundamental "right of privacy" implicit in the Fourteenth

Amendment's Due Process Clause. . . . [Quoting from Griswold v. Connecticut (1965).]

Cases subsequent to *Griswold* and *Loving* have routinely categorized the decision to marry as among the personal decisions protected by the right of privacy. See generally Whalen v. Roe (1977). For example . . . in Carey v. Population Services International (1977), we declared:

> While the outer limits of [the right of personal privacy] have not been marked by the Court, it is clear that among the decisions that an individual may make without unjustified government interference are personal decisions relating to marriage, *Loving*; procreation, *Skinner*; contraception, Eisenstadt v. Baird [1972] (White, J., concurring in result); family relationships, Prince v. Massachusetts (1944); and child rearing and education, Pierce v. Society of Sisters (1925); *Meyer*. . . .

It is not surprising that the decision to marry has been placed on the same level of importance as decisions relating to procreation, childbirth, child rearing, and family relationships. As the facts of this case illustrate, it would make little sense to recognize a right of privacy with respect to other matters of family life and not with respect to the decision to enter the relationship that is the foundation of the family in our society. The woman whom appellee desired to marry had a fundamental right to seek an abortion of their expected child, see Roe v. Wade (1973), or to bring the child into life to suffer the myriad social, if not economic, disabilities that the status of illegitimacy brings. Surely, a decision to marry and raise the child in a traditional family setting must receive equivalent protection. And, if appellee's right to procreate means anything at all, it must imply some right to enter the only relationship in which the State of Wisconsin allows sexual relations legally to take place.

By reaffirming the fundamental character of the right to marry, we do not mean to suggest that every state regulation which relates in any way to the incidents of or prerequisites for marriage must be subjected to rigorous scrutiny. To the contrary, reasonable regulations that do not significantly interfere with decisions to enter into the marital relationship may legitimately be imposed. The statutory classification at issue here, however, clearly does interfere directly and substantially with the right to marry.

Under the challenged statute, no Wisconsin resident in the affected class may marry in Wisconsin or elsewhere without a court order, and marriages contracted in violation of the statute are both void and punishable as criminal offenses. Some of those in the affected class, like appellee, will never be able to obtain the necessary court order, because they either lack the financial means to meet their support obligations or cannot prove that their children will not become public charges. These persons are absolutely prevented from getting married. Many others, able in theory to satisfy the statute's requirements, will be sufficiently burdened by having to do so that they will in effect be coerced into forgoing their right to marry. And even those who can be persuaded to meet the statute's requirements suffer a serious intrusion into their freedom of choice in an area in which we have held such freedom to be fundamental.

III

When a statutory classification significantly interferes with the exercise of a fundamental right, it cannot be upheld unless it is supported by sufficiently important state interests and is closely tailored to effectuate only those interests. See, e.g., *Carey; Memorial Hospital;* San Antonio v. Rodriguez (1973); Bullock v. Carter (1972). Appellant asserts that two interests are served by the challenged statute: the permission-to-marry proceeding furnishes an opportunity to counsel the applicant as to the necessity of fulfilling his prior support obligations; and the welfare of the out-of-custody children is protected. We may accept for present purposes that these are legitimate and substantial interests, but, since the means selected by the State for achieving these interests unnecessarily impinge on the right to marry, the statute cannot be sustained.

. . . The statute actually enacted, however, does not expressly require or provide for any counseling whatsoever, nor for any automatic granting of permission to marry by the court, and thus it can hardly be justified as a means for ensuring counseling of the persons within its coverage. Even assuming that counseling does take place—a fact as to which there is no evidence in the record—this interest obviously cannot support the withholding of court permission to marry once counseling is completed.

With regard to safeguarding the welfare of the out-of-custody children, appellant's brief does not make clear the connection between the State's interest and the statute's requirements. At argument, appellant's counsel suggested that, since permission to marry cannot be granted unless the applicant shows that he has satisfied his court-determined support obligations to the prior children and that those children will not become public charges, the statute provides incentive for the applicant to make support payments to his children. This "collection device" rationale cannot justify the statute's broad infringement on the right to marry.

First, with respect to individuals who are unable to meet the statutory requirements, the statute merely prevents the applicant from getting married, without delivering any money at all into the hands of the applicant's prior children. More importantly, regardless of the applicant's ability or willingness to meet the statutory requirements, the State already has numerous other means for exacting compliance with support obligations, means that are at least as effective as the instant statute's and yet do not impinge upon the right to marry.

. . . .

There is also some suggestion that § 245.10 protects the ability of marriage applicants to meet support obligations to prior children by preventing the applicants from incurring new support obligations. But the challenged provisions of § 245.10 are grossly underinclusive with respect to this purpose, since they do not limit in any way new financial commitments by the applicant other than those arising out of the contemplated marriage. The statutory classification is substantially overinclusive as well: Given the possibility that the new spouse will actually better the applicant's financial situation, by contributing income from a job or otherwise, the statute in many cases may prevent affected individuals from improving their ability to satisfy their prior support obligations. And, although it is true that the applicant will incur support obligations to any children born during the contemplated marriage, preventing the marriage may only result in the children being born out of wedlock, as in fact occurred in appellee's case. Since the support obligation is the same whether the child is born in or out of wedlock, the net result of preventing the marriage is simply more illegitimate children. . . .

Affirmed.

Mr. Chief Justice **BURGER**, concurring. . . .

Mr. Justice **STEWART**, concurring in the judgment.

. . . The Equal Protection Clause deals not with substantive rights or freedoms but with invidiously discriminatory classifications. *San Antonio* (concurring opinion). The paradigm of its violation is, of course, classification by race.

Like almost any law, the Wisconsin statute now before us affects some people and does not affect others. But to say that it thereby creates "classifications" in the equal protection sense strikes me as little short of fantasy. The problem in this case is not one of discriminatory classifications, but of unwarranted encroachment upon a constitutionally protected freedom. I think that the Wisconsin statute is unconstitutional because it exceeds the bounds of permissible state regulation of marriage, and invades the sphere of liberty protected by the Due Process Clause of the Fourteenth Amendment. . . .

In an opinion of the Court half a century ago, Mr. Justice Holmes described an equal protection claim as "the usual last resort of constitutional arguments." Buck v. Bell [1927]. Today equal protection doctrine has become the Court's chief instrument for invalidating state laws. Yet, in a case like this one, the doctrine is no more than substantive due process by another name.

Although the Court purports to examine the bases for legislative classifications and to compare the treatment of legislatively defined groups, it actually erects substantive limitations on what States may do. Thus, the effect of the Court's decision in this case is not to require Wisconsin to draw its legislative classifications with greater precision or to afford similar treatment to similarly situated persons. Rather, the message of the Court's opinion is that Wisconsin may not use its control over marriage to achieve the objectives of the state statute.

Such restrictions on basic governmental power are at the heart of substantive due process.

The Court is understandably reluctant to rely on substantive due process. But to embrace the essence of that doctrine under the guise of equal protection serves no purpose but obfuscation. . . .

To conceal this appropriate inquiry invites mechanical or thoughtless application of misfocused doctrine. To bring it into the open forces a healthy and responsible recognition of the nature and purpose of the extreme power we wield when, in invalidating a state law in the name of the Constitution, we invalidate pro tanto the process of representative democracy in one of the sovereign States of the Union.

Mr. Justice **POWELL**, concurring in the judgment. . . .

I

On several occasions, the Court has acknowledged the importance of the marriage relationship to the maintenance of values essential to organized society. "This Court has long recognized that freedom of personal choice in matters of marriage and family life is one of the liberties protected by the Due Process Clause of the Fourteenth Amendment." Cleveland Board of Education v. LaFleur (1974). Our decisions indicate that the guarantee of personal privacy or autonomy secured against unjustifiable governmental interference by the Due Process Clause "has some extension to activities relating to marriage," *Loving.*
. . .

Thus, it is fair to say that there is a right of marital and familial privacy which places some substantive limits on the regulatory power of government. But the Court has yet to hold that all regulation touching upon marriage implicates a "fundamental right" triggering the most exacting judicial scrutiny.

The principal authority cited by the majority is *Loving.* Although *Loving* speaks of the "freedom to marry" as "one of the vital personal rights essential to the orderly pursuit of happiness by free men," the Court focused on the miscegenation statute before it. Mr. Chief Justice Warren stated:

> To deny this fundamental freedom on so unsupportable a basis as the racial classifications embodied in these statutes, classifications so directly subversive of the principle of equality at the heart of the Fourteenth Amendment, is surely to deprive all the State's citizens of liberty without due process of law. The Fourteenth Amendment requires that the freedom of choice to marry not be restricted by invidious racial discriminations. . . .

Thus, *Loving* involved a denial of a "fundamental freedom" on a wholly unsupportable basis—the use of classifications "directly subversive of the principle of equality at the heart of the Fourteenth Amendment. . . ." It does not speak to the level of judicial scrutiny of, or governmental justification for, "supportable" restrictions on the "fundamental freedom" of individuals to marry or divorce.

In my view, analysis must start from the recognition of domestic relations as "an area that has long been regarded as a virtually exclusive province of the States." Sosna v. Iowa (1975). . . . A "compelling state purpose" inquiry would cast doubt on the network of restrictions that the States have fashioned to govern marriage and divorce.

II

State power over domestic relations is not without constitutional limits. The Due Process Clause requires a showing of justification "when the government intrudes on choices concerning family living arrangements" in a manner which is contrary to deeply rooted traditions. Moore v. East Cleveland (1977) (plurality opinion). Due process constraints also limit the extent to which the State may monopolize the process of ordering certain human relationships while excluding the truly indigent from that process. Boddie v. Connecticut (1971). Furthermore, under the Equal Protection Clause the means chosen by the State in this case must bear " 'a fair and substantial relation" to the object of the legislation. Reed v. Reed (1971); Craig v. Boren (1976) (Powell, J., concurring).

The Wisconsin measure in this case does not pass muster under either due process or equal protection standards. . . .

Mr. Justice **STEVENS,** concurring in the judgment. . . .

Mr. Justice **REHNQUIST,** dissenting.

I substantially agree with my Brother Powell's reasons for rejecting the Court's conclusion that marriage is the sort of "fundamental right" which must invariably trigger the strictest judicial scrutiny. I disagree with his imposition of an "intermediate" standard of review, which leads him to conclude that the statute, though generally valid as an "additional collection mechanism" offends the Constitution by its "failure to make provision for those without the means to comply with child support obligations." . . . I would view this legislative judgment in the light of the traditional presumption of validity. I think that under the Equal Protection Clause the statute need pass only the "rational basis test," Dandridge v. Williams (1970), and that under the Due Process Clause it need only be shown that it bears a rational relation to a constitutionally permissible objective. Williamson v. Lee Optical Co. (1955); Ferguson v. Skrupa (1963) (Harlan, J., concurring). The statute so viewed is a permissible exercise of the State's power to regulate family life and to assure the support of minor children, despite its possible imprecision in the extreme cases envisioned in the concurring opinions.

Earlier this Term the traditional standard of review was applied in Califano v. Jobst (1977) despite the claim that the statute there in question burdened the exercise of the right to marry. The extreme situation considered there involved a permanently disabled appellee whose benefits under the Social Security Act had been terminated because of his marriage to an equally disabled woman who was not, however, a beneficiary under the Act. This Court recognized that Congress, in granting the original benefit, could reasonably assume that a disabled adult child remained dependent upon his parents for support. The Court concluded that, upon a beneficiary's marriage, Congress could terminate his benefits, because "there can be no question about the validity of the assumption that a married person is less likely to be dependent on his parents for support than one who is unmarried." Although that assumption had been proved false as applied in that individual case, the statute was nevertheless rational. "The broad legislative classification must be judged by reference to characteristics typical of the affected classes rather than by focusing on selected, atypical examples."

The analysis applied in *Jobst* is equally applicable here. . . . Because of the limited amount of funds available for the support of needy children, the State has an exceptionally strong interest in securing as much support as their parents are able to pay. Nor does the extent of the burden imposed by this statute so differentiate it from that considered in *Jobst* as to warrant a different result. In the case of some applicants, this statute makes the proposed marriage legally impossible for financial reasons; in a similar number of extreme cases, the Social Security Act makes the proposed marriage practically impossible for the same reasons. I cannot conclude that such a difference justifies the application of a heightened standard of review to the statute in question here. In short, I conclude that the statute, despite its imperfections, is sufficiently rational to satisfy the demands of the Fourteenth Amendment. . . .

Editors' Notes

(1) **Query:** To what degree is Justice Stewart's criticism of the Court's use of "fundamental rights" and equal protection valid? Did the justices in *Zablocki* and in earlier rulings such as *Skinner* (1942; reprinted above, p. 868) and *Shapiro* (1969; reprinted above, p. 873) decide the cases because of denials of equal protection or because of violation of fundamental rights? Can one make an intellectually meaningful distinction here?

(2) **Query:** In his concurrence, was Powell adopting Marshall's argument about continua as expressed in *San Antonio* or was he merely using a middle-tier as in Craig v. Boren (1976; reprinted above, p. 844)?

"The guarantee of equal protection . . . is not a source
of substantive rights or liberties, but rather a right to be
free from invidious discrimination in statutory classifications and other governmental activity."

HARRIS v. McRAE
448 U.S. 297, 100 S.Ct. 2671, 65 L.Ed.2d 784 (1980).

Roe v. Wade (1973; reprinted below, p. 1109) held that a woman has a
constitutional right to choose an abortion during at least the first three months
of her pregnancy. In the Medicaid Program, enacted in 1965 at Title XIX of
the Social Security Act, Congress had provided for federal assistance to states
that set up programs to help pay the costs for medical care of the poor. Thus,
following Wade, federal money became available to the states to pay for poor
women to have abortions. Between 1976 and 1980, however, Congress each
year attached a rider—known as "the Hyde Amendment"—to the appropriations bill limiting the circumstances under which federal money could be used
to subsidize abortions. The terms of those limitations varied from year to year;
in fiscal 1980, the rider allowed federal funding only when the pregnancy was
the result of rape or threatened the life of the mother.

Maher v. Roe (1977) upheld Connecticut's limiting state financing of
abortions to those "medically necessary," but did not discuss the Hyde
Amendment. A year earlier, Cora McRae, a pregnant woman otherwise
eligible for benefits under Medicaid, had filed suit in a federal district court,
alleging violation of her rights under the First, Fourth, Fifth, and Ninth amendments. The suit was later joined by other pregnant women and interested
parties. The district court invalidated the Hyde Amendment, and the government appealed directly to the Supreme Court.

Mr. Justice **STEWART** delivered the opinion of the Court. . . .

II

It is well settled that if a case may be decided on either statutory or
constitutional grounds, this Court, for sound jurisprudential reasons,
will inquire first into the statutory question. This practice reflects the
deeply rooted doctrine "that we ought not to pass on questions of
constitutionality . . . unless such adjudication is unavoidable."
Spector Motor Co. v. McLaughlin [1944]. . . . [The Court concluded
that] Title XIX does not require a participating State to pay for those
medically necessary abortions for which federal reimbursement is unavailable under the Hyde Amendment.

III

[Next] we must consider the constitutional validity of the Hyde
Amendment. . . .

It is well settled that, quite apart from the guarantee of equal
protection, if a law "impinges upon a fundamental right explicitly or
implicitly secured by the Constitution [it] is presumptively unconstitutional." Mobile v. Bolden [1980] (plurality opinion). Accordingly, before turning to the equal protection issue in this case, we examine
whether the Hyde Amendment violates any substantive rights secured
by the Constitution.

A

We address first the appellees' argument that the Hyde Amendment, by restricting the availability of certain medically necessary abortions under Medicaid, impinges on the "liberty" protected by the Due Process Clause as recognized in Roe v. Wade [1973] and its progeny. . . . The constitutional underpinning of *Wade* was a recognition that the "liberty" protected by the Due Process Clause of the Fourteenth Amendment includes not only the freedoms explicitly mentioned in the Bill of Rights, but also a freedom of personal choice in certain matters of marriage and family life. This implicit constitutional liberty, the Court in *Wade* held, includes the freedom of a woman to decide whether to terminate a pregnancy. . . .

In Maher v. Roe [1977], the Court was presented with the question whether the scope of personal constitutional freedom recognized in *Wade* included an entitlement to Medicaid payments for abortions that are not medically necessary. At issue in *Maher* was a Connecticut welfare regulation under which Medicaid recipients received payments for medical services incident to childbirth, but not for medical services incident to nontherapeutic abortions. . . .

. . . The doctrine of *Wade*, the Court held in *Maher*, . . . did not translate into a constitutional obligation of Connecticut to subsidize abortions. [T]he Court cited the "basic difference between direct state interference with a protected activity and state encouragement of an alternative activity consonant with legislative policy. Constitutional concerns are greatest when the State attempts to impose its will by force of law; the State's power to encourage actions deemed to be in the public interest is necessarily far broader." . . .

The Hyde Amendment, like the Connecticut welfare regulation at issue in *Maher*, places no governmental obstacle in the path of a woman who chooses to terminate her pregnancy, but rather, by means of unequal subsidization of abortion and other medical services, encourages alternative activity deemed in the public interest. The present case does differ factually from *Maher* insofar as that case involved a failure to fund nontherapeutic abortions, whereas the Hyde Amendment withholds funding of certain medically necessary abortions. Accordingly, the appellees argue that because the Hyde Amendment affects a significant interest not present or asserted in *Maher*—the interest of a woman in protecting her health during pregnancy—and because that interest lies at the core of the personal constitutional freedom recognized in *Wade*, the present case is constitutionally different from *Maher*. . . .

. . . [R]egardless of whether the freedom of a woman to choose to terminate her pregnancy for health reasons lies at the core or the periphery of the due process liberty recognized in *Wade*, it simply does not follow that a woman's freedom of choice carries with it a constitutional entitlement to the financial resources to avail herself of the full range of protected choices. . . . The financial constraints that restrict an indigent woman's ability to enjoy the full range of constitutionally protected freedom of choice are the product not of governmental restrictions on access to abortions, but rather of her indigency. Although Congress has opted to subsidize medically necessary services generally, but not certain medically necessary abortions, the fact remains that the Hyde Amendment leaves an indigent woman with at least the same range of choice in deciding whether to obtain a medically necessary abortion as she would have had if Congress had chosen to subsidize no health care costs at all. . . .

. . . To translate the limitation on governmental power implicit in the Due Process Clause into an affirmative funding obligation would require Congress to subsidize the medically necessary abortion of an indigent woman even if Congress had not enacted a Medicaid program to subsidize other medically necessary services. Nothing in the Due Process Clause supports such in extraordinary result. Whether freedom of choice that is constitutionally protected warrants federal subsidization is a question for Congress to answer, not a matter of constitutional entitlement. Accordingly, we conclude that the Hyde Amendment does not impinge on the due process liberty recognized in *Wade.*

B

The appellees also argue that the Hyde Amendment contravenes rights secured by the Religion Clauses of the First Amendment. . . . [They argue that it] violates the Establishment Clause because it incorporates into law the doctrines of the Roman Catholic Church concerning the sinfulness of abortion and the time at which life commences. Moreover, insofar as a woman's decision to seek a medically necessary abortion may be a product of her religious beliefs under certain Protestant and Jewish tenets, the appellees assert that the funding limitations of the Hyde Amendment impinge on the freedom of religion guaranteed by the Free Exercise Clause.

. . . [T]he Hyde Amendment does not run afoul of the Establishment Clause. Although neither a State nor the Federal Government can constitutionally "pass laws which aid one religion, aid all religions, or prefer one religion over another," Everson v. Board of Education [1947], it does not follow that a statute violates the Establishment Clause because it "happens to coincide or harmonize with the tenets of some or all religions." McGowan v. Maryland [1961]. That the Judeo-Christian religions oppose stealing does not mean that a State or the Federal Government may not consistent with the Establishment Clause enact law prohibiting larceny. The Hyde Amendment . . . is as much a reflection of "traditionalist" values toward abortion, as it is an embodiment of the views of any particular religion. . . .

C

It remains to be determined whether the Hyde Amendment violates the equal protection component of the Fifth Amendment. This challenge is premised on the fact that, although federal reimbursement is available under Medicaid for medically necessary services generally, the Hyde Amendment does not permit federal reimbursement of all medically necessary abortions. . . .

The guarantee of equal protection . . . is not a source of substantive rights or liberties, but rather a right to be free from invidious discrimination in statutory classifications and other governmental activity. It is well-settled that where a statutory classification does not itself impinge on a right or liberty protected by the Constitution, the validity of classification must be sustained unless "the classification rests on grounds wholly irrelevant to the achievement of [any legitimate governmental] objective." *McGowan*. This presumption of constitutional validity, however, disappears if a statutory classification is predicated on criteria that are, in a constitutional sense, "suspect," the principal example of which is a classification based on race, e.g., Brown v. Board of Education [1954].

. . . [W]e have already concluded that the Hyde Amendment violates no constitutionally protected substantive rights. We now conclude as well that it is not predicated on a constitutionally suspect classification. In reaching this conclusion, we again draw guidance from the Court's decision in *Maher* . . . :

> In a sense, every denial of welfare to an indigent creates a wealth classification as compared to nonindigents who are able to pay for the desired goods or services. But this Court has never held that financial need alone identifies a suspect class for purposes of equal protection analysis." San Antonio School Dist. v. Rodriguez [1973]; Dandridge v. Williams [1970]. . . .

. . . Here, as in *Maher,* the principal impact of the Hyde Amendment falls on the indigent. But that fact does not itself render the funding restriction constitutionally invalid, for this Court has held repeatedly that poverty, standing alone, is not a suspect classification. . . .

2

The remaining question then is whether the Hyde Amendment is rationally related to a legitimate governmental objective. . . .

In *Wade,* the Court recognized that the State has "an important and legitimate interest in protecting the potentiality of human life." . . . Moreover, in *Maher,* the Court held that Connecticut's decision to fund the costs associated with childbirth but not those associated with nontherapeutic abortions was a rational means of advancing the legitimate state interest in protecting potential life by encouraging childbirth.

It follows that the Hyde Amendment, by encouraging childbirth except in the most urgent circumstances, is rationally related to the legitimate governmental objective of protecting potential life. By subsidizing the medical expenses of indigent women who carry their pregnancies to term while not subsidizing the comparable expenses of

women who undergo abortions (except those whose lives are threatened), Congress has established incentives that make childbirth a more
attractive alternative than abortion for persons eligible for Medicaid.
. . . Nor is it irrational that Congress has authorized federal reimbursement for medically necessary services generally, but not for certain medically necessary abortions. Abortion is inherently different
from other medical procedures, because no other procedure involves the
purposeful termination of a potential life. . . . [I]t is not the mission of this Court or any other to decide whether the balance of
competing interests reflected in the Hyde Amendment is wise social
policy. If that were our mission, not every Justice who has subscribed
to the judgment of the Court today could have done so. But we cannot,
in the name of the Constitution, overturn duly enacted statutes simply
"because they may be unwise, improvident or out of harmony with a
particular school of thought." Williamson v. Lee Optical Co. [1955].
Rather, "when an issue involves policy choices as sensitive as those
implicated [here] . . . the appropriate forum for their resolution in a
democracy is the legislature." Maher. . . .

[Reversed.]

Mr. Justice **WHITE,** concurring. . . .

Mr. Justice **BRENNAN,** with whom Mr. Justice **MARSHALL** and Mr.
    Justice **BLACKMUN** join, dissenting.

I agree entirely with my Brother Stevens. . . . I write separately to express my continuing disagreement with the Court's mis-
characterization of the nature of the fundamental right recognized in
Wade, and its misconception of the manner in which that right is
infringed by federal and state legislation withdrawing all funding for
medically necessary abortions. . . .

. . . Wade and its progeny established that the pregnant woman
has a right to be free from state interference with her choice to have an
abortion. . . . The proposition for which these cases stand thus is
not that the State is under an affirmative obligation to ensure access to
abortions for all who may desire them; it is that the State must refrain
from wielding its enormous power and influence in a manner that
might burden the pregnant woman's freedom to choose whether to have
an abortion. The Hyde Amendment's denial of public funds for medically necessary abortions plainly intrudes upon this constitutionally
protected decision, for both by design and in effect it serves to coerce
indigent pregnant women to bear children that they would otherwise
elect not to have.

When viewed in the context of the Medicaid program to which it is
appended, it is obvious that the Hyde Amendment is nothing less than
an attempt by Congress to circumvent the dictates of the Constitution
and achieve indirectly what Wade said it could not do directly. . . .

[It] is a transparent attempt by the Legislative Branch to impose
the political majority's judgment of the morally acceptable and socially

desirable preference on a sensitive and intimate decision that the Constitution entrusts to the individual. Worse yet, the Hyde Amendment does not foist that majoritarian viewpoint with equal measure upon everyone in our Nation, rich and poor alike; rather, it imposes that viewpoint only upon that segment of our society which, because of its position of political powerlessness, is least able to defend its privacy rights from the encroachments of state-mandated morality. The instant legislation thus calls for more exacting judicial review than in most other cases. "When elected leaders cower before public pressure, this Court, more than ever, must not shirk its duty to enforce the Constitution for the benefit of the poor and powerless." Beal v. Doe (1977) (Marshall, J., dissenting). Though it may not be this Court's mission "to decide whether the balance of competing interests reflected in the Hyde Amendment is wise social policy," it most assuredly is our responsibility to vindicate the pregnant woman's constitutional right to decide whether to bear children free from governmental intrusion.

. . .

    . . . [W]hat the Court fails to appreciate is that it is not simply the woman's indigency that interferes with her freedom of choice, but the combination of her own poverty and the government's unequal subsidization of abortion and childbirth.

    A poor woman in the early stages of pregnancy confronts two alternatives: she may elect either to carry the fetus to term or to have an abortion. In the abstract, of course, this choice is hers alone.

. . .

    . . . [But] as a practical matter, many poverty-stricken women will choose to carry their pregnancy to term simply because the government provides funds for the associated medical services, even though these same women would have chosen to have an abortion if the government had also paid for that option, or indeed if the government had stayed out of the picture altogether and had defrayed the costs of neither procedure.

    The fundamental flaw in the Court's due process analysis, then, is its failure to acknowledge that the discriminatory distribution of the benefits of governmental largesse can discourage the exercise of fundamental liberties just as effectively as can an outright denial of those rights through criminal and regulatory sanctions. Implicit in the Court's reasoning is the notion that as long as the government is not obligated to provide its citizens with certain benefits or privileges, it may condition the grant of such benefits on the recipient's relinquishment of his constitutional rights.

    . . . [W]e have heretofore never hesitated to invalidate any scheme of granting or withholding financial benefits that incidentally or intentionally burdens one manner of exercising a constitutionally protected choice. . . .

Mr. Justice **MARSHALL** dissenting.

. . . In *Maher* . . . I expressed my fear "that the Court's decisions will be an invitation to public officials, already under extraordinary pressure from well-financed and carefully orchestrated lobbying campaigns, to approve more such restrictions" on governmental funding for abortion (dissenting).

That fear has proved justified. Under the Hyde Amendment, federal funding is denied for abortions that are medically necessary and that are necessary to avert severe and permanent damage to the health of the mother. . . . As my Brother Stevens has demonstrated, the premise underlying the Hyde Amendment was repudiated in *Wade.* . . . The Court's decision today marks a retreat from *Wade* and represents a cruel blow to the most powerless members of our society. I dissent. . . .

II

The Court resolves the equal protection issue in this case through a relentlessly formalistic catechism. . . .

I continue to believe that the rigid "two-tiered" approach is inappropriate and that the Constitution requires a more exacting standard of review than mere rationality in cases such as this one. Further, in my judgment the Hyde Amendment cannot pass constitutional muster even under the rational-basis standard of review.

A

This case is perhaps the most dramatic illustration to date of the deficiencies in the Court's obsolete "two-tiered" approach to the Equal Protection Clause. . . .

. . . Heightened scrutiny of legislative classifications [is] designed to protect groups "saddled with such disabilities or subjected to such a history of purposeful unequal treatment, or relegated to such a position of political powerlessness as to command extraordinary protection from the majoritarian political process." *San Antonio.* And while it is now clear that traditional "strict scrutiny" is unavailable to protect the poor against classifications that disfavor them, *Dandridge,* I do not believe that legislation that imposes a crushing burden on indigent women can be treated with the same deference given to legislation distinguishing among business interests ["more than able to protect themselves in the political process."]

B

The Hyde Amendment . . . distinguishes between medically necessary abortions and other medically necessary expenses. . . . [S]uch classifications must be assessed by weighing " 'the importance of the governmental benefits denied, the character of the class, and the asserted state interests.' " Under that approach, the Hyde Amendment is clearly invalid.

As in *Maher,* the governmental benefits at issue here are "of absolutely vital importance in the lives of the recipients." An indigent woman denied governmental funding for a medically necessary abortion is confronted with two grotesque choices. First, she may seek to obtain "an illegal abortion that poses a serious threat to her health and even her life." Alternatively, she may attempt to bear the child, a course that may both significantly threaten her health and eliminate any chance she might have had "to control the direction of her own life."

The class burdened by the Hyde Amendment consists of indigent women, a substantial proportion of whom are members of minority races. . . . In my view, the fact that the burden of the Hyde Amendment falls exclusively on financially destitute women suggests "a special condition, which tends seriously to curtail the operation of those political processes ordinarily to be relied upon to protect minorities, and which may call for a correspondingly more searching judicial inquiry." United States v. Carolene Products Co., n. 4 (1938). For this reason, I continue to believe that "a showing that state action has a devastating impact on the lives of minority racial groups must be relevant" for purposes of equal protection analysis. Jefferson v. Hackney (1972) (Marshall, J., dissenting).

. . . [T]he asserted state interest in protecting potential life is insufficient to "outweigh the deprivation or serious discouragement of a vital constitutional right of especial importance to poor and minority women." . . .

The governmental interest in the present case is substantially weaker than in *Maher*, for under the Hyde Amendment funding is refused even in cases in which normal childbirth will not result: one can scarcely speak of "normal childbirth" in cases where the fetus will die shortly after birth, or in which the mother's life will be shortened or her health otherwise gravely impaired by the birth. . . . I am unable to see how even a minimally rational legislature could conclude that the interest in fetal life outweighs the brutal effect of the Hyde Amendment on indigent women. . . .

C

Although I would abandon the strict-scrutiny/rational-basis dichotomy in equal protection analysis, it is by no means necessary to reject that traditional approach to conclude, as I do, that the Hyde Amendment is a denial of equal protection. . . .

The Court treats this case as though it were controlled by *Maher*. To the contrary, this case is the mirror image of *Maher*. The result in *Maher* turned on the fact that the legislation there under consideration discouraged only nontherapeutic, or medically unnecessary, abortions. In the Court's view, denial of Medicaid funding for nontherapeutic abortions was not a denial of equal protection because Medicaid funds were available only for medically necessary procedures. Thus the plaintiffs were seeking benefits which were not available to others similarly situated . . . [But respondents here] are protesting their exclusion from a benefit that is available to all others similarly situated. This, it need hardly be said, is a crucial difference for equal protection purposes.

Under Title XIX and the Hyde Amendment, funding is available for essentially all necessary medical treatment for the poor. Respondents have met the statutory requirements for eligibility, but they are excluded because the treatment that is medically necessary involves the exercise of a fundamental right, the right to choose an abortion. . . . In such circumstances the Hyde Amendment must be invalidated because it does not meet even the rational-basis standard of review. . . .

Mr. Justice **BLACKMUN**, dissenting. . . .

Mr. Justice **STEVENS**, dissenting.

"The federal sovereign, like the States, must govern impartially. . . ." Hampton v. Mow Sun Wong (1976). When the sovereign provides a special benefit or a special protection for a class of persons, it must define the membership in the class by neutral criteria; it may not make special exceptions for reasons that are constitutionally insufficient.

. . . Individuals who satisfy two neutral statutory criteria— financial need and medical need—are entitled to equal access to [the pool of benefits under Title XIX]. The question is whether certain persons who satisfy those criteria may be denied access to benefits solely because they must exercise the constitutional right to have an abortion in order to obtain the medical care they need. Our prior cases plainly dictate the answer to that question. . . .

If a woman has a constitutional right to place a higher value on avoiding either serious harm to her own health or perhaps an abnormal childbirth than on protecting potential life, the exercise of that right cannot provide the basis for the denial of a benefit to which she would otherwise be entitled. The Court's sterile equal protection analysis evades this critical though simple point. The Court focuses exclusively on the "legitimate interest in protecting the potential life of the fetus." . . . [But] *Wade* squarely held that the States may not protect that interest when a conflict with the interest in a pregnant woman's health exists. . . .

Nor can it be argued that the exclusion of this type of medically necessary treatment of the indigent can be justified on fiscal grounds. . . . [T]he cost of an abortion is only a small fraction of the costs associated with childbirth. Thus, the decision to tolerate harm to indigent persons who need an abortion in order to avoid "serious and long-lasting health damage" is one that is financed by draining money out of the pool that is used to fund all other necessary medical procedures. Unlike most invidious classifications, this discrimination harms not only its direct victims but also the remainder of the class of needy persons that the pool was designed to benefit. . . .

. . . In my judgment, these amendments constitute an unjustifiable, and indeed blatant, violation of the sovereign's duty to govern impartially. . . .

Editors' Notes

(1) **Query:** There is a striking similarity between Stewart's reasoning in Harris v. McRae and Harlan's dissenting opinion in Griffin v. Illinois (1955), the grandfather of modern cases involving wealth as a classification. There the Court invalidated as a denial of equal protection a state law that required indigent prisoners to pay for transcripts of their trials in order to appeal their convictions. Harlan wrote: "Nor is this a case where the State's own action has prevented a defendant from appealing. All that Illinois has done is to fail to alleviate the consequences of the differences [in wealth] that exist wholly apart from any state action." Is there a difference relevant to constitutional interpretation between requiring an indigent prisoner to pay for his transcript as a condition for appealing his conviction and requiring an indigent pregnant woman whose life is not threatened by her pregnancy and whose pregnancy was not caused by rape to pay for an abortion if she chooses one?

(2) **Query:** How convincing as a matter of constitutional interpretation— as opposed to wise or just public policy—is Brennan's argument that it violates equal protection for the government to subsidize a live birth but not an abortion?

(3) For a recent analysis of the problems that *McRae* raises, see Laurence H. Tribe, "The Abortion Funding Conundrum," 99 *Harv.L.Rev.* 330 (1985).

IV. A NEW MODEL? REASONABLENESS "WITH BITE" AND WITHOUT PRESUMPTION?

"If the State is to deny a discrete group of innocent children the free public education that it offers to other children residing within its borders, that denial must be justified by a showing that it furthers some substantial state interest."

PLYLER v. DOE
457 U.S. 202, 102 S.Ct. 2382, 72 L.Ed.2d 786 (1982).

Faced with an increasing number of illegal aliens crossing from Mexico, Texas in 1975 added § 21.031 to its Educational Code, withholding from local school boards state funds for the education of children who were "not legally admitted" into the United States. Sec. 21.031 further authorized local boards to deny enrollment to children of illegal aliens. A series of class actions filed in U.S. district courts challenged the statute as a denial of equal protection. Those courts and the Court of Appeals for the Fifth Circuit held it unconstitutional. Texas appealed.

Justice **BRENNAN** delivered the opinion of the Court. . . .

II

. . . . Appellants argue . . . that undocumented aliens, because of their immigration status, are not "persons within the jurisdiction" of . . . Texas, and that therefore they have no right to the equal protection of Texas law. We reject this argument. . . . [E]ven aliens whose presence in this country is unlawful have long been recognized as "persons" guaranteed due process of law by the Fifth and Fourteenth Amendments. Yick Wo v. Hopkins (1886). Indeed, we have clearly held that the Fifth Amendment protects aliens whose presence in this country is unlawful from invidious discrimination by the Federal Government.[1] Mathews v. Diaz (1976).

Appellants seek to distinguish our prior cases, emphasizing that the Equal Protection Clause directs a State to afford its protection to persons *within its jurisdiction,* while the Due Process Clauses of the Fifth and Fourteenth Amendments contain no such . . . phrase. . . . We have never suggested that the class of persons who might avail themselves of the equal protection guarantee is less than coextensive with that entitled to due process. To the contrary, we have recognized that both provisions . . . protect an identical class of persons, and to reach every exercise of state authority. . . .

There is simply no support for appellant's suggestion that "due process" is somehow of greater stature than "equal protection" and therefore available to a larger class of persons. To the contrary, each aspect of the Fourteenth Amendment reflects an elementary limitation on state power. To permit a State to employ the phrase "within its jurisdiction" in order to identify subclasses of persons whom it would define as beyond its jurisdiction . . . would undermine the principal purpose for which the Equal Protection Clause was incorporated. . . . [It] was intended to work nothing less than the abolition of all caste-based and invidious class-based legislation. That objective is fundamentally at odds with the power the State asserts here. . . .

III . . .

. . . . A legislature must have substantial latitude to establish classifications that roughly approximate the nature of the problem perceived, that accommodate competing concerns both public and private, and that account for limitations on the practical ability of the State to remedy every ill. In applying the Equal Protection Clause to most forms of state action, we thus seek only the assurance that the classification . . . bears some fair relationship to a legitimate public purpose.

But we would not be faithful to our obligations under the Fourteenth Amendment if we applied so deferential a standard to every classification. The Equal Protection Clause was intended as a restriction on state legislative action inconsistent with elemental constitution-

---

1. It would be incongruous to hold that the United States . . . is barred from invidious discrimination with respect to unlawful aliens, while exempting the States from a similar limitation. . . . [Footnote by the Court.]

al premises. Thus we have treated as presumptively invidious those classifications that disadvantage a "suspect class,"[2] or that impinge upon the exercise of a "fundamental right. . . ."[3] In addition, we have recognized that certain forms of legislative classification, while not facially invidious, nonetheless give rise to recurring constitutional difficulties; in these limited circumstances we have sought the assurance that the classification reflects a reasoned judgment consistent with the ideal of equal protection by inquiring whether it may fairly be viewed as furthering a substantial interest of the state. We turn to a consideration of the standard appropriate for the evaluation of § 21.031.

A

Sheer incapability or lax enforcement of the laws barring entry into this country, coupled with the failure to establish an effective bar to the employment of undocumented aliens, has resulted in the creation of a substantial "shadow population" of illegal immigrants . . . within our borders . . . [raising] the specter of a permanent caste . . . [whose existence] presents most difficult problems for a Nation that prides itself on adherence to principles of equality under law.[4]

The children who are plaintiffs in these cases are special members of this underclass. Persuasive arguments support the view that a State may withhold its beneficence from those whose very presence within the United States is the product of their own unlawful conduct. These arguments do not apply with the same force to classifications imposing disabilities on the minor *children* of such illegal entrants. . . . Even if the State found it expedient to control the conduct of adults by acting against their children, legislation directing the onus of a parent's misconduct against his children does not comport with fundamental conceptions of justice.

2. Several formulations might explain our treatment of certain classifications as "suspect." Some . . . are more likely than others to reflect deep-seated prejudice . . . [and are] easily recognized as incompatible with the constitutional understanding that each person is to be judged individually and to be entitled to equal justice under the law. Classifications treated as suspect tend to be irrelevant to any proper legislative goal. See McLaughlin v. Florida (1964); Hirabayashi v. United States (1943). Finally, certain groups . . . have historically been "relegated to such a position of political powerlessness as to command extraordinary protection from the majoritarian political process." San Antonio v. Rodriguez (1973); see United States v. Carolene Products Co. (1938). . . . Legislation imposing special disabilities upon groups disfavored by virtue of circumstances beyond their control suggests the kind of "class or caste" treatment that the Fourteenth Amendment was designed to abolish. [Footnote by the Court.]

3. In determining whether a class-based denial of a particular right is deserving of strict scrutiny . . . we look to the Constitution to see if the right infringed has its source, explicitly or implicitly therein. But we have also recognized the fundamentality of participation in state "elections on an equal basis with other citizens in the jurisdiction," Dunn v. Blumstein (1972), even though "the right to vote, *per se*, is not a constitutionally protected right." *San Antonio.* With respect to suffrage, we have explained the need for strict scrutiny as arising from the significance of the franchise as the guardian of all other rights. See Harper v. Virginia (1966); Reynolds v. Sims (1964); Yick Wo v. Hopkins (1886). [Footnote by the Court.]

4. We reject the claim that "illegal aliens" are a "suspect class." . . . [Footnote by the Court.]

[V]isiting . . . condemnation on the head of an infant is illogical and
unjust. Moreover, imposing disabilities on the . . . child is contrary
to the basic concept of our system that legal burdens should bear some
relationship to individual responsibility or wrongdoing. Obviously, no
child is responsible for his birth and penalizing the . . . child is an
ineffectual—as well as unjust—way of deterring the parent. Weber v.
Aetna Casualty & Surety Co. (1972).

Of course, undocumented status is not irrelevant to any proper
legislative goal. Nor is undocumented status an absolutely immutable
characteristic since it is the product of conscious, indeed unlawful,
action. But § 21.031 is directed against children, and imposes its
discriminatory burden on the basis of a legal characteristic over which
children can have little control. It is thus difficult to conceive of a
rational justification for penalizing these children for their presence
within the United States. Yet that appears to be precisely the effect of
§ 21.031.

Public education is not a "right" granted to individuals by the
Constitution. San Antonio v. Rodriguez (1973). But neither is it
merely some governmental "benefit" indistinguishable from other
forms of social welfare legislation. Both the importance of education in
maintaining our basic institutions, and the lasting impact of its deprivation on the child, mark the distinction. . . . [E]ducation provides
the basic tools by which individuals might lead economically productive
lives to the benefit of us all. In sum, education has a fundamental role
in maintaining the fabric of our society. We cannot ignore the significant social costs borne by our Nation when select groups are denied the
means to absorb the values and skills upon which our social order rests.
. . . The inestimable toll of that deprivation on the social, economic,
intellectual, and psychological well-being of the individual, and the
obstacle it poses to individual achievement, makes it most difficult to
reconcile the cost or the principle of a status-based denial of basic
education with the framework of equality embodied in the Equal
Protection Class. . . .

B

These well-settled principles allow us to determine the proper level
of deference to be afforded § 21.031. Undocumented aliens cannot be
treated as a suspect class because their presence in this country in
violation of federal law is not a "constitutional irrelevancy." Nor is
education a fundamental right; a State need not justify by compelling
necessity every variation in the manner in which education is provided
to its population. *San Antonio.* But more is involved in these cases.
. . . In determining the rationality of § 21.031, we may appropriately take into account its costs to the Nation and to the innocent children
who are its victims. In light of these countervailing costs, the discrimination contained in § 21.031 can hardly be considered rational unless it
furthers some substantial goal of the State.

IV

It is the State's principal argument, and apparently the view of the dissenting Justices, that the undocumented status of these children . . . establishes a sufficient rational basis for denying them benefits that a State might choose to afford other residents. The State notes that while other aliens are admitted "on an equality of legal privileges with all citizens under non-discriminatory laws," Takahashi v. Fish & Game Comm'n. (1948), the asserted right of these children to an education can claim no implicit congressional imprimatur. Indeed, in the State's view, Congress' apparent disapproval of the presence of these children within the United States . . . provides authority for [Texas's] decision to impose upon them special disabilities. . . . [W]e agree that the courts must be attentive to congressional policy; the exercise of congressional power might well affect the State's prerogatives to afford differential treatment to a particular class of aliens. But we are unable to find in the congressional immigration scheme any statement of policy that might weigh significantly in arriving at an equal protection balance concerning the State's authority to deprive these children of an education. . . .

V

Appellants argue that the classification . . . furthers an interest in the "preservation of the state's limited resources for the education of its lawful residents." Of course, a concern for preservation of resources standing alone can hardly justify the classification used in allocating those resources. Graham v. Richardson (1971). Apart from the asserted state prerogative to act against undocumented status—an asserted prerogative that carries only minimal force in the circumstances of these cases—we discern three colorable state interests that might support § 21.031.

First, appellants . . . suggest that the State may . . . protect itself from an influx of illegal immigrants. While a State might have an interest in mitigating the potentially harsh economic effects of sudden shifts in population, § 21.031 hardly offers an effective method of dealing with an urgent demographic or economic problem. There is no evidence in the record suggesting that illegal entrants impose any significant burden on the State's economy. . . . [E]ven making the doubtful assumption that the net impact of illegal aliens on the economy is negative, we think it clear that "[c]harging tuition to undocumented children constitutes a ludicrously ineffectual attempt to stem the tide of illegal immigration," at least when compared with the alternative of prohibiting the employment of illegal aliens.

Second, while . . . a State may "not . . . reduce expenditures for education by barring [some arbitrarily chosen class of] children from its schools," Shapiro v. Thompson (1969), appellants suggest that undocumented children are appropriately singled out for exclusion because of the special burdens they impose on the State's ability to provide high-quality public education. But the record in no way supports the claim that exclusion of undocumented children is likely to improve the overall quality of education in the State. . . . Of course, even if improvement in the quality of education were a likely result of barring some *number* of children from the schools of the State, the State must support its selection of *this* group as the appropriate target for exclusion. In terms of educational cost and need, however, undocumented children are "basically indistinguishable" from legally resident alien children.

Finally, appellants suggest that undocumented children are appropriately singled out because their unlawful presence within the United States renders them less likely than other children to remain within the boundaries of the State, and to put their education to productive social or political use within the State. . . . The State has no assurance that any child, citizen or not, will employ the education provided by the State within the confines of the State's borders. . . . It is difficult to understand precisely what the State hopes to achieve by promoting the creation and perpetuation of a subclass of illiterates within our boundaries, surely adding to the problems and costs of unemployment, welfare, and crime. It is thus clear that whatever savings might be achieved by denying these children an education, they are wholly insubstantial in relation to the costs involved to these children, the State, and the Nation.

VI

If the State is to deny a discrete group of innocent children the free public education that it offers to other children residing within its borders, that denial must be justified by a showing that it furthers some substantial state interest. No such showing was made here.

Affirmed.

Justice **MARSHALL,** concurring. . . .

While I join the Court's opinion, I do so without in any way retreating from my [dissenting] opinion in *San Antonio.* I continue to believe that an individual's interest in education is fundamental. . . . Furthermore, I believe that the facts of these cases demonstrate the wisdom of rejecting a rigidified approach to equal protection analysis, and of employing an approach that allows for varying levels of scrutiny depending upon "the constitutional and societal importance of the interest adversely affected and the recognized invidiousness of the basis upon which the particular classification is drawn."

Justice **BLACKMUN,** concurring. . . .

Like Justice Powell, I believe that the children involved in this litigation "should not be left on the streets uneducated." I write separately, however, because in my view the nature of the interest at stake is crucial to the proper resolution of these cases. . . .

[T]he Court's experience has demonstrated that the *San Antonio* formulation does not settle every issue of "fundamental rights" arising under the Equal Protection Clause. Only a pedant would insist that there are *no* meaningful distinctions among the multitude of social and political interests regulated by the States, and *San Antonio* does not stand for quite so absolute a proposition. . . .

Justice **POWELL,** concurring. . . .

The classification in question severely disadvantages children who are the victims of a combination of circumstances. . . .

Our review in cases such as these is properly heightened. [Trimble v. Gordon (1977).] Cf. Craig v. Boren (1976). The classification at issue deprives a group of children of the opportunity for education afforded all other children simply because they have been assigned a legal status due to a violation of law by their parents. These children thus have been singled out for a lifelong penalty and stigma. A legislative classification that threatens the creation of an underclass of future citizens and residents cannot be reconciled with one of the fundamental purposes of the Fourteenth Amendment. In these unique circumstances, the Court properly may require that the State's interests be substantial and that the means bear a "fair and substantial relation" to these interests. See Lalli v. Lalli (1978). . . .

Chief Justice **BURGER,** with whom Justice **WHITE,** Justice **REHNQUIST,** and Justice **O'CONNOR** join, dissenting.

Were it our business to set the Nation's social policy, I would agree without hesitation that it is senseless for an enlightened society to deprive any children—including illegal aliens—of an elementary education. . . . However, the Constitution does not constitute us as "Platonic Guardians" nor does it vest in this Court the authority to strike down laws because they do not meet our standards of desirable social policy, "wisdom," or "common sense." See TVA v. Hill (1978). We trespass on the assigned function of the political branches under our structure of limited and separated powers when we assume a policymaking role as the Court does today. . . .

I . . .

The dispositive issue in these cases . . . is whether, for purposes of allocating its finite resources, a state has a legitimate reason to differentiate between persons who are lawfully within the state and those who are unlawfully there. The distinction . . . Texas has drawn—based not only upon its own legitimate interests but on classifications established by the Federal Government in its immigration laws and policies—is not unconstitutional.

A . . .

The Court first suggests that these illegal alien children, although not a suspect class, are entitled to special solicitude under the Equal

Protection Clause because they lack "control" over or "responsibility" for their unlawful entry into this country. Similarly, the Court appears to take the position that § 21.031 is presumptively "irrational" because it has the effect of imposing "penalties" on "innocent" children. However, the Equal Protection Clause does not preclude legislators from classifying among persons on the basis of factors over which individuals . . . lack "control." . . . The Equal Protection Clause protects against arbitrary and irrational classifications, and invidious discrimination stemming from prejudice and hostility; it is not an all-encompassing "equalizer" designed to eradicate every distinction for which persons are not "responsible."

The Court does not presume to suggest that appellees' purported lack of culpability for their illegal status prevents them from being deported or otherwise "penalized" under federal law. Yet would deportation be any less a "penalty" than denial of privileges provided to legal residents? Illegality of presence in the United States does not—and need not—depend on some amorphous concept of "guilt" or "innocence" concerning an alien's entry. Similarly, a state's use of federal immigration status as a basis for legislative classification is not necessarily rendered suspect for its failure to take such factors into account.

. . . This Court has recognized that in allocating governmental benefits to a given class of aliens, one "may take into account the character of the relationship between the alien and this country." Mathews v. Diaz (1976). . . . When that relationship is a federally prohibited one, there can, of course, be no presumption that a state has a constitutional duty to include illegal aliens among the recipients of its governmental benefits.

The second strand of the Court's analysis rests on the premise that, although public education is not a constitutionally guaranteed right, "neither is it merely some governmental 'benefit' indistinguishable from other forms of social welfare legislation." Whatever meaning or relevance this opaque observation might have in some other context, it simply has no bearing on the issues at hand. . . .

The importance of education is beyond dispute. Yet we have held repeatedly that the importance of a governmental service does not elevate it to the status of a "fundamental right" for purposes of equal protection analysis. In *San Antonio,* Justice Powell, speaking for the Court, expressly rejected the proposition that state laws dealing with public education are subject to special scrutiny under the Equal Protection Clause. Moreover, the Court points to no meaningful way to distinguish between education and other governmental benefits in this context. Is the Court suggesting that education is more "fundamental" than food, shelter, or medical care?

The Equal Protection Clause . . . does not mandate a constitutional hierarchy of governmental services. . . . The fact that the distinction is drawn in legislation affecting access to public education— as opposed to . . . other important governmental benefits, such as public assistance, health care, or housing—cannot make a difference in the level of scrutiny applied.

B

. . . [O]ur inquiry should focus on and be limited to whether the legislative classification at issue bears a rational relationship to a legitimate state purpose. Vance v. Bradley (1979); Dandridge v. Williams (1970).

The State contends primarily that § 21.031 serves to prevent undue depletion of its limited revenues available for education, and to preserve the fiscal integrity of the State's school-financing system against an ever-increasing flood of illegal aliens. . . . Of course such fiscal concerns alone could not justify discrimination against a suspect class or an arbitrary and irrational denial of benefits to a particular group of persons. Yet I assume no Member of this Court would argue that prudent conservation of finite state revenues is *per se* an illegitimate goal. Indeed, the numerous classifications this Court has sustained in social welfare legislation were invariably related to the limited amount of revenues available to spend on any given program. . . . See, e.g., Jefferson v. Hackney (1972); *Dandridge.* The significant question here is whether the requirement of tuition from illegal aliens who attend the public schools . . . is a rational and reasonable means of furthering the State's legitimate fiscal ends. . . .

. . . [I]t simply is not "irrational" for a state to conclude that it does not have the same responsibility to provide benefits for persons whose very presence in the state . . . is illegal as it does to provide for persons lawfully here. . . . The Court has failed to offer even a plausible explanation why illegality of residence in this country is not a factor that may legitimately bear upon the bona fides of state residence and entitlement to the benefits of lawful residence. . . .

The Court maintains—as if this were the issue—that "barring undocumented children from local schools would not necessarily improve the quality of education provided in those schools." However, the legitimacy of barring illegal aliens from programs such as Medicare or Medicaid does not depend on a showing that the barrier would "improve the quality" of medical care given to persons lawfully entitled to participate in such programs. . . . The State need not show . . . that the incremental cost of educating illegal aliens will send it into bankruptcy, or have a "grave impact on the quality of education"; that is not dispositive under a "rational basis" scrutiny. . . .

II

. . . Today's cases . . . present yet another example of unwarranted judicial action which in the long run tends to contribute to the weakening of our political processes.

. . . While the "specter of a permanent caste" of illegal Mexican residents of the United States is indeed a disturbing one, it is but one segment of a larger problem, which is for the political branches to solve.

I find it difficult to believe that Congress would long tolerate such a self-destructive result. . . .

Editors' Notes

(1) **Query:** To what extent does Brennan's majority opinion in *Plyler* represent a new model of interpretation of the constitutional command of equal protection? Is this model what Prof. Gerald Gunther would call a rational basis test with bite? (See his "In Search of Evolving Doctrine on a Changing Court," 86 *Harv.L.Rev.* 1 [1972].) To what extent is it merely a refinement on Marshall's doctrine of continua as explained in his dissents to *San Antonio* (above, p. 858), Harris v. McRae (reprinted above, p. 898), and his dissenting opinion in *Dandridge* (reprinted above, p. 884)? Or is it merely an application of "heightened scrutiny" in the manner of Craig v. Boren (1976) reprinted above, p. 844)?

(2) **Query:** Does Justice Blackmun's concurring opinion indicate that he has become sympathetic to if not a convert to Marshall's doctrine of continua?

(3) **Query:** Note how in footnote 2 and accompanying text Brennan conflates suspect class and suspect classification. What differences would separate analyses under these two concepts make here?

> **"Because mental retardation is a characteristic that the government may legitimately take into account in a wide range of decisions, and because both state and federal governments have recently committed themselves to assisting the retarded, we will not presume that any given legislative action, even one that disadvantages retarded individuals, is rooted in considerations that the Constitution will not tolerate."—Justice WHITE**

> **". . . [T]he Court does not label its handiwork heightened scrutiny, and perhaps the method employed must hereafter be called 'second order' rational basis review. . . ."—Justice MARSHALL**

CLEBURNE v. CLEBURNE LIVING CENTER
___ U.S. ___, 105 S.Ct. 3249, 87 L.Ed.2d 313 (1985).

Cleburne, Texas, acting pursuant to a municipal zoning ordinance requiring special permits for construction of "[h]ospitals for the insane or feeble-minded, or alcoholic [sic] or drug addicts, or penal or correctional institutions," denied Cleburne Living Center (CLC) such a permit for the operation of a group home for the mentally retarded. CLC filed suit in federal district court, alleging that the zoning ordinance discriminated against the mentally retarded in violation of the Equal Protection Clause. After the district court, applying the rational basis standard, upheld the ordinance on its face and as applied, the court of appeals, holding that mental retardation was a "quasi-suspect" classification that triggered intermediate or heightened scrutiny, reversed in both respects. The Supreme Court granted certiorari.

Mr. Justice **WHITE** delivered the opinion of the Court. . . .

II

The Equal Protection Clause of the Fourteenth Amendment . . . is essentially a direction that all persons similarly situated should be treated alike. Plyler v. Doe (1982). Section 5 of the Amendment empowers Congress to enforce this mandate, but absent controlling congressional direction, the courts have themselves devised standards for determining the validity of state legislation or other official action that is challenged as denying equal protection. The general rule is that legislation is presumed to be valid and will be sustained if the classification drawn by the statute is rationally related to a legitimate state interest. . . . When social or economic legislation is at issue, the Equal Protection Clause allows the states wide latitude, United States Railroad Retirement Board v. Fritz [1980]; New Orleans v. Dukes [1976], and the Constitution presumes that even improvident decisions will eventually be rectified by the democratic processes.

The general rule gives way, however, when a statute classifies by race, alienage or national origin. These factors are so seldom relevant to the achievement of any legitimate state interest that laws grounded in such considerations are deemed to reflect prejudice and antipathy—a view that those in the burdened class are not as worthy or deserving as others. For these reasons and because such discrimination is unlikely to be soon rectified by legislative means, these laws are subjected to strict scrutiny and will be sustained only if they are suitably tailored to serve a compelling state interest. McLaughlin v. Florida (1964); Graham v. Richardson (1971). Similar oversight by the courts is due when state laws impinge on personal rights protected by the Constitution. Kramer v. Union Free School District No. 15 (1969); Shapiro v. Thompson (1969); Skinner v. Oklahoma (1942).

Legislative classifications based on gender also call for a heightened standard of review. . . .   [S]tatutes distributing benefits and burdens between the sexes in different ways very likely reflect outmoded notions of the relative capabilities of men and women. A gender classification fails unless it is substantially related to a sufficiently important governmental interest. Mississippi University for Women v. Hogan (1982); Craig v. Boren (1976). Because illegitimacy is beyond the individual's control and bears "no relation to the individual's ability to participate in and contribute to society," Mathews v. Lucas (1976), official discriminations resting on that characteristic are also subject to somewhat heightened review. . . .   Mills v. Habluetzel (1982).

We have declined, however, to extend heightened review to differential treatment based on age:

> While the treatment of the aged in this Nation has not been wholly free of discrimination, such persons, unlike, say, those who have been discriminated against on the basis of race or national origin, have not experienced a "history of purposeful unequal treatment" or been subjected to unique disabilities on the basis of stereotyped characteris-

tics not truly indicative of their abilities.   Massachusetts Board of
Retirement v. Murgia (1976).

The lesson of *Murgia* is that where individuals in the group
affected by a law have distinguishing characteristics relevant to interests the state has the authority to implement, the courts have been
very reluctant, as they should be in our federal system and with our
respect for the separation of powers, to closely scrutinize legislative
choices as to whether, how and to what extent those interests should be
pursued.   In such cases, the Equal Protection Clause requires only a
rational means to serve a legitimate end.

III

. . . [T]he Court of Appeals erred in holding mental retardation a
quasi-suspect classification calling for a more exacting standard of
judicial review than is normally accorded economic and social legislation.   First, it is undeniable . . . that those who are mentally retarded have a reduced ability to cope with and function in the everyday
world. . . .   They are thus different, immutably so, in relevant
respects, and the states' interest in dealing with and providing for them
is plainly a legitimate one.[1]   How this large and diversified group is to
be treated under the law is a difficult and often a technical matter, very
much a task for legislators guided by qualified professionals and not by
the perhaps ill-informed opinions of the judiciary.   Heightened scrutiny
inevitably involves substantive judgments about legislative decisions,
and we doubt that the predicate for such judicial oversight is present
where the classification deals with mental retardation.

Second, the distinctive legislative response, both national and state,
to the plight of those who are mentally retarded demonstrates . . .
that the lawmakers have been addressing their difficulties in a manner
that belies a continuing antipathy or prejudice and a corresponding
need for more intrusive oversight by the judiciary.   Thus, the federal
government has not only outlawed discrimination against the mentally
retarded in federally funded programs, but it has also provided the
retarded with the right to receive "appropriate treatment, services, and
habilitation" in a setting that is "least restrictive of [their] personal
liberty."   In addition, the government has conditioned federal education funds on a State's assurance that retarded children will enjoy an
education that, "to the maximum extent appropriate," is integrated
with that of non-mentally retarded children.   The government has also
facilitated the hiring of the mentally retarded into the federal civil

---

1. As Dean Ely has observed:

Surely one has to feel sorry for a person disabled by something he or she can't do
anything about, but I'm not aware of any reason to suppose that elected officials are
unusually unlikely to share that feeling.   Moreover, classifications based on physical
disability and intelligence are typically accepted as legitimate, even by judges and
commentators who assert that immutability is relevant.   The explanation, when one
is given, is that *those* characteristics (unlike the one the commentator is trying to
render suspect) are often relevant to legitimate purposes.   At that point there's not
much left of the immutability theory, is there?   J. Ely, *Democracy and Distrust* 150
(1980) (footnote omitted).

See also id., at 154–155.   [Footnote by the Court.]

service by exempting them from the requirement of competitive examination. The State of Texas has similarly enacted legislation that acknowledges the special status of the mentally retarded by conferring certain rights upon them, such as "the right to live in the least restrictive setting appropriate to [their] individual needs and abilities," including "the right to live . . . in a group home."

Such legislation thus singling out the retarded for special treatment reflects the real and undeniable differences between the retarded and others. That a civilized and decent society expects and approves such legislation indicates that governmental consideration of those differences in the vast majority of situations is not only legitimate but desirable. It may be, as CLC contends, that legislation designed to benefit, rather than disadvantage, the retarded would generally withstand examination under a test of heightened scrutiny. The relevant inquiry, however, is whether heightened scrutiny is constitutionally mandated in the first instance. Even assuming that many of these laws could be shown to be substantially related to an important governmental purpose, merely requiring the legislature to justify its efforts in these terms may lead it to refrain from acting at all. Much recent legislation intended to benefit the retarded also assumes the need for measures that might be perceived to disadvantage them. . . . Especially given the wide variation in the abilities and needs of the retarded themselves, governmental bodies must have a certain amount of flexibility and freedom from judicial oversight in shaping and limiting their remedial efforts.

Third, the legislative response . . . negates any claim that the mentally retarded are politically powerless in the sense that they have no ability to attract the attention of the lawmakers. Any minority can be said to be powerless to assert direct control over the legislature, but if that were a criterion for higher level scrutiny by the courts, much economic and social legislation would now be suspect.

Fourth, if the large and amorphous class of the mentally retarded were deemed quasi-suspect . . . , it would be difficult to find a principled way to distinguish a variety of other groups who have perhaps immutable disabilities setting them off from others, who cannot themselves mandate the desired legislative responses, and who can claim some degree of prejudice from at least part of the public at large. One need mention in this respect only the aging, the disabled, the mentally ill, and the infirm. We are reluctant to set out on that course, and we decline to do so.

Doubtless, there have been and there will continue to be instances of discrimination against the retarded that are in fact invidious, and that are properly subject to judicial correction under constitutional norms. But the appropriate method of reaching such instances is not to create a new quasi-suspect classification and subject all governmental action based on that classification to more searching evaluation. Rather, we should look to the likelihood that governmental action premised on a particular classification is valid as a general matter, not merely to the specifics of the case before us. Because mental retardation is a characteristic that the government may legitimately take into account in a wide range of decisions, and because both state and federal governments have recently committed themselves to assisting the retarded, we will not presume that any given legislative action, even one that disadvantages retarded individuals, is rooted in considerations that the Constitution will not tolerate.

Our refusal to recognize the retarded as a quasi-suspect class does not leave them entirely unprotected from invidious discrimination. To withstand equal protection review, legislation that distinguishes between the mentally retarded and others must be rationally related to a legitimate governmental purpose. This standard, we believe, affords government the latitude necessary both to pursue policies designed to assist the retarded in realizing their full potential, and to freely and efficiently engage in activities that burden the retarded in what is essentially an incidental manner. The State may not rely on a classification whose relationship to an asserted goal is so attenuated as to render the distinction arbitrary or irrational. See Zobel v. Williams (1982); United States Department of Agriculture v. Moreno (1973). Furthermore, some objectives—such as "a bare . . . desire to harm a politically unpopular group," *Moreno*—are not legitimate state interests. Beyond that, the mentally retarded, like others, have and retain their substantive constitutional rights in addition to the right to be treated equally by the law.

IV

We turn to the issue of the validity of the zoning ordinance insofar as it requires a special use permit for homes for the mentally retarded. We inquire first whether requiring a special use permit for the Featherston home in the circumstances here deprives respondents of the equal protection of the laws. If it does, there will be no occasion to decide whether the special use permit provision is facially invalid where the mentally retarded are involved, or to put it another way, whether the city may never insist on a special use permit for a home for the mentally retarded in an R–3 zone. This is the preferred course of adjudication since it enables courts to avoid making unnecessarily broad constitutional judgments. . . .

The constitutional issue is clearly posed. . . . May the city require the permit for this facility when other care and multiple dwelling facilities are freely permitted?

It is true . . . that the mentally retarded as a group are indeed different from others not sharing their misfortune. . . . But this difference is largely irrelevant unless the Featherston home and those who would occupy it would threaten legitimate interests of the city in a way that other permitted uses such as boarding houses and hospitals would not. [In] our view the record does not reveal any rational basis for believing that the Featherston home would pose any special threat to the city's legitimate interests. . . .

The District Court found that the City Council's insistence on the permit rested on several factors. First, the Council was concerned with the negative attitude of the majority of property owners located within 200 feet of the Featherston facility, as well as with the fears of elderly residents of the neighborhood. But mere negative attitudes, or fear, unsubstantiated by factors which are properly cognizable in a zoning proceeding, are not permissible bases for treating a home for the mentally retarded differently from apartment houses, multiple dwellings, and the like. It is plain that the electorate as a whole, whether by referendum or otherwise, could not order city action violative of the Equal Protection Clause, Lucas v. Forty-Fourth General Assembly of Colorado (1964), and the City may not avoid the strictures of that Clause by deferring to the wishes or objections of some fraction of the body politic. "Private biases may be outside the reach of the law, but the law cannot, directly or indirectly, give them effect." Palmore v. Sidoti (1984).

Second, the Council had two objections to the location of the facility. It was concerned that the facility was across the street from a junior high school, and it feared that the students might harass the occupants of the Featherston home. But the school itself is attended by about 30 mentally retarded students, and denying a permit based on such vague, undifferentiated fears is again permitting some portion of the community to validate what would otherwise be an equal protection violation. The other objection to the home's location was that it was located on "a five hundred year flood plain." This concern with the possibility of a flood, however, can hardly be based on a distinction between the Featherston home and, for example, nursing homes, homes for convalescents or the aged, or sanitariums or hospitals, any of which could be located on the Featherston site without obtaining a special use permit. The same may be said of another concern of the Council— doubts about the legal responsibility for actions which the mentally retarded might take. . . .

Fourth, the Council was concerned with the size of the home and the number of people that would occupy it. . . . [But] there would be no restrictions on the number of people who could occupy this home as a boarding house, nursing home, family dwelling, fraternity house, or dormitory. The question is whether it is rational to treat the mentally retarded differently. It is true that they suffer disability not shared by others; but why this difference warrants a density regulation that others need not observe is not at all apparent. . . .

In the courts below the city also urged that the ordinance is aimed at avoiding concentration of population and at lessening congestion of the streets. These concerns [and] . . . the expressed worry about fire hazards, the serenity of the neighborhood, and the avoidance of danger to other residents fail rationally to justify singling out a home such as 201 Featherston for the special use permit, yet imposing no such restrictions on the many other uses freely permitted in the neighborhood.

The short of it is that requiring the permit in this case appears to us to rest on an irrational prejudice against the mentally retarded.

. . .

The judgment of the Court of Appeals is affirmed insofar as it invalidates the zoning ordinance as applied to the Featherston home. The judgment is otherwise vacated.

It is so ordered.

Mr. Justice **STEVENS**, with whom The Chief Justice [**BURGER**] joins, concurring.

The Court of Appeals disposed of this case as if a critical question to be decided were which of three clearly defined standards of equal protection review should be applied to a legislative classification discriminating against the mentally retarded. In fact, our cases have not delineated three—or even one or two—such well defined standards.[1] Rather, our cases reflect a continuum of judgmental responses to differing classifications which have been explained in opinions by terms ranging from "strict scrutiny" at one extreme to "rational basis" at the other. I have never been persuaded that these so called "standards" adequately explain the decisional process.[2] Cases involving classifications based on alienage, illegal residency, illegitimacy, gender, age, or . . . mental retardation, do not fit well into sharply defined classifications.

. . . In my own approach to these cases, I have always asked myself whether I could find a "rational basis" for the classification at issue. The term "rational," of course, includes a requirement that an impartial lawmaker could logically believe that the classification would serve a legitimate public purpose that transcends the harm to the members of the disadvantaged class. Thus, the word "rational"—for me at least—includes elements of legitimacy and neutrality that must always characterize the performance of the sovereign's duty to govern impartially.

The rational basis test, properly understood, adequately explains why a law that deprives a person of the right to vote because his skin has a different pigmentation than that of other voters violates the Equal Protection Clause. It would be utterly irrational to limit the franchise on the basis of height or weight; it is equally invalid to limit it on the basis of skin color. None of these attributes has any bearing at all on the citizen's willingness or ability to exercise that civil right. We do not need to apply a special standard, or to apply "strict scrutiny," or even "heightened scrutiny," to decide such cases.

---

1. In United States Railroad Retirement Board v. Fritz (1980), after citing 11 cases applying the rational basis standard, the Court stated: "The most arrogant legal scholar would not claim that all of these cases applied a uniform or consistent test under equal protection principles." [Footnote by the Justice Stevens.]

2. Cf. San Antonio v. Rodriguez (1973) (Marshall, J., dissenting, joined by Douglas, J.) (criticizing "the Court's rigidified approach to equal protection analysis"). [Footnote by Justice Stevens.]

In every equal protection case, we have to ask certain basic questions. What class is harmed by the legislation, and has it been subjected to a "tradition of disfavor" by our laws? What is the public purpose that is being served by the law? What is the characteristic of the disadvantaged class that justifies the disparate treatment? In most cases the answer to these questions will tell us whether the statute has a "rational basis." The answers will result in the virtually automatic invalidation of racial classifications and in the validation of most economic classifications, but they will provide differing results in cases involving classifications based on alienage, gender, or illegitimacy. But that is not because we apply an "intermediate standard of review" in these cases; rather it is because the characteristics of these groups are sometimes relevant and sometimes irrelevant to a valid public purpose, or, more specifically, to the purpose that the challenged laws purportedly intended to serve.

Every law that places the mentally retarded in a special class is not presumptively irrational. The differences between mentally retarded persons and those with greater mental capacity are obviously relevant to certain legislative decisions. . . .

. . . The record convinces me that this permit was required because of the irrational fears of neighboring property owners, rather than for the protection of the mentally retarded persons who would reside in respondent's home.

. . . I cannot believe that a rational member of this disadvantaged class could ever approve of the discriminatory application of the city's ordinance in this case.

Accordingly, I join the opinion of the Court.

Mr. Justice **MARSHALL**, with whom Mr. Justice **BRENNAN** and Mr. Justice **BLACKMUN** join, concurring in the judgment in part and dissenting in part.

The Court holds that all retarded individuals cannot be grouped together as the "feebleminded" and deemed presumptively unfit to live in a community. Underlying this holding is the principle that mental retardation *per se* cannot be a proxy for depriving retarded people of their rights and interests without regard to variations in individual ability. With this holding and principle I agree. The equal protection clause requires attention to the capacities and needs of retarded people as individuals.

. . . Because I dissent from [the Court's] novel and truncated remedy, and because I cannot accept [its] disclaimer that no "more exacting standard" than ordinary rational basis review is being applied, I write separately.

I

. . . [T]he Court's heightened scrutiny discussion is . . . puzzling given that Cleburne's ordinance is invalidated only after being subjected to precisely the sort of probing inquiry associated with heightened scrutiny. To be sure, the Court does not label its handiwork heightened scrutiny, and perhaps the method employed must hereafter be called "second order" rational basis review rather than "heightened scrutiny." But however labelled, the rational basis test invoked today is most assuredly not the rational basis test of Williamson v. Lee Optical (1955) and [its] progeny. . . .

The refusal to acknowledge that something more than minimum rationality review is at work here is . . . unfortunate in at least two respects. The suggestion that the traditional rational basis test allows this sort of searching inquiry creates precedent for this Court and lower courts to subject economic and commercial classifications to similar and searching "ordinary" rational basis review—a small and regrettable step back toward the days of Lochner v. New York (1905). Moreover, by failing to articulate the factors that justify today's "second order" rational basis review, the Court provides no principled foundation for determining when more searching inquiry is to be invoked. . . .

II

I have long believed the level of scrutiny employed in an equal protection case should vary with "the constitutional and societal importance of the interest adversely affected and the recognized invidiousness of the basis upon which the particular classification is drawn." San Antonio v. Rodriguez (1973) (Marshall, J., dissenting). See also Plyler v. Doe (1982) (Marshall, J., concurring); Dandridge v. Williams (1970) (Marshall, J., dissenting). When a zoning ordinance works to exclude the retarded from all residential districts in a community, these two considerations require that the ordinance be convincingly justified as substantially furthering legitimate and important purposes. . . .

[An extended application of this framework led Marshall to conclude that] Cleburne's vague generalizations for classifying the "feeble minded" with drug addicts, alcoholics, and the insane, and excluding them where the elderly, the ill, the boarder, and the transient are allowed, are not substantial or important enough to overcome the suspicion that the ordinance rests on impermissible assumptions or outmoded and perhaps invidious stereotypes.

III

. . . [T]he Court offers several justifications as to why the retarded do not warrant heightened judicial solicitude. These justifications, however, find no support in our heightened scrutiny precedents and cannot withstand logical analysis.

. . . First, heightened scrutiny is said to be inapplicable where *individuals* in a group have distinguishing characteristics that legislatures properly may take into account in some circumstances. [It] is also purportedly inappropriate when many legislative classifications affecting the *group* are likely to be valid. . . .

Our . . . precedents belie the claim that a characteristic must virtually always be irrelevant to warrant heightened scrutiny. . . . Heightened but not strict scrutiny is considered appropriate in areas such as gender, illegitimacy, or alienage because the Court views the trait as relevant under some circumstances but not others. That view—indeed the very concept of heightened, as opposed to strict, scrutiny—is flatly inconsistent with the notion that heightened scrutiny should not apply to the retarded because "mental retardation is a characteristic that the government may legitimately take into account in a wide range of decisions." Because the government also may not take this characteristic into account in many circumstances, such as those presented here, careful review is required to separate the permissible from the invalid in classifications relying on retardation. . . .

Potentially discriminatory classifications exist only where some constitutional basis can be found for presuming that equal rights are required. Discrimination, in the Fourteenth Amendment sense, connotes a substantive constitutional judgment that two individuals or groups are entitled to be treated equally with respect to some thing. With regard to economic and commercial matters, no basis for such a conclusion exists, for as Justice Holmes urged the *Lochner* Court, the Fourteenth Amendment was not "intended to embody a particular economic theory. . . ." *Lochner* (Holmes, J., dissenting). As a matter of substantive policy, therefore, government is free to move in any direction, or to change directions, in the economic and commercial sphere. The structure of economic and commercial life is a matter of political compromise, not constitutional principle, and no norm of equality requires that there be as many opticians as optometrists, see *Williamson,* or new businesses as old, see New Orleans v. Dukes [1976].

But the Fourteenth Amendment does prohibit other results under virtually all circumstances, such as castes created by law along racial or ethnic lines, and significantly constrains the range of permissible government choices where gender or illegitimacy, for example, are concerned. Where such constraints . . . are present, and where history teaches they have systemically been ignored, a "more searching judicial inquiry" is required. United States v. Carolene Products Co. n. 4 (1938).

That more searching inquiry, be it called heightened scrutiny or "second order" rational basis review, is a method of approaching certain classifications skeptically, with judgment suspended until the facts are in and the evidence considered. . . . Heightened scrutiny does not allow courts to second guess reasoned legislative or professional judgments tailored to the unique needs of a group like the retarded, but it does seek to assure that the hostility or thoughtlessness with which there is reason to be concerned has not carried the day. . . .[1]

1. No single talisman can define those groups likely to be the target of classifications offensive to the Fourteenth Amendment and therefore warranting heightened or strict scrutiny; experience, not abstract logic, must be the primary guide. The "political powerlessness" of a group may be relevant, *Rodriguez,* but that factor is neither necessary, as the gender cases demonstrate, nor sufficient, as the example of minors

IV

In light of the scrutiny that should be applied here, Cleburne's ordinance sweeps too broadly to dispel the suspicion that it rests on a bare desire to treat the retarded as outsiders, pariahs who do not belong in the community. The Court, while disclaiming that special scrutiny is necessary or warranted, reaches the same conclusion. Rather than striking the ordinance down, however, the Court invalidates it merely as applied to respondents. I must dissent from the novel proposition that "the preferred course of adjudication" is to leave standing a legislative act resting on "irrational prejudice," thereby forcing individuals in the group discriminated against to continue to run the act's gauntlet.

The Court appears to act out of a belief that the ordinance might be "rational" as applied to some subgroup of the retarded under some circumstances, such as those utterly without the capacity to live in a community, and that the ordinance should not be invalidated *in toto* if it is capable of ever being validly applied. But the issue is not "whether the city may never insist on a special use permit for the mentally retarded in an R–3 zone." The issue is whether the city may require a permit pursuant to a blunderbuss ordinance drafted many years ago to exclude all the "feeble-minded," or whether the city must enact a new ordinance carefully tailored to the exclusion of some well defined subgroup of retarded people in circumstances in which exclusion might reasonably further legitimate city purposes.

. . . [T]he Court's as-applied remedy relegates future retarded applicants to the standardless discretion of low-level officials who have already shown an all too willing readiness to be captured by the "vague, undifferentiated fears" of ignorant or frightened residents.

Invalidating on its face the ordinance's special treatment of the "feebleminded," in contrast, would place the responsibility for tailoring

---

illustrates. . . . Similarly, immutability of the trait at issue may be relevant, but many immutable characteristics, such as height or blindness, are valid bases of governmental action and classifications under a variety of circumstances.

The political powerlessness of a group and the immutability of its defining trait are relevant insofar as they point to a social and cultural isolation that gives the majority little reason to respect or be concerned with that group's interests and needs. Statutes discriminating against the young have not been common nor need be feared because those who do vote and legislate were once themselves young, typically have children of their own, and certainly interact regularly with minors. Their social integration means that minors, unlike discrete and insular minorities, tend to be treated in legislative arenas with full concern and respect, despite their formal and complete exclusion from the electoral process.

The discreteness and insularity warranting a "more searching judicial inquiry," *Carolene Products*, must therefore be viewed from a social and cultural perspective as well as a political one. To this task judges are well suited, for the lessons of history and experience are surely the best guide as to when, and with respect to what interests, society is likely to stigmatize individuals as members of an inferior caste or view them as not belonging to the community. Because prejudice spawns prejudice, and stereotypes produce limitations that confirm the stereotype on which they are based, a history of unequal treatment requires sensitivity to the prospect that its vestiges endure. In separating those groups that are discrete and insular from those that are not, as in many important legal distinctions, "a page of history is worth a volume of logic." New York Trust Co. v. Eisner (1921) (Holmes, J.). [Footnote by Justice Marshall.]

and updating Cleburne's unconstitutional ordinance where it belongs: with the legislative arm of the City of Cleburne. . . . [T]he city should not be allowed to keep its ordinance on the books intact and thereby shift to the courts the responsibility to confront the complex empirical and policy questions involved in updating statutes affecting the mentally retarded. A legislative solution would yield standards and provide the sort of certainty to retarded applicants and administrative officials that case-by-case judicial rulings cannot provide. Retarded applicants should not have to continue to attempt to surmount Cleburne's vastly overbroad ordinance. . . .

To my knowledge, the Court has never before treated an equal protection challenge to a statute on an as applied basis. When statutes rest on impermissibly overbroad generalizations, our cases have invalidated the presumption on its face. We do not instead leave to the courts the task of redrafting the statute through an ongoing and cumbersome process of "as applied" constitutional rulings. . . . When a presumption is unconstitutionally overbroad, the preferred course of adjudication is to strike it down. . . .

Editors' Notes

(1) **Query:** Does *Cleburne* move beyond *Plyler* in articulating a standard of "rationality with bite"? Is Marshall correct in suggesting that the Court is in fact only using a "second order rational basis" standard that amounts to heightened or intermediate scrutiny? Are his fears that the Court may have taken "a small and regrettable step back toward the days of *Lochner*" [v. New York (1905; reprinted below, p. 975)] justified?

(2) **Query:** Does Stevens' opinion here further develop or merely reiterate his argument in Craig v. Boren (1976; reprinted above, p. 844)? What is the difference between Stevens' conception of the proper single standard and Marshall's notion of a spectrum of standards? If they differ, which is more defensible as a coherent jurisprudence?

(3) **Query:** To what extent do *Plyler* and *Cleburne* represent efforts to cope simultaneously with questions of WHO and HOW?

E

Discovering Fundamental Rights

Building on the general discussion in Chapter 8 of HOW to interpret the Constitution, Section C of this Part of the book examined a theory of representative democracy as providing a purposive *mode* of constitutional interpretation. Section D took up a second such *mode,* equality of citizenship, a concern that democratic and constitutional theory to some extent, though perhaps for different reasons, share. Now we move to a purposive *mode* lying at the heart of constitutionalism, called "fundamental rights."[1]

I. FUNDAMENTAL RIGHTS AS A PURPOSIVE MODE

A. The Interpretive Standards of Fundamental Rights

For fundamental rights, a valid policy must meet not only the procedural rules demanded by representative democracy—that is, be the product of free and open political processes—it must also meet substantive standards. Essentially, it must respect individual rights as explicitly and implicitly guaranteed by the Constitution. And here the concept "constitution" includes more than the black letter of the document. The touchstone for the legitimacy of a public policy is its respect for the individual's "liberty," "autonomy," and "dignity."

The connection between fundamental rights and constitutionalism is both direct and obvious. As we saw in Chapter 2, however, a "pure constitutionalist" is much more rare than a "pure representative democrat." Constitutional democrats, however, are numerous. These interpreters share much of the concern of representative democrats for open political processes and broad-based political participation. They also share with constitutionalists deep concern for fundamental rights and a broad definition of "the constitution." Because they are heavily represented among commentators, judges, and other public officials, we shall pit the arguments of constitutional democrats

---

1. Much of the literature of constitutional interpretation uses "fundamental rights" and "fundamental values" interchangeably; see, for example, John Hart Ely, *Democracy and Distrust* (Cambridge, Mass.: Harvard University Press, 1980), chap. 3. But the first term is narrower than the second, since rights might be only specific reflections of more abstract values and not all values need be associated with rights. For the sake of clarity, we shall maintain a distinction between the two concepts. The chapters in this Section focus on "fundamental rights"; when we refer to "fundamental values" we shall be speaking more abstractly.

rather than of pure constitutionalists against the opponents of fundamental rights.

B.   Criticisms of the *Mode*

The initial and most critical problem with this interpretive *mode*
lies in the fuzziness of its rules of recognition.   How does an
interpreter discover "fundamental rights"?   And how does he or she
justify (validate) their status as "fundamental"?   Literalists, positivists,
and democratic theorists do not necessarily deny that certain rights are
fundamental;   their usual justification is that the plain words of the
document single some rights out, as, for example, the First Amendment does freedom of religion.   As an interpretive *mode,* however,
fundamental rights does not limit itself to the document's words.   As
Edward S. Corwin summed up the argument, "These rights are not
fundamental because they find mention in the written instrument;
they find mention there because they are fundamental." [2]

Although heavily dependent on constitutionalist theory, fundamental rights also rests in part on the words of the document,
especially those of the Ninth Amendment, "The enumeration in the
Constitution, of certain rights, shall not be construed to deny or
disparage others retained by the people," and of the Fifth and
Fourteenth amendments' protecting "life, liberty, and property"
against government's acting "without due process of law."

But these clauses are as open-ended as the guarantee of equal
protection.   Their interpretation demands a degree of judgment and
discretion that democratic theorists and even some constitutional
democrats would reserve to elected officials.   Thus the in-
determinacy of fundamental rights generates problems of WHO shall
interpret as well as HOW to interpret.   Beyond worry that wrong
decisions will be made about which rights to protect and which not to
protect, is concern that the wrong officials will make those inevitably
controversial and consequential determinations and interfere with the
execution of the people's will as expressed at the ballot box.   The fear
is that of judicial power running amok.   And, as we have several times
mentioned in referring to the period 1890–1937 and Chapter 15 will
explain in detail, that fear is not the product of paranoid imaginations.

For most of half a century, judges saw the right to acquire, use,
and dispose of property, including the "property" one has in his or
her own labor, as *the* fundamental right and read the economic theory
of laissez faire into the Constitution.   For much of that era, judicial
supremacy was a reality, and substantive due process was its most
powerful instrument.   As we have noted before, the word "process"
refers to procedure; thus "due process" meant normal legal procedure.   Substantive due process, on the other hand, holds that some
forms of liberty are so fundamental that government may not abridge

---

2. "The Basic Doctrine of American Constitutional Law," reprinted in Alpheus Thomas
Mason and Gerald Garvey, eds., *American Constitutional History: Essays by Edward S. Corwin* (New
York: Harper & Row, 1964), p. 26 (originally published in 12 *Mich.L.Rev.* 247 [1914]).

them by any process (procedure) whatever. It makes the clauses in the Fifth and Fourteenth amendments forbidding the federal or state governments to deprive any person of "life, liberty or property, without due process of law" read:

> Neither the state nor the federal government may take away certain liberties no matter what procedures are used.

Substantive due process, as John Hart Ely has remarked, "is a contradiction in terms—sort of like 'green pastel redness.' . . . By the same token, 'procedural due process' is redundant." [3] But the justices, having refused in the Slaughter-House Cases (1873; reprinted above, p. 435) to infer much of significance from the privileges or immunities clause of the Fourteenth Amendment, needed some tie to the constitutional document to protect what they thought were fundamental rights against state infractions. And they chose the due process clause. Constitutional interpretation seems stuck with the concept.

Since 1937 and more particularly since *Carolene Products* (1938; reprinted above, p. 482), the Court has turned its attention to rights other than those to property and freedom of contract. Section C of this book analyzed the rights to participate freely in open political processes that Stone included in paragraph 2 of footnote 4 of *Carolene Products,* and Section D those to equal treatment he included under paragraph 3. This Section treats those rights arguably included in paragraph 1. Each of those rights is no less consequential than property for the political system, and each is no less controversial.

Dissenting in *Griswold* against the Court's reading a right to privacy into the Constitution, Justice Black expressed the basic objection to using the due process clause to employ fundamental rights as a *mode* of interpretation:

> The due process argument . . . is based . . . on the premise that this Court is vested with power to invalidate all state laws that it considers to be arbitrary, capricious, unreasonable, or oppressive, or this Court's belief that a particular state law has no "rational or justifying" purpose, or is offensive to a "sense of fairness and justice." If these formulas based on "natural justice," or others which mean the same thing, are to prevail, they require judges to determine what is or is not constitutional on the basis of their own appraisal of what laws are unwise or unnecessary. The power to make such decisions is of course that of a legislative body.

Ely echoes Black's assertions and says more generally that, as an interpretive *mode,* fundamental rights means little more than the imposition of judges' personal values: "the fact that it's done with mirrors shouldn't count as a defense." [4]

---

3. Ely, supra note 1, p. 16.

4. Ibid., p. 70.

C. The Defenders Reply: The Judges

This objection points to a flaw that representative democrats, constitutional democrats, and constitutionalists alike would deem fatal, for the rule of law is not the rule of whim, whether executive, legislative, or judicial. But the response of interpreters who favor fundamental rights is that the objection is invalid; this *mode* does not leave judges free to impose their personal values, or at least any more free than do other interpretive *modes*.

Arguments supporting this reply have varied in intellectual power. Justice Cardozo spoke of grounding notions of fundamentality in the "traditions and [collective] conscience of our people"[5] and in "the very essence of a scheme of ordered liberty."[6] Felix Frankfurter thought that judicial choices, if "deeply rooted in reason," were effectively bounded by "the deposit of history," "the traditions and conscience of our people," and the "decencies of civilized conduct," all of which could be discovered by a "disinterested inquiry pursued in the spirit of science, on a balanced order of facts exactly and fairly stated, on the detached consideration of conflicting claims."[7] Earl Warren's comment about the standards of "cruel and unusual punishments" was part of his concept of fundamental rights as reflections of "the evolving standards of decency that mark the progress of a maturing society."[8]

In his dissenting opinion in Poe v. Ullman (1961; reprinted above, p. 106), John Marshall Harlan, II, tried his hand at explaining how judges translated "due process" into substantive fundamental rights:

> The best that can be said is that, through the course of this Court's decisions, [due process] has represented the balance which our Nation, built upon postulates of respect for the liberty of the individual, has struck between that liberty and the demands of organized society. If the supplying of content to this Constitutional concept has of necessity been a rational process, it certainly has not been one where judges have felt free to roam where unguided speculation might take them. The balance of which I speak is the balance struck by this country, having regard to what history teaches are the traditions from which it developed as well as the traditions from which it broke. . . . No formula could serve as a substitute, in this area, for judgment and restraint.

In Rochin v. California (1952; reprinted above, p. 100), Douglas joined Black in condemning "the accordion-like qualities" of substantive due process in particular and the fundamental rights *mode* (which Black misconstrued as a form of natural law) in general. Later,

---

5. Snyder v. Massachusetts (1934).

6. Palko v. Connecticut (1937; reprinted above, p. 94).

7. Rochin v. California (1952; reprinted above, p. 100).

8. Trop v. Dulles (1958; reprinted above, p. 144).

however, Douglas, to Black's dismay, became a convert to fundamental rights, though he tried to anchor decisions in the document and to do so in clauses other than due process. In *Griswold,* for example, he used textual structuralism to find a right of privacy in the "penumbra" of the First, Third, Fourth, and Ninth amendments as well as in self-incrimination clause of the Fifth.

Justice Goldberg's interpretive strategy was different. Concurring in *Griswold,* he agreed that "the concept of liberty protects those personal rights that are fundamental, and is not confined to the specific terms of the Bill of Rights." His principal textual grounding was the Ninth Amendment, whose "language and history," he claimed, "reveal that the Framers . . . believed that there are additional fundamental rights, protected from governmental infringement, which exist alongside those fundamental rights specifically mentioned in the first eight amendments." But, he added, he did not view that amendment as

> an independent source of rights protected from infringement by either the States or the Federal Government. Rather, the Ninth Amendment . . . simply shows the intent of the Constitution's authors that other fundamental personal rights should not be denied such protection or disparaged in any other way simply because they are not specifically listed. . . .

This usage is novel, but how it solves the problem of judicial discretion is not obvious, unless it is to claim that the framers meant judges to have discretion.

Thurgood Marshall has also tried to find textual moorings firmer than due process for unlisted fundamental rights. As he explained in his dissent in San Antonio v. Rodriguez (1973; reprinted above, p. 858):

> The task in every case should be to determine the extent to which constitutionally guaranteed rights are dependent upon interests not mentioned in the Constitution. As the nexus between the specific constitutional guarantee and the nonconstitutional interest draws closer, the nonconstitutional interest becomes more fundamental and the degree of judicial scrutiny applied . . . must be adjusted accordingly.

D. The Defenders Reply: The Commentators

Constitutional commentators offer a different and somewhat broader set of responses. On the one hand, they point out that alternative *modes* of interpretation suffer from similar problems of indeterminancy. Textual analysis solves some but hardly all problems and if anything supports fundamental rights as an interpretive *mode.* The plain words of the Ninth Amendment specifically say that the listing of some rights does not put others on a lower plane. Thus literalists face a cruel dilemma: The document tells them to look beyond the document. It is no accident, proponents of fundamental rights chortle, that many literalists ignore the plain words of the Ninth Amendment. Hugo Black, for instance, dismissed it as "a recent discovery" even though it had been in the constitutional document for 173 years.

John Hart Ely is more subtle in trying to outflank the Ninth Amendment. Addressing the WHO interrogative, he claims it is not directed toward judges but toward elected officials. Why its plain words deflect it from judicial concern any more than other clauses of the Bill of Rights, especially the First, which begins "Congress shall make no law," is something Ely finds it difficult to explain. What he does explain very convincingly, however, is that excluding the Ninth Amendment from the judicial ambit enables a theory of democracy to fit the Constitution more closely and so supports reinforcing representative democracy as *the* proper interpretative *mode*. But this argument, proponents of fundamental rights retort, reasons that because the analytical model does not fit reality, it is reality and not the model that is wrong.

Historical analysis, insofar as it quests for intent of the framers, fails on its own terms for it seeks a collective state of mind that may well not have existed and in any event is beyond our power to recapture; insofar as it looks at development over time, it is much more likely to find several patterns among which interpreters must choose than to discover a single bright thread. Structural analysis is often useful but it, too, requires wide discretion, as does prudential analysis. Like historical analysis, doctrinal analysis will probably produce a variety of models from which an interpreter must select.

As we have seen in the chapters in Section C, reinforcing representative democracy also requires an interpreter to make important choices, not least of which is to read democratic theory into the Constitution. Indeed, Laurence H. Tribe argues that that interpretive *mode* is merely a particular aspect of a fundamental values *mode* (as is fundamental rights): An interpreter chooses self-government through political participation as *the* fundamental value of the polity and proceeds from there.[9]

More positively, proponents of fundamental rights assert that the Constitution is based on two political theories, constitutionalism as well as democracy, and the interpretive *mode* of fundamental rights is necessary to understanding and construing the document as well as the larger constitution.

However one evaluates these arguments and counterarguments, it is essential to recognize that interpretation inevitably involves judgment and judgment inevitably brings power to whoever possesses it. Proponents of fundamental rights are correct to underline the wide range of discretion that the other interpretive *modes* require, but

---

9. "The Puzzling Persistence of Process-Based Constitutional Theories," 89 *Yale L.J.* 1063 (1980); reprinted as chap. 2 to his *Constitutional Choices* (Cambridge, Mass.: Harvard University Press, 1985).

reading constitutionalist theory into the Constitution represents just as great—democratic theorists would say greater—discretion as reading democratic theory into the Constitution.

II. THE PLAN OF CHAPTERS 15–17

The most logical way to analyze fundamental rights as a *mode* of constitutional interpretation would seem to be to start with the plain words of the constitutional document and analyze the fate of a fundamental right such as freedom of religion, then proceed outward to less textually entrenched rights such as property, to those "implicit" in the document and claiming beatification by tradition, such as marriage, and ultimately to those, such as privacy, that some interpreters believe constitutionalism requires. Unfortunately, American constitutional development has not proceeded so logically. In deciding the first cases—see, for example, Calder v. Bull (1798; reprinted above, p. 86)—judges immediately leaped beyond the text to theories of constitutionalism and notions of natural law and natural rights. The Court abandoned that approach in the second decade of the nineteenth century, just as, more slowly and less completely, it withdrew from open use of fundamental rights.

When, near the end of the century, the Court returned to problems of fundamental rights, both the justices and commentators couched analyses largely in terms of property or of putative liberties, such as freedom of contract, closely connected to property. The core problem was individual liberty and autonomy but the context was property—how much control over an individual's economic freedom, even to work for starvation wages, could government exert without infringing, even in the name of benevolence, the autonomy that constitutionalism says is the goal of the state?

Because many current concepts and much juridical vocabulary of fundamental rights developed in the battle over property, economic liberty, and due process of law—as did many of the scars that still mark the Supreme Court's institutional psyche—understanding past struggles over economic rights is essential to understanding more recent struggles about fundamental rights outside the economic sphere. Thus this Section begins with a chapter that focuses on the problems generated for constitutional interpretation when property is—or is not—held to be a fundamental right. Only then does Chapter 16 proceed to a more textually secure right, that to freedom of religion. Last, Chapter 17 takes up a set of claims to rights relating to privacy and personal liberty, most of which are at least as strongly based in visions of the polity's transcendent structure and underlying political theories as in the text of the constitutional document.

SELECTED BIBLIOGRAPHY

Ball, Milner S. *The Promise of American Law* (Athens, Ga.: University of Georgia Press, 1981).

Barber, Sotiorios A. *On What the Constitution Means* (Baltimore: Johns Hopkins University Press, 1984).

Benedict, Michael Les. "To Secure These Rights: Rights, Democracy, and Judicial Review in the Anglo-American Constitutional Heritage," 42 *Ohio St.L.J.* 69 (1982).

Black, Hugo L. *A Constitutional Faith* (New York: Knopf, 1969).

Brest, Paul. "The Fundamental Rights Controversy," 90 *Yale L.J.* 1063 (1981).

————. "Interpretation and Interest," 34 *Stan.L.Rev.* 765 (1982). (a reply to Fiss, listed below.)

Choper, Jesse H. *Judicial Review and the National Political Process* (Chicago: University of Chicago Press, 1980), espec. Chaps. 1–2.

Corwin, Edward S. "The Basic Doctrine of American Constitutional Law," 12 *Mich.L.Rev.* 247 (1914); reprinted in Alpheus Thomas Mason and Gerald Garvey, eds., *American Constitutional History: Essays by Edward S. Corwin* (New York: Harper & Row, 1964).

Ely, John H. *Democracy and Distrust* (Cambridge, Mass.: Harvard University Press, 1980), espec. chap. 3.

Fiss, Owen. "Objectivity and Interpretation," 43 *Stan.L.Rev.* 739 (1982).

Flathman, Richard. *The Practice of Rights* (Cambridge: Cambridge University Press, 1976).

Fleming, James E. "A Critique of John Hart Ely's Quest for the Ultimate Constitutional Interpretivism of Representative Democracy," 80 *Mich.L.Rev.* 634 (1982).

Hazard, Geoffrey C., Jr. "Comment: Commentary on the 'Fundamental Values' Controversy," 90 *Yale L.J.* 1110 (1981). (A comment on Brest, 90 *Yale L.J.* 1063.)

Miller, Arthur S. "Toward a Definition of 'the' Constitution," 8 *U. of Dayton L.Rev.* 633 (1983).

Murphy, Walter F. "Constitutional Interpretation: Text, Values, and Processes," 9 *Reviews in Am. Hist.* 7 (1981).

Parker, Richard D. "The Past of Constitutional Theory—And its Future," 42 *Ohio St.L.J.* 223 (1982).

Pennock, J. Roland, and John W. Chapman, eds. *Constitutionalism* (New York: New York University Press, 1979) (*Nomos,* vol. 20).

————. *Human Rights* (New York: New York University Press, 1979) (*Nomos,* vol. 23).

————. *Liberal Democracy* (New York: New York University Press, 1979) (*Nomos,* vol. 25).

Perry, Michael J. *The Constitution, the Courts, and Human Rights* (New Haven, Conn.: Yale University Press, 1982).

Richards, David A.J. "Moral Philosophy and the Search for Fundamental Values in Constitutional Law," 42 *Ohio St.L.J.* 319 (1982).

Smith, Rogers M. "The Constitution and Autonomy," 60 *Tex.L.Rev.* 175 (1982).

Tribe, Laurence H. "The Puzzling Persistence of Process-Based Constitutional Theories," 89 *Yale L.J.* 1063 (1980); reprinted in *Constitutional Choices* (Cambridge, Mass,: Harvard University Press, 1985).

————. *American Constitutional Law* (Mineola, N.Y.: Foundation Press, 1978), chaps. 11, 14–15.

15

The Right to Property: To Individual Autonomy and Back

As we saw in Chapter 2, the framers of the Constitution believed that legislatures, if checked only by popular election, threatened the institution of private property. Not unnaturally, then, the document that emerged from the Philadelphia Convention was studded with actual and potential limitations on state authority to tax, regulate trade, enact bankruptcy laws, coin money, refuse to recognize legal transactions in other states, and impair the obligation of contracts. The Fifth Amendment later included an additional pair of restrictions on the power of the federal government over property, a ban against depriving persons of rights to property "without due process of law," and a requirement that "just compensation" be paid for private property taken for public use.

A desire to safeguard the goods they had accumulated and expected to accumulate, an acquisitive spirit, and perhaps even greed all pushed the Framers, who were men of money and means, to try to keep government as well as private individuals away from their property. They exemplified as well as believed John Locke's statement in his *Second Treatise of Civil Government* (1690) that the "great and *chief end* " of society "*is the Preservation of their property.*" (Emphasis in original; reprinted below, p. 949.)

I. PROPERTY AS A CIVIL RIGHT

At the outset, we should note three points important to a discussion of property as a fundamental constitutional right. First of all, the word "property" in the seventeenth and eighteenth centuries often—but not always—had a broader meaning than it does today. We speak of property in the sense of tangible goods. Earlier generations could use the word to encompass much more. For Locke, property primarily referred to a man's right "in his own person" to use his labor as he saw fit. In his *Second Treatise,* he had spoken of men uniting to form civil society for "the mutual *preservation* of their Lives, Liberties and Estates, which I call by the general name, *Property.*" (Reprinted below, p. 949.) Even James Madison, who generally used property in the narrower, modern sense, could say that

> a man has a property in his opinions and the free communication of
> them, ... in his religious opinions, and in the profession and

938

> practice dictated by them. . . . In a word, as a man is said to
> have a right to his property, he may be equally said to have a
> property in his rights.[1]

In this broader sense, a right to property is shorthand for an expanse
of personal freedoms that need only be tangentially related, if at all, to
economic activity.

The second point is that, although the situation would soon
change, for America's founding generation *the* tangible productive
property was usually land. The society was basically agricultural, the
population heavily composed of those who worked their own land,
artisans ("mechanics") and shopkeepers who traded with farmers, and
small-scale merchants who bought their crops. All of these people
may have had a few "hired hands," but land was plentiful and cheap,
and the frontier was constantly beckoning. Only in the Plantation
South was there anything like the huge modern factory, where masses
of people worked for an owner. Thus productive property was
something that just about every healthy, male adult could possess and
exploit with his own labor. His relationships with other members of
the community were direct and face to face. In these respects, the
change from eighteenth to twentieth century America is radical.

Third, people then as now recognized that a right to exclusive use
of some tangible property is essential to autonomy, indeed to survival.
Without a minimal amount of food, water, clothing, and medicine, a
human being quickly dies. And to the extent that a person is
dependent on another for the necessities of life, that person is not
autonomous. He or she cannot make independent decisions about
self expression, the religious, social, and economic choices life
presents, or the politics of representative democracy. Franklin
Roosevelt was only speaking ancient wisdom when he said that
"Necessitous men are not free men." [2] In *Federalist* No. 79, Alexander Hamilton had written that *"a power over a man's subsistence amounts
to a power over his will."* (Emphasis in original.) On this point, at
least, Jefferson was in full agreement:

> Dependence begets subservience and venality, suffocates the germ
> of virtue, and prepares fit tools for the designs of ambition. . . .
> The mobs of great cities add just so much strength to the support of
> pure government, as sores do to the strength of the human body. It
> is the manners and spirit of a people which preserve a republic in
> vigour.[3]

A few years earlier, Jefferson had proposed that, to make its people
truly independent, Virginia should give to "every person of full age"

---

1. "Property," *National Gazette,* March 29, 1792; reprinted in Marvin Meyers, ed., *The Mind
of the Founder* (Indianapolis, Ind.: Bobbs-Merrill, 1973), pp. 243–244.

2. Speech of January 11, 1944; quoted in Edward S. Corwin, *Liberty Against Government*
(Baton Rouge, La.: Louisiana State University Press, 1948), p. 4.

3. *Notes on Virginia* (1782), in Andrew A. Lipscomb, ed., *The Writings of Thomas Jefferson*
(Washington, D.C.: The Thomas Jefferson Memorial Association, 1903), II, 229.

enough land to total fifty acres and that women should have a right to inherit equal to men.[4]

Psychological expectations change the content of "necessities" across time and culture. Even Jefferson "came to appreciate the political and economic advantage, if not the virtue, of commerce and urban growth. . . ."[5] And few people in a modern society are likely to be completely autonomous in the sense of having enough land—or knowing what to do with it if they had it—or other resources to be self sufficient. Even so, there is a vast difference between, on the one hand, the impersonal interdependence that middle class American now experiences and, on the other, the abject personal dependence that a factory worker in the 1890s or a share cropper in the 1930s suffered or a migrant agricultural worker or illegal alien suffers in the 1980s, just as there is a vast difference between wanting for cake and wanting for bread.

When the Constitution was drafted, the connection between property and autonomy in the political sphere was more apparent than it is today. Voting then was usually done publicly and orally, and so employers could check on employees and creditors on debtors to ensure that they voted "correctly." The linkage between economic power and individual autonomy remains strong, despite institutional changes and far greater prosperity. And that bond may not merely be negative. In *Federalist* No. 10, Madison described the right to property as arising from "diversity in the faculties of men" and asserted that "protection of those faculties is the first object of government." (Reprinted below, p. 952.) The existence of a strong and positive relation between a right to private property and human productivity remains an important part of the American credo, periodically reinforced by failures of Soviet collectives and by eastern European nations' and mainland China's creepings toward more and more private ownership.

II. THE DEVELOPMENT OF SUBSTANTIVE DUE PROCESS

A. The Transformation of American Law

For the generation of 1787, property was a natural right. And if men were to be able to use their property, they had to have an equal right to makes pledges about their property—to contract. Thus the right to contract was of the same sacredness as the right to property itself, and the obligation to keep one's contracts was a duty required by the natural right to property. Early judicial opinions—for example, those of Marshall and Johnson in Fletcher v. Peck (1810; reprinted below, p. 956)—show just how fundamental many members of that

4. "The Virginia Constitution: Third Draft of Jefferson," Julian P. Boyd, ed., *The Papers of Thomas Jefferson* (Princeton, N.J.: Princeton University Press, 1950), I, 358.

5. Stanley N. Katz, "Thomas Jefferson and the Right to Property in Revolutionary America," 19 *J. of Law and Economics* 467, 487 (1976).

age thought property and contract were. Johnson, for instance, would have held that even the Deity had to respect the obligation of contracts, though the justice did not mention how he would enforce his writ.

By the time of the Charles River Bridge case (1837; reprinted below, p. 960), however, notions of property's functions and to a lesser extent contract's obligations had changed from those of the founding period. Judges were willing to tolerate more state intervention,[6] usually in the interests of new economic groups of merchants and capitalists as opposed to those of farmers and other landholders. "While the rights of private property are safely guarded," Chief Justice Roger Brooke Taney said for the Court, "we must not forget that the community also have rights, and that the happiness and well being of every citizen depends on their faithful preservation."

In fact, Taney was preferring one form of private property over another, not choosing rights of the community over those of the individual. He was presiding over a massive transformation—a shift of which he did not fully approve—from the legal economy of an agricultural society to that of a capitalist nation. Morton J. Horwitz summarizes the changes:

> As the spirit of economic development began to take hold of American society in the early years of the nineteenth century . . . the idea of property underwent a fundamental transformation—from a static agrarian conception entitling an owner to undisturbed enjoyment, to a dynamic, instrumental, and more abstract view of property that emphasized the newly paramount virtues of productive use and development. By the time of the Civil War, the basic change in legal conceptions about property was completed.[7]

Entrepreneurs and merchants allied with lawyers, Horwitz argues, to encourage state intervention to help the new capitalism. On the one hand, these groups persuaded state legislatures to use tax money and public lands to subsidize mills, canals, and railroads. On the other hand, they persuaded legislatures to delegate to them the state's power of eminent domain, the authority to seize private property for "public use." That "public use," of course, would be for "civic improvements" that these entrepreneurs were constructing for their private gain.

---

6. Note, however, that *Dred Scott* (1857) declared the Missouri Compromise, an Act of Congress, unconstitutional because it denied slave holders "substantive due process" in outlawing slavery in some of the territories.

7. *The Transformation of American Law, 1780–1860* (Cambridge, Mass.: Harvard University Press, 1977), p. 31. Horwitz' thesis has not been universally accepted. For sharp critiques, see espec.: A.W.B. Simpson, "The Horwitz Thesis and the History of Contracts," 46 *U.Chi.L.Rev.* 533 (1979); Gary T. Schwartz, "Tort Law and the Economy in Nineteenth Century America: A Reinterpretation," 90 *Yale L.J.* 1717 (1981); Stephen Presser, "Revising the Conservative Tradition," 52 *N.Y.U.L.Rev.* 700 (1977); Tony Freyer, "Reassessing the Impact of Eminent Domain," 1981 *Wisc.L.Rev.* 1263.

B. The Grangers, the ABA, and Social Darwinism

The avarice and ruthlessness of the new alliance caused periodic popular reactions, from Jacksonian democracy through the Grangers, the Populists, the Progressives, and eventually the New Deal.   In part, Chief Justice Taney's defense of states rights was a Jacksonian affirmation of state power—the state police power—to regulate these new corporations.   But the great victory came a dozen years after the Civil War, when in Munn v. Illinois (1877; reprinted below, p. 966) the Grangers won the Court's constitutional approval of state legislative authority to regulate the prices that owners of grain elevators could charge farmers to store their grain.

Munn struck terror into the business alliance by showing how the state power it had so carefully cultivated could be turned against capital.   The counterattack was swift, deadly, and, ironically "conservative" in tone, urging not continuing legal changes but protecting changes effected by the previous generation—in effect, guarding the new status quo.   Among the first moves to counter *Munn* was the founding of the American Bar Association in 1878, an organization that soon became, in Corwin's words, "a juristic sewing circle for mutual education in the gospel of *laissez faire.*" [8]   Blocking all governmental regulation of business may have been its ultimate aim; but the ABA had as its intermediate goal the reversal of *Munn,* and toward those ends began a campaign to "educate" both lawyers and judges.

The times were propitious.   In a series of essays and speeches and his *Social Statics* (1866), Herbert Spencer was preaching a doctrine called "Social Darwinism" that fit well with economic laissez faire and a constitutional right to own, use, and dispose of private property without governmental regulation.   As Darwin taught biological evolution, so Spencer and his followers taught social evolution: If left to themselves, the best of mankind, "the fittest," would survive and prosper.   If government intervened beyond keeping public order and protecting private property, the morally weak would also survive and impede the march of progress.   Life was a dog-eat-dog battle.   The kindest and most efficient course for government was to let the economic struggle be played out on its own terms—that is, those terms that, thanks to the recent transformation of American law, gave legal advantage to business interests over those of labor, railroads over farmers, and bankers over just about everybody.

Spencer was immensely popular and influential in the last quarter of the nineteenth century and well into the twentieth, exercising, Henry Steele Commager says, "such sovereignty over America as George III had never enjoyed." [9]   Other writers, like Charles W. Eliot of Harvard, Nicholas Murray Butler at Columbia, and, most

---

8. Supra note 2, p. 138. Corwin relied heavily on what is still among the most important works on the incorporation of laissez faire into American constitutional law, Benjamin R. Twiss, *Lawyers and the Constitution* (Princeton, N.J.: Princeton University Press, 1942).

9. *The American Mind* (New Haven, Conn.: Yale University Press, 1950), p. 87.

eloquently of all, William Graham Sumner of Yale, lent academic prestige to the spread of Spencer's good news that competition was "a law of nature," the reward of liberty was progress, and the price of mitigating the economic struggle was "the survival of the unfittest" and the destruction of liberty.[10]

More positively, "the Gospel of Wealth" transformed acquisitiveness into civic duty and religious virtue. "[T]he acquisition of property is required by love," Mark Hopkins, president of Williams College, wrote in 1868, "because it is a powerful means of benefitting others." "Godliness is in league with riches," Episcopalian Bishop William Lawrence said at the turn of the century. "Material prosperity is helping to make the national character sweeter, more joyous, more unselfish, more Christlike." Earlier, the Rev. Russell H. Conwell, who was to become president of Temple University, had urged young people "get rich, get rich!" To "make money honestly," he claimed, "is to preach the gospel. . . . Money is power and you ought to be reasonably ambitious to have it. You ought to because you can do more good with it than without it. . . . If you can honestly attain unto riches . . . it is your Christian and godly duty to do so." [11]

There were, of course, dissenting voices who warned that the economic theory of laissez faire was self-serving, the sociology of Social Darwinism fallacious, the theology of wealth a cruel sacrilege, and the effects of all three destructive to the lives of millions of farmers, workers, and their families. And, as we have mentioned, there were occasional counteralliances, like those of the Populists and the Progressives, who managed to dull some of capitalism's harsher edges, but not until the Great Depression of 1929 and the New Deal would wide scale and long term reform succeed.

In the legal sphere, Thomas Cooley's *Treatise on Constitutional Limitations* (1868) and Christopher G. Tiedeman's *Treatise on the Limitations of Police Power in the United States* (1886) were the most influential books of their time. Cooley anticipated the development of property as *the* fundamental constitutional value, liberty as the primary constitutional right, and substantive due process as the instrument for their accomplishment; but Tiedeman "deserves credit for [their] crystalization into a fixed and pervading doctrine." [12]

C. The Judges Respond

The influence on judges developed slowly. The first great victory came in 1885 when the Court held that corporations were

---

10. See the excellent analyses in A.J. Beitzinger, *A History of American Political Thought* (New York: Dodd, Mead, 1972), chap. 19; and Alpheus Thomas Mason and Gordon E. Baker, eds., *Free Government in the Making* (4th ed.; New York: Oxford University Press, 1985), chap. 14.

11. Quoted in Mason and Baker, supra note 10, pp. 522–523.

12. Clyde E. Jacobs, *Law Writers and the Courts* (Berkeley, Cal.: University of California Press, 1954), p. 62.

"persons" protected by the Fourteenth Amendment.[13] In 1890 Chicago, Milwaukee, and St. Paul Ry. v. Minnesota gutted *Munn* by ruling that the fairness of rates that businesses could charge was ultimately a judicial not a legislative question. In 1895, three landmark decisions solidified laissez faire. United States v. E.C. Knight held that the Sherman Antitrust Act could not reach a sugar manufacturer who produced more than 95 per cent of the sugar sold in the United States because manufacturing was local commerce, beyond the scope of congressional power. Pollock v. Farmers' Loan & Trust Co. held the income tax unconstitutional, in spite of precedents as old as 1796[14] and as recent as 1881.[15]

The third case, In re Debs, struck a serious blow at labor unions by ruling that the President could seek an injunction to prevent a railroad strike and that the district judge could summarily punish for contempt of court the labor leader whose union violated the injunction. Later decisions extended the liability of unions under the Sherman Act by holding them liable for triple damages [16] and invalidated both federal and state statutes outlawing so-called "yellow dog" contracts, under which owners obliged workers, as a condition of employment, to pledge not to join a union.[17]

In 1897, Allgeyer v. Louisiana summed up the Court's new jurisprudence, explaining WHAT the Constitution included as well as HOW the judges were interpreting it:

> The liberty mentioned in that [fourteenth] amendment means not only the right of the citizen to be free from the mere physical restraint of his person . . . but the term is deemed to embrace the right of the citizen to be free in the enjoyment of all his faculties; to be free to use them in all lawful ways: to live and work where he will; to earn his livelihood by any lawful calling; to pursue any livelihood or avocation, and for that purpose to enter into all contracts which may be proper, necessary and essential to his carrying out to a successful conclusion the purposes above mentioned.

Of this litany, it was the last right, that of contract, which the Court considered paramount. Interestingly, the list did not mention such freedoms as those of speech, press, and religion. The justices would not begin to protect these until well into the 1920s.

The paradigm case of laissez faire and substantive due process was Lochner v. New York (1905; reprinted below, p. 975), in which the Court by a 5–4 vote held that a state law limiting bakers to no more than a 60-hour work week was "a mere meddlesome interference" with freedom of contract. As we shall see in the head- and endnotes to the cases reprinted in this chapter, the judicial record was not

---

13. Santa Clara County v. South Pacific Rr.

14. Hylton v. United States.

15. Springer v. United States.

16. For example, Loewe v. Lawlor (1908) (the Danbury Hatters' Case).

17. Adair v. United States (1908); Coppage v. Kansas (1915).

uniform during the period 1890–1937, but generally the justices used the due process clause of the Fourteenth Amendment to strike down state regulations of business and the Tenth Amendment to strike down federal regulations.

D. The End of Freedom of Contract

The climax came during the years 1935–36, when a majority of the justices waged full-scale war against the New Deal's efforts to regulate business and labor. As Justice Stone wrote his sister at the close of the 1935 term:

> Our latest exploit was a holding by a divided vote that there was no power in a state to regulate minimum wages for women. Since the court last week said that this could not be done by the national government, as the matter was local, and it is said that it cannot be done by local government even though it is local, we have tied Uncle Sam up in a hard knot.[18]

The knot, of course, did not stay tied. Stinging dissents from Stone and sometimes Brandeis and Cardozo, along with an occasional protest from Charles Evans Hughes, ate at the majority's self-confidence. The crushing blow, however, came from Roosevelt's stunning victory at the polls in November, 1936, winning in every state except Maine and Vermont. "Looking back," Justice Owen J. Roberts commented fifteen years later, "it is difficult to see how the Court could have resisted the popular urge for uniform standards throughout the country—for what in effect was a unified economy." [19]

By early December 1936, the justices began to capitulate. Roberts changed his mind first on the constitutionality of state regulation of wages (see West Coast Hotel v. Parrish [1937; reprinted below, p. 987),[20] then on the reach of the commerce clause,[21] and later on the authority of the federal government to tax in order to regulate.[22] Because these changes began in December, 1936 in the justices' secret

---

18. Quoted in Alpheus Thomas Mason, *Harlan Fiske Stone* (New York: Viking, 1956), p. 426.

19. *The Court and the Constitution* (Cambridge, Mass.: Harvard University Press, 1951), p. 61.

20. In 1936 Roberts provided the fifth vote in Morehead v. New York to invalidate a state law regulating wages and less than a year later the fifth vote in *Parrish* upholding a practically identical law. He left with Frankfurter a memorandum, which Frankfurter later published, trying to explain away his apparent shift. "Mr. Justice Roberts," 104 *U.Pa.L.Rev.* 311 (1955), reprinted in Philip Elman, ed., *Of Law and Men: Papers and Addresses of Felix Frankfurter* (New York: Harcourt, Brace, 1956). For a full length study of Roberts, see Charles A. Leonard, *A Search for a Judicial Philosophy* (Port Washington, N.Y.: Kennikat Press, 1971).

21. During the war against the New Deal, Roberts joined the majority in several cases construing the commerce clause narrowly, most espec. Schecter Poultry Co. v. United States (1935) and Carter v. Carter Coal Co. (1936); in the spring of 1937 he provided the fifth vote for a very broad interpretation of the commerce clause in NLRB v. Jones & Laughlin and also joined even broader interpretations in United States v. Darby Lumber Co. (1941) and Wickard v. Filburn (1942).

22. He wrote the opinion for the Court in United States v. Butler (1935), one of narrowest interpretations of federal taxing power in the Court's history but later joined in broad interpretations and even wrote the opinion in one, Mulford v. Smith (1939).

conferences, months before they were publicly announced, Roosevelt
had no way of knowing that he was winning the war.   In February,
1937, he launched his plan to add one justice to the Court for each
member over 70 who did not retire, up to a maximum number of
fifteen.   Given the advanced age of many of the justices, Roosevelt
would have immediately had six nominations.   Ultimately, the Court-
packing bill failed to pass either house of Congress; but, when the
Court's shift became public that spring, it seemed that the justices had
retreated under fire.   References to the about-face in *West Coast Hotel*
as "the switch in time that saved nine" implied more than an outburst
of judicial prudence.

III. PROPERTY, AUTONOMY, AND CONSTITUTIONAL INTERPRETATION

During the period 1890--1937, a majority of the justices were
typically ready to play the role of guardians of constitutionalism
against the onslaughts of democracy, to discover fundamental rights in
the breadth of "liberty" and the interstices of "due process."   It was
in reaction to the early signs of this role that James Bradley Thayer
had in 1893 created his "doctrine of the clear mistake," (reprinted
above, p. 476), and partially in reaction that a half century later
Harlan F. Stone formulated his famous footnote in *Carolene Products*
(1938; reprinted above, p. 482).   Felix Frankfurter endorsed Thayer's thesis, and Hugo L. Black began insisting on literal interpretation
and, though an ardent civil libertarian, opposed the Court's finding
fundamental rights outside the four corners of the document.

For a time after what Corwin called "the constitutional revolution" of 1937,[23] the justices relegated economic freedoms to a very
low rung on the hierarchy of constitutional values, as we saw in the
cases dealing with equal protection and business interests in Chapter
13 and shall see again in Ferguson v. Skrupa (1963; reprinted below,
p. 995) and Hawaiian Housing Authority v. Midkiff (1984; reprinted
below, p. 997).   Yet the connection between property and autonomy
remains real.   William O. Douglas could argue in 1955 that "no right
is more precious" than the right to earn a living.[24]   Eight years later
he added:

> Man's liberty is, of course, often related to his property rights.
> The home and its privacy are property interests.   Ownership of a
> press is essential to the freedom granted [sic] newspapers,
> magazines, pamphlets, and books.   Ownership of a cathedral or
> church is basic to the exercise of religion by those whose faith
> brings them together in congregations.[25]

23. *Constitutional Revolution, Ltd.* (Claremont, Cal.: Claremont Colleges Press, 1941).

24. Barsky v. Board of Regents (1955).

25. *Anatomy of Liberty* (New York: Trident Press, 1963), p. 87.

In 1972, Justice Stewart noted for the Court:

[T]he dichotomy between personal liberties and property rights is a false one. Property does not have rights. People have rights. The right to enjoy property without unlawful deprivation, no less than the right to speak or the right to travel, is in truth a "personal" right, whether the "property" in question be a welfare check, a home, or a savings account. In fact, a fundamental interdependence exists between the personal right to liberty and the personal right to property. Neither could have meaning without the other.[26]

If, then, the linkage between economic liberty and individual autonomy is close and protecting individual autonomy is one of the two chief goals of constitutionalism, what was the "mistake" in the Court's constitutional interpretation during the period 1890–1937? What are the implications of this linkage for future constitutional interpretation? Some commentators now speak of the "new property"[27]—governmental largesse in such forms as welfare payments, subsidies to farmers, guaranteed loans, free public education, and research grants. Does constitutionalism require that government, in a modern version of Jefferson's scheme to distribute public lands, guarantee each citizen a sufficient share of this new property to provide a minimal standard of living and so ensure a large degree of autonomy?

Or does constitutionalism's other chief goal, preserving individual dignity, require government to leave citizens alone to struggle to achieve as much autonomy as his or her talents and inner drive permit? To what extent was William O. Douglas speaking "good constitutionalism" when he said "So far as the Bill of Rights is concerned, the individual is on his own when it comes to the pursuit of happiness"?[28] Would guaranteeing a minimal standard of living imply that individuals who accepted such grants were not capable of self-sufficiency?

What about the demands of democratic theory here? Does it require that citizens must have, if not equality of resources, at least access to those necessary for a minimum standard of living so they can exercise their civic rights and responsibilities? Providing such a minimum would, of course, entail some redistribution of property beyond what the current tax structure attempts.

If the emphasis is on rights and duties of democratic citizenship, what about access to less tangible goods? In his dissent in San Antonio v. Rodriguez (1973; reprinted above, p. 858), Thurgood Marshall argued that to communicate intelligently, to organize effectively, and to vote wisely all require considerable education. Beyond the high school level, education, in turn, is expensive, if not in direct monetary outlays for tuition, books, food, and housing, at least in

---

26. Lynch v. Household Finance Corp.

27. See espec. Charles A. Reich, "The New Property," 73 *Yale L.J.* 733 (1964).

28. "The Bill of Rights Is Not Enough," in Edmund Cahn, ed., *The Great Rights* (New York: Macmillan, 1963), pp. 146–147.

opportunity costs. The person attending college or graduate school could be working and earning money—an opportunity that the wealthy but not the poor can easily forgo. Does democracy, then, require government to provide enough free education, even to subsiding students, so as to all enable people to perform *effectively* as citizens? The Court's answer in *San Antonio,* of course, was no; but did the majority misread democratic theory?

SELECTED BIBLIOGRAPHY

Ackerman, Bruce A. *Property and the Constitution* (New Haven: Yale University Press, 1977).

————. *Social Justice in the Liberal State* (New Haven: Yale University Press, 1980).

Corwin, Edward S. *Liberty Against Government* (Baton Rouge: Louisiana State University Press, 1948).

Dworkin, Ronald. *A Matter of Principle* (Cambridge, Mass.: Harvard University Press, 1985), espec. chap. 12.

Faulkner, Robert K. *The Jurisprudence of John Marshall* (Princeton, N.J.: Princeton University Press, 1968).

Goldwin, Robert A., and William A. Schambra, eds. *How Capitalistic Is the Constitution?* (Washington, D.C.: The American Enterprise Institute for Public Policy Research, 1982).

Hamilton, Walton. "The Path of Due Process," in Conyers Read, ed., *The Constitution Reconsidered* (New York: Columbia University Press, 1938).

Hofstadter, Richard. *Social Darwinism in American Thought* (rev. ed.; Boston: Beacon Press, 1955).

Horwitz, Morton J. *The Transformation of American Law 1780–1860* (Cambridge: Harvard University Press, 1977).

McCurdy, Charles W. "Justice Field and the Jurisprudence of Government-Business Relations: Some Parameters of Laissez Faire Constitutionalism, 1863–1897," 61 *J. of Am. Hist.* 970 (1975); reprinted in Lawrence M. Friedman and Harry N. Scheiber, eds., *American Law and the Constitutional Order* (Cambridge, Mass.: Harvard University Press, 1978).

MacPherson, C.B. "Human Rights as Property Rights," *Dissent* (Winter, 1977), pp. 72–77.

Michelman, Frank I. "Welfare Rights in a Constitutional Democracy," 1979 *Wash.U.L.Q.* 659.

Murphy, Walter F. *Congress and the Court* (Chicago: University of Chicago Press, 1962), chap. 3.

Nozick, Robert. *Anarchy, State, and Utopia* (New York: Basic Books, 1974), espec. chap. 7.

Paul, Arnold M. *The Conservative Crisis and the Rule of Law: Attitudes of Bench and Bar, 1887–1895* (Ithaca, N.Y.: Cornell University Press, 1960).

Pennock, J. Roland, and John W. Chapman, eds. *Property* (New York: New York University Press, 1980) (*Nomos,* vol. XXII).

Radin, M.J. "Property and Personhood, 34 *Stan.L.Rev.* 957 (1982).

Rawls, John. *A Theory of Justice* (Cambridge, Mass.: The Belknap Press of Harvard University Press, 1971), espec. chap. 5.

Reich, Charles A. "The New Property," 73 *Yale L.J.* 733 (1964).

Scheiber, Harry N. "The Road to *Munn,*" 5 *Perspectives in Am. Hist.* 329 (1971).

Siegen, Bernard H. *Economic Liberties and the Constitution* (Chicago: University of Chicago Press, 1981).

Simpson, A.W.B. "The Horwitz Thesis and the History of Contracts," 46 *U.Chi.L.Rev.* 533 (1979).

Twiss, Benjamin R. *Lawyers and the Constitution* (Princeton, N.J.: Princeton University Press, 1942).

Van Alstyne, William. "The Recrudescence of Property Rights as the Foremost Principle of Civil Liberties," 43 *Law & Cont. Probs.* 66 (1980).

"The great and *chief end* therefore, of Mens uniting into Commonwealths, and putting themselves under Government, *is the Preservation of their Property.*"

PROPERTY AND THE ENDS OF POLITICAL SOCIETY *
John Locke.

27. Though the Earth, and all inferior Creatures be common to all Men, yet every Man has a *Property* in his own *Person*. This no Body has any Right to but himself. The *Labour* of his Body, and the *Work* of his Hands, we may say, are properly his. Whatsoever then he removes out of the State that Nature hath provided, and left it in, he hath mixed his *Labour* with, and joyned to it something that is his own, and thereby makes it his *Property*. It being by him removed from the common state Nature placed it in, hath by this *labour* something annexed to it, that excludes the common right of other Men. For this *Labour* being the unquestionable Property of the Labourer, no Man but he can have a right to what that is once joyned to, at least where there is enough, and as good left in common for others. . . .

31. It will perhaps be objected to this, That if gathering the Acorns, or other Fruits of the Earth, &c. makes a right to them, then

---

* John Locke, *The Second Treatise of Civil Government* (1690), chapters V, IX.

any one may *ingross* as much as he will. To which I Answer, Not so. The same Law of Nature, that does by this means give us Property, does also *bound* that *Property* too. . . . As much as any one can make use of to any advantage of life before it spoils; so much he may by his labour fix a Property in. Whatever is beyond this, is more than his share, and belongs to others. . . .

32. But the *chief matter of Property* being now . . . the *Earth it self* . . . I think it is plain, that *Property* in that too is acquired as the former. *As much Land* as a Man Tills, Plants, Improves, Cultivates, and can use the Product of, so much is his *Property*. He by his Labour does, as it were, inclose it from the Common. Nor will it invalidate his right to say, Every body else has an equal Title to it; and therefore he cannot appropriate, he cannot inclose, without the Consent of all his Fellow-Commoners, all Mankind. . . .

33. Nor was this *appropriation* of any parcel of *Land*, by improving it, any prejudice to any other Man, since there was still enough, and as good left; and more than the yet unprovided could use. . . . No Body could think himself injur'd by the drinking of another Man, though he took a good Draught, who had a whole River of the same Water left him to quench his thirst. And the Case of Land and Water, where there is enough of both, is perfectly the same. . . .

36. The measure of Property, Nature has well set, by the Extent of Mens *Labour, and the Conveniency of Life:* No Mans Labour could subdue, or appropriate all: nor could his Enjoyment consume more than a small part; so that it was impossible for any Man, this way, to intrench upon the right of another, or acquire, to himself, a Property, to the Prejudice of his Neighbour, who would still have room, for as good, and as large a Possession (after the other had taken out his) as before it was appropriated. This *measure* did confine every Man's *Possession*, to a very moderate Proportion. . . . And the same *measure* may be allowed still, without prejudice to any Body, as full as the World seems. For supposing a Man, or Family, in the state they were, at first peopling of the World by the Children of *Adam*, or *Noah;* let him plant in some in-land, vacant places of *America*, we shall find that the *Possessions* he could make himself upon the *measures* we have given, would not be very large, nor, even to this day, prejudice the rest of Mankind, or give them reason to complain, or think themselves injured. . . . That the same *Rule of Propriety*, (*viz.*) that every Man should have as much as he could make use of, would hold still in the World, without straitning any body, since there is Land enough in the World to suffice double the Inhabitants had not the *Invention of Money*, and the tacit Agreement of Men to put a value on it, introduced (by Consent) larger Possessions, and a Right to them. . . .

46. . . . Again if he would give us Nuts for a piece of Metal, pleased with its colour, or exchanged his Sheep for Shells, or Wool for a sparkling Pebble or a Diamond, and keep those by him all his Life, he invaded not the Right of others, he might heap up as much of these durable things as he pleased; the *exceeding of the bounds of his* just

Property not lying in the largeness of his Possession, but the perishing of any thing uselesly in it. . . .

47. And thus *came in the use of Money,* some lasting thing that Men might keep without spoiling, and that by mutual consent Men would take in exchange for the truly useful, but perishable Supports of Life. . . .

50. But since Gold and Silver, being little useful to the Life of Man in proportion to Food, Rayment, and Carriage, has its *value* only from the consent of Men, whereof Labour yet makes, in great part, *the measure,* it is plain, that Men have agreed to disproportionate and unequal Possession of the Earth, they having by a tacit and voluntary consent found out a way, how a man may fairly possess more land than he himself can use the product of, by receiving in exchange for the overplus, Gold and Silver, which may be hoarded up without injury to any one, these metalls not spoileing or decaying in the hands of the possessor. . . .

123. If Man in the State of Nature be so free . . ., [i]f he be absolute Lord of his own Person and Possessions, equal to the greatest, and subject to no Body, why will he part with his Freedom? Why will he give up this Empire, and subject himself to the Dominion and Controul of any other Power? To which 'tis obvious to Answer, that though in the state of Nature he hath such a right, yet the Enjoyment of it is very uncertain, and constantly exposed to the Invasion of others. For all being Kings as much as he, every Man his Equal, and the greater part no strict Observers of Equity and Justice, the enjoyment of the property he has in this state is very unsafe, very unsecure. This makes him willing to quit a Condition, which however free, is full of fears and continual dangers: And 'tis not without reason, that he seeks out, and is willing to joyn in Society with others who are already united, or have a mind to unite for the mutual *Preservation* of their Lives, Liberties and Estates, which I call by the general Name *Property.*

124. The great and *chief end* therefore, of Mens uniting into Commonwealths, and putting themselves under Government, *is the Preservation of their Property.* To which in the state of Nature there are many things wanting.

First, There wants an *establish'd,* settled, known *Law,* received and allowed by common consent to be the Standard of Right and Wrong, and the common measure to decide all Controversies between them. For though, the Law of Nature be plain and intelligible to all rational Creatures; yet Men being biassed by their Interest, as well as ignorant for want of study of it, are not apt to allow of it as a Law binding to them in the application of it to their particular Cases.

125. *Secondly,* In the State of Nature there wants a *known and indifferent Judge,* with Authority to determine all differences according to the established Law. For every one in that state being both Judge and Executioner of the Law of Nature, Men being partial to themselves, Passion and Revenge is very apt to carry them too far, and with too

much heat, in their own Cases, as well as negligence and unconcerned-
ness, to make them too remiss, in other Mens.

126. *Thirdly,* In the state of Nature there often wants *Power* to
back and support the Sentence when right, and to *give* it due *Execution.*
They who by any Injustice offended, will seldom fail, where they are
able, by force to make good their Injustice: such resistance many times
makes the punishment dangerous, and frequently destructive, to those
who attempt it. . . .

128. For in the State of Nature . . . a Man has two Powers.

The first is to do whatsoever he thinks fit for the preservation of
himself and others within the permission of the *Law of Nature:* by
which Law common to them all, he and all the rest of *Mankind are one
Community.* . . . And were it not for the corruption, and vitious-
ness of degenerate Men, there would be no need of any other. . . .

The other power a Man has in the State of Nature, is the *power to
punish the Crimes* committed against that Law. Both these he gives
up, when he joyns in a . . . particular Political Society, and incorporates into any Commonwealth, separate from the rest of Mankind.
. . .

131. But though Men when they enter into Society, give up the
Equality, Liberty, and Executive Power they had in the State of
Nature, into the hands of the Society, to be so far disposed of by the
Legislative, as the good of the Society shall require; yet it being only
with an intention in every one the better to preserve himself his
Liberty and Property . . . the power of the Society, or *Legislative*
constituted by them, *can never be suppos'd to extend farther than the
common good;* but is obliged to secure every ones Property by providing
against those three defects above-mentioned, that made the State of
Nature so unsafe and uneasie. And so whoever has the Legislative or
Supream Power of any Common-wealth, is bound to govern by establish'd *standing Laws,* promulgated and known to the People, and not by
Extemporary Decrees; by *indifferent* and upright *Judges,* who are to
decide Controversies by those Laws; And to imploy the force of the
Community at home, *only in the Execution of such Laws,* or abroad to
prevent or redress Foreign Injuries, and secure the Community from
Inroads and Invasion. And all this to be directed to no other *end,* but
the *Peace, Safety,* and *publick good* of the People.

"The diversity in the faculties of men from which the
rights of property originate, is . . . an insuperable obstacle to a uniformity of interests. The protection of
these faculties is the first object of Government."

THE FEDERALIST NO. 10
James Madison.

Among the numerous advantages promised by a well constructed
Union, none deserves to be more accurately developed than its tenden-

cy to break and control the violence of faction. The friend of popular
governments, never finds himself so much alarmed for their character
and fate, as when he contemplates their propensity to this dangerous
vice. . . . The instability, injustice and confusion introduced into
the public councils, have in truth been the mortal diseases under which
popular governments have every where perished. . . .

By a faction I understand a number of citizens, whether amounting
to a majority or minority of the whole, who are united and actuated by
some common impulse of passion, or of interest, adverse to the rights of
other citizens, or to the permanent and aggregate interests of the
community.

There are two methods of curing the mischiefs of faction: the one,
by removing its causes; the other, by controling its effects.

There are again two methods of removing the causes of faction: the
one by destroying the liberty which is essential to its existence; the
other, by giving to every citizen the same opinions, the same passions,
and the same interests.

It could never be more truly said than of the first remedy, that it is
worse than the disease. Liberty is to faction, what air is to fire, an
aliment without which it instantly expires. But it could not be a less
folly to abolish liberty, which is essential to political life, because it
nourishes faction, than it would be to wish the annihilation of air,
which is essential to animal life, because it imparts to fire its destructive agency.

The second expedient is as impracticable, as the first would be
unwise. As long as the reason of man continues fallible, and he is at
liberty to exercise it, different opinions will be formed. As long as the
connection subsists between his reason and his self-love, his opinions
and his passions will have a reciprocal influence on each other. . . .
The diversity in the faculties of men from which the rights of property
originate, is not less an insuperable obstacle to a uniformity of interests. The protection of these faculties is the first object of Government.
From the protection of different and unequal faculties of acquiring
property, the possession of different degrees and kinds of property
immediately results: and from the influence of these on the sentiments
and views of the respective proprietors, ensues a division of the society
into different interests and parties.

The latent causes of faction are thus sown in the nature of man.
. . . So strong is this propensity of mankind to fall into mutual
animosities, that where no substantial occasion presents itself, the most
frivolous and fanciful distinctions have been sufficient to kindle their
unfriendly passions, and excite their most violent conflicts. But the
most common and durable source of factions, has been the various and
unequal distribution of property. Those who hold, and those who are
without property, have ever formed distinct interests in society. Those
who are creditors, and those who are debtors, fall under a like discrimination. A landed interest, a manufacturing interest, a mercantile
interest, a monied interest, with many lesser interests, grow up of

necessity in civilized nations, and divide them into different classes, actuated by different sentiments and views. The regulation of these various and interfering interests forms the principal task of modern Legislation. . . .

No man is allowed to be a judge in his own cause; because his interest would certainly bias his judgment, and, not improbably, corrupt his integrity. With equal, nay with greater reason, a body of men, are unfit to be both judges and parties, at the same time; yet, what are many of the most important acts of legislation, but so many judicial determinations . . . concerning the rights of large bodies of citizens; and what are the different classes of legislators, but advocates and parties to the causes which they determine? Is a law proposed concerning private debts? It is a question to which the creditors are parties on one side, and the debtors on the other. Justice ought to hold the balance between them. Yet the parties are and must be themselves the judges; and the most numerous party, or, in other words, the most powerful faction must be expected to prevail. . . . The apportionment of taxes on the various descriptions of property, is an act which seems to require the most exact impartiality; yet, there is perhaps no legislative act in which greater opportunity and temptation are given to a predominant party, to trample on the rules of justice. . . .

It is in vain to say, that enlightened statesmen will be able to adjust these clashing interests, and render them all subservient to the public good. Enlightened statesmen will not always be at the helm: Nor, in many cases, can such an adjustment be made at all, without taking into view indirect and remote considerations, which will rarely prevail over the immediate interest which one party may find in disregarding the rights of another, or the good of the whole.

The inference to which we are brought, is, that the *causes* of faction cannot be removed; and that relief is only to be sought in the means of controlling its *effects*.

If a faction consists of less than a majority, relief is supplied by the republican principle, which enables the majority to defeat its sinister views by regular vote. . . . When a majority is included in a faction, the form of popular government on the other hand enables it to sacrifice to its ruling passion or interest, both the public good and the rights of other citizens. To secure the public good, and private rights, against the danger of such a faction, and at the same time to preserve the spirit and the form of popular government, is then the great object to which our enquiries are directed. . . .

By what means is this object attainable? Evidently by one of two only. Either the existence of the same passion or interest in a majority at the same time, must be prevented; or the majority, having such coexistent passion or interest, must be rendered, by their number and local situation, unable to concert and carry into effect schemes of oppression. If the impulse and the opportunity be suffered to coincide, we well know that neither moral nor religious motives can be relied on as an adequate control. . . .

. . . . [A] pure Democracy, by which I mean, a Society, consisting of a small number of citizens, who assemble and administer the Government in person, can admit of no cure for the mischiefs of faction. A common passion or interest will, in almost every case, be felt by a majority of the whole . . . and there is nothing to check the inducements to sacrifice the weaker party, or an obnoxious individual. Hence it is, that such Democracies have ever been spectacles of turbulence and contention; have ever been found incompatible with personal security, or the rights of property; and have in general been as short in their lives, as they have been violent in their deaths. Theoretic politicians, who have patronized this species of Government, have erroneously supposed, that by reducing mankind to a perfect equality in their political rights, they would, at the same time, be perfectly equalized and assimilated in their possessions, their opinions, and their passions.

A Republic, by which I mean a Government in which the scheme of representation takes place, opens a different prospect, and promises the cure for which we are seeking. . . .

The two great points of difference between a Democracy and a Republic are, first, the delegation of the Government, in the latter, to a small number of citizens elected by the rest: secondly, the greater number of citizens, and greater sphere of country, over which the latter may be extended.

The effect of the first difference is . . . to refine and enlarge the public views, by passing them through the medium of a chosen body of citizens, whose wisdom may best discern the true interest of their country, and whose patriotism and love of justice, will be least likely to sacrifice it to temporary or partial considerations. . . . On the other hand, the effect may be inverted. Men of factious tempers, of local prejudices, or of sinister designs, may by intrigue, by corruption or by other means, first obtain the suffrages, and then betray the interests of the people. The question resulting is, whether small or extensive Republics are most favorable to the election of proper guardians of the public weal: and it is clearly decided in favor of the latter by two obvious considerations.

In the first place it is to be remarked that however small the Republic may be, the Representatives must be raised to a certain number, in order to guard against the cabals of a few; and that however large it may be, they must be limited to a certain number, in order to guard against the confusion of a multitude. Hence the number of Representatives in the two cases, not being in proportion to that of the Constituents, and being proportionally greatest in the small Republic, it follows, that if the proportion of fit characters, be not less, in the large than in the small Republic, the former will present a greater option, and consequently a greater probability of a fit choice.

In the next place, as each Representative will be chosen by a greater number of citizens in the large than in the small Republic, it will be more difficult for unworthy candidates to practise with success the vicious arts, by which elections are too often carried. . . .

The other point of difference is, the greater number of citizens and extent of territory which may be brought within the compass of Republican, than of Democratic Government; and it is this circumstance principally which renders factious combinations less to be dreaded in the former, than in the latter. The smaller the society, the fewer probably will be the distinct parties and interests composing it; the fewer the distinct parties and interests, the more frequently will a majority be found of the same party; and the smaller the number of individuals composing a majority, and the smaller the compass within which they are placed, the more easily will they concert and execute their plans of oppression. Extend the sphere, and you take in a greater variety of parties and interests; you make it less probable that a majority of the whole will have a common motive to invade the rights of other citizens; or if such a common motive exists, it will be more difficult for all who feel it to discover their own strength, and to act in unison with each other. Besides other impediments . . . where there is a consciousness of unjust or dishonorable purposes, communication is always checked by distrust, in proportion to the number whose concurrence is necessary.

The influence of factious leaders may kindle a flame within their particular States, but will be unable to spread a general conflagration through the other States. . . . A rage for paper money, for an abolition of debts, for an equal division of property, or for any other improper or wicked project, will be less apt to pervade the whole body of the Union than a particular member of it. . . .

"What motive, then, for implying in words which import a general prohibition to impair the obligation of contracts, an exception in favor of the right to impair the obligations of those contracts into which the state may enter?"

FLETCHER v. PECK

10 U.S. (6 Cranch) 87, 3 L.Ed. 162 (1810).

In 1795, a group of speculators bribed the Georgia legislature to grant them, at less than a penny and a half an acre, the so-called Yazoo Land Tract, some 35 million acres in what is now Mississippi. In 1796, after a great public outcry, a newly elected legislature annulled the grant, directing named state officers to come to the capitol

> with the several records, documents, and deeds . . . and which records and documents shall then and there be expunged from the faces and indexes of the books of record of the State, and the enrolled law or usurped act shall then be publicly burnt, in order that no trace of so unconstitutional, vile, and fraudulent a transaction, other than the infamy attached to it by this law, shall remain in the public offices. . . .

Further, the legislature ordered all county officers responsible for recording deeds to bring deeds resulting from the grant of 1795 to local courts and destroy them.

This case, a friendly suit to untangle what had become a massive legal as well as political mess, was between two private citizens. Robert Fletcher of New Hampshire, who had purchased land in the Yazoo Tract from John Peck of Massachusetts—who, in turn, had bought it from one of the original speculators—asked a U.S. circuit court to order return of the money he had paid Peck because, if the grant of 1795 was invalid, the sale was void. That court, however, sustained the legality of the sale, and Fletcher obtained a writ of error from the U.S. Supreme Court.

MARSHALL, Ch. J., delivered the opinion of the court. . . .

The question, whether a law be void for its repugnancy to the constitution, is, at all times, a question of much delicacy, which ought seldom, if ever, to be decided in the affirmative, in a doubtful case. The court, when impelled by duty to render such a judgment, would be unworthy of its station, could it be unmindful of the solemn obligations which that station imposes. But it is not on slight implication and vague conjecture, that the legislature is to be pronounced to have transcended its powers, and its acts to be considered as void. The opposition between the constitution and the law should be such that the judge feels a clear and strong conviction of their incompatibility with each other. . . .

If a suit be brought to set aside a conveyance obtained by fraud, and the fraud be clearly proved, the conveyance will be set aside, as between the parties; but the rights of third persons, who are purchasers without notice, for a valuable consideration, cannot be disregarded. Titles which, according to every legal test, are perfect, are acquired with that confidence which is inspired by the opinion that the purchaser is safe. If there be any concealed defect, arising from the conduct of those who had held the property long before he acquired it, of which he had no notice, that concealed defect cannot be set up against him. He has paid his money for a title good at law, he is innocent, whatever may be the guilt of others, and equity will not subject him to the penalties attached to that guilt. All titles would be insecure, and the intercourse between man and man would be very seriously obstructed, if this principle be overturned. . . .

Is the power of the legislature competent to the annihilation of such title . . .? The principle asserted is, that one legislature is competent to repeal any act which a former legislature was competent to pass; and that one legislature cannot abridge the powers of a succeeding legislature. The correctness of this principle, so far as respects general legislation, can never be controverted. But, if an act be done under a law, a succeeding legislature cannot undo it. The past cannot be recalled by the most absolute power. . . . When, then, a law is in its nature a contract, when absolute rights have vested under that contract, a repeal of the law cannot divest those rights; and the act of annulling them, if legitimate, is rendered so by a power applicable to the case of every individual in the community.

It may well be doubted, whether the nature of society and of government does not prescribe some limits to the legislative power; and if any be prescribed, where are they to be found, if the property of an individual, fairly and honestly acquired, may be seized without compensation? To the legislature, all legislative power is granted; but the question, whether the act of transferring the property of an individual to the public, be in the nature of the legislative power, is well worthy of serious reflection. It is the peculiar province of the legislature, to prescribe general rules for the government of society; the application of those rules to individuals in society would seem to be the duty of other departments. How far the power of giving the law may involve every other power, in cases where the constitution is silent, never has been, and perhaps never can be, definitely stated.

The validity of this rescinding act, then, might well be doubted, were Georgia a single sovereign power. But Georgia cannot be viewed as a single, unconnected, sovereign power, on whose legislature no other restrictions are imposed than may be found in its own constitution. She is a part of a large empire; she is a member of the American union; and that union has a constitution, the supremacy of which all acknowledge, and which imposes limits to the legislatures of the several states. . . . The constitution of the United States declares that no state shall pass any bill of attainder, *ex post facto* law, or law impairing the obligation of contracts.

Does the case now under consideration come within this prohibitory section of the constitution? In considering this very interesting question, we immediately ask ourselves, what is a contract? Is a grant a contract? A contract is a compact between two or more parties. . . . The contract between Georgia and the purchasers was executed by the grant. A contract . . . contains obligations binding on the parties. A grant, in its own nature, amounts to an extinguishment of the right of the grantor, and implies a contract not to re-assert that right. A party is, therefore, always estopped by his own grant.

Since, then, in fact, a grant is a contract executed, the obligation of which still continues, and since the constitution uses the general term contract . . . it must be construed to comprehend [grants]. . . .

If, under a fair construction of the constitution, grants are comprehended under the term contracts, is a grant from the state excluded from the operation of the provision?. . . . The words themselves contain no such distinction. They are general, and are applicable to contracts of every description. If contracts made with the state are to be exempted from their operation, the exception must arise from the character of the contracting party, not from the words which are employed.

Whatever respect might have been felt for the state sovereignties, it is not to be disguised, that the framers of the constitution viewed, with some apprehension, the violent acts which might grow out of the feelings of the moment; and that the people of the United States, in adopting that instrument, have manifested a determination to shield themselves and their property from the effects of those sudden and strong passions to which men are exposed. The restrictions on the legislative power of the states are obviously founded in this sentiment; and the constitution of the United States contains what may be deemed a bill of rights for the people of each state.

. . . What motive, then, for implying, in words which import a general prohibition to impair the obligation of contracts, an exception in favor of the right to impair the obligation of those contracts into which the state may enter?

The state legislatures can pass no *ex post facto* law. An *ex post facto* law is one which renders an act punishable in a manner in which it was not punishable when it was committed. Such a law may inflict penalties on the person, or may inflict pecuniary penalties which swell the public treasury. The legislature is then prohibited from passing a law by which a man's estate, or any part of it, shall be seized for a crime which was not declared, by some previous law, to render him liable to that punishment. Why, then, should violence be done to the natural meaning of words for the purpose of leaving to the legislature the power of seizing, for public use, the estate of an individual, in the form of a law annulling the title by which he holds that estate? The court can perceive no sufficient grounds for making this distinction. This rescinding act would have the effect of an *ex post facto* law. It forfeits the estate of Fletcher for a crime not committed by himself, but by those from whom he purchased. This cannot be effected in the form of an *ex post facto* law, or bill of attainder; why then, is it allowable in the form of a law annulling the original grant? . . .

It is, then, the unanimous opinion of the court, that, in this case, the estate having passed into the hands of a purchaser for a valuable consideration, without notice, the state of Georgia was restrained, either by general principles which are common to our free institutions, or by the particular provisions of the constitution of the United States, from passing a law whereby the estate of the plaintiff in the premises so purchased could be constitutionally and legally impaired and rendered null and void. . . .   *Affirmed.*

JOHNSON, J.

In this case, I entertain . . . an opinion different from that which has been delivered by the court.

I do not hesitate to declare, that a state does not possess the power of revoking its own grants. But I do it, on a general principle, on the reason and nature of things; a principle which will impose laws even on the Deity. . . .

The right of jurisdiction is essentially connected to, or rather identified with, the national sovereignty. To part with it, is to commit a species of political suicide. . . . But it is not so with the interests or property of a nation. Its possessions nationally are in no wise necessary to its political existence; they are entirely accidental, and may be parted with, in every respect, similarly to those of the individuals who compose the community. When the legislature have once conveyed their interest or property in any subject to the individual, they have lost all control over it; have nothing to act upon; it has passed from them; is vested in the individual; becomes intimately blended with his existence, as essentially so as the blood that circulates through his system. . . .

I have thrown out these ideas, that I may have it distinctly understood, that my opinion on this point is not founded on the provision in the constitution of the United States, relative to laws impairing the obligation of contracts. . . .

Editors' Notes

(1) **Query:** To what extent did Marshall base his opinion on "general principles which are common to our free institutions" and to what extent on "the particular provisions of the constitution"? Is the former distinguishable from the sort of theory of natural rights Chase applied in Calder v. Bull (1798; reprinted above, p. 86)? Is the latter different from the legal positivism that Iredell espoused in *Calder* and Black in *Griswold* (1965; reprinted above, p. 113)? To what extent are these various *modes* of interpretation logically compatible? How does Justice Johnson's opinion relate to these lines of reasoning?

(2) Congress and the executive were also deeply involved in the settlement of this controversy. During the period 1798–1803, federal commissioners worked out an agreement under which Georgia gave its title to the Yazoo territory to the United States in exchange for $1,250,000 and assumption of all the claims that resulted from the rescinding act of 1796. It was not, however, until 1814 that Congress passed an act allowing claimants to be repaid, either in cash or land, as they chose.

(3) For excellent accounts of the Yazoo controversy, see: C. Peter Magrath, *Yazoo: Law and Politics in the New Republic* (New York: W.W. Norton & Co., 1966); Albert J. Beveridge, *The Life of John Marshall* (Boston: Houghton Mifflin Co., 1919), III, chap. 10; and George Lee Haskins and Herbert A. Johnson, *Foundations of Power: John Marshall, 1801–15* (New York: Macmillan, 1981), pp. 336–353.

"While the rights of private property are sacredly guarded, we must not forget that the community also have rights. . . ."

CHARLES RIVER BRIDGE v. WARREN BRIDGE
36 U.S. (11 Pet.) 420, 9 L.Ed. 773 (1837).

In 1640 Massachusetts Bay Colony gave Harvard College the right to operate a ferry across the Charles River between Boston and Charlestown.

The arrangement was unsatisfactory to the college and the community; and, in 1785, the Commonwealth of Massachusetts chartered a corporation to build a toll bridge to replace the ferry. The corporation was to pay Harvard an annual fee of $666.66 until 1856. For decades the bridge operated profitably, earning more than $800,000 between 1786 and 1827. Then in 1828 the state chartered a new corporation to build a second bridge. Not only was this structure to be located only a few hundred yards from the old but, as soon as tolls paid off its costs of construction plus 5 per cent, it was to be free to the public.

The Charles River Bridge Co. sued in a state court to invalidate the new charter. Among its claims was that the law of 1828 unconstitutionally impaired the obligation of the grant of 1785 which, according to Fletcher v. Peck (1810; reprinted above, p. 956) and the Dartmouth College Case (1819), was a contract. The state courts upheld the constitutionality of the new charter—the highest court dividing equally on the question—and the Charles River Bridge Co. obtained a writ of error from the U.S. Supreme Court.

The Court first heard argument in March, 1831, but, because of absences and divisions among the justices, several times ordered reargument. Final argument came in 1837, shortly after Roger Brooke Taney, Andrew Jackson's nominee, had replaced John Marshall as Chief Justice. Marshall wanted to adhere to the doctrine of *Fletcher* and *Dartmouth College*, but Taney had different views.

Mr. Chief Justice **TANEY** delivered the opinion of the court.

The questions involved in this case are of the gravest character, and the court have given to them the most anxious and deliberate consideration. The value of the right claimed by the plaintiffs is large in amount . . . and the questions which have been raised as to the power of the several states, in relation to the corporations they have chartered, are pregnant with important consequences; not only to the individuals who are concerned in the corporate franchises, but to the communities in which they exist. The court are fully sensible that it is their duty, in exercising the high powers conferred on them by the constitution of the United States, to deal with these great and extensive interests with the utmost caution; guarding, as far as they have the power to do so, the rights of property, and at the same time carefully abstaining from any encroachment on the rights reserved to the states. . . .

Much has been said in the argument of the principles of construction by which this law is to be expounded, and what undertakings, on the part of the state may be implied. The court think there can be no serious difficulty on that head. It is the grant of certain franchises by the public to a private corporation, and in a matter where the public interest is concerned. The rule of construction in such cases is well settled, both in England, and by the decisions of our own tribunals. In . . . the case of the Proprietors of the Stourbridge Canal against Wheely and others, the court say,

> the canal having been made under an act of parliament, the rights of the plaintiffs are derived entirely from that act. This, like many other cases, is a bargain between a company of adventurers and the public,

the terms of which are expressed in the statute; and the rule of construction in all such cases, is . . . that any ambiguity in the terms of the contract, must operate against the adventurers, and in favour of the public, and the plaintiffs can claim nothing that is not clearly given them by the act. . . .

Borrowing, as we have done, our system of jurisprudence from the English law; and having adopted, in every other case, civil and criminal, its rules for the construction of statutes; is there any thing in our local situation, or in the nature of our political institutions, which should lead us to depart from the principle where corporations are concerned? . . . We think not. . . .

But we are not now left to determine, for the first time, the rules by which public grants are to be construed in this country. The subject has already been considered in this court; and the rule of construction, above stated, fully established. In the case of the United States v. Arredondo [1832], the leading cases upon this subject are collected . . . and the principle recognized, that in grants by the public, nothing passes by implication. . . .

. . . [T]he object and end of all government is to promote the happiness and prosperity of the community . . . and it can never be assumed, that the government intended to diminish its power of accomplishing the end for which it was created and in a country like ours, free, active, and enterprising, continually advancing in numbers and wealth; new channels of communication are daily found necessary, both for travel and trade; and are essential to the comfort, convenience, and prosperity of the people. A state ought never to be presumed to surrender this power, because, like the taxing power, the whole community have an interest in preserving it undiminished. And when a corporation alleges, that a state has surrendered for seventy years, its power of improvement and public accommodation, in a great and important line of travel, along which a vast number of its citizens must daily pass; the community have a right to insist . . . "that its abandonment ought not to be presumed, in a case, in which the deliberate purpose of the state to abandon it does not appear." The continued existence of a government would be of no great value, if by implications and presumptions, it was disarmed of the powers necessary to accomplish the ends of its creation. . . . While the rights of private property are sacredly guarded, we must not forget that the community also have rights, and that the happiness and well being of every citizen depends on their faithful preservation.

Adopting the rule of construction above stated . . . we proceed to apply it to the charter of 1785, to the proprietors of the Charles river bridge. . . . It confers on them the ordinary faculties of a corporation, for the purpose of building the bridge; and establishes certain rates of toll, which the company are authorized to take. This is the whole grant. There is no exclusive privilege given to them over the waters of Charles river, above or below their bridge. No right to erect another bridge themselves, nor to prevent other persons from erecting one. No engagement from the state, that another shall not be erected;

and no undertaking not to sanction competition, nor to make improvements that may diminish the amount of its income. Upon all these subjects the charter is silent. . . .

. . . Can such an agreement be implied? The rule of construction before stated is an answer to the question. . . .

Indeed, the practice and usage of almost every state in the Union . . . is opposed to the doctrine contended for on the part of the plaintiffs in error. Turnpike roads have been made in succession, on the same line of travel; the later ones interfering materially with the profits of the first. These corporations have, in some instances, been utterly ruined by the introduction of newer and better modes of transportation, and travelling. In some cases, rail roads have rendered the turnpike roads on the same line of travel so entirely useless, that the franchise of the turnpike corporation is not worth preserving. Yet in none of these cases have the corporation supposed that their privileges were invaded, or any contract violated on the part of the state. . . . We cannot deal thus with the rights reserved to the states; and by legal intendments and mere technical reasoning, take away from them any portion of that power over their own internal police and improvement, which is so necessary to their well being and prosperity.

And what would be the fruits of this doctrine of implied contracts on the part of the states, and of property in a line of travel by a corporation, if it should now be sanctioned by this court? . . . If it is to be found in the charter to this bridge, the same process of reasoning must discover it, in the various acts which have been passed, within the last forty years, for turnpike companies. . . . If this court should establish the principles now contended for, what is to become of the numerous rail roads established on the same line of travel with turnpike companies; and which have rendered the franchises of the turnpike corporations of no value? Let it once be understood that such charters carry with them these implied contracts, and give this unknown and undefined property in a line of travelling; and you will soon find the old turnpike corporations awakening from their sleep, and calling upon this court to put down the improvements which have taken their place. The millions of property which have been invested in rail roads and canals, upon lines of travel which had been before occupied by turnpike corporations, will be put in jeopardy. We shall be thrown back to the improvements of the last century . . . until . . . the old turnpike corporations . . . shall consent to permit these states to avail themselves of the lights of modern science, and to partake of the benefit of those improvements which are now adding to the wealth and prosperity, and the convenience and comfort, of every other part of the civilized world. . . . This court are not prepared to sanction principles which must lead to such results. . . .

[*Affirmed.*]

Mr. Justice **M'LEAN**. . . .

. . . I am in favour of dismissing the bill for want of jurisdiction.

Mr. Justice **STORY,** dissenting. . . .

The present . . . is not the case of a royal grant, but of a legislative grant, by a public statute. The rules of the common law in relation to royal grants have, therefore, in reality, nothing to do with the case. We are to give this act of incorporation a rational and fair construction, according to the general rules which govern in all cases of the exposition of public statutes. We are to ascertain the legislative intent; and that once ascertained, it is our duty to give it a full and liberal operation. The books are full of cases to this effect. . . .

. . . [W]here the terms of a grant are to impose burdens upon the public, or to create a restraint injurious to the public interests, there is sound reason for interpreting the terms, if ambiguous, in favour of the public. But at the same time . . . there is not the slightest reason for saying, even in such a case, that the grant is not to be construed favourably to the grantee, so as to secure him in the enjoyment of what is actually granted. . . .

. . . Our legislatures neither have, nor affect to have any royal prerogatives. There is no provision in the constitution authorizing their grants to be construed differently from the grants of private persons, in regard to the like subject matter. The policy of the common law, which gave the crown so many exclusive privileges, and extraordinary claims . . . was founded in a good measure, if not altogether, upon the divine right of kings, or at least upon a sense of their exalted dignity and preeminence over all subjects. . . . [Yet t]hey were always construed according to common sense and common reason, upon their language and their intent. . . . Is it not at least as important in our free governments, that a citizen should have as much security for his rights and estate derived from the grants of the legislature, as he would have in England? What solid ground is there to say, that the words of a grant in the mouth of a citizen, shall mean one thing, and in the mouth of the legislature shall mean another thing? That in regard to the grant of a citizen, every word shall in case of any question of interpretation or implication be construed against him, and in regard to the grant of the government, every word shall be construed in its favour? . . .

But it has been argued . . . that if grants of this nature are to be construed liberally . . . it will interpose an effectual barrier against all general improvements of the country. . . . For my own part, I can conceive of no surer plan to arrest all public improvements, founded on private capital and enterprise, than to make the outlay of that capital uncertain, and questionable both as to security, and as to productiveness. No man will hazard his capital in any enterprise, in which, if there be a loss, it must be borne exclusively by himself; and if there be success, he has not the slightest security of enjoying the rewards of that success for a single moment. . . .

Mr. Justice **THOMPSON**.

The opinion delivered by my brother, Mr. Justice Story, I have read over, and deliberately considered. On this full consideration, I concur entirely in all the principles and reasonings contained in it. . . .

Editors' Notes

(1) As explained in the introductory essay to this chapter, Morton J. Horwitz, *The Transformation of American Law, 1780–1860* (Cambridge: Harvard University Press, 1977), argues that, during the first decades of the nineteenth century, the American law of property underwent a dramatic transformation from a static, agrarian conception of a right to quiet enjoyment to one that benefitted venturesome new groups of merchants, industrialists, and entrepreneurs—"a dynamic, instrumental, and more abstract view of property that emphasized the newly paramount virtues of productive use and development." (P. 31.) Thus, for Horwitz, *Charles River Bridge* "represented the last great contest in America between two different models of economic development." (P. 134.) Story spoke for the old order, Taney for the new. Horwitz' general thesis has been hotly contested. See the literature cited in fn. 7 to the introductory essay to this chapter.

(2) After the decision, Daniel Webster, who had argued the case for the Charles River Bridge Co., sensed the change that Horwitz was to describe: "The decision of the Court will have completely overturned, in my judgment, a great provision of the Constitution." Quoted in Charles Warren, *The Supreme Court in United States History* (Boston: Little, Brown and Co., 1926), II, p. 25n.

(3) Story felt the same change as Webster and wrote to Justice McLean: "There will not, I fear, ever in our day, be any case in which a law of a State or of Congress will be declared unconstitutional; for the old constitutional doctrines are fast fading away, and a change has come over the public mind from which I augur little good." Quoted in Warren, II, p. 28. During Story's remaining eight years on the bench, the Supreme Court declared seven state statutes unconstitutional, though none under the contract clause. (During his previous 26 years on the Court, the justices had held 16 state statutes unconstitutional, a somewhat lower annual average but a much higher mortality rate of laws challenged.) The Court was not to declare an act of Congress unconstitutional until Dred Scott v. Sanford (1857); so during Story's entire tenure, the Court never declared an act of Congress unconstitutional.

(4) For a study tracing the decline of the contracts clause as a bulwark of property rights, see: Benjamin F. Wright, *The Contract Clause of the Constitution* (Cambridge, Mass.: Harvard University Press, 1938). Despite the general demise of the contracts clause, the Court has several times in recent years used it to invalidate state statutes: United States Trust Co. v. New Jersey (1977); and Allied Structural Steel Co. v. Spannaus (1978). See Bernard Schwartz, "Old Wine in New Bottles? The Renaissance of the Contracts Clause," 1979 *Sup.Ct.Rev.* 95; and C. Herman Pritchett, *Constitutional Civil Liberties* (Englewood Cliffs, N.J.: Prentice-Hall, 1984), pp. 284–289.

"For protection against abuses by legislatures the people must resort to the polls, not to the courts."

MUNN v. ILLINOIS
94 U.S. (4 Otto) 113, 24 L.Ed. 77 (1877).

The Grangers were an agrarian reform movement that gathered force in the Midwest after the Civil War in reaction against the new corporations whom, the farmers felt, were stealing their land for railroad rights-of-way, then overcharging them to haul their goods to market, and further overcharging them to store their crops in grain elevators while awaiting sale. Chicago was, of course, a central market, and a few companies had what amounted to monopolistic control over storage elevators. They unashamedly used that power to charge exorbitant rates and to speculate with other people's property. The New constitution that Illinois adopted in 1870 declared grain elevators to be "public warehouses" and authorized the legislature to regulate the business of grain storage. Under this authority, the legislature in 1871 passed a comprehensive regulatory act that, among other things, required a license to operate a grain elevator and fixed charges for storage. Munn and Scott, a particularly unscrupulous firm, were fined $100 for violating the statute. When news of the company's other illegal activities leaked out, the firm went bankrupt. Its successors, however, appealed the judgment, claiming that the state had deprived their company of its property "without due process of law." The operators lost in the Illinois courts but obtained a writ of error from the U.S. Supreme Court.

Mr. Chief Justice **WAITE** delivered the opinion of the court. . . .

Every statute is presumed to be constitutional. The courts ought not to declare one to be unconstitutional, unless it is clearly so. If there is doubt, the expressed will of the legislature should be sustained.

The Constitution contains no definition of the word "deprive," as used in the Fourteenth Amendment. To determine its signification, therefore, it is necessary to ascertain the effect which usage has given it, when employed in the same or a like connection.

While this provision of the amendment is new in the Constitution of the United States, as a limitation upon the powers of the States, it is old as a principle of civilized government. It is found in Magna Charta, and, in substance if not in form, in nearly or quite all the constitutions that have been from time to time adopted by the several States of the Union. By the Fifth Amendment, it was introduced into the Constitution of the United States as a limitation upon the powers of the national government, and by the Fourteenth, as a guaranty against any encroachment upon an acknowledged right of citizenship by the legislatures of the States. . . .

When one becomes a member of society, he necessarily parts with some rights or privileges which, as an individual not affected by his relations to others, he might retain. . . . This does not confer power upon the whole people to control rights which are purely and exclusively private . . . but it does authorize the establishment of laws requiring each citizen to so conduct himself, and so use his own property, as not

unnecessarily to injure another. This is the very essence of government.
. . . From this source come the police powers, which as was said by
Mr. Chief Justice Taney in the *License Cases* [1847], "are nothing more
or less than the powers of government inherent in every sovereignty,
. . . the power to govern men and things." Under these powers the
government regulates the conduct of its citizens one towards another,
and the manner in which each shall use his own property, when such
regulation becomes necessary for the public good. In their exercise it
has been customary in England from time immemorial, and in this
country from its first colonization, to regulate ferries, common carriers,
hackmen, bakers, millers, wharfingers, innkeepers, &c. and in so doing to
fix a maximum of charge to be made for services rendered, accommodations furnished, and articles sold. . . . [I]t has never yet been successfully contended that such legislation came within any of the constitutional prohibitions against interference with private property. With the
Fifth Amendment in force, Congress, in 1820, conferred power upon the
city of Washington "to regulate . . . the rates of wharfage at private
wharves, . . . the sweeping of chimneys, and to fix the rates of fees
therefor, . . . and the weight and quality of bread," . . . and, in
1848, "to make all necessary regulations respecting hackney carriages
and the rates of fare of the same, and the rates of hauling by cartmen,
wagoners, carmen, and draymen, and the rates of commission of auction-
eers." . . .

From this it is apparent that, down to the time of the adoption of
the Fourteenth Amendment, it was not supposed that statutes regulating the use, or even the price of the use, of private property necessarily
deprived an owner of his property without due process of law. Under
some circumstances they may, but not under all. The amendment does
not change the law in this particular: it simply prevents the States
from doing that which will operate as such a deprivation.

This brings us to inquire as to the principles upon which this power
of regulation rests. . . .

. . . Looking, then, to the common law, from whence came the
right which the Constitution protects, we find that when private property is "affected with a public interest, it ceases to be *juris privati*
only." This was said by Lord Chief Justice Hale more than two
hundred years ago . . . and has been accepted without objection as an
essential element in the law of property ever since. Property does
become clothed with a public interest when used in a manner to make
it of public consequence, and affect the community at large. When,
therefore, one devotes his property to a use in which the public has an
interest, he, in effect, grants to the public an interest in that use, and
must submit to be controlled by the public for the common good, to the
extent of the interest he has thus created. He may withdraw his grant
by discontinuing the use; but, so long as he maintains the use, he must
submit to the control. . . .

. . . Enough has already been said to show that, when private
property is devoted to a public use, it is subject to public regulation. It

remains only to ascertain whether the warehouses of these plaintiffs in
error . . . come within the operation of this principle.

. . . [I]t appears that "the great producing region of the West and
North-west sends its grain by water and rail to Chicago, where the
greater part of it is shipped by vessel for transportation to the seaboard
by the Great Lakes, and some of it is forwarded by railway to the
Eastern ports. . . . The grain warehouses or elevators in Chicago
are immense structures, holding from 300,000 to 1,000,000 bushels at
one time. . . . They are located with the river harbor on one side
and the railway tracks on the other; and the grain is run through them
from car to vessel, or boat to car. . . . It has been found impossible
to preserve each owner's grain separate, and this has given rise to a
system of inspection and grading, by which the grain of different
owners is mixed, and receipts issued for the number of bushels which
are negotiable, and redeemable in like kind, upon demand. . . ."

. . . [A]lthough in 1874 there were in Chicago fourteen warehouses adapted to this particular business, and owned by about thirty
persons, nine business firms controlled them, and . . . the prices
charged and received for storage were such "as have been from year to
year agreed upon and established by the different elevators or warehouses in the city of Chicago. . . ." Thus it is apparent that all the
elevating facilities through which these vast productions "of seven or
eight great States of the West" must pass on the way "to four or five of
the States on the seashore" may be a "virtual" monopoly.

Under such circumstances it is difficult to see why, if the common
carrier, or the miller, or the ferryman, or the innkeeper, or the
wharfinger, or the baker, or the cartman, or the hackney-coachman,
pursues a public employment and exercises "a sort of public office,"
these plaintiffs in error do not. They stand . . . in the very "gateway
of commerce," and take toll from all who pass. Their business most
certainly "tends to a common charge, and is become a thing of public
interest and use." . . . Certainly, if any business can be clothed
"with a public interest, and cease to be *juris privati* only," this has
been. It may not be made so by the operation of the Constitution of
Illinois or this statute, but it is by the facts.

. . . For our purposes we must assume that, if a state of facts
could exist that would justify such legislation, it actually did exist when
the statute now under consideration was passed. For us the question is
one of power, not of expediency. If no state of circumstances could
exist to justify such a statute, then we may declare this one void,
because in excess of the legislative power of the State. But if it could,
we must presume it did. Of the propriety of legislative interference
within the scope of legislative power, the legislature is the exclusive
judge.

Neither is it a matter of any moment that no precedent can be
found for a statute precisely like this. It is conceded that the business
is one of recent origin. . . . It presents, therefore, a case for the
application of a long-known and well-established principle in social

science, and this statute simply extends the law so as to meet this new development of commercial progress. There is no attempt to compel these owners to grant the public an interest in their property, but to declare their obligations, if they use it in this particular manner. . . .

It is insisted, however, that the owner of property is entitled to a reasonable compensation for its use, even though it be clothed with a public interest, and that what is reasonable is a judicial and not a legislative question.

As has already been shown, the practice has been otherwise. In countries where the common law prevails, it has been customary from time immemorial for the legislature to declare what shall be a reasonable compensation under such circumstances, or, perhaps more properly speaking, to fix a maximum beyond which any charge made would be unreasonable. Undoubtedly, in mere private contracts, relating to matters in which the public has no interest, what is reasonable must be ascertained judicially. But this is because the legislature has no control over such a contract. . . . Rights of property which have been created by the common law cannot be taken away without due process; but the law itself, as a rule of conduct, may be changed at the will, or even at the whim, of the legislature, unless prevented by constitutional limitations. . . .

We know that this is a power which may be abused; but that is no argument against its existence. For protection against abuses by legislatures the people must resort to the polls, not to the courts. . . .

Judgment Affirmed.

Mr. Justice **FIELD.**

. . . The principle upon which the opinion of the majority proceeds is, in my judgment, subversive of the rights of private property.
. . .

The declaration of the [Illinois] Constitution of 1870, that private buildings used for private purposes shall be deemed public institutions, does not make them so. The receipt and storage of grain in a building erected by private means for that purpose does not constitute the building a public warehouse. There is no magic in the language, though used by a constitutional convention, which can change a private business into a public one. . . . A tailor's or a shoemaker's shop would still retain its private character, even though the assembled wisdom of the State should declare . . . that such a place was a public workshop. . . . One might as well attempt to change the nature of colors, by giving them a new designation. The defendants were no more public warehousemen . . . than the merchant who sells his merchandise to the public is a public merchant, or the blacksmith who shoes horses for the public is a public blacksmith; and it is a strange notion that by calling them so they would be brought under legislative control. . . .

. . . . When Sir Matthew Hale, and the sages of the law in his day, spoke of property as affected by a public interest, and ceasing from that cause to be *juris privati* solely, ... they referred to property dedicated by the owner to public uses, or to property the use of which was granted by the government, or in connection with which special privileges were conferred. Unless the property was thus dedicated, or some right bestowed by the government was held with the property, either by specific grant or by prescription of so long a time as to imply a grant originally, the property was not affected by any public interest so as to be taken out of the category of property held in private right. But it is not in any such sense that the terms "clothing property with a public interest" are used in this case. From the nature of the business under consideration—the storage of grain—which, in any sense in which the words can be used, is a private business, in which the public are interested only as they are interested in the storage of other products of the soil, or in articles of manufacture, it is clear that the court intended to declare that, whenever one devotes his property to a business which is useful to the public,—"affects the community at large,"—the legislature can regulate the compensation which the owner may receive for its use, and for his own services in connection with it. . . . .

If this be sound law, if there be no protection, either in the principles upon which our republican government is founded, or in the prohibitions of the Constitution against such invasion of private rights, all property and all business in the State are held at the mercy of a majority of its legislature. The public has no greater interest in the use of buildings for the storage of grain than it has in the use of buildings for the residences of families . . . and, according to the doctrine announced, the legislature may fix the rent of all tenements used for residence, without reference to the cost of their erection. If the owner does not like the rates prescribed, he may cease renting his houses. He has granted to the public, says the court, an interest in the use of the buildings, and "he may withdraw his grant by discontinuing the use; but, so long as he maintains the use, he must submit to the control." . . . [T]here is hardly an enterprise or business engaging the attention and labor of any considerable portion of the community, in which the public has not an interest in the sense in which that term is used by the court in its opinion; and the doctrine which allows the legislature to interfere with and regulate the charges which the owners of property thus employed shall make for its use . . . has never before been asserted, so far as I am aware, by any judicial tribunal in the United States. . . . .

. . . . The provision [of the Fourteenth Amendment] . . . places property under the same protection as life and liberty. Except by due process of law, no State can deprive any person of either. The provision has been supposed to secure to every individual the essential conditions for the pursuit of happiness; and for that reason has not been heretofore, and should never be, construed in any narrow or restricted sense.

No State "shall deprive any person of life, liberty, or property without due process of law. . . ." By the term "life" . . . something more is meant than mere animal existence. The inhibition against its deprivation extends to all those limbs and faculties by which life is enjoyed. The provision equally prohibits the mutilation of the body by the amputation of an arm or leg, or the putting out of an eye, or the destruction of any other organ of the body through which the soul communicates with the outer world. The deprivation not only of life, but of whatever God has given to every one with life, for its growth and enjoyment, is prohibited . . . if its efficacy be not frittered away by judicial decision.

By the term "liberty" . . . something more is meant than mere freedom from physical restraint or the bounds of a prison. It means freedom to go where one may choose, and to act in such manner, not inconsistent with the equal rights of others, as his judgment may dictate for the promotion of his happiness; that is, to pursue such callings and avocations as may be most suitable to develop his capacities, and give to them their highest enjoyment.

The same liberal construction which is required for the protection of life and liberty, in all particulars in which life and liberty are of any value, should be applied to the protection of private property. . . .

. . . The legislation in question is nothing less than a bold assertion of absolute power by the State to control at its discretion the property and business of the citizen, and fix the compensation he shall receive. The will of the legislature is made the condition upon which the owner shall receive the fruits of his property and the just reward of his labor, industry, and enterprise. "That government," says Story, "can scarcely be deemed to be free where the rights of property are left solely dependent upon the will of a legislative body without any restraint. The fundamental maxims of a free government seem to require that the rights of personal liberty and private property should be held sacred," Wilkeson v. Leland . . . [1829]. The decision of the court in this case gives unrestrained license to legislative will. . . .

. . . But I deny the power of any legislature under our government to fix the price which one shall receive for his property of any kind. If the power can be exercised as to one article, it may as to all articles, and the prices of every thing, from a calico gown to a city mansion, may be the subject of legislative direction. . . .

Mr. Justice **STRONG**. . . .

I concur in what [Mr. Justice **FIELD**] has said.

Editors' Notes

(1) The doctrine "affected with a public interest" sounds strange to modern ears, but it was widely used in nineteenth century law. See Harry N. Scheiber, "The Road to *Munn*," 5 *Perspectives in Am. Hist.* 329 (1971).

(2) Compare the individualistic philosophy of Field's dissent here with his dissent in the Slaughter-House Cases (1873; reprinted above, p. 435).

(3) *Munn* heartened the Grangers but it shocked and angered many more wealthy economic and political interest groups. See the introductory essay to this chapter, pp. 942–943 for that reaction.

Munn did not challenge the new conception of dynamic, productive use of property. Rather it built on that concept to legitimate legislative action that imposed *duties* on the sorts of people who had expanded their rights to property, on grounds that these people were performing public functions. By 1895, however, the doctrine of laissez faire had become the dominant constitutional jurisprudence. The justices were to use the Tenth Amendment to strike down federal regulations and the Fourteenth's due process clause to invalidate state statutes. To understand these cases involving substantive due process in the economic sphere and later decisions involving substantive due process in other areas, such as privacy—see, for example, Griswold v. Connecticut (1965; reprinted above, p. 113) and Roe v. Wade (1973; reprinted below, p. 1109)—one must keep in mind that more than economic interests were in conflict in the earlier cases. There were also clashes between very different visions of what society was actually like, what it was becoming, what it should become, and what the goal of individual autonomy meant and required in those actual and potential worlds.

"No legislature can bargain away the public health or the public morals."

STONE v. MISSISSIPPI

101 U.S. (11 Otto) 814, 25 L.Ed. 1079 (1880).

In 1867 Mississippi granted a 25-year charter to a lottery company for an initial fee of $5,000 and an annual tax of $1,000. The following year, however, the state adopted a new constitution, one clause of which forbade the legislature to authorize lotteries or the sale of lottery tickets. In 1870 the legislature enacted a statute which, in effect, repealed the charter of 1867. In 1874 the state attorney general began legal proceedings against the company, and Mississippi courts ruled that it could no longer do business within the state. The company then obtained a writ of error from the U.S. Supreme Court.

Mr. Chief Justice **WAITE** delivered the opinion of the court. . . .

It is now too late to contend that any contract which a State actually enters into when granting a charter to a private corporation is not within the protection of the clause in the Constitution of the United States that prohibits States from passing laws impairing the obligation of contracts. . . . The doctrines of Trustees of Dartmouth College v. Woodward [1819] have become so imbedded in the jurisprudence of the United States as to make them to all intents and purposes a part of the Constitution itself. In this connection, however, it is to be kept in mind that it is not the charter which is protected, but only any contract the charter may contain. If there is no contract, there is nothing in the grant on which the Constitution can act. Consequently, the first inquiry in this class of cases always is, whether a contract has in fact been entered into, and if so, what its obligations are.

In the present case the question is whether the State of Mississippi, in its sovereign capacity, did by the charter now under consideration bind itself irrevocably by a contract. . . . There can be no dispute but that . . . the legislature of the State chartered a lottery company . . . for twenty-five years. . . . If the legislature that granted this charter had the power to bind the people of the State and all succeeding legislatures to allow the corporation to continue its corporate business during the whole term of its authorized existence, there is no doubt about the sufficiency of the language employed to effect that object, although there was an evident purpose to conceal the vice of the transaction by the phrases that were used. Whether the alleged contract exists, therefore, or not, depends on the authority of the legislature to bind the State and the people of the State in that way.

All agree that the legislature cannot bargain away the police power of a State. . . . Many attempts have been made in this court and elsewhere to define the police power, but never with entire success. It is always easier to determine whether a particular case comes within the general scope of the power, than to give an abstract definition of the power itself which will be in all respects accurate. No one denies, however, that it extends to all matters affecting the public health or the public morals. Beer Company v. Massachusetts [1878]; Patterson v. Kentucky [1878]. Neither can it be denied that lotteries are proper subjects for the exercise of this power. When the government is untrammelled by any claim of vested rights or chartered privileges, no one has ever supposed that lotteries could not lawfully be suppressed, and those who manage them punished severely as violators of the rules of social morality. . . .

The question is therefore directly presented, whether, in view of these facts, the legislature of a State can, by the charter of a lottery company, defeat the will of the people, authoritatively expressed, in relation to the further continuance of such business in their midst. We think it cannot. No legislature can bargain away the public health or the public morals. The people themselves cannot do it, much less their servants. . . . Government is organized with a view to their preservation, and cannot divest itself of the power to provide for them. For this purpose the largest legislative discretion is allowed, and the discretion cannot be parted with any more than the power itself. *Beer Company.* . . .

In *Dartmouth College* . . . Chief Justice Marshall . . . was careful to say . . . "that the framers of the Constitution did not intend to restrain States in the regulation of their civil institutions, adopted for internal government, and that the instrument they have given us is not to be so construed." The present case, we think, comes within this limitation. . . .

. . . [T]he power of governing is a trust committed by the people to the government, no part of which can be granted away. The people, in their sovereign capacity, have established their agencies for the preservation of the public health and the public morals, and the protection of public and private rights. These several agencies can govern according to their discretion, if within the scope of their general authority, while in power; but they cannot give away nor sell the discretion of those that are to come after them, in respect to matters the government of which, from the very nature of things, must "vary with varying circumstances." . . .

The contracts which the Constitution protects are those that relate to property rights, not governmental. It is not always easy to tell on which side of the line which separates governmental from property rights a particular case is to be put; but in respect to lotteries there can be no difficulty. . . . They are species of gambling, and wrong in their influences. They disturb the checks and balances of a well-ordered community. . . . Certainly the right to suppress them is governmental, to be exercised at all times by those in power, at their discretion. Any one, therefore, who accepts a lottery charter does so with the implied understanding that the people, in their sovereign capacity, and through their properly constituted agencies, may resume it at any time when the public good shall require, whether it be paid for or not. . . .

Judgment affirmed.

Editors' Notes

(1) **Query:** In *Stone* where does the Court find an "implied understanding" that a contract with a state regarding lotteries—or any other subject—can be modified by the state? In the words of the constitutional document? In reasoned inference from those words? In the "intent of the framers"? In previous decisions? In some theory of democracy or constitutionalism?

(2) During Marshall's era, the contracts clause was the principal judicial instrument for protecting property rights. *Stone,* however, dealt a powerful blow to the holding in Fletcher v. Peck (1810; reprinted above, p. 956) and *Dartmouth College* (1819) that state grants were contracts for constitutional purposes. Home Building & Loan Assn v. Blaisdell (1934; reprinted above, p. 136), weakened the contract clause as a limitation on state power to modify contracts between private citizens. More than forty years after *Blaisdell,* the Court suddenly struck down two state statutes and reminded the world that the "Contract Clause remains part of the Constitution. It is not a dead letter." United States Trust Co. v. New Jersey (1977); Allied Structural Steel Co. v. Spannaus (1978). See the literature cited in the Editors' Note 4 to *Charles River Bridge* (1837), at p. 960.

"Statutes of the nature of that under review . . . are mere meddlesome interferences with the rights of the individual. . . ."

LOCHNER v. NEW YORK

198 U.S. 45, 25 S.Ct. 539, 49 L.Ed. 937 (1905).

Mr. Justice **PECKHAM** . . . delivered the opinion of the Court.

The indictment . . . charges that the plaintiff in error violated . . . the labor law of the State of New York, in that he wrongfully and unlawfully required and permitted an employé working for him to work more than sixty hours in one week. . . . The mandate of the statute that "no employé shall be required or permitted to work," is the substantial equivalent of an enactment that "no employé shall contract or agree to work," more than ten hours per day, and as there is no provision for special emergencies the statute is mandatory in all cases. It is not an act merely fixing the number of hours which shall constitute a legal day's work, but an absolute prohibition upon the employer, permitting, under any circumstances, more than ten hours work to be done in his establishment. The employé may desire to earn the extra money, which would arise from his working more than the prescribed time, but this statute forbids the employer from permitting the employé to earn it.

The statute necessarily interferes with the right of contract between the employer and employés, concerning the number of hours in which the latter may labor in the bakery of the employer. The general right to make a contract in relation to his business is part of the liberty of the individual protected by the Fourteenth Amendment of the Federal Constitution. Allgeyer v. Louisiana [1897]. Under that provision no State can deprive any person of life, liberty or property without due process of law. The right to purchase or to sell labor is part of the liberty protected by this amendment, unless there are circumstances which exclude the right. There are, however, certain powers, existing in the sovereignty of each State in the Union, somewhat vaguely termed police powers, the exact description and limitation of which have not been attempted by the courts. Those powers . . . relate to the safety, health, morals and general welfare of the public. Both property and liberty are held on such reasonable conditions as may be imposed by the governing power of the State in the exercise of those powers, and with such conditions the Fourteenth Amendment was not designed to interfere. Mugler v. Kansas [1887]; In re Kemmler [1878]; Crowley v. Christensen [1890]; In re Converse [1891].

The State, therefore, has power to prevent the individual from making certain kinds of contracts. . . . Contracts in violation of a statute, either of the Federal or state government, or a contract to let one's property for immoral purposes, or to do any other unlawful act, could obtain no protection from the Federal Constitution, as coming under the liberty of person or of free contract. Therefore, when the State . . . in the assumed exercise of its police powers, has passed an act which seriously limits the right to labor or the right of contract in regard to their means of livelihood between persons . . . it becomes of great importance to determine which shall prevail—the right of the individual to labor for such time as he may choose, or the right of the State to prevent the individual from laboring . . . beyond a certain time prescribed by the State.

This court has recognized the existence and upheld the exercise of the police powers of the States in many cases. . . .

It must, of course, be conceded that there is a limit to the valid exercise of the police power by the State. . . . Otherwise the Fourteenth Amendment would have no efficacy and the legislatures of the States would have unbounded power, and it would be enough to say that any piece of legislation was enacted to conserve the morals, the health or the safety of the people. . . . The claim of the police power would be a mere pretext—become another and delusive name for the supreme sovereignty of the State to be exercised free from constitutional restraint. . . . In every case that comes before this court, therefore, where legislation of this character is concerned and where the protection of the Federal Constitution is sought, the question necessarily arises: Is this a fair, reasonable and appropriate exercise of the police power of the State . . . ? Of course the liberty of contract relating to labor includes both parties to it. The one has as much right to purchase as the other to sell labor.

This is not a question of substituting the judgment of the court for that of the legislature. If the act be within the power of the State it is valid, although the judgment of the court might be totally opposed to the enactment of such a law. But the question would still remain: Is it within the police power of the State? and that question must be answered by the court.

It is a question of which of two powers or rights shall prevail—the power of the State to legislate or the right of the individual to liberty of person and freedom of contract. . . .

. . . There is no reasonable ground for interfering with the liberty of person or the right of free contract, by determining the hours of labor, in the occupation of a baker. There is no contention that bakers as a class are not equal in intelligence and capacity to men in other trades or manual occupations, or that they are not able to assert their rights and care for themselves without the protecting arm of the State, interfering with their independence of judgment and of action. They are in no sense wards of the State. Viewed in the light of a purely labor law, with no reference whatever to the question of health, we think that a law like the one before us involves neither the safety, the morals nor the welfare of the public, and that the interest of the public is not in the slightest degree affected by such an act. The law must be upheld, if at all, as a law pertaining to the health of the individual engaged in the occupation of a baker. . . . Clean and wholesome bread does not depend upon whether the baker works but ten hours per day or only sixty hours a week. The limitation of the hours of labor does not come within the police power on that ground. . . .

We think that there can be no fair doubt that the trade of a baker, in and of itself, is not an unhealthy one to that degree which would authorize the legislature to interfere with the right to labor, and with the right of free contract on the part of the individual, either as employer or employé. . . . It might be safely affirmed that almost all occupations more or less affect the health. . . . But are we all, on that account, at the mercy of legislative majorities? A printer, a tinsmith, a locksmith, a carpenter, a cabinetmaker, a dry goods clerk, a bank's, a lawyer's or a physician's clerk, or a clerk in almost any kind of business, would all come under the power of the legislature, on this assumption. . . .

It is also urged . . . that it is to the interest of the State that its population should be strong and robust, and therefore any legislation which may be said to tend to make people healthy must be valid as health laws, enacted under the police power. If this be a valid argument . . . it follows that the protection of the Federal Constitution from undue interference with liberty of person and freedom of contract is visionary. . . . Scarcely any law but might find shelter under such assumptions. . . . Not only the hours of employés, but the hours of employers, could be regulated, and doctors, lawyers, scientists, all professional men, as well as athletes and artisans, could be forbidden to fatigue their brains and bodies by prolonged hours of exercise. . . . We mention these extreme cases because the contention is extreme. We do not believe in the soundness of the views which uphold this law. On the contrary, we think that such a law as this, although passed in the assumed exercise of the police power, and as relating to the public health, or the health of the employés named, is not within the meaning of that power, and is invalid. The act is . . . an illegal interference with the rights of individuals, both employers and employés, to make such contracts regarding labor upon such terms as they may think best. . . . Statutes of the nature of that under review . . . are mere meddlesome interferences with the rights of the individual. . . .

This interference on the part of the legislatures of the several States with the ordinary trades and occupations of the people seems to be on the increase. . . .

It is impossible to shut our eyes to the fact that many of the laws of this character, while passed under what is claimed to be the police power for the purpose of protecting the public health or welfare, are, in reality, passed from other motives. . . . The purpose of a statute must be determined from the natural and legal effect of the language employed; and whether or not it is repugnant to the Constitution of the United States must be determined from the natural effect of such statutes when put into operation, and not from their proclaimed purpose. . . . The court looks beyond the mere letter of the law in such cases. Yick Wo v. Hopkins [1886].

It is manifest to us that . . . the real object and purpose were simply to regulate the hours of labor between the master and his employés . . . in a private business, not dangerous in any degree to morals or in any real and substantial degree, to the health of the employés. Under such circumstances the freedom of the master and employé to contract with each other . . . cannot be prohibited or interfered with, without violating the Federal Constitution. . . .

Reversed.

Mr. Justice **HARLAN,** with whom Mr. Justice **WHITE** and Mr. Justice **DAY** concurred, dissenting. . . .

Granting . . . that there is a liberty of contract which cannot be violated even under the sanction of direct legislative enactment, but assuming, as according to settled law we may assume, that such liberty of contract is subject to such regulations as the State may reasonably prescribe for the common good and the well-being of society, what are the conditions under which the judiciary may declare such regulations to be in excess of legislative authority and void? Upon this point there is no room for dispute; for, the rule is universal that a legislative enactment, Federal or state, is never to be disregarded or held invalid unless it be, beyond question, plainly and palpably in excess of legislative power. . . . If there be doubt as to the validity of the statute, that doubt must therefore be resolved in favor of its validity . . . leaving the legislature to meet the responsibility for unwise legislation. If the end which the legislature seeks to accomplish be one to which its power extends, and if the means employed to that end, although not the wisest or best, are yet not plainly and palpably unauthorized by law, then the court cannot interfere. In other words, when the validity of a statute is questioned, the burden of proof, so to speak, is upon those who assert it to be unconstitutional. McCulloch v. Maryland [1819].

Let these principles be applied to the present case. . . .

It is plain that this statute was enacted in order to protect the physical well-being of those who work in bakery and confectionery establishments. . . . [T]he statute must be taken as expressing the belief of the people of New York that, as a general rule . . . labor in excess of sixty hours during a week in such establishments may endanger the health of those who thus labor. Whether or not this be wise legislation it is not the province of the court to inquire. Under our systems of government the courts are not concerned with the wisdom or policy of legislation. . . . I find it impossible, in view of common experience, to say that there is here no real or substantial relation between the means employed by the State and the end sought to be accomplished by its legislation. . . . Nor can I say that the statute has no appropriate or direct connection with that protection to health which each State owes to her citizens . . . or that it is not promotive of the health of the employés in question . . . or that the regulation prescribed by the State is utterly unreasonable and extravagant or wholly arbitrary. . . . Still less can I say that the statute is, beyond question, a plain, palpable invasion of rights secured by the fundamental law. . . .

Mr. Justice **HOLMES** dissenting. . . .

This case is decided upon an economic theory which a large part of the country does not entertain. If it were a question whether I agreed with that theory, I should desire to study it further and long before making up my mind. But I do not conceive that to be my duty, because I strongly believe that my agreement or disagreement has nothing to do with the right of a majority to embody their opinions in law. It is settled by various decisions of this court that state constitutions and state laws may regulate life in many ways which we as legislators might think as injudicious or if you like as tyrannical as this, and which equally with this interfere with the liberty to contract. Sunday laws and usury laws are ancient examples. . . . The liberty of the citizen to do as he likes so long as he does not interfere with the liberty of others to do the same, which has been a shibboleth for some well-known writers, is interfered with by school laws, by the Post Office, by every state or municipal institution which takes his money for purposes thought desirable, whether he likes it or not. The Fourteenth Amendment does not enact Mr. Herbert Spencer's Social Statics. The other day we sustained the Massachusetts vaccination law. Jacobson v. Massachusetts [1905].

United States and state statutes and decisions cutting down the liberty to contract by way of combination are familiar to this court. Northern Securities Co. v. United States [1904]. Two years ago we upheld the prohibition of sales of stock on margins or for future delivery in the constitution of California. Otis v. Parker [1903]. The decision sustaining an eight hour law for miners is still recent. Holden v. Hardy [1898]. Some of those laws embody convictions or prejudices which judges are likely to share. Some may not. But a constitution is not intended to embody a particular economic theory, whether of paternalism and the organic relation of the citizen to the State or of *laissez faire*. It is made for people of fundamentally differing views, and the accident of our finding certain opinions natural and familiar or novel and even shocking ought not to conclude our judgment upon the question whether statutes embodying them conflict with the Constitution of the United States.

General propositions do not decide concrete cases. The decision will depend on a judgment or intuition more subtle than any articulate major premise. . . . Every opinion tends to become a law. I think that the word liberty in the Fourteenth Amendment is perverted when it is held to prevent the natural outcome of a dominant opinion, unless it can be said that a rational and fair man necessarily would admit that the statute proposed would infringe fundamental principles as they have been understood by the traditions of our people and our law. It does not need research to show that no such sweeping condemnation can be passed upon the statute before us. A reasonable man might think it a proper measure on the score of health. Men whom I certainly could not pronounce unreasonable would uphold it as a first instalment of a general regulation of the hours of work. . . .

Editors' Notes

(1) **Query:** How persuasive is Holmes's claim that "a constitution is not intended to embody a particular economic theory"? Does a constitution necessarily embody a political theory or combination of political theories? What, for constitutional interpretation, is the relationship between economic and political theory? (See the dissent of Justice Harlan, II, in Harper v. Virginia [1966; reprinted above, p. 151].)

(2) **Query:** Aside from the Dred Scott Case (1857) and Korematsu v. United States (1944; reprinted below, p. 1197) *Lochner* is perhaps the most infamous case in American constitutional history. "To Lochner" or "to Lochnerize" has become a term of opprobrium referring to judges' reading their personal preferences about fundamental rights into the Constitution. To what extent are the Court's critics correct when they claim that any discovery of unlisted fundamental rights involves "Lochnering"?

(3) **Query:** Does the notion of "substantive due process" affect both HOW to interpret and WHAT is to be interpreted so as to change the due process clauses in the Fifth and Fourteenth amendments to read "due substance" of law? Cf. Henry P. Monaghan, "Our Perfect Constitution," 56 *N.Y.U.L.Rev.* 353 (1981).

"[F]reedom of contract is . . . the general rule and restraint the exception. . . ."

ADKINS v. CHILDREN'S HOSPITAL
261 U.S. 525, 43 S.Ct. 394, 67 L.Ed. 785 (1923).

Lochner stirred a reaction among liberals much as *Munn* had among the new alliance for capitalism. The National Consumers League retained a prominent Boston attorney, Louis D. Brandeis, to defend the legislation the Progressive movement had managed to get on the statute books to protect workers. The immediate result was an instrument known as the Brandeis Brief, a legal argument that justified such statutes by amassing hard social and economic data to show the nature of the problem and the reasonableness of the regulation rather than by construing abstract constitutional doctrines or explaining away earlier decisions. Brandeis first used this instrument in Muller v. Oregon (1908) and won a unanimous ruling sustaining, "without questioning in any respect the decision in Lochner v. New York," the validity of an Oregon law limiting the hours that women could work in laundries. Bunting v. Oregon (1917)—Brandeis was then on the Supreme Court and a young lawyer named Felix Frankfurter had taken his place as advocate—upheld a law setting maximum hours for both men and women.

Bunting, however, was a temporary high water mark for the constitutionality of progressive legislation. During oral argument in Adams v. Tanner (1917), Chief Justice Edward Douglass White picked up the Brandeis Brief dealing with abuses by private employment agencies and remarked that he could easily compile a document twice as thick that would justify outlawing the legal profession. By a 6–3 vote, the Court then struck down the state statute that forbade private employment agencies to charge job seekers fees for finding them work. The validity of a state minimum wage law for women divided the justices 4–4 in Stettler v. O'Hara. Equal division meant that the lower court's decision, which happened to be in favor of the constitutionality of the act, stood; equal division also meant, however, that *Stettler* had no authority as a precedent of the Supreme Court.

Another opportunity to settle the issue of regulation of wages arose when a hospital and a female employee obtained an injunction against enforcement of an Act of Congress that had created a board to set minimum wages for women and minors in the District of Columbia. The board appealed to the Supreme Court.

Mr. Justice **SUTHERLAND** delivered the opinion of the Court. .   .   .

The judicial duty of passing upon the constitutionality of an act of Congress is one of great gravity and delicacy. The statute here in question has successfully borne the scrutiny of the legislative branch of the government, which, by enacting it, has affirmed its validity; and that determination must be given great weight. This Court, by an unbroken line of decisions from Chief Justice Marshall to the present day, has steadily adhered to the rule that every possible presumption is in favor of the validity of an act of Congress until overcome beyond rational doubt. But if by clear and indubitable demonstration a statute be opposed to the Constitution we have no choice but to say so. The Constitution, by its own terms, is the supreme law of the land, emanating from the people, the repository of ultimate sovereignty under our form of government. A congressional statute, on the other hand, is the act of an agency of this sovereign authority and if it conflict with the Constitution must fall; for that which is not supreme must yield to that which is. To hold it invalid (if it be invalid) is a plain exercise of the judicial power—that power vested in courts to enable them to administer justice according to law. From the authority to ascertain and determine the law in a given case, there necessarily results, in case of conflict, the duty to declare and enforce the rule of the supreme law and reject that of an inferior act of legislation which, transcending the Constitution, is of no effect and binding on no one. This is not the exercise of a substantive power to review and nullify acts of Congress, for no such substantive power exists. It is simply a necessary concomitant of the power to hear and dispose of a case or controversy properly before the court, to the determination of which must be brought the test and measure of the law.

That the right to contract about one's affairs is a part of the liberty of the individual protected by this [the Due Process] clause, is settled by the decisions of this Court and is no longer open to question. Allgeyer v. Louisiana [1897]; Coppage v. Kansas [1915]; Adair v. United States [1908]; *Lochner*; *Muller*.

There is, of course, no such thing as absolute freedom of contract. It is subject to a great variety of restraints. But freedom of contract is, nevertheless, the general rule and restraint the exception; and the exercise of legislative authority to abridge it can be justified only by the existence of exceptional circumstances. Whether these circumstances

exist in the present case constitutes the question to be answered.
. . .

In the *Muller Case* the validity of an Oregon statute, forbidding the
employment of any female in certain industries more than ten hours
during any one day was upheld. The decision proceeded upon the
theory that the difference between the sexes may justify a different
rule respecting hours of labor in the case of women than in the case of
men. It is pointed out that these consist in differences of physical
structure, especially in respect of the maternal functions, and also in
the fact that historically woman has always been dependent upon man,
who has established his control by superior physical strength. . . .
But the ancient inequality of the sexes, otherwise than physical, . . .
has continued "with diminishing intensity." In view of the great—not
to say revolutionary—changes which have taken place . . . in the
contractual, political and civil status of women, culminating in the
Nineteenth Amendment, it is not unreasonable to say that these
differences have now come almost, if not quite, to the vanishing point.
In this aspect of the matter, while the physical differences must be
recognized in appropriate cases, and legislation fixing hours or conditions of work may properly take them into account, we cannot accept
the doctrine that women of mature age, *sui juris,* require or may be
subjected to restrictions upon their liberty of contract which could not
lawfully be imposed in the case of men under similar circumstances.
To do so would be to ignore all the implications to be drawn from the
present day trend of legislation, as well as that of common thought and
usage, by which woman is accorded emancipation from the old doctrine
that she must be given special protection or be subjected to special
restraint in her contractual and civil relationships. . . .

The essential characteristics of the statute now under consideration, which differentiate it from the laws fixing hours of labor, will be
made to appear as we proceed. It is sufficient now to point out that the
latter . . . deal with incidents of the employment having no necessary effect upon the heart of the contract, that is, the amount of wages
to be paid and received. A law forbidding work to continue beyond a
given number of hours leaves the parties free to contract about wages
and thereby equalize whatever additional burdens may be imposed
upon the employer as a result of the restrictions as to hours, by an
adjustment in respect to the amount of wages. Enough has been said
to show that the authority to fix hours of labor cannot be exercised
except in respect of those occupations where work of long continued
duration is detrimental to health. This Court has been careful in every
case where the question has been raised, to place its decision upon this
limited authority of the legislature to regulate hours of labor and to
disclaim any purpose to uphold the legislation as fixing wages, thus
recognizing an essential difference between the two. It seems plain
that these decisions afford no real support for any form of law establishing minimum wages.

If now . . . we examine and analyze the statute in question, we shall see that it differs from them in every material respect. It is not a law dealing with any business charged with a public interest or with public work, or to meet and tide over a temporary emergency. It has nothing to do with the character, methods or periods of wage payments. It does not prescribe hours of labor or conditions under which labor is to be done. It is not for the protection of persons under legal disability or for the prevention of fraud. It is simply and exclusively a price-fixing law, confined to adult women . . . who are legally as capable of contracting for themselves as men. It forbids two parties having lawful capacity . . . to freely contract with one another in respect of the price for which one shall render service to the other in a purely private employment where both are willing, perhaps anxious, to agree, even though the consequence may be to oblige one to surrender a desirable engagement and the other to dispense with the services of a desirable employee. The price fixed by the board need have no relation to the capacity or earning power of the employee, the number of hours which may happen to constitute the day's work, the character of the place where the work is to be done, or the circumstances or surroundings of the employment. . . . It is based wholly on the opinions of the members of the board and their advisers—perhaps an average of their opinions, if they do not precisely agree—as to what will be necessary to provide a living for a woman, keep her in health and preserve her morals. It applies to any and every occupation in the District, without regard to its nature or the character of the work. . . .

The law takes account of the necessities of only one party to the contract. It ignores the necessities of the employer by compelling him to pay not less than a certain sum, not only whether the employee is capable of earning it, but irrespective of the ability of his business to sustain the burden, generously leaving him, of course, the privilege of abandoning his business as an alternative for going on at a loss. . . . It therefore undertakes to solve but one-half of the problem. The other half is the establishment of a corresponding standard of efficiency, and this forms no part of the policy of the legislation, although in practice the former half without the latter must lead to ultimate failure, in accordance with the inexorable law that no one can continue indefinitely to take out more than he puts in without ultimately exhausting the supply. . . . To the extent that the sum fixed exceeds the fair value of the services rendered, it amounts to a compulsory exaction from the employer for the support of a partially indigent person, for whose condition there rests upon him no peculiar responsibility, and therefore, in effect, arbitrarily shifts to his shoulders a burden which, if it belongs to anybody, belongs to society as a whole. . . .

. . . The ethical right of every worker, man or woman, to a living wage may be conceded. . . . [B]ut the fallacy of the proposed method of attaining it is that it assumes that every employer is bound at all events to furnish it. The moral requirement implicit in every contract of employment, viz, that the amount to be paid and the service

to be rendered shall bear to each other some relation of just equiva-
lence, is completely ignored. . . .

We are asked, upon the one hand, to consider the fact that several
States have adopted similar statutes, and we are invited, upon the other
hand, to give weight to the fact that three times as many States,
presumably as well informed and as anxious to promote the health and
morals of their people, have refrained from enacting such legislation.
We have also been furnished with a large number of printed opinions
approving the policy of the minimum wage, and our own reading has
disclosed a large number to the contrary. These are all proper enough
for the consideration of the lawmaking bodies, since their tendency is to
establish the desirability or undesirability of the legislation; but they
reflect no legitimate light upon the question of its validity, and that is
what we are called upon to decide. The elucidation of that question
cannot be aided by counting heads.

It is said that great benefits have resulted from the operation of
such statutes. . . . They may be, and quite probably are, due to
other causes. We cannot close our eyes to the notorious fact that
earnings everywhere in all occupations have greatly increased . . .
quite as much or more among men as among women and in occupations
outside the reach of the law as in those governed by it. No real test of
the economic value of the law can be had during periods of maximum
employment. . . .

Finally, it may be said that if, in the interest of the public welfare,
the police power may be invoked to justify the fixing of a minimum
wage, it may, when the public welfare is thought to require it, be
invoked to justify a maximum wage. The power to fix high wages
connotes, by like course of reasoning, the power to fix low wages.
. . .

. . . To sustain the individual freedom of action contemplated by
the Constitution, is not to strike down the common good but to exalt it;
for surely the good of society as a whole cannot be better served than by
the preservation against arbitrary restraint of the liberties of its
constituent members. . . .

Affirmed.

Mr. Justice **BRANDEIS** took no part in the consideration or decision of
these cases.

Mr. Chief Justice **TAFT,** dissenting. . . .

The boundary of the police power beyond which its exercise becomes an invasion of the guaranty of liberty under the Fifth and
Fourteenth Amendments to the Constitution is not easy to mark. Our
Court has been laboriously engaged in pricking out a line in successive
cases. We must be careful . . . to follow that line as well as we can
and not to depart from it by suggesting a distinction that is formal
rather than real.

. . . . [I]t is a disputable question in the field of political economy how far a statutory requirement of maximum hours or minimum wages may be a useful remedy. . . . But it is not the function of this Court to hold congressional acts invalid simply because they are passed to carry out economic views which the Court believes to be unwise or unsound.

The right of the legislature under the Fifth and Fourteenth Amendments to limit the hours of employment on the score of the health of the employee, it seems to me, has been firmly established.

. . . .

. . . . It is impossible for me to reconcile the *Bunting Case* and the *Lochner Case* and I have always supposed that the *Lochner Case* was thus overruled *sub silentio.* Yet the opinion of the Court herein in support of its conclusion quotes from the opinion in the *Lochner Case* as one which has been sometimes distinguished but never overruled. Certainly there was no attempt to distinguish it in the *Bunting Case.*

However, the opinion herein does not overrule the *Bunting Case* in express terms, and therefore I assume that the conclusion in this case rests on the distinction between a minimum of wages and a maximum of hours in the limiting of liberty to contract. . . . In absolute freedom of contract the one term is as important as the other, for both enter equally into the consideration given and received, a restriction as to one is not any greater in essence than the other, and is of the same kind. One is the multiplier and the other the multiplicand.

If it be said that long hours of labor have a more direct effect upon the health of the employee than the low wage, there is very respectable authority from close observers, disclosed in the record and in the literature on the subject quoted at length in the briefs, that they are equally harmful in this regard. Congress took this view and we can not say it was not warranted in so doing.

With deference to the very able opinion of the Court . . . it appears to me to exaggerate the importance of the wage term of the contract of employment as more inviolate than its other terms. Its conclusion seems influenced by the fear that the concession of the power to impose a minimum wage must carry with it a concession of the power to fix a maximum wage. This, I submit, is a *non sequitur.* A line of distinction like the one under discussion in this case is, as the opinion elsewhere admits, a matter of degree and practical experience and not of pure logic. Certainly the wide difference between prescribing a minimum wage and a maximum wage could as a matter of degree and experience be easily affirmed.

I am authorized to say that Mr. Justice **SANFORD** concurs in this opinion.

Mr. Justice **HOLMES,** dissenting. . . .

. . . . [T]he power of Congress seems absolutely free from doubt. The end, to remove conditions leading to ill health, immorality and the deterioration of the race, no one would deny to be within the scope of constitutional legislation. The means are means that have the approval of Congress, of many States, and of those governments from which we have learned our greatest lessons. When so many intelligent persons, who have studied the matter more than any of us can, have thought that the means are effective and are worth the price, it seems to me impossible to deny that the belief reasonably may be held by reasonable men. . . . [I]n the present instance the only objection that can be urged is found within the vague contours of the Fifth Amendment, prohibiting the depriving any person of liberty or property without due process of law. . . .

The earlier decisions upon the same words in the Fourteenth Amendment began within our memory and went no farther than an unpretentious assertion of the liberty to follow the ordinary callings. Later that innocuous generality was expanded into the dogma, Liberty of Contract. Contract is not specially mentioned in the text that we have to construe. It is merely an example of doing what you want to do, embodied in the word liberty. But pretty much all law consists in forbidding men to do some things that they want to do, and contract is no more exempt from law than other acts. Without enumerating all the restrictive laws that have been upheld I will mention a few that seem to me to have interfered with liberty of contract quite as seriously and directly as the one before us. Usury laws prohibit contracts by which a man receives more than so much interest for the money that he lends. Statutes of frauds restrict many contracts to certain forms. Some Sunday laws prohibit practically all contracts during one-seventh of our whole life. Insurance rates may be regulated. . . .

I confess that I do not understand the principle on which the power to fix a minimum for the wages of women can be denied by those who admit the power to fix a maximum for their hours of work. . . . The bargain is equally affected whichever half you regulate. Muller v. Oregon, I take it, is as good law today as it was in 1908. It will need more than the Nineteenth Amendment to convince me that there are no differences between men and women, or that legislation cannot take those differences into account. I should not hesitate to take them into account if I thought it necessary to sustain this act. Quong Wing v. Kirkendall [1912]. But after *Bunting*, I had supposed that it was not necessary, and that *Lochner* would be allowed a deserved repose.

The criterion of constitutionality is not whether we believe the law to be for the public good. We certainly cannot be prepared to deny that a reasonable man reasonably might have that belief in view of the legislation of Great Britain, Victoria and a number of the States of this Union. The belief is fortified by a very remarkable collection of documents submitted on behalf of the appellants, material here, I conceive, only as showing that the belief reasonably may be held. . . .

Editors' Notes

(1) **Query:** In the third sentence of that part of his opinion reprinted here, Sutherland said:

> This Court, by an unbroken line of decisions from Chief Justice Marshall to the present day, has steadily adhered to the rule that every possible presumption is in favor of the validity of an act of Congress until overcome by rational doubt.

Two paragraphs later, however, he also said:

> [F]reedom of contract is . . . the general rule and restraint the exception; and the exercise of legislative authority to abridge it can be justified only by the existence of exceptional circumstances.

Can these two sentences be reconciled? To what extent is the Court tacitly using a rule similar to that of strict scrutiny where fundamental rights are involved, with the fundamental right here being freedom of contract?

(2) **Query:** If one disagrees with Sutherland in *Adkins,* how can one distinguish between the nature of the fundamental right protected here and those guarded in, for example, Skinner v. Oklahoma (1942; reprinted above, p. 868), Shapiro v. Thompson (1969; reprinted above, p. 873), or the other decisions reprinted in Sec. III of Chapter 14? Those guarded by *Griswold* (1965; reprinted above, p. 113), Roe v. Wade (1973; reprinted below, p. 1109), and other cases reprinted in Chapter 17?

(3) **Query:** If one agrees with Sutherland in *Adkins,* does one also have to accept the jurisprudence behind, if not the specific decisions applying, strict scrutiny?

(4) For the genesis of the Brandeis Brief, see: Clement E. Vose, "The National Consumers' League and the Brandeis Brief," 1 *Midw. J. of Pol. Sci.* 267 (1957); and Alpheus Thomas Mason, *Brandeis: A Free Man's Life* (New York: Viking, 1946), chap. 16.

"[T]he Constitution does not recognize an absolute and uncontrollable liberty."

WEST COAST HOTEL v. PARRISH
300 U.S. 379, 57 S.Ct. 578, 81 L.Ed. 703 (1937).

Lochner and *Adkins* stood as barriers against state regulation of economic affairs; but other decisions—most recently before West Coast Hotel v. Parrish, Nebbia v. New York (1934)—indicated a more tolerant judicial attitude. The Court had also given mixed signals about federal regulations of the economy. Hammer v. Dagenhart (1918) had invalidated a statute curtailing shipment in interstate commerce of goods mined or produced by child labor. As in the Sugar Trust Case (1895), the majority held that neither mining nor manufacturing was commerce. The Court ignored the "necessary and proper clause" and gave a misleading paraphrase of the Tenth Amendment:

> In interpreting the Constitution it must never be forgotten that the nation is made up of States to which are entrusted the powers of

local government. And to them and to the people the powers not expressly [sic] delegated to the national government are reserved.

Hammer, however, was an extreme decision. During the 1920s the Court, though seldom warmly receptive, sustained most federal statutes attacked as exceeding the commerce power.

Then the New Deal's rash of regulation rekindled judicial hostility. During 1935 and 1936, the Court struck down much of the legislation Franklin Roosevelt had pushed through Congress. The usual explanation was that, in attempting to regulate conditions of labor, the federal government was exceeding its authority under the commerce clause and invading power the Tenth Amendment reserved to the states.

On the other hand, in the spring of 1936, Morehead v. New York held, 5–4, that a state law establishing minimum wages and maximum hours violated liberty of contract. In the fall, Roosevelt won in a landslide election. Three weeks before the election, the justices denied a rehearing in *Morehead.* Six weeks after, they heard argument in West Coast Hotel v. Parrish, a challenge to a statute from the state of Washington that was almost identical to the one from New York that *Morehead* had voided. At the conference, Owen J. Roberts, who had supplied the fifth vote in *Morehead,* now voted to sustain Washington's statute. Chief Justice Hughes, who had dissented in *Morehead,* assigned himself the task of writing the opinion of the Court. His work was not finished until March, and by then Roosevelt's campaign for his Court-packing bill was well under way.

Mr. Chief Justice **HUGHES** delivered the opinion of the Court. . . .

The appellant conducts a hotel. The appellee Elsie Parrish was employed as a chambermaid and (with her husband) brought this suit to recover the difference between the wages paid her and the minimum wage fixed pursuant to the state law. The minimum wage was $14.50 per week of 48 hours. The appellant challenged the act as repugnant to the due process clause of the Fourteenth Amendment of the Constitution of the United States. The Supreme Court of the State, reversing the trial court, sustained the statute. . . . This case is here on appeal.

The appellant relies upon the decision of this Court in Adkins v. Children's Hospital. . . . [C]ounsel for the appellees attempted to distinguish the *Adkins* case. . . . That effort at distinction is obviously futile. . . .

. . . Morehead v. New York . . . [1936] held the New York minimum wage act for women to be invalid. . . . [T]he Court of Appeals of New York had said that it found no material difference between the two statutes, and this Court held that the "meaning of the statute" as fixed by the decision of the state court "must be accepted here as if the meaning had been specifically expressed in the enactment." . . . That view led to the affirmance by this Court of the judgment in the *Morehead* case, as the Court considered that the only question before it was whether the *Adkins* case was distinguishable and that reconsideration of that decision had not been sought. . . .

. . . The Supreme Court of Washington has upheld that minimum wage statute of that State. It has decided that the statute is a reasonable exercise of the police power. . . . In reaching that conclusion the state court has invoked principles long established by this Court in the application of the Fourteenth Amendment. The state court has refused to regard . . . *Adkins* . . . as determinative and has pointed to our decisions both before and since that case as justifying its position. We are of the opinion that this ruling . . . demands . . . reexamination of the *Adkins* case. The importance of the question, in which many States have similar laws are concerned, the close division by which the decision in the *Adkins* case was reached, and the economic conditions which have supervened, and in the light of which the reasonableness of the exercise of the protective power of the State must be considered, make it not only appropriate, but . . . imperative, that . . . the subject receive fresh consideration. . . .

The principle which must control our decision is not in doubt. The constitutional provision invoked is the due process clause of the Fourteenth Amendment governing the States, as the due process clause invoked in the *Adkins* case governed Congress. In each case the violation alleged by those attacking minimum wage regulation for women is deprivation of freedom of contract. What is this freedom? The Constitution does not speak of freedom of contract. It speaks of liberty and prohibits the deprivation of liberty without due process of law. In prohibiting that deprivation the Constitution does not recognize an absolute and uncontrollable liberty. Liberty in each of its phases has its history and connotation. But the liberty safeguarded is liberty in a social organization which requires the protection of law against the evils which menace the health, safety, morals and welfare of the people. Liberty under the Constitution is thus necessarily subject to the restraints of due process, and regulation which is reasonable in relation to its subject and is adopted in the interests of the community is due process.

This essential limitation of liberty in general governs freedom of contract in particular. More than twenty-five years ago we set forth the applicable principlespm. . .: ". . . [f]reedom of contract is a qualified and not an absolute right. There is no absolute freedom to do as one wills or to contract as one chooses. . . . Liberty implies the absence of arbitrary restraint, not immunity from reasonable regulations and prohibitions imposed in the interests of the community." Chicago, B. & Q, R. Co. v. McGuire [1911].

This power under the Constitution to restrict freedom of contract has had many illustrations. . . . Thus statutes have been sustained limiting employment in underground mines and smelters to eight hours [per] day; in forbidding the payment of seamen's wages in advance; in prohibiting contracts limiting liability for injuries to employees; in limiting hours of work of employees in manufacturing establishments; and in maintaining workmen's compensation laws. In dealing with the relation of employer and employed, the legislature has necessarily a

wide field of discretion in order that there may be suitable protection of
health and safety, and that peace and good order may be promoted
through regulations designed to insure wholesome conditions of work
and freedom from oppression. . . .

The point that has been strongly stressed that adult employees
should be deemed competent to make their own contracts was decisively met nearly forty years ago in Holden v. Hardy [1898] where we
pointed out the inequality in the footing of the parties . . . .:

> The legislature has also recognized . . . that the proprietors of these
> establishments and their operatives do not stand upon an equality, and
> that their interests are, to a certain extent, conflicting. The former
> naturally desire to obtain as much labor as possible from their employ-
> ees, while the latter are often induced by the fear of discharge to
> conform to regulations which their judgment, fairly exercised, would
> pronounce to be detrimental to their health or strength. . . . In
> such cases self-interest is often an unsafe guide, and the legislature
> may properly interpose its authority.

And we added that the fact "that both parties are of full age and
competent to contract does not necessarily deprive the State of the power
to interfere where the parties do not stand upon an equality, or where the
public health demands that one party to the contract shall be protected
against himself." "The State still retains an interest in his welfare,
however reckless he may be . . . .. [W]hen the individual health, safety
and welfare are sacrificed or neglected, the State must suffer."

. . . This established principle is peculiarly applicable in relation
to the employment of women in whose protection the State has a
special interest. That phase of the subject received elaborate consideration in Muller v. Oregon (1908), where the constitutional authority of
the State to limit the working hours of women was sustained. We
emphasized the consideration that "woman's physical structure and the
performance of maternal functions place her at a disadvantage in the
struggle for subsistence" and that her physical well being "becomes an
object of public interest and care in order to preserve the strength and
vigor of the race." We emphasized the need of protecting women
against oppression despite her possession of contractual rights. . . .

This array of precedents and the principles they applied were
thought by the dissenting Justices in the Adkins case to demand that
the minimum wage statute be sustained. The validity of the distinction
made by the Court between a minimum wage and a maximum of hours
in limiting liberty of contract was especially challenged. . . . That
challenge persists and is without any satisfactory answer. As Chief
Justice Taft observed [dissenting in Adkins]: ". . . One is the multiplier and the other the multiplicand." . . .

The minimum wage . . . under the Washington statute is fixed
after full consideration by representatives of employers, employees and
the public. It may be assumed that the minimum wage is fixed in
consideration of the services that are performed in the particular
occupations under normal conditions. . . . The statement of Mr.
Justice Holmes in the Adkins case is pertinent: "This statute does not

compel anybody to pay anything. It simply forbids employment at rates below those fixed as the minimum requirement of health and right living. It is safe to assume that women will not be employed at even the lowest wages allowed unless they earn them, or unless the employer's business can sustain the burden. . . ."

We think that . . . the *Adkins* case was a departure from the true application of the principles governing the regulation by the State of the relation of employer and employed. Those principles have been reenforced by our subsequent decisions. Thus in Radice v. New York [1924] we sustained the New York statute which restricted the employment of women in restaurants at night. . . . In Nebbia v. New York [1934] dealing with . . . the general subject of the regulation of the use of private property and of the making of private contracts . . . we again declared that if such laws "have a reasonable relation to a proper legislative purpose, and are neither arbitrary nor discriminatory, the requirements of due process are satisfied"; that "with the wisdom of the policy adopted, with the adequacy or practicability of the law enacted to forward it, the courts are both incompetent and unauthorized to deal"; . . . that the legislature is primarily the judge of the necessity of such an enactment, that every possible presumption is in favor of its validity. . . .

. . . [We] find it impossible to reconcile that ruling [*Adkins*] with these well-considered declarations. What can be closer to the public interest than the health of women and their protection from unscrupulous and overreaching employers? And if the protection of women is a legitimate end of the exercise of state power, how can it be said that the requirement of the payment of a minimum wage fairly fixed in order to meet the very necessities of existence is not an admissible means to that end? . . .

. . . [A]doption of similar requirements by many States evidences a deepseated conviction both as to the presence of the evil and as to the means adapted to check it. Legislative response to that conviction cannot be regarded as arbitrary or capricious, and that is all we have to decide. . . .

There is an additional and compelling consideration which recent economic experience has brought into a strong light. The exploitation of a class of workers who are in an unequal position with respect to bargaining power and are thus relatively defenseless against the denial of a living wage is not only detrimental to their health and well being but casts a direct burden for their support upon the community. What these workers lose in wages the taxpayers are called upon to pay. The bare cost of living must be met. We may take judicial notice of the unparalleled demands for relief which arose during the recent period of depression and still continue to an alarming extent despite the degree of economic recovery which has been achieved. . . .

The community is not bound to provide what is in effect a subsidy for unconscionable employers. . . . The argument that the legislation in question constitutes an arbitrary discrimination, because it does not extend to men is unavailing. This Court has frequently held that the legislative authority . . . is not bound to extend its regulation to all cases which it might possibly reach. The legislature "is free to recognize degrees of harm and it may confine its restrictions to those classes of cases where the need is deemed to be clearest." . . .

. . . Adkins v. Children's Hospital should be, and it is, overruled. The judgment of the Supreme Court of the State of Washington is

Affirmed.

Mr. Justice **SUTHERLAND**, dissenting:

Mr. Justice **VAN DEVANTER**, Mr. Justice **McREYNOLDS,** Mr. Justice **BUTLER** and I think the judgment of the court below should be reversed. . . .

Under our form of government, where the written Constitution, by its own terms, is the supreme law, some agency, of necessity, must have the power to say the final word as to the validity of a statute assailed as unconstitutional. The Constitution makes it clear that the power has been intrusted to this court when the question arises in a controversy within its jurisdiction; and so long as the power remains there, its exercise cannot be avoided without betrayal of the trust.

It has been pointed out many times . . . that this judicial duty is one of gravity and delicacy; and that rational doubts must be resolved in favor of the constitutionality of the statute. But whose doubts, and by whom resolved? Undoubtedly it is the duty of a member of the court, in the process of reaching a right conclusion, to give due weight to the opposing views of his associates; but in the end, the question . . . is not whether such views seem sound to those who entertain them, but whether they convince him that the statute is constitutional or engender in his mind a rational doubt upon that issue. The oath which he takes as a judge is not a composite oath, but an individual one. And in passing upon the validity of a statute, he discharges a duty imposed upon *him,* which cannot be consummated justly by an automatic acceptance of the views of others which have neither convinced, nor created a reasonable doubt in, his mind. If upon a question so important he thus surrender his deliberate judgment, he stands forsworn. He cannot subordinate his convictions to that extent and keep faith with his oath or retain his judicial and moral independence.

The suggestion that the only check upon the exercise of the judicial power . . . is the judge's own faculty of self-restraint, is both ill considered and mischievous. Self-restraint belongs in the domain of will and not of judgment. The check upon the judge is that imposed by his oath of office, by the Constitution and by his own conscientious and informed convictions; and since he has the duty to make up his own mind and adjudge accordingly, it is hard to see how there could be any other restraint. . . .

It is urged that the question involved should now receive fresh consideration, among other reasons, because of "the economic conditions which have supervened"; but the meaning of the Constitution does not change with the ebb and flow of economic events. We frequently are told in more general words that the Constitution must be construed in the light of the present. If by that it is meant that the Constitution is made up of living words that apply to every new condition which they include, the statement is quite true. But to say . . . that the words of the Constitution mean today what they did not mean when written—that is, that they do not apply to a situation now to which they would have applied then—is to rob that instrument of the essential element which continues it in force as the people have made it until they, and not their official agents, have made it otherwise. . . .

The judicial function is that of interpretation; it does not include the power of amendment under the guise of interpretation. To miss the point of difference between the two is to miss all that the phrase "supreme law of the land" stands for. . . .

If the Constitution, intelligently and reasonably construed in the light of these principles, stands in the way of desirable legislation, the . . . remedy in that situation—and the only true remedy—is to amend the Constitution. . . .

The people by their Constitution created three separate, distinct, independent and coequal departments of government. The governmental structure rests, and was intended to rest, not upon any one or upon any two, but upon all three of these fundamental pillars. It seems unnecessary to repeat . . . that the powers of these departments are different and are to be exercised independently. . . . Each is answerable to its creator . . . not to another agent. The view, therefore, of the Executive and of Congress that an act is constitutional is persuasive in a high degree; but it is not controlling.

. . . [T]he Washington statute . . . is in every substantial respect identical with the statute involved in the *Adkins* case. . . . And if the *Adkins* case was properly decided, as we . . . think it was, it necessarily follows that the Washington statute is invalid.

In support of minimum-wage legislation it has been urged . . . that great benefits will result in favor of underpaid labor. . . .

But with these speculations we have nothing to do. We are concerned only with the question of constitutionality. . . .

Editors' Notes

(1) As the headnote suggests, *Parrish* removed much of the justification for Roosevelt's "Court-packing plan." Soon after, Justice Willis Van Devanter announced his retirement, further weakening support for the bill by giving FDR his first opportunity to nominate a justice. But while Van Devanter was still on the bench—and over his dissents along with those of the others in the minority in *Parrish* —the Court began to lift the other barrier to governmental regulation of economic relations, the Tenth Amendment as a restriction on federal control over commerce. The first decisions, NLRB v. Jones & Laughlin, Corp., NLRB v. Fruehauf Trailer Co., and NLRB v. Friedman-Harry Marks, came a few

weeks after *Parrish.*   There the Court sustained the Wagner Act's regulation of labor relations in a large steel conglomerate, a medium sized truck factory, and a small clothing plant.   The Court had, as Edward S. Corwin said, begun a "constitutional revolution."   *Constitutional Revolution, Ltd.* (Claremont, Cal.: Claremont Colleges Press, 1941).   Not until National League of Cities v. Usery (1976; reprinted above, p. 449) were the justices again to invalidate a federal statute as exceeding congressional control over commerce, and *Usery* had a short and troubled life before being interred by Garcia v. San Antonio Metroplitan Transit Authority (1985; reprinted above, p. 461).

(2) The reference in Sutherland's dissent on p. 992 is to Stone's dissent in United States v. Butler (1936).   There, in his most eloquent protest against how far afield of the Constitution he felt the majority were roaming to invalidate the New Deal, Stone—in an opinion in which Brandeis and Cardozo joined and FDR loved to quote—wrote:

> . . . The power of courts to declare a statute unconstitutional is subject to two guiding principles of decision. . . .   One is that courts are concerned only with the power to enact statutes, not with their wisdom.   The other is that while unconstitutional exercise of power by the executive and legislative branches of government is subject to judicial restraint, the only check upon our own exercise of power is our own sense of self-restraint.   For the removal of unwise laws from the statute books appeal lies not to the courts but to the ballot and to the processes of democratic government. . . .
>
> A tortured construction of the Constitution is not to be justified by recourse to extreme examples . . . which might occur if courts could not prevent [them].   Courts are not the only agency of government that must be assumed to have the capacity to govern.   Congress and the courts both unhappily may falter or be mistaken in the performance of their constitutional duty.   But interpretation of our great charter of government which proceeds on any assumption that the responsibility for the preservation of our institutions is the exclusive concern of any one of the three branches of government, or that it alone can save them from destruction, is far more likely, in the long run, "to obliterate the constituent members . . ." than the frank recognition that language, even of a constitution, may mean what it says; that the power to tax and spend includes the power to relieve a nation-wide economic maladjustment by conditional gifts of money.

"The day is gone when this Court uses the Due Process Clause of the Fourteenth Amendment to strike down state laws, regulatory of business and industrial conditions, because they may be unwise, improvident, or out of harmony with a particular school of thought."

WILLIAMSON v. LEE OPTICAL CO.
348 U.S. 483, 75 S.Ct. 461, 99 L.Ed. 563 (1955).

Oklahoma enacted a complex statute regulating visual care, reducing drastically the scope of optician's lawful activities and correspondingly enlarging those phases of visual care that could be performed only by ophthalmologists or optometrists. Lee Optical Co. claimed that, by taking away the company's business, the statute deprived the owners of their property without due process and denied them equal protection of the laws. The Supreme Court rejected both arguments in the opinion reprinted above, p. 763.

"Whether the legislature takes for its textbook Adam Smith, Herbert Spencer, Lord Keynes, or some other is no concern of ours."

FERGUSON v. SKRUPA

372 U.S. 726, 83 S.Ct. 1028, 10 L.Ed.2d 93 (1963).

Kansas law forbade anyone to engage in "debt adjusting"—defined as consolidating the debts of another and, for a fee, arranging to have them paid off—except as part of the licensed practice of law. Skrupa, a "credit adviser" whose business fell within the statutory prohibition, attacked the statute in a special federal three-judge district court, claiming that Kansas had deprived him of his property—his right to carry on a legitimate business—without due process. That court agreed and enjoined enforcement of the act. Kansas appealed to the Supreme Court.

Mr. Justice **BLACK** delivered the opinion of the Court. . . .

. . . Under the system of government created by our Constitution, it is up to legislatures, not courts, to decide on the wisdom and utility of legislation. There was a time when the Due Process Clause was used by this Court to strike down laws which were thought unreasonable, that is, unwise or incompatible with some particular economic or social philosophy. In this manner the Due Process Clause was used, for example, to nullify laws prescribing maximum hours for work in bakeries, Lochner v. New York (1905), outlawing "yellow dog" contracts, Coppage v. Kansas (1915), setting minimum wages for women, Adkins v. Children's Hospital (1923), and fixing the weight of loaves of bread, Jay Burns Baking Co. v. Bryan (1924). This intrusion by the judiciary into the realm of legislative value judgments was strongly objected to at the time, particularly by Mr. Justice Holmes and Mr. Justice Brandeis. Dissenting from the Court's invalidating a state statute which regulated the resale price of theatre and other tickets, Mr. Justice Holmes said, "I think the proper course is to recognize that a state legislature can do whatever it sees fit to do unless it is restrained by some express prohibition in the Constitution of the United States or of the State, and that Courts should be careful not to extend such prohibitions beyond their obvious meaning by reading into them conceptions of public policy that the particular Court may happen to entertain."

And in an earlier case he had emphasized that, "The criterion of constitutionality is not whether we believe the law to be for the public good."

The doctrine that prevailed in *Lochner, Coppage, Adkins, Burns,* and like cases—that due process authorizes courts to hold laws unconstitutional when they believe the legislature has acted unwisely—has long since been discarded. We have returned to the original constitutional proposition that courts do not substitute their social and economic beliefs for the judgment of legislative bodies, who are elected to pass laws. As this Court stated in a unanimous opinion in 1941, "We are not concerned . . . with the wisdom, need, or appropriateness of the legislation." Olsen v. Nebraska (1955). Legislative bodies have broad scope to experiment with economic problems, and this Court does not sit to "subject the State to an intolerable supervision hostile to the basic principles of our Government and wholly beyond the protection which the general clause of the Fourteenth Amendment was intended to secure." It is now settled that States "have power to legislate against what are found to be injurious practices in their internal commercial and business affairs, so long as their laws do not run afoul of some specific federal constitutional prohibition, or of some valid federal law."

. . . We conclude that the Kansas Legislature was free to decide for itself that legislation was needed to deal with the business of debt adjusting. Unquestionably, there are arguments showing that the business of debt adjusting has social utility, but such arguments are properly addressed to the legislature, not to us. We refuse to sit as a "super-legislature to weigh the wisdom of legislation," and we emphatically refuse to go back to the time when courts used the Due Process Clause "to strike down state laws, regulatory of business and industrial conditions, because they may be unwise, improvident, or out of harmony with a particular school of thought." [Williamson v. Lee Optical (1955).] Nor are we able or willing to draw lines by calling a law "prohibitory" or "regulatory." Whether the legislature takes for its textbook Adam Smith, Herbert Spencer, Lord Keynes, or some other is no concern of ours. The Kansas debt adjusting statute may be wise or unwise. But relief, if any be needed, lies not with us but with the body constituted to pass laws for the State of Kansas. . . .

Reversed.

Mr. Justice **HARLAN** concurs in this judgment on the ground that this state measure bears a rational relationship to a constitutionally permissible objective. See Williamson v. Lee Optical [1955].

Editors' Note

(1) **Query:** Would the Court have been so tolerant if Kansas had taken Karl Marx for "its textbook"?

(2) **Query:** Justice Black confidently announced in *Ferguson* in 1963 that the Court had "long since" discarded substantive due process in the economic field. Two years later in *Griswold* (reprinted above, p. 113), he thought the Court was adopting another form of the same doctrine, and he protested

bitterly. Can one convincingly distinguish between the reasoning of *Lochner* (reprinted above, p. 975) and *Griswold*?

———

"[T]he Court has made it clear that it will not substitute its judgment for a legislature's judgment as to what constitutes [taking of private property for] a public use 'unless the use be palpably without reasonable foundation.'"

HAWAII HOUSING AUTHORITY v. MIDKIFF
467 U.S. 229, 104 S.Ct. 2321, 81 L.Ed.2d 186 (1984).

In the mid-1960s, an investigation by the Hawaiian legislature showed that 72 persons held more than 90 per cent of the privately owned land in the state. These people leased land to those who wished to build their own homes. Claiming that this concentration of ownership was inflating real estate prices and contributing to public unrest, the legislature passed the Land Reform Act of 1967. This statute authorized the Hawaiian Housing Authority, when asked by people leasing the land on which they lived, to condemn large tracts of land occupied by single family homes, pay the land owner(s) a fair price as determined either by negotiation between the lessors and the lessees or by arbitration, and resell the land to the home owners at the purchase price, though with the proviso that no person could so purchase more than one lot.

In 1977, the HHA began condemnation procedures under the Land Reform Act and ordered Frank E. Midkiff and others to negotiate with some of their lessees over the value of land occupied by those lessees. When those negotiations broke down, the HHA ordered arbitration. Midkiff et al. refused and sued in a federal district court for an injunction against enforcement of the Act. The district judge upheld the statute as constitutional, but the Court of Appeals for the Ninth Circuit reversed, saying the Act was "a naked attempt on the part of Hawaii to take the private property of A and transfer it to B solely for B's private use and benefit." Hawaii then appealed to the Supreme Court.

Justice **O'CONNOR** delivered the opinion of the Court. . . .

III

The majority of the Court of Appeals . . . determined that the Act violates the "public use" requirement of the Fifth and Fourteenth Amendments. . . .

A

The starting point for our analysis of the Act's constitutionality is the Court's decision in Berman v. Parker (1954). In *Berman*, the Court held constitutional the District of Columbia Redevelopment Act of 1945. That Act provided both for the comprehensive use of the eminent domain power to redevelop slum areas and for the possible sale or lease of the condemned lands to private interests. In discussing whether the takings authorized by that Act were for a "public use," the Court stated

We deal, in other words, with what traditionally has been known as the police power. An attempt to define its reach or trace its outer limits is fruitless, for each case must turn on its own facts. The definition is essentially the product of legislative determinations addressed to the purposes of government, purposes neither abstractly nor historically capable of complete definition. Subject to specific constitutional limitations, when the legislature has spoken, the public interest has been declared in terms well-nigh conclusive. In such cases the legislature, not the judiciary, is the main guardian of the public needs to be served by social legislation, whether it be Congress legislating concerning the District of Columbia . . . or the States legislating concerning local affairs. . . . This principle admits of no exception merely because the power of eminent domain is involved. . . .

The Court explicitly recognized the breadth of the principle it was announcing, noting:

Once the object is within the authority of Congress, the right to realize it through the exercise of eminent domain is clear. For the power of eminent domain is merely the means to the end. . . . Once the object is within the authority of Congress, the means by which it will be attained is also for Congress to determine. Here one of the means chosen is the use of private enterprise for redevelopment of the area. Appellants argue that this makes the project a taking from one businessman for the benefit of another businessman. But the means of executing the project are for Congress and Congress alone to determine, once the public purpose has been established.

The "public use" requirement is thus coterminous with the scope of a sovereign's police powers.

There is, of course, a role for courts to play in reviewing a legislature's judgment of what constitutes a public use, even when the eminent domain power is equated with the police power. But the Court in *Berman* made clear that it is "an extremely narrow" one. The Court in *Berman* cited with approval the Court's decision in Old Dominion Co. v. United States (1925), which held that deference to the legislature's "public use" determination is required "until it is shown to involve an impossibility." . . . In short, the Court has made clear that it will not substitute its judgment for a legislature's judgment as to what constitutes a public use "unless the use be palpably without reasonable foundation." United States v. Gettysburg Electric R. Co. (1896).

To be sure, the Court's cases have repeatedly stated that "one person's property may not be taken for the benefit of another private person without a justifying public purpose, even though compensation be paid." Thompson v. Consolidated Gas Corp. (1937). Thus, in Missouri Pacific R. Co. v. Nebraska (1896), where the "order in question was not, *and was not claimed to be*, . . . a taking of private property for a public use under the right of eminent domain," (Emphasis added) the Court invalidated a compensated taking of property for lack of a justifying public purpose. But where the exercise of the eminent domain power is rationally related to a conceivable public purpose, the Court has never held a compensated taking to be proscribed by the Public Use Clause. See *Berman;* Block v. Hirsh (1921).

On this basis, we have no trouble concluding that the Hawaii Act is constitutional. The people of Hawaii have attempted, much as the settlers of the original 13 Colonies did,[1] to reduce the perceived social and economic evils of a land oligopoly traceable to their monarchs. The land oligopoly has, according to the Hawaii Legislature, created artificial deterrents to the normal functioning of the State's residential land market and forced thousands of individual homeowners to lease, rather than buy, the land underneath their homes. Regulating oligopoly and the evils associated with it is a classic exercise of a State's police powers. See Exxon Corp. v. Governor of Maryland (1978); Block v. Hirsh. We cannot disapprove of Hawaii's exercise of this power.

Nor can we condemn as irrational the Act's approach to correcting the land oligopoly problem. The Act presumes that when a sufficiently large number of persons declare that they are willing but unable to buy lots at fair prices the land market is malfunctioning. When such a malfunction is signalled, the Act authorizes HHA to condemn lots in the relevant tract. The Act limits the number of lots any one tenant can purchase and authorizes HHA to use public funds to ensure that the market dilution goals will be achieved. This is a comprehensive and rational approach to identifying and correcting market failure.

Of course, this Act, like any other, may not be successful in achieving its intended goals. But "whether *in fact* the provision will accomplish its objectives is not the question: the [constitutional requirement] is satisfied if . . . the . . . [state] Legislature *rationally could have believed* that the [Act] would promote its objective." Western & Southern Life Ins. Co. v. State Bd. of Equalization (1981). . . . When the legislature's purpose is legitimate and its means are not irrational, our cases make clear that empirical debates over the wisdom of takings—no less than debates over the wisdom of other kinds of socioeconomic legislation—are not to be carried out in the federal courts. Redistribution of fees simple to correct deficiencies in the market determined by the state legislature to be attributable to land oligopoly is a rational exercise of the eminent domain power. Therefore, the Hawaii statute must pass the scrutiny of the Public Use Clause.

B

The Court of Appeals read . . . our "public use" cases, especially *Berman,* as requiring that government possess and use property at some point during a taking. Since Hawaiian lessees retain possession of the property for private use throughout the condemnation process, the court found that the Act exacted takings for private use. Second, it determined that these cases involved only "the review of . . . *congressional* determination[s] that there was a public use, *not* the review of . . . state legislative determination[s]." Because state legislative determinations are involved in the instant cases, the Court of Appeals

---

1. After the American Revolution, the colonists in several states took steps to eradicate the feudal incidents with which large proprietors had encumbered land in the colonies. . . . [Footnote by the Court.]

decided that more rigorous judicial scrutiny of the public use determinations was appropriate. . . .

The mere fact that property taken outright by eminent domain is transferred in the first instance to private beneficiaries does not condemn that taking as having only a private purpose. The Court long ago rejected any literal requirement that condemned property be put into use for the general public. "It is not essential that the entire community, nor even any considerable portion, . . . directly enjoy or participate in any improvement in order [for it] to constitute a public use." Rindge Co. v. Los Angeles [1923]. "[W]hat in its immediate aspect [is] only a private transaction may . . . be raised by its class or character to a public affair." *Block*. As the unique way titles were held in Hawaii skewed the land market, exercise of the power of eminent domain was justified. The Act advances its purposes without the State taking actual possession of the land. In such cases, government does not itself have to use property to legitimate the taking; it is only the taking's purpose, and not its mechanics, that must pass scrutiny under the Public Use Clause.

Similarly, the fact that a state legislature, and not the Congress, made the public use determination does not mean that judicial deference is less appropriate.[2] Judicial deference is required because, in our system of government, legislatures are better able to assess what public purposes should be advanced by an exercise of the taking power. State legislatures are as capable as Congress of making such determinations within their respective spheres of authority. See *Berman*. Thus, if a legislature, state or federal, determines there are substantial reasons for an exercise of the taking power, courts must defer to its determination that the taking will serve a public use.

IV

The State of Hawaii has never denied that the Constitution forbids even a compensated taking of property when executed for no reason other than to confer a private benefit on a particular private party. A purely private taking could not withstand the scrutiny of the public use requirement; it would serve no legitimate purpose of government and would thus be void. But no purely private taking is involved in this case. The Hawaii Legislature enacted its Land Reform Act not to benefit a particular class of identifiable individuals but to attack certain perceived evils of concentrated property ownership in Hawaii—a legitimate public purpose. Use of the condemnation power to achieve this purpose is not irrational. Since we assume for purposes of this appeal that the weighty demand of just compensation has been met, the

---

2. It is worth noting that the Fourteenth Amendment does not itself contain an independent "public use" requirement. Rather, that requirement is made binding on the states only by the incorporation of the Fifth Amendment's Eminent Domain Clause through the Fourteenth Amendment's Due Process Clause. See Chicago, Burlington & Quincy R. Co. v. Chicago (1897). It would be ironic to find that state legislation is subject to greater scrutiny under the incorporated "public use" requirement than is congressional legislation under the express mandate of the Fifth Amendment. [Footnote by the Court.]

requirements of the Fifth and Fourteenth Amendments have been
satisfied. . . .

[Reversed.]

Justice **MARSHALL** took no part in the consideration or decision of
these cases.

Editors' Notes

(1) **Query:** In footnote 2 Justice O'Connor argued that the Court should
accord state legislatures the same deference as Congress because the
Fourteenth Amendment "incorporated" the Fifth's eminent domain clause and
so provided the same constitutional text to interpret. Is this form of reasoning
based on plain words? Notwithstanding the answer to that query, is this a
convincing reason for equal deference? To what extent do considerations of
federalism—and of WHO interprets, state or national officials—come into play?
What did James Bradley Thayer say about the comparative deference judges
owe to Congress and state legislatures? See his article, reprinted above at p.
476. More generally, what would democratic theory say? Constitutionalism?
Is O'Connor's argument in the body of her opinion about the functional
capabilities of courts and legislatures more persuasive on the question of
deference? See the analysis of the underlying problems in Charles L. Black,
Structure and Relationship in Constitutional Law (Baton Rouge, La.: Louisiana
State University Press, 1969), chap. 3.

(2) **Query:** After *Hawaii Housing Authority,* is there any judicially enforceable limit to a state's authority to redistribute private property as long as it
provides just compensation to the former owners? For other important
decisions in accord with *HHA,* see: Penn Central v. New York (1978) and a
case from the Supreme Court of Michigan, Poletown v. Detroit (1981).

16

Autonomy and the Fundamental Right to Religious Freedom

From the problems of property we turn to what should be a much simpler issue for constitutional interpretation, religious freedom. Here is a right that, like freedom of speech and press, provides an ideal case for fundamentality. First of all, the plain words of the constitutional document are very plain indeed: "Congress shall make no law respecting the establishment of religion or prohibiting the free exercise thereof. . . ." Incorporation of some of the Bill of Rights into the Fourteenth Amendment has applied this restriction to the states. Even John Hart Ely, the arch advocate of representative democracy and thus of a process-perfecting *mode* of constitutional interpretation, concedes that the document's clear command requires an active judicial role in protecting the substantive right to religious liberty.[1]

The document's words, at least as far as "free exercise" is concerned, are congruent with the political theories of democracy and constitutionalism. The latter's exaltation of individual autonomy and dignity demands that government leave matters of religion to the citizen's own conscience. For democratic theory, the issue is not so evident; but one can make a powerful structural argument, as do some of the opinions we read—most strikingly, West Virginia v. Barnette (1943; reprinted below, p. 1027)—that free expression of religious views is closely tied to free expression generally. Government cannot inhibit one without impeding the other. In fact, much of constitutional law regarding freedom of communication comes from litigation brought by Jehovah's Witnesses to protect their free exercise of religion. (See, for instance, Cantwell v. Connecticut [1940; reprinted below, p. 1014].)

Threads of political tradition are in accord with these other sources of constitutional law. Americans frequently congratulate themselves on having separated church and state and established

---

1. *Democracy and Distrust* (Cambridge, Mass.: Harvard University Press, 1980), p. 94. In part, Ely derives this exception to his general rule from the document's plain words; in part, however, he also finds it in the "intent of the framers": "[P]art of the explanation of the Free Exercise Clause has to be that for the framers religion was an important substantive value they wanted to put significantly beyond the reach of at least the federal legislature."

religious toleration as integral elements of their cultural heritage. Although religious bigotry has been a part of the American past and remains an ugly part of its present, the ideal has been and remains that of religious freedom. And, as a practical matter, the existence of a dozen large religious denominations and thousands of smaller ones usually makes it politically inexpedient for elected politicians openly to prefer one religion over another or, again openly, to trample on religious freedoms.

We have, then, a general, if somewhat scarred, pattern: Constitutional language, constitutional and democratic theory, tradition, and political expediency all respect religious liberty as a fundamental right. Thus there would seem to be no serious problem here for constitutional interpretation.

I. THE INTERPRETIVE PROBLEMS

A. What Constitutes Establishment?

As is so often the case, however, pluralistic checks may not function effectively; and those seemingly clear words, theories, and traditions may blur when they confront specific problems. When does government "establish" a religion? Only when it makes one religion that of the state, as governments often did in the eighteenth century when the Bill of Rights was adopted? Or does government violate the ban when it gives real but less favorable treatment to one religion or only to some religions?

What about government's aiding all religions? Does it violate the ban to allow any sect that wishes to offer religious instruction in public schools for students who freely opt to attend? Eight justices said yes, one said no.[2] Does allowing "released time" for public school students to attend religious instruction off school property but during school hours constitute establishment? Six justices said no, three said yes.[3] Does purchasing books on non-religious subjects for children attending public and private, including sectarian, schools? Six justices said no, three said yes.[4] Does supplying instructional material and equipment to public and private, including sectarian, schools? The Court unanimously said yes, but divided four different ways in explaining its response.[5] Does providing free buses for all children whether attending public or religious schools? Five justices said no, four said yes.[6] Do grants to private colleges including those with religious affiliations? Five justices said no, four said yes.[7] Does exempting religious institutions from tax laws and donations to

---

2. McCullom v. Board (1948).

3. Zorach v. Clauson (1952).

4. Board of Education v. Allen (1968).

5. Meek v. Pittinger (1975).

6. Everson v. Ewing Township (1947).

7. Roemer v. Maryland (1976).

churches from donors' taxable incomes? Seven justices said no, one said yes.[8] Does a state's allowing parents of children in private, including religious, schools tax deductions for part of the tuition? Five justices said no, four said yes.[9] Does a city's building a creche at Christmas? Five justices said no, four said yes.[10]

B. Free Exercise and the Police Power

The meaning of the "free exercise" clause is equally clouded. May government force a religious pacifist to take up a gun and serve in the armed forces? Eight justices said yes in Gillette v. United States (1971; reprinted below, p. 1054). May government outlaw a religiously ordained practice of polygamy and even forbid believers to vote? All nine justices said yes in Davis v. Beason (1890; reprinted below, p. 1010). May it forbid religious rituals involving snake handling or hallucinogenic drugs?[11] May it force Jehovah's Witnesses, who believe that blood transfusions violate the Biblical ban against drinking blood, to submit to such a procedure when needed to save their lives? To save their children's lives?[12] What if a sect preaches the necessity of killing its opponents? May government take action against it?

C. Tensions Between Clauses

When we consider the two clauses in tandem, problems multiply. At first glance the two seem directed toward the common goal of religious freedom, the first by forbidding government to tax or otherwise regulate its citizens in order to support religions of which they do not approve, the second by allowing citizens to practice or not practice their religious beliefs, according to their own individual consciences. As the Court has admitted, however, either clause, "if

---

8. Walz v. Tax Commissioner (1970).

9. Mueller v. Allen (1983).

10. Lynch v. Donnelly (1984).

11. In Pack v. Tennessee (1976), the U.S. Supreme Court denied certiorari to review a decision by the Supreme Court of Tennessee upholding an injunction against snake handling as a public nuisance. In People v. Woody (1964) the Supreme Court of California reversed the convictions of Navajo Indians for using Peyote in religious ceremonies.

12. Earlier American decisions tended to grant hospitals' requests for court orders to give transfusions to save lives. See, for example, Application of Georgetown College (1964; U.S. Court of Appeals for the Dist. of Col.); John F. Kennedy Memorial Hosp. v. Heston (1971). But there is a growing movement among judges not to intervene. See the discussion by the Supreme Court of New Jersey in In re Karen Quinlan (1976). See also Norman L. Cantor, "A Person's Decision to Decline Life-Saving Medical Treatment," 26 *Rutgers L.Rev.* 228 (1973). The older rule that courts will intervene to allow hospitals to administer life-saving care to children—for example, the New Jersey Supreme Court's ruling in Raleigh Fitkin-Paul Memorial Hospital v. Anderson (1964)—seems to be giving way, at least where the question of quality of life of the child is at stake, as with retarded children suffering from illnesses that are incurable or curable only after long and expensive treatment, to an attitude that parents should have ultimate authority.

expanded to a logical extreme, would tend to clash with the other." [13]
Even under circumstances far short of logical extremes, the two may
send out conflicting messages, as several cases reprinted in this chapter
demonstrate. (See espec. Thomas v. Review Board [1981; reprinted
below, p. 1068].) To require a pacifist to serve in the armed forces
may violate his right to free exercise; to give him an exemption
because of his religious beliefs might "establish" his religion. "The
problem," C. Herman Pritchett has said, "is that too much coercion
may deny free exercise, while exemption from coercion in response to
religious objections may be favoritism amounting to establishment." [14]

II. POSSIBLE SOLUTIONS: THE *TECHNIQUES* OF INTERPRETATION

A. Literalism

Some *techniques* of constitutional interpretation offer scant help
here—or perhaps they offer too much. Literalism, for example,
presents a very simple solution. The First Amendment guarantees
"free exercise" of religion, not merely "free belief" in religion, and it
specifies "no law," not merely "no unreasonable law." Thus all
regulations that impinge on the practice of religion seem to be invalid.
But can "free exercise" of religion confer a right to inflict on others
the consequences of that exercise? Or an exemption from the civic
duties that all other citizens must bear?

And, of course, the potential clash between the words of the
establishment and free exercise clauses often becomes actual, as with
the military draft or when government provides chaplains for people
in the armed forces. Not to provide the means for these people to
practice their religion could mean denying them free exercise; bringing clergy to them—or them to clergy—would certainly help religion,
perhaps to the point of establishment.

B. "Intent of the Framers"

"Intent of the framers" provides little additional nourishment.
The amendment Madison introduced was quite different from that
which Congress approved and the states ratified:

> The civil rights of none shall be abridged on account of
> religious belief or worship, nor shall any national religion be
> established, nor shall the full and equal rights of conscience be in
> any manner, or on any pretext, infringed.

But even this proposal is full of ambiguity. How much action, for
example, would "worship" include? Use of Peyote, as in the reli-

---

13. *Walz.* Concurring in Abington School Dist. v. Schempp (1963), Justice Brennan
visualized a more harmonious relationship between the two clauses. For a similar argument, see
Leo Pfeffer, "Freedom and/or Separation," 64 *Minn.L.Rev.* 561 (1980). See also Thomas v.
Review Board (1981; reprinted below, p. 1068), espec. Justice Rehnquist's dis. op.

14. *The American Constitution* (3rd ed.; New York: McGraw-Hill, 1977), p. 391.

gious ceremonies of some Indians in the Southwest? Snake handling? Human sacrifice? At least Madison would have made some of the awkward business of incorporation through the Fourteenth Amendment unnecessary:

> No State shall violate the equal rights of conscience, or the freedom of the press, or the trial by jury in criminal cases.

Congress's changing Madison's proposals does not tell us much about the meaning of the words actually adopted, other than that they were not aimed at the states. At times, however, the Court has sought support from a letter that Jefferson wrote in 1802 [15] and from the Statute on Religious Liberty that he had drafted for Virginia in 1779. In the letter he asserted that the Amendment erected "a wall of separation between church and State." The Statute, widely reprinted in the United States and Europe, read:

> Whereas Almighty God hath created the mind free. . . . *Be it enacted by the General Assembly,* that no man shall be compelled to frequent or support any religious worship, place or ministry whatsoever, nor shall be enforced, restrained, molested, or burthened in his body or goods, nor shall otherwise suffer on account of his religious opinions or belief; but that all men shall be free to profess, and by argument to maintain, their opinion in matters of religion, and the same shall in no wise diminish, enlarge or affect their civil capacities.

Even accepting the Court's unsubstantiated assertion in Reynolds v. United States (1878) that this statute provided the model for those who recast Madison's draft, voted for the revised version in Congress, and ratified it in the state legislatures, does not solve modern problems. As do the words of the Amendment, the statute expresses general principles with which few Americans would disagree but around whose application there is sharp dispute.

C. Deductive Inference

Deductive inference suffers from its usual limitation: What appears to one interpreter to be a reasonable inference may appear quite unreasonable to another. One need only read Davis v. Beason (reprinted below, p. 1010), upholding the imprisonment of a Mormon for daring to try to vote, to see that what judges of that era thought was "deduction" from general constitutional principles now seems more like gross religious bigotry further tainted by bad anthropology.

D. Stare Decisis

Stare decisis offers no help at all in illuminating the original understanding, if any, for the initial cases reached the Supreme Court nearly a century after adoption of the First Amendment. Neverthe-

---

15. Jefferson's reply to the address of the Committee of the Danbury Baptists Association, January 1, 1802; Andrew A. Lipscomb, ed., *The Writings of Thomas Jefferson* (Washington, D.C.: The Thomas Jefferson Memorial Association, 1903), XVI, 282.

less, stare decisis does collect the wisdom of the Court as an institution. That heritage, however, could be charitably described as a mixed bag. Justice Rehnquist's dissent in Thomas v. Review Board (1981; reprinted below, p. 1068) forms a biting indictment of constitutional interpretation in this area. The justices have followed a tortuous course which, the Court has admitted, "sacrifices clarity and predictability for flexibility. . . ."[16] For example, in establishment cases the justices have abandoned Jefferson's "wall of separation" in favor of a new metaphor, equally unanchored in the text: "a blurred, indistinct and variable barrier, depending on all the circumstances of a particular relationship."[17]

E. Balancing

Balancing offers its usual attractions and drawbacks. Empirically, it seems to fit the justices' meanderings, but that fit hardly constitutes a strong argument for balancing's use as a guiding framework for future decisions. The typical failures of this *technique* of interpretation—lack of relative weights among interests and constitutional clauses and absence of any indication about how the "scale" is calibrated—are especially evident in the Court's work here.

F. Structural Analysis

Structural analysis seems to hold out greater promise. Philip B. Kurland suggested in 1961 that the two clauses should be read together as unit, forbidding government's using religion as a standard for action or inaction.[18] Justice Harlan took over this approach, though without converting the Court to its gospel.[19] But, as Pritchett has commented,

> the Kurland-Harlan position, while attractive in its simplicity, would prevent any accommodation of religious claims such as the Court approved in releasing the Amish from school attendance laws[20] and would render invalid the exemption granted by Congress in 1965 to the Amish—who believe that any form of insurance shows a lack of faith in God—from the social security system.[21]

III. ANOTHER SOLUTION: FUNDAMENTAL RIGHTS, STRUCTURALISM, AND POLITICAL THEORY

There is something important in what Kurland and Harlan argued, but they were using structural analysis more as what Chapter 8

---

16. Comm'n for Public Education v. Regan (1980).

17. Lemon v. Kurtz*man* (1971).

18. "Of Church and State and the Supreme Court," 29 *U. of Chi.L.Rev.* 1 (1961).

19. See his separate opinions in Bd. of Education v. Allen (1968) and *Walz.*

20. Wisconsin v. Yoder (1972; reprinted below, p. 1046).

21. *Constitutional Civil Liberties* (Englewood Cliffs, N.J.: Prentice-Hall, 1984), p. 155. For another critique of the Kurland-Harlan position, see John H. Garvey, "Freedom and Equality in the Religion Clauses," 1981 *Sup.Ct.Rev.* 193, 218–221.

(at pp. 289–313) called a *technique* of interpretation, rather than a broader *mode*. It is not likely that an interpreter can resolve the tensions between the two clauses without first establishing the place of a fundamental right to religious freedom within a larger structure—whether of the document or "the document plus"—of constitutional values. For religious liberty not only has internal tensions, on occasion it also conflicts with other very important rights and values. The Flag Salute Cases of 1940 and 1943 (reprinted below at pp. 1017 and 1027) provided what Felix Frankfurter termed "an illustration of what the Greeks thousands of years ago recognized as a tragic issue, namely, the clash of rights, not the clash of wrongs." [22] The state thought it had a compelling public interest in promoting national loyalty; the children (or at least their parents) thought that saluting the flag violated the First Commandment's ban against worshipping "graven images."

Similar tragedies have played on the Court's dramatic stage: The refusal of the Amish to educate their children beyond grammar school lest their religious faith be corrupted by secular, materialistic values pitted against the authority of the state to educate all citizens (Wisconsin v. Yoder [1972; reprinted below, p. 1046]); the consciences of those whose religious beliefs allow them to fight only in "just" wars pitted against the authority of Congress to raise armies and more generally the value of national self-preservation (Gillette v. United States [1971; reprinted below, p. 1054]); or the belief of some Christian Fundamentalists that God has forbidden racial intermarriage, and therefore they must require social separation of the races within their private schools pitted against the authority of the government to eradicate all vestiges of racial discrimination (Bob Jones University v. United States [1983; reprinted below, p. 1075]).

What systematic, defensible constitutional interpretation must have is a general scheme in which to arrange these fundamental rights and the larger values they reflect so that choices among them may be principled rather than ad hoc. To discover, or perhaps to construct, such a hierarchy requires a broad sort of structural analysis, one that includes but goes beyond the words of the constitutional document. Perhaps it requires, as much of constitutional interpretation does, the discovery, construction, or reconstruction of a complex political philosophy.

IV. RELIGIOUS FREEDOM AND AMERICAN CONSTITUTIONALISM

The First Amendment has achieved, albeit slowly and imperfectly, Madison's hope for the entire Bill of Rights, that they "acquire by degrees the character of fundamental maxims of free Government, and as they become incorporated with the National sentiment,

---

22. Felix Frankfurter to Harlan F. Stone, May 27, 1940; reprinted as part of the *Gobitis* case, below, at p. —.

counteract the impulses of interest and passion." [23]   It has become so internalized within the American civic consciousness that it is unlikely that any legislator or administrator would attempt the sort of establishment or persecution with which Madison's generation was familiar; and it is certain that no appellate court would hesitate to invalidate any such effort.

On the other hand, more subtle forms of oppression, especially if directed at small, unpopular sects, are still possible.   The reality of this possibility became evident in 1984, when the Supreme Court, despite para. 3 of the *Carolene Products* footnote and despite its feverish defense of equal justice in other areas, denied certiorari when Rev. Sun Myung Moon, head of the controversial Unification Church, sought review of his conviction for tax fraud in using church funds for private purposes.[24]   This sort of use—or allegations of its use— presents a perennial problem.   "I would not be standing here today," Moon claimed, "if my skin were white or my religion were Presbyterian." [25]   Perhaps he was wrong, but it is noteworthy that IRS chose to prosecute a wealthy, foreign religious leader with relatively few followers, while ignoring the financial scandal in the archdiocese of Chicago when for years the Cardinal, to the embarrassment of his clergy and laity as well as the Vatican, treated donations as private property.   IRS has turned a similarly blind eye toward the multi-million dollar enterprises conducted by various white, native-born Protestant divines on radio and television.[26]

The First Amendment sets bounds on current controversies, but it by no means eliminates them.   Perhaps the failures of constitutional interpretation here are inevitable: However far apart one might keep church and state, it is impossible completely to separate religion and politics as long as they both compete for people's minds and loyalties.

SELECTED BIBLIOGRAPHY

Baker, John W. "Belief and Action: Limitations on the Free Exercise of Religion," in Jaye B. Hensel, ed., *Church, State, and Politics* (Washington D.C.: The Roscoe Pound-American Trial Lawyers Foundation, 1981).

Berns, Walter. *The First Amendment and the Future of American Democracy* (New York: Basic Books, 1976).

Giannella, Donald A.   "The Religious Liberty Guarantee," 80 *Harv. L.Rev.* 1311 (1967).

23. To Jefferson, Oct. 17, 1788; reprinted in Marvin Meyers, ed., *The Mind of the Framer* (Indianapolis, Ind.: Bobbs-Merrill, 1973), p. 207.

24. Moon v. United States.

25. *New York Times,* Nov. 5, 1981 (advertisement).

26. In the 1940s, the federal government's prosecution of the leader of the "I am" Cult showed the morass into which such efforts could sink. See United States v. Ballard (1944) and Ballard v. United States (1946).

Howe, Mark DeWolfe. *The Garden and the Wilderness: Religion and Government in American Constitutional History* (Chicago: University of Chicago Press, 1965).

Kurland, Philip. *Religion and the Law* (Chicago: Aldine, 1962).

Manwaring, David R. *Render unto Caesar: The Flag-Salute Controversy* (Chicago: University of Chicago Press, 1962).

Marty, Martin E. *A Nation of Believers* (Chicago: University of Chicago Press, 1976).

Morgan, Richard E. *The Supreme Court and Religion* (New York: The Free Press, 1972)

Note. "Toward a Constitutional Definition of Religion," 91 *Harv.L. Rev.* 1056 (1978).

Pfeffer, Leo. *God, Caesar, and the Constitution* (Boston: Beacon Press, 1975).

Pritchett, C. Herman. *Constitutional Civil Liberties* (Englewood Cliffs, N.J.: Prentice-Hall, 1984), chap. 7.

Smith, Michael E. "The Special Place of Religion in the Constitution," 1983 *Sup.Ct.Rev.* 83.

Sorauf, Frank J. *The Wall of Separation* (Princeton, N.J.: Princeton University Press, 1976).

Tribe, Laurence H. *American Constitutional Law* (Mineola, N.Y.: Foundation Press, 1978), chap. 14.

"However free the exercise of religion may be, it must be subordinate to the criminal laws of the country. . . ."

DAVIS v. BEASON

133 U.S. 333, 10 S.Ct. 299, 33 L.Ed. 637 (1890).

As part of a continuing campaign against Mormons—most of whom had migrated to Utah under Brigham Young—Congress forbade polygamy in the territories. Reynolds v. United States (1878) unanimously sustained this statute as applied to the Territory of Utah, against Mormon's claims that it interfered with their free exercise of religion. Branding polygamy "odious" to western culture, the Court said:

Congress was deprived of all legislative power over mere opinion, but was left free to reach actions which were in violation of social duties or subversive of good order. . . . Laws are made for the government of actions, and while they cannot interfere with mere religious belief and opinions, they may with practices. Suppose one believed that human sacrifices were a necessary part of worship, would it be seriously contended that the civil government under which he lived could not interfere to prevent a sacrifice?

Later, the Territory of Idaho limited the right to vote to adult males of sound mind who had not been convicted of treason, bribery, or other felony and who would swear not only that they were not themselves practicing polygamy but also that they were not members of an organization that "advises, counsels, or encourages" anyone "to commit the crime of bigamy or polygamy." Samuel Davis, a Mormon, was convicted for conspiring with others to swear falsely to this oath. He appealed to the Supreme Court.

Mr. Justice **FIELD**, after stating the case, delivered the opinion of the Court.

. . . Bigamy and polygamy are crimes by the laws of all civilized and Christian countries. They are crimes by the laws of the United States, and they are crimes by the laws of Idaho. They tend to destroy the purity of the marriage relation, to disturb the peace of families, to degrade woman and to debase man. Few crimes are more pernicious to the best interests of society and receive more general or more deserved punishment. To extend exemption from punishment for such crimes would be to shock the moral judgment of the community. To call their advocacy a tenet of religion is to offend the common sense of mankind. If they are crimes, then to teach, advise and counsel their practice is to aid in their commission, and such teaching and counselling are themselves criminal and proper subjects of punishment, as aiding and abetting crime are in all other cases.

The term "religion" has reference to one's views of his relations to his Creator, and to the obligations they impose of reverence for his being and character, and of obedience to his will. It is often confounded with the *cultus* or form of worship of a particular sect, but is distinguishable from the latter. The first amendment to the Constitution, in declaring that Congress shall make no law respecting the establishment of religion, or forbidding the free exercise thereof, was intended to allow every one under the jurisdiction of the United States to entertain such notions respecting his relations to his Maker and the duties they impose as may be approved by his judgment and conscience, and to exhibit his sentiments in such form of worship as he may think proper, not injurious to the equal rights of others, and to prohibit legislation for the support of any religious tenets, or the modes of worship of any sect. The oppressive measures adopted, and the cruelties and punishments inflicted by the governments of Europe for many ages, to compel parties to conform, in their religious beliefs and modes of worship, to the views of the most numerous sect, and the folly of attempting in that way to control the mental operations of persons, and enforce an outward conformity to a prescribed standard, led to the adoption of the amendment in question. It was never intended or supposed that the amendment could be invoked as a protection against legislation for the punishment of acts inimical to the peace, good order and morals of society. With man's relations to his Maker and the obligations he may think they impose, and the manner in which an expression shall be made by him of his belief on those subjects, no interference can be permitted, provided always the laws of society, designed to secure its peace and prosperity, and the morals of its people, are not interfered with. However free the exercise of religion may be, it must be subordinate to the criminal laws of the country, passed with reference to actions regarded by general consent as properly the subjects of punitive legislation. There have been sects which denied as a part of their religious tenets that there should be any marriage tie, and advocated promiscuous intercourse of the sexes as prompted by the passions of its members. And history discloses the fact that the necessity of human sacrifices, on special occasions, has been a tenet of many sects. Should a sect of either of these kinds ever find its way into this country, swift punishment would follow the carrying into effect of its doctrines, and no heed would be given to the pretence that, as religious beliefs, their supporters could be protected in their exercise by the Constitution of the United States. Probably never before in the history of this country has it been seriously contended that the whole punitive power of the government for acts, recognized by the general consent of the Christian world in modern times as proper matters for prohibitory legislation, must be suspended in order that the tenets of a religious sect encouraging crime may be carried out without hindrance. . . .

It is assumed by counsel of the petitioner, that because no mode of worship can be established or religious tenets enforced in this country, therefore any form of worship may be followed and any tenets, however destructive of society, may be held and advocated, if asserted to be a part of the religious doctrines of those advocating and practising them. But nothing is further from the truth. Whilst legislation for the establishment of a religion is forbidden, and its free exercise permitted, it does not follow that everything which may be so called can be tolerated. Crime is not the less odious because sanctioned by what any particular sect may designate as religion. . . .

. . . In our judgment, § 501 of the Revised Statutes of Idaho Territory . . . is not open to any constitutional or legal objection. With the exception of persons under guardianship or of unsound mind, it simply excludes from the privilege of voting, or of holding any office of honor, trust or profit, those who have been convicted of certain offences, and those who advocate a practical resistance to the laws of the Territory and justify and approve the commission of crimes forbidden by it. . . .

The judgment of the court below is therefore

Affirmed.

Editors' Notes

(1) **Query:** *Davis* raises two immediate questions, neither of which apparently occurred to Field, who considered himself, where most aspects of liberty were concerned and especially those of property and contract, to be a great constitutionalist: (i) What does it leave of a constitutional right to free exercise, as contrasted with a democratic right to participate in the political processes and to share in the community's judgment about what is or is not objectionable? Or, in terms of *Carolene Products,* what protections did Field leave to "discrete and insular" religious minorities against the prejudices of hostile majorities? And (ii) What democratic rights did Mormons have under this law? Once it was in place, they lost the right to vote. To retrieve that right, they would have had to surrender their religious affiliation.

(2) This statute and case were only parts of a long persecution of Mormons, one that initially forced them, under the leadership of Brigham Young, to flee from the Middle West to found a new home in Utah. The laws against the practice of their religion followed them. In 1882 Congress denied the right to vote to any citizen in the territories (Utah was not yet a state) who practiced polygamy. Five years later, Congress annulled the Mormon Church's corporate charter and declared most of its property forfeit. The Supreme Court affirmed in The Late Corporation of the Church of Jesus Christ of Latter Day Saints v. United States (1890). Referring to polygamy as a "barbarous practice" and a "nefarious" doctrine "contrary to the spirit of Christianity," the justices, speaking through Justice Brewer, Field's nephew, ruled the government's action constitutional. They abruptly dismissed as a "sophistical plea" the Mormons' claim to freedom of religion: "No doubt the Thugs of India imagined that their belief in the right of assassination was a religious belief; but their thinking did not make it so."

In 1890 the Mormon Church abandoned the teaching and practice of polygamy, but some fundamentalist groups refused to accept the change; and occasional legal problems still arise. As recently as 1946, the Supreme Court sustained the conviction under the Mann Act, outlawing transporting women across state lines for "immoral" purposes, of a Mormon who traveled on a vacation with several of his wives. Cleveland v. United States.

For scholarly studies of the Mormons' travails, see Klaus J. Hansen, *Mormonism and the American Experience* (Chicago: University of Chicago Press, 1981); and Marvin S. Hill and James B. Allen, eds., *Mormonism and American Culture* (New York: Harper & Row, 1972).

(3) In keeping with its general jurisprudence, the justices have pretty much given up the role of Grand Inquisitor and no longer equate their personal views about "the spirit of Christianity" as a criterion for judging rights protected under the First Amendment. See, for example, Thomas v. Review Bd. (1981; reprinted below, p. 1068):

> The determination of what is a "religious" belief is more often than not a difficult and delicate task. . . . However, the resolution of that question is not to turn upon a judicial perception of the particular belief or practice in question; religious beliefs need not be acceptable, logical, consistent, or comprehensible to others in order to merit First Amendment protection. . . . Courts are not arbiters of scriptural interpretation.

"The essential characteristic of these liberties is, that
under their shield many types of life, character, opinion
and belief can develop unmolested and unobstructed."

CANTWELL v. CONNECTICUT
310 U.S. 296, 60 S.Ct. 900, 84 L.Ed. 1213 (1940).

On Palm Sunday, 1938, Newton Cantwell and his two sons Jesse and
Russell, all Jehovah's Witnesses, went from house to house and also stopped
people in the street in a heavily Catholic neighborhood in New Haven, offering
to play a phonograph record and to sell religious literature. The message on
the record and in some of the literature not only explained the Witnesses'
beliefs but also attacked the Catholic Church as "the Whore of Babylon." The
Cantwells were arrested and convicted on the third and fifth counts of charges
lodged against them. The third count alleged violation of a statute forbidding
solicitation of funds for any "religious, charitable or philanthropic cause . . .
unless such cause shall have been approved by the secretary of the public
welfare council." The fifth count alleged incitement to breach of peace in that
Jesse Cantwell played his record for two men who became angry at its attack
on Catholicism and threatened to punch him. At that point Jesse retreated
without further discussion. The state supreme court sustained the convictions,
and the Cantwells appealed to the U.S. Supreme Court.

Mr. Justice **ROBERTS** delivered the opinion of the Court. . . .

First. We hold that the statute, as construed and applied to the
appellants, deprives them of their liberty without due process of law in
contravention of the Fourteenth Amendment. The fundamental concept of liberty embodied in that Amendment embraces the liberties
guaranteed by the First Amendment. The First Amendment declares
that Congress shall make no law respecting an establishment of religion or prohibiting the free exercise thereof. The Fourteenth Amendment has rendered the legislatures of the states as incompetent as
Congress to enact such laws. The constitutional inhibition of legislation on the subject of religion has a double aspect. On the one hand, it
forestalls compulsion by law of the acceptance of any creed or the
practice of any form of worship. Freedom of conscience and freedom to
adhere to such religious organization or form of worship as the individual may choose cannot be restricted by law. On the other hand, it
safeguards the free exercise of the chosen form of religion. Thus the
Amendment embraces two concepts,—freedom to believe and freedom
to act. The first is absolute but, in the nature of things, the second
cannot be. Conduct remains subject to regulation for the protection of
society. The freedom to act must have appropriate definition to preserve the enforcement of that protection. In every case the power to
regulate must be so exercised as not, in attaining a permissible end,
unduly to infringe the protected freedom. No one would contest the
proposition that a state may not, by statute, wholly deny the right to
preach or to disseminate religious views. Plainly such a previous and
absolute restraint would violate the terms of the guaranty. It is

equally clear that a state may by general and nondiscriminatory legislation regulate the times, the places, and the manner of soliciting upon its streets, and of holding meetings thereon; and may in other respects safeguard the peace, good order and comfort of the community, without unconstitutionally invading the liberties protected by the Fourteenth Amendment. . . .

The general regulation, in the public interest, of solicitation, which does not involve any religious test and does not unreasonably obstruct or delay the collection of funds, is not open to any constitutional objection, even though the collection be for a religious purpose. . . .

It will be noted, however, that the Act requires an application to the secretary of the public welfare council of the State; that he is empowered to determine whether the cause is a religious one, and that the issue of a certificate depends upon his affirmative action. If he finds that the cause is not that of religion, to solicit for it becomes a crime. He is not to issue a certificate as a matter of course. His decision to issue or refuse it involves appraisal of facts, the exercise of judgment, and the formation of an opinion. He is authorized to withhold his approval if he determines that the cause is not a religious one. Such a censorship of religion as the means of determining its right to survive is a denial of liberty protected by the First Amendment and included in the liberty which is within the protection of the Fourteenth. . . .

. . . [A]vailability of a judicial remedy for abuses in the system of licensing still leaves that system one of previous restraint which, in the field of free speech and press, we have held inadmissible. A statute authorizing previous restraint upon the exercise of the guaranteed freedom by judicial decision after trial is as obnoxious to the Constitution as one providing for like restraint by administrative action.

Nothing we have said is intended even remotely to imply that, under the cloak of religion, persons may, with impunity, commit frauds upon the public. Certainly penal laws are available to punish such conduct. Even the exercise of religion may be at some slight inconvenience in order that the state may protect its citizens from injury. Without doubt a state may protect its citizens from fraudulent solicitation by requiring a stranger in the community, before permitting him publicly to solicit funds for any purpose, to establish his identity and his authority to act for the cause which he purports to represent. The state is likewise free to regulate the time and manner of solicitation generally, in the interest of public safety, peace, comfort or convenience. But to condition the solicitation of aid for the perpetuation of religious views or systems upon a license, the grant of which rests in the exercise of a determination by state authority as to what is a religious cause, is to lay a forbidden burden upon the exercise of liberty protected by the Constitution.

Second. We hold that, in the circumstances disclosed, the conviction of Jesse Cantwell on the fifth count must be set aside. Decision as to the lawfulness of the conviction demands the weighing of two conflicting interests. The fundamental law declares the interest of the United States that the free exercise of religion be not prohibited and that freedom to communicate information and opinion be not abridged. The state of Connecticut has an obvious interest in the preservation and protection of peace and good order within her borders. We must determine whether the alleged protection of the State's interest, means to which end would, in the absence of limitation by the federal Constitution, lie wholly within the State's discretion, has been pressed, in this instance, to a point where it has come into fatal collision with the overriding interest protected by the federal compact. . . .

The offense known as breach of the peace embraces a great variety of conduct destroying or menacing public order and tranquillity. It includes not only violent acts but acts and words likely to produce violence in others. No one would have the hardihood to suggest that the principle of freedom of speech sanctions incitement to riot or that religious liberty connotes the privilege to exhort others to physical attack upon those belonging to another sect. When clear and present danger of riot, disorder, interference with traffic upon the public streets, or other immediate threat to public safety, peace, or order, appears, the power of the state to prevent or punish is obvious. Equally obvious is it that a state may not unduly suppress free communication of views, religious or other, under the guise of conserving desirable conditions. Here we have a situation analogous to a conviction under a statute sweeping in a great variety of conduct under a general and indefinite characterization, and leaving to the executive and judicial branches too wide a discretion in its application. . . .

The record played by Cantwell embodies a general attack on all organized religious systems as instruments of Satan and injurious to man; it then singles out the Roman Catholic Church for strictures couched in terms which naturally would offend not only persons of that persuasion, but all others who respect the honestly held religious faith of their fellows. The hearers were in fact highly offended. . . .

We find in the instant case no assault or threatening of bodily harm, no truculent bearing, no intentional discourtesy, no personal abuse. On the contrary, we find only an effort to persuade a willing listener to buy a book or to contribute money in the interest of what Cantwell, however misguided others may think him, conceived to be true religion.

In the realm of religious faith, and in that of political belief, sharp differences arise. In both fields the tenets of one man may seem the rankest error to his neighbor. To persuade others to his own point of view, the pleader, as we know, at times, resorts to exaggeration, to vilification of men who have been, or are, prominent in church or state, and even to false statement. But the people of this nation have ordained in the light of history, that, in spite of the probability of excesses and abuses, these liberties are, in the long view, essential to enlightened opinion and right conduct on the part of the citizens of a democracy.

The essential characteristic of these liberties is, that under their shield many types of life, character, opinion and belief can develop unmolested and unobstructed. Nowhere is this shield more necessary than in our own country for a people composed of many races and of many creeds. There are limits to the exercise of these liberties. The danger in these times from the coercive activities of those who in the delusion of racial or religious conceit would incite violence and breaches of the peace in order to deprive others of their equal right to the exercise of their liberties, is emphasized by events familiar to all. These and other transgressions of those limits the states appropriately may punish. . . .

Although the contents of the record not unnaturally aroused animosity, we think that, in the absence of a statute narrowly drawn to define and punish specific conduct as constituting a clear and present danger to a substantial interest of the State, the petitioner's communication, considered in the light of the constitutional guaranties, raised no such clear and present menace to public peace and order as to render him liable to conviction of the common law offense in question.

. . . .

Reversed.

Editors' Notes

(1) **Query:** Did Roberts' opinion treat free exercise as a "fundamental right" or merely as an "ordinary right" to be balanced against the authority of the state to maintain public order? How would (or should) the Court's treatment of a "fundamental right" differ from that of its treatment of an "ordinary right"?

(2) *Cantwell* is the leading case interpreting the First and Fourteenth amendments to limit governmental authority to regulate dissemination of information on public streets to "time, place, and manner." *Cantwell* and its descendants bar government's restricting the content of the information a speaker/writer wishes to communicate. For analyses of this "two-track" framework, see Laurence H. Tribe, *American Constitutional Law* (Mineola, N.Y.: Foundation Press, 1978), chap. 12; John Hart Ely, *Democracy and Distrust* (Cambridge, Mass.: Harvard University Press, 1980), chap. 5; and John Rawls, "The Basic Liberties and Their Priority," 3 *The Tanner Lectures on Human Values* 1 (1982).

———

"[T]o the legislature no less than to courts is committed the guardianship of deeply-cherished liberties."

MINERSVILLE SCHOOL DISTRICT v. GOBITIS

310 U.S. 586, 60 S.Ct. 1010, 84 L.Ed. 1375 (1940).

Minersville, Pennsylvania, had a long established *custom* of opening each day at public schools with a flag saluting ceremony. In October, 1935, Lillian and William Gobitis, two children of the Jehovah's Witnesses' faith, refused to salute the flag because the ceremony violated their religious scruples: The First Commandment forbids worshipping "a graven image." After unsuccessfully negotiating with the students' father, the local school superintendent asked the state attorney general if the school board could require the flag salute. The attorney general said it could, and Minersville's school board adopted a resolution ordering the ceremony and providing that failure to participate would constitute "an act of insubordination and shall be dealt with accordingly."

Immediately after adoption of the resolution, the superintendent expelled the Gobitis children. Mr. Gobitis sought help from the Witnesses' national headquarters; and, almost eighteen months later, the Witnesses' national legal counsel filed suit for Gobitis in a federal district court, claiming that requiring the salute violated the First and Fourteenth Amendments and asking for an injunction against its enforcement. The district court agreed, and the court of appeals affirmed. The board then obtained certiorari from the Supreme Court.

The Saturday after oral argument, the justices met in conference to discuss and vote on the case. According to Justice Frank Murphy's notes, Chief Justice Hughes opened the debate:

> It is the requirement of the [salute] that is objected to. We can't say this requirement is contrary to state law. . . . [T]he question here is one of the free exercise of religion.
>
> Religious scruples or belief will not give a citizen immunity from payment of taxes or instruction in military science. As Justice Cardozo has said, "The right of private judgment has never yet been exalted above the powers and the compulsion of the agencies of government." *
>
> Consider the nature of the requirement. If the requirement is aimed at religion, then it lies outside the sphere of regulation because the [First] Amendment prohibits such regulation. So I must first inquire—is it a reasonable regulation that the state asks? On the proper needs of a social order a state can require not devotions, not family prayers or religious observances . . . but if the state acts in its proper sphere the scruples of the individual cannot avoid the proper state power.
>
> So let's look at it. The pledge of allegiance. The gesture is objected to as a token of loyalty to the flag.
>
> As I see it the state can insist on inculcation of loyalty. It would be extraordinary if this country and the state could not provide for the respect for the flag of our land. It has nothing to do with religion— indeed it has to do with freedom of religion.
>
> Who is entitled to a judgment on the general effect of what is required? Almost anything the state might do may be [an] offense to

---

* **Eds.' Note:** We have slightly edited Murphy's notes to quote exactly from Cardozo's concur. op. in Hamilton v. Regents (1934), upholding compulsory military training at a state university against a pacifist's claim of free exercise. Hughes often brought into the conference either copies of the U.S. Reports or quotations from them. Murphy actually wrote "etc." to summarize what Hughes quoted from Cardozo. Again, we warn that Murphy took notes, not a verbatim record.

many people. If the legislature has judgment there is room for the belief to the effect that judgment would be good.

I come up to this case like a skittish horse to a brass band. . . . There is nothing that I have more profound belief in than religious freedom so I must bring myself to view this case on the question of state power.

There is no [il]legitimate impingement on religious belief here. What is required of those who salute the flag is a legitimate object [of state power].

We have no jurisdiction as to the wisdom of this. We have to deal with state power and consider whether this is a proper exercise or not. I don't want to be dogmatic about this, but I simply cannot believe that the state has not the power to inculcate this social objective.

According to Justice Douglas' recollection, no one disputed Hughes at the Conference; the vote was 7–0 to sustain the constitutionality of requiring the salute. Two justices, Harlan Fiske Stone and Hugo L. Black, passed, i.e., did not vote. Chief Justice Hughes assigned the task of writing the opinion of the Court to Felix Frankfurter, who had been anxious, for several reasons, to do that job. After Frankfurter circulated his opinion, all but two members of the Court joined in it. McReynolds decided to note simply that he concurred in the result, and Stone hesitated. Eventually he told his brethren that he was deeply troubled and circulated the draft of a dissent. A week before the Court announced its decision, Frankfurter sent a message to Stone:

May 27, 1940

Dear Stone:

Were No. 690 [Minersville School District v. Gobitis] an ordinary case I should let the opinion speak for itself. But that you should entertain doubts has naturally stirred me to an anxious re-examination of my own views, even though I can assure you that nothing has weighed as much on my conscience, since I have come on this Court, as has this case. . . . After all, the vulgar intrusion of law in the domain of conscience is for me a very sensitive area. For various reasons . . . a good part of my mature life has thrown whatever weight it has had against foolish and harsh manifestations of coercion and for the amplest expression of dissident views, however absurd or offensive these may have been to my own notions of rationality and decency. . . .

But no one has more clearly in his mind than you, that even when it comes to these ultimate civil liberties . . . we are not in the domain of absolutes. Here, also, we have an illustration of what the Greeks thousands of years ago recognized as a tragic issue, namely, the clash of rights, not the clash of wrongs. For resolving such clash we have no calculus. But there is for me, and I know also for you, a great make-weight for dealing with this problem, namely, that we are not the primary resolvers of the clash. We are not exercising an independent judgment; we are sitting in judgment upon the judgment of the legislature. I am aware of the important distinction which you so skillfully adumbrated in your footnote 4 (particularly the second paragraph of it) in the *Carolene Products Co.* case. I agree with that distinction; I regard it as basic. I have taken over that distinction in its central aspect . . . in the present opinion by insisting on the importance of keeping open all those channels of free expression by which undesirable legislation may be removed, and keeping unobstructed all forms of protests against what are deemed invasions of conscience. . . .

What weighs with me strongly in this case is my anxiety that, while we lean in the direction of the libertarian aspect, we do not exercise our judicial power unduly, and as though we ourselves were legislators by holding too tight a rein on the organs of popular government. In other words, I want to avoid the mistake comparable to that made by those whom we criticized when dealing with the control of property. I hope I am aware of the different interests that are compendiously summarized by opposing "liberty" to "property." But I also know that the generalizations implied in these summaries are also inaccurate and hardly correspond to the complicated realities of an advanced society. I cannot rid myself of the notion that it is not fantastic, although I think foolish and perhaps worse, for school authorities to believe . . . that to allow exemption to some of the children goes far towards disrupting the whole patriotic exercise. . . .

For time and circumstances are surely not irrelevant considerations in resolving the conflicts that we do have to resolve in this particular case. . . . You may have noticed that in my opinion I did not rely on the prior adjudications by this Court of this question. I dealt with the matter as I believe it should have been dealt with, as though it were a new question. But certainly it is relevant to make the adjustment that we have to make within the framework of the present circumstances and those that are clearly ahead of us. . . . [T]his case would have a tail of implications as to legislative power that is certainly debatable and might easily be invoked far beyond the size of the immediate kite, were it to deny the very minimum exaction, however foolish as to the Gobitis children, of expression of faith in the heritage and purposes of our country.

For my intention . . . was to use this opinion as a vehicle for preaching the true democratic faith of not relying on the Court for the impossible task of assuring a vigorous, mature, self-protecting and tolerant democracy by bringing the responsibility for a combination of firmness and toleration directly home where it belongs—to the people and their representatives themselves.

I have tried in this opinion really to act on what will, as a matter of history, be a lodestar for due regard between legislative and judicial powers, to wit, your dissent in the *Butler* case * . . . . The duty of compulsion [in the flag salute requirement] being as minimal as it is for an act, the normal legislative authorization of which certainly cannot be denied, and all channels of affirmative free expression being open to both children and parents, I cannot resist the conviction

---

* **Eds.' Note:** The relevant part of Stone's dissent in United States v. Butler (1936) is quoted in Eds.' Note (2) to West Coast Hotel v. Parrish (1937; reprinted above, p. 987).

that we ought to let the legislative judgment stand and put the responsibility for its exercise where it belongs. . . .

Faithfully yours,
Felix Frankfurter

Stone remained unconvinced, and the judgment came down on June 3, 1940, as the Nazi army, which had just swept across Holland and Belgium, was in the process of crushing France.

Mr. Justice **FRANKFURTER** delivered the opinion of the Court. . . .

Centuries of strife over the erection of particular dogmas as exclusive or all-comprehending faiths led to the inclusion of a guarantee for religious freedom in the Bill of Rights. The First Amendment, and the Fourteenth through its absorption of the First, sought to guard against repetition of those bitter religious struggles by prohibiting the establishment of a state religion and by securing to every sect the free exercise of its faith. So pervasive is the acceptance of this precious right that its scope is brought into question, as here, only when the conscience of individuals collides with the felt necessities of society.

Certainly the affirmative pursuit of one's convictions about the ultimate mystery of the universe and man's relation to it is placed beyond the reach of law. Government may not interfere with organized or individual expression of belief or disbelief. Propagation of belief—or even of disbelief in the supernatural—is protected, whether in church or chapel, mosque or synagogue, tabernacle or meeting-house. Likewise the Constitution assures generous immunity to the individual from imposition of penalties for offending, in the course of his own religious activities, the religious views of others, be they a minority or those who are dominant in government. Cantwell v. Connecticut [1940].

But the manifold character of man's relations may bring his conception of religious duty into conflict with the secular interests of his fellow-men. When does the constitutional guarantee compel exemption from doing what society thinks necessary for the promotion of some great common end, or from a penalty for conduct which appears dangerous to the general good? To state the problem is to recall the truth that no single principle can answer all of life's complexities. The right to freedom of religious belief, however dissident and however obnoxious to the cherished beliefs of others—even of a majority—is itself the denial of an absolute. But to affirm that the freedom to follow conscience has itself no limits in the life of a society would deny that very plurality of principles which, as a matter of history, underlies protection of religious toleration. . . . Our present task then, as so often the case with courts, is to reconcile two rights in order to prevent either from destroying the other. But, because in safeguarding conscience we are dealing with interests so subtle and so dear, every possible leeway should be given to the claims of religious faith.

In the judicial enforcement of religious freedom we are concerned with a historic concept. . . . The religious liberty which the Constitution protects has never excluded legislation of general scope not directed against doctrinal loyalties of particular sects. Judicial nullification of legislation cannot be justified by attributing to the framers of the Bill of Rights views for which there is no historic warrant. Conscientious scruples have not, in the course of the long struggle for religious toleration, relieved the individual from obedience to a general law not aimed at the promotion or restriction of religious beliefs. The mere possession of religious convictions which contradict the relevant concerns of a political society does not relieve the citizen from the discharge of political responsibilities. The necessity for this adjustment has again and again been recognized. In a number of situations the exertion of political authority has been sustained, while basic considerations of religious freedom have been left inviolate. Reynolds v. United States [1878]; Davis v. Beason [1890]; Selective Draft Law Cases [1918]; Hamilton v. University of California [1934]. In all these cases the general laws in question, upheld in their application to those who refused obedience from religious conviction, were manifestations of specific powers of government deemed by the legislature essential to secure and maintain that orderly, tranquil, and free society without which religious toleration itself is unattainable. Nor does the freedom of speech assured by Due Process move in a more absolute circle of immunity than that enjoyed by religious freedom. . . . We are dealing with an interest inferior to none in the hierarchy of legal values. National unity is the basis of national security. To deny the legislature the right to select appropriate means for its attainment presents a totally different order of problem from that of the propriety of subordinating the possible ugliness of littered streets to the free expression of opinion through distribution of handbills. Compare Schneider v. Irvington [1939].

Situations like the present are phases of the profoundest problem confronting a democracy—the problem which Lincoln cast in memorable dilemma: "Must a government of necessity be too *strong* for the liberties of its people, or too *weak* to maintain its own existence?" No mere textual reading or logical talisman can solve the dilemma. And when the issue demands judicial determination, it is not the personal notion of judges of what wise adjustment requires which must prevail. . . .

. . . [S]pecific activities of government presuppose the existence of an organized political society. The ultimate foundation of a free society is the binding tie of cohesive sentiment. Such a sentiment is fostered by all those agencies of the mind and spirit which may serve to gather up the traditions of a people, transmit them from generation to generation, and thereby create that continuity of a treasured common life which constitutes a civilization. "We live by symbols." The flag is the symbol of our national unity, transcending all internal differences, however large, within the framework of the Constitution. . . .

The case before us must be viewed as though the legislature of Pennsylvania had itself formally directed the flag-salute for the children of Minersville; had made no exemption for children whose parents were possessed of conscientious scruples like those of the Gobitis family; and had indicated its belief in the desirable ends to be secured by having its public school children share a common experience at those periods of development when their minds are supposedly receptive to its assimilation. . . . The precise issue, then, for us to decide is whether the legislatures of the various states and the authorities in a thousand counties and school districts of this country are barred from determining the appropriateness of various means to evoke that unifying sentiment without which there can ultimately be no liberties, civil or religious. To stigmatize legislative judgment in providing for this universal gesture of respect for the symbol of our national life in the setting of the common school as a lawless inroad on that freedom of conscience which the Constitution protects, would amount to no less than the pronouncement of pedagogical and psychological dogma in a field where courts possess no marked and certainly no controlling competence. The influences which help toward a common feeling for the common country are manifold. Some may seem harsh and others no doubt are foolish. Surely, however, the end is legitimate. And the effective means for its attainment are still so uncertain and so unauthenticated by science as to preclude us from putting the widely prevalent belief in flag-saluting beyond the pale of legislative power.
. . .

The wisdom of training children in patriotic impulses by those compulsions which necessarily pervade so much of the educational process is not for our independent judgment. . . . [T]he courtroom is not the arena for debating issues of educational policy. It is not our province to choose among competing considerations in the subtle process of securing effective loyalty to the traditional ideals of democracy, while respecting at the same time individual idiosyncracies among a people so diversified in racial origins and religious allegiances. So to hold would in effect make us the school board for the country. That authority has not been given to this Court, nor should we assume it.
. . .

. . . Except where the trangression of constitutional liberty is too plain for argument, personal freedom is best maintained—so long as the remedial channels of the democratic process remain open and unobstructed—when it is ingrained in a people's habits and not enforced against popular policy by the coercion of adjudicated law. That the flag-salute is an allowable portion of a school program for those who do not invoke conscientious scruples is surely not debatable. But for us to insist that, though the ceremony may be required, exceptional immunity must be given to dissidents, is to maintain that there is no basis for a legislative judgment that such an exemption might introduce elements of difficulty into the school discipline, might cast doubts in the

minds of the other children which would themselves weaken the effect
of the exercise.

The preciousness of the family relation, the authority and independence which give dignity to parenthood, indeed the enjoyment of all
freedom, presuppose the kind of ordered society which is summarized
by our flag. A society which is dedicated to the preservation of these
ultimate values of civilization may in self-protection utilize the educational process for inculcating those almost unconscious feelings which
bind men together in a comprehending loyalty, whatever may be their
lesser differences and difficulties. That is to say, the process may be
utilized so long as men's right to believe as they please, to win others to
their way of belief, and their right to assemble in their chosen places of
worship for the devotional ceremonies of their faith, are all fully
respected.

Judicial review, itself a limitation on popular government, is a
fundamental part of our constitutional scheme. But to the legislature
no less than to courts is committed the guardianship of deeply-cherished liberties. See Missouri K. & T.R. Co. v. May [1904]. Where all
the effective means of inducing political changes are left free from
interference, education in the abandonment of foolish legislation is
itself a training in liberty. To fight out the wise use of legislative
authority in the forum of public opinion and before legislative assemblies rather than to transfer such a contest to the judicial arena, serves
to vindicate the self-confidence of a free people.

Reversed.

Mr. Justice **McREYNOLDS** concurs in the result.

Mr. Justice **STONE**, dissenting. . . .

The law which is . . . sustained is unique in the history of Anglo-
American legislation. It does more than suppress freedom of speech
and more than prohibit the free exercise of religion. . . . For by
this law the state seeks to coerce these children to express a sentiment
which, as they interpret it, they do not entertain, and which violates
their deepest religious convictions. . . .

Concededly the constitutional guaranties of personal liberty are not
always absolutes. Government has a right to survive and powers
conferred upon it are not necessarily set at naught by the express
prohibitions of the Bill of Rights. . . . But it is a long step, and one
which I am unable to take, to the position that government may, as a
supposed educational measure and as a means of disciplining the
young, compel public affirmations which violate their religious conscience.

The very fact that we have constitutional guaranties of civil liberties and the specificity of their command where freedom of speech and
of religion are concerned require some accommodation of the powers
which government normally exercises . . . to the constitutional demand that those liberties be protected against the action of government

itself. The state concededly has power to require and control the education of its citizens, but it cannot by a general law compelling attendance at public schools preclude attendance at a private school adequate in its instruction, where the parent seeks to secure for the child the benefits of religious instruction not provided by the public school. Pierce v. Society of Sisters [1925]. And only recently we have held that the state's authority to control its public streets by generally applicable regulations is not an absolute to which free speech must yield, and cannot be made the medium of its suppression, Hague v. Committee of Industrial Organization [1939], any more than can its authority to penalize littering of the streets by a general law be used to suppress the distribution of handbills as a means of communicating ideas to their recipients. Schneider v. Irvington [1939].

. . . [W]here there are competing demands of the interests of government and of liberty under the Constitution, and where the performance of governmental functions is brought into conflict with specific constitutional restrictions, there must, when that is possible, be reasonable accommodation between them so as to preserve the essentials of both and . . . it is the function of courts to determine whether such accommodation is reasonably possible. In the cases just mentioned the Court was of opinion that there were ways enough to secure the legitimate state end without infringing the asserted immunity, or that the inconvenience caused by the inability to secure that end satisfactorily through other means, did not outweigh freedom of speech or religion. So here, even if we believe that such compulsions will contribute to national unity, there are other ways to teach loyalty and patriotism which are the sources of national unity, than by compelling the pupil to affirm that which he does not believe and by commanding a form of affirmance which violates his religious convictions. . . .

. . . The very essence of the liberty which [the Bill of Rights] guarantee is the freedom of the individual from compulsion as to what he shall think and what he shall say, at least where the compulsion is to bear false witness to his religion. If these guaranties are to have any meaning they must, I think, be deemed to withhold from the state any authority to compel belief or the expression of it where that expression violates religious convictions, whatever may be the legislative view of the desirability of such compulsion.

History teaches us that there have been but few infringements of personal liberty by the state which have not been justified, as they are here, in the name of righteousness and the public good, and few which have not been directed, as they are now, at politically helpless minorities. The framers were not unaware that under the system which they created most governmental curtailments of personal liberty would have the support of a legislative judgment that the public interest would be better served by its curtailment than by its constitutional protection. I cannot conceive that in prescribing, as limitations upon the powers of government, the freedom of the mind and spirit secured by the explicit guaranties of freedom of speech and religion, they intended or rightly could have left any latitude for a legislative judgment that the compulsory expression of belief which violates religious convictions would better serve the public interest than their protection. The Constitution may well elicit expressions of loyalty to it and to the government which it created, but it does not command such expressions or otherwise give any indication that compulsory expressions of loyalty play any such part in our scheme of government as to override the constitutional protection of freedom of speech and religion. And while such expressions of loyalty, when voluntarily given, may promote national unity, it is quite another matter to say that their compulsory expression by children in violation of their own and their parents' religious convictions can be regarded as playing so important a part in our national unity as to leave school boards free to exact it despite the constitutional guaranty of freedom of religion. The very terms of the Bill of Rights preclude, it seems to me, any reconciliation of such compulsions with the constitutional guaranties by a legislative declaration that they are more important to the public welfare than the Bill of Rights. . . .

. . . I am not persuaded that we should refrain from passing upon the legislative judgment "as long as the remedial channels of the democratic process remain open and unobstructed." This seems to me no more than the surrender of the constitutional protection of the liberty of small minorities to the popular will. We have previously pointed to the importance of a searching judicial inquiry into the legislative judgment in situations where prejudice against discrete and insular minorities may tend to curtail the operation of those political processes ordinarily to be relied on to protect minorities. See United States v. Carolene Products Co. [1938]. And until now we have not hesitated similarly to scrutinize legislation restricting the civil liberty of racial and religious minorities although no political process was affected. Meyer v. Nebraska [1923]; *Pierce*. Here we have such a small minority entertaining in good faith a religious belief, which is such a departure from the usual course of human conduct, that most persons are disposed to regard it with little toleration or concern. In such circumstances careful scrutiny of legislative efforts to secure conformity of belief and opinion by a compulsory affirmation of the desired belief, is especially needful if civil rights are to receive any protection. Tested by this standard, I am not prepared to say that the right of this small and helpless minority . . . to refrain from an expression obnoxious to their religion, is to be overborne by the interest of the state in maintaining discipline in the schools.

The Constitution expresses more than the conviction of the people that democratic processes must be preserved at all costs. It is also an expression of faith and a command that freedom of mind and spirit must be preserved, which government must obey, if it is to adhere to that justice and moderation without which no free government can exist. For this reason it would seem that legislation which operates to repress the religious freedom of small minorities, which is admittedly within the scope of the protection of the Bill of Rights, must at least be subject to the same judicial scrutiny as legislation which we have recently held to infringe the constitutional liberty of religious and racial minorities.   .   .   .

Editors' Notes

(1) **Query:** Frankfurter said that the "case before us must be viewed as though the legislature of Pennsylvania had itself formally directed the flag-salute.   .   .   ." Does that claim comport with the facts of the case? What difference for constitutional interpretation would it have made had Frankfurter said the "case before us concerns an administrative regulation adopted by a local school board"? See Richard Danzig, "How Questions Begot Answers in Felix Frankfurter's First Flag Salute Opinion," 1977 *Sup.Ct.Rev.* 257. For a general discussion of different deference due to various levels of government, see Charles L. Black, *Structure and Relationship in Constitutional Law* (Baton Rouge: Louisiana State University Press, 1969), chap. 3.

(2) **Query:** In his letter to Stone, Frankfurter claimed to be following Stone's footnote in United States v. Carolene Products (1938; reprinted above, p. 482). To what extent was that claim valid? To what extent was Stone himself following that note? In short, is the jurisprudence of *Carolene Products* only that of reinforcing representative democracy and protecting small minorities who are badly disadvantaged politically or does it also include a dimension of fundamental rights?

"The very purpose of a Bill of Rights was to withdraw certain subjects from the vicissitudes of political controversy."

WEST VIRGINIA v. BARNETTE
319 U.S. 624, 63 S.Ct. 1178, 87 L.Ed. 1628 (1943).

Justices Black, Douglas, and Murphy had joined the majority in Minersville v. Gobitis (1940) with uneasy feelings. A series of later events increased their doubts. First, many commentators in law reviews, educational journals, and even newspapers were highly critical of the decision. Second, during the next few years there was increased persecution of the Witnesses by local officials and private citizens. Third, Black, Douglas, and Murphy began to part with Frankfurter on personal and, more importantly, on jurisprudential grounds. They had come to believe in the necessity of the Court's playing a positive role in protecting the Bill of Rights and saw Frankfurter, as Douglas said two decades later, as "deeply and passionately devoted to the British system, to the supremacy of the legislative branch." In 1942, when the Court sustained a local licensing tax applied to Witnesses who were trying to distribute religious pamphlets, Black, Douglas, and Murphy noted in dissent: "This is but another step in the direction which Minersville School Dist. v. Gobitis . . . took against the same religious minority and is a logical extension of the principles upon which that decision rested. Since we joined in the opinion in the Gobitis

Case, we think it is appropriate to state that we now believe that it was also wrongly decided." Jones v. Opelika (1942).

These defections meant that there would be at least four votes to overturn *Gobitis* if the issue ever came before the Court again. Moreover, two other members of the majority in *Gobitis,* Hughes and McReynolds, retired and were replaced by Robert H. Jackson and Wiley Rutledge, both of whom were rumored to have been hostile to the ruling in *Gobitis.*

Hayden Covington, national counsel for the Witnesses, decided to present the Court with an opportunity to reconsider its ruling. His choice of a target for a test case was West Virginia, whose state board of education, following *Gobitis,* had required a ceremony similar to Minersville's. A special three-judge district court noted the changes of heart and personnel on the U.S. Supreme Court and enjoined enforcement of West Virginia's policy. The state appealed to the Supreme Court.

Mr. Justice **JACKSON** delivered the opinion of the Court. . . .

The freedom asserted by these appellees does not bring them into collision with rights asserted by any other individual. It is such conflicts which most frequently require intervention of the State to determine where the rights of one end and those of another begin. But the refusal of these persons to participate in the ceremony does not interfere with or deny rights of others to do so. Nor is there any question in this case that their behavior is peaceable and orderly. The sole conflict is between authority and rights of the individual. The State asserts power to condition access to public education on making a prescribed sign and profession and at the same time to coerce attendance by punishing both parent and child. The latter stand on a right of self-determination in matters that touch individual opinion and personal attitude. . . .

There is no doubt that, in connection with the pledges, the flag salute is a form of utterance. Symbolism is a primitive but effective way of communicating ideas. The use of an emblem or flag to symbolize some system, idea, institution, or personality, is a short cut from mind to mind. Causes and nations, political parties, lodges and ecclesiastical groups seek to knit the loyalty of their followings to a flag or banner, a color or design. The State announces rank, function, and authority through crowns and maces, uniforms and black robes; the church speaks through the Cross, the Crucifix, the altar and shrine, and clerical raiment. Symbols of State often convey political ideas just as religious symbols come to convey theological ones. Associated with many of these symbols are appropriate gestures of acceptance or respect: a salute, a bowed or bared head, a bended knee. A person gets from a symbol the meaning he puts into it, and what is one man's comfort and inspiration is another's jest and scorn. . . .

It is also to be noted that the compulsory flag salute and pledge requires affirmation of a belief and an attitude of mind. . . . It is now a commonplace that censorship or suppression of expression of opinion is tolerated by our Constitution only when the expression presents a clear and present danger of action of a kind the State is empowered to prevent and punish. It would seem that involuntary affirmation could be commanded only on even more immediate and urgent grounds than silence. But here the power of compulsion is invoked without any allegation that remaining passive during a flag salute ritual creates a clear and present danger that would justify an effort even to muffle expression. To sustain the compulsory flag salute we are required to say that a Bill of Rights which guards the individual's right to speak his own mind, left it open to public authorities to compel him to utter what is not in his mind. . . .

The *Gobitis* opinion reasoned that this is a field "where courts possess no marked and certainly no controlling competence," that it is committed to the legislatures as well as the courts to guard cherished liberties and that it is constitutionally appropriate to "fight out the wise use of legislative authority in the forum of public opinion and before legislative assemblies rather than to transfer such a contest to the judicial arena," since all the "effective means of inducing political changes are left free."

Lastly, and this is the very heart of the *Gobitis* opinion, it reasoned that "national unity is the basis of national security," that the authorities have "the right to select appropriate means for its attainment," and hence reaches the conclusion that such compulsory measures toward "national unity" are constitutional. Upon the verity of this assumption depends our answer in this case.

Struggles to coerce uniformity of sentiment in support of some end thought essential to their time and country have been waged by many good as well as by evil men. Nationalism is a relatively recent phenomenon but at other times and places the ends have been racial or territorial security, support of a dynasty or regime, and particular plans for saving souls. . . . Probably no deeper division of our people could proceed from any provocation than from finding it necessary to choose what doctrine and whose program public educational officials shall compel youth to unite in embracing. . . . Those who begin coercive elimination of dissent soon find themselves exterminating dissenters. Compulsory unification of opinion achieves only the unanimity of the graveyard.

It seems trite but necessary to say that the First Amendment to our Constitution was designed to avoid these ends by avoiding these beginnings. . . . We set up government by consent of the governed, and the Bill of Rights denies those in power to coerce that consent. Authority here is to be controlled by public opinion, not public opinion by authority.

The very purpose of a Bill of Rights was to withdraw certain subjects from the vicissitudes of political controversy, to place them beyond the reach of majorities and officials and to establish them as legal principles to be applied by the courts. One's right to life, liberty, and property, to free speech, a free press, freedom of worship and assembly, and other fundamental rights may not be submitted to vote; they depend on the outcome of no elections.

In weighing arguments of the parties it is important to distinguish between the due process clause of the Fourteenth Amendment as an instrument for transmitting the principles of the First Amendment and those cases in which it is applied for its own sake. The test of legislation which collides with the Fourteenth Amendment, because it also collides with the principles of the First, is much more definite than the test when only the Fourteenth is involved. Much of the vagueness of the due process clause disappears when the specific prohibitions of the First become its standard. The right of a State to regulate, for example, a public utility may well include, so far as the due process test is concerned, power to impose all of the restrictions which a legislature may have a "rational basis" for adopting. But freedoms of speech and of press, of assembly, and of worship may not be infringed on such slender grounds. They are susceptible of restriction only to prevent grave and immediate danger to interests which the state may lawfully protect. It is important to note that while it is the Fourteenth Amendment which bears directly upon the State it is the more specific limiting principles of the First Amendment that finally govern this case.

Nor does our duty to apply the Bill of Rights to assertions of official authority depend upon our possession of marked competence in the field where the invasion of rights occurs. True, the task of translating the majestic generalities of the Bill of Rights, conceived as part of the pattern of liberal government in the eighteenth century, into concrete restraints on officials dealing with the problems of the twentieth century, is one to disturb self-confidence. . . . But we act in these matters not by authority of our competence but by force of our commissions. We cannot, because of modest estimates of our competence in such specialties as public education, withhold the judgment that history authenticates as the function of this Court when liberty is infringed.

. . . [F]reedom to differ is not limited to things that do not matter much. That would be a mere shadow of freedom. The test of its substance is the right to differ as to things that touch the heart of the existing order.

If there is any fixed star in our constitutional constellation, it is that no official, high or petty, can prescribe what shall be orthodox in politics, nationalism, religion, or other matters of opinion or force citizens to confess by word or act their faith therein. . . .

The decision of this Court in *Gobitis* and the holdings of those few *per curiam* decisions which preceded and foreshadowed it are overruled, and the judgment enjoining enforcement of the West Virginia Regulation is

Affirmed.

Mr. Justice **BLACK** and Mr. Justice **DOUGLAS** concurring. . . .

Mr. Justice **ROBERTS** and Mr. Justice **REED** adhere to the views expressed by the Court in *Gobitis*. . . .

Mr. Justice **FRANKFURTER**, dissenting.

One who belongs to the most vilified and persecuted minority in history is not likely to be insensible to the freedoms guaranteed by our Constitution. Were my purely personal attitude relevant I should wholeheartedly associate myself with the general libertarian views in the Court's opinion, representing as they do the thought and action of a lifetime. But as judges we are neither Jew nor Gentile, neither Catholic nor agnostic. We owe equal attachment to the Constitution and are equally bound by our judicial obligations whether we derive our citizenship from the earliest or the latest immigrants to these shores. As a member of this Court I am not justified in writing my private notions of policy into the Constitution, no matter how deeply I may cherish them or how mischievous I may deem their disregard. The duty of a judge . . . is not that of the ordinary person. It can never be emphasized too much that one's own opinion about the wisdom or evil of a law should be excluded altogether when one is doing one's duty on the bench. The only opinion of our own even looking in that direction that is material is our opinion whether legislators could in reason have enacted such a law. In the light of all the circumstances, including the history of this question in this Court, it would require more daring than I possess to deny that reasonable legislators could have taken the action which is before us for review. . . .

The admonition that judicial self-restraint alone limits arbitrary exercise of our authority is relevant every time we are asked to nullify legislation. The Constitution does not give us greater veto power when dealing with one phase of "liberty" than with another. . . . In neither situation is our function comparable to that of a legislature or are we free to act as though we were a super-legislature. Judicial self-restraint is equally necessary whenever an exercise of political or legislative power is challenged. There is no warrant in the constitutional basis of this Court's authority for attributing different roles to it depending upon the nature of the challenge to the legislation. Our power does not vary according to the particular provision of the Bill of Rights which is invoked. The right not to have property taken without just compensation has, so far as the scope of judicial power is concerned, the same constitutional dignity as the right to be protected against unreasonable searches and seizures, and the latter has no less claim than freedom of the press or freedom of speech or religious freedom. In no instance is this Court the primary protector of the particular liberty that is invoked. . . .

. . . [R]esponsibility for legislation lies with legislatures, answerable as they are directly to the people, and this Court's only and very narrow function is to determine whether within the broad grant of authority vested in legislatures they have exercised a judgment for which reasonable justification can be offered. . . .

The reason why from the beginning even the narrow judicial authority to nullify legislation has been viewed with a jealous eye is that it serves to prevent the full play of the democratic process. The

fact that it may be an undemocratic aspect of our scheme of government does not call for its rejection or its disuse. But it is the best of
reasons, as this Court has frequently recognized, for the greatest
caution in its use. . . .

. . . If the avowed or intrinsic legislative purpose is either to
promote or to discourage some religious community or creed, it is
clearly within the constitutional restrictions imposed on legislatures
and cannot stand. But it by no means follows that legislative power is
wanting whenever a general non-discriminatory civil regulation in fact
touches conscientious scruples or religious beliefs . . . Regard for
such scruples or beliefs undoubtedly presents one of the most reasonable claims for the exertion of legislative accommodation. . . . But
the real question is, who is to make such accommodations, the courts or
the legislature?

This is no dry, technical matter. It cuts deep into one's conception
of the democratic process—it concerns no less the practical differences
between the means for making these accommodations that are open to
courts and to legislatures. A court can only strike down. It can only
say "This or that law is void." It cannot modify or qualify, it cannot
make exceptions to a general requirement. And it strikes down not
merely for a day. At least the finding of unconstitutionality ought not
to have ephemeral significance unless the Constitution is to be reduced
to the fugitive importance of mere legislation. When we are dealing
with the Constitution of the United States, and more particularly with
the great safeguards of the Bill of Rights, we are dealing with principles
of liberty and justice "so rooted in the traditions and conscience of our
people as to be ranked as fundamental"—something without which "a
fair and enlightened system of justice would be impossible." Palko v.
Connecticut [1937]. If the function of this Court is to be essentially no
different from that of a legislature . . . then indeed judges should not
have life tenure and they should be made directly responsible to the
electorate. . . .

The subjection of dissidents to the general requirement of saluting
the flag, as a measure conducive to the training of children in good
citizenship, is very far from being the first instance of exacting obedience to general laws that have offended deep religious scruples. Compulsory vaccination, food inspection regulations, the obligation to bear
arms, testimonial duties, compulsory medical treatment—these are but
illustrations of conduct that has often been compelled in the enforcement of legislation of general applicability even though the religious
consciences of particular individuals rebelled at the exaction.

Law is concerned with external behavior and not with the inner
life of man. It rests in large measure upon compulsion. Socrates lives
in history partly because he gave his life for the conviction that duty of
obedience to secular law does not presuppose consent to its enactment
or belief in its virtue. The consent upon which free government rests is
the consent that comes from sharing in the process of making and
unmaking laws. The state is not shut out from a domain because the

individual conscience may deny the state's claim. The individual conscience may profess what faith it chooses. It may affirm and promote that faith—in the language of the Constitution, it may "exercise" it freely—but it cannot thereby restrict community action through political organs in matters of community concern, so long as the action is not asserted in a discriminatory way either openly or by stealth. One may have the right to practice one's religion and at the same time owe the duty of formal obedience to laws that run counter to one's beliefs. . . .

One's conception of the Constitution cannot be severed from one's conception of a judge's function in applying it. The Court has no reason for existence if it merely reflects the pressures of the day. Our system is built on the faith that men set apart for this special function, freed from the influences of immediacy and from the deflections of worldly ambition, will become able to take a view of longer range than the period of responsibility entrusted to Congress and legislatures. We are dealing with matters as to which legislators and voters have conflicting views. Are we as judges to impose our strong convictions on where wisdom lies? . . .

Of course patriotism can not be enforced by the flag salute. But neither can the liberal spirit be enforced by judicial invalidation of illiberal legislation. Our constant preoccupation with the constitutionality of legislation rather than with its wisdom tends to preoccupation of the American mind with a false value. The tendency of focussing attention on constitutionality is to make constitutionality synonymous with wisdom, to regard a law as all right if it is constitutional. Such an attitude is a great enemy of liberalism. Particularly in legislation affecting freedom of thought and freedom of speech much which should offend a free-spirited society is constitutional. Reliance for the most precious interests of civilization, therefore, must be found outside of their vindication in courts of law. Only a persistent positive translation of the faith of a free society into the convictions and habits and actions of a community is the ultimate reliance against unabated temptations to fetter the human spirit.

Editors' Notes

(1) **Query:** Are there basic differences between Stone's dissent in *Gobitis* and Jackson's opinion for the Court in *Barnette*? To what extent did Jackson use a "fundamental rights" *mode* of constitutional interpretation and to what extent did he use "reinforcing representative democracy"? To what degree are the two *modes* compatible?

(2) For the background and aftermath of the Flag Salute Cases, see Alpheus Thomas Mason, *Harlan Fiske Stone* (New York: Viking, 1956), chap. 31; and David R. Manwaring, *Render unto Caesar* (Chicago: University of Chicago Press, 1962).

(3) New Hampshire had the motto "Live Free or Die" on its license plates. A pair of Jehovah's Witnesses who found this creed offensive to their pacifist

religious beliefs covered up the motto. After being twice convicted in state courts for defacing a license, they obtained an injunction from a federal court against further enforcement of the statute. Starting from *Barnette* 's proposition that "the right of freedom of thought protected by the First Amendment against state action includes both the right to speak freely and the right to refrain from speaking at all," the Supreme Court, 5–4, affirmed. Wooley v. Maynard (1977).

———

"A democratic society rests, for its continuance, upon the healthy, well-rounded growth of young people into full maturity as citizens. . . ."

PRINCE v. MASSACHUSETTS
312 U.S. 158, 64 S.Ct. 438, 88 L.Ed. 645 (1944).

Sec. 69 of Chap. 149 of the General Laws of Massachusetts forbade boys under 12 and girls under 18 to sell newspapers or periodicals in public places and punished anyone who assisted children in such activities. Sarah Prince, a Jehovah's Witness, was convicted under § 69 for allowing her ward, a 9-year old girl, named Betty Simmons, to accompany her in preaching and distributing religious literature. After losing in the state appellate system, Prince appealed to the U.S. Supreme Court.

Mr. Justice **RUTLEDGE** delivered the opinion of the Court. . . .

. . . [T]wo claimed liberties are at stake. One is the parent's, to bring up the child in the way he should go, which for appellant means to teach him the tenets and the practices of their faith. The other freedom is the child's, to observe these; and among them is "to preach the gospel . . . by public distribution" of "Watchtower" and "Consolation," in conformity with the scripture: "A little child shall lead them."

If by this position appellant seeks for freedom of conscience a broader protection than for freedom of the mind, it may be doubted that any of the great liberties insured by the First Article [of Amendment] can be given higher place than the others. All have preferred position in our basic scheme. Schneider v. Irvington [1939]; Cantwell v. Connecticut [1940]. All are interwoven there together. . . . They cannot be altogether parted in law more than in life.

To make accommodation between these freedoms and an exercise of state authority always is delicate. It hardly could be more so than in such a clash as this case presents. On one side is the obviously earnest claim for freedom of conscience and religious practice. With it is allied the parent's claim to authority in her own household and in the rearing of her children. Against these sacred private interests, basic in a democracy, stand the interests of society to protect the welfare of children, and the state's assertion of authority to that end, made here in a manner conceded valid if only secular things were involved. The last is no mere corporate concern of official authority. It is the interest of youth itself, and of the whole community, that children be both safeguarded from abuses and given opportunities for growth into free and independent well-developed men and citizens. Between contrary pulls of such weight, the safest and most objective recourse is to the lines already marked out, not precisely but for guides, in narrowing the no man's land where this battle has gone on.

The rights of children to exercise their religion, and of parents to give them religious training and to encourage them in the practice of religious belief, as against preponderant sentiment and assertion of state power voicing it, have had recognition here, most recently in West Virginia State Bd. of Edu. v. Barnette [1943]. Previously in Pierce v. Society of Sisters [1925], this Court had sustained the parent's authority to provide religious with secular schooling, and the child's right to receive it, as against the state's requirement of attendance at public schools. And in Meyer v. Nebraska [1923], children's rights to receive teaching in languages other than the nation's common tongue were guarded against the state's encroachment. It is cardinal with us that the custody, care and nurture of the child reside first in the parents, whose primary function and freedom include preparation for obligations the state can neither supply nor hinder. And it is in recognition of this that these decisions have respected the private realm of family life which the state cannot enter.

But the family itself is not beyond regulation in the public interest, as against a claim of religious liberty. Reynolds v. United States [1878]; Davis v. Beason [1890]. Acting to guard the general interest in youth's well being, the state as parens patriae may restrict the parent's control by requiring school attendance, regulating or prohibiting the child's labor, and in many other ways. Its authority is not nullified merely because the parent grounds his claim to control the child's course of conduct on religion or conscience. Thus, he cannot claim freedom from compulsory vaccination for the child more than for himself on religious grounds. The right to practice religion freely does not include liberty to expose the community or the child to communicable disease or the latter to ill health or death. . . . The catalogue need not be lengthened. . . .

But it is said the state cannot do so here. This, first, because when state action impinges upon a claimed religious freedom, it must fall unless shown to be necessary for or conducive to the child's protection against some clear and present danger . . . and, it is added, there was no such showing here. The child's presence on the street, with her guardian, distributing or offering to distribute the magazines, it is urged, was in no way harmful to her, nor in any event more so than the presence of many other children at the same time and place, engaged in shopping and other activities not prohibited. Accordingly, in view of the preferred position the freedoms of the First Article [of Amendment] occupy, the statute in its present application must fall. It cannot be sustained by any presumption of validity. Cf. *Schneider*. And, finally, it is said, the statute is, as to children, an absolute prohibition, not merely a reasonable regulation, of the denounced activity.

Concededly a statute or ordinance identical in terms with § 69, except that it is applicable to adults or all persons generally, would be invalid. Kim-Young v. California [1939]; Jamison v. Texas [1943]; Murdock v. Pennsylvania [1943]; Martin v. Struthers [1943]. But the mere fact a state could not wholly prohibit this form of adult activity does not mean it cannot do so for children. Such a conclusion granted would mean that a state could impose no greater limitation upon child labor than upon adult labor. Or, if an adult were free to enter dance halls, saloons, and disreputable places generally, in order to discharge his conceived religious duty to admonish or dissuade persons from frequenting such places, so would be a child with similar convictions and objectives, if not alone then in the parent's company, against the state's command.

The state's authority over children's activities is broader than over like actions of adults. This is peculiarly true of public activities and in matters of employment. A democratic society rests, for its continuance, upon the healthy, well-rounded growth of young people into full maturity as citizens, with all that implies. It may secure this against impeding restraints and dangers within a broad range of selection. Among evils most appropriate for such action are the crippling effects of child employment. . . .

It is true children have rights, in common with older people, in the primary use of highways. But even in such use streets afford dangers for them not affecting adults. And in other uses, whether in work or in other things, this difference may be magnified. This is so not only when children are unaccompanied but certainly to some extent when they are with their parents. What may be wholly permissible for adults therefore may not be so for children, either with or without their parents' presence.

Street preaching, whether oral or by handing out literature, is not the primary use of the highway, even for adults. While for them it cannot be wholly prohibited, it can be regulated within reasonable limits in accommodation to the primary and other incidental uses. . . .

. . . The zealous though lawful exercise of the right to engage in propagandizing the community, whether in religious, political or other matters, may and at times does create situations difficult enough for adults to cope with and wholly inappropriate for children, especially of tender years, to face. Other harmful possibilities could be stated, of emotional excitement and psychological or physical injury. Parents may be free to become martyrs themselves. But it does not follow they are free, in identical circumstances, to make martyrs of their children before they have reached the age of full and legal discretion when they can make that choice for themselves. Massachusetts has determined that an absolute prohibition, though one limited to streets and public places and to the incidental uses proscribed, is necessary to accomplish its legitimate objectives. Its power to attain them is broad enough to reach these peripheral instances in which the parent's supervision may reduce but cannot eliminate entirely the ill effects of the prohibited conduct. . . .

Affirmed.

Mr. Justice **MURPHY,** dissenting. . . .

As the opinion of the Court demonstrates, the power of the state lawfully to control the religious and other activities of children is greater than its power over similar activities of adults. But that fact is no more decisive of the issue posed by this case than is the obvious fact that the family itself is subject to reasonable regulation in the public interest. We are concerned solely with the reasonableness of this particular prohibition of religious activity by children.

In dealing with the validity of statutes which directly or indirectly infringe religious freedom and the right of parents to encourage their children in the practice of a religious belief, we are not aided by any strong presumption of the constitutionality of such legislation. United States v. Carolene Products Co. [1938]. On the contrary, the human freedoms enumerated in the First Amendment and carried over into the Fourteenth Amendment are to be presumed to be invulnerable and any attempt to sweep away those freedoms is prima facie invalid. It follows that any restriction or prohibition must be justified by those who deny that the freedoms have been unlawfully invaded. . . .

The burden in this instance, however, is not met by vague references to the reasonableness underlying child labor legislation in general. The great interest of the state in shielding minors from the evil vicissitudes of early life does not warrant every limitation on their religious training and activities. The reasonableness that justifies the prohibition of the ordinary distribution of literature in the public streets by children is not necessarily the reasonableness that justifies such a drastic restriction when the distribution is part of their religious faith. Murdock v. Pennsylvania [1943]. If the right of a child to practice its religion in that manner is to be forbidden by constitutional means, there must be convincing proof that such a practice constitutes a grave and immediate danger to the state or to the health, morals or welfare of the child. West Virginia State Bd. of Edu. v. Barnette [1943]. The vital freedom of religion, which is "of the very essence of a scheme of ordered liberty," Palko v. Connecticut [1937], cannot be erased by slender references to the state's power to restrict the more secular activities of children.

The state, in my opinion, has completely failed to sustain its burden of proving the existence of any grave or immediate danger to any interest which it may lawfully protect. There is no proof that Betty Simmons' mode of worship constituted a serious menace to the public. It was carried on in an orderly, lawful manner at a public street corner. . . . The sidewalk, no less than the cathedral or the evangelist's tent, is a proper place, under the Constitution, for the orderly worship of God. Such use of the streets is as necessary to the Jehovah's Witnesses, the Salvation Army and others who practice religion without benefit of conventional shelters as is the use of the streets for purposes of passage. . . .

. . . [T]here is not the slightest indication in this record, or in sources subject to judicial notice, that children engaged in distributing literature pursuant to their religious beliefs have been or are likely to be subject to any of the harmful "diverse influences of the street." Indeed, if probabilities are to be indulged in, the likelihood is that children engaged in serious religious endeavor are immune from such influences. Gambling, truancy, irregular eating and sleeping habits, and the more serious vices are not consistent with the high moral character ordinarily displayed by children fulfilling religious obligations. Moreover, Jehovah's Witness children invariably make their distributions in groups subject at all times to adult or parental control, as was done in this case. The dangers are thus exceedingly remote, to say the least. And the fact that the zealous exercise of the right to propagandize the community may result in violent or disorderly situations difficult for children to face is no excuse for prohibiting the exercise of that right.

No chapter in human history has been so largely written in terms of persecution and intolerance as the one dealing with religious freedom. From ancient times to the present day, the ingenuity of man has known no limits in its ability to forge weapons of oppression for use against those who dare to express or practice unorthodox religious beliefs. And the Jehovah's Witnesses are living proof of the fact that even in this nation, conceived as it was in the ideals of freedom, the right to practice religion in unconventional ways is still far from secure. Theirs is a militant and unpopular faith, pursued with a fanatical zeal. They have suffered brutal beatings; their property has been destroyed; they have been harassed at every turn by the resurrection and enforcement of little used ordinances and statutes. . . . To them, along with other present-day religious minorities, befalls the burden of testing our devotion to the ideals and constitutional guarantees of religious freedom. . . . Religious freedom is too sacred a right to be restricted or prohibited in any degree without convincing proof that a legitimate interest of the state is in grave danger.

Mr. Justice **JACKSON**. . . .

> The mere fact that the religious literature is "sold" by itinerant preachers rather than "donated" does not transform evangelism into a commercial enterprise. If it did, then the passing of the collection plate in church would make the church service a commercial project. The constitutional rights of those spreading their religious beliefs through the spoken and printed word are not to be gauged by standards governing retailers or wholesalers of books. Murdock v. Pennsylvania [1943].

It is difficult for me to believe that going upon the streets to accost the public is the same thing for application of public law as withdrawing to a private structure for religious worship. But if worship in the churches and the activity of Jehovah's Witnesses on the streets "occupy the same high estate" and have the "same claim to protection" it would seem that child labor laws may be applied to both if to either. If the *Murdock* doctrine stands along with today's decision, a foundation is laid for any state interference in the indoctrination and participation of children in religion, provided it is done in the name of their health and welfare.

This case brings to the surface the real basis of disagreement among members of this Court in previous Jehovah's Witness cases. Our basic difference seems to be as to the method of establishing limitations which of necessity bound religious freedom.

My own view may be shortly put:

I think the limits begin to operate whenever activities begin to affect or collide with liberties of others or of the public. Religious activities which concern only members of the faith are and ought to be free—as nearly absolutely free as anything can be. But beyond these, many religious denominations or sects engage in collateral and secular activities intended to obtain means from unbelievers to sustain the worshippers and their leaders. They raise money, not merely by passing the plate to those who voluntarily attend services or by contributions by their own people, but by solicitations and drives addressed to the public by holding public dinners and entertainments, by various kinds of sales and Bingo games and lotteries. All such money-raising activities on a public scale are, I think, Caesar's affairs and may be regulated by the state so long as it does not discriminate . . . and the regulation is not arbitrary and capricious, in violation of other provisions of the Constitution.

The Court in the Murdock Case rejected this principle. . . . Instead, the Court now draws a line based on age that cuts across both true exercise of religion and auxiliary secular activities. . . .

Mr. Justice **ROBERTS** and Mr. Justice **FRANKFURTER** join in this opinion.

Editors' Notes

(1) **Query:** Rutledge referred to freedom of conscience and freedom of the mind as "sacred private interests, basic in a democracy." But are these rights basic to a theory of representative, majoritarian democracy? What answer do Frankfurter's opinions for the Court in *Gobitis* (above p. 1021) and his dissent in *Barnette* (above, p. 1031) offer?

(2) **Query:** In the first paragraph of his dissent reprinted here, Murphy said: "We are concerned solely with the reasonableness of this particular prohibition of religious activity by children." Recalling the usual use of reasonableness in the essays and cases in Chapters 13 and 14 on equal protection, does § 69 not easily meet this test of constitutionality?

"[I]f the State regulates conduct by enacting a general law within its power, the purpose and effect of which is to advance the State's secular goals, the statute is valid despite its indirect burden on religious observance unless the State may accomplish its purpose by means which do not impose such a burden."—Chief Justice WARREN

"The question is whether a State can impose criminal sanctions on those who . . . worship on a different day or do not share the religious scruples of the majority."— Justice DOUGLAS

BRAUNFELD v. BROWN
366 U.S. 599, 81 S.Ct. 1144, 6 L.Ed.2d 563 (1961).

This case presented one of a series of challenges to state laws requiring certain businesses to be closed on Sundays. A special three-judge federal district court had dismissed a suit brought by Jewish merchants, and they appealed to the Supreme Court.

Mr. Chief Justice **WARREN** announced the judgment of the Court and an opinion in which Mr. Justice **BLACK,** Mr. Justice **CLARK,** and Mr. Justice **WHITTAKER** concur. . . .

Appellants contend that the enforcement against them of the Pennsylvania statute will prohibit the free exercise of their religion because, due to the statute's compulsion to close on Sunday, appellants will suffer substantial economic loss, to the benefit of their non-Sabbatarian competitors, if appellants also continue their Sabbath observance by closing their businesses on Saturday; that this result will either compel appellants to give up their Sabbath observance, a basic tenet of the Orthodox Jewish faith, or will put appellants at a serious economic disadvantage if they continue to adhere to their Sabbath. Appellants also assert that the statute will operate so as to hinder the Orthodox Jewish faith in gaining new adherents. . . .

In McGowan v. Maryland [1961] we noted the significance that this Court has attributed to the development of religious freedom in Virginia in determining the scope of the First Amendment's protection. We observed that when Virginia passed its Declaration of Rights in 1776, providing that "all men are equally entitled to the free exercise of religion," Virginia repealed its laws which in any way penalized "maintaining any opinions in matters of religion, forbearing to repair to church, or the exercising any mode of worship whatsoever." But Virginia retained its laws prohibiting Sunday labor.

We also took cognizance, in *McGowan,* of the evolution of Sunday Closing Laws from wholly religious sanctions to legislation concerned with the establishment of a day of community tranquility, respite and recreation, a day when the atmosphere is one of calm and relaxation rather than one of commercialism, as it is during the other six days of the week. . . .

Concededly, appellants . . . will be burdened economically by the State's day of rest mandate; and appellants point out that their religion requires them to refrain from work on Saturday as well. Our inquiry then is whether, in these circumstances, the First and Fourteenth Amendments forbid application of the Sunday Closing Law to appellants.

Certain aspects of religious exercise cannot, in any way, be restricted or burdened by either federal or state legislation. Compulsion by law of the acceptance of any creed or the practice of any form of worship is strictly forbidden. The freedom to hold religious beliefs and opinions is absolute. Cantwell v. Connecticut [1940]; Reynolds v. United States [1878]. Thus, in West Virginia State Board of Education v. Barnette [1945], this Court held that state action compelling school children to salute the flag, on pain of expulsion from public school, was contrary to the First and Fourteenth Amendments when applied to those students whose religious beliefs forbade saluting a flag. But this is not the case at bar; the statute before us does not make criminal the holding of any religious belief or opinion, nor does it force anyone to embrace any religious belief or to say or believe anything in conflict with his religious tenets.

However, the freedom to act, even when the action is in accord with one's religious convictions, is not totally free from legislative restrictions. *Cantwell.* As pointed out in *Reynolds*, legislative power may reach people's actions when they are found to be in violation of important social duties or subversive of good order, even when the actions are demanded by one's religion. . . .

Thus, in *Reynolds*, this Court upheld the polygamy conviction of a member of the Mormon faith despite the fact that an accepted doctrine of his church then imposed upon its male members the *duty* to practice polygamy. And, in Prince v. Massachusetts [1944], this Court upheld a statute making it a crime for a girl under eighteen years of age to sell any newspapers, periodicals or merchandise in public places despite the fact that a child of the Jehovah's Witnesses faith believed that it was her religious *duty* to perform this work.

It is to be noted that, in the two cases just mentioned, the religious practices themselves conflicted with the public interest. In such cases, to make accommodation between the religious action and an exercise of state authority is a particularly delicate task . . . because resolution in favor of the State results in the choice to the individual of either abandoning his religious principle or facing criminal prosecution.

But . . . the statute at bar does not make unlawful any religious practices of appellants; the Sunday law simply regulates a secular activity and, as applied to appellants, operates so as to make the practice of their religious beliefs more expensive. Furthermore, the law's effect does not inconvenience all members of the Orthodox Jewish faith but only those who believe it necessary to work on Sunday. And even these are not faced with as serious a choice as forsaking their religious practices or subjecting themselves to criminal prosecution.

Fully recognizing that the alternatives open to appellants and others similarly situated . . . may well result in some financial sacrifice in order to observe their religious beliefs, still the option is wholly different than when the legislation attempts to make a religious practice itself unlawful.

To strike down, without the most critical scrutiny, legislation which imposes only an indirect burden on the exercise of religion . . . would radically restrict the operating latitude of the legislature. Statutes which tax income and limit the amount which may be deducted for religious contributions impose an indirect economic burden on the observance of the religion of the citizen whose religion requires him to donate a greater amount to his church; statutes which require the courts to be closed on Saturday and Sunday impose a similar indirect burden on the observance of the religion of the trial lawyer whose religion requires him to rest on a weekday. The list of legislation of this nature is nearly limitless.

Needless to say, when entering the area of religious freedom, we must be fully cognizant of the particular protection that the Constitution has accorded it. Abhorrence of religious persecution and intolerance is a basic part of our heritage. But we are a cosmopolitan nation made up of people of almost every conceivable religious preference. These denominations number almost three hundred. . . . Consequently, it cannot be expected, much less required, that legislators enact no law regulating conduct that may in some way result in an economic disadvantage to some religious sects and not to others because of the special practices of the various religions. We do not believe that such an effect is an absolute test for determining whether the legislation violates the freedom of religion protected by the First Amendment.

Of course, to hold unassailable all legislation regulating conduct which imposes solely an indirect burden on the observance of religion would be a gross oversimplification. If the purpose or effect of a law is to impede the observance of one or all religions or is to discriminate invidiously between religions, that law is constitutionally invalid even though the burden may be characterized as being only indirect. But if the State regulates conduct by enacting a general law within its power, the purpose and effect of which is to advance the State's secular goals, the statute is valid despite its indirect burden on religious observance unless the State may accomplish its purpose by means which do not impose such a burden. . . .

As we pointed out in *McGowan*, we cannot find a State without power to provide a weekly respite from all labor and, at the same time, to set one day of the week apart from the others as a day of rest, repose, recreation and tranquillity—a day when the hectic tempo of everyday existence ceases and a more pleasant atmosphere is created, a day which all members of the family and community have the opportunity to spend and enjoy together, a day on which people may visit friends and relatives who are not available during working days, a day when the weekly laborer may best regenerate himself. . . .

Also, in *McGowan,* we examined several suggested alternative means by which . . . the State might accomplish its secular goals without even remotely or incidentally affecting religious freedom. We found there that a State might well find that those alternatives would not accomplish bringing about a general day of rest. . . .

However, appellants advance yet another means at the State's disposal which they would find unobjectionable. They contend that the State should cut an exception from the Sunday labor proscription for those people who, because of religious conviction, observe a day of rest other than Sunday. . . .

A number of States provide such an exemption, and this may well be the wiser solution to the problem. But our concern is not with the wisdom of legislation but with its constitutional limitation. Thus, reason and experience teach that to permit the exemption might well undermine the State's goal of providing a day that, as best possible, eliminates the atmosphere of commercial noise and activity. Although not dispositive of the issue, enforcement problems would be more difficult since there would be two or more days to police rather than one and it would be more difficult to observe whether violations were occurring. . . . For all of these reasons, we cannot say that the Pennsylvania statute before us is invalid, either on its face or as applied.

Mr. Justice **HARLAN** concurs in the judgment. Mr. Justice **BREN-NAN** and Mr. Justice **STEWART** concur in our disposition of appellants' claims under the Establishment Clause and the Equal Protection Clause. Mr. Justice **FRANKFURTER** and Mr. Justice **HARLAN** have rejected appellants' claim under the Free Exercise Clause in a separate opinion.* . . .

Accordingly, the decision is

Affirmed.

Mr. Justice **DOUGLAS,** dissenting.

The question is not whether one day out of seven can be imposed by a State as a day of rest. The question is not whether Sunday can by force of custom and habit be retained as a day of rest. The question is whether a State can impose criminal sanctions on those who . . . worship on a different day or do not share the religious scruples of the majority.

If the "free exercise" of religion were subject to reasonable regulations, as it is under some constitutions, or if all laws "respecting the establishment of religion" were not proscribed, I could understand how rational men, representing a predominantly Christian civilization, might think these Sunday laws did not unreasonably interfere with anyone's free exercise of religion. . . .

But that is not the premise from which we start. . . .

---

* **Eds.' Note:** In a companion case, McGowan v. Maryland (1961).

The First Amendment commands government to have no interest in theology or ritual; it admonishes government to be interested in allowing religious freedom to flourish—whether the result is to produce Catholics, Jews, or Protestants, or turn the people toward the path of Buddah, or to end in a predominantly Moslem nation, or to produce in the long run atheists or agnostics. On matters of this kind government must be neutral. . . . Certainly the "free exercise" clause does not require that everyone embrace the theology of some church or of some faith, or observe the religious practices of any majority or minority sect. . . .

Mr. Justice **BRENNAN,** concurring and dissenting. . . .

. . . I dissent . . . as to the claim that Pennsylvania has [not] prohibited the free exercise of appellants' religion.

The Court has demonstrated that public need for a weekly surcease from worldly labor. . . . I would approach this case differently, from the point of view of the individuals whose liberty is—concededly— curtailed by these enactments. For the values of the First Amendment, as embodied in the Fourteenth, look primarily towards the preservation of personal liberty, rather than towards the fulfillment of collective goals. . . .

. . . [T]he issue in this case . . . is whether a State may put an individual to a choice between his business and his religion. The Court today holds that it may. But I dissent. . . .

The first question to be resolved . . . concerns the appropriate standard of constitutional adjudication in cases in which a statute is assertedly in conflict with the First Amendment. . . . The Court in such cases is not confined to the narrow inquiry whether the challenged law is rationally related to some legitimate legislative end. Nor is the case decided by a finding that the State's interest is substantial and important, as well as rationally justifiable. This canon of adjudication was clearly stated by Mr. Justice Jackson, speaking for the Court in West Virginia State Board of Education v. Barnette:

> . . . The test of legislation which collides with the Fourteenth Amendment, because it also collides with the principles of the First, is much more definite than the test when only the Fourteenth is in- volved. . . . The right of a State to regulate, for example, a public utility may well include . . . power to impose all of the restrictions which a legislature may have a 'rational basis' for adopting. But freedoms of speech and of press, of assembly, and of worship may not be infringed on such slender grounds. They are susceptible of restric- tion only to prevent grave and immediate danger to interests which the State may lawfully protect. . . .

This exacting standard has been consistently applied by this Court as the test of legislation under all clauses of the First Amendment. . . . For religious freedom—the freedom to believe and to practice strange and, it may be, foreign creeds—has classically been one of the highest values of our society. . . . The honored place of religious freedom in our constitutional hierarchy, . . . foreshadowed by a prescient footnote in United States v. Carolene Products Co. (1938), must now be taken to be settled. Or at least so it appeared until today. For in this case the Court seems to say, without so much as a deferential nod towards that high place which we have accorded religious freedom in the past, that any substantial state interest will justify encroachments on religious practice, at least if those encroachments are cloaked in the guise of some nonreligious public purpose.

Admittedly, these laws do not compel overt affirmation of a repugnant belief, as in *Barnette*, nor do they prohibit outright any of appellants' religious practices, as did the federal law upheld in Reynolds v. United States. But their effect is that appellants may not simultaneously practice their religion and their trade, without being hampered by a substantial competitive disadvantage. Their effect is that no one may at one and the same time be an Orthodox Jew and compete effectively with his Sunday-observing fellow tradesmen. This clog upon the exercise of religion, this state-imposed burden on Orthodox Judaism, has exactly the same economic effect as a tax levied upon the sale of religious literature. And yet, such a tax, when applied in the form of an excise or license fee, was held invalid in Follett v. McCormick [1944]. All this the Court, as I read its opinion, concedes.

What, then, is the compelling state interest which impels the Commonwealth of Pennsylvania to impede appellants' freedom of worship? What overbalancing need is so weighty in the constitutional scale that it justifies this substantial, though indirect, limitation of appellants' freedom? It is not the desire to stamp out a practice deeply abhorred by society, such as polygamy, as in *Reynolds*, for the custom of resting one day a week is universally honored, as the Court has amply shown. Nor is it the State's traditional protection of children, as in Prince v. Massachusetts, for appellants are reasoning and fully autonomous adults. It is not even the interest in seeking that everyone rests one day a week, for appellants' religion requires that they take such a rest. It is the mere convenience of having everyone rest on the same day. . . .

It is true, I suppose, that the granting of such an exemption would make Sundays a little noisier, and the task of police and prosecutor a little more difficult. It is also true that a majority—21—of the 34 States which have general Sunday regulations have exemptions of this kind. We are not told that those States are significantly noisier, or that their police are significantly more burdened, than Pennsylvania's.

. . .

In fine, the Court, in my view, has exalted administrative convenience to a constitutional level high enough to justify making one religion economically disadvantageous. . . . The Court forgets, I think, a warning uttered during the congressional discussion of the First Amendment itself: ". . . the rights of conscience are, in their nature, of peculiar delicacy, and will little bear the gentlest touch of governmental hand. . . ." . . .

Mr. Justice **STEWART**, dissenting.

I agree with substantially all that Mr. Justice Brennan has written.
.   .   .

Editors' Notes

(1) Sherbert v. Verner (1963) to some extent undercut the substantive holding in *Braunfeld.* In an opinion written by Brennan, the Court held, with Warren joining the majority, that a denial of unemployment benefits to a Seventh Day Adventist who refused to take any job that required her to work on Saturdays violated free exercise. Despite the vote of 7–2, Brennan had difficulty in mustering a majority behind his opinion. See Bernard Schwartz, *Super Chief* (New York: New York University Press, 1983), pp. 468–470. Stewart concurred separately, expressing concern about the Court's creating a conflict between the establishment and free exercise clauses. For further analysis of this problem, see Rehnquist's dis. op. in Thomas v. Review Bd. (1981; reprinted below, p. 1068).

(2) For the background and aftermath of *Braunfeld* and its companion cases, see Candida Lund, "Religion and Commerce," in C. Herman Pritchett and Alan F. Westin, eds., *The Third Branch of Government* (New York: Harcourt, Brace & World, 1963); for a comparative study of Sunday Closing laws in Canada and the United States, see Jerome A. Barron, "Sunday in North America," 79 *Harv.L.Rev.* 42 (1965).

"[A] State's interest in universal education . . . is not totally free from a balancing process when it impinges on fundamental rights and interests. . . ."

WISCONSIN v. YODER
406 U.S. 205, 92 S.Ct. 1526, 32 L.Ed.2d 15 (1972).

Wisconsin prosecuted three Old Order Amish parents who kept their teen-age children at home, in violation of a state law requiring education of children up to age sixteen. The Amish explained that they believe in the religious necessity of living a simple farm life in harmony with nature. They are willing to send their children to grammar school but consider it morally dangerous to expose teenagers to the culture and values of secular society. The trial court convicted the parents, but Wisconsin's Supreme Court reversed, holding that compulsory attendance violated the right of the Old Order Amish to free exercise of religion. The state obtained certiorari from the U.S. Supreme Court.

Mr. Chief Justice **BURGER** delivered the opinion of the Court. . . .

I

There is no doubt as to the power of a State, having a high responsibility for education of its citizens, to impose reasonable regulations for the control and duration of basic education. See, e.g., Pierce v.

Society of Sisters [1925]. Providing public schools ranks at the very apex of the function of a State. Yet even this paramount responsibility was, in *Pierce*, made to yield to the right of parents to provide an equivalent education in a privately operated system. . . . As that case suggests, the values of parental direction of the religious upbringing and education of their children in their early and formative years have a high place in our society. . . . Thus, a State's interest in universal education . . . is not totally free from a balancing process when it impinges on fundamental rights and interests, such as those specifically protected by the Free Exercise Clause of the First Amendment, and the traditional interest of parents with respect to the religious upbringing of their children so long as they, in the words of *Pierce*, "prepare [them] for additional obligations."

. . . [F]or Wisconsin to compel school attendance beyond the eighth grade against a claim that such attendance interferes with the practice of a legitimate religious belief, it must appear either that the State does not deny the free exercise of religious belief by its requirement, or that there is a state interest of sufficient magnitude to override the interest claiming protection under the Free Exercise Clause. Long before there was general acknowledgment of the need for universal formal education, the Religion Clauses had specifically and firmly fixed the right to free exercise of religious beliefs, and buttressing this fundamental right was an equally firm, even if less explicit, prohibition against the establishment of any religion by government.

. . .

The essence of all that has been said and written on the subject is that only those interests of the highest order and those not otherwise served can overbalance legitimate claims to the free exercise of religion. We can accept it as settled, therefore, that, however strong the State's interest in universal compulsory education, it is by no means absolute to the exclusion of all other interests. E.g. Sherbert v. Verner (1963); McGowan v. Maryland (1961) (separate opinion of Frankfurter, J.); Prince v. Massachusetts (1944).

II

. . . . In evaluating those claims we must be careful to determine whether the Amish religious faith and their mode of life are . . . inseparable and interdependent. A way of life, however virtuous and admirable, may not be interposed as a barrier to reasonable state regulation of education if it is based on purely secular considerations; to have the protection of the Religion Clauses, the claims must be rooted in religious belief. Although a determination of what is a "religious" belief or practice entitled to constitutional protection may present a most delicate question, the very concept of ordered liberty precludes allowing every person to make his own standards on matters of conduct in which society as a whole has important interests. Thus, if the Amish asserted their claims because of their subjective evaluation and rejection of the contemporary secular values accepted by the majority, much as Thoreau rejected the social values of his time and isolated himself at Walden Pond, their claims would not rest on a religious basis. Thoreau's choice was philosophical and personal rather than religious, and such belief does not rise to the demands of the Religion Clauses.

. . . [W]e see that the record in this case abundantly supports the claim that the traditional way of life of the Amish is not merely a matter of personal preference, but one of deep religious conviction, shared by an organized group, and intimately related to daily living. . . . Moreover, for the Old Order Amish, religion is not simply a matter of theocratic belief. As the expert witnesses explained, the Old Order Amish religion pervades and determines virtually their entire way of life. . . .

. . . The conclusion is inescapable that secondary schooling, by exposing Amish children to worldly influences in terms of attitudes, goals, and values contrary to beliefs, and by substantially interfering with the religious development of the Amish child and his integration into the way of life of the Amish faith community at the crucial adolescent stage of development, contravenes the basic religious tenets and practice of the Amish faith, both as to the parent and the child. . . .

III . . .

Wisconsin concedes that under the Religion Clauses religious beliefs are absolutely free from the State's control, but it argues that "actions," even though religiously grounded, are outside the protection of the First Amendment. But our decisions have rejected the idea that religiously grounded conduct is always outside the protection of the Free Exercise Clause. It is true that activities of individuals, even when religiously based, are often subject to regulation by the States in the exercise of their undoubted power to promote the health, safety, and general welfare, or the Federal Government in the exercise of its delegated powers. See, e.g., Gillette v. United States [1971]; Braunfeld v. Brown [1961]; *Prince*; Reynolds v. United States [1878]. But to agree that religiously grounded conduct must often be subject to the broad police power of the State is not to deny that there are areas of conduct protected by the Free Exercise Clause of the First Amendment and thus beyond the power of the State to control. . . .

Nor can this case be disposed of on the grounds that Wisconsin's requirement for school attendance to age 16 applies uniformly . . . or that it is motivated by legitimate secular concerns. A regulation neutral on its face may, in its application, nonetheless offend the constitutional requirement for governmental neutrality if it unduly burdens the free exercise of religion. *Sherbert*. By preserving doctrinal flexibility and recognizing the need for a sensible and realistic application of the Religion Clauses "we have been able to chart a course that preserved the autonomy and freedom of religious bodies while avoiding any semblance of established religion. This is a 'tight rope' and one that we have successfully traversed." Walz v. Tax Commission [1970].

We turn, then, to the State's broader contention that its interest in its system of compulsory education is so compelling that even the established religious practices of the Amish must give way. . . .

The State advances two primary arguments. . . . It notes . . . that some degree of education is necessary to prepare citizens to participate effectively and intelligently in our open political system. . . . Further, education prepares individuals to be self-reliant and self-sufficient participants in society. We accept these propositions.

However, the evidence adduced by the Amish . . . is persuasively to the effect that an additional one or two years of formal high school for Amish children in place of their long-established program of informal vocational education would do little to serve those interests. . . . It is one thing to say that compulsory education for a year or two beyond the eighth grade may be necessary when its goal is the preparation of the child for life in modern society as the majority live, but it is quite another if the goal of education be viewed as the preparation of the child for life in the separated agrarian community that is the keystone of the Amish faith. See Meyer v. Nebraska [1923].

We must not forget that in the Middle Ages important values of the civilization of the Western World were preserved by members of religious orders who isolated themselves from all worldly influences against great obstacles. There can be no assumption that today's majority is "right" and the Amish and others like them are "wrong." A way of life that is odd or even erratic but interferes with no rights or interests of others is not to be condemned because it is different.

The State, however, supports its interest in providing an additional one or two years of compulsory high school education to Amish children because of the possibility that some such children will choose to leave the Amish community, and that if this occurs they will be ill-equipped for life. . . . However, on this record, that argument is highly speculative. . . .

Insofar as the State's claim rests on the view that a brief additional period of formal education is imperative to enable the Amish to participate effectively and intelligently in our democratic process, it must fall. The Amish alternative to formal secondary school education has enabled them to function effectively in their day-to-day life . . . for more than 200 years in this country. In itself this is strong evidence that they are capable of fulfilling the social and political responsibilities of citizenship without compelled attendance beyond the eighth grade at the price of jeopardizing their free exercise of religious belief. . . .

IV

Finally, the State, on authority of *Prince*, argues that a decision exempting Amish children from the State's requirement fails to recognize the substantive right of the Amish child to a secondary education, and fails to give due regard to the power of the State as parens patriae to extend the benefit of secondary education to children regardless of the wishes of their parents.   Taken at its broadest sweep, the Court's language in *Prince* might be read to give support to the State's position. However, the Court was not confronted in *Prince* with a situation comparable to that of the Amish as revealed in this record.   .   .   . The Court later took great care to confine *Prince* to a narrow scope in *Sherbert*.

This case, of course, is not one in which any harm to the physical or mental health of the child or to the public safety, peace, order, or welfare has been demonstrated or may be properly inferred.   The record is to the contrary.   .   .   .

Contrary to the suggestion of the dissenting opinion of Mr. Justice Douglas, our holding today in no degree depends on the assertion of the religious interest of the child as contrasted with that of the parents.   It is the parents who are subject to prosecution here for failing to cause their children to attend school, and it is their right of free exercise, not that of their children, that must determine Wisconsin's power to impose criminal penalties on the parent.   .   .   .   The children are not parties to this litigation.   .   .   .

Our holding in no way determines the proper resolution of possible competing interests of parents, children, and the State in an appropriate state court proceeding.   .   .   .

V . . .

Nothing we hold is intended to undermine the general applicability of the State's compulsory school-attendance statutes or to limit the power of the State to promulgate reasonable standards that, while not impairing the free exercise of religion, provide for continuing agricultural vocational education under parental and church guidance by the Old Order Amish or others similarly situated.   .   .   .

Affirmed.

Mr. Justice **POWELL** and Mr. Justice **REHNQUIST** took no part in the consideration or decision of this case.

Mr. Justice **STEWART**, with whom Mr. Justice **BRENNAN** joins, concurring.   .   .   .

Mr. Justice **WHITE**, with whom Mr. Justice **BRENNAN** and Mr. Justice **STEWART** join, concurring.   .   .   .

Mr. Justice **DOUGLAS** dissenting in part.

I

I agree with the Court that the religious scruples of the Amish are opposed to the education of their children beyond the grade schools, yet I disagree with the Court's conclusion that the matter is within the dispensation of parents alone. The Court's analysis assumes that the only interests at stake in the case are those of the Amish parents on the one hand, and those of the State on the other. The difficulty with this approach is that . . . the parents are seeking to vindicate not only their own free exercise claims, but also those of their high-school-age children. . . .

First, respondents' motion to dismiss in the trial court expressly asserts, not only the religious liberty of the adults, but also that of the children. . . .

. . . If the parents in this case are allowed a religious exemption, the inevitable effect is to impose the parents' notions of religious duty upon their children. Where the child is mature enough to express potentially conflicting desires, it would be an invasion of the child's rights to permit such an imposition without canvassing his views. . . . As the child has no other effective forum, it is in this litigation that his rights should be considered. And, if an Amish child desires to attend high school, and is mature enough to have that desire respected, the State may well be able to override the parents' religiously motivated objections.

Religion is an individual experience. It is not necessary, nor even appropriate, for every Amish child to express his views on the subject in a prosecution of a single adult. Crucial, however, are the views of the child whose parent is the subject of the suit. . . .

II . . .

These children are "persons" within the meaning of the Bill of Rights. We have so held over and over again. . . .

On this important and vital matter of education, I think the children should be entitled to be heard. While the parents, absent dissent, normally speak for the entire family, the education of the child is a matter on which the child will often have decided views. He may want to be a pianist or an astronaut or an oceanographer. To do so he will have to break from the Amish tradition.[1]

It is the future of the student, not the future of the parents, that is imperiled by today's decision. If a parent keeps his child out of school beyond the grade school, then the child will be forever barred from entry into the new and amazing world of diversity that we have today. . . . It is the student's judgment, not his parents', that is essential if we are to give full meaning to what we have said about the Bill of Rights. . . .

III . . .

The Court rightly rejects the notion that actions, even though religiously grounded, are always outside the protection of the Free

---

1. A significant number of Amish children do leave the Old Order. Professor Hostetler notes that "[t]he loss of members is very limited in some Amish districts and considerable in others." J. Hostetler, *Amish Society* 226 (1968). In one Pennsylvania church, he observed a defection rate of 30%. . . . Rates up to 50% have been reported by others. . . . [Footnote by Justice Douglas.]

Exercise Clause of the First Amendment. In so ruling, the Court departs from the teaching of *Reynolds*.

. . . What we do today, at least in this respect, opens the way to give organized religion a broader base than it has ever enjoyed; and it even promises that in time *Reynolds* will be overruled.

In another way, however, the Court retreats when in reference to Henry Thoreau it says his "choice was philosophical and personal rather than religious, and such belief does not rise to the demands of the Religion Clauses." That is contrary to what we held in United States v. Seeger [1965] where we were concerned with the meaning of the words "religious training and belief" in the Selective Service Act, which were the basis of many conscientious objector claims. We said:

> Within that phrase would come all sincere religious beliefs which are based upon a power or being, or upon a faith, to which all else is subordinate or upon which all else is ultimately dependent. The test might be stated in these words: A sincere and meaningful belief which occupies in the life of its possessor a place parallel to that filled by the God of those admittedly qualifying for the exemption comes within the statutory definition. . . .

Welsh v. United States [1970] was in the same vein. . . .

I adhere to these exalted views of "religion" and see no acceptable alternative to them now that we have become a Nation of many religions and sects, representing all of the diversities of the human race. . . .

Editors' Notes

(1) **Query**: Chief Justice Burger claimed to have "balanced" interests here. What strengths and weaknesses of balancing as a *technique* of constitutional interpretation are evident in his opinion? (One should reread Douglas' opinion before trying to answer.)

(2) **Query**: To what extent does *Yoder* modify *Prince* (above, p. 1034) and Davis v. Beason (above, p. 1010) and the other Mormon cases mentioned in the headnote and Eds.' Note (2) to *Davis*? To pass constitutional muster now, would state and federal laws against polygamy have to make exceptions for members of religious sects that advocate polygamy? *Yoder* notwithstanding, would such an exemption give a preference to one religion over another?

(3) **Query**: Because the Amish forbid acceptance of insurance benefits— caring for one another, they reason, is a religious duty—some members have refused to pay social security taxes. Respecting this view, Congress in 1965 exempted from the social security tax on the self-employed anyone who is

> a member of a recognized religious sect or division thereof and is an adherent of established tenets or teachings of such sect or division opposed to acceptance of the benefits of any public or private insurance. . . . 26 U.S.C. § 1402(g).

Does this exemption constitute a preference for some religions over others? For religion over non-religion?

United States v. Lee (1982) unanimously held that the Amish must pay social security taxes on employers and employees. The Court conceded that the tax conflicted with the religious beliefs of the Amish but ruled that the government's interest in uniform collection of taxes was compelling.

Editors' Note

CONSCIENTIOUS OBJECTION

Compulsory military service presents the most dramatic clash between the claims of Caesar and God. Despite the First Amendment's bold proclamation, the United States was slow to recognize claims of conscience when pitted against perceptions of national security. During the early years, it was the states, not bound by the First Amendment, who insisted on the primacy of Caesar's call to join the militia. The first national draft came during the Civil War, and Congress showed itself equally insensitive. One should note that the basic authority of Congress to raise an army by conscription was controversial. On his deathbed in 1864, Chief Justice Roger Brooke Taney wrote an unpublished opinion denying such authority. And the first ruling by the Supreme Court did not come until 1918, in the Selective Draft Law Cases. The opinion stated a conclusion rather than reasoned toward a reconciliation of Article I's grant of authority "to raise and support armies" and the Thirteenth Amendment's prohibition of "involuntary servitude."

During World War I, the draft act exempted any member of a "well-recognized religious sect or organization [then] organized and existing and whose existing creed or principles [forbade] its members to participate in war in any form. . . ." The Secretary of War interpreted the statute to include "personal scruples against war," but the history of the administration of the act was often ungenerous.

Between the two world wars, over eloquent dissents by Holmes, Hughes, and Stone, the Supreme Court several times interpreted the naturalization act to deny citizenship to aliens who were conscientious objectors. United States v. Schwimmer (1929); United States v. Macintosh (1931); and United States v. Bland (1931). In 1946, however, the Court changed its interpretation of the statute and eliminated the ban. Girouard v. United States.

During World War II, Congress again allowed conscientious exemption from the draft, dropping the requirement that an objector had to belong to a recognized religion. It was sufficient that his objection be based on "religious training and belief." In 1948, Congress further modified the law to define "religious training and belief" as "an individual's belief in a relation to a Supreme Being involving duties superior to those arising from any human relation, but [not including] essentially political, sociological, or philosophical views or a merely personal moral code."

During the war in Vietnam, the Court avoided the constitutional question whether Congress had violated the First Amendment by giving preference to religion over non-religion by interpreting the statute to include a "sincere and meaningful belief which occupies in the life of its possessor a place parallel to that filled by the God of" theologically motivated objectors. United States v. Seeger (1965); Welsh v. United States (1970). In vain, Justice Harlan protested that the Court had "performed a lobotomy and completely transformed the statute. . . ."

The Court's surgery could not avoid all constitutional problems. Some religious sects, such as the Quakers, oppose war in any form. Roman Catholicism, however, instructs its adherents that they may participate in wars, but only in "just wars," raising yet another possibility of a complex clash between fundamental values: On the one hand, the fundamental rights to free exercise of religion and freedom from governmental preference among religions, and on the other hand, the fundamental necessity of national security.

Among the more useful studies of the problems of conscientious objection are: James Finn, ed., *A Conflict of Loyalties: The Case for Selective Conscientious Objection* (New York: Pegasus, 1968); Lillian Schlissel, *Conscience in America: A Documentary History of Conscientious Objection in America* (New York: Dutton, 1968); Paul Ramsey, *The Just War* (New York: Scribner's, 1968); John A. Rohr, *Prophets without Honor: Public Policy and the Selective Conscientious Objector* (Nashville: Abington Press, 1974). It is no accident that three of these four books were published during the peak of the war in Vietnam.

————

"Neutrality in matters of religion is not inconsistent with 'benevolence' by way of exemption from onerous duties, so long as an exemption is tailored broadly enough that it reflects valid secular purposes."

GILLETTE v. UNITED STATES; NEGRE v. LARSEN

401 U.S. 437, 91 S.Ct. 828, 28 L.Ed.2d 168 (1971).

Sec. 6(j) of the Selective Service Act of 1967 provided:

Nothing contained in this title . . . shall be construed to require any person to be subject to combatant training and service in the armed forces . . . who, by reasons of religious training and belief, is conscientiously opposed to participation in war in any form.

Guy Gillette claimed a draft exemption under § 6(j) not because he was "opposed to participation in war in any form," but because he was opposed to participation in wars, such as that in Vietnam, that violated his conscience. (United States v. Seeger [1965] had interpreted "religious training and belief" to include general considerations of conscience not connected to formal religion.) His draft board denied the exemption, and Gillette refused to report for induction. He was convicted in a U.S. district court for this refusal, and the court of appeals affirmed. He sought and obtained certiorari from the U.S. Supreme Court.

Louis Negre, a Catholic, claimed status as a conscientious objector after his induction in the army, basing his claim on his religion's tenet that to fight in an unjust war is to participate in murder. The Army rejected his application, and he began habeas corpus proceedings in a U.S. district court. The judge denied his petition, and the court of appeals affirmed. The Supreme Court granted certiorari and heard and decided Negre's case along with Gillette's.

Mr. Justice **MARSHALL** delivered the opinion of the Court. . . .

. . . . Petitioners contend that Congress interferes with free exercise of religion by failing to relieve objectors to a particular war from military service, when the objection is religious or conscientious in nature. While the two religious clauses—pertaining to "free exercise" and "establishment" of religion—overlap and interact in many ways, it is best to focus first on petitioners' other contention, that § 6(j) is a law respecting the establishment of religion. For despite free exercise overtones, the gist of the constitutional complaint is that § 6(j) impermissibly discriminates among types of religious belief and affiliation.

. . . [P]etitioners ask how their claims to relief from military service can be permitted to fail, while other "religious" claims are upheld by the Act. It is a fact that § 6(j), properly construed, has this effect. Yet we cannot conclude in mechanical fashion, or at all, that the section works an establishment of religion.

An attack founded on disparate treatment of "religious" claims invokes what is perhaps the central purpose of the Establishment Clause—the purpose of ensuring governmental neutrality in matters of religion. See Epperson v. Arkansas (1968); Everson v. Board of Education (1947). . . . And as a general matter it is surely true that the Establishment Clause prohibits government from abandoning secular purposes in order to put an imprimatur on one religion, or on religion as such, or to favor the adherents of any sect or religious organization. See Engel v. Vitale (1962); Torcaso v. Watkins (1961). The metaphor of a "wall" or impassable barrier between Church and State, taken too literally, may mislead constitutional analysis, see Walz v. Tax Commission [1970]; Zorach v. Clauson (1952), but the Establishment Clause stands at least for the proposition that when Government activities touch on the religious sphere, they must be secular in purpose, evenhanded in operation, and neutral in primary impact. Abington School District v. Schempp [1963] (Brennan, J., concurring) (Goldberg, J., concurring).

A

The critical weakness of petitioners' establishment claim arises from the fact that § 6(j), on its face, simply does not discriminate on the basis of religious affiliation or religious belief, apart of course from beliefs concerning war. The section says that anyone who is conscientiously opposed to all war shall be relieved of military service. The specified objection must have a grounding in "religious training and belief," but no particular sectarian affiliation or theological position is required. . . . Congress has framed the conscientious objector exemption in broad terms compatible with "its long-established policy of not picking and choosing among religious beliefs." United States v. Seeger [1965].

Thus, there is no occasion to consider the claim that when Congress grants a benefit expressly to adherents of one *religion*, courts must either nullify the grant or somehow extend the benefit to cover all religions. For § 6(j) does not single out any religious organization or religious creed for special treatment. . . .

Properly phrased, petitioners' contention is that the special statutory status accorded conscientious objection to all war, but not objection to a particular war, works a de facto discrimination among religions. This happens, say petitioners, because some religious faiths themselves distinguish between personal participation in "just" and in "unjust" wars, commending the former and forbidding the latter, and therefore adherents of some religious faiths—and individuals whose personal beliefs of a religious nature include the distinction—cannot object to all wars consistently with what is regarded as the true imperative of conscience. Of course, this contention of de facto religious discrimination, rendering § 6(j) fatally underinclusive, cannot simply be brushed aside. The question of governmental neutrality is not concluded by the observation that § 6(j) on its face makes no discrimination between religions, for the Establishment Clause forbids subtle departures from neutrality, "religious gerrymanders," as well as obvious abuses. Still a claimant alleging "gerrymander" must be able to show the absence of a neutral, secular basis for the lines government has drawn. For the reasons that follow, we believe that petitioners have failed to make the requisite showing with respect to § 6(j).

Section 6(j) serves a number of valid purposes having nothing to do with a design to foster or favor any sect, religion, or cluster of religions. There are considerations of a pragmatic nature, such as the hopelessness of converting a sincere conscientious objector into an effective fighting man, but no doubt the section reflects as well the view that "in the forum of conscience, duty to a moral power higher than the State has always been maintained." United States v. Macintosh [1931] (Hughes, C.J., dissenting). See *Seeger*. We have noted that the legislative materials show congressional concern for the hard choice that conscription would impose on conscientious objectors to war, as well as respect for the value of conscientious action and for the principle of supremacy of conscience.

. . . The point is that these affirmative purposes are neutral in the sense of the Establishment Clause. Quite apart from the question whether the Free Exercise Clause might require some sort of exemption, it is hardly impermissible for Congress to attempt to accommodate free exercise values, in line with "our happy tradition" of "avoiding unnecessary clashes with the dictates of conscience." *Macintosh*. "Neutrality" in matters of religion is not inconsistent with "benevolence" by way of exemptions from onerous duties, *Walz*, so long as an exemption is tailored broadly enough that it reflects valid secular purposes. In the draft area for 30 years the exempting provision has focused on individual conscientious belief, not on sectarian affiliation. The relevant individual belief is simply objection to all war, not adherence to any extraneous theological viewpoint. And while the objection must have roots in conscience and personality that are "religious" in nature, this requirement has never been construed to elevate conventional piety or religiosity of any kind above the imperatives of a personal faith.

In this state of affairs it is impossible to say that § 6(j) intrudes upon "voluntarism" in religious life, or that the congressional purpose in enacting § 6(j) is to promote or foster those religious organizations that traditionally have taught the duty to abstain from participation in any war. A claimant, seeking judicial protection for his own conscientious beliefs, would be hard put to argue that § 6(j) encourages membership in putatively "favored" religious organizations, for the painful dilemma of the sincere conscientious objector arises precisely because he feels himself bound in conscience not to compromise his beliefs or affiliations.

B

We conclude not only that the affirmative purposes underlying § 6(j) are neutral and secular, but also that valid neutral reasons exist for limiting the exemption to objectors to all war, and that the section therefore cannot be said to reflect a religious preference.

Apart from the Government's need for manpower, perhaps the central interest involved in the administration of conscription laws is the interest in maintaining a fair system for determining "who serves when not all serve." When the Government exacts so much, the importance of fair, evenhanded, and uniform decisionmaking is obviously intensified. . . .

A virtually limitless variety of beliefs are subsumable under the rubric, "objection to a particular war." All the factors that might go into nonconscientious dissent from policy, also might appear as the concrete basis of an objection that has roots as well in conscience and religion. Indeed, over the realm of possible situations, opposition to a particular war may more likely be political and nonconscientious, than otherwise. . . . The difficulties of sorting the two, with a sure hand, are considerable. Moreover, the belief that a particular war at a particular time is unjust is by its nature changeable and subject to nullification by changing events. . . .

. . . [P]etitioners make no attempt to provide a careful definition of the claim to exemption that they ask the courts to carve out and protect. They do not explain why objection to a particular conflict—much less an objection that focuses on a particular facet of a conflict—should excuse the objector from all military service whatever, even from military operations that are connected with the conflict at hand in remote or tenuous ways. They suggest no solution to the problems arising from the fact that altered circumstances may quickly render the objection to military service moot.

To view the problem of fairness and evenhanded decisionmaking, in the present context, as merely a commonplace chore of weeding out "spurious claims," is to minimize substantial difficulties of real concern to a responsible legislative body. . . .

Ours is a Nation of enormous heterogeneity in respect of political views, moral codes, and religious persuasions. It does not bespeak an establishing of religion for Congress to forgo the enterprise of distinguishing those whose dissent has some conscientious basis from those who simply dissent. . . . There is even a danger of unintended religious discrimination—a danger that a claim's chances of success would be greater the more familiar or salient the claim's connection with conventional religiosity could be made to appear. . . . While the danger of erratic decisionmaking unfortunately exists in any system of conscription that takes individual differences into account, no doubt the dangers would be enhanced if a conscientious objection of indeterminate scope were honored in theory. . . .

Tacit at least in the Government's view of the instant cases is the contention that the limits of § 6(j) serve an overriding interest in protecting the integrity of democratic decisionmaking against claims to individual noncompliance. . . .

. . . [I]t is not inconsistent with orderly democratic government for individuals to be exempted by law, on account of special characteristics, from general duties of a burdensome nature. But real dangers . . . might arise if an exemption were made available that in its nature could not be administered fairly and uniformly over the run of relevant fact situations. Should it be thought that those who go to war are chosen unfairly or capriciously, then a mood of bitterness and cynicism might corrode the spirit of public service and the values of willing performance of a citizen's duties that are the very heart of free government.

III

Petitioners' remaining contention is that Congress interferes with the free exercise of religion by conscripting persons who oppose a particular war on grounds of conscience and religion. . . .

. . . [O]ur analysis of § 6(j) for Establishment Clause purposes has revealed governmental interests of a kind and weight sufficient to justify under the Free Exercise Clause the impact of the conscription laws on those who object to particular wars.

Our cases do not at their farthest reach support the proposition that a stance of conscientious opposition relieves an objector from any colliding duty fixed by a democratic government. See Cantwell v. Connecticut (1940); Jacobson v. Massachusetts (1905). To be sure, the Free Exercise Clause bars "governmental regulation of religious *beliefs* as such," Sherbert v. Verner (1963), or interference with the dissemination of religious ideas. See Fowler v. Rhode Island (1953); Follett v. McCormack (1944); Murdock v. Pennsylvania (1943). It prohibits misuse of secular governmental programs "to impede the observance of one or all religions or . . . to discriminate invidiously between religions, . . . even though the burden may be characterized as being only indirect." Braunfeld v. Brown [1961]. And even as to neutral prohibitory or regulatory laws having secular aims, the Free Exercise Clause may condemn certain applications clashing with imperatives of religion and conscience, when the burden on First Amendment values is not justifiable in terms of the Government's valid aims. See id., *Sherbert*. However, the impact of conscription on objectors to particular wars is far from unjustified. The conscription laws, applied to such persons as to others, are not designed to interfere with any religious ritual or practice, and do not work a penalty against any theological position. The incidental burdens felt by persons in petitioners' position are strictly justified by substantial governmental interests that relate directly to the very impacts questioned. And more broadly, of course, there is the Government's interest in procuring the manpower necessary for military purposes, pursuant to the constitutional grant of power to Congress to raise and support armies. . . .

Affirmed.

Mr. Justice **BLACK** concurs in the Court's judgment and in [portions] of the opinion of the Court.

Mr. Justice **DOUGLAS,** dissenting in Gillette v. United States. . . .

The question, Can a conscientious objector, whether his objection be rooted in "religion" or in moral values, be required to kill? has never been answered by the Court. Hamilton v. Regents [1934] did no more than hold that the Fourteenth Amendment did not require a State to make its university available to one who would not take military training. *Macintosh* denied naturalization to a person who "would not promise in advance to bear arms in defense of the United States unless he believed the war to be morally justified." The question of compelling a man to kill against his conscience was not squarely involved. Most of the talk in the majority opinion concerned "serving in the armed forces of the Nation in time of war." Such service can, of course, take place in noncombatant roles. The ruling was that such service is "dependent upon the will of Congress and not upon the scruples of the individual, except as Congress provides." The dicta of the Court in the *Macintosh* case squint towards the denial of Gillette's claim, though as I have said, the issue was not squarely presented.

Yet if dicta are to be our guide, my choice is the dicta of Chief Justice Hughes who, dissenting in *Macintosh*, spoke as well for Justices Holmes, Brandeis, and Stone:

> Nor is there ground, in my opinion, for the exclusion of Professor Macintosh because his conscientious scruples have particular reference to wars believed to be unjust. There is nothing new in such an attitude. Among the most eminent statesmen here and abroad have been those who condemned the action of their country in entering into wars they thought to be unjustified. Agreements for the renunciation of war presuppose a preponderant public sentiment against wars of aggression. If, while recognizing the power of Congress, the mere holding of religious or conscientious scruples against all wars should not disqualify a citizen from holding office in this country, or an

applicant otherwise qualified from being admitted to citizenship, there would seem to be no reason why a reservation of religious or conscientious objection to participation in wars believed to be unjust should constitute such a disqualification. . . .

I think the Hughes view is the constitutional view. It is true that the First Amendment speaks of the free exercise of religion, not of the free exercise of conscience or belief. Yet conscience and belief are the main ingredients of First Amendment rights. They are the bedrock of free speech as well as religion. The implied First Amendment right of "conscience" is certainly as high as the "right of association" which we recognized in Shelton v. Tucker [1960]. . . .

But the constitutional infirmity in the present Act seems obvious once "conscience" is the guide. As Chief Justice Hughes said in *Macintosh*:

> But, in the forum of conscience, duty to a moral power higher than the State has always been maintained. The reservation of that supreme obligation, as a matter of principle, would unquestionably be made by many of our conscientious and law-abiding citizens. The essence of religion is belief in a relation to God involving duties superior to those arising from any human relation.

The law as written is a species of those which show an invidious discrimination in favor of religious persons and against others with like scruples. Mr. Justice Black once said: "The First Amendment has lost much if the religious follower and the atheist are no longer to be judicially regarded as entitled to equal justice under law." *Zorach* (dissenting). We said as much in our recent decision in *Epperson*, where we struck down as unconstitutional a state law prohibiting the teaching of the doctrine of evolution in the public schools:

> Government in our democracy, state and national, must be neutral in matters of religious theory, doctrine, and practice. It may not be hostile to any religion or to the advocacy of no-religion; and it may not aid, foster, or promote one religion or religious theory against another or even against the militant opposite. The First Amendment mandates governmental neutrality between religion and religion, and between religion and nonreligion. . . .

While there is no Equal Protection Clause in the Fifth Amendment, our decisions are clear that invidious classifications violate due process. Bolling v. Sharpe [1954]. . . . A classification of "conscience" based on a "religion" and a "conscience" based on more generalized, philosophical grounds is equally invidious by reason of our First Amendment standards.

I had assumed that the welfare of the single human soul was the ultimate test of the vitality of the First Amendment. . . .

Mr. Justice **DOUGLAS**, dissenting in Negre v. Larsen. . . .

Under the doctrines of the Catholic Church a person has a moral duty to take part in wars declared by his government so long as they comply with the tests of his church for just wars. Conversely, a Catholic has a moral duty not to participate in unjust wars.

The Fifth Commandment, "Thou shall not kill," provides a basis for the distinction between just and unjust wars. In the 16th century Francisco Victoria, Dominican master of the University of Salamanca . . . elaborated on the distinction. "If a subject is convinced of the injustice of a war, he ought not to serve in it, even on the command of his prince. This is clear, for no one can authorize the killing of an innocent person." . . . Well over 400 years later, today, the Baltimore Catechism makes an exception to the Fifth Commandment for a "soldier fighting a just war."

No one can tell a Catholic that this or that war is either just or unjust. This is a personal decision that an individual must make on the basis of his own conscience after studying the facts.

Like the distinction between just and unjust wars, the duty to obey conscience is not a new doctrine in the Catholic Church. When told to stop preaching by the Sanhedrin, to which they were subordinate by law, "Peter and the apostles answered and said, 'We must obey God rather than men.'" That duty has not changed. Pope Paul VI has expressed it as follows: "On his part, man perceives and acknowledges the imperatives of the divine law through the mediation of conscience. In all his activity a man is bound to follow his conscience, in order that he may come to God, the end and purpose of life." . . .

. . . The full impact of the horrors of modern war were emphasized in the *Pastoral Constitution* announced by Vatican II:

> The development of armaments by modern science has immeasurably magnified the horrors and wickedness of war. Warfare conducted with these weapons can inflict immense and indiscriminate havoc which goes far beyond the bounds of legitimate defense. Indeed, if the kind of weapons now stocked in the arsenals of the great powers were to be employed to the fullest, the result would be the almost complete reciprocal slaughter of one side by the other, not to speak of the widespread devastation that would follow in the world and the deadly after-effects resulting from the use of such arms. . . .
>
> . . .
>
> [I]t is one thing to wage a war of self-defense; it is quite another to seek to impose domination on another nation. . . .

The *Pastoral Constitution* announced that "[e]very act of war directed to the indiscriminate destruction of whole cities or vast areas with their inhabitants is a crime against God and man which merits firm and unequivocal condemnation." . . .

For the reasons I have stated in my dissent in the *Gillette* case decided this day, I would reverse the judgment.

Editors' Notes

(1) **Query**: Is it fair to say that the Selective Service Act and *Gillette* protect the free exercise of Quakers and members of other pacifist sects, but not of Catholics and members of other sects who believe in selective conscientious objection? Are there, as Justice Douglas claimed, serious problems of equal protection here? Are the establishment and free exercise clauses guarantees of equal protection as far as religious matters are concerned? Do all variations on the strict-scrutiny test require judges to treat classifications by religion as suspect? Given Justice Marshall's views about race as a suspect classification, would he have been likely to vote to sustain draft legislation, apparently neutral on its face, that imposed heavier burdens on blacks than on whites? Why would he sustain legislation that imposed heavier burdens on Catholics than on main-line Protestants?

(2) **Query**: But, is it possible for a person affiliated with the Judeo-Christian ethic or who considers him/herself to be a humanitarian (or a "secular humanist") *not* to be at least a selective conscientious objector? To what extent did the fear that we are all selective CO's cause Marshall and his colleagues to put such heavy emphasis on problems of administration, a consideration that it has repeatedly said in equal protection cases is not compelling when it affects a fundamental right or employs a suspect classification? Do we have here another shift of the question to WHO shall interpret, with the Court giving way to Congress and the President on matters falling under the war powers?

"[W]e support the right of selective conscientious objection as a moral conclusion which can be validly drawn from the classical moral teaching of just-war theory."

STATEMENT BY THE ADMINISTRATIVE BOARD OF THE UNITED STATES CATHOLIC CONFERENCE
(1980).

The Military Service Act authorizes the President to order males between the ages of 18 and 26 to register for possible military service. In 1980, President Carter ordered registration to begin again, the first time since conscription ended at the close of the war in Vietnam. This decision was controversial—see Rostker v. Goldberg (1981) for a challenge to the MSA's exclusion of females. Among the reactions it provoked was a declaration by the Administrative Board of the organization of Roman Catholic Bishops in the United States.

. . . The questions of registration and conscription for military service are part of the broader political-moral issue of war and peace in the nuclear age. But registration and conscription bear so directly on the moral decision making of citizens that they require specific attention. . . .

We recognize, of course, that the questions of registration and conscription arise, as Vatican II [the Second Vatican Council] said, "because war has not been rooted out of human affairs." In the face of the sad truth of this statement, our response as teachers in the church must be the same as that of all popes of this century. We call in season and out of season for the international community to turn from war and to do the works of peace. The primary obligation of the nuclear age is to banish resort to force from the daily affairs of nations and peoples. From Pius XII to John Paul II the cry of the church and the prayer of all believers is a reiteration of the words of Paul VI: "No more war, war never again!" This must remain our primary response to war today.

Only in the context of this statement can we consider the question of what is the legitimate role of governments and the responsibilities of citizens regarding military conscription. We see registration, conscription and participation in military service as moral questions as well as political issues. Our perspective on these issues is shaped by Catholic moral teaching on the role of the state and the rights and responsibilities of citizens when both citizen and state are confronted by questions of war and peace.

With Vatican II we recognize that "as long as the danger of war remains and there is no competent and sufficiently powerful authority at the international level, governments cannot be denied the right to legitimate defense once every means of peaceful settlement has been exhausted." This principle acknowledges the right of the state to call citizens to acts of "legitimate defense." To this right there corresponds the duty each citizen has to contribute to the common good of society, including, as an essential element, the defense of society. Both the right of the state and the responsibility of the citizen are governed by moral principles which seek to protect the welfare of society and to preserve inviolate the conscience of the citizen.

The moral right of the state to use force is severely limited both in terms of the reasons for which force is employed and the means to be used. While acknowledging the duty of the state to defend society and its correlative right to use force in certain circumstances, we also affirm the Catholic teaching that the state's decision to use force should always be morally scrutinized by citizens asked to support the decision or to participate in war. From the perspective of the citizen, the moral scrutiny of every use of force can produce a posture of responsible participation in the government's decision, or conscientious objection to some reasons for using force, some methods of using force or even some specific branches of the service because of the missions they may be asked to perform. . . .

In light of these general principles, we are led to the following specific positions:

1. *Registration:* We acknowledge the right of the state to register citizens for the purpose of military conscription, both in peacetime and in times of national emergency. . . .

2. *Military Conscription:* We are opposed to any re-institution of military conscription except in the case of a national defense emergency. . . .

3. *Conscientious Objection:* We regard this question in all its dimensions as a central element in Catholic teaching on the morality of war. First, we support the right of conscientious objection, as a valid moral position, derived from the Gospel and Catholic teaching, and recognized as well in U.S. civil law. The legal protection provided conscientious objectors is a commendable part of our political system which must be preserved in any policy of conscription.

Second, we support the right of selective conscientious objection as a moral conclusion which can be validly derived from the classical moral teaching of just-war theory. The position of selective conscientious objection has not yet found expression in our legal system, but a means should be found to give this legitimate moral position a secure legal status. The experience of the Vietnam War highlighted the moral and political significance of precisely this question. We are sure of the moral validity of selective conscientious objection; we would welcome a dialogue with legislators, lawyers, ethicists and other religious leaders about how to transpose this moral position into effective legal language. . . .

Editors' Notes

(1) This statement was by no means the first time American Catholic bishops had proclaimed a moral right to selective conscientious objection. In November 1968, for example, when the war in Vietnam was near its peak, the Conference issued a pastoral letter, "Human Life in Our Day," affirming a moral right to conscientious objection and calling on Congress to modify the Selective Service Act not only to allow selective conscientious objectors to refuse "to serve in wars they consider unjust" but also to decline to serve "in branches of service (e.g., the strategic nuclear forces) which would subject them to the performance of actions contrary to deeply held moral convictions about indiscriminate killing."

(2) By 1982, some Catholic bishops' opposition to war, and more particularly to threats of use or even possession of nuclear arms, had moved far beyond earlier statements. Seventeen bishops signed a letter questioning whether any nuclear conflict could qualify as a "just war." Archbishop John Quinn of San Francisco wrote: "The teaching of the church is clear. Nuclear weapons and the arms race must be condemned as immoral." As more and more clergy of all faiths questioned the morality of serving in forces that had nuclear weapons, Archbishop Raymond Hunthausen of Seattle announced he was refusing to pay part of his income tax as a protest against American nuclear armaments. Then in May 1983, American Catholic bishops, speaking as a group, issued a Pastoral Document on War and Peace subtitled "The Challenge of Peace." In it, the bishops stressed that all human beings were members of the same family, reiterated their endorsement of selective conscientious objection, and reminded their people that "no state may demand blind obedience." Disobedience by the military of immoral orders, the bishops claimed, was "not an act of cowardice or treason but one of courage and patriotism." What was new in the pastoral was an institutional attack on the morality of nuclear deterrence as a national policy. Such a doctrine, the

bishops said, was moral only as a stop-gap measure to keep the peace while proceeding with disarmament.

Needless to say, the Reagan administration was disappointed and angry. Thus the stage is set for continued political conflict that is likely to lead to a challenge of *Gillette* as ruling constitutional interpretation.

"The withholding of educational benefits involves only an incidental burden upon appellee's free exercise of religion—if, indeed, any burden exists at all."

JOHNSON v. ROBISON
415 U.S. 361, 94 S.Ct. 1160, 39 L.Ed.2d 389 (1974).

The Veterans' Readjustment Act of 1966 (the GI Bill) limited its benefits to those who had served on active duty in the armed forces. William Robison, a conscientious objector who had completed two years of alternate, non-military service required by the draft act, instituted a class action for himself and other COs against the Veterans Administration, seeking a declaratory judgment that, so limited, the GI Bill violated the First Amendment's free exercise clause and the Fifth Amendment's implicit guarantee of equal protection. The district court sustained the statute under the First Amendment, but held it invidiously discriminated, contrary to the Fifth Amendment. The Veterans Administration appealed directly to the Supreme Court.

Mr. Justice **BRENNAN** delivered the opinion of the Court. . . .

Unlike many state and federal statutes that come before us, Congress in this statute has responsibly revealed its express legislative objectives in § 1651 of the Act and no other objective is claimed:

> The Congress of the United States hereby declares that the education program created by this chapter is for the purpose of (1) enhancing and making more attractive service in the Armed Forces of the United States, (2) extending the benefits of a higher education to qualified and deserving young persons who might not otherwise be able to afford such an education, (3) providing vocational readjustment and restoring lost educational opportunities to those service men and women whose careers have been interrupted or impeded by reason of active duty after January 31, 1955, and (4) aiding such persons in attaining the vocational and educational status which they might normally have aspired to and obtained had they not served their country.

Legislation to further these objectives is plainly within Congress' Art. I, § 8, power "to raise and support Armies." Our task is therefore narrowed to the determination of whether there is some ground of difference having a fair and substantial relation to at least one of the stated purposes justifying the different treatment accorded veterans who served on active duty in the Armed Forces, and conscientious objectors who performed alternative civilian service.

The District Court reasoned that objectives (2), (3), and (4) of § 1651 are basically variations on a single theme reflecting a congressional purpose to "eliminate the educational gaps between persons who served their country and those who did not." . . .

The error in this rationale is that it states too broadly the congressional objective reflected in (2), (3), and (4) of § 1651. The wording of those sections, in conjunction with the attendant legislative history, makes clear that Congress' purpose in enacting the Veterans' Readjustment Benefits Act of 1966 was . . . primarily . . . to compensate for the disruption that military service causes to civilian lives. In other words, the aim of the Act was to assist those who served on active duty in the Armed Forces to "readjust" to civilian life. Indeed . . . "the very name of the statute—the Veterans' Readjustment Benefits Act— emphasizes congressional concern with the veteran's need for assistance in readjusting to civilian life."

Of course, merely labeling the class of beneficiaries under the Act as those having served on active duty in the Armed Services cannot rationalize a statutory discrimination against conscientious objectors who have performed alternative civilian service, if, in fact, the lives of the latter were equally disrupted and equally in need of readjustment. See Richardson v. Belcher (1971). . . . Congress expressly recognized that significant differences exist between military service veterans and alternative service performers, particularly in respect of the Act's purpose to provide benefits to assist in readjusting to civilian life. These differences "afford the basis for a different treatment within a constitutional framework," McGinnis v. Royster (1973).

First, the disruption caused by military service is quantitatively greater than that caused by alternative civilian service. A conscientious objector performing alternative service is obligated to work for two years. Service in the Armed Forces, on the other hand, involves a six-year commitment. While active duty may be limited to two years, the military veteran remains subject to an Active Reserve and then Standby Reserve obligation after release from active duty. This additional military service obligation was emphasized by Congress as a significant reason for providing veterans' readjustment benefits. . . .

Second, the disruptions suffered by military veterans and alternative service performers are qualitatively different. Military veterans suffer a far greater loss of personal freedom during their service careers. Uprooted from civilian life, the military veteran becomes part of the military establishment, subject to its discipline and potentially hazardous duty. . . . The Senate Report accompanying the Act states:

> The major part of the burden caused by these cold war conditions quite obviously falls upon those of our youths who are called to extended tours of active military service. *It is they who must serve in the Armed Forces throughout troubled parts of the world, thereby subjecting themselves to the mental and physical hazards as well as the economic and family detriments which are peculiar to military service and which do not exist in normal civil life.* It is they who, upon

separation from service, find themselves far, far behind those in their age group whose lives have not been disrupted by military service. . . . [Emphasis added.]

Congress' reliance upon these differences between military and civilian service is highlighted by the inclusion of Class I-A-O conscientious objectors, who serve in the military in noncombatant roles, within the class of beneficiaries entitled to educational benefits under the Act.

These quantitative and qualitative distinctions, expressly recognized by Congress, form a rational basis for Congress' classification limiting educational benefits to military service veterans as a means of helping them readjust to civilian life; alternative service performers are not required to leave civilian life to perform their service.

The statutory classification also bears a rational relationship to objective (1) of § 1651, that of "enhancing and making more attractive service in the Armed Forces of the United States." By providing educational benefits to *all* military veterans who serve on active duty Congress expressed its judgment that such benefits would make military service more attractive to enlistees and draftees alike. Appellee concedes . . . that this objective is rationally promoted by providing educational benefits to those who *enlist*. But, appellee argues, there is no rational basis for extending educational benefits to *draftees* who serve in the military and not to draftees who perform civilian alternative service, since neither group is induced by educational benefits to enlist. . . .

The two groups of draftees are, in fact, not similarly circumstanced. To be sure, a draftee, by definition, does not find educational benefits sufficient incentive to enlist. But, military service with educational benefits is obviously more attractive to a draftee than military service without educational benefits. . . . Furthermore, once drafted, educational benefits may help make military service more palatable to a draftee and thus reduce a draftee's unwillingness to be a soldier.

. . .

Finally, appellee . . . contends that the Act's denial of benefits to alternative service conscientious objectors interferes with his free exercise of religion by increasing the price he must pay for adherence to his religious beliefs. That contention must be rejected in light of our decision in Gillette v. United States (1971). . . .

. . . The withholding of educational benefits involves only an incidental burden upon appellee's free exercise of religion—if, indeed, any burden exists at all. . . . Appellee and his class were not included in the class of beneficiaries, not because of any legislative design to interfere with their free exercise of religion, but because to do so would not rationally promote the Act's purposes. Thus, in light of *Gillette,* the Government's substantial interest in raising and supporting armies, Art. I, § 8, is "a kind and weight" clearly sufficient to sustain the challenged legislation, for the burden upon appellee's free exercise of religion—the denial of the economic value of veterans' educational benefits under the Act—is not nearly of the same order or magnitude as the infringement upon free exercise of religion suffered by petitioners in *Gillette.* See also Wisconsin v. Yoder (1972).

Reversed.

Mr. Justice **DOUGLAS,** dissenting. . . .

. . . [T]he discrimination against a man with religious scruples seems apparent. . . . Full benefits are available to occupants of safe desk jobs and the thousands of veterans who performed civilian type duties at home and for whom the rigors of the "war" were far from "totally disruptive," to use the Government's phrase. The benefits are provided, though the draftee did not serve overseas but lived with his family in a civilian community and worked from nine until five as a file clerk on a military base or attended college courses in his off-duty hours. No condition of hazardous duty was attached to the educational assistance program. As Senator Yarborough said, the benefits would accrue even to those who never served overseas. . . .

But the line drawn in the Act is between Class I–O conscientious objectors who performed alternative civilian service and all other draftees. Such conscientious objectors get no educational benefits whatsoever. It is, indeed, demeaning to those who have religious scruples against shouldering arms to suggest, as the Government does, that those religious scruples must be susceptible of compromise before they will be protected. The urge to forego religious scruples to gain a monetary advantage would certainly be a burden on the Free Exercise Clause in cases of those who were spiritually weak. But that was not the test in Sherbert [v. Verner (1963)] or Girouard [v. United States (1945)]. We deal with people whose religious scruples are unwaivering. Those who would die at the stake for their religious scruples may not constitutionally be penalized for the Government by the exaction of penalties because of their free exercise of religion. Where Government places a price on the free exercise of one's religious scruples it crosses the forbidden line. The issue of "coercive effects" . . . is irrelevant. Government, as I read the Constitution and the Bill of Rights, may not place a penalty on anyone for asserting his religious scruples. . . .

"Courts are not arbiters of scriptural interpretation."

THOMAS v. REVIEW BOARD
450 U.S. 707, 101 S.Ct. 1425, 67 L.Ed.2d 624 (1981).

Eddie Thomas, a foundry worker in Indiana, was transferred from making steel sheeting to producing gun turrets for tanks. He felt that, as a Jehovah's Witness and a pacifist, he could not engage in such work and requested another transfer. The company refused, and Thomas quit his job. When he applied for unemployment benefits, the state administrative review board ruled that Indiana law did not cover those who left work for personal, even religious reasons. The state supreme court affirmed the ruling and expressed doubts

about the religious grounding of Thomas' decision to leave his job. He
obtained certiorari from the U.S. Supreme Court.

Mr. Chief Justice **BURGER** delivered the opinion of the Court. . . .

II

Only beliefs rooted in religion are protected by the Free Exercise
clause, which, by its terms, gives special protection to the exercise of
religion. Sherbert v. Verner [1963]; Wisconsin v. Yoder (1972). The
determination of what is a "religious" belief or practice is more often
than not a difficult and delicate task. . . . However, the resolution
of that question is not to turn upon a judicial perception of the
particular belief or practice in question; religious beliefs need not be
acceptable, logical, consistent, or comprehensible to others in order to
merit First Amendment protection.

In support of his claim for benefits, Thomas testified:

"Q. And then when it comes to actually producing the tank itself, ham-
mering it out; that you will not do. . . .
"A. That's right, that's right when . . . I'm daily faced with the knowledge that these are tanks. . . . I really could not, you know, conscientiously continue to work with armaments. It would be against all of the
. . . religious principles that . . . I have come to learn. . . ."

Based upon this and other testimony, the referee held that Thomas
"quit due to his religious convictions." The Review Board adopted that
finding, and the finding is not challenged in this Court.

The Indiana Supreme Court apparently took a different view of the
record. It concluded that "although the claimant's reasons for quitting
were described as religious, it was unclear what his belief was, and
what the religious basis of his belief was." In that court's view,
Thomas had made a merely "personal philosophical choice rather than
a religious choice."

In reaching its conclusion, the Indiana court seems to have placed
considerable reliance on the facts that Thomas was "struggling" with
his beliefs and that he was not able to "articulate" his belief precisely.
It noted, for example, that Thomas admitted before the referee that he
would not object to

working for United States Steel or Inland Steel . . . produc[ing] the
raw product necessary for the production of any kind of tank . . .
[because I] would not be a direct party to whoever they shipped it to
[and] would not be . . . chargeable in . . . conscience. . . .

The court found this position inconsistent with Thomas' stated opposition to participation in the production of armaments. But, Thomas'
statements reveal no more than that he found work in the roll foundry
sufficiently insulated from producing weapons of war. We see, therefore, that Thomas drew a line, and it is not for us to say that the line he
drew was an unreasonable one. Courts should not undertake to dissect
religious beliefs because the believer admits that he is "struggling"

with his position or because his beliefs are not articulated with the clarity and precision that a more sophisticated person might employ.

The Indiana court also appears to have given significant weight to the fact that another Jehovah's Witness had no scruples about working on tank turrets. . . . Intrafaith differences of that kind are not uncommon among followers of a particular creed, and the judicial process is singularly ill equipped to resolve such differences in relation to the Religion Clauses. One can, of course, imagine an asserted claim so bizarre, so clearly nonreligious in motivation, as not to be entitled to protection under the Free Exercise Clause; but that is not the case here, and the guarantee of free exercise is not limited to beliefs which are shared by all of the members of a religious sect. Particularly in this sensitive area, it is not within the judicial function and judicial competence to inquire whether the petitioner or his fellow worker more correctly perceived the commands of their common faith. Courts are not arbiters of scriptural interpretation.

. . . On this record, it is clear that Thomas terminated his employment for religious reasons.

III

A

More than 30 years ago, the Court held that a person may not be compelled to choose between the exercise of a First Amendment right and participation in an otherwise available public program. A state may not

> exclude individual Catholics, Lutherans, Mohammedans, Baptists, Jews, Methodists, Non-believers, Presbyterians, or the members of any other faith, because of their faith, or lack of it, from receiving the benefits of public welfare legislation. Everson v. Board of Education (1947).

Later, in *Sherbert,* the Court examined South Carolina's attempt to deny unemployment compensation benefits to a Sabbatarian who declined to work on Saturday. In sustaining her right to receive benefits, the Court held:

> The ruling . . . forces her to choose between following the precepts of her religion and forfeiting benefits, on the one hand, and abandoning one of the precepts of her religion in order to accept work, on the other hand. Governmental imposition of such a burden puts the same kind of burden upon the free exercise of religion as would a fine imposed against [her] for her Saturday worship. . . .

The respondent Review Board argues, and the Indiana Supreme Court held, that the burden upon religion here is only the indirect consequence of public welfare legislation that the state clearly has authority to enact. . . . Indiana requires applicants for unemployment compensation to show that they left work for "good cause in connection with the work." . . .

A similar argument was made and rejected in *Sherbert,* however. It is true that, as in *Sherbert,* the Indiana law does not *compel* a violation of conscience. But, "this is only the beginning, not the end, of our inquiry." In a variety of ways we have said that "a regulation neutral on its face may, in its application, nonetheless offend the constitutional requirement for governmental neutrality if it unduly burdens the free exercise of religion." *Yoder*.

Here, as in *Sherbert*, the employee was put to a choice between fidelity to religious belief or cessation of work; the coercieve impact on Thomas is indistinguishable from *Sherbert*. . . . Where the state conditions receipt of an important benefit upon conduct proscribed by a religious faith, or where it denies such a benefit because of conduct mandated by religious belief, thereby putting substantial pressure on an adherent to modify his behavior and to violate his beliefs, a burden upon religion exists. While the compulsion may be indirect, the infringement upon free exercise is nonetheless substantial. . . .

B

The mere fact that the petitioner's religious practice is burdened by a governmental program does not mean that an exemption accommodating his practice must be granted. The state may justify an inroad on religious liberty by showing that it is the least restrictive means of achieving some compelling state interest. However, it is still true that "[t]he essence of all that has been said and written on the subject is that only those interests of the highest order can overbalance legitimate claims to the free exercise of religion." *Yoder*.

The purposes urged to sustain the disqualifying provision of the Indiana unemployment compensation scheme are two-fold: (1) to avoid the widespread unemployment and the consequent burden on the fund resulting if people were permitted to leave jobs for "personal" reasons; and (2) to avoid a detailed probing by employers into job applicants' religious beliefs. These are by no means unimportant considerations. When the focus of the inquiry is properly narrowed, however, we must conclude that the interests advanced by the state do not justify the burden placed on free exercise of religion.

There is no evidence in the record to indicate that the number of people who find themselves in the predicament of choosing between benefits and religious beliefs is large enough to create "widespread unemployment," or even to seriously affect unemployment—and no such claim was advanced by the Review Board. Similarly, although detailed inquiry by employers into applicants' religious beliefs is undesirable, there is no evidence in the record to indicate that such inquiries will occur in Indiana, or that they have occurred in any of the states that extend benefits to people in the petitioner's position. Nor is there any reason to believe that the number of people terminating employment for religious reasons will be so great as to motivate employers to make such inquiries.

Neither of the interests advanced is sufficiently compelling to justify the burden upon Thomas' religious liberty. Accordingly, Thomas is entitled to receive benefits unless, as the state contends and the Indiana court held, such payment would violate the Establishment Clause.

IV

The respondent contends that to compel benefit payments to Thomas involves the state in fostering a religious faith. There is, in a sense, a "benefit" to Thomas deriving from his religious beliefs, but this manifests no more than the tension between the two Religious Clauses which the Court resolved in *Sherbert:*

> In holding as we do, plainly we are not fostering the 'establishment' of the Seventh Day Adventist religion in South Carolina, for the extension of unemployment benefits to Sabbatarians in common with Sunday worshippers reflects nothing more than the governmental obligation of neutrality in the face of religious differences, and does not represent that involvement of religious with secular institutions which it is the object of the Establishment Clause to forestall. . . .

Reversed.

Justice **BLACKMUN** joins Parts . . . II and III of the Court's opinion. As to Part IV thereof, he concurs in the result.

Justice **REHNQUIST**, dissenting. . . .

I

The Court correctly acknowledges that there is a "tension" between the Free Exercise and Establishment Clauses of the First Amendment of the United States Constitution. Although the relationship of the two clauses has been the subject of much commentary, the "tension" is of fairly recent vintage, unknown at the time of the framing and adoption of the First Amendment. The causes of the tension, it seems to me, are three-fold. First, the growth of social welfare legislation during the latter part of the 20th century has greatly magnified the potential for conflict between the two clauses, since such legislation touches the individual at so many points in his life. Second, the decision by this Court that the First Amendment was "incorporated" into the Fourteenth Amendment and thereby made applicable against the States, Stromberg v. California (1931); Cantwell v. Connecticut (1940), similarly multiplied the number of instances in which the "tension" might arise. The third, and perhaps most important, cause of the tension is our overly expansive interpretation of *both* clauses. By broadly construing both clauses, the Court has constantly narrowed the channel between the Scylla and Charybdis through which any state or federal action must pass in order to survive constitutional scrutiny.

None of these developments could have been foreseen by those who framed and adopted the First Amendment. The First Amendment was adopted well before the growth of much social welfare legislation and at a time when the Federal Government was in a real sense considered a government of limited delegated powers. . . . Moreover, as originally enacted, the First Amendment applied only to the Federal Gov-

ernment, not the government of the States. Barron v. Baltimore (1833).
The Framers could hardly anticipate *Barron* being superseded by the
"selective incorporation" doctrine adopted by the Court. . . .

II

The decision today illustrates how far astray the Court has gone in
interpreting the Free Exercise and Establishment Clauses of the First
Amendment. Although the Court holds that a State is constitutionally
required to provide direct financial assistance to persons solely on the
basis of their religious beliefs and recognizes the "tension" between the
two clauses, it does little to help resolve that tension or to offer
meaningful guidance to other courts which must decide cases like this
on a day-by-day basis. Instead, it simply asserts that there is no
Establishment Clause violation here and leaves tension between the
two Religion Clauses to be resolved on a case-by-case basis. . . . I
believe that the "tension" is largely of this Court's own making, and
would diminish almost to the vanishing point if the clauses were
properly interpreted.

Just as it did in *Sherbert*, the Court today reads the Free Exercise
Clause more broadly than is warranted. As to the proper interpretation of the Free Exercise Clause, I would accept the decision of Braunfeld v. Brown (1961), and the dissent in *Sherbert*. In *Braunfeld*, we held
that Sunday Closing laws do not violate the First Amendment rights of
Sabbatarians. Chief Justice Warren explained that the statute did not
make unlawful any religious practices of appellants; it simply made
the practice of their religious beliefs more expensive. . . . Likewise
in this case, it cannot be said that the State discriminated against
Thomas on the basis of his religious beliefs or that he was denied
benefits *because* he was a Jehovah's Witness. Where, as here, a State
has enacted a general statute, the purpose and effect of which is to
advance the State's secular goals, the Free Exercise Clause does not in
my view require the State to conform that statute to the dictates of
religious conscience of any group. . . .

The Court's treatment of the Establishment Clause is equally
unsatisfying. . . . I would agree that the Establishment Clause,
properly interpreted, would not be violated if Indiana voluntarily chose
to grant unemployment benefits to those persons who left their jobs for
religious reasons. But I also believe that the decision below is inconsistent with many of our prior Establishment Clause cases. Those cases,
if faithfully applied, would require us to hold that such voluntary
action by a State *did* violate the Establishment Clause.

. . . In *Everson*, the Court stated that the Establishment Clause
bespeaks a "government . . . stripped of all power . . . to support,
or otherwise assist any or all religions . . .," and no State "can
pass laws which aid one religion [or] all religions." In Torcaso v.
Watkins (1961), the Court asserted that the government cannot "constitutionally pass laws or impose requirements which aid all religions as
against non-believers." And in School District of Abington Township v.

Schempp (1963), the Court adopted Justice Rutledge's words in *Everson* that the Establishment Clause forbids "every form of public aid or support for religion." See also Engel v. Vitale (1962).

In recent years the Court has moved away from the mechanistic "no-aid-to-religion" approach to the Establishment Clause and has stated a three-part test to determine the constitutionality of governmental aid to religion. See Lemon v. Kurtzman (1971); Committee for Public Education & Religious Liberty v. Nyquist (1973). First, the statute must serve a secular legislative purpose. Second, it must have a "primary effect" that neither advances nor inhibits religion. And third, the State and its administration must avoid excessive entanglement with religion. Walz v. Tax Commission (1970).

It is not surprising that the Court today makes no attempt to apply those principles to the facts of this case. If Indiana were to legislate what the Court today requires—an unemployment compensation law which permitted benefits to be granted to those persons who quit their jobs for religious reasons—the statute would "plainly" violate the Establishment Clause as interpreted in such cases as *Lemon* and *Nyquist*. First, although the unemployment statute as a whole would be enacted to serve a secular legislative purpose, the proviso would clearly serve only a religious purpose. It would grant financial benefits for the sole purpose of accommodating religious beliefs. Second, there can be little doubt that the primary effect on the proviso would be to "advance" religion by facilitating the exercise of religious belief. Third, any statute including such a proviso would surely "entangle" the State in religion. . . . By granting financial benefits to persons solely on the basis of their religious beliefs, the State must necessarily inquire whether the claimant's belief is "religious" and whether it is sincerely held. Otherwise any dissatisfied employee may leave his job without cause and claim that he did so because his own particular beliefs required it.

It is unclear from the Court's opinion whether it has temporarily retreated from its expansive view of the Establishment Clause, or wholly abandoned it. I would welcome the latter. . . .

. . . I believe that Justice Stewart, dissenting in *Schempp*, accurately stated the reach of the Establishment Clause. He explained that the Establishment Clause is limited to "government support of proselytizing activities of religious sects by throwing the weight of secular authorities behind the dissemination of religious tenets." . . . Conversely, governmental assistance which does not have the effect of "inducing" religious belief, but instead merely "accommodates" or implements an independent religious choice does not impermissibly involve the government in religious choices and therefore does not violate the Establishment Clause of the First Amendment. I would think that in this case, as in *Sherbert*, had the state voluntarily chosen to pay unemployment compensation benefits to persons who left their jobs for religious reasons, such aid would be constitutionally permissible because it redounds directly to the benefit of the individual. . . .

Editors' Notes

(1) **Query:** Chief Justice Burger said in *Thomas:* "Where the state conditions receipt of an important benefit upon conduct proscribed by a religious faith, or where it denies such a benefit because of conduct mandated by religious belief . . . a burden upon religion exists." How can one reconcile that assertion with Gillette v. United States (1971) and Johnson v. Robison (1974)?

(2) **Query:** To what extent has the Court in these cases treated religious freedom as a fundamental right? Has it been groping for scales along which to measure threats against that right (for instance, removal of unemployment benefits, denial of GI Bill, or obligation to fight in a war that one's religious conscience deems murder) along with the relative importance of various countervailing governmental interests? Or are the CO cases merely examples of ad hoc balancing? What other explanations for these rulings can one suggest?

"On occasion this Court has found certain governmental interests so compelling as to allow even regulations prohibiting religiously based conduct."

BOB JONES UNIVERSITY v. UNITED STATES
461 U.S. 574, 103 S.Ct. 2017, 76 L.Ed.2d 157 (1983).

In 1970 a special three-judge district court enjoined the Internal Revenue Service from according tax-exempt status to private schools in Mississippi that discriminated because of race in admitting students (Green v. Connally). The Supreme Court affirmed per curiam, without opinion (Coit v. Green (1971)). Following those decisions, IRS issued Revenue Bulletin 71–447 denying tax exempt status to all private schools practicing racial discrimination. This ruling denied exemption to the finances of the schools themselves under § 501(c)(3) of the Internal Revenue Code, making them liable to federal taxes, and also excluded donations by private individuals from tax deductions under § 170 of the Code. Neither section of the Code mentioned racial discrimination as a basis for denying exemption, but IRS and the three-judge district court reasoned that racial discrimination was so directly contrary to public policy as, even in the absence of explicit statutory language, to exclude its practitioners from claiming to be charitable organizations aiding the public welfare.

Bob Jones University, located in Greenville, S.C., is a non-denominational, fundamentalist Christian institution whose purposes are both religious and educational. Its rules require all faculty to be devout Christians, and the Bible (as the University interprets it) to provide the guiding principles of education. The school's regulations carefully prescribe codes of conduct for students. Until 1975, BJU was open only to whites, but after the Court of Appeals for the Fourth Circuit held that a federal statute enacted pursuant to the Thirteenth Amendment outlawed racial exclusion practiced even by private schools—the

Supreme Court affirmed in Runyon v. McCrary (1976)—BJU began to admit unmarried blacks, but with certain restrictions:

There is to be no interracial dating

1. Students who are partners in an interracial marriage will be expelled.

2. Students who are members of or affiliated with any group or organization which holds as one of its goals or advocates interracial marriage will be expelled.

3. Students who date outside their own race will be expelled.

4. Students who espouse, promote, or encourage others to violate the University's dating rules and regulations will be expelled.

This policy was based on a belief that God forbids racial intermarriage.

In 1970 IRS informed BJU it was losing its status as a tax exempt institution. The University then began a long series of legal actions that in 1980 resulted in a decision by the Court of Appeals for the Fourth Circuit that the University had no statutory or constitutional right to a tax exemption. BJU sought and obtained certiorari. Before oral argument, the Reagan administration announced that it agreed with Bob Jones University's interpretation of the Revenue Code, but the Supreme Court refused to dismiss the case. Instead, it appointed William T. Coleman, a prominent black attorney and former cabinet official under Richard M. Nixon, to argue the case as amicus curiae.

Chief Justice **BURGER** delivered the opinion of the Court. . . .

II . . .

B

We are bound to approach these questions with full awareness that determinations of public benefit and public policy are sensitive matters with serious implications for the institutions affected; a declaration that a given institution is not "charitable" should be made only where there can be no doubt that the activity involved is contrary to a fundamental public policy. But there can no longer be any doubt that racial discrimination in education violates deeply and widely accepted views of elementary justice. Prior to 1954, public education in many places still was conducted under the pall of Plessy v. Ferguson, (1896); racial segregation in primary and secondary education prevailed in many parts of the country. This Court's decision in Brown v. Board of Education (1954) signalled an end to that era. Over the past quarter of a century, every pronouncement of this Court and myriad Acts of Congress and Executive Orders attest a firm national policy to prohibit racial segregation and discrimination in public education.

An unbroken line of cases following *Brown* establishes beyond doubt this Court's view that racial discrimination in education violates a most fundamental national public policy, as well as rights of individuals. . . .

. . . . Congress, in Titles IV and VI of the Civil Rights Act of 1964, clearly expressed its agreement that racial discrimination in education violates a fundamental public policy. Other sections of that Act, and numerous enactments since then, testify to the public policy against racial discrimination. See, e.g., the Voting Rights Act of 1965; Title VIII of the Civil Rights Act of 1968; the Emergency School Aid Act of 1972 (repealed effective Sept. 30, 1979; replaced by similar provisions in the Emergency School Aid Act of 1978).

The Executive Branch has consistently placed its support behind eradication of racial discrimination. . . .

Few social or political issues in our history have been more vigorously debated and more extensively ventilated than the issue of racial discrimination, particularly in education. Given the stress and anguish of the history of efforts to escape from the shackles of the "separate but equal" doctrine of *Plessy*, it cannot be said that educational institutions that, for whatever reasons, practice racial discrimination, are institutions exercising "beneficial and stabilizing influences in community life," Walz v. Tax Comm'n (1970), or should be encouraged by having all taxpayers share in their support by way of special tax status.

There can thus be no question that the interpretation of § 170 and § 501(c)(3) announced by the IRS in 1970 was correct. . . . It would be wholly incompatible with the concepts underlying tax exemption to grant the benefit of tax-exempt status to racially discriminatory educational entities, which "exer[t] a pervasive influence on the entire educational process." Norwood v. Harrison [1973]. Whatever may be the rationale for such private schools' policies, and however sincere the rationale may be, racial discrimination in education is contrary to public policy. Racially discriminatory educational institutions cannot be viewed as conferring a public benefit within the "charitable" concept discussed earlier, or within the Congressional intent underlying § 170 and § 501(c)(3).

C

Petitioners contend that . . . only Congress can alter the scope of § 170 and § 501(c)(3). Petitioners accordingly argue that the IRS overstepped its lawful bounds in issuing its 1970 and 1971 rulings. . . .

D

The actions of Congress since 1970 leave no doubt that the IRS reached the correct conclusion in exercising its authority. . . . [F]or a dozen years Congress has been made aware—acutely aware—of the IRS rulings of 1970 and 1971. . . .

Sincere adherents advocating contrary views have ventilated the subject for well over three decades. Failure of Congress to modify the IRS rulings of 1970 and 1971, of which Congress was, by its own studies and by public discourse, constantly reminded; and Congress' awareness of the denial of tax-exempt status for racially discriminatory schools when enacting other and related legislation make out an unusually strong case of legislative acquiescence in and ratification by implication of the 1970 and 1971 rulings.

Ordinarily, and quite appropriately, courts are slow to attribute significance to the failure of Congress to act on particular legislation. Here, however, we do not have an ordinary claim of legislative acquiescence. Only one month after the IRS announced its position in 1970, Congress held its first hearings on this precise issue. . . . Exhaustive hearings have been held on the issue at various times since then. These include hearings in February 1982, after we granted review in this case. . . .

. . . [T]he non-action here is significant. During the past 12 years there have been no fewer than 13 bills introduced to overturn the IRS interpretation of § 501(c)(3). Not one of these bills has emerged from any committee, although Congress has enacted numerous other amendments to § 501 during this same period. . . . It is hardly conceivable that Congress—and in this setting, any Member of Congress—was not abundantly aware of what was going on. In view of its prolonged and acute awareness of so important an issue, Congress' failure to act on the bills proposed on this subject provides added support for concluding that Congress acquiesced in the IRS rulings of 1970 and 1971. . . .

The evidence of Congressional approval of the policy embodied in [the] Revenue Ruling goes well beyond the failure of Congress to act on legislative proposals. Congress affirmatively manifested its acquiescence in the IRS policy when it enacted the present § 501(i) of the Code. . . . That provision denies tax-exempt status to social clubs whose charters or policy statements provide for "discrimination against any person on the basis of race, color, or religion." Both the House and Senate committee reports on that bill articulated the national policy against granting tax exemptions to racially discriminatory private clubs.

Even more significant is the fact that both reports focus on this Court's affirmance of Green v. Connally [1971] as having established that "discrimination on account of race is inconsistent with an *educational institution's* tax exempt status." (Emphasis added.). . . .

III

Petitioners contend that, even if the Commissioner's policy is valid as to nonreligious private schools, that policy cannot constitutionally be applied to schools that engage in racial discrimination on the basis of sincerely held religious beliefs. As to such schools, it is argued that the IRS construction of § 170 and § 501(c)(3) violates their free exercise rights under the Religion Clauses of the First Amendment. This contention presents claims not heretofore considered by this Court in precisely this context.

This Court has long held the Free Exercise Clause of the First Amendment an absolute prohibition against governmental regulation of religious beliefs, Wisconsin v. Yoder (1972); Sherbert v. Verner (1963); Cantwell v. Connecticut (1940). As interpreted by this Court, moreover, the Free Exercise Clause provides substantial protection for lawful conduct grounded in religious belief, see *Yoder*, Thomas v. Review Board (1981). However, "[n]ot all burdens on religion are unconstitutional. . . . The state may justify a limitation on religious liberty by showing that it is essential to accomplish an overriding governmental interest." United States v. Lee (1982).

On occasion this Court has found certain governmental interests so compelling as to allow even regulations prohibiting religiously based conduct. In Prince v. Massachusetts, (1944), for example, the Court held that neutrally cast child labor laws prohibiting sale of printed materials on public streets could be applied to prohibit children from dispensing religious literature. . . . See also Reynolds v. United States (1878); *Lee*; Gillette v. United States (1971). Denial of tax benefits will inevitably have a substantial impact on the operation of private religious schools, but will not prevent those schools from observing their religious tenets.

The governmental interest at stake here is compelling. . . . [T]he Government has a fundamental, overriding interest in eradicating racial discrimination in education. . . . That governmental interest substantially outweighs whatever burden denial of tax benefits places on petitioners' exercise of their religious beliefs. The interests asserted by petitioners cannot be accommodated with that compelling governmental interest, see *Lee*, and no "less restrictive means," see *Thomas*, are available to achieve the governmental interest.[1] . . .

[*Affirmed.*]

Justice **POWELL,** concurring in part and concurring in the judgment.

I join the Court's judgment, along with part III of its opinion holding that the denial of tax exemptions to petitioners does not violate the First Amendment. I write separately because I am troubled by the broader implications of the Court's opinion with respect to the authority of the Internal Revenue Service (IRS) and its construction of §§ 170(c) and 501(c)(3) of the Internal Revenue Code. . . .

Justice **REHNQUIST,** dissenting. . . .

I have no disagreement with the Court's finding that there is a strong national policy in this country opposed to racial discrimination. I agree with the Court that Congress has the power to further this policy by denying § 501(c)(3) status to organizations that practice racial discrimination. But as of yet Congress has failed to do so. Whatever

---

1. Bob Jones University also contends that denial of tax exemption violates the Establishment Clause by preferring religions whose tenets do not require racial discrimination over those which believe racial intermixing is forbidden. It is well settled that neither a State nor the Federal Government may pass laws which "prefer one religion over another," Everson v. Board of Education (1947), but "[i]t is equally true" that a regulation does not violate the Establishment Clause merely because it "happens to coincide or harmonize with the tenets of some or all religions." McGowan v. Maryland (1961). See Harris v. McRae (1980). The IRS policy at issue here is founded on a "neutral, secular basis," *Gillette*, and does not violate the Establishment Clause. . . . [Footnote by the Court.]

the reasons for the failure, this Court should not legislate for Congress.
. . .

Editors' Notes

(1) **Query:** We return to a now familiar pair of questions: (a) Is Burger's formula for testing the constitutionality of the Revenue Code (as interpreted by IRS and the three-judge district Court in *Green*) merely the strict scrutiny test from equal protection as applied to statutes that touch on fundamental rights? (b) To what extent is the test that Burger used merely a form of balancing?

(2) **Query:** All the justices identified hostility toward racial discriminations as a prominent national public policy. Granted the correctness of this claim, is there also a prominent national public policy to the effect that people should be able, when neither public money nor violation of ordinary criminal law is involved, to practice their religion as their consciences direct? Does Burger make a convincing case that racial equality is a more important constitutional value than freedom of conscience? What shape would such an argument, to be convincing, take?

(3) **Query:** Can one make the case that public money is involved in Bob Jones' claim to be tax exempt? Even so, would that "fact" give constitutional preference to the value of racial equality over the value of freedom of conscience? See Mayer G. Freed and Daniel D. Polsby, "Race, Religion, and Public Policy: Bob Jones University v. United States," 1983 *Supreme Court Review* I; also Paul B. Stephan III, "Bob Jones University v. United States: Public Policy in Search of Tax Policy," ibid. 33.

(4) Allen v. Wright (1984) held 5–3 that a group of black parents lacked standing to challenge decisions by IRS to give tax immune status to private schools practicing racial discrimination. In effect, the parents were claiming that the Reagan administration was not enforcing the law as interpreted by *Bob Jones.* Speaking through Justice O'Connor, the Court held the "abstract stigmatic injury" the parents asserted their children suffered was insufficient to confer standing. Justices Brennan, Blackmun, and Stevens dissented; Marshall did not participate.

17

Individual Autonomy: Privacy, Personhood, and Personal Liberty

Most of us would agree that the rights to worship or not worship as one chooses, to express oneself freely, and to secure enough personal property to achieve a meaningful degree of independence are all essential to autonomy and dignity. It is equally essential that a human being have control over his or her own bodily integrity as well as over a certain amount of surrounding physical and psychological space into which no one may enter uninvited. Some commentators have referred to this cluster of rights as relating to "personhood," to "privacy," or to "personal liberty." Laurence H. Tribe describes the underlying thought:

> The very idea of a fundamental right of personhood rests on the conviction that, even though one's identity is constantly and profoundly shaped by . . . one's social environment, the "personhood" resulting from this process is sufficiently "one's own" to be deemed fundamental in confronting the one entity that retains a monopoly over legitimate violence—the government. Thus active coercion by government to alter a person's being, or deliberate neglect by government which permits a being to suffer, are conceived as qualitatively different from the passive, incremental coercion that shapes all life. . . .[1]

Whatever name one puts on this concept, it is intrinsic to any operative notion of constitutionalism. "The right to be let alone," William O. Douglas once said, "is indeed the beginning of all freedom."[2]

Closely allied is the notion of "equal concern and respect" from government,[3] an equal "respect that is owed to persons irrespective of their social position."[4] It is, constitutionalism argues, precisely these broad rights to equal dignity and personal liberty that limited government protects—*government* to protect each citizen against encroach-

---

1. *American Constitutional Law* (Mineola, N.Y.: Foundation Press, 1978), p. 890.

2. Pollack v. PUC, dis. op., (1952).

3. Ronald Dworkin, *Taking Rights Seriously* (Cambridge, Mass.: Harvard University Press, 1977), p. 180, and chaps. 6 and 12 generally.

4. John Rawls, *A Theory of Justice* (Cambridge, Mass.: Harvard University Press, 1971), p. 511.

ments by foreign nations or fellow citizens, *limited* government to prevent public officials from invading that private sphere.

The principal textual anchors of the unlisted rights to personal liberty have been the due process clauses of the Fifth and Fourteenth amendments and the Ninth's command that the "enumeration in the Constitution, of certain rights, shall not be construed to deny or disparage others retained by the people." And a constitutional democrat would insist that the term "command" here is exact, for, according to the rules of syntax and grammar, this sentence, like that of the First Amendment, is not declarative but imperative in mood.

I. WHAT IS THE CONSTITUTION?

If few people raised in Western culture deny the importance of rights to privacy, personhood, and personal liberty, they may disagree sharply about the source of those rights as well as about who has authority to declare and define them—in sum about the WHAT and WHO as well as the HOW of constitutional interpretation. One might plausibly argue that these rights originate in the Constitution— in the document's plain words, in its clear implications, in its "architectural scheme," in its "penumbras," in the way the larger political system has developed, or in the theory of constitutionalism that undergirds both the document and the system. Or one might argue, as Justice Rehnquist does in "The Notion of a Living Constitution" (reprinted above, p. 163), that the source of these rights, except when they are specifically listed in the document, is not in the Constitution at all but in the people's will made binding on society through formal enactments by popularly elected officials.

There are still those who look for the source of these rights in a higher law than the Constitution. In the 1950s, as he began to abandon the positivism that he had once shared with Hugo Black, Justice Douglas made a series of off-the-bench statements that laid bare some of the theological underpinnings of his constitutional jurisprudence. "In our scheme of things," he wrote in 1954, "the rights of men are unalienable. They come from the Creator, not from a president, a legislator, or a court."[5] "Man," he reiterated in 1958, "is a child of God, entitled to dignified treatment."[6] Then, in 1963, two years before Griswold v. Connecticut (1965; reprinted above, p. 113) and its announcement that a right to privacy hovered in the "penumbras" of the Bill of Rights, he spoke even more emphatically:

> Men do not acquire rights from the government; one man does not give another rights. Man gets his rights from the Creator. They come to him because of the divine spark in every human being.[7]

---

5. *An Almanac of Liberty* (Garden City, N.Y.: Doubleday, 1954), p. 5.

6. *The Right of the People* (Garden City, N.Y.: Doubleday, 1958), p. 145.

7. *The Anatomy of Liberty* (New York: Trident Press, 1963), p. 2. For Douglas' change from positivism to natural rights, see Kenneth L. Karst, "The Return of the Natural-Law-Due-Process Formula," 16 *U.C.L.A.L.Rev.* 716 (1969).

More recently, other justices have returned to Jefferson's constitutionalist argument from natural rights. Justice Stevens, dissenting in Meachum v. Fanno (1976), wrote:

> I had thought it self-evident that all men were endowed by their Creator with liberty as one of the cardinal unalienable rights. It is that basic freedom which the Due Process Clause protects, rather than the particular rights or privileges conferred by specific laws or regulations.

A year later, writing for the Court, Justice Brennan said that the family's right to privacy "has its source . . . not in state law, but in intrinsic human rights." [8]

All these sorts of arguments, from Rehnquist's positivism to Douglas' theology, are still very much alive. As we saw in Chapter 4 and have seen throughout this book, the choice an interpreter makes here is as crucial as it is controversial. And, despite disagreements over sources, the Court has tended to find a plethora of unlisted rights in notions of "the Constitution" broader than the plain words of the document. The justices have often viewed the constitutional document as mapping only the "core of a much wider region of private rights, which, though not reduced to black and white, are as fully entitled to the protection of government as if defined in the minutest detail." [9]

This attitude goes back to the Constitution's early days. Justice Chase in Calder v. Bull (1798; reprinted above, p. 86) and Marshall and Johnson in Fletcher v. Peck (1810; reprinted above, p. 956) exemplify what could be called the traditional constitutionalist view. There have been challenges by justices like Hugo Black,[10] but the debate within the Court, though acerbic, has typically focused on whether this or that unlisted right is constitutionally protected, not on whether any unlisted rights deserve such status.

The issue of incorporation of the Bill of Rights in the Fourteenth Amendment (see above, pp. 98–100) has concerned not only whether some listed rights are more or less fundamental than others, but also whether some unlisted rights are so fundamental as to be "of the very essence of a scheme of ordered liberty." (Palko v. Connecticut [1937; reprinted above, p. 94].) Over the years, the Court has recognized at least the following unlisted rights as fundamental:

---

8. Smith v. Organization of Foster Families (1977).

9. Edward S. Corwin, "The Basic Doctrine of American Constitutional Law," 12 *Mich.L.Rev.* 247 (1912); reprinted in Alpheus Thomas Mason and Gerald Garvey, eds., *American Constitutional History* (New York: Harper & Row, 1964).

10. Speaking for the Court in San Antonio v. Rodriguez (1973; reprinted above p. 858), Justice Powell spoke of fundamental rights as those "explicitly or implicitly guaranteed by the Constitution." (See Justice Marshall's response, at p. 863.) Putting aside questions of what "the Constitution" and "implicitly guaranteed" mean in this context, Powell in his opinion in Moore v. East Cleveland (1977; reprinted below, p. 1145) unequivocally endorsed the fundamentality of unlisted constitutional rights.

Fundamental

(1) To retain American citizenship, despite even criminal activities, until explicitly and voluntarily renouncing it; [11]

(2) To receive equal protection not only from the states but also from the federal government. [12]

(3) To vote, subject only to reasonable restrictions to prevent fraud, and to cast a ballot equal in weight to those of other citizens; [13]

(4) To have a presumption of innocence and to demand proof beyond a reasonable doubt before being convicted of crime; [14]

(5) To use the federal courts and other governmental institutions and to urge others to use these processes to protect their interests; [15]

(6) To associate with others; [16]

(7) To enjoy a zone of privacy; [17]

(8) To travel within the United States; [18]

(9) To marry or not to marry [19] and to make one's own choice about having children; [20]

(10) To educate one's children as long as one meets certain minimum standards set by the state; [21]

(11) To choose and follow a profession; [22]

(12) To attend and report on criminal trials. [23]

II.   WHO SHALL INTERPRET?

Protecting privacy, personhood, and personal liberty frequently involves a paradox. For government, even limited government, to safeguard this cluster of rights leaves them less than absolute and to some degree restricts their orbit. Privacy, even of the home, cannot mean that a householder may conduct criminal activities in the base-

---

11. Afroyim v. Rusk (1967; reprinted below, p. 1093).

12. See the cases analyzed and reprinted in Chapters 13 and 14.

13. See the cases analyzed and reprinted in Chapter 12.

14. In re Winship (1970; reprinted below, p. 1101); Estelle v. Williams (1976); Taylor v. Kentucky (1978); Sandstrom v. Montana (1979); Jackson v. Virginia (1979). Schall v. Martin (1984), however, upheld pretrial detention for juveniles who, in the opinion of the juvenile judge, present a serious risk of committing an offense before trial.

15. Slaughter-House Cases (1873; reprinted above, p. 435); NAACP v. Button (1963; reprinted above, p. 723).

16. De Jonge v. Oregon (1937); NAACP v. Alabama (1958; reprinted above, p. 646).

17. Griswold v. Connecticut (1965; reprinted above, p. 113). Palmer v. Hudson (1984), however, held that prisoners have no right to privacy even in their cells.

18. Crandall v. Nevada (1868; reprinted above, p. 426); Shapiro v. Thompson (1969; reprinted above, p. 873).

19. Loving v. Virginia (1967; reprinted above p. 777) and Zablocki v. Redhail (1978; reprinted above, p. 890).

20. *Griswold;* Eisenstadt v. Baird (1972); Carey v. Population Services (1977); and Roe v. Wade (1973; reprinted below, p. 1109).

21. Pierce v. Society of Sisters (1925; reprinted below, p. 1144).

22. For example: Allgeyer v. Louisiana (1897); Meyer v. Nebraska (1923; reprinted below, p. 1089); Gibson v. Berryhill (1973).

23. Richmond Newspapers v. Virginia (1980; reprinted above, p. 587).

ment of his or her castle.[24]   One's right to personal liberty has to stop short of a right to drive an automobile on a public highway after consuming intoxicating quantities of alcohol or ingesting other hallucinogens.   "In this world as it is," Lord Devlin has written, "no man can be free unless he lives under the protection of a free society."[25] And the price of protecting liberty includes some restraints on liberty.

"Some restraints" means choices about the breadth, depth, and shape of the private sphere as well as the dimensions of the public sphere.   In the context of constitutional interpretation, this requirement returns us to the critical question of WHO shall interpret—who may legitimately make these sorts of fundamental choices.

James Bradley Thayer's "doctrine of the clear mistake" (reprinted above, p. 476), which Justice Felix Frankfurter endorsed (see his concur. op. in Dennis v. United States [1951; reprinted above, p. 510]), would solve the problem for judges by virtual abdication where congressional authority is involved.   Thayer, in effect, concluded that constitutional interpretation is basically a task for elected national officials.   The proper judicial role is only to determine if the political branches of the federal government have acted rationally in their choices.   The practical results of this doctrine would be two-fold: First, private citizens would have little judicial defense against congressional or presidential action, though they could appeal to the courts against state decisions.   Second, most of the burden of constitutional interpretation would fall on senators, congressmen, and presidents; and they would have to seek a more substantive theory to justify their interpretations, since Thayer's doctrine only allocates responsibility.

Broader theories of representative democracy like John Hart Ely's[26] justify judges taking an active role in defining and enforcing only political participation, equality of government's treatment of its subjects, and such rights as are specifically listed in the constitutional document.   Elected officials would define all other rights.   Thus most unlisted rights would depend on changing public moods to a degree unacceptable to many constitutional democrats.

And here, of course, we are again on another familiar battlefield. Public officials and commentators who stress the constitutionalism in a system of constitutional democracy tend to accept, as did Gouverneur Morris, "the judicial power" as "that fortress of the Constitution" and judges as its "noble guards,"[27] and so to endorse a creative judicial role in defining the nature and scope of unlisted rights.   As with the question of WHAT is the Constitution, some judges like James Wilson and William H. Rehnquist and more persistently Hugo Black have challenged the Court's authority to carry on such tasks, but the Court

---

24.   Whether acts legitimate within the privacy of one's home would be criminal if performed outside the home is another question.   See Stanley v. Georgia (1969).

25.   Patrick Devlin, *The Enforcement of Morals* (London: Oxford University Press, 1965), p. 100.

26.   *Democracy and Distrust* (Cambridge, Mass.: Harvard University Press, 1980).

27.   Senate Debates of 1802; reprinted above, p. 203.

has tended to accept, if not to explicate, a role as the principal (though hardly exclusive) interpreter of the Constitution.

Still, the debate goes on, though in truncated form. Dissenting in an abortion case, Akron v. Akron Center for Reproductive Health (1983; reprinted below, p. 1122), Justice O'Connor quoted Louis Powell, author of the majority opinion in *Akron,* quoting Oliver Wendell Holmes:

> In determining whether the State imposes an "undue burden" [on a woman's right to choose an abortion], we must keep in mind that when we are concerned with extremely sensitive issues, such as the one involved here, "the appropriate forum for their resolution in a democracy is the legislature. We should not forget that 'legislatures are ultimate guardians of the liberties and welfare of the people in quite as great a degree as the courts.'"

III. HOW TO INTERPRET?

HOW one interprets is clearly critical to this enterprise. A positivist theory of constitutional meaning based on plain words, even if augmented by a search for original intent, would impose on interpreters a form of intellectual schizophrenia. In very positive terms, the Ninth Amendment orders interpreters not to act as narrow legal positivists. And that command carries out Madison's precise purpose—though it is dangerous to generalize from *his* purpose to that of a majority of those who supported the amendment.

As usual, the *techniques* of constitutional interpretation do not offer definitive answers. We have already seen that the document itself says precious little about WHO should be its authoritative interpreter(s). Substantively, plain words beyond the Ninth Amendment offer small aid in determining WHAT is included in the Constitution's meaning beyond the document's explicit terms. Concepts such as "liberty" may include, as Brandeis once said, "all fundamental rights," [28] but that inclusion is not evident from the words themselves. Original intent in its broadest sense of a search for overarching purpose rather than the specific historical meaning of a particular clause or phrase would probably, though not conclusively, point toward constitutionalism's goals.

Stare decisis could offer similar support. Because the Court has been using a *mode* of fundamental values since before John Marshall, a justice could cite those previous instances as justifications for doing so again. Moreover, stare decisis might provide authority, however weak, for reaffirming the fundamentality of particular unlisted rights. For example, Justice Potter Stewart, writing for the Court in United States v. Guest (1966), conceded that the right to travel "finds no explicit mention in the Constitution"; but, he immediately added, "freedom to travel throughout the United States has long been recognized as a basic right under the Constitution." Stewart offered

---

28. Whitney v. California, concur. op. (1927; reprinted above, p. 503).

no explanation why such a right was "basic." He merely appended references to more previous cases which he said settled the issue.[29]

Deductive inference is always of some use. Here it would be most effective if joined in a polygamous marriage with the interpretive *modes* of fundamental rights and structural analysis. For one can make the argument, as Douglas did for the Court in *Griswold,* that by examining "the architectural scheme"[30] of the Constitution, an interpreter can discover certain fundamental rights in the document's penumbras. Or, one can reason, as Marshall did in his dissent in San Antonio v. Rodriguez (1973; reprinted above, p. 858), that certain unlisted rights are so closely connected with enumerated rights as to be necessary to the vitality of the latter.

The intrinsic difficulty confronting a search for the constitutional legitmacy of rights of personal liberty is exactly that of the *mode* of fundamental rights: As articulated by judges and commentators, it has been an open-ended quest. Formulas such as a "disinterested inquiry pursued in the spirit of science"[31] into "history and tradition"[32] do little to straighten what an eighteenth century critic called "the Crooked Cord of a Judge's Discretion in matters of the greatest moment and value."[33] As Justice White protested in Moore v. East Cleveland (1977; reprinted below, p. 1145): "What the deeply rooted traditions of the country are is arguable; which of them deserve the protection of the Due Process Clause is even more debatable."

Serious reservations about judges' performing such creative interpretation need not be rooted in democratic theory. In a pluralistic society such as that of the United States, disagreements with the practical wisdom and moral values that inform judges' choices are inevitable. It would hardly be irrational to be disturbed by judges' finding within "the Constitution" a right to abortion (Roe v. Wade [1973; reprinted below, p. 1109]), or their not finding a right to a decent reputation (Paul v. Davis [1976; reprinted below, p. 1161]) to be within the Constitution's scope.

If, however, definiteness were the sole criterion for choosing among *modes* and *techniques* of constitutional interpretation, all but the most banal would fail. More important, discarding the *mode* of fundamental rights would mean discarding much of constitutionalism itself. The difficulties outlined here and in the cases that follow present constitutional interpretation with a challenge: HOW to maintain protection for rights essential to autonomy and dignity without

29. He omitted the most obvious, Crandall v. Nevada (1868; reprinted above, p. 426).

30. "Stare Decisis," 4 *The Record of the Association of the Bar of the City of New York* 152, 157 (1949).

31. Rochin v. California (1952; reprinted above, p. 100).

32. *Griswold,* Harlan, J., concur. op.

33. Quoted in Morton J. Horwitz, *The Transformation of American Law, 1780–1860* (Cambridge, Mass.: Harvard University Press, 1977), p. 13.

allowing the "crooked cord" of judicial discretion to become a noose around society's neck.

SELECTED BIBLIOGRAPHY

Ball, Milner S. *The Promise of American Law* (Athens, Ga.: University of Georgia Press, 1981).

Barber, Sotirios A. *On What the Constitution Means* (Baltimore: Johns Hopkins University Press, 1984), espec. chaps. 4–6.

Benedict, Michael Les. "To Secure These Rights: Rights, Democracy, and Judicial Review in the Anglo-American Constitutional Heritage," 42 *Ohio St.L.J.* 69 (1982).

Bobbitt, Phillip. *Constitutional Fate* (New York: Oxford University Press, 1982), espec. Bk. II.

Brest, Paul. "The Fundamental Rights Controversy," 90 *Yale L.J.* 1063 (1981).

Choper, Jesse H. *Judicial Review and the National Political Process* (Chicago: University of Chicago Press, 1980), espec. Chaps. 1–2.

Corwin, Edward S. "The Basic Doctrine of American Constitutional Law," 12 *Mich.L.Rev.* 247 (1914); reprinted in Alpheus Thomas Mason and Gerald Garvey, eds., *American Constitutional History: Essays by Edward S. Corwin* (New York: Harper & Row, 1964).

Craven, J. Braxton, Jr. "The Right to be Let Alone," 1976 *Duke L.J.* 699.

Ely, John H. *Democracy and Distrust* (Cambridge, Mass.: Harvard University Press, 1980), espec. chap. 3.

Fried, Charles. "Privacy," 77 *Yale L.J.* 475 (1968).

Karst, Kenneth L. "Freedom of Intimate Association," 89 *Yale L.J.* 624 (1980).

Lusky, Louis. "Invasion of Privacy: A Clarification of Concepts," 72 *Colum.L.Rev.* 693 (1972).

O'Brien, David M. *Privacy, Law, and Public Policy* (New York: Praeger, 1979).

Pennock, J. Roland, and John W. Chapman, eds. *Privacy* (New York: Atherton, 1971).

Perry, Michael J. *The Constitution, the Courts, and Human Rights* (New Haven, Conn.: Yale University Press, 1982).

Richards, David A.J. "Sexual Autonomy and the Constitutional Right to Privacy," 30 *Hastings L.J.* 957 (1979).

Smith, Rogers M. "The Constitution and Autonomy," 60 *Tex.L.Rev.* 175 (1982).

Wilkinson, J. Harvie, III, and G. Edward White. "Constitutional Protection for Personal Liberties," 62 *Corn.L.Rev.* 563 (1977).

I. GENERAL LIBERTY

"[T]he individual has certain fundamental rights which must be respected."

MEYER v. NEBRASKA

262 U.S. 390, 43 S.Ct. 625, 67 L.Ed. 1042 (1923).

As part of a general xenophobia that pulsed in America during the first and second decades of this century and more particularly of anti-German feeling engendered by World War I, Nebraska in 1919 enacted a statute forbidding teaching in, or the teaching of, a modern language other than English to pupils who had not successfully completed eight years of schooling. Meyer, a parochial school instructor, was convicted for violating this act by teaching German to a ten year old boy. After the state supreme court sustained his conviction, Meyer sought and obtained review by the U.S. Supreme Court.

Mr. Justice **McREYNOLDS** delivered the opinion of the Court. . . .

The problem for our determination is whether the statute as construed and applied unreasonably infringes the liberty guaranteed to the plaintiff in error by the Fourteenth Amendment. "No State shall . . . deprive any person of life, liberty, or property, without due process of law."

While this Court has not attempted to define with exactness the liberty thus guaranteed, the term has received much consideration and some of the included things have been definitely stated. Without doubt, it denotes not merely freedom from bodily restraint but also the right of the individual to contract, to engage in any of the common occupations of life, to acquire useful knowledge, to marry, establish a home and bring up children, to worship God according to the dictates of his own conscience, and generally to enjoy those privileges long recognized at common law as essential to the orderly pursuit of happiness by free men. Slaughter-House Cases [1873]; Yick Wo v. Hopkins [1886]; Minnesota v. Barber [1890]; Allgeyer v. Louisiana [1897]; Lochner v. New York [1905]; Twining v. New Jersey [1908]; Truax v. Raich [1915]; Adams v. Tanner [1917]; Truax v. Corrigan [1921]; Adkins v. Children's Hospital [1923]. The established doctrine is that this liberty may not be interfered with, under the guise of protecting the public interest, by legislative action which is arbitrary or without reasonable relation to some purpose within the competency of the State to effect. Determination by the legislature of what constitutes proper exercise of police power is not final or conclusive but is subject to supervision by the courts. Lawton v. Steele [1894].

The American people have always regarded education and acquisition of knowledge as matters of supreme importance which should be diligently promoted. . . . Corresponding to the right of control, it is the natural duty of the parent to give his children education suitable to their station in life; and nearly all the States, including Nebraska, enforce this obligation by compulsory laws.

Practically, education of the young is only possible in schools conducted by especially qualified persons who devote themselves thereto. The calling always has been regarded as useful and honorable, essential, indeed, to the public welfare. Mere knowledge of the German language cannot reasonably be regarded as harmful. Heretofore it has been commonly looked upon as helpful and desirable. Plaintiff in error taught this language in school as part of his occupation. His right thus to teach and the right of parents to engage him so to instruct their children, we think, are within the liberty of the Amendment.

. . .

That the State may do much, go very far, indeed, in order to improve the quality of its citizens, physically, mentally and morally, is clear; but the individual has certain fundamental rights which must be respected. The protection of the Constitution extends to all, to those who speak other languages as well as to those born with English on the tongue. Perhaps it would be highly advantageous if all had ready understanding of our ordinary speech, but this cannot be coerced by methods which conflict with the Constitution—a desirable end cannot be promoted by prohibited means.

For the welfare of his Ideal Commonwealth, Plato suggested a law which should provide:

> That the wives of our guardians are to be common, and their children are to be common, and no parent is to know his own child, nor any child his parent. . . . The proper officers will take the offspring of the good parents to the pen or fold, and there they will deposit them with certain nurses who dwell in a separate quarter; but the offspring of the inferior, or of the better when they chance to be deformed, will be put away in some mysterious, unknown place, as they should be.

In order to submerge the individual and develop ideal citizens, Sparta assembled the males at seven into barracks and intrusted their subsequent education and training to official guardians. Although such measures have been deliberately approved by men of great genius, their ideas touching the relation between individual and State were wholly different from those upon which our institutions rest; and it hardly will be affirmed that any legislature could impose such restrictions upon the people of a State without doing violence to both letter and spirit of the Constitution.

The desire of the legislature to foster a homogeneous people with American ideals prepared readily to understand current discussions of civic matters is easy to appreciate. Unfortunate experiences during the late war and aversion toward every characteristic of truculent adversaries were certainly enough to quicken that aspiration. But the means adopted, we think, exceed the limitations upon the power of the State and conflict with rights assured to plaintiff in error. The interference is plain enough and no adequate reason therefor in time of peace and domestic tranquility has been shown.

The power of the State to compel attendance at some school and to make reasonable regulations for all schools, including a requirement that they shall give instructions in English, is not questioned. Nor has challenge been made of the State's power to prescribe a curriculum for institutions which it supports. *Adams* pointed out that mere abuse incident to an occupation ordinarily useful is not enough to justify its abolition, although regulation may be entirely proper. No emergency has arisen which renders knowledge by a child of some language other than English so clearly harmful as to justify its inhibition with the consequent infringement of rights long freely enjoyed. We are constrained to conclude that the statute as applied is arbitrary and without reasonable relation to any end within the competency of the State.

As the statute undertakes to interfere only with teaching which involves a modern language, leaving complete freedom as to other matters, there seems no adequate foundation for the suggestion that the purpose was to protect the child's health by limiting his mental activities. It is well known that proficiency in a foreign language seldom comes to one not instructed at an early age, and experience shows that this is not injurious to the health, morals or understanding of the ordinary child. .   .   .

Reversed.

Mr. Justice **HOLMES,** dissenting.

We all agree .   .   . that it is desirable that all the citizens of the United States should speak a common tongue, and therefore that the end aimed at by the statute is a lawful and proper one. The only question is whether the means adopted deprive teachers of the liberty secured to them by the Fourteenth Amendment. .   .   . I cannot bring my mind to believe that in some circumstances and circumstances existing it is said in Nebraska, the statute might not be regarded as a reasonable or even necessary method of reaching the desired result. The part of the act with which we are concerned deals with the teaching of young children. Youth is the time when familiarity with a language is established and if there are sections in the State where a child would hear only Polish or French or German spoken at home I am not prepared to say that it is unreasonable to provide that in his early years he shall hear and speak only English at school. But if it is reasonable it is not an undue restriction of the liberty either of teacher or scholar. No one would doubt that a teacher might be forbidden to teach many things, and the only criterion of his liberty under the Constitution that I can think of is "whether, considering the end in view, the statute passes the bounds of reason and assumes the character of a merely arbitrary fiat." Purity Extract & Tonic Co. v. Lynch [1912]. Hebe v. Shaw [1919]. Jacob Ruppert v. Caffey [1920]. I think I appreciate the objection to the law but it appears to me to present a question upon which men reasonably might differ and therefore I am unable to say that the Constitution of the United States prevents the experiment being tried. .   .   .

Mr. Justice **SUTHERLAND** concurs in this opinion.

Editors' Notes

(1) **Query:** In explaining the meaning of the word "liberty" in the Four-teenth Amendment was McReynolds merely using deductive inference as a *technique* of constitutional interpretation? Does "liberty" imply a constitution-ally protected "right to teach"? The "natural duty of the parent" to educate his or her children?

(2) **Query:** What interpretive *mode(s)* and/or *technique(s)* did Holmes use? Stone claimed to have borrowed heavily from Holmes and Brandeis for his own jurisprudence. How does Holmes' jurisprudence, as he explained it here and in his dissent in Lochner v. New York (1905; reprinted above, p. 975), differ from *Carolene Products* (1938; reprinted above, p. 482)? From Thayer's (reprinted above, p. 476)?

(3) Holmes' dissent surprised many people. He was still groping his way toward a distinction between judicial deference toward governmental regula-tion of economic affairs and governmental regulation of ideas. Brandeis, the son of German-speaking immigrants, did not join Holmes in his dissent, but the only immigrant on the Court, Sutherland, did. Sutherland, of course, was an ardent defender of economic laissez faire and the author of the Court's opinion in Adkins v. Childrens Hospital (1923; reprinted above, p. 980).

(4) Like Sutherland, McReynolds was one of the justices most closely associated with economic laissez faire; and the Court after 1937 spent a good deal of time undoing the constitutional jurisprudence that he and his brethren had constructed. In the plurality opinion in Moore v. East Cleveland (1977; reprinted below, p. 1145), Justice Powell cited *Meyer* and Pierce v. Society of Sisters (1925; reprinted below, p. 1144) to support a decision defending rights of the extended family against a municipal zoning ordinance. Quoting Harlan's dissent in Poe v. Ullman (1961; reprinted above, p. 106) to the effect that the American constitutional tradition is a "living thing" and that a decision "which builds on what has survived is likely to be sound," Powell added a footnote:

> This explains why *Meyer* and *Pierce* have survived and enjoyed
> frequent reaffirmance, while other substantive due process cases of
> the same era have been repudiated—including a number written, as
> were *Meyer* and *Pierce,* by Mr. Justice McReynolds.

(5) For the background of *Meyer,* see Orville H. Zabel, *God and Caesar in Nebraska* (Lincoln: University of Nebraska Press, 1955).

(6) Bartels v. Iowa (1923) consolidated several rulings the same day as *Meyer,* invalidating similar laws from Iowa and Ohio. *Pierce* struck down an Oregon law that required parents to send their children between the ages of 8 and 16 to *public* schools.

II. THE RIGHT TO CITIZENSHIP: THE
RIGHT TO HAVE RIGHTS

"Citizenship is not a license that expires upon misbehavior. . . . As long as a person does not voluntarily renounce or abandon his citizenship . . . his fundamental right of citizenship is secure."

TROP v. DULLES
356 U.S. 86, 78 S.Ct. 590, 2 L.Ed.2d 630 (1958).

This case, invalidating a federal statute that revoked American citizenship for desertion in time of war, is reprinted above, at p. 144. Note there was no opinion for the Court.

"The very nature of our free government makes it completely incongruous to have a rule of law under which a group of citizens temporarily in office can deprive another group of citizens of their citizenship."

AFROYIM v. RUSK
387 U.S. 253, 87 S.Ct. 1660, 18 L.Ed.2d 757 (1967).

Sec. 401(e) of the Nationality Act of 1940 provided for loss of citizenship for any American who voted "in a political election in a foreign state." On the same day in 1958 that it decided Trop v. Dulles, the Court sustained, 5–4, in Perez v. Brownell the constitutionality of § 401(e). Several years later, when Beys Afroyim, a naturalized American citizen who had been living in Israel for a decade, applied for renewal of his passport, the State Department refused on grounds that he had voted in Israeli elections. Afroyim sued in a federal district court, but lost there as well as in the court of appeals. He then obtained certiorari.

Mr. Justice **BLACK** delivered the opinion of the Court. . . .

Petitioner, relying on the same contentions about voluntary renunciation of citizenship which this Court rejected in upholding § 401(e) in *Perez*, urges us to reconsider that case, adopt the view of the minority there, and overrule it. That case, decided by a 5–4 vote almost 10 years ago, has been a source of controversy and confusion ever since. . . . Moreover, in the other cases decided with and since *Perez*, this Court has consistently invalidated on a case-by-case basis various other statutory sections providing for involuntary expatriation. It has done so on various grounds and has refused to hold that citizens can be expatriated without their voluntary renunciation of citizenship. These cases, as well as many commentators, have cast great doubt upon the soundness of *Perez*. Under these circumstances, we granted certiorari to reconsider it. . . .

The fundamental issue before this Court . . . is whether Congress can consistently with the Fourteenth Amendment enact a law stripping

an American of his citizenship which he has never voluntarily re-
nounced or given up. The majority in *Perez* held that Congress could
do this. . . . That conclusion was reached by this chain of reasoning: Congress has an implied power to deal with foreign affairs as an
indispensable attribute of sovereignty; this implied power, plus the
Necessary and Proper Clause, empowers Congress to regulate voting by
American citizens in foreign elections; involuntary expatriation is
within the "ample scope" of "appropriate modes" Congress can adopt to
effectuate its general regulatory power[;] "there is nothing in the . . .
Fourteenth Amendment to warrant drawing from it a restriction upon
the power otherwise possessed by Congress to withdraw citizenship" . . . .

First we reject the idea expressed in *Perez* that, aside from the
Fourteenth Amendment, Congress has any general power, express or
implied, to take away an American citizen's citizenship without his
assent. This power cannot . . . be sustained as an implied attribute
of sovereignty possessed by all nations. Other nations are governed by
their own constitutions, if any, and we can draw no support from theirs.
In our country the people are sovereign and the Government cannot
sever its relationship to the people by taking away their citizenship.
Our Constitution governs us and we must never forget that our Constitution limits the Government to those powers specifically granted or
those that are necessary and proper to carry out the specifically
granted ones. The Constitution, of course, grants Congress no express
power to strip people of their citizenship. . . . And even before the
adoption of the Fourteenth Amendment, views were expressed in Congress and by this Court that under the Constitution the Government
was granted no power, even under its express power to pass a uniform
rule of naturalization, to determine what conduct should and should
not result in the loss of citizenship. . . .

Although these legislative and judicial statements may be regarded
as inconclusive . . . [1] any doubt as to whether prior to the passage of
the Fourteenth Amendment Congress had the power to deprive a
person against his will of citizenship once obtained should have been
removed by the unequivocal terms of the Amendment itself. It provides its own constitutional rule in language calculated completely to
control the status of citizenship: "All persons born or naturalized in
the United States . . . are citizens of the United States. . . ."
There is no indication in these words of a fleeting citizenship, good at
the moment it is acquired but subject to destruction by the Government
at any time. Rather the Amendment can most reasonably be read as
defining a citizenship which a citizen keeps unless he voluntarily
relinquishes it. Once acquired, this Fourteenth Amendment citizenship was not to be shifted, canceled, or diluted at the will of the Federal
Government, the States, or any other governmental unit.

---

1. The dissenting opinion here points to the fact that a Civil War Congress passed two
Acts designed to deprive military deserters to the Southern side of the rights of
citizenship. Measures of this kind passed in those days of emotional stress and hostility
are by no means the most reliable criteria for determining what the Constitution means.
[Footnote by the Court.]

It is true that the chief interest of the people in giving permanence and security to citizenship in the Fourteenth Amendment was the desire to protect Negroes. The Dred Scott [v. Sanford] decision [1857] had shortly before greatly disturbed many people about the status of Negro citizenship. But the Civil Rights Act of 1866 had already attempted to confer citizenship on all persons born or naturalized in the United States. Nevertheless, when the Fourteenth Amendment passed the House without containing any definition of citizenship, the sponsors of the Amendment in the Senate insisted on inserting a constitutional definition and grant of citizenship. They expressed fears that the citizenship so recently conferred on Negroes by the Civil Rights Act could be just as easily taken away from them by subsequent Congresses. . . . Senator Howard, who sponsored the Amendment in the Senate, thus explained the purpose of the clause:

> It settles the great question of citizenship and removes all doubt as to what persons are or are not citizens of the United States. . . . We desired to put this question of citizenship and the rights of citizens . . . under the civil rights bill beyond the legislative power. . . .

This undeniable purpose of the Fourteenth Amendment to make citizenship of Negroes permanent and secure would be frustrated by holding that the Government can rob a citizen of his citizenship without his consent by simply proceeding to act under an implied general power to regulate foreign affairs or some other power generally granted. Though the framers of the Amendment were not particularly concerned with the problem of expatriation, it seems undeniable from the language they used that they wanted to put citizenship beyond the power of any governmental unit to destroy. In 1868, two years after the Fourteenth Amendment had been proposed, Congress specifically considered the subject of expatriation. Several bills were introduced to impose involuntary expatriation on citizens who committed certain acts. With little discussion, these proposals were defeated. . . .

The entire legislative history of the 1868 Act makes it abundantly clear that there was a strong feeling in the Congress that the only way the citizenship it conferred could be lost was by the voluntary renunciation or abandonment by the citizen himself. And this was the unequivocal statement of the Court in the case of United States v. Wong Kim Ark [1898]. . . . The Court . . . held that Congress could not do anything to abridge or affect [Ark's] citizenship conferred by the Fourteenth Amendment. Quoting Chief Justice Marshall's well-considered and oft-repeated dictum in Osborn [v. Bank of the U.S. (1824)] to the effect that Congress under the power of naturalization has "a power to confer citizenship, not a power to take it away," the Court said:

> Congress having no power to abridge the rights conferred by the Constitution upon those who have become naturalized citizens by virtue of acts of Congress, a fortiori no act . . . of Congress . . . can affect citizenship acquired as a birthright, by virtue of the Constitution itself. . . .

. . . [T]he Government is without power to rob a citizen of his citizenship under § 401(e).[2]

Because the legislative history of the Fourteenth Amendment and of the expatriation proposals which preceded and followed it, like most other legislative history, contains many statements from which conflicting inferences can be drawn, our holding might be unwarranted if it rested entirely or principally upon that legislative history. But it does not. Our holding we think is the only one that can stand in view of the language and the purpose of the Fourteenth Amendment, and our construction of that Amendment, we believe, comports more nearly than *Perez* with the principles of liberty and equal justice to all that the entire Fourteenth Amendment was adopted to guarantee. Citizenship is no light trifle to be jeopardized any moment Congress decides to do so under the name of one of its general or implied grants of power. In some instances, loss of citizenship can mean that a man is left without the protection of citizenship in any country in the world—as a man without a country. Citizenship in this Nation is a part of a cooperative affair. Its citizenry is the country and the country is its citizenry. The very nature of our free government makes it completely incongruous to have a rule of law under which a group of citizens temporarily in office can deprive another group of citizens of their citizenship. We hold that the Fourteenth Amendment was designed to, and does, protect every citizen of this Nation against a congressional forcible destruction of his citizenship, whatever his creed, color, or race. Our holding does no more than to give to this citizen that which is his own, a constitutional right to remain a citizen in a free country unless he voluntarily relinquishes that citizenship.

Perez is overruled. The judgment is

Reversed.

Mr. Justice **HARLAN,** whom Mr. Justice **CLARK,** Mr. Justice **STEWART,** and Mr. Justice **WHITE** join, dissenting. . . .

I . . .

The pertinent evidence for the period prior to the adoption of the Fourteenth Amendment can . . . be summarized as follows. The Court's conclusion today is supported only by the statements, associated at least in part with a now abandoned view of citizenship, of three individual Congressmen, and by the ambiguous and inapposite dictum from *Osborn.* Inconsistent with the Court's position are statements from individual Congressmen in 1794, and Congress' passage in 1864 and 1865 of legislation which expressly authorized the expatriation of unwilling citizens. It may be that legislation adopted in the heat of war should be discounted in part by its origins, but, even if this is done, it is surely plain that the Court's conclusion is entirely unwarranted by the available historical evidence for the period prior to the passage of

---

2. Of course . . . naturalization unlawfully procured can be set aside. See, e.g., Knauer v. United States [1946]; Baumgartner v. United States [1941]; Schneiderman v. United States [1943]. [Footnote by the Court.]

the Fourteenth Amendment. The evidence suggests, to the contrary, that Congress in 1865 understood that it had authority, at least in some circumstances, to deprive a citizen of his nationality.

II

The evidence with which the Court supports its thesis that the Citizenship Clause of the Fourteenth Amendment was intended to lay at rest any doubts of Congress' inability to expatriate without the citizen's consent is no more persuasive. . . .

The Amendment as initially approved by the House contained nothing which described or defined citizenship. The issue did not as such even arise in the House debates. . . .

In the Senate, however, it was evidently feared that unless citizenship were defined, or some more general classification substituted, freedmen might, on the premise that they were not citizens, be excluded from the Amendment's protection. Senator Stewart thus offered an amendment which would have inserted into § 1 a definition of citizenship, and Senator Wade urged as an alternative the elimination of the term "citizen" from the Amendment's first section. After a caucus of the chief supporters of the Amendment, Senator Howard announced on their behalf that they favored the addition of the present Citizenship Clause.

The debate upon the clause was essentially cursory in both Houses, but there are several clear indications of its intended effect. Its sponsors evidently shared the fears of Senators Stewart and Wade that unless citizenship were defined, freedmen might, under the reasoning of the *Dred Scott* decision, be excluded by the courts from the scope of the Amendment. . . . It was suggested, moreover, that it would, by creating a basis for federal citizenship which was indisputably independent of state citizenship, preclude any effort by state legislatures to circumvent the Amendment by denying freedmen state citizenship. Nothing in the debates, however, supports the Court's assertion that the clause was intended to deny Congress its authority to expatriate unwilling citizens. . . .

The narrow, essentially definitional purpose of the Citizenship Clause is reflected in the clear declarations in the debates that the clause would not revise the prevailing incidents of citizenship. Senator Henderson of Missouri thus stated specifically his understanding that the "section will leave citizenship where it now is." Senator Howard, in the first of the statements relied upon, in part, by the Court, said quite unreservedly that "This amendment [the Citizenship Clause] which I have offered is simply declaratory of what I regard as the law of the land already, that every person born within the limits of the United States, and subject to their jurisdiction, is . . . a citizen of the United States." Henderson had been present at the Senate's consideration both of the Wade-Davis bill and of the Enrollment Act [the two bills passed by Congress in 1864 and 1865 that would have removed American citizenship from certain Confederates and deserters from the Union Army], and had voted at least for the Wade-Davis bill. Howard was a member of the Senate when both bills were passed, and had actively participated in the debates upon the Enrollment Act. . . . Howard certainly never expressed to the Senate any doubt either of their wisdom or of their constitutionality. It would be extraordinary if these prominent supporters of the Citizenship Clause could have imagined . . . that it would entirely withdraw a power twice recently exercised by Congress in their presence.

There is, however, even more positive evidence that the Court's construction of the clause is not that intended by its draftsmen. Between the two brief statements from Senator Howard relied upon by the Court, Howard, in response to a question, said the following:

> I take it for granted that after a man becomes a citizen of the United States under the Constitution he cannot cease to be citizen, *except by expatriation* or *the commission of some crime by which his citizenship shall be forfeited.* [Emphasis added.]

It would be difficult to imagine a more unqualified rejection of the Court's position; Senator Howard, the clause's sponsor, very plainly believed that it would leave unimpaired Congress' power to deprive unwilling citizens of their citizenship.

Additional confirmation of the expectations of the clause's draftsmen may be found in the legislative history, wholly overlooked by the Court, of the Act for the Relief of certain Soldiers and Sailors, adopted in 1867. The Act, debated by Congress within 12 months of its passage of the Fourteenth Amendment, provided an exception from the provisions of § 21 of the Enrollment Act of 1865 for those who had deserted from the Union forces after the termination of general hostilities. Had the Citizenship Clause been understood to have the effect now given it by the Court, surely this would have been clearly reflected in the debates. . . . Nothing of the sort occurred. . . .

There is, moreover, still further evidence. . . . While the debate on the Act of 1868 was still in progress, negotiations were completed on the first of a series of bilateral expatriation treaties, which "initiated this country's policy of automatic divestment of citizenship for specified conduct affecting our foreign relations." . . . Seven such treaties were negotiated in 1868 and 1869 alone; each was ratified by the Senate. If, as the Court now suggests, it was "abundantly clear" to Congress in 1868 that the Citizenship Clause had taken from its hands the power of expatriation, it is quite difficult to understand why these conventions were negotiated, or why, once negotiated, they were not immediately repudiated by the Senate.

Further, the executive authorities of the United States repeatedly acted, in the 40 years following 1868, upon the premise that a citizen might automatically be deemed to have expatriated himself by conduct short of a voluntary renunciation of citizenship; individual citizens were, as the Court indicated in *Perez*, regularly held on this basis to have lost their citizenship. Interested Members of Congress, and others, could scarcely have been unaware of the practice. . . .

It seems to me apparent that the historical evidence . . . irresistibly suggests that the draftsmen of the Fourteenth Amendment did not intend, and could not have expected, that the Citizenship Clause would deprive Congress of authority which it had, to their knowledge, only recently twice exercised. The construction demanded by the pertinent historical evidence, and entirely consistent with the clause's terms and purposes, is instead that it declares to whom citizenship, as a consequence either of birth or of naturalization, initially attaches. The clause thus served at the time of its passage both to overturn *Dred Scott* and to provide a foundation for federal citizenship entirely independent of state citizenship. . . . But nothing in the history, purposes, or language of the clause suggests that it forbids Congress in all circumstances to withdraw the citizenship of an unwilling citizen. To the contrary, it was expected, and should now be understood, to leave Congress at liberty to expatriate a citizen if the expatriation is an appropriate exercise of a power otherwise given to Congress by the Constitution, and if the methods and terms of expatriation adopted by Congress are consistent with the Constitution's other relevant commands.

. . . Once obtained, citizenship is of course protected from arbitrary withdrawal by the constraints placed around Congress' powers by the Constitution. . . . [But the] construction now placed on the Citizenship Clause rests, in the last analysis, simply on the Court's ipse dixit, evincing little more, it is quite apparent, than the present majority's own distaste for the expatriation power. . . .

Editors' Notes

(1) **Queries:** What is the scope of "the Constitution" as Black sees it here? Only the document? What *modes* and *techniques* of constitutional interpretation did Black use to justify his decision? How effectively did he use any of them? To what extent did he rely on his usual appeal to the "plain words" of the Constitution? Does "intent of the framers of the Fourteenth Amendment" help his argument? The "purpose" of that amendment? Long and unbroken tradition? To what extent was Black's opinion based on "structural analysis," either in the narrow sense of the Constitution as document or in the broader sense of the evolving political system? To what degree and in what ways did Black's jurisprudence as stated here differ from Warren's in Trop v. Dulles (1958; reprinted above, p. 144)? From his own in Griswold v. Connecticut (1965; reprinted above, p. 113)? Is there a firmer textual basis for a right to citizenship than for a right to privacy?

(2) **Queries:** What *mode(s)* and/or *techniques* of interpretation does Harlan use? How convincing is his opinion when pitted against Black's? Against Warren's in *Trop*? Granting, for the sake of argument, that Harlan was correct about the specific historical "intent of the framers" of the Fourteenth Amendment, given what have since become the ruthless uses of revocation of citizenship (see the discussion of Nazi policies in the Eds.' Notes to Trop v. Dulles, above at p. 144) and the consequences of statelessness in our world, how authoritative a source for constitutional interpretation is that "original intent"?

(3) Fedorenko v. United States (1981) reaffirmed federal authority to revoke the citizenship of a naturalized alien who had fraudulently obtained naturalization. (See fn. 2 to Black's opinion in *Afroyim*.) Fedorenko had given false answers to important questions when initially applying for a visa to enter the United States. During World War II, he had been a Russian soldier; but he concealed from immigration officials the fact that, after being captured by the Germans, he had become a guard at Treblinka, a death camp in which the Nazis murdered several hundred thousand Jews. For the majority, Justice Marshall tersely disposed of the constitutional issue:

> On the one hand, our decisions have recognized that the right to acquire American citizenship is a precious one, and that once citizenship has been acquired, its loss can have severe and unsettling consequences. . . . For these reasons, we have held that the Government "carries a heavy burden of proof in proceeding to divest a naturalized citizen of his citizenship." . . .
>
> At the same time, our cases have also recognized that there must be strict compliance with all the congressionally imposed prerequisites to the acquisition of citizenship. Failure to comply with any of these conditions renders the certificate of citizenship "illegally procured," and naturalization that is unlawfully procured can be set aside.

The sole reference to *Afroyim* in the majority opinion was to fn. 2, "naturalization unlawfully procured can be set aside." White and Stevens dissented on statutory grounds.

(4) See also the discussion of the Court's denial of certiorari in Longstaff v. INS (1984), in fn. 3 to the Introductory Essay to Chapter 14, above at p. 830, and below in the Eds.' Notes (5) and (6) to Doe v. Commonwealth's Attorney (1976), at p. 1161. INS began deportation proceedings against Longstaff because when he was admitted to the United States nineteen years earlier he had not admitted he was homosexual. His background became public knowledge when he applied for citizenship.

III. THE RIGHT TO PHYSICAL FREEDOM

"The Constitution of the United States is a law for rulers and people, equally in war and in peace, and covers with the shield of its protection all classes of men, at all times, and under all circumstances."

EX PARTE MILLIGAN
71 U.S. (4 Wall.) 2, 18 L.Ed. 281 (1866).

This decision, invalidating President Lincoln's use of courts martial during the Civil War to try civilians, is reprinted below, p. 1190.

"It is . . . important in our free society that every individual going about his ordinary affairs have confidence that his government cannot adjudge him guilty of a criminal offense without convincing a proper factfinder of his guilt with utmost certainty."

IN RE WINSHIP
397 U.S. 358, 90 S.Ct. 1068, 25 L.Ed.2d 368 (1970).

A New York statute allowed family courts trying juveniles on criminal charges to convict on the basis of "a preponderance of the evidence" rather than requiring "proof beyond a reasonable doubt." Following the statutory procedure, a family court convicted Samuel Winship, a twelve year old boy, of stealing $112 and sentenced him to six years in a reformatory. On appeal, state courts sustained the constitutionality of the statute; Winship then appealed to the U.S. Supreme Court.

Mr. Justice **BRENNAN** delivered the opinion of the Court. . . .

I

The requirement that guilt of a criminal charge be established by proof beyond a reasonable doubt dates at least from our early years as a Nation. The "demand for a higher degree of persuasion in criminal cases was recurrently expressed from ancient times, [though] its crystallization into the formula 'beyond a reasonable doubt' seems to have occurred as late as 1798. It is now accepted in common law jurisdictions as the measure of persuasion by which the prosecution must convince the trier of all the essential elements of guilt." C. McCormick, *Evidence* § 321, pp. 681–682 (1954). Although virtually unanimous adherence to the reasonable-doubt standard in common-law jurisdictions may not conclusively establish it as a requirement of due process, such adherence does "reflect a profound judgment about the way in which law should be enforced and justice administered." Duncan v. Louisiana (1968).

Expressions in many opinions of this Court indicate that it has long been assumed that proof of a criminal charge beyond a reasonable doubt is constitutionally required. See, for example, Miles v. United States (1881); Davis v. United States (1895); Holt v. United States (1910); Wilson v. United States (1914); Brinegar v. United States (1949); Leland v. Oregon (1952); Holland v. United States (1954); Speiser v. Randall (1958). . . . Mr. Justice Frankfurter stated that "[i]t is the duty of the Government to establish . . . guilt beyond a reasonable doubt. This notion—basic in our law and rightly one of the boasts of a free society—is a requirement and a safeguard of due process of law in the historic, procedural content of 'due process.'" *Leland* (dissenting opinion). In a similar vein, the Court said in *Brinegar* that "[g]uilt in a criminal case must be proved beyond a reasonable doubt and by evidence confined to that which long experience in the common-law tradition, to some extent embodied in the

Constitution, has crystallized into rules of evidence consistent with that standard. These rules are historically grounded rights of our system, developed to safeguard men from dubious and unjust convictions, with resulting forfeitures of life, liberty and property." Davis v. United States stated that the requirement is implicit in "constitutions . . . [which] recognize the fundamental principles that are deemed essential for the protection of life and liberty." . . .

The reasonable-doubt standard plays a vital role in the American scheme of criminal procedure. It is a prime instrument for reducing the risk of convictions resting on factual error. The standard provides concrete substance for the presumption of innocence—that bedrock "axiomatic and elementary" principle whose "enforcement lies at the foundation of the administration of our criminal law." Coffin v. United States [1895]. . . .

. . . The accused during a criminal prosecution has at stake interests of immense importance, both because of the possibility that he may lose his liberty upon conviction and because of the certainty that he would be stigmatized by the conviction. Accordingly, a society that values the good name and freedom of every individual should not condemn a man for commission of a crime when there is reasonable doubt about his guilt. . . .

Moreover, use of the reasonable-doubt standard is indispensable to command the respect and confidence of the community in applications of the criminal law. It is critical that the moral force of the criminal law not be diluted by a standard of proof that leaves people in doubt whether innocent men are being condemned. It is also important in our free society that every individual going about his ordinary affairs have confidence that his government cannot adjudge him guilty of a criminal offense without convincing a proper factfinder of his guilt with utmost certainty.

Lest there remain any doubt about the constitutional stature of the reasonable-doubt standard, we explicitly hold that the Due Process Clause protects the accused against conviction except upon proof beyond a reasonable doubt of every fact necessary to constitute the crime with which he is charged. . . .

[The Court went on to hold that this constitutional right, like those of notice of charges, to counsel, to confront and crossexamine witnesses, and not to incriminate oneself, that In re Gault (1967) recognized, applied to juvenile cases in family courts as well as to proceedings against adults in criminal courts.]

[*Reversed.*]

Mr. Justice **HARLAN**, concurring. . . .

In this context, I view the requirement of proof beyond a reasonable doubt in a criminal case as bottomed on a fundamental value determination of our society that it is far worse to convict an innocent man than to let a guilty man go free. It is only because of the nearly complete and long-standing acceptance of the reasonable-doubt standard by the States in criminal trials that the Court has not before today had to hold explicitly that due process, as an expression of fundamental procedural fairness, requires a more stringent standard for criminal trials than for ordinary civil litigation. . . .

Mr. Chief Justice **BURGER**, with whom Mr. Justice **STEWART** joins, dissenting. . . .

Mr. Justice **BLACK**, dissenting.

The majority states that "many opinions of this Court indicate that it has long been assumed that proof of a criminal charge beyond a reasonable doubt is constitutionally required." . . . I have joined in some of those opinions, as well as the dissenting opinion of Mr. Justice Frankfurter in *Leland*. The Court has never clearly held, however, that proof beyond a reasonable doubt is either expressly or impliedly commanded by any provision of the Constitution. The Bill of Rights, which in my view is made fully applicable to the States by the Fourteenth Amendment, see Adamson v. California (1947) (dissenting opinion), does by express language provide for, among other things, a right to counsel in criminal trials, a right to indictment, and the right of a defendant to be informed of the nature of the charges against him. And in two places the Constitution provides for trial by jury, but nowhere in that document is there any statement that conviction of crime requires proof of guilt beyond a reasonable doubt. The Constitution thus goes into some detail to spell out what kind of trial a defendant charged with crime should have, and I believe the Court has no power to add to or subtract from the procedures set forth by the Founders. I realize that it is far easier to substitute individual judges' ideas of "fairness" for the fairness prescribed by the Constitution, but I shall not at any time surrender my belief that that document itself should be our guide, not our own concept of what is fair, decent, and right. That this old "shock-the-conscience" test is what the Court is relying on, rather than the words of the Constitution, is clearly enough revealed by the reference of the majority to "fair treatment" and to the statement by the dissenting judges in the New York Court of Appeals that failure to require proof beyond a reasonable doubt amounts to a "lack of fundamental fairness." As I have said time and time again, I prefer to put my faith in the words of the written Constitution itself rather than to rely on the shifting, day-to-day standards of fairness of individual judges. . . .

It can be, and has been, argued that when this Court strikes down a legislative act because it offends the idea of "fundamental fairness," it furthers the basic thrust of our Bill of Rights by protecting individual freedom. But that argument ignores the effect of such decisions on perhaps the most fundamental individual liberty of our people—the right of each man to participate in the self-government of his society. Our Federal Government was set up as one of limited powers, but it was also given broad power to do all that was "necessary and proper" to carry out its basic purpose of governing the Nation, so long as those powers were not exercised contrary to the limitations set forth in the Constitution. And the States, to the extent they are not restrained by the provisions in that document, were to be left free to govern themselves in accordance with their own views of fairness and decency. . . . The people, through their elected representatives, may of course be wrong in making those determinations, but the right of self-government that our Constitution preserves is just as important as any of the specific individual freedoms preserved in the Bill of Rights. The liberty of government by the people, in my opinion, should never be denied by this Court except when the decision of the people as stated in laws passed by their chosen representatives, conflicts with the express or necessarily implied commands of our Constitution. . . .

Editors' Notes

(1) **Query**: How do the interpretive *modes* and *techniques* that Brennan and Black use in this case differ? How do Harlan's differ from Brennan's and Black's? To what extent is Black debating the majority on the question of WHO shall interpret the Constitution? To what degree do the three interrogatives WHAT, WHO, and HOW shade into each other here?

(2) **Query**: Where does Harlan find the "fundamental value determination of our society that it is far worse to convict an innocent man than to let a guilty man go free"? If this value has been so fundamental, why, as Black in effect asks, is it not plainly written in the constitutional document?

(3) **Query**: Does Black's insistence on the "plain words" of the document conflict with Ronald Dworkin's distinction between "concepts" and "conceptions" (reprinted above, p. 168)? Does Black's insistence on the Court's not going beyond the document's plain words square with his opinion in Afroyim v. Rusk (1967; reprinted above, p. 1093)?

(4) **Query**: In Louisville v. Thompson (1960), Black wrote the opinion for the Court holding that the due process clause precluded conviction of a person without evidence of his or her guilt. Are plain words any more dispositive of that issue than of proof "beyond a reasonable doubt"?

(5) Jackson v. Virginia (1979) distinguished between the "necessity of proof beyond a reasonable doubt" and "presumption of innocence" and held that both are rights protected by the due process clauses of the Fifth and Fourteenth Amendments. For other cases expounding on this principle, see Estelle v. Williams (1976) and Sandstrom v. Montana (1979). Schall v. Martin (1984) held, however, that a juvenile judge may incarcerate for a brief period an accused juvenile whom the judge thinks likely to commit a crime before coming to trial. See generally C. Herman Pritchett, *Constitutional Civil Liberties* (Englewood Cliffs, N.J.: Prentice-Hall, 1984), pp. 230–231.

IV. THE RIGHT TO BODILY INTEGRITY

"There are manifold restraints to which every person is necessarily subject for the common good."

JACOBSON v. MASSACHUSETTS
197 U.S. 11, 25 S.Ct. 358, 49 L.Ed. 643 (1905).

This case, upholding a local ordinance requiring vaccinations against Smallpox, is reprinted above, p. 91.

———

"The principle that sustains compulsory vaccination is broad enough to cover cutting the Fallopian tubes."

BUCK v. BELL
274 U.S. 200, 74 S.Ct. 584, 71 L.Ed. 1000 (1927).

Mr. Justice **HOLMES** delivered the opinion of the Court. . . .

Carrie Buck is a feeble minded white woman who was committed to the State mental hospital. She was the daughter of a feeble minded mother in the same institution, and the mother of an illegitimate feeble minded child.* She was eighteen years old at the time of the trial of her case in the Circuit Court, in the latter part of 1924. An Act of Virginia recites that the health of the patient and the welfare of society may be promoted in certain cases by the sterilization of mental defectives, under careful safeguard, &c.; that the sterilization may be effected in males by vasectomy and in females by salpingectomy, without serious pain or substantial danger to life; that the Commonwealth is supporting in various institutions many defective persons who if now discharged would become a menace but if incapable of procreating might be discharged with safety and become self-supporting with benefit to themselves and to society; and that experience has shown that heredity plays an important part in the transmission of insanity, imbecility, &c. The statute then enacts that whenever the superintendent of certain institutions . . . shall be of opinion that it is for the best interests of the patients and of society that an inmate under his care should be sexually sterilized, he may have the operation performed upon any patient afflicted with hereditary forms of insanity, imbecility, etc., on complying with the very careful provisions by which the act protects the patients from possible abuse. . . .

[Holmes then detailed the procedures the act required, including notice, appointment of a guardian, and a hearing.]

 . . . There can be no doubt that so far as procedure is concerned the rights of the patient are most carefully considered, and as every step in this case was taken in scrupulous compliance with the statute

---

* **Eds.' Note:** In fact, Carrie Buck's daughter was not feeble minded.

and after months of observation, there is no doubt that in that respect the plaintiff in error has had due process of law.

The attack is not upon the procedure but upon the substantive law. It seems to be contended that in no circumstances could such an order be justified. It certainly is contended that the order cannot be justified upon the existing grounds. The judgment finds the facts that have been recited and that Carrie Buck "is the probable potential parent of socially inadequate offspring, likewise afflicted, that she may be sexually sterilized without detriment to her general health and that her welfare and that of society will be promoted by her sterilization," and thereupon makes the order. In view of the general declarations of the legislature and the specific findings of the Court, obviously we cannot say as matter of law that the grounds do not exist, and if they exist they justify the result. We have seen more than once that the public welfare may call upon the best citizens for their lives. It would be strange if it could not call upon those who already sap the strength of the State for these lesser sacrifices, often not felt to be such by those concerned, in order to prevent our being swamped with incompetence. It is better for all the world, if instead of waiting to execute degenerate offspring for crime, or to let them starve for their imbecility, society can prevent those who are manifestly unfit from continuing their kind. The principle that sustains compulsory vaccination is broad enough to cover cutting the Fallopian tubes. Jacobson v. Massachusetts [1905]. Three generations of imbeciles are enough.

But, it is said, however it might be if this reasoning were applied generally, it fails when it is confined to the small number who are in the institutions named and is not applied to the multitudes outside. It is the usual last resort of constitutional arguments to point out shortcomings of this sort. But the answer is that the law does all that is needed when it does all that it can, indicates a policy, applies it to all within the lines, and seeks to bring within the lines all similarly situated so far and so fast as its means allow. Of course so far as the operations enable those who otherwise must be kept confined to be returned to the world, and thus open the asylum to others, the equality aimed at will be more nearly reached.

Judgment affirmed.

Mr. Justice **BUTLER** dissents.

Editors' Notes

(1) **Query:** What mode(s) of constitutional interpretation did Holmes apply here?

Why were there no dissenting opinions from McReynolds, who was so eloquent in Meyer v. Nebraska (1923; reprinted above, p. 1089) in defense of the rights "to marry, establish a home and bring up children," or George Sutherland the great exponent in Adkins v. Children's Hospital (1923; reprinted above, p. 980) of individual autonomy in the economic sphere? Only

Pierce Butler dissented and he did so without opinion. Commentators usually attribute his opposition to his Catholicism. See the discussion in David J. Danelski, *A Supreme Court Justice Is Appointed* (New York: Random House, 1964), pp. 189–190.

(2) Holmes had given his personal views on eugenics a dozen years before Buck v. Bell:

> I believe that the wholesale social regeneration which so many now seem to expect, if it can be helped by conscious, co-ordinated human effort, cannot be affected appreciably by tinkering with the institutions of property, but only by taking in hand life and trying to build a race. That would be my starting point for an ideal for the law. [Quoted in Walter Berns, "Buck v. Bell: Due Process of Law?" 6 *West.Pol.Q.* 762 (1953).]

At the time of the litigation, Holmes wrote to a friend that he "took pleasure" in sustaining Virginia's law. James B. Peabody, ed., *The Holmes-Einstein Letters* (New York: St. Martins, 1964), p. 267. Berns presents an interesting analysis of *Buck,* showing that it was a friendly suit designed to test the constitutionality of Virginia's law rather than a genuine conflict. See also Clement E. Vose, *Constitutional Change: Amendment Politics and Supreme Court Litigation Since 1900* (Lexington, Mass.: Lexington Books, 1972); and Elliot A. Brown, "Cases Histories, Interest Group Litigation, and Mr. Justice Holmes," 24 *Emory L.J.* 1037 (1975).

(3) **Query:** To what extent did Skinner v. Oklahoma (1942; reprinted above, p. 868) modify *Buck?* In 1969 the Court almost had an opportunity to answer this question. The justices noted probable jurisdiction in Cavitt v. Nebraska, a challenge to a statute permitting mental institutions to condition release on the patient's being sterilized. While the case was pending, the state changed its law in a deliberate effort to moot the controversy. The U.S. Supreme Court then dismissed the appeal (1970). See Vose, supra, p. 19.

(4) O'Connor v. Donaldson (1975) unanimously held that

> A finding of 'mental illness' alone cannot justify a State's locking up a person against his will and keeping him indefinitely in simple custodial confinement. . . . [T]here is still no constitutional basis for confining such persons involuntarily if they are dangerous to no one and can live safely in freedom.

The ability of the patient to procreate was not an issue in the case. Youngberg v. Romeo (1982) held that a mentally retarded person involuntarily committed to a state mental institution has a due process right to freedom from unreasonable restraint, to safe conditions of confinement, and to "minimumly adequate training" to allow him to enjoy these "liberty interests." Mills v. Rogers (1982) ruled that mental patients at a state hospital had constitutionally protected "liberty interests" to refuse "antipsychotic" drugs (sometimes called "major tranquillizers" or "mind altering" drugs).

(5) Congress has passed a series of statutes to protect the interests of mental patients, retarded persons, and handicapped adults as well as children. The Court, however, has tended to interpret these statutes narrowly. Pennhurst v. Halderman (1981), for example, interpreted the Developmentally Disabled Assistance and Bill of Rights Act of 1975 (42 U.S.C. § 6010) as not creating any substantive rights for mentally handicapped persons to "appropri-

ate treatment" in the "least restrictive environment." Even though he concurred in the judgment, Blackmun thought the Court's opinion set "the odd and
perhaps dangerous precedent of ascribing no meaning to a congressional
enactment. . . ." For details, see espec. C. Herman Pritchett, *Constitutional Civil Liberties* (Englewood Cliffs, N.J.: Prentice-Hall, 1984), pp. 235, 331;
and Judith A. Baer, *Equality under the Constitution* (Ithaca, N.Y.: Cornell
University Press, 1983), chap. 8.

(6) In Cleburne v. Cleburne Living Center (1985; reprinted above, p. 916),
the Court held that classifications based on mental retardation are neither
suspect nor "quasi-suspect" warranting heightened judicial scrutiny. The
Court suggested that recent federal and state legislation attempting to amelio-
rate the condition of the mentally retarded "belie[d] a continuing antipathy or
prejudice" against such persons.

(7) Danger to bodily integrity does not always come from biased legislators or calloused administrators. Stump v. Sparkman (1978) involved a suit by
a young woman against an Indiana judge who, by his own fiat and without legal
authority, had ordered her sterilized when she had been a teen-ager. The
Supreme Court ruled 5–3 that, however wrong the judge's act, federal statutes
did not make him liable for damages to the young woman or the man she later
married.

(8) In the Matter of Lee Ann Grady (1981) presented the Supreme Court
of New Jersey with a variation on *Buck.* In *Grady,* the parents and physician
of a 19-year old woman suffering from Down's Syndrome—her IQ was less
than 40—sought to have her sterilized. The hospital refused and the family
sued. The state supreme court held that the constitutional right to privacy
(see Griswold v. Connecticut [1965; reprinted above, p. 113]; and Roe v.
Wade [1973; reprinted below, p. 1109]) included a right to sterilization, but
that the decision to exercise that right for a mentally retarded person would
have to be made by a judge, not by parents or guardians. The judge, the
court said, must weigh many factors, including the risks of pregnancy, the
dangers to the retarded person's health of a pregnancy and of sterilization, the
feasibility of less drastic means of contraception, and a showing that those
who sought the sterilization were seeking it for the good of the retarded person
and not for their own or the public's convenience. See George J. Annas,
"Sterilization of the Mentally Retarded," 11 *The Hastings Center Report* 18
(August, 1981), and literature cited.

(9) Welfare officials, frustrated in their dealings with the poor, have
occasionally come close to carrying out informal policies of mandatory sterilization, sometimes with the support of lower court judges. See Julius Paul,
"The Return of Punitive Sterilization Proposals: Current Attacks on Illegitimacy
and the AFDC Program," 3 *Law & Soc. Rev.* 77 (1968).

"We are dealing here with legislation which involves one of the basic civil rights of man. . . . [S]trict scrutiny of the classification which a state makes in a sterilization law is essential, lest . . . invidious discriminations are made against groups or types of individuals in violation of the constitutional guaranty of just and equal laws."

SKINNER v. OKLAHOMA
316 U.S. 535, 62 S.Ct. 1110, 86 L.Ed. 1655 (1942).

This case, which invalidated a state statute requiring some habitual criminals to be sterilized, is reprinted above, p. 868.

"This is conduct that shocks the conscience."

ROCHIN v. CALIFORNIA
342 U.S. 165, 72 S.Ct. 205, 96 L.Ed. 183 (1952).

This decision, holding that use by police of a stomach pump to regain evidence that a suspect had swallowed, violated the due process clause of the Fourteenth Amendment, is reprinted above, p. 100.

"[S]pecific guarantees in the Bill of Rights have penumbras, formed by emanations from those guarantees that help give them life and substance."

GRISWOLD v. CONNECTICUT
381 U.S. 479, 85 S.Ct. 1678, 14 L.Ed.2d 510 (1965).

This ruling, striking down a Connecticut statute that made it a crime to use or to aid, abet, or counsel use of "any drug, medicinal article or instrument for the purpose of preventing conception," is reprinted above, at p. 113.

"The right of privacy . . . is broad enough to encompass a woman's decision whether or not to terminate her pregnancy."

ROE v. WADE
410 U.S. 113, 93 S.Ct. 705, 35 L.Ed.2d 147 (1973).

Mr. Justice **BLACKMUN** delivered the opinion of the Court. . . .

We forthwith acknowledge our awareness of the sensitive and emotional nature of the abortion controversy, of the vigorous opposing views, even among physicians, and of the deep and seemingly absolute convictions that the subject inspires. One's philosophy, one's experiences, one's exposure to the raw edges of human existence, one's religious training, one's attitudes toward life and family and their values, and the moral standards one establishes and seeks to observe, are all likely to influence and to color one's thinking and conclusions about abortion.

In addition, population growth, pollution, poverty, and racial overtones tend to complicate and not to simplify the problem.

Our task, of course, is to resolve the issue by constitutional measurement free of emotion and of predilection. We seek earnestly to do this, and, because we do, we have inquired into, and in this opinion place some emphasis upon, medical and medical-legal history and what that history reveals about man's attitudes toward the abortive procedure over the centuries. We bear in mind, too, Mr. Justice Holmes' admonition in his now vindicated dissent in Lochner v. New York (1905).

> [The Constitution] is made for people of fundamentally differing views, and the accident of our finding certain opinions natural and familiar or novel and even shocking ought not to conclude our judgment upon the question whether statutes embodying them conflict with the Constitution of the United States.

I

The Texas statutes . . . make it a crime to "procure an abortion," as therein defined, or to attempt one, except with respect to "an abortion procured or attempted by medical advice for the purpose of saving the life of the mother." Similar statutes are in existence in a majority of the States. . . .

VI

It perhaps is not generally appreciated that the restrictive criminal abortion laws in effect in a majority of States today are of relatively recent vintage. Those laws . . . are not of ancient or even of common law origin. Instead, they derive from statutory changes effected, for the most part, in the latter half of the 19th century.

1. *Ancient attitudes.* . . . We are told that at the time of the Persian Empire abortifacients were known and that criminal abortions were severely punished. We are also told, however, that abortion was practiced in Greek times as well as in the Roman Era, and that "it was resorted to without scruple." The Ephesian, Soranos, often described as the greatest of the ancient gynecologists, appears to have been generally opposed to Rome's prevailing free-abortion practices. . . . Greek and Roman law afforded little protection to the unborn. If abortion was prosecuted in some places, it seems to have been based on a concept of a violation of the father's right to his offspring. Ancient religion did not bar abortion.

2. *The Hippocratic Oath.* What then of the famous Oath that has stood so long as the ethical guide of the medical profession and that bears the name of the great Greek (460(?)–377(?) B.C.), who has been described as the Father of Medicine . . ., who dominated the medical

schools of his time, and who typified the sum of the medical knowledge of the past? The Oath varies somewhat according to the particular translation, but in any translation the content is clear: "I will give no deadly medicine to anyone if asked, nor suggest any such counsel; and in like manner I will not give to a woman a pessary to produce abortion. . . ."

. . . [T]he Oath . . . represents the apex of development of strict ethical concepts in medicine, and its influence endures to this day. Why did not the authority of Hippocrates dissuade abortion practice in his time and that of Rome? The late Dr. Edelstein provides us with a theory: The Oath was not uncontested even in Hippocrates' day; only the Pythagorean school of philosophers frowned upon the related act of suicide. Most Greek thinkers, on the other hand, commended abortion, at least prior to viability. See Plato, Republic, V, 461; Aristotle, Politics, VII, 1335 b 25. For the Pythagoreans, however, it was a matter of dogma. For them the embryo was animate from the moment of conception, and abortion meant destruction of a living being.

. . .

Edelstein then concludes that the Oath originated in a group representing only a small segment of Greek opinion and that it certainly was not accepted by all ancient physicians. . . .

3. *The common law.* It is undisputed that at the common law, abortion performed before "quickening"—the first recognizable movement of the fetus in utero, appearing usually from the 16th to the 18th week of pregnancy—was not an indictable offense. The absence of a common law crime for pre-quickening abortion appears to have developed from a confluence of earlier philosophical, theological, and civil and canon law concepts of when life begins. These disciplines variously approached the question in terms of the point at which the embryo or fetus became "formed" or recognizably human, or in terms of when a "person" came into being, that is, infused with a "soul" or "animated." A loose consensus evolved in early English law that these events occurred at some point between conception and live birth. This was "mediate animation." Although Christian theology and the canon law came to fix the point of animation at 40 days for a male and 80 days for a female, a view that persisted until the 19th century, there was otherwise little agreement about the precise time of formation or animation. There was agreement, however, that prior to this point the fetus was to be regarded as part of the mother and its destruction, therefore, was not homicide. . . .

Whether abortion of a quick fetus was a felony at common law, or even a lesser crime, is still disputed. Bracton, writing early in the 13th century, thought it homicide. But the later and predominant view, following the great common law scholars, has been that it was at most a lesser offense. In a frequently cited passage, Coke took the position that abortion of a woman "quick with childe" is "a great misprision and no murder." Blackstone followed, saying that while abortion after quickening had once been considered manslaughter (though not murder), "modern law" took a less severe view. A recent view of the

common law precedents argues, however, that those precedents contradict Coke and that even post-quickening abortion was never established
as a common law crime. This is of some importance because while
most American courts ruled . . . that abortion of an unquickened
fetus was not criminal under their received common law, others followed Coke in stating that abortion of a quick fetus was a "misprision,"
a term they translated to mean "misdemeanor." That their reliance on
Coke on this aspect of the law was uncritical and, apparently in all the
reported cases, dictum . . . makes it now appear doubtful that abortion was ever firmly established as a common law crime even with
respect to the destruction of a quick fetus.

4. *The English statutory law.* England's first criminal abortion
statute came in 1803. It made abortion of a quick fetus a capital crime
but . . . provided lesser penalties for the felony of abortion before
quickening. . . . This contrast was continued in the general revision of 1828. It disappeared, however, together with the death penalty
in 1837 and did not reappear in the Offenses Against the Person Act of
1861 that formed the core of English anti-abortion law until the
liberalizing reforms of 1967. . . .

Recently Parliament enacted a new abortion law. . . . The Act
permits a licensed physician to perform an abortion where two other
licensed physicians agree (a) "that the continuance of the pregnancy
would involve risk to the life of the pregnant woman, or of injury to the
physical or mental health of the pregnant woman or any existing
children of her family, greater than if the pregnancy were terminated,"
or (b) "that there is a substantial risk that if the child were born it
would suffer from such physical or mental abnormalities as to be
seriously handicapped." The Act also provides that, in making this
determination, "account may be taken of the pregnant woman's actual
or reasonably foreseeable environment." It also permits a physician,
without the concurrence of others, to terminate a pregnancy where he
is of the good faith opinion that the abortion "is immediately necessary
to save the life or to prevent grave permanent injury to the physical or
mental health of the pregnant woman."

5. *The American law.* In this country the law in effect in all but
a few States until mid-19th century was the pre-existing English
common law. . . . It was not until after the War Between the
States that legislation began generally to replace the common law.
Most of these initial statutes dealt severely with abortion after quickening but were lenient with it before quickening. . . .

Gradually, in the middle and late 19th century the quickening
distinction disappeared from the statutory law of most States and the
degree of the offense and the penalties were increased. By the end of
the 1950's a large majority of the States banned abortion, however and
whenever performed, unless done to save or preserve the life of the
mother. . . . In the past several years, however, a trend toward
liberalization of abortion statutes has resulted in adoption, by about
one-third of the States, of less stringent laws. . . .

It is thus apparent that at common law, at the time of the adoption of our Constitution, and throughout the major portion of the 19th century, abortion was viewed with less disfavor than under most American statutes currently in effect. Phrasing it another way, a woman enjoyed a substantially broader right to terminate a pregnancy than she does in most States today. . . .

6. *The position of the American Medical Association.* The anti-abortion mood prevalent in this country in the late 19th century was shared by the medical profession. Indeed, the attitude of the profession may have played a significant role in the enactment of stringent criminal abortion legislation during that period. . . .

An AMA Committee on Criminal Abortion was appointed in May 1857. It presented its report in [1859]. . . . The Committee then offered, and the Association adopted, resolutions protesting "against such unwarrantable destruction of human life," calling upon state legislatures to revise their abortion laws, and requesting the cooperation of state medical societies "in pressing the subject." . . .

In 1871 a long and vivid report was submitted by the Committee on Criminal Abortion. . . . It proffered resolutions, adopted by the Association . . . recommending, among other things, that it "be unlawful and unprofessional for any physician to induce abortion or premature labor, without the concurrent opinion of at least one respectable consulting physician, and then always with a view to the safety of the child—if that be possible," and calling "the attention of the clergy of all denominations to the perverted views of morality entertained by a large class of females—aye and men also, of this important question."

Except for periodic condemnation of the criminal abortionist, no further formal AMA action took place until 1967. In that year the Committee on Human Reproduction urged the adoption of a stated policy of opposition to induced abortion, except when there is "documented medical evidence" of a threat to the health or life of the mother, or that the child "may be born with incapacitating physical deformity or mental deficiency," or that a pregnancy "resulting from legally established statutory or forcible rape or incest may constitute a threat to the mental or physical health of the patient," and two other physicians "chosen because of their recognized professional competence have examined the patient and have concurred in writing," and the procedure "is performed in a hospital accredited by the Joint Commission on Accreditation of Hospitals." . . . This recommendation was adopted by the House of Delegates. . . .

In 1970 . . . a reference committee noted "polarization of the medical profession on this controversial issue". . . . On June 25, 1970, the House of Delegates adopted preambles and most of the resolutions proposed by the reference committee. The preambles emphasized "the best interests of the patient," "sound clinical judgment," and "informed patient consent," in contrast to "mere acquiescence to the patient's demand." The resolutions asserted that abortion is a medical procedure that should be performed by a licensed physician in an accredited hospital only after consultation with two other physicians and in conformity with state law, and that no party to the procedure should be required to violate personally held moral principles. . . .

VII

Three reasons have been advanced to explain historically the enactment of criminal abortion laws in the 19th century and to justify their continued existence.

It has been argued occasionally that these laws were the product of a Victorian social concern to discourage illicit sexual conduct. Texas, however, does not advance this justification . . . and it appears that no court or commentator has taken the argument seriously. . . .

A second reason is concerned with abortion as a medical procedure. When most criminal abortion laws were first enacted, the procedure was a hazardous one for the woman. This was particularly true prior to the development of antisepsis. . . . Abortion mortality was high. Even after 1900, and perhaps until as late as the development of antibiotics in the 1940's, standard modern techniques such as dilation and curettage were not nearly so safe as they are today. Thus it has been argued that a State's real concern in enacting a criminal abortion law was to protect the pregnant woman, that is, to restrain her from submitting to a procedure that placed her life in serious jeopardy.

Modern medical techniques have altered this situation. . . . Mortality rates for women undergoing early abortions, where the procedure is legal, appear to be as low as or lower than the rates for normal childbirth. Consequently, any interest of the State in protecting the woman from an inherently hazardous procedure . . . has largely disappeared. Of course, important state interests in the area of health and medical standards do remain. The State has a legitimate interest in seeing to it that abortion, like any other medical procedure, is performed under circumstances that insure maximum safety for the patient. . . . The prevalence of high mortality rates at illegal "abortion mills" strengthens, rather than weakens, the State's interest in regulating the conditions under which abortions are performed. Moreover, the risk to the woman increases as her pregnancy continues. Thus the State retains a definite interest in protecting the woman's own health and safety when an abortion is proposed at a late stage of pregnancy.

The third reason is the State's interest—some phrase it in terms of duty—in protecting prenatal life. Some of the argument for this justification rests on the theory that a new human life is present from the moment of conception. The State's interest and general obligation to protect life then extends, it is argued, to prenatal life. Only when the life of the pregnant mother herself is at stake, balanced against the life she carries within her, should the interest of the embryo or fetus not prevail. Logically, of course, a legitimate state interest in this area need not stand or fall on acceptance of the belief that life begins at conception or at some other point prior to live birth. In assessing the State's interest, recognition may be given to the less rigid claim that as long as at least potential life is involved, the State may assert interests beyond the protection of the pregnant woman alone. . . .

VIII

The Constitution does not explicitly mention any right of privacy. In a line of decisions, however, . . . the Court has recognized that a right of personal privacy, or a guarantee of certain areas or zones of privacy, does exist under the Constitution. In varying contexts the Court or individual Justices have indeed found at least the roots of that right in the First Amendment, Stanley v. Georgia (1969); in the Fourth and Fifth Amendments, Terry v. Ohio (1968), Katz v. United States (1967), Boyd v. United States (1867), see Olmstead v. United States (1928) (Brandeis, J., dissenting); in the penumbras of the Bill of Rights, Griswold v. Connecticut (1965); in the Ninth Amendment, id. (Goldberg, J., concurring); or in the concept of ordered liberty guaranteed by the first section of the Fourteenth Amendment, see Meyer v. Nebraska (1923). These decisions make it clear that only personal rights that can be deemed "fundamental" or "implicit in the concept of ordered liberty," Palko v. Connecticut (1937), are included in this guarantee of personal privacy. They also make it clear that the right has some extension to activities relating to marriage, Loving v. Virginia (1967); procreation, Skinner v. Oklahoma (1942); contraception, Eisenstadt v. Baird [1972]; family relationships, Prince v. Massachusetts (1944); and child rearing and education, Pierce v. Society of Sisters (1925), *Meyer*.

This right of privacy, whether it be found in the Fourteenth Amendment's concept of personal liberty and restrictions upon state action, as we feel it is, or, as the District Court determined, in the Ninth Amendment's reservation of rights to the people, is broad enough to encompass a woman's decision whether or not to terminate her pregnancy. The detriment that the State would impose upon the pregnant woman by denying this choice altogether is apparent. Specific and direct harm medically diagnosable even in early pregnancy may be involved. Maternity, or additional offspring, may force upon the woman a distressful life and future. Psychological harm may be imminent. Mental and physical health may be taxed by child care. There is also the distress, for all concerned, associated with the unwanted child, and there is the problem of bringing a child into a family already unable, psychologically and otherwise, to care for it. In other cases . . . the additional difficulties and continuing stigma of unwed motherhood may be involved. All these are factors the woman and her responsible physician necessarily will consider in consultation.

. . . [A]ppellant and some amici argue that the woman's right is absolute. . . . With this we do not agree. . . . The Court's decisions recognizing a right of privacy also acknowledge that some state regulation in areas protected by that right is appropriate. . . . [A] state may properly assert important interests in safe-guarding health, in maintaining medical standards, and in protecting potential life. At some point in pregnancy, these respective interests become sufficiently compelling to sustain regulation of the factors that govern the abortion decision. . . .

We therefore conclude that the right of personal privacy includes the abortion decision, but that this right is not unqualified and must be considered against important state interests in regulation. . . .

Fundamental

Where certain "fundamental rights" are involved, the Court has held that regulation limiting these rights may be justified only by a "compelling state interest," Kramer v. Union Free School District (1969); Shapiro v. Thompson (1969); Sherbert v. Verner (1963), and that legislative enactments must be narrowly drawn to express only the legitimate state interests at stake. *Griswold*; Aptheker v. Secretary of State (1964); Cantwell v. Connecticut (1940). . . .

IX . . .

A

The appellee and certain amici argue that the fetus is a "person" within the language and meaning of the Fourteenth Amendment. . . . If this suggestion of personhood is established, the appellant's case, of course, collapses, for the fetus' right to life is then guaranteed specifically by the amendment. . . . On the other hand, the appellee conceded on reargument that no case could be cited that holds that a fetus is a person within the meaning of the Fourteenth Amendment.

The Constitution does not define "person" in so many words. Sec. I of the Fourteenth Amendment contains three references to "person". . . . "Person" is used in other places in the Constitution. . . . But in nearly all these instances, the use of the word is such that it has application only post-natally. None indicates, with any assurance, that it has any possible pre-natal application.

All this, together with our observation . . . that throughout the major portion of the 19th century prevailing legal abortion practices were far freer than they are today, persuades us that the word "person," as used in the Fourteenth Amendment, does not include the unborn. . . .

This conclusion, however, does not of itself fully answer the contentions raised by Texas, and we pass on to other considerations.

B

The pregnant woman cannot be isolated in her privacy. She carries an embryo and, later, a fetus. . . . The situation therefore is inherently different from marital intimacy, or bedroom possession of obscene material, or marriage, or procreation, or education. . . . [I]t is reasonable and appropriate for a State to decide that at some point in time another interest, that of health of the mother or that of potential human life, becomes significantly involved. The woman's privacy is no longer sole and any right of privacy she possesses must be measured accordingly.

Texas urges that, apart from the Fourteenth Amendment, life begins at conception and is present throughout pregnancy, and that, therefore, the State has a compelling interest in protecting that life

from and after conception. We need not resolve the difficult question
of when life begins. When those trained in the respective disciplines of
medicine, philosophy, and theology are unable to arrive at any consensus, the judiciary, at this point in the development of man's knowledge,
is not in a position to speculate as to the answer.

It should be sufficient to note briefly the wide divergence of
thinking on this most sensitive and difficult question. There has
always been strong support for the view that life does not begin until
live birth. . . .

In the areas other than criminal abortion the law has been reluctant to endorse any theory that life, as we recognize it, begins before
live birth or to accord legal rights to the unborn except in narrowly
defined situations and except when the rights are contingent upon live
birth. . . . In most States recovery is said to be permitted only if
the fetus was viable or at least quick when the injuries were sustained,
though few courts have squarely so held. In a recent development,
generally opposed by the commentators, some States permit the parents
of a stillborn child to maintain an action for wrongful death because of
prenatal injuries. Such an action, however, would appear to be one to
vindicate the parents' interest and is thus consistent with the view that
the fetus, at most, represents only the potentiality of life. Similarly,
unborn children have been recognized as acquiring rights or interests
by way of inheritance or other devolution of property, and have been
represented by guardians ad litem. Perfection of the interests involved, again, has generally been contingent upon live birth. In short,
the unborn have never been recognized in the law as persons in the
whole sense.

In view of all this, we do not agree that, by adopting one theory of
life, Texas may override the rights of the pregnant woman. . . .

With respect to the State's important and legitimate interest in the
health of the mother, the "compelling" point, in the light of present
medical knowledge, is at approximately the end of the first trimester.
This is so because of the now established medical fact . . . that until
the end of the first trimester mortality in abortion may be less than
mortality in normal childbirth. It follows that, from and after this
point, a state may regulate the abortion procedure to the extent that
the regulation reasonably relates to the preservation and protection of
maternal health. . . .

This means, on the one hand, that, for the period of pregnancy
prior to this "compelling" point, the attending physician, in consultation with his patient, is free to determine, without regulation by the
State, that in his judgment the patient's pregnancy should be terminated. If that decision is reached, the judgment may be effectuated by an
abortion free of interference by the State.

With respect to the State's important and legitimate interest in
potential life, the "compelling" point is at viability. This is so because
the fetus then presumably has the capability of meaningful life outside
the mother's womb. State regulation protective of fetal life after
viability thus has both logical and biological justifications. If the State

is interested in protecting fetal life after viability, it may go so far as to proscribe abortion during that period except when it is necessary to preserve the life or health of the mother.

Measured against these standards, Art. 1196 of the Texas Penal Code . . . sweeps too broadly. The statute makes no distinction between abortions performed early in pregnancy and those performed later, and it limits to a single reason, "saving" the mother's life, the legal justification for the procedure. The statute, therefore, cannot survive the constitutional attack made upon it here. . . .

Mr. Chief Justice **BURGER,** concurring. . . .

Mr. Justice **DOUGLAS,** concurring. . . .

Mr. Justice **STEWART,** concurring. . . .

Mr. Justice **WHITE,** with whom Mr. Justice **REHNQUIST** joins, dissenting. . . .

. . . . I find nothing in the language or history of the Constitution to support the Court's judgment. The Court simply fashions and announces a new constitutional right for pregnant mothers and, with scarcely any reason or authority for its action, invests that right with sufficient substance to override most existing state abortion statutes. The upshot is that the people and the legislatures of the 50 States are constitutionally disentitled to weigh the relative importance of the continued existence and development of the fetus on the one hand against a spectrum of possible impacts on the mother on the other hand. As an exercise of raw judicial power, the Court perhaps has authority to do what it does today; but in my view its judgment is an improvident and extravagant exercise of the power of judicial review that the Constitution extends to this Court.

The Court apparently values the convenience of the pregnant mother more than the continued existence and development of the life or potential life which she carries. Whether or not I might agree with that marshalling of values, I can in no event join the Court's judgment because I find no constitutional warrant for imposing such an order of priorities on the people and legislatures of the States. In a sensitive area such as this, involving as it does issues over which reasonable men may easily and heatedly differ, I cannot accept the Court's exercise of its clear power of choice by interposing a constitutional barrier to state efforts to protect human life and by investing mothers and doctors with the constitutionally protected right to exterminate it. This issue, for the most part, should be left with the people and to the political processes the people have devised to govern their affairs. . . .

Mr. Justice **REHNQUIST,** dissenting. . . .

. . . . I have difficulty in concluding, as the Court does, that the right of "privacy" is involved in this case. Texas . . . bars the performance of a medical abortion by a licensed physician on a plaintiff such as Roe. A transaction resulting in an operation such as this is not "private" in the ordinary usage of that word. Nor is the "privacy" which the Court finds here even a distant relative of the freedom from searches and seizures protected by the Fourth Amendment to the Constitution which the Court has referred to as embodying a right to privacy. . . .

If the Court means by the term "privacy" no more than that the claim of a person to be free from unwanted state regulation of consensual transactions may be a form of "liberty" protected by the Fourteenth Amendment, there is no doubt that similar claims have been upheld in our earlier decisions on the basis of that liberty. I agree . . . that the "liberty," against deprivation of which without due process the Fourteenth Amendment protects, embraces more than the rights found in the Bill of Rights. But that liberty is not guaranteed absolutely against deprivation, but only against deprivation without due process of law. The test traditionally applied in the area of social and economic legislation is whether or not a law such as that challenged has a rational relation to a valid state objective. Williamson v. Lee Optical Co. (1955). If the Texas statute were to prohibit an abortion even where the mother's life is in jeopardy, I have little doubt that such a statute would lack a rational relation to a valid state objective under the test stated in *Williamson*. . . . But the Court's sweeping invalidation of any restrictions on abortion during the first trimester is impossible to justify under that standard, and the conscious weighing of competing factors which the Court's opinion apparently substitutes for the established test is far more appropriate to a legislative judgment than to a judicial one. . . .

While the Court's opinion quotes from the dissent of Mr. Justice Holmes in *Lochner*, the result it reaches is more closely attuned to the majority opinion of Mr. Justice Peckham in that case. As in *Lochner* and similar cases applying substantive due process standards, . . . adoption of the compelling state interest standard will inevitably require this Court to examine the legislative policies and pass on the wisdom of these policies in the very process of deciding whether a particular state interest put forward may or may not be "compelling." The decision here to break the term of pregnancy into three distinct terms and to outline the permissible restrictions the State may impose in each one, for example, partakes more of judicial legislation than it does of a determination of the intent of the drafters of the Fourteenth Amendment.

The fact that a majority of the States, reflecting, after all, the majority sentiment in those States, have had restrictions on abortions for at least a century, it seems to me, is a strong indication that the asserted right to an abortion is not "so rooted in the traditions and conscience of our people as to be ranked as fundamental," Snyder v. Massachusetts (1934). Even today, when society's views on abortion are changing, the very existence of the debate is evidence that the "right" to an abortion is not so universally accepted.   .   .   .

To reach its result the Court necessarily has had to find within the scope of the Fourteenth Amendment a right that was apparently completely unknown to the drafters of the Amendment.   .   .   .   By the time of the adoption of the Fourteenth Amendment in 1868 there were at least 36 laws enacted by state or territorial legislatures limiting abortion.   While many States have amended or updated their laws, 21 of the laws on the books in 1868 remain in effect today.   Indeed, the Texas statute struck down today was, as the majority notes, first enacted in 1857 and "has remained substantially unchanged to the present time."   .   .   .

There apparently was no question concerning the validity of this provision or of any of the other state statutes when the Fourteenth Amendment was adopted.   The only conclusion possible from this history is that the drafters did not intend to have the Fourteenth Amendment withdraw from the States the power to legislate with respect to this matter.   .   .   .

Editors' Notes

(1) **Query:** How is the history of the law of abortion that Blackmun chronicled in Part VI of his opinion relevant to his reasoning? Did Rehnquist's reliance on "intent of the framers" rebut Blackmun's argument or did it miss his point?

(2) **Query:** How did Blackmun reason from a right of privacy, "found in the Fourteenth Amendment's concept of personal liberty and restrictions upon state action," to a right to abortion? What constitutional justification did he offer for dividing a pregnancy—and the strength of a woman's right to privacy in her decision to have an abortion—into trimesters?

(3) **Query:** In his concur. op., Burger underlined Blackmun's point that the right to abortion was not unlimited by specifically saying the Court was not holding that "abortion on demand" was a constitutional right. To what extent do the logical implications of the Court's opinion in *Roe* support that claim?

(4) **Query:** Does the Court's ruling that a fetus is not a person comport with a "fundamental rights" *mode* of interpretation? Or is such a *mode* agnostic with respect to the definition of who or what is a person entitled to fundamental rights? See the discussion of "person" in the Introductory Essay to this chapter.

(5) On the day that *Roe* came down, the Court also decided Doe v. Bolton. Again speaking through Blackmun, the Court stressed that *Roe* "sets forth our conclusion that a woman does not have an absolute constitutional right to an abortion of her demand." Nevertheless, the justices also emphasized that a woman had a limited right which the state could not unconstitutionally burden, and that Georgia's requirements that (a) abortion be performed only in accredited hospitals; (b) the procedure be approved by a special committee of physicians; (c) two other physicians concur in the attending physician's recommendation for an abortion; and (d) the patient be a state resident were all unconstitutional burdens on that right.

(6) These rulings, of course, are among the most controversial of this century. They were followed by a spate of additional decisions as well as efforts to overturn them by constitutional amendment—see, for example, *Hearings* on S. 158, reprinted above, p. 247—to limit their effect by restricting use of federal money—see Harris v. McRae (1980; reprinted above, p. 898)— and attempts to outflank them by new legislation. For the latter, see the analysis in C. Herman Pritchett, *Constitutional Civil Liberties* (Englewood Cliffs, N.J.: Prentice-Hall, 1984), pp. 319–322; H.L. v. Matheson (1981); and Akron v. Akron Center for Reproductive Health (1983; reprinted below, p. 1122).

(7) **Query:** After *Roe,* the Department of Health, Education, and Welfare changed its traditional interpretation of "dependent child" to exclude the unborn. Burns v. Alcala (1975) sustained this new interpretation. Only Marshall dissented. Compare his dissent against what he considered limitations on the right to abortion in *Harris.* Is it consistent to maintain that a fetus is a "dependent child" and at the same time that a woman has a right to abortion even when her own life is not threatened by her pregnancy?

(8) Louisiana Medical Examiners v. Rosen (1975) gave *Roe* retroactive effect by invalidating a state abortion statute under which a physician had been suspended in 1969. Bigelow v. Virginia (1975) struck down on First Amendment grounds a statute making it illegal for out-of-state abortion clinics to advertise in Virginia.

(9) Rep. Bella Abzug reprinted many articles on abortion antedating *Roe* in 118 *Cong.Rec.* H3833–H3970 (daily ed., May 2, 1972). See also: Daniel Callahan, *Abortion: Law, Choice, and Morality* (New York: Macmillan, 1970); Lawrence Lader, *Abortion II: Making the Revolution* (Boston: Beacon, 1966); and John T. Noonan, Jr., ed., *The Morality of Abortion* (Cambridge: Harvard University Press, 1970).

(10) *Roe* and its progeny have sired a vast number of legal, ethical, and theological analyses. Some of this material is collected in U.S. Senate, Subcommittee on the Separation of Powers, *Hearings on S. 158,* 97th Cong., 1st Sess. (1981), 2 vols. See also James T. Burtchaell, ed., *Abortion Parley* (Kansas City: Andrews & McMeel, 1980); James T. Burtchaell, *Rachel Weeping* (Kansas City: Andrews & McMeel, 1981); Marshall Cohen et al., eds., *The Rights and Wrongs of Abortion* (Princeton N.J.: Princeton University Press, 1974); John Hart Ely, "The Wages of Crying Wolf," 82 *Yale L.J.* 920 (1973); Joel Feinberg, ed., *The Problem of Abortion* (Belmont, Calif.: Wadsworth, 1973); Wolfgang Friedman, "Interferences with Human Life: Jurisprudential Reflections," 70 *Col.L.Rev.* 1058 (1970); Edward Marnier et al., eds., *Abortion: New Directions for Policy Studies* (Notre Dame, Ind.: University of Notre Dame Press, 1977); Bernard N. Nathanson, *Aborting America* (New York: Doubleday, 1979); John T. Noonan, Jr., "Abortion: The Case for a Constitutional Amendment," *New Oxford Rev.* (Jan., 1978), p. 4; Paul Ramsey, *Ethics at the Edges of Life* (New Haven Conn.: Yale University Press, 1978), chaps. 1–3; Donald H. Regan, "Rewriting *Roe v. Wade,*" 77 *Mich.L.Rev.* 1569 (1979); Sacred Congregation for the Doctrine of the Faith, "Declaration on Procured Abortion," *L'Osservatore Romano* (English language ed.), Dec. 5, 1974; Gilbert Y. Steiner, ed., *The Abortion Dispute and the American System* (Washington, D.C.: The Brookings Institution, 1983); Laurence H. Tribe, *American Constitutional Law* (Mineola, N.Y.: Foundation Press, 1978), § 15–10. Walter

F. Murphy and Joseph Tanenhaus, eds., *Comparative Constitutional Law* (New York: St. Martin's, 1977), chap. 12, reprints cases from Canada and West Germany as well as the United States and includes a long bibliography. For a fictionalized account of the justices' struggling over the legal, political, and moral issues surrounding the constitutionality of laws against abortion, see Walter F. Murphy, *The Vicar of Christ* (New York: Macmillan, 1979), Part II, chap. 9.

"[S]tare decisis, while perhaps never entirely persuasive on a constitutional question, is a doctrine that demands respect in a society governed by the rule of law. We respect it today and reaffirm *Roe*."

AKRON v. AKRON CENTER FOR REPRODUCTIVE HEALTH
462 U.S. 416, 103 S.Ct. 2481, 76 L.Ed.2d 687 (1983).

In 1978 Akron adopted a comprehensive ordinance regulating abortions, including: (1) § 1870.03 requiring that all abortions after the first trimester be performed in accredited hospitals; (2) § 1870.05 setting up procedures for notifying, before abortions, the parents of unmarried minors; (3) § 1870.06 mandating that "the attending physician," before an abortion, make certain specified statements, inter alia, that "the unborn child is a human life from the moment of conception," and describing the characteristics of the fetus, the dangers of abortion, and the public services available to help women through pregnancy; and (4) § 1870.07 ordering, except in an emergency, a 24-hour delay between the time the woman signed a consent form and the abortion was performed.

Three corporations that ran abortion clinics in Akron and a physician who specialized in that work filed suit in a federal district court, asking for an injunction against enforcement of the various regulations. The district court upheld some provisions, but struck down others. Both sides appealed portions of that decision. The court of appeals affirmed in part and reversed in part. Both sides then sought and obtained certiorari.

Justice **POWELL** delivered the opinion of the Court. . . .

These cases come to us a decade after we held in Roe v. Wade (1973) that the right to privacy, grounded in the concept of personal liberty guaranteed by the Constitution, encompasses a woman's right to decide whether to terminate her pregnancy. Legislative responses to the Court's decision have required us on several occasions, and again today, to define the limits of a State's authority to regulate the performance of abortions. And arguments continue to be made, in these cases and elsewhere, that we erred in interpreting the Constitution. Nonetheless, the doctrine of stare decisis, while perhaps never entirely persuasive on a constitutional question, is a doctrine that demands respect in a society governed by the rule of law.[1] We respect it today and reaffirm *Roe*. . . .

Today, however, the dissenting opinion rejects the basic premise of *Roe* and its progeny. The dissent stops short of arguing flatly that *Roe* should be overruled. Rather, it adopts reasoning that, for all practical purposes, would accomplish precisely that result. . . .

In sum, it appears that the dissent would uphold virtually any abortion regulation under a rational-basis test. It also appears that even where heightened scrutiny is deemed appropriate, the dissent would uphold virtually any abortion-inhibiting regulation because of the State's interest in preserving potential human life. . . . This analysis is wholly incompatible with the fundamental right recognized in *Roe*.

II

In *Roe*, the Court held that the "right of privacy, . . . founded in the Fourteenth Amendment's concept of personal liberty and restrictions upon state action, . . . is broad enough to encompass a woman's decision whether or not to terminate her pregnancy." Although the Constitution does not specifically identify this right, the history of this Court's constitutional adjudication leaves no doubt that "the full scope of the liberty guaranteed by the Due Process Clause cannot be found in or limited by the precise terms of the specific guarantees elsewhere provided in the Constitution." Poe v. Ullman (1961) (Harlan, J., dissenting from dismissal of appeal). Central among these protected liberties is an individual's "freedom of personal choice in matters of marriage and family life." *Roe* (Stewart, J., concurring). See, e.g., Eisenstadt v. Baird (1972); Loving v. Virginia (1967); Griswold v. Connecticut (1965); Pierce v. Society of Sisters (1925); Meyer v. Nebraska (1923). The decision in *Roe* was based firmly on this long-recognized and essential element of personal liberty.

The Court also has recognized, because abortion is a medical procedure, that the full vindication of the woman's fundamental right necessarily requires that her physician be given "the room he needs to make his best medical judgment." Doe v. Bolton (1973). See Whalen v. Roe (1977). The physician's exercise of this medical judgment encompasses both assisting the woman in the decisionmaking process and implementing her decision should she choose abortion. See Colautti v. Franklin (1979).

At the same time, the Court in *Roe* acknowledged that the woman's fundamental right "is not unqualified and must be considered against important state interests in abortion." But restrictive state regulation

---

1. There are especially compelling reasons for adhering to stare decisis in applying the principles of *Roe*. That case was considered with special care. It was argued during the 1971 Term, and reargued—with extensive briefing—the following Term. The decision was joined by the Chief Justice and six other Justices. Since *Roe* was decided . . . the Court repeatedly and consistently has accepted and applied the basic principle that a woman has a fundamental right to make the highly personal choice whether or not to terminate her pregnancy. . . . [Footnote by the Court.]

of the right to choose abortion, as with other fundamental rights subject to searching judicial examination, must be supported by a compelling state interest. We have recognized two such interests that may justify state regulation of abortions.[2]

First, a State has an "important and legitimate interest in protecting the potentiality of human life." Although the interest exists "throughout the course of the woman's pregnancy," Beal v. Doe (1977), it becomes compelling only at viability, the point at which the fetus "has the capability of meaningful life outside the mother's womb," Roe. At viability this interest in protecting the potential life of the unborn child is so important that the State may proscribe abortions altogether, "except when it is necessary to preserve the life or health of the mother." Roe.

Second, because a State has a legitimate concern with the health of women who undergo abortions, "a State may properly assert important interests in safeguarding health [and] in maintaining medical standards." We held in Roe, however, that this health interest does not become compelling until "approximately the end of the first trimester" of pregnancy. Until that time, a pregnant woman must be permitted, in consultation with her physician, to decide to have an abortion and to effectuate that decision "free of interference by the State."

This does not mean that a State never may enact a regulation touching on the woman's abortion right during the first weeks of pregnancy. Certain regulations that have no significant impact on the woman's exercise of her right may be permissible where justified by important state health objectives. In Danforth, we unanimously upheld two Missouri statutory provisions, applicable to the first trimester, requiring the woman to provide her informed written consent to the abortion and the physician to keep certain records, even though comparable requirements were not imposed on most other medical procedures. The decisive factor was that the State met its burden of demonstrating that these regulations furthered important health-related State concerns. But even these minor regulations on the abortion procedure during the first trimester may not interfere with physician-patient consultation or with the woman's choice between abortion and childbirth.

From approximately the end of the first trimester of pregnancy, the State "may regulate the abortion procedure to the extent that the regulation reasonably relates to the preservation and protection of maternal health." Roe. The State's discretion to regulate on this basis does not, however, permit it to adopt abortion regulations that depart from accepted medical practice. We have rejected a State's attempt to

---

2. In addition, the Court repeatedly has recognized that, in view of the unique status of children under the law, the States have a "significant" interest in certain abortion regulations aimed at protecting children "that is not present in the case of an adult." Planned Parenthood v. Danforth (1976). See H.L. v. Matheson (1981). . . . A majority of the Court, however, has indicated that these state and parental interests must give way to the constitutional right of a mature minor or of an immature minor whose best interests are contrary to parental involvement. See, e.g., Matheson (Powell, J., concurring) (Marshall, J., dissenting). . . . [Footnote by the Court.]

ban a particular second-trimester abortion procedure, where the ban would have increased the costs and limited the availability of abortions without promoting important health benefits. See *Danforth*. . . .

III

Section 1870.03 of the Akron ordinance requires that any abortion performed "upon a pregnant woman subsequent to the end of the first trimester of her pregnancy" must be "performed in a hospital." A "hospital" is "a general hospital or special hospital devoted to gynecology or obstetrics which is accredited by the Joint Commission on Accreditation of Hospitals or by the American Osteopathic Association." § 1870.1(B). Accreditation by these organizations requires compliance with comprehensive standards governing a wide variety of health and surgical services. The ordinance thus prevents the performance of abortions in outpatient facilities that are not part of an acute-care, full-service hospital. . . .

. . . [W]e now hold that § 1807.03 is unconstitutional.

A . . .

We reaffirm today that a State's interest in health regulation becomes compelling at approximately the end of the first trimester. The existence of a compelling state interest in health, however, is only the beginning of the inquiry. The State's regulation may be upheld only if it is reasonably designed to further that state interest. See *Doe*. . . .

B

There can be no doubt that § 1870.03's second-trimester hospitalization requirement places a significant obstacle in the path of women seeking an abortion. A primary burden created by the requirement is additional cost to the woman. . . . [A] second-trimester abortion costs more than twice as much in a hospital as in a clinic. . . . It therefore is apparent that a second-trimester hospitalization requirement may significantly limit a woman's ability to obtain an abortion.

Akron does not contend that § 1870.03 imposes only an insignificant burden on women's access to abortion, but rather defends it as a reasonable health regulation. This position had strong support at the time of *Roe*, as hospitalization for second-trimester abortions was recommended by the American Public Health Association (APHA) and the American College of Obstetricians and Gynecologists (ACOG). Since then, however, the safety of second-trimester abortions has increased dramatically. The principal reason is that the D[ilation] & E[vacuation] procedure is now widely and successfully used for second-trimester abortions. . . .

. . . [E]xperience indicates that D & E may be performed safely on an outpatient basis in appropriate nonhospital facilities. The evidence is strong enough to have convinced the APHA to abandon its prior recommendation of hospitalization for all second-trimester abortions. . . . Similarly, the ACOG no longer suggests that all second-trimester abortions be performed in a hospital. . . .

These developments, and the professional commentary supporting them, constitute impressive evidence that—at least during the early weeks of the second trimester—D & E abortions may be performed as safely in an outpatient clinic as in a full-service hospital. We conclude, therefore, that "present medical knowledge," *Roe*, convincingly undercuts Akron's justification for requiring that *all* second-trimester abortions be performed in a hospital. . . .

IV

We turn next to § 1870.05(B), the provision prohibiting a physician from performing an abortion on a minor pregnant woman under the age of 15 unless he obtains "the informed written consent of one of her parents or her legal guardian" or unless the minor obtains "an order from a court having jurisdiction over her that the abortion be performed or induced." . . .

The relevant legal standards are not in dispute. The Court has held that "the State may not impose a blanket provision . . . requiring the consent of a parent or person in loco parentis as a condition for abortion of an unmarried minor." *Danforth*. In Bellotti v. Baird (1979) (*Bellotti* II), a majority of the Court indicated that a State's interest in protecting immature minors will sustain a requirement of a consent substitute, either parental or judicial. [Plurality opinion of four Justices.] The *Bellotti* II plurality cautioned, however, that the State must provide an alternative procedure whereby a pregnant minor may demonstrate that she is sufficiently mature to make the abortion decision herself or that, despite her immaturity, an abortion would be in her best interests. Under these decisions, it is clear that Akron may not make a blanket determination that *all* minors under the age of 15 are too immature to make this decision or that an abortion never may be in the minor's best interests without parental approval.

Akron's ordinance does not create expressly the alternative procedure required by *Bellotti* II. . . .

V

The Akron ordinance provides that no abortion shall be performed except "with the informed written consent of the pregnant woman, . . . given freely and without coercion." § 1870.06(A). Furthermore, "in order to insure that the consent for an abortion is truly informed consent," the woman must be "orally informed by her attending physician" of the status of her pregnancy, the development of her fetus, the date of possible viability, the physical and emotional complications that may result from an abortion, and the availability of agencies to provide her with assistance and information with respect to birth control, adoption, and childbirth. § 1870.06(B). In addition, the attending physician must inform her "of the particular risks associated with her own pregnancy and the abortion technique to be employed . . . [and] other information which in his own medical judgment is relevant to her decision as to whether to have an abortion or carry her pregnancy to term." § 1870.06(C). . . .

A

In *Danforth*, we upheld a Missouri law requiring a pregnant woman to "certif[y] in writing her consent to the abortion and that her consent is informed and freely given and is not the result of coercion." We explained:

> The decision to abort . . . is an important, and often a stressful one, and it is desirable and imperative that it be made with full knowledge of its nature and consequences. The woman is the one primarily concerned, and her awareness of the decision and its significance may be assured, constitutionally, by the State to the extent of requiring her prior written consent. . . .

The validity of an informed consent requirement thus rests on the State's interest in protecting the health of the pregnant woman. The decision to have an abortion has "implications far broader than those associated with most other kinds of medical treatment," *Bellotti* II (plurality opinion), and thus the State legitimately may seek to ensure that it has been made "in the light of all attendant circumstances—psychological and emotional as well as physical—that might be relevant to the well-being of the patient." This does not mean, however, that a State has unreviewable authority to decide what information a woman must be given before she chooses to have an abortion. It remains primarily the responsibility of the physician to ensure that appropriate information is conveyed to his patient, depending on her particular circumstances. *Danforth*'s recognition of the State's interest in ensuring that this information be given will not justify abortion regulations designed to influence the woman's informed choice between abortion or childbirth.

B

Viewing the city's regulations in this light, we believe that § 1870.06(B) attempts to extend the State's interest in ensuring "informed consent" beyond permissible limits. First, it is fair to say that much of the information required is designed not to inform the woman's consent but rather to persuade her to withhold it altogether. Subsection (3) requires the physician to inform his patient that "the unborn child is a human life from the moment of conception," a requirement inconsistent with the Court's holding in *Roe* that a State may not adopt one theory of when life begins to justify its regulation of abortions. Moreover, much of the detailed description of "the anatomical and physiological characteristics of the particular unborn child" required by subsection (3) would involve at best speculation by the physician. And subsection (5), that begins with the dubious statement that "abortion is a major surgical procedure" and proceeds to describe numerous possible physical and psychological complications of abortion, is a "parade of horribles" intended to suggest that abortion is a particularly dangerous procedure.

An additional, and equally decisive, objection to § 1870.06(B) is its intrusion upon the discretion of the pregnant woman's physician. . . . For example, even if the physician believes that some of the risks outlined in subsection (5) are nonexistent for a particular patient, he remains obligated to describe them to her. . . . By insisting upon recitation of a lengthy and inflexible list of information, Akron unreasonably has placed "obstacles in the path of the doctor upon whom [the woman is] entitled to rely for advice in connection with her decision." *Whalen.*

C

Section 1870.06(C) presents a different question. Under this provision, the "attending physician" must inform the woman

> of the particular risks associated with her own pregnancy and the abortion technique to be employed including providing her with at least a general description of the medical instructions to be followed subsequent to the abortion in order to insure her safe recovery, and shall in addition provide her with such other information which in his own medical judgment is relevant to her decision as to whether to have an abortion or carry her pregnancy to term.

The information required clearly is related to maternal health and to the State's legitimate purpose in requiring informed consent. . . .

We are not convinced, however, that there is as vital a state need for insisting that the physician performing the abortion, or for that matter any physician, personally counsel the patient in the absence of a request. The State's interest is in ensuring that the woman's consent is informed and unpressured; the critical factor is whether she obtains the necessary information and counseling from a qualified person, not the identity of the person from whom she obtains it. . . . [O]n the record before us we cannot say that the woman's consent to the abortion will not be informed if a physician delegates the counseling task to another qualified individual.

In so holding, we do not suggest that the State is powerless to vindicate its interest in making certain the "important" and "stressful" decision to abort "is made with full knowledge of its nature and consequences." *Danforth.* Nor do we imply that a physician may abdicate his essential role as the person ultimately responsible for the medical aspects of the decision to perform the abortion. A State may define the physician's responsibility to include verification that adequate counseling has been provided and that the woman's consent is informed. In addition, the State may establish reasonable minimum qualifications for those people who perform the primary counseling function. . . .

VI

The Akron ordinance prohibits a physician from performing an abortion until 24 hours after the pregnant woman signs a consent form. § 1870.07. . . .

We find that Akron has failed to demonstrate that any legitimate state interest is furthered by an arbitrary and inflexible waiting period. There is no evidence suggesting that the abortion procedure will be performed more safely. Nor are we convinced that the State's legitimate concern that the woman's decision be informed is reasonably served by requiring a 24-hour delay as a matter of course. . . .

Justice **O'CONNOR,** with whom Justice **WHITE** and Justice **REHNQUIST** join, dissenting.

 . . . [I]t is apparent from the Court's opinion that neither sound constitutional theory nor our need to decide cases based on the application of neutral principles can accommodate an analytical framework that varies according to the "stages" of pregnancy, where those stages, and their concomitant standards of review, differ according to the level of medical technology available when a particular challenge to state regulation occurs. The Court's analysis of the Akron regulations is inconsistent both with the methods of analysis employed in previous cases dealing with abortion, and with the Court's approach to fundamental rights in other areas.

 Our recent cases indicate that a regulation imposed on "a lawful abortion 'is not unconstitutional unless it unduly burdens the right to seek an abortion.' " Maher v. Roe (1977). See also Harris v. McRae (1980). In my view, this "unduly burdensome" standard should be applied to the challenged regulations throughout the entire pregnancy without reference to the particular "stage" of pregnancy involved. If the particular regulation does not "unduly burden[ ]" the fundamental right, *Maher,* then our evaluation of that regulation is limited to our determination that the regulation rationally relates to a legitimate state purpose. Irrespective of what we may believe is wise or prudent policy in this difficult area, "the Constitution does not constitute us as 'Platonic Guardians' nor does it vest in this Court the authority to strike down laws because they do not meet our standards of desirable social policy, 'wisdom,' or 'common sense.' " Plyler v. Doe (1982) (Burger, C.J., dissenting).

I

 The trimester or "three-stage" approach adopted by the Court in *Roe* . . . cannot be supported as a legitimate or useful framework for accommodating the woman's right and the State's interests. The decision of the Court today graphically illustrates why the trimester approach is a completely unworkable method of accommodating the conflicting personal rights and compelling state interests that are involved in the abortion context.

 . . . [T]he State's compelling interest in maternal health changes as medical technology changes, and any health regulation must not "depart from accepted medical practice." In applying this standard, the Court holds that "the safety of second-trimester abortions has increased dramatically" since 1973, when *Roe* was decided. Although a regulation such as one requiring that all second-trimester abortions be performed in hospitals "had strong support" in 1973 "as a reasonable health regulation," this regulation can no longer stand because, according to the Court's diligent research into medical and scientific literature, the dilation and evacuation procedure (D & E), used in 1973 only for first-trimester abortions, "is now widely and successfully used for second trimester abortions." . . .

It is not difficult to see that despite the Court's purported adherence to the trimester approach adopted in *Roe*, the lines drawn in that decision have now been "blurred" because of what the Court accepts as technological advancement in the safety of abortion procedure. . . . [T]he State must continuously and conscientiously study contemporary medical and scientific literature in order to determine whether the effect of a particular regulation is to "depart from accepted medical practice" insofar as particular procedures and particular periods within the trimester are concerned. Assuming that legislative bodies are able to engage in this exacting task, it is difficult to believe that our Constitution *requires* that they do it as a prelude to protecting the health of their citizens. It is even more difficult to believe that this Court, without the resources available to those bodies entrusted with making legislative choices, believes itself competent to make these inquiries and to revise these standards every time the American College of Obstetricians and Gynecologists (ACOG) or similar group revises its views about what is and what is not appropriate medical procedure in this area. . . .

Just as improvements in medical technology inevitably will move *forward* the point at which the State may regulate for reasons of maternal health, different technological improvements will move *backward* the point of viability at which the State may proscribe abortions except when necessary to preserve the life and health of the mother.

In 1973, viability before 28 weeks was considered unusual. . . . However, recent studies have demonstrated increasingly earlier fetal viability. It is certainly reasonable to believe that fetal viability in the first trimester of pregnancy may be possible in the not too distant future. Indeed, the Court has explicitly acknowledged that *Roe* left the point of viability "flexible for anticipated advancements in medical skill." *Colautti*. . . .

The *Roe* framework, then, is clearly on a collision course with itself. . . . [I]t is clear that the trimester approach violates the fundamental aspiration of judicial decision making through the application of neutral principles "sufficiently absolute to give them roots throughout the community and continuity over significant periods of time. . . ." A. Cox, *The Role of the Supreme Court in American Government* 114 (1976). The *Roe* framework is inherently tied to the state of medical technology that exists whenever particular litigation ensues. Although legislatures are better suited to make the necessary factual judgments in this area, the Court's framework forces legislatures, as a matter of constitutional law, to speculate about what constitutes "accepted medical practice" at any given time. Without the necessary expertise or ability, courts must then pretend to act as science review boards and examine those legislative judgments.

The Court adheres to the *Roe* framework because the doctrine of stare decisis "demands respect in a society governed by the rule of law." Although respect for stare decisis cannot be challenged, "this Court's considered practice [is] not to apply stare decisis as rigidly in constitutional as in nonconstitutional cases." Glidden Company v. Zdanok (1962). Although we must be mindful of the "desirability of continuity of decision in constitutional questions . . . when convinced of former error, this Court has never felt constrained to follow precedent. In constitutional questions, when correction depends on amendment and not upon legislative action this Court throughout its history has freely exercised its power to reexamine the basis of its constitutional decisions." Smith v. Allwright (1944).

Even assuming that there is a fundamental right to terminate pregnancy in some situations, there is no justification in law or logic for the trimester framework adopted in *Roe* and employed by the Court today on the basis of stare decisis. For the reasons stated above, that framework is clearly an unworkable means of balancing the fundamental right and the compelling state interests that are indisputably implicated.

II

The Court in *Roe* correctly realized that the State has important interests "in the areas of health and medical standards" and that "[t]he State has a legitimate interest in seeing to it that abortion, like any other medical procedure, is performed under circumstances that insure maximum safety for the patient." The Court also recognized that the State has "*another* important and legitimate interest in protecting the potentiality of human life." (Emphasis in original.) I agree completely that the State has these interests, but in my view, the point at which these interests become compelling does not depend on the trimester of pregnancy. Rather, these interests are present *throughout* pregnancy.
. . .

The fallacy inherent in the *Roe* framework is apparent: just because the State has a compelling interest in ensuring maternal safety once an abortion may be more dangerous in childbirth, it simply does not follow that the State has no interest before that point. . . .

The state interest in potential human life is likewise extant throughout pregnancy. In *Roe,* the Court held that although the State had an important and legitimate interest in protecting potential life, that interest could not become compelling until the point at which the fetus was viable. The difficulty with this analysis is clear: *potential* life is no less potential in the first weeks of pregnancy than it is at viability or afterward. At any stage in pregnancy, there is the *potential* for human life. Although the Court refused to "resolve the difficult question of when life begins," the Court chose the point of

viability—when the fetus is *capable* of life independent of its mother—
to permit the complete proscription of abortion. The choice of viability
as the point at which the state interest in *potential* life becomes
compelling is no less arbitrary than choosing any point before viability
or any point afterward. . . .

III

Although the State possesses compelling interests in the protection
of potential human life and in maternal health throughout pregnancy,
not every regulation that the State imposes must be measured against
the State's compelling interests and examined with strict scrutiny.
". . . *Roe* did not declare an unqualified 'constitutional right to an
abortion' . . . . Rather, the right protects the woman from unduly
burdensome interference with her freedom to decide whether to terminate her pregnancy." *Maher.* The Court and its individual Justices
have repeatedly utilized the "unduly burdensome" standard in abortion
cases.

The requirement that state interference "infringe substantially" or
"heavily burden" a right before heightened scrutiny is applied is not
novel in our fundamental-rights jurisprudence, or restricted to the
abortion context. In San Antonio Independent School District v. Rodriguez (1973), we observed that we apply "strict judicial scrutiny" only
when legislation may be said to have " 'deprived,' 'infringed,' or 'interfered' with the free exercise of some such fundamental personal right
or liberty." If the impact of the regulation does not rise to the level
appropriate for our strict scrutiny, then our inquiry is limited to
whether the state law bears "some rational relationship to legitimate
state purposes." Even in the First Amendment context, we have
required in some circumstances that state laws "infringe substantially"
on protected conduct, Gibson v. Florida Legislative Investigation Committee (1963), or that there be "a significant encroachment upon
personal liberty," Bates v. City of Little Rock (1960).

In Carey v. Population Services International (1977), we eschewed
the notion that state law had to meet the exacting "compelling state
interest" test " 'whenever it implicates sexual freedom.' " Rather, we
required that before the "strict scrutiny" standard was employed, it
was necessary that the state law "impose[ ] a significant burden" on a
protected right or that it "burden an individual's right to prevent
conception or terminate pregnancy by *substantially* limiting access to
the means of effectuating that decision. . . ." (Emphasis added.)
The Court stressed that, "even a burdensome regulation may be validated by a sufficiently compelling state interest." . . .

Indeed, the Court today follows this approach. Although the Court
does not use the expression "undue burden," the Court recognizes that
even a "significant obstacle" can be justified by a "reasonable" regulation.

The "undue burden" required in the abortion cases represents the
required threshold inquiry that must be conducted before this Court

can require a State to justify its legislative actions under the exacting "compelling state interest" standard. . . .

The "unduly burdensome" standard is particularly appropriate in the abortion context because of the *nature* and *scope* of the right that is involved. The privacy right involved in the abortion context "cannot be said to be absolute." *Roe.* "*Roe* did not declare an unqualified 'constitutional right to an abortion.'" *Maher.* Rather, the *Roe* right is intended to protect against state action "drastically limiting the availability and safety of the desired service," against the imposition of an "absolute obstacle" on the abortion decision, *Danforth,* or against "official interference" and "coercive restraint" imposed on the abortion decision, *Harris* (White, J., concurring). That a state regulation may "inhibit" abortions to some degree does not require that we find that the regulation is invalid. See H.L. v. Matheson (1981). . . .

In determining whether the State imposes an "undue burden," we must keep in mind that when we are concerned with extremely sensitive issues, such as the one involved here, "the appropriate forum for their resolution in a democracy is the legislature. We should not forget that 'legislatures are ultimate guardians of the liberties and welfare of the people in quite as great a degree as the courts.' Missouri, K. & T.R. Co. v. May (1904) (Holmes, J.)." *Maher.* This does not mean that in determining whether a regulation imposes an "undue burden" on the *Roe* right that we defer to the judgments made by state legislatures. "The point is, rather, that when we face a complex problem with many hard questions and few easy answers we do well to pay careful attention to how the other branches of Government have addressed the same problem." Columbia Broadcasting System, Inc. v. Democratic National Committee (1973).

We must always be mindful that "[t]he Constitution does not compel a state to fine-tune its statutes so as to encourage or facilitate abortions. To the contrary, state action 'encouraging childbirth except in the most urgent circumstances' is 'rationally related to the legitimate government objective of protecting potential life.'" *Harris.*

. . . .

[Justice O'Connor then examined each of the regulations and found all were rationally related to the compelling governmental interest in preserving potential human life and did not impose "an undue burden" on the right to abortion.]

Editors' Notes

(1) **Query:** Both Powell and O'Connor claimed to be defenders of stare decisis. Which used it more properly? To what extent is that interpretive *technique* useful in settling the basic questions of *Akron*?

(2) **Query:** Did O'Connor use a fundamental rights *mode* of interpretation or did she use a variant of balancing? Or both? Are they in fact compatible with each other? Did O'Connor accept a woman's fundamental right to an

abortion? See fn. 1 to Powell's opinion for the Court. Did Powell himself use or merely presume a fundamental rights *mode* of interpretation?

(3) **Query:** To what extent were Powell and O'Connor debating the question of WHO shall interpret?

(4) **Query:** Powell, following *Roe,* said that government cannot impose a theory of when human life begins. But, by denying that a fetus is a person, do not *Roe* and *Akron* impose a theory, indeed a theory supposedly grounded in the Constitution, that at least until viability a fetus is not a human life?

(5) The Court decided two other abortion cases the same day as *Akron.* Planned Parenthood v. Ashcroft invalidated Missouri's requirement that abortions after 12 weeks of pregnancy be performed in hospitals but sustained, over the dissents of Justices Blackmun, Brennan, Marshall, and Stevens, provisions mandating: (1) a pathology report for each abortion; (2) the presence of a second physician where the fetus is viable; and (3) where "unemancipated minors" are involved, the written permission of one parent or guardian or of a juvenile court. Simopoulos v. Virginia sustained a state statute requiring that second trimester abortions be performed in a hospital or licensed clinic.

(6) For an elaboration of Justice O'Connor's argument that *Roe* is at war with itself, see Daniel Callahan, "How Technology is Reframing the Abortion Debate," 16 *Hastings Center Report* 33 (1986).

"[T]he presumption of innocence . . . has no application to a determination of the rights of a pretrial detainee during his confinement before his trial has even begun."

BELL v. WOLFISH

441 U.S. 520, 99 S.Ct. 1861, 60 L.Ed.2d 447 (1979).

"Pre-trial detainees," who are typically people accused of crimes but unable to post bail, being held at the federal government's Metropolitan Correction Center (MCC) in New York City, which also houses convicted prisoners, brought a class action seeking to enjoin certain policies of the institution as depriving them of their liberty without due process and of violating the "cruel and unusual punishments" clause of the Eighth Amendment. The U.S. district court—upheld by the Court of Appeals for the Second Circuit solely on grounds of due process—enjoined the MCC from (1) "double bunking"—placing two detainees in a cell designed for one; (2) not allowing detainees to receive books unless sent directly from a publisher or book club; (3) blocking packages containing food or personal items; (4) requiring detainees to leave their cells when guards conducted their unannounced searches of those cells; and (5) subjecting detainees to a "strip search" that included visual examination of "body cavities" after they had met with visitors, even under closely supervised conditions. The Court of Appeals ruled that the MCC failed to show a "compelling necessity" for such repressive measures. The federal government obtained certiorari.

Mr. Justice **REHNQUIST** delivered the opinion of the Court. . . .

II . . .

A

The presumption of innocence is a doctrine that allocates the burden of proof in criminal trials; it also may serve as an admonishment to the jury to judge an accused's guilt or innocence solely on the evidence adduced at trial and not on the basis of suspicions that may arise from the fact of his arrest, indictment, or custody, or from other matters not introduced as proof at trial. Taylor v. Kentucky (1978); see Estelle v. Williams (1976); In re Winship (1970); 9 J. Wigmore, Evidence § 2511 (3d ed. 1940). . . . Without question, the presumption of innocence plays an important role in our criminal justice system. . . . But it has no application to a determination of the rights of a pretrial detainee during confinement before his trial has even begun.

. . . We do not doubt that the Due Process Clause protects a detainee from certain conditions and restrictions of pretrial detainment. Nonetheless, that Clause provides no basis for application of a compelling-necessity standard to conditions of pretrial confinement that are not alleged to infringe any other, more specific guarantee of the Constitution.

. . . [W]hat is at issue when an aspect of pretrial detention that is not alleged to violate any express guarantee of the Constitution is challenged, is the detainee's right to be free from punishment and his understandable desire to be as comfortable as possible during his confinement, both of which may conceivably coalesce at some point.

. . . [T]his desire simply does not rise to the level of those fundamental liberty interests delineated in cases such as Roe v. Wade (1973); Eisenstadt v. Baird (1972); Stanley v. Illinois (1972); Griswold v. Connecticut (1965); Meyer v. Nebraska (1923).

B

In evaluating the constitutionality of conditions or restrictions of pretrial detention that implicate only the protection against deprivation of liberty without due process of law, we think that the proper inquiry is whether those conditions amount to punishment of the detainee. For under the Due Process Clause, a detainee may not be punished prior to an adjudication of guilt in accordance with due process of law. . . .

. . . Absent a showing of an expressed intent to punish on the part of detention facility officials, that determination generally will turn on "whether an alternative purpose to which [the restriction] may rationally be connected is assignable for it, and whether it appears excessive in relation to the alternative purpose assigned [to it]." Kennedy v. Mendoza-Martinez [1963]. Thus, if a particular condition or restriction of pretrial detention is reasonably related to a legitimate governmental objective, it does not, without more, amount to "punishment." Conversely, if a restriction or condition is not reasonably related to a legitimate goal—if it is arbitrary or purposeless—a court permissibly may infer that the purpose of the governmental action is punishment that may not constitutionally be inflicted upon detainees qua detainees. Courts must be mindful that these inquiries spring from constitutional requirements and that judicial answers to them must reflect that fact rather than a court's idea of how best to operate a detention facility.

One further point requires discussion. The petitioners assert, and respondents concede, that the "essential objective of pretrial confine-ment is to insure the detainees' presence at trial." While this interest undoubtedly justifies the original decision to confine an individual in some manner, we do not accept respondents' argument that the Govern-ment's interest in ensuring the detainee's presence at trial is the *only* objective that may justify restraints and conditions once the decision is lawfully made to confine a person. . . . The Government also has legitimate interests that stem from its need to manage the facility in which the individual is detained. These legitimate operational con-cerns may require administrative measures that go beyond those that are, strictly speaking, necessary to ensure that the detainee shows up at trial. For example, the Government must be able to take steps to maintain security and order at the institution and make certain no weapons or illicit drugs reach detainees. Restraints that are reasona-bly related to the institution's interest in maintaining jail security do not, without more, constitute unconstitutional punishment, even if they are discomforting and are restrictions that the detainee would not have experienced had he been released while awaiting trial. . . .

C

. . . [W]e are convinced as a matter of law that "double-bunking" as practiced at the MCC did not amount to punishment and did not, therefore, violate respondents' rights under the Due Process Clause of the Fifth Amendment. . . .

. . . We disagree with both the District Court and the Court of Appeals that there is some sort of "one man, one cell" principle lurking in the Due Process Clause of the Fifth Amendment. While confining a given number of people in a given amount of space in such a manner as to cause them to endure genuine privations and hardship over an extended period of time might raise serious questions under the Due Process Clause as to whether those conditions amounted to punishment, nothing even approaching such hardship is shown by this record. . . .

[The Court went on to hold rational: (1) the ban on receiving books unless sent by a publisher or book club because of the risks of drugs, weapons, or other contraband being hidden in the covers (moreover, MCC had its own library, and the ban was nondiscriminatory—that is, it was not related to the content of books, only to sources of shipment); (2) the ban on packages for similar reasons; and (3) the requirement that detainees remain outside their rooms during unannounced search-es.]

D

Inmates at all Bureau of Prisons facilities, including the MCC, are required to expose their body cavities for visual inspection as a part of a strip search conducted after every contact visit with a person from outside the institution.[1] Corrections officials testified that visual cavity searches were necessary not only to discover but also to deter the smuggling of weapons, drugs, and other contraband into the institution.

. . .

Admittedly, this practice instinctively gives us the most pause. However, assuming for present purposes that inmates, both convicted prisoners and pretrial detainees, retain some Fourth Amendment rights upon commitment to a corrections facility, we nonetheless conclude that these searches do not violate that Amendment. The Fourth Amendment prohibits only unreasonable searches, and under the cir-cumstances, we do not believe that these searches are unreasonable.

The test of reasonableness under the Fourth Amendment is not capable of precise definition or mechanical application. In each case it requires a balancing of the need for the particular search against the invasion of personal rights that the search entails. Courts must consid-er the scope of the particular intrusion, the manner in which it is conducted, the justification for initiating it, and the place in which it is conducted. A detention facility is a unique place fraught with serious security dangers. Smuggling of money, drugs, weapons, and other contraband is all too common an occurrence. And inmate attempts to secrete these items into the facility by concealing them in body cavities are documented in this record and in other cases. That there has been only one instance where an MCC inmate was discovered attempting to smuggle contraband into the institution on his person may be more a testament to the effectiveness of this search technique as a deterrent than to any lack of interest on the part of the inmates to secrete and import such items when the opportunity arises.

We do not underestimate the degree to which these searches may invade the personal privacy of inmates. Nor do we doubt . . . that on occasion a security guard may conduct the search in an abusive fashion. Such abuse cannot be condoned. The searches must be conducted in a reasonable manner. But we deal here with the question whether visual body-cavity inspections as contemplated by the MCC rules can *ever* be conducted on less than probable cause. Balancing the significant and legitimate security interests of the institution against the privacy interests of the inmates, we conclude that they can. . . .

[Reversed.]

---

1. If the inmate is a male, he must lift his genitals and bend over to spread his buttocks for visual inspection. The vaginal and anal cavities of female inmates also are visually inspected. The inmate is not touched by security personnel at any time during the *visual* search procedure. [Footnote by the Court.]

Mr. Justice **POWELL,** concurring in part and dissenting in part.

I join the opinion of the Court except the discussion and holding with respect to body-cavity searches. In view of the serious intrusion on one's privacy occasioned by such a search, I think at least some level of cause, such as a reasonable suspicion, should be required to justify the anal and genital searches described in this case. I therefore dissent on this issue.

Mr. Justice **MARSHALL,** dissenting.

The Court holds that the Government may burden pretrial detainees with almost any restriction, provided detention officials do not proclaim a punitive intent or impose conditions that are "arbitrary or purposeless." As if this standard were not sufficiently ineffectual, the Court dilutes it further by according virtually unlimited deference to detention officials' justifications for particular impositions. Conspicuously lacking from this analysis is any meaningful consideration of the most relevant factor, the impact that restrictions may have on inmates. Such an approach is unsupportable given that all of these detainees are presumptively innocent and many are confined solely because they cannot afford bail.

In my view, the Court's holding . . . precludes effective judicial review of the conditions of pretrial confinement. More fundamentally, I believe the proper inquiry in this context is not whether a particular restraint can be labeled "punishment." Rather, as with other due process challenges, the inquiry should be whether the governmental interests served by any given restriction outweigh the individual deprivations suffered.

I . . .

B

Although the Court professes to go beyond the direct inquiry regarding intent and to determine whether a particular imposition is rationally related to a nonpunitive purpose, this exercise is at best a formality. Almost any restriction on detainees, including, as the Court concedes, chains and shackles, can be found to have some rational relation to institutional security, or more broadly, to "the effective management of the detention facility." Yet this toothless standard applies irrespective of the excessiveness of the restraint or the nature of the rights infringed.

Moreover, the Court has not in fact reviewed the rationality of detention officials' decisions. . . . Instead, the majority affords "wide-ranging" deference to those officials "in the adoption and execution of policies and practices that in their judgment are needed to preserve internal order and discipline and to maintain institutional security." Reasoning that security considerations in pretrial detention facilities are little different than in prisons, the Court concludes that cases requiring substantial deference to prison administrators' determinations on security-related issues are equally applicable in the present context.

Yet as the Court implicitly acknowledges, the rights of detainees, who have not been adjudicated guilty of a crime, are necessarily more extensive than those of prisoners "who have been found to have violated one or more of the criminal laws established by society for its orderly governance." Jones v. North Carolina Prisoners' Union (1977). Judicial tolerance of substantial impositions on detainees must be concomitantly less. However, by blindly deferring to administrative judgments on the rational basis for particular restrictions, the Court effectively delegates to detention officials the decision whether pretrial detainees have been punished. This, in my view, is an abdication of an unquestionably judicial function.

II

Even had the Court properly applied the punishment test, I could not agree to its use in this context. It simply does not advance analysis to determine whether a given deprivation imposed on detainees constitutes "punishment." For in terms of the nature of the imposition and the impact on detainees, pretrial incarceration, although necessary to secure defendants' presence at trial, is essentially indistinguishable from punishment. The detainee is involuntarily confined and deprived of the freedom "to be with his family and friends and to form the other enduring attachments of normal life," Morrissey v. Brewer (1972). Indeed, this Court has previously recognized that incarceration is an "infamous punishment." Flemming v. Nestor [1960]; see also Wong Wing v. United States (1896); Ingraham v. Wright (1977). . . .

A test that balances the deprivations involved against the state interests assertedly served would be more consistent with the import of the Due Process Clause. Such an approach would be sensitive to the tangible physical and psychological harm that a particular disability inflicts on detainees and to the nature of the less tangible, but significant, individual interests at stake. The greater the imposition on detainees, the heavier the burden of justification the Government would bear. See Bates v. Little Rock [1960].

When assessing the restrictions on detainees, we must consider the cumulative impact of restraints imposed during confinement. Incarceration of itself clearly represents a profound infringement of liberty, and each additional imposition increases the severity of that initial deprivation. Since any restraint thus has a serious effect on detainees, I believe the Government must bear a more rigorous burden of justification than the rational-basis standard mandates. At a minimum, I would require a showing that a restriction is substantially necessary to jail administration. Where the imposition is of particular gravity, that is, where it implicates interests of fundamental importance or inflicts significant harms, the Government should demonstrate that the restriction serves a compelling necessity of jail administration.

[Marshall argued that the trial court should conduct further hearings on double bunking but that the restrictions on receiving books and packages as well as the way in which searches of cells were conducted all failed the proper constitutional test.]

III . . .

D

In my view, the body-cavity searches of MCC inmates represent one of the most grievous offenses against personal dignity and common decency.   After every contact visit with someone from outside the facility, including defense attorneys, an inmate must remove all of his or her clothing, bend over, spread the buttocks, and display the anal cavity for inspection by a correctional officer.   Women inmates must assume a suitable posture for vaginal inspection, while men must raise their genitals.   And, as the Court neglects to note, because of time pressures, this humiliating spectacle is frequently conducted in the presence of other inmates.

The District Court found that the stripping was "unpleasant, embarrassing, and humiliating."   A psychiatrist testified that the practice placed inmates in the most degrading position possible, a conclusion amply corroborated by the testimony of the inmates themselves.   There was evidence, moreover, that these searches engendered among detainees fears of sexual assault, were the occasion for actual threats of physical abuse by guards, and caused some inmates to forgo personal visits.

Not surprisingly, the Government asserts a security justification for such inspections.   These searches are necessary, it argues, to prevent inmates from smuggling contraband into the facility.   In crediting this justification despite the contrary findings of the two courts below, the Court overlooks the critical facts.   As respondents point out, inmates are required to wear one-piece jumpsuits with zippers in the front.   To insert an object into the vaginal or anal cavity, an inmate would have to remove the jumpsuit, at least from the upper torso.   Since contact visits occur in a glass enclosed room and are continuously monitored by corrections officers, such a feat would seem extraordinarily difficult.   There was medical testimony, moreover, that inserting an object into the rectum is painful and "would require time and opportunity which is not available in the visiting areas," and that visual inspection would probably not detect an object once inserted.   Additionally, before entering the visiting room, visitors and their packages are searched thoroughly by a metal detector and fluoroscope, and by hand.   Correction officers may require that visitors leave packages or handbags with guards until the visit is over.   Only by blinding itself to the facts presented on this record can the Court accept the Government's security rationale.

Without question, these searches are an imposition of sufficient gravity to invoke the compelling-necessity standard.   It is equally indisputable that they cannot meet that standard.   Indeed, the procedure is so unnecessarily degrading that it "shocks the conscience." Rochin v. California (1952).   Even in *Rochin,* the police had reason to believe that the petitioner had swallowed contraband. Here, the searches are employed absent any suspicion of wrongdoing. . . .

Mr. Justice **STEVENS**, with whom Mr. Justice **BRENNAN** joins, dissenting.

This is not an equal protection case. An empirical judgment that most persons formally accused of criminal conduct are probably guilty would provide a rational basis for a set of rules that treat them like convicts until they establish their innocence. No matter how rational such an approach might be . . . it is obnoxious to the concept of individual freedom protected by the Due Process Clause. If ever accepted in this country, it would work a fundamental change in the character of our free society.

Nor is this an Eighth Amendment case. That provision of the Constitution protects individuals convicted of crimes from punishment that is cruel and unusual. The pretrial detainees whose rights are at stake in this case, however, are innocent men and women who have been convicted of no crimes. Their claim is not that they have been subjected to cruel and unusual punishment in violation of the Eighth Amendment, but that to subject them to any form of punishment at all is an unconstitutional deprivation of their liberty.

This is a due process case. The most significant—and I venture to suggest the most enduring—part of the Court's opinion today is its recognition of this initial constitutional premise. The Court squarely holds that "under the Due Process Clause, a detainee may not be punished prior to an adjudication of guilt in accordance with due process of law."

This right to be free of punishment is not expressly embodied in any provision in the Bill of Rights. Nor is the source of this right found in any statute. The source of this fundamental freedom is the word "liberty" itself as used in the Due Process Clause, and as informed by "history, reason, the past course of decisions," and the judgment and experience of "those whom the Constitution entrusted" with interpreting that word. Anti-Fascist Committee v. McGrath (Frankfurter, J., concurring) [1952]. See Leis v. Flynt (Stevens, J., dissenting) [1979].

In my opinion, this latter proposition is obvious and indisputable. Nonetheless, it is worthy of emphasis because the Court has now accepted it in principle. In recent years, the Court has mistakenly implied that the concept of liberty encompasses only those rights that are either created by statute or regulation or are protected by an express provision of the Bill of Rights. Today, however, without the help of any statute, regulation, or express provision of the Constitution, the Court has derived the innocent person's right not to be punished from the Due Process Clause itself. It has accordingly abandoned its parsimonious definition of the "liberty" protected by the majestic words of the Clause. I concur in that abandonment. It is with regard to the scope of this fundamental right that we part company. . . .

I . . .

[A] careful reading of the Court's opinion reveals that it has attenuated the detainee's constitutional protection against punishment into nothing more than a prohibition against irrational classifications or barbaric treatment. Having recognized in theory that the source of that protection is the Due Process Clause, the Court has in practice defined its scope in the far more permissive terms of equal protection and Eighth Amendment analysis. . . .

II

When measured against an objective standard, it is clear that the four rules discussed in . . . the Court's opinion are punitive in character. All of these rules were designed to forestall the potential harm that might result from smuggling money, drugs, or weapons into the institution. Such items, it is feared, might be secreted in hardcover books, packages of food or clothing, or body cavities. . . .

There is no question that jail administrators have a legitimate interest in preventing smuggling. But it is equally clear that that interest is being served here in a way that punishes many if not all of the detainees.

The challenged practices concededly deprive detainees of fundamental rights and privileges of citizenship beyond simply the right to leave. The Court recognizes this premise, but it dismisses its significance by asserting that detainees may be subjected to the " 'withdrawal or limitation' " of fundamental rights. I disagree. The withdrawal of rights is itself among the most basic punishments that society can exact, for such a withdrawal qualifies the subject's citizenship and violates his dignity. Without question that kind of harm is an "affirmative disability" that "has historically been regarded as a punishment." . . .

In contrast to these severe harms to the individual, the interests served by these rules appear insubstantial. . . .

The body-cavity search—clearly the greatest personal indignity— may be the least justifiable measure of all. After every contact visit a body-cavity search is mandated by the rule. The District Court's finding that these searches have failed in practice to produce any demonstrable improvement in security is hardly surprising. Detainees and their visitors are in full view during all visits, and are fully clad. To insert contraband in one's private body cavities during such a visit would indeed be "an imposing challenge to nerves and agility." . . . Moreover, as the District Court explicitly found, less severe alternatives are available to ensure that contraband is not transferred during visits. Weapons and other dangerous instruments, the items of greatest legitimate concern, may be discovered by the use of metal detecting devices or other equipment commonly used for airline security. In addition, inmates are required, even apart from the body-cavity searches, to disrobe, to have their clothing inspected, and to present open hands and arms to reveal the absence of any concealed objects. These alternative procedures, the District Court found, "amply satisf[y]" the demands of security. In my judgment, there is no basis in this record to disagree.

It may well be, as the Court finds, that the rules at issue here were not adopted by administrators eager to punish those detained at MCC. The rules can all be explained as the easiest way for administrators to ensure security in the jail. But the easiest course for jail officials is not always one that our Constitution allows them to take. If fundamental rights are withdrawn and severe harms are indiscriminately inflicted on detainees merely to secure minimal savings in time and effort for administrators, the guarantee of due process is violated.

In my judgment, each of the rules at issue here is unconstitutional. The four rules do indiscriminately inflict harm on all pretrial detainees in MCC. They are all either unnecessary or excessively harmful, particularly when judged against our historic respect for the dignity of the free citizen. . . . Absent probable cause to believe that a specific individual detainee poses a special security risk, none of these practices would be considered necessary, or even arguably reasonable, if the pretrial detainees were confined in a facility separate and apart from convicted prisoners. . . .

Editors' Notes

(1) **Query:** Both Rehnquist and Marshall claimed to use the *technique* of balancing. How do their tests differ? How does each differ from that used by Stevens? How does Marshall's differ, if at all, from that which he tried to persuade the Court to apply when faced with questions of legislative classifications affecting fundamental rights?

(2) **Query:** Would an argument from plain words by either the Court or the dissenters be persuasive in this case? To what extent did Stevens directly, and Rehnquist and Marshall indirectly, address the WHAT interrogative?

(3) **Query:** Was Marshall correct when he argued that Rehnquist's opinion abdicates to prison administrators the authority to interpret the Constitution for prisoners and detainees? How does Rehnquist's implicit view in *Wolfish* about WHO should interpret compare with the views he expressed in his article "The Notion of a Living Constitution" (reprinted above, p. 163)?

(4) Hudson v. Palmer (1984) held, 5–4, that "privacy rights for prisoners in their individual cells simply cannot be reconciled with the concept of incarceration and the needs and objectives of penal institutions."

V. THE RIGHT TO FAMILY INTEGRITY

"The child is not the mere creature of the state. . . ."

PIERCE v. SOCIETY OF SISTERS
268 U.S. 510, 45 S.Ct. 571, 69 L.Ed. 1070 (1925).

In 1922 Oregon enacted a law that required parents to send all their children between the ages of 8 and 16, with limited exceptions for those who were not normal or were receiving private instruction, to public schools. The Society of Sisters of Holy Names, a Catholic religious order that operated several parochial schools in Oregon, and the Hill Military Academy, a private school, brought suit in a federal district court for an injunction against enforcement of the act. The state defended the statute as a reasonable means of insuring that its citizens would be educated and as a means of insuring separation of church and state. The district court granted the writ and Oregon appealed.

Mr. Justice **McREYNOLDS** delivered the opinion of the Court. . . .

Under the doctrine of Meyer v. Nebraska [1923], we think it entirely plain that the Act of 1922 unreasonably interferes with the liberty of parents and guardians to direct the upbringing and education of children under their control. As often heretofore pointed out, rights guaranteed by the Constitution may not be abridged by legislation which has no reasonable relation to some purpose within the competency of the state. The fundamental theory upon which all governments in this Union repose excludes any general power of the state to standardize its children by forcing them to accept instruction from public teachers only. The child is not the mere creature of the state; those who nurture him and direct his destiny have the right, coupled with the high duty, to recognize and prepare him for additional obligations.

Appellees are corporations, and therefore, it is said, they cannot claim for themselves the liberty which the 14th Amendment guarantees. Accepted in the proper sense, this is true. But they have business and property for which they claim protection. These are threatened with destruction through the unwarranted compulsion which appellants are exercising over present and prospective patrons of their schools. And this court has gone very far to protect against loss threatened by such action. Truax v. Raich [1915]; Truax v. Corrigan [1921]; Terrace v. Thompson [1923]. . . .

[Affirmed.]

Editors' Notes

(1) The decision was apparently unanimous. Holmes did not repeat his objections to Meyer v. Nebraska (1923; reprinted above, p. 1091). He may have followed his usual practice of not dissenting a second time.

(2) McReynolds apparently based the decision on the rights of parents to educate their children, but the suit was brought by private corporations, as he conceded. Obviously, the question of standing gave neither him nor his brethren any pause.

(3) Like *Meyer, Pierce* provides a marvelous example of the merger of economic liberty with other kinds of personal liberty under the general concept of individual autonomy.

"Acting to guard the general interest in youth's well being, the state as parens patriae may restrict the parent's control by requiring school attendance, regulating or prohibiting child labor, and in many other ways."

PRINCE v. MASSACHUSETTS
312 U.S. 158, 64 S.Ct. 438, 88 L.Ed. 645 (1944).

This opinion, upholding the constitutionality of a state law that forbade minors to sell newspapers or periodicals on the public streets even against a challenge by a Jehovah's Witness missionary who allowed her young ward to accompany her while distributing religious literature, is reprinted above at p. 1034.

"[T]he Constitution protects the sanctity of the family precisely because the institution of the family is deeply rooted in this Nation's history and tradition."—Justice POWELL

"The Judiciary . . . is most vulnerable and comes nearest to illegitimacy when it deals with judge-made constitutional law having little or no cognizable roots in the language or even the design of the Constitution."—Justice WHITE

MOORE v. EAST CLEVELAND
431 U.S. 494, 97 S.Ct. 1932, 52 L.Ed.2d 531 (1977)

An ordinance of East Cleveland, Ohio, limited occupancy of each dwelling unit to members of a single family, with "family" defined essentially as the nuclear family of parents and their children. The ordinance also provided an administrative procedure to request variances. Without following this procedure, Inez Moore shared her home with her son and two grandsons who were cousins rather than brothers. She was convicted for violating the ordinance and state appellate courts affirmed her conviction. She then appealed to the U.S. Supreme Court.

Mr. Justice **POWELL** announced the judgment of the Court and delivered an opinion in which Mr. Justice **BRENNAN,** Mr. Justice **MARSHALL,** and Mr. Justice **BLACKMUN** joined. . . .

II

The city argues that our decision in Village of Belle Terre v. Boraas (1974) requires us to sustain the ordinance attacked here. Belle Terre, like East Cleveland, imposed limits on the types of groups that could occupy a single dwelling unit. Applying the constitutional standard announced in this Court's leading land-use case, Euclid v. Ambler (1926), we sustained the Belle Terre ordinance on the ground that it bore a rational relationship to permissible state objectives.

But one overriding factor sets this case apart from *Belle Terre*. The ordinance there affected only *unrelated* individuals. It expressly allowed all who were related by "blood, adoption, or marriage" to live together, and in sustaining the ordinance we were careful to note that it promoted "family needs" and "family values." . . . East Cleveland, in contrast, has chosen to regulate the occupancy of its housing by slicing deeply into the family itself. This is no mere incidental result of the ordinance. On its face it selects certain categories of relatives who may live together and declares that others may not. . . .

When a city undertakes such intrusive regulation of the family, neither *Belle Terre* nor *Euclid* governs; the usual judicial deference to the legislature is inappropriate. "This Court has long recognized that freedom of personal choice in matters of marriage and family life is one of the liberties protected by the Due Process Clause of the Fourteenth Amendment." Cleveland Board of Education v. LaFleur (1974). A host of cases, tracing their lineage to Meyer v. Nebraska (1923) and Pierce v. Society of Sisters (1925), have consistently acknowledged a "private realm of family life which the state cannot enter." Prince v. Massachusetts (1944). See, e.g., Roe v. Wade (1973); Wisconsin v. Yoder (1972); Stanley v. Illinois (1972); Ginsburg v. New York (1968); Griswold v. Connecticut (1965); Poe v. Ullman (1961) (Harlan, J., dissenting); cf. Loving v. Virginia (1967); May v. Anderson (1953); Skinner v. Oklahoma (1942). Of course, the family is not beyond regulation. See *Prince*. But when the government intrudes on choices concerning family living arrangements, this Court must examine carefully the importance of the governmental interests advanced and the extent to which they are served by the challenged regulation. See *Poe* (Harlan, J., dissenting).

When thus examined, this ordinance cannot survive. The city seeks to justify it as a means of preventing overcrowding, minimizing traffic and parking congestion, and avoiding an undue financial burden on East Cleveland's school system. Although these are legitimate goals, the ordinance before us serves them marginally, at best. For example, the ordinance permits any family consisting only of husband, wife, and unmarried children to live together, even if the family contains a half dozen licensed drivers, each with his or her own car. At the same time it forbids an adult brother and sister to share a household, even if both faithfully use public transportation. . . .

III

The city would distinguish the cases based on *Meyer* and *Pierce.* It . . . suggests that any constitutional right to live together as a family extends only to the nuclear family—essentially a couple and its dependent children.

To be sure, these cases did not expressly consider the family relationship presented here. . . . But unless we close our eyes to the basic reasons why certain rights associated with the family have been accorded shelter under the Fourteenth Amendment's Due Process Clause, we cannot avoid applying the force and rationale of these precedents to the family choice involved in this case.

Understanding those reasons requires careful attention to this Court's function under the Due Process Clause. Mr. Justice Harlan described it eloquently:

> Due process has not been reduced to any formula; its content cannot be determined by reference to any code. The best that can be said is that . . . it has represented the balance which our Nation, built upon postulates of respect for the liberty of the individual, has struck between that liberty and the demands of organized society. If the supplying of content to this Constitutional concept has of necessity been a rational process, it certainly has not been one where judges have felt free to roam where unguided speculation might take them. The balance . . . is the balance struck by this country, having regard to what history teaches are the traditions from which it developed as well as the traditions from which it broke. That tradition is a living thing. A decision of this Court which radically departs from it could not long survive, while a decision which builds on what has survived is likely to be sound. No formula could serve as a substitute, in this area, for judgment and restraint.
>
> . . . [T]he full scope of the liberty guaranteed by the Due Process Clause cannot be found in or limited by the precise terms of the specific guarantees elsewhere provided in the Constitution. This 'liberty' is not a series of isolated points pricked out in terms of the taking of property; the freedom of speech, press, and religion; the right to keep and bear arms; the freedom from unreasonable searches and seizures; and so on. It is a rational continuum which, broadly speaking, includes a freedom from all substantial arbitrary impositions and purposeless restraints, . . . and which also recognizes, what a reasonable and sensitive judgment must, that certain interests require particularly careful scrutiny of the state needs asserted to justify their abridgment. *Poe* (dissenting opinion).

Substantive due process has at times been a treacherous field for this Court. There *are* risks when the judicial branch gives enhanced protection to certain substantive liberties without the guidance of the more specific provisions of the Bill of Rights. As the history of the Lochner [v. New York (1905)] era demonstrates, there is reason for concern lest the only limits to such judicial intervention become the predilections of those who happen at the time to be Members of this Court. That history counsels caution and restraint. But it does not counsel abandonment, nor does it require what the city urges here:

cutting off any protection of family rights at the first convenient, if arbitrary boundary—the boundary of the nuclear family.

Appropriate limits on substantive due process come not from drawing arbitrary lines but rather from careful "respect for the teachings of history [and] solid recognition of the basic values that underlie our society." *Griswold* (Harlan, J., concurring). Our decisions establish that the Constitution protects the sanctity of the family precisely because the institution of the family is deeply rooted in this Nation's history and tradition. It is through the family that we inculcate and pass down many of our most cherished values, moral and cultural.

Ours is by no means a tradition limited to respect for the bonds uniting the members of the nuclear family. The tradition of uncles, aunts, cousins, and especially grandparents sharing a household along with parents and children has roots equally venerable and equally deserving of constitutional recognition. . . . Even if conditions of modern society have brought about a decline in extended family households, they have not erased the accumulated wisdom of civilization, gained over the centuries and honored throughout our history, that supports a larger conception of the family. . . .

Whether or not such a household is established because of personal tragedy, the choice of relatives in this degree of kinship to live together may not lightly be denied by the State. *Pierce* struck down an Oregon law requiring all children to attend the State's public schools, holding that the Constitution "excludes any general power of the State to standardize its children by forcing them to accept instruction from public teachers only." By the same token the Constitution prevents East Cleveland from standardizing its children—and its adults—by forcing all to live in certain narrowly defined family patterns.

Reversed.

Mr. Justice **BRENNAN,** with whom Mr. Justice **MARSHALL** joins, concurring. . . .

Mr. Justice **STEVENS** concurring in the judgment.

. . . [T]he critical question . . . is whether East Cleveland's housing ordinance is a permissible restriction on appellant's right to use her own property as she sees fit.

Long before the original States adopted the Constitution, the common law protected an owner's right to decide how best to use his own property. This basic right has always been limited by the law of nuisance which proscribes uses that impair the enjoyment of other property in the vicinity. But the question whether an individual owner's use could be further limited by a municipality's comprehensive zoning plan was not finally decided until this century.

The holding in *Euclid*, that a city could use its police power . . . to create and implement a comprehensive plan for the use . . . of land in the community, vastly diminished the rights of individual property owners. It did not, however, totally extinguish those rights. On the contrary, that case expressly recognized that the broad zoning power must be exercised within constitutional limits. . . .

There appears to be no precedent for an ordinance which excludes any of an owner's relatives from the group of persons who may occupy his residence on a permanent basis. Nor does there appear to be any justification for such a restriction on an owner's use of his property. The city has failed totally to explain the need for a rule which would allow a homeowner to have two grandchildren live with her if they are brothers, but not if they are cousins. Since this ordinance has not been shown to have any "substantial relation to the public health, safety, morals or general welfare" of the city of East Cleveland, and since it cuts so deeply into a fundamental right normally associated with the ownership of residential property—that of an owner to decide who may reside on his or her property—it must fall under the limited standard of review of zoning decisions which this Court preserved in *Euclid*. Under that standard, East Cleveland's unprecedented ordinance constitutes a taking of property without due process and without just compensation. . . .

Mr. Chief Justice **BURGER,** dissenting.

It is unnecessary for me to reach the difficult constitutional issue this case presents. Appellant's deliberate refusal to use a plainly adequate administrative remedy provided by the city should foreclose her from pressing in this Court any constitutional objections to the city's zoning ordinance. Considerations of federalism and comity, as well as the finite capacity of federal courts, support this position. In courts, as in hospitals, two bodies cannot occupy the same space at the same time; when any case comes here which could have been disposed of long ago at the local level, it takes the place of some other case, which, having no alternative remedy, might well have been given [that place]. . . .

. . . [T]here is [a] powerful additional reason why exhaustion should be enforced in this case. We deal here with federal judicial review of an administrative determination by a subdivision of the State of Ohio. When the question before a federal court is whether to enforce exhaustion of state administrative remedies, interests of federalism and comity make the analysis strikingly similar to that appropriate when the question is whether federal courts should abstain from interference with ongoing state judicial proceedings. In both situations federal courts are being requested to act in ways lacking deference to, and perhaps harmful to, important state interests in order to vindicate rights which can be protected in the state system as well as in the federal. The policies underlying this Court's refusals to jeopardize important state objectives needlessly in Huffman v. Pursue, Ltd. [1975]; Juidice v. Vail (1977); and Trainor v. Hernandez (1977) argue strongly against action which encourages evasion and undermining of other important state interests embodied in regulatory procedures.

When the State asserts its sovereignty through the administrative process, no less than when it proceeds judicially, "federal courts . . . should abide by standards of restraint that go well beyond those of private equity jurisprudence." *Huffman;* cf. Younger v. Harris (1971). . . . Where, as here, state law affords an appropriate "doorstep" vehicle for vindication of the claims underlying those rights, federal courts should not be called upon unless those remedies have been utilized. No litigant has a right to force a constitutional adjudication by eschewing the only forum in which adequate nonconstitutional relief is possible. . . . We should now make clear that the finite resources of this Court are not available unless the litigant has first pursued all adequate and available administrative remedies. . . .

Mr. Justice **STEWART,** with whom Mr. Justice **REHNQUIST** joins, dissenting. . . .

The *Belle Terre* decision . . . disposes of the appellant's contentions to the extent they focus not on her blood relationships with her sons and grandsons but on more general notions about the "privacy of the home." . . .

To suggest that the biological fact of common ancestry necessarily gives related persons constitutional rights of association superior to those of unrelated persons is to misunderstand the nature of the associational freedoms that the Constitution has been understood to protect. Freedom of association has been constitutionally recognized because it is often indispensable to effectuation of explicit First Amendment guarantees. See NAACP v. Alabama [1958]; Bates v. Little Rock [1960]; Shelton v. Tucker [1960]; NAACP v. Button [1963]; Railroad Trainmen v. Virginia [1964]; Kusper v. Pontikes [1973]; cf. Edwards v. South Carolina [1963]. But the scope of the associational right, until now, at least, has been limited to the constitutional need that created it; obviously not every "association" is for First Amendment purposes or serves to promote the ideological freedom that the First Amendment was designed to protect.

The "association" in this case is not for any purpose relating to the promotion of speech, assembly, the press, or religion. And wherever the outer boundaries of constitutional protection of freedom of association may eventually turn out to be, they surely do not extend to those who assert no interest other than the gratification, convenience, and economy of sharing the same residence.

The appellant is considerably closer to the constitutional mark in asserting that the East Cleveland ordinance intrudes upon "the private realm of family life which the state cannot enter." *Prince.* Several decisions of the Court have identified specific aspects of what might broadly be termed "private family life" that are constitutionally protected against state interference. See, e.g., *Roe* (woman's right to decide whether to terminate pregnancy); *Loving* (freedom to marry person of another race); *Griswold*; Eisenstadt v. Baird [1972] (right to use contraceptives); *Pierce* (parents' right to send children to private schools); *Meyer* (parents' right to have children instructed in foreign language).

Although the appellant's desire to share a single-dwelling unit also involves "private family life" in a sense, that desire can hardly be equated with any of the interests protected in the cases just cited. . . .

. . . When the Court has found that the Fourteenth Amendment placed a substantive limitation on a State's power to regulate, it has been in those rare cases in which the personal interests at issue have been deemed "'implicit in the concept of ordered liberty.'" The interest that the appellant may have in permanently sharing a single kitchen and a suite of contiguous rooms with some of her relatives simply does not rise to that level. To equate this interest with the fundamental decisions to marry and to bear and raise children is to extend the limited substantive contours of the Due Process Clause beyond recognition. . . .

. . . I do not think East Cleveland's definition of "family" offends the Constitution. The city has undisputed power to ordain single-family residential occupancy. *Belle Terre*; *Euclid*. And that power plainly carries with it the power to say what a "family" is. Here the city has defined "family" to include not only father, mother, and dependent children, but several other close relatives as well. The definition is rationally designed to carry out the legitimate governmental purposes identified in the *Belle Terre* opinion. . . .

Mr. Justice **WHITE**, dissenting. . . .

I

The emphasis of the Due Process Clause is on "process." As Mr. Justice Harlan once observed, it has been "ably and insistently argued in response to what were felt to be abuses by this Court of its reviewing power," that the Due Process Clause should be limited "to a guarantee of procedural fairness." *Poe* (dissenting opinion). These arguments had seemed "persuasive" to Justices Brandeis and Holmes, Whitney v. California (1927), but they recognized that the Due Process Clause, by virtue of case-to-case "judicial inclusion and exclusion," Davidson v. New Orleans (1878), had been construed to proscribe matters of substance, as well as inadequate procedures, and to protect from invasion by the States "all fundamental rights comprised within the term liberty."

Mr. Justice Black also recognized that the Fourteenth Amendment had substantive as well as procedural content. But believing that its reach should not extend beyond the specific provisions of the Bill of Rights, see Adamson v. California (1947) (dissenting opinion), he never embraced the idea that the Due Process Clause empowered the courts to strike down merely unreasonable or arbitrary legislation, nor did he

accept Mr. Justice Harlan's consistent view. See Griswold v. Connecticut. Writing at length in dissent in *Poe*, Mr. Justice Harlan stated the
essence of his position. . . .

[Justice White quoted at length the same passage that Justice
Powell did, above, p. 106.]

This construction was far too open ended for Mr. Justice Black.
For him, *Meyer* and *Pierce* were as suspect as *Lochner*; Coppage v.
Kansas (1915); and Adkins v. Children's Hospital (1923). In his view,
Ferguson v. Skrupa (1963), should have finally disposed of them all.
But neither *Meyer* nor *Pierce* has been overruled, and recently there
have been decisions of the same genre—*Roe*; *Loving*; *Griswold*; and
Eisenstadt. Not all of these decisions purport to rest on substantive
due process grounds, but all represented substantial reinterpretations
of the Constitution.

Although the Court regularly proceeds on the assumption that the
Due Process Clause has more than a procedural dimension, we must
always bear in mind that the substantive content of the Clause is
suggested neither by its language nor by preconstitutional history; that
content is nothing more than the accumulated product of judicial
interpretation. . . . This is not to suggest . . . that any of these
cases should be overruled, or that the process by which they were
decided was illegitimate or even unacceptable, but only to underline
Mr. Justice Black's constant reminder to his colleagues that the Court
has no license to invalidate legislation which it thinks merely arbitrary
or unreasonable. . . .

. . . That the Court has ample precedent for the creation of new
constitutional rights should not lead it to repeat the process at will.
The Judiciary, including this Court, is the most vulnerable and comes
nearest to illegitimacy when it deals with judge-made constitutional
law having little or no cognizable roots in the language or even the
design of the Constitution. Realizing that the present construction of
the Due Process Clause represents a major judicial gloss on its terms, as
well as on the anticipation of the Framers, and that much of the
underpinning for the broad, substantive application of the Clause
disappeared in the conflict between the Executive and the Judiciary in
the 1930's and 1940's, the Court should be extremely reluctant to
breathe still further substantive content into the Due Process Clause so
as to strike down legislation adopted by a State or city to promote its
welfare. Whenever the Judiciary does so, it unavoidably pre-empts for
itself another part of the governance of the country without express
constitutional authority.

II . . .

It would not be consistent with prior cases to restrict the liberties
protected by the Due Process Clause to those fundamental interests
"implicit in the concept of ordered liberty." Palko v. Connecticut
(1937), from which this much-quoted phrase is taken, is not to the
contrary. *Palko* was a criminal case, and the issue was thus not
whether a protected liberty interest was at stake but what protective

process was "due" that interest. . . . Nor do I think the broader view of "liberty" is inconsistent with or foreclosed by the dicta in *Roe* and Paul v. Davis (1976). These cases at most assert that only fundamental liberties will be given *substantive* protection; and they may be understood as merely identifying certain fundamental interests that the Court has deemed deserving of a heightened degree of protection under the Due Process Clause. . . .

The term "liberty" is not, therefore, to be given a crabbed construction. I have no more difficulty than Mr. Justice Powell apparently does in concluding that appellant in this case properly asserts a liberty interest within the meaning of the Due Process Clause. The question is not one of liberty vel non. Rather, there being no procedural issue at stake, the issue is whether the precise interest involved . . . is entitled to such substantive protection under the Due Process Clause that this ordinance must be held invalid.

III

. . . I see the doctrine [of substantive due process] as taking several forms under the cases, each differing in the severity of review and the degree of protection offered to the individual. First, a court may merely assure itself that there is in fact a duly enacted law which proscribes the conduct sought to be prevented or sanctioned. In criminal cases, this approach is exemplified by the refusal of courts to enforce vague statutes that no reasonable person could understand. . . . There is no such problem here.

Second is the general principle that "liberty may not be interfered with, under the guise of protecting the public interest, by legislative action which is arbitrary or without reasonable relation to some purpose within the competency of the State to effect." *Meyer.* This means-end test appears to require that any statute restrictive of liberty have an ascertainable purpose and represent a rational means to achieve that purpose, whatever the nature of the liberty interest involved. This approach was part of the substantive due process doctrine prevalent earlier in the century, and it made serious inroads on the presumption of constitutionality supposedly accorded to state and federal legislation. But with Nebbia v. New York (1934), and other cases of the 1930's and 1940's such as West Coast Hotel Co. v. Parrish [1937] the courts came to demand far less from and to accord far more deference to legislative judgments. This was particularly true with respect to legislation seeking to control or regulate the economic life of the State or Nation. Even so, "while the legislative judgment on economic and business matters is 'well-nigh conclusive' . . . , it is not beyond judicial inquiry." *Poe* (Douglas, J., dissenting). . . .

There are various "liberties," however, which require that infringing legislation be given closer judicial scrutiny, not only with respect to existence of a purpose and the means employed, but also with respect to the importance of the purpose itself relative to the invaded interest. Some interests would appear almost impregnable to invasion, such as the freedoms of speech, press, and religion, and the freedom from cruel and unusual punishments. Other interests, for example, the right of association, the right to vote, and various claims sometimes referred to under the general rubric of the right to privacy, also weigh very heavily against state claims of authority to regulate. . . .

. . . Under our cases, the Due Process Clause extends substantial protection to various phases of family life, but none requires that the claim made here be sustained. I cannot believe that the interest in residing with more than one set of grandchildren is one that calls for any kind of heightened protection under the Due Process Clause. . . . The present claim is hardly one of which it could be said that "neither liberty nor justice would exist if it were sacrificed." *Palko.*

Mr. Justice Powell would apparently construe the Due Process Clause to protect from all but quite important state regulatory interests any right or privilege that in his estimate is deeply rooted in the country's traditions. For me, this suggests a far too expansive charter for this Court. . . . What the deeply rooted traditions of the country are is arguable; which of them deserve the protection of the Due Process Clause is even more debatable. The suggested view would broaden enormously the horizons of the Clause; and, if the interest involved here is any measure of what the States would be forbidden to regulate, the courts would be substantively weighing and very likely invalidating a wide range of measures that Congress and state legislatures think appropriate to respond to a changing economic and social order.

Mrs. Moore's interest in having the offspring of more than one dependent son live with her qualifies as a liberty protected by the Due Process Clause; but, because of the nature of that particular interest, the demands of the Clause are satisfied once the Court is assured that the challenged proscription is the product of a duly enacted or promulgated statute, ordinance, or regulation and that it is not wholly lacking in purpose or utility. . . .

Editors' Notes

(1) **Query:** Justice Stewart saw the right of association as limited to democratic purposes. What claims, if any, does constitutionalism have here?

(2) **Query:** At root, how different was Justice White's *mode* of constitutional interpretation from Powell's? From Stewart's? To what extent did Stevens avoid White's objections to Powell's reasoning?

(3) **Query:** Do the differences among the justices about HOW to interpret the Constitution depend on different views about WHAT is the Constitution and WHO shall interpret? Compare the tone of White's statement that "[t]he Judiciary . . . is most vulnerable and comes nearest to illegitimacy when it deals with judge-made constitutional law having little or no cognizable roots in the language or even the design of the Constitution" with the Court's claim in the Little Rock Case (Cooper v. Aaron [1958; reprinted above, p. 281]) that

"the federal judiciary is supreme in the exposition of the law of the Constitution."

(4) For the status of the family as a unit in American constitutional law and politics, see: Robert A. Burt, "The Constitution of the Family," 1979 *Sup. Ct.Rev.* 329; James S. Fishkin, *Justice, Equal Opportunity, and the Family* (New Haven, Conn.: Yale University Press, 1983); and Stanley N. Katz, "Legal History and Family History," 21 *Bost.C.L.Rev.* 1025 (1980); Laurence H. Tribe, *American Constitutional Law* (Mineola, N.Y.: Foundation Press, 1978), pp. 985–990.

(5) Questions of state power and family integrity have frequently arisen in the context of disputes about a woman's right to have an abortion. Planned Parenthood of Central Missouri v. Danforth (1976) invalidated a state requirement that a married woman obtain her husband's consent before obtaining an abortion, and Bellotti v. Baird (1976) struck down a state requirement that unmarried, minor females get parental consent. On the other hand, H.L. v. Matheson (1981) upheld Utah's requirement that, before performing an abortion on an unmarried minor, a doctor notify "if possible" her parents or husband. Taking the statute as on its face not applying to females who were "mature and emancipated," the Court said that " 'constitutional interpretation has consistently recognized the parents' claim to authority in their own household to direct the rearing of their children is basic in the structure of our society.' " (Quoting Ginsberg v. New York [1968].) The majority, speaking through Chief Justice Burger, found the statute served the important state interests of furthering "family integrity and protecting adolescents." Brennan, Marshall, and Blackmun dissented. They did not dispute the importance of the family as a traditional value, but warned that many families did not fit the ideal and that parental reaction, especially when the pregnancy was the result of incest, might result in physical and emotional abuse, withdrawal of financial support, or force the daughter either to have an abortion from an unlicensed person or bear the child to term.

"When a statutory classification significantly interferes with the exercise of a fundamental right, it cannot be upheld unless it is supported by sufficiently important state interests and is closely tailored to effectuate only those interests."

ZABLOCKI v. REDHAIL
434 U.S. 374, 98 S.Ct. 673, 54 L.Ed.2d 618 (1978).

This decision, striking down a state law that prohibited people who had fallen behind in court-ordered child support to marry, is reprinted above, at p. 890.

VI. THE RIGHT TO SEXUAL CHOICE

"[I]f the state has the burden of proving that it has a legitimate interest in the subject of the statute, or that the statute is rationally supportable, then Virginia has completely fulfilled this obligation."—Bryan, U.S. Senior Circuit Judge

"The judgment is affirmed."—U.S. Supreme Court

DOE v. COMMONWEALTH'S ATTORNEY
403 F.Supp. 1199 (E.D.Va.1975).

Two male homosexuals filed suit in a federal district court, attacking the constitutionality of § 18.1–212 of the Virginia Code, which made it a crime, even for consenting adults acting in private, to engage in homosexual relations. As then required by jurisdictional statutes, a special three-judge district court heard the case.

BRYAN, Senior Circuit Judge. . . .

Our decision is that on its face and in the circumstances here . . . [§ 18.1–212] is not unconstitutional. No judgment is made upon the wisdom or policy of the statute. It is simply that we cannot say that the statute offends the Bill of Rights or any other of the Amendments. . . .

I

Precedents cited to us as *contra* rest exclusively on the precept that the Constitution condemns State legislation that trespasses upon the privacy of the incidents of marriage, upon the sanctity of the home, or upon the nurture of family life. This and only this concern has been the justification for nullification of State regulation in this area. . . .

In Griswold v. Connecticut (1965) the Court has most recently announced its views on the question here. Striking down a State statute forbidding the use of contraceptives, the ruling was put on the right of marital privacy . . . and was also put on the sanctity of the home and family. . . .

That *Griswold* is premised on the right of privacy and that homosexual intimacy is denunciable by the State is unequivocally demonstrated by Mr. Justice Goldberg in his concurrence in his adoption of Mr. Justice Harlan's dissenting statement in Poe v. Ullman (1961):

> Adultery, *homosexuality* and the like are sexual intimacies *which the State forbids* . . . but the intimacy of husband and wife is necessarily an essential and accepted feature of the institution of marriage, an institution which the State not only must allow, but which always and in every age it has fostered and protected. *It is one thing when the State exerts its power either to forbid extra-marital sexuality* . . . or to say who may marry, but it is quite another when, having acknowledged a marriage and the intimacies inherent in it, it undertakes to

regulate by means of the criminal law the details of that intimacy. (Emphasis added.)

Equally forceful is the succeeding paragraph of Justice Harlan:

[T]he intrusion of the whole machinery of the criminal law into the very heart of marital privacy, requiring husband and wife to render account before a criminal tribunal of their uses of that intimacy is surely *a very different thing indeed from punishing those who establish intimacies which the law has always forbidden and which can have no claim to social protection.* . . . (Emphasis added.)

Justice Harlan's words are nonetheless commanding merely because they were written in dissent. To begin with . . . they were authentically approved in *Griswold.* Moreover, he was not differing with the majority there on the merits of the substantive case but only as to the procedural reason of its dismissal. At all events, the Justice's exegesis is that of a jurist of widely acknowledged superior stature and weighty whatever its context.

With his standing what he had further to say in *Poe* is worthy of high regard. On the plaintiffs' effort presently to shield the practice of homosexuality from State incrimination by according it immunity when committed in private as against public exercise, the Justice said this:

Indeed to attempt a line between public behavior and that which is purely consensual or solitary would be to withdraw from community concern a range of subjects with which every society in civilized times has found it necessary to deal. The laws regarding marriage which provide both when the sexual powers may be used and the legal and societal context in which children are born and brought up, as well as *laws forbidding adultery, fornication and homosexual practices which express the negative of the proposition,* confining sexuality to lawful marriage, form a pattern so deeply pressed into the substance of our social life that any Constitutional doctrine in this area must build upon that basis. (Emphasis added.) . . .

Many states have long had, and still have, statutes and decisional law criminalizing conduct depicted in the Virginia legislation. . . .

II

With no authoritative judicial bar to the proscription of homosexuality—since it is obviously no portion of marriage, home or family life—the next question is whether there is any ground for barring Virginia from branding it as criminal. If a State determines that punishment therefor, even when committed in the home, is appropriate in the promotion of morality and decency, it is not for the courts to say that the State is not free to do so. In short, it is an inquiry addressable only to the State's Legislature.

Furthermore, if the State has the burden of proving that it has a legitimate interest in the subject of the statute or that the statute is rationally supportable, Virginia has completely fulfilled this obligation.

Fundamentally the State action is simply directed to the suppression of crime, whether committed in public or in private.   .   .   .

Moreover, to sustain its action, the State is not required to show that moral delinquency actually results from homosexuality.   It is enough for upholding the legislation to establish that the conduct is likely to end in a contribution to moral delinquency.   .   .   .

Although a questionable law is not removed from question by the lapse of any prescriptive period, the longevity of the Virginia statute does testify to the State's interest and its legitimacy.   It   .   .   . has ancestry going back to Judaic and Christian law.   The immediate parentage may be readily traced to the Code of Virginia of 1792.   All the while the law has been kept alive, as evidenced by the periodic amendments.   .   .   .

In sum, we believe that the sodomy statute   .   .   . has rational basis of State interest demonstrably legitimate and mirrored in the cited decisional law of the Supreme Court.   Indeed, the Court has treated as free of infirmity a State law with a background similar to the Virginia enactment in suit.   .   .   .

MERHIGE, District Judge, dissenting.

   .   .   . In   .   .   . the absence of any legitimate interest or rational basis to support the statute's application we must, without regard to our own proclivities and reluctance to judicially bar the state proscription of homosexuality, hold the statute as it applies to the plaintiffs to be violative of their rights under the Due Process Clause of the Fourteenth Amendment.   .   .   .   The Supreme Court decision in *Griswold* is   .   .   . premised on the right of privacy, but I fear my brothers have misapplied its precedent value through an apparent over-adherence to its factual circumstances.

The Supreme Court has consistently held that the Due Process Clause of the Fourteenth Amendment protects the right of individuals to make personal choices, unfettered by arbitrary and purposeless restraints, in the private matters of marriage and procreation.   Roe v. Wade [1973].   See also *Griswold* (Harlan, J. concurring).   I view those cases as standing for the principle that every individual has a right to be free from unwarranted governmental intrusion into one's decisions on private matters of intimate concern.   A mature individual's choice of an adult sexual partner, in the privacy of his or her own home, would appear to me to be a decision of the utmost private and intimate concern.   Private consensual sex acts between adults are matters, absent evidence that they are harmful, in which the state has no legitimate interest.

To say, as the majority does, that the right of privacy   .   .   . is limited to matters of marital, home or family life is unwarranted under the law.   Such a contention places a distinction in marital-nonmarital matters which is inconsistent with current Supreme Court opinions and is unsupportable.

In my view, the reliance of the majority on Mr. Justice Harlan's dissenting statement in *Poe* is misplaced. An analysis of the cases indicates that in 1965 when *Griswold,* which invalidated a statute prohibiting the use of contraceptives by married couples, was decided, at least three of the Court . . . would not have been willing to attach the right of privacy to homosexual conduct. In my view, *Griswold* applied the right of privacy to its particular factual situation. That the right of privacy is not limited to the facts of *Griswold* is demonstrated by later Supreme Court decisions. After *Griswold,* by virtue of Eisenstadt v. Baird (1972), the legal viability of a marital-nonmarital distinction in private sexual acts if not eliminated, was at the very least seriously impaired. In *Eisenstadt* the Court declined to restrict the right of privacy in sexual matters to married couples:

> Yet the marital couple is not an independent entity with a mind and heart of its own, but an association of two individuals each with a separate intellectual and emotional makeup. If the right of privacy means anything, it is the right of the *individual,* married or single, to be free from unwarranted governmental intrusion into matters so fundamentally affecting a person as the decision whether to bear or beget a child.

In significantly diminishing the importance of the marital-nonmarital distinction, the Court to a great extent vitiated any implication that the state can . . . forbid extra-marital sexuality. . . .
    . . . *Eisenstadt* . . . clearly demonstrates that the right to privacy in sexual relationships is not limited to the marital relationship. Both *Roe* and *Eisenstadt* cogently demonstrate that intimate personal decisions or private matters of substantial importance to the well-being of the individuals involved are protected by the Due Process Clause. The right to select consenting adult sexual partners must be considered within this category. The exercise of that right, whether heterosexual or homosexual, should not be proscribed by state regulation absent compelling justification.

This approach does not unqualifiedly sanction personal whim. If the activity in question involves more than one participant, as in the instant case, each must be capable of consenting, and each must in fact consent to the conduct for the right of privacy to attach. For example, if one of the participants in homosexual contact is a minor, or force is used to coerce one of the participants to yield, the right will not attach. Similarly, the right of privacy cannot be extended to protect conduct that takes place in publicly frequented areas. . . .

The defendants [the State] . . . made no tender of any evidence which even impliedly demonstrated that homosexuality causes society any significant harm. No effort was made by the defendants to establish either a rational basis or a compelling state interest in the proscription. . . . To suggest, as defendants do, that the prohibition of homosexual conduct will in some manner encourage new heterosexual marriages and prevent the dissolution of existing ones is unworthy of judicial response. . . .

On the basis of this record one can only conclude that the sole basis of the proscription of homosexuality was what the majority refers to as the promotion of morality and decency. As salutary a legislative goal as this may be, I can find no authority for intrusion by the state into the private dwelling of a citizen. . . . Whether the guarantee of personal privacy springs from the First, Fourth, Fifth, Ninth, the penumbra of the Bill of Rights, or, as I believe, in the concept of liberty guaranteed by the first section of the Fourteenth Amendment, the Supreme Court has made it clear that fundamental rights of such an intimate facet of an individual's life as sex, absent circumstances warranting intrusion by the state, are to be respected. My brothers, I respectfully suggest, have by today's ruling misinterpreted the issue—the issue centers not around morality or decency, but the constitutional right of privacy. . . .

Editors' Notes

(1) In a Per Curiam decision, without opinion, the U.S. Supreme Court affirmed the judgment of the District Court (Doe v. Commonwealth's Attorney [1976]). Justices Brennan, Marshall, and Stevens, however, indicated that they would note probable jurisdiction and set the case down for oral argument.

(2) At the time this case began, federal jurisdictional statutes required that suits to enjoin enforcement of state laws be heard before special district courts, staffed by three judges. Except for a few special kinds of litigation, such as suits to reapportion states or those arising under the Civil Rights Acts of 1964 or the Voting Rights Acts of 1965, Congress in 1976 repealed this requirement. In this instance, Judge Merhige was the only active member of the bench. The other two members were retired judges called back to service to hear this case. The heavy burden of federal dockets makes this practice quite common.

(3) A "summary" affirmance as here means that the decision of the lower court stands but does not mean that the Supreme Court accepts the lower court's reasoning. In Carey v. Population Services (1977), Brennan denied that the Court had "definitively" settled the issue of state regulation of private sexual conduct. (Brennan, of course, had dissented in *Doe*; and, although he wrote the opinion of the Court in *Carey*, only four justices concurred in the section of his opinion in which this statement occurred.) Dissenting in *Carey*, Rehnquist cited *Doe* and said "the facial constitutional validity of criminal statutes prohibiting certain consensual acts has been 'definitively' established." Notwithstanding Rehnquist's comment, the Court granted certiorari in Bowers v. Hardwick (1986).

(4) **Query:** Is Judge Bryan's standard of "legitimate state interest" or that "the statute is rationally supportable" consistent with the standards required by the Supreme Court when state legislation impinges on such "fundamental rights" as privacy? See such cases as Skinner v. Oklahoma (1942; reprinted above, p. 868) and Akron v. Akron Center for Reproductive Health (1983; reprinted above, p. 1122).

(5) In Wainwright v. Stone (1973), two males, one convicted for "copulating per os and per anum," the other for copulating "per anum," attacked as unconstitutional the Florida statute under which they had been tried. Speaking

only to the claim that the law was void for vagueness, the Supreme Court unanimously sustained the convictions. The immigration laws still forbid homosexual aliens to come into the United States. See Longstaff v. INS (1984), denying certiorari in a case where the Immigration and Naturalization Service had begun deportation proceedings against a resident alien who applied for citizenship because at the time of his entry into the United States he had not noted he was a homosexual.

(6) Despite *Doe, Wainwright,* and *Longstaff,* there has been a trend in American law toward repealing, amending, or interpreting statutes proscribing homosexual conduct so as to make exceptions for relations between consenting adults. Enforcement of laws punishing homosexual activity is haphazard, encouraging blackmail at least as much as adherence to particular moral standards. In July, 1975 the U.S. Civil Service Commission published a set of rules governing standards for hiring and promoting which were to apply equally to homosexuals and heterosexuals. For general discussions of the right to privacy and sexual freedom, see: Kenneth Karst, "The Freedom of Intimate Association," 89 *Yale L.J.* 624 (1980); David A.J. Richards, "Sexual Autonomy and the Constitutional Right to Privacy," 30 *Hastings L.J.* 957 (1979); J. Harvie Wilkinson, III, and G. Edward White, "Constitutional Protection for Personal Lifestyles," 62 *Cornell L.Rev.* 563 (1977).

VII. THE RIGHT TO REPUTATION

"[W]e hold that the right of reputation . . . is neither 'liberty' nor 'property' guaranteed against state deprivation without due process of law."

PAUL v. DAVIS
424 U.S. 693, 96 S.Ct. 1155, 47 L.Ed.2d 405 (1976).

Two local police departments in Kentucky sent flyers to all businesses in the area giving names and photographs of shoplifters who, the police said, were "known to be active in this criminal field." Among those so included was Edward Charles Davis, III. He had, in fact, once been arrested by a store's private guard but had pleaded not guilty to shoplifting, and the judge had dismissed the charge.

After the flyer came out, Davis filed suit in a federal district court under 42 U.S.C. § 1983.* Alleging that the public claim by the police that he was a criminal deprived him, without due process of law, of his right to liberty in a decent reputation, he asked for a declaration of his constitutional rights, an injunction against further distribution of the flyer, and monetary damages. The district judge dismissed the suit as not stating a cause of action under § 1983. The Court of Appeals for the Sixth Circuit reversed. The police then sought and obtained certiorari.

---

* Eds.' Note: 42 U.S.Code § 1983 provides: "Every person who, under color of any statute, ordinance, regulation, custom or usage of any State or Territory subjects, or causes to be subjected, any citizen of the United States or other person within the jurisdiction thereof to the deprivation of rights, privileges, or immunities secured by the Constitution and laws shall be liable to the injured party in an action at law, suit in equity, or other proper proceeding for redress."

Mr. Justice **REHNQUIST** delivered the opinion of the Court. . . .

I

Respondent's . . . complaint asserted that the "active shoplifter" designation would inhibit him from entering business establishments for fear of being suspected of shoplifting and possibly apprehended, and would seriously impair his future employment opportunities. Accepting that such consequences may flow from the flyer in question, respondent's complaint would appear to state a classical claim for defamation actionable in the courts of virtually every State. . . .

Respondent brought his action, however . . . in a United States District Court. . . . He asserted . . . a claim that he had been deprived of rights secured to him by the Fourteenth Amendment. . . .

If respondent's view is to prevail, a person arrested by law enforcement officers who announce that they believe such person to be responsible for a particular crime . . . presumably obtains a claim against such officers under § 1983. And since it is surely far more clear from the language of the Fourteenth Amendment that "life" is protected against state deprivation than it is that reputation is protected against state injury, it would be difficult to see why the survivors of an innocent bystander mistakenly shot by a policeman or negligently killed by a sheriff driving a government vehicle would not have claims equally cognizable under § 1983.

It is hard to perceive any logical stopping place to such a line of reasoning. . . . We think it would come as a great surprise to those who drafted and shepherded the adoption of that Amendment to learn that it worked such a result, and a study of our decisions convinces us they do not support the construction urged by respondent.

II

The result reached by the Court of Appeals . . . must be bottomed on one of two premises. The first is that the Due Process Clause of the Fourteenth Amendment and § 1983 make actionable many wrongs inflicted by government employees which had heretofore been thought to give rise only to state-law tort claims. The second premise is that the infliction by state officials of a "stigma" to one's reputation is somehow different in kind from the infliction by the same official of harm or injury to other interests protected by state law, so that an injury to reputation is actionable under § 1983 and the Fourteenth Amendment even if other such harms are not. We examine each of these premises in turn.

A

The first premise would be contrary to pronouncements in our cases. In the leading case of Screws v. United States (1945), the Court considered the proper application of the criminal counterpart of § 1983. In his opinion for the Court plurality in that case, Mr. Justice Douglas observed:

> Violation of local law does not necessarily mean that federal rights have been invaded. The fact that a prisoner is assaulted, injured, or even murdered by state officials does not necessarily mean that he is deprived of any right protected or secured by the Constitution or laws of the United States.

After recognizing that Congress' power to make criminal the conduct of state officials under the aegis of the Fourteenth Amendment was not unlimited because that Amendment "did not alter the basic relations between the States and the national government," the plurality opinion observed that Congress should not be understood to have attempted

> to make all torts of state officials federal crimes. It brought within [the criminal provision] only specified acts done "under color" of law and then only those acts which deprived a person of some right secured by the Constitution or laws of the United States.

This understanding of the limited effect of the Fourteenth Amendment was not lost in the Court's decision in Monroe v. Pape (1961). There the Court was careful to point out that the complaint stated a cause of action under the Fourteenth Amendment because it alleged an unreasonable search and seizure violative of the guarantee "contained in the Fourth Amendment (and) made applicable to the States by reason of the Due Process Clause of the Fourteenth Amendment." [Davis], however, has pointed to no specific constitutional guarantee safeguarding the interest he asserts has been invaded.

Rather, he apparently believes that the Fourteenth Amendment's Due Process Clause should *ex proprio vigore* * extend to him a right to be free of injury wherever the State may be characterized as the tortfeasor. But such a reading would make of the Fourteenth Amendment a font of tort law to be superimposed upon whatever systems may already be administered by the States. . . . [T]he procedural guarantees of the Due Process Clause cannot be the source for such law.

B

The Second premise . . .—that the infliction by state officials of a "stigma" to one's reputation is somehow different in kind from infliction by a state official of harm to other interests protected by state law—is equally untenable. The words "liberty" and "property" as used in the Fourteenth Amendment do not in terms single out reputation . . . for special protection. . . . While . . . a number of our prior cases pointed out the frequently drastic effect of the "stigma" which may result from defamation by the government . . . this line of cases does not establish the proposition that reputation alone, apart from some more tangible interests such as employment, is either "liberty" or "property" by itself sufficient to invoke the procedural protection of the Due Process Clause. . . . The Court of Appeals, in reaching a contrary conclusion, relied primarily upon Wisconsin v.

---

* **Eds.' Note:** "By its own force."

Constantineau (1971). We think the correct import of that decision, however, must be derived from an examination of the precedents upon which it relied, as well as consideration of the other decisions by this Court, before and after *Constantineau*. . . . While not uniform in their treatment of the subject, we think that the weight of our decisions establishes no constitutional doctrine converting every defamation by a public official into a deprivation of liberty within the meaning of the Due Process Clause of the Fifth or Fourteenth Amendment.

In United States v. Lovett (1946), the Court held that an Act of Congress which specifically forbade payment of any salary or compensation to three named Government agency employees was an unconstitutional bill of attainder. . . . The Court, while recognizing that the underlying charge [of subversive activities] upon which Congress' action was premised "stigmatized [the employees'] reputation and seriously impaired their chance to earn a living," also made it clear that "[w]hat is involved here is a congressional proscription of [these employees] prohibiting their ever holding a government job."

Subsequently, in Joint Anti-Fascist Refugee Comm. v. McGrath (1951), the Court examined the validity of the Attorney General's designation of certain organizations as "Communist". . . . There was no majority opinion in the case. . . . [But] at least six [justices] . . . viewed any "stigma" imposed by official action of the Attorney General . . . as an insufficient basis for invoking the Due Process Clause of the Fifth Amendment.

In Wieman v. Updegraff (1952), the Court again recognized the potential "badge of infamy" . . . from being branded disloyal by the government. . . . But it did not hold this sufficient by itself to invoke the procedural guarantees of the Fourteenth Amendment; indeed, the Court expressly refused to pass upon the procedural due process claims. . . .

. . . [T]he Court returned to consider further the requirements of procedural due process in this area in the case of Cafeteria Workers v. McElroy (1961). Holding that the discharge of an employee of a Government contractor in the circumstances there presented comported with the due process required by the Fifth Amendment, the Court observed:

> [T]his is not a case where government action has operated to bestow a badge of disloyalty or infamy *with an attendant foreclosure from other employment opportunity*. (Emphasis supplied.)

Two things appear from the line of cases. . . . The Court has recognized the serious damage that could be inflicted by branding a government employee as "disloyal," and thereby stigmatizing his good name. But the Court has never held that the mere defamation . . . was sufficient to invoke the guarantees of procedural due process absent an accompanying loss of government employment. . . .

It was against this backdrop that the Court in 1971 decided *Constantineau*. There the Court held that a Wisconsin statute authorizing "posting" was unconstitutional because it failed to provide procedural safeguards of notice and an opportunity to be heard, prior to an individual's being "posted." Under the statute "posting" consisted of forbidding in writing the sale or delivery of alcoholic beverages to certain persons who were determined to have become hazards . . . by reason of their "excessive drinking." . . .

There is undoubtedly language in *Constantineau* which is sufficiently ambiguous to justify the reliance upon it by the Court of Appeals:

> Yet certainly where the state attaches "a badge of infamy" to the citizen, due process comes into play. . . .
>
> Where a person's good name, reputation, honor, or integrity is at stake *because of what the government is doing to him,* notice and an opportunity to be heard are essential. (Emphasis supplied.)

. . . We should not read this language as significantly broadening those [earlier] holdings . . . if there is any other possible interpretation of *Constantineau*'s language. We believe there is.

We think that the italicized language . . . referred to the fact that the governmental action . . . deprived the individual of a right previously held under state law—the right to purchase or obtain liquor. . . . "Posting," therefore, significantly altered his status as a matter of state law, and it was that alteration of legal status which, combined with the injury resulting from the defamation, justified the invocation of procedural safeguards. . . . [W]e do not think that such defamation, standing alone, deprived Constantineau of any "liberty" protected by the procedural guarantees of the Fourteenth Amendment.

This conclusion is reinforced by . . . Board of Regents v. Roth (1972). There we noted that "the range of interests protected by procedural due process is not infinite" and that with respect to property interests they are

> of course . . . not created by the Constitution. Rather, they are created and their dimensions are defined by existing rules or understandings that stem from an independent source such as state law.
>
> . . .

While *Roth* recognized that governmental action defaming an individual . . . could entitle the person to notice and an opportunity to be heard as to the defamation, its language is quite inconsistent with any notion that a defamation perpetrated by a government official but unconnected with any refusal to rehire would be actionable under the Fourteenth Amendment. . . .

This conclusion is quite consistent with our most recent holding . . ., Goss v. Lopez (1975), that suspension from school based upon charges of misconduct could trigger the procedural guarantees of the Fourteenth Amendment. While the Court noted that charges of misconduct could seriously damage the student's reputation . . . it also took care to point out that Ohio law conferred a right upon all children to attend school and that the act of the school officials suspending the student . . . resulted in a denial or deprivation of that right.

III

It is apparent from our decisions that there exists a variety of interests which are difficult of definition but are nevertheless comprehended within the meaning of either "liberty" or "property" as meant in the Due Process Clause. These interests attain this constitutional status by virtue of the fact that they have been initially recognized and protected by state law; and we have repeatedly ruled that the procedural guarantees of the Fourteenth Amendment apply whenever the State seeks to remove or significantly alter that protected status. In Bell v. Burson (1971), for example, the State by issuing drivers' licenses recognized in its citizens a right to operate a vehicle on the highways of the State. The Court held that the State could not withdraw this right without giving petitioner due process. In Morissey v. Brewer (1972), the State afforded parolees the right to remain at liberty as long as the conditions of their parole were not violated. Before the State could alter the status of a parolee because of alleged violations of these conditions, we held that the Fourteenth Amendment's guarantee of due process of law required procedural safeguards.

In each of these cases . . . a right or status previously recognized by state law was distinctly altered or extinguished. . . . But the interest in reputation alone . . . is quite different from the "liberty" or "property" recognized in those decisions. Kentucky law does not extend to respondent any legal guarantee of present enjoyment of reputation which has been altered as a result of petitioners' actions. Rather his interest in reputation is simply one of a number which the State may protect against injury. . . . And any harm or injury to that interest, even where as here inflicted by an officer of the State, does not result in a deprivation of any "liberty" or "property" recognized by state or federal law, nor has it worked any change of respondent's status as theretofore recognized under the State's laws. For these reasons we hold that the interest in reputation asserted in this case in neither "liberty" nor "property" guaranteed against state deprivation without due process of law. . . .

IV

Respondent . . . also alleged a violation of a "right to privacy. . . ."

While there is no "right of privacy" found in any specific guarantee of the Constitution, the Court has recognized that "zones of privacy" may be created by more specific constitutional guarantees. . . . See Roe v. Wade (1973). Respondent's case, however, comes within none of these areas. He does not seek to suppress evidence seized in the course of an unreasonable search. And our other "right of privacy" cases . . . deal generally with substantive aspects of the Fourteenth Amendment. In *Roe* the Court pointed out that the personal rights found in this guarantee of personal privacy must be limited to those which are "fundamental" or "implicit in the concept of ordered liberty" as described in Palko v. Connecticut (1937). The activities detailed as being within this definition were . . . matters relating to marriage, procreation, contraception, family relationships, and child rearing and education. . . .

Respondent's claim is far afield from this line of decisions. He claims constitutional protection against the disclosure of the fact of his arrest on a shoplifting charge. His claim is based, not upon any challenge to the State's ability to restrict his freedom of action in a sphere contended to be "private," but instead on a claim that the State may not publicize a record of an official act such as an arrest. . . .

Reversed.

Mr. Justice **STEVENS** took no part in the consideration or decision in this case.

Mr. Justice **BRENNAN,** with whom Mr. Justice **MARSHALL** concurs and Mr. Justice **WHITE** concurs in part, dissenting.

. . . The Court today holds that police officials, acting in their official capacities as law enforcers, may on their own initiative and without trial constitutionally condemn innocent individuals as criminals and thereby brand them with one of the most stigmatizing and debilitating labels in our society. If there are no constitutional restraints on such oppressive behavior, the safeguards constitutionally accorded an accused in a criminal trial are rendered a sham. . . . The Court accomplishes this result by excluding a person's interest in his good name and reputation from all constitutional protection. . . . The result . . . is demonstrably inconsistent with our prior case law and unduly restrictive in its construction of our precious Bill of Rights. . . .

. . . [I]t is first necessary to dispel some misconceptions apparent in the Court's opinion. . . . [T]he implication . . . that the existence vel non [or not] of a state remedy . . . is relevant to the determination whether there is a cause of action under § 1983, is wholly unfounded. "It is no answer that the State has a law which if enforced would give relief. The federal remedy is supplementary to the state remedy, and the latter need not be first sought and refused before the federal one is invoked." Monroe v. Pape (1961). . . .

Equally irrelevant is the Court's statement that "[c]oncededly if the same allegations had been made about respondent by a private individual, he would have nothing more than a claim for defamation under state law." . . . The action complained of here is "state action" allegedly in violation of the Fourteenth Amendment. . . .

. . . An official's actions are not "under color of" law merely because he is an official; an off-duty policeman's discipline of his own children, for example, would not constitute conduct "under color of" law. The essential element of this type of § 1983 action is abuse of his official position. . . . [T]he police officials here concede that their conduct was intentional and was undertaken in their official capacities.

Therefore, beyond peradventure, it is action taken under color of law and it is disingenuous for the Court to argue that respondent is seeking to convert § 1983 into a generalized font of tort law. . . .

The stark fact is that the police here have officially imposed on respondent the stigmatizing label "criminal" without the salutary and constitutionally mandated safeguards of a criminal trial. The Court concedes that this action will have deleterious consequences for respondent. . . .[1] [N]othing in the record appears to suggest the existence at that time [of Davis's arrest] of even constitutionally sufficient probable cause for that single arrest on a shoplifting charge. Nevertheless, petitioners had 1,000 flyers printed . . . proclaiming that the individuals identified by name and picture were "subjects known to be active in this criminal field [shoplifting]," and trumpeting the "fact" that each page depicted "Active Shoplifters" (emphasis supplied). . . .

. . . [T]he Court by mere fiat and with no analysis wholly excludes personal interest in reputation from the ambit of "life, liberty, or property" under the Fifth and Fourteenth Amendments, thus rendering due process concerns never applicable to the official stigmatization, however arbitrary, of an individual. The logical and disturbing corollary of this holding is that no due process infirmities would inhere in a statute constituting a commission to conduct ex parte trials of individuals, so long as the only official judgment pronounced was limited to the public condemnation and branding of a person as a Communist, a traitor, an "active murderer," a homosexual, or any other mark that "merely" carries social opprobrium. The potential of today's decision is frightening for a free people. That decision surely finds no support in our relevant constitutional jurisprudence.

"In a Constitution for a free people, there can be no doubt that the meaning of 'liberty' must be broad indeed. See, e.g., Bolling v. Sharpe [1954]; Stanley v. Illinois [1972]." Board of Regents v. Roth (1972). "Without doubt, it denotes not merely freedom from bodily restraint but also the right of the individual . . . generally to enjoy those privileges long recognized . . . as essential to the orderly pursuit of happiness by free men." Meyer v. Nebraska (1923). Certainly the enjoyment of one's good name and reputation has been recognized repeatedly in our cases as being among the most cherished rights enjoyed by a free people, and therefore as falling within the concept of personal "liberty."

---

1. Petitioners [police] testified:

"Q. And you didn't limit this to persons who had been convicted of the offense of shoplifting, is that correct?
"A. That's correct. . . .
"Q. Now, my question is what is the basis for your conclusion that a person—a person who has been arrested for the offense of shoplifting is an active shoplifter?
"A. The very fact that he's been arrested for the charge of shoplifting and evidence presented to that effect.
"Q. And this is not based on any findings of the court?
"A. No, sir." . . .

[Footnote by Justice Brennan.]

[A]s Mr. Justice Stewart has reminded us, the individual's right to his own good name "reflects no more than our basic concept of the essential dignity and worth of every human being—a concept at the root of any decent system of ordered liberty. The protection of private personality, like the protection of life itself, is left primarily to the individual States under the Ninth and Tenth Amendments. But this does not mean that the right is entitled to any less recognition by this Court as a basic of our constitutional system." Rosenblatt v. Baer (1966) (concurring opinion). Gertz v. Robert Welch, Inc. (1974).[2]

We have consistently held that

"[w]here a person's good name, reputation, honor or integrity is at stake because of what the government is doing to him, notice and an opportunity to be heard are essential." Wisconsin v. Constantineau [1971]. . . .   Board of Regents v. Roth (1972). . . .

Today's decision marks a clear retreat from Jenkins v. McKeithen (1969), a case closely akin to the factual pattern of the instant case, and yet essentially ignored by the Court. *Jenkins,* which was also an action brought under § 1983, both recognized that the public branding of an individual implicates interests cognizable as either "liberty" or "property," and held that such public condemnation cannot be accomplished without procedural safeguards designed to eliminate arbitrary or capricious executive action. . . .   [A]lthough the Court was divided on the particular procedural safeguards that would be necessary in particular circumstances, the common point of agreement, and the one that the Court today inexplicably rejects, was that the official characterization of an individual as a criminal affects a constitutional "liberty" interest. . . .

Moreover, *Constantineau* . . . did not rely at all on the fact asserted by the Court today as controlling—namely . . . that "posting" denied Ms. Constantineau the right to purchase alcohol for a year. Rather, *Constantineau* stated: "The *only* issue present here is whether the label or characterization given a person by 'posting,' though a mark of serious illness to some, is to others such a stigma or badge of disgrace that procedural due process requires notice and an opportunity to be heard." (Emphasis supplied.) . . .

I had always thought that one of this Court's most important roles is to provide a formidable bulwark against governmental violation of the constitutional safeguards securing in our free society the legitimate expectations of every person to innate human dignity and sense of worth. It is a regrettable abdication of that role and a saddening denigration of our majestic Bill of Rights when the Court tolerates arbitrary and capricious official conduct branding an individual as a criminal without compliance with constitutional procedures designed to

2. It is strange that the Court should hold that the interest in one's good name and reputation is not embraced within the concept of "liberty" or "property" under the Fourteenth Amendment, and yet hold that that same interest, when recognized under state law, is sufficient to overcome the specific protections of the First Amendment. See, e.g., Gertz v. Robert Welch, Inc. (1974); Time, Inc. v. Firestone (1976). [Footnote by Justice Brennan.]

ensure the fair and impartial ascertainment of criminal culpability. Today's decision must surely be a short-lived aberration.

Editors' Notes

(1) **Query:** Is there a contradiction in a political system's endorsing the concepts of human dignity and autonomy and at the same time allowing public officials to destroy the reputations of citizens without following any sort of legal process? Does Rehnquist leave the right to a reputation without federal legal protection?

(2) **Query:** From his article "The Notion of a Living Constitution," would one have expected Rehnquist to be sympathetic to the interpretive *mode* of fundamental rights? What *mode* did he use here? Insofar as he and Brennan each used the *technique* of stare decisis, who had the better of the argument?

(3) **Query:** Brennan referred to Rehnquist's opinion for the Court in Time v. Firestone (1976; reprinted above, p. 606), holding that a private citizen's right to reputation may take precedence over a magazine's First Amendment right to freedom of the press. How can one square Rehnquist's opinions in these two cases?

(4) Some commentators have suggested either that the fear of additional burdens on the federal judiciary moved some of the justices to join Rehnquist in *Paul* or that considerations of federalism and deference to state judges were dominant. See Laurence H. Tribe, *American Constitutional Law* (Mineola, N.Y.: Foundation Press, 1978), pp. 970–972.

(5) Ingraham v. Wright (1977) held, 5–4, that corporal punishment of children in the Dade County, Fla., school system was not a cruel and unusual punishment in the constitutional sense. In dissent, Stevens expressed the view that *Paul* "may have been correctly decided on an incorrect rationale." Perhaps, he wrote,

> the Court will one day agree with Mr. Justice Brennan's appraisal of the constitutional interest at stake in [*Paul*] and nevertheless conclude that an adequate state remedy may prevent every state-inflicted injury to a person's reputation from violating 42 U.S.C. § 1983.

What was Stevens' point?

(6) For an analysis of cases dealing with the concept of "liberty," see Ernest H. Schopler, "Annotation: Supreme Court's Views as to the Concept of 'Liberty' under Due Process Clauses of Fifth and Fourteenth Amendments," 47 L.Ed.2d 975 (1977).

V

Constitutional Democracy in the Crucible of Crisis

Chapter 18: Constitutional Interpretation and Emergency Powers

The essays, cases, notes, and queries in this book have stressed the necessity, importance, and complexity of constitutional interpretation. As practiced in the United States over the past two centuries, this enterprise, despite recurrent failures, has enjoyed a great measure of success. The country prospers; there is a greater degree of both constitutionalism and democracy in the system than there was in 1787. Not since the Civil War has there been a widespread, fundamental challenge to the very nature of the political system. Still, no one who experienced the domestic crises of the New Deal in the 1930s, of the Red Scare during the Cold War, or of the Civil Rights Movement during the 1950s and '60s can claim to have lived in times of constitutional calm. And there is no assurance that this enterprise will continue to be successful in preserving constitutional democracy.

There are additional kinds of crisis, those brought on by war or terrorism. Looking back with the omniscience of hindsight, it is easy to judge that dire threats to national security have been rare; but honesty would compel us to acknowledge that had we lived in other times, our perceptions of those events might have been different. And, the world in which we now live is rife with war and rumors of war, of terrorism and threats of terrorism. It is likely that, when future crises occur, decision makers will act even more swiftly in self-defense but not necessarily more wisely than have their predecessors.

A precipitate response, of course, generates its own kind of crisis, a crisis of legitimacy for the entire political system and its ideals, as Korematsu v. United States (1944; reprinted below p. 1197)[1] so dreadfully illustrates. Perhaps the most difficult problem that will confront future constitutional interpreters is that of how to save both the country and the Constitution.

---

1. See also the analysis of this case in Chapter 3.

18

Constitutional Interpretation
and Emergency Powers

The problems of constitutional interpretation discussed in previous chapters take on added urgency when an emergency strikes. During severe crises, immediate actions usually appear necessary, and it may be inconvenient for government to respect individual rights or democratic processes. Further, fastidious regard for either may endanger the nation's survival. "It is in vain," Madison wrote in *Federalist* No. 41,

> to oppose constitutional barriers to the impulse of self-preservation. It is worse than in vain; because it plants in the Constitution itself necessary usurpations of power, every precedent of which is a germ of unnecessary and multiplied repetitions.

Hamilton was even more blunt. "These powers," he wrote in *Federalist* No. 23 about national defense, "ought to exist without limitation, *because it is impossible to foresee or define the extent and variety of the means which may be necessary* to *satisfy them.*" (Italics in original.) He continued:

> The circumstances that endanger the safety of nations are infinite, and for this reason no constitutional shackles can wisely be imposed on the power to which the care of it is committed. This power ought to be co-extensive with all the possible combinations of such circumstances; and ought to be under the direction of the same councils which are appointed to preside over the common defense.

Despite his opposition to the Alien and Sedition Acts (see the Kentucky Resolutions, reprinted above p. 261), Jefferson's general views on emergency powers were rather close to those of Hamilton. Because of his insistence on "strict construction" of the Constitution, Jefferson did not advocate taking a broad view of governmental powers to cope with emergencies, but argued that obligation to the Constitution was subject to a higher law:

> A strict observance of the written laws is doubtless *one* of the high duties of a good citizen, but it is not *the highest.* The laws of necessity, of self-preservation, of saving our country when in danger, are of higher obligation.[1]

Lincoln was equally candid in justifying his use of courts martial to try civilians:

---

1. Letter to J.B. Colvin, Sept. 20, 1810; reprinted below, p. 1181.

Was it possible to lose the nation, and yet preserve the constitution? By general law life *and* limb must be protected; yet often a limb must be amputated to save a life; but a life is never wisely given to save a limb. I felt that measures, otherwise unconstitutional, might become lawful, by becoming indispensable to the preservation of the constitution, through the preservation of the nation.[2]

A defender of Jefferson and Lincoln could argue that they were using structural and prudential *modes* of interpretation: To preserve the Constitution's viability, they were willing to sanction temporary violations of some of the document's specific terms. A critic might reply that, at least in this narrow context, Jefferson and Lincoln were arguing that the Constitution "constitutes" us as a people only in good times and thus is a trivial element in our public life. Indeed the Supreme Court gave just such a response to Lincoln in Ex parte Milligan (1866; reprinted below, p. 1190): "The Constitution of the United States is a law for rulers and people, equally in war and in peace, and covers with the shield of its protection all classes of men, at all times, and under all circumstances."

I. PRESERVING THE CONSTITUTION AND THE NATION

The choice, of course, need not be simply between the stark alternatives of flouting the Constitution and rigidly adhering to every comma of the document's text. A subtle interpretation of even these opposing claims might discern a wide middle ground. One might, for example: (1) avoid at least the appearance of violating the Constitution by ignoring it; (2) suspend some or all of its guarantees; or (3) interpret it so as to accommodate conflicting values.

A. Ignoring the Constitution

By ignoring the Constitution, one asks WHY interpret or WHEN to interpret? and decides it is prudent not to do so, at least at this time. Jefferson chose such a solution in 1803 when he purchased the Louisiana Territory despite his conviction that the national government lacked authority to acquire new lands. "It appears to me," Thomas Paine wrote him, "to be one of those cases with which the Constitution has nothing to do" [3]—in effect, speaking to the question of WHAT and limiting the Constitution's reach. Jefferson's solution was different, though he also spoke to the question of WHAT more than he realized. Perceiving a grave danger to national security in foreign control of the mouth of the Mississippi—the Napoleonic wars were raging in Europe, and the territory had been traded between France and Spain—and presented with an opportunity to remove that

---

2. To A.G. Hodges, April 4, 1864; Roy P. Basler, ed., *The Collected Works of Abraham Lincoln* (New Brunswick, N.J.: Rutgers University Press, 1953), VII, 281.

3. Quoted in Dumas Malone, *Jefferson the President: First Term, 1801–1805* (Boston: Little, Brown, 1970), p. 318.

peril as well as to acquire an empire at a bargain price, he signed the treaty and urged his supporters in the Senate to consent to it "with as little debate as possible, & particularly so far as respects the constitutional difficulty." He then explained his reasoning:

> Our peculiar security is in possession of a written Constitution. Let us not make it a blank paper by construction. I say the same as to the opinion of those who consider the grant of the treaty making power as boundless. If it is, we have no Constitution. . . . Let us go on then perfecting it, by adding, by way of amendment to the Constitution, those powers which time & trial show are still wanting.[4]

Ignoring the Constitution may be a more frequent occurrence than Americans imagine. Especially during the years of Richard Nixon's presidency but also under earlier presidents, the CIA, FBI, and IRS often spied on, harassed, and sometimes silenced political dissidents. Most notorious was the FBI's obsession with Martin Luther King. Recognizing the black civil rights leader's magnetic popular appeal, J. Edgar Hoover reasoned that if King abandoned his advocacy of non-violence and brotherly love, he could start a revolution. Therefore, the Director of the FBI concluded, the shrewd tactic would be to discredit him so he could never pose a threat. "No holds were barred," the investigator in charge of the operation admitted. Agents followed King, tapped his telephone, and bugged his hotel rooms. They even threatened to make public allegedly damaging tapes unless he committed suicide.[5]

Walter Sullivan, then Assistant Director of the FBI, conceded that the campaign against King had not been "an isolated phenomenon . . . . this was the practice of the Bureau down through the years." He added:

> [N]ever once did I hear anybody, including myself, raise the question, is this course of action which we have agreed upon lawful, is it legal, is it ethical or moral? We never gave any thought to this realm of reasoning. . . .[6]

Nor, of course, did anyone give any thought to the query: "Is it constitutional?"

This sordid history confirms the claim of Chapter 1 that one of the primary reasons for interpreting the Constitution is to reaffirm commitment to it. The kindest comment one can make about these people, from President to junior clerk, is that that they did not take their oaths of allegiance to the Constitution seriously because they

---

4. To Senator Wilson Cary Nicholas, Sept. 7, 1803; reprinted in Paul L. Ford, ed., *The Works of Thomas Jefferson* (New York: Putnam's, 1905), X, 10–11n. As noted below, Jefferson wrote out several drafts of a constitutional amendment, but never formally proposed such a change.

5. See the 7 volumes of *Hearings* and 6 volumes of the *Final Report* of the Church Committee: U.S. Senate, Select Committee to Study Governmental Operations with Respect to Intelligence Activities, 94th Cong., 2d sess. (1975–76); Book III of the *Final Report* contains a 106 page summary of the FBI's efforts to "get" Dr. King.

6. Quoted in Church Committee, *Final Report*, supra note 5, III, 135.

never bothered to think about it, much less interpret it. Thus, while one can admire the purity of Jefferson's motives and his resolve—on which he never acted—to seek a constitutional amendment to ratify what he thought was a necessary but unconstitutional act,[7] his decision to ignore the Constitution set a dangerous precedent.

B. Suspending the Constitution

Another solution involves suspending some constitutional provisions during emergencies. The document itself provides for suspension of several safeguards for individual rights.[8] The most important, Article I, § 9 reads:

> The privilege of the writ of habeas corpus shall not be suspended, unless when in cases of rebellion or invasion the public safety may require it.

Habeas corpus, of course, is an order from a judge to the official—civilian or military—who has custody of a prisoner, directing the custodian to bring the prisoner into court and explain to the judge the justification for detention. Its primary function is to prevent arbitrary arrest and imprisonment.

Despite Article I's limited authorization, suspension of habeas corpus hardly disposes of all constitutional questions. (See Ex parte Merryman [1861; reprinted below, p. 1184]; Lincoln's Message to Congress of July 4, 1861 [reprinted below, p. 1187], and Ex parte Milligan [1866; reprinted below, p. 1190].) First, one confronts the question of WHO. Does the location of this power in Article I mean that only Congress—subject to the usual presidential veto—can authorize suspension? Or can the President do so on his own to fulfill the obligations imposed on him by Article II to "take care that the laws be faithfully executed" and to "protect and defend the Constitution"? What role, if any, does the Constitution leave to judges in deciding such matters? If the proper institution suspends the writ, may judges legitimately inquire into whether "the public safety" in fact requires that action?

Whatever the answer to the WHO interrogatory, HOW does an interpreter—legislative, executive, or judicial—decide when suspension is legitimate? What are the standards? Indeed, are there any standards beyond a decision maker's (mis)perception of peril during hectic moments of crisis? Further, assuming an initial suspension was legitimate, HOW does one determine the length of time it remains valid?

---

7. Ford reprints several of Jefferson's drafts of a possible constitutional amendment; supra note 4, X, 3–12.

8. See, for example, the Third Amendment, allowing quartering of troops in civilian homes during wartime, "in a manner prescribed by law"; and the Fifth Amendment, suspending the right to indictment by grand jury of members of the militia "when in actual service in time of war or public danger," and allowing government to take, "with just compensation," private property for public use.

The effects of suspension of habeas corpus are potentially immense. If the writ does not run, there is no easy way to review any aspect of military rule. The President could try any person accused of *any* crime before military tribunals. Thus an accused could lose not only protection against arbitrary arrest and imprisonment, but also such rights as those to indictment by grand jury and trial by jury presided over by a judge appointed for good behavior. These results do not automatically follow from suspension of habeas corpus—the President would also have to declare martial law—but habeas corpus is the most effective, though not the sole, defense of these and other rights.

These rippling effects lead to a further question. In an emergency, might the federal government suspend operation of all provisions of the constitutional document? The history of such actions in other constitutional democracies—Weimar Germany before the rise of Hitler, for example—does not radiate happy omens. Yet it is not unreasonable to argue that a crisis, brought on for instance by nuclear war or terrorism, could overwhelm the usual governmental processes and trigger, as Madison and Jefferson feared, destructive violations of the Constitution—a fate possibly worse than suspension. Nevertheless, even some who argue that total suspension may be necessary have attached a limitation: Under truly extraordinary conditions, government might legitimately suspend the Constitution, but it could not legitimately suspend its commitment to constitutionalism. That is, the government must continue to observe such basic requirements as respect for the worth and dignity of each citizen, though it may, as a temporary measure, suspend any or all of the document's specific limitations.[9]

C. Interpreting the Constitution

It might also be possible to interpret the constitutional document as delegating broad emergency powers. During the first World War, Charles Evans Hughes claimed that "we have a *fighting* constitution" and the power to wage war "is a power to wage war successfully."[10] Clearly the framers contemplated emergencies. The Preamble lists "the common defense" and "domestic tranquility" among the nation's fundamental objectives; and Article I specifically delegates to Congress authority to establish armed forces, punish piracy (an ancient form of terrorism), declare war, and call out the militia to repel invasions or insurrections. Moreover, Article IV guarantees each state a republican form of government and imposes on the federal

---

9. John E. Finn, "Constitutional Crises and the Limits of Human Foresight," unpub. Ph.D. diss., Princeton University, 1986. For a quite different analysis, but one receptive to the notion that a temporary "constitutional dictatorship" may be the least of evils in the real world, see Carl J. Friedrich, *Constitutional Government and Democracy* (4th ed.; Waltham, Mass.: Blaisdell, 1968), chap. 25.

10. "War Powers under the Constitution," 42 *Am. Bar Ass'n Rep.* 232, 238 (1917). Hughes had resigned from the Court in 1916 to run against Woodrow Wilson in the presidential election of that year. He returned to the Court as Chief Justice in 1930.

government additional obligations to repel invasions of the states and put down insurrections there. These provisions, Justice Frankfurter wrote in Korematsu v. United States (1944; reprinted below, p. 1197), "are as much part of the Constitution as provisions looking to a nation at peace."

The various *approaches* to and *modes* of interpretation discussed in Chapter 8 provide some help in finding meaning in and limits to these powers. Interpreters who viewed the Constitution as fixed or as changing would probably differ somewhat, but it is difficult to tell how much. Even Justice Sutherland, the archspokesman for a fixed Constitution, conceded that:

> The provisions of the federal Constitution, undoubtedly, are pliable in the sense that in appropriate cases they have the capacity of bringing within their grasp every new condition. But their *meaning* is changeless; it is only their *application* which is extensible. (Minnesota Moratorium Case [1934; reprinted above, p. 136].)

And here, one could plausibly contend, the country would face only variations, albeit dramatic ones, in application to the problems with which the framers were familiar.

The continuum of *approaches* represented by differences between viewing the Constitution as a set of commands and as a vision of the good society we aspire to could—but not necessarily would—offer quite distinct responses to interpretations of the scope of emergency powers. Much would depend on the particular vision of the society to which an interpreter saw the Constitution as authoritatively directing the nation.

A third continuum of *approaches,* textualism versus transcendence, might be more decisive. Textualism, as we just saw, could well support a claim to broad emergency powers, but one that would fall far short of acknowledging authority to suspend the entire Constitution. The direction a transcendent *approach* would take would depend largely on the documents, practices, and theories the interpreter considered part of "the Constitution." An interpreter might well see the principle, "The survival of the people is the highest law" as standing behind the Preamble's goal of "a more perfect union . . . [for] ourselves and our posterity." Such a principle could easily accommodate partial or total, if temporary, suspension of the Constitution.

Certainly most "transcendent" *approaches* would include either or both democratic and constitutionalist theory. While neither democratic nor constitutionalist theory looks on a constitution as a suicide pact, each would be wary of governmental action that encroached on rights it considered fundamental—for democratic theory, those to open political processes; for constitutionalism, those relating to privacy and autonomy.

One can envision a transcendent *approach* that stressed constitutional theory taking a very narrow view, as *Milligan* did, of emergency powers that infringe on some provisions of the Bill of Rights. A transcendent *approach* that stressed democratic theory would probably take a wider view of governmental power, on the premise that the political processes were open and the electorate could always influence and at the next election change the government if it wished. On the other hand, if emergency powers curtailed political freedom, democratic theory might well require a very different reaction, for then the principal check on tyranny would be gone.

In using any or all of these *approaches,* the interpreter's willingness to employ a prudential *mode* would be critical. And the simple fact is that, in times of dire crisis, most interpreters have been more concerned with prudence than with *jus. Milligan* sounds a ringing hymn of praise to constitutionalism, but its stirring rhetoric came *after* the Civil War. When the bullets were flying, the justices were careful not to take a public stance against Lincoln's court-martialing civilians. So, too, *during* World War II, the justices agonized over Hirabayashi v. United States (1943) and Korematsu v. United States (1944; reprinted below, p. 1197); but, in the name of "military necessity," they legitimated the government's harsh and discriminatory treatment of American citizens of Japanese ancestry. *After* the war, when confronted with a case concerning martial law in Hawaii during a time when the military had excellent reasons to fear invasion, the Court leaped to the defense of civil liberties.[11]

This interpretive schizophrenia led Clinton Rossiter to conclude that we have two constitutions, one for peace and one for national emergencies.[12] There is something in that conclusion. When interpreters "accommodate" the claims of necessity against those of constitutionalism or democracy, the winner has typically, though not always, been emergency powers.[13] And later, when the crisis has passed, the claim of necessity sometimes turns out to fraudulent, as it was in *Korematsu,* and in prosecution of alleged subversives during the Adams administration and World War I, deportation of evil foreigners after that war, and "witch hunts" for communists during the Cold War and for radicals who were so subversive as to campaign against Richard Nixon during the years from 1968 until 1974.

II. *INTER ARMES SILENT LEGES?*

Of all the problems the polity faces, the claims of emergency powers put its commitment to the Constitution to the severest test. The American record is certainly better than that of most nations. We have never suspended the Constitution in its entirety and only rarely invoked Article I's explicit authorization of suspension of habeas corpus. Yet our record of hysterical mistreatment in the name of survival is hardly one that can be squared with a Constitution that

---

11. Duncan v. Kanhanamoku (1946).

12. *The Supreme Court and the Commander in Chief,* expanded ed. with Richard P. Longaker (Ithaca, N.Y.: Cornell University Press, 1976).

13. United States v. United States District Court (1972; reprinted below, p. 1205) is one of the most significant exceptions.

seeks to enshrine human dignity and the life of reason as national ideals. A century after *Milligan*, Earl Warren preached for the Court a sermon whose message has been often ignored:

> "[N]ational defense" cannot be deemed an end in itself. . . . Implicit in the term . . . is the notion of defending those values and ideas which set this Nation apart. . . . It would indeed be ironic if, in the name of national defense, we would sanction the subversion of one of those liberties . . . which makes the defense of the Nation worthwhile.[14]

Yet that irony abounds.

The usual response is that deviations have been few and temporary, and the system has survived to right its wrongs. We must, as good democrats, trust those whom we elected to use emergency power to cope with crises that threaten the survival of the nation and to do so not merely not to further their own careers, but for the common good. But democratic theorists might remember that truly free political processes require that all public issues be open to debate, a condition that did not obtain in 1944 when Thomas E. Dewey agreed not to discuss what happened at Pearl Harbor or in 1948 or 1952 when one made a prima facie case against oneself of being a "pink, fellow travelling, comsymp" if one dared to question the claim that the United States was confronted by a monolithic world communist movement directed from Moscow.

Constitutionalists need only remember *Korematsu* to devalue the way in which the political process will protect a hated minority. They could quote Jefferson when he faced the partisan prosecutions of the Adams administration: "In questions of power then let no more be heard of confidence in man, but bind him down from mischief by the chains of the Constitution." [15] Constitutionalists, however, might also remember that explicit guarantees, under the oversight of an independent judiciary, did no more to protect the Nisei against concentration camps than did the political processes.

Any discussion of emergency power takes place in a strange, if not brave, new world. The age of missiles and stars wars means that any dichotomy between "ordinary times" and emergencies is useless, for "ordinary times" no longer exist. Our civilization is constantly threatened by terrorism and war. The first challenges the basic values of constitutionalism and democracy by taking advantage of liberty to destroy liberty; the second makes the planet itself hostage to a MAD international system sated with thermonuclear weapons. Thus an effort to conceptualize crisis as a temporary state of affairs dashes to pieces against the cruel reef of reality: We now live in a constant state of siege, at some times the danger is more threatening than at other times; but the end looms never more than minutes away. It is with that fact that constitutional democracy must come to grips if it is to

---

14. United States v. Robel (1967).

15. Kentucky Resolutions (1798; reprinted above, p. 261).

remain more than an artifact of a soon to be forgotten—or obliterated—past.

SELECTED BIBLIOGRAPHY

Barber, Sotirios A. *On What the Constitution Means* (Baltimore, Md.: Johns Hopkins University Press, 1984), chap. 4.

Bessette, Joseph M., and Jeffrey Tulis, *The Presidency in the Constitutional Order* (Baton Rouge, La.: Louisiana State University Press, 1981).

Corwin, Edward S. *The Presidency: Office and Powers* (4th ed.; New York: New York University Press, 1957), chap. 6.

———. *Of Presidential Prerogative* (Whittier, Cal.: Whittier College, 1954).

Fairman, Charles. *The Law of Martial Rule* (2d. ed.; Chicago: University of Chicago Press, 1943).

Friedrich, Carl J. *Constitutional Government and Democracy* (4th ed.; Waltham, Mass.: Blaisdell, 1968), chap. 25.

Genovese, Michael A. *The Supreme Court, the Constitution, and Presidential Power* (Lanham, Md.: University Press of America, 1980).

Pritchett, C. Herman. *Constitutional Law of the Federal System* (Englewood Cliffs, N.J.: Prentice Hall, 1984). chap. 17.

Pyle, Christopher H., and Richard M. Pious, *The President, Congress, and the Constitution* (New York: The Free Press, 1984), chaps. 4–5.

Rossiter, Clinton. *Constitutional Dictatorship* (Princeton, N.J.: Princeton University Press, 1948).

———. *The Supreme Court and the Commander in Chief,* expanded ed., with Richard P. Longaker (Ithaca, N.Y.: Cornell University Press, 1976).

Winterton, George. "The Concept of Extra-Constitutional Executive Power in Domestic Affairs," 7 *Hastings Con.L.Q.* 7 (1979).

"To lose our country by a scrupulous adherence to written law, would be to lose the law itself, with life, liberty, property and all those who are enjoying them with us; thus absurdly sacrificing the end to the means."

THOMAS JEFFERSON TO J.B. COLVIN *
1810.

As the introductory essay to this chapter pointed out, as President, Jefferson believed that the federal government lacked constitutional authority to acquire foreign lands. On the other hand, he saw ownership of the Louisiana Territory as critical to national security. His solution to the dilemma was not to interpret the Constitution at all but to ignore it—to purchase the territory but not to justify the act as constitutional. This strategy was successful, in part because many officials did not share Jefferson's belief that the Constitution did not allow acquisition of foreign land. Even in retirement, however, the larger question of fidelity to law in time of crisis continued to dog him.

Monticello, September 20, 1810

SIR . . .

The question you propose, whether circumstances do not sometimes occur, which make it a duty in officers of high trust, to assume authorities beyond the law, is easy of solution in principle, but sometimes embarrassing in practice. A strict observance of the written laws is doubtless *one* of the high duties of a good citizen, but it is not *the highest*. The laws of necessity, of self-preservation, of saving our country when in danger, are of higher obligation. To lose our country by a scrupulous adherence to written law, would be to lose the law itself, with life, liberty, property and all those who are enjoying them with us; thus absurdly sacrificing the end to the means. When, in the battle of Germantown, General Washington's army was annoyed from Chew's house, he did not hesitate to plant his cannon against it, although the property of a citizen. When he besieged Yorktown, he leveled the suburbs, feeling that the laws of property must be postponed to the safety of the nation. While the army was before York, the Governor of Virginia took horses, carriages, provisions and even men by force, to enable that army to stay together till it could master the public enemy; and he was justified. A ship at sea in distress for provisions, meets another having abundance, yet refusing a supply; the law of self-preservation authorizes the distressed to take a supply by force. In all these cases, the unwritten laws of necessity, of self-preservation, and of the public safety, control the written laws of *meum* and *tuum*. . . .

* Andrew A. Lipscomb, ed., *The Writings of Thomas Jefferson* (Washington, D.C.: The Thomas Jefferson Memorial Ass'n, 1903), XII, 418–422.

.   .   . After the affair of the *Chesapeake*,* we thought war a very possible result. Our magazines were illy provided with some necessary articles, nor had any appropriations been made for their purchase. We ventured, however, to provide them, and to place our country in safety; and stating the case to Congress, they sanctioned the act.

To proceed to the conspiracy of Burr, and particularly to General Wilkinson's situation in New Orleans. In judging this case, we are bound to consider the state of the information, correct and incorrect, which he then possessed. He expected Burr and his band from above, a British fleet from below, and he knew there was a formidable conspiracy within the city. Under these circumstances, was he justifiable, 1st, in seizing notorious conspirators? On this there can be but two opinions: one, of the guilty and their accomplices; the other, that of all honest men. 2d. In sending them to the seat of government, when the written law gave them a right to trial in the territory? The danger of their rescue, of their continuing their machinations, the tardiness and weakness of the law, apathy of the judges, active patronage of the whole tribe of lawyers, unknown disposition of the juries, an hourly expectation of the enemy, salvation of the city, and of the Union itself, which would have been convulsed to its centre, had that conspiracy succeeded; all these constituted a law of necessity and self-preservation, and rendered the *salus populi* supreme over the written law. The officer who is called to act on this superior ground, does indeed risk himself on the justice of the controlling powers of the Constitution, and his station makes it his duty to incur that risk. But those controlling powers, and his fellow citizens generally, are bound to judge according to the circumstances under which he acted. They are not to transfer the information of this place or moment to the time and place of his action; but to put themselves into his situation. We knew here that there never was danger of a British fleet from below, and that Burr's band was crushed before it reached the Mississippi. But General Wilkinson's information was very different, and he could act on no other.*

From these examples and principles you may see what I think on the question proposed. They do not go to the case of persons charged with petty duties, where consequences are trifling, and time allowed for a legal course, nor to authorize them to take such cases out of the written law. In these, the example of overleaping the law is of greater evil than a strict adherence to its imperfect provisions. It is incumbent

---

* **Eds.' Note:** In 1807, just off Norfolk, Va., a British warship attacked and disabled the American frigate *Chesapeake,* boarded her, and took off seamen whom the British alleged had earlier deserted from the royal navy. The circumstances of the attack—the British ship had come close aboard under the pretense of asking the *Chesapeake* to accept mail—as well as the kidnapping of American seamen and the death of others during the attack—provoked loud demands for war.

* **Eds.' Note:** The situation was more complex that Jefferson knew. Modern research in the Spanish archives in Madrid has shown that General Wilkinson was on the payroll of the Spanish government, who wanted Burr's expedition stopped before he took over territory that Spain then claimed. Thus Wilkinson probably well knew that the "information" he was sending to Jefferson was false.

on those only who accept of great charges, to risk themselves on great occasions, when the safety of the nation, or some of its very high interests are at stake. An officer is bound to obey orders; yet he would be a bad one who should do it in cases for which they were not intended, and which involved the most important consequences. The line of discrimination between cases may be difficult; but the good officer is bound to draw it at his own peril, and throw himself on the justice of his country and the rectitude of his motives. . . .

"He certainly does not faithfully execute the laws, if he takes upon himself legislative power, by suspending the writ of habeas corpus, and the judicial power also, by arresting and imprisoning a person without due process of law."

EX PARTE MERRYMAN

17 Fed.Cases 145 (No. 9,487; U.S.Cir.Ct., 1861).

At 2 a.m. on May 25, 1861, Union troops entered the home of John Merryman outside of Baltimore—which had recently experienced pro-Southern riots—arrested him for helping destroy several railroad bridges, and brought him to Fort McHenry. Merryman was a prominent local citizen, a state legislator, a member of a state unit of cavalry, and strongly Confederate in his sympathies. The military allowed him to see his attorney, who filed suit the next day in the U.S. circuit court (then the name of the federal courts that conducted trials in serious cases) in Baltimore for habeas corpus. As was also then required by law, Supreme Court justices "rode circuit"—presided at circuit court. Baltimore fell within the jurisdiction of Chief Justice Roger Brooke Taney. He issued the writ, ordering General George Cadwalader, commanding Fort McHenry, to come to court with Merryman on May 27 and justify the detention.

The General did not appear, but sent a letter explaining that Merryman was guilty of treasonous acts and also that the President had authorized him (Cadwalader) to suspend the writ of habeas corpus. Furious, Taney issued a writ of attachment (arrest) against the General. On May 28, the marshal returned to court and explained he had tried to serve the writ but had been denied entrance to the fort. Taney then inquired why the marshal had not summoned a posse, and the marshal explained that such a remedy was likely to be ineffective against federal troops. Still frustrated, the Chief Justice ruled that the President had no authority to suspend the writ and thus could not authorize anyone else to do so.*

TANEY, Circuit Justice. . . .

As the case comes before me . . . I understand that the president not only claims the right to suspend the writ of habeas corpus himself, at his discretion, but to delegate that discretionary power to a military

---

* **Eds.' Note:** When he had been Attorney General, Taney had drafted Andrew Jackson's veto of the bank bill (reprinted above, p. 225), which asserted an independent presidential power to interpret the Constitution.

officer, and to leave it to him to determine whether he will or will not obey judicial process that may be served upon him.   No official notice has been given to the courts of justice, or to the public, by proclamation or otherwise, that the president claimed this power, and had exercised it in the manner stated in the return.   And I certainly listened to it with some surprise, for I had supposed it to be one of those points of constitutional law upon which there was no difference of opinion, and that it was admitted on all hands, that the privilege of the writ could not be suspended, except by act of congress.   .   .   .

The clause of the constitution, which authorizes the suspension of the privilege of the writ of habeas corpus, is in the 9th section of the first article.   This article is devoted to the legislative department of the United States, and has not the slightest reference to the executive department.   It begins by providing "that all legislative powers therein granted, shall be vested in a congress of the United States, which shall consist of a senate and house of representatives."   And after prescribing the manner in which these two branches of the legislative department shall be chosen, it proceeds to enumerate specifically the legislative powers which it thereby grants [and legislative powers which it expressly prohibits]; and at the conclusion of this specification, a clause is inserted giving congress "the power to make all laws which shall be necessary and proper for carrying into execution the foregoing powers, and all other powers vested by this constitution in the government of the United States, or in any department or officer thereof."   .   .   .

It is true, that .   .   . congress is, of necessity, the judge of whether the public safety does or does not require it [suspension of the writ of habeas corpus]; and their judgment is conclusive.   But the introduction of these words is a standing admonition to the legislative body of the danger of suspending it, and of the extreme caution they should exercise, before they give the government of the United States such power over the liberty of a citizen.

It is the second article of the constitution that provides for the organization of the executive department, enumerates the powers conferred on it, and prescribes its duties.   And if the high power over the liberty of the citizen now claimed, was intended to be conferred on the president, it would undoubtedly be found in plain words in this article; but there is not a word in it that can furnish the slightest ground to justify the exercise of the power.   .   .   .

The only power, therefore, which the president possesses, where the "life, liberty or property" of a private citizen is concerned, is the power and duty prescribed in the third section of the second article, which requires "that he shall take care that the laws shall be faithfully executed."   He is not authorized to execute them himself, or through agents or officers, civil or military, appointed by himself, but he is to take care that they be faithfully carried into execution, as they are expounded and adjudged by the co-ordinate branch of the government to which that duty is assigned by the constitution.   It is thus made his duty to come in aid of the judicial authority, if it shall be resisted by a force too strong to be overcome without the assistance of the executive arm; but in exercising this power he acts in subordination to judicial authority, assisting it to execute its process and enforce its judgments.

With such provisions in the constitution, expressed in language too clear to be misunderstood by any one, I can see no ground whatever for supposing that the president, in any emergency, or in any state of things, can authorize the suspension of the privileges of the writ of habeas corpus, or the arrest of a citizen, except in aid of the judicial power. He certainly does not faithfully execute the laws, if he takes upon himself legislative power, by suspending the writ of habeas corpus, and the judicial power also, by arresting and imprisoning a person without due process of law.

Nor can any argument be drawn from the nature of sovereignty, or the necessity of government, for self-defence in times of tumult and danger. The government of the United States is one of delegated and limited powers; it derives its existence and authority altogether from the constitution, and neither of its branches, executive, legislative or judicial, can exercise any of the powers of government beyond those specified and granted; for the tenth article of the amendments to the constitution, in express terms, provides that "the powers not delegated to the United States by the constitution, nor prohibited by it to the states, are reserved to the states, respectively, or to the people." . . .

. . . Chief Justice Marshall, in delivering the opinion of the supreme court in the case of Ex parte Bollman and Swartwout [1807] uses this decisive language . . . : "If at any time, the public safety should require the suspension of the powers vested by this act in the courts of the United States, it is for the legislature to say so. That question depends on political considerations, on which the legislature is to decide; until the legislative will be expressed, this court can only see its duty, and must obey the laws." I can add nothing to these clear and emphatic words of my great predecessor.

But the documents before me show, that the military authority in this case has gone far beyond the mere suspension of the privilege of the writ of habeas corpus. It has, by force of arms, thrust aside the judicial authorities and officers to whom the constitution has confided the power and duty of interpreting and administering the laws, and substituted a military government in its place, to be administered and executed by military officers. For, at the time these proceedings were had against John Merryman, the district judge of Maryland, the commissioner appointed under the act of congress, the district attorney and the marshal, all resided in the city of Baltimore, a few miles only from the home of the prisoner. Up to that time, there had never been the slightest resistance or obstruction to the process of any court or judicial officer of the United States, in Maryland, except by the military authority. And if a military officer, or any other person, had reason to believe that the prisoner had committed any offence against the laws of the United States, it was his duty to give information of the fact and the evidence to support it, to the district attorney. . . .

The constitution provides, as I have before said, that "no person shall be deprived of life, liberty or property, without due process of law." It declares that "the right of the people to be secure in their persons, houses, papers and effects, against unreasonable searches and seizures, shall not be violated; and no warrant shall issue, but upon probable cause, supported by oath or affirmation, and particularly describing the place to be searched, and the persons or things to be seized." It provides that the party accused shall be entitled to a speedy trial in a court of justice.

These great and fundamental laws, which congress itself could not suspend, have been disregarded and suspended, like the writ of habeas corpus, by a military order, supported by force of arms. Such is the case now before me, and I can only say that if the authority which the constitution has confided to the judiciary department and judicial officers, may thus, upon any pretext or under any circumstances, be usurped by the military power, at its discretion, the people of the United States are no longer living under a government of laws, but every citizen holds life, liberty and property at the will and pleasure of the army officer in whose military district he may happen to be found.

In such a case, my duty was too plain to be mistaken. I have exercised all the power which the constitution and laws confer upon me, but that power has been resisted by a force too strong for me to overcome. It is possible that the officer who has incurred this grave responsibility may have misunderstood his instructions, and exceeded the authority intended to be given him; I shall, therefore, order all the proceedings in this case, with my opinion, to be filed and recorded in the circuit court of the United States for the district of Maryland, and direct the clerk to transmit a copy, under seal, to the president of the United States. It will then remain for that high officer, in fulfillment of his constitutional obligation to "take care that the laws be faithfully executed," to determine what measures he will take to cause the civil process of the United States to be respected and enforced.

Editors' Notes

(1) Lincoln's administration did not acknowledge that Taney's ruling had imposed any obligation, but it quietly transferred jurisdiction of the case to the regular civilian courts. A grand jury indicted Merryman for conspiracy to commit treason. He was released on bail and never tried.

(2) For the background and aftermath of *Merryman,* see Carl B. Swisher, *The Taney Period, 1836–1864* (New York: Macmillan, 1974), chaps. 33 and 35.

"[A]re all the laws, *but one,* to go unexecuted, and the government itself go to pieces, lest that one be violated?"

LINCOLN'S MESSAGE TO CONGRESS*
July 4, 1861.

Lincoln received Taney's opinion in *Merryman,* but he did not respond directly. Instead, he took up the issue of emergency powers in a more general way in a special message to Congress six weeks later.

Fellow-citizens of the Senate and House of Representatives:

Having been convened on an extraordinary occasion, as authorized by the Constitution, your attention is not called to any ordinary subject of legislation.

At the beginning of the present Presidential term, four months ago, the functions of the Federal Government were found to be generally suspended within the several States of South Carolina, Georgia, Alabama, Mississippi, Louisiana, and Florida, excepting only those of the Post Office Department.

Within these States, all the Forts, Arsenals, Dock-yards, Custom-houses, and the like, including the movable and stationary property in, and about them, had been seized, and were held in open hostility to this Government, excepting only Forts Pickens, Taylor, and Jefferson, on, and near the Florida coast, and Fort Sumter, in Charleston harbor, South Carolina. The Forts thus seized had been put in improved condition; new ones had been built; and armed forces had been organized, and were organizing, all avowedly with the same hostile purpose.

The Forts remaining in the possession of the Federal government, in, and near, these States, were either besieged or menaced by warlike preparations; and especially Fort Sumter was nearly surrounded by well-protected hostile batteries, with guns equal in quality to the best of its own, and outnumbering the latter as perhaps ten to one. A disproportionate share, of the Federal muskets and rifles, had somehow found their way into these States, and had been seized, to be used against the government. Accumulations of the public revenue, lying within them, had been seized for the same object. The Navy was scattered in distant seas; leaving but a very small part of it within the immediate reach of the government. Officers of the Federal Army and Navy, had resigned in great numbers; and, of those resigning, a large proportion had taken up arms against the government. Simultaneously, and in connection, with all this, the purpose to sever the Federal Union, was openly avowed. In accordance with this purpose, an ordinance had been adopted in each of these States, declaring the States, respectively, to be separated from the National Union. A formula for instituting a combined government of these states had been promulgat-

---

ed; and this illegal organization, in the character of confederate States was already invoking recognition, aid, and intervention, from Foreign Powers.

Finding this condition of things, and believing it to be an imperative duty upon the incoming Executive, to prevent, if possible, the consummation of such attempt to destroy the Federal Union, a choice of means to that end became indispensable. This choice was made; and was declared in the Inaugural address. The policy chosen looked to the exhaustion of all peaceful measures, before a resort to any stronger ones. It sought only to hold the public places and property, not already wrested from the Government, and to collect the revenue; relying for the rest, on time, discussion, and the ballot-box. It promised a continuance of the mails, at government expense, to the very people who were resisting the government; and it gave repeated pledges against any disturbance to any of the people, or any of their rights. Of all that which a president might constitutionally, and justifiably, do in such a case, everything was foreborne, without which, it was believed possible to keep the government on foot. . . .

. . . . By the affair at Fort Sumter, with its surrounding circumstances, that point [of conflict] was reached. Then, and thereby, the assailants of the Government, began the conflict of arms, without a gun in sight, or in expectancy, to return their fire, save only the few in the Fort, sent to that harbor, years before, for their own protection, and still ready to give that protection, in whatever was lawful. In this act, discarding all else, they have forced upon the country, the distinct issue: "Immediate dissolution, or blood."

And this issue embraces more than the fate of these United States. It presents to the whole family of man, the question, whether a constitutional republic, or a democracy—a government of the people, by the same people—can, or cannot, maintain its territorial integrity, against its own domestic foes. It presents the question, whether discontented individuals, too few in numbers to control administration, according to organic law, in any case, can always, upon the pretences made in this case, or on any other pretences, or arbitrarily, without any pretence, break up their Government, and thus practically put an end to free government upon the earth. It forces us to ask: "Is there, in all republics, this inherent, and fatal weakness?" "Must a government, of necessity, be too *strong* for the liberties of its own people, or too *weak* to maintain its own existence?"

So viewing the issue, no choice was left but to call out the war power of the Government; and so to resist force, employed for its destruction, by force, for its preservation. . . .

Soon after the first call for militia, it was considered a duty to authorize the Commanding General, in proper cases, according to his discretion, to suspend the privilege of the writ of habeas corpus; or, in other words, to arrest, and detain, without resort to the ordinary processes and forms of law, such individuals as he might deem dangerous to the public safety. This authority has purposely been exercised but very sparingly. Nevertheless, the legality and propriety of what has been done under it, are questioned; and the attention of the country has been called to the proposition that one who is sworn to "take care that the laws be faithfully executed," should not himself violate them. Of course some consideration was given to the questions of power, and propriety, before this matter was acted upon. The whole of the laws which were required to be faithfully executed, were being resisted, and failing of execution, in nearly one-third of the States. Must they be allowed to finally fail of execution, even had it been perfectly clear, that by the use of the means necessary to their execution, some single law, made in such extreme tenderness of the citizen's liberty, that practically, it relieves more of the guilty, than of the innocent, should, to a very limited extent, be violated? To state the question more directly, are all the laws, *but one,* to go unexecuted, and the government itself go to pieces, lest that one be violated? Even in such a case, would not the official oath be broken, if the government should be overthrown, when it was believed that disregarding the single law, would tend to preserve it? But it was not believed that this question was presented. It was not believed that any law was violated. The provision of the Constitution that "The privilege of the writ of habeas corpus, shall not be suspended unless when, in cases of rebellion or invasion, the public safety may require it," is equivalent to a provision—is a provision—that such privilege may be suspended when, in cases of rebellion, or invasion, the public safety *does* require it. It was decided that we have a case of rebellion, and that the public safety does require the qualified suspension of the privilege of the writ which was authorized to be made. Now it is insisted that Congress, and not the Executive, is vested with this power. But the Constitution itself, is silent as to which, or who, is to exercise the power; and as the provision was plainly made for a dangerous emergency, it cannot be believed the framers of the instrument intended, that in every case, the danger should run its course, until Congress could be called together; the very assembling of which might be prevented, as was intended in this case, by the rebellion.

No more extended argument is now offered; as an opinion, at some length, will probably be presented by the Attorney General. Whether there shall be any legislation upon the subject, and if any, what, is submitted entirely to the better judgment of Congress. . . .

Editors' Note

In August 1861, Congress gave retrospective approval to Lincoln's suspension of habeas corpus but did not authorize future presidential suspensions. Lincoln again acted on his own in September, 1862. In March, 1863, Congress finally authorized the President to use his own judgment in suspending habeas corpus (12 Stat. 755), but imposed certain restrictions when the President exercised this authority within states loyal to the Union. See the discussion in the concur. op. of Chief Justice Chase in Ex parte Milligan (1866;

reprinted below, p. 1190). For a general discussion, see Charles Fairman, *Reconstruction and Reunion, 1864–1868* (New York: Macmillan, 1971), chaps. 4–5.

———

"The Constitution of the United States is a law for rulers and people, equally in war and in peace. . . ."

EX PARTE MILLIGAN
71 U.S. (4 Wall.) 2, 18 L.Ed. 281 (1866).

Early in the Civil War, Lambdin P. Milligan, a citizen of Indiana, had been a "Peace Democrat"—one who believed the South should be allowed to leave the Union in peace. Later he became a "major general" in "the Sons of Liberty," a group who planned to raid military prisons in the Midwest and release thousands of Confederate prisoners of war. In October, 1864, before the raids could begin, federal troops arrested Milligan. He was tried by a military commission and sentenced to be hanged. Lincoln had suspended habeas corpus in the area, but Milligan's counsel applied to the nearest federal circuit court for the writ. The two judges—one was Justice David Davis, who had been among Lincoln's managers during the presidential campaign of 1864—certified the case to the Supreme Court.

Mr. Justice **DAVIS** delivered the opinion of the Court. . . .

The importance of the main question presented by this record cannot be overstated, for it involves the very framework of the government and the fundamental principles of American liberty.

During the late wicked Rebellion the temper of the times did not allow that calmness in deliberation and discussion so necessary to a correct conclusion of a purely judicial question. Then, considerations of safety were mingled with the exercise of power, and feelings and interests prevailed which are happily terminated. Now that the public safety is assured, this question, as well as all others, can be discussed and decided without passion. . . .

The controlling question in the case is this: . . . had the Military Commission . . . jurisdiction, legally, to try and sentence [Milligan]? Milligan, not a resident of one of the rebellious states, or a prisoner of war, but a citizen of Indiana for twenty years past, and never in the military or naval service, is, while at his home, arrested by the military . . . imprisoned and . . . tried, convicted, and sentenced to be hanged by a military commission, organized under the direction of the military commander of the military district of Indiana. Had this tribunal the legal power and authority to try and punish this man?

No graver question was ever considered by this court, nor one which more nearly concerns the rights of the whole people; for it is the birthright of every American citizen when charged with crime, to be tried and punished according to law. . . . The decision of this question does not depend on argument or judicial precedents. . . . These precedents inform us of the extent of the struggle to preserve

liberty and to relieve those in civil life from military trials. The
founders of our government were familiar with the history of that
struggle; and secured in a written Constitution every right which the
people had wrested from power during a contest of ages. . . .

. . . . The Constitution of the United States is a law for rulers and
people, equally in war and in peace, and covers with the shield of its
protection all classes of men, at all times, and under all circumstances.
No doctrine, involving more pernicious consequences, was ever invented
by the wit of man than that any of its provisions can be suspended
during any of the great exigencies of government. Such a doctrine
leads directly to anarchy or despotism, but the theory of necessity on
which it is based is false; for the government, within the Constitution,
has all the powers granted to it which are necessary to preserve its
existence, as has been happily proved by the result of the great effort to
throw off its just authority. . . .

Every trial involves the exercise of judicial power; and from what
source did the Military Commission that tried him derive their authority? Certainly no part of the judicial power of the country was conferred on them; because the Constitution expressly vests it "in one
Supreme Court and such inferior courts as the Congress may from time
to time ordain and establish," and it is not pretended that the commission was a court ordained and established by Congress. They cannot
justify on the mandate of the President; because he is controlled by
law, and has his appropriate sphere of duty, which is to execute, not to
make, the laws. . . .

But it is said that the jurisdiction is complete under the "laws and
usages of war."

It can serve no useful purpose to inquire what those laws and
usages are . . . . [T]hey can never be applied to citizens in states
which have upheld the authority of the government, and where the
courts are open and their process unobstructed. This court has judicial
knowledge that in Indiana the Federal authority was always unop-
posed, and its courts always open to hear criminal accusations and
redress grievances; and no usage of war could sanction a military trial
there for any offense whatever of a citizen in civil life in nowise
connected with the military service. Congress could grant no such
power; and to the honor of our national legislature be it said, it has
never been provoked by the state of the country even to attempt its
exercise. One of the plainest constitutional provisions was, therefore,
infringed when Milligan was tried by a court not ordained and established by Congress, and not composed of judges appointed during good
behavior. . . .

Another guarantee of freedom was broken when Milligan was
denied a trial by jury. The great minds of the country have differed on
the correct interpretation to be given to various provisions of the
Federal Constitution . . . but until recently no one ever doubted that
the right of trial by jury was fortified in the organic law against the
power of attack. It is now assailed; but if ideas can be expressed in

words, and language has any meaning, this right—one of the most valuable in a free country—is preserved to every one accused of crime who is not attached to the Army or Navy or Militia in actual service. . . .

. . . This privilege is a vital principle, underlying the whole administration of criminal justice; it is not held by sufferance, and cannot be frittered away on any plea of state or political necessity. When peace prevails . . . there is no difficulty in preserving the safeguards of liberty; for the ordinary modes of trial are never neglected . . . but if society is disturbed by civil commotion—if the passions of men are aroused and the restraints of law weakened, if not disregarded—these safeguards need, and should receive, the watchful care of those entrusted with the guardianship of the Constitution and laws. In no other way can we transmit to posterity unimpaired the blessings of liberty, consecrated by the sacrifices of the Revolution.

It is claimed that martial law covers with its broad mantle the proceedings of this Military Commission. The proposition is this: That in a time of war the commander of an armed force . . . has the power, within the lines of his military district, to suspend all civil rights and their remedies, and subject citizens as well as soldiers to the rule of his will; and in the exercise of his lawful authority cannot be restrained, except by his superior officer or the President of the United States.

If this position is sound . . . then when war exists, foreign or domestic, and the country is subdivided into military departments for mere convenience, the commander of one of them can, if he chooses . . . with the approval of the Executive, substitute military force for and to the exclusion of the laws, and punish all persons, as he thinks right and proper, without fixed or certain rules.

The statement of this proposition shows its importance; for, if true, republican government is a failure, and there is an end of liberty regulated by law. . . . Civil liberty and this kind of martial law cannot endure together . . . . [O]ne or the other must perish.

This nation . . . cannot always remain at peace, and has no right to expect that it will always have wise and humane rulers. . . . Wicked men, ambitious of power, with hatred of liberty and contempt of law, may fill the place once occupied by Washington and Lincoln; and if this is conceded, and the calamities of war again befall us, the dangers to human liberty are frightful to contemplate. If our fathers had failed to provide for just such a contingency, they would have been false to the trust reposed in them. . . .

. . . [T]here are occasions when martial rule can be properly applied. If, in foreign invasion or civil war, the courts are actually closed, and it is impossible to administer criminal justice according to law, then, in the theater of actual military operations, where war really prevails, there is a necessity to furnish a substitute for the civil authority. . . . As necessity creates the rule, so it limits its duration; for, if this government is continued after the courts are reinstated, it is a gross usurpation of power. Martial rule can never exist where the courts are open, and in the proper and unobstructed exercise of their jurisdiction. It is also confined to the locality of actual war.

. . .

It is proper to say, although Milligan's trial and conviction by a military commission was illegal, yet, if guilty of the crimes imputed to him, and his guilt had been ascertained by an established court and impartial jury, he deserved severe punishment. . . .

Mr. Chief Justice **CHASE**. . . .

The act of Congress of March 3d, 1863, comprises all the legislation which seems to require consideration in this connection. The constitutionality of this act has not been questioned and is not doubted.

The first section authorized the suspension, during the Rebellion, of the writ of *habeas corpus* throughout the United States by the President. The two next sections limited this authority in important respects.

The second section required that lists of all persons, being citizens of states in which the administration of the laws had continued unimpaired in the Federal courts, who were then held or might thereafter be held as prisoners of the United States, under the authority of the President, otherwise than as prisoners of war, should be furnished to the judges of the Circuit and District Courts. The lists transmitted to the judges were to contain the names of all persons, residing within their respective jurisdictions, charged with violation of national law. And it was required, in cases where the grand jury in attendance upon any of these courts should terminate its session without proceeding by indictment or otherwise against any prisoner named in the list, that the judge of the court should forthwith make an order that such prisoner desiring a discharge, should be brought before him or the court to be discharged, on entering into recognizance, if required, to keep the peace and for good behavior, or to appear, as the court might direct, to be further dealt with according to law. Every officer of the United States having custody of such prisoners was required to obey and execute the judge's order, under penalty, for refusal or delay, of fine and imprisonment.

The third section provided, in case lists of persons other than prisoners of war then held in confinement, or thereafter arrested, should not be furnished within twenty days after the passage of the act, or, in cases of subsequent arrest, within twenty days after the time of arrest, that any citizen after the termination of a session of the grand jury without indictment or presentment, might, by petition alleging the facts and verified by oath, obtain the judge's order of discharge in favor of any person so imprisoned, on the terms and conditions prescribed in the second section.

It was made the duty of the District Attorney of the United States to attend examinations on petitions for discharge.

It was under this act that Milligan petitioned the Circuit Court for the District of Indiana for discharge from imprisonment.

The holding of the Circuit and District Courts of the United States in Indiana had been uninterrupted. The administration of the laws in the Federal courts had remained unimpaired. Milligan was imprisoned under the authority of the President, and was not a prisoner of war. No list of prisoners had been furnished to the judges, either of the District or Circuit Courts, as required by the law. A grand jury had attended the Circuit Courts of the Indiana district, while Milligan was there imprisoned, and had closed its session without finding any indictment or presentment or otherwise proceeding against the prisoner.

His case was thus brought within the precise letter and intent of the act of Congress. . . .

The first question, therefore—Ought the writ to issue? must be answered in the affirmative.

And it is equally clear that he was entitled to the discharge prayed for.

It must be borne in mind that the prayer of the petition was not for an absolute discharge, but to be delivered from military custody and imprisonment, and if found probably guilty of any offence, to be turned over to the proper tribunal for inquiry and punishment; or, if not found thus probably guilty, to be discharged altogether.

And the express terms of the act of Congress required this action of the court. . . .

An affirmative answer must, therefore, be given to the second question, namely: Ought Milligan to be discharged according to the prayer of the petition?

That the third question, namely: Had the military commission in Indiana, under the facts stated, jurisdiction to try and sentence Milligan? must be answered negatively is an unavoidable inference from affirmative answers to the other two.

But the opinion . . . [of the Court] goes further and . . . asserts not only that the military commission held in Indiana was not authorized by Congress but that it was not in the power of Congress to authorize it. . . .

We cannot agree. . . .

We think that Congress had power, though not exercised, to authorize the military commission which was held in Indiana. . . .

The Constitution itself provides for military government as well as for civil government. And we do not understand it to be claimed that the civil safeguards of the Constitution have application in cases within the proper sphere of the former. . . .

Where peace exists the laws of peace must prevail. . . . [W]hen the nation is involved in war, and some portions of the country are invaded, and all are exposed to invasion, it is within the power of Congress to determine in what states or districts such great and imminent public danger exists as justifies the authorization of military tribunals for the trial of crimes and offenses against the discipline or security of the army or against the public safety.

In Indiana, for example, at the time of the arrest of Milligan and his co-conspirators . . . the state was a military district, was the theatre of military operations, had been actually invaded, and was constantly threatened with invasion. It appears, also, that a powerful secret association, composed of citizens and others, existed within the state, under military organization, conspiring against the draft, and plotting insurrection, the liberation of the prisoners of war at various depots, the seizure of the state and national arsenals, armed coopera- tion with the enemy, and war against the national government.

We cannot doubt that, in such a time of public danger, Congress had power, under the Constitution, to provide for the organization of a military commission, and for trial by that commission of persons engaged in this conspiracy. The fact that the Federal courts were open was regarded by Congress as a sufficient reason for not exercising the power; but that fact could not deprive Congress of the right to exercise it. Those courts might be open and undisturbed in the execution of their functions, and yet wholly incompetent to avert threatened danger, or to punish, with adequate promptitude and certainty, the guilty conspirators. . . .

We have no apprehension that this power, under our American system of government, in which all official authority is derived from the people, and exercised under direct responsibility to the people, is more likely to be abused than the power to regulate commerce, or the power to borrow money. And we are unwilling to give our assent by silence to expressions of opinion which seem to us calculated, though not intended, to cripple the constitutional powers of the government, and to augment the public dangers in times of invasion and rebellion.

Mr. Justice **WAYNE,** Mr. Justice **SWAYNE,** and Mr. Justice **MILLER** concur with me in these views.

Editors' Notes

(1) **Query:** How did Davis and Chase differ on the question of WHO shall interpret? On the issue of emergency powers?

(2) Milligan's execution had been stayed pending the outcome of his appeal, and President Johnson commuted his sentence to life imprisonment before the Supreme Court heard the case. After the Court's decision, Milligan was released and never tried. In 1868 he sued the commanding general and won a nominal award. See Charles Warren, *The Supreme Court in United States History* (Rev. ed.; Boston: Little Brown, 1926), II, 427n. The most authoritative accounts of constitutional problems during the Civil War and Reconstruction are: Harold Hyman, *A More Perfect Union* (New York: Knopf, 1973); Carl B. Swisher, *The Taney Period, 1836–1864* (New York: Macmillan, 1974), chaps. 32–37; Charles Fairman, *Reconstruction and Reunion, 1864–1888* (New York: Macmillan, 1974), I, chaps. 1–13.

(3) In 1863–64, the Court had almost become embroiled in a similar controversy. Clement L. Vallandigham, a prominent Ohio politician and "supreme commander" of the Sons of Liberty, the organization in which Milligan was a "major general," had been arrested by the military for sedition. He was convicted and sentenced to imprisonment until the end of the war. He then unsuccessfully petitioned the U.S. circuit court for writ of habeas corpus. Before the Supreme Court could hear the appeal, Lincoln commuted the sentence to banishment and had Vallandigham taken behind Confederate lines and released. The justices were not anxious to take on the President during the middle of the war, and they held that they were without jurisdiction in the case. Ex parte Vallandigham (1864).

(4) *Milligan* triggered a direct confrontation with Congress. Radical Republicans had enacted a series of Reconstruction Acts that provided for military tribunals to try Southern civilians, and Radical leaders saw *Milligan* as a menace to their entire program. "That decision," Thaddeus Stevens thundered, "although in terms perhaps not as infamous as the *Dred Scott* decision, is yet far more dangerous in its operations upon the lives and liberties of the loyal men of this country. . . . That decision has unsheathed the dagger of the assassin. . . ." Congressman John Bingham, one of the principal architects of the Fourteenth Amendment, stated that if the Court persisted in its error, Congress would "defy judicial usurpation" and propose a constitutional amendment for "the abolition of the tribunal itself." The opponents of Reconstruction saw *Milligan* as an opportunity, and a case, Ex parte McCardle (1869; reprinted above, p. 361) quickly appeared on the docket.

(5) In Ex parte Quirin (1942), the Supreme Court unanimously sustained the authority of the federal government to try by military commission eight German saboteurs who had landed in the United States by submarine. After the war, the Court refused to intervene to stop trials of Axis leaders by special military courts. In re Yamashita (1946) and Hirota v. MacArthur (1948). See also Johnson v. Eisentrager (1950).

(6) After the attack on Pearl Harbor in 1941, the governor of Hawaii (then a territory) suspended habeas corpus and placed the islands under martial law. The President approved the governor's action and designated the commanding general in the area to exercise all normal executive and judicial powers. The local U.S. district judge, however, ruled that the courts were open and that, on the basis of *Milligan,* he would issue writs. The general forbade the judge to do so, and the judge held the general in contempt of court and fined him $5,000. An emissary from the Department of Justice had to negotiate a compromise that eventually led to a pair of cases being taken to the Supreme Court. The justices decided the cases after the war and ruled in favor of the judge. But the Court avoided the constitutional issue and held that the governor had exceeded his statutory authority. Duncan v. Kahanamoku (1946).

(7) Dependents of American military personnel living abroad cannot be tried by courts martial, despite executive agreements with the host country and despite the fact that local jurisdictions might deprive defendants of more procedural safeguards than would military tribunals. Reid v. Covert (1957); Kinsella v. Kruger (1957); and Kinsella v. United States ex rel. Singleton (1960). Nor can American citizens who are living abroad as civilian employees

of the armed forces be tried by courts martial. McElroy v. United States ex rel. Guagliardo (1960); Grisham v. Hagan (1960).

" '[W]e cannot reject as unfounded the judgment of the military authorities and of Congress that there were disloyal members of that population. . . .' "

KOREMATSU v. UNITED STATES
323 U.S. 214, 65 S.Ct. 193, 89 L.Ed. 194 (1944).

Chapter 3, pp. 62–73, elaborated the background of this case in some detail. Several months after the attack on Pearl Harbor, Congress made it a crime for persons of Japanese ancestry to enter or remain in zones designated by the President. Pursuant to this authority, the Commanding General of the west coast region ordered all such persons to report to relocation centers for internment in concentration camps. Fred Korematsu, an American citizen of Japanese descent, defied this order, was arrested, and convicted. He obtained certiorari from the Supreme Court.

Mr. Justice **BLACK** delivered the opinion of the Court. . . .

It should be noted . . . that all legal restrictions which curtail the civil rights of a single racial group are immediately suspect. That is not to say that all such restrictions are unconstitutional. It is to say that courts must subject them to more rigid scrutiny. Pressing public necessity may sometimes justify the existence of such restrictions; racial antagonism never can. . . .

In light of the principles we announced in Hirabayashi [v. United States (1943)], we are unable to conclude that it was beyond the war power of Congress and the Executive to exclude those of Japanese ancestry from the West Coast war area. . . . True, exclusion from . . . one's home . . . is a far greater deprivation than constant confinement to the home from 8 P.M. to 6 A.M. . . . But exclusion from a threatened area, no less than curfew, has a definite and close relationship to the prevention of espionage and sabotage. The military authorities, charged with the primary responsibility of defending our shores, concluded that curfew provided inadequate protection and ordered exclusion. They did so . . . in accordance with congressional authority to the military to say who should, and who should not, remain in the threatened areas. . . .

Here, as in *Hirabayashi*, "we cannot reject as unfounded the judgment of the military authorities and of Congress that there were disloyal members of that population. . . ."

. . . It was because we could not reject the finding of the military authorities that it was impossible to bring about an immediate segregation of the disloyal from the loyal that we sustained the validity of the curfew order as applying to the whole group. In the instant case, temporary exclusion of the entire group was rested by the military on the same ground. . . .

. . . That there were members of the group who retained loyalties to Japan has been confirmed by investigations made subsequent to the exclusion. Approximately five thousand American citizens of Japanese ancestry refused to swear unqualified allegiance to the United States and to renounce allegiance to the Japanese Emperor, and several thousand evacuees requested repatriation to Japan.

We uphold the exclusion order as of the time it was made and when the petitioner violated it. . . .

. . . [W]e are not unmindful of the hardships imposed by it upon a large group of American citizens. . . . But hardships are part of war, and war is an aggregation of hardships. Compulsory exclusion of large groups of citizens from their homes, except under circumstances of direst emergency and peril, is inconsistent with our basic governmental institutions. But when under conditions of modern warfare our shores are threatened by hostile forces, the power to protect must be commensurate with the threatened danger. . . .

We are thus being asked to pass at this time upon the whole subsequent detention program in both assembly and relocation centers, although the only issues framed at the trial related to petitioner's remaining in the prohibited area in violation of the exclusion order. Had petitioner here left the prohibited area and gone to an assembly center we cannot say either as a matter of fact or law, that his presence in that center would have resulted in his detention in a relocation center.* Some who did report to the assembly center were not sent to relocation centers, but were released upon condition that they remain outside the prohibited zone until the military orders were modified or lifted. . . .

Since the petitioner has not been convicted of failing to report or to remain in an assembly or relocation center, we cannot in this case determine the validity of those separate provisions of the order. . . .

Some of the members of the Court are of the view that evacuation and detention in an assembly center were inseparable. . . . The power to exclude includes the power to do it by force if necessary. And any forcible measure must necessarily entail some degree of detention or restraint whatever method of removal is selected. But whichever view is taken, it results in holding that the order under which petitioner was convicted was valid.

It is said that we are dealing here with the case of imprisonment of a citizen in a concentration camp solely because of his ancestry. . . . Our task would be simple were this a case involving the imprisonment of a loyal citizen in a concentration camp because of racial prejudice. Regardless of the true nature of the assembly and relocation centers— and we deem it unjustifiable to call them concentration camps with all the ugly connotations that term implies—we are dealing specifically

---

* **Eds.' Note:** In its brief, the Department of Justice conceded that had Korematsu obeyed the army's order he would have been placed in a detention camp.

with nothing but an exclusion order. To cast this case into outlines of racial prejudice, without reference to the real military dangers which were presented, merely confuses the issue. Korematsu was not excluded from the Military Area because of hostility to him or his race. He *was* excluded because we are at war with the Japanese Empire, because the properly constituted military authorities feared an invasion of our West Coast and felt constrained to take proper security measures, because they decided that the military urgency of the situation demanded that all citizens of Japanese ancestry be segregated from the West Coast temporarily, and finally, because Congress, reposing its confidence in this time of war in our military leaders—as inevitably it must—determined that they should have the power to do just this. There was evidence of disloyalty on the part of some, the military authorities considered that the need for action was great, and time was short. We cannot—by availing ourselves of the calm perspective of hindsight—now say that at that time these actions were unjustified.

Affirmed.

Mr. Justice **FRANKFURTER,** concurring. . . .

The provisions of the Constitution which confer on the Congress and the President powers to . . . wage war are as much part of the Constitution as provisions looking to a nation at peace. . . . Therefore the validity of action under the war power must be judged wholly in the context of war. That action is not to be stigmatized as lawless because like action in times of peace would be lawless. To talk about a military order that expresses an allowable judgment of war needs by those entrusted with the duty of conducting war as "an unconstitutional order" is to suffuse a part of the Constitution with an atmosphere of unconstitutionality. The respective spheres of action of military authorities and of judges are of course very different. But within their sphere, military authorities are no more outside the bounds of obedience to the Constitution than are judges within theirs. . . . If a military order . . . does not transcend the means appropriate for conducting war, such action by the military is as constitutional as would be any authorized action by the Interstate Commerce Commission within the limits of the constitutional power to regulate commerce. . . . To find that the Constitution does not forbid the military measures now complained of does not carry with it approval of that which Congress and the Executive did. That is their business, not ours.

Mr. Justice **ROBERTS:**

I dissent, because I think the indisputable facts exhibit a clear violation of Constitutional rights. . . . [E]xclusion was but a part of an over-all plan for forceable detention. . . . The two conflicting orders, one of which commanded him to stay and the other which commanded him to go, were nothing but a cleverly devised trap to accomplish the real purpose of the [military] authority, which was to lock him up in a concentration camp. . . . Why should we set up a figmentary and artificial situation instead of addressing ourselves to the actualities of the case? .   .   .

Mr. Justice **MURPHY**, dissenting:

This exclusion .   .   . goes over "the very brink of constitutional power" and falls into the ugly abyss of racism.

In dealing with matters relating to the prosecution and progress of a war, we must accord great respect .   .   . to the judgments of the military authorities.   .   .   .

At the same time, however, it is essential that there be limits to military discretion.   .   .   .

The judicial test of whether the Government, on a plea of military necessity, can validly deprive an individual of any of his constitutional rights is whether the deprivation is reasonably related to a public danger that is so "immediate, imminent, and impending" as not to admit of delay and not to permit the intervention of ordinary constitutional processes to alleviate the danger.   .   .   .   Civilian Exclusion Order No. 34 .   .   . clearly does not meet that test. Being an obvious racial discrimination, the order deprives all those within its scope of the equal protection of the laws as guaranteed by the Fifth Amendment. It further deprives these individuals of their constitutional rights to live and work where they will, to establish a home where they choose and to move about freely. In excommunicating them without benefit of hearings, this order also deprives them of all their constitutional rights to procedural due process. Yet no reasonable relation to an "immediate, imminent, and impending" public danger is evident to support this racial restriction.   .   .   .

It must be conceded that the military and naval situation in the spring of 1942 was such as to generate a very real fear of invasion of the Pacific Coast, accompanied by fears of sabotage and espionage in that area. The military command was therefore justified in adopting all reasonable means necessary to combat these dangers. In adjudging the military action taken in light of the then apparent dangers, we must not erect too high or too meticulous standards; it is necessary only that the action have some reasonable relation to the removal of the dangers.   .   .   .   But the exclusion .   .   . of all persons with Japanese blood in their veins has no such reasonable relation .   .   . because the exclusion order necessarily must rely for its reasonableness upon the assumption that *all* persons of Japanese ancestry may have a dangerous tendency to commit sabotage and espionage and to aid our Japanese enemy in other ways.   .   .   .

That this forced exclusion was the result in good measure of this erroneous assumption of racial guilt rather than bona fide military necessity is evidenced by the Commanding General's Final Report on the evacuation from the Pacific Coast area. In it he refers to all individuals of Japanese descent as "subversive," as belonging to "an enemy race" whose "racial strains are undiluted," and as constituting "over 112,000 potential enemies .   .   . at large today" along the Pacific

Coast. In support of this blanket condemnation of all persons of Japanese descent, however, no reliable evidence is cited. . . .

Justification . . . is sought instead, mainly upon questionable racial and sociological grounds not ordinarily within the realm of expert military judgment, supplemented by certain semi-military conclusions drawn from an unwarranted use of circumstantial evidence. Individuals of Japanese ancestry are condemned because they are said to be "a large, unassimilated, tightly knit racial group, bound to an enemy nation by strong ties of race, culture, custom and religion." They are claimed to be given to "emperor worshipping ceremonies" and to "dual citizenship." Japanese language schools and allegedly pro-Japanese organizations are cited as evidence of possible group disloyalty, together with facts as to certain persons being educated and residing at length in Japan. It is intimated that many of these individuals deliberately resided "adjacent to strategic points," thus enabling them "to carry into execution a tremendous program of sabotage on a mass scale should any considerable number of them have been inclined to do so." The need for protective custody is also asserted. The report refers without identity to "numerous incidents of violence" as well as to other admittedly unverified or cumulative incidents. From this, plus certain other events not shown to have been connected with the Japanese Americans, it is concluded that the "situation was fraught with danger to the Japanese population itself" and that the general public "was ready to take matters into its own hands." Finally, it is intimated, though not directly charged or proved, that persons of Japanese ancestry were responsible for three minor isolated shellings and bombings of the Pacific Coast area, as well as for unidentified radio transmissions and night signalling.

The main reasons . . . appear . . . to be largely an accumulation of much of the misinformation, half-truths and insinuations that for years have been directed against Japanese Americans by people with racial and economic prejudices—the same people who have been among the foremost advocates of the evacuation. A military judgment based upon such racial and sociological considerations is not entitled to the great weight ordinarily given the judgments based upon strictly military considerations. Especially is this so when every charge relative to race, religion, culture, geographical location, and legal and economic status has been substantially discredited by independent studies made by experts in these matters. . . .

I dissent, therefore, from this legalization of racism. Racial discrimination in any form and in any degree has no justifiable part whatever in our democratic way of life. It is unattractive in any setting but it is utterly revolting among a free people who have embraced the principles set forth in the Constitution of the United States. . . .

Mr. Justice **JACKSON,** dissenting.

Now if any fundamental assumption underlies our system, it is that guilt is personal and not inheritable. . . . But here is an attempt to make an otherwise innocent act a crime merely because this prisoner is the son of parents as to whom he had no choice, and belongs to a race from which there is no way to resign. . . .

. . . [T]he "law" which this prisoner is convicted of disregarding is not found in an act of Congress, but in a military order. Neither the Act of Congress nor the Executive Order of the President, nor both together, would afford a basis for the conviction. . . . And it is said that if the military commander had reasonable military grounds for promulgating the orders, they are constitutional and become law, and the Court is required to enforce them. . . .

It would be impracticable and dangerous idealism to expect or insist that each specific military command in an area of probable operations will conform to conventional tests of constitutionality. . . . The armed services must protect a society, not merely its Constitution. The very essence of the military job is to marshal physical force, to remove every obstacle to its effectiveness, to give it every strategic advantage. Defense measures will not, and often should not, be held within the limits that bind civil authority in peace. . . .

But if we cannot confine military expedients by the Constitution, neither would I distort the Constitution to approve all that the military may deem expedient. . . . I cannot say . . . that the orders of General DeWitt were not reasonably expedient military precautions, nor could I say that they were. But even if they were permissible military procedures, I deny that it follows that they are constitutional. If, as the Court holds, it does follow, then we may as well say that any military order will be constitutional and have done with it. . . .

Much is said of the danger to liberty from the Army program. . . . But a judicial construction of the due process clause that will sustain this order is a far more subtle blow to liberty. . . . A military order, however unconstitutional, is not apt to last longer than the military emergency. Even during that period a succeeding commander may revoke it all. But once a judicial opinion rationalizes such an order to show that it conforms to the Constitution, or rather rationalizes the Constitution to show that the Constitution sanctions such an order, the Court for all time has validated the principle of racial discrimination in criminal procedure and of transplanting American citizens. The principle then lies about like a loaded weapon ready for the hand of any authority that can bring forward a plausible claim of an urgent need. . . . All who observe the work of courts are familiar with what Judge Cardozo described as "the tendency of a principle to expand itself to the limit of its logic." A military commander may overstep the bounds of constitutionality, and it is an incident. But if we review and approve, that passing incident becomes the doctrine of the Constitution. There it has a generative power of its own, and all that it creates will be in its own image. Nothing better illustrates this danger than does the Court's opinion in this case.

It argues that we are bound to uphold the conviction of Korematsu because we upheld one in *Hirabayashi.* . . .

In that case we were urged to consider only the curfew feature. . . . We yielded, and the Chief Justice guarded the opinion as carefully as language will do. He said: ". . . We decide only the issue as we have defined it—we decide only that the *curfew order* as applied, and at the time it was applied, was within the boundaries of the war power." . . . Now the principle of racial discrimination is pushed from support of mild measures to very harsh ones, and from temporary deprivations to indeterminate ones. And the precedent which it is said requires us to do so is *Hirabayashi.* The Court is now saying that in *Hirabayashi* we did decide the very things we there said we were not deciding. Because we said that these citizens could be made to stay in their homes during the hours of dark, it is said we must require them to leave home entirely; and if that, we are told they may also be taken into custody for deportation; and if that, it is argued they may also be held for some undetermined time in detention camps. How far the principle of this case would be extended before plausible reasons would play out, I do not know.

I should hold that a civil court cannot be made to enforce an order which violates constitutional limitations even if it is a reasonable exercise of military authority. The courts can exercise only the judicial power, can apply only law, and must abide by the Constitution, or they cease to be civil courts and become instruments of military policy.

. . . I would not lead people to rely on this Court for a review that seems to me wholly delusive. . . . If the people ever let command of the war power fall into irresponsible and unscrupulous hands, the courts wield no power equal to its restraint. The chief restraint upon those who command the physical forces of the country . . . must be their responsibility to the political judgments of their contemporaries and to the moral judgments of history.

My duties as a justice . . . do not require me to make a military judgment as to whether General DeWitt's evacuation and detention program was a reasonable military necessity. I do not suggest that the courts should have attempted to interfere with the Army in carrying out its task. But I do not think they may be asked to execute a military expedient that has no place in law under the Constitution. I would reverse the judgment and discharge the prisoner.

Editors' Notes

(1) In 1983, Korematsu asked the U.S. District Court in San Francisco, in which he had been convicted, to vacate his conviction, on grounds that the government's claims of danger from Nisei had been false. The Department of Justice filed a brief that, according to the district judge, was "tantamount to a confession of error." The judge granted Korematsu's request and the conviction was finally expunged from his record.

(2) Compare the way in which the Court scrutinized the military's claim of necessity in *Korematsu,* decided in 1944, when the war was still going on in both Europe and Asia, with its much tougher attitude in 1946, when, a year after the end of the war, it decided Duncan v. Kanhanamoku, discussed in Eds.' Note 6 to Ex parte Milligan, above, p. 1190.

(3) To what extent was Black's opinion consistent with his usual textual *approach* to interpretation, his usual interpretive *modes* of verbal and historical analyses, and his usual *technique* of literalism? How did he and Frankfurter differ in justifying the decision to uphold Korematsu's conviction? Compare these two opinions with those by the same justices in Rochin v. California (1952; reprinted above, p. 100).

(4) Jackson's dissent has been called "an essay in judicial nihilism." To what extent is that charge accurate?

(5) In 1948, in a minor spasm of guilt, Congress passed the Japanese-Americans Evacuation Claims Act, allowing Nisei to file for "loss of real or personal property," not compensated by insurance, resulting from the evacuation. 50 U.S.C.App. § 1981ff. The government eventually paid out about $37 million of the $148 million claimed. The Federal Reserve Bank in San Francisco estimated the actual losses at $400 million. See Commission on Wartime Relocation and Internment of Civilians, *Report: Personal Justice Denied* (Washington, D.C.: Government Printing Office, 1982), chap. 4.

(6) In addition to the *Report* cited in Note 5, the best studies of the relocation program's origins, effects, and constitutional as well as human problems are: Morton Grodzins, *Americans Betrayed* (Chicago: University of Chicago Press, 1949); Jacobus tenBroek et al., *Prejudice, War, and the Constitution* (Berkeley, Cal.: University of California Press, 1954); Alpheus Thomas Mason, *Harlan Fiske Stone* (New York: Viking, 1956), chap. 40; J. Woodford Howard, *Mr. Justice Murphy* (Princeton, N.J.: Princeton University Press, 1968), chaps. 12–13; and Peter Irons, *Justice at War* (New York: Oxford University Press, 1983).

"Even though 'theater of war' be an expanding concept, we cannot with faithfulness to our constitutional system hold that the Commander in Chief of the Armed Forces has the ultimate power as such to take possession of private property in order to keep labor disputes from stopping production."

YOUNGSTOWN SHEET & TUBE CO. v. SAWYER
343 U.S. 579, 72 S.Ct. 863, 96 L.Ed. 1153 (1952).

This case, involving the authority of the President, acting without congressional authorization, to seize and operate steel mills to prevent a strike that would have crippled production of ammunition during the Korean War, is reprinted above at p. 339.

"We cannot accept the Government's argument that internal security matters are too subtle and complex for judicial evaluation."

UNITED STATES v. UNITED STATES DISTRICT COURT
407 U.S. 297, 92 S.Ct. 2125, 32 L.Ed.2d 752 (1972).

The United States charged three people with conspiring to destroy government property and one of the three with dynamiting a CIA office. During
pretrial proceedings, the defendants asked the judge to order the government
to produce information gathered against them by electronic surveillance to
determine if the government's case was "tainted" by illegally obtained evidence. The Nixon administration conceded that it had used wiretaps without
obtaining a warrant as required by Title III of the Omnibus Crime Control and
Safe Streets Act, but asserted that the President's inherent power to protect
national security was sufficient authority for such, even though the source of
danger was domestic not foreign.
      The district judge held that the wiretaps, without a warrant, violated the
Fourth Amendment. The Court of Appeals for the Sixth Circuit agreed, and
the government sought and obtained certiorari.

Mr. Justice **POWELL** delivered the opinion of the Court. . . .
      The issue before us is an important one for the people of our
country and their Government. It involves the delicate question of the
President's power . . . to authorize electronic surveillance in internal
security matters without prior judicial approval. Successive Presidents
for more than one-quarter of a century have authorized such surveillance in varying degrees, without guidance from the Congress or a
definitive decision of this Court. This case brings the issue here for the
first time. Its resolution is a matter of national concern, requiring
sensitivity both to the Government's right to protect itself from unlawful subversion and attack and to the citizen's right to be secure in his
privacy against unreasonable Government intrusion. . . .

                                    I

      Title III of the Omnibus Crime Control and Safe Streets Act, 18
U.S.C. §§ 2510–2520, authorizes the use of electronic surveillance for
classes of crimes carefully specified. . . . Such surveillance is subject to prior court order. Section 2518 sets forth the detailed and
particularized application necessary to obtain such an order as well as
carefully circumscribed conditions for its use. The Act represents a
comprehensive attempt by Congress to promote more effective control
of crime while protecting the privacy of individual thought and expression. Much of Title III was drawn to meet the constitutional requirements for electronic surveillance enunciated by this Court in Berger v.
New York (1967) and Katz v. United States (1967).
      Together with the elaborate surveillance requirements in Title III,
there is the following proviso, 18 U.S.C. § 2511(3):

Nothing contained in this chapter or in section 605 of the Communications Act of 1934 shall limit the constitutional power of the President to take such measures as he deems necessary to protect the Nation against actual or potential attack or other hostile acts of a foreign power, to obtain foreign intelligence information deemed essential to the security of the United States, or to protect national security information against foreign intelligence activities. *Nor shall anything contained in this chapter be deemed to limit the constitutional power of the President to take such measures as he deems necessary to protect the United States against the overthrow of the Government by force or other unlawful means, or against any other clear and present danger to the structure or existence of the Government.* . . . (Emphasis supplied.)

The Government relies on § 2511(3). It argues that "in excepting national security surveillances from the Act's warrant requirement Congress recognized the President's authority to conduct such surveillances without prior judicial approval." The section thus is viewed as a recognition or affirmance of a constitutional authority in the President to conduct warrantless domestic security surveillance such as that involved in this case.

We think the language of § 2511(3), as well as the legislative history of the statute, refutes this interpretation. . . . At most, this [language] is an implicit recognition that the President does have certain powers in the specified areas. Few would doubt this. . . . But so far as the use of the President's electronic surveillance power is concerned, the language is essentially neutral.

Section 2511(3) certainly confers no power. . . . It merely provides that the Act shall not be interpreted to limit or disturb such power as the President may have under the Constitution. In short, Congress simply left presidential powers where it found them.

The language of subsection (3), here involved, is to be contrasted with the language of the exceptions set forth in the preceding subsection. Rather than stating that warrantless presidential uses of electronic surveillance "shall not be unlawful" and thus employing the standard language of exception, subsection (3) merely disclaims any intention "to limit the constitutional power of the President."

The express grant of authority to conduct surveillances is found in § 2516, which authorizes the Attorney General to make application to a federal judge when surveillance may provide evidence of certain offenses. These offenses are described with meticulous care and specificity.

Where the Act authorizes surveillance, the procedure to be followed is specified in § 2518. Subsection (1) thereof requires application to a judge of competent jurisdiction for a prior order of approval, and states in detail the information required in such application. Subsection (3) prescribes the necessary elements of probable cause which the judge must find before issuing an order authorizing an interception. Subsection (4) sets forth the required contents of such an order. Subsection (5) sets strict time limits on an order. Provision is made in subsection (7) for "an emergency situation" found to exist by the

Attorney General (or by the principal prosecuting attorney of a State) "with respect to conspiratorial activities threatening the national security interest." In such a situation, emergency surveillance may be conducted "if an application for an order approving the interception is made . . . within forty-eight hours." If such an order is not obtained, or the application therefor is denied, the interception is deemed to be a violation of the Act.

In view of these and other interrelated provisions delineating permissible interceptions of particular criminal activity upon carefully specified conditions, it would have been incongruous for Congress to have legislated with respect to the important and complex area of national security in a single brief and nebulous paragraph. This would not comport with the sensitivity of the problem involved or with the extraordinary care Congress exercised in drafting other sections of the Act. We therefore think the conclusion inescapable that Congress only intended to make clear that the Act simply did not legislate with respect to national security surveillances.

The legislative history of § 2511(3) supports this interpretation. . . .

II

It is important at the outset to emphasize the limited nature of the question before the Court. This case raises no constitutional challenge to electronic surveillance as specifically authorized by Title III of the [Act]. Nor is there any question or doubt as to the necessity of obtaining a warrant in the surveillance of crimes unrelated to the national security interest. *Katz*; *Berger*. Further, the instant case requires no judgment on the scope of the President's surveillance power with respect to the activities of foreign powers, within or without his country. . . . There is no evidence of any involvement, directly or indirectly, of a foreign power.

Our present inquiry, though important, is therefore a narrow one. It addresses a question left open by *Katz*:

> Whether safeguards other than prior authorization by a magistrate would satisfy the Fourth Amendment in a situation involving the national security. . . .

. . . We begin the inquiry by noting that the President of the United States has the fundamental duty, under Art II, § 1, of the Constitution, to "preserve, protect, and defend the Constitution of the United States." Implicit in that duty is the power to protect our Government against those who would subvert or overthrow it by unlawful means. In the discharge of this duty, the President—through the Attorney General—may find it necessary to employ electronic surveillance to obtain intelligence information on the plans of those who plot unlawful acts against the Government. The use of such surveillance in internal security cases has been sanctioned more or less continuously by various Presidents and Attorneys General since July 1946. . . .*

. . . The covertness and complexity of potential unlawful conduct against the Government and the necessary dependency of many conspirators upon the telephone make electronic surveillance an effective investigatory instrument in certain circumstances. The marked acceleration in technological developments and sophistication in their use have resulted in new techniques for the planning, commission, and concealment of criminal activities. It would be contrary to the public interest for Government to deny to itself the prudent and lawful employment of those very techniques which are employed against the Government and its law-abiding citizens.

It has been said that "[t]he most basic function of any government is to provide for the security of the individual and of his property." Miranda v. Arizona (1966) (White, J., dissenting). And unless Government safeguards its own capacity to function and to preserve the security of its people, society itself could become so disordered that all rights and liberties would be endangered. . . .

But a recognition of these elementary truths does not make the employment by Government of electronic surveillance a welcome development—even when employed with restraint and under judicial supervision. There is, understandably, a deep-seated uneasiness and apprehension that this capability will be used to intrude upon cherished privacy of law-abiding citizens. We look to the Bill of Rights to safeguard this privacy. Though physical entry of the home is the chief evil against which the wording of the Fourth Amendment is directed, its broader spirit now shields private speech from unreasonable surveillance. *Katz*; *Berger*; Silverman v. United States (1961). Our decision in *Katz* refused to lock the Fourth Amendment into instances of actual physical trespass. Rather, the Amendment governs "not only the seizure of tangible items, but extends as well to the recording of oral statements . . . without any 'technical trespass under . . . local property law.'" That decision implicitly recognized that the broad and unsuspected governmental incursions into conversational privacy which electronic surveillance entails necessitate the application of Fourth Amendment safeguards.

National security cases, moreover, often reflect a convergence of First and Fourth Amendment values not present in cases of "ordinary" crime. Though the investigative duty of the executive may be stronger in such cases, so also is there greater jeopardy to constitutionally protected speech. . . . History abundantly documents the tendency of Government—however benevolent and benign its motives—to view with suspicion those who most fervently dispute its policies. Fourth Amendment protections become the more necessary when the targets of official surveillance may be those suspected of unorthodoxy in their political beliefs. The danger to political dissent is acute where the Government attempts to act under so vague a concept as the power to

---

* **Eds.' Note:** In fact since 1940.

protect "domestic security." Given the difficulty of defining the domestic security interest, the danger of abuse in acting to protect that interest becomes apparent. . . . The price of lawful public dissent must not be a dread of subjection to an unchecked surveillance power. Nor must the fear of unauthorized official eavesdropping deter vigorous citizen dissent and discussion of Government action in private conversation. For private dissent, no less than open public discourse, is essential to our free society.

III

As the Fourth Amendment is not absolute in its terms, our task is to examine and balance the basic values at stake in this case: the duty of Government to protect the domestic security, and the potential danger posed by unreasonable surveillance to individual privacy and free expression. If the legitimate need of Government to safeguard domestic security requires the use of electronic surveillance, the question is whether the needs of citizens for privacy and free expression may not be better protected by requiring a warrant before such surveillance is undertaken. We must also ask whether a warrant requirement would unduly frustrate the efforts of Government to protect itself from acts of subversion and overthrow directed against it.

Though the Fourth Amendment speaks broadly of "unreasonable searches and seizures," the definition of "reasonableness" turns, at least in part, on the more specific commands of the warrant clause. . . . [That clause] . . . has been "a valued part of our constitutional law for decades. . . . It is not an inconvenience to be somehow 'weighed' against the claims of police efficiency. It is, or should be, an important working part of our machinery of government." . . .

These Fourth Amendment freedoms cannot properly be guaranteed if domestic security surveillances may be conducted solely within the discretion of the executive branch. The Fourth Amendment does not contemplate the executive officers of Government as neutral and disinterested magistrates. Their duty and responsibility is to enforce the laws, to investigate, and to prosecute. *Katz.* But those charged with this investigative and prosecutorial duty should not be the sole judges of when to utilize constitutionally sensitive means in pursuing their tasks. The historical judgment, which the Fourth Amendment accepts, is that unreviewed executive discretion may yield too readily to pressures to obtain incriminating evidence and overlook potential invasions of privacy and protected speech.

It may well be that, in the instant case, the Government's surveillance . . . was a reasonable one which readily would have gained prior judicial approval. . . . The Fourth Amendment contemplates a prior judicial judgment, not the risk that executive discretion may be reasonably exercised. This judicial role accords with our basic constitutional doctrine that individual freedoms will best be preserved through a separation of powers and division of functions among the different branches and levels of Government. The independent check upon executive discretion is not satisfied, as the Government argues, by "extremely limited" post-surveillance judicial review. Indeed, post-surveillance review would never reach the surveillances which failed to result in prosecutions. Prior review by a neutral and detached magistrate is the time-tested means of effectuating Fourth Amendment rights. Beck v. Ohio (1964).

It is true that there have been some exceptions to the warrant requirement. But those exceptions are few in number and carefully delineated, *Katz*; in general, they serve the legitimate needs of law enforcement officers to protect their own well-being and preserve evidence from destruction. . . .

The Government argues that . . . the requirement of prior judicial review would obstruct the President in the discharge of his constitutional duty to protect domestic security. We are told further that these surveillances are directed primarily to the collecting and maintaining of intelligence with respect to subversive forces, and are not an attempt to gather evidence for specific criminal prosecutions. It is said that this type of surveillance should not be subject to traditional warrant requirements which were established to govern investigation of criminal activity. . . .

As a final reason for exemption from a warrant requirement, the Government believes that disclosure to a magistrate of all or even a significant portion of the information involved in domestic security surveillances "would create serious potential dangers to the national security and to the lives of informants and agents. . . ."

These contentions in behalf of a complete exemption from the warrant requirement, when urged on behalf of the President and the national security in its domestic implications, merit the most careful consideration. We certainly do not reject them lightly, especially at a time of worldwide ferment. . . .

But we do not think a case has been made for the requested departure from Fourth Amendment standards. The circumstances described do not justify complete exemption of domestic security surveillance from prior judicial scrutiny. Official surveillance, whether its purpose be criminal investigation or ongoing intelligence gathering, risks infringement of constitutionally protected privacy of speech. Security surveillances are especially sensitive because of the inherent vagueness of the domestic security concept, the necessarily broad and continuing nature of intelligence gathering, and the temptation to utilize such surveillances to oversee political dissent. We recognize . . . the constitutional basis of the President's domestic security role, but we think it must be exercised in a manner compatible with the Fourth Amendment. In this case we hold that this requires an appropriate prior warrant procedure.

We cannot accept the Government's argument that internal security matters are too subtle and complex for judicial evaluation. Courts regularly deal with the most difficult issues of our society. There is no reason to believe that federal judges will be insensitive to or uncomprehending of the issues involved in domestic security cases. . . .

Nor do we believe prior judicial approval will fracture the secrecy essential to official intelligence gathering. The investigation of criminal activity has long involved imparting sensitive information to judicial officers who have respected the confidentialities involved. . . . Title III of the [Act] already has imposed this responsibility on the judiciary in connection with such crimes as espionage, sabotage, and treason, each of which may involve domestic as well as foreign security threats. Moreover, a warrant application involves no public or adversary proceedings: it is an ex parte request before a magistrate or judge. . . .

Thus, we conclude that the Government's concerns do not justify departure in this case from the customary Fourth Amendment requirement of judicial approval prior to initiation of a search or surveillance. Although some added burden will be imposed upon the Attorney General, this inconvenience is justified in a free society to protect constitutional values. . . .

IV

We emphasize . . . the scope of our decision. As stated at the outset, this case involves only the domestic aspects of national security. We have not addressed, and express no opinion as to, the issues which may be involved with respect to activities of foreign powers or their agents. . . .

The judgment of the Court of Appeals is hereby

Affirmed.

The Chief Justice [**BURGER**] concurs in the result.

Mr. Justice **REHNQUIST** took no part in the consideration or decision of this case.

Mr. Justice **DOUGLAS**, concurring. . . .

Mr. Justice **WHITE** concurring in the judgment. . . .

Editors' Notes

(1) **Query:** In Part III of his opinion Powell said that the Court must "balance the basic values at stake." Does he carry through this task so as to meet Chapter 8's criticisms of balancing as a *technique* of interpretation?

(2) Laird v. Tatum (1972), argued a month after and decided a week after *U.S. District Court,* involved a class action for an injunction against Army intelligence surveillance of people accused of no crime but suspected of political radicalism. Plaintiffs claimed that this intimate watch on their lives had "a chilling effect" on freedoms protected by the First Amendment. By a 5–4 vote, the Court held that the plaintiffs lacked "standing to sue"—that is, they had not shown real injury to a specifically guaranteed legal right.

APPENDIX A

WHEN May a Litigant Invoke the Constitution?

Citizens of the United States regularly invoke the Constitution as an authoritative ground for political arguments. Even if we restrict the interrogative WHEN to legislative or executive officials, the answer is sweeping, for governmental work inevitably involves frequent interpretation of the Constitution.

As the American constitutional system has developed, however, for better or worse (see Part III concerning the interrogative, WHO are the Authoritative Interpreters?), judges have taken a special role as regularized interpreters of the Constitution. The more specific question of this Appendix, therefore, poses the interrogative: WHEN may a *litigant,* a person suing or being sued in a court, invoke the Constitution as legally compelling? Here we are concerned with a narrower question about the rules that judges, especially justices of the U.S. Supreme Court, have created to regulate access to their authority to interpret the Constitution.

Besides its rather narrow original jurisdiction to hear cases in the first instance, the Supreme Court combines three appellate functions that might conceivably have been separated among different courts or, in some respects, not given to courts at all: (1) It performs as the nation's *high court of appeals,* with the capacity to assure substantive uniformity and procedural consistency in the application of federal law by the nation's courts. (2) It serves as the *ultimate judicial interpreter of federal legislation,* inquiring into the meaning of congressionally mandated public policy. And (3) it has assumed the role of *final court of constitutional review,* ascertaining the conformity of governmental actions with the Court's interpretation of the Constitution.

Although these three functions may overlap to a greater or lesser extent depending on the case, the first two functions occupy the greatest portion of the Court's workload and are frequently conducted without resort to the role of constitutional reviewer. This third role, however, involves the Court in most public controversy about its power. It is important to note that it is this role that serves as the focus of our treatment of the Supreme Court in this book. It is access to this function that the Court has sought most assiduously to control through the devices of the interrogative WHEN.

Two forces—one of practical political power and the other of normative political theory—combine to require judges to pay a marked degree of deference to the decisions of elected officials. Nevertheless, it is important to understand that the rules judges have constructed around the jurisdictional clauses of the constitutional document and congressional statutes insure that whatever the correct response to the issue of deference may be, a decision to respond at all remains firmly under the control of judges.

1213

One can compare judicial power to diplomacy in international relations. And nowhere are the prudential aspects of judicial power more evident than in deciding whether to interpret the Constitution. Once the justices decide that they will interpret it, they often confront serious clashes between the logical imperatives of the Constitution taken as a body of legal norms and the compelling demands of practical government. Sometimes it may seem wiser to leave resolution of competing demands to other officials—at least for a time.

The Supreme Court's procedures allow it some simple controls over timing. The justices can carry a case over for argument in the term after agreeing to hear it, announce their decision many months later or merely order reargument, remand it to the trial court for clarification of the record, or decide on procedural rather than substantive grounds. There are other, more complex, means of control. But to understand those, one must know something of the sinuosities of federal jurisdiction and judicial organization.

I. FEDERAL JURISDICTION

A. General

Most succinctly, the term "jurisdiction," means the power to say what the law is. Chapter 3 noted that judges lack a self-starter and have only limited jurisdiction or authority to hear and decide cases. Article III of the constitutional document, as modified by the Eleventh Amendment, provides an outline of federal jurisdiction. The two organizing factors are the nature of the controversy and the status of the parties to the dispute:

1. *Nature of the Controversy.* The case must involve:

    a. Interpretation of the U.S. Constitution or a federal statute or treaty;

    b. Admiralty or maritime law.

2. *Status of the Parties.* One of the parties must be:

    c. The United States government or any of its offices or officers;

    d. A diplomatic or consular representative of a foreign nation;

    e. A state government suing:

        (i) Another state;

        (ii) A citizen of another state;

        (iii) A foreign government or its subjects;

    f. A citizen of one state suing a citizen of another state;

    g. An American citizen suing a foreign government or a citizen of a foreign nation;

    h. A citizen of one state suing a citizen of his own state where both claim land under grants of different states.

Presence of any one of these elements (a through h) poses a federal question, which (subject to congressional regulations and judge-made rules) federal courts may decide.

B. Mandatory Jurisdiction

Article III says that "the judicial power shall extend" to all of these kinds of cases "in law and equity." This sentence is imperative in mood, and Justice Story in Martin v. Hunter's Lessee (1816; reprinted above, at p. 266) and some later commentators[1] have claimed that Congress was obliged to establish lower federal courts and confer jurisdiction upon them. Nevertheless, the working principle of federal judges has been that, except for the original jurisdiction of the Supreme Court, jurisdiction flows to federal courts not directly from the Constitution but indirectly through congressional statutes.[2]

In creating national courts, Congress did not give federal judges anything like full authority over these sorts of cases until after the Civil War, and even today it has not completely filled in Article III's outline. Moreover, Congress has granted federal courts *exclusive* jurisdiction in only a few areas—either geographic (such as the District of Columbia) or topical (such as interpretation of congressional statutes regulating bankruptcy, patents, taxes, and most aspects of federal criminal law). A private citizen who initiates a lawsuit raising a federal question typically has a choice of beginning in a state or federal court.

C. Law and Equity

The phrase "in law and equity" refers to different kinds of litigation. Cases in law are those brought either under the common law (the law judges have made through accretion of precedent) or statutes (legislative acts regulating civil or criminal matters).

Courts of equity do not use juries, but their principal difference with courts of law lies in the nature of the remedies then offer. *Law* mainly provides *compensatory* justice. For private litigants, monetary damages will be the ususal remedy, jail sentences or fines if the government secures a criminal conviction. *Equity,* on the other hand, provides *preventive* justice. It can order a defendant not to act, to cease acting, or to undo the effects of previous action. Its most common remedy is the injunction, an order directed to a named person or persons, including government officials, forbidding them from certain behavior. Sometimes an injunction is quite simple, as when it prohibits an official from enforcing a particular statute. Sometimes, it can be complicated, as when it in effect requires state officials to redraw the lines of electoral districts.

In the Judiciary Act of 1789, Congress accomplished a sweeping innovation by establishing one set of federal courts to function both as

---

1. Julius Goebel, *History of the Supreme Court of the United States: Antecedents and Beginnings to 1801* (New York: Macmillan, 1971), pp. 246–47. Henry J. Friendly, *Federal Jurisdiction* (New York: Columbia University Press, 1973), p. 2, disagrees.

2. See espec. Cary v. Curtis (1845): "[T]he organization of the judicial power, definition and distribution of the subjects of jurisdiction in the federal tribunals, and the modes of their actions and authority, have been, and of right must be, the work of the legislature."

courts of law and equity. This dual capacity not only requires fewer judges, it also allows litigants to combine proceedings—for example, to file a single suit for an injunction to prevent further injury as well as for money to compensate for past injury. Most states have copied this reform, though many only in this century.

D. Cases and Controversies

Article III limits federal jurisdiction to "cases" and "controversies." These are words of art, technical terms that refer to a real dispute (as distinguished from a friendly quarrel or an academic debate) between two parties in which one person has injured or threatened a legally protected right of the other with immediate injury. Repeatedly, the Court has said that federal judges may not answer hypothetical questions or make decisions that will have no practical effect. The requirement that there be a "case" or "controversy" is the reason that justices give for refusing to render advisory opinions.

II. THE ORGANIZATION OF FEDERAL COURTS

Federal jurisdiction is divided into two kinds: *original,* authority to hear and decide cases as a court of first instance, that is, to hold trials; and *appellate,* authority to review decisions of lower courts. Article III specifies that the Supreme Court shall have original jurisdiction in cases involving foreign diplomats and those to which a state is a party. "In all other cases before mentioned, the Supreme Court shall have appellate jurisdiction, both as to law and fact, with such exceptions, and under such regulations as the Congress shall make."

This section focuses on the ways in which Congress has organized federal courts to exercise the power conferred by Article III.

A. Legislative Courts

There is an important difference between courts Congress has established under Articl III and those it has created under powers given under Article I, for example, to govern territories. The latter are "special" or "legislative" courts.[3] They have limited jurisdiction, and their judges may serve for specific terms rather than during "good behavior." The best known legislative tribunals are the Tax Court, which hears appeals from the Internal Revenue Service, and the Court of Military Appeals, which reviews courts martial.

---

3. See John Marshall's opinion for the Court in American Ins. Co. v. Canter (1828); and discussion in Henry M. Hart, Herbert Wechsler, et al., *The Federal Courts and the Federal System* (2d ed.; Mineola, N.Y.: The Foundation Press, 1973), pp. 375–418; and Martin H. Redish, *Federal Jurisdiction* (Indianapolis: Bobbs-Merrill, 1980), chap. 2.

B. Constitutional Courts

The term "constitutional courts" here refers to the courts Congress has created under Article III. Judges who staff these courts must be nominated by the President, confirmed by the Senate, and can be removed only by impeachment and conviction. Their jurisdiction is limited to the kinds of cases and controversies described above. Congress has vested most federal jurisdiction in three layers of courts: district courts, courts of appeals, and the Supreme Court.

1. *District Courts.* Most federal civil and criminal cases begin at this level. There are currently 91 such courts in the United States, at least one in each state, the District of Columbia, and Puerto Rico. Usually a single judge presides, though as many as 32 may be attached to the courts. Here trials are held and juries deliberate. Almost 200,000 cases a year are filed in these courts. Many of these, however, are settled between the parties without trial and, in criminal cases, by bargains between the defendant and the U.S. Attorney. Nevertheless, dockets are typically crowded and civil suits may take several years to come to trial.

In a nontechnical sense, district courts also sit as appellate tribunals when they hear petitions for habeas corpus from prisoners convicted in state courts. Normally, a person convicted in a state court who wishes to appeal must first utilize the review provided by state law. Afterward, the prisoner may ask the U.S. Supreme Court to take the case. If this effort fails, there is yet another chance: a petition to a federal district court for habeas corpus, alleging a federal constitutional flaw in the state trial.

The district judge must then examine the record and pass on the merits of the case. These petitions are usually frivolous, but occasionally a judge finds serious error and frees the prisoner. The losing side in the district court may appeal to the appropriate U.S. court of appeals, and the loser there may seek review by the Supreme Court.

Some cases reprinted in this book have been appeals from three-judge district courts. These are special tribunals convened to hear a particular controversy; they have no life beyond the case that called them into existence. To prevent a single federal judge from issuing an injunction against enforcement of a state statute, Congress in 1911 required such suits to be heard by a three-judge district court, at least one of whose members had to be a judge from the court of appeals. In 1937, Congress imposed a similar requirement on suits against enforcement of federal statutes.

Three-judge courts caused a great strain on judicial energies. In 1976 Congress eliminated these tribunals except for a few situations such as apportionment cases or enforcement of the Civil Rights Acts of 1964 and 1965. As in the past, the loser in these courts can obtain review by direct appeal to the Supreme Court.

2. *Courts of Appeal.* Losing litigants have one appeal as a matter of right. Congress has divided the areas served by district courts into

eleven circuits. One of these includes only the District of Columbia. The others, which are numbered, sweep across the country in a fashion that often reflects bargains among legislators rather than fully rational divisions of territory.

Every justice of the Supreme Court carries the additional title of circuit judge and is assigned to at least one circuit. Some justices try to visit their assigned areas but seldom can they hear cases there. Justices, however, may sit as circuit judges in their own chambers in Washington to hear cases that require immediate action. Usually these involve "staying," or delaying the effect of, lower court orders until the Supreme Court can decide the cases.

Currently, 140 judges staff the circuit courts. Only five are assigned to the First Circuit and 23 to the Fifth, indicating disparities in caseloads. Normally three judges, assigned by the chief judge of the circuit, hear each case, though in rare instances the entire court sits *en banc.* Almost all cases are appeals from district courts, though the Court of Appeals for the District of Columbia also reviews orders of some federal administrative agencies.

3. *The Supreme Court.* The Supreme Court sits at the apex of a twin system of courts. The justices have appellate jurisdiction over all cases from U.S. courts of appeals and some legislative tribunals, as well as decisions of the highest state courts involving federal questions. This jurisdiction, however, does not extend to interpreting state law but only to judging the conformity of that law with the Constitution, statutes, or treaties of the United States. Federal courts take state laws to mean what the highest state court says they mean. Even, for example, if a state constitution replicates the wording or substance of a provision of the U.S. Constitution, federal courts will take the state constitution to mean what the highest state court says it means rather than what the U.S. Supreme Court has said the same provision of the federal Constitution means. If no state court has yet interpreted a state statute or constitutional provision, federal judges either will not decide the issue until state courts have had an opportunity to interpret it or, if an immediate ruling is necessary, will follow state interpretations of similar acts or clauses.

The Supreme Court also has some original jurisdiction. Most of these cases are disputes between states over such matters as boundaries and allocations of water resources. The Court usually appoints a "special master" to hold hearings, collect evidence, and present recommendations. The final decision, however, belongs to the justices themselves.

C. The Appellate Jurisdiction of the Supreme Court

Cases come to the Court for review in one of three ways: *certification, appeal,* or *certiorari.*

1. *Certification.* Under this seldom-used procedure, a court of appeals or the Court of Claims "certifies" to the Supreme Court that a case poses an issue of such difficulty that the lower court needs instruction. Only questions of law, not of fact, can be certified. The Supreme Court may, however, require a court of appeals (though not

the Court of Claims) to send the record of the case up so that the justices can decide the basic dispute rather than merely answer a legal question.

  2. *Appeal.* A losing litigant may appeal a case when:
    a. A federal court declares:
        (i) a state statute invalid under the Constitution, laws, or treaties of the United States;
        (ii) a federal statute unconstitutional.
    b. A special three-judge district court has decided a case.
    c. A state court declares:
        (i) a federal statute or treaty unconstitutional;
        (ii) a state statute valid against a challenge that it violates the federal Constitution.

Supposedly, the court to which one takes an appeal is obliged to hear it, unless the reasons for requesting review are patently frivolous. But as Chief Justice Warren publicly admitted, it is "only accurate to a degree to say that our jurisdiction in cases on appeal is obligatory as distinguished from discretionary on certiorari."[4] In practice, the Court dismisses a large percentage of appeals with only the Delphic explanation: "for want of a substantial federal question." In effect, then, the justices treat appeals in much the same way as petitions for certiorari.[5]

  If the Court dismisses an appeal, the lower court's decision stands. Moreover, despite the effectively discretionary nature of granting an appeal, the Court has held that, unlike a denial of certiorari, a decision to dismiss for want of a substantial federal question is a decision on the merits of a case. That means that it can be cited as a precedent before the Supreme Court and lower courts; and lower courts at least are bound to follow it.[6]

  3. *Certiorari.* Petitions for a writ of certiorari form the main avenue to the Court's appellate jurisdiction. Unless their circumstances fit the categories of appeals, losers in courts of appeals or the highest state courts, providing they raise federal questions, who want the Supreme Court to review their cases must petition for certiorari. In recent years the Court has been receiving about 4,000 such petitions and has been granting less than 150.

  Chapter 3 described in more detail the way the Court handles those petitions. Granting or denying the writ is completely within the Court's discretion. It takes a vote of only four justices to grant, although a majority of the justices may later "DIG" the writ—that is, "dismiss" it as "improvidently granted." Denial of the writ means that the lower court's decision stands; but because of the wide variety

---

4. Quoted in Frederick B. Wiener, "The Supreme Court's New Rules," 68 *Harv.L.Rev.* 20, 51 (1954).

5. Doris Marie Provine, *Case Selection in the United States Supreme Court* (Chicago: University of Chicago Press, 1980), p. 14. The commission headed by Prof. Paul Freund reached the same conclusion; *Report of the Study Group on the Caseload of the Supreme Court* (Washington, D.C.: Federal Judicial Center, 1972), p. 25. Justice Douglas, however, implied the contrary: "The Supreme Court and its Case Load," 45 *Corn.L.Q.* 410 (1960).

6. Hicks v. Miranda (1975).

of reasons that might be involved, the Court's refusing certiorari is not a decision on the merits and has no value as a precedent.

Rule 17 of the Supreme Court Rules explicitly states that "certiorari is not a matter of right, but of judicial discretion, and will be granted only where there are special and important reasons therefor." Rule 17 then outlines *some* of the circumstances the justices consider important in evaluating petitions:

(a) Where a federal court of appeals has rendered a decision in conflict with the decision of another court of appeals on the same matter; or has decided a federal question in a way in conflict with a state court of last resort; or has so far departed from the accepted and usual course of judicial proceedings, or so far sanctioned such a departure by a lower court, as to call for an exercise of this Court's power of supervision.

(b) When a state court of last resort has decided a federal question in a way in conflict with the decision of another state court of last resort or of a federal court of appeals.

(c) When a state court or a federal court of appeals has decided an important question of federal law which has not been, but should be, settled by this Court, or has decided a federal question in a way in conflict with applicable decisions of this Court.

These considerations are hardly exhaustive. Furthermore, several studies [7] have demonstrated that the justices often ignore these factors and seem quite concerned with others.

III. THE WORKLOAD OF THE SUPREME COURT

Some of the justices have complained in recent years about the staggering burden of their caseload. Despite some disagreement among the justices about how difficult it is to separate important from unimportant petitions for review,[8] most people find the prospect of facing more than 4,000 cases each year awesome; and Congress, prodded by Chief Justice Burger, has considered many proposals for reform. Those that have received most support entail creation of a National Court of Appeals to act as a filter between the Supreme Court and the highest state courts or existing courts of appeal. While there have been several variations on this plan,[9] the new court's essential function would be to settle some disputes, refuse review of others, and send yet others on to the Supreme Court. So far, none of these plans has been able to gather sufficient support to get out of committee in either house of Congress.

---

7. See espec. Joseph Tanenhaus et al., "The Supreme Court's Certiorari Jurisdiction: Cue Theory," in Glendon A. Schubert, ed., *Judicial Decision-Making* (New York: The Free Press, 1963); S. Sidney Ulmer et al., "The Decision to Grant or Deny Certiorari," 6 *Law & Soc.Rev.* 637 (1972); and the spate of articles by Fowler Harper and co-authors that appeared in the *U. of Pa.L.Rev.* from 1950–55. See also the literature cited in the notes to chap. 1, Provine, supra note 5.

8. For example: William O. Douglas, supra note 5; and his dis. op. in Tidewater Oil v. United States (1972).

9. See Note, "Of High Designs: A Compendium of Proposals to Reduce the Workload of the Supreme Court," 97 *Harv.L.Rev.* 307 (1983).

APPENDIX B

Table of U.S. Supreme Court Justices

The table shows the positions on the Court as numbered columns, so that lines of succession can be followed. The first column represents the Chief Justice. Each justice's political party affiliation and state are provided. In instances where a justice serves until a year prior to the year in which his successor takes office, his final year of service is given in italics in the numbered column representing his position on the Court.

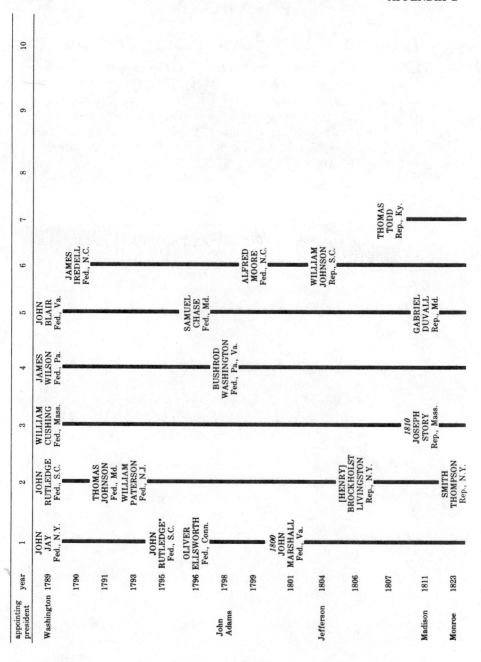

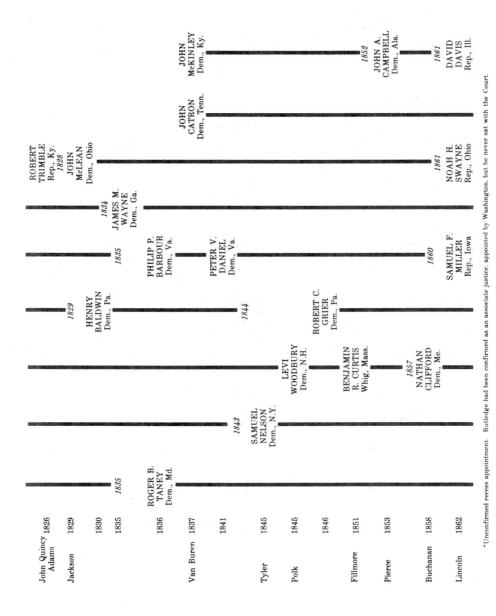

*Unconfirmed recess appointment. Rutledge had been confirmed as an associate justice, appointed by Washington, but he never sat with the Court.

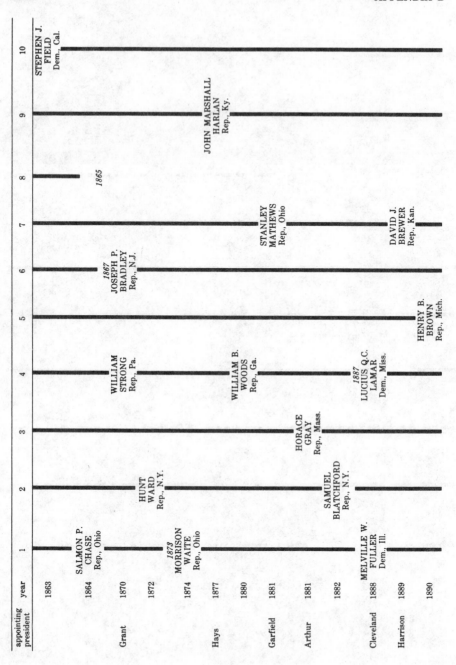

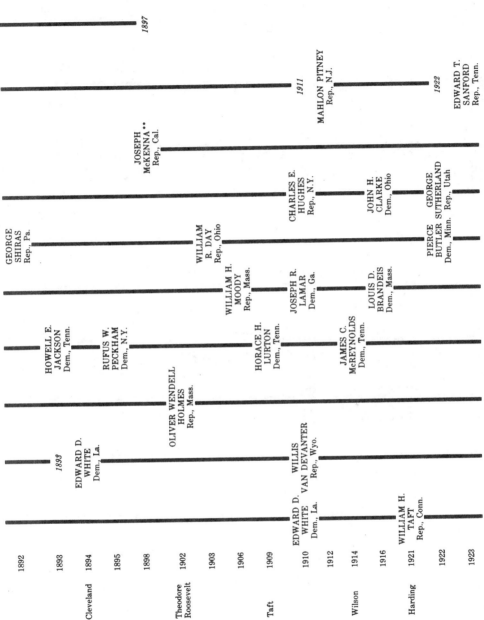

** McKenna was appointed to fill the vacancy created by the resignation of Field in 1897. Congress had established a tenth seat (to which Field was appointed) in 1863, but in 1866 provided that no vacancies among associate justices could be filled until their number was reduced to fewer than six, leaving a seven-member Court. The sixth and eighth seats on the Court were left vacant after the deaths of Wayne in 1867 and Catron in 1865. Congress increased the Court's membership to nine again in 1869.

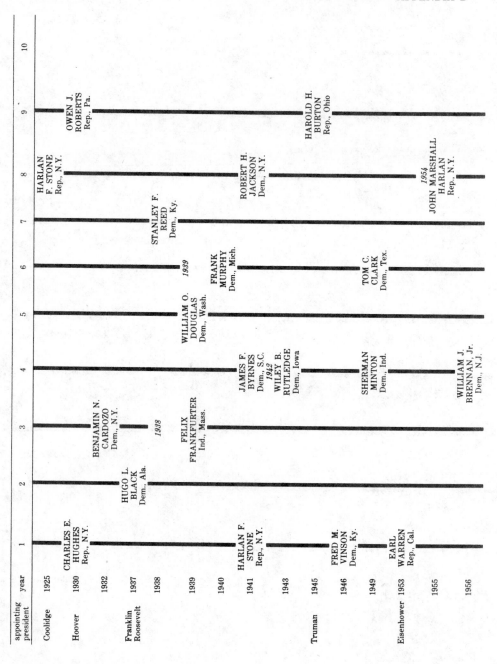

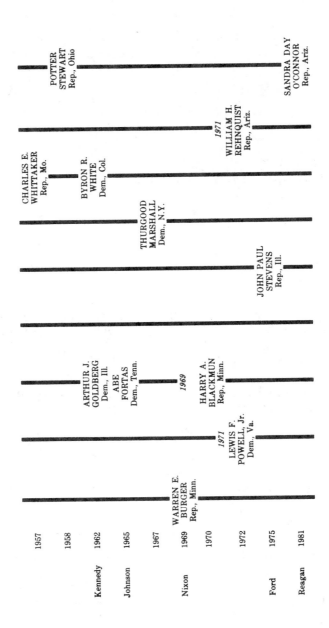

APPENDIX C

The Constitution of the United States of America

We the People of the United States, in Order to form a more perfect Union, establish Justice, insure domestic Tranquility, provide for the common defence, promote the general Welfare, and secure the Blessings of Liberty to ourselves and our Posterity, do ordain and establish this Constitution for the United States of America.

Article I

SECTION 1

All legislative Powers herein granted shall be vested in a Congress of the United States, which shall consist of a Senate and House of Representatives.

SECTION 2

The House of Representatives shall be composed of Members chosen every second Year by the People of the several States, and the Electors in each State shall have the Qualifications requisite for Electors of the most numerous Branch of the State Legislature.

No Person shall be a Representative who shall not have attained to the Age of twenty five Years, and been seven Years a Citizen of the United States, and who shall not, when elected, be an Inhabitant of that State in which he shall be chosen.

Representatives and direct Taxes shall be apportioned among the several States which may be included within this Union, according to their respective Numbers, which shall be determined by adding to the whole Number of free Persons, including those bound to Service for a Term of Years, and excluding Indians not taxed, three fifths of all other Persons. The actual Enumeration shall be made within three Years after the first Meeting of the Congress of the United States, and within every subsequent Term of ten Years, in such Manner as they shall by Law direct. The Number of Representatives shall not exceed one for every thirty Thousand, but each State shall have at Least one Representative; and until such enumeration shall be made, the State of New Hampshire shall be entitled to chuse three, Massachusetts eight, Rhode Island and Providence Plantations one, Connecticut five, New-York six, New Jersey four, Pennsylvania eight, Delaware one, Maryland six, Virginia ten, North Carolina five, South Carolina five, and Georgia three.

When vacancies happen in the Representation from any State, the Executive Authority thereof shall issue Writs of Election to fill such Vacancies.

The House of Representatives shall chuse their Speaker and other Officers; and shall have the sole Power of Impeachment.

SECTION 3

The Senate of the United States shall be composed of two Senators from each State, chosen by the Legislature thereof, for six Years; and each Senator shall have one Vote.

Immediately after they shall be assembled in Consequence of the first Election, they shall be divided as equally as may be into three Classes. The Seats of the Senators of the first Class shall be vacated at the Expiration of the second Year, of the second Class at the Expiration of the fourth Year, and of the third Class at the Expiration of the sixth Year, so that one third may be chosen every second Year; and if Vacancies happen by Resignation, or otherwise, during the Recess of the Legislature of any State, the Executive thereof may make temporary Appointments until the next Meeting of the Legislature, which shall then fill such Vacancies.

No Person shall be a Senator who shall not have attained to the Age of thirty Years, and been nine Years a Citizen of the United States, and who shall not, when elected, be an Inhabitant of that State for which he shall be chosen.

The Vice President of the United States shall be President of the Senate, but shall have no Vote, unless they be equally divided.

The Senate shall chuse their other Officers, and also a President pro tempore, in the Absence of the Vice President, or when he shall exercise the Office of President of the United States.

The Senate shall have the sole Power to try all Impeachments. When sitting for that Purpose, they shall be on Oath or Affirmation. When the President of the United States is tried the Chief Justice shall preside: And no Person shall be convicted without the Concurrence of two thirds of the Members present.

Judgment in Cases of Impeachment shall not extend further than to removal from Office, and disqualification to hold and enjoy any Office of honor, Trust or Profit under the United States: but the Party convicted shall nevertheless be liable and subject to Indictment, Trial, Judgment and Punishment, according to Law.

SECTION 4

The Times, Places and Manner of holding Elections for Senators and Representatives, shall be prescribed in each State by the Legislature thereof; but the Congress may at any time by Law make or alter such Regulations, except as to the Places of chusing Senators.

The Congress shall assemble at least once in every Year, and such Meeting shall be on the first Monday in December, unless they shall by Law appoint a different Day.

SECTION 5

Each House shall be the Judge of the Elections, Returns and Qualifications of its own Members, and a Majority of each shall constitute a Quorum to do Business; but a smaller Number may adjourn from day to day, and may be authorized to compel the Attendance of absent Members, in such Manner, and under such Penalties as each House may provide.

Each House may determine the Rules of its Proceedings, punish its Members for disorderly Behaviour, and, with the Concurrence of two thirds, expel a Member.

Each House shall keep a Journal of its Proceedings, and from time to time publish the same, excepting such Parts as may in their Judgment require Secrecy; and the Yeas and Nays of the Members of either House on any question shall, at the Desire of one fifth of those Present, be entered on the Journal.

Neither House, during the Session of Congress, shall, without the Consent of the other, adjourn for more than three days, nor to any other Place than that in which the two Houses shall be sitting.

SECTION 6

The Senators and Representatives shall receive a Compensation for their Services, to be ascertained by Law, and paid out of the Treasury of the United States. They shall in all Cases, except Treason, Felony and Breach of the Peace, be privileged from Arrest during their Attendance at the Session of their respective Houses, and in going to and returning from the same; and for any Speech or Debate in either House, they shall not be questioned in any other Place.

No Senator or Representative shall, during the Time for which he was elected, be appointed to any civil Office under the Authority of the United States, which shall have been created, or the Emoluments whereof shall have been encreased during such time; and no Person holding any Office under the United States, shall be a Member of either House during his Continuance in Office.

SECTION 7

All Bills for raising Revenue shall originate in the House of Representatives; but the Senate may propose or concur with amendments as on other Bills.

Every Bill which shall have passed the House of Representatives and the Senate, shall, before it become a Law, be presented to the President of the United States; If he approve he shall sign it, but if not he shall return it, with his Objections to that House in which it shall have originated, who shall enter the Objections at large on their Journal, and proceed to reconsider it. If after such Reconsideration two thirds of that House shall agree to pass the Bill, it shall be sent, together with the Objections, to the other House, by which it shall likewise be reconsidered, and if approved by two thirds of that House, it shall become a Law. But in all such Cases the Votes of both Houses shall be determined by Yeas and Nays, and the Names of the Persons voting for and against the Bill shall be entered on the Journal of each

House respectively. If any Bill shall not be returned by the President within ten Days (Sunday excepted) after it shall have been presented to him, the Same shall be a Law, in like Manner as if he had signed it, unless the Congress by their Adjournment prevent its Return, in which Case it shall not be a Law.

Every Order, Resolution, or Vote to which the Concurrence of the Senate and House of Representatives may be necessary (except on a question of Adjournment) shall be presented to the President of the United States; and before the Same shall take Effect, shall be approved by him, or being disapproved by him, shall be repassed by two thirds of the Senate and House of Representatives, according to the Rules and Limitations prescribed in the Case of a Bill.

SECTION 8

The Congress shall have Power To lay and collect Taxes, Duties, Imposts and Excises, to pay the Debts and provide for the common Defence and general Welfare of the United States; but all Duties, Imposts and Excises shall be uniform throughout the United States;

To borrow Money on the credit of the United States;

To regulate Commerce with foreign Nations, and among the several States, and with the Indian Tribes;

To establish an uniform Rule of Naturalization, and uniform Laws on the subject of Bankruptcies throughout the United States;

To coin Money, regulate the Value thereof, and of foreign Coin, and fix the Standard of Weights and Measures;

To provide for the Punishment of counterfeiting the Securities and current Coin of the United States;

To establish Post Offices and post Roads;

To promote the Progress of Science and useful Arts, by securing for limited Times to Authors and Inventors the exclusive Right to their respective Writings and Discoveries;

To constitute Tribunals inferior to the supreme Court;

To define and punish Piracies and Felonies committed on the high Seas, and Offences against the Law of Nations;

To declare War, grant Letters of Marque and Reprisal, and make Rules concerning Captures on Land and Water;

To raise and support Armies, but no Appropriation of Money to that Use shall be for a longer Term than two Years;

To provide and maintain a Navy;

To make Rules for the Government and Regulation of the land and naval Forces;

To provide for calling forth the Militia to execute the Laws of the Union, suppress Insurrections and repel Invasions;

To provide for organizing, arming, and disciplining, the Militia, and for governing such Part of them as may be employed in the Service of the United States, reserving to the States respectively, the Appointment of the Officers, and the Authority of training the Militia according to the discipline prescribed by Congress;

To exercise exclusive Legislation in all Cases whatsoever, over such District (not exceeding ten Miles square) as may, by Cession of particular States, and the Acceptance of Congress, become the Seat of the Government of the United States, and to exercise like Authority over all Places purchased by the Consent of the Legislature of the State in which the Same shall be, for the Erection of Forts, Magazines, Arsenals, dock-Yards, and other needful Buildings;—And

To make all Laws which shall be necessary and proper for carrying into Execution the foregoing Powers, and all other Powers vested by this Constitution in the Government of the United States, or in any Department or Officer thereof.

SECTION 9

The Migration or Importation of such Persons as any of the States now existing shall think proper to admit, shall not be prohibited by the Congress prior to the Year one thousand eight hundred and eight, but a Tax or duty may be imposed on such Importation, not exceeding ten dollars for each Person.

The Privilege of the Writ of Habeas Corpus shall not be suspended, unless when in Cases of Rebellion or Invasion the public Safety may require it.

No Bill of Attainder or ex post facto Law shall be passed.

No Capitation, or other direct, Tax shall be laid, unless in Proportion to the Census or Enumeration herein before directed to be taken.

No Tax or Duty shall be laid on Articles exported from any State.

No Preference shall be given by any Regulation of Commerce or Revenue to the Ports of one State over those of another; nor shall Vessels bound to, or from, one State, be obliged to enter, clear or pay Duties in another.

No Money shall be drawn from the Treasury, but in Consequence of Appropriations made by Law; and a regular Statement and Account of the Receipts and Expenditures of all public Money shall be published from time to time.

No Title of Nobility shall be granted by the United States: And no Person holding any Office of Profit or Trust under them, shall, without the Consent of the Congress, accept of any present, Emolument, Office, or Title, of any kind whatever, from any King, Prince or foreign State.

SECTION 10

No State shall enter into any Treaty, Alliance, or Confederation; grant Letters of Marque and Reprisal; coin Money; emit Bills of Credit; make any Thing but gold and silver Coin a Tender in Payment of Debts; pass any Bill of Attainder, ex post facto Law, or Law impairing the Obligation of Contracts, or grant any Title of Nobility.

No State shall, without the Consent of the Congress, lay any Imposts or Duties on Imports or Exports, except what may be absolutely necessary for executing its inspection Laws: and the net Produce of all Duties and Imposts, laid by any State on Imports or Exports, shall be for the Use of the Treasury of the United States; and all such Laws shall be subject to the Revision and Controul of the Congress.

No State shall, without the Consent of Congress, lay any Duty of Tonnage, keep Troops, or Ships of War in time of Peace, enter into any Agreement or Compact with another State, or with a foreign Power, or engage in War, unless actually invaded, or in such imminent Danger as will not admit of delay.

Article II

SECTION 1

The executive Power shall be vested in a President of the United States of America. He shall hold his Office during the Term of four Years, and, together with the Vice President, chosen for the same Term, be elected, as follows

Each State shall appoint, in such Manner as the Legislature thereof may direct, a Number of Electors, equal to the whole Number of Senators and Representatives to which the State may be entitled in the Congress: but no Senator or Representative, or Person holding an Office of Trust or Profit under the United States, shall be appointed an Elector.

The Electors shall meet in their respective States, and vote by Ballot for two Persons, of whom one at least shall not be an Inhabitant of the same State with themselves. And they shall make a List of all the Persons voted for, and of the Number of Votes for each; which List they shall sign and certify, and transmit sealed to the Seat of the Government of the United States, directed to the President of the Senate. The President of the Senate shall, in the Presence of the Senate and House of Representatives, open all the Certificates, and the Votes shall then be counted. The Person having the greatest Number of Votes shall be the President, if such Number be a Majority of the whole Number of Electors appointed; and if there be more than one who have such Majority, and have an equal Number of Votes, then the House of Representatives shall immediately chuse by Ballot one of them for President; and if no Person have a Majority, then from the five highest on the List the said House shall in like Manner chuse the President. But in chusing the President, the Votes shall be taken by States, the Representation from each State having one Vote; a quorum for this Purpose shall consist of a Member or Members from two thirds of the States, and a Majority of all the States shall be necessary to a Choice. In every Case, after the Choice of the President, the Person having the greatest Number of Votes of the Electors shall be the Vice President. But if there should remain two or more who have equal Votes, the Senate shall chuse from them by Ballot the Vice President.

The Congress may determine the Time of chusing the Electors, and the Day on which they shall give their Votes; which Day shall be the same throughout the United States.

No Person except a natural born Citizen, or a Citizen of the United States, at the time of the Adoption of this Constitution, shall be eligible to the Office of President; neither shall any Person be eligible to that Office who shall not have attained to the Age of thirty five Years, and been fourteen Years a Resident within the United States.

In Case of the Removal of the President from Office, or of his Death, Resignation, or Inability to discharge the Powers and Duties of the said Office, the Same shall devolve on the Vice President, and the Congress may by Law provide for the Case of Removal, Death, Resignation or Inability, both of the President and Vice President, declaring what Officer shall then act as President, and such Officer shall act accordingly, until the Disability be removed, or a President shall be elected.

The President shall, at stated Times, receive for his Services, a Compensation, which shall neither be encreased nor diminished during the Period for which he shall have been elected, and he shall not receive within that Period any other Emolument from the United States, or any of them.

Before he enter on the Execution of his Office, he shall take the following Oath or Affirmation:—"I do solemnly swear (or affirm) that I will faithfully execute the Office of President of the United States, and will to the best of my Ability, preserve, protect and defend the Constitution of the United States."

SECTION 2

The President shall be Commander in Chief of the Army and Navy of the United States, and of the Militia of the several States, when called into the actual Service of the United States; he may require the Opinion, in writing, of the principal Officer in each of the executive Departments, upon any Subject relating to the Duties of their respective Offices, and he shall have Power to grant Reprieves and Pardons for Offences against the United States, except in Cases of Impeachment.

He shall have Power, by and with the Advice and Consent of the Senate, to make Treaties, provided two thirds of the Senators present concur; and he shall nominate, and by and with the Advice and Consent of the Senate, shall appoint Ambassadors, other public Ministers and Consuls, Judges of the supreme Court, and all other Officers of the United States, whose Appointments are not herein otherwise provided for, and which shall be established by Law: but the Congress may by Law vest the Appointment of such inferior Officers, as they think proper, in the President alone, in the Courts of Law, or in the Heads of Departments.

The President shall have Power to fill up all Vacancies that may happen during the Recess of the Senate, by granting Commissions which shall expire at the End of their next Session.

SECTION 3

He shall from time to time give to the Congress Information of the State of the Union, and recommend to their Consideration such Measures as he shall judge necessary and expedient; he may, on extraordinary Occasions, convene both Houses, or either of them, and in Case of Disagreement between them, with Respect to the Time of Adjournment, he may adjourn them to such Time as he shall think proper; he shall receive Ambassadors and other public Ministers; he shall take Care that the Laws be faithfully executed, and shall Commission all the Officers of the United States.

SECTION 4

The President, Vice President and all Civil Officers of the United States, shall be removed from Office on Impeachment for, and Conviction of, Treason, Bribery, or other high Crimes and Misdemeanors.

Article III

SECTION 1

The judicial Power of the United States, shall be vested in one supreme Court, and in such inferior Courts as the Congress may from time to time ordain and establish. The Judges, both of the supreme and inferior Courts, shall hold their Offices during good Behaviour, and shall, at stated Times, receive for their Services, a Compensation, which shall not be diminished during their Continuance in Office.

SECTION 2

The judicial Power shall extend to all Cases, in Law and Equity, arising under this Constitution, the Laws of the United States, and Treaties made, or which shall be made, under their Authority;—to all Cases affecting Ambassadors, other public Ministers and Consuls;—to all Cases of admiralty and maritime Jurisdiction;—to Controversies to which the United States shall be a Party;—to Controversies between two or more States;—between a State and Citizens of another State;—between Citizens of different States;—between Citizens of the same State claiming Lands under Grants of different States, and between a State, or the Citizens thereof, and foreign States, Citizens or Subjects.

In all Cases affecting Ambassadors, other public Ministers and Consuls, and those in which a State shall be Party, the Supreme Court shall have original Jurisdiction. In all the other Cases before mentioned, the supreme Court shall have appellate Jurisdiction, both as to

Law and Fact, with such Exceptions, and under such Regulations as the Congress shall make.

The Trial of all Crimes, except in Cases of Impeachment, shall be by Jury; and such Trial shall be held in the State where the said Crimes shall have been committed; but when not committed within any State, the Trial shall be at such Place or Places as the Congress may by Law have directed.

SECTION 3

Treason against the United States, shall consist only in levying War against them, or in adhering to their Enemies, giving them Aid and Comfort. No Person shall be convicted of Treason unless on the Testimony of two Witnesses to the same overt Act, or on Confession in open Court.

The Congress shall have Power to declare the Punishment of Treason, but no Attainder of Treason shall work Corruption of Blood, or Forfeiture except during the Life of the Person attainted.

Article IV

SECTION 1

Full Faith and Credit shall be given in each State to the public Acts, Records, and judicial Proceedings of every other State. And the Congress may by general Laws prescribe the Manner in which such Acts, Records and Proceedings shall be proved, and the Effect thereof.

SECTION 2

The Citizens of each State shall be entitled to all Privileges and Immunities of Citizens in the several States.

A Person charged in any State with Treason, Felony, or other Crime, who shall flee from Justice, and be found in another State, shall on Demand of the executive Authority of the State from which he fled, be delivered up, to be removed to the State having Jurisdiction of the Crime.

No Person held to Service or Labour in one State, under the Laws thereof, escaping into another, shall, in Consequence of any Law or Regulation therein, be discharged from such Service or Labour, but shall be delivered up on Claim of the Party to whom such Service or Labour may be due.

SECTION 3

New States may be admitted by the Congress into this Union; but no new State shall be formed or erected within the Jurisdiction of any other State; nor any State be formed by the Junction of two or more States, or Parts of States, without the Consent of the Legislatures of the States concerned as well as of the Congress.

The Congress shall have Power to dispose of and make all needful Rules and Regulations respecting the Territory or other Property belonging to the United States; and nothing in this Constitution shall be so construed as to Prejudice any Claims of the United States, or of any particular State.

SECTION 4

The United States shall guarantee to every State in this Union a Republican Form of Government, and shall protect each of them against Invasion; and on Application of the Legislature, or of the Executive (when the Legislature cannot be convened) against domestic Violence.

Article V

The Congress, whenever two thirds of both Houses shall deem it necessary, shall propose Amendments to this Constitution, or, on the Application of the Legislatures of two thirds of the several States, shall call a Convention for proposing Amendments, which, in either Case, shall be valid to all Intents and Purposes, as Part of this Constitution, when ratified by the Legislatures of three fourths of the several States, or by Conventions in three fourths thereof, as the one or the other Mode of Ratification may be proposed by the Congress; Provided that no Amendment which may be made prior to the Year One thousand eight hundred and eight shall in any Manner affect the first and fourth Clauses in the Ninth Section of the first Article; and that no State, without its Consent, shall be deprived of its equal Suffrage in the Senate.

Article VI

All Debts contracted and Engagements entered into, before the Adoption of this Constitution, shall be as valid against the United States under this Constitution, as under the Confederation.

This Constitution, and the Laws of the United States which shall be made in Pursuance thereof; and all Treaties made, or which shall be made, under the Authority of the United States, shall be the supreme Law of the Land; and the Judges in every State shall be bound thereby, any Thing in the Constitution or Laws of any State to the Contrary notwithstanding.

The Senators and Representatives before mentioned, and the Members of the several State Legislatures, and all executive and judicial Officers, both of the United States and of the several States, shall be bound by Oath or Affirmation, to support this Constitution; but no religious Test shall ever be required as a Qualification to any Office or public Trust under the United States.

Article VII

The Ratification of the Conventions of nine States, shall be sufficient for the Establishment of this Constitution between the States so ratifying the Same.

* * *

Articles in Addition to, and Amendment of, the Constitution of the United States of America, Proposed by Congress, and Ratified by the Several States, Pursuant to the Fifth Article of the Original Constitution

Amendment I [1791]

Congress shall make no law respecting an establishment of religion, or prohibiting the free exercise thereof; or abridging the freedom of speech, or of the press; or the right of the people peaceably to assemble, and to petition the Government for a redress of grievances.

Amendment II [1791]

A well regulated Militia, being necessary to the security of a free State, the right of the people to keep and bear Arms, shall not be infringed.

Amendment III [1791]

No Soldier shall, in time of peace be quartered in any house, without the consent of the Owner, nor in time of war, but in a manner to be prescribed by law.

Amendment IV [1791]

The right of the people to be secure in their persons, houses, papers, and effects, against unreasonable searches and seizures, shall not be violated, and no Warrants shall issue, but upon probable cause, supported by Oath or affirmation, and particularly describing the place to be searched, and the persons or things to be seized.

Amendment V [1791]

No person shall be held to answer for a capital, or otherwise infamous crime, unless on a presentment or indictment of a Grand Jury, except in cases arising in the land or naval forces, or in the Militia, when in actual service in time of War or public danger; nor shall any person be subject for the same offence to be twice put in jeopardy of life or limb; nor shall be compelled in any criminal case to be a witness against himself, nor be deprived of life, liberty, or property, without due process of law; nor shall private property be taken for public use, without just compensation.

Amendment VI [1791]

In all criminal prosecutions, the accused shall enjoy the right to a speedy and public trial, by an impartial jury of the State and district wherein the crime shall have been committed, which district shall have been previously ascertained by law, and to be informed of the nature and cause of the accusation; to be confronted with the witnesses against him; to have compulsory process for obtaining Witnesses in his favor, and to have the Assistance of Counsel for his defence.

Amendment VII [1791]

In Suits at common law, where the value in controversy shall exceed twenty dollars, the right of trial by jury shall be preserved, and no fact tried by a jury, shall be otherwise re-examined in any Court of the United States, than according to the rules of the common law.

Amendment VIII [1791]

Excessive bail shall not be required, nor excessive fines imposed, nor cruel and unusual punishments inflicted.

Amendment IX [1791]

The enumeration in the Constitution, of certain rights, shall not be construed to deny or disparage others retained by the people.

Amendment X [1791]

The powers not delegated to the United States by the Constitution, nor prohibited by it to the States, are reserved to the States respectively, or to the people.

Amendment XI [1798]

The Judicial power of the United States shall not be construed to extend to any suit in law or equity, commenced or prosecuted against one of the United States by Citizens of another State, or by Citizens or Subjects of any Foreign State.

Amendment XII [1804]

The Electors shall meet in their respective states and vote by ballot for President and Vice-President, one of whom, at least, shall not be an inhabitant of the same state with themselves; they shall name in their ballots the person voted for as President, and in distinct ballots the person voted for as Vice-President, and they shall make distinct lists of all persons voted for as President, and of all persons voted for as Vice-President, and of the number of votes for each, which lists they shall sign and certify, and transmit sealed to the seat of the government of the United States, directed to the President of the

Senate;—The President of the Senate shall, in the presence of the Senate and House of Representatives, open all the certificates and the votes shall then be counted;—The person having the greatest number of votes for President, shall be the President, if such number be a majority of the whole number of Electors appointed; and if no person have such majority, then from the persons having the highest numbers not exceeding three on the list of those voted for as President, the House of Representatives shall choose immediately, by ballot, the President. But in choosing the President, the votes shall be taken by states, the representation from each state having one vote; a quorum for this purpose shall consist of a member or members from two-thirds of the states, and a majority of all the states shall be necessary to a choice. And if the House of Representatives shall not choose a President whenever the right of choice shall devolve upon them, before the fourth day of March next following, then the Vice-President shall act as President, as in the case of the death or other constitutional disability of the President—The person having the greatest number of votes as Vice-President, shall be the Vice-President, if such number be a majority of the whole number of Electors appointed, and if no person have a majority, then from the two highest numbers on the list, the Senate shall choose the Vice-President; a quorum for the purpose shall consist of two-thirds of the whole number of Senators, and a majority of the whole number shall be necessary to a choice. But no person constitutionally ineligible to the office of President shall be eligible to that of Vice-President of the United States.

Amendment XIII [1865]

SECTION 1

Neither slavery nor involuntary servitude, except as a punishment for crime whereof the party shall have been duly convicted, shall exist within the United States, or any place subject to their jurisdiction.

SECTION 2

Congress shall have power to enforce this article by appropriate legislation.

Amendment XIV [1868]

SECTION 1

All persons born or naturalized in the United States and subject to the jurisdiction thereof, are citizens of the United States and of the State wherein they reside. No State shall make or enforce any law which shall abridge the privileges or immunities of citizens of the United States; nor shall any State deprive any person of life, liberty, or property, without due process of law; nor deny to any person within its jurisdiction the equal protection of the laws.

SECTION 2

Representatives shall be apportioned among the several States according to their respective numbers, counting the whole number of persons in each State, excluding Indians not taxed. But when the right to vote at any election for the choice of electors for President and Vice President of the United States, Representatives in Congress, the Executive and Judicial officers of a State, or the members of the Legislature thereof, is denied to any of the male inhabitants of such State, being twenty-one years of age, and citizens of the United States, or in any way abridged, except for participation in rebellion, or other crime, the basis of representation therein shall be reduced in the proportion which the number of such male citizens shall bear to the whole number of male citizens twenty-one years of age in such State.

SECTION 3

No person shall be a Senator or Representative in Congress, or elector of President and Vice President, or hold any office, civil or military, under the United States, or under any State, who, having previously taken an oath, as a member of Congress, or as an officer of the United States, or as a member of any State legislature, or as an executive or judicial officer of any State, to support the Constitution of the United States, shall have engaged in insurrection or rebellion against the same, or given aid or comfort to the enemies thereof. But Congress may by a vote of two-thirds of each House, remove such disability.

SECTION 4

The validity of the public debt of the United States, authorized by law, including debts incurred for payment of pensions and bounties for services in suppressing insurrection or rebellion, shall not be questioned. But neither the United States nor any State shall assume or pay any debt or obligation incurred in aid of insurrection or rebellion against the United States, or any claim for the loss of emancipation of any slave; but all such debts, obligations and claims shall be held illegal and void.

SECTION 5

The Congress shall have power to enforce, by appropriate legislation, the provisions of this article.

Amendment XV [1870]

SECTION 1

The right of citizens of the United States to vote shall not be denied or abridged by the United States or by any State on account of race, color, or previous condition of servitude.

SECTION 2

The Congress shall have power to enforce this article by appropriate legislation.

Amendment XVI [1913]

The Congress shall have power to lay and collect taxes on incomes, from whatever source derived, without apportionment among the several States, and without regard to any census or enumeration.

Amendment XVII [1913]

The Senate of the United States shall be composed of two Senators from each State, elected by the people thereof, for six years; and each Senator shall have one vote. The electors in each State shall have the qualifications requisite for electors of the most numerous branch of the State legislatures.

When vacancies happen in the representation of any State in the Senate, the executive authority of such State shall issue writs of election to fill such vacancies: *Provided,* That the legislature of any State may empower the executive thereof to make temporary appointments until the people fill the vacancies by election as the legislature may direct.

This amendment shall not be so construed as to affect the election or term of any Senator chosen before it becomes valid as part of the Constitution.

Amendment XVIII [1919]

SECTION 1

After one year from the ratification of this article the manufacture, sale, or transportation of intoxicating liquors within, the importation thereof into, or the exportation thereof from the United States and all territory subject to the jurisdiction thereof for beverage purposes is hereby prohibited.

SECTION 2

The Congress and the several States shall have concurrent power to enforce this article by appropriate legislation.

SECTION 3

This article shall be inoperative unless it shall have been ratified as an amendment to the Constitution by the legislatures of the several States, as provided in the Constitution, within seven years from the date of the submission hereof to the States by the Congress.

Amendment XIX [1920]

The right of citizens of the United States to vote shall not be denied or abridged by the United States or by any State on account of sex.

Congress shall have power to enforce this article by appropriate legislation.

Amendment XX [1933]

SECTION 1

The terms of the President and Vice President shall end at noon on the 20th day of January, and the terms of Senators and Representatives at noon on the 3d day of January, of the years in which such terms would have ended if this article had not been ratified; and the terms of their successors shall then begin.

SECTION 2

The Congress shall assemble at least once in every year, and such meeting shall begin at noon on the 3d day of January, unless they shall by law appoint a different day.

SECTION 3

If, at the time fixed for the beginning of the term of the President, the President elect shall have died, the Vice President elect shall become President. If a President shall not have been chosen before the time fixed for the beginning of his term, or if the President elect shall have failed to qualify, then the Vice President elect shall act as President until a President shall have qualified; and the Congress may by law provide for the case wherein neither a President elect nor a Vice President elect shall have qualified, declaring who shall then act as President, or the manner in which one who is to act shall be selected, and such person shall act accordingly until a President or Vice President shall have qualified.

SECTION 4

The Congress may by law provide for the case of the death of any of the persons from whom the House of Representatives may choose a President whenever the right of choice shall have devolved upon them, and for the case of the death of any of the persons from whom the Senate may choose a Vice President whenever the right of choice shall have devolved upon them.

SECTION 5

Sections 1 and 2 shall take effect on the 15th day of October following the ratification of this article.

SECTION 6

This article shall be inoperative unless it shall have been ratified as an amendment to the Constitution by the legislatures of three-fourths of the several States within seven years from the date of its submission.

Amendment XXI [1933]

SECTION 1

The eighteenth article of amendment to the Constitution of the United States is hereby repealed.

SECTION 2

The transportation or importation into any State, Territory, or possession of the United States for delivery or use therein of intoxicating liquors, in violation of the laws thereof, is hereby prohibited.

SECTION 3

This article shall be inoperative unless it shall have been ratified as an amendment to the Constitution by conventions in the several States, as provided in the Constitution, within seven years from the date of the submission hereof to the States by the Congress.

Amendment XXII [1951]

SECTION 1

No person shall be elected to the office of the President more than twice, and no person who has held the office of President, or acted as President, for more than two years of a term to which some other person was elected President shall be elected to the office of the President more than once. But this Article shall not apply to any person holding the office of President when this Article was proposed by the Congress, and shall not prevent any person who may be holding the office of President, or acting as President, during the term within which this Article becomes operative from holding the office of President or acting as President during the remainder of such term.

SECTION 2

This article shall be inoperative unless it shall have been ratified as an amendment to the Constitution by the legislatures of three-fourths of the several States within seven years from the date of its submission to the States by the Congress.

Amendment XXIII [1961]

SECTION 1

The District constituting the seat of Government of the United States shall appoint in such manner as the Congress may direct:

A number of electors of President and Vice President equal to the whole number of Senators and Representatives in Congress to which the District would be entitled if it were a State, but in no event more than the least populous State; they shall be in addition to those appointed by the States, but they shall be considered, for the purposes of the election of President and Vice President, to be electors appointed by a State; and they shall meet in the District and perform such duties as provided by the twelfth article of amendment.

SECTION 2

The Congress shall have power to enforce this article by appropriate legislation.

Amendment XXIV [1964]

SECTION 1

The right of citizens of the United States to vote in any primary or other election for President or Vice President, for electors for President or Vice President, or for Senator or Representative in Congress, shall not be denied or abridged by the United States or any State by reason of failure to pay any poll tax or other tax.

SECTION 2

The Congress shall have power to enforce this article by appropriate legislation.

Amendment XXV [1967]

SECTION 1

In case of the removal of the President from office or of his death or resignation, the Vice President shall become President.

SECTION 2

Whenever there is a vacancy in the office of the Vice President, the President shall nominate a Vice President who shall take office upon confirmation by a majority vote of both Houses of Congress.

SECTION 3

Whenever the President transmits to the President pro tempore of the Senate and the Speaker of the House of Representatives his written declaration that he is unable to discharge the powers and duties of his office, and until he transmits to them a written declaration to the contrary, such powers and duties shall be discharged by the Vice President as Acting President.

SECTION 4

Whenever the Vice President and a majority of either the principal officers of the executive departments or of such other body as Congress may by law provide, transmit to the President pro tempore of the Senate and the Speaker of the House of Representatives their written declaration that the President is unable to discharge the powers and duties of his office, the Vice President shall immediately assume the powers and duties of the office as Acting President.

Thereafter, when the President transmits to the President pro tempore of the Senate and the Speaker of the House of Representatives his written declaration that no inability exists, he shall resume the powers and duties of his office unless the Vice President and a majority of either the principal officers of the executive department or of such other body as Congress may by law provide, transmit within four days to the President pro tempore of the Senate and the Speaker of the House of Representatives their written declaration that the President is unable to discharge the powers and duties of his office. Thereupon Congress shall decide the issue, assembling within forty-eight hours for that purpose if not in session. If the Congress, within twenty-one days after receipt of the latter written declaration, or, if Congress is not in session, within twenty-one days after Congress is required to assemble, determines by two-thirds vote of both Houses that the President is unable to discharge the powers and duties of his office, the Vice President shall continue to discharge the same as Acting President; otherwise, the President shall resume the powers and duties of his office.

Amendment XXVI [1971]

SECTION 1

The right of citizens of the United States, who are eighteen years of age or older, to vote shall not be denied or abridged by the United States or by any State on account of age.

SECTION 2

The Congress shall have power to enforce this article by appropriate legislation.

TABLE OF CASES

Principal cases are in italic type. Cases cited or discussed are in roman. References are to pages. If a case is cited more than once in a principal case, generally only the first citation is listed.

1247

*

INDEX

References are to Pages